Methods for Achieving Your Purpose in Writing

The Bedford Reader centers on common ways of thinking and writing about all kinds of subjects, from everyday experiences to public policies to scientific theories. Whatever your purpose in writing, one or more of these ways of thinking — or methods of development — can help you discover and shape your ideas in individual paragraphs or entire papers.

The following list connects various purposes you may have for writing and the methods for achieving those purposes. The blue boxes along the right edge of the page correspond to tabs on later pages where each method is explained.

PURPOSE	METHOD
To tell a story about your subject, possibly to enlighten readers or to explain something to them	**Narration**
To help readers understand your subject through the evidence of their senses — sight, hearing, touch, smell, taste	**Description**
To explain your subject with instances that show readers its nature or character	**Example**
To explain or evaluate your subject by helping readers see the similarities and differences between it and another subject	**Comparison and Contrast**
To inform readers how to do something or how something works — how a sequence of actions leads to a particular result	**Process Analysis**
To explain a conclusion about your subject by showing readers the subject's parts or elements	**Division or Analysis**
To help readers see order in your subject by understanding the kinds or groups it can be sorted into	**Classification**
To tell readers the reasons for or consequences of your subject, explaining why or what if	**Cause and Effect**
To show readers the meaning of your subject — its boundaries and its distinctions from other subjects	**Definition**
To have readers consider your opinion about your subject or your proposal for it	**Argument and Persuasion**

THE BEDFORD READER

Thirteenth Edition

X. J. Kennedy

Dorothy M. Kennedy

Jane E. Aaron

Ellen Kuhl Repetto

bedford/st.martin's
Macmillan Learning
Boston | New York

For Bedford/St. Martin's

Vice President, Editorial, Macmillan Learning Humanities: Edwin Hill
Editorial Director, English: Karen S. Henry
Senior Publisher for Composition, Business and Technical Writing, Developmental Writing:
   Leasa Burton
Executive Editor: John E. Sullivan III
Developmental Editor: Sherry Mooney
Production Editor: Louis C. Bruno Jr.
Media Producer: Rand Thomas
Publishing Services Manager: Andrea Cava
Senior Production Supervisor: Jennifer Wetzel
Executive Marketing Manager: Joy Fisher Williams
Assistant Editor: Jennifer Prince
Project Management: Jouve
Senior Photo Editor: Martha Friedman
Photo Researcher: Julie Tesser
Permissions Editor: Kalina Ingham
Senior Art Director: Anna Palchik
Text Design: Anna Palchik, Dorothy Bungert/EriBen Graphics, and Jean Hammond
Cover Design: William Boardman
Cover Image: Dariush M / Shutterstock
Composition: Jouve
Printing and Binding: LSC Communications

Manufactured in the United States of America.

1   0   9   8   7   6

f   e   d   c   b   a

For information, write: Bedford/St. Martin's, 75 Arlington Street, Boston, MA 02116
   (617-399-4000)

ISBN 978-1-319-03051-3 (Student Edition)
ISBN 978-1-319-07276-6 (Instructor's Edition)
ISBN 978-1-319-06568-3 (High School Edition)

ACKNOWLEDGMENTS
Text acknowledgments and copyrights appear at the back of the book on pages 693–96, which constitute an extension of the copyright page. Art acknowledgments and copyrights appear on the same pages as the art selections they cover.

PREFACE FOR INSTRUCTORS

"A writer" says Saul Bellow, "is a reader moved to emulate." In a nutshell, the aim of *The Bedford Reader* is to move students to be writers, through reading and emulating the good writing of others.

Like its popular predecessors, this thirteenth edition pursues that aim both rhetorically and thematically. We present the rhetorical methods realistically, as we ourselves use them — as instinctive forms that assist invention and fruition and as flexible forms that mix easily for any purpose a writer may have. Further, we make numerous thematic connections among selections, both to spark students' interest in reading and to show how different writers tackle similar subjects with unique results.

Filling in this outline is a wealth of features, new and enduring.

NEW FEATURES

ENGAGING NEW READINGS BY REMARKABLE WRITERS As always, we have been enthralled with freshening the book's selections. In searching for essays academic yet lively, we discovered exceptional rhetorical models that will, we trust, also capture students' interest. The twenty-eight new selections include classic pieces by writers such as N. Scott Momaday and Joan Didion; recent works by established favorites such as Diane Ackerman, Malcolm Gladwell, and Marion Winik; and contributions from contemporary voices such as Issa Rae, Brian Doyle, and Colson Whitehead.

FOCUS ON STUDENT WORK *The Bedford Reader* now features more student writing than any other textbook of its kind. Twenty-four models of exemplary college work (ten of them new to this edition) include samples of a student's critical reading and response; ten annotated examples of student writing in academic genres such as lab reports, field observations, and policy proposals; eleven essays given the same treatment as the professional writing; and two new annotatated research papers.

A GREATER EMPHASIS ON THE CONNECTION BETWEEN READING AND WRITING More than ever, *The Bedford Reader* demonstrates that critical reading and academic writing are related processes that naturally inform and build off each other. At the request of instructors who use the book, we have thoroughly revised and reorganized the material on academic reading and writing in Part One, with increased attention throughout the text to writing in response to sources, whether one or many.

- **A stronger focus on reading to write.** Offering more guidance on active and critical reading than any other rhetorical reader, we stress the inter-connectedness of reading and writing in Chapter 1, with a clearer over-view of annotating texts and a new discussion of writing in response as a component of critical thinking.

- **Expanded coverage of key writing topics.** Chapter 2 now examines the writing situation in more detail, clarifying the distinctions between writ-ing to reflect, entertain, explain, or persuade, and explaining how an awareness of purpose and audience influences a writer's choices. Placing fresh emphasis on supporting a thesis with ideas gleaned from reading, the chapter also features a newly integrated discussion of synthesizing evidence, with multiple examples of acceptable and unacceptable sum-maries, paraphrases, and quotations.

- **Examples of writing that responds to reading.** In addition to the essay-in-progress that concludes Chapter 2, *The Bedford Reader* for the first time features multiple student and professional essays that respond, directly or indirectly, to other works in the book. Student writer Rachel O'Connor, for instance, shares her critical reading of Shirley Jackson's "The Lottery," and composition instructor Barbara B. Parsons offers a rhetorical analysis of Brent Staples's "Black Men and Public Space." Janelle Asselin makes a point-by-point rebuttal of an argument presented by Chuck Dixon and Paul Rivoche, while Jon Overton counters Brianne Richson's call for trigger warnings on syllabi. And Luis Alberto Urrea, in "Barrio Walden," reveals how he was influenced by the writings of Henry David Thoreau, "What I Lived For" in particular.

- **A new Appendix, "Finding and Documenting Sources,"** gathers the details on research and source citation where students are most likely to look for guidance. Freshened guidelines emphasize asking questions, finding and evaluating sources, creating annotated bibliographies, and avoiding plagiarism; and updated help with documenting sources reflects the most recent versions of both MLA style and APA style, offering dozens of current models and new annotated student essays for each. Ten additional examples of documented writing are spread throughout the book.

A FRESH TAKE ON THE WRITERS' COMMENTS ON WRITING   After their essays, more than half of the book's writers offer comments on everything from reading to grammar to how they developed the particular piece we reprint. Besides providing rock-solid advice, these comments — eighteen of them new — prove that for the pros, too, writing is usually a challenge. New notes following the comments highlight the writers' key points, telling students where in the book they can find additional resources and suggesting how they might apply the insights to their own work.

For easy access, the "Writers on Writing" commentaries are listed in a new Directory under the topics they address. Look up *Revision*, for instance, and find that Junot Díaz, Shirley Jackson, Anne Lamott, and Colson Whitehead, among others, have something to say about this crucial stage of the writing process.

TRADEMARK FEATURES

EXCELLENT SELECTIONS BY WELL-KNOWN AUTHORS   All of them models of exceptional writing, the essays in *The Bedford Reader* vary in authorship, topic, even length and format. We offer clear and interesting applications of the methods of development by noted writers such as Anna Quindlen, Brent Staples, Amy Tan, and David Sedaris. Half the selections are by women, and a third touch on cultural diversity. They range in subject from family to science, from language to psychology, from food to politics.

EXTENSIVE THEMATIC CONNECTIONS   *The Bedford Reader* provides substantial opportunities for topical class discussion and writing. A pair of essays in each chapter addresses the same subject, from the ordinary (embarrassment) to the controversial (privilege). Eight of those pairings are new, and the thoroughly refreshed chapter on argument now includes a new essay pair and two casebooks (one new) consisting of three selections apiece. At least one "Connections" writing topic after every selection suggests links to other selections in the book. And an alternate table of contents arranges the book's selections under more than three dozen topics and academic disciplines (nine new).

REALISTIC TREATMENT OF THE RHETORICAL METHODS   *The Bedford Reader* treats the methods of development not as empty forms but as tools for inventing, for shaping, and, ultimately, for accomplishing a purpose.

- **A practical guide.** The chapters on reading and writing in Part One and the introductions to the rhetorical methods in Part Two are simple and clear, with many explanations and suggestions distilled into bulleted lists and boxed guidelines so that students can easily follow and use the book's advice on their own. Each chapter introduction links the method to the range of purposes it can serve and gives step-by-step guidance for writing and revising. (For quick reference, the purpose/method links also appear inside the front cover, where they are keyed to the marginal page tabs that appear in each chapter introduction.)

- **A "Focus" box in every rhetorical chapter** highlights an element of writing that is especially relevant to that method — for example, verbs in narration, concrete words in description, parallelism in comparison and contrast, and tone in argument and persuasion. To show these elements in context, most selections include a question about them.

- **Annotated examples** of a textbook passage and a college writing assignment end each chapter introduction to demonstrate academic applications of the methods across the disciplines.

- **An emphasis on mixing the methods** takes the realistic approach even further. We show how writers freely combine methods to achieve their purposes: Each rhetorical introduction discusses how that method might work with others, and at least one "Other Methods" question after every selection helps students analyze how methods work together. Most significantly, Part Three provides an anthology of works by celebrated writers that specifically illustrate mixed methods. The headnotes for these selections point to where each method comes into play.

ABUNDANT EDITORIAL APPARATUS   As always, we've surrounded the selections with a wealth of material designed to get students reading, thinking, and writing. To help structure students' critical approach to the selections, each one is preceded by a headnote on the author and one on the selection itself, which outlines the selection's cultural and historical contexts. Each selection is followed by sets of questions on meaning, writing strategy, and language and at least five writing suggestions. One writing suggestion encourages students to explore their responses in their journals; another suggests how to develop the journal writing into an essay; and others emphasize critical writing, research, and connections among selections.

Besides the aids provided with every selection, the book also includes additional writing topics at the end of every rhetorical chapter (with several new suggestions in each), a Glossary of Useful Terms that defines key terms used in the book (all those printed in SMALL CAPITAL LETTERS), and a comprehensive index that alphabetizes not only authors and titles but also all important topics (including the elements of composition).

ATTENTION TO GENRE *The Bedford Reader* is still the only rhetorical reader to show students how they can apply the methods of development to various genres of writing. Integrated discussions throughout Part One introduce students to the concept of genre and help them understand how purpose, audience, and convention affect a writer's choices. And in each rhetorical chapter in Part Two, an annotated sample of a student-written document demonstrates a specific application of method to genre, with brief guidelines for writing different kinds of projects. Three of these documents — a criminal justice report, a critical reading of literature, and a policy proposal — are new to this edition.

ENGAGING VISUAL DIMENSION *The Bedford Reader* emphasizes the visual as well as the verbal. Chapter 1, on reading, provides a short course in thinking critically about images, with a photograph serving as a case study. Each rhetorical chapter then opens with a striking image — an ad, a photograph, a drawing — (a third of them new) with accompanying text and questions to invite students' own critical reading and show how the rhetorical methods work visually. Finally, several of the book's selections either take images as their starting points or use illustrations to explain or highlight key ideas.

EXTENSIVE INSTRUCTOR'S MANUAL Available as a separate manual, online on the book page at *macmillanlearning.com*, or bound into the instructor's edition, *Notes and Resources for Teaching The Bedford Reader* suggests ways to integrate journaling and collaboration into writing classes; discusses uses for the book's chapters on critical reading, academic writing, and research and documentation; and provides tips on using visuals and multimedia selections in a writing course. In addition, *Notes and Resources* discusses every method, every selection (with new multimedia resource suggestions and with possible answers provided for all questions), and every "Writers on Writing" feature.

TWO VERSIONS *The Bedford Reader* has a sibling. A shorter edition, *The Brief Bedford Reader*, features fifty essays instead of sixty-eight, including four selections (rather than eight) in Part Three.

ADDITIONAL RESOURCES

Bedford/St. Martin's offers multiple resources that can help you and your students get even more out of *The Bedford Reader* and your course. To learn more about or to order any of the following products at a significant discount, contact your Bedford/St. Martin's sales representative or find *The Bedford Reader* book page on *macmillanlearning.com*.

E-BOOK OPTION   *The Bedford Reader* is also available as an e-book. For details, visit *macmillanlearning.com/ebooks*.

LAUNCHPAD SOLO FOR READERS AND WRITERS   Offering instruction tailored to individual students' unique needs, *LaunchPad Solo for Readers and Writers* features several innovative digital tools.

- **Reading comprehension quizzes** for every selection in *The Bedford Reader*.
- **Pre-built units that support a learning arc.** Each unit includes a pre-test, multimedia instruction and assessment, help for multilingual writers, and a post-test that assesses what students have learned about critical reading, the writing process, using sources, grammar, style, and mechanics.
- **Video introductions** offer overviews of many unit topics and illustrate the concepts at hand.
- **Adaptive quizzing for targeted learning.** Most units include Learning-Curve, game-like quizzing that focuses on the areas in which each student needs the most help.
- **The ability to monitor student progress.** Instructors can use the Gradebook to see which students are on track and which need additional help.

Order ISBN 978-1-319-09775-2 to package *LaunchPad Solo for Readers and Writers* with *The Bedford Reader*, or visit *macmillanlearning.com/catalog/readwrite* for more information.

WRITER'S HELP 2.0   Built on research with more than 1,600 student writers, this online writing resource helps students find answers whether they are searching for advice on their own or as part of an assignment. The smart search feature leads to trusted content from best-selling handbooks, even when students use novice terms such as *flow* and *getting unstuck*. And Writer's Help 2.0 includes LearningCurve, game-like quizzing that adapts to what students already know and helps them focus on what they need to learn, as well as reading comprehension quizzes for every essay in *The Bedford Reader*.

Order ISBN 978-1-319-09779-0 to package *Writer's Help 2.0, Hacker Version* or ISBN 978-1-319-09780-6 for *Writer's Help 2.0, Lunsford Version* with *The Bedford Reader*; students who rent or buy a used book can purchase access at *macmillanlearning.com/writershelp2*. Instructor access is free. For technical support, visit *macmillanlearning.com/getsupport*.

PORTFOLIOS The third edition of *Portfolio Keeping*, by Nedra Reynolds and Elizabeth Davis, provides all the information students need to use the portfolio method successfully in a writing course. *Portfolio Teaching*, a companion guide for instructors, provides practical support for you and your writing-program administrator. Contact your sales representative for a package ISBN.

JOIN OUR COMMUNITY! *The Macmillan English Community* is now the home for all Bedford/St. Martin's professional resources, featuring Bedford *Bits*, a popular blog site offering new ideas for the composition classroom and composition teachers. Connect and converse with a growing team of Bedford authors and top scholars who blog on *Bits*: Andrea Lunsford, Nancy Sommers, Steve Bernhardt, Traci Gardner, Barclay Barrios, Jack Solomon, Susan Bernstein, Elizabeth Wardle, Doug Downs, Liz Losh, Jonathan Alexander, and Donna Winchell. In addition, you'll find an expanding collection of additional resources that support your teaching. Download titles from the publisher's professional resource series to support your teaching, review projects in the pipeline, sign up for professional development webinars, start a discussion, ask a question, and follow your favorite members. Visit *community .macmillan.com* to join the conversation.

ACKNOWLEDGMENTS

Hundreds of teachers and students over the years have helped us shape *The Bedford Reader*. For this edition, the following teachers offered insights from their experiences that encouraged worthy changes: Debra Benedetti, Piermont Community and Technical College; Mary Bodelson, Anoka Ramsey Community College; Elizabeth Cochrane, Harper College; Cinder Cooper, Montgomery College; Joseph Couch, Montgomery College; Rebecca Eades, Volunteer State Community College; Lori Fox, Art Institute of California at Sacramento; Mary Hart, University of Mount Olive; David James, Houston Community College System–Northwest College; Michael Johnson, Muskegon Community College; Claire Kageyama, Houston Community College; Mary Anne Keefer, Lord Fairfax Community College–Fauquier Campus; Tamara Kuzmenkov, Tacoma Community College; Laura La Flair, Belmont Abbey College; Aggie Mendoza, Nashville State Community College; Jeanni Pruitt, Northeast Texas Community College; Larry Silverman, Seattle Central College; Miriam Simon, Montgomery College; Robert Sternberg, American

International College; Brenda Tuberville, Rogers State University; Linda Webster, Sam Houston State University; Benjamin West, State University of New York at Delhi; Dianna M. Woods, Northeast Texas Community College; and Scott Wrobel, Anoka Ramsey Community College.

We are as ever deeply in debt to the creative people at and around Bedford/St. Martin's. Leasa Burton, Steve Scipione, John Sullivan, Maura Shea, and Karen Henry contributed insight and support. Sherry Mooney, developing the book, was an invaluable collaborator: She helped to plan and implement the revisions and new features, hunted for readings, researched and drafted some of the apparatus, and calmly steered the ship through unexpected storms. Jennifer Prince ably assisted, especially in reaching out to student writers and coordinating the inclusion of their essays. William Boardman created the refreshing new cover. Louis Bruno planned and oversaw the production of the book. And Kevin Bradley, with remarkable patience and flexibility, transformed the raw manuscript into the book you hold.

CONTENTS

A writer with multiple sclerosis thinks she knows why the media carry so few images of people like herself with disabilities: Viewers might conclude, correctly, that "there is something ordinary about disability itself."

The great Civil War generals Ulysses S. Grant and Robert E. Lee clearly personified their opposing traditions. But what they had in common was more vital by far.

Trying to buy a skirt in a US department store leads the author, a Moroccan Muslim, to compare the relative disadvantages of women in Western and Muslim countries. Who's actually worse off?

This popular philosopher considers the uncanny similarities between the tabloid news of today and the Greek dramas of ancient history.

Visual Images: *A Man Drives into His Family Home to Punish His Wife,* video still by BBC News; *Medea Kills Her Son to Punish Her Husband,* painted vase by unknown artist

Visual Image: *Workers Making Dolls,* photograph by Wally McNamee

WRITING

For those who struggle with writer's block, this writer recommends quieting their inner voices and just getting words down, no matter how terrible the effort.

PAIRED
SELECTIONS

"Be nebulous. Scratch that, be amphibological." With tongue firmly in cheek, a college student offers writing tips for his peers.

Visual Image: *Mounted Nazi Troops on the Lookout for Likely Polish Children,* photograph

Considering social pressures to compete in every aspect of life, a sports writer cautions that athletic obsession with "masculinity and power" handicaps us all.

What gives an ancient legend the power to infiltrate contemporary popular culture? A filmmaker and a novelist, coauthors of a best-selling vampire trilogy, have a theory.

To model critical analysis for her writing students, a college teacher examines the classic essay "Black Men and Public Space" by Brent Staples (Chap. 5) — and finds a striking resonance for contemporary readers.

Visual Image: *How the Poor, the Middle Class, and the Rich Spend Their Money,* table by National Public Radio

FAILURES TO COMMUNICATE

PAIRED SELECTIONS

Sometimes an apology is not an apology, observes an expert on communication. Men and women would get along better, she says, if they understood each other's codes of speech.

For a writing seminar, a pre-med student investigates some "startling" recent discoveries in neuroscience — and is deeply encouraged by what he learns.

CONTENTS BY THEME AND DISCIPLINE

BUSINESS AND ECONOMICS

CHILDHOOD

CLASS

COMMUNICATION AND LANGUAGE

COMMUNITY

COMPUTER TECHNOLOGY

CRIME

DEATH

DIVERSITY

EDUCATION

ETHICS

FAMILY

FOOD

GENDER AND SEXUALITY

HEALTH AND DISABILITY

HISTORY

HUMOR AND SATIRE

INTERNATIONAL STUDIES

MYTH AND LEGEND

THE NATURAL ENVIRONMENT

PHILOSOPHY

POPULAR CULTURE

PSYCHOLOGY

READING AND WRITING

SCIENCE

SELF-DISCOVERY

SOCIAL CUSTOMS

SPORTS AND LEISURE

VIOLENCE

WAR AND CONFLICT

WORK

HOW (AND WHY) TO USE THIS BOOK

Many prophets have predicted the doom of words on paper, and they may yet be proved correct. Already, many of us are reading books and magazines mainly on mobile devices and communicating mostly by text messages. But even if we do discard paper and pens, the basic aims and methods of writing will not fundamentally change. Whether in print or on screen, we will need to explain our thoughts to others plainly and forcefully.

Our aim with *The Bedford Reader* is to provide you with ample and varied resources that will help you develop your skills as a reader and writer. In this academic toolbox, you'll find not only interesting models of good writing but also useful advice, reference guides, ideas for writing, and practical strategies that you can apply to your own work.

THE SELECTIONS

Essays

In this book, we trust, you'll find many selections you will enjoy and want to discuss. *The Bedford Reader* features work by some of the finest nonfiction writers and even a few famous literary figures.

The selections deal with more than just writing; they cut broadly across a college curriculum. You'll find professional essays and textbook paragraphs on science, history, business, culture, technology, sports, and politics. Some writers recall their childhoods, their problems and challenges. Some explore academic concerns such as the goals of education and the physics of mass movement. Some touch on matters likely to spark debate: free speech, class privilege, race relations, child labor. Some writers are serious; others, funny. In all, these selections mirror the kinds of reading you will meet in your other courses. Such reading is the intellectual storehouse of well-informed people with lively minds — who, to be sure, aren't found only on college campuses.

We have chosen the essays with one main purpose in mind: to show you how good writers write. Don't be discouraged if at first you find an immense gap in quality between Joan Didion's writing and yours. Of course there's a gap: Didion is an immortal with a unique style that she perfected over half a century. You don't have to judge your efforts by comparison. The idea is to gain whatever writing techniques you can. If you're going to learn from other writers, why not go to the best of them?

Student Examples

You can glean many skills by reading the work of seasoned writers, but you can also learn from your peers. Students, too, produce writing worth studying, as proved by Scott Beltran, Andrea Roman, Koji Frahm, and many others. In every chapter in Part Two, you'll find student pieces among the professional selections, at least one of them annotated to show you how the writers' strategies work. These examples vary in subject, approach, and GENRE, but every one of them shows how much student writers can achieve with a little inspiration and effort.

Visuals

The selections in *The Bedford Reader* go beyond the written word. Much of what we "read" in the world is visual information, as in paintings and drawings, or visual-with-verbal information, as in advertisements and cartoons. In all, we include eighteen visual works. Some of them are subjects of writing, as when a writer analyzes a news photo or a bar graph. Other visual works stand free, offering themselves to be understood, interpreted, and perhaps enjoyed, just as prose and fiction do. To help you get the most from these images, we offer advice on reading visuals, with a sample analysis of a photograph, in Chapter 1.

We combine visual material with written texts to further a key aim of *The Bedford Reader*: to encourage you to think critically about what you see, hear, and read. Like everyone else, you face a daily barrage of words and pictures. Mulling over the views of the writers, artists, and others represented in this book — figuring out their motives and strategies, agreeing or disagreeing with their ideas — will help you learn to manage, digest, and use in your own writing whatever media you encounter.

THE METHODS OF DEVELOPMENT

The selections in *The Bedford Reader* fall into distinct sections. In Part Two, the heart of the book, each of ten chapters explains a familiar method of developing ideas, such as NARRATION, DESCRIPTION, EXAMPLE, CAUSE AND EFFECT, or DEFINITION. These methods are extraordinarily useful tools for achieving your PURPOSE in writing, whatever that purpose may be. They can help you discover what you know, what you need to know, how to think critically about your subject, and how to shape your ideas.

An introduction to each chapter outlines the method, explains its uses, and shows how you can apply it to your own writing. The reading selections that follow illustrate the method at work. Examining these selections, you'll discover two important facts about the methods of development. First, they are flexible: Two people can use the same method for quite different ends, and just about any method can point a way into just about any subject in any medium.

The second fact about the methods of development is this: A writer never sticks to just one method all the way through a piece of writing. Even when one method predominates, you'll see the writer pick up another method, let it shape a paragraph or more, and then move on to yet another method — all to achieve some overriding aim. Part Three offers an anthology of classic and contemporary selections that illustrate how, in most writing, the methods work together.

THE PRACTICAL GUIDANCE

Overviews of Reading, Writing, and Research

The selections in *The Bedford Reader* are meant to be enjoyed, but also to give you ideas for your own writing. We include two chapters in Part One to help you build your critical reading and writing skills as you work with the readings. You might want to read these chapters straight through as a general guide or turn back to them as necessary for reference, or both.

Chapter 1 explains the connection between reading and writing, outlines the goals of CRITICAL READING, and provides concrete advice for approaching written and visual works with an open, questioning mind. To demonstrate what academic reading entails, we include a sample essay and accompany it with one student's notes and with our own interpretations of the writer's meanings and strategies.

In Chapter 2 we walk you through the stages of the writing process, following the same student as she works from rough idea to final draft. Like the first chapter, this one features bulleted points and boxed checklists to help you find the information you need. It addresses in particular the challenges of ACADEMIC WRITING, whether in responding to individual selections or developing an idea with reference to multiple works. It also includes a brief overview of common editing challenges and shows you how to solve them.

The Appendix goes over the basics of finding and using sources in academic writing. It offers dozens of citation models for both MLA and APA styles and includes two annotated student research papers.

Reading Questions and Writing Prompts

Following every essay in *The Bedford Reader*, you'll find a battery of questions that can help you analyze the selection and respond to it. First, a suggestion for responding in your JOURNAL to what you've just read encourages you to think about the writer's themes and your reactions to them. Next, you'll find critical reading questions that can help you read beneath the surface of the work, teasing out the elements that contribute to the writer's success and even those that don't. (You can see a sample of how these questions work when we analyze Nancy Mairs's essay "Disability," starting on p. 12.)

After these questions are at least four suggestions for writing, including one that proposes turning your journal entry into an essay, one that links the selection with one or two others in the book, and one that asks you to read the selection and write about it with your critical faculties alert. Additional suggestions for writing appear at the end of each chapter. We intend these prompts not as rigid taskmasters but as helpful guides. Certainly you can respond to them exactly as written, but if they spark other insights for you, by all means pursue your inspiration. Writing is always best when it comes from a real interest in the subject and a desire to write about it.

Glossary and Index

In this introduction and throughout the following chapters, certain words appear in CAPITAL LETTERS. These are key terms helpful in discussing both the selections in this book and the reading and writing you do. If you'd like to see such a term defined and illustrated, you can find it in the Glossary of Useful Terms on pages 668–82. The Glossary offers more than just brief definitions. It is there to provide you with further explanation, examples, and support.

You can also find the help you need by consulting the Index, located at the back of the book. Say you're revising a draft and your instructor has commented that your essay needs a clearer thesis, but you're not sure what that means or what to do. Look up THESIS, and you'll discover exactly where in *The Bedford Reader* you can find advice for clarifying and expressing your main idea.

THE WRITERS ON WRITING

A final word. The writers represented in this book did not produce their readable and informative texts on the first try, as if by magic, leaving the rest of us to cope with writer's block, awkward sentences, and all the other difficulties of writing. As proof, we visit their workshops. Following more than half the selections are comments by their writers, revealing how they write (or wrote), offering their tricks, setting forth things they admire about good writing. Accompanying the comments are tips on how you can apply the writers' insights to your own work, and a directory at the back of the book points you toward their advice on such practical matters as drafting, finding your point, and revising. No doubt you'll notice some contradictions in these comments: The writers disagree about when and how to think about readers, about whether outlines have any value, about whether style follows subject or vice versa. The reason for the differences of opinion is, simply, that no two writers follow the same path to finished work. Even the same writer may take a left instead of the customary right turn if the writing situation demands a change. A key aim of providing the writers' statements is to suggest the sheer variety of routes open to you, the many approaches to writing and strategies for succeeding at it.

Let's get started then.

ACADEMIC READING AND WRITING

1

CRITICAL READING

Reading and writing are interconnected. Deepen your mastery of one, and you deepen your mastery of the other. The experience of carefully reading an excellent writer, noticing not only what the writer has to say but also the quality of its saying, rubs off (if you are patient and perceptive) on your own writing. For any writer, then, reading is indispensable. It turns up fresh ideas; it stocks the mind with information, understanding, and examples; it instills critical awareness of one's own surroundings.

Whatever career you enter, reading will be an integral part of your work. You may be trying to understand a new company policy, seeking the truth in a campaign ad, researching a scientific development, or looking for pointers to sharpen your skills. Such reading, like writing itself, demands effort. Unlike the casual reading you might do to pass the time or entertain yourself, CRITICAL READING involves looking beneath the surface of a text, seeking to understand the creator's intentions, the strategies for achieving them, and their effects. This book offers dozens of selections that reward critical reading and can teach you how to become a better writer. To learn from a selection, plan to spend an hour or two in its company. Seek out some quiet place — a library, a study cubicle, your room. Switch off the music and the phone. The fewer the distractions, the easier your task will be and the more you'll enjoy it.

How do you read critically? Exactly how, that is, do you engage with a work, master its complexities, learn from it, and respond? To find out, we'll model critical-thinking processes that you can apply to the written and visual selections in this book, taking a close look at an essay and a photograph for examples.

READING ACTIVELY

Previewing

Critical reading starts before you read the first word of a piece of writing. You take stock of what's before you, locating clues to the work's content and the writer's biases. Whenever you approach a written work, make a point of assessing these features beforehand:

- **The title.** Effective titles do more than lure readers in; they also hint at what to expect from a work. Often the title will tell you the writer's subject, as with Anna Quindlen's "Homeless." Sometimes the title immediately states the main point the writer will make: "I Want a Wife." Some titles spell out the method a writer proposes to follow: "Grant and Lee: A Study in Contrasts." And the title may reveal the writer's attitude toward the material, as "Live Free and Starve" does.

- **The author.** Whatever you know or can learn about a writer — upbringing, special training, previous publications, outlook, ideology — can often help you predict something about a work. Is the writer a political conservative or a liberal? a feminist? an athlete? an internationally renowned philosopher? a popular comedian? By knowing something about the background or beliefs of a writer, you may guess beforehand a little of what he or she will say.

- **The genre.** Identifying the type, or GENRE, of a work can tell you much about the writer's intentions and likely strategies. Genres vary widely; they include critical analyses, business reports, works of literature, humor pieces, and newspaper columns — among many others. The conventions of a given genre necessarily direct a writer's choices. For instance, you can assume that a scholarly article will take an academic tone, lay out arguments and evidence carefully, and cite other published works. The same approach in a personal narrative, however, would confuse most readers.

- **Where the work was published.** Clearly, it matters to a writer's credibility whether an article called "Creatures of the Dark Oceans" appears in a science magazine or in a supermarket tabloid. But no less important, knowing where a work first appeared can tell you for whom the writer was writing. Good writers, as you will see, develop an awareness of their AUDIENCE and shape their messages to appeal to particular readers' interests and needs.

- **When the work was published.** Knowing the year a work appeared may give you another key to understanding it. A 2017 article on ocean creatures will contain statements of fact more advanced and reliable than an essay printed in 1917 — although the older work might offer valuable information and insights, too.

To help provide such prereading knowledge, this book supplies biographical information about the writers and tells you something about the sources and original contexts of the selections, in notes just before each essay. It can be tempting to skip over such introductory materials, but we encourage you to look at them. Doing so will help you become a more efficient reader in the end.

Annotating

To learn from other writers how to write well, you'll want to read the essays in this book multiple times. On the first reading, focus on what the author has to say, without getting hung up on every particular. If you encounter any words or concepts that you don't know, take them in stride; you can always circle them and look them up later. Begin by getting a feel for the gist of the essay; later, you will examine the details and strategies that make it work.

In giving an essay a second or third going-over, critical readers find a pencil (or stylus) indispensable. A pencil in hand concentrates the attention wonderfully, and, as often happens with writing, it can lead to unexpected connections. (Some readers favor highlighting key words or lines, but you can't use color alone to note *why* a word or an idea is important.)

You can annotate your own material in several ways, developing a personal system that works best for you:

- **Underline essential ideas**, and double-underline repeated points or concepts.
- **Mark key passages** with checks or vertical lines.
- **Write questions** in the margins.
- **Note associations** with other works you've read, seen, or heard.
- **Vent your feelings** ("Bull!" "Yes!" "Says who?").

If you can't annotate what you're reading — because it's borrowed or your device doesn't have that functionality — make your notes on a separate sheet of paper or in an electronic bookmark or file.

Writing while reading helps you uncover the hidden workings of an essay, so that you, as much as any expert, can judge its effectiveness. You'll develop an opinion about what you read, and you'll want to express it. While reading this way, you're being a writer. Your pencil marks or keystrokes will jog your memory, too, when you review for a test, take part in class discussion, or write about what you've read.

To show what a reader's annotations on an essay might look like, we give you Nancy Mairs's "Disability" with a student's marginal notes, written over the course of several readings. The same student, Rosie Anaya, wrote an essay spurred by the ideas she found in reading Mairs's work; it appears at the end of the next chapter.

NANCY MAIRS

A self-described "radical feminist, pacifist, and cripple," Nancy Mairs aims to "speak the 'unspeakable.'" Her poetry, memoirs, and essays deal with many sensitive subjects, including her struggles with multiple sclerosis. Born in Long Beach, California, in 1943, Mairs grew up in New Hampshire and Massachusetts. She received a BA from Wheaton College and an MFA in creative writing and a PhD in English literature from the University of Arizona. While working on her advanced degrees, Mairs taught high-school and college writing courses. Her second book of poetry, *In All the Rooms of the Yellow House* (1984), received a Western States Arts Foundation book award. Mairs's essays are collected in several volumes, including *Carnal Acts* (1990), *Waist High in the World* (1996), *A Troubled Guest* (2001), and *A Dynamic God* (2007). In 2008 she received the Arizona Literary Treasure Award. In addition to working as a writer, Mairs is a public speaker and a research associate with the Southwest Institute for Research on Women.

Disability

As a writer afflicted with multiple sclerosis, Mairs is in a unique position to examine how the culture responds to people with disabilities. In this essay from *Carnal Acts*, she examines media depictions of disability and argues with her usual unsentimental candor that the media must treat disability as normal. The essay was first published in 1987 in the *New York Times*. To what extent is Mairs's critique still valid today?

For months now I've been consciously searching for repre- [1]
sentations of myself in the media, especially television. I know
I'd recognize this self because of certain distinctive, though not
unique, features: I am a forty-three-year-old woman crippled with
multiple sclerosis; although I can still totter short distances with
the aid of a brace and a cane, more and more of the time I ride in
a wheelchair. Because of these appliances and my peculiar gait,
I'm easy to spot even in a crowd. So when I tell you I haven't
noticed any women like me on television, you can believe me.

Actually, last summer I did see a woman with multiple scle- [2]
rosis portrayed on one of those medical dramas that offer an
illness-of-the-week like the daily special at your local diner. In
fact, that was the whole point of the show: that this poor young
woman had MS. She was terribly upset (understandably, I assure
you) by the diagnosis, and her response was to plan a trip to
Kenya while she was still physically capable of making it, against
the advice of the young, fit, handsome doctor who had fallen in
love with her. And she almost did it. At least, she got as far as
a taxi to the airport, hotly pursued by the doctor. But at the last
she succumbed to his blandishments and fled the taxi into his
manly protective embrace. No escape to Kenya for this cripple.

Capitulation into the arms of a man who uses his medi- [3]
cal powers to strip one of even the urge toward independence
is hardly the sort of representation I had in mind. But even if
the situation had been sensitively handled, according to the
woman her right to her own adventures, it wouldn't have been
what I'm looking for. Such a television show, as well as films
like *Duet for One* and *Children of a Lesser God*, in taking disability
as its major premise, excludes the complexities that round out
a character and make her whole. It's not about a woman who
happens to be physically disabled; it's about physical disability as
the determining factor of a woman's existence.

Take it from me, physical disability looms pretty large in [4]
one's life. But it doesn't devour one wholly. I'm not, for instance,
Ms. MS, a walking, talking embodiment of a chronic incur-
able degenerative disease. In most ways I'm just like every other
woman of my age, nationality, and socioeconomic background.
I menstruate, so I have to buy tampons. I worry about smoker's
breath, so I buy mouthwash. I smear my wrinkling skin with
lotions. I put bleach in the washer so my family's undies won't

"myself" = a person with a disability living a full life

!

Wait, I've seen characters with wheelchairs. Plenty.

A movie shows disability defining a woman's life.

emotions

again!

Also The Soloist, *and* A Beautiful Mind

The complaint: these shows miss the point

Details have a point

she buys things the advertisers sell.

be dingy. I drive a car, talk on the telephone, get runs in my pantyhose, eat pizza. In most ways, that is, I'm the advertisers' dream: Ms. Great American Consumer. And yet the advertisers, who determine nowadays who will get represented publicly and who will not, deny the existence of me and my kind absolutely.

Ads don't show disability either — still true?

I once asked a local advertiser why he didn't include dis- 5 abled people in his spots. His response seemed direct enough: "We don't want to give people the idea that our product is just for the handicapped." But tell me truly now: If you saw me pouring out puppy biscuits, would you think these kibbles were only for the puppies of the cripples? If you saw my blind niece ordering a Coke, would you switch to Pepsi lest you be struck sightless? No, I think the advertiser's excuse masked a deeper and more anx- ious rationale: To depict disabled people in the ordinary activities of daily life is to admit that there is something ordinary about disability itself, that it may enter anybody's life. If it is effaced completely, or at least isolated as a separate "problem," so that it remains at a safe distance from other human issues, then the viewer won't feel threatened by her or his own physical vulnerability.

Hah! Snarky.
emotions

✓ scary thought

effaced? (means erased, or made to disappear)

This kind of effacement or isolation has painful, even dan- 6 gerous consequences, however. For the disabled person, these include self-degradation and a subtle kind of self-alienation not unlike that experienced by other minorities. Socialized human beings love to conform, to study others and then mold themselves to the contours of those whose images, for good reasons or bad, they come to love. Imagine a life in which feasible others — others you can hope to be like — don't exist. At the least you might conclude that there is something queer about you, something ugly or foolish or shameful. In the extreme, you might feel as though you don't exist, in any meaningful social sense, at all. Everyone else is "there," sucking breath mints and splashing cologne and swigging wine coolers. You're "not there." And if not there, nowhere.

effects — IMPORTANT

emotions

What about individuality?

emotions

But this denial of disability imperils even you who are able- 7 bodied, and not just by shrinking your insight into the physically and emotionally complex world you live in. Some disabled people call you TAPs, or Temporarily Abled Persons. The fact is that ours is the only minority you can join involuntarily, without warning, at any time. And if you live long enough, as you're

Problem affects people without disabilities too — interesting point.

✓

increasingly likely to do, you may well join it. The transition will probably be difficult from a physical point of view no matter what. But it will be a good bit easier <u>psychologically</u> if you are accustomed to seeing disability as a normal characteristic, one that complicates but does not ruin human existence. Achieving this integration, for disabled and able-bodied people alike, requires that we insert disability daily into our field of vision: quietly, naturally, in the small and common scenes of our ordinary lives. *main idea*

DEVELOPING AN UNDERSTANDING

Apart from your specific notes on an essay, you'll also need a place to work out your comprehension using the strategies and detailed analyses discussed below and on the following pages. For such responses, you may find a JOURNAL handy. It can be a repository of your ideas, a comfortable place to record thoughts about what you read. You may be surprised to find that the more you write in an unstructured way, the more you'll have to say when it's time to write a structured essay.

Summarizing

It's good practice, especially with more difficult essays, to SUMMARIZE the content in writing to be sure you understand it or, as often happens, to come to understand it. (We're suggesting here that you write summaries for yourself, but the technique is also useful when you discuss other people's works in your writing, as shown on pp. 43–44.)

In summarizing a work of writing, you digest, *in your own words*, what the author says: You take the essence of the author's meaning, without the supporting evidence and other details that make the whole convincing or interesting. If the work is short, you may want to make this a two-step procedure: First write a summary sentence for every paragraph or related group of paragraphs; then summarize those sentences in two or three others that capture the heart of the author's meaning.

Here is a two-step summary of "Disability." (The numbers in parentheses refer to paragraph numbers in the essay.) First, the longer version:

(1) Mairs searches the media in vain for depictions of women like herself with disabilities. (2) One TV movie showed a woman recently diagnosed with multiple sclerosis, but she chose dependence over independence. (3) Such shows oversimplify people with disabilities by making disability

central to their lives. (4) People with disabilities live lives and consume goods like everyone else, but the media ignore them. (5) Showing disability as ordinary would remind nondisabled viewers that they are vulnerable. (6) The media's exclusion of others like themselves deprives people with disabilities of role models and makes them feel undesirable or invisible. (7) Nondisabled viewers lose an understanding that could enrich them and would help them adjust to disability of their own.

Now the short summary:

> Mairs believes that the media, by failing to depict disability as ordinary, both marginalize viewers with disabilities and impair the outlook and coping skills of the "Temporarily Abled."

Thinking Critically

Summarizing will start you toward understanding the author's meaning, but it is just a first step. Once you comprehend the gist of a text, you're ready to examine its deeper meanings and intentions and apply them to your own work and life. (A TEXT may be a written document, but it may also be a photograph, an experiment, a conversation, a work of art, a Web site, or any other form of communication.)

We're talking here about critical thinking — not "negative," the common conception of *critical*, but "thorough, thoughtful, inquisitive, judgment forming." When you approach something critically, you harness your faculties, your fund of knowledge, and your experiences to understand, appreciate, and evaluate the text. Critical thinking is a process involving several overlapping operations: analysis, inference, synthesis, and evaluation.

Analysis

A way of thinking so essential that it has its own chapter in this book (Chap. 8), ANALYSIS separates an item into its parts. Say you're listening to a new song by a band you like: Without thinking much about it, you isolate melodies, lyrics, and instrumentals. Critical readers analyze essays more consciously, by looking at an author's main idea, support for that idea, special writing strategies, and other elements. To show you how the beginnings of such an analysis might look, we examine these elements in "Disability" later in this chapter.

Inference

Next you draw conclusions about a work based on your store of information and experience, your knowledge of the creator's background and biases, and your analysis. Say that after listening to the new song, you conclude

> ### CHECKLIST FOR CRITICAL READING
>
> ✔ **Analyze.** Examine the elements of the work, such as thesis, purpose and audience, genre, evidence, structure, and language.
>
> ✔ **Infer.** Interpret the underlying meanings of the elements and the assumptions and intentions of the author.
>
> ✔ **Synthesize.** Form an idea about how the elements function together to produce a whole and to deliver a message.
>
> ✔ **Evaluate.** Judge the quality, significance, or value of the work.

that it reveals the band's interest in the Caribbean soca scene. Now you are using INFERENCE. When you infer, you add to the work, making explicit what was only implicit.

Inference is especially important in discovering a writer's ASSUMPTIONS: opinions or beliefs, often unstated, that direct the writer's ideas, supporting evidence, writing strategies, and language choices. A writer who favors gun control, for instance, may assume without saying so that an individual's rights may be infringed for the good of the community. A writer who opposes gun control might assume the opposite, that an individual's right is superior to the community's good.

Synthesis

During SYNTHESIS, you use your special aptitudes, interests, and training to reconstitute a text so that it now contains not just the original elements but also your sense of their underpinnings, relationships, and implications. What is the band trying to accomplish with its new song? Has the musical style changed? Answering such questions leads you to link elements into a whole or to link two or more wholes.

Synthesis is the core of much academic writing. Sometimes you'll respond directly to a text, or you'll use it as a springboard to another subject. Sometimes you'll show how two or more texts resemble each other or how they differ. Sometimes you'll draw on many texts to answer a question or support an argument. In all these cases, you'll put your reading to use to develop your own ideas.

Evaluation

When you EVALUATE, you determine the adequacy, significance, or value of a work: Is the band getting better or just standing still? In evaluating an essay you answer a question such as whether you are moved as the author intended, whether the author has proved a case, or whether the effort was even worthwhile. Not all critical thinking involves evaluation, however;

often you (and your teachers) will be satisfied with analyzing, inferring, and synthesizing ideas without judging a text's overall merit.

Using this book, you'll learn to think critically about an essay by considering what the author's purpose and main idea are, how clear they are, and how well supported. You'll isolate which writing techniques the author has used to special advantage, what hits you as particularly fresh, clever, or wise — and what *doesn't* work, too. You'll discover exactly what the writer is saying, how he or she says it, and whether, in the end, it was worth saying. In class discussions and in writing, you'll tell others what you think and why.

ANALYZING ESSAYS

To help you in your critical reading, questions after every selection in this book direct your attention to specific elements of the writer's work. Here we introduce the three categories of questions — on meaning, writing strategy, and language — and show how they might be applied to Nancy Mairs's "Disability" (p. 12).

QUESTIONS FOR ANALYZING AN ESSAY

MEANING

✔ **What is the thesis,** or main point? Where is stated?

✔ **What is the writer's purpose?** What does the essay try to acomplish?

WRITING STRATEGY

✔ **Who is the intended audience?** What assumptions does the writer make about readers' knowledge, perspectives, and interests?

✔ **How are supporting details structured?** What methods does the writer use to organize ideas? How does the writer achieve unity and coherence?

✔ **What evidence does the writer provide** to support the main idea? Is it sufficient and compelling?

LANGUAGE

✔ **What is the overall tone of the essay?** Is it appropriate, given the writer's purpose and audience?

✔ **How effective are the writer's words?** Are their meanings clear? What connotations do they hold?

✔ **Does the writer use any figures of speech,** such as metaphor, simile, hyperbole, personification, or irony? How well do they lend meaning and vibrancy to the writer's thoughts?

Meaning

By *meaning*, we're getting at what the words say literally, of course, but also what they imply and, more generally, what the author's aims are. When reading an essay, look especially for the THESIS and try to determine the author's PURPOSE for writing.

- **Thesis.** Every essay has — or should have — a point, a main idea the writer wants to communicate. Many writers come right out and sum up this idea in a sentence or two, a THESIS STATEMENT. They may provide it in the first or second paragraph, give it somewhere in the middle of the essay, or hold it for the end. Mairs, for instance, develops her thesis over the course of the essay and then states it in paragraph 7:

  Achieving this integration [of seeing disability as normal], for disabled and able-bodied people alike, requires that we insert disability daily into our field of vision: quietly, naturally, in the small and common scenes of our ordinary lives.

  Sometimes a writer will not state his or her thesis outright at all, although it remains in the background controlling the work and can be inferred by a critical reader. If you find yourself confused about a writer's point — "What *is* this about?" — it will be up to you to figure out what the author is trying to say.

- **Purpose.** By *purpose*, we mean the writer's apparent reason for writing: what he or she was trying to achieve. In making a simple statement of a writer's purpose, we might say that a person writes *to reflect* on an experience or observation, *to entertain* readers, *to explain* something to them, or *to persuade* them. To state a purpose more fully, we might say that a writer writes not just to persuade, for instance, but to motivate readers to accept a particular idea or take a specific action. In the case of "Disability," it seems that Mairs's purpose is twofold: to explain her view of the media and to convince readers that lack of representation hurts people without disabilities as much as it does people with disabilities.

Writing Strategy

Almost all writing is a *transaction* between a writer and an audience, maybe one reader, maybe millions. To the extent that writers hold our interest, make us think, and convince us to accept a thesis, it pays to ask, "How do they succeed?" (When writers bore or anger us, we ask why they fail.) Conscious writers make choices intended to get readers on their side so that they can achieve their purpose. These choices are what we mean by STRATEGY in writing.

- **Audience.** We can tell much about a writer's intended audience from the context in which the piece was first published. And when we know something of the audience, we can better analyze the writer's decisions, from the choice of supporting details to the use of a particular tone. Mairs's original audience, for instance, was the readers of the *New York Times*, as the introduction to "Disability" on page 12 informs us. She could assume educated readers with diverse interests who are not themselves disabled or even familiar with disability. So she fills them in, taking pains to describe her disability (par. 1) and her life (4). For her thoughtful but somewhat blinkered audience, Mairs mixes a blend of plain talk, humor, and insistence to give them the facts they need, win them over with common humanity, and convey the gravity of the problem.

- **Method.** A crucial part of a writer's strategy is how he or she develops ideas to achieve a particular purpose or purposes. As Chapters 3–12 of this book illustrate, a writer may draw on one or more familiar methods of development to make those ideas concrete and convincing. Mairs, for instance, uses COMPARISON AND CONTRAST to show similarities and differences between herself and nondisabled people (pars. 1, 4, 5). She offers EXAMPLES: of dramas she dislikes (2–3), of products she buys (4), and of ads in which people with disabilities might appear (5). With DESCRIPTION she shows the flavor of her life (4) and the feelings she has experienced (6). And with CAUSE AND EFFECT she explains why disability is ignored by the media (5) and what that does to people with disabilities (6) and those without (7). Overall, Mairs uses these methods to build an ARGUMENT, asserting and defending an opinion.

- **Evidence.** Typically, each method of development benefits from — and lends itself to — different kinds of support. For this EVIDENCE, the writer may use facts, reasons, examples, expert opinions — whatever best delivers the point. (We have more to say about the uses of evidence in the introductions to Chapters 3–12.) Mairs draws on several types of evidence to develop her claims, including personal experiences and emotions (pars. 1, 4, 5), details to support her generalizations (2, 4, 5), and the opinion of an advertiser (5).

- **Structure.** A writer must mold and arrange ideas to capture, hold, and direct readers' interest. Writing that we find clear and convincing almost always has UNITY (everything relates to the main idea) and COHERENCE (the relations between parts are clear). All the parts fit together logi-cally. In "Disability," Mairs first introduces herself and establishes her complaint (pars. 1–5). Then she explains and argues the negative effects of "effacement" on people with disabilities (6) and the positive effects that normalizing disability would have on people who are not presently disabled (7). As often occurs in arguments, Mairs's organization builds to her main idea, her thesis, which readers might find difficult to accept at the outset.

Language

To examine the element of language is to go even more deeply into an essay and how it was made. A writer's tone, voice, and choice of words in particular not only express meaning but also convey the writer's attitudes and elicit those attitudes from readers.

- **Tone.** The TONE of a piece of writing is the equivalent of tone of voice in speaking. Whether it's angry, sarcastic, or sad, joking or serious, tone carries almost as much information about a writer's purpose as the words themselves do. Mairs's tone mixes lightness with gravity, humor with intensity. Sometimes she uses IRONY, saying one thing but meaning another, as in "If you saw my blind niece ordering a Coke, would you switch to Pepsi lest you be struck sightless?" (par. 5). She's blunt, too, revealing intimate details about her life. Honest and wry, Mairs invites us to see the media's exclusion as ridiculous and then leads us to her uncom-fortable conclusion.

- **Word choice.** Tone comes in part from DICTION, a writer's choices regard-ing words and sentence structures — academic, casual, or otherwise. Mairs is a writer whose diction is rich and varied. Expressions from com-mon speech, such as "what I'm looking for" (par. 3), lend her prose vigor and naturalness. At the same time, Mairs is serious about her argument, so she puts it in serious terms, such as "denial of disability imperils even you who are able-bodied" (7). Pay attention also to the CONNOTATIONS of words — their implied meanings and associations. Such subtle nuances can have a profound effect on both a writer's meaning and readers' under-standing of it. In "Disability," the word with the strongest connotations may be "cripple" (2, 5) because it calls up insensitivity: By using this word, Mairs stresses her frankness but also suggests that negative attitudes deter-mine what images the media present.

- **Imagery.** One final use of language is worth noting: those concrete words and phrases that appeal to readers' senses. Such IMAGES might be straightforward, as in Mairs's portrayal of herself as someone who "can still totter short distances with the aid of a brace and a cane" (par. 1). But often writers use FIGURES OF SPEECH, bits of colorful language that capture meaning or attitude better than literal words can. For instance, Mairs says that people "study others and then mold themselves to the contours of those whose images . . . they come to love" (6). That figure of speech is a *metaphor*, stating that one thing (behavioral change) is another (physical change). Elsewhere Mairs uses *simile*, stating that one thing is *like* another ("an illness-of-the-week like the daily special at your local diner," 2), and *understatement* ("physical disability looms pretty large in one's life," 4). More examples of figures of speech appear in the Glossary of Useful Terms, page 675.

Many of the reading questions in this book point to figures of speech, to oddities of tone, to particulars of diction, or to troublesome or unfamiliar words. Writers have few traits more valuable than a fondness for words and a willingness to experiment with them.

EXAMINING VISUAL IMAGES

We often forget that a visual text, just as much as a written work, was created for a reason. No matter what it is — advertisement, infographic, painting, video, photograph, cartoon — an image originated with a person or persons who had a purpose, an intention for how that image should look and how viewers should respond to it.

In their origins, then, visual images are not much different from written texts, and they are no less open to critical thinking that will uncover their meanings and effects. To a great extent, the method for critically "reading" visuals parallels the one for essays outlined earlier in this chapter. In short, as the checklist on the facing page indicates, you start with an overview of the image and then analyze its elements, make inferences, synthesize, and evaluate.

As you do when reading written works, always write while examining a visual image or images. Jotting down responses, questions, and other notes will not only help you remember what you were thinking but also jog further thoughts into being.

To show the critical method in action, we'll look closely at the photograph on page 24. Further examples of visual works appear elsewhere in this book as well: For images that support written works, see pages 151 (a painting),

QUESTIONS FOR EXAMINING AN IMAGE

THE BIG PICTURE

✔ **What is the source of the work?** Who was the intended audience?

✔ **What does the work show overall?** What appears to be happening?

✔ **Why was the work created** — to educate, to sell, to shock, to entertain?

ANALYSIS

✔ **Which elements of the image stand out?** What is distinctive about each?

✔ **What does the composition of the image emphasize?** What is pushed to the background or the sides?

INFERENCE

✔ **What do the elements of the work suggest** about the creator's intentions and assumptions?

✔ **If words accompany the work, what do they say?** How are they sized and placed in relation to the visual elements? How do the written and visual parts interact?

SYNTHESIS

✔ **What general appeal does the work make to viewers?** For instance, does it emphasize logic, emotion, or value?

✔ **What feelings, memories, moods, or ideas does the work summon from viewers' own store of experiences?** Why would its creator try to establish these associations?

EVALUATION

✔ **Does the work fulfill its creator's intentions?** Was it worth creating?

✔ **How does the work affect you?** Are you moved? amused? bored? offended?

243 and 316 (photographs), 410–13 (drawings), 417 (a bar graph), and 501 (a comic). And Chapters 3–12 each open with a visual that gives you a chance to try critical viewing on your own.

Seeing the Big Picture

To examine any visual representation, it helps first to get an overview, a sense of the whole and its context. On such a first glance, consider who created it — for instance, a painter, a teacher, an advertiser — when it was created, and why.

Robin Nelson

The photograph above was taken by photojournalist Robin Nelson near the Watts Bar nuclear power plant in Spring City, Tennessee, for a 2011 photo essay in *Mother Jones*, a magazine known for its progressive outlook. The year before, an earthquake and tsunami had destroyed nuclear reactors in Japan, causing global alarm. Nelson's picture shows a solitary older man fishing from a boat with his hands resting on its steering wheel; the Chicamauga Reservoir and two cooling towers appear in the background. (The tower on the left has operated since 1996; a new reactor for the other tower was under construction at the time of the photograph and was slated to begin operation within a year.)

Taking a Critical Look

After you've gained an overview of an image, you can start making the kinds of deeper inquiry — analysis, inference, synthesis, and evaluation — that serve as the foundation of any critical reading, whatever form the text may take.

Analysis

To analyze a visual work, focus on the elements that contribute to the whole — not just the people, animals, or objects depicted but also artistic elements such as lighting, color, shape, and balance. Notice which elements stand out and what seems to be emphasized. If spoken or written words accompany the work, examine their relation to the visual components as well as what they say.

In Nelson's photograph, the dominant elements are the towers and the man, whose smile suggests contentment. A fishing rod and line occupy the center of the image, visually connecting the man, the towers, and the water. The pole points at the sun in the upper left corner. The sun reflects off the water and puts parts of the man in shadow; the towers are reflected in the water as well. A line of trees runs across the midline of the photo, highlighting the natural environment. The sky is clear, with one cloud floating in the upper right. And in the foreground we see what appear to be a container for bait and a cooler.

Inference

Identifying the elements of a visual leads you to consider what they mean and how the image's creator has selected and arranged them so that viewers will respond in certain ways. You make explicit what may only be implicit in the work — the creator's intentions and assumptions.

We can guess at Robin Nelson's intentions for the photograph. On the one hand, it seems to support nuclear power as harmless: The bright sun, clear sky, sparkling water, and lush trees imply an unspoiled environment, and the man appears unworried about fishing near the plant. On the other hand, Nelson would know that most readers of *Mother Jones* are concerned about the safety of nuclear power and that the cooling towers alone would raise red flags for many; certainly the cloud in the otherwise clear sky and the deep shadow obscuring most of the fisherman hint at danger. The photographer may see these opposites as reflecting the controversy over nuclear power.

Synthesis

Linking the elements and your inferences about them will move you into a new conception of a visual representation: your own conclusions about its overall message and effect.

As we see it, Nelson's photograph represents Americans' mixed feelings about nuclear power. The looming towers, the cloud, and the shadowing seem ominous, suggesting risks facing the area around the plant and the country as a whole. The beauty of the scenery evokes our appreciation of nature; the implied pleasure of fishing evokes our approval as it intensifies our concerns for the man's safety. The juxtaposition of the power plant, the environment, and a single human being seems to represent the intersecting forces of nature and society and the complex implications of nuclear energy for both.

Evaluation

Often in criticizing visual works, you'll take one step beyond synthesis to judge the quality, significance, or value of the work.

Robin Nelson's photograph seems to us masterful in delivering a message. As Nelson seems to have intended, he distills strong, contradictory feelings about nuclear power and environmental protection into a deceptively simple image of a man fishing. Viewers' own biases, positive or negative, will affect their responses to Nelson's image and the meanings they derive from it.

READING TO WRITE

As we said at the start of this chapter, reading and writing are interconnected. Not only will reading the work of other writers help you develop your skills as a communicator, but much of the reading you do will result in writing. You might be prompted to write by an assignment for a class, or you might be moved to respond for your own reasons, perhaps to express your agreement with — or outrage at — an opinion posted online, or simply to work out your thoughts for yourself. Responding to texts in some way — the natural outcome of reading them critically — will occupy much of your academic career.

Building Knowledge

In college you will read and write in many disciplines — history, psychology, chemistry, and so on — each with its own subjects, approaches, and genres for shaping ideas and information. As varied as your readings may be, however, they will all share the goals and requirements of ACADEMIC WRITING: The writers build and exchange knowledge by thinking critically and writing effectively about what they read, see, hear, or do.

For a taste of such academic knowledge building, you can take a look at any of the selections in this book that synthesize information and ideas gleaned from a SOURCE or sources — such as Rachel O'Connor's critical reading of Shirley Jackson's short story "The Lottery" (p. 307), Barbara B. Parsons's evaluation of Brent Staples's essay "Black Men and Public Space" (p. 337), Laila Ayad's examination of a historical photograph (p. 315), Marie Javdani's study of the global effects of the drug trade (p. 403), Malcolm Gladwell's take on why most students are better off not going to Ivy League colleges (p. 422), Chuck Dixon and Paul Rivoche's assessment of the current state of superhero comics (p. 500) and Janelle Asselin's retort (p. 505), Luis Alberto Urrea's response to Henry David Thoreau's *Walden* (p. 596), Margaret Lundberg's environmental argument for vegetarianism (p. 645), or Eric Kim's overview of recent developments in neuroscience (p. 661).

You may notice that regardless of discipline, these essays follow certain conventions of academic writing:

- **Each writer presents a clearly stated thesis** — a debatable idea about a subject — and attempts to gain readers' agreement with it.

- **The writers provide evidence to support the thesis,** drawing on one or more texts, or works that can be examined or interpreted.

- **The writers analyze meaning, infer assumptions, and synthesize texts with their own views.** Academic writers do not merely summarize sources; they grapple with them — in short, they read and write critically.

- **They assume an educated audience** — one that can be counted on to read critically in turn. The writers express their ideas clearly, provide the information readers need to analyze those ideas, and organize points and evidence effectively. Further, they approach their subjects seriously and discuss evidence and opposing views fairly.

- **The essays acknowledge the use of sources,** often using in-text citations and a bibliography in a format appropriate for the discipline.

This book will show you how to achieve your own academic writing by responding directly to what you read (below), integrating evidence ethically and effectively (Chap. 2), and orchestrating — and documenting — multiple sources to develop and support your ideas (Appendix).

Forming a Response

The essay by Rosie Anaya at the end of the next chapter (p. 58) illustrates one genre of academic writing, the critical response: Anaya summarizes Nancy Mairs's essay "Disability" (p. 12), explores its implications, and uses it as a springboard to her own related subject, which she supports with personal observation and experience.

Just as Anaya responds to Mairs's essay, so you can respond to any essay in this book, or for that matter to any text you read, see, or hear. Using evidence from the text, from your own experiences, and sometimes from additional sources, you can take a variety of approaches to writing about what you read:

- **Agree with and extend the author's ideas,** providing additional examples or exploring related ideas.
- **Agree with the author on some points,** but disagree on others.
- **Disagree with the author** on one or more key points.

- **Explain how the author achieves a particular** EFFECT, such as enlisting your sympathy or sparking your anger.
- **Judge the overall effectiveness of the essay** — for instance, how well the writer supports the thesis, whether the argument is convincing, or whether the author succeeds in his or her stated or unstated purpose.

These suggestions assume that you are responding to a single work, but of course you may take on two or even more works at the same time. You might, for instance, use the method of comparison and contrast to show how two stories are alike or different, or find your own way between competing arguments on an issue.

Some works you read will spark an immediate reaction, maybe because you disagree or agree strongly right from the start. Other works may require a more gradual entry into the author's meaning and what you think about it. At the same time, you may have an assignment that narrows the scope of your response — for instance, by asking you to look at tone or some other element of the work or by asking you to agree or disagree with the author's thesis.

Whatever your initial reaction or your assignment, you can use the tools discussed in this chapter to generate and structure your response: summary, analysis, inference, synthesis, and evaluation. As you work out a response, you'll certainly need to make notes of some sort: For instance, Rosie Anaya's annotations on Mairs's essay on pages 12–15 include questions raised while reading, highlights of key quotations, summaries of Mairs's ideas, interpretations of their meanings, and the beginnings of Anaya's ideas in response. Such notes may grow increasingly focused as you refine your response and return to the work to interpret it further and gather additional passages to discuss.

Knowledge builds as you bring your own perspectives to bear on what others have written, making your own contributions to what has come before. By reading carefully and writing thoughtfully in response, you're well on your way to becoming an academic writer yourself.

2

THE WRITING PROCESS

The CRITICAL THINKING discussed in the previous chapter will serve you in just about every role you'll play in life — consumer, voter, friend, parent. As a student and a worker, though, you'll find critical thinking especially important as the foundation for writing. Whether to demonstrate your competence or to contribute to discussions and projects, writing will be the main way you communicate with teachers, supervisors, and peers.

Writing is no snap: As this book's Writers on Writing attest, not even professionals can produce thoughtful, detailed, attention-getting prose in a single draft. Writing well demands, and rewards, a willingness to work recursively — to begin tentatively and then to double back, to welcome change and endure frustration, to recognize progress and move forward.

This recursive writing process is not really a single process at all, not even for an individual writer. Some people work out meticulous plans ahead of time; others prefer to just start writing; still others will work one way for one project and a different way for another. Generally, though, writers do move through distinct stages between initial idea and finished work: discovery, drafting, revising, and editing.

In examining these stages, we'll have the help of a student, Rosie Anaya, who wrote an essay for this book responding to Nancy Mairs's essay "Disability." Along with the finished essay (pp. 58–60), Anaya also shares her notes and multiple drafts.

ASSESSING THE WRITING SITUATION

Any writing you do will occur in a specific situation. What are you writing about? Whom are you writing for? Why are you writing about this subject to these people? What will they expect of you? Subject, audience, and purpose are the main components of the writing situation, discussed in detail in this section. We also touch on another component, genre (or type of writing), which relates to audience and purpose.

Subject

The SUBJECT of a work is what it is about, or the general topic. Your subject may be specified or at least suggested in an assignment. "Discuss one of the works we've read this semester in its historical and social context," reads a literature assignment; "Can you draw up a proposal for holiday staffing?" asks your boss. If you're left to your own devices and nothing occurs to you, try the discovery techniques explained on pages 32–34 to find a topic that interests you.

In this book we provide ideas that will also give you practice in working with assignments. After each reading selection, a variety of writing prompts suggest possible subjects; more writing topics conclude each chapter. You may not wish to take any of our suggestions exactly as worded; they may merely inspire your own thoughts — and thus what you want to say.

Audience

We looked at AUDIENCE in the previous chapter as a way of understanding the decisions other writers make. When *you* are doing the writing, considering audience moves from informative to necessary.

You can conceive of your audience generally — for instance, your classmates, subscribers to a particular newspaper or blog, members of the city council. Usually, though, you'll want to think about the characteristics of readers that will affect how they respond to you:

- **Who will read your work?** What in the makeup of readers will influence their responses? How old are they? Are they educated? Do they share your values? Are they likely to have some misconceptions about your subject?

- **What do readers need to know?** To get them to understand you or agree with you, how much background should you provide? How thoroughly must you support your ideas? What kinds of evidence will be most effective?

Knowing whom you're addressing and why tells you what approach to take, what EVIDENCE to gather, how to arrange ideas, even what words to use. Imagine, for instance, that you are writing two reviews of a new movie, one for students who read the campus newspaper, the other for amateur and professional filmmakers who read the trade journal *Millimeter*. For the first audience, you might write about the actors, the plot, and especially dramatic scenes. You might judge the film and urge your readers to see it — or to avoid it. Writing for *Millimeter*, you might discuss special effects, shooting techniques, problems in editing and in mixing picture and sound. In this review, you might use more specialized and technical terms. An awareness of the interests and knowledge of your readers, in each case, would help you decide how to write.

Purpose

While you are considering readers' backgrounds and inclinations, you'll also be refining your PURPOSE. As we discussed earlier (p. 19), writers generally write with one of four broad goals in mind:

- **To reflect** on an experience, an observation, or an idea. Reflective writing is most common in personal journals or diaries, but writers often mull over their thoughts for others to read, especially in essays that draw on NARRATION or DESCRIPTION.

- **To entertain** others, perhaps by relating a thrilling event or by poking fun at a subject. Fiction is often meant to entertain, of course, but so are Web comics, many popular blogs, celebrity gossip magazines, and several of the selections in this book.

- **To explain** something, typically by sharing information gleaned from experience or investigation. Such is the case with most newspapers and textbooks, for instance, as well as science and business reports, research papers, or biographies.

- **To persuade** members of an audience to accept an idea or take a particular action. Almost all writing offers an ARGUMENT of some sort, whether explicitly or implicitly. Opinion pieces and proposals are the most obvious examples; most academic writing seeks to convince readers of the validity of a THESIS, or debatable assertion, as well.

You may know your basic purpose for writing early on — whether you want to explain something about your subject or argue something about it, for instance. To be most helpful, though, your idea of purpose should include what you want readers to think or do as a result of reading your writing, as in the following examples:

> To explain two therapies for autism in young children so that parents and educators can weigh the options
>
> To defend term limits for state legislators so that voters who are undecided on the issue will support limits
>
> To analyze Shakespeare's *Macbeth* so that theatergoers see the strengths as well as the flaws of the title character
>
> To propose an online system for scheduling work shifts so that company managers decide to implement it

We have more to say about purpose in the introductions to the rhetorical methods (Chaps. 3–12). Each method, such as EXAMPLE and CAUSE AND EFFECT, offers useful tools for achieving your purposes in writing.

Genre

Closely tied to audience and purpose is the type of writing, the GENRE, that you will use to shape your ideas. Your assignment might specify the genre: Have you been asked to write a personal narrative? a critical analysis? an argumentative response? These and other genres have distinctive features — such as organization, kinds of evidence, and even TONE — that readers expect.

You will find many examples of different genres in this book. In a sense each method of development (CLASSIFICATION, DEFINITION, and so on) is itself a genre, and its conventions and strategies are covered in the chapter devoted to it (Chaps. 3–12). Each chapter introduction also shows the method at work in a specific academic genre, such as a field observation or a review. And the book's selections illustrate a range of genres, from personal reflection and memoir to objective reporting and critical evaluation. The best way to learn about genres and readers' expectations is to read widely and attentively.

DISCOVERING IDEAS

During the initial phase of the writing process, you'll feel your way into an assignment. This DISCOVERY period is the time when you critically examine any TEXT that is part of the assignment and begin to generate ideas. When writing about selections in this book, you'll be reading and rereading and writing, coming to understand the work, figuring out what you think of it, figuring out what you have to *say* about it.

From marginal notes to jotted phrases, lists, or half-finished paragraphs of response, the discovery stage should always be a writing stage. You may even produce a rough draft. The important thing is to let yourself go: Do not, above all, concern yourself with making beautiful sentences or correcting errors. Such self-consciousness at this stage will only jam the flow of thoughts. Several techniques can help you open up, among them writing in a journal, freewriting, and exploring the methods of development.

Keeping a Journal

A JOURNAL is a record of your thoughts *for yourself*. You can keep a journal on paper or on a computer or mobile device. When you write in it, you don't have to worry about being understood by a reader or making mistakes: You are free to get your thoughts down however you want.

Kept faithfully — say, for ten or fifteen minutes a day — a journal can limber up your writing muscles, giving you more confidence and flexibility. It can also provide a place to work out personal difficulties, explore half-formed ideas, make connections between courses, or respond to reading. (For examples of one student's journal notes, see p. 53.)

Freewriting

Another technique for limbering up, usually in response to a specific writing assignment rather than as a regular habit, is *freewriting*. When freewriting, you write without stopping for ten or fifteen minutes, not halting to reread, criticize, edit, or admire. You can use partial sentences, abbreviations, question marks for uncertain words. If you can't think of anything to write about, jot "can't think" over and over until new words come. (They will.)

You can use this technique to find a subject for writing or to explore ideas on a subject you already have. When you've finished, you can separate the promising passages from the dead ends, and then use those promising bits as the starting place for more freewriting or perhaps a freely written first draft.

Exploring the Methods of Development

In Part Two of this book each of the ten chapters explains a familiar method of developing ideas. In the discovery stage, approaching your subject with these methods in mind can reveal its potential:

- **Narration.** Tell a story about the subject, possibly to enlighten or entertain readers or to explain something to them. Answer the journalist's questions: who, what, when, where, why, how?
- **Description.** Explain or evoke the subject by focusing on its look, sound, feel, smell, taste — the evidence of the senses.

- **Example.** Point to instances, or illustrations, of the subject that clarify and support your idea about it.
- **Comparison and contrast.** Set the subject beside something else, noting similarities or differences or both, for the purpose of either explaining or evaluating.
- **Process analysis.** Explain step by step how to do something or how something works — in other words, how a sequence of actions leads to a particular result.
- **Division or analysis.** Slice the subject into its parts or elements in order to show how they relate and to explain your conclusions about the subject.
- **Classification.** Show resemblances and differences among many related subjects, or the many forms of a subject, by sorting them into kinds or groups.
- **Cause and effect.** Explain why or what if, showing reasons for or consequences of the subject.
- **Definition.** Trace a boundary around the subject to pin down its meaning.
- **Argument and persuasion.** Formulate an opinion or make a proposal about the subject.

You can use the methods of development singly or together to find direction, ideas, and supporting details. Say you already have a sense of your purpose for writing: Then you can search the methods for one or more that will help you achieve that purpose by revealing and focusing your ideas. Or say you're still in the dark about your purpose: Then you can apply each method of development systematically to throw light on your subject, helping you see it from many possible angles.

DRAFTING

Sooner or later, the discovery stage yields to DRAFTING: writing out sentences and paragraphs, linking thoughts, focusing them. For most writers, drafting is the occasion for exploring ideas, filling in the details to support them, beginning to work out the shape and aim of the whole. A few suggestions for drafting:

- **Give yourself time,** at least a couple of hours.
- **Find a quiet place to work,** somewhere you won't be disturbed.
- **Stay loose** so that you can wander down intriguing avenues or consider changing direction altogether.
- **Keep your eyes on what's ahead,** not on possible errors, "wrong" words, or bumpy sentences. This is an important message that many inexperienced writers miss: It's okay to make mistakes. You can fix them later.

Expect to draft in fits and starts, working in chunks and fleshing out points as you go. And don't feel compelled to follow a straight path from beginning to end. If the opening paragraph is giving you trouble, skip it until later. In fact, most writers find that drafting is easier and more productive if they work on the body of the essay first, leaving the introduction and conclusion until everything else has been worked out.

Focusing on a Thesis

Your essay will need to center on a THESIS, a core idea to which everything else relates. When you write with a clear-cut thesis in mind, you head toward a goal. Without the focus of a thesis, an essay wanders and irritates and falls flat. With a focus, a draft is much more likely to click.

You may start a project with a thesis already in mind, or your idea might take shape as you proceed through the writing process. Sometimes you may have to write one or more drafts to know exactly what your point is. But early on, try to express your main idea in a sentence or two, called a THESIS STATE-MENT, like these from essays in this book:

> That first encounter, and those that followed, signified that a vast, unnerv-ing gulf lay between nighttime pedestrians — particularly women — and me.
> — Brent Staples, "Black Men and Public Space"

> Inanimate objects are classified into three major categories — those that don't work, those that break down and those that get lost.
> — Russell Baker, "The Plot against People"

> A bill [to prohibit import of goods produced with children's labor] is of no use unless it goes hand in hand with programs that will offer a new life to these newly released children.
> — Chitra Divakaruni, "Live Free and Starve"

As these diverse examples reveal, a thesis shapes an essay. It gives the writer a clearly defined aim, focusing otherwise scattered thoughts and providing a center around which the details and supporting points can gather.

An effective thesis statement, like the ones above, has a few important qualities:

- **It asserts an opinion, taking a position on the subject.** A good thesis state-ment moves beyond facts or vague generalities, as in "That first encounter was troubling" or "This bill is a bad idea."
- **It projects a single, focused idea.** A thesis statement may have parts (such as Baker's three categories of objects), but those parts should all relate to a single, central point.

- **It accurately forecasts the scope of the essay,** neither taking on too much nor leaving out essential parts.
- **It hints at the writer's purpose.** From their thesis statements, we can tell that Staples and Baker mean to explain, whereas Divakaruni intends mainly to persuade.

Every single essay in this book has a thesis because a central, controlling idea is a requirement of good writing. As you will see, writers have great flexibility in presenting a thesis statement — how long it might be, where it appears, even whether it appears. For your own writing, we advise stating your thesis explicitly and putting it near the beginning of your essay — at least until you've gained experience as a writer. The stated thesis will help you check that you have the necessary focus, and the early placement will tell your readers what to expect from your writing. We offer additional suggestions for focusing your thesis and crafting your thesis statement, with examples, later in this chapter (pp. 40–41) and in each of the introductions to the methods of development (Chaps. 3–12).

Supporting the Thesis

The BODY of an essay consists of the subpoints and supporting evidence that develop the main idea. In some way, each sentence and paragraph should serve to support your thesis by making it clear and explicit to readers. You will likely need to experiment and explore your thoughts before they fully take shape, tackling your essay in multiple drafts and filling in (or taking out) details as you go, adjusting your thesis to fit your ideas. Most writers do.

Developing Ideas

You may have gotten a start at expressing your thoughts in the discovery stage, in which case you can build on what you've already written in your journal or during freewriting sessions. Or you may find yourself staring at a blank screen. In either case, it's usually best to focus first on the parts you're most comfortable with, keeping your thesis, your purpose, and your audience in mind.

Earlier we saw that the methods of development can help you discover ideas about a subject (see pp. 33–34). They can also help you find, present, and structure evidence as you draft. Suppose, for example, that you set out to explain what makes a certain singer unique. You want to discuss her voice, her music, her lyrics, her style. While putting your ideas down, it strikes you that you can best illustrate the singer's distinctions by showing the differences between her and another singer. To achieve your purpose, then, you draw on the method of COMPARISON AND CONTRAST; and as you proceed, the method prompts you to notice differences you had missed.

Each method typically benefits from — and lends itself to — a particular kind of support. Narration and description might draw on personal experience, for instance, while a CAUSE-AND-EFFECT or PROCESS ANALYSIS may require objective information such as verifiable facts. Give the methods a try. See how flexible they are, coming into play as you need them to develop parts of your essay.

Organizing the Evidence

How you ORGANIZE your evidence depends on your purpose and your audience: What is your aim? What do you want readers to think or feel? What's the best way to achieve that? For instance, anyone writing a proposal to solve a problem wants to cover all the reasonable solutions and make a case for one or more. But one writer might bring readers gradually to her favored solution by first discussing and rejecting the alternatives, while another might grab readers' attention by focusing right away on his own solution, dispensing with alternatives only near the end. In either case, the choices aren't random but depend on the writer's understanding of readers — their assumptions, their biases, and their purposes for reading.

Some methods of development lend themselves to familiar patterns of organization, which we discuss in the introductions to Chapters 3–12. In a narrative essay or a process analysis, for instance, you would probably put events in CHRONOLOGICAL ORDER. Other methods require that you put more thought into how you arrange your points. In an essay developed by example, you might use a CLIMACTIC ORDER, starting with the weakest point and ending with the most compelling one (or vice versa). And a descriptive essay might take a SPATIAL ORDER, following details the way an eye might scan a scene: left to right, near to far, and so forth.

Some writers like to plan the order of their points in advance, perhaps with a rough outline or simply a list of points to cover. If concerns about the organization leave you feeling stuck or frustrated, however, focus instead on getting your ideas into sentences and paragraphs; you can rearrange things in revision.

Shaping the Introduction and Conclusion

The opening and closing paragraphs of an essay serve as bookends for the thoughts and information presented in the body. The INTRODUCTION identifies and narrows the subject for readers, capturing their interest and giving them a reason to continue reading. The CONCLUSION creates a sense of completion, bringing readers back to the main idea and satisfying them that you have accomplished what you set out to do as a writer.

Because of the importance of these paragraphs, and because it is difficult to set up and close out material that has not yet been drafted, most writers find that it works best to turn to the introduction and conclusion *after* the rest of the essay has begun to take shape.

The Introduction

The opening paragraph or paragraphs of an essay invite readers in. At a minimum, your introduction will state the subject and lead to your main idea, often presented in a thesis statement. But an effective introduction also grabs readers' attention and inspires them to read on.

Introductions vary in length, depending on their purpose. A research paper may need several paragraphs to set forth its central idea and its plan of organization; a brief, informal essay may need only a sentence or two for an introduction. Whether long or short, a good introduction tells readers no more than they need to know when they begin reading.

Here are a few possible ways to open an essay effectively:

- **Present startling facts** about your subject.
- **Tell an** ANECDOTE, a brief story that illustrates your subject.
- **Give background information** so that readers will understand your subject or see why it is important.
- **Begin with an arresting quotation** that sets up your subject or previews your main idea.
- **Ask a challenging question.** (In your essay, you'll go on to answer it.)

Whatever technique you try, strive to make a good first impression and establish a positive, engaging tone, taking care to match the voice in the body of your essay. Avoid beginning with a hedge such as *It seems important to understand why* . . . ; and stay away from mechanical phrasing such as *In this essay, I will explain* . . . or *The purpose of this paper is to show.* . . . Such openings bore readers and give them little incentive to read on.

The Conclusion

A conclusion is purposefully crafted to give a sense of unity to the whole essay. The best conclusions evolve naturally out of what has gone before and convince readers that the essay is indeed at an end, not that the writer has run out of steam.

Conclusions vary in type and length depending on the nature and scope of the essay. A long research paper may require several paragraphs of summary to review and emphasize the main points. A short essay, however, may benefit from a few brief closing sentences.

Although there are no set formulas for closing, consider these options:

- **Restate the thesis of your essay,** and possibly summarize your main points.
- **Mention the broader implications** or significance of your topic.
- **Give a final example,** pulling all the parts of your discussion together.
- **Offer a prediction** for the future.
- **End with the most important point,** or the culmination of your essay's development.
- **Suggest how readers can apply the information you have provided** in their own lives or work.
- **End with a bit of drama or flourish.** Tell an anecdote, offer an appropriate quotation, ask a question, make a final insightful remark, circle back to the introduction. Keep in mind, however, that an ending shouldn't sound false and gimmicky. It truly has to conclude.

In concluding an essay, beware of diminishing the impact of your writing by finishing on a weak note. Resist the urge to apologize for what you have or have not written, or to cram in a final detail that would have been better placed elsewhere.

REVISING

If it helps to get you writing, you may want to view a draft as a kind of dialog with readers, fulfilling their expectations, answering the questions you imagine they would ask. But some writers save this kind of thinking for the next stage, REVISION. Literally "re-seeing," revision involves stepping outside the intense circle of you-and-the-material to see the work as a reader will, with whatever qualities you imagine that reader to have.

The first task of revising is to step back and view your draft as a whole, looking at the big picture and ignoring details like grammar and spelling. Let a draft sit for a while before you come back to revise it: at least a few hours, ideally a day or more. When you return with fresh eyes and a refreshed mind, you'll be in a better position to see what works, what doesn't, and what needs your attention. The checklist on the next page and the ensuing discussion can guide you to the big-picture view. Specific revision guidelines for each method of development appear in the introductions to Chapters 3–12.

> ### QUESTIONS FOR REVISION
>
> ✔ **Will my purpose be clear to readers?** Have I achieved it?
>
> ✔ **What are readers' expectations for this kind of writing?** Have I met them?
>
> ✔ **What is my thesis?** Have I supported it for readers? Is my thesis statement clear and to the point?
>
> ✔ **Is the essay unified?** Can readers see how all parts relate to the thesis?
>
> ✔ **Have I developed my points well?** Have I supplied enough details, examples, and other specifics so that readers can understand me and follow my reasoning?
>
> ✔ **Is the essay coherent?** Can readers see how the parts relate?
>
> ✔ **Is the organization clear?** Can readers follow it?

Purpose and Genre

Earlier we looked at purpose and genre as important considerations in planning an essay. They are even more important in revision. Like many writers, in the discovery and experimentation of drafting you may lose track of your original direction. Did you set out to write a critical analysis of a reading but end up with a summary? Did you rely on personal experience when you were supposed to integrate evidence from sources? Did you set out to persuade readers but not get beyond explanation? That's okay. You've jumped the first hurdle simply by putting your thoughts into words. Now you can add, delete, and reorganize until your purpose will be clear to readers and you meet their expectations for how it should be fulfilled.

Thesis

As you've developed your ideas and your draft, you've also been developing your thesis, the main idea that you want to get across to readers. The thesis may be stated up front or hover in the background, but it should be clear to readers and the rest of the essay should support it. Almost always, you will need to revise your thesis as your ideas take form and your purpose for writing becomes clear to you. You may find that you need to adjust your thesis to reflect what you ended up writing in your draft, or you may need to rework your supporting ideas so that they adequately develop your thesis.

Pay attention, too, to your thesis statement itself. Few writers craft a perfect statement on the first try. In each of the following pairs, for example, the draft statement is too vague to work as a hook: It conveys the writer's general opinion but not its basis. Each revised statement clarifies the point.

DRAFT   The sculpture is a beautiful piece of work.

REVISED   Although it may not be obvious at first, this smooth bronze sculpture unites urban and natural elements to represent the city dweller's relationship with nature.

DRAFT   The sculpture is a waste of money.

REVISED   The huge bronze sculpture in the middle of McBean Park demonstrates that so-called public art may actually undermine the public interest.

When you revise, make a point of checking your thesis and your thesis statement against the guidelines listed earlier in this chapter (pp. 35–36) and discussed in the introduction to every method chapter in Part Two. You want to ensure that your thesis takes an arguable position on your subject, that it focuses on a single idea, that it reflects the actual content of your essay, and that it gives a sense of your purpose for writing.

Unity

Drafting freely, as you should, can easily take you into some of the byways of your topic. A goal of revision, then, is to deal with digressions so that your essay has UNITY, with every paragraph relating to the thesis and every sentence in a paragraph relating to a single idea, often expressed in a TOPIC SENTENCE. You may choose to cut a digression altogether or to rework it so that it connects to the main idea. Sometimes you may find that a digression is really what you want to write about and then opt to recast your thesis instead. For more help, see "Focus on Paragraph and Essay Unity" on page 442.

Development

While some points in your draft may have to be sacrificed for the sake of unity, others will probably want more attention. Be sure that any general statements you make are backed up with evidence: details, examples, analysis, information from sources, whatever it takes to show readers that your point is valid. The introductions to the methods in Chapters 3–12 offer suggestions for developing specific kinds of essays; take a look, too, at "Focus on Paragraph Development" on page 349.

Coherence

Drafting ideas into sentences can be halting work, and a first draft can seem jumbled as a result. In revision, you want to help readers follow your thoughts by improving COHERENCE: the clear flow and relation of parts.

You can achieve coherence through your use of paragraphs, transitions, and organization.

PARAGRAPHS help readers grasp related information in an essay by developing one supporting point at a time: All of the sentences hang together, defining, explaining, illustrating, or supporting one central idea. Check all your paragraphs to be sure that each sentence connects with the one preceding and that readers will see the connection without having to stop and reread. One way to clarify such connections is with TRANSITIONS: linking words and phrases such as *in addition*, *moreover*, and *at the same time*. (We have more to say about transitions in "Focus on Paragraph Coherence" on p. 305.)

Be sure, too, that each paragraph follows logically from those before it and leads clearly to those that follow, and that any material from your reading and other sources is integrated logically and smoothly (see the next section). Constructing an outline of what you've written can help you see how well your thoughts hold together. Expect to experiment, moving paragraphs around, deleting some and adding others, before everything clicks into place.

INTEGRATING READING

Writing about what you have read will occupy you for much of your college career, as you rely on books, periodical articles, interviews, Web sites, and other materials to establish and extend your own contributions to academic conversations. The selections in this book, for instance, can serve as sources for your writing: You might analyze them, respond to them, or use them to support your own ideas. Such SYNTHESIS, as we note in Chapter 1, is the core of academic writing. Much of your synthesis of others' work will come as you present evidence from your reading and integrate that evidence into your own text. An important goal of revision, then, is to ensure that you have used such materials honestly and effectively.

Exercising Caution

When you write with sources, your readers expect you to distinguish your own contributions from those of others, honestly acknowledging material that originated elsewhere. To do otherwise — to deliberately or accidentally copy another's idea, data, or wording without acknowledgment — is considered stealing. Called PLAGIARISM, this theft is a serious offense.

Plagiarism is often a result of careless note taking or drafting. The simplest way to avoid problems is always to acknowledge your sources, clearly marking the boundaries between your ideas and those picked up from other writers. Integrate source materials carefully, following the suggestions provided on the following pages. And cite your sources in an appropriate documentation style, such as MLA for English or APA for the social sciences. (See the Appendix for detailed guidelines and documentation models.)

Summarizing, Paraphrasing, and Quoting

As you revise, make sure you have used the ideas and information in sources to support your own ideas, not to direct or overwhelm them. Depending on the importance and complexity of source material, you might summarize it, paraphrase it, or quote it directly. *All summaries, paraphrases, and quotations must be acknowledged in source citations.*

Summary

In a SUMMARY you use your own words to condense a paragraph, an entire article, or even a book into a few lines that convey the source's essential meaning. We discussed summarizing as a reading technique on pages 15–16, and the advice and examples there apply here as well. When responding to a text, you might use a brief summary to catch readers up on the gist of the author's argument or a significant point in the argument. Here, for example, is a summary of Anna Quindlen's "Homeless," which appears on pages 184–86:

> SUMMARY   Quindlen argues that reducing homeless people to the abstract issue of homelessness can obscure the fundamental problem of the homeless individual: He or she needs a home (184–86).

Notice that a summary identifies the source's author and page numbers and uses words that are *not* the author's. A summary that picks up any of the author's distinctive language or neglects to acknowledge that the idea is borrowed from a source counts as plagiarism and must be rewritten. In an early draft of "Mental Illness on Television" (p. 58), for instance, Rosie Anaya inadvertently plagiarized this passage from Nancy Mairs's "Disability":

> ORIGINAL QUOTATION   "But this [media] denial of disability imperils even you who are able-bodied, and not just by shrinking your insight into the physically and emotionally complex world you live in. Some disabled people call you TAPs, or Temporarily Abled Persons. The fact is that ours is the only minority you can join involuntarily, without warning, at any time. . . . The transition will probably be difficult from a physical point of view no matter what. But it will be a good bit easier psychologically if you are accustomed to seeing disability as a normal characteristic, one that complicates but does not ruin human existence."

> PLAGIARISM   Media misrepresentation of disability hurts not only viewers with disabilities but also Temporarily Abled Persons.

In forgetting to name Mairs as the source and in using the phrase "Temporarily Abled Persons" without quotation marks, Anaya stole Mairs's idea. Here is her revision:

> ACCEPTABLE SUMMARY   Mairs argues that media misrepresentation of disability hurts not only viewers with disabilities but also "Temporarily Abled Persons," or those without disabilities (13–15).

Paraphrase

When you PARAPHRASE, you restate a specific passage in your own words. Paraphrase adheres more closely than summary to the source author's line of thought, so it's useful for presenting an author's ideas or data in detail. Generally, use paraphrase rather than quotation for this purpose, since paraphrase shows that you're in command of your evidence and lets your own voice come through. Here is a quotation from Quindlen's essay and a paraphrase of it:

> ORIGINAL QUOTATION   "Homes have stopped being homes. Now they are real estate."

> PARAPHRASE   Quindlen points out that people's dwellings seem to have lost their emotional hold and to have become just investments (185).

As with a summary, note that a paraphrase cites the original author and page number. And like a summary, a paraphrase must express the original idea in an entirely new way, both in word choice and in sentence structure. The following attempt to paraphrase a line from an essay by David Cole slips into plagiarism through sloppiness:

> ORIGINAL QUOTATION   "We stand to be collectively judged by our treatment of immigrants, who may appear to be 'other' now but in a generation will be 'us.'"

> PLAGIARISM   Cole argues that we will be judged as a group by how we treat immigrants, who seem to be different now but eventually will be the same as us (110).

Even though the writer identifies Cole as the source and provides a page number, much of the language and the sentence structure are also Cole's. It's not enough to change a few words — such as "collectively" to "as a group," "they may appear to be 'other'" to "they may seem different," and "in a generation" to "eventually." In contrast, this acceptable paraphrase restates Cole's point in completely new language *and* a new sentence structure:

> ACCEPTABLE PARAPHRASE   Cole argues that the way the United States deals with immigrants now will come back to haunt it when those immigrants eventually become part of mainstream society (110).

Quotation

Quotations from sources can both support and enliven your own ideas — *if* you choose them well. When analyzing a source such as an essay in this book, you may need to quote some passages in order to give the flavor of the author's words and evidence for your analysis. Too many quotations, however, will clutter your essay and detract from your voice. Select quotations that are relevant to the point you are making, that are concise and pithy, and that use lively, bold, or original language. Sentences that lack distinction — for example, a statement providing statistics on immigration rates — should be paraphrased.

Always enclose quotations in quotation marks and cite the source author and page number. For a blatant example of plagiarism, look at the following use of a quotation from Anna Quindlen's "Homeless":

ORIGINAL QUOTATION   "It has been customary to take people's pain and lessen our own participation in it by turning it into an issue, not a collection of human beings."

PLAGIARISM   As a society we tend to lessen our participation in other people's pain by turning it into an issue.

By not acknowledging Quindlen at all, the writer takes claim for her idea and for much of her wording. A source citation would help — at least the idea would be credited — but still the expression of the idea would be stolen because there's no indication that the language is Quindlen's. Here is a revision with citation and quotation marks:

ACCEPTABLE QUOTATION   Quindlen suggests that our tendency "to take people's pain and lessen our own participation in it by turning it into an issue" dehumanizes homeless people (186).

You may adapt quotations to fit your sentences, provided you make clear how you've changed them. If you omit something from a quoted passage, signal the omission with the three spaced periods of an ellipsis mark as shown:

In Quindlen's view, "the thing that seems most wrong with the world . . . right now is that there are so many people with no homes" (185).

If you need to insert words or phrases into a quotation to clarify the author's meaning or make the quotation flow with your own language, show that the insertion is yours by enclosing it in brackets:

Quindlen points out that "we work around [the problem], just as we walk around" the homeless people we encounter (186).

Synthesizing Ideas

When you write about a text, your perspective on it will be your thesis — the main point you have in response to the text or as a result of examining it. As you develop and revise your essay, keep your ideas front and center, pulling in material from the text as needed for support. In each paragraph, your idea should come first and, usually, last: State the idea, use evidence from the reading to support it, and then interpret the evidence.

You can see a paragraph structured like this in Rosie Anaya's essay "Mental Illness on Television" at the end of this chapter:

SYNTHESIS

However, in depicting one type of disability, the media are, if anything, worse than they were three decades ago. Mairs doesn't address mental illness, but it falls squarely into the misrepresentation she criticizes. It has never been shown, in Mairs's words, "as a normal characteristic, one that complicates but does not ruin human existence" (15). Thus people who cope with a psychological disability such as depression, bipolar disorder, or obsessive-compulsive disorder as part of their lives do not see themselves in the media. And those who don't have a psychological disability now but may someday do not see that mental illness is usually a condition one can live with.

> Anaya's idea

> Evidence from Mairs's text

> Anaya's interpretation of Mairs's idea

Understand that synthesis is more than summary, which just distills what the text says or shows. Summary has its uses, especially in understanding a writer's ideas (p. 15) and in presenting evidence from source material (p. 43), but it should not substitute for your own ideas. Contrast the preceding paragraph from Anaya's essay with the following early draft passage in which Anaya uses summary to present evidence:

SUMMARY

Mairs argues that media misrepresentation of disability hurts not only viewers with disabilities but also those without disabilities (14). The media either ignore disability altogether or present it as the defining characteristic of a person's life (13–14). In doing so, they deny "Temporarily Abled Persons" the opportunity to see disability as something common that may be difficult to adjust to but does not destroy one's life (14–15).

> Mairs's idea

> Mairs's idea

> Mairs's idea

With synthesis, you're always making it clear to readers what *your* idea is and how the evidence from your reading supports that idea. To achieve this clarity, you want to fit evidence from other texts into your sentences and show what you make of it. In this passage, the writer drops a quotation awkwardly into her paragraph and doesn't clarify how it relates to her idea:

NOT INTEGRATED   Homelessness affects real people. "[W]e work around it, just as we walk around it when it is lying on the sidewalk or sitting in the bus terminal — the problem, that is" (Quindlen 186).

In the revision below, the writer uses "but" and the SIGNAL PHRASE "as Quindlen points out" to link the quotation to the writer's idea and to identify the source author:

INTEGRATED   Homelessness affects real people, but, as Quindlen points out, "we work around it, just as we walk around it when it is lying on the sidewalk or sitting in the bus terminal — the problem, that is" (186).

A final note: Whether you are synthesizing information and ideas from one text or several, remember that all source material must be acknowledged with in-text citations and a list of works cited or references at the end of your paper. The Appendix at the back of this book (pp. 623–67) provides detailed guidelines and ample models for both the MLA and APA styles of documenting sources.

EDITING

You will find that you produce better work when you approach revision as at least a two-step process. First revise, focusing on fundamental, whole-essay matters such as purpose, organization, and synthesis. Only then turn to EDITING, focusing on surface issues such as grammar and word choice to improve the flow of your writing and to fix the mistakes that tend to get in the way of readers' understanding.

The checklist below covers the most common opportunities and problems, which are explained on the pages following. Because some challenges tend to pop up more often when writing with a particular method, you'll find additional help in the introductions to Chapters 3–12, in boxes labeled "Focus on . . ." that highlight specific issues and provide tips for solving them.

QUESTIONS FOR EDITING

✔ **Are my language and tone appropriate** for my purpose, audience, and genre?

✔ **Do my words say what I mean,** and are they as vivid as I can make them?

✔ **Are my sentences smooth and concise?** Do they use emphasis, parallelism, variety, and other techniques to clarify meaning and hold readers' interest?

✔ **Are my sentences grammatically sound?** In particular, have I avoided sentence fragments, run-on sentences, comma splices, mismatched subjects and verbs, unclear pronouns, unclear modifiers, and inconsistencies?

✔ **Are any words misspelled?**

Effective Language

Many of us, when we draft, fall back on the familiar language we use when chatting with friends: We might rely on COLLOQUIAL EXPRESSIONS such as *get into* and *freak out* or slip into texting shortcuts such as *u* for "you" and *idk* for "I don't know." This strategy can help us to put ideas together without getting sidetracked by details. But patterns of casual communication are usually too imprecise for college writing, where word choices can dramatically affect how readers understand your ideas.

As a critical reader, you take note of writers' language and consider how their choices affect the meaning and impact of their work (see pp. 21–22). As a writer, you should devote similar attention to your own choices, adapting your general language and your specific words to reflect your purpose, your meaning, and your audience.

A few guidelines:

- **Adopt a relatively formal voice.** Replace overly casual or emotional language with standard English DICTION and a neutral TONE. (Refer to pp. 672 and 681 of the Glossary and to "Focus on Tone" on p. 490.)

- **Choose an appropriate point of view.** In most academic writing, you should prefer the more objective third PERSON (*he, she, it, they*) over the first person (*I*) or the second person (*you*). There are exceptions, of course: A personal narrative written without *I* would ring strange to most ears, and a how-to process analysis often addresses readers as *you*.

- **Check that words have the meanings you intend.** The DENOTATION of a word is its dictionary meaning — for example, *affection* means "caring regard." A CONNOTATION, in contrast, is an emotional association that a word produces in readers, as *passion* evokes intensity or *obsession* evokes compulsion. Using a word with the wrong denotation muddies meaning, while using words with strong connotations can shape readers' responses to your ideas — for good or for ill.

- **Use concrete and specific words.** Effective writing balances ABSTRACT and GENERAL words, which provide outlines of ideas and things, with CONCRETE and SPECIFIC words, which limit and sharpen. You need abstract and general words such as *old* and *transportation* for broad statements that convey concepts or refer to entire groups. But you also need concrete and specific words such as *crumbling* and *streetcar line* to make meaning precise and vivid. See "Focus on Specific and Concrete Language" on page 118.

- **Be creative.** You can make your writing more lively and forceful with FIGURES OF SPEECH, expressions that imply meanings beyond or different from their literal meanings, such as *curled tight like a rosebud* or *feelings trampled to dirt*. Be careful not to resort to CLICHÉS, worn phrases that have lost their power (*hour of need, thin as a rail*), or to combine figures of speech into confusing or absurd images, such as *The players flooded the soccer field like bulls ready for a fight*.

Clear and Engaging Sentences

Effective sentences are the product of careful attention to meaning and readability. Editing for emphasis, parallelism, and variety will ensure that readers can follow your ideas without difficulty and stay interested in what you have to say.

Emphasis

While drafting, simply getting ideas down in sentence form can be challenge enough. But once the ideas are down, it becomes apparent that some are more important than others. Editing for emphasis offers an opportunity to clarify those relationships for readers. As you do so, focus on the following changes:

- **Put verbs in the active voice.** A verb in the ACTIVE VOICE expresses action by the subject (*He recorded a new song*), whereas a verb in the PASSIVE VOICE expresses action done *to* the subject (*A new song was recorded*, or, adding who did the action, *A new song was recorded by him*). The active voice is usually more emphatic and therefore easier to follow. See "Focus on Verbs" on page 69.

- **Simplify wordy sentences.** Unnecessary padding deflates readers' interest. Weed out any empty phrases or meaningless repetition:

  WORDY The nature of social-networking sites is such that they reconnect lost and distant friends but can also for all intents and purposes dredge up old relationships, relationships that were better left forgotten.

  CONCISE Social-networking sites reconnect lost and distant friends but can also dredge up old relationships that were better left forgotten.

  See also "Focus on Clarity and Conciseness" on page 394.

- **Combine sentences.** You can often clarify meaning by merging sentences. Use *coordination* to combine and balance equally important ideas, joining them with *and, but, or, nor, for, so,* or *yet*:

  UNEMPHATIC Many restaurant meals are high in fat. Their sodium content is also high. To diners they seem harmless.

  EMPHATIC Many restaurant meals are high in fat and sodium, but to diners they seem harmless.

Use *subordination* to de-emphasize less important ideas, placing minor information in modifying words or word groups:

UNEMPHATIC Restaurant menus sometimes label certain options. They use the label "healthy." These options are lower in fat and sodium.

EMPHATIC Restaurant menus sometimes label <u>as "healthy"</u> the options <u>that</u> <u>are lower in fat and sodium.</u>

Parallelism

Another way to clarify meaning is to give parallel structure to related words, phrases, and sentences. PARALLELISM is the use of similar grammatical forms for elements of similar importance, either within or among sentences.

PARALLELISM WITHIN A SENTENCE Binge drinking can <u>worsen heart disease</u> and <u>cause liver failure.</u>

PARALLELISM AMONG SENTENCES Binge drinking has less well-known effects, too. <u>It can cause</u> brain damage. <u>It can raise</u> blood sugar to diabetic levels. And <u>it can reduce</u> the body's ability to fight off infections.

Readers tend to stumble over elements that seem equally important but are not in parallel form. As you edit, look for groups of related ideas and make a point of expressing them consistently:

NONPARALLEL Even occasional binges can cause serious problems, from <u>the experience of blackouts</u> to <u>getting arrested</u> to <u>injury.</u>

PARALLEL Even occasional binges can cause serious problems, from <u>blackouts</u> to <u>arrests</u> to <u>injuries.</u>

For more on parallel structure, see "Focus on Parallelism" on page 202.

Sentence Variety

Sentence after sentence with the same length and structure can be stiff and dull. By varying sentences, you can hold readers' interest while also achieving the emphasis you want. The techniques to achieve variety include adjusting the lengths of sentences and varying their beginnings. For examples and specifics, see "Focus on Sentence Variety" on page 162.

Common Errors

Writers sometimes think of grammar as a set of rules that exist solely to give nitpickers a chance to point out mistakes. But basic errors can undermine an otherwise excellent piece of writing by distracting readers or creating confusion. The guidelines here can help you catch some of the most common problems.

Sentence Fragments

A *sentence fragment* is a word group that is punctuated like a sentence but is not a complete sentence. Experienced writers sometimes use fragments for effect, but readers usually stumble over incomplete sentences. For the sake of clarity, make sure every sentence has a subject and a verb and expresses a complete thought:

FRAGMENT Snowboarding a relatively young sport.

COMPLETE Snowboarding is a relatively young sport.

FRAGMENT Many ski resorts banned snowboards at first. Believing they were dangerous and destructive.

COMPLETE Many ski resorts banned snowboards at first, believing they were dangerous and destructive.

Run-on Sentences and Comma Splices

When two or more sentences run together with no punctuation between them, they create a *run-on sentence.* When they run together with only a comma between them, they create a *comma splice.* Writers usually correct these errors by separating the sentences with a period, with a semicolon, or with a comma along with *and, but, or, nor, for, so,* or *yet:*

RUN-ON Snowboarding has become a mainstream sport riders are now as common as skiers on the slopes.

COMMA SPLICE Snowboarding has become a mainstream sport, riders are now as common as skiers on the slopes.

EDITED Snowboarding has become a mainstream sport. Riders are now as common as skiers on the slopes.

EDITED Snowboarding has become a mainstream sport; riders are now as common as skiers on the slopes.

EDITED Snowboarding has become a mainstream sport, and riders are now as common as skiers on the slopes.

Subject-Verb Agreement

Most writers know to use singular verbs with singular subjects and plural verbs with plural subjects, but matching subjects and verbs can sometimes be tricky. Watch especially for these situations:

- **Don't mistake a noun that follows the subject for the actual subject.** In the examples below, the subject is *appearance,* not *snowboarders* or *Olympics:*

MISMATCHED The appearance of snowboarders in the Olympics prove their status as true athletes.

MATCHED The appearance of snowboarders in the Olympics proves their status as true athletes.

- **With subjects joined by** and **, use a plural verb.** Compound word groups are treated as plural even if the word closest to the verb is singular:

  MISMATCHED The cross course and the half-pipe shows the sport's versatility.

  MATCHED The cross course and the half-pipe show the sport's versatility.

Pronouns

We tend to use pronouns without thinking much about them. Problems occur when usage that feels natural in speech causes confusion in writing:

- **Check that each pronoun refers clearly to an appropriate noun.** Rewrite sentences in which the reference is vague or only implied:

  VAGUE Students asked the administration to add more parking spaces, but it had no effect.

  CLEAR Students asked the administration to add more parking spaces, but their pleas had no effect.

  IMPLIED Although commuter parking is hard to find, they keep driving to campus.

  CLEAR Although commuters know that parking is hard to find, they keep driving to campus.

- **Take care with indefinite pronouns.** Although people often use pronouns such as *anybody, anyone, everyone,* and *somebody* to mean "many" or "all," these indefinite pronouns are technically singular, not plural:

  MISMATCHED Everyone should change their passwords frequently.

  MATCHED Everyone should change his or her passwords frequently.

  MATCHED All computer users should change their passwords frequently.

Misplaced and Dangling Modifiers

A *modifier* describes another word or group of words in a sentence. Make sure that modifiers clearly describe the intended words. Misplaced and dangling modifiers can be awkward or even unintentionally amusing:

  MISPLACED I swam away as the jellyfish approached in fear of being stung.

  CLEAR In fear of being stung, I swam away as the jellyfish approached.

  DANGLING Floating in the ocean, the clouds drifted by.

  CLEAR Floating in the ocean, I watched as the clouds drifted by.

Shifts

Be consistent in your use of verb tense (past, present, and so on), person (*I, you, he/she/it, they*), and voice (active or passive). Unnecessary shifts can confuse readers. For details, see "Focus on Verbs" on page 69 and "Focus on Consistency" on page 258.

AN ESSAY-IN-PROGRESS

In the following pages, you have a chance to follow Rosie Anaya as she develops an essay through journal writing and several drafts. She began the writing process early, while reading and annotating Nancy Mairs's "Disability" (p. 12). Inspired by Mairs's argument, Anaya writes about another group that has been "effaced" by the media.

Discovering Ideas and Drafting

Journal Notes on Reading

Haven't the media gotten better about showing people with disabilities since Mairs wrote this essay? Lots of TV shows have characters who just happen to use wheelchairs. But I see why she has a problem: I would be bothered, too, if I didn't see people like me represented. I would feel left out, probably hurt, maybe angry.

Mairs is doing more: Invisibility is a problem for healthy people too — anybody could become disabled and wouldn't know that people with disabilities live full, normal lives.

Interesting that she mentions emotions so many times: The references to feelings and psychology raise a question about people with mental disabilities, like depression or schizophrenia. How are *they* represented by the media? Definitely *not* as regular people: Stories in the news about emotionally disturbed people who go over the edge and hurt or even kill people. And *Criminal Minds* etc. always using some kind of psychological disorder to explain a crime.

Except the problem with mental illness isn't just invisibility — it's negative stereotyping. What if you're represented as a danger to yourself and others? That's got to be worse.

First Draft

Nancy Mairs is upset with television and movies that don't show physical disability as a feature of normal life. She says the media shows disability consuming a character's life or it doesn't show disability at all, and she wants to see "representations of myself in the media, especially television" (p. no.).

Mairs makes a convincing argument that the media should portray physical disability as part of everyday life because "effacement" leaves the rest of us unprepared to cope in the case that we should eventually become disabled ourselves. As she explains it, anybody could become disabled, but because we rarely see people with disabilities living full, normal lives on tv, we assume that becoming disabled means life is pretty much over (p. no.). It's been three decades since Mairs wrote her essay, and she seems to have gotten her wish. Plenty of characters on television today who have a disability are not defined by it. But psychological disabilities are disabilities too, and they have never been shown "as a normal characteristic, one that complicates but does not ruin human existence" (p. no.).

Television routinely portrays people with mental illness as threats to them-selves and to others. Think about all those stories on the evening news about a man suffering from schizophrenia who went on a shooting spree before turning his gun on himself, or a mother who drowned her own children in the throes of depression, or a bipolar teenager who commits suicide. Such events are tragic, no doubt, but although the vast majority of people with these illnesses hurt nobody, the news implies that they're all potential killers.

Fictional shows, too, are always using some kind of psychological disorder to explain why someone committed a crime. On *Criminal Minds* a woman with "inter-mittent explosive disorder" impulsively kills multiple people after she is released from a psychiatric hospital and stops taking her medication. On *Rizzoli and Isles* a serial abductor's actions are blamed on "a long history of mental illness" that started with depression after he saw his father kill his mother and developed a perverse need to recreate their relationship with victims of his own. And the entire premise of *Dexter* is that the trauma of witnessing his mother's brutal murder turned the title character into a serial killer. Dexter is an obsessive-compulsive killer who jus-tifies his impulses by killing only other killers. Early in the series, viewers learned that his nemesis, the "Ice Truck Killer," who at one point was engaged to Dexter's adopted sister and then tried to kill her, was actually his long-lost brother. Every season featured a different enemy, and each one of them had some kind of stated or implied mental illness: The "Doomsday Killer" of season six, for example, was a psychotic divinity student who went off his meds and suffered from delusions.

It is my belief that the presentation of psychological disability may do worse than the "effacement" of disability that bothered Mairs. People with mental illness are discouraged from seeking help and are sent deeper into isolation and despair. This negative stereotype hurts us all.

Revising

Anaya's first draft was a good start. She found an idea worth pursuing and explored her thoughts. But as with any first draft, her essay needed work. To improve it, Anaya revised extensively, cutting digressions in some places and adding support in others. Her revised draft, you'll see, responds to "Disability" more directly, spells out Mairs's points and Anaya's own ideas in more detail, and builds more thoroughly on what Mairs had to say.

Revised Draft

Mental Illness on Television

In her essay "Disability" Nancy Mairs ~~is upset with~~ argues that television and movies ~~that don't~~ fail to show physical disability as a feature of normal life. ~~She~~ Instead, Mairs says, the media shows disability consuming a character's life or it doesn't show disability at all~~, and she wants to see "representations of myself in the media, especially television" (p. no. ~~13). But Mairs wrote her essay in 1987. Since then the situation has actually improved for physical disability. At the same time, another group — those with mental illness — have come to suffer even worse representation.

~~Mairs makes a convincing argument~~ Mairs's purpose in writing her essay was to persuade her readers that the media should portray physical disability as part of everyday life because ~~"effacement"~~ otherwise it denies or misrepresents disability, and it leaves ~~the rest of us~~ "Temporarily Abled Persons" (those without disability, for now) unprepared to cope in the case that ~~we~~ they should eventually become disabled ~~ourselves~~ themselves (14-15). ~~As she explains it, anybody could become disabled, but because we rarely see people with disabilities living full, normal lives on tv, we assume that becoming disabled means life is pretty much over (p. no.). It's been three decades since Mairs wrote her essay, and~~ Three decades later, Mairs ~~she~~ seems to have gotten her wish. Plenty of characters on television today who have a disability are not defined by it. Lawyer and superhero Matt Murdoch on *Daredevil* is blind. Daphne Vasquez on *Switched at Birth* (as well as many of her friends and their

Uses a less abrupt, more formal tone.

Deletes a quotation to remove a side issue and tighten the introduction.

Adds a thesis statement.

Explains Mairs's idea more clearly.

Provides page numbers in Mairs's essay.

Adds examples to support the assertion about TV today.

parents) is deaf. Security analyst Patton Plame of *NCIS: New Orleans* uses a wheelchair equipped with a computer to help his team solve crimes, Joe Swanson of *Family Guy* is also paraplegic. A current ad campaign for TJ Maxx features a wheelchair dance team, and Amy Purdy, an athlete with two prosthetic feet, is featured on a TV spot for Toyota. The media still has a long way to go in representing physical disability, but it has made progress.

However, the media depiction of one type of disability is, if anything, worse than it was three decades ago. Although Mairs doesn't address mental illness in "Disability," mental illness falls squarely into the misrepresentation she criticizes. ~~But p~~Psychological disabilities are disabilities too, ~~and~~ but they have never been shown "as a normal characteristic, one that complicates but does not ruin human existence" (~~p. no.~~ 15). People who cope with a disability such as depression, bipolar disorder, or obsessive-compulsive disorder as parts of their lives do not see themselves in the media; those who don't have a psychological disability now but may someday do not see that mental illness is usually a condition they can live with.

> Adds a transition to tighten the connection with Mairs's essay.

> More fully develops the idea about mental illness as a "normal characteristic."

The depictions of mental illness actually go beyond Mairs's concerns, as the media actually exploits it. Television routinely portrays people with mental illness as threats to themselves and to others. Think about all those stories on the evening news about a man suffering from schizophrenia who went on a shooting spree before turning his gun on himself, or a mother who drowned her own children in the throes of depression, or a bipolar teenager who commits suicide. ~~Such events are tragic, no doubt, but although the vast majority of people with these illnesses hurt nobody, the news implies that they're all potential killers.~~ Fictional shows, too, are always using some kind of psychological disorder to explain why someone committed a crime. On *Criminal Minds* a woman with "intermittent explosive disorder" impulsively kills multiple people after she is released from a psychiatric hospital and stops taking her medication~~,~~ and ~~O~~on *Rizzoli and Isles* a serial abductor's actions are blamed on "a long history of mental illness" beginning ~~that started~~ with depression. ~~after he saw his father kill his mother and developed a perverse need to recreate their relationship with victims of his own. And the entire~~

> Adds a transition to link back to Mairs and the thesis.

> Combines related paragraphs ("Fictional shows" used to start a new paragraph).

~~premise of *Dexter* is that the trauma of witnessing his mother's brutal murder turned the title character into a serial killer. Dexter is an obsessive-compulsive killer who justifies his impulses by killing only other killers. Early in the series, viewers learned that his nemesis, the "Ice Truck Killer," who at one point was engaged to Dexter's adopted sister and then tried to kill her, is actually his long-lost brother. Every season has featured a different enemy, and each one of them has had some kind of stated or implied mental illness: The "Doomsday Killer" of season six, for example, was a psychotic divinity student who went off his meds and suffered from delusions.~~

Removes digressions and simplifies examples to improve unity.

These programs highlight mental illness to get viewers' attention. But the media is also telling us that the proper response to people with mental illness is to be afraid of them. Mairs argues that invisibility in the media can cause people with disabilities to feel unattractive or inappropriate (14). It is my belief that the presentation of psychological disability may do worse. ~~than the "effacement" of disability that bothered Mairs.~~ People with mental illness are discouraged from seeking help and are sent deeper into isolation and despair. Those feelings are often cited as the fuel for violent outbursts, but ironically the media portrays such violence as inevitable with mental illness. ~~This negative stereotype hurts us all.~~

Expands paragraph to link to Mairs's essay and lend authority to Anaya's point.

More complex and varied depictions of all kinds of impairments, both physical and mental, will weaken the negative stereotypes that are harmful to all of us. With mental illness especially, we would all be better served if psychological disability was portrayed by the media as a part of everyday life. It's not a crime.

Provides a new conclusion that explains why the topic is important and ends with a flourish.

Works Cited

Adds a list of works cited. (See pp. 635–45.)

"Breath Play." *Criminal Minds*, season 10, episode 17, CBS, 11 Mar. 2015. *Netflix*, www.netflix.com/search/criminalminds. Accessed 19 July 2015.

"Deadly Harvest." *Rizzoli and Isles*, season 6, episode 3, TNT, 23 July 2015.

Mairs, Nancy. "Disability." *The Bedford Reader*, edited by X. J. Kennedy et al., 13th ed., Bedford/St. Martin's, 2017, pp. 12-15.

TJ Maxx. Advertisement. Fox, 21 July 2015.

Toyota. Advertisement. TNT, 23 July 2015.

Editing

With her thesis clarified, the connections between her argument and Mairs's tightened, and her ideas more fully developed, Anaya was satisfied that her essay was much improved and just about finished. She still had some work to do, though. In editing, she corrected errors, cleaned up awkward sentences, and added explanations. Here we show you her changes to one paragraph.

Edited Paragraph

Mairs's purpose in ~~writing her essay~~ "Disability" ~~was~~ is to persuade ~~her~~ readers that the media should portray physical disability as part of everyday life because otherwise ~~it denies~~ they deny or misrepresent~~s~~ disability~~,~~ and ~~it~~ leave~~s~~ "Temporarily Abled Persons" (those without disability, for now) unprepared to cope ~~in the case that they should eventually~~ if they become disabled ~~themselves~~ (14-15). Three decades later, Mairs seems to have gotten her wish~~. Plenty of~~ for characters ~~on television today~~ who have a disability but are not defined by it. Lawyer and superhero Matt Murdoch on *Daredevil* is blind. ~~Daphne Vasquez~~ Several characters on *Switched at Birth* ~~(as well as many of her friends and their parents) is~~ are deaf. Security analyst Patton Plame of *NCIS: New Orleans* uses a wheelchair equipped with a computer to help his team solve crimes~~,~~. Police officer Joe Swanson of *Family Guy* is also paraplegic. A current ad campaign for TJ Maxx features a wheelchair dance team, and ~~Amy Purdy, an athlete with two prosthetic feet, is featured on~~ a TV spot for Toyota highlights Amy Purdy, an athlete with two prosthetic feet. The media still ~~has~~ have a long way to go in representing physical disability, but ~~it has~~ they have made progress.

Right-margin annotations:

Reduces wordiness; corrects tense shift.

Corrects pronoun-antecedent and subject-verb agreement (*media* is plural).

Reduces wordiness.

Adds coordination for emphasis.

Reduces wordiness.

Fixes comma splice.

Eliminates passive voice and creates parallelism.

Corrects subject-verb and pronoun-antecedent agreement.

Final Draft

Mental Illness on Television

In her essay "Disability," Nancy Mairs argues that the media, such as television and movies, fail to show physical disability as a feature of normal life. Instead, Mairs says, they show disability consuming a character's life or they don't show disability at all. Mairs wrote her essay in 1987, and since then

Right-margin annotation:

Introduction summarizes Mairs's essay and sets up Anaya's thesis.

the situation has actually improved for depiction of physical disability. At the same time, another group — those with mental illness — has come to suffer even worse representation.

Thesis statement establishes Anaya's main idea.

Mairs's purpose in "Disability" is to persuade readers that the media should portray physical disability as part of everyday life because otherwise they deny or misrepresent disability and leave "Temporarily Abled Persons" (those without disability, for now) unprepared to cope if they become disabled (14-15). Three decades later, Mairs seems to have gotten her wish for characters who have a disability but are not defined by it. Lawyer and superhero Matt Murdoch on *Daredevil* is blind. Several characters on *Switched at Birth* are deaf. Security analyst Patton Plame of *NCIS: New Orleans* uses a wheelchair equipped with a computer to help his team solve crimes. Police officer Joe Swanson of *Family Guy* is also paraplegic. A current ad campaign for TJ Maxx features a wheelchair dance team, and a TV spot for Toyota highlights Amy Purdy, an athlete with two prosthetic feet. The media still have a long way to go in representing physical disability, but they have made progress.

Page numbers in parentheses refer to "Works Cited" at end of paper.

Examples provide support for Anaya's analysis.

However, in depicting one type of disability, the media are, if anything, worse than they were three decades ago. Mairs doesn't address mental illness, but it falls squarely into the misrepresentation she criticizes. It has never been shown, in Mairs's words, "as a normal characteristic, one that complicates but does not ruin human existence" (15). Thus people who cope with a psychological disability such as depression, bipolar disorder, or obsessive-compulsive disorder as part of their lives do not see themselves in the media. And those who don't have a psychological disability now but may someday do not see that mental illness is usually a condition one can live with.

Comparison and contrast extend Mairs's idea to Anaya's new subject.

Follow-up comments explain what the quotation contributes to Anaya's thesis.

Unfortunately, the depictions of mental illness also go beyond Mairs's concerns, because the media actually exploit it. Television routinely portrays people with mental illness as threats to themselves and to others. TV news often features stories about a man suffering from schizophrenia who goes on a shooting spree before turning his gun on himself, a mother with depression who drowns her own children, or a teenager with bipolar disorder who commits suicide. Fictional programs,

Topic sentence introduces new idea.

Examples provide evidence for Anaya's point.

especially crime dramas, regularly use mental illness to develop their plots. On *Criminal Minds* a woman with "intermittent explosive disorder" impulsively kills multiple people after she is released from a psychiatric hospital and stops taking her medication, and on *Rizzoli and Isles* a serial abductor's actions are blamed on "a long history of mental illness" beginning with depression. These programs and many others like them highlight mental illness to get viewers' attention, and they strongly imply that the proper response is fear. Mairs argues that the invisibility of physical disability in the media can cause people with disabilities to feel unattractive or inappropriate (14), but the presentation of psychological disability may do worse. It can prevent people with mental illness from seeking help and send them deeper into isolation and despair. Those feelings are often cited as the fuel for violent outbursts, but ironically the media portray such violence as inevitable with mental illness.

    Seeing more complex and varied depictions of people living with all kinds of impairments, physical and mental, can weaken the negative stereotypes that are harmful to all of us. With mental illness especially, we would all be better served if the media would make an effort to portray psychological disability as a part of everyday life, not a crime.

Paraphrase explains one of Mairs's points in Anaya's own words.

Cause-and-effect analysis applies Mairs's idea to Anaya's thesis.

Conclusion reasserts the thesis and explains the broader implications of the subject.

Works Cited

"Breath Play." *Criminal Minds*, season 10, episode 17, CBS, 11 Mar. 2015. *Netflix*, www.netflix.com/search/criminalminds. Accessed 19 July 2015.

"Deadly Harvest." *Rizzoli and Isles*, season 6, episode 3, TNT, 23 July 2015.

Mairs, Nancy. "Disability." *The Bedford Reader*, edited by X. J. Kennedy et al., 13th ed., Bedford/St. Martin's, 2017, pp. 12-15.

TJ Maxx. Advertisement. Fox, 21 July 2015.

Toyota. Advertisement. TNT, 23 July 2015.

List of "Works Cited" at the end of the paper gives complete publication information for Anaya's sources. (See pp. 635–45.)

PART TWO

THE METHODS

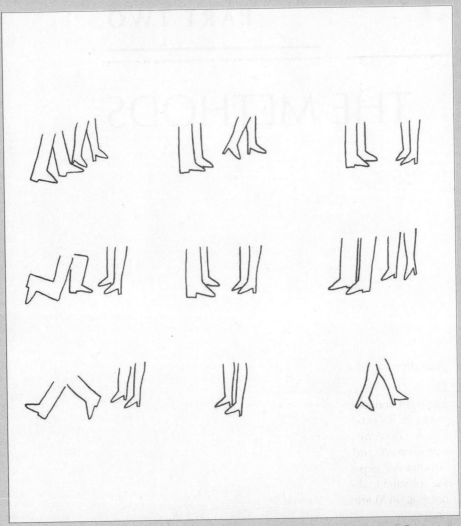

3

NARRATION

Telling a Story

◀ **Narration in a drawing**

Demetri Martin is a popular stand-up comedian known for intelligent wit and for the clever graphs and drawings he incorporates into his act. He has published two books of such artwork: *This Is a Book by Demetri Martin* (2011), which also includes comic essays, and *Point Your Face at This* (2013). "Reality is a concept that depends on where you point your face," he says in the epigraph to the second book — an idea illustrated with this drawing. In Martin's trademark simple style, the sketch focuses on just the lower legs of two people to tell a brief narrative, or story. What experience is depicted here? What do the details in each part of the sequence tell us about the characters, and what do they contribute to the narrative? What effect does Martin achieve by not showing the couple more fully? How does the unusual perspective shape your understanding of what has happened?

THE METHOD

"What happened?" you ask a friend who sports a swollen black eye. Unless he merely grunts, "A golf ball," he may answer you with a narrative — a story, true or fictional.

"Okay," he sighs, "you know The Tenth Round? That gym down by the docks that smells like formaldehyde? Last night I heard they were giving away $500 to anybody who could stand up for three minutes against this karate expert, the Masked Samurai. And so . . ."

You lean forward. At least, you lean forward *if* you love a story. Most of us do, particularly if the story tells us of people in action or in conflict, and if it is told briskly, vividly, or with insight into the human condition. NARRATION, or storytelling, is therefore a powerful method by which to engage and hold the attention of listeners — readers as well. A little of its tremendous power flows to the blogger who encapsulates events in a critical social moment, and to the lawyer who pulls together the threads of a compelling case.

The term *narrative* takes in abundant territory. A narrative may be short or long, factual or imagined, as artless as a tale told in a locker room or as artful as a novel by Toni Morrison. A narrative may instruct and inform, or simply entertain. It may set forth some point or message, or it may be no more significant than a horror tale that aims to curdle your blood. Because narration can both put across ideas and hold attention, the ability to tell a story — on paper, as well as in conversation — may be one of the most useful skills you can acquire.

THE PROCESS

Purpose and Shape

At least a hundred times a year, you probably turn to narration, not always to tell an entertaining story, but often to report information or to illustrate an idea. Every good story has a purpose, because a narrative without a point is bound to irritate readers.

In academic writing, you will use mainly brief narratives, or ANECDOTES, that recount single incidents as a way of supporting an explanation or argument with the flesh and blood of real life. That is, although a narrative can run from the beginning of an essay to the end, as those later in this chapter do, more often in your writing a narrative will be only a part of what you have to say. It will serve a larger purpose. For instance, say you're writing about therapies for autism and you want readers to see how one particular method works. In a paragraph or so, you can narrate a session you observed between a child and his teacher. Your purpose will determine which of the session's events you relate — not every action and exchange but the ones that, in your eyes, convey the essence of the therapy and make it interesting for readers.

The Thesis

In writing a news story, a reporter often begins by placing the main event in the opening paragraph (called the *lead*) so that readers get the essentials up front. Similarly, in using an anecdote to explain something or to argue a point, you'll want to tell readers directly what the story demonstrates. But in most other kinds of narration, whether fiction or nonfiction, whether to entertain or to make an idea clear, the storyteller refrains from revealing the gist of the story, its point, right at the beginning.

In fact, many narratives do not contain a THESIS STATEMENT, an assertion of the idea behind the story, because such a statement can rob the reader of the very pleasure of narration, the excitement of seeing a story build. That doesn't mean the story lacks a thesis, however — far from it. The writer has every obligation to construct the narrative as if a thesis statement shows the way at the start, even when it doesn't.

By the end of the story, that thesis should become obvious, as the writer builds toward a memorable CONCLUSION. Most storytellers end with a bang if they can, often by surprising the reader with a final moment of IRONY, or an unexpected twist to the tale. In the drawing that opens this chapter, for instance, Demetri Martin shows a marriage proposal that ends in a breakup. For another example, take specific notice in this chapter of Shirley Jackson's ending for "The Lottery" (*after* you've read the whole story, that is). The final impact need not be as dramatic as Martin's or Jackson's, either. As Junot Díaz demonstrates in his narrative in this chapter, you can achieve a lot just by working up to your point, and stating your thesis at the very end. You can sometimes make your point just by saving the best incident — the most dramatic or the funniest — for last.

The Narrator in the Story

Every story has a NARRATOR, the person telling the tale. The narrator's role in relation to the story determines the POINT OF VIEW, or angle of seeing, that shapes the telling. Generally, writers use different points of view to tell different kinds of stories.

- **Narratives that report personal experience:** Whether you are telling of a real or a fictional event, your narrator will be the one who was there. The telling will probably be SUBJECTIVE: You will use the first PERSON ("I did this; we did that") and choose details and language to express the feelings of the narrator — your own feelings when you are recounting your actual experience or the imagined feelings of a character you have invented. Of course, any experience told in the first person can use some artful telling and structuring, as the personal narratives in this chapter — by Amy Tan, Naomi Shihab Nye, Jonathan Bethards, and Maya Angelou — all demonstrate.

- **Narratives that report others' experiences:** When a story isn't your own but someone else's, you proceed differently as narrator. You use the third person, *he, she, it,* or *they*: "The experimenter did this; she did that." Your approach may be subjective, building in the real or imagined feelings of the person experiencing the events — as Junot Díaz does in this chapter, reporting his mother's story. Or your approach may be OBJECTIVE, sticking to the facts as observed by you or by others. In objective narration — typical of writing such as news stories, history books, lab reports, and some fiction — you show what transpired as accurately and dispassionately as possible. In this chapter you can see objective narration in the police log by Scott Beltran and in the short story by Shirley Jackson.

A final element of the narrator's place in the story is verb tense, whether present (*I stare, she stares*) or past (*I stared, she stared*). The present tense is often tempting because it gives events a sense of immediacy. Told as though everything were happening right now, the story of the Masked Samurai might begin: "I duck between the ropes and step into the ring. My heart is thudding fast." But the present tense can seem artificial because we're used to reading stories in the past tense, and it can be difficult to sustain throughout an entire narrative. (See p. 258 on consistency in tenses.) The past tense may be more removed, but it is still powerful: Just look at Maya Angelou's gripping "Champion of the World," beginning on page 94.

What to Emphasize

Discovery of Details

Whether you tell of your own experience or of someone else's, even if it is brief, you need a whole story to tell. If the story is complex, do some searching and discovering in writing. One trusty method to test your memory (or to make sure you have all the necessary elements of a story) is that of a news reporter. Ask yourself:

- **What happened?**
- **Who took part?**

- **When?**
- **Where?**
- **Why did it happen?**
- **How did it happen?**

Journalists call this handy list of questions "the five *W*'s and the *H*." The *H* — *how* — isn't merely another way of asking what happened. It means: In exactly what way or under what circumstances? If the event was a break-in, how was it done — with an ax or with a bulldozer?

Scene versus Summary

If you have prepared well — searching your memory or doing some research — you'll have far more information on hand than you can use in your narrative. You'll need to choose carefully, to pick out just those events and details that will accomplish your purpose with your readers.

A key decision is to choose between the two main strategies of narration:

- **Tell a story by SCENE, visualizing each event as vividly and precisely as if you were there.** Think of the scene as if it were in a film, with your reader sitting before the screen. This is the strategy Shirley Jackson uses in her account of a tense crowd's behavior as, gathered in a small town square, they anticipate who will be at the center of an annual tradition (in "The Lottery," p. 100). Instead of just mentioning people, you portray them. You recall dialog as best you can, or you invent some that could have been spoken. You include DESCRIPTION (a mode of writing to be dealt with fully in the next chapter). You might prolong one scene for an entire essay, or you could draw a scene in only two or three sentences (as Scott Beltran does in his police log on pp. 71–73).

- **Tell a story by SUMMARY, relating events concisely.** Instead of depicting people and their surroundings in great detail, you set down just the essentials of what happened. Such is the strategy Junot Díaz uses in "The Dreamer" (p. 88) to tell of his mother's childhood determination to get an education. Most of us employ this method in the everyday stories we tell, for it takes less time and fewer words. When chosen well, the economy of a story told in summary may be as effective as the lavish detail of a story told in scenes.

As always, your choice of a strategy depends on your answers to the questions you ask yourself: What is my purpose? Who is my audience? Whether to flesh out a scene fully, how much detail to include — these choices depend on what you seek to do and on how much your audience needs to know to follow you. You may find that you want to use both strategies in telling a single story, passing briskly from one scene to the next, distilling events of lesser importance. Were you to write, let's say, the story of your grandfather's emigration from Cuba, you might just summarize his decision to leave Cuba and his settlement in Florida. These summaries could frame and emphasize a detailed telling of the events that you consider essential and most interesting — his nighttime escape, his harrowing voyage in a small boat, his surprising welcome by immigration authorities.

Dialog

In this book we are primarily concerned with the kind of writing you do every day in college: nonfiction writing in which you explain ideas, organize information you have learned, analyze other people's ideas, or argue a case. In fiction, though, we find an enormously popular and appealing use of narration and certain devices of storytelling from which all writers can learn. For these reasons, this chapter includes one celebrated short story by a master storyteller, Shirley Jackson. But fiction and fact barely separate Jackson's tale and the equally compelling true stories in this chapter. All of the authors strive to make people and events come alive for us. Many of them also use a tool that academic writers generally do not: DIALOG. Reported speech, in quotation marks, is invaluable for revealing characters' feelings, as Amy Tan, Naomi Shihab Nye, Jonathan Bethards, and Maya Angelou all demonstrate with their tales from real life.

Organization

In any kind of narration, the simplest approach is to set down events in CHRONOLOGICAL ORDER, following the sequence in which they occurred. To do so is to have your story already organized for you.

Chronological order is an excellent pattern to follow unless you can see some special advantage in violating it. Ask: What am I trying to do? If you are trying to capture your readers' attention right away, you might begin *in medias res* (Latin, "in the middle of things") and open with a colorful, dramatic event, even though it took place late in the chronology. If trying for dramatic effect, you might save the most exciting or impressive event for last, even though it actually happened early. By this means, you can keep your readers in suspense for as long as possible. (You can return to earlier events in a FLASHBACK, an earlier scene recalled.) Let your purpose be your guide.

No matter what order you choose, either following chronology or departing from it, make sure your audience can follow it. The sequence of events has to be clear. This calls for TRANSITIONS that mark time, whether they are brief phrases that point out exactly when each event happened ("seven years later," "a moment earlier") or whole sentences that announce an event and clearly locate it in time ("Passing by the gym on Friday evening, I noticed the sign: 'Go Three Minutes with the Masked Samurai and Win $500.' "). See *Transitions* in the Glossary for a list of possibilities.

FOCUS ON VERBS

Narration depends heavily on verbs to clarify and enliven events. Strong verbs sharpen meaning and encourage you to add other informative details:

WEAK   The wind <u>made</u> an awful noise.

STRONG   The wind <u>roared</u> around the house and <u>rattled</u> the trees.

Forms of *make* (as in the example above) and forms of *be* (as in the next example) can sap the life from narration:

WEAK   The noises <u>were</u> alarming to us.

STRONG   The noises <u>alarmed</u> us.

Verbs in the ACTIVE VOICE (the subject does the action) usually pack more power into fewer words than verbs in the PASSIVE VOICE (the subject is acted upon):

WEAK PASSIVE   We <u>were besieged</u> in the basement by the wind, as the water at our feet <u>was swelled</u> by the rain.

STRONG ACTIVE   The wind <u>besieged</u> us in the basement, as the rain <u>swelled</u> the water at our feet.

While strengthening verbs, also ensure that they're consistent in tense. The tense you choose for relating events, present or past, should not shift unnecessarily.

INCONSISTENT TENSES   We <u>held</u> a frantic conference to consider our options. It <u>takes</u> only a minute to decide to stay put.

CONSISTENT TENSE   We <u>held</u> a frantic conference to consider our options. It <u>took</u> only a minute to decide to stay put.

See page 49 for further discussion of passive versus active verbs and page 258 for advice on avoiding shifts in tense.

```
┌─────────────────────────────────────────────────────────────────────┐
│              CHECKLIST FOR REVISING A NARRATIVE                      │
```

✔ **Thesis.** What is the point of your narrative? Will it be clear to readers by the end? Even if you don't provide a thesis statement, your story should focus on a central idea. If you can't risk readers' misunderstanding — if, for instance, you're using narration to support an argument or explain a concept — then have you stated your thesis outright?

✔ **Point of view.** Is your narrator's position in the story appropriate for your purpose and consistent throughout? Check for awkward or confusing shifts in point of view (subjective or objective; first or third person) and in the tenses of verbs (present to past or vice versa).

✔ **Selection of events.** Have you selected and emphasized events to suit your audience and fulfill your purpose? Tell the important parts of the story in the greatest detail. Summarize the less important, connective events.

✔ **Organization.** If your organization is not strictly chronological (first event to last), do you have a compelling reason for altering it? If you start somewhere other than the beginning of the story or use flashbacks at any point, will your readers benefit from your creativity?

✔ **Transitions.** Have you used transitions to help clarify the order of events and their duration?

✔ **Dialog.** If you have used dialog, quoting participants in the story, is it appropriate for your purpose? Is it concise, telling only the important, revealing lines? Does the language sound like spoken English?

✔ **Verbs.** Do strong, active verbs move your narrative from event to event? Are verb tenses consistent?

NARRATION IN ACADEMIC WRITING

A Geology Textbook

In this paragraph from *The Earth: An Introduction to Physical Geology*, the authors Edward J. Tarbuck and Frederick K. Lutgens use narration to illustrate a powerful geological occurrence. Following a paragraph that explains landslides more generally, this narrative places the reader at a historic event.

The news media periodically relate the terrifying and often grim details of landslides. On <u>May 31, 1970</u>, one such event occurred when a gigantic rock avalanche buried more than 20,000 people in Yungay and Ranrahirca, Peru. There was little warning of the impending disaster; it began and ended in just <u>a matter of a few minutes</u>. The avalanche started 14 kilometers from Yungay, near the summit of 6,700-meter-high Nevados Huascaran, the loftiest

Generalization illustrated by narrative

Anecdote helps explain landslides:

• Sudden beginning

peak in the Peruvian Andes. Triggered by the ground motion from a strong offshore earthquake, a huge mass of rock and ice broke free from the precipitous north face of the mountain. <u>After plunging nearly one kilometer</u>, the material pulverized on impact and immediately began rushing down the mountainside, made fluid by trapped air and melted ice. The initial mass ripped loose additional millions of tons of debris <u>as it roared downhill</u>. The shock waves produced by the event created thunderlike noise and stripped nearby hillsides of vegetation. Although the material followed a previously eroded gorge, a portion of the debris jumped a 200–300-meter-high bedrock ridge that had protected Yungay from past rock avalanches and buried the entire city. <u>After inundating another town in its path</u>, Ranrahirca, the mass of debris <u>finally</u> reached the bottom of the valley where its momentum carried it across the Rio Santa and tens of meters up the opposite bank.

• Fast movement

• Irresistible force

Transitions (<u>underlined</u>) clarify sequence and pace of events

A Police Log

What is it like to work in law enforcement? What takes place on a typical shift? What procedures are the police expected to follow, and why? To learn the answers to such questions, criminal justice students — and sometimes civilians — are often given the opportunity to ride along on patrol with seasoned officers and observe their activities.

Whatever else the risks and rewards of the job, policing involves a good deal of paperwork. Every incident must be recorded in writing — sometimes in formal reports, but more often in simple activity logs. Kept by all police departments and often published in local newspapers, such logs provide straightforward public records of calls for help, motor vehicle stops, interactions with suspected criminals, and similar events. Always in chronological order, these narratives are generally presented as briefly and objectively as possible, written in the past tense and third-person point of view, and limited to the facts of each case: what happened, who was involved, where and when the events took place. Even so, as novelist Brian Doyle observes (p. 182), police logs offer some of the most engaging writing produced for general readers.

For an introductory criminal justice class at Lone Star College–Montgomery in Texas, student Scott Beltran went on a Saturday-night ride-along with the Crime Reduction Unit (CRU) of the Houston Police Department. Like the officers themselves, he kept an activity log through the shift. He also ANALYZED each event to better understand the experience. The final report he wrote and turned in to his instructor is excerpted on the following pages.

2000: CRU Roll Call. Two Sergeants take muster to make sure all officers are present and accounted for. After muster they discuss any intelligence on open cases they're actively investigating, and then they formulate a strategy to decide what part of town to focus their efforts. . . .

Narrative opens with beginning of shift

Chronological order

2030–2130: Officer Smith and I teamed up with one other unit and began conducting sweeps of previously identified drug trafficking locations. . . . During these sweeps, the officers were on alert for any type of suspicious activity, such as loitering, and they approached everyone in the area for at least some sort of brief questioning, but almost no one was detained or arrested. Officer Smith explained that these sweeps were done not only to make arrests, but also to establish HPD's presence in high-crime areas and to get the word out that Houston Police are proactively working to stop crime.

Time markers (in military time) clarify sequence and pace of events

Narration by summary

2200: We responded to an "officer needs assistance" call in the 800 block of N. Shepherd Drive. When we arrived there was one other unit on the scene; they already had two males and a female in custody. One male and the female were being detained for possession of crack cocaine, and the other male was being held for a parole violation warrant. After some investigation . . . it was determined that there were possibly more drugs in the suspect's apartment. The officers asked for, and were granted, consent to search the apartment. The officers asked the suspect to sign a "Consent to Search" form, which she did voluntarily. This was witnessed and signed by two other officers. After a quick search of the residence, the officers located a small amount of marijuana, a chemical mixing beaker, and a hot plate that appeared to have been used to cook, or make drugs. These items were seized and the suspects were charged with possession of a controlled substance. . . . All three suspects were transported to the central police station in downtown Houston. . . .

Narration by scene

Past tense

Objective, third-person point of view

0030: Officer Smith initiated a stop of a black Dodge Charger for the windows being tinted too dark. While running the driver's license through the system he determined that the driver was wanted out of Louisiana for a felony warrant, but the warrant stipulated arrest-in-state only. Officer Smith attempted to

Narration by scene

contact the agency that issued the warrant to determine if they wanted him to make the arrest. While he was waiting for the Louisiana agency to return his phone call, Officer Smith made contact with the passenger, the owner of the vehicle, and got consent to search the car. A search was completed and nothing illegal was found. Because he still hadn't gotten in touch with a supervisor in Louisiana, he took down all of the suspect's information and released him. . . .

0400: While traveling northbound we came upon a vehicle stopped at a red light in the 6500 block of the Gulf Freeway. With our windows rolled up we could still easily hear the vehicle's stereo system playing at a high volume. Officer Smith initiated a stop of the vehicle for violation of a city noise ordinance. After the vehicle pulled off the road we observed the driver making obvious furtive gestures while reaching toward the passenger seat. Officer Smith made contact with the driver and noticed that he was acting very nervous and appeared to be under the influence of some type of stimulant. Officer Smith removed the driver from the vehicle to investigate further. The driver admitted that he had been using cocaine and that he had a small amount still in the car. . . . Officer Smith placed a call to the District Attorney's office to make sure they would accept charges. The DA did accept the charges and the suspect was charged with Felony Possession of a Controlled Substance and booked into the central police station.

Narration by scene

0530: All of the Officers in the CRU met back at the station for an end of shift muster and de-briefing.

Narration concludes with the end of shift

AMY TAN

Amy Tan is a gifted storyteller whose first novel, *The Joy Luck Club* (1989), met with critical acclaim and huge success. The relationships it details between immigrant Chinese mothers and their Chinese American daughters came from Tan's firsthand experience. She was born in 1952 in Oakland, California, the daughter of immigrants who had fled China's civil war in the late 1940s. She majored in English and linguistics at San José State University, where she received a BA in 1973 and an MA in 1974. After two more years of graduate work, Tan became a consultant in language development for disabled children and then a freelancer writing reports and speeches for business corporations. Bored with such work, Tan began writing fiction to explore her ethnic ambivalence and to find her voice. Since *The Joy Luck Club*, she has published several more novels — most recently *The Valley of Amazement* (2013) — as well as children's books and *The Opposite of Fate* (2003), a collection of autobiographical essays. She is also a founding member of the Rock Bottom Remainders, a "literary garage band" made up of popular writers.

Fish Cheeks

In Tan's novel *The Bonesetter's Daughter* (2001), one of the characters says, "Good manners are not enough. . . . They are not the same as a good heart." Much of Tan's writing explores those tensions between keeping up appearances and having true intentions. In the brief narrative that follows, the author deftly portrays the contradictory feelings of a girl with feet in different cultures. The essay first appeared in *Seventeen*, a magazine for teenage girls and young women, in 1987.

For another entertaining story about a cultural misunderstanding, read the next essay, Naomi Shihab Nye's "Museum."

I fell in love with the minister's son the winter I turned fourteen. He was 1 not Chinese, but as white as Mary in the manger. For Christmas I prayed for this blond-haired boy, Robert, and a slim new American nose.

When I found out that my parents had invited the minister's family over 2 for Christmas Eve dinner, I cried. What would Robert think of our shabby Chinese Christmas? What would he think of our noisy Chinese relatives who lacked proper American manners? What terrible disappointment would he feel upon seeing not a roasted turkey and sweet potatoes but Chinese food?

On Christmas Eve I saw that my mother had outdone herself in creating   3
a strange menu. She was pulling black veins out of the backs of fleshy prawns.
The kitchen was littered with appalling mounds of raw food: A slimy rock cod
with bulging eyes that pleaded not to be thrown into a pan of hot oil. Tofu,
which looked like stacked wedges of rubbery white sponges. A bowl soaking
dried fungus back to life. A plate of squid, their backs crisscrossed with knife
markings so they resembled bicycle tires.

And then they arrived — the minister's family and all my relatives in a   4
clamor of doorbells and rumpled Christmas packages. Robert grunted hello,
and I pretended he was not worthy of existence.

Dinner threw me deeper into despair. My relatives licked the ends of their   5
chopsticks and reached across the table, dipping them into the dozen or so
plates of food. Robert and his family waited patiently for platters to be passed
to them. My relatives murmured with pleasure when my mother brought out
the whole steamed fish. Robert grimaced. Then my father poked his chopsticks
just below the fish eye and plucked out the soft meat. "Amy, your favorite," he
said, offering me the tender fish cheek. I wanted to disappear.

At the end of the meal my father leaned back and belched loudly, thank-   6
ing my mother for her fine cooking. "It's a polite Chinese custom to show you
are satisfied," explained my father to our astonished guests. Robert was looking down at his plate with a reddened face. The minister managed to muster
up a quiet burp. I was stunned into silence for the rest of the night.

After everyone had gone, my mother said to me, "You want to be the   7
same as American girls on the outside." She handed me an early gift. It was a
miniskirt in beige tweed. "But inside you must always be Chinese. You must be
proud you are different. Your only shame is to have shame."

And even though I didn't agree with her then, I knew that she understood   8
how much I had suffered during the evening's dinner. It wasn't until many
years later — long after I had gotten over my crush on Robert — that I was
able to fully appreciate her lesson and the true purpose behind our particular
menu. For Christmas Eve that year, she had chosen all my favorite foods.

Journal Writing

Do you sympathize with the shame Tan feels because of her family's differences from
their non-Chinese guests? Or do you think she should have been more proud to share
her family's customs? Think of an occasion when, for whatever reason, you were
acutely aware of being different. How did you react? Did you try to hide your difference in order to fit in, or did you reveal or celebrate your uniqueness?

Questions on Meaning

1. Why does Tan cry when she finds out that the boy she is in love with is coming to dinner?

2. Why does Tan's mother go out of her way to prepare a disturbingly traditional Chinese dinner for her daughter and guests? What one sentence best sums up the lesson Tan was not able to understand until years later?

3. How does the fourteen-year-old Tan feel about her Chinese background? about her mother?

4. What is Tan's PURPOSE in writing this essay? Does she just want to entertain readers, or might she have a weightier goal?

Questions on Writing Strategy

1. How does Tan draw the reader into her story right from the beginning?

2. How does Tan use TRANSITIONS both to drive and to clarify her narrative?

3. What is the IRONY of the last sentence of the essay?

4. **OTHER METHODS** Paragraph 3 is a passage of pure DESCRIPTION. Why does Tan linger over the food? What is the EFFECT of this paragraph?

Questions on Language

1. The simile about Mary in the second sentence of the essay is surprising. Why? Why is it amusing? (See FIGURES OF SPEECH in the Glossary for a definition of *simile*.)

2. How does the narrator's age affect the TONE of this essay? Give EXAMPLES of language particularly appropriate to a fourteen-year-old.

3. In which paragraph does Tan use strong verbs most effectively?

4. Make sure you know the meanings of the following words: prawns, tofu (par. 3); clamor (4); grimaced (5); muster (6).

Suggestions for Writing

1. **FROM JOURNAL TO ESSAY** Using Tan's essay as a model, write a brief narrative based on your journal sketch (p. 75) about a time when you felt different from others. Try to imitate the way Tan integrates the external events of the dinner with her own feelings about what is going on. Your story may be humorous, like Tan's, or more serious.

2. Take a perspective like that of the minister's son, Robert: Write a narrative essay about a time when you had to adjust to participating in a culture different from your own. It could be a meal, a wedding or other rite of passage, a religious ceremony, a trip to another country. What did you learn from your experience, about yourself and others?

3. **CRITICAL WRITING** From this essay one can INFER two very different sets of ASSUMPTIONS about the extent to which immigrants should seek to integrate themselves into the culture of their adopted country. Take either of these positions, in favor of or against assimilation (cultural integration), and make an ARGUMENT for your case.

4. **CONNECTIONS** Both Amy Tan and Naomi Shihab Nye, in "Museum" (next page), write about embarrassment, but their POINTS OF VIEW are not the same: Tan's is a teenager's lament about not fitting in; Nye's is an adult's celebration of a past mistake. In an essay, ANALYZE the two authors' uses of narration to convey their perspectives. What details do they focus on? What internal thoughts do they report? Is one essay more effective than the other? Why, or why not?

NAOMI SHIHAB NYE

Naomi Shihab Nye is an accomplished writer of poetry, fiction, and prose for young readers and adults alike. Born in 1952 in St. Louis, Missouri, she earned a BA in English and world religions from Trinity University in 1974 and teaches as a visiting writer at schools and colleges across the country. Growing up, Nye was enchanted by the lyricism of her father's Palestinian folktales and her mother's American lullabies; she published her first poem in a children's magazine when she was seven years old. Since then, Nye's entranced and entrancing writing has appeared regularly in *The Horn Book*, *The Texas Observer*, *World Literature Today*, and other magazines and in her wide-ranging books, including *Habibi* (1997), a young-adult novel based on Nye's own time living in Jerusalem as a teenager; *Sitti's Secrets* (1994) and *Benito's Dream Bottle* (1995), picture books for children; and *Honeybee* (2008), poems and essays for adults. She has also compiled or translated several anthologies of world and student poetry, among them *This Same Sky* (1992) and *Salting the Ocean* (2000). In 2010 Nye was elected a chancellor of the Academy of American Poets. She lives in San Antonio, Texas, and enjoys singing.

Museum

Themes of human connection and cultural exchange run throughout Nye's work. In this story from *Honeybee*, she leads us fleeing giddily from an honest mistake. Like all of her writing, this romp shows Nye's unparalleled exuberance for everyday life and her skill at expressing it.

The preceding essay, Amy Tan's "Fish Cheeks," also tells a tale of embarrassment.

I was 17, and my family had just moved to San Antonio. A local magazine 1 featured an alluring article about a museum called the McNay, an old mansion once the home of an eccentric many-times-married watercolorist named Marian Koogler McNay. She had deeded it to the community to become a museum upon her death. I asked my friend Sally, who drove a cute little convertible and had moved to Texas a year before we did, if she wanted to go there. Sally said, "Sure." She was a good friend that way. We had made up a few words in our own language and could dissolve into laughter just by saying them. Our mothers thought we were a bit odd. On a sunny Saturday afternoon, we drove over to Broadway. Sally asked, "Do you have the address of this place?"

"No," I said, "just drive very slowly and I'll recognize it, there was a picture in the magazine." I peered in both directions and pointed, saying, "There, there it is, pull in!" The parking lot under some palm trees was pretty empty. We entered, excited. The museum was free. Right away, the spirit of the arched doorways, carved window frames, and elegant artwork overtook us. Sally went left; I went right. A group of people seated in some chairs in the lobby stopped talking and stared at us.

"May I help you?" a man said. "No," I said. "We're fine." I didn't like to   2
talk to people in museums. Tours and docents got on my nerves. What if they talked a long time about a painting you weren't that interested in? I took a deep breath, and moved on to another painting — fireworks over a patio in Mexico, maybe? There weren't very good tags in this museum. In fact, there weren't any. I stood back and gazed. Sally had gone upstairs. The people in the lobby had stopped chatting. They seemed very nosy, keeping their eyes on me with irritating curiosity. What was their problem? I turned down a hall-way. Bougainvilleas and azaleas pressed up right against the windows. Maybe we should have brought a picnic. Where was the Moorish courtyard? I saw some nice sculptures in another room, and a small couch. This would be a great place for reading. Above the couch hung a radiant print by Paul Klee,[1] my favorite artist, blues and pinks merging softly in his own wonderful way. I stepped closer. Suddenly I became aware of a man from the lobby standing behind me in the doorway.

"Where do you think you are?" he asked. I turned sharply. "The McNay   3
Art Museum!" He smiled then, and shook his head. "Sorry to tell you. The McNay is three blocks over, on New Braunfels Street. Take a right when you go out of our driveway, then another right." "What is this place?" I asked, still confused. He said, "Well, we thought it was our home." My heart jolted. I raced past him to the bottom of the staircase and called out, "Sally! Come down immediately! Urgent!" I remember being tempted to shout something in our private language, but we didn't have a word for this. Sally came to the top of the stairs smiling happily and said, "You have to come up here, there's some really good stuff! And there are old beds too!" "No, Sally, no," I said, as if she were a dog, or a baby. "Get down here. Speed it up. This is an emergency." She stepped elegantly down the stairs as if in a museum trance, looking puzzled. I just couldn't tell her out loud in front of those people what we had done. I actually pushed her toward the front door, waving my hand at the family in

[1] Paul Klee (1879–1940) was a Swiss artist in the German Expressionist school, known for his childish yet sophisticated imagery. — EDS.

the chairs, saying, "Sorry, ohmygod, please forgive us, you have a really nice place." Sally stared at me in the parking lot. When I told her, she covered her mouth and doubled over with laughter, shaking. We were still in their yard. I imagined them inside looking out the windows at us. She couldn't believe how long they let us look around without saying anything, either. "That was really friendly of them!" "Get in the car," I said sternly. "This is mortifying."

The real McNay was fabulous, splendid, but we felt a little nervous the   4 whole time we were there. Van Gogh, Picasso, Tamayo.[2] This time, there were tags. This time, we stayed together, in case anything else weird happened.

We never told anyone.   5

Thirty years later, a nice-looking woman approached me in a public place.   6 "Excuse me," she said. "I need to ask a strange question. Did you ever, by any chance, enter a residence, long ago, thinking it was the McNay Museum?"

Thirty years later, my cheeks still burned. "Yes. But how do you know?   7 I never told anyone."

"That was my home. I was a teenager sitting with my family talking in the   8 living room. Before you came over, I never realized what a beautiful place I lived in. I never felt lucky before. You thought it was a museum. My feelings changed about my parents after that too. They had good taste. I have always wanted to thank you."

Journal Writing

Why do you suppose Nye remembers in such vivid detail a minor event that happened more than thirty years ago? What small embarrassments or misadventures from your youth seem momentous even now? List these incidents, along with some notes about their importance.

Questions on Meaning

1. What is Nye's PURPOSE in this essay? Obviously, she wants to entertain readers, but does she have another purpose as well?

2. How does Nye explain why she and her friend walked into the home of strangers and wandered around? What do you imagine the family thought was going on?

---

[2] All groundbreaking modern artists. Cubist Pablo Picasso (1881–1973) was Spanish; Post-Impressionist Vincent van Gogh (1853–90) was Dutch; Surrealist Rufino Tamayo (1899–1991) was Mexican. — EDS.

3. What does the incident represent for Nye? What does it represent for the daughter of the household? How did the teenager's feelings about herself and her parents change after the other teenagers left the house, and why?

4. In your own words, try to express Nye's THESIS, or the moral of her story.

Questions on Writing Strategy

1. Does Nye narrate primarily by summary or by scene? How effective do you find
   her choice?

2. Discuss the author's POINT OF VIEW. Is her perspective that of a seventeen-year-old
   or that of an adult writer reflecting on her experience?

3. Nye writes poetry and books both for children and for adult readers. Who seems
   to be the intended AUDIENCE for this story? Why do you think so?

4. **OTHER METHODS** "Museum" implicitly COMPARES AND CONTRASTS Nye's and
   the family's appreciation for luxury and fine art. What are some of the differences
   (and similarities) that Nye implies?

Questions on Language

1. Look up any of the following words that you don't already know: eccentric
   (par. 1); docents, bougainvilleas, azaleas, Moorish (2); mortifying (3).

2. Nye uses short and simple sentences through most of this essay. Why do you suppose that is? What does "Museum" gain (or lose) from lack of sentence variety?
   (If necessary, see pp. 49–53 and 162 on sentence structure.)

3. How does Nye use DIALOG to make the story easy to follow?

4. "Our mothers thought we were a bit odd," Nye writes in the first paragraph. Pick
   out a few other instances of understatement in the essay. What is their effect? (For
   an explanation of *understatement*, look under FIGURES OF SPEECH in the Glossary.)

Suggestions for Writing

1. **FROM JOURNAL TO ESSAY** Choose one embarrassing incident from the list of experiences you wrote for your journal, and narrate the incident as vividly as you can.
   Include the details: Where did the event take place? What did people say? How
   were they dressed? What was the weather like? Follow Nye's model in putting
   CONCRETE IMAGES to work for an idea, in this case an idea about the significance
   of the incident to you then and now.

2. Nye and her friend were clearly amused when they discovered their mistake, but
   entering a private home uninvited — even unintentionally — can have serious
   consequences. Many states, including Texas, authorize homeowners to use deadly
   force against intruders regardless of immediate threat to their own safety. Write a
   serious argumentative essay that addresses the issue of gun rights and self-defense.
   To what extent should homeowners be allowed to shoot first and ask questions

later in the case of home invasion? What about someone on the street who simply feels threatened? Under what circumstances, if any, should personal freedoms
be limited in the name of public safety? (You might want to do some research on
what's known as the "castle doctrine" and on "stand your ground" laws to learn
more about the issue.) Be sure to include evidence to support your opinion and
to ARGUE your position calmly and rationally. You could, if you wish, include
ANECDOTES — whether based on Nye's story or other incidents you know of — to
help develop your argument.

3. **CRITICAL WRITING** Using your answer to the second Question on Meaning
    (p. 80) as a starting point, tell Nye's story from the father's or the daughter's
    point of view. What do you imagine they were talking about when Naomi and
    Sally walked in? What did they think was happening? Were they amused, or do
    you suppose they felt annoyed, even frightened? What lessons did they take from
    the incident? You could take a humorous approach, as Nye does, or you could
    choose to be more serious.

4. **CONNECTIONS** Write an essay about the humor gained from IRONY, relying on
    Nye's essay and Amy Tan's "Fish Cheeks" (p. 74). Why is irony often funny?
    What qualities does self-effacing humor have? Quote and PARAPHRASE from Nye's
    and Tan's essays for your support.

Naomi Shihab Nye on Writing

In an interview with Nye for *Pif Magazine*, Rachel Barenblatt asked, "What is
your advice to writers, especially young writers who are just starting out?" This
was her response:

Number one: Read, Read, and then Read some more. Always Read. Find
the voices that speak most to *you*. This is your pleasure and blessing, as well
as responsibility!

It is crucial to make one's own writing circle — friends, either close or
far, with whom you trade work and discuss it — as a kind of support system,
place-of-conversation, and energy. Find those people, even a few, with whom
you can share and discuss your works — then do it. Keep the papers flowing
among you. Work does not get into the world by itself. We must help it. . . .
Let that circle be sustenance.

There is so much goodness happening in the world of writing today. And
there is plenty of *room* and appetite for new writers. I think there always was.
Don't let anybody tell you otherwise. Attend all the readings you can, and get
involved in giving some, if you like to do that. Be part of your own writing
community. Often the first step in doing this is simply to let yourself become
identified as One Who Cares About Writing!

My motto early on was "Rest and be kind, you don't have to prove anything" — Jack Kerouac's advice about writing — I still think it's true. But working always felt like resting to me.

The Bedford Reader on Writing

Naomi Shihab Nye's advice to beginning writers echoes our own. For more on how reading can make you a better writer, see Chapter 1 on Critical Reading, especially "Reading to Write" on pages 26–28. You can learn about the roles of AUDIENCE and PURPOSE in writing on pages 19–20 and 30–32. And for additional tips on writing freely without trying "to prove anything," see "Drafting," on pages 34–39.

JONATHAN BETHARDS

Jonathan Bethards was born in 1978 in Lodi, California, and grew up in nearby Stockton. After graduating from Lincoln High School he trained and worked as an emergency medical technician (EMT) until he was sidelined by an injury on the job. He now attends San Joaquin Delta College as he seeks ideas for a new career. A "big-time sports fan," Bethards enjoys the outdoors and photography.

Code Three

In this heart-pounding narrative, Bethards relates the experience of first respond-ers on a particularly tense ambulance call. "Code Three" was featured in the 2015 edition of *Delta Winds*, San Joaquin Delta College's annual anthology of exemplary student writing.

The man's family stood around us in a circle; I could feel their eyes on us   1
as we worked feverishly under the blazing afternoon sun. "This isn't going to work," I thought to myself. I glanced over at my partner, Oscar, and I could tell he was thinking the same thing. We didn't have much time left until we had to call it, but neither of us was letting up yet. This was definitely not how I saw my first shift back from vacation going.

My time as an Emergency Medical Technician (EMT) on a 911 ambu-   2
lance may have lasted for only five years, but they were very interesting years. I will freely admit that a majority of our shifts were spent just hanging out at quarters; but some days we would just get slammed, and this was looking like one of those days.

After an afternoon full of the usual calls, mainly non-life threatening,   3
and with the temperature soaring in the low 100s, Oscar and I were ready for a short nap in the cool confines of our quarters. We were a few blocks away from our air-conditioned station when we heard exactly what we didn't want to hear: "Unit Ninety-Two, are you clear for a Code Three call?" I cringed as I picked up the microphone from the radio and responded, "Unit Ninety-Two is clear and available." Dispatch proceeded to have my unit and Stockton Fire Engine Six sent out to a "man down" call in the middle of the street. I told Dispatch we were en route and gunned the engine as Oscar flipped the sirens and lights on. Code Three driving isn't nearly as fun as it may look; legally we're only supposed to go fifteen miles per hour over the limit. We have to watch out for all the numbskulls and space cadets on the road as we navigate our way to the call.

We reached the scene at about the same time as the SFD; I quickly ran   4
around the back of the rig and threw the monitor, airway bag, and our main bag

on the gurney. I yanked the gurney out of the rig and made my way through a large group of people standing around a man lying in the street. I looked down at my partner, who had been assessing the patient, and read his body language and hand signals. This was not going to be an easy call. The man, who was in his late fifties and had an extensive medical history, was non-responsive and had no discernable pulse. As I hooked him up to the monitor, we could all see why he was non-responsive: He was in respiratory arrest and ventricular fibrillation. In other words, this man was in a world of hurt.

My partner and the fire medic were getting ready to deploy the defibrillation paddles and the fire EMT was doing chest compressions as I readied an IV setup and prepared the epinephrine; I had been in this situation before and knew we would need these at a minimum. Upon seeing my partner apply gel to the paddles and the man's chest, a woman became hysterical. The fire captain was putting forth a valiant effort to restrain her but was failing. The rest of the family started to become increasingly confrontational and angry. "Why the hell aren't you doing anything?" I heard from behind me. "Get off your asses and FIX him or . . . or so help me I'll SUE you," screamed the woman, who was now engaged in some serious hand fighting with the captain. Now, clearly we were trying to help the patient, but when panic and love combine, a situation can change from stressful to violent in an instant.   5

The fire medic got the IV in on the first try and was now trying to get an airway into the lungs. This was not an easy job as he had to keep stopping to clear the patient while Oscar defibrillated him, pushing another round of epinephrine into the IV, or holding the patient's increasingly agitated family members back so we could do our job. On his third attempt, the medic got an airway, and almost simultaneously we heard an unmistakable sound. It was the sweetest sound I think that I had ever heard. It was the slow but steady beeping of the patient's heart, represented by a beautiful normal sinus rhythm on our monitor.   6

Oscar and I, sweat pouring down our faces, exchanged a quick smile and then looked over at the fire crew. They were equally soaked in sweat and were smiling even wider than we were. "Why did you stop?" screamed the woman. "Why are you all smiling like a bunch of jackasses? MY HUSBAND IS DYING!" The fire captain had finally had enough and gripped the woman by her fleshy arms. "Ma'am! Your husband isn't dying: We got him back!" That was it for the woman and her family; they all broke down and cried and started thanking us in between sobs.   7

The patient, though not out of the woods, was doing far better than he was when we arrived on the scene; after all, he was breathing on his own and his heart, though slow, was beating on its own. I couldn't believe it; this was the first patient we'd revived who hadn't immediately crashed again. As we   8 loaded him into the rig for transport to Saint Joseph's, he opened his eyes and tried to say something. "Sir," I said, "don't try to talk. You have a tube down your throat. You're going to be okay, and your family is going to meet us at the emergency room." Tears started to roll down the man's cheeks, and he looked me right in the eye. I could tell that he was trying to thank me. "You're welcome," I said as I choked back tears of my own and put my hand over his: "We were just doing our jobs, sir."

Journal Writing

At one point or another, most of us have had at least one interaction with emergency personnel — EMTs like Bethards, paramedics, hospital staff, police, firefighters, lifeguards, and the like. Think of one such instance in your life, either as the person needing help or as a bystander. In your journal, recall as much about the event as you can, using the five journalist's questions (pp. 66–67) to prompt your memory. What happened, and where? Who was in trouble, and why? How did things turn out?

Questions on Meaning

1. What would you say is the writer's PURPOSE in this essay? Is it primarily to entertain readers with an exciting story, or does he seem to have another purpose as well? How can you tell?

2. What actually happened to the man to prompt a 911 call? Does Bethards provide enough explanation for readers to know? Is it necessary to understand the details of the patient's condition to understand the rest of the story?

3. Why did the situation threaten to become violent? How does Bethards explain the wife's behavior?

4. Bethards does not state a THESIS. In your own words, what is the controlling idea of his narrative?

Questions on Writing Strategy

1. What POINT OF VIEW does Bethards take as a narrator?

2. What is the EFFECT of Bethards's opening paragraph? Why does he begin his narrative in the middle?

3. "Code Three" is a particularly gripping student narrative. How does Bethards create SUSPENSE through the essay?

4. **OTHER METHODS** Where does Bethards use PROCESS ANALYSIS to explain events for an AUDIENCE of laypeople not trained in medical procedures?

Questions on Language

1. Be sure you know how to define the following terms: confines, en route (par. 3); gurney, discernable, respiratory arrest, ventricular fibrillation (4); deploy, defibrillation, epinephrine, valiant (5); agitated (6).

2. Bethards mixes occupational JARGON and COLLOQUIAL EXPRESSIONS, such as when he writes, "He was in respiratory arrest and ventricular fibrillation. In other words, this man was in a world of hurt" (par. 4). Find a few additional examples. Is this use of language appropriate? Is it effective? Why, or why not?

3. Explain the contradiction in the concluding statement, "We were just doing our jobs, sir" (par. 8). Can you find other examples of paradox in what Bethards says? How is this paradox related to his apparent view of the job? (See FIGURES OF SPEECH in the Glossary for a definition of *paradox*.)

Suggestions for Writing

1. **FROM JOURNAL TO ESSAY** Turn your journal notes into a narrative about an encounter with emergency providers from the perspective of a person needing help (or, if you weren't the person in trouble, from a bystander's point of view). Like Bethards does, try to convey the urgency of the situation and to build suspense so that readers care about the outcome.

2. In an essay that combines narration and process analysis, write about a memorable experience you have had at work or while volunteering. What was the job? Was the work anything like you expected? What moments stand out in your memory, and why? Try to use colorful language and specific details to help readers share in your experience.

3. **CRITICAL WRITING** EVALUATE the effectiveness of Bethards's narrative. What do you think of his choice of details? His pacing? His TONE? How successful is the author's attempt to convey the tensions and rewards of working as an emergency responder? Did his story hold your interest? Does the essay have any weaknesses, in your view? Why, or why not?

4. **CONNECTIONS** In his police "Ride-Along Report" (p. 71), Scott Beltran also presents a narrative based on the experiences of first responders, but he writes in a different GENRE for different reasons. In a paragraph, distill the events Bethards recounts into an objective activity log for the public record. Compare the two versions of his story, and then explain how genre, purpose, and audience influence the structure and effect of a narrative.

JUNOT DÍAZ

Junot Díaz is a writer well loved for his unique voice and unflinching fiction, which typically involves young Dominicans struggling with obstacles. Born in 1968 in Santo Domingo, Dominican Republic, he immigrated to New Jersey with his family in 1975. As a poor child who had trouble speaking English and who felt like an outsider, Díaz immersed himself in comic books and science fiction and discovered that writing helped him cope with his difficulties. He earned degrees in literature and history from Rutgers University in 1992 and an MFA in creative writing from Cornell University in 1995. Díaz's critically acclaimed work includes the collections of short stories *Drown* (1996) and *This Is How You Lose Her* (2012) and the novel *The Brief Wondrous Life of Oscar Wao* (2007), which centers on the brutalities of Dominican history and an awkward boy's struggles to adapt. Díaz won a National Book Critics Circle Award and a Pulitzer Prize for that novel; he has also been recognized with a PEN/Malamud Award, a Dayton Literary Peace Prize, an O. Henry Prize, and a Guggenheim Fellowship. He received a MacArthur "genius" grant in 2012. A frequent contributor to *The New Yorker* and the fiction editor at the *Boston Review*, Díaz teaches writing at the Massachusetts Institute of Technology.

The Dreamer

In this essay Díaz relates a remarkable episode of his mother's life in the Dominican Republic. In expressing his admiration for her determination to learn, Díaz hints at the myriad ways a young girl's daring has influenced his own life and work. "The Dreamer" first appeared in *More*, a women's magazine, in 2011.

I think of my mother, of course. She's one of those ironwill rarely speak   1
figures that haunt. See her in New Jersey, in the house with the squirrels in the back that she feeds sparingly (they shouldn't get fat) and that she chides when she thinks they're acting up. You wouldn't know it looking at her in that kitchen, but she grew up one of those poor Third World–country girls. The brutalized backbone of our world. The kind of Dominican girl who was destined never to get off the mountain or out of the *campo*.[1] Her own mother a straight-haired terror. Expected her to work on the family farm until she died or was married off, but my mother in those small spaces between the work cultivated dreams, that unbreakable habit of the young. When the field hands were hurt or fell ill, she was the one who cared for them. Opened in her a horizon. A dream of being a nurse in the capital, where she heard that every

---

[1] Spanish, "countryside." — EDS.

block had electricity. But to be a nurse, you needed education, and while there were some girls who attended the one-room school at the base of the hill, my mother was not one of them. Her mother, my grandmother, demanded that she stay on the farm, that she stay a mule. No one more threatened by the thought of an educated girl than my grandmother. Any time my mother was caught near the schoolhouse, my grandmother gave her a beating. And not the beatings of the First World but the beatings of the Third — which you do not so easily shake off.

So the months passed and the horizon started to dim, and that's the way it should have stayed, but then the world, so far away, intervened. For his own complicated reasons the dictator of that time, Trujillo,[2] passed a mandatory-education act stipulating that all Dominican children under the age of fifteen had to be in school and not stuck out in the fields. All children. Any parent keeping a child from school would be imprisoned! Nothing short of the threat of a year inside a Trujillo prison could snap the resistance that rural Dominicans had to the idea of educating their young.   2

My mother heard about the law, of course. And she brooded on it. The house, like all other houses in the Dominican Republic, had a portrait of Trujillo hanging in it. I guess my mother figured if anyone was going to protect her from my grandmother's wrath, it was going to be him.   3

She'd only learn later how little our dictator protected her or anyone else.   4

The news of the school came at a crucial time. My mother's family was preparing for its seasonal move up higher into the hills, in the mist-soaked highlands where the coffee was waiting, but my mother had other plans. Two days before the move, she got down on her knees beside a stagnant puddle of water, put her mouth in it and drank deeply.   5

She was so sick that the family decided to head into the hills without her. The coffee could not wait. My mother was left with a cousin, and as soon as my grandmother was out of sight, my mother, bent over double from the stomach pains, hobbled down to the schoolhouse and reported my grandmother.   6

I want to go to school, was what she told the teacher.   7

What should have happened was that the teacher should have laughed and sent her poor ass back to the hills to pick coffee. But as it turned out, the teacher was an idealistic young woman from the capital — God bless all idealistic educators — and she took my mother's claim seriously. Went to the police, who *always* took Trujillo's laws seriously, and so when my grandmother came back to fetch her daughter, she found my mother attending school.   8

---

[2] General Rafael Trujillo took over rule of the Dominican Republic in a 1930 military coup. His regime was characterized by violent oppression and lasted until he was assassinated in 1961. — Eds.

And when she tried to drag my mother up to the hills, the police put her   9
in handcuffs, and that was that.

"Your grandmother beat me almost every day," my mother explained, "but   10
I got my education."

She never did become a nurse, my mother. Immigration got in the way   11
of that horizon — once in the United States, my mother never could master
English, no matter how hard she tried, and my God, did she try. But strange
how things work — her son became a reader and a writer, practices she
encouraged as much as possible. I write professionally now, and life is long and
complicated, and who knows how things might have turned out under different circumstances, but I do believe that who I am as an artist, everything that
I've ever written, was possible because a seven-year-old girl up in the hills of
Azua knelt before a puddle, found courage in herself and drank. Every time
I'm in trouble in my art, I try to think of that girl. I think of that thirst, of that
courage. I think of her.

Journal Writing

Díaz writes that his mother was severely beaten by her own mother, and distinguishes
"the beatings of the First World [from] the beatings of the Third — which you do not
so easily shake off" (par. 1). How do you react to this distinction? Why would beatings
in developing countries be especially brutal? Do degrees of abuse matter? Why would
any parent beat a child? And why wouldn't families, neighbors, or authority figures
(such as teachers) step in to stop the abuse? Explore your thoughts on any of these
questions in your journal.

Questions on Meaning

1. Why does Díaz admire his mother as he does? What does her experience represent to him?

2. Does Díaz have a THESIS? In which sentence or sentences does he state the point
   of his story most directly?

3. What would you say is Díaz's PURPOSE in this essay? Is it simply to inform readers
   about his mother's quest for an education, or does he seem to have another purpose in mind?

4. "She'd only learn later how little our dictator protected her or anyone else," Díaz
   writes in paragraph 4. What does he mean? Based on this statement and other
   references to Rafael Trujillo in the essay, what can you INFER about life in the
   Dominican Republic under his dictatorship?

Questions on Writing Strategy

1. Take note of the first and last sentences in "The Dreamer." How are they related, and what is their effect?

2. In telling his mother's story, does Díaz take mostly an objective or a subjective POINT OF VIEW? How effective do you find his choice?

3. This essay originally appeared in a women's magazine. What evidence in the text reveals that Díaz was writing for an AUDIENCE of female readers?

4. **OTHER METHODS** Explain the CAUSE-AND-EFFECT relationships Díaz outlines in his narrative. What actions — and whose — made it possible for his mother to attend school? What impact did her education have on her life? on his?

Questions on Language

1. Be sure you know how to define the following words: ironwill, chides, cultivated (par. 1); intervened, stipulating (2); brooded (3); stagnant (5).

2. In what sense does Díaz use the word *horizon* (pars. 1, 2, and 11)? What makes this IMAGE particularly appropriate to the story's meaning?

3. The first paragraph of this essay is loaded with sentence fragments, such as "The brutalized backbone of our world." Where else do you find incomplete sentences? What do they contribute to (or take away from) Díaz's VOICE and the effectiveness of his narrative?

4. Díaz quotes his mother twice. Why do you suppose he uses quotation marks around her words in paragraph 10 but not in paragraph 7?

Suggestions for Writing

1. **FROM JOURNAL TO ESSAY** Building on your journal entry, compose an essay that examines one of the causes or effects of child abuse, in the United States or elsewhere. If you have had some experience with abuse (as a counselor, a bystander, a victim, or an abuser) and you care to write about it, you might develop your thesis based on your experience and observation; otherwise, draw on information you have gleaned from the media and your reading, being sure to acknowledge any sources you use.

2. Using Díaz's essay as a model, compose an essay in which you contemplate and explain your sense of identity. How do you define yourself? Has any one person had a significant effect on who you are? How so?

3. **CRITICAL WRITING** Write an essay in which you ANALYZE Díaz's use of language in this essay or a portion of it. How would you characterize his DICTION? What are some especially creative uses of language? What overall EFFECT does Díaz create with the language he uses?

4. **CONNECTIONS** In "Live Free and Starve" (p. 398), Chitra Divakaruni also writes about children in desperate circumstances. Write an essay that COMPARES AND

CONTRASTS Díaz's and Divakaruni's attitudes toward child labor. Taken together, what do these two authors seem to believe is the best recourse for a family struggling in poverty? What do they suggest are a parent's responsibilities to children? a community's? a government's? What is each writer saying about the role of education in particular? How do you respond to their ideas?

Junot Díaz on Writing

In a 2009 essay for Oprah Winfrey's O magazine, Díaz tells the story of how, in his mind, he became a writer. It begins with failure. He had drafted seventy-five pages of his second book, then got stuck. "It wasn't that I couldn't write," he explains. "I wrote every day. I actually worked really hard at writing. At my desk by seven a.m., would work a full eight and more. Scribbled at the dinner table, in bed, on the toilet, on the No. 6 train, at Shea Stadium. I did everything I could. But none of it worked. . . . I wrote and I wrote and I wrote, but nothing I produced was worth a damn."

Díaz goes on to say that he kept trying all the same. "Want to talk about stubborn? I kept at it for five straight years. Five damn years. Every day failing for five years? I'm a pretty stubborn, pretty hard-hearted character, but those five years of fail did a number on my psyche. On me. Five years, sixty months? It just about wiped me out." Frustrated and despondent, he considered pursuing another line of work: "I knew I couldn't go on much more the way I was going. I just couldn't. . . . So I put the manuscript away. All the hundreds of failed pages, boxed and hidden in a closet. I think I cried as I did it."

"I slipped into my new morose half-life," Díaz recalls. "Started preparing for my next stage, back to school in September." And then, on a sleepless night, "sickened that I was giving up, but even more frightened by the thought of having to return to the writing," Díaz pulled the pages out of storage. "I figured if I could find one good thing in the pages I would go back to it," he explains. "Spent the whole night reading everything I had written, and guess what? It was still terrible. In fact with the new distance the lameness was even worse than I'd thought. . . . I didn't have the heart to go on. But I guess I did. . . . I separated the seventy-five pages that were worthy from the mountain of loss, sat at my desk, and despite every part of me shrieking no no no no, I jumped back down the rabbit hole again." And after five more years of struggle and regular bouts "of being utterly, dismayingly lost," he finally completed *The Brief Wondrous Life of Oscar Wao*.

"That," concludes Díaz, is his "tale in a nutshell. Not the tale of how I came to write my novel but rather of how I became a writer. Because, in truth, I didn't become a writer the first time I put pen to paper or when I finished my first book (easy) or my second one (hard). You see, in my view a writer is a writer not because she writes well and easily, because she has amazing talent, because everything she does is golden. In my view a writer is a writer because even when there is no hope, even when nothing you do shows any sign of promise, you keep writing anyway. Wasn't until that night when I was faced with all those lousy pages that I realized, really realized, what it was exactly that I am."

The *Bedford Reader* on Writing

Díaz seems to have inherited a good streak of his mother's determination and willingness to make personal sacrifices — as indeed he suggests in "The Dreamer." Although you probably can't imagine discarding hundreds of pages of manuscript during REVISION, you can surely empathize with the frustrations of failed writing and the agony of starting over. Have you ever, like Díaz, tossed out most of a DRAFT? How might "one good thing" justify, or even require, starting over? See our suggestions in "Revising," pages 39–42.

MAYA ANGELOU

Maya Angelou was born Marguerite Johnson in St. Louis in 1928. After an unpleasantly eventful youth by her account ("from a broken family, raped at eight, unwed mother at sixteen"), she went on to join a dance company, act in the off-Broadway play *The Blacks* and the television series *Roots*, write several books of poetry, produce a TV series on Africa, serve as a coordinator for the Southern Christian Leadership Conference, win the Presidential Medals of Arts and of Freedom, teach American studies at Wake Forest University, write and deliver the inaugural poem ("On the Pulse of Morning") for President Clinton, and be inducted into the National Women's Hall of Fame. Angelou is the author of thirty best-selling works but is probably best known for the six books of her searching, frank, and joyful autobiography — from *I Know Why the Caged Bird Sings* (1970) through *A Song Flung Up to Heaven* (2002). She died in 2014 at her home in Winston-Salem, North Carolina.

Champion of the World

"Champion of the World" is the nineteenth chapter in *I Know Why the Caged Bird Sings;* the title is a phrase taken from the chapter. Remembering her childhood, the writer tells how she and her older brother, Bailey, grew up in a town in Arkansas. The center of their lives was Grandmother and Uncle Willie's store. On the night of this story, in the late 1930s, the African American community gathers in the store to listen to a boxing match on the radio. Joe Louis, the "Brown Bomber," who was a hero to black people, is defending his heavyweight title against a white contender. (Louis successfully defended his title twenty-five times, a record that stands today.) Angelou's telling of the event both entertains us and explains what it was like to be African American in a certain time and place.

The last inch of space was filled, yet people continued to wedge themselves along the walls of the Store. Uncle Willie had turned the radio up to its last notch so that youngsters on the porch wouldn't miss a word. Women sat on kitchen chairs, dining-room chairs, stools, and upturned wooden boxes. Small children and babies perched on every lap available and men leaned on the shelves or on each other. 1

The apprehensive mood was shot through with shafts of gaiety, as a black sky is streaked with lightning. 2

"I ain't worried 'bout this fight. Joe's gonna whip that cracker like it's open season." 3

"He gone whip him till that white boy call him Momma." 4

At last the talking finished and the string-along songs about razor blades were over and the fight began. 5

"A quick jab to the head." In the Store the crowd grunted. "A left to the   6
head and a right and another left." One of the listeners cackled like a hen and
was quieted.

"They're in a clinch, Louis is trying to fight his way out."   7

Some bitter comedian on the porch said, "That white man don't mind   8
hugging that niggah now, I betcha."

"The referee is moving in to break them up, but Louis finally pushed the   9
contender away and it's an uppercut to the chin. The contender is hanging
on, now he's backing away. Louis catches him with a short left to the jaw."

A tide of murmuring assent poured out the door and into the yard.   10

"Another left and another left. Louis is saving that mighty right . . ." The   11
mutter in the Store had grown into a baby roar and it was pierced by the clang of
a bell and the announcer's "That's the bell for round three, ladies and gentlemen."

As I pushed my way into the Store I wondered if the announcer gave any   12
thought to the fact that he was addressing as "ladies and gentlemen" all the
Negroes around the world who sat sweating and praying, glued to their "Master's voice."[1]

There were only a few calls for RC Colas, Dr Peppers, and Hires root beer.   13
The real festivities would begin after the fight. Then even the old Christian
ladies who taught their children and tried themselves to practice turning the
other cheek would buy soft drinks, and if the Brown Bomber's victory was a
particularly bloody one they would order peanut patties and Baby Ruths also.

Bailey and I laid the coins on top of the cash register. Uncle Willie didn't   14
allow us to ring up sales during a fight. It was too noisy and might shake up the
atmosphere. When the gong rang for the next round we pushed through the
near-sacred quiet to the herd of children outside.

"He's got Louis against the ropes and now it's a left to the body and a right   15
to the ribs. Another right to the body, it looks like it was low . . . Yes, ladies
and gentlemen, the referee is signaling but the contender keeps raining the
blows on Louis. It's another to the body, and it looks like Louis is going down."

My race groaned. It was our people falling. It was another lynching, yet   16
another Black man hanging on a tree. One more woman ambushed and raped.
A Black boy whipped and maimed. It was hounds on the trail of a man running through slimy swamps. It was a white woman slapping her maid for being
forgetful.

The men in the Store stood away from the walls and at attention. Women   17
greedily clutched the babes on their laps while on the porch the shufflings

---

[1] "His Master's Voice," accompanied by a picture of a little dog listening to a phonograph,
was a familiar advertising slogan. (The picture still appears on some RCA recordings.) — Eds.

and smiles, flirtings and pinching of a few minutes before were gone. This might be the end of the world. If Joe lost we were back in slavery and beyond help. It would all be true, the accusations that we were lower types of human beings. Only a little higher than apes. True that we were stupid and ugly and lazy and dirty and, unlucky and worst of all, that God Himself hated us and ordained us to be hewers of wood and drawers of water, forever and ever, world without end.

We didn't breathe. We didn't hope. We waited.   18

"He's off the ropes, ladies and gentlemen. He's moving towards the cen-   19
ter of the ring." There was no time to be relieved. The worst might still happen.

"And now it looks like Joe is mad. He's caught Carnera with a left hook   20
to the head and a right to the head. It's a left jab to the body and another left to the head. There's a left cross and a right to the head. The contender's right eye is bleeding and he can't seem to keep his block up. Louis is penetrating every block. The referee is moving in, but Louis sends a left to the body and it's an uppercut to the chin and the contender is dropping. He's on the canvas, ladies and gentlemen."

Babies slid to the floor as women stood up and men leaned toward the   21
radio.

"Here's the referee. He's counting. One, two, three, four, five, six, seven . . .   22
Is the contender trying to get up again?"

All the men in the store shouted, "no."   23

" — eight, nine, ten." There were a few sounds from the audience, but   24
they seemed to be holding themselves in against tremendous pressure.

"The fight is all over, ladies and gentlemen. Let's get the microphone over   25
to the referee . . . Here he is. He's got the Brown Bomber's hand, he's holding it up . . . Here he is . . ."

Then the voice, husky and familiar, came to wash over us — "The win-   26
nah, and still heavyweight champeen of the world . . . Joe Louis."

Champion of the world. A Black boy. Some Black mother's son. He was   27
the strongest man in the world. People drank Coca-Colas like ambrosia and ate candy bars like Christmas. Some of the men went behind the Store and poured white lightning in their soft-drink bottles, and a few of the bigger boys followed them. Those who were not chased away came back blowing their breath in front of themselves like proud smokers.

It would take an hour or more before the people would leave the Store   28
and head for home. Those who lived too far had made arrangements to stay in town. It wouldn't do for a Black man and his family to be caught on a lonely country road on a night when Joe Louis had proved that we were the strongest people in the world.

Journal Writing

How do you respond to the group identification and solidarity that Angelou writes about in this essay? What groups do you belong to, and how do you know you're a member? Consider groups based on race, ethnic background, religion, sports, hobbies, politics, friendship, kinship, or any other ties.

Questions on Meaning

1. What do you take to be the author's PURPOSE in telling this story?

2. What connection does Angelou make between the outcome of the fight and the pride of African Americans? To what degree do you think the author's view is shared by the others in the store listening to the broadcast?

3. To what extent are the statements in paragraphs 16 and 17 to be taken literally? What function do they serve in Angelou's narrative?

4. Primo Carnera was probably *not* the Brown Bomber's opponent on the night Maya Angelou recalls. Louis fought Carnera only once, on June 25, 1935, and it was not a title match. Does the author's apparent error detract from her story?

Questions on Writing Strategy

1. What details in the opening paragraphs indicate that an event of crucial importance is about to take place?

2. How does Angelou build up SUSPENSE in her account of the fight? At what point were you able to predict the winner?

3. Comment on the IRONY in Angelou's final paragraph.

4. What EFFECT does the author's use of direct quotation have on her narrative?

5. **OTHER METHODS** Besides narration, Angelou also relies heavily on the method of DESCRIPTION. Analyze how narration depends on description in paragraph 27 alone.

Questions on Language

1. Explain what the author means by "string-along songs about razor blades" (par. 5).

2. Point to some examples in the essay of Angelou's use of strong verbs.

3. How does Angelou's use of NONSTANDARD ENGLISH contribute to her narrative?

4. Be sure you know the meanings of these words: apprehensive (par. 2); assent (10); ambushed, maimed (16); ordained (17); ambrosia, white lightning (27).

Suggestions for Writing

1. **FROM JOURNAL TO ESSAY** From your journal entry, choose one of the groups you belong to and explore your sense of membership through a narrative that tells of an incident that occurred when that sense was strong. Try to make the incident

come alive for your readers with vivid details, dialog, and tight sequencing of events.

2. Write an essay based on some childhood experience of your own, still vivid in your memory.

3. **CRITICAL WRITING** Angelou does not directly describe relations between African Americans and whites, yet her essay implies quite a lot. Write a brief essay about what you can INFER from the exaggeration of paragraphs 16–17 and the obliqueness of paragraph 28. Focus on Angelou's details and the language she uses to present them.

4. **CONNECTIONS** Angelou's "Champion of the World" and Amy Tan's "Fish Cheeks" (p. 74) both tell stories of feeling like outsiders in predominantly white America. COMPARE AND CONTRAST the two writers' perceptions of what sets them apart from the dominant culture. How does the event each reports affect that sense of difference? Use specific examples from both essays as your EVIDENCE.

Maya Angelou on Writing

Maya Angelou's writings have shown great variety: She has done notable work as an autobiographer, poet, short-story writer, screenwriter, journalist, and song lyricist. Asked by interviewer Sheila Weller, "Do you start each project with a specific idea?" Angelou replied:

It starts with a definite subject, but it might end with something entirely different. When I start a project, the first thing I do is write down, in longhand, everything I know about the subject, every thought I've ever had on it. This may be twelve or fourteen pages. Then I read it back through, for quite a few days, and find — given that subject — what its rhythm is. 'Cause everything in the universe has a rhythm. So if it's free form, it still has a rhythm. And once I hear the rhythm of the piece, then I try to find out what are the salient points that I must make. And then it begins to take shape.

I try to set myself up in each chapter by saying: "This is what I want to go from — from B to, say, G-sharp. Or from D to L." And then I find the hook. It's like the knitting, where, after you knit a certain amount, there's one thread that begins to pull. You know, you can see it right along the cloth. Well, in writing, I think: "Now where is that one hook, that one little thread?" It may be a sentence. If I can catch that, then I'm home free. It's the one that tells me where I'm going. It may not even turn out to be in the final chapter. I may throw it out later or change it. But if I follow it through, it leads me right out.

The Bedford Reader on Writing

What response would you give someone who asked, "Doesn't Angelou's approach to writing take more time and thought than it's worth?" Freewriting, or putting down many pages' worth of random thoughts before starting a project — as Angelou does and as we recommend on page 33 — may seem an excessive amount of toil. But Angelou invites the observation that the more work you do before you write, the easier it is once you begin writing in earnest. For our advice on discovering ideas about a SUBJECT, see pages 32–34. And for help on finding a "hook," or THESIS, for a narrative, turn to page 65 in this chapter.

SHIRLEY JACKSON

Shirley Jackson was a fiction writer best known for horror stories that probe the dark side of human nature and social behavior. But she also wrote humorously about domestic life, a subject she knew well as a wife and the mother of four children. Born in 1916 in California, Jackson moved as a teenager to upstate New York, and graduated from Syracuse University in 1940. She started writing as a young girl and was highly disciplined and productive all her life. She began publishing stories in 1941, and eventually her fiction appeared in *The New Yorker*, *Harper's*, *Good Housekeeping*, and many other magazines. Her tales of family life appeared in two books, *Life among the Savages* (1953) and *Raising Demons* (1957). Her suspense novels, which were more significant to her, included *The Haunting of Hill House* (1959) and *We Have Always Lived in the Castle* (1962). After Jackson died in 1965, her husband, the literary critic Stanley Edgar Hyman, published two volumes of her stories, novels, and lectures: *The Magic of Shirley Jackson* (1966) and *Come Along with Me* (1968).

The Lottery

By far Jackson's best-known work and indeed one of the best-known short stories ever written, "The Lottery" first appeared in *The New Yorker* in 1948 to loud applause and louder cries of outrage. The time was just after World War II, when Nazi concentration camps and the dropping of atomic bombs had revealed the horrors of organized human cruelty. Jackson's husband, denying that her work purveyed "neurotic fantasies," argued instead that it was fitting "for our distressing world." Is the story still relevant today?

The morning of June 27th was clear and sunny, with the fresh warmth 1
of a full-summer day; the flowers were blossoming profusely and the grass was richly green. The people of the village began to gather in the square, between the post office and the bank, around ten o'clock; in some towns there were so many people that the lottery took two days and had to be started on June 26th, but in this village, where there were only about three hundred people, the whole lottery took less than two hours, so it could begin at ten o'clock in the morning and still be through in time to allow the villagers to get home for noon dinner.

The children assembled first, of course. School was recently over for the 2
summer, and the feeling of liberty sat uneasily on most of them; they tended to gather together quietly for a while before they broke into boisterous play, and their talk was still of the classroom and the teacher, of books and reprimands. Bobby Martin had already stuffed his pockets full of stones, and the other

boys soon followed his example, selecting the smoothest and roundest stones; Bobby and Harry Jones and Dickie Delacroix — the villagers pronounced this name "Dellacroy" — eventually made a great pile of stones in one corner of the square and guarded it against the raids of the other boys. The girls stood aside, talking among themselves, looking over their shoulders at the boys, and the very small children rolled in the dust or clung to the hands of their older brothers or sisters.

Soon the men began to gather, surveying their own children, speaking 3 of planting and rain, tractors and taxes. They stood together, away from the pile of stones in the corner, and their jokes were quiet and they smiled rather than laughed. The women, wearing faded house dresses and sweaters, came shortly after their menfolk. They greeted one another and exchanged bits of gossip as they went to join their husbands. Soon the women, standing by their husbands, began to call to their children, and the children came reluctantly, having to be called four or five times. Bobby Martin ducked under his mother's grasping hand and ran, laughing, back to the pile of stones. His father spoke up sharply, and Bobby came quickly and took his place between his father and his oldest brother.

The lottery was conducted — as were the square dances, the teenage 4 club, the Halloween program — by Mr. Summers, who had time and energy to devote to civic activities. He was a round-faced, jovial man and he ran the coal business, and people were sorry for him, because he had no children and his wife was a scold. When he arrived in the square, carrying the black wooden box, there was a murmur of conversation among the villagers, and he waved and called, "Little late today, folks." The postmaster, Mr. Graves, followed him, carrying a three-legged stool, and the stool was put in the center of the square and Mr. Summers set the black box down on it. The villagers kept their distance, leaving a space between themselves and the stool, and when Mr. Summers said, "Some of you fellows want to give me a hand?" there was a hesitation before two men, Mr. Martin and his oldest son, Baxter, came forward to hold the box steady on the stool while Mr. Summers stirred up the papers inside it.

The original paraphernalia for the lottery had been lost long ago, and the 5 black box now resting on the stool had been put into use even before Old Man Warner, the oldest man in town, was born. Mr. Summers spoke frequently to the villagers about making a new box, but no one liked to upset even as much tradition as was represented by the black box. There was a story that the present box had been made with some pieces of the box that had preceded it, the one that had been constructed when the first people settled down to make a village here. Every year, after the lottery, Mr. Summers began talking again about a new box, but every year the subject was allowed to fade off without anything's being done. The black box grew shabbier each year; by now it was no longer completely black but splintered badly along one side to show the original wood color, and in some places faded or stained.

Mr. Martin and his oldest son, Baxter, held the black box securely on   6
the stool until Mr. Summers had stirred the papers thoroughly with his hand. Because so much of the ritual had been forgotten or discarded, Mr. Summers had been successful in having slips of paper substituted for the chips of wood that had been used for generations. Chips of wood, Mr. Summers had argued, had been all very well when the village was tiny, but now that the population was more than three hundred and likely to keep on growing, it was necessary to use something that would fit more easily into the black box. The night before the lottery, Mr. Summers and Mr. Graves made up the slips of paper and put them in the box, and it was then taken to the safe of Mr. Summers's coal company and locked up until Mr. Summers was ready to take it to the square next morning. The rest of the year, the box was put away, sometimes one place, sometimes another; it had spent one year in Mr. Graves's barn and another year underfoot in the post office, and sometimes it was set on a shelf in the Martin grocery and left there.

There was a great deal of fussing to be done before Mr. Summers declared   7
the lottery open. There were the lists to make up — of heads of families, heads of households in each family, members of each household in each family. There was the proper swearing-in of Mr. Summers by the postmaster, as the official of the lottery; at one time, some people remembered, there had been a recital of some sort, performed by the official of the lottery, a perfunctory, tuneless chant that had been rattled off duly each year; some people believed that the official of the lottery used to stand just so when he said or sang it, others believed that he was supposed to walk among the people, but years and years ago this part of the ritual had been allowed to lapse. There had been, also, a ritual salute, which the official of the lottery had had to use in address-ing each person who came up to draw from the box, but this also had changed with time, until now it was felt necessary only for the official to speak to each person approaching. Mr. Summers was very good at all this; in his clean white shirt and blue jeans, with one hand resting carelessly on the black box, he seemed very proper and important as he talked interminably to Mr. Graves and the Martins.

Just as Mr. Summers finally left off talking and turned to the assembled   8
villagers, Mrs. Hutchinson came hurriedly along the path to the square, her sweater thrown over her shoulders, and slid into place in the back of the crowd. "Clean forgot what day it was," she said to Mrs. Delacroix, who stood next to her, and they both laughed softly. "Thought my old man was out back stacking wood," Mrs. Hutchinson went on, "and then I looked out the window

and the kids was gone, and then I remembered it was the twenty-seventh and came a-running." She dried her hands on her apron, and Mrs. Delacroix said, "You're in time, though. They're still talking away up there."

Mrs. Hutchinson craned her neck to see through the crowd and found her husband and children standing near the front. She tapped Mrs. Delacroix on the arm as a farewell and began to make her way through the crowd. The people separated good-humoredly to let her through; two or three people said, in voices just loud enough to be heard across the crowd, "Here comes your Missus, Hutchinson," and "Bill, she made it after all." Mrs. Hutchinson reached her husband, and Mr. Summers, who had been waiting, said cheerfully, "Thought we were going to have to get on without you, Tessie." Mrs. Hutchinson said, grinning, "Wouldn't have me leave m'dishes in the sink, now, would you, Joe?" and soft laughter ran through the crowd as the people stirred back into position after Mrs. Hutchinson's arrival. 9

"Well now," Mr. Summers said soberly, "guess we better get started, get this over with, so's we can go back to work. Anybody ain't here?" 10

"Dunbar," several people said. "Dunbar, Dunbar." 11

Mr. Summers consulted his list. "Clyde Dunbar," he said. "That's right. He's broke his leg, hasn't he? Who's drawing for him?" 12

"Me, I guess," a woman said, and Mr. Summers turned to look at her. "Wife draws for her husband," Mr. Summers said. "Don't you have a grown boy to do it for you, Janey?" Although Mr. Summers and everyone else in the village knew the answer perfectly well, it was the business of the official of the lottery to ask such questions formally. Mr. Summers waited with an expression of polite interest while Mrs. Dunbar answered. 13

"Horace's not but sixteen yet," Mrs. Dunbar said regretfully. "Guess I gotta fill in for the old man this year." 14

"Right," Mr. Summers said. He made a note on the list he was holding. Then he asked, "Watson boy drawing this year?" 15

A tall boy in the crowd raised his hand. "Here," he said. "I'm drawing for m'mother and me." He blinked his eyes nervously and ducked his head as several voices in the crowd said things like "Good fellow, Jack," and "Glad to see your mother's got a man to do it." 16

"Well," Mr. Summers said, "guess that's everyone. Old Man Warner make it?" 17

"Here," a voice said, and Mr. Summers nodded. 18

A sudden hush fell on the crowd as Mr. Summers cleared his throat and looked at the list. "All ready?" he called. "Now, I'll read the names — heads of families first — and the men come up and take a paper out of the box. Keep the paper folded in your hand without looking at it until everyone has had a turn. Everything clear?" 19

The people had done it so many times that they only half listened to the directions, most of them were quiet, wetting their lips, not looking around. Then Mr. Summers raised one hand high and said, "Adams." A man disengaged himself from the crowd and came forward. "Hi, Steve," Mr. Summers said, and Mr. Adams said, "Hi, Joe." They grinned at one another humorlessly and nervously. Then Mr. Adams reached into the black box and took out a folded paper. He held it firmly by one corner as he turned and went hastily back to his place in the crowd, where he stood a little apart from his family, not looking down at his hand.

"Allen," Mr. Summers said, "Anderson. . . . Bentham."   21

"Seems like there's no time at all between lotteries anymore," Mrs. Delacroix   22
said to Mrs. Graves in the back row. "Seems like we got through with the last one
only last week."

"Time sure goes fast," Mrs. Graves said.   23

"Clark. . . . Delacroix."   24

"There goes my old man," Mrs. Delacroix said. She held her breath while   25
her husband went forward.

"Dunbar," Mr. Summers said, and Mrs. Dunbar went steadily to the box   26
while one of the women said, "Go on, Janey," and another said, "There she goes."

"We're next," Mrs. Graves said. She watched while Mr. Graves came   27
around from the side of the box, greeted Mr. Summers gravely, and selected
a slip of paper from the box. By now, all through the crowd there were men
holding the small folded papers in their large hands, turning them over and
over nervously. Mrs. Dunbar and her two sons stood together, Mrs. Dunbar
holding the slip of paper.

"Harburt. . . . Hutchinson."   28

"Get up there, Bill," Mrs. Hutchinson said, and the people near her   29
laughed.

"Jones."   30

"They do say," Mr. Adams said to Old Man Warner, who stood next to   31
him, "that over in the north village they're talking of giving up the lottery."

Old Man Warner snorted. "Pack of crazy fools," he said. "Listening to the   32
young folks, nothing's good enough for *them*. Next thing you know, they'll be
wanting to go back to living in caves, nobody work anymore, live *that* way
for a while. Used to be a saying about 'Lottery in June, corn be heavy soon.'
First thing you know, we'd all be eating stewed chickweed and acorns. There's
always been a lottery," he added petulantly. "Bad enough to see young Joe
Summers up there joking with everybody."

"Some places have already quit lotteries," Mrs. Adams said.   33

"Nothing but trouble in *that*," Old Man Warner said stoutly. "Pack of   34
young fools."

"Martin." And Bobby Martin watched his father go forward. "Overdyke. . . . 35
Percy."

"I wish they'd hurry," Mrs. Dunbar said to her older son. "I wish they'd hurry." 36

"They're almost through," her son said. 37

"You get ready to run tell Dad," Mrs. Dunbar said. 38

Mr. Summers called his own name and then stepped forward precisely and 39
selected a slip from the box. Then he called, "Warner."

"Seventy-seventh year I been in the lottery," Old Man Warner said as he 40
went through the crowd. "Seventy-seventh time."

"Watson." The tall boy came awkwardly through the crowd. Someone 41
said, "Don't be nervous, Jack," and Mr. Summers said, "Take your time, son."

"Zanini." 42

After that, there was a long pause, a breathless pause, until Mr. Summers, 43
holding his slip of paper in the air, said, "All right, fellows." For a minute,
no one moved, and then all the slips of paper were opened. Suddenly, all the
women began to speak at once, saying, "Who is it?" "Who's got it?" "Is it the
Dunbars?" "Is it the Watsons?" Then the voices began to say, "It's Hutchinson.
It's Bill," "Bill Hutchinson's got it."

"Go tell your father," Mrs. Dunbar said to her older son. 44

People began to look around to see the Hutchinsons. Bill Hutchinson 45
was standing quiet, staring down at the paper in his hand. Suddenly, Tessie
Hutchinson shouted to Mr. Summers, "You didn't give him time enough to
take any paper he wanted. I saw you. It wasn't fair!"

"Be a good sport, Tessie," Mrs. Delacroix called, and Mrs. Graves said, 46
"All of us took the same chance."

"Shut up, Tessie," Bill Hutchinson said. 47

"Well, everyone," Mr. Summers said, "that was done pretty fast, and now 48
we've got to be hurrying a little more to get done in time." He consulted his
next list. "Bill," he said, "you draw for the Hutchinson family. You got any
other households in the Hutchinsons?"

"There's Don and Eva," Mrs. Hutchinson yelled. "Make *them* take their 49
chance!"

"Daughters draw with their husbands' families, Tessie," Mr. Summers said 50
gently. "You know that as well as anyone else."

"It wasn't *fair*," Tessie said. 51

"I guess not, Joe," Bill Hutchinson said regretfully. "My daughter draws with 52
her husband's family, that's only fair. And I've got no other family except the kids."

"Then, as far as drawing for families is concerned, it's you," Mr. Summers 53
said in explanation, "and as far as drawing for households is concerned, that's
you, too. Right?"

"Right," Bill Hutchinson said.   54

"How many kids, Bill?" Mr. Summers asked formally.   55

"Three," Bill Hutchinson said. "There's Bill, Jr., and Nancy, and little   56
Dave. And Tessie and me."

"All right, then," Mr. Summers said. "Harry, you got their tickets back?"   57

Mr. Graves nodded and held up the slips of paper. "Put them in the box,   58
then," Mr. Summers directed. "Take Bill's and put it in."

"I think we ought to start over," Mrs. Hutchinson said, as quietly as she   59
could. "I tell you it wasn't *fair*. You didn't give him time enough to choose.
Everybody saw that."

Mr. Graves had selected the five slips and put them in the box, and he   60
dropped all the papers but those onto the ground, where the breeze caught
them and lifted them off.

"Listen, everybody," Mrs. Hutchinson was saying to the people around   61
her.

"Ready, Bill?" Mr. Summers asked, and Bill Hutchinson, with one quick   62
glance around at his wife and children, nodded.

"Remember," Mr. Summers said, "take the slips and keep them folded   63
until each person has taken one. Harry, you help little Dave." Mr. Graves took
the hand of the little boy, who came willingly with him up to the box. "Take
a paper out of the box, Davy," Mr. Summers said. Davy put his hand into the
box and laughed. "Take just *one* paper," Mr. Summers said. "Harry, you hold
it for him." Mr. Graves took the child's hand and removed the folded paper
from the tight fist and held it while little Dave stood next to him and looked
up at him wonderingly.

"Nancy next," Mr. Summers said. Nancy was twelve, and her school   64
friends breathed heavily as she went forward, switching her skirt, and took
a slip daintily from the box. "Bill, Jr.," Mr. Summers said, and Billy, his face
red and his feet overlarge, nearly knocked the box over as he got a paper out.
"Tessie," Mr. Summers said. She hesitated for a minute, looking around defi-
antly, and then set her lips and went up to the box. She snatched a paper out
and held it behind her.

"Bill," Mr. Summers said, and Bill Hutchinson reached into the box and   65
felt around, bringing his hand out at last with the slip of paper in it.

The crowd was quiet. A girl whispered, "I hope it's not Nancy," and the   66
sound of the whisper reached the edges of the crowd.

"It's not the way it used to be," Old Man Warner said clearly. "People ain't   67
the way they used to be."

"All right," Mr. Summers said. "Open the papers. Harry, you open little   68
Dave's."

Mr. Graves opened the slip of paper and there was a general sigh through 69
the crowd as he held it up and everyone could see that it was blank. Nancy
and Bill, Jr., opened theirs at the same time, and both beamed and laughed,
turning around to the crowd and holding their slips of paper above their heads.

"Tessie," Mr. Summers said. There was a pause, and then Mr. Summers 70
looked at Bill Hutchinson, and Bill unfolded his paper and showed it. It was
blank.

"It's Tessie," Mr. Summers said, and his voice was hushed. "Show us her 71
paper, Bill."

Bill Hutchinson went over to his wife and forced the slip of paper out of 72
her hand. It had a black spot on it, the black spot Mr. Summers had made the
night before with the heavy pencil in the coal-company office. Bill Hutchinson held it up and there was a stir in the crowd.

"All right, folks," Mr. Summers said. "Let's finish quickly." 73

Although the villagers had forgotten the ritual and lost the original black 74
box, they still remembered to use stones. The pile of stones the boys had made
earlier was ready; there were stones on the ground with the blowing scraps of
paper that had come out of the box. Mrs. Delacroix selected a stone so large
she had to pick it up with both hands and turned to Mrs. Dunbar. "Come on,"
she said. "Hurry up."

Mrs. Dunbar had small stones in both hands, and she said, gasping for 75
breath, "I can't run at all. You'll have to go ahead and I'll catch up with you."

The children had stones already, and someone gave little Davy Hutchin- 76
son a few pebbles.

Tessie Hutchinson was in the center of a cleared space by now, and she 77
held her hands out desperately as the villagers moved in on her. "It isn't fair,"
she said. A stone hit her on the side of the head.

Old Man Warner was saying, "Come on, come on, everyone." Steve 78
Adams was in front of the crowd of villagers, with Mrs. Graves beside him.

"It isn't fair, it isn't right," Mrs. Hutchinson screamed and then they were 79
upon her.

Journal Writing

Think about rituals in which you participate, such as those involving holidays, meals,
religious observances, family vacations, sporting events — anything that is repeated
and traditional. List some of these in your journal and write about their significance
to you.

Questions on Meaning

1. The PURPOSE of all fiction might be taken as entertainment or self-expression. Does Jackson have any other purpose in "The Lottery"?
2. When does the reader know what is actually going to occur?
3. Describe this story's community on the basis of what Jackson says of it.
4. What do the villagers' attitudes toward the black box indicate about their feelings toward the lottery?

Questions on Writing Strategy

1. Jackson uses the third PERSON (*he, she, it, they*) to narrate the story, and she does not enter the minds of her characters. Why do you think she keeps this distant POINT OF VIEW?
2. On your first reading of the story, what did you make of the references to rocks in paragraphs 2–3? Do you think they effectively forecast the ending?
3. Jackson has a character introduce a controversial notion in paragraph 31. Why does she do this?
4. **OTHER METHODS** Jackson is exploring — or inviting us to explore — CAUSES AND EFFECTS. Why do the villagers participate in the lottery every year? What does paragraph 32 hint might have been the original reason for it?

Questions on Language

1. Dialog provides much information not stated elsewhere in the story. Give three examples of such information about the community and its interactions.
2. Check a dictionary for definitions of the following words: profusely (par. 1); boisterous, reprimands (2); jovial, scold (4); paraphernalia (5); perfunctory, duly, interminably (7); petulantly (32).
3. In paragraph 64 we read that Mrs. Hutchinson "snatched" the paper out of the box. What does this verb suggest about her attitude?
4. Jackson admits to setting the story in her Vermont village in the present time (that is, 1948). Judging from the names of the villagers, where did these people's ancestors originally come from? What do you make of the names Delacroix and Zanini? What is their significance?
5. Unlike much fiction, "The Lottery" contains few FIGURES OF SPEECH. Why do you think this is?

Suggestions for Writing

1. **FROM JOURNAL TO ESSAY** Choose one of the rituals you wrote about in your journal (p. 107), and compose a narrative about the last time you participated in this ritual. Use DESCRIPTION and dialog to convey the significance of the ritual and your own and other participants' attitudes toward it.

2. In his 1974 book *Obedience to Authority*, the psychologist Stanley Milgram reported and analyzed the results of a study he had conducted that caused a furor among psychologists and the general public. Under orders from white-coated "experimenters," many subjects administered what they believed to be life-threatening electric shocks to other people whom they could hear but not see. In fact, the "victims" were actors and received no shocks, but the subjects thought otherwise and many continued to administer stronger and stronger "shocks" when ordered to do so. Find *Obedience to Authority* in the library and COMPARE AND CONTRAST the circumstances of Milgram's experiment with those of Jackson's lottery. For instance, who or what is the order-giving authority in the lottery? What is the significance of seeing or not seeing one's victim?

3. **CRITICAL WRITING** Jackson has said that a common response she received to "The Lottery" was "What does this story mean?" (She never answered the question.) In an essay, interpret the meaning of the story as *you* understand it. (What does it say, for instance, about conformity, guilt, or good and evil?) You will have to INFER meaning from such features as Jackson's TONE as narrator, the villagers' dialog, and, of course, the events of the story. Your essay should be supported with specific EVIDENCE from the story. (For a sample of another student's interpretation of "The Lottery," see Rachel O'Connor's critical analysis on p. 307.)

4. **CONNECTIONS** Although very different from Jackson's story, Firoozeh Dumas's essay "Sweet, Sour, and Resentful" (p. 275) also focuses on observing a tradition. Taken together, what do these two pieces seem to say about the benefits and the dangers of adhering to tradition? Write an essay in which you explore the pros and cons of maintaining rituals, giving examples from these selections and from your own experience.

Shirley Jackson on Writing

Come Along with Me, a posthumous collection of her work, contains a lecture by Shirley Jackson titled "Biography of a Story" — specifically a biography of "The Lottery." Far from being born in cruelty or cynicism, the story had quite benign origins. Jackson wrote the story, she recalled, "on a bright June morning when summer seemed to have come at last, with blue skies and warm sun and no heavenly signs to warn me that my morning's work was anything but just another story. The idea had come to me while I was pushing my daughter up the hill in her stroller — it was, as I say, a warm morning, and the hill was steep, and beside my daughter the stroller held the day's groceries — and perhaps the effort of that last fifty yards up the hill put an edge on the story; at any rate, I had the idea fairly clearly in my mind when I put my daughter in her playpen and the frozen vegetables in the refrigerator, and, writing the story, I found that it went quickly and easily, moving from beginning to end without pause. As a matter of fact, when I read it over later I decided that except for one or two minor corrections, it needed no changes, and the story I finally typed up and sent off to my agent the next day was almost word for word the original draft. This, as any writer of stories can tell you, is not a usual thing. All I know is that when I came to read the story over I felt strongly that I didn't want to fuss with it. I didn't think it was perfect, but I didn't want to fuss with it. It was, I thought, a serious, straightforward story, and I was pleased and a little surprised at the ease with which it had been written; I was reasonably proud of it, and hoped that my agent would sell it to some magazine and I would have the gratification of seeing it in print."

After the story was published, however, Jackson was surprised to find both it and herself the subject of "bewilderment, speculation, and plain old-fashioned abuse." She wrote that "one of the most terrifying aspects of publishing stories and books is the realization that they are going to be read, and read by strangers. I had never fully realized this before, although I had of course in my imagination dwelt lovingly upon the thought of the millions and millions of people who were going to be uplifted and enriched and delighted by the stories I wrote. It had simply never occurred to me that these millions and millions of people might be so far from being uplifted that they would sit down and write me letters I was downright scared to open; of the three-hundred-odd letters that I received that summer I can count only thirteen that spoke kindly to me, and they were mostly from friends."

Jackson's favorite letter was one concluding, "Our brothers feel that Miss Jackson is a true prophet and disciple of the true gospel of the redeeming light. When will the next revelation be published?" Jackson's answer: "Never. I am out of the lottery business for good."

The Bedford Reader on Writing

As Jackson observes, inspiration often comes when least expected — while walking, in the shower, asleep. Notice, though, that Jackson didn't wait for inspiration to actually *write*: She sat right down and began work. For our advice on finding ideas and drafting productively, see pages 32–39. And for tips on anticipating readers' reactions to your writing, see pages 30–31.

ADDITIONAL WRITING TOPICS

Narration

1. Write a narrative with one of the following as your subject. It may be (as your instructor may advise) either a first-PERSON memoir or a story written in the third person, observing the experience of someone else. Decide before you begin what your PURPOSE is and whether you are writing (1) an anecdote, (2) an essay consisting mainly of a single narrative, or (3) an essay that includes more than one story.

   A lesson you learned the hard way
   A trip into unfamiliar territory
   An embarrassing moment that taught you something
   A monumental misunderstanding
   An accident
   An adventure or misadventure
   A friendship
   An unexpected encounter
   A loss that lingers
   A moment of triumph
   A story about a famous person
   A legend from family history
   A conflict or contest
   A fierce storm
   A historical event of significance

2. Tell a true story of your early or recent school days, either humorous or serious, relating a struggle you experienced (or still experience) in school.

3. Write a fictional narrative, set in the past, present, or future, of a ritual that demonstrates something about the people who participate in it. The ritual can be, but need not be, as sinister as Shirley Jackson's lottery; yours could concern bathing, eating, dating, going to school, driving, growing older.

Note: Writing topics combining narration and description appear on page 157.

Photograph: Margaret Morton © OmbraLuce LLC

4

DESCRIPTION

Writing with Your Senses

◀ **Description in a photograph**

Margaret Morton photographs homeless communities in New York City. This photograph, titled *Doug and Mizan's House, East River*, depicts a makeshift dwelling on a Manhattan riverbank. Consider Morton's photograph as a work of description — revealing a thing through the perceptions of the senses. What do you see through her eyes? What is the house made of? What do the overhanging structure on the upper left and the bridge behind the house add to the impression of the house? If you were standing in the picture, in front of the house, what might you hear or smell? If you touched the house, what textures might you feel? What main idea do you think Morton wants this photograph to convey?

THE METHOD

Like narration, DESCRIPTION is a familiar method of expression, already a working part of your life. In any chat, you probably do your share of describing. You depict in words someone you've met by describing her clothes, the look on her face, the way she walks. You describe somewhere you've been, something you admire, something you just can't stand. In a message to a friend back home, you describe your college (concrete buildings, crowded walks, pigeons scuttling); or perhaps you describe your brand-new secondhand car, from the glitter of its hubcaps to the odd antiques wedged in its seat cushions. You can hardly go a day without describing (or hearing described) some person, place, or thing. Small wonder, then, that in written discourse description is almost as indispensable as words.

Description reports the testimony of your senses. It invites your readers to imagine that they, too, not only see but perhaps also hear, taste, smell, and touch the subject you describe. Usually, you write a description for either of two PURPOSES:

- **Convey information without bias,** using description that is OBJECTIVE (or *impartial*, *public*, or *functional*). You describe your subject so clearly and exactly that your reader will understand it or recognize it, and you leave your emotions out. The description in academic writing is usually objective: A biology report on a particular species of frog, for instance, might detail the animal's appearance (four-inch-wide body, bright-orange skin with light-brown spots), its sounds (hoarse clucks), and its feel (smooth, slippery). In writing an objective description your purpose is not to share your feelings. You are trying to make the frog or the subject easily recognized.

- **Convey perceptions with feeling,** using description that is SUBJECTIVE (or *emotional*, *personal*, or *impressionistic*). This is the kind included in a magazine advertisement for a new car. It's what you write in your message to a friend setting forth what your college is like — whether you are pleased or displeased with it. In this kind of description, you may use biases and personal feelings — in fact, they are essential.

For a splendid example of subjective description, read the following passenger's-eye view of a storm at sea by Charles Dickens. Notice how the writer's words convey the terror of the event:

> Imagine the ship herself, with every pulse and artery of her huge body swollen and bursting . . . sworn to go on or die. Imagine the wind howling, the sea roaring, the rain beating; all in furious array against her. Picture the sky both dark and wild, and the clouds in fearful sympathy with the waves,

making another ocean in the air. Add to all this the clattering on deck and down below; the tread of hurried feet; the loud hoarse shouts of seamen; the gurgling in and out of water through the scuppers; with every now and then the striking of a heavy sea upon the planks above, with the deep, dead, heavy sound of thunder heard within a vault; and there is the head wind of that January morning.

Think of what a starkly different description of the very same storm the captain might set down — objectively — in the ship's log: "At 0600 hours, watch reported a wind from due north of 70 knots. Whitecaps were noticed, in height two ells above the bow. Below deck water was reported to have entered the bilge. . . ." But Dickens, not content simply to record information, strives to ensure that his emotions are clear.

Description is usually found in the company of other methods of writing. Often, for instance, it will enliven NARRATION and make the people in the story and the setting unmistakably clear. Writing a PROCESS ANALYSIS in her essay "Sweet, Sour, and Resentful" (p. 275), Firoozeh Dumas begins with a description of her family's hometown in Iran. Description will help a writer in examining the EFFECTS of a storm or in COMPARING AND CONTRASTING two paintings. Keep description in mind when you try expository and argumentative writing. The method is key to clarity and to readers' interest.

THE PROCESS

Purpose and Audience

Understand, first of all, why you are writing about your subject and thus what kind of description is called for. Is it appropriate to perceive and report without emotion or bias — and thus write an objective description? Or is it appropriate to express your personal feelings as well as your perceptions — and thus write a subjective description?

Give some thought also to your AUDIENCE. What do your readers need to be told, if they are to share the perceptions you would have them share? If, let's say, you are describing a downtown street on a Saturday night for an audience of fellow students who live in the same city, then you need not dwell on the street's familiar geography. What must you tell? Only those details that make the place different on a Saturday night. But if you are remembering your home city, and writing for readers who don't know it, you'll need to establish a few central landmarks to sketch (in their minds) an unfamiliar street on a Saturday night.

Before you begin to write a description, go look at your subject. If that is not possible, your next best course is to spend a few minutes imagining the

Description

subject until, in your mind's eye, you can see every speck of it. Then, having fixed your subject in mind, ask yourself which of its features you'll need to report to your particular audience, for your particular purpose. Ask yourself, "What am I out to accomplish?"

Dominant Impression and Thesis

When you consider your aim in describing, you'll begin to see what impression you intend your subject to make on readers. Let your description, as a whole, convey this one DOMINANT IMPRESSION. If you are writing a subjective description of an old house, laying weight on its spooky atmosphere to make readers shiver, then you might mention its squeaking bats and its shadowy halls. If, however, you are describing the house in a classified ad, for an audience of possible buyers, you might focus instead on its eat-in kitchen, working fireplace, and proximity to public transportation. Details have to be carefully selected. Feel no obligation to include every perceptible detail. To do so would only invite chaos — or perhaps, for the reader, tedium. Pick out the features that matter most.

Your dominant impression is like the THESIS of your description — the main idea about your subject that you want readers to take away with them. When you use description to explain or to argue, it's usually a good strategy to state that dominant impression outright, tying it to your essay's thesis or a part of it. In the biology report on a species of frog, for instance, you might preface your description with a statement like this one:

> A number of unique features distinguish this frog from others in the order Anura.

Or in an argument in favor of cleaning a local toxic-waste site, you might begin with a description of the site and then state your point about it:

> This landscape is as poisonous as it looks, for underneath its barren crust are enough toxic chemicals to sicken an entire village.

When you use subjective description more for its own sake — to show the reader a place or a person, to evoke feelings — you needn't always state your dominant impression as a THESIS STATEMENT, as long as the impression is there dictating the details.

Organization

To help them arrange the details of a description, many writers rely on their POINT OF VIEW — the physical angle from which they're perceiving and describing. As an observer who stays put and observes steadily, you can make a carefully planned inspection tour of your subject, using SPATIAL ORDER (from left to right, from near to far, from top to bottom, from center to periphery), or perhaps moving from prominent objects to tiny ones, from dull to bright, from commonplace to extraordinary — or vice versa.

The plan for you is the one that best fulfills your purpose, arranging details so that the reader receives the exact impression you mean to convey. If you were to describe, for instance, a chapel in the middle of a desert, you might begin with the details of the lonely terrain. Then, as if approaching the chapel with the aid of a zoom lens, you might detail its exterior before going on inside. That might be a workable method *if* you wanted to create the dominant impression of the chapel as an island of beauty in the midst of desolation. Say, however, that you had a different impression in mind: to emphasize the spirituality of the chapel's interior. You might then begin your description inside the structure, perhaps with its most prominent feature, the stained glass windows. You might mention the surrounding desert later in your description, but only incidentally.

Whatever pattern you follow, stick with it all the way through so that your arrangement causes no difficulty for the reader. In describing the chapel, you wouldn't necessarily proceed in the way you explored the structure in person, first noting its isolation, then entering and studying its windows, then going outside again to see what the walls were made of, then moving back inside to look at the artwork. Instead, you would lead the reader around and through (or through and around) the structure in an organized manner. Even if a scene is chaotic, the prose should be orderly.

Details

Luckily, to write a memorable description, you don't need a ferocious storm or any other awe-inspiring subject. As Brad Manning and N. Scott Momaday demonstrate later in this chapter, you can write about your family as effectively as you write about a hurricane. The secret is in the vividness, the evocativeness of the details. Momaday, for instance, uses many IMAGES to call up concrete sensory experiences, including FIGURES OF SPEECH (expressions that do not mean literally what they say). Using *metaphor*, he writes that "the walls have closed in upon my grandmother's house" to express his change in perception when he returns to the house as an adult. And using *simile*, Momaday describes grasshoppers "popping up like corn" to bring a sense of stinging suddenness to life for his readers.

FOCUS ON SPECIFIC AND CONCRETE LANGUAGE

When you write effective description, you'll convey your subject as exactly as possible. You may use figures of speech, as discussed above, and you'll definitely rely on language that is *specific* (tied to actual things) and *concrete* (tied to the senses of sight, hearing, touch, smell, and taste). Such language enables readers to behold with the mind's eye — and to feel with the mind's fingertips.

The first sentence below shows a writer's first-draft attempt to describe something she saw. After editing, the second sentence is much more vivid.

VAGUE   Beautiful, scented wildflowers were in the field.

CONCRETE AND SPECIFIC   Backlighted by the sun and smelling faintly sweet, an acre of tiny lavender flowers spread away from me.

When editing your description, keep a sharp eye out for vague words such as *delicious*, *handsome*, *loud*, and *short* that force readers to create their own impressions or, worse, leave them with no impression at all. Using details that call on readers' sensory experiences, tell why delicious or why handsome, how loud or how short. When stuck for a word, conjure up your subject and see it, hear it, touch it, smell it, taste it.

Note that *concrete* and *specific* do not mean "fancy": Good description does not demand five-dollar words when nickel equivalents are just as informative. The writer who uses *rubiginous* instead of *rusty red* actually says less because fewer readers will understand the less common word and all readers will sense a writer showing off.

CHECKLIST FOR REVISING A DESCRIPTION

✔ **Subjective or objective.** Is the description appropriately subjective (emphasizing feelings) or objective (unemotional) for your purpose?

✔ **Dominant impression.** What is your dominant impression of the subject? If you haven't stated it, will your readers be able to pinpoint it accurately?

✔ **Point of view and organization.** Do your point of view and organization work together to make the subject clear for readers? Are they consistent?

✔ **Details.** Have you provided all of the details — and just those details — needed to convey your dominant impression? What needs expanding? What needs condensing or cutting?

✔ **Specific and concrete language.** Have you used words that express your meaning exactly and appeal to the senses of sight, hearing, touch, taste, and smell?

DESCRIPTION IN ACADEMIC WRITING

An Art History Textbook

Description interprets a familiar painting in the following paragraphs from *Janson's History of Art* by H. W. Janson et al. The details "translate" the painting, creating a bridge between the reader and the text's reproduction of the work.

While working on *The Battle of Anghiari*, Leonardo painted his most famous portrait, the *Mona Lisa*. The delicate *sfumato* already noted in the *Madonna of the Rocks* is here so perfected that it seemed miraculous to the artist's contemporaries. The forms are built from layers of glazes so gossamer-thin that the entire panel seems to glow with a gentle light from within. But the fame of the *Mona Lisa* comes not from this pictorial subtlety alone; even more intriguing is the psychological fascination of the sitter's personality. Why, among all the smiling faces ever painted, has this particular one been singled out as "mysterious"? Perhaps the reason is that, as a portrait, the picture does not fit our expectations. The features are too individual for Leonardo to have simply depicted an ideal type, yet the element of idealization is so strong that it blurs the sitter's character. Once again the artist has brought two opposites into harmonious balance. The smile, too, may be read in two ways: as the echo of a momentary mood, and as a timeless, symbolic expression (somewhat like the "Archaic smile" of the Greeks . . .). Clearly, the *Mona Lisa* embodies a quality of maternal tenderness which was to Leonardo the essence of womanhood. Even the landscape in the background, composed mainly of rocks and water, suggests elemental generative forces.

(Sfumato: soft gradations of light and dark)

Main idea (topic sentence) of the paragraph, supported by description of "pictorial subtlety" (above) and "psychological fascination" (below)

Details (underlined) contribute to dominant impression

A Field Observation

In many of your classes, particularly those in the social sciences, you will be asked to observe people or phenomena in particular settings and to describe what your senses perceive. A systematic observation may produce evidence for an ARGUMENT, as when a writer describes the listlessness of kittens in an animal shelter to encourage support for a spay-and-neuter program. Just as often, however, an observation results in an objective report providing information from which readers draw their own conclusions. Like any description, such a field report emphasizes details and uses concrete language to convey the writer's perceptions. Because the writer's purpose is to inform, the report takes a neutral, third-PERSON (*he, she, they*) point of view, uses unemotional language, and refrains from interpretation or opinion — or withholds such analysis for a separate section near the end.

For an education class in child development, Nick Fiorelli spent a morning in a private preschool, observing the teachers' techniques and the children's behaviors and taking note of how they interacted. The paragraphs below, excerpted from his finished report, "Teaching Methodologies at Child's Play Preschool," describe both the classroom itself and some of the activities Fiorelli witnessed. The full report goes on to outline the educational philosophies and developmental theories that inform the school's approach, with additional examples and descriptions from Fiorelli's visit.

The preschool's Web site explains that it draws on elements of Waldorf, Montessori, Reggio Emillia, and other educational models. This background was evident in the large and colorful classroom, which included separate interest areas for different activities. The room was also open and well lit, with long windows that looked out on a playground and an expansive lawn. The walls of the room were decorated with students' paintings and drawings. Colored rugs, floor tiles, or rubber mats indicated the boundaries of each activity area.

Background information sets the stage

Organization moves from the periphery to the center, then around the room's distinct areas

Dominant impression: structured creativity

At first, the general atmosphere appeared noisy and unstructured, but a sense of order emerged within a few minutes of observation. At a sturdy wooden art table, two students used safety scissors to cut shapes from sheets of red construction paper. Behind them, a child in a red smock stood at a small wooden easel and painted with a foam brush. Another strung multicolored beads on a string. Next to the art table, two children at a sensory station poured wet sand and rocks through an oversize funnel into a miniature sandbox, while a third filled a clear plastic tank with water from a blue enameled pail. A teacher moved between the two tables, encouraging the students and asking questions about their play. In the back of the room, at a literacy area with a thick blue rug and low yellow bookshelves, six students lolled on beanbag chairs, pillows, and a low brown couch, listening to a teacher read a story from an illustrated children's book. She paused on each page to help the children connect the pictures with the story.

Concrete details contribute to the dominant impression

BRAD MANNING

Brad Manning was born in Little Rock, Arkansas, in 1967 and grew up near Charlottesville, Virginia. While a student at Harvard University he played intramural sports and wrote articles and reviews for the *Harvard Independent*. He graduated in 1990 with a BA in history and religion. Now living in Charlottesville, Manning is a psychiatrist specializing in the treatment of children and adolescents.

Arm Wrestling with My Father

In this essay written for his freshman composition course, Manning explores his physical contact with his father over the years, perceiving gradual changes that are, he realizes, inevitable. For Manning, description provides a way to express his feelings about his father and to comment on relations between sons and fathers. In the essay after Manning's, N. Scott Momaday uses description for similar ends, but his subject is his grandmother.

"Now you say when" is what he always said before an arm-wrestling match. 1 He liked to put the responsibility on me, knowing that he would always control the outcome. "When!" I'd shout, and it would start. And I would tense up, concentrating and straining and trying to push his wrist down to the carpet with all my weight and strength. But Dad would always win; I always had to lose. "Want to try it again?" he would ask, grinning. He would see my downcast eyes, my reddened, sweating face, and sense my intensity. And with squinting eyes he would laugh at me, a high laugh, through his perfect white teeth. Too bitter to smile, I would not answer or look at him, but I would just roll over on my back and frown at the ceiling. I never thought it was funny at all.

That was the way I felt for a number of years during my teens, after I 2 had lost my enjoyment of arm wrestling and before I had given up that same intense desire to beat my father. Ours had always been a physical relationship, I suppose, one determined by athleticism and strength. We never communicated as well in speech or in writing as in a strong hug, battling to make the other gasp for breath. I could never find him at one of my orchestra concerts. But at my lacrosse games, he would be there in the stands, with an angry look, ready to coach me after the game on how I could do better. He never helped me write a paper or a poem. Instead, he would take me outside and show me a new move for my game, in the hope that I would score a couple of goals and gain confidence in my ability. Dad knew almost nothing about lacrosse and his movements were all wrong and sad to watch. But at those times I could just feel how hard he was trying to communicate, to help me, to show the love he had for me, the love I could only assume was there.

His words were physical. The truth is, I have never read a card or a letter 3 written in his hand because he never wrote to me. Never. Mom wrote me all the cards and letters when I was away from home. The closest my father ever came, that I recall, was in a newspaper clipping Mom had sent with a letter. He had gone through and underlined all the important words about the dangers of not wearing a bicycle helmet. Our communication was physical, and that is why we did things like arm wrestle. To get down on the floor and grapple, arm against arm, was like having a conversation.

This ritual of father-son competition in fact had started early in my life, 4 back when Dad started the matches with his arm almost horizontal, his wrist an inch from defeat, and still won. I remember in those battles how my tiny shoulders would press over our locked hands, my whole upper body pushing down in hope of winning that single inch from his calm, unmoving forearm. "Say when," he'd repeat, killing my concentration and causing me to squeal, "I did, I did!" And so he'd grin with his eyes fixed on me, not seeming to notice his own arm, which would begin to rise slowly from its starting position. My greatest efforts could not slow it down. As soon as my hopes had disappeared I'd start to cheat and use both hands. But the arm would continue to move steadily along its arc toward the carpet. My brother, if he was watching, would sometimes join in against the arm. He once even wrapped his little legs around our embattled wrists and pulled back with everything he had. But he did not have much and, regardless of the opposition, the man would win. My arm would lie at rest, pressed into the carpet beneath a solid, immovable arm. In that pinned position, I could only giggle, happy to have such a strong father.

My feelings have changed, though. I don't giggle anymore, at least not 5 around my father. And I don't feel pressured to compete with him the way I thought necessary for years. Now my father is not really so strong as he used to be and I am getting stronger. This change in strength comes at a time when I am growing faster mentally than at any time before. I am becoming less my father and more myself. And as a result, there is less of a need to be set apart from him and his command. I am no longer a rebel in the household, wanting to stand up against the master with clenched fists and tensing jaws, trying to impress him with my education or my views on religion. I am no longer a challenger, quick to correct his verbal mistakes, determined to beat him whenever possible in physical competition.

I am not sure when it was that I began to feel less competitive with my 6
father, but it all became clearer to me one day this past January. I was home
in Virginia for a week between exams, and Dad had stayed home from work
because the house was snowed in deep. It was then that I learned something I
never could have guessed.

I don't recall who suggested arm wrestling that day. We hadn't done it for 7
a long time, for months. But there we were, lying flat on the carpet, face to
face, extending our right arms. Our arms were different. His still resembled
a fat tree branch, one which had leveled my wrist to the ground countless
times before. It was hairy and white with some pink moles scattered about.
It looked strong, to be sure, though not so strong as it had in past years. I
expect that back in his youth it had looked even stronger. In high school he
had played halfback and had been voted "best-built body" of the senior class.
Between college semesters he had worked on road crews and on Louisiana
dredges. I admired him for that. I had begun to row crew in college and that
accounted for some small buildup along the muscle lines, but it did not seem
to be enough. The arm I extended was lanky and featureless. Even so, he
insisted that he would lose the match, that he was certain I'd win. I had to
ignore this, however, because it was something he always said, whether or not
he believed it himself.

Our warm palms came together, much the same way we had shaken 8
hands the day before at the airport. Fingers twisted and wrapped about once
again, testing for a better grip. Elbows slid up and back making their little
indentations on the itchy carpet. My eyes pinched closed in concentration
as I tried to center as much of my thought as possible on the match. Arm
wrestling, I knew, was a competition that depended less on talent and experience than on one's mental control and confidence. I looked up into his eyes
and was ready. He looked back, smiled at me, and said softly (did he sound
nervous?), "You say when."

It was not a long match. I had expected him to be stronger, faster. I was 9
conditioned to lose and would have accepted defeat easily. However, after
some struggle, his arm yielded to my efforts and began to move unsteadily
toward the carpet. I worked against his arm with all the strength I could find.
He was working hard as well, straining, breathing heavily. It seemed that this
time was different, that I was going to win. Then something occurred to me,
something unexpected. I discovered that I was feeling sorry for my father. I
wanted to win but I did not want to see him lose.

It was like the thrill I had once experienced as a young boy at my grand- 10
father's lake house in Louisiana when I hooked my first big fish. There was
that sudden tug that made me leap. The red bobber was sucked down beneath
the surface and I pulled back against it, reeling it in excitedly. But when my

cousin caught sight of the fish and shouted out, "It's a keeper," I realized that I would be happier for the fish if it were let go rather than grilled for dinner. Arm wrestling my father was now like this, like hooking "Big Joe," the old fish that Lake Quachita holds but you can never catch, and when you finally think you've got him, you want to let him go, cut the line, keep the legend alive.

Perhaps at that point I could have given up, letting my father win. But it 11 was so fast and absorbing. How could I have learned so quickly how it would feel to have overpowered the arm that had protected and provided for me all of my life? His arms have always protected me and the family. Whenever I am near him I am unafraid, knowing his arms are ready to catch me and keep me safe, the way they caught my mother one time when she fainted halfway across the room, the way he carried me, full grown, up and down the stairs when I had mononucleosis, the way he once held my feet as I stood on his shoulders to put up a new basketball net. My mother may have had the words or the touch that sustained our family, but his were the arms that protected us. And his were the arms now that I had pushed to the carpet, first the right arm, then the left.

I might have preferred him to be always the stronger, the one who carries 12 me. But this wish is impossible now; our roles have begun to switch. I do not know if I will ever physically carry my father as he has carried me, though I fear that someday I may have that responsibility. More than once this year I have hesitated before answering the phone late at night, fearing my mother's voice calling me back to help carry his wood coffin. When I am home with him and he mentions a sharp pain in his chest, I imagine him collapsing onto the floor. And in that second vision I see me rushing to him, lifting him onto my shoulders, and running.

A week after our match, we parted at the airport. The arm-wrestling match 13 was by that time mostly forgotten. My thoughts were on school. I had been awake most of the night studying for my last exam, and by that morning I was already back into my college-student manner of reserve and detachment. To say goodbye, I kissed and hugged my mother and I prepared to shake my father's hand. A handshake had always seemed easier to handle than a hug. His hugs had always been powerful ones, intended I suppose to give me strength. They made me suck in my breath and struggle for control, and the way he would pound his hand on my back made rumbles in my ears. So I offered a handshake; but he offered a hug. I accepted it, bracing myself for the impact. Once our arms were wrapped around each other, however, I sensed a different message. His embrace was softer, longer than before. I remember how it surprised me and how I gave an embarrassed laugh as if to apologize to anyone watching.

I got on the airplane and my father and mother were gone. But as the 14 plane lifted my throat was hurting with sadness. I realized then that Dad must have learned something as well, and what he had said to me in that last hug was that he loved me. Love was a rare expression between us, so I had denied it at first. As the plane turned north, I had a sudden wish to go back to Dad and embrace his arms with all the love I felt for him. I wanted to hold him for a long time and to speak with him silently, telling him how happy I was, telling him all my feelings, in that language we shared.

In his hug, Dad had tried to tell me something he himself had discovered.   15
I hope he tries again. Maybe this spring, when he sees his first crew match, he'll advise me on how to improve my stroke. Maybe he has started doing pushups to rebuild his strength and challenge me to another match — if this were true, I know I would feel less challenged than loved. Or maybe, rather than any of this, he'll just send me a card.

Journal Writing

Manning expresses conflicting feelings about his father. How do you respond to his conflict? When have you felt strongly mixed emotions about a person or an event, such as a relative, friend, breakup, ceremony, move? Write a paragraph or two exploring your feelings.

Questions on Meaning

1. In paragraph 3 Manning says that his father's "words were physical." What does this mean?

2. After his most recent trip home, Manning says, "I realized then that Dad must have learned something as well" (par. 14). What is it that father and son have each learned?

3. Manning says in the last paragraph that he "would feel less challenged than loved" if his father challenged him to a rematch. Does this statement suggest that he did not feel loved earlier? Why, or why not?

4. What do you think is Manning's PURPOSE in this essay? Does he want to express love for his father, or is there something more as well?

Questions on Writing Strategy

1. Why does Manning start his essay with a match that leaves him "too bitter to smile" and then move backward to earlier bouts of arm wrestling?

2. In the last paragraph Manning suggests that his father might work harder at competing with him and pushing him to be competitive, or he might just send his

son a card. Why does Manning present both of these options? Are we supposed to know which will happen?

3. Explain the fishing ANALOGY Manning uses in paragraph 10.

4. **OTHER METHODS** Manning's essay is as much a NARRATIVE as a description: The author gives brief stories, like video clips, to show the dynamic of his relationship with his father. Look at the story in paragraph 4. How does Manning mix elements of both methods to convey his powerlessness?

Questions on Language

1. Manning uses the word *competition* throughout this essay. Why is this a more accurate word than *conflict* to describe Manning's relationship with his father?

2. What is the EFFECT of "the arm" in this sentence from paragraph 4: "But the arm would continue to move steadily along its arc toward the carpet"?

3. In paragraph 9 Manning writes, "I wanted to win but I did not want to see him lose." What does this apparent contradiction mean?

4. If any of these words is unfamiliar, look it up in a dictionary: embattled (par. 4); dredges, crew (7); conditioned (9); mononucleosis (11).

Suggestions for Writing

1. **FROM JOURNAL TO ESSAY** Expand your journal entry (p. 125) into a descriptive essay that brings to life your mixed feelings about a person or an event. Focus less on the circumstances and happenings than on emotions, both positive and negative.

2. Write an essay that describes your relationship with a parent or another close adult. You may want to focus on just one aspect of your relationship, or one especially vivid moment, in order to give yourself the space and time to build many sensory details into your description.

3. Arm wrestling is a highly competitive sport with a long history. Research the sport in the library or on the Internet. Then write a brief essay that traces its history and explains its current standing.

4. **CRITICAL WRITING** In paragraph 12 Manning says that "our roles have begun to switch." Does this seem like an inevitable switch, or one that this father and son have been working to achieve? Use EVIDENCE from Manning's essay to support your answer. Also consider whether Manning and his father would respond the same way to this question.

5. **CONNECTIONS** Like "Arm Wrestling with My Father," the next essay, N. Scott Momaday's "The Way to Rainy Mountain," depicts the lasting influence of a family member. In an essay, COMPARE AND CONTRAST the two essays on this point. What conclusions do the authors draw about aging and maturity? How do they resolve their conflicts with older generations?

Brad Manning on Writing

For this book, Brad Manning offered some valuable concrete advice on writing as a student.

You hear this a lot, but writing takes a long time. For me, this is especially true. The only difference between the "Arm Wrestling" essay and all the other essays I wrote in college (and the only reason it's in this book and not thrown away) is that I rewrote it six or seven times over a period of weeks.

If I have something to write, I need to start early. In college, I had a bad habit of putting off papers until 10 p.m. the night before they were due and spending a desperate night typing whatever ideas the coffee inspired. But putting off papers didn't just lower my writing quality; it robbed me of a good time.

I like starting early because I can jot down notes over a stretch of days; then I type them up fast, ignoring typos; I print the notes with narrow margins, cut them up, and divide them into piles that seem to fit together; then it helps to get away for a day and come back all fresh so I can throw away the corny ideas. Finally, I sit on the floor and make an outline with all the cutouts of paper, trying at the same time to work out some clear purpose for the essay.

When the writing starts, I often get hung up most on trying to "sound" like a good writer. If you're like me and came to college from a shy family that never discussed much over dinner, you might think your best shot is to sound like a famous writer like T. S. Eliot and you might try to sneak in words that aren't really your own like *ephemeral* or *the lilacs smelled like springtime*. But the last thing you really want a reader thinking is how good or bad a writer you are.

Also, in the essay on arm wrestling, I got hung up thinking I had to make my conflict with my father somehow "universal." So in an early draft I wrote in a classical allusion — Aeneas lifting his old father up onto his shoulders and carrying him out of the burning city of Troy.[1] I'd read that story in high school and guessed one classical allusion might make the reader think I knew a lot more. But Aeneas didn't help the essay much, and I'm glad my teacher warned me off trying to universalize. He told me to write just what was true for me.

But that was hard, too, and still is — especially in the first draft. I don't know anyone who enjoys the first draft. If you do, I envy you. But in my early drafts, I always get this sensation like I have to impress somebody and

---

[1] In the *Aeneid*, by the Roman poet Virgil (70–19 BC), the mythic hero Aeneas escapes from the city of Troy when it is sacked by the Greeks and goes on to found Rome. — EDS.

I end up overanalyzing the effects of every word I am about to write. This self-consciousness may be unavoidable (I get self-conscious calling L.L. Bean to order a shirt), but, in this respect, writing is great for shy people because you can edit all you want, all day long, until it finally sounds right. I never feel that I am being myself until the third or fourth draft, and it's only then that it gets personal and starts to be fun.

When I said that putting off papers robbed me of a good time, I really meant it. Writing the essay about my father turned out to be a high point in my life. And on top of having a good time with it, I now have a record of what happened. And my ten-month-old son, when he grows up, can read things about his grandfather and father that he'd probably not have learned any other way.

The Bedford Reader on Writing

Brad Manning has some good advice for other college writers, especially about taking the time to plan (pp. 30–32), organize (p. 37), and revise (pp. 39–42) a draft, often many times over. For guidelines on how to edit your writing as he did, especially to establish and maintain your own VOICE, refer to pages 47–53 of Chapter 2.

disperse the tribe. Forbidden without cause the essential act of their faith, having seen the wild herds slaughtered and left to rot upon the ground, the Kiowas backed away forever from the medicine tree. That was July 20, 1890, at the great bend of the Washita. My grandmother was there. Without bitterness, and for as long as she lived, she bore a vision of deicide.[7]

Now that I can have her only in memory, I see my grandmother in the   10 several postures that were peculiar to her: standing at the wood stove on a winter morning and turning meat in a great iron skillet; sitting at the south window, bent above her beadwork, and afterwards, when her vision failed, looking down for a long time into the fold of her hands; going out upon a cane, very slowly as she did when the weight of age came upon her; praying. I remember her most often at prayer. She made long, rambling prayers out of suffering and hope, having seen many things. I was never sure that I had the right to hear, so exclusive were they of all mere custom and company. The last time I saw her she prayed standing by the side of her bed at night, naked to the waist, the light of a kerosene lamp moving upon her dark skin. Her long, black hair, always drawn and braided in the day, lay upon her shoulders and against her breasts like a shawl. I do not speak Kiowa, and I never understood her prayers, but there was something inherently sad in the sound, some merest hesitation upon the syllables of sorrow. She began in a high and descending pitch, exhausting her breath to silence; then again and again — and always the same intensity of effort, of something that is, and is not, like urgency in the human voice. Transported so in the dancing light among the shadows of her room, she seemed beyond the reach of time. But that was illusion; I think I knew then that I should not see her again.

Houses are like sentinels in the plain, old keepers of the weather watch.   11 There, in a very little while, wood takes on the appearance of great age. All colors wear soon away in the wind and rain, and then the wood is burned gray and the grain appears and the nails turn red with rust. The windowpanes are black and opaque; you imagine there is nothing within, and indeed there are many ghosts, bones given up to the land. They stand here and there against the sky, and you approach them for a longer time than you expect. They belong in the distance; it is their domain.

Once there was a lot of sound in my grandmother's house, a lot of com-   12 ing and going, feasting and talk. The summers there were full of excitement and reunion. The Kiowas are a summer people; they abide the cold and keep to themselves, but when the season turns and the land becomes warm and vital they cannot hold still; an old love of going returns upon them. The aged visitors who came to my grandmother's house when I was a child were made

[7] The killing of a divine being or beings (from Latin words meaning "god" and "kill"). — EDS.

of lean and leather, and they bore themselves upright. They wore great black hats and bright ample shirts that shook in the wind. They rubbed fat upon their hair and wound their braids with strips of colored cloth. Some of them painted their faces and carried the scars of old and cherished enmities. They were an old council of warlords, come to remind and be reminded of who they were. Their wives and daughters served them well. The women might indulge themselves; gossip was at once the mark and compensation of their servitude. They made loud and elaborate talk among themselves, full of jest and gesture, fright and false alarm. They went abroad in fringed and flowered shawls, bright beadwork and German silver. They were at home in the kitchen, and they prepared meals that were banquets.

There were frequent prayer meetings, and great nocturnal feasts. When I 13 was a child I played with my cousins outside, where the lamp-light fell upon the ground and the singing of the old people rose up around us and carried away into the darkness. There were a lot of good things to eat, a lot of laughter and surprise. And afterwards, when the quiet returned, I lay down with my grandmother and could hear the frogs away by the river and feel the motion of the air.

Now there is a funeral silence in the rooms, the endless wake of some 14 final word. The walls have closed in upon my grandmother's house. When I returned to it in mourning, I saw for the first time in my life how small it was. It was late at night, and there was a white moon, nearly full. I sat for a long time on the stone steps by the kitchen door. From there I could see out across the land; I could see the long row of trees by the creek, the low light upon the rolling plains, and the stars of the Big Dipper. Once I looked at the moon and caught sight of a strange thing. A cricket had perched upon the handrail, only a few inches away from me. My line of vision was such that the creature filled the moon like a fossil. It had gone there, I thought, to live and die, for there, of all places, was its small definition made whole and eternal. A warm wind rose up and purled like the longing within me.

The next morning I awoke at dawn and went out on the dirt road to 15 Rainy Mountain. It was already hot, and the grasshoppers began to fill the air. Still, it was early in the morning, and the birds sang out of the shadows. The long yellow grass on the mountain shone in the bright light, and a scissortail hied above the land. There, where it ought to be, at the end of a long and legendary way, was my grandmother's grave. Here and there on the dark stones were ancestral names. Looking back once, I saw the mountain and came away.

Journal Writing

"The Way to Rainy Mountain" is about Momaday's associations between his grandmother and Rainy Mountain. Think of somebody special to you and a specific place that you associate with this person. Jot down as many details about the person and place as you can.

Questions on Meaning

1. What is the significance of Momaday's statement that the Kiowas "reckoned their stature by the distance they could see" (par. 6)? How does this statement relate to the ultimate fate of the Kiowas?

2. Remembering his grandmother, Momaday writes, "She made long, rambling prayers out of suffering and hope, having seen many things" (par. 10). What is the key point here, and how does the concept of prayer connect with the essay as a whole?

3. What do you think Momaday's main idea is? What thread links all the essay's parts?

4. What seems to be Momaday's PURPOSE in writing this essay? Can we read this as more than a personal story about a visit to his grandmother's grave?

Questions on Writing Strategy

1. Who is Momaday's AUDIENCE? Do you think he is writing for other Kiowa descendants? for non-Indians? for others who have lost an older relative?

2. "Loneliness is an aspect of the land," Momaday writes (par. 1). To what extent do you think this sentence captures the DOMINANT IMPRESSION of the essay? If you perceive a different impression, what is it?

3. How does Momaday organize his essay? (It may help to plot the structure by preparing a rough outline.) How effective do you find this organization, and why?

4. Would you characterize Momaday's description as SUBJECTIVE or OBJECTIVE? What about his use of language suggests one over the other?

5. **OTHER METHODS** Besides description, Momaday relies on mixing other methods, such as NARRATION, EXAMPLE, COMPARISON AND CONTRAST, and CAUSE AND EFFECT. What is the purpose of the comparison in paragraphs 12–14?

Questions on Language

1. If you do not know the meanings of the following words, look them up in a dictionary: anvil (par. 1); infirm (2); preeminently, pillage, affliction (3); nomadic (4); cleavages (6); lees, profusion, deity, caldron (7); engender, tenuous (8); reverence, consummate (9); inherently (10); purled (14); hied (15).

2. Momaday uses many vivid FIGURES OF SPEECH. Locate at least one use each of metaphor, simile, and hyperbole (review these terms in the Glossary if necessary). What does each of these figures convey?

3. Momaday's first and last paragraphs present contrasting IMAGES of Rainy Mountain and the surrounding plain: At first, "the prairie is an anvil's edge" and the "grass turns brittle and brown"; in the end, "the birds sang out of the shadows" and the "long yellow grass on the mountain shone in the bright light." How does this contrast serve Momaday's purpose?

4. Notice Momaday's use of PARALLELISM in describing the visitors to his grandmother's house (par. 12) — for instance, "They wore. . . . They rubbed. . . . They made. . . ." What does the parallelism convey about the people being described?

Suggestions for Writing

1. **FROM JOURNAL TO ESSAY** Develop your journal entry (p. 135) into an essay that describes both the person and the place, using concrete and specific details to make the connection between them clear to your readers.

2. Momaday writes about his ancestors and a way of life very different from that of the present. For this assignment you may need to investigate your family's history. Write an essay that describes your ancestors' way of life. (Your ancestors may be as recent as your grandparents or as distant as your research allows.) Who were these people? How did they live? How does that way of life differ from the way you and your family live now? Be specific in your description and comparison, providing concrete details and examples for clarity.

3. One of Momaday's underlying themes in this essay is the difficulties American Indians often face on reservations. Do some research about the conditions of reservation life. Then write an essay in which you report your findings.

4. **CRITICAL WRITING** In an essay, ANALYZE Momaday's attitudes toward the Kiowas as revealed in the language he uses to describe them. Support your THESIS (your central idea about Momaday's attitudes) with specific quotations from the essay.

5. **CONNECTIONS** Both Momaday and Manning write about traditions and the evolution of relationships in their families. Write an essay that contrasts the sense of continuity in Manning's essay with the sense of loss and change in Momaday's. Are there also similarities in the feelings and influences they describe?

N. Scott Momaday on Writing

In an interview for *Sequoia* magazine in 1975, N. Scott Momaday was asked by William T. Morgan, Jr., whether he saw himself as a "spokesman" for American Indians.

No, and it's something I don't think about very often. I don't identify with any group of writers, and I don't think of myself as being a spokesman for the Indian people. That would be presumptuous, it seems to me. . . . When I write I find it a very private kind of thing, and I like to keep it that way. You know, I would be uncomfortable I think if I were trying to express the views of other people. When I write I write out of my own experience, and out of my own ideas of that experience, and I'm not concerned to write the history of a people except as that history bears on me directly. When I was writing *The Way to Rainy Mountain*, for example, I was dealing with something that belongs to the Indian world, and the Kiowa people as a whole, but I wasn't concerned with that so much as I was concerned with the fact that it meant this to me — this is how I as a person felt about it. And I want my writing to reflect myself in certain ways — that is my first concern.

The Bedford Reader on Writing

Momaday insists on a personal approach to ACADEMIC WRITING, a habit that some teachers caution against (see, for example, our comments regarding the uses of the first-PERSON *I* on p. 48). But Momaday demonstrates particular mastery of SYNTHESIS, bringing in other people's perspectives while keeping his own ideas at the center. See pages 42–47 for advice on integrating evidence without losing your distinctive VOICE, as Momaday does in "The Way to Rainy Mountain."

DIANE ACKERMAN

Diane Ackerman is a poet and essayist who writes extensively on the natural world. She was born in Waukegan, Illinois, in 1948 and grew up mostly in gritty Allentown, Pennsylvania. She studied English at Penn State (BA, 1970) and, after completing an MFA (1973) and PhD (1978) at Cornell University, took up travel, college teaching, and constant writing. A former staff writer for *The New Yorker*, Ackerman is consistently praised for her detailed scientific observations, expressed with a poet's knack for sensuous language and a child's sense of wonder. She has published several books of poetry, including *The Planets: A Cosmic Pastoral* (1976) and *I Praise My Destroyer* (1998), and more than a dozen works of exuberant nonfiction ranging from memoir to philosophy to anthropology, most notably *A Natural History of the Senses* (1991) and *The Zookeeper's Wife* (2008). Ackerman is also a regular contributor to *Smithsonian*, *National Geographic*, *Parnassus*, and many other magazines and literary journals. She lives in Ithaca, New York, where she is an avid gardener and cyclist.

Black Marble

Ackerman's latest book, *The Human Age: The World Shaped by Us* (2014), offers a refreshingly optimistic take on the causes and implications of our changing environment. Suggesting that the world has entered a new geological era and calling it the *Anthropocene*, or "Human Age," Ackerman insists that "our relationship with nature has changed . . . radically, irreversibly, but by no means all for the bad." In this chapter from the book, she imagines what travelers from outer space might encounter as they approach the Earth — and what we might make of their observations.

As our spaceship enters the roulette wheel of a new solar system, hope starts building its fragile crystals once again. Disappointment has dogged our travels, but we are nomads with restless minds, and this sun resembles our own middle-aged star. Like ours, it rules a tidy jumble of planets looping in atypical orbits, some unfurling a pageant of seasons, others hard-hearted, monotone, and remote. They're a strange assortment for siblings, with many small straggling hangers-on, but we've encountered odder night-fellows, and variety is their lure. One fizzy giant trails dozens of sycophantic moons; another floats inside a white cocoon. We weave between rocky, hard-boiled worlds, swing by a blimp tugging a retinue of jagged moons, dodge the diffuse rubble of asteroids, skirt a hothouse of acid clouds and phantom light. 1

Slowing to a hyperglide, we admire all the dappled colors, mammoth canyons of razor-backed rust, ice-spewing volcanoes, fountains fifty miles high, 2 hydrocarbon lakes, scarlet welts and scourges, drooling oceans of frozen methane, light daggers, magma flows, sulfur rain, and many other intrigues of climate and geology. Yet there's no sign of living, breathing life forms anywhere. We are such a lonely species. Maybe this solar system will be the harbor where we find others like ourselves, curious, questing beings of unknown ardor or bloom. Life will have whittled them to fit their world, it doesn't matter how.

One more planet to survey, and then it's on to the next port of call.   3

On a small water planet flocked over by clouds, sequins sparkle every-   4
where. Racing toward it with abandon, we give in to its pull, and orbit in step with nightfall shadowing the world, transfixed by the embroidery of gold and white lights — from clusters and ribbons to willful circles and grids. *Crafted* lights, not natural auroras or lightning, but *designed*, and too many, too regular, too rare to ignore.

In 2003, aboard the Space Station, Don Pettit[1] felt his heart pin-wheel   5
whenever he viewed Earth's cities at night. *If only everyone could see Earth like this*, he thought, *they'd marvel at how far we've come, and they'd understand what we share.* A born tinkerer, he used spare parts he found in the Space Station to photograph the spinning planet with pristine clarity, as if it were sitting still. When he returned home he stitched the photographs together into a video montage, an orbital tour of Earth's cities at night, which he posted on *YouTube.* His voice-over identifies each glowing spiderweb as we sail toward it with him, as if we too were peering out of a Space Station window: "Zurich, Switzerland; Milan, Italy; Madrid, Spain.

"Cities at night are caught in a triangle," he says with awe tugging at his   6
voice, "between culture, geography, and technology. . . . Cities in Europe display a characteristic network of roads that radiate outwards. . . . London, with a tour down the English coast to Bristol. Cairo, Egypt, with the Nile River seen as a dark shape running south to north, the Pyramids of Giza are well lit at night . . . Tel Aviv on the left, Jerusalem on the right . . ."

Glowing gold, green, and yellow, the Middle Eastern cities seem especially   7
lustrous. He points out India's hallmark — village lights dotted over the countryside, softly glowing as through a veil. Then we fly above Manila, where geometrical lights define the waterfront. The dragon-shaped lights of Hong Kong flutter under us, and the southeast tip of South Korea. In the welling darkness of the Korea Strait, a band of dazzling white grains is a fleet of fishing boats shining high-intensity xenon lamps as lures.

[1] Don Pettit (born 1955) is an American astronaut, chemical engineer, and NASA photographer. He worked aboard the International Space Station from November 2002 to May 2003. — Eds.

"There's Tokyo, Brisbane, the San Francisco Bay, Houston," Pettit notes.   8

We don't intend our cities to be so beautiful from space. They're human-   9
ity's electric fingerprints on the planet, the chrome-yellow energy that flows
through city veins. Dwarfed by the infinite dome of space with its majestic
coliseum of stars, we've created our own constellations on the ground and
named them after our triumphs, enterprises, myths, and leaders. Copenhagen
("Merchants Harbor"), Amsterdam ("A Dam on the Amstel River"), Ottawa
("Traders"), Bogotá ("Planted Fields"), Cotonou ("Mouth of the River of
Death"), Canberra ("Meeting Place"), Fleissenberg ("Castle of Diligence"),
Ouagadougou ("Where People Get Honor and Respect"), Athens (City of
Athena, Greek goddess of wisdom). We play out our lives amid a festival of
lights. The story the lights tell would be unmistakable to any space traveler:
some bold life form has criss-crossed the planet with an exuberance of cities,
favoring settlements along the coast and beside flowing water, and connecting
them all with a labyrinth of brilliantly lit roads, so that even without a map
the outlines of the continents loom and you can spot the meandering rivers.

The silent message of this spectacle is timely, strange, and wonderful.   10
We've tattooed the planet with our doings. Our handiwork is visible everywhere, which NASA has captured with graphic poignancy in *Black Marble*,
its December 7, 2012, portrait of Earth ablaze at night. A companion to the
famous *Blue Marble* photograph of Earth that appeared forty years ago, this
radical new self-portrait promises to awaken and inspire us just as mightily.

On December 7, 1972, the crew of *Apollo 17*, the last manned lunar mis-   11
sion, shot the *Blue Marble* photograph of the whole Earth floating against the
black velvet of space. Africa and Europe were eye-catching under swirling
white clouds, but the predominant color was blue. This was the one picture
from the Apollo missions that dramatically expanded our way of thinking. It
showed us how small the planet is in the vast sprawl of space, how entwined
and spontaneous its habitats are. Despite all the wars and hostilities, when
viewed from space Earth had no national borders, no military zones, no visible
fences. One could see how storm systems swirling above the Amazon might
affect the grain yield half a planet away in China. An Indian Ocean hurricane,
swirling at the top of the photo, had pummeled India with whirlwinds and
floods only two days before. Because it was nearly winter solstice, the white
lantern of Antarctica glowed. The entire atmosphere of the planet — all the
air we breathe, the sky we fly through, even the ozone layer — was visible as
the thinnest rind.

Released during a time of growing environmental concern, it became an   12
emblem of global consciousness, the most widely distributed photo in human
history. It gave us an image to float in the lagoon of the mind's eye. It helped
us embrace something too immense to focus on as a single intricately known

and intricately unknown organism. Now we could see Earth in one eye-gulp, the way we gaze on a loved one. We could paste the image into our *Homo sapiens* family album. Here was a view of every friend, every loved one and acquaintance, every path ever traveled, all together in one place. No wonder it adorned so many college dorm rooms. As the ultimate group portrait, it helped us understand our global kinship and cosmic address. It proclaimed our shared destiny.

NASA's new image of city lights, a panorama of the continents emblazoned with pulsating beacons, startles and transforms our gaze once again. Ours is the only planet in our solar system that glitters at night. Earth is 4.5 billion years old, and for eons the nighttime planet was dark. In a little over two hundred years we've wired up the world and turned on the lights, as if we signed the planet in luminous ink. In another forty years our scrawl won't look the same. There are so many of us who find urban life magnetic that our cities no longer simply sprawl — they've begun to grow exponentially. Millions of us pack up, leave jobs and neighbors behind, and migrate to the city every year, joining nearly two-thirds of all the people on Earth. In the future, more and more clusters will appear, with even wider lattices and curtains of lights connecting them. Many display our curious tastes and habits. A harlequin thread drawn from Moscow to Vladivostok and dipping into China is the Trans-Siberian Railway. A golden streak through a profound darkness, the Nile River pours between the Aswan Dam and the Mediterranean Sea. A trellis connecting bright dots is the US interstate highway system. The whole continent of Antarctica is still invisible at night. The vast deserts of Mongolia, Africa, Arabia, Australia, and the United States look almost as dark. So, too, teeming jungles in Africa and South America, the colossal arc of the Himalayas, and the rich northern forests of Canada and Russia. But shopping centers and seaports sizzle with light, as if they're frying electrons. The single brightest spot on the entire planet isn't Jerusalem or the Pyramids of Giza, though those do sparkle, but a more secular temple of neon, the Las Vegas Strip. 13

Newer settlements in the American West tend to be boxy, with streets that bolt north-south and east-west, before trickling into darkness at the fringes of town. In big cities like Tokyo, the crooked, meandering lines of the oldest neighborhoods glow mantis-green from mercury vapor streetlights, while the newer streets wrapped around them shine orange from modern sodium vapor lamps. 14

Our shimmering cities tell all (including us) that Earth's inhabitants are thinkers, builders and rearrangers who like to bunch together in hivelike settlements, and for some reason — bad night vision, primal fear, sheer vanity, to scare predators, or as a form of group adornment — we bedeck them all with garlands of light. 15

Journal Writing

Imagine you're an alien visiting Earth for the first time, and that the spaceship has touched down in the neighborhood you currently occupy (or, if you prefer, in a region you have lived in or visited in the past). Look around and describe what you find, absorbing as much as you can and taking nothing for granted. Consider, for instance, the area's physical attributes, any movements you perceive, subtle or overpowering scents, the weather, and any human alterations to the natural surroundings such as roads, buildings, and power lines. Jot down your impressions in your journal.

Questions on Meaning

1. What DOMINANT IMPRESSION does Ackerman create of the Earth as viewed from space at night?

2. What would you say is Ackerman's PURPOSE in this essay? Does she express her purpose in a THESIS STATEMENT, or is it implied?

3. What does Ackerman mean when she says in paragraph 2, "Life will have whittled them to fit their world, it doesn't matter how"? Where in the essay does she return to this notion, and why?

4. In what ways does light serve as a SYMBOL for Ackerman?

Questions on Writing Strategy

1. Reread the first four paragraphs of the essay closely. What sense do you make of Ackerman's introduction? What is the EFFECT of opening the way she does?

2. How does Ackerman organize her description?

3. What does Ackerman seem to ASSUME about the interests and knowledge of her AUDIENCE? To what extent do you fit her assumptions?

4. Ackerman's description is based on viewing online SOURCES. What are they? What strategies does she use to SYNTHESIZE information and ideas from her sources without losing her own voice? How well does she succeed?

5. **OTHER METHODS** Where in the essay does Ackerman use COMPARISON AND CONTRAST to explain her meaning to readers? What does the method contribute to her essay?

Questions on Language

1. Ackerman uses an abundance of FIGURES OF SPEECH in this essay, most notably metaphor, but also simile and personification. Find at least two or three examples of each and comment on their effectiveness.

2. How would you characterize Ackerman's DICTION and TONE? Is her language appropriate given her subject? Why, or why not?

3. Ackerman uses a number of words that may not be familiar to you. Consult a dictionary if you need help defining the following: nomads, atypical, sycophantic, retinue, diffuse (par. 1); hyperglide, hydrocarbon, scourges, magma, ardor (2); transfixed, auroras (4); pristine, orbital (5); lustrous, xenon (7); coliseum, enterprises, exuberance, labyrinth (9); poignancy (10); lunar, entwined, solstice, ozone (11); lagoon, *Homo sapiens* (12); luminous, exponentially, lattices, harlequin, colossal, secular (13); mantis (14); primal (15). From what field(s) of academic study does much of her vocabulary derive?

Suggestions for Writing

1. **FROM JOURNAL TO ESSAY** Working from your journal entry (p. 142), write an essay that describes a particular aspect of your corner of the planet Earth from the perspective of someone experiencing it for the first time. Draw on as many of the five senses as you like, but make your description as lively as possible, letting your feelings influence your selection of details, what you say about them, and the dominant impression you create.

2. Go online and find the *Blue Marble* and *Black Marble* photographs that Ackerman describes so subjectively. Pick one (or both) of the photographs, and in a paragraph or essay of your own, describe it as *objectively* as possible, leaving emotions out of your description and focusing on the observable details.

3. **CRITICAL WRITING** Using your response to the first Question on Language (p. 142) as a starting point, analyze Ackerman's use of sensory IMAGES in "Black Marble." How does the abundant imagery and figurative language help convey her ideas about a changing environment? What else do the images contribute to the essay?

4. **CONNECTIONS** Like Ackerman, *National Geographic*, in "Wild Weather" (p. 388), Randall Munroe, in "Everybody Jump" (p. 410), and Margaret Lundberg, in "Eating Green" (p. 645) address the issue of human impacts on the planet. While Ackerman suggests such impacts might be beneficial, Munroe believes they are negligible, Lundberg asserts that they are damaging, and *National Geographic* implies they are catastrophic. What do you think? Write a brief essay about your view of one aspect of the environment. Do you regard energy consumption, carbon emissions, climate change, overpopulation, or dwindling natural resources as critical problems? Do you believe that governments are taking adequate steps to protect the environment? Do you believe that the actions of individuals can make a difference? Your essay may but need not be an ARGUMENT: That is, you could explain your answer to any of these questions or argue a specific point. Either way, choose a narrow focus and use examples and details to support your ideas, drawing on evidence from any of these selections as appropriate.

SVEN BIRKERTS

Born in Pontiac, Michigan, in 1951 to immigrants from Latvia, Sven Birkerts grew up near Detroit "wrestling," as he once put it, "with the ghosts of another culture." For much of his childhood he heard only Latvian at home and was regularly regaled with stories of a happier life in northern Europe before World War II. Birkerts was a voracious reader in his youth and studied literature at the University of Michigan, earning a bachelor's degree in 1973. He stumbled on his career as a literary critic in the early 1980s while working as a bookstore clerk. On a whim he wrote a review of a novel for his own enjoyment and submitted it to a journal; to his surprise the amateur effort led to regular assignments. Birkerts's essays have been collected in several volumes, starting with *An Artificial Wilderness: Essays on Twentieth-Century Literature* (1987) and including *The Gutenberg Elegies: The Fate of Reading in an Electronic Age* (1994), *The Art of Time in Memoir: Then, Again* (2008), *The Other Walk* (2011), and *Changing the Subject: Art and Attention in the Internet Age* (2015). He has also taught college writing and is a co-author of two literature textbooks. Often praised for his lack of pretention, Birkerts is known for his skill at distilling complex thoughts into simple prose. He lives in Arlington, Massachusetts, a suburb of Boston.

Ladder

Birkerts's book *The Other Walk* (2011) mixes critical analysis and personal reflection and was praised by *Publisher's Weekly* for "the humor and insights conveyed in [its] enchanting and well-crafted essays," such as the one we include here. In "Ladder," Birkerts describes with precision and embarrassment what it felt like to discover a crippling phobia at a most inopportune time.

It was already there when I came around the side of the house. I saw it in 1 that sidelong way you register one thing while looking for another. I was trying to find the man I'd spoken to on the phone, who had hired me for the day, and there he was, cross-legged on the grass, wearing a bright white T-shirt, with a full head of silvery hair, camera hair, though he didn't really look like the kind of older man who would go to all the trouble. But maybe he was, because when he heard me coming and turned full-face I saw he was handsome, lady-killer handsome the way some older men are, and these men are always vain. He was cleaning paintbrushes — they were neatly lined up on a sheet of newspaper — and he didn't get up. He had strong-looking arms, maybe even an old-style tattoo. I was looking, staring, at his face, but not so distracted that I didn't take in the other thing. Off to my right, propped up against the side of the house, going up and up in sections, was the tallest ladder I'd ever seen. I felt a bump in my stomach. I hadn't even really turned yet, or followed the ladder up into the light to see where the ends were propped against the highest gable. I was still making my way across the grass, and the man, I don't remember his name anymore, was squinting up and saluting me, or maybe lifting his arm to block the sun, saying, "Here to do some work?" I nodded and said I was. That was the deal. I'd been living on the edge all winter in our little seaside Maine town, buying dented canned goods at discount and even signing on one day with my girlfriend, Sally, to deliver phone books in nearby Biddeford, the mill town in which every other person was named Pelletier or Thibodeaux — and we were required to check off the right recipient and address. Thibodeaux, Thibodeaux, Thibodeaux . . . We quit after a day. Next I'd put up a sign in our little cracker-box post office offering my odd-job services for a laughably low hourly rate. My logic: who could resist?

And now it was one of the first real spring days and this man had called 2 with a job, and my attention was evenly split between the shock of his sea-soned movie-star looks and my growing awareness of that ladder. Did I already know how it was with me and heights? How could I not? I was in my early twenties and had done enough playing in trees and high places as a kid to have an idea. I'd always been a reluctant climber, though maybe I'd later chalked it off as a fear outgrown — as if a decade of not testing the edge would have made it go away. I don't know. I only know that the man — my boss — walked me over to where the ladder stood flat on its grips and showed me my bucket and brushes and handed me a rag that I tucked into my belt. But just before he did that — this comes back with close-up clarity — he reached his thumb and forefinger into the two corners of his mouth and took out his teeth. Out. The whole apparatus. He pulled it from his mouth and held it up like one of those party jokes that you wind with a key. I looked away — I felt embarrassed — and when I glanced back I must have done a double take. Impossible. His face had completely fallen in on itself — the strong jaw was gone, the mouth was crimped like the top of a string bag. I watched as he bent down and set the teeth on another sheet of newspaper in the grass.

When he straightened up, I was face-to-face with an old man with a thick, 3 groomed head of silver hair. I don't know if he had any idea of the effect he had just achieved. He was standing with me by the ladder, telling me to make sure I got enough paint onto the wood, and I was nodding, agreeing, and already registering — I'm sure of it — that first nervous heaviness in my legs, and that tightness in the chest that starts you drawing deep breaths as if a good deep rush of air will make everything better. And then I was on the ladder, starting, a few rungs up, hauling the bucket with my left hand, the shore in sight, the ground still an easy jump. I had that instinct, or instruction, picked up somewhere, to keep my gaze straight ahead, taking in the lapping shingles row by row, the voice that said, "Don't look, just climb." Which I did, so carefully, every bit of my focus on my legs and hands, and on keeping the line of the vertical steady — no twists or turns, just plant the foot on the rung and pull with my one free arm, the right arm, the other gripping the bucket, which I was to hang on a hook next to where I painted — and I was already telling myself the facts of the matter, that people did this all the time, everywhere; that the ladder was strong, well planted at the base; and that little wobbles would naturally be magnified as sensations, that there was no real danger, and that even if I were to fall — *I would not fall* — it would be nothing more than a bad bump and some embarrassment at this point. So I stepped and pulled and steadied and watched myself in slow blurry sections pass by the frame of the first big window, which I knew was about halfway up.

But here the ordinary sequence stops. This upward progress was not hap-   4
pening in units anymore, never mind the rungs lined up ahead of me. Some-where between one step and another the time stream balked, then stopped and started backing up. Every movement was suddenly breaking into its parts, the one arm aware of itself lifting, wrapping its fingers around the metal of the next rung, the other hand feeling in its joints the cut of the handle, the weight of the bucket, the weathered shingles mere inches away now gathering into the clearest detail: nail heads, streaks and smears and hardened little droplets of ancient paint, the ribbing of the wood grain visible under the color. "Don't look down, just climb." And I could feel it then, on my skin, up the armholes, the April wind, sweetly cool even in the spots of full sun, which I knew with-out looking was moving in and out behind the clouds. The moment of the shift. It comes now. I hear myself breathing and realize that I've stopped. I don't remember stopping, but all at once I know that I've been staring and staring at the same few warps and scratches. How long? I don't know. The window below me rattles in the breeze, I hear it. Suddenly I can't help myself: I turn my head just slightly to the left and I look down. Mainly to see if the man, my boss, is still there somewhere, but also because I need to know where I am. I feel a kind of thud as the scene clicks in. Ground, grass. He's not any-where on the left side. Nor — I've moved my head so carefully, as if that little action could make a difference — on the other. The lawn falls away in either direction, empty. I am halfway up the side of the tallest house I've ever seen, and I'm alone. And that little twist of the neck was like breaking the seal. The calm, the focus, whatever story I was telling myself up here, is gone. I take in the great wide lawn, and over there, tiny as a kit for dolls, the newspaper with its row of tiny brushes lined up, and one corner flipping up in the breeze. That repeating movement makes me feel sick, that and the ground all at once so far away, the wind now pulling at the back of my shirt, and I feel the fingers of my right hand tighten their grasp and my chest and stomach push in harder against the rungs. What have I done? I can't unsee the distance down, or lose

the sense of the ladder shrinking away to nothing below me and above me. My hand hurts where I hold the metal, and now my knees go soft, just like that. I have the weight of the bucket in my other hand. For the first time I think, *Let it go, just drop it* — drop it and reach up with that hand, as if maybe with both hands gripping I can make it down. But somehow I can't make myself loosen my hold on the bucket, or do anything. Except close my eyes. Close my eyes and start to count, slowly: *One thousand one, one thousand two* . . . I don't know how high I get, but after enough numbers I feel something in me settle, I say to myself, *OK now,* and as I say that I get my fingers to go loose, and then without ever taking them away from the ladder I slide them, along the rung to the right-hand side, and then down the metal slowly, clutching between thumb and forefinger, until I reach the nearer rung, which I grab, and as I do that I let my left leg loose to find the lower support, and this I find, and lower the other leg, foot, shuddering my torso inch by inch down along the rungs, and again repeating the whole sequence, gaining just the first slight ease as the ground lifts slightly toward me, again, again, until I reach the first rung and take the backward step to earth, almost crazy with reaching it, bending to set the bucket down, letting go my other grip and straightening slowly up . . . and only then becoming aware of the man standing right in back of me. He's arrived from somewhere, and I know he's seen the whole of it, and at the same time I can feel that the fingers of my left hand, free from the clutch and the weight, are shaking. But I have no doubt, no question. Standing there, I notice where the shadows — mine, his — break from the grass against the side of the house, and I say to him without turning around, "I can't go up that high. I didn't know it before." I wait for a moment. When I finally turn and meet his eye, he shrugs, saying basically, *What can you do?* He's wearing a painter's cap now, flecked with white paint, and I see that he has put the teeth back in — and he looks good, not quite Paul Newman,[1] but very handsome. Obviously a lady-killer.

Journal Writing

Using Birkerts's essay as a springboard, consider any irrational fears that you may have. Are you afraid of heights, for instance, or snakes or spiders or tight spaces? Does any one instance involving your phobia stand out in your memory? Write about the experience in your journal.

[1] Paul Newman (1925–2008) was a movie actor famous for striking good looks that seemed to improve as he aged. — Eds.

Questions on Meaning

1. How would you describe the writer's PURPOSE in this essay? What DOMINANT IMPRESSION does Birkerts create?

2. In describing turning his head while high up during his climb, Birkert says, "that little twist of the neck was like breaking the seal" (par. 4)? What do you think he means? What phenomenon does "breaking the seal" ALLUDE to?

3. Why did the author seek out odd jobs like a day of house painting? How do those circumstances hint at the deeper implications of his fear?

4. Why is Birkerts terrified by the ladder? What does it represent to him?

Questions on Writing Strategy

1. What strategy does Birkerts use to connect with his readers? How well does he succeed, in your estimation?

2. What point of view does Birkerts take, and how does he arrange the details of his description?

3. What is the intended EFFECT of the unusually long final paragraph?

4. **OTHER METHODS** Where does Birkerts use COMPARISON AND CONTRAST? What do these passages contribute to the essay?

Questions on Language

1. Consult a dictionary if you are unsure of the meaning of any of the following: sidelong, vain, gable (par. 1); lapping (3); balked (4).

2. In paragraph 1 Birkerts describes his boss as "lady-killer handsome." What does that mean? Where in his essay does Birkerts come back to this idea, and what is the effect of the repetition?

3. Point to a few instances in the essay that make particularly effective use of CONCRETE details and sensory IMAGES to convey Birkerts's feelings.

Suggestions for Writing

1. **FROM JOURNAL TO ESSAY** Write an essay on the experience you explored in your journal, using SUBJECTIVE description to convey the effect a phobia had on you.

2. Have you ever initiated a course of action but then, as events unfolded, lost control of the situation? What happened, and how did you respond? Write a NARRATIVE essay in which you relate your experience.

3. Think of some job you have held, whether something temporary like a day of house painting or more structured work for a regular employer. What was the job? Did you do it because you wanted to, because you needed the income, or for some other reason? How do you feel about working? Write about your work experience,

using PROCESS ANALYSIS to explain the mechanics of the job to a new or future employee. Or, if you wish, use description and narration to convey the effect the experience had on you.

4. **CRITICAL WRITING** In an essay, ANALYZE the image that Birkerts presents of himself. Consider specific examples of his language and TONE, along with what he says about himself and his implied attitude toward traditional measures of masculinity.

5. **CONNECTIONS** Both Sven Birkerts's "Ladder" and Kellie Young's "The Under-current" (p. 189) examine how the writers react to anxiety. Write an essay that considers the extent to which attitude affects a person's ability to cope with fears and worries, using these two essays and your own experience for examples and EVIDENCE.

JOYCE CAROL OATES

One of America's most respected and prolific contemporary authors, Joyce Carol Oates was born in 1938 in Lockport, New York. After graduating from Syracuse University in 1960, she earned an MA from the University of Wisconsin. In 1963 she published her first book, a collection of short stories, and she has published an average of two books a year since then. With the novel *them* (1969), Oates became one of the youngest writers to receive the National Book Award for fiction. Other notable novels include *Wonderland* (1971), *Black Water* (1992), *Blonde* (2000), *A Fair Maiden* (2010), and *The Man without a Shadow* (2016). Oates has also written more than a dozen volumes of poetry, a score of plays, and several works of nonfiction, including memoir, literary criticism, and a study of boxing. Her many awards include the 2010 National Humanities Medal and the 2012 PEN Center USA Award for Lifetime Achievement. Oates teaches writing and literature at Princeton University.

Edward Hopper's *Nighthawks*, 1942

First published in Oates's poetry collection *The Time Traveler* (1989), this poem responds to a well-known painting by the American artist Edward Hopper (1882–1967). The painting, *Nighthawks*, is reproduced on the facing page, both in full view and in detail.

> The three men are fully clothed, long sleeves,　　　　1
> even hats, though it's indoors, and brightly lit,
> and there's a woman. The woman is wearing
> a short-sleeved red dress cut to expose her arms,
> a curve of her creamy chest; she's contemplating　　5
> a cigarette in her right hand, thinking that
> her companion has finally left his wife but
> can she trust him? Her heavy-lidded eyes,
> pouty lipsticked mouth, she has the redhead's
> true pallor like skim milk, damned good-looking　　10
> and she guesses she knows it but what exactly
> has it gotten her so far, and where? — he'll start
> to feel guilty in a few days, she knows
> the signs, an actual smell, sweaty, rancid, like
> dirty socks; he'll slip away to make telephone calls　　15
> and she swears she isn't going to go through that
> again, isn't going to break down crying or begging
> nor is she going to scream at him, she's finished

Edward Hopper, *Nighthawks* 1942, Oil on canvas, Friends of American Art Collection, The Art Institute of Chicago / Superstock / Superstock

with all that. And he's silent beside her,
not the kind to talk much but he's thinking   20
thank God he made the right move at last,
he's a little dazed like a man in a dream —
is this a dream? — so much that's wide, still,
mute, horizontal, and the counterman in white,
stooped as he is and unmoving, and the man   25
on the other stool unmoving except to sip
his coffee; but he's feeling pretty good,
it's primarily relief, this time he's sure
as hell going to make it work, he owes it to her
and to himself, Christ's sake. And she's thinking   30
the light in this place is too bright, probably
not very flattering, she hates it when her lipstick
wears off and her makeup gets caked, she'd like
to use a ladies' room but there isn't one here
and Jesus how long before a gas station opens? —   35
it's the middle of the night and she has a feeling
time is never going to budge. This time
though she isn't going to demean herself —
he starts in about his wife, his kids, how
he let them down, they trusted him and he let   40
them down, she'll slam out of the goddamned room
and if he calls her *Sugar* or *Baby* in that voice,
running his hands over her like he has the right,
she'll slap his face hard, *You know I hate that: Stop!*
And he'll stop. He'd better. The angrier   45
she gets the stiller she is, hasn't said a word
for the past ten minutes, not a strand
of her hair stirs, and it smells a little like ashes
or like the henna she uses to brighten it, but
the smell is faint or anyway, crazy for her   50
like he is, he doesn't notice, or mind —
burying his hot face in her neck, between her cool
breasts, or her legs — wherever she'll have him,
and whenever. She's still contemplating
the cigarette burning in her hand,   55
the counterman is still stooped gaping
at her, and he doesn't mind that, why not,
as long as she doesn't look back, in fact
he's thinking he's the luckiest man in the world
so why isn't he happier?   60

Journal Writing

In this poem Oates describes what she sees in Hopper's painting and also what she imagines, particularly about the woman. Most of us have unobtrusively observed strangers in a public place and imagined what they were thinking or what was going on between them. Write a paragraph or two on why such observation can be interesting or what it can (or can't) reveal.

Questions on Meaning

1. What story does Oates imagine about the couple in *Nighthawks*? How are the man's and the woman's thoughts different?

2. Line 23 of the poem asks, "*is this a dream?*" Who is posing this question? What about the painting is dreamlike?

3. Throughout the poem, Oates emphasizes the silence and stillness of the scene in the restaurant — for instance, "The angrier / she gets the stiller she is, hasn't / said a word / for the past ten minutes" (lines 45–47). What meanings about the painting and the people in it might Oates be emphasizing?

Questions on Writing Strategy

1. Where in the poem does Oates use CONCRETE language to describe what can actually be seen in the painting, as opposed to what she imagines? How does she use the former to support the latter? What does the mixture suggest about Oates's PURPOSE?

2. The thoughts of the woman include some vivid sensory images. What are some examples? How do these thoughts contrast with the man's?

3. What techniques of sentence structure does Oates use in lines 12–19 and 30–45 to suggest the woman's rising anger?

4. **OTHER METHODS** Where does Oates use NARRATION in the poem? Where does she imply a narrative? Why is narration important to her analysis of Hopper's painting?

Questions on Language

1. Oates uses just a few words that might be unfamiliar. Make sure you know the meanings of contemplating (line 5); rancid (14); budge (37); demean (38); henna (49).

2. The man's and woman's thoughts are peppered with strong language that some might find offensive. What does this language suggest about how Oates sees the characters?

3. In lines 27–28 Oates writes that the man is "feeling pretty good, / it's primarily relief." How does the word "relief" undercut the notion of "feeling pretty good"?

Suggestions for Writing

1. **FROM JOURNAL TO ESSAY** Find a public place where you can observe strangers unobtrusively from a distance — a park, for example, or a plaza, campus quad, dining hall, restaurant, bus, train. Take notes about what you observe — what your subjects look like, how they behave, how they interact with each other. Then write an essay based on your notes that incorporates both actual description of your subjects and what the details lead you to imagine they are thinking to themselves and saying to each other. Make sure the link between actual and imaginary is clear to your readers.

2. In a local gallery or museum, in a library art book, or on a Web site such as *WebMuseum* (*ibiblio.org/wm/paint*), find a painting that seems to you particularly intriguing or appealing. Then write a prose essay or a poem that expresses the painting's appeal to you. You may but need not imitate Oates by focusing on the thoughts of any figures in the painting. Describe the details of the painting and how they work together to create meaning for you. If you write a poem, don't worry about the technical aspects of poetry (meter, rhyme, and the rest). Think instead about your choice of words and IMAGES, building the poem through description.

3. **CRITICAL WRITING** Throughout her poem Oates interweaves description of the painting and its figures with what she imagines the figures are thinking. Mark each kind of material in the poem, and then examine the shifts from one to the other. How does Oates make readers aware that she is moving from one to the other? Are the shifts always clear? If not, are the blurrings deliberate or a mistake? What do you think of this technique overall?

4. **CONNECTIONS** In "But What Do You Mean?" (p. 353), Deborah Tannen outlines differences in the ways women and men communicate. Read that essay, and ANALYZE which of the differences seem to apply to Hopper's woman and man, either as Oates imagines them or as you see them. In an essay, explain how Tannen might view each as typifying his or her gender.

Joyce Carol Oates on Writing

For a 1997 book titled *Introspections: American Poets on One of Their Own Poems*, Joyce Carol Oates did us the valuable service of writing an essay about her poem "Edward Hopper's *Nighthawks*, 1942." She tells us why and how the painting sparked her own work of imagination.

The attempt to give concrete expression to a very amorphous impression is the insurmountable difficulty in painting.

These words of Edward Hopper's apply to all forms of art, of course. Certainly to poetry. How to evoke, in mere words, the powerful, inchoate flood of emotions that constitute "real life"? How to take the reader into the poet's innermost self, where the poet's language becomes the reader's, if only for a quicksilver moment? This is the great challenge of art, which even to fail in requires faith.

Insomniac nights began for me when I was a young teenager. Those long, lonely stretches of time when no one else in the house was awake (so far as I knew); the romance of solitude and self-sufficiency in which time seems not to pass or passes so slowly it will never bring dawn.

Always there was an air of mystery in the insomniac night. What profound thoughts and visions came to me! How strangely detached from the day-self I became! Dawn brought the familiar world, and the familiar self; a "self" that was obliged to accommodate others' expectations, and was, indeed, defined by others, predominantly adults. *Yes but you don't know me*, I would think by day, in adolescent secrecy and defiance. *You don't really know me!*

Many of Edward Hopper's paintings evoke the insomniac's uncanny vision, none more forcefully than *Nighthawks*, which both portrays insomniacs and evokes their solitude in the viewer. In this famous painting, "reality" has undergone some sort of subtle yet drastic alteration. The immense field of detail that would strike the eye has been reduced to smooth, streamlined surfaces; people and objects are enhanced, as on a lighted stage; not life but a nostalgia for life, a memory of life, is the true subject. Men and women in Hopper's paintings are somnambulists, if not mannequins, stiffly posed, with faces of the kind that populate our dreams, at which we dare not look too closely for fear of seeing the faces dissolve.

Here is, not the world, but a memory of it. For all dreams are memory: cobbled-together sights, sounds, impressions, snatches of previous experience. The dream-vision is the perpetual present, yet its contents relate only to the past.

There is little of Eros in Hopper's puritanical vision, *Nighthawks* being the rare exception. The poem enters the painting as a way of animating what cannot be animated; a way of delving into the painting's mystery. *Who are these people, what has brought them together, are they in fact together?* At the time of writing the poem I hadn't read Gail Levin's definitive biography of Hopper, and did not know how Hopper had made himself into the most methodical and premeditated of artists, continuously seeking, with his wife Jo (who would have posed for the redheaded nighthawk), scenes and tableaux to paint. Many of Hopper's canvases are elaborately posed, and their suggestion of movie stills is not accidental. This is a visual art purposefully evoking narrative, or at least the opening strategies of narrative, in which a scene is "set," "characters" are presented, often in ambiguous relationships.

Nighthawks is a work of silence. Here is an Eros of stasis, and of melancholy. It is an uncommonly beautiful painting of stark, separate, sculpted forms, in heightened juxtapositions, brightly lit and yet infinitely mysterious. The poem slips into it with no transition, as we "wake" in a dream, yearning to make the frozen narrative come alive; but finally thwarted by the painting's measured void of a world, in which silence outweighs the human voice, and the barriers between human beings are impenetrable. So the poem ends as it begins, circling upon its lovers' obsessions, achieving no crisis, no confrontation, no epiphany, no release, time forever frozen in the insomniac night.

The Bedford Reader on Writing

Oates's comments on the "great challenge of art" demonstrate just how much insight a writer can gain by applying close examination and ANALYSIS to a visual text. To learn how to take a similar approach of CRITICAL READING with a work of fine art — or any other visual image — read pages 22–26 (closely).

ADDITIONAL WRITING TOPICS

Description

1. Try this in-class writing experiment. Describe another person in the room so clearly and unmistakably that when you read your description aloud, your subject will be recognized. (Be OBJECTIVE. No insulting descriptions, please!)

2. Write a paragraph describing one subject from each of the following categories. It will be up to you to make the general subject refer to a particular person, place, or thing. Write at least one paragraph as an objective description and at least one as a SUBJECTIVE description.

PERSON

A friend or roommate
A rap, pop, or country musician
A parent or grandparent
A child you know
A prominent politician
A historical figure

THING

A city or rural bus
A favorite toy or gadget
A painting or photograph
A foggy day
A season of the year
A musical instrument

PLACE

An office
A classroom
A college campus
A peaceful spot
A waiting room
A lake or pond

3. In a brief essay, describe your ideal place — perhaps an apartment or dorm room, a home office, a restaurant, a gym, a store, a garden, a dance club, a theater. With concrete details, try to make the ideal seem actual.

Narration and Description

4. Use a combination of NARRATION and description to develop any one of the following topics, or a topic they suggest for you:

Your first day on the job or at college
A vacation
Returning to an old neighborhood
Getting lost
An encounter with a wild animal
Delivering bad (or good) news

LOW-ENERGY DRINKS

LeLIEVRE

5

EXAMPLE

Pointing to Instances

◀ **Examples in a cartoon**

This cartoon by Glen Le Lievre, first published in *The New Yorker*, uses the method of example in a complex way. Most simply, the drawings propose instances of the general category stated in the title — imaginary "low-energy drinks." At the same time, the humor of the examples comes from their contrast with real caffeine-laced high-energy drinks such as Red Bull, Monster Energy, Xtreme Shock Fruit Punch, and Zippfizz Liquid Shot. Whom are these drinks marketed to? (Consider visiting a grocery store or a gas station minimart to see some samples up close.) Whom does their marketing ignore? How would you express the general idea of Le Lievre's cartoon?

THE METHOD

"There have been many women runners of distinction," a writer begins, and quickly goes on, "among them Joan Benoit Samuelson, Florence Griffith Joyner, Grete Waitz, Uta Pippig, and Marla Runyan."

You have just seen examples at work. An EXAMPLE (from the Latin *exemplum*: "one thing selected from among many") is an instance that reveals a whole type. By selecting an example, a writer shows the nature or character of the group from which it is taken. In a written essay, examples will often serve to illustrate a general statement, or GENERALIZATION. Here, for instance, the writer Linda Wolfe makes a point about the food fetishes of Roman emperors (Domitian and Claudius ruled in the first century AD).

> The emperors used their gastronomical concerns to indicate their contempt of the country and the whole task of governing it. Domitian humiliated his cabinet by forcing them to attend him at his villa to help solve a serious problem. When they arrived he kept them waiting for hours. The problem, it finally appeared, was that the emperor had just purchased a giant fish, too large for any dish he owned, and he needed the learned brains of his ministers to decide whether the fish should be minced or whether a larger pot should be sought. The emperor Claudius one day rode hurriedly to the Senate and demanded they deliberate the importance of a life without pork. Another time he sat in his tribunal ostensibly administering justice but actually allowing the litigants to argue and orate while he grew dreamy, interrupting the discussions only to announce, "Meat pies are wonderful. We shall have them for dinner."

Wolfe might have allowed the opening sentence of her paragraph — the TOPIC SENTENCE — to remain a vague generalization. Instead, she supports it with three examples, each a brief story of an emperor's contemptuous behavior. With these examples, Wolfe not only explains and supports her generalization but also animates it.

The method of giving examples — of illustrating what you're saying with a "for instance" — is not merely helpful to all kinds of writing; it is essential. Writers who bore us, or lose us completely, often have an ample supply of ideas; their trouble is that they never pull their ideas down from the clouds. A dull writer, for instance, might declare, "The emperors used food to humiliate their governments," and then, instead of giving examples, go on, "They also manipulated their families," or something — adding still another large, unillustrated idea. Specific examples are *needed* elements in effective prose. Not only do they make ideas understandable, but they also keep readers from falling asleep.

Example **161**

THE PROCESS

The Generalization and the Thesis

Examples illustrate a generalization, such as Linda Wolfe's opening statement about the Roman emperors. Any example essay is bound to have such a generalization as its THESIS, expressed in a THESIS STATEMENT. Here are examples from the essays in this chapter:

> That first encounter, and those that followed, signified that a vast, unnerving gulf lay between nighttime pedestrians — particularly women — and me.
> — Brent Staples, "Black Men and Public Space"

> The truth is, I slip in and out of my black consciousness, as if I'm in a racial coma. Sometimes, I'm so deep in my anger, my irritation, my need to stir change, that I can't see anything outside of the lens of race. At other times I feel guilty about my apathy.
> — Issa Rae, "The Struggle"

> I think we love animals as images because we miss them in the flesh, and I think we love them as images because they matter to us spiritually in ways we cannot hope to articulate.
> — Brian Doyle, "A Note on Mascots"

> Sometimes I think we would be better off [in dealing with social problems such as homelessness] if we forgot about the broad strokes and concentrated on the details.
> — Anna Quindlen, "Homeless"

The thesis statement establishes the backbone, the central idea, of an essay developed by example. Then the specifics flesh the idea out for readers, bringing it to life.

The Examples

An essay developed by example will often start with a random observation. That is, you'll see something — a man pilfering a dollar from a child's lemonade stand, a friend copying another friend's homework, a roommate downloading pirated movies — and your observation will suggest a generalization (perhaps a statement about the problem of stealing). But a mere example or two probably won't demonstrate your generalization for readers and thus won't achieve your PURPOSE in writing. For that you'll need a range of instances.

Where do you find more? In anything you know — or care to learn. Start close to home. Seek examples in your own immediate knowledge and experience. Explore your conversations with others, your studies, and the storehouse of information you have gathered from books, newspapers, radio, TV, and the Internet as well as from popular hearsay: proverbs and sayings, popular songs, bits of wisdom you've heard voiced in your family.

Now and again, you may feel an irresistible temptation to make up an example out of thin air. Suppose you have to write about the benefits — any benefits — that rocket science has conferred on society. You might imagine one such benefit: the prospect of one day being able to vacation in outer space and drift about like a soap bubble. That imagined benefit would be all right, but it is obviously a conjecture that you dreamed up. An example from fact or experience is likely to carry more weight. Do a little digging on the Internet or in recent books and magazines. Your reader will feel better informed to be told that science — specifically, the NASA space program — has produced useful inventions. You add:

> Among these are the smoke detector, originally developed as Skylab equipment; the inflatable air bag to protect drivers and pilots, designed to cushion astronauts in splashdowns; a walking chair that enables paraplegics to mount stairs and travel over uneven ground, derived from the moonwalkers' surface buggy; and the technique of cryosurgery, the removal of cancerous tissue by fast freezing.

By using specific examples like these, you render the idea of "benefits to society" more concrete and more definite. Such examples are not mere decoration for your essay; they are necessary if you are to hold your readers' attention and convince them that you are worth listening to.

When giving examples, you'll find other methods useful. Sometimes, as in the paragraph by Linda Wolfe, an example takes the form of a NARRATIVE (Chap. 3): an ANECDOTE or a case history. Sometimes an example embodies a vivid DESCRIPTION of a person, place, or thing (Chap. 4).

Lazy writers think, "Oh well, I can't come up with any example here — I'll just leave it to the reader to find one." The flaw in this ASSUMPTION is that the reader may be as lazy as the writer. As a result, a perfectly good idea may be left suspended in the stratosphere.

FOCUS ON SENTENCE VARIETY

While accumulating and detailing examples during drafting — both essential tasks for a successful essay — you may find yourself writing strings of similar sentences:

Example   **163**

Example

UNVARIED   One example of a movie that deals with chronic illness is *Rockingham Place*. Another example is *The Beating Heart*. Another is *Tree of Life*. These three movies treat misunderstood or little-known diseases in a way that increases the viewer's sympathy and understanding. *Rockingham Place* deals with a little boy who suffers from cystic fibrosis. *The Beating Heart* deals with a mother of four who is weakening from multiple sclerosis. *Tree of Life* deals with brothers who are both struggling with muscular dystrophy. All three movies show complex, struggling human beings caught blamelessly in desperate circumstances.

The writer of this paragraph was clearly pushing to add examples and to expand them, but the resulting passage needs editing so that the writer's labor isn't so obvious. In the more readable and interesting revision, the sentences vary in structure, group similar details, and distinguish the specifics from the generalizations:

VARIED   Three movies dealing with disease are *Rockingham Place*, *The Beating Heart*, and *Tree of Life*. In these movies people with little-known or misunderstood diseases become subjects for the viewer's sympathy and understanding. A little boy suffering from cystic fibrosis, a mother weakening from multiple sclerosis, a pair of brothers coping with muscular dystrophy — these complex, struggling human beings are caught blamelessly in desperate circumstances.

As you review your draft, be alert to repetitive sentence structures and look for opportunities to change them: Try coordinating and subordinating ideas, varying the beginnings and endings of sentences, shortening some and lengthening others (see pp. 49–50).

CHECKLIST FOR REVISING AN EXAMPLE ESSAY

✔ **Generalization.** What general statement do your examples illustrate? Will it be clear to readers what ties the examples together?

✔ **Support.** Do you have enough examples to establish your generalization, or will readers be left needing more?

✔ **Specifics.** Are your examples detailed? Does each one capture some aspect of the generalization?

✔ **Relevance.** Do all your examples relate to your generalization? Should any be cut because they go off track?

✔ **Sentence variety.** Have you varied sentence structures for clarity and interest?

EXAMPLES IN ACADEMIC WRITING

An Economics Textbook

The following paragraph from *Microeconomics*, by Lewis C. Solmon, appears amid the author's explanation of how markets work. To dispel what might seem like clouds of theory, the author here brings an abstract principle down to earth with a concrete and detailed example.

The primary function of the market is to bring together suppliers and demanders so that they can trade with one another. Buyers and sellers do not necessarily have to be in face-to-face contact; they can signal their desires and intentions through various intermediaries. | *Generalization to be illustrated*

For example, the demand for green beans in California is not expressed directly by the green bean consumers to the green bean growers. People who want green beans buy them at a grocery store; the store orders them from a vegetable wholesaler; the wholesaler buys them from a bean cooperative, whose manager tells local farmers of the size of the current demand for green beans. The demanders of green beans are able to signal their demand schedule to the original suppliers, the farmers who raise the beans, without any personal communication between the two parties. | *Single extended example*

A Job-Application Letter

To obtain the kinds of jobs a college education prepares you for, you'll submit a résumé that presents your previous work experience, your education, and your qualifications for a specific career field. To capture the prospective employer's interest, you'll introduce yourself and your résumé with a cover letter.

Rather than merely repeat or summarize the contents of a résumé, a job-application letter highlights the connections between your background and the employer's need for someone with particular training and skills. Typically brief and tightly focused on the job in question, an application letter aims to persuade the reader to look at the accompanying résumé and then to follow up with an interview.

When college junior Kharron Reid was applying for a summer internship implementing computer networks for businesses, he put together a résumé tailored for a specific opportunity posted at his school's placement office. (See the résumé on p. 352.) His cover letter, opposite, pulls out examples from the résumé to support the statement (in the second-to-last paragraph) that "my education and my hands-on experience with network development have prepared me for the opening you have."

Example 165

137 Chester St., Apt. E
Allston, MA 02134
February 21, 2017

Dolores Jackson
Human Resources Director
E-line Systems
75 Arondale Avenue
Boston, MA 02114

Dear Ms. Jackson:

I am applying for the network development internship in your information technology department, advertised in the career services office of Boston University.

Introduction states purpose of letter

I have considerable experience in network development from summer internships at NBS Systems and at Pioneer Networking. At NBS I planned and laid the physical platforms and configured the software for seven WANs on Windows Server 2016. At Pioneer, I laid the physical platforms and configured the software to connect eight workstations into a LAN. Both internships gave me experience in every stage of network development.

Generalization about experience

Two examples of experience

In my three years in Boston University's School of Management, I have concentrated on developing skills in business administration and information systems. I have completed courses in organizational behavior, computer science (including programming), and networking and data communications. At the same time, I have become proficient in Unix, Windows 10/8, Windows Server 2016/2012, and Red Hat Enterprise Linux.

Generalization about education and skills

Two sets of examples about education and skills

As the enclosed résumé indicates, my education and my hands-on experience with network development have prepared me for the opening you have.

Concluding paragraphs summarize qualifications, refer reader to résumé, and invite a response

I am available for an interview at your convenience. Please call me at (617) 555–4009 or e-mail me at kreid@bu.edu.

Sincerely,

Kharron Reid

Kharron Reid

BRENT STAPLES

Brent Staples is a member of the editorial board of the *New York Times*, where he writes on culture, politics, and special education, advocating for children with learning disabilities. Born in 1951 in Chester, Pennsylvania, Staples has a BA in behavioral science from Widener University in Chester and a PhD in psychology from the University of Chicago. Before joining the *New York Times* in 1985, he worked for the *Chicago Sun-Times*, the *Chicago Reader*, *Chicago* magazine, and *Down Beat* magazine. He has also taught psychology and contributed to the *New York Times Magazine*, *New York Woman*, *Ms.*, *Harper's*, and other periodicals.

Black Men and Public Space

"Black Men and Public Space" first appeared in the December 1986 issue of *Harper's* magazine and was then published, in a slightly different version, in Staples's memoir, *Parallel Time: Growing Up in Black and White* (1994). To explain a recurring experience of African American men, Staples relates incidents when he has been "an avid night walker" in the urban landscape. Sometimes his only defense against others' stereotypes is to whistle.

In the essay following this one, "The Struggle," Issa Rae offers a contemporary woman's counterpoint to Staples's perspective.

My first victim was a woman — white, well dressed, probably in her late   1
twenties. I came upon her late one evening on a deserted street in Hyde Park, a relatively affluent neighborhood in an otherwise mean, impoverished section of Chicago. As I swung onto the avenue behind her, there seemed to be a discreet, uninflammatory distance between us. Not so. She cast back a worried glance. To her, the youngish black man — a broad six feet two inches with a beard and billowing hair, both hands shoved into the pockets of a bulky military jacket — seemed menacingly close. After a few more quick glimpses, she picked up her pace and was soon running in earnest. Within seconds she disappeared into a cross street.

That was more than a decade ago. I was twenty-two years old, a graduate   2
student newly arrived at the University of Chicago. It was in the echo of that terrified woman's footfalls that I first began to know the unwieldy inheritance I'd come into — the ability to alter public space in ugly ways. It was clear that she thought herself the quarry of a mugger, a rapist, or worse. Suffering a bout

of insomnia, however, I was stalking sleep, not defenseless wayfarers. As a softy who is scarcely able to take a knife to a raw chicken — let alone hold one to a person's throat — I was surprised, embarrassed, and dismayed all at once. Her flight made me feel like an accomplice in tyranny. It also made it clear that I was indistinguishable from the muggers who occasionally seeped into the area from the surrounding ghetto. That first encounter, and those that followed, signified that a vast, unnerving gulf lay between nighttime pedestrians — particularly women — and me. And I soon gathered that being perceived as dangerous is a hazard in itself. I only needed to turn a corner into a dicey situation, or crowd some frightened, armed person in a foyer somewhere, or make an errant move after being pulled over by a policeman. Where fear and weapons meet — and they often do in urban America — there is always the possibility of death.

In that first year, my first away from my hometown, I was to become thoroughly familiar with the language of fear. At dark, shadowy intersections, I could cross in front of a car stopped at a traffic light and elicit the *thunk, thunk, thunk, thunk* of the driver — black, white, male, or female — hammering down the door locks. On less traveled streets after dark, I grew accustomed to but never comfortable with people crossing to the other side of the street rather than pass me. Then there were the standard unpleasantries with policemen, doormen, bouncers, cabdrivers, and others whose business it is to screen out troublesome individuals *before* there is any nastiness.

I moved to New York nearly two years ago and I have remained an avid night walker. In central Manhattan, the near-constant crowd cover minimizes tense one-on-one street encounters. Elsewhere — in SoHo, for example, where sidewalks are narrow and tightly spaced buildings shut out the sky — things can get very taut indeed.

After dark, on the warrenlike streets of Brooklyn where I live, I often see women who fear the worst from me. They seem to have set their faces on neutral, and with their purse straps strung across their chests bandolier-style, they forge ahead as though bracing themselves against being tackled. I understand, of course, that the danger they perceive is not a hallucination. Women are particularly vulnerable to street violence, and young black males are drastically overrepresented among the perpetrators of that violence. Yet these truths are no solace against the kind of alienation that comes of being ever the suspect, a fearsome entity with whom pedestrians avoid making eye contact.

It is not altogether clear to me how I reached the ripe old age of twenty-two without being conscious of the lethality nighttime pedestrians attributed to me. Perhaps it was because in Chester, Pennsylvania, the small, angry industrial town where I came of age in the 1960s, I was scarcely noticeable against a backdrop of gang warfare, street knifings, and murders. I grew up one of the good boys, had perhaps a half-dozen fistfights. In retrospect, my shyness of combat has clear sources.

As a boy, I saw countless tough guys locked away; I have since buried several, too. They were babies, really — a teenage cousin, a brother of twenty-two, a childhood friend in his mid-twenties — all gone down in episodes of bravado played out in the streets. I came to doubt the virtues of intimidation early on. I chose, perhaps unconsciously, to remain a shadow — timid, but a survivor. 7

The fearsomeness mistakenly attributed to me in public places often has a perilous flavor. The most frightening of these confusions occurred in the late 1970s and early 1980s, when I worked as a journalist in Chicago. One day, rushing into the office of a magazine I was writing for with a deadline story in hand, I was mistaken for a burglar. The office manager called security and, with an ad hoc posse, pursued me through the labyrinthine halls, nearly to my editor's door. I had no way of proving who I was. I could only move briskly toward the company of someone who knew me. 8

Another time I was on assignment for a local paper and killing time before an interview. I entered a jewelry store on the city's affluent Near North Side. The proprietor excused herself and returned with an enormous red Doberman pinscher straining at the end of a leash. She stood, the dog extended toward me, silent to my questions, her eyes bulging nearly out of her head. I took a cursory look around, nodded, and bade her good night. 9

Relatively speaking, however, I never fared as badly as another black male journalist. He went to nearby Waukegan, Illinois, a couple of summers ago to work on a story about a murderer who was born there. Mistaking the reporter for the killer, police officers hauled him from his car at gunpoint and but for his press credentials would probably have tried to book him. Such episodes are not uncommon. Black men trade tales like this all the time. 10

Over the years, I learned to smother the rage I felt at so often being taken for a criminal. Not to do so would surely have led to madness. I now take precautions to make myself less threatening. I move about with care, particularly late in the evening. I give a wide berth to nervous people on subway platforms during the wee hours, particularly when I have exchanged business clothes for jeans. If I happen to be entering a building behind some people who appear skittish, I may walk by, letting them clear the lobby before I return, so as not to seem to be following them. I have been calm and extremely congenial on those rare occasions when I've been pulled over by the police. 11

And on late-evening constitutionals I employ what has proved to be an excellent tension-reducing measure: I whistle melodies from Beethoven and 12

Vivaldi and the more popular classical composers. Even steely New Yorkers hunching toward nighttime destinations seem to relax, and occasionally they even join in the tune. Virtually everybody seems to sense that a mugger wouldn't be warbling bright, sunny selections from Vivaldi's *Four Seasons*. It is my equivalent of the cowbell that hikers wear when they know they are in bear country.

Journal Writing

Staples explains how he perceives himself altering public space. Write in your journal about a time when you felt as if *you* altered public space — in other words, you changed people's attitudes or behavior just by being in a place or entering a situation. If you haven't had this experience, write about a time when you saw someone else alter public space in this way.

Questions on Meaning

1. What is the PURPOSE of this essay? Do you think Staples believes that he (or other African American men) will cease "to alter public space in ugly ways" (par. 2) in the near future? Does he suggest any long-term solution for "the kind of alienation that comes of being ever the suspect" (5)?

2. In paragraph 5 Staples says he understands that the danger women fear when they see him "is not a hallucination." Do you take this to mean that Staples perceives himself to be dangerous? Explain.

3. Staples says, "I chose, perhaps unconsciously, to remain a shadow — timid, but a survivor" (par. 7). What are the usual CONNOTATIONS of the word *survivor*? Is "timid" one of them? How can you explain this apparent discrepancy?

Questions on Writing Strategy

1. The concept of altering public space is relatively abstract. How does Staples convince you that this phenomenon really takes place?

2. Staples employs a large number of examples in a fairly short essay. How does he avoid having the piece sound like a list? How does he establish COHERENCE among all these examples? (Look, for example, at details and TRANSITIONS.)

3. **OTHER METHODS** Many of Staples's examples are actually ANECDOTES — brief NARRATIVES. The opening paragraph is especially notable. Why is it so effective?

Questions on Language

1. What does the author accomplish by using the word *victim* in the essay's opening line? Is the word used literally? What TONE does it set for the essay?

2. Be sure you know how to define the following words, as used in this essay: affluent, uninflammatory (par. 1); unwieldy, tyranny, pedestrians (2); intimidation (7); congenial (11); constitutionals (12).

3. The word *dicey* (par. 2) comes from British slang. Without looking it up in your dictionary, can you figure out its meaning from the context in which it appears?

Suggestions for Writing

1. **FROM JOURNAL TO ESSAY**　Write an essay narrating your experience of either altering public space yourself or being a witness when someone else did so. What changes did you observe in people's behavior? Was your behavior similarly affected? In retrospect, do you think your reactions were justified?

2. Write an essay using examples to show how a trait of your own or of someone you know well always seems to affect people, whether positively or negatively.

3. The ironic term "driving while black" expresses the common perception that African American drivers are more likely than white drivers to be pulled over by police for minor infractions — or no infraction at all. Research and write an essay about the accuracy of this perception in one state or municipality: Is there truth to it? If African Americans have been discriminated against, what, if anything, has been done to address the problem?

4. **CRITICAL WRITING**　Consider, more broadly than Staples does, what it means to alter public space. Staples would rather not have the power to do so, but it *is* a power, and it could perhaps be positive in some circumstances (wielded by a street performer, for instance, or the architect of a beautiful new building on campus). Write an essay that expands on Staples's idea and examines the pros and cons of altering public space. Use specific examples as your EVIDENCE.

5. **CONNECTIONS**　Like Brent Staples, Issa Rae, in "The Struggle" (p. 173), considers misplaced expectations of African Americans. In an essay, examine the POINTS OF VIEW of these two authors. How does point of view affect each author's selection of details and tone?

Brent Staples on Writing

In comments written especially for this book, Brent Staples talks about the writing of "Black Men and Public Space": "I was only partly aware of how I felt when I began this essay. I knew only that I had this collection of experiences (facts) and that I felt uneasy with them. I sketched out the experiences one by one and strung them together. The bridge to the essay — what I wanted to say, but did not know when I started — sprang into life quite unexpectedly as I sat looking over these experiences. The crucial sentence comes right after the opening anecdote, in which my first 'victim' runs away from me: 'It was in the echo of that terrified woman's footfalls that I first began to know the unwieldy inheritance I'd come into — the ability to alter public space in ugly ways.' 'Aha!' I said. 'This is why I feel bothered and hurt and frustrated when this happens. I don't want people to think I'm stalking them. I want some fresh air. I want to stretch my legs. I want to be as anonymous as any other person out for a walk in the night.'"

A news reporter and editor by training and trade, Staples sees much similarity between the writing of a personal essay like "Black Men and Public Space" and the writing of, say, a murder story for a daily newspaper. "The newspaper murder," he says, "begins with standard newspaper information: the fact that the man was found dead in an alley in such-and-such a section of the city; his name, occupation, and where he lived; that he died of gunshot wounds to such-and-such a part of his body; that arrests were or were not made; that such-and-such a weapon was found at the scene; that the police have established no motive; etc.

"Personal essays take a different tack, but they, too, begin as assemblies of facts. In 'Black Men and Public Space,' I start out with an anecdote that crystallizes the issue I want to discuss — what it is like to be viewed as a criminal all the time. I devise a sentence that serves this purpose and also catches the reader's attention: 'My first victim was a woman — white, well dressed, probably in her late twenties.' The piece gives examples that are meant to illustrate the same point and discusses what those examples mean.

"The newspaper story stacks its details in a specified way, with each piece taking a prescribed place in a prescribed order. The personal essay begins often with a flourish, an anecdote, or the recounting of a crucial experience, then goes off to consider related experiences and their meanings. But both pieces rely on reporting. Both are built of facts. Reporting is the act of finding and analyzing facts.

"A fact can be a state of the world — a date, the color of someone's eyes, the arc of a body that flies through the air after having been struck by a car. A fact can also be a feeling — sorrow, grief, confusion, the sense of being pleased, offended, or frustrated. 'Black Men and Public Space' explores the relationship between two sets of facts: (1) the way people cast worried glances at me and sometimes run away from me on the streets after dark, and (2) the frustration and anger I feel at being made an object of fear as I try to go about my business in the city."

Personal essays and news stories share one other quality as well, Staples thinks: They affect the writer even when the writing is finished. "The discoveries I made in 'Black Men and Public Space' continued long after the essay was published. Writing about the experiences gave me access to a whole range of internal concerns and ideas, much the way a well-reported news story opens the door onto a given neighborhood, situation, or set of issues."

The Bedford Reader on Writing

Staples provides an enlightening illustration of how writing generates ideas, rather than merely recording them. As often happens, he discovered his THESIS by writing about his subject, that is, by working out his examples and finding the connecting threads in the process. And as Staples observes, although personal essays and newspaper stories are different GENRES, both types of writing rely on gathering EVIDENCE first, before starting to draft. For tips on "finding and analyzing facts" for your own writing, see "Developing Ideas" in Chapter 2, pages 36–37.

ISSA RAE

Jo-Issa Rae Diop was born in 1985 and raised in Potomac, Maryland, and Los Angeles, California, with extended stays with family in Senegal (a country in West Africa). Frustrated by the lack of positive roles for black women in television and film, she started producing and acting in her own online programming while a student at Stanford University, adopted the screen name Issa Rae in 2008, and created the award-winning Web series *The Misadventures of Awkward Black Girl* shortly out of college with funding from a Kickstarter campaign. The popular comedy follows a self-deprecating introvert, "J," as she navigates the pitfalls of social interaction; it has captured more than twenty million views and the attention of traditional media outlets including *Elle*, *Forbes*, *Essence*, MSNBC, and HBO. Rae's first book of memoir and essays, also titled *The Misadventures of Awkward Black Girl*, was published in 2015. She lives in Los Angeles.

The Struggle

In this selection from her book, Rae tackles the fraught subject of race with characteristically acerbic wit. While Brent Staples in the previous essay expresses embarrassment at strangers' reactions to his skin color, Rae has a different problem with stereotypes: Her peers don't think she's "black enough."

I don't remember the exact day I demilitarized from my blackness. It's all 1 a blur and since I'm fairly certain that militants never forget, and I forget stuff *all* the time, I guess I wasn't meant to be one.

I love being black; that's not a problem. The problem is that I don't 2 want to always *talk* about it because honestly, talking about being "black" is extremely tiring. I don't know how Al Sharpton and Jesse Jackson do it. I know why Cornel West and Tavis Smiley do it.[1] They *love* the attention and the groupies. But the rest of these people who talk, think, and breathe race every single day — how? Just how? Aren't they exhausted?

The pressure to contribute to these conversations now that we have a 3 black president is even more infuriating.

"What do you think about what's going on in the world? And how our 4 black president is handling it?" asks a race baiter.

"It's all good, I guess," I want to answer, apathetically, with a Kanye shrug. 5 "I'm over it." But am I really? Could I be even if I wanted to?

[1] The Reverend Jesse Jackson (1941–) and Baptist minister Al Sharpton (1954–) are prominent civil rights activists; Dr. Cornel West (1953–) is a public intellectual and college professor; Tavis Smiley (1964–) is a talk show host. — Eds.

Even now, I feel obligated to write about race. It's as though it's expected   6
of me to acknowledge what we all already know. The truth is, I slip in and out
of my black consciousness, as if I'm in a racial coma. Sometimes, I'm so deep
in my anger, my irritation, my need to stir change, that I can't see anything
outside of the lens of race.

At other times I feel guilty about my apathy. But then I think, *isn't this*   7
what those who came before me fought for? The right *not* to have to deal with
race? If faced with a choice between fighting until the death for freedom and
civil rights and living life without any acknowledgment of race, they'd choose
the latter.

Growing up as a young black girl in Potomac, Maryland, was easy. I never   8
really had to put much thought into my race, and neither did anybody else.
I had a Rainbow Coalition of friends of all ethnicities, and we would carelessly skip around our elementary school like the powerless version of Captain
Planet's Planeteers. I knew I was black. I knew there was a history that accompanied my skin color and my parents taught me to be proud of it. End of story.

All that changed when my family moved to Los Angeles and placed me   9
in a middle school where my blackness was constantly questioned — and
not even necessarily in the traditional sense, i.e., "You talk white, Oreo girl"
or "You can't dance, white girl." Those claims were arguable, for the most
part. My biggest frustration in the challenge to prove my "blackness" usually
stemmed from two very annoying, very repetitive situations.

SITUATION #1: "I'm not even black, and I'm blacker than you." It's one   10
thing when other African Americans try to call me out on my race card, but
when people outside my ethnicity have the audacity to question how "down" I
am because of the bleak, stereotypical picture pop culture has painted of black
women, it's a whole other thing. Unacceptable. I can recall a time when I was
having a heated discussion with a white, male classmate of mine. Our eighth-
grade class was on a museum field trip as the bus driver blasted Puff Daddy's
"Been around the World" to drown us out.

It began as a passive competition of lyrics, as we each silently listened for   11
who would mess up first. By the second verse, our lazy rap-whispers escalated
to an aggressive volume, accompanied by rigorous side-eyes by the time we
got to, "Playa please, I'm the macaroni with the cheese," and I felt threatened.
Was this fool seriously trying to outrap me? And why did I care? After the
song ended, he offered his opinion: "Puff Daddy is wack, yo." How dare he?
Not only was I angry, but I felt as if he had insulted my own father (who did I
think I was? Puff Daughter?).

"Puff Daddy is tight," I retorted. He rolled his eyes and said, "Have you   12
heard of [insert Underground rapper]? Now, *he's* dope." I hadn't heard of him,
but I couldn't let this white boy defeat me in rap music knowledge, especially

as others started to listen. "Yeah, I know him. He's not dope," I lied, for the sake of saving face. Perhaps because he saw through me or because he actually felt strongly about this particular artist, he asked me to name which songs I thought were "not dope." Panic set in as I found myself exposed, then — "You don't even know him, huh? Have you even heard of [insert Random Underground rapper]?"

As he continued to rattle off the names of make-believe-sounding MCs,   13
delighted that he had one-upped me, he managed to make me feel as though my credibility as a black person relied on my knowledge of hip-hop culture. My identity had been reduced to the Bad Boy label clique as this boy seemingly claimed my black card as his own.

Of course, as I grew older and Ma$e found his calling as a reverend, I real-   14
ized there was more to being black than a knowledge of rap music, and that I didn't have to live up to this pop cultural archetype. I began to take pride in the fact that I couldn't be reduced to a stereotype and that I didn't have to be. This leads me to my next situation.

SITUATION #2: "Black people don't do that." Or so I'm told by a black   15
person. These, too, are derived from (mostly negative) stereotypes shaped by popular culture. The difference is that in these situations, we black people are the ones buying into these stereotypes.

When I was a teenager, for example, others questioned my blackness   16
because some of the life choices I made weren't considered to be "black" choices: joining the swim team when it is a known fact that "black people don't swim," or choosing to become a vegetarian when blacks clearly love chicken. These choices and the various positive and negative responses to them helped to broaden my own perspective on blackness and, eventually, caused me to spurn these self-imposed limitations. But not before embarrassing the hell out of myself in a poor attempt to prove I was "down." I'll never forget submitting a school project in "Ebonics" for my seventh-grade English class, just to prove that I could talk *and* write "black." I was trying to prove it to myself just as much as I was to everyone around me.

Even in my early adulthood, post-college, I'd overtip to demonstrate I was   17
one of the good ones. Only recently have I come to ask, *What am I trying to prove and to whom am I proving it?* Today, I haven't completely rid myself of the feeling that I'm still working through Du Bois's double consciousness.[2]

For the majority of my life I cared too much about how my blackness   18
was perceived, but *now?* At this very moment? I couldn't care less. Call it

---

[2] In *The Souls of Black Folk* (1903), the sociologist and historian W. E. B. Du Bois famously proposed that African Americans struggle to reconcile the conflict of belonging simultaneously to two cultures in opposition to each other, a mental state he called *double consciousness*. — EDS.

maturation or denial or self-hatred — I give no f%^&s. And it feels great. I've decided to focus only on the positivity of being black, and especially of being a black woman. Am I supposed to feel oppressed? Because I don't. Is racism supposed to hurt me? That's so 1950s. Should I feel marginalized? I prefer to think of myself as belonging to an "exclusive" club.

While experiencing both types of situations — being made to feel not   19
black enough by "down" white people on one hand and not black enough by the blacks in the so-called know on the other — has played a role in shaping a more comfortably black me, in the end, I have to ask: Who is to say what we do and don't do? What we can and can't do? The very definition of "black-ness" is as broad as that of "whiteness," yet the media seemingly always tries to find a specific, limited definition. As CNN produces news specials about us, and white and Latino rappers feel culturally dignified in using the N-word, our collective grasp of "blackness" is becoming more and elusive. And that may not be a bad thing.

Journal Writing

Rae shares examples of times when her perception of her "blackness" did not match the expectations of those around her. Think of a defining characteristic you hold for yourself — your race, perhaps, or your gender, your sexual orientation, your nation-ality, your sports affiliations, your career aspirations, and so forth. Has your sense of who and what you are ever been challenged by others? How, and why? List some such instances in your journal.

Questions on Meaning

1. Rae opens her essay by saying she is tired of discussing race. What, then, would you say was her PURPOSE in writing? Does she have a THESIS?

2. To whom does Rae feel she needs to prove her "blackness"? How do you know?

3. How does Rae characterize society's expectations for black people, especially black women? What does she blame as the source of these stereotypes?

Questions on Writing Strategy

1. "The Struggle" contains one extended example and several brief examples. How does Rae organize them? What is the effect of grouping these "situations" as she does?

2. What ASSUMPTIONS about her readers are evident in Rae's choice of ALLUSIONS, particularly in paragraphs 10–14? Do you need to be familiar with the musicians she mentions to understand her point?

3. **OTHER METHODS**   Rae's essay is in some ways an attempt at DEFINITION. What do her examples of being "not black enough" (par. 19) contribute to that attempt?

Questions on Language

1. Consider Rae's DICTION, especially her use of slang and references to racial slurs such as "Oreo" (par. 9) and "N-word" (19). What is the EFFECT of such language? Where in the essay, if at all, does Rae explain her decision to use it?

2. The words "black" and "blackness" often appear in quotation marks in this essay. Why? What does Rae intend by employing this device?

3. Be sure you know how to define the following words: demilitarized (par. 1); apathetically (5); coalition (8); rigorous (11); archetype (14); Ebonics (16); maturation (18).

Suggestions for Writing

1. **FROM JOURNAL TO ESSAY**   Building on the episodes you recorded in your journal, write about a time or times when others made you think deeply about who you are and how you present yourself to the world. Use Rae's work as a model: Incorporate concrete examples into your essay and try to address the larger social implications of your reflection.

2. Consider an incident from your childhood that has stuck with you. You might choose an embarrassing or frustrating moment, as Rae did in writing about her school-bus rap battle, or a proud or defining event, such as a sports victory or a sudden understanding of a truth. Write a personal reflection, that, like Rae's essay, explains how your understanding of the incident has changed now that you are older.

3. **CRITICAL WRITING**   In an essay, examine Rae's TONE. Is it consistent throughout? Are there passages where she seems self-pitying? mocking? determined? resigned? triumphant? What is the overall tone of the essay? Is it effective? Why?

4. **CONNECTIONS**   COMPARE AND CONTRAST Issa Rae's and Brent Staples's (p. 166) perceptions of "blackness" and of the stereotypes that have been assigned to them. Use specific passages from each essay to support your comparison.

BRIAN DOYLE

Widely admired for his breathless reflections on spirituality, human connection, and the natural world, Brian Doyle defies boundaries of genre and style. Born in 1956 in New York City, he graduated from the University of Notre Dame in 1978, worked for *US Catholic Magazine* and *Boston College Magazine*, and is now the editor of *Portland*, an award-winning quarterly publication for the University of Portland. A frequent contributor to that magazine and to many others, including *The Atlantic Monthly, Orion, The Sun,* and *Harper's,* Doyle has published two nonfiction books on family and faith, four novels, and multiple collections of short fiction, poetry, and essays, among them *Leaping: Revelations and Epiphanies* (2003), *Grace Notes* (2011), and *So Very Much the Best of Us: Songs of Praise in Prose* (2015) — all consistently lauded for their high quality and Doyle's unique voice. He describes himself as a "shambling shuffling mumbling grumbling muttering muddled maundering meandering male being" with a "deep and abiding love" for his wife, his three children, and basketball.

A Note on Mascots

Whatever he writes, Doyle has a reputation for crafting prose that is unusually poetic; in fact, he calls many of his own works "proems." In this piece from *Children and Other Wild Animals* (2014), he uses examples to ponder the meaning of animals — some of them imaginary or simply odd — standing in as representatives of college sports teams.

The first sports team I remember loving as a child, in the dim dewy days 1 when I was two or three years old and just waking up to things that were not milk and mama and dirt and dogs, was the Fighting Irish of the University of Notre Dame, who were on television every day, it seemed, in our bustling brick Irish Catholic house; and then, inasmuch as I was hatched and coddled near Manhattan, there were Metropolitans and Knickerbockers and Rangers and Islanders; and then, as I shuffled shyly into high school, there were, for the first time, snarling and roaring mammalian mascots, notably the Cougars of my own alma mater, which was plopped in marshlands where I doubt a cougar had been seen for three hundred years; but right about then I started paying attention to how we fetishize animals as symbols for our athletic adventures, and I have become only more attentive since, for I have spent nearly thirty years now working for colleges and universities, and you could earn a degree in zoology just by reading the college sports news, where roar and fly and sprint and lope and canter and gallop and prowl animals from anteater to wasp — among them, interestingly, armadillos, bees, boll weevils, herons, owls, koalas, turtles, moose, penguins, gulls, sea lions, and squirrels, none of which seem especially intimidating or prepossessing, although I know a man in North Carolina who once lost a fistfight with a heron, and certainly many of us have run away from angry bees and moose, and surely there are some among us who could relate stories of furious boll weevils, but perhaps this is not the time, although anyone who *has* a story like that should see me right after class.

There are vast numbers of canids (coyotes, foxes, huskies, salukis, 2 wolves), felids (lions, tigers, panthers, lynx, bobcats), ruminants (bulls, chargers, broncs, broncos, and bronchoes, though no bronchials), mustelids (badgers, wolverine, otters), and denizens of the deep (dolphins, gators, sharks, sailfish, and "seawolves," or orca). There are two colleges which have an aggrieved camel as their mascot. There are schools represented by snakes and tomcats. There is a school whose symbol is a frog and one whose mascot is a large clam and one whose mascot famously is a slug. There is a school whose mascot is the black fly. There are the Fighting Turtles of the College of Insurance in New York. There are schools represented by lemmings and scorpions and spiders. There are the Fighting Stormy Petrels of Oglethorpe University in Georgia. There is a school represented by an animal that has never yet been seen in the Americas, the bearcat of Asia, although perhaps that is meant to be a wolverine, which did once inhabit southern Ohio, and may still live in Cincinnati, which has tough neighborhoods. The most popular mascot appears to be the eagle, especially if you count the fifteen schools represented by golden eagles, which brings us to a round total of eighty-two schools symbolized by a bird Benjamin Franklin considered "a bird of bad moral character, too lazy to fish for himself . . . like those among men who live by sharping & robbing he is generally poor and often very lousy. Besides he is a rank coward . . ." But the two schools that Franklin helped establish are nicknamed the Quakers and the Diplomats, so we can safely ignore Ben on this matter.

And this is not even to delve into the mysterious world of fantastical 3 fauna — blue bears and blue tigers, crimson hawks, trolls, dragons and firebirds, griffins and griffons and gryphons, delta devils and jersey devils (there are a *lot* of devils, which says something interesting), jayhawks and kohawks and duhawks, green eagles and phoenixes, thunderhawks and thunderwolves, the mind reels, and then there is the whole subset of nicknamery that has to do with botany, as evidenced most memorably by the Fighting Violets of New York University, on which image we had better pull this whole essay to the side of the road and sit silently for a moment.

Beyond all the obvious reasons we choose animals as symbols for our 4 sporting teams — their incredible energy and muscle, grace and strength, intelligence and verve, our ancient conviction of their power and magic, ancient associations as clan signs and tribal totems, even more ancient shivers perhaps of fear at animals who hunted and ate us, not to mention the way their images look cool on letterhead and sweatshirts and pennants and fund-raising appeals — there is something else, something so deep and revelatory about human beings that I think we do not admit it because it is too sad. I think we love animals as images because we miss them in the flesh, and I think we love them as images because they matter to us spiritually in ways we cannot hope to articulate. The vast majority of us will never see a cougar or a wolverine, not to mention a boll weevil, but even wearing one on a shirt, or shouting the miracle of its name in a stadium, or grinning to see its rippling beauty on the window of a car, gives us a tiny subtle crucial electric jolt in the heart, connects us somehow to what we used to be with animals, which was thrilled and terrified. We've lost the salt of that feeling forever, but even a hint of it matters immensely to us as animals too. Maybe that's what we miss the most — the feeling that they are our cousins, and not clans of creatures who once filled the earth and now are shreds of memory, mere symbols, beings who used to be.

Journal Writing

Doyle provides quite a few examples of the many school mascots he has encountered over the years, as well as a reflection on why, generally, we select animals to represent our sports teams. Choose your favorite of the mascots he names and in your journal brainstorm possible explanations for why that particular mascot might be a good choice for a college or university.

Questions on Meaning

1. What do you take to be Doyle's PURPOSE with "A Note on Mascots"? Is it meant to be a straightforward essay, do you think, or more like a poem? Why do you think so?

2. Why does Doyle cite Benjamin Franklin's thoughts on eagles (par. 2)? What might have been the impact if he had chosen to quote, say, a naturalist or sports enthusiast instead?

3. Doyle observes of mascots that "there are a *lot* of devils, which says something interesting" (par. 3). What does he mean? What exactly does it say?

4. How does Doyle explain the appeal of animal mascots? What is his THESIS? Why does he wait until the final paragraph to state it?

Questions on Writing Strategy

1. Examine Doyle's sentences. How varied are they? Taken as a whole, what is the EFFECT of their structures and length?

2. Doyle concludes the first paragraph by dropping the reader into a classroom setting that should be familiar to you. Why? Where else in the essay does he employ a similar strategy? What do these lines reveal about his imagined AUDIENCE?

3. **OTHER METHODS**   Explain how Doyle uses CLASSIFICATION to organize his examples. What does the method contribute to his purpose?

Questions on Language

1. Be sure you know how to define the following words: zoology, boll weevils, prepossessing (par. 1); canids, ruminants, mustelids, denizens (2); fauna, botany (3); verve, totems (4).

2. Doyle's style in this piece is unusual in that he mixes scientific language with the first person (*I* and *we*). Does this POINT OF VIEW seem appropriate, given the author's subject and purpose? Why, or why not? How does it affect his TONE?

3. Doyle identifies several "Fighting" mascots. List them for yourself. What makes these names funny?

4. In his comments on writing (next page), Doyle stresses the importance of using "energized" verbs. Point to any particularly strong verbs you find in "A Note on Mascots." What makes them effective?

Suggestions for Writing

1. **FROM JOURNAL TO ESSAY**   Expand your journal entry into an ARGUMENT proposing that your school should adopt a new mascot. Remember to select several convincing examples to support your choice.

2. Besides sports, where else do you often see animals represented for some purpose beyond their literal existence? Consider Halloween costumes, toys, and television shows, for instance. Do the representations you have observed seem to be fulfilling a longing, such as the one Doyle describes in "A Note on Mascots"? If so, how? If not, what purpose do they seem to serve? Write a reflective essay that contemplates these questions.

3. **CRITICAL WRITING**   Select one of the plants or animals that Doyle highlights and research its current population and habitat. Is Doyle correct that the mascot you chose is something rare that most people will not casually encounter? Have any conservation efforts been made on behalf of the mascot you selected (plants, as well as animals, can be endangered)? How might being a mascot help preserve awareness of the plant or animal you selected? If you chose a mascot that is common or not threatened, make a case for its continuing value as a SYMBOL.

4. **CONNECTIONS**   As a fan, Doyle expresses a certain amount of reverence for sports and their icons. In "Jock Culture" (p. 324), on the other hand, sportswriter

Robert Lipsyte argues that athleticism in general fuels unhealthy competition in the working environment. In an essay, consider how Doyle's admiration of sports mascots supports or contradicts Lipsyte's analysis of the implications of Jock Culture for individuals and society.

Brian Doyle on Writing

In a weekly blog for *The American Scholar*, the magazine of the Phi Beta Kappa honor society, Doyle writes about "stories that nourish and sustain us, and the small miracles of everyday life." In August of 2013 he used the space to reflect on how, and why, he became a writer by trade.

"How did you become a writer?" is a question asked of me surprisingly often when I visit schools, which I much enjoy not only as part of my overarching subtle devious plan to get on the good side of the children who will soon run the world, but also for the consistent entertainment of their artlessly honest questions (the best ever: *Is that your real nose?*), and for the sometimes deeply piercing depth of our conversations; we have suddenly spoken of death and miracles and loss and love, while we were supposed to be talking about writing and literature; and I have wept in front of them, and they have wept in front of me; which seems to me a sweet gift, to be trusted that much.

But in almost every class I am asked how I became a writer, and after I make my usual joke about it being a benign neurosis, as my late friend George Higgins[1] once told me, I usually talk about my dad. My dad was a newspaperman, and still is, at age 92, a man of great grace and patience and dignity, and he taught me immensely valuable lessons. If you wish to be a writer, *write*, he would say. There are people who talk about writing and then there are people who sit down and type. Writing is fast typing. Also you must read like you are starving for ink. Read widely. Read everything. . . . Note how people get their voices and hearts and stories down on the page. Also get a job; eating is a good habit and you will never make enough of a living as a writer to support a family. Be honest with yourself about the size of your gift. Expect no money but be diligent about sending pieces out for publication. All money is gravy. A piece is not finished until it is off your desk and onto an editor's desk. Write hard and then edit yourself hard. Look carefully at your verbs to see if they can be energized.

---

[1] George V. Higgins (1939–99) was an American newspaper columnist, lawyer, and college professor who wrote several best-selling crime novels. — Eds.

The best writers do not write about themselves but about everyone else. The best writers are great listeners. Learn to ask a question and then shut your mouth and listen. Use silence as a journalistic tool; people are uncomfortable with it and will leap to fill the holes, often telling you more than they wanted to. . . . Everyone has sweet sad brave wonderful stories; give them a chance to tell their stories. So many people do not get the chance. Listening is the greatest literary art. Your ears are your best tools. No one is dull or boring. Anyone who thinks so is an idiot.

Many fine writers do not get credit for the quality of their prose because they were famous for something else: Lincoln, for example. The best writing is witness. The lowest form of writing is mere catharsis.[2] Persuasive writing generally isn't. The finest writers in newspapers are often sports and police reporters. When in doubt about a line or a passage, cut it. All writing can be improved by a judicious editor. . . .

Do not let writing be a special event; let it be a normal part of your day. It *is* normal. We are all storytellers and story-attentive beings. Otherwise we would never be loved or have a country or a religion. You do not need a sabbatical or a grant to write a book. Write a little bit every day. You will be surprised how deep the muck gets at the end of the year, but at that point you can cut out the dull parts, elevate your verbs, delete mere catharsis, celebrate witness, find the right title, and send it off to be published. Any questions?

The Bedford Reader on Writing

As we stress throughout this book, but especially on pages 26–28, Doyle encourages aspiring writers to read and read often, and to keep a JOURNAL, writing "a little bit every day." Notice, too, the importance he places on EDITING, especially for strong verbs and unnecessary phrases; for our advice on these subjects see "Focus on Verbs," page 69, and "Focus on Clarity and Conciseness," p. 394.

---

[2] Doyle uses the word *catharsis* in its meaning of a cleansing purge, or the release of emotion. — EDS.

ANNA QUINDLEN

Anna Quindlen was born in 1953 and graduated from Barnard College in 1974. She worked as a reporter for the *New York Post* and the *New York Times* before taking over the latter's "About New York" column, eventually serving as the paper's deputy metropolitan editor and creating her own weekly column. Quindlen later wrote a twice-weekly op-ed column for the *Times* on social and political issues, earning a Pulitzer Prize for commentary in 1992. She also wrote a biweekly column for *Newsweek* magazine. Quindlen's essays and columns are collected in *Living Out Loud* (1988), *Thinking Out Loud* (1993), and *Loud and Clear* (2004). Her memoir, *Lots of Candles, Plenty of Cake*, appeared in 2012. Quindlen has also published two books for children, three books of non-fiction with a how-to bent, and seven successful novels, most recently *Still Life with Bread Crumbs* (2014). She lives in New York City.

Homeless

In this essay from *Living Out Loud*, Quindlen mingles a reporter's respect for details with a keen sense of empathy, using examples to explore a persistent social issue. When Quindlen wrote, in 1987, homelessness had become a severe and highly visible problem in New York City and elsewhere in the United States. The problem has not abated since then: Using government data, the National Alliance to End Homelessness estimates that more than half a million Americans are homeless on any given day.

Her name was Ann, and we met in the Port Authority Bus Terminal 1 several Januarys ago. I was doing a story on homeless people. She said I was wasting my time talking to her; she was just passing through, although she'd been passing through for more than two weeks. To prove to me that this was true, she rummaged through a tote bag and a manila envelope and finally unfolded a sheet of typing paper and brought out her photographs.

They were not pictures of family, or friends, or even a dog or cat, its eyes 2 brown-red in the flashbulb's light. They were pictures of a house. It was like a thousand houses in a hundred towns, not suburb, not city, but somewhere in between, with aluminum siding and a chain-link fence, a narrow driveway running up to a one-car garage and a patch of backyard. The house was yellow. I looked on the back for a date or a name, but neither was there. There was no need for discussion. I knew what she was trying to tell me, for it was something I had often felt. She was not adrift, alone, anonymous, although her bags and her raincoat with the grime shadowing its creases had made me believe she was. She had a house, or at least once upon a time had had one.

Inside were curtains, a couch, a stove, potholders. You are where you live. She was somebody.

I've never been very good at looking at the big picture, taking the global 3
view, and I've always been a person with an overactive sense of place, the legacy of an Irish grandfather. So it is natural that the thing that seems most wrong with the world to me right now is that there are so many people with no homes. I'm not simply talking about shelter from the elements, or three square meals a day or a mailing address to which the welfare people can send the check — although I know that all these are important for survival. I'm talking about a home, about precisely those kinds of feelings that have wound up in cross-stitch and French knots on samplers over the years.

Home is where the heart is. There's no place like it. I love my home with 4
a ferocity totally out of proportion to its appearance or location. I love dumb things about it: the hot-water heater, the plastic rack you drain dishes in, the roof over my head, which occasionally leaks. And yet it is precisely those dumb things that make it what it is — a place of certainty, stability, predictability, privacy, for me and for my family. It is where I live. What more can you say about a place than that? That is everything.

Yet it is something that we have been edging away from gradually during 5
my lifetime and the lifetimes of my parents and grandparents. There was a time when where you lived often was where you worked and where you grew the food you ate and even where you were buried. When that era passed, where you lived at least was where your parents had lived and where you would live with your children when you became enfeebled. Then, suddenly where you lived was where you lived for three years, until you could move on to something else and something else again.

And so we have come to something else again, to children who do not 6
understand what it means to go to their rooms because they have never had a room, to men and women whose fantasy is a wall they can paint a color of their own choosing, to old people reduced to sitting on molded plastic chairs, their skin blue-white in the lights of a bus station, who pull pictures of houses out of their bags. Homes have stopped being homes. Now they are real estate.

People find it curious that those without homes would rather sleep sitting up 7
on benches or huddled in doorways than go to shelters. Certainly some prefer to do so because they are emotionally ill, because they have been locked in before and they are damned if they will be locked in again. Others are afraid of the violence and trouble they may find there. But some seem to want something that is not available in shelters, and they will not compromise, not for a cot, or oatmeal, or a shower with special soap that kills the bugs. "One room," a woman with a baby who was sleeping on her sister's floor, once told me, "painted blue." That was the crux of it; not size or location, but pride of ownership. Painted blue.

This is a difficult problem, and some wise and compassionate people are   8
working hard at it. But in the main I think we work around it, just as we walk
around it when it is lying on the sidewalk or sitting in the bus terminal —
the problem, that is. It has been customary to take people's pain and lessen
our own participation in it by turning it into an issue, not a collection of
human beings. We turn an adjective into a noun: the poor, not poor people;
the homeless, not Ann or the man who lives in the box or the woman who
sleeps on the subway grate.

Sometimes I think we would be better off if we forgot about the broad   9
strokes and concentrated on the details. Here is a woman without a bureau.
There is a man with no mirror, no wall to hang it on. They are not the homeless. They are people who have no homes. No drawer that holds the spoons.
No window to look out upon the world. My God. That is everything.

Journal Writing

What does the word *home* mean to you? Does it involve material things, privacy,
family, a sense of permanence? In your journal, explore your ideas about this word.

Questions on Meaning

1. What is Quindlen's THESIS?
2. What distinction is Quindlen making in her CONCLUSION with the sentences
   "They are not the homeless. They are people who have no homes"?
3. Why does Quindlen believe that having a home is essential?

Questions on Writing Strategy

1. Why do you think Quindlen begins with the story of Ann? How else might
   Quindlen have begun her essay?
2. What is the EFFECT of Quindlen's examples about her own home?
3. What key ASSUMPTIONS does the author make about her AUDIENCE? Are the
   assumptions reasonable? Where does she specifically address an assumption that
   might undermine her view?
4. How does Quindlen vary the sentences in paragraph 7 that give examples of why
   homeless people avoid shelters?
5. **OTHER METHODS** Quindlen uses examples to support an ARGUMENT. What
   position does she want readers to recognize and accept?

Questions on Language

1. What is the effect of "My God" in the last paragraph?

2. How might Quindlen be said to give new meaning to the old CLICHÉ "Home is where the heart is" (par. 4)?

3. What is meant by "crux" (par. 7)? Where does the word come from?

Suggestions for Writing

1. **FROM JOURNAL TO ESSAY**   Write an essay that gives a detailed DEFINITION of *home* by using your own home, hometown, or experiences with homes as supporting examples. (See Chap. 11 if you need help with definition.)

2. Have you ever moved from one place to another? What sort of experience was it? Write an essay about leaving an old home and moving to a new one. Was there an activity or a piece of furniture that helped ease the transition?

3. Write an essay on the problem of homelessness in your town or city. Use examples to support your view of the problem and a possible solution.

4. **CRITICAL WRITING**   Write a brief essay in which you agree or disagree with Quindlen's assertion that a home is "everything." Can one, for instance, be a fulfilled person without a home? In your answer, take account of the values that might underlie an attachment to home; Quindlen mentions "certainty, stability, predictability, privacy" (par. 4), but there are others, including some (such as fear of change) that are less positive.

5. **CONNECTIONS**   Quindlen makes an emphatic distinction between "the homeless" and "people who have no homes" (par. 9). Read William Lutz's "The World of Doublespeak" (p. 363), which examines how language can be used to distort our perceptions of unpleasant truths. Drawing on what he and Quindlen have to say, write an essay that explores how the way we label a problem like homelessness influences what solutions we may (or may not) be able to find.

Anna Quindlen on Writing

Anna Quindlen started her writing career as a newspaper reporter. "I had wanted to be a writer for most of my life," she recalls in the introduction to her book *Living Out Loud*, "and in the service of the writing I became a reporter. For many years I was able to observe, even to feel, life vividly, but at secondhand. I was able to stand over the chalk outline of a body on a sidewalk dappled with black blood; to stand behind the glass and look down into an operating theater where one man was placing a heart in the yawning chest of another; to sit in the park on the first day of summer and find myself professionally obligated to record all the glories of it. Every day I found answers: who, what, when, where, and why."

Quindlen was a good reporter, but the business of finding answers did not satisfy her personally. "In my own life," she continues, "I had only questions." Then she switched from reporter to columnist at the *New York Times*. It was "exhilarating," she says, that "my work became a reflection of my life. After years of being a professional observer of other people's lives, I was given the opportunity to be a professional observer of my own. I was permitted — and permitted myself — to write a column, not about my answers, but about my questions. Never did I make so much sense of my life as I did then, for it was inevitable that as a writer I would find out most clearly what I thought, and what I only thought I thought, when I saw it written down. . . . After years of feeling secondhand, of feeling the pain of the widow, the joy of the winner, I was able to allow myself to feel those emotions for myself."

The Bedford Reader on Writing

While Brent Staples (p. 170) and Brian Doyle (p. 182) in this chapter both stress the strategies and techniques essay writers can learn from newspaper reporters, Quindlen seems to stress the opposite. For her, GENRE and PURPOSE (see pp. 31–32) impose restrictions as much as they open up possibilities. What did she feel she could accomplish in a column that she could not accomplish in a news article? What evidence of this difference do you see in her essay "Homeless"?

KELLIE YOUNG

Kellie Young was born and raised in Honolulu, Hawaii, where she attended the Iolani School and volunteered at hospitals over summer breaks. At the Massachusetts Institute of Technology, she worked as a student researcher in the school's biomedical and chemical engineering labs, served as copresident of the Southeast Asian Service Leadership Network, and played on the water polo team. Young graduated in 2011 with a BS in chemical-biological engineering and went on to earn a medical degree from the University of California at San Francisco. She is now a physician. An avid reader, Young also loves movies, kites, and ketchup.

The Undercurrent

Young wrote the following essay in her sophomore year in response to a writing assignment that prompted her to reflect on events or emotions that shaped her into the person she is. Focusing on a legacy of incessant and sometimes irrational worries, Young examines her mother's enduring influence on her own thoughts and actions. "The Undercurrent" was selected for the 2010 edition of *Angles*, MIT's annual anthology of exemplary student writing.

> *The future destiny of a child is always the work of the mother.*
> — Napoleon Bonaparte

The tires crunch heavily over the rocky path, crackling in the still 1 morning air. The truck's headlights flood the darkness in front of us, slicing through the heavy veil to illuminate an unpaved road overshadowed with sweeping branches. When the car has gone as far as it can, we kill the engine and let the silence engulf us. We slip off our seats, tuck our surfboards under our arms, and creep through the trees until the sharp rocks beneath our feet smooth out into fine sand. Only black shadows on the beach, we are utterly and completely alone, blending in with the deepness of the sky and sea.

Quickly, before the sun rises. 2

Hannah rushes out to meet the black water, her body and board collid- 3 ing recklessly onto the rough surf. I hesitate before leaping in after her. My stomach flips as the cold Pacific swallows me up, but even more striking is my mother's voice that begins to scream in my mind, freezing me in the water.

You're going to get swept out by the undertow! You're going to get eaten alive by 4 *a tiger shark! The coral is poisonous! Get one shard in your toe and you're going to have to chop it off — the entire thing! What are you thinking? Do you want to die? Come home!*

"I'm going to be fine, this is fine, nothing's wrong, everything's okay," I ⁵
chant in time to my thrumming heart, as my arms pull me further from home.
I paddle away from my mother, but her voice only becomes muted, a humming
background that does not fade until my arms are outstretched on a perfect
wave, greeting the day.

My mother's voice has been a constant presence throughout my life, from ⁶
when I was little ("Kellie, get down from that stool! You're going to fall off
and break your leg!") up through high school ("No, you cannot go to that
concert — what if someone starts a mosh pit and you get crushed?"). My life's
roadmap is littered with my mother's interjections and fears about the horrible
things that can happen in life. Everything constitutes a risk, and as sentient
beings, we should know better than to take those risks that could (and would!)
prematurely cut short our lives. No one better embraces Murphy's Law[1] than
my mother. Her love is thick and binding, and as my mother, she has always
felt responsible for my personal safety; her love constantly drew me back
("Kellie, did you hear what I said?").

How could I *not* hear? ⁷

Her cautious attitude toward me was not unfounded. When I was young, ⁸
I was the maverick. I launched into situations without hesitation, tackling all
obstacles, physical or otherwise, by tucking my chin down and charging forward. Once in December, when I was twelve, a great and wonderful lightning
storm blacked out the bright afternoon sky. Angry, gray clouds blotted out all
semblance of time and the rain fell so thick I could not make out my neighbor's plumeria tree growing just outside my window. Naturally I ran outside. I
slammed the front door behind me, welcoming this phenomenon by whooping
and hollering down the street. I had never seen lightning so close before; the
electric charge in the air felt energizing. It was only after my T-shirt stuck to
my chest and shivers trembled through my body that I discovered the locked
door. My parents found their cold and slightly sick child shivering on the front
steps when they pulled into their driveway later that day.

My thoughtlessness was a danger to myself, my mother concluded, and ⁹
she determined that if I lacked the capacity to think ahead, she would do it for
me. Now whenever I see electric storms, I imagine those poor souls unlucky
enough to be struck down by those lightning bolts of doom.

My mother's reach, however, has always extended far beyond natural ¹⁰
disasters and the obvious everyday life-threatening situations. I have often
imagined a rapist or mugger waiting in the shadows to attack me as I walked

---

[1] Murphy's Law is a fundamental principle normally associated with pessimists. The law
basically says that if anything can go wrong, it will. There is a sense of doom and uncontrollable
fate associated with the law and its principles ("Murphy's Law").

by myself on a sidewalk of a lonely street. Even if I were with a bunch of friends at the mall, my mother's voice would scream at me to stay away from all suspicious-looking adults. If I accidentally looked into strangers' eyes, crazy, irrational thoughts would immediately flood my mind. They were kidnappers, ready to seize me and hold me for an obscenely large ransom, which my parents would have to pay to retrieve their most beloved daughter, forcing the entire family into the utter depths of poverty. Public restrooms were equally dangerous. The toilet seat was swarming with germs so terrible that if I were unfortunate enough to touch the seat with my bare skin, I would contract a disease and die too quickly for doctors to make a saving diagnosis. It would be a tragic death, and at my funeral my mother would cry out in sorrow, "If only she had used a toilet seat cover!" My induced vigilance in public restroom hygiene has called for excessive amounts of the finite paper resources in the stall. For this I am certain that I am on the hit list of countless custodians under the alias: "girl who clogged the toilet with twenty seat covers and yards of toilet paper."

I often feel overwhelmed with the number of decisions that seem to over- 11
run my life, each demanding an extraordinary amount of thought and contemplation. With my mother's voice insisting on caution, I often find myself torn between several paths, trying to project which road will lead me to the best outcome. Once an ingenious, spontaneous idea strikes me, it is abruptly and violently reeled back in. My friends often throw up their hands in despair as I wage war with a restaurant menu. Often I stare between the listed options, calculating the value of each potential meal according to price, nutritional content, and taste, before ordering. "Yes, that is my final answer." After living eighteen years in a house filled with my mother's warnings and cautionary instructions, I unconsciously had begun incorporating her perspective into my own.

Whereas I had been the somewhat unwilling recipient of this seeming 12
oversensitivity, my mother's situation as a child-adult fostered the growth of these ideals for the survival of her family in a new world. When my grandfather immigrated to paradise with his first wife, he found that life did not simply improve with tropical sunshine and democracy. When his first spouse died, leaving behind four teenagers, he returned to China and brought my grandmother and my mom back home with him to Hawaii. With my grandmother taking care of the first family, my mother was left to care for herself and her three younger sisters. She was brilliant at juggling work at her father's general store in rainy Manoa and schoolwork, graduating from high school as the top mathematics scholar. Her decisions were all based on taking care of her family, making sure lunches were packed, laces tied, and her sisters equipped with everything her family could afford. In fact, my mom and dad's first date was

picking up my aunt from school. My mother's hardships taught her to be cautious and to make wise choices.

Having everything (two parents who do not believe in corporal punishment, a financially stable home, abundant opportunities for obtaining a good education), I am buffered from the reality that so educated my mother. Our middle-class status put me at the bottom of this learning curve. Since I could not be poor, my mother made her voice my teacher, hoping I could learn from her what she had learned from life. "Are you listening to me, Kellie?"   13

The home is now empty. All three of my older siblings are in medical school and one is even married. I am the youngest of her followers and am so far from home (a twelve-hour flight with stopovers, six time zones, an ocean, a continent away). In the winter, when I stare out my window at the grey, frozen courtyard covered in brown snow, my mother is staring out of our home window at the brilliant, bright blue sky hanging over the sparkling Pacific Ocean.   14

At the end of summer 2007 when I was at the airport, not at all ready for MIT, my mother checked (four times) the gate and boarding time, even though I had already checked (four times). Separated by towering metal detectors and the mob of people being herded through them, my mom and I shouted our parting farewells. However, our real good-bye was minutes before I turned my phone off for boarding in the form of a text message: "Don't fall asleep at your connection. Someone might steal your laptop. Love you."   15

My mother's voice in my head is something I cannot shake or hide from, but neither is it confining or oppressing. I can sneak out in the morning to surf dawn patrol and meet the eyes of strangers in malls or bars. However, I make these decisions fully aware, consciously, and carefully. Even with so many miles between us now, she is everywhere I go; she is the undercurrent pulling my thoughts, her thoughts, to the forefront of my mind. She slows down my recklessness, throwing caution and wisdom back into the whirlwind of my mind. Although at times her/my fears catch me, freezing me momentarily before I leap, she is me, and her voice steers me clear of jumps I realize I cannot make.   16

When my dad is working at the office, my mom sometimes comes home early by herself. All her life, she has always looked after someone, making sure shoelaces are tied and lunches packed. Looking at her spotless house, which in my younger years was fondly nicknamed "pigsty," she likes to call me to talk about her day, my day, and what I should be doing with my life ("Are you studying for the MCATs?"). Occasionally the line phases into static, the airwaves between Boston and Honolulu too filled with distance, and when it's over, my mom will always be frantic on the other end saying, "Kellie? Hello? Can you hear me? Are you still listening?"   17

"Yup, still listening, go ahead."   18

Work Cited
"Murphy's Law." *Word Net*, Princeton University, 2010, wordnetweb.princeton
.edu/perl/webwn?s=murphy%27s+law.

Journal Writing

Young writes about the strong influence her mother has had on her thoughts, on her actions, and on her very sense of who she is. Who has been the strongest influence in your life? It might be a parent, or perhaps another relative, a friend, a religious figure, a celebrity of some sort. Think about what this person has meant to you and how he or she has influenced you, in ways both good and bad. Jot down your musings in your journal.

Questions on Meaning

1. What do you make of the title of this essay? What is an undercurrent, and what does it have to do with Young's subject? (If necessary, look up *undercurrent* in a dictionary.)

2. What would you say is Young's PURPOSE in this essay? Is it primarily to entertain readers by depicting an obsession, or does Young seem to have another purpose in mind?

3. Young explains some of the reasons for her mother's constant worrying in paragraph 12. PARAPHRASE the background information she provides. What circumstances brought Young's mother to Hawaii? Why was she, as a girl, responsible for taking care of three children?

4. What is Young's THESIS? Does she seem to consider her mother's influence on her mostly negative or mostly positive? Explain.

Questions on Writing Strategy

1. Why do you think Young opens her essay as she does? What is the EFFECT of this introduction?

2. What assumptions does the author make about her AUDIENCE?

3. "The Undercurrent" includes quite a few examples. How does Young maintain UNITY and COHERENCE in her essay?

4. **OTHER METHODS**   Where in the essay does Young use NARRATION to relate stories about her experiences? What do these ANECDOTES contribute to her point?

Questions on Language

1. Why does Young quote her mother so extensively? What would the essay lose without this DIALOG?

2. Point to some instances of hyperbole in the essay. (For a definition of *hyperbole*, see FIGURES OF SPEECH in the Glossary.) What does Young's language contribute to her TONE?

3. Find definitions of the following words: interjections, sentient (par. 6); maverick, plumeria (8); induced, vigilance, hygiene, finite (10); ingenious (11); corporal, buffered (13).

4. Why do you think Young repeats the parenthetical phrase "(four times)" in paragraph 15?

Suggestions for Writing

1. **FROM JOURNAL TO ESSAY**   Drawing on your journal entry (p. 193) and using your experiences as EVIDENCE, write an essay that explains the influence of a particular person on your identity and behavior. Your essay may be serious or humorous, but it should include plenty of details and focus on CAUSE AND EFFECT.

2. The ability to read other people's and our own thoughts is a key element of emotional intelligence, a relatively new concept that is often evoked in the fields of psychology and education to help people improve their work and life skills. Search your library catalog and databases for books and articles about emotional intelligence; then write a brief DEFINITION of the concept. Consider as well your own emotional intelligence and how you could improve it.

3. **CRITICAL WRITING**   ANALYZE Young's use of humor in this essay. What is it that makes her essay funny? In particular, consider her use of hyperbole, irony, and humorous IMAGES. You might also do some library or Internet research on humor writing to further support your analysis.

4. **CONNECTIONS**   Young's essay is one of several in this book that explore the experience of growing away from one's parents; other essays include Amy Tan's "Fish Cheeks" (p. 74), Brad Manning's "Arm Wrestling with My Father" (p. 121), Firoozeh Dumas's "Sweet, Sour, and Resentful" (p. 275), and Judith Ortiz Cofer's "The Cruel Country" (p. 310). Looking at one or two of these essays along with Young's, compare and contrast the authors' relationships with their parents. How are the parents themselves and the authors' feelings similar or different? Use quotations or paraphrases from the essays as evidence for your ideas.

ADDITIONAL WRITING TOPICS

Example

1. Select one of the following general statements, or set forth a general statement of your own that one of these inspires. Making it your central idea (or THESIS), support it in an essay full of examples. Draw your examples from your reading, your studies, your conversations, or your own experience.

   Text messaging has many advantages (or many disadvantages) over making a phone call.
   Individual consumers can (or cannot) help slow down global climate change.
   Friendships don't always start off easily.
   Spending (or saving) is necessary to the nation's economy.
   Each family has its own distinctive culture.
   Certain games, closely inspected, promote violence.
   Graphic novels have become a serious form of literary art.
   Most people can triumph over crushing difficulties.
   Churchgoers aren't perfect.
   Online articles use misleading titles to get readers to click on the stories.
   Local foods, in season, are best for everyone (or not).
   Ordinary lives sometimes give rise to legends.
   Some people are born winners (or losers).
   Music can change lives.
   Certain machines *do* have personalities.
   Some road signs lead drivers astray.

2. In a brief essay, make a GENERALIZATION about the fears, joys, or contradictions that members of minority groups seem to share. To illustrate your generalization, draw examples from personal experience, from outside reading, or from two or three of the essays in this book by the following authors: Nancy Mairs (p. 12), Amy Tan (p. 74), Junot Díaz (p. 88), N. Scott Momaday (p. 129), Brent Staples (p. 166), Issa Rae (p. 173), Andrea Roman (p. 215), Fatema Mernissi (p. 233), Firoozeh Dumas (p. 275), Tal Fortgang (p. 446), Roxane Gay (p. 453), Dagoberto Gilb (p. 465), and Linda Chavez (p. 495).

I WAS SPARTAN TO MY FATHER'S ATHENIAN.

MODERN TO HIS VICTORIAN.

BUTCH TO HIS NELLY.

UTILITARIAN TO HIS AESTHETE.

6

COMPARISON
AND CONTRAST

Setting Things Side by Side

◀ **Comparison and contrast in a graphic memoir**

In the highly praised and influential *Fun Home* (2006), comic artist Alison Bechdel explores the complications of growing up the lesbian daughter of a closeted gay man while living in a nineteenth-century house that held the family's funeral business. In this panel, from the first chapter of the book, she compares herself with her father on four points: politics (ancient Sparta, in Greece, was a warrior society; neighboring Athens focused on education and the arts), cultural sensibilities, gender stereotypes, and values. What striking and not-so-striking differences do you notice? What is the most obvious similarity? What are some more subtle similarities? How would you summarize the conflict Bechdel portrays?

THE METHOD

Which team do you place your money on, the Giants or the Patriots? To go to school full-time or part-time: What are the rewards and drawbacks of each way of life? How do the Republican and the Democratic platforms stack up against each other? In what ways are the psychological theories of Carl Jung like or unlike those of Sigmund Freud? Should we pass laws to regulate medical marijuana or just let recreational use run wild? These are questions that may be addressed by the dual method of COMPARISON AND CONTRAST. In comparing, you point to similar features of the subjects; in contrasting, to different features. (The features themselves you identify by the method of DIVISION or ANALYSIS; see Chap. 8.)

In practice, comparison and contrast are usually inseparable because two subjects are generally neither entirely alike nor entirely unlike. When Bruce Catton sets out to portray the Civil War generals Ulysses S. Grant and Robert E. Lee (p. 227), he considers both their similarities and their differences. Often, as in this case, the similarities make the subjects comparable at all and the differences make comparison worthwhile.

Uses of Comparison and Contrast

Comparison and contrast are especially helpful in academic writing. You can use the method in expository writing to illuminate two or more subjects and demonstrate that you understand your material thoroughly. And in an argument in which you support one of two possible choices, a careful and detailed comparison and contrast may be extremely convincing as you show why you prefer one thing to another, one course of action to another, one idea to another.

Because comparison and contrast reveal knowledge about the subjects under investigation, you will also often be asked to use the method in exams that call for essay answers. Sometimes the examiner will come right out and say, "Compare and contrast nineteenth-century methods of treating drug addiction with those of the present day." Sometimes, however, comparison and contrast won't even be mentioned by name; instead, the examiner may ask, "What resemblances do you find between John Updike's short story 'A & P' and the Grimm fairy tale 'Godfather Death'?" Or, "Explain the relative desirability of holding a franchise against going into business as an independent proprietor." But those — as you realize when you begin to plan your reply — are just other ways of asking you to compare and contrast.

Purposes

A good essay in comparing and contrasting serves a PURPOSE. Most of the time, the writer of such an essay has one of two purposes in mind:

- **To explain the similarities and differences between two things,** the writer shows each of the subjects distinctly by considering both, side by side. With such a purpose, the writer doesn't necessarily find one of the subjects better than the other. In his essay on Grant and Lee, Bruce Catton does not favor either general but concludes that each reflected strong currents of American history.

- **To choose between two things, or EVALUATE them,** the writer shows how one of the subjects is better than the other on the basis of some standard: Which of two films more convincingly captures the experience of being a teenager? Which of two chemical processes works better to clean waste water? To answer either question, the writer has to consider the features of both subjects — both the positive and the negative — and then choose the subject whose positive features more clearly predominate.

THE PROCESS

Subjects for Comparison

Comparison usually works best with two of a kind: two means of reading for the visually impaired, two films on the same theme, two processes for cleaning waste water, two mystery writers, two schools of political thought. When you find yourself considering two subjects side by side or preferring one subject over another, you have already embarked on comparison and contrast. Just be sure that your two subjects display a clear basis for comparison. In other words, they should have something significant in common.

It can sometimes be effective, however, to find similarities between evidently unlike subjects — a city and a country town, say — and a special form of comparison, ANALOGY, equates two very unlike things, explaining one in terms of the other. In an analogy you might explain how the human eye works by comparing it to a simple camera, or you might explain the forces in a thunderstorm by comparing them to armies in battle. In "Tragedy" (p. 240), the pop philosopher Alain de Botton explains the civilizing functions of tabloid news stories by equating them with ancient Greek dramas.

In any comparison, you must have a valid reason for bringing the two things together — that is, the similarities and differences must be significant enough to warrant examination. In a comparison of a city and a country town, for instance, the features must extend beyond the obvious — that people live in them, that both have streets and shops — and venture into likenesses that are more meaningful — perhaps that both places create a sense of community that residents depend on, for instance.

Basis for Comparison and Thesis

Beginning to identify the shared and dissimilar features of your subjects will get you started, but the comparison won't be manageable for you or interesting to your readers unless you also limit it. You would be overly ambitious to try to compare and contrast the Russian way of life with the American way of life in five hundred words; you couldn't include all the important similarities and differences. In a brief paper, you would be wise to select a single basis for comparison: to show, for instance, how representative day-care centers in Russia and the United States are both like and unlike each other.

This basis for comparison will eventually underpin the THESIS of your essay — the claim you have to make about the similarities and dissimilarities of two things or about one thing's superiority over another. Here, from essays in this chapter, are THESIS STATEMENTS that clearly lay out what's being compared and why:

> Neat people are lazier and meaner than sloppy people.
> — Suzanne Britt, "Neat People vs. Sloppy People"

> One would think that language would create the biggest barriers for immigrants but in my mother's case, the biggest obstacles were the small cultural differences.
> — Andrea Roman, "We're Not . . ."

> They were two strong men, these oddly different generals, and they represented the strengths of two conflicting currents that, through them, had come into collision.
> — Bruce Catton, "Grant and Lee: A Study in Contrasts"

Notice that each author not only identifies his or her subjects (neat and sloppy people, cultural differences, two generals) but also previews the purpose of the comparison, whether to evaluate (Britt) or to explain (Roman and Catton).

Organization

Even with a limited basis for comparison, the method of comparison and contrast can be tricky without some planning. We suggest that you make an outline (formal or informal), using one of two organizations described below: subject by subject or point by point.

Say you're writing an essay on two guitarists, Jed and Jake. Your purpose is to explain the distinctive identities of the two players, and your thesis statement might be the following:

Jed and Jake are both excellent guitarists whose differences in style reflect their training.

Here are the two ways you might arrange the BODY of your comparison:

- **Subject by subject.** Set forth all your facts about Jed; then do the same for Jake. Next, sum up their similarities and differences. In your conclusion, state what you think you have shown.

  1. *Jed*
     Training
     Choice of instrument
     Technical dexterity
     Playing style

  2. *Jake*
     Training
     Choice of instrument
     Technical dexterity
     Playing style

  This procedure works well for a paper of a few paragraphs, but for a longer one, it has a built-in disadvantage: Readers need to remember all the facts about subject 1 while they read about subject 2. If the essay is long and lists many facts, a subject-by-subject arrangement may be difficult to hold in mind.

- **Point by point.** Usually more workable in writing a long paper than the first method, the second scheme is to compare and contrast as you go. You consider one point at a time, taking up your two subjects alternately. In this way, you continually bring the subjects together, perhaps in every paragraph. Notice the differences in the outline:

  1. *Training*
     Jed: self-taught
     Jake: classically trained

  2. *Choice of instrument*
     Jed: electric
     Jake: acoustic

  3. *Technical dexterity*
     Jed: highly skilled
     Jake: highly skilled

4. *Playing style*
   Jed: rapid-fire
   Jake: impressionistic

For either organizing scheme, your conclusion might be as follows: "Although similar in skills, the two differ greatly in aims and in personalities. Jed is better suited to a local club and Jake to a concert hall."

By the way, a subject-by-subject organization works most efficiently for a *pair* of subjects. If you want to write about *three* guitarists, you might first consider Jed and Jake, then Jake and Josh, then Josh and Jed — but it would probably be easier to compare and contrast all three point by point.

Balance and Flexibility

An outline will help you see the shape of your paper and keep your points in mind as you draft. A trick of comparison and contrast will be to balance the treatment of both subjects while allowing them to breathe. You do have to give the subjects equivalence: You can't discuss Jed's on-stage manner without discussing Jake's, too. If you have nothing to say about Jake's on-stage manner, then you might as well omit the point. A surefire loser is the paper that proposes to compare and contrast two subjects but then proceeds to discuss quite different elements in each: Jed's playing style and Jake's choice of material, Jed's fondness for Italian food and Jake's hobby of antique-car collecting. The writer of such a paper doesn't compare and contrast the two musicians at all, but engages in two entirely separate discussions.

Balance your subjects' features, but don't let your outline constrain you too tightly. The reader of a mechanically written comparison-and-contrast essay comes to feel like a weary tennis spectator whose head has to swivel from side to side: now Jed, now Jake; now Jed again, now back to Jake. You need to mention the same features of both subjects, it is true, but no law says *how* you must mention them. You need not follow your outline in lockstep order, or cover similarities and differences at precisely the same length (none of the authors later in this chapter do), or spend a hundred words on Jed's fingering skill just because you spend a hundred words on Jake's. As you write, keep casting your thoughts upon a living, particular world — not twisting and squeezing that world into a rigid scheme.

FOCUS ON PARALLELISM

With several points of comparison and alternating subjects, a comparison will be easier for your readers to follow if you emphasize likenesses and differences in your wording. Take advantage of the technique of parallelism discussed in Chapter 2 (p. 50). PARALLELISM — the use of similar grammatical structures for elements of similar importance — balances a comparison and clarifies the relations between elements. At the same time, lack of parallelism can distract or confuse readers.

To make the elements of a comparison parallel, repeat the forms of related words, phrases, and sentences:

NONPARALLEL Harris expects dieters who follow his plan to limit bread, dairy, and meat, while Marconi's diet forbids few foods.

PARALLEL Harris's diet limits bread, dairy, and meat, while Marconi's diet forbids few foods.

NONPARALLEL Harris emphasizes self-denial, but when following Marconi's plan you can eat whatever you want in moderation.

PARALLEL Harris emphasizes self-denial, but Marconi stresses moderation.

NONPARALLEL If you want to lose weight quickly, choose Harris's diet. You'll have more success keeping the weight off if you follow Marconi's plan.

PARALLEL If you want to lose weight quickly, choose Harris's diet. If you want to keep the weight off, follow Marconi's plan.

CHECKLIST FOR REVISING
A COMPARISON-AND-CONTRAST ESSAY

✔ **Purpose.** What is the aim of your comparison: to explain two (or more) subjects or to evaluate them? Will the purpose be clear to readers from the start?

✔ **Subjects.** Are the subjects enough alike, sharing enough features, to make comparison worthwhile?

✔ **Thesis.** Does your thesis establish a limited basis for comparison so that you have room and time to cover all the relevant similarities and differences?

✔ **Organization.** Does your arrangement of material, whether subject by subject or point by point, do justice to your subjects and help readers follow the comparison?

✔ **Balance and flexibility.** Have you covered the same features of both subjects? At the same time, have you avoided a rigid back-and-forth movement that could bore or exhaust a reader?

✔ **Parallelism.** Have you used parallel structure to clarify the subjects and points you are discussing?

COMPARISON AND CONTRAST IN ACADEMIC WRITING

A Communications Textbook

Taken from Steven McCornack's *Reflect and Relate*, the following point-by-point comparison explains a key difference between men and women. The in-text citations, in APA style (see pp. 651–61 of the Appendix), refer readers to a list of sources provided at the end of McCornack's textbook.

Immediately after birth, we begin a lifelong process of gender socialization, learning from others what it means personally, interpersonally, and culturally to be "male" or "female." Girls are typically taught feminine behaviors, such as sensitivity to one's own and others' emotions, nurturance, and compassion (Lippa, 2002). Boys are usually taught masculine behaviors, learning about assertiveness, competitiveness, and independence from others. As a result of gender socialization, men and women often end up forming comparatively different self-concepts (Cross & Madson, 1997). For example, women are more likely than men to perceive themselves as connected to others and to assess themselves based on the quality of these interpersonal connections. Men are more likely than women to think of themselves as a composite of their individual achievements, abilities, and beliefs — viewing themselves as separate from other people. At the same time, the existence of these differences doesn't mean that all men and all women think of themselves in identical ways. Many men and women appreciate and embrace both feminine and masculine characteristics in their self-concepts.

> Point-by-point comparison supporting this topic sentence
>
> 1. First point: Learned behaviors
>   - Girls
>   - Boys
>
> 2. Second point: Self-concepts
>   - Women
>   - Men

A Review

If you browse the Web or flip through any newspaper or magazine, you're bound to spot a review: a writer's assessment of anything from a restaurant to a scholarly book. Commonly assigned in college, too, reviews rely mainly on ANALYSIS to identify and interpret the elements of a subject. But because a review evaluates quality, writers naturally turn to comparison and contrast as well, weighing two or more products, works, or ideas to determine their relative worth. Such a comparison takes its evidence from the subjects themselves, as in descriptions of paintings in an exhibit or quotations from written works.

For a course in popular culture, Charlotte Pak wrote a review of singer Beyoncé Knowles's solo career. Pak chose her subject because "Single Ladies (Put a Ring on It)" bolstered Beyoncé's reputation as a champion of women. Although Pak enjoyed the song, she was bothered by some of the implications in its lyrics, and she decided to investigate the singer's work for similar themes. In the paragraphs below, excerpted from her full review, Pak compares "Single Ladies" with a popular song from the 1960s, with unexpected results.

Critics and fans often view Beyoncé as one of the leaders in the "strong woman" style that encourages female independence, equality, and self-worth. These listeners offer her 2009 hit "Single Ladies (Put a Ring on It)" as a symbol of how far women have come since the 1950s and 1960s. But this and other songs by Beyoncé just seem strong when in fact they present women who are no more independent than the ones portrayed half a century ago.

Basis for comparison: portrayals of women's strength

Subject-by-subject organization supporting this claim

A classic example of the older style is the Dixie Cups' 1964 hit "Chapel of Love." The refrain of the song is familiar even today: "Goin' to the chapel and we're / Gonna get married / . . . Goin' to the chapel of love." The song itself seems sentimental and even naive on the surface. In a sweet, dreamy voice, the female singer imagines marital bliss, as "Birds all sing as if they knew / Today's the day we'll say 'I do.' " She sings of marriage as the fulfillment of her life, implying her dependence on a man. Yet despite the tone and the sentimentality, the song also suggests equality between the singer and her husband-to-be within the bounds of traditional marriage: "I'll be his and he'll be mine." The possession is mutual. Two independent individuals will say "I do."

1. Representative older song: "Chapel of Love" by the Dixie Cups

• Quotations from song

• Interpretation

In contrast, the singer in Beyoncé's "Single Ladies" seems pleased to be free from an ex-boyfriend. She dances with another man in a club while her ex jealously watches: "Don't pay him any attention / 'Cause you had your turn and now you're gonna learn / What it really feels like to miss me." Her tone is feisty and no-nonsense, the voice of a sophisticated and independent woman. Yet she remains preoccupied with her ex-boyfriend and still sees herself through his eyes. In the song's chorus — "If you like it then you shoulda put a ring on it" — the "it" suggests that she has a sense of herself as an object to be possessed rather than an independent being. That suggestion is explicit in the lines "Pull me into your arms, / Say I'm the one you own." The wimpy "Chapel of Love" at least offers an image of equality. "Single Ladies" misleads by casting dependency as strength.

2. Representative Beyoncé song: "Single Ladies (Put a Ring on It)"

• Quotations from song

• Interpretation

Concluding sentences express judgment

DAVID SEDARIS

Winner of the Thurber Prize for American Humor, David Sedaris was born in 1957 and grew up in North Carolina. After graduating from the School of the Art Institute of Chicago in 1987, Sedaris taught writing there part-time and then moved to New York City, where he took various odd jobs. One of these jobs — a stint as a department-store Christmas elf — provided Sedaris with material for "The Santaland Diaries," the essay that launched his career as a humorist after he read it on National Public Radio's *Morning Edition* in 1993. Since then, Sedaris has contributed numerous commentaries to public radio's *Morning Edition* and *This American Life*, and his work appears frequently in *The New Yorker*, *Esquire*, and other magazines. He has published eight collections of essays and fiction, including *Naked* (1997), *Dress Your Family in Corduroy and Denim* (2004), *When You Are Engulfed in Flames* (2008), and *Let's Explore Diabetes with Owls* (2013). Sedaris frequently tours and gives readings of his essays and works in progress; in 2013 he adapted his story "C.O.G.," about an apple-picking job in Oregon, into the script for a feature film. He lives in rural England.

Remembering My Childhood on the Continent of Africa

Many of Sedaris's essays locate comedy in exaggerated depictions of his basically normal North Carolina childhood. In this essay from *Me Talk Pretty One Day* (2000), Sedaris highlights that normality by contrasting it with the distinctly unusual childhood of his partner. For another approach to a similar subject, see the next essay, by student writer Andrea Roman.

When Hugh was in the fifth grade, his class took a field trip to an Ethiopian 1 slaughterhouse. He was living in Addis Ababa at the time, and the slaughterhouse was chosen because, he says, "it was convenient."

This was a school system in which the matter of proximity outweighed 2 such petty concerns as what may or may not be appropriate for a busload of eleven-year-olds. "What?" I asked. "Were there no autopsies scheduled at the local morgue? Was the federal prison just a bit too far out of the way?"

Hugh defends his former school, saying, "Well, isn't that the whole point 3 of a field trip? To see something new?"

"Technically yes, but . . ." 4

"All right then," he says. "So we saw some new things." 5

One of his field trips was literally a trip to a field where the class watched   6
a wrinkled man fill his mouth with rotten goat meat and feed it to a pack of
waiting hyenas. On another occasion they were taken to examine the blood-
ied bedroom curtains hanging in the palace of the former dictator. There were
tamer trips, to textile factories and sugar refineries, but my favorite is always
the slaughterhouse. It wasn't a big company, just a small rural enterprise run
by a couple of brothers operating out of a low-ceilinged concrete building.
Following a brief lecture on the importance of proper sanitation, a small white
piglet was herded into the room, its dainty hooves clicking against the concrete floor. The class gathered in a circle to get a better look at the animal,
who seemed delighted with the attention he was getting. He turned from face
to face and was looking up at Hugh when one of the brothers drew a pistol
from his back pocket, held it against the animal's temple, and shot the piglet,
execution-style. Blood spattered, frightened children wept, and the man with
the gun offered the teacher and bus driver some meat from a freshly slaughtered goat.

When I'm told such stories, it's all I can do to hold back my feelings of   7
jealousy. An Ethiopian slaughterhouse. Some people have all the luck. When
I was in elementary school, the best we ever got was a trip to Old Salem
or Colonial Williamsburg, one of those preserved brick villages where time
supposedly stands still and someone earns his living as a town crier. There
was always a blacksmith, a group of wandering patriots, and a collection of
bonneted women hawking corn bread or gingersnaps made "the ol'-fashioned
way." Every now and then you might come across a doer of bad deeds serving
time in the stocks, but that was generally as exciting as it got.

Certain events are parallel, but compared with Hugh's, my childhood was   8
unspeakably dull. When I was seven years old, my family moved to North
Carolina. When he was seven years old, Hugh's family moved to the Congo.
We had a collie and a house cat. They had a monkey and two horses named
Charlie Brown and Satan. I threw stones at stop signs. Hugh threw stones
at crocodiles. The verbs are the same, but he definitely wins the prize when
it comes to nouns and objects. An eventful day for my mother might have
involved a trip to the dry cleaner or a conversation with the potato-chip
deliveryman. Asked one ordinary Congo afternoon what she'd done with her
day, Hugh's mother answered that she and a fellow member of the Ladies'
Club had visited a leper colony on the outskirts of Kinshasa. No reason was
given for the expedition, though chances are she was staking it out for a future
field trip.

Due to his upbringing, Hugh sits through inane movies never realizing   9
that they're often based on inane television shows. There were no poker-faced
sitcom martians in his part of Africa, no oil-rich hillbillies or aproned brides

trying to wean themselves from the practice of witchcraft. From time to time a movie would arrive packed in a dented canister, the film scratched and faded from its slow trip around the world. The theater consisted of a few dozen folding chairs arranged before a bedsheet or the blank wall of a vacant hangar out near the airstrip. Occasionally a man would sell warm soft drinks out of a cardboard box, but that was it in terms of concessions.

When I was young, I went to the theater at the nearby shopping center   10
and watched a movie about a talking Volkswagen. I believe the little car had a taste for mischief but I can't be certain, as both the movie and the afternoon proved unremarkable and have faded from my memory. Hugh saw the same movie a few years after it was released. His family had left the Congo by this time and were living in Ethiopia. Like me, Hugh saw the movie by himself on a weekend afternoon. Unlike me, he left the theater two hours later, to find a dead man hanging from a telephone pole at the far end of the unpaved parking lot. None of the people who'd seen the movie seemed to care about the dead man. They stared at him for a moment or two and then headed home, saying they'd never seen anything as crazy as that talking Volkswagen. His father was late picking him up, so Hugh just stood there for an hour, watching the dead man dangle and turn in the breeze. The death was not reported in the newspaper, and when Hugh related the story to his friends, they said, "You saw the movie about the talking car?"

I could have done without the flies and the primitive theaters, but   11
I wouldn't have minded growing up with a houseful of servants. In North Carolina it wasn't unusual to have a once-a-week maid, but Hugh's family had houseboys, a word that never fails to charge my imagination. They had cooks and drivers, and guards who occupied a gatehouse, armed with machetes. Seeing as I had regularly petitioned my parents for an electric fence, the business with the guards strikes me as the last word in quiet sophistication. Having protection suggests that you are important. Having that protection paid for by the government is even better, as it suggests your safety is of interest to someone other than yourself.

Hugh's father was a career officer with the US State Department, and   12
every morning a black sedan carried him off to the embassy. I'm told it's not as glamorous as it sounds, but in terms of fun for the entire family, I'm fairly confident that it beats the sack race at the annual IBM picnic. By the age of three, Hugh was already carrying a diplomatic passport. The rules that applied to others did not apply to him. No tickets, no arrests, no luggage search: He was officially licensed to act like a brat. Being an American, it was expected of him, and who was he to deny the world an occasional tantrum?

They weren't rich, but what Hugh's family lacked financially they more   13
than made up for with the sort of exoticism that works wonders at cocktail

parties, leading always to the remark "That sounds fascinating." It's a compliment one rarely receives when describing an adolescence spent drinking Icees at the North Hills Mall. No fifteen-foot python ever wandered onto my school's basketball court. I begged, I prayed nightly, but it just never happened. Neither did I get to witness a military coup in which forces sympathetic to the colonel arrived late at night to assassinate my next-door neighbor. Hugh had been at the Addis Ababa teen club when the electricity was cut off and soldiers arrived to evacuate the building. He and his friends had to hide in the back of a jeep and cover themselves with blankets during the ride home. It's something that sticks in his mind for one reason or another.

Among my personal highlights is the memory of having my picture taken   14
with Uncle Paul, the legally blind host of a Raleigh children's television show. Among Hugh's is the memory of having his picture taken with Buzz Aldrin on the last leg of the astronaut's world tour. The man who had walked on the moon placed his hand on Hugh's shoulder and offered to sign his autograph book. The man who led Wake County schoolchildren in afternoon song turned at the sound of my voice and asked, "So what's your name, princess?"

When I was fourteen years old, I was sent to spend ten days with my   15
maternal grandmother in western New York State. She was a small and private woman named Billie, and though she never came right out and asked, I had the distinct impression she had no idea who I was. It was the way she looked at me, squinting through her glasses while chewing on her lower lip. That, coupled with the fact that she never once called me by name. "Oh," she'd say, "are you still here?" She was just beginning her long struggle with Alzheimer's disease, and each time I entered the room, I felt the need to reintroduce myself and set her at ease. "Hi, it's me. Sharon's boy, David. I was just in the kitchen admiring your collection of ceramic toads." Aside from a few trips to summer camp, this was the longest I'd ever been away from home and I like to think I was toughened by the experience.

About the same time I was frightening my grandmother, Hugh and his   16
family were packing their belongings for a move to Somalia. There were no English-speaking schools in Mogadishu, so, after a few months spent lying around the family compound with his pet monkey, Hugh was sent back to Ethiopia to live with a beer enthusiast his father had met at a cocktail party. Mr. Hoyt installed security systems in foreign embassies. He and his family gave Hugh a room. They invited him to join them at the table, but that was as far as they extended themselves. No one ever asked him when his birthday was, so when the day came, he kept it to himself. There was no telephone service between Ethiopia and Somalia, and letters to his parents were sent to Washington and then forwarded on to Mogadishu, meaning that his news was more than a month old by the time they got it. I suppose it wasn't much

different than living as a foreign-exchange student. Young people do it all the time, but to me it sounds awful. The Hoyts had two sons about Hugh's age who were always saying things like "Hey that's *our* sofa you're sitting on" and "Hands off that ornamental stein. It doesn't belong to you."

He'd been living with these people for a year when he overheard Mr. Hoyt   17
tell a friend that he and his family would soon be moving to Munich, Germany, the beer capital of the world.

"And that worried me," Hugh said, "because it meant I'd have to find   18
some other place to live."

Where I come from, finding shelter is a problem the average teenager   19
might confidently leave to his parents. It was just something that came with having a mom and a dad. Worried that he might be sent to live with his grandparents in Kentucky, Hugh turned to the school's guidance counselor, who knew of a family whose son had recently left for college. And so he spent another year living with strangers and not mentioning his birthday. While I wouldn't have wanted to do it myself, I can't help but envy the sense of fortitude he gained from the experience. After graduating from college, he moved to France knowing only the phrase "Do you speak French?" — a question guaranteed to get you nowhere unless you also speak the language.

While living in Africa, Hugh and his family took frequent vacations,   20
often in the company of their monkey. The Nairobi Hilton, some suite of high-ceilinged rooms in Cairo or Khartoum: These are the places his people recall when gathered at a common table. "Was that the summer we spent in Beirut or, no, I'm thinking of the time we sailed from Cyprus and took the *Orient Express* to Istanbul."

Theirs was the life I dreamt about during my vacations in eastern North   21
Carolina. Hugh's family was hobnobbing with chiefs and sultans while I ate hush puppies at the Sanitary Fish Market in Morehead City, a beach towel wrapped like a hijab around my head. Someone unknown to me was very likely standing in a muddy ditch and dreaming of an evening spent sitting in a clean family restaurant, drinking iced tea and working his way through an extra-large seaman's platter, but that did not concern me, as it meant I should have been happy with what I had. Rather than surrender to my bitterness, I have learned to take satisfaction in the life that Hugh has led. His stories have, over time, become my own. I say this with no trace of a kumbaya.[1] There is no spiritual symbiosis; I'm just a petty thief who lifts his memories the same way I'll take a handful of change left on his dresser. When my own experiences fall short of the mark, I just go out and spend some of his. It is

[1] From the gospel-folk song with the line "Kumbaya, my Lord, kumbaya," meaning "Come by here." Probably because of its popularity in folk music, the word now also has negative connotations of passivity or touchy-feely spiritualism. — EDS.

with pleasure that I sometimes recall the dead man's purpled face or the report of the handgun ringing in my ears as I studied the blood pooling beneath the dead white piglet. On the way back from the slaughterhouse, we stopped for Cokes in the village of Mojo, where the gas-station owner had arranged a few tables and chairs beneath a dying canopy of vines. It was late afternoon by the time we returned to school, where a second bus carried me to the foot of Coffeeboard Road. Once there, I walked through a grove of eucalyptus trees and alongside a bald pasture of starving cattle, past the guard napping in his gatehouse, and into the waiting arms of my monkey.

Journal Writing

Hugh's experiences living with strangers gave him a "sense of fortitude" (par. 19), according to Sedaris. Have you ever gone through a difficult experience that left you somehow stronger? Write about the struggle in your journal. Was the trouble caused by family relationships? Educational or employment obstacles? Travel experiences? Something else?

Questions on Meaning

1. What is the subject of Sedaris's comparison and contrast in this essay?

2. What do you think is the THESIS of this essay? Take into account both Sedaris's obvious envy of Hugh's childhood and his awareness that Hugh's life was often lonely and insecure. Is the thesis stated or only implied?

3. There is a certain amount of IRONY in Sedaris's envy of Hugh's childhood. What is this irony? How does Sedaris make this irony explicit in paragraph 21?

Questions on Writing Strategy

1. Does Sedaris develop his comparison and contrast subject by subject or point by point? Briefly outline the essay to explain your answer.

2. Point to some of the TRANSITIONS Sedaris uses in moving between his and Hugh's lives.

3. Sedaris refers to Hugh's monkey in paragraphs 8, 16, 20, and 21. In what sense does he use the monkey as a SYMBOL?

4. The first five paragraphs of the essay include a conversation between Sedaris and Hugh about Hugh's childhood. Why do you think the author opened the essay this way?

5. **OTHER METHODS**   How does Sedaris use NARRATION to develop his comparison and contrast?

Questions on Language

1. How does Sedaris use PARALLEL STRUCTURE in paragraph 8 to highlight the contrast between himself and Hugh? How does he then point up this parallelism?

2. Sedaris offers the image of himself as a "petty thief" in paragraph 21. What is the effect of this IMAGE?

3. Sedaris's language in this essay is notably SPECIFIC and CONCRETE. Point to examples of such language just in paragraph 6.

4. Consult a dictionary if necessary to learn the meanings of the following words: proximity, petty (par. 2); hyenas (6); hawking, stocks (7); leper (8); hangar (9); machetes (11); diplomatic (12); exoticism, coup, evacuate (13); ornamental, stein (16); fortitude (19); hobnobbing, symbiosis, report, canopy, eucalyptus (21).

Suggestions for Writing

1. **FROM JOURNAL TO ESSAY** Starting from your journal entry (p. 211), write an essay about a difficult experience that shows how it changed you, whether for better or for worse. How are you different now than before? What did the experience teach you?

2. In your library or on the Internet, locate and read reviews of Sedaris's book *Me Talk Pretty One Day*, the source of "Remembering My Childhood," or of another essay collection by Sedaris. Write an essay in which you SYNTHESIZE the reviewers' responses to Sedaris's work.

3. **CRITICAL WRITING** How seriously does Sedaris want the readers of his essay to take him? Write an essay in which you analyze his TONE, citing specific passages from the text to support your conclusions.

4. **CONNECTIONS** Andrea Roman, in "We're Not . . ." (p. 215), writes about a childhood unlike Sedaris's or Hugh's. In an essay, consider how Sedaris and Roman might view each other's childhoods.

David Sedaris on Writing

In "Day In, Day Out," an essay in *Let's Explore Diabetes with Owls*, Sedaris explains why he started keeping a diary and how it has become essential to his work as a writer. He begins by describing an afternoon transcribing snippets from a newspaper with a friend's young son, who interrupts to ask him, "But why? . . . What's the point?" Sedaris goes on:

That's a question I've asked myself every day since September 5, 1977. I hadn't known on September 4 that the following afternoon, I would start keeping a diary, or that it would consume me for the next thirty-five years and counting. It wasn't something I'd been putting off, but once I began, I knew that I had to keep doing it. I knew as well that what I was writing was not a journal, but an old-fashioned, girlish, Keep-Out-This-Means-You diary. Often the terms are used interchangeably, though I've never understood why. Both have the word "day" at their root, but a journal, in my opinion, is a repository of ideas — your brain on the page. A diary, by contrast, is your heart. As for "journal*ing*," a verb that cropped up at around the same time as "scrapbook-ing," that just means you're spooky and have way too much time on your hands.

A few things have changed since that first entry in 1977, but I've never wavered in my devotion, skipping, on average, maybe one or two days a year. It's not that I think my life is important or that future generations might care to know that on June 6, 2009, a woman with a deaf, drug-addicted mother-in-law taught me to say "I need you to stop being an [expletive]" in sign language. Perhaps it just feeds into my compulsive nature, the need to do the exact same thing at the exact same time every morning. Some diary sessions are longer than others, but the length has more to do with my mood than with what's been going on. I met [actor] Gene Hackman once, and wrote three hundred words about it. Six weeks later I watched a centipede attack and kill a worm and filled two pages. And I really *like* Gene Hackman. . . .

Over a given three-month period, there may be fifty bits worth noting, and six that, with a little work, I might consider reading out loud. . . . Here is a passenger on the Eurostar from Paris to London, an American woman in a sand-colored vest hitting her teenage granddaughter with a guidebook until the girl cries. "You are a very lazy, very selfish person," she scolds. "Nothing like your sister."

If I sit down six months or a year or five years from now and decide to put this into an essay, I'll no doubt berate myself for not adding more details. What sort of shoes was the granddaughter wearing? What was the name of the book the old woman was hitting her with? But if you added every detail of everything that struck you as curious or spectacular, you'd have no time for anything else. As it is, I seem to be pushing it. Hugh and I will go on a trip, and while he's out, walking the streets of Manila or Reykjavik or wherever we happen to be, I'm back at the hotel, writing about an argument we'd over-heard in the breakfast room. It's not lost on me that I'm so busy recording life, I don't have time to live it. I've become like one of those people I hate, the sort who go to a museum and, instead of looking at the magnificent Brueghel, take a picture of it, reducing it from art to proof. It's not "Look what Brueghel did, painted this masterpiece" but "Look what *I* did, went to Rotterdam and stood in front of a Brueghel painting!"

Were I to leave the hotel *without* writing in my diary, though, I'd feel too antsy and incomplete to enjoy myself. Even if what I'm recording is of no consequence, I've got to put it down on paper.

The Bedford Reader on Writing

Sedaris insists on making a distinction between a diary and a JOURNAL, but his practice of keeping daily notes fits neatly with our suggestions, on pages 4 and 33 and in every set of journal prompts (such as those following "Remembering My Childhood on the Continent of Africa"), to write informally on a regular basis. As Sedaris shows us, the observations and ideas sketched out quickly for oneself can often be transformed into full essays — even months or years later.

ANDREA ROMAN

The daughter of Bolivian immigrants, Andrea Roman was born in 1992 in Washington, DC, and grew up in Rockville, Maryland. She attended Saint Andrews Episcopal School, where she was captain of the varsity girls' soccer team and a volunteer medical translator. As a political science major at Boston College, she volunteered as a Big Sister and served on the cabinet for the school's Organization of Latin American Affairs. Roman graduated in 2014 and is now pursuing a master's degree in education at the University of Pennsylvania, where she works with Teach for America and remains "extremely devoted" to Caporales, a popular Bolivian folk dance.

"We're Not . . ."

Roman wrote "We're Not . . ." at the end of a first-year writing seminar. She revised it with feedback from her classmates and saw it selected for *Fresh Ink*, Boston College's annual collection of student writing. Assigned to write a personal account of a significant event in her life, she chose to focus on a series of disagreements with her mother. Like David Sedaris in the previous essay, Roman compares two distinct cultures, both of them important to the writer's identity.

"No somos pobres, Andrea. Para qué tienes que prestar ropa?"[1] These were 1 words I heard continually from my mother as I grew up. My parents, being immigrants from Bolivia during the eighties, experienced a complete culture clash when they arrived in America. One would think that language would create the biggest barriers for immigrants but in my mother's case, the biggest obstacles were the small cultural differences. Sooner or later, this became a generic formula for strict rules given by my parents: "We're not _____, Andrea. Why do you have to _____?" Typically, the first blank was filled in by the word "American," while the second invariably changed. My mother could not understand that certain unacceptable actions in our culture were quite acceptable here in the States.

I was eleven years old when I first showed up at my house with an article 2 of clothing that was not mine. I had spilled hot chocolate all over my sweater

---

[1] Spanish, "We're not poor, Andrea. Why do you have to borrow clothes?" — EDS.

during lunch that day. Luckily, my best friend Emily had an extra zip-up in her locker. As any good friend would do, she offered me her sweater to wear for the rest of the day since it was the middle of December. Logically, I accepted the sweater with gratitude and went on with my day as if nothing strange had happened. Little did I know, when my mother picked me up from school, I would receive the familiar speech about how embarrassing my act had been.

"De quien es esa chompa?!" Those were the very first words that came out   3
of my mother's mouth. Not a breath, not an intake of air, just these words in a ridiculing tone: "Whose sweater is that?!" I remained clueless and answered the question, simply, "Emily's." Immediately after my answer, my mother gave me one of the longest speeches I have ever heard. "We're not poor, Andrea. Why do you have to borrow clothes? I buy you clothes. You have sweaters. You wore one this morning!" I could not grasp the magnitude of my mother's anger or disturbance as I did not see what the big deal was in borrowing a sweater. Kids in my class did it all the time without any problem. They'd borrow a sweater one day and give it back the other. It was as simple as that — but not to my mother. "In Bolivia," my mother said, "we do not borrow clothes from other people. It is seen as an insult to the family in saying that we cannot afford to take care of our family. It's a want of an unnecessary thing seeing as you already have your own." The speech went on and on, usually repeating the same points, until I finally got a word in: "I stained my sweater. I had nothing to wear and was cold. I just don't see why it's such a big deal." Boy, was that a mistake. Talking back to my mother was the worst thing I could have done. The second I got home I got a good deep mouth-washing with dishwasher soap as punishment.

"We're not American, Andrea. Why do you want a sleepover?" Sleepovers   4
were a big no to my family. In fact, they were unheard of. "You want to sleep where?" If my girlfriends were having a slumber party over the weekend, I knew better than to ask for permission. I learned this through multiple attempts and failed experiences: *"Mami, puedo ir a dormir donde la Caroline este viernes, porfa?"* *"Para qué?"* Great. Every time I asked to sleep over at a friend's house my mother's response was always, "Why?"

So I would then respond, "Because all my friends are sleeping over and it's   5
going to be fun and her parents said we could all spend the night."

"Mmm, then no."   6

"Pero por qué???"   7

"Te dije que no."[2]   8

And just like that my attempt to go to a sleepover would end.   9

---

[2] Spanish, "I told you no." — Eds.

"We're not American, Andrea. We don't do that in Bolivia. Everyone has   10
their own house for a reason. If you want to go over to Caroline's your father
will gladly take you and pick you up later tonight, but don't try to convince
him to stay over because it just won't work."

I suppose my mother letting me go to Caroline's for some time was better than   11
nothing, yet I always longed for that sleepover. Growing up, I quickly learned
that what my mother said was the rule in the household. After several attempts
to attend a sleepover, I gave up — not because I didn't want to sleep over, but
because I began to understand why my mother didn't want me to stay over.

Sunday, 1:00 p.m. My family is just getting out of church and deciding   12
where to go for lunch, when all of a sudden I remember that a six-page paper
is due in class on Monday. I assume I had a stunned look on my face, because
my mother asked what was wrong.

"Oh, nothing. I just remembered that I have an essay due tomorrow, so   13
I'll probably have to start working on that rather soon, if that influences our
lunch decision."

"You mean to say that you left all your homework due Monday to do   14
today?"

"Yeah . . ."   15

"Why would you do that? Don't you know Sunday is family day? A day to   16
worship God and be thankful for family?"

"Yes . . ."   17

"Okay then, so you don't have any work due tomorrow right?"   18

"No, Mami, I just said I have an essay due."   19

"Sundays are not the day to leave homework for. That's why you get Friday   20
and Saturday. You have two days to complete it; there is no reason why you
need Sunday, too."

Geesh. My mother sure did accumulate rules over the years.   21

"Okay, Mami, but I really have to do this essay now."   22

"Well you should have thought of that sooner, no?"   23

Silence overtook the car on our way home and I could feel the disappoint-   24
ment on my mother's face.

When I first arrived at Boston College, I immediately knew that my con-   25
servative cultural position would have to become more open-minded. I knew
that not everyone had grown up with strict Bolivian parents, as I had. I would
not have to lose my cultural identity, however.

As I lay in my new bed for the very first time in an unfamiliar room filled   26
with familiar things, I started to ask myself the same question that my hall
mates confronted me with: "Why do you have such a big American flag?" This

question constantly arose when I met someone. Why *did* I have an American flag next to my Bolivian one? My mother instilled Bolivian values in me; Bolivian culture was the only thing I had ever been exposed to, and I loved it. I had just bought this American flag a week before move-in day for my room decorations.

Through my mother's multiple rules, I had become comfortable enough 27 with my identity and culture that showing pride in another country would not take away from my heritage. I now borrow clothes, have sleepovers, and do a ton of work on Sundays, but I have not left behind that little Bolivian girl who received the mouth-washing with dishwasher soap, no matter what flag hangs on my wall.

Journal Writing

Write about a time when you were punished for an act that you didn't think was a "big deal." What did you do, and what was the punishment? Was it fair? How did the situation make you feel about your action? about whoever punished you? about yourself? about others involved, such as anyone who may have gotten you into trouble?

Questions on Meaning

1. What is Roman's THESIS? Where does she state it?

2. What seems to be Roman's PURPOSE in this essay? Does she mean to explain or to evaluate? How can you tell?

3. Why was Roman's mother so upset that her daughter borrowed a sweater from a classmate? What prompted her to wash Roman's mouth with soap?

4. Why does Roman hang two flags on the wall of her dorm room? What do they represent to her?

Questions on Writing Strategy

1. What is the function of the extra spaces between certain paragraphs in Roman's essay? What do they indicate?

2. Roman organizes her essay point by point. What points does she compare? What is her basis of comparison?

3. To whom does Roman seem to be writing? Why do you think so?

4. What is notable about Roman's concluding paragraph?

5. **OTHER METHODS** Roman uses NARRATION to relate three telling episodes involving her mother. What does the dialog contribute to her essay?

Questions on Language

1. How does Roman ensure that English-speaking readers will understand the Spanish phrases she quotes in her essay? Are any statements left unclear to you?

2. Where in the essay does Roman include variations on her mother's complaint "We're not _____, Andrea. Why do you have to _____?" (par. 1)? What is the EFFECT of this repetition?

3. Consult a dictionary if necessary to learn the meanings of the following words: invariably (par. 1), magnitude (3), accumulate (21), instilled (26), heritage (27).

Suggestions for Writing

1. **FROM JOURNAL TO ESSAY** Based on your journal entry, write an essay in which you narrate your experience (or, perhaps, experiences) with being punished while growing up. As you plan and draft your essay, try to draw a larger point about the results of the punishment(s) on your sense of fairness. What did you learn about yourself and the world around you?

2. Roman writes of differences with her mother that frustrated her but that also helped form her sense of identity. In a narrative and descriptive essay, relate some aspect of a relationship with a parent or other figure of authority that you found troubling or even maddening at the time but that now seems to have shaped you in positive ways. Did a parent (or someone else) push you to study when you wanted to play sports or hang out with your friends? make you attend religious services when they seemed unimportant to you? refuse to let you participate in certain activities? try to direct you onto a path that you didn't care to take?

3. **CRITICAL WRITING** Roman attributes many of her mother's attitudes to her Bolivian heritage. As an extension of the previous assignment, consider whether Roman's experiences are particular to Bolivian American families or are common in all families, whatever their ethnicity. Are conflicts between children and their parents inevitable, do you think? Why, or why not?

4. **CONNECTIONS** Much as David Sedaris, in the previous essay, expresses envy for his partner's more exotic childhood in Africa, Roman reveals a certain amount of envy for her classmates' less restrictive American upbringings. Write an essay in which you compare and contrast your own experiences with those of someone you've envied. What in that person's life was attractive to you? Have your feelings, like Sedaris's and Roman's, changed over time? Why, or why not?

Andrea Roman on Writing

Asked how she chose the SUBJECT for "We're Not . . . ," Andrea Roman answered, "I had a lot of difficulty in deciding what to write about because truthfully, I didn't think I was all that interesting." Away from her family, she was painfully homesick and seriously contemplated moving back. Being assigned to write about an event in her life prompted Roman to think about why she was having such a hard time adjusting to college. "After a lot of self-reflection," she says, she pinpointed the source of her discomfort: While at home her "school-life was separate from home-life," at college "school *was* home." For the first time, she felt her "two cultures were colliding." The effort to "integrate" her "American and Bolivian lives," she decided, was a struggle worth exploring in writing.

Roman wrote two drafts and then, with "amazing help" from her teacher and her classmates, was able to "refine and refocus the most important aspects" of her experience. "They informed me of the parts they found most interesting," she explains, "so that I could expand on those specific ideas and events." By the time she was finished, she was gratified to discover that writing had "guided" her "in understanding and embracing the difficult time" she was having. Roman encourages other writers to always ask for feedback as well, particularly when writing about their own lives. "You lived through the story," she points out, "but no one else did. An outsider's perspective can highlight ambiguity and confusion" and help you "be as clear as possible."

The best advice Roman ever received? "Don't hold back, be true, and let yourself go." She explains why this mantra has proven so useful: "Our personal experiences and inspirations can never be taken away from us, and we should not shy away from telling our stories. If we do not share our obstacles and adversities, they will be lost and unheard. When you try to write what you think the audience wants, a feeling of forcedness is apparent. Inversely, when you write truthfully, genuineness becomes evident."

The Bedford Reader on Writing

Roman's experience bears out a lesson that many beginning writers have trouble grasping: DRAFTING provides an opportunity to explore a subject for yourself, to "let yourself go" and discover what you think. REVISION is the time to rework an essay with a particular AUDIENCE in mind. For help identifying the most interesting parts of your drafts and developing those ideas with specifics, you can always turn to your peers — and to pages 39–42 of this book.

SUZANNE BRITT

Suzanne Britt was born in Winston-Salem, North Carolina, and studied at Salem College and Washington University, where she earned an MA in English. Britt has written for *Sky Magazine*, the *New York Times*, *Newsweek*, the *Boston Globe*, and many other publications. Her poems have been published in the *Denver Quarterly*, the *Southern Poetry Review*, and similar literary magazines. Britt teaches English at Meredith College in North Carolina and has published a history of the college and two English textbooks. Her other books are collections of her essays: *Skinny People Are Dull and Crunchy like Carrots* (1982) and *Show and Tell* (1983).

Neat People vs. Sloppy People

"Neat People vs. Sloppy People" appears in Britt's collection *Show and Tell*. Mingling humor with seriousness (as she often does), Britt has called the book a report on her journey into "the awful cave of self: You shout your name and voices come back in exultant response, telling you their names." In this essay, Britt uses comparison mainly to entertain by showing us aspects of our own selves, awful or not.

I've finally figured out the difference between neat people and sloppy people. The distinction is, as always, moral. Neat people are lazier and meaner than sloppy people.

Sloppy people, you see, are not really sloppy. Their sloppiness is merely the unfortunate consequence of their extreme moral rectitude. Sloppy people carry in their mind's eye a heavenly vision, a precise plan, that is so stupendous, so perfect, it can't be achieved in this world or the next.

Sloppy people live in Never-Never Land. Someday is their métier. Someday they are planning to alphabetize all their books and set up home catalogs. Someday they will go through their wardrobes and mark certain items for tentative mending and certain items for passing on to relatives of similar shape and size. Someday sloppy people will make family scrapbooks into which they will put newspaper clippings, postcards, locks of hair, and the dried corsage from their senior prom. Someday they will file everything on the surface of their desks, including the cash receipts from coffee purchases at the snack shop. Someday they will sit down and read all the back issues of *The New Yorker*.

For all these noble reasons and more, sloppy people never get neat. They aim too high and wide. They save everything, planning someday to file, order, and straighten out the world. But while these ambitious plans take clearer and clearer shape in their heads, the books spill from the shelves onto the floor, the clothes pile up in the hamper and closet, the family mementos accumulate in every drawer, the surface of the desk is buried under mounds of paper, and the unread magazines threaten to reach the ceiling.

Sloppy people can't bear to part with anything. They give loving atten- 5 tion to every detail. When sloppy people say they're going to tackle the sur- face of a desk, they really mean it. Not a paper will go unturned; not a rubber band will go unboxed. Four hours or two weeks into the excavation, the desk looks exactly the same, primarily because the sloppy person is meticulously creating new piles of papers with new headings and scrupulously stopping to read all the old book catalogs before he throws them away. A neat person would just bulldoze the desk.

Neat people are bums and clods at heart. They have cavalier attitudes 6 toward possessions, including family heirlooms. Everything is just another dust-catcher to them. If anything collects dust, it's got to go and that's that. Neat people will toy with the idea of throwing the children out of the house just to cut down on the clutter.

Neat people don't care about process. They like results. What they want 7 to do is get the whole thing over with so they can sit down and watch the rass- lin' on TV. Neat people operate on two unvarying principles: Never handle any item twice, and throw everything away.

The only thing messy in a neat person's house is the trash can. The min- 8 ute something comes to a neat person's hand, he will look at it, try to decide if it has immediate use and, finding none, throw it in the trash.

Neat people are especially vicious with mail. They never go through their 9 mail unless they are standing directly over a trash can. If the trash can is beside the mailbox, even better. All ads, catalogs, pleas for charitable contributions, church bulletins, and money-saving coupons go straight into the trash can without being opened. All letters from home, postcards from Europe, bills, and paychecks are opened, immediately responded to, then dropped in the trash can. Neat people keep their receipts only for tax purposes. That's it. No sentimental salvaging of birthday cards or the last letter a dying relative ever wrote. Into the trash it goes.

Neat people place neatness above everything, even economics. They are 10 incredibly wasteful. Neat people throw away several toys every time they walk through the den. I knew a neat person once who threw away a perfectly good dish drainer because it had mold on it. The drainer was too much trouble to wash. And neat people sell their furniture when they move. They will sell a La-Z-Boy recliner while you are reclining in it.

Neat people are no good to borrow from. Neat people buy everything in 11 expensive little single portions. They get their flour and sugar in two-pound bags. They wouldn't consider clipping a coupon, saving a leftover, reusing plastic nondairy whipped cream containers, or rinsing off tin foil and draping it over the unmoldy dish drainer. You can never borrow a neat person's newspaper to see what's playing at the movies. Neat people have the paper all wadded up and in the trash by 7:05 a.m.

Neat people cut a clean swath through the organic as well as the inorganic   12 world. People, animals, and things are all one to them. They are so insensitive. After they've finished with the pantry, the medicine cabinet, and the attic, they will throw out the red geranium (too many leaves), sell the dog (too many fleas), and send the children off to boarding school (too many scuff-marks on the hardwood floors).

Journal Writing

Britt suggests that grouping people according to oppositions, such as neat versus sloppy, reveals other things about them. Write about the oppositions you use to evaluate people. Smart versus dumb? Fit versus out of shape? Rich versus poor? Outgoing versus shy? Open-minded versus narrow-minded? Something else?

Questions on Meaning

1. "Suzanne Britt believes that neat people are lazy, mean, petty, callous, wasteful, and insensitive." How would you respond to this statement?

2. Is the author's main PURPOSE to make fun of neat people, to assess the habits of neat and sloppy people, to help neat and sloppy people get along better, to defend sloppy people, to amuse and entertain, or to prove that neat people are morally inferior to sloppy people? Discuss.

3. What is meant by "as always" in the sentence "The distinction is, as always, moral" (par. 1)? Does the author seem to be suggesting that any and all distinctions between people are moral?

Questions on Writing Strategy

1. What is the general TONE of this essay? What words and phrases help you determine that tone?

2. Britt mentions no similarities between neat and sloppy people. Does that mean this is not a good comparison-and-contrast essay? Why might a writer deliberately focus on differences and give very little or no time to similarities?

3. How does Britt use repetition to clarify her comparison?

4. Consider the following GENERALIZATIONS: "For all these noble reasons and more, sloppy people never get neat" (par. 4) and "The only thing messy in a neat person's house is the trash can" (8). How can you tell that these statements are generalizations? Look for other generalizations in the essay. What is the EFFECT of using so many?

5. **OTHER METHODS**   Although filled with generalizations, Britt's essay does not lack for EXAMPLES. Study the examples in paragraph 11, and explain how they do and don't work the way they should: to bring the generalizations about people down to earth.

Questions on Language

1. Consult your dictionary for definitions of these words: rectitude (par. 2); métier, tentative (3); accumulate (4); excavation, meticulously, scrupulously (5); salvaging (9).

2. How do you understand the use of the word *noble* in the first sentence of paragraph 4? Is it meant literally? Are there other words in the essay that appear to be written in a similar tone?

Suggestions for Writing

1. **FROM JOURNAL TO ESSAY**   From your journal entry (p. 223), choose your favorite opposition for evaluating people, and write an essay in which you compare and contrast those who pass your "test" with those who fail it. You may choose to write a tongue-in-cheek essay, as Britt does, or a serious one.

2. Write an essay in which you compare and contrast two apparently dissimilar groups of people: for example, blue-collar workers and white-collar workers, people who send a lot of text messages and people who don't bother with them, cyclists and football players, readers and TV watchers, or any other variation you choose. Your approach may be either lighthearted or serious, but make sure you come to some conclusion about your subjects. Which group do you favor? Why?

3. **CRITICAL WRITING**   Britt's essay is remarkable for its exaggeration of the two types. Write a brief essay analyzing and contrasting the ways Britt characterizes sloppy people and neat people. Be sure to consider the CONNOTATIONS of the words, such as "moral rectitude" for sloppy people (par. 2) and "cavalier" for neat people (6).

4. **CONNECTIONS**   Write an essay about the humor gained from exaggeration, relying on Britt's essay, Russell Baker's "The Plot against People" (p. 373), and Randall Munroe's "Everybody Jump" (p. 410). Why is exaggeration often funny? What qualities does humorous exaggeration have? Quote and PARAPHRASE from all three essays for your support.

Suzanne Britt on Writing

Asked to tell how she writes, Suzanne Britt contributed the following comment for this book.

The question "How do you write?" gets a snappy, snappish response from me. The first commandment is "Live!" And the second is like unto it: "Pay attention!" I don't mean that you have to live high or fast or deep or wise or broad. And I certainly don't mean you have to live true and upright. I just mean that you have to suck out all the marrow of whatever you do, whether it's picking the lint off the navy-blue suit you'll be wearing to Cousin Ione's funeral or popping an Aunt Jemima frozen waffle into the toaster oven or lying between sand dunes, watching the way the sea oats slice the azure sky. The ominous question put to me by students on all occasions of possible account-ability is "Will this count?" My answer is rock bottom and hard: "Everything counts," I say, and silence falls like prayers across the room.

The same is true of writing. Everything counts. Despair is good. Numb-ness can be excellent. Misery is fine. Ecstasy will work — or pain or sorrow or passion. The only thing that won't work is indifference. A writer refuses to be shocked and appalled by anything going or coming, rising or falling, singing or soundless. The only thing that shocks me, truth to tell, is indifference. How dare you not fight for the right to the crispy end piece on the standing-rib roast? How dare you let the fragrance of Joy go by without taking a whiff of it? How dare you not see the old woman in the snap-front housedress and the rolled-down socks, carrying her Polident and Charmin in a canvas tote that says, simply, elegantly, Le Bag?

After you have lived, paid attention, seen connections, felt the harmony, writhed under the dissonance, fixed a Diet Coke, popped a big stick of Juicy Fruit in your mouth, gathered your life around you as a mother hen gathers her brood, as a queen settles the folds in her purple robes, you are ready to write. And what you will write about, even if you have one of those teachers who makes you write about, say, Guatemala, will be something very exclusive and intimate — something just between you and Guatemala. All you have to find out is what that small intimacy might be. It is there. And having found it, you have to make it count.

There is no rest for a writer. But there is no boredom either. A Sunday morning with a bottle of extra-strength aspirin within easy reach and an ice bag on your head can serve you very well in writing. So can a fly buzzing at your ear or a heart-stopping siren in the night or an interminable afternoon in a biology lab in front of a frog's innards.

All you need, really, is the audacity to believe, with your whole being, that if you tell it right, tell it truly, tell it so we can all see it, the "it" will play in Peoria, Poughkeepsie, Pompeii, or Podunk. In the South we call that conviction, that audacity, an act of faith. But you can call it writing.

The Bedford Reader on Writing

What advice would *we* give a student assigned to write a paper about, say, Guatemala? Like Britt, we suggest that you study the SUBJECT long enough to find some personal connection or interest in it, ask questions, and do some RESEARCH to find the answers. For more on how, see "Discovering Ideas" in Chapter 2 (pp. 32–34) and "Using the Library" in the Appendix (p. 624).

BRUCE CATTON

Bruce Catton (1899–1978) was one of America's best-known historians of the American Civil War. As a boy in Benzonia, Michigan, Catton acted out historical battles on local playing fields. In his memoir *Waiting for the Morning Train* (1972), he recalls how he would listen by the hour to the memories of Union army veterans. His studies at Oberlin College were interrupted by service in World War I, and he never finished his bachelor's degree. Instead, he worked as a reporter, columnist, and editorial writer for the *Cleveland Plain Dealer* and other newspapers, then became a speechwriter and information director for government agencies. Of Catton's eighteen books, seventeen were written after he turned fifty. *A Stillness at Appomattox* (1953) won him both a Pulitzer Prize for history and a National Book Award; other notable works include *This Hallowed Ground* (1956) and *Gettysburg: The Final Fury* (1974). From 1954 until his death, Catton edited *American Heritage*, a magazine of history. President Gerald Ford awarded him a Medal of Freedom for his life's accomplishment.

Grant and Lee: A Study in Contrasts

"Grant and Lee: A Study in Contrasts" first appeared in *The American Story*, a book of essays written by eminent historians for interested general readers. Ulysses S. Grant and Robert E. Lee were opposing generals of the Civil War, Grant commanding forces of the North and Lee commanding forces of the South (called the Confederacy). The war lasted from 1861 to 1865, ending with Lee's surrender to Grant during the meeting Catton describes. Contrasting the two great generals allows Catton to portray not only two very different men but also the conflicting traditions they represented. Catton's essay builds toward the conclusion that, in one outstanding way, the two leaders were more than a little alike.

When Ulysses S. Grant and Robert E. Lee met in the parlor of a modest house at Appomattox Court House, Virginia, on April 9, 1865, to work out the terms for the surrender of Lee's Army of Northern Virginia, a great chapter in American life came to a close, and a great new chapter began. 1

These men were bringing the Civil War to its virtual finish. To be sure, other armies had yet to surrender, and for a few days the fugitive Confederate government would struggle desperately and vainly, trying to find some way to go on living now that its chief support was gone. But in effect it was all over when Grant and Lee signed the papers. And the little room where they wrote out the terms was the scene of one of the poignant, dramatic contrasts in American history. 2

227

They were two strong men, these oddly different generals, and they 3
represented the strengths of two conflicting currents that, through them, had
come into final collision.

Back of Robert E. Lee was the notion that the old aristocratic concept 4
might somehow survive and be dominant in American life.

Lee was tidewater Virginia, and in his background were family, culture, 5
and tradition . . . the age of chivalry transplanted to a New World which was
making its own legends and its own myths. He embodied a way of life that had
come down through the age of knighthood and the English country squire.
America was a land that was beginning all over again, dedicated to nothing
much more complicated than the rather hazy belief that all men had equal
rights, and should have an equal chance in the world. In such a land Lee stood
for the feeling that it was somehow of advantage to human society to have a
pronounced inequality in the social structure. There should be a leisure class,
backed by ownership of land; in turn, society itself should be keyed to the land
as the chief source of wealth and influence. It would bring forth (according to
this ideal) a class of men with a strong sense of obligation to the community;
men who lived not to gain advantage for themselves, but to meet the solemn
obligations which had been laid on them by the very fact that they were privileged. From them the country would get its leadership; to them it could look
for the higher values — of thought, of conduct, of personal deportment — to
give it strength and virtue.

Lee embodied the noblest elements of this aristocratic ideal. Through 6
him, the landed nobility justified itself. For four years, the Southern states had
fought a desperate war to uphold the ideals for which Lee stood. In the end,
it almost seemed as if the Confederacy fought for Lee; as if he himself was the
Confederacy . . . the best thing that the way of life for which the Confederacy
stood could ever have to offer. He had passed into legend before Appomattox.
Thousands of tired, underfed, poorly clothed Confederate soldiers, long since
past the simple enthusiasm of the early days of the struggle, somehow considered Lee the symbol of everything for which they had been willing to die. But
they could not quite put this feeling into words. If the Lost Cause, sanctified
by so much heroism and so many deaths, had a living justification, its justification was General Lee.

Grant, the son of a tanner on the Western frontier, was everything Lee 7
was not. He had come up the hard way, and embodied nothing in particular
except the eternal toughness and sinewy fiber of the men who grew up beyond
the mountains. He was one of a body of men who owed reverence and obeisance to no one, who were self-reliant to a fault, who cared hardly anything
for the past but who had a sharp eye for the future.

These frontier men were the precise opposites of the tidewater aristocrats. 8
Back of them, in the great surge that had taken people over the Alleghenies
and into the opening Western country, there was a deep, implicit dissatisfaction with a past that had settled into grooves. They stood for democracy, not
from any reasoned conclusion about the proper ordering of human society, but
simply because they had grown up in the middle of democracy and knew how
it worked. Their society might have privileges, but they would be privileges
each man had won for himself. Forms and patterns meant nothing. No man
was born to anything, except perhaps to a chance to show how far he could
rise. Life was competition.

Yet along with this feeling had come a deep sense of belonging to a 9
national community. The Westerner who developed a farm, opened a shop, or
set up in business as a trader could hope to prosper only as his own community
prospered — and his community ran from the Atlantic to the Pacific and from
Canada down to Mexico. If the land was settled, with towns and highways
and accessible markets, he could better himself. He saw his fate in terms of the
nation's own destiny. As its horizons expanded, so did his. He had, in other
words, an acute dollars-and-cents stake in the continued growth and development of his country.

And that, perhaps, is where the contrast between Grant and Lee becomes 10
most striking. The Virginia aristocrat, inevitably, saw himself in relation to his
own region. He lived in a static society which could endure almost anything
except change. Instinctively, his first loyalty would go to the locality in which
that society existed. He would fight to the limit of endurance to defend it,
because in defending it he was defending everything that gave his own life its
deepest meaning.

The Westerner, on the other hand, would fight with an equal tenacity 11
for the broader concept of society. He fought so because everything he lived
by was tied to growth, expansion, and a constantly widening horizon. What
he lived by would survive or fall with the nation itself. He could not possibly
stand by unmoved in the face of an attempt to destroy the Union. He would
combat it with everything he had, because he could only see it as an effort to
cut the ground out from under his feet.

So Grant and Lee were in complete contrast, representing two diametri- 12
cally opposed elements in American life. Grant was the modern man emerging; beyond him, ready to come on the stage, was the great age of steel and
machinery, of crowded cities and a restless, burgeoning vitality. Lee might
have ridden down from the old age of chivalry, lance in hand, silken banner
fluttering over his head. Each man was the perfect champion of his cause,
drawing both his strengths and his weaknesses from the people he led.

Yet it was not all contrast, after all. Different as they were — in   13
background, in personality, in underlying aspiration — these two great soldiers had much in common. Under everything else, they were marvelous
fighters. Furthermore, their fighting qualities were really very much alike.

Each man had, to begin with, the great virtue of utter tenacity and fidel-   14
ity. Grant fought his way down the Mississippi Valley in spite of acute personal discouragement and profound military handicaps. Lee hung on in the
trenches at Petersburg after hope itself had died. In each man there was an
indomitable quality . . . the born fighter's refusal to give up as long as he can
still remain on his feet and lift his two fists.

Daring and resourcefulness they had, too; the ability to think faster   15
and move faster than the enemy. These were the qualities which gave Lee
the dazzling campaigns of Second Manassas and Chancellorsville and won
Vicksburg for Grant.

Lastly, and perhaps greatest of all, there was the ability, at the end, to turn   16
quickly from war to peace once the fighting was over. Out of the way these
two men behaved at Appomattox came the possibility of a peace of reconciliation. It was a possibility not wholly realized, in the years to come, but which
did, in the end, help the two sections to become one nation again . . . after
a war whose bitterness might have seemed to make such a reunion wholly
impossible. No part of either man's life became him more than the part he
played in their brief meeting in the McLean house at Appomattox. Their
behavior there put all succeeding generations of Americans in their debt. Two
great Americans, Grant and Lee — very different, yet under everything very
much alike. Their encounter at Appomattox was one of the great moments of
American history.

Journal Writing

How do you respond to the opposing political beliefs represented by Grant and Lee?
During the American Civil War, nearly every citizen had an opinion and chose sides.
Do you think Americans today commit themselves as strongly to political and social
causes? In your journal, explain why, or why not.

Questions on Meaning

1. What is Catton's PURPOSE in writing: to describe the meeting of two generals at a
   famous moment in history, to explain how the two men stood for opposing social
   forces in America, or to show how the two differed in personality?

2. SUMMARIZE the background and the way of life that produced Robert E. Lee; then do the same for Ulysses S. Grant. According to Catton, what ideals did each man represent?

3. In the historian's view, what essential traits did the two men have in common? Which trait does Catton think most important of all? For what reason?

4. How does this essay help you understand why Grant and Lee were such determined fighters?

Questions on Writing Strategy

1. From the content of this essay, and from knowing where it first appeared, what can you INFER about Catton's original AUDIENCE? At what places in "Grant and Lee: A Study in Contrasts" does the writer expect of his readers a familiarity with US history?

2. What EFFECT does the writer achieve by setting both his INTRODUCTION and his CONCLUSION in Appomattox?

3. For what reasons does Catton contrast the two generals *before* he compares them? Suppose he had reversed his outline, and had dealt first with Grant's and Lee's mutual resemblances. Why would his essay have been less effective?

4. Closely read the first sentence of every paragraph and underline each word or phrase in it that serves as a TRANSITION. Then review your underlinings. How much COHERENCE has Catton given his essay?

5. What is the TONE of this essay — that is, what is the writer's attitude toward his two subjects? Is Catton poking fun at Lee by imagining the Confederate general as a knight of the Middle Ages, "lance in hand, silken banner fluttering over his head" (par. 12)?

6. **OTHER METHODS**   In identifying "two conflicting currents," Catton uses CLAS-SIFICATION to sort Civil War–era Americans into two groups represented by Lee and Grant. Catton then uses ANALYSIS to tease out the characteristics of each current, each type. How do classification and analysis serve Catton's comparison and contrast?

Questions on Language

1. In his opening paragraph, Catton uses a metaphor: American life is a book containing chapters. Find other FIGURES OF SPEECH in his essay (consulting the Glossary if you need help). What do the figures of speech contribute?

2. What information do you glean from "Lee was tidewater Virginia" (par. 5)?

3. Look up *poignant* in the dictionary. Why is it such a fitting word in paragraph 2? Why wouldn't *touching*, *sad*, or *teary* have been as good?

4. Define *aristocratic* (pars. 4 and 6), *obeisance* (7), and *indomitable* (14) as Catton uses them, based solely on their context in the essay.

Suggestions for Writing

1. **FROM JOURNAL TO ESSAY** Using your journal entry (p. 230) as a starting point, write an essay that offers an explanation for public participation in or commitment to political and social causes today. What fires people up or turns them off? To help focus your essay, zero in on a specific issue, such as education, government spending, health insurance, or terrorism.

2. In your thinking and your attitudes, whom do you more closely resemble — Grant or Lee? Compare and contrast your outlook with that of one of these famous Americans or the other. (A serious tone for this topic isn't required.)

3. Catton writes with respect for the Confederacy and its values as they were exemplified in Robert E. Lee's background and beliefs. The flag that Lee fought under is currently the subject of much heated debate, as some argue that it represents hatred and violence against African Americans, while others insist that it represents Southern tradition and heritage. What is your take on the issue? Should any states or institutions, for instance, fly the Confederate flag on public land? Should individuals display it on their private property or on their persons? Why do you feel the way you do? Present your argument in a brief essay, taking care to consider both sides of the debate.

4. **CRITICAL WRITING** Although slavery, along with other issues, helped precipitate the Civil War, Catton in this particular essay does not deal with it. Perhaps he assumes that his readers will supply the missing context themselves. Is this a fair ASSUMPTION? If Catton had recalled the facts of slavery, would he have undermined any of his assertions about Lee? (Though the general of the pro-slavery Confederacy, Lee was personally opposed to slavery.) In a brief essay, judge whether or not the omission of slavery weakens the essay, and explain why.

5. **CONNECTIONS** Catton contrasts Robert E. Lee's and Ulysses S. Grant's ideas about the privileges and obligations inherent in aristocracy and democracy, respectively. Tal Fortgang, in "Checking My Privilege" (p. 446), and Roxane Gay, in "Peculiar Benefits" (p. 453), also examine the notion that some people enjoy built-in advantages in American society. In a brief essay full of specific examples, discuss whether the "two diametrically opposed elements in American life" (as Catton calls them in par. 12) still exist in the country today. Is there any "advantage to human society to have a pronounced inequality in the social structure," as Lee believed (5)? Or is it true, as Grant exemplified, that nobody "was born to anything, except perhaps to a chance to show how far he could rise" (8)?

FATEMA MERNISSI

A teacher, writer, and feminist sociologist, Fatema Mernissi was born in 1940 in Fez, Morocco, and educated at the University of Mohammed V in Rabat, the Sorbonne in Paris, and Brandeis University in Massachusetts, from which she earned a PhD. Mernissi soon established herself as both a scholar and a lively writer on women's studies, religion, history, and sociology. She writes in French, English, and Arabic, and her books have been translated into several other languages. Her English titles include *Beyond the Veil: Male-Female Dynamics in Modern Muslim Society* (1975, revised in 1987), *Islam and Democracy: Fear of the Modern World* (1992, revised in 2002 and 2011), *Dreams of Trespass: Tales of a Harem Girlhood* (1994), and *Women's Rebellion and Islamic Memory* (1996). A professor and research scholar at the University of Mohammed V, Mernissi has also taught at Harvard University and the University of California at Berkeley. She received the Prince of Asturias Award for Literature in 2003 and is currently studying how the Internet and other communications technologies affect Muslim societies.

Size 6: The Western Women's Harem

Mernissi was raised in a harem, an enclave of women and children within a traditional Muslim household, off-limits to men. Traveling outside the Middle East, she encounters common Western misconceptions of a harem as either a "peaceful pleasure-garden" or an "orgiastic feast" in which "men reign supreme over obedient women" — when in fact Muslim men and women both acknowledge the inequality of the harem and women resist men in any way they can. In *Scheherazade Goes West: Different Cultures, Different Harems* (2001), Mernissi explores the "mystery of the Western harem," trying to understand why outsiders imagine harem women as totally compliant and unthreatening to men. In the last chapter of the book, excerpted here, Mernissi finds her answer.

Note that Mernissi provides source citations for the book she quotes in paragraph 20. The citations are in the format of *The Chicago Manual of Style*.

It was during my unsuccessful attempt to buy a cotton skirt in an American department store that I was told my hips were too large to fit into a size 6. That distressing experience made me realize how the image of beauty in the West can hurt and humiliate a woman as much as the veil does when enforced by the state police in extremist nations such as Iran, Afghanistan, or Saudi Arabia. Yes, that day I stumbled onto one of the keys to the enigma of passive beauty in Western harem fantasies. The elegant saleslady in the American store looked at me without moving from her desk and said that she had no skirt my size. "In this whole big store, there is no skirt for me?" I said. "You

1

are joking." I felt very suspicious and thought that she just might be too tired
to help me. I could understand that. But then the saleswoman added a condescending judgment, which sounded to me like an imam's fatwa.[1] It left no
room for discussion:

"You are too big!" she said.   2

"I am too big compared to what?" I asked, looking at her intently, because   3
I realized that I was facing a critical cultural gap here.

"Compared to a size 6," came the saleslady's reply.   4

Her voice had a clear-cut edge to it that is typical of those who enforce   5
religious laws. "Size 4 and 6 are the norm," she went on, encouraged by my
bewildered look. "Deviant sizes such as the one you need can be bought in
special stores."

That was the first time that I had ever heard such nonsense about my size.   6
In the Moroccan streets, men's flattering comments regarding my particularly
generous hips have for decades led me to believe that the entire planet shared
their convictions. It is true that with advancing age, I have been hearing fewer
and fewer flattering comments when walking in the medina, and sometimes
the silence around me in the bazaars is deafening. But since my face has never
met with the local beauty standards, and I have often had to defend myself
against remarks such as *zirafa* (giraffe), because of my long neck, I learned long
ago not to rely too much on the outside world for my sense of self-worth. In
fact, paradoxically, as I discovered when I went to Rabat as a student, it was
the self-reliance that I had developed to protect myself against "beauty black-
mail" that made me attractive to others. My male fellow students could not
believe that I did not give a damn about what they thought about my body.
"You know, my dear," I would say in response to one of them, "all I need to
survive is bread, olives, and sardines. That you think my neck is too long is
your problem, not mine."

In any case, when it comes to beauty and compliments, nothing is too   7
serious or definite in the medina, where everything can be negotiated. But
things seemed to be different in that American department store. In fact, I
have to confess that I lost my usual self-confidence in that New York environment. Not that I am always sure of myself, but I don't walk around the
Moroccan streets or down the university corridors wondering what people are
thinking about me. Of course, when I hear a compliment, my ego expands
like a cheese soufflé, but on the whole, I don't expect to hear much from
others. Some mornings, I feel ugly because I am sick or tired; others, I feel
wonderful because it is sunny out or I have written a good paragraph. But suddenly, in that peaceful American store that I had entered so triumphantly, as

[1] An *imam* is a Muslim leader. A *fatwa* is a Muslim legal opinion or ruling. — EDS.

a sovereign consumer ready to spend money, I felt savagely attacked. My hips, until then the sign of a relaxed and uninhibited maturity, were suddenly being condemned as a deformity. . . .

"And who says that everyone must be a size 6?" I joked to the saleslady   8
that day, deliberately neglecting to mention size 4, which is the size of my skinny twelve-year-old niece.

At that point, the saleslady suddenly gave me an anxious look. "The norm   9
is everywhere, my dear," she said. "It's all over, in the magazines, on television, in the ads. You can't escape it. There is Calvin Klein, Ralph Lauren, Gianni Versace, Giorgio Armani, Mario Valentino, Salvatore Ferragamo, Christian Dior, Yves Saint-Laurent, Christian Lacroix, and Jean-Paul Gaultier. Big department stores go by the norm." She paused and then concluded, "If they sold size 14 or 16, which is probably what you need, they would go bankrupt."

She stopped for a minute and then stared at me, intrigued. "Where on   10
earth do you come from? I am sorry I can't help you. Really, I am." And she looked it too. She seemed, all of a sudden, interested, and brushed off another woman who was seeking her attention with a cutting, "Get someone else to help you, I'm busy." Only then did I notice that she was probably my age, in her late fifties. But unlike me, she had the thin body of an adolescent girl. Her knee-length, navy blue, Chanel dress had a white silk collar reminiscent of the subdued elegance of aristocratic French Catholic schoolgirls at the turn of the century. A pearl-studded belt emphasized the slimness of her waist. With her meticulously styled short hair and sophisticated makeup, she looked half my age at first glance.

"I come from a country where there is no size for women's clothes," I told   11
her. "I buy my own material and the neighborhood seamstress or craftsman makes me the silk or leather skirt I want. They just take my measurements each time I see them. Neither the seamstress nor I know exactly what size my new skirt is. We discover it together in the making. No one cares about my size in Morocco as long as I pay taxes on time. Actually, I don't know what my size is, to tell you the truth."

The saleswoman laughed merrily and said that I should advertise my   12
country as a paradise for stressed working women. "You mean you don't watch your weight?" she inquired, with a tinge of disbelief in her voice. And then, after a brief moment of silence, she added in a lower register, as if talking to herself: "Many women working in highly paid fashion-related jobs could lose their positions if they didn't keep to a strict diet."

Her words sounded so simple, but the threat they implied was so cruel   13
that I realized for the first time that maybe "size 6" is a more violent restriction imposed on women than is the Muslim veil. Quickly I said good-bye so as not to make any more demands on the saleslady's time or involve her in

any more unwelcome, confidential exchanges about age-discriminating salary cuts. A surveillance camera was probably watching us both.

Yes, I thought as I wandered off, I have finally found the answer to my   14 harem enigma. Unlike the Muslim man, who uses space to establish male domination by excluding women from the public arena, the Western man manipulates time and light. He declares that in order to be beautiful, a woman must look fourteen years old. If she dares to look fifty, or worse, sixty, she is beyond the pale. By putting the spotlight on the female child and framing her as the ideal of beauty, he condemns the mature woman to invisibility. In fact, the modern Western man enforces Immanuel Kant's[2] nineteenth-century theories: To be beautiful, women have to appear childish and brainless. When a woman looks mature and self-assertive, or allows her hips to expand, she is condemned as ugly. Thus, the walls of the European harem separate youthful beauty from ugly maturity.

These Western attitudes, I thought, are even more dangerous and cun-   15 ning than the Muslim ones because the weapon used against women is time. Time is less visible, more fluid than space. The Western man uses images and spotlights to freeze female beauty within an idealized childhood, and forces women to perceive aging — that normal unfolding of the years — as a shameful devaluation. "Here I am, transformed into a dinosaur," I caught myself saying aloud as I went up and down the rows of skirts in the store, hoping to prove the saleslady wrong — to no avail. This Western time-defined veil is even crazier than the space-defined one enforced by the ayatollahs.[3]

The violence embodied in the Western harem is less visible than in the   16 Eastern harem because aging is not attacked directly, but rather masked as an aesthetic choice. Yes, I suddenly felt not only very ugly but also quite useless in that store, where, if you had big hips, you were simply out of the picture. You drifted into the fringes of nothingness. By putting the spotlight on the prepubescent female, the Western man veils the older, more mature woman, wrapping her in shrouds of ugliness. This idea gives me the chills because it tattoos the invisible harem directly onto a woman's skin. Chinese footbinding worked the same way: Men declared beautiful only those women who had small, childlike feet. Chinese men did not force women to bandage their feet to keep them from developing normally — all they did was to define the beauty ideal. In feudal China, a beautiful woman was the one who voluntarily sacrificed her right to unhindered physical movement by mutilating her own feet, and thereby proving that her main goal in life was to please men. Similarly, in the Western world, I was expected to shrink my hips into a size 6 if I wanted

---

[2] Kant (1724–1804) was a German philosopher. — EDS.
[3] Among Shiite Muslims, the authorities who interpret religious law. — EDS.

to find a decent skirt tailored for a beautiful woman. We Muslim women have only one month of fasting, Ramadan, but the poor Western woman who diets has to fast twelve months out of the year. *"Quelle horreur,"*[4] I kept repeating to myself, while looking around at the American women shopping. All those my age looked like youthful teenagers. . . .

Now, at last, the mystery of my Western harem made sense. Framing youth   17
as beauty and condemning maturity is the weapon used against women in the West just as limiting access to public space is the weapon used in the East. The objective remains identical in both cultures: to make women feel unwelcome, inadequate, and ugly.

The power of the Western man resides in dictating what women should   18
wear and how they should look. He controls the whole fashion industry, from cosmetics to underwear. The West, I realized, was the only part of the world where women's fashion is a man's business. In places like Morocco, where you design your own clothes and discuss them with craftsmen and -women, fash-ion is your own business. Not so in the West. . . .

But how does the system function? I wondered. Why do women accept it?   19

Of all the possible explanations, I like that of the French sociologist Pierre   20
Bourdieu the best. In his latest book, *La Domination Masculine*, he proposes something he calls *"la violence symbolique"*: "Symbolic violence is a form of power which is hammered directly on the body, and as if by magic, without any apparent physical constraint. But this magic operates only because it activates the codes pounded in the deepest layers of the body."[5] Reading Bourdieu, I had the impression that I finally understood Western man's psyche better. The cosmetic and fashion industries are only the tip of the iceberg, he states, which is why women are so ready to adhere to their dictates. Something else is going on on a far deeper level. Otherwise, why would women belittle themselves spontaneously? Why, argues Bourdieu, would women make their lives more difficult, for example, by preferring men who are taller or older than they are? "The majority of French women wish to have a husband who is older and also, which seems consistent, bigger as far as size is concerned," writes Bourdieu.[6] Caught in the enchanted submission characteristic of the symbolic violence inscribed in the mysterious layers of the flesh, women relinquish what he calls "les signes ordinaires de la hiérarchie sexuelle," the ordinary signs of sexual hierarchy, such as old age and a larger body. By so doing, explains Bourdieu, women spontaneously accept the subservient position. It is this spontaneity Bourdieu describes as magic enchantment.[7]

[4] French, "What a horror." — EDS.
[5] Pierre Bourdieu, *La Domination Masculine* (Paris: Editions du Seuil, 1998), p. 44.
[6] Ibid., p. 41.
[7] Ibid., p. 42.

Once I understood how this magic submission worked, I became very   21
happy that the conservative ayatollahs do not know about it yet. If they did,
they would readily switch to its sophisticated methods, because they are so
much more effective. To deprive me of food is definitely the best way to para-
lyze my thinking capabilities. . . .

"I thank you, Allah, for sparing me the tyranny of the 'size 6 harem,'"   22
I repeatedly said to myself while seated on the Paris-Casablanca flight, on my
way back home at last. "I am so happy that the conservative male elite does
not know about it. Imagine the fundamentalists switching from the veil to
forcing women to fit size 6."

How can you stage a credible political demonstration and shout in the   23
streets that your human rights have been violated when you cannot find the
right skirt?

Journal Writing

Within your peer group, what constitutes the norm of physical attractiveness for
women and for men? (Don't focus on the ideal here, but on what is expected for a person not to be considered *un*attractive.) Are the norms similar for women and for men?

Questions on Meaning

1. What two subjects does Mernissi compare? Where does she state her THESIS initially, and where does she later restate and expand on it? What does Mernissi
   conclude is the same about the two subjects?

2. What is the saleswoman's initial attitude toward Mernissi? How does her attitude
   seem to change, and how does this change contribute to Mernissi's point?

3. Why does Mernissi believe Western attitudes toward women are "more dangerous and cunning than the Muslim ones" (par. 15)?

Questions on Writing Strategy

1. What is the PURPOSE of paragraphs 6–7? What do these paragraphs contribute to
   Mernissi's larger point?

2. What two further comparisons does Mernissi make in paragraph 16? What
   TRANSITIONS does she use to signal the shift of subject within these comparisons?

3. **OTHER METHODS** Mernissi devotes considerable attention to a NARRATIVE of her
   adventure in the department store. Why does she tell this story in such detail?
   What does it contribute to the essay?

Questions on Language

1. What are the CONNOTATIONS of the saleswoman's word *deviant* (par. 5)?

2. Why is the metaphor of the veil in paragraph 16 especially appropriate? (See FIGURES OF SPEECH in the Glossary if you need a definition of *metaphor*.)

3. Consult a dictionary if you are unsure of the meanings of any of the following: enigma (par. 1); generous, medina, bazaars, paradoxically (6); soufflé, sovereign (7); subdued (10); cunning, devaluation (15); aesthetic, prepubescent, unhindered, mutilating (16).

Suggestions for Writing

1. **FROM JOURNAL TO ESSAY**   Based on your journal entry, draft an essay in which you compare and contrast standards of attractiveness for women and men within your peer group. Be sure to consider how strictly the standards are applied in each case.

2. Write an essay about a time when your self-confidence was shaken because of how someone else treated or spoke to you. Like Mernissi, explain why you had been confident of yourself before this encounter and what effect it had on you.

3. Mernissi comes from Morocco. Put her essay in context by researching the history and culture of that country. Then write an essay in which you discuss what you have learned. How is Morocco different from the more "extremist nations" Mernissi refers to in paragraph 1?

4. **CRITICAL WRITING**   Respond to Mernissi's essay. Do you agree with her views about "the tyranny of the 'size 6 harem' " (par. 22)? Does Mernissi provide enough EVIDENCE to convince you of her views? Even if you agree with her take on her department-store experience, do you think her conclusions apply across the board, as she implies? For instance, do they apply among the poor and working class as well as among the affluent? Write an essay that ANALYZES and EVALUATES Mernissi's thesis and the support for it.

5. **CONNECTIONS**   When Mernissi asks who declared size 6 to be the norm in the United States, the sales clerk implicates the media: "The norm is everywhere, my dear. . . . It's all over, in the magazines, on television, in the ads. You can't escape it" (par. 9). In "*Facebook* Is Using You" (p. 541), Lori Andrews also touches on the power of advertising, explaining how the social networking site's business model compromises consumers' privacy and with it their liberties. Using examples from both selections as well as from your own experience and observations, write an essay exploring a positive or a negative EFFECT of advertising on individuals. You might do some library or Internet research to further support your point.

ALAIN DE BOTTON

Alain de Botton is a journalist whom the *Houston Chronicle* has credited with creating his "own subgenre of nonfiction, one that examines the preoccupations of everyday life . . . through the lens of philosophy." He was born in 1969 in Zurich, Switzerland, emigrated to England in 1981, and earned degrees in history and philosophy from Caius College, Cambridge (1991) and King's College London (1992). For a time de Botton directed the graduate philosophy program at London University but decided that the academic world was too rigid and stifling for his tastes. As a writer, de Botton debuted as an experimental novelist in the mid-1990s before inventing the distinct blend of criticism and self-help for which he is known. He has published a dozen such books on subjects ranging from art and architecture to love and sex, including *Status Anxiety* (1994), *How Proust Can Change Your Life* (1997), *The Pleasures and Sorrows of Work* (2006), *Religion for Atheists* (2012), and, most recently, *The News: A User's Manual* (2014). As a producer, he has adapted several of his books into documentaries for PBS and the BBC and recorded lectures for *YouTube*. In 2008 de Botton founded (and still helps to run) the School of Life, an international offering of classes, workshops, and therapies "dedicated to a new vision of education" and designed to foster emotional intelligence in its students. He lives in London.

Tragedy

This essay, a self-contained section of *The News: A User's Manual*, illustrates de Botton's knack for distilling heady concepts for general readers. As he does throughout the book, the author takes a critical look at contemporary journalistic practices. In this case, our self-help philosopher examines the tendency of newspapers and broadcasters to fixate on the most gruesome of tragedies, finding in ancient Greek dramas a possible purpose in telling such stories.

A Manhattan doctor plunged 30 stories to his death from his Upper East Side high-rise yesterday in an apparent suicide, police and witnesses said. The body of Dr. Sheldon "Shelly" Steinbach, 68, an anesthesiologist, slammed into a second-floor balcony at the building, at 246 E. 63rd St., at 9:35 a.m. "I heard a large bang, and we looked outside and saw him. His body just exploded," said resident Jonathan Kershner, 25, who lives two floors above where the doctor landed. "Then a doorman came by saying a woman was looking for her husband," Kershner added. Steinbach had a *Twitter* page but had not updated it since October 2011. The personal description on his account reads: "I am an anesthesiologist in New York City and am having a great day. Married. Love aerobic activities and music."

— *New York Post*

Every time we connect with the news, we can be sure that we will be 1 confronted by graphic accounts of some of the most appalling eventualities that can befall our species: A depressed man leaps out of the window, a mother poisons her children, a teacher rapes his pupil, a husband beheads his wife, a teenager shoots his classmates. The news leads us very reliably into the crucible of human horror.

A decent impulse is to look away and to insist that such deaths and trau- 2 mas are simply too sad and too private to be subjected to a stranger's gaze. Any curiosity seems, from this perspective, to be a particularly shameful and modern kind of pathology.

Motivated by fears of intrusion, the more serious news organizations 3 typically adopt a reserved tone in their reports on the sorts of events that severely test any faith one might still have in the reasonableness and decency of mankind.

They leave it to their less dignified colleagues, unfettered by scruples, to 4 evoke the truly vivid details of the latest outrages: to give us a close-up view of the body after it fell from the balcony, the bedroom where the little child was tied up or the carving knife with the spouse's blood still on its blade. Their reward for being willing to undertake such investigations is the occasionally guilty but concerted and lucrative interest of many millions of readers and viewers.

It isn't hard to characterize the interest of the public in horror stories as 5 tasteless and unproductive. But beneath the surface banality, we should allow that we are often — in confused and inarticulate ways — attempting to get at something important. When immersing ourselves in blood-soaked narratives, we are not always solely in search of entertainment or distraction; we are not always being merely prurient or callously appropriating intensities of feeling that our own lives have failed to provide.

We may also be looking to expose ourselves to barbaric tales to help us 6 retain a tighter hold on our more civilized selves — and in particular, to nur- ture our always ephemeral reserves of patience, self-control, forgiveness and empathy.

Rather than just inveigh moralistically against our fascination with hei- 7 nous events, the challenge should be to tweak how they are reported — in order that they better release their important, yet too often latent, emotional and societal benefits.

Every year, at the end of March, the citizens of ancient Athens would 8 gather under open skies on the southern slopes of the Acropolis in the Theater of Dionysus and there listen to the latest works by the great tragedians of

their city. The plot lines of these plays were unmitigatingly macabre, easily
matching anything our own news could provide: A man kills his father, mar-
ries his mother and gouges out his own eyes (*Oedipus Rex*); a man has his
daughter murdered as part of a plan to revenge the infidelity of his brother's
wife (*Iphigenia*); a mother murders her two children to spoil her unfaithful
husband's plans to start a new family with another woman (*Medea*).[1]

Rather than regarding these stories as grotesque spectacles that all right-   9
minded people should avoid, in his *Poetics* of c. 335 BC, the philosopher Aristotle looked generously upon the human fascination with them. He proposed
that, when they are well written and artfully staged, such stories can become
crucial resources for the emotional and moral education of a whole society.
Despite the barbarity they describe, they themselves can function as civilizing
forces.

But in order for this to happen, in order for a *horror* (a meaningless   10
narration of revolting events) to turn into what Aristotle called a *tragedy*
(an educative tale fashioned from abominations), the philosopher thought
it was vital that the plot should be well arranged and the motives and the
personalities of the characters properly outlined to us. Extreme dramatic
skill would be required in order for the audience to spontaneously reach a
point at which it recognized that the apparently unhinged protagonist of the
story, who had acted impetuously, arrogantly and blindly, who had perhaps
killed others and destroyed his own reputation and life, the person whom
one might at first (had one come across the story in the news) dismissed as
nothing but a maniac, was, in the final analysis, rather like us in certain key
ways. A work of tragedy would rise to its true moral and edifying possibilities when the audience looked upon the hero's ghastly errors and crimes and
was left with no option but to reach the terrifying conclusion: "How easily
I, too, might have done the same." Tragedy's task was to demonstrate the
ease with which an essentially decent and likeable person could end up
generating hell.

If we were entirely sane, if madness did not have a serious grip on one   11
side of us, other people's tragedies would hold a great deal less interest for us.
While we circle gruesome stories in the media, we may at a highly unconscious
level be exploring shocking but important questions: "If things got really out
of hand late one night, and I was feeling wound up and tired and insecure,
might I be capable of killing my partner?" "If I was divorced and my spouse

---

[1] All three are classical Greek dramas. *Oedipus Rex*, by Sophocles (c. 496–406 BC), was first
performed around 429 BC. *Iphigenia* and *Medea* were penned by Euripides (c. 480–406 BC) and
debuted in 405 BC and 431 BC, respectively. — EDS.

Cascade News

A man drives into his family home to punish his wife, Manchester, 2012.

Erich Lessing / Art Resource, NY

Medea kills her son to punish her husband, Greek jar, c. 330 BC.

Our fascination with crimes may be part of an unconscious effort to make sure we never commit them.

was keeping my children from me, would I ever be able to kill them in a form of twisted revenge?" "Could I ever start chatting with a minor on the Internet and, without quite realizing the enormity of what I was doing, end up trying to seduce him or her?"

For civilization to proceed, we naturally need the answers to be a firm   12
no in all cases. There is a serious task for the news here: The disasters we are introduced to should be framed in order to give us the maximum encouragement to practice *not* doing the things that the more chaotic parts of us would — under extreme circumstances — be attracted to exploring. We may never actually fling our children off a bridge at the end of our access day or shoot our partner dead during an argument, but we are all, at times, emotionally in the space where these sorts of things can happen. Tragedies remind us how badly we need to keep controlling ourselves by showing us what happens when people don't.

Tragedies shouldn't only help us to be good, they should also prompt us   13
to be kind. How likely we are to be sympathetic to someone who kills their spouse or children depends in large part on how their story happens to be told to us: what information we are given about them, how we are introduced to their motives and with what degree of insight and complexity their psyches are laid before us.

In Greek tragedies, a Chorus regularly interrupts events to direct sen-   14
timents and richly contextualize characters' actions. It tends to speak with solemn respect about the protagonists, whatever the sins they have committed. Such sensitivity ensures that few audience members are likely to leave a performance of *Oedipus Rex* dismissing the unfortunate central character as a "loser" or "psycho."

The news is less careful in its narrations; and our judgements are — as a   15
result — far more intemperate and nastier:

> A Teesside doctor who downloaded more than 1,300 child porn images, including scenes of torture, has been jailed. Police found the "sickening" images on the laptop of James Taylor, 31, from Wensleydale Gardens, Thornaby. The doctor, who worked at Pinderfields Hospital in Wakefield, earlier admitted looking at indecent images of children. Taylor was sentenced to a year and a day in prison by a judge at Teesside Crown Court on Friday and was banned from working with children for life.
>
> — BBC

At first glance, the doctor seems to deserve no sympathy whatsoever. But our decision about how we consider him is crucially dependent on how the facts of his case are presented to us. We could sympathize with more or less anyone if their story was told to us in a certain way — *and we wouldn't necessarily be wrong to do so* (as Dostoevsky or Jesus would have reminded us).[2]

In the context of news reporting, this claim seems contentious, even dangerous, because we have to juggle two ideas which sound opposing: that we can sympathize with a criminal and at the same time firmly condemn his or her crime. The news is tacitly convinced that its audience wouldn't be able to pull off this conceptual feat, and that any sympathy it might express would lead the audience to want to open up the prisons and let murderers roam the streets. It hence remains steadfast in its refusal to undertake the narrative and psychological maneuvers required to humanize criminals. Instead it rushes through their stories. A performance of *Oedipus Rex* might last an hour and a half; the news story in which the doctor appears is 304 words long.

Inevitably, a feeling of outrage is likely to be at its height when we confront the headline "Doctor had 'sickening' child porn." But, as we read on, our certainty might be challenged. Towards the end of the piece, we learn, "Ordering Taylor to sign the Sex Offenders Register for 10 years, the judge said: 'As a result of this conviction no doubt your career will come to an end.'" We might feel a chill at the thought of how seven long years of medical school had come to this. The article gives a hint of the panic the doctor must have felt: "The court was told Taylor initially denied being responsible, but later admitted, during police interviews, that he had downloaded the images." And the enormous price that he has subsequently had to pay: "Stephen Rich, defending, told Judge George Moorhouse that Taylor's wife and newborn baby had left him and that his life had collapsed."

An addendum informs us that while in prison, the man tried to commit suicide. All this is no less sad than the plot line of *Madame Bovary* or *Hamlet* — and, let's argue, the character of the doctor is not fundamentally any worse; Hamlet is, after all, a murderer and Emma Bovary is guilty of extreme child cruelty.[3] We consider them "tragic" figures — that is, entitled to a degree of complex understanding — because we imagine that there must have been something unusually noble and dignified about their nature and circumstances. But really it is only the generosity of spirit of Flaubert and Shakespeare that elevates Bovary and Hamlet above the ordinary criminal and dissuades us from judging them as harshly as we might the imprisoned doctor.

16

17

18

[2] Russian author Fyodor Dostoevsky (1821–81) is known especially for the philosophical novels *The Brothers Karamazov* (1880) and *Crime and Punishment* (1886), both of which examine questions of murder and morality. — EDS.

[3] *Hamlet*, by William Shakespeare (1564–1616), was first published in print form in 1603. *Madame Bovary*, by French novelist Gustave Flaubert (1821–80), appeared in 1856. — EDS.

When reporting on a tragedy, the news tends to make dreadful conduct   19
seem unique to a particular person. It resists the wider resonance and the more
helpful conclusion: that we are all a hair's breadth away from catastrophe.
This knowledge should, if properly absorbed, sink us into a mood of reflective,
mature sadness. We are more implicated than we might like to believe in the
misdeeds of other members of our species. A lack of a serious criminal record
is in large measure a matter of luck and good circumstance, not proof of an
incorruptible nature. A clean conscience is the preserve of those without sufficient imagination. Were life, or what the Greeks termed the gods, ever really
to test us, we would almost surely be found wanting — an awareness upon
which a measure of understanding towards the guilty should be founded.

The tragedians of ancient Greece never forgot this. They liked to tell us   20
how vicious, stupid, sexual, enraged and blind we could be, but they allowed
room for complex compassion as well. Through the examples they leave us,
we are coaxed into accepting that we are members of a noble but hideously
flawed species; capable of performing amazing feats, ably practicing medicine
or parenting with love for many years, and then of turning around and blowing
up our existence with a single rash move. We should be scared. The ancient
Greeks saw tragic plays once a year, at a specific time, within a particular context and with some knowledge of the works' larger purpose.

By contrast, we take in tragic news stories almost every day, but we rarely   21
recognize them as belonging to a coherent narrative cycle with a distinctive
moral to impart. The news doesn't help us to place in a single genre all those
incidents in which self-control is lost and the monster within is released. It
doesn't, as it should, gather all its varied tales of horror under the unified
heading of "Tragedy" and then narrate them in such a way that we can more
easily recognize our own smoldering tendencies in the demented actions of
the bloody protagonists.

Much of the news is in the end an account of people around the globe,   22
in all sorts of positions, getting things very wrong. They fail to master their
emotions, contain their obsessions, judge right from wrong and act decently
when there is still time. We shouldn't waste their failures. The news, like
literature and history, can serve as that most vital of instruments, a "life simu-
lator" — which is to say, a machine that inserts us into a variety of scenarios
stretching far beyond anything we might ordinarily have to cope with and
that affords us a chance safely, and at our leisure, to hone our best responses.

Yet too often the news doesn't help us to learn from the experiences of our   23
wretched brethren; it doesn't actively try to spare us and our societies the full
force of error at every new turn. If a good life demands that we learn from, and
imitate, the example of inspiring figures, it also requires us to undertake close

study of those whose behavior should profoundly scare, horrify and warn us. These are two sides of the same coin of growth and development, and it lies within the remit of the news, if not yet on its agenda, to help us with both.

Journal Writing

In his conclusion de Botton remarks that a lot "of the news is in the end an account of people around the globe, in all sorts of positions, getting things very wrong" (par. 22). In your journal, reflect on some things you have gotten wrong. When is the last time you remember slipping up? What was the most significant mistake you ever made? Could it have destroyed you or someone else, or were the potential consequences less serious? What actually happened?

Questions on Meaning

1. What is the PURPOSE of de Botton's essay? Does he seek to justify sloppy or sensationalistic journalism? to defend readers who are drawn to gruesome stories? something else? How do you know?

2. How OBJECTIVE is de Botton's portrayal of contemporary news and Greek tragedy? Does he seem to prefer one GENRE over the other?

3. Does de Botton have a THESIS? Explain the central idea of his essay. What is the basis for comparison?

4. Summarize de Botton's comparison and contrast. What do news reports and Greek tragedies have in common? How are they different? What does de Botton see as the major problem with the reporting he describes?

5. The author refers to three ancient plays (*Oedipus Rex*, *Iphigenia*, and *Medea*) and mentions a few other works of philosophy and literature (such as Aristotle's *Poetics*, Shakespeare's *Hamlet*, and Flaubert's *Madame Bovary*). Does he seem to expect that his audience will understand these ALLUSIONS? Do readers need to be familiar with the texts de Botton cites to understand his comparison or appreciate his meaning?

Questions on Writing Strategy

1. De Botton's comparison is organized point by point — similarities in basic plots, then differences in the writers' sensitivity to context and their audiences' capacity for empathy. What is the EFFECT of this organization? Or, from another angle, what would have been the effect of a subject-by-subject organization — just contemporary news, then just Greek tragedies (or vice versa)?

2. How does de Botton indicate when he's changing points of comparison?

3. "Tragedy" includes two visuals. What do the parallels in the pictures of a video frame and a vase contribute to de Botton's comparison?

4. **OTHER METHODS** Take note of de Botton's reliance on Aristotle's ANALYSIS of drama (pars. 9–10) to support his own interpretation of the news. What, according to the ancient philosopher, are the major elements of tragedy? How is it distinct from horror?

Questions on Language

1. Consult a dictionary if you are unable to determine the meanings of the following words from their context in de Botton's essay: crucible (par. 1); pathology (2); unfettered, scruples, lucrative (4); banality, prurient (5); ephemeral, empathy (6); inveigh, latent (7); unmitigatingly, macabre (8); abominations, protagonist, impetuously, edifying (10); psyches (13); tacitly, steadfast (16); brethren (23).

2. This essay opens with some particularly graphic IMAGES from crime reports. What do you take to be de Botton's intended effect of including such disturbing language? How well does he succeed, in your estimation?

3. The author includes several quotations from newspapers but only SUMMARIZES the plays he cites. Why do you think that is?

4. How would you characterize de Botton's DICTION and TONE? What does his language contribute to the overall effectiveness of his comparison?

Suggestions for Writing

1. **FROM JOURNAL TO ESSAY** Do you agree with de Botton that most people have the capacity to lose control and fall victim to the kinds of mistakes that make headlines? How common are the kinds of stories he relates? What are your attitudes toward them? Do you tend to sympathize with the characters, for instance, or are you more likely to judge them? Drawing on the mistakes you recalled in your journal (p. 247) for inspiration, write an essay in which you consider the average person's likelihood of committing a heinous crime. Who does these things? Why? What should a civilized society do about it?

2. Analyze the similarities and differences between two characters in your favorite play, film, or TV show. Which aspects of their personalities make them work well together, within the context in which they appear? Which characteristics work against each other, and therefore provide the necessary conflict to hold the reader's or viewer's attention?

3. **CRITICAL WRITING** Find a recent newspaper story of the gruesome sort de Botton discusses and analyze it using his basis of comparison. Does the reporter, for instance, rush through the details, or does the report provide the kind of background and context that humanizes a subject? Are readers given a reason to sympathize with the perpetrator and learn from his or her example, or is the story mere spectacle? How well does the article conform to the careful style of

writing de Botton would like to see more of in the news? Quote, paraphrase, and summarize the story as appropriate to support your conclusions.

4. **CONNECTIONS** Christopher Beam, in "Blood Loss" (p. 416), also criticizes the news media. But where de Botton believes that crime reports, thoughtfully crafted, can make us better people, Beam suggests that they may actually incite violence and mayhem. What do you think? How much power do the media — newspapers, magazines, television, the Internet — hold over individuals' thoughts and behaviors? Are some forms of reporting more influential than others? Do news accounts affect world events, or merely record them? Taking evidence from both essays as well as your own reading, experience, and observation, write an essay that examines the state of journalism today.

Alain de Botton on Writing

As a generalist, Alain de Botton is known for writing on whatever subjects capture his imagination: His books have examined love, fine art, literature, religion, work, airports, journalism, and more. In a 2014 interview for the *Deloitte Review*, Scott Wilson asked him, "Does wielding such an obviously wide, diverse lens through which to observe, think, and write demand some sort of a process to getting stuff done?" The author responded:

Yes. Broadly speaking, my discipline base is the humanities. So I feed off history, psychology, philosophy, sociology. I'm not a scientist; I'm not an economist. I look at a number of areas related to, let's say, emotional satisfaction or well-being, which encompasses lots of different areas. So it can go as widely as architecture because architecture and the spaces we inhabit are part of what contribute to well-being. Overall I think it's about getting to grips with a topic and trying to find out what belongs to that topic. Really what I'm trying to do is to work out what ideas belong where. It's a chance to structure an order to a topic. So, if I'm writing about architecture, I want to try and gather all my thoughts that are around space and aesthetics and the psychology of location. I want to try and get all those ideas in there. And so the working process starts off relatively freeform and fluid and I'm just trying to get to the main idea. The best analogy is again with architecture. You start with a sketch. You then build it up into detailed plans. You then go into the actual construction of the thing. You put down the main bones and supporting pillars, and then at the very end, you're tidying and decorating the little details, the minor things. So it's very similar to putting up a building except you're putting up chapter three rather than a floor.

The Bedford Reader on Writing

In describing his method of exploring a topic, finding the main idea, planning, drafting, revising, and editing, de Botton likens writing to architecture, one of his favorite academic disciplines. What do you make of this ANALOGY? How else is writing similar to constructing a building? For a concrete overview of the foundations of writing and the stages within it, see Chapter 2, especially pages 30–53.

ADDITIONAL WRITING TOPICS
Comparison and Contrast

1. In an essay replete with EXAMPLES, compare and contrast the two subjects in any one of the following pairs:

   Toys marketed to girls and boys
   Vampires and zombies
   A photograph and a painting
   The special skills of two basketball players
   High school and college
   Introverts and extraverts
   Liberals and conservatives: their opposing views of the role of government
   How city dwellers and country dwellers spend their leisure time
   The presentation styles of two popular comedians
   Science and the humanities

2. Approach a comparison-and-contrast essay on one of the following general subjects by explaining why you prefer one thing to the other:

   Vehicles: hybrid and electric engines; sedans and SUVs; American and Asian; Asian and European
   Smartphone platforms: Apple and Android
   Two buildings on campus or in town
   Two baseball teams
   Two horror movie franchises
   Television when you were a child and television today
   High art and low art
   Malls and main streets
   Two sports
   A vegetarian (or vegan) diet and a meat-based diet

3. Write an essay in which you compare a reality (what actually exists) with an ideal (what should exist). Some possible topics:

   The affordable car
   Available living quarters
   Parenthood
   A job
   A personal relationship
   A companion animal
   The college curriculum
   Public transportation
   Financial aid for college students
   Political candidates

7

PROCESS ANALYSIS

Explaining Step by Step

◀ **Process analysis in a photograph**

In a factory in Shenzhen, China, workers create dolls for export to the United States. This single image catches several steps in the doll-making process. At the very back of the assembly line, flat, unstuffed dolls begin the journey past the ranks of workers who stuff the body parts, using material prepared by other workers on the sides. A supervisor, hands behind his or her back, oversees the process. What do you think the photographer, Wally McNamee, wants viewers to understand about this process? What do you imagine the workers themselves think about it?

THE METHOD

A chemist working for a soft-drink firm is asked to improve on a competitor's product, Hydra Sports Water. First, she chemically tests a sample to figure out what's in the drink. This is the method of DIVISION or ANALYSIS, the separation of something into its parts in order to understand it (see the next chapter). Then the chemist writes a report telling her boss how to make a drink like Hydra Sports Water, but better. This recipe is a special kind of analysis, called PROCESS ANALYSIS: explaining step by step how to do something or how something is done.

Like any type of analysis, process analysis divides a subject into its components: It divides a continuous action into stages. Processes much larger and more involved than the making of a sports drink may also be analyzed. When geologists explain how a formation such as the Grand Canyon developed — a process taking several hundred million years — they describe the successive layers of sediment deposited by oceans, floods, and wind; then the great uplift of the entire region by underground forces; and then the erosion, visible to us today, by the Colorado River and its tributaries, by little streams and flash floods, by crumbling and falling rock, and by wind. Exactly what are the geologists doing in this explanation? They are taking a complicated event (or process) and dividing it into parts. They are telling us what happened first, second, and third, and what is still happening today.

Because it is useful in explaining what is complicated, process analysis is a favorite method of scientists such as chemists and geologists. The method, however, may be useful to anybody. Two PURPOSES of process analysis are very familiar to you:

- **A *directive process analysis* explains how to do something or how to make something.** You make use of it when you read a set of instructions for taking an exam or for assembling a new bookcase ("Lay part A on a flat surface and, using two of the lock tabs provided, attach part B on the left . . .").

- **An *informative process analysis* explains how something is done or how it takes place.** You see it in textbook descriptions of how atoms behave when they split, how lions hunt, and how a fertilized egg develops into a child.

In this chapter, you will find examples of both kinds of process analysis — both the "how to" and the "how." For instance, Anne Lamott and Koji Frahm offer their own directives for writing successfully, while Jessica Mitford spellbindingly explains how corpses are embalmed.

Sometimes process analysis is used imaginatively. Foreseeing that eventually the sun will burn out and all life on Earth will perish, an astronomer who cannot possibly behold the end of the world nevertheless can write a process analysis of it. An exercise in learned guesswork, such an essay divides a vast and almost inconceivable event into stages that, taken one at a time, become clearer and more readily imaginable. Whether it is useful or useless (but fun or scary to imagine), an effective process analysis can grip readers and even hold them fascinated. Say you were proposing a change in the procedures for course registration at your school. You could argue your point until you were out of words, but you would get nowhere if you failed to tell your readers exactly how the new process would work: That's what makes your proposal sing.

Readers, it seems, have an unslakable thirst for process analysis. Leaf through any magazine, and you will find that instructions abound. You may see, for instance, articles telling you how to do a magic trick, make a difficult decision, build muscle, overcome anxiety, and score at stock trading. Less practical, but not necessarily less interesting, are the informative articles: how brain surgeons work, how diamonds are formed, how cities fight crime. Every issue of the *New York Times Book Review* features an entire best-seller list devoted to "Advice, How-to, and Miscellaneous," including books on how to make money in real estate, how to lose weight, how to find a good mate, and how to lose a bad one. Evidently, if anything can still make a busy person crack open a book, it is a step-by-step explanation of how he or she can be a success at living.

THE PROCESS

Here are suggestions for writing an effective process analysis of your own. (In fact, what you are about to read is itself a process analysis.)

1. **Understand clearly the process you are about to analyze.** Think it through. This preliminary survey will make the task of writing far easier for you.

2. **Consider your thesis.** What is the point of your process analysis? Why are you bothering to tell readers about it? The THESIS STATEMENT for a process analysis need do no more than say what the subject is and maybe outline its essential stages, as in this example:

   The main stages in writing a process analysis are listing the steps in the process, drafting to explain the steps, and revising to clarify the steps.

But your readers will surely appreciate something livelier and more pointed, something that says "You can use this" or "This may surprise you" or "Listen up." Here are two thesis statements from essays in this chapter:

Almost all good writing begins with terrible first efforts. You need to start somewhere.

— Anne Lamott, "The Crummy First Draft"

[In a mortuary the body] is in short order sprayed, sliced, pierced, pickled, trussed, trimmed, creamed, waxed, painted, rouged, and neatly dressed — transformed from a common corpse into a Beautiful Memory Picture.

— Jessica Mitford, "Behind the Formaldehyde Curtain"

3. **Think about preparatory steps.** If the reader should do something before beginning the process, list these steps. For instance, you might begin, "Assemble the needed equipment: a 20-milliliter beaker, a 5-milliliter burette, safety gloves, and safety goggles."

4. **List the steps or stages in the process.** Try setting them down in CHRONOLOGICAL ORDER, one at a time — if this is possible. Some processes, however, do not happen in an orderly sequence, but occur all at once. If, for instance, you are writing an account of a typical earthquake, what do you mention first? The shifting of underground rock strata? cracks in the earth? falling houses? bursting water mains? toppling trees? mangled cars? casualties? For this subject the method of CLASSIFICATION (Chap. 9) might come to your aid. You might sort out apparently simultaneous events into categories: injury to people; damage to homes, to land, to public property.

5. **Check the completeness and order of the steps.** Make sure your list includes *all* the steps in the right order. Sometimes a stage of a process may contain a number of smaller stages. Make sure none has been left out. If any seems particularly tricky or complicated, underline it on your list to remind yourself when you write your essay to slow down and detail it with extra care.

6. **Define your terms.** Ask yourself, "Do I need any specialized or technical terms?" If so, be sure to define them. You'll sympathize with your reader if you have ever tried to assemble a bicycle according to a directive that begins, "Position sleeve casing on wheel center in fork with shaft in tongue groove, and gently but forcibly tap in pal-nut head."

7. **Use time-markers or** TRANSITIONS. These words or phrases indicate *when* one stage of a process stops and the next begins, and they greatly aid your reader in following you. Consider, for example, the following paragraph, in which plain medical prose makes good use of helpful time-markers (underlined). (The paragraph is adapted from *Pregnancy and Birth: A Book for Expectant Parents*, by Alan Frank Guttmacher.)

> In the human, <u>thirty-six hours after</u> the egg is fertilized, a two-cell egg appears. A twelve-cell development takes place in <u>seventy-two hours</u>. The egg is <u>still</u> round and has increased little in diameter. In this respect it is like a real estate development. <u>At first</u> a road bisects the whole area, <u>then</u> a cross road divides it into quarters, and <u>later</u> other roads divide it into eighths and twelfths. This happens without the taking of any more land, simply by subdivision of the original tract. <u>On the third or fourth day</u>, the egg passes from the Fallopian tube into the uterus. <u>By the fifth day</u> the original single large cell has subdivided into sixty small cells and floats about the slitlike uterine cavity <u>a day or two longer, then</u> adheres to the cavity's inner lining. <u>By the twelfth day</u> the human egg is already firmly implanted. Impregnation is <u>now</u> completed, <u>as yet</u> unbeknown to the woman. <u>At present</u>, she has not even had time to miss her first menstrual period, and other symptoms of pregnancy are <u>still several days distant</u>.

Brief as these time-markers are, they define each stage of the human egg's journey. When using time-markers, vary them so that they won't seem mechanical. If you can, avoid the monotonous repetition of a fixed phrase (*In the fourteenth stage . . . , In the fifteenth stage . . .*). Even boring time-markers, though, are better than none at all. Words and phrases such as *in the beginning, first, second, next, then, after that, three seconds later, at the same time*, and *finally* can help a process move smoothly in the telling and lodge firmly in the reader's mind.

8. **Be specific.** When you write a first draft, explain your process analysis in generous detail, even at the risk of being wordy. When you revise, it will be easier to delete than to amplify.

9. **Revise.** When your essay is finished, reread it carefully against the checklist on page 259. You might also enlist a friend's help. If your process analysis is directive ("How to Eat an Ice-Cream Cone without Dribbling"), see if your friend can follow the instructions without difficulty. If your process analysis is informative ("How a New Word Enters the Dictionary"), ask whether the process unfolds as clearly in his or her mind as it does in yours.

FOCUS ON CONSISTENCY

While drafting a process analysis, you may start off with subjects or verbs in one form and then shift to another form because the original choice feels awkward. In directive analyses, shifts occur most often with the subjects *a person* and *one*:

> INCONSISTENT   To keep the car from rolling while changing the tire, one should first set the car's emergency brake. Then you should block the three other tires with objects like rocks or chunks of wood.

In informative analyses, shifts usually occur from singular to plural as a way to get around *he* when the meaning includes males and females:

> INCONSISTENT   The poll worker first checks each voter against the registration list. Then they ask the voter to sign another list.

To repair inconsistencies, start with a subject that is both comfortable and sustainable:

> CONSISTENT   To keep the car from rolling while changing the tire, you should set the car's emergency brake. Then you should block the three other tires with objects like rocks or chunks of wood.

> CONSISTENT   Poll workers first check each voter against the registration list. Then they ask the voter to sign another list.

Sometimes, writers try to avoid naming or shifting subjects by using PASSIVE verbs that don't require actors:

> INCONSISTENT   To keep the car from rolling while changing the tire, one should first set the car's emergency brake. Then the three other tires should be blocked with objects like rocks or chunks of wood.

> INCONSISTENT   Poll workers first check each voter against the registration list. Then the voter is asked to sign another list.

In directive analyses, avoid passive verbs by using *you*, as shown in the consistent example above, or by using the commanding form of verbs, in which *you* is understood as the subject:

> CONSISTENT   To keep the car from rolling while changing the tire, first set the car's emergency brake. Then block the three other tires with objects like rocks or chunks of wood.

In informative analyses, passive verbs may be necessary if you don't know who the actor is or want to emphasize the action over the actor. But identifying the actor is generally clearer and more concise:

> CONSISTENT   Poll workers first check each voter against the registration list. Then they ask the voter to sign another list.

CHECKLIST FOR REVISING A PROCESS ANALYSIS

✔ **Thesis.** Does your process analysis have a point? Have you made sure readers know what it is?

✔ **Organization.** Have you arranged the steps of your process in a clear chronological order? If steps occur simultaneously, have you grouped them so that readers perceive some order?

✔ **Completeness.** Have you included all the necessary steps and explained each one fully? Is it clear how each one contributes to the result?

✔ **Definitions.** Have you explained the meanings of any terms your readers may not know?

✔ **Transitions.** Do time-markers distinguish the steps of your process and clarify their sequence?

✔ **Consistency.** Have you maintained comfortable, consistent, and clear subjects and verb forms?

PROCESS ANALYSIS IN ACADEMIC WRITING

A Psychology Textbook

This passage on our descent into sleep comes from a section in *Psychology*, by Carole Wade and Carol Tavris, on "the most perplexing of all our biological rhythms." Before this paragraph the authors review the history of sleep research; after it they continue to analyze the night-long process that follows this initial descent.

When you first climb into bed, close your eyes, and relax, your brain emits bursts of *alpha waves*. On an EEG recording, alpha waves have a regular, slow rhythm and high amplitude (height). Gradually, these waves slow down even further, and you drift into the Land of Nod, passing through four stages, each deeper than the previous one.

Steps preceding the process

Process to be explained with informative analysis

Stage 1. Your brain waves become small and irregular, and you feel yourself drifting on the edge of consciousness, in a state of light sleep. If awakened, you may recall fantasies or a few visual images.

Step 1

Stage 2. Your brain emits occasional short bursts of rapid, high-peaking waves called *sleep spindles*. Minor noises probably won't disturb you.

Step 2

Stage 3. In addition to the waves that are characteristic of stage 2, your brain occasionally emits *delta waves*, very slow waves with very high peaks. Your breathing and pulse have slowed down, your muscles are relaxed, and you are hard to waken.

Step 3

Stage 4. Delta waves have now largely taken over, and you are in deep sleep. It will take vigorous shaking or a loud noise to awaken you. Oddly, though, if you walk in your sleep, this is when you are likely to do so.

Step 4

A Lab Report

When scientists conduct experiments to test their hypotheses, or theories, they almost always write reports outlining the processes they followed so that other researchers can attempt to duplicate the outcomes. Laboratory reports are straightforward and objective and are generally organized under standardized headings, such as *Purpose, Materials, Procedure,* and *Results.* They often include tables, figures, and calculations pertaining to the experiment. Most writers of lab reports put the focus on the experiment by keeping themselves in the background: They avoid *I* or *we* and use the PASSIVE VOICE of verbs (*the solution was heated,* as opposed to *we heated the solution*). The passive voice is not universal, however. Most lab assignments you receive in college will include detailed instructions for writing up the experiment and its results, so the best writing strategy is to follow those instructions to the letter.

For a first-year chemistry experiment, Victor Khoury used mostly household materials to extract and isolate deoxyribonucleic acid (DNA) from an onion. Found in all plants and animals, DNA is the molecule that holds the genetic information needed to create and direct living organisms. Khoury's instructor intended the experiment to teach students basic techniques and interactions in chemistry and to help them understand genetics at a molecular level. In the following excerpt from his lab report, Khoury explains the procedure and the main result.

Procedure

A small onion was coarsely chopped and placed in a 1000-ml measuring cup along with 100 ml of a solution consisting of 10 ml of liquid dishwashing detergent, 1.5 g of table salt, and distilled water. The solution was intended to dissolve the proteins and lipids binding the cell membranes of the onion. The onion pieces were next pressed with the back of a spoon for 30 seconds to break the onion structure down into a mash.

Step 1

Reason for step

Step 2

Reason for step

The measuring cup was then placed in a pan of preheated 58°C water for 13 minutes to further separate the DNA from the walls of the onion cells. For the first 7 minutes, the onion was continuously pressed with a spoon. After 13 minutes of heating, the cup of mixture was then placed in a pan of ice water and the mixture was pressed and stirred for 5 minutes to cool it and to slow enzyme activity that would otherwise break down the DNA. The onion mixture was then placed in a coffee filter over a lab beaker and stored for 1 hour in a 4°C refrigerator in order to filter and further cool the solution.

After refrigeration, the filtered solution was stirred for 30 seconds and 10 ml were poured into a clean vial. A toothpick dipped in meat tenderizer was placed into the onion solution so that the enzymes in the tenderizer would further separate any remaining proteins from the DNA. Then refrigerated ethyl alcohol was poured into the vial until it formed a 1-cm layer on top of the onion solution.

Results

After the solution sat for 2 minutes, the DNA precipitated into the alcohol layer. The DNA was long, white, and stringy, with a gelatinous texture. This experiment demonstrated that DNA can be extracted and isolated using a process of homogenization and deproteinization. . . .

Step 3

Reason for step

Step 4

Reason for step

Step 5
Reason for step

Steps 6, 7, and 8

Reason for steps
Step 9

Discussion of results

Process Analysis

ANNE LAMOTT

Born in San Francisco in 1954, Anne Lamott is a novelist and essayist whom *Amazon* once characterized as "your run-of-the-mill recovering alcoholic and drug addict, born-again Christian, left-wing liberal, and single mother who just so happens to have written *New York Times*–best-selling books." Those books, including *Bird by Bird* (1994), *Traveling Mercies* (1999), *Blue Shoe* (2002), *Imperfect Birds* (2010), and *Small Victories* (2014), touch on subjects ranging from fiction to family to faith and have earned Lamott a devoted following. Her biweekly diary for *Salon*, "Word by Word," ran from 1996 to 1999 and was voted "The Best of the Web" by *Time* magazine. Lamott has taught at the University of California, Davis, and at writing workshops across the country. She lives in northern California.

The Crummy First Draft

Lamott's *Bird by Bird* is an inspiring and often very funny guide to writing. In this excerpt from the book, Lamott advises others how to begin writing by silencing their noisy inner critics.

In the next essay, "How to Write an *A* Paper," college student Koji Frahm offers a different take on succeeding as a writer.

For me and most of the other writers I know, writing is not rapturous. In fact, the only way I can get anything written at all is to write really, really crummy first drafts. 1

The first draft is the child's draft, where you let it all pour out and then let it romp all over the place, knowing that no one is going to see it and that you can shape it later. You just let this childlike part of you channel whatever voices and visions come through and onto the page. If one of the characters wants to say "Well, so what, Mr. Poopy Pants?" you let her. No one is going to see it. If the kid wants to get into really sentimental, weepy, emotional territory, you let him. Just get it all down on paper, because there may be something great in those six crazy pages that you would never have gotten to by more rational, grown-up means. There may be something in the very last line of the very last paragraph on page six that you just love, that is so beautiful or wild that you now know what you're supposed to be writing about, more or less, or in what direction you might go — but there was no way to get to this without first getting through the first five and a half pages. 2

I used to write food reviews for *California* magazine before it folded. (My   3
writing food reviews had nothing to do with the magazine folding, although
every single review did cause a couple of canceled subscriptions. Some readers
took umbrage at my comparing mounds of vegetable puree with various
ex-presidents' brains.) These reviews always took two days to write. First I'd go
to a restaurant several times with a few opinionated, articulate friends in tow.
I'd sit there writing down everything anyone said that was at all interesting or
funny. Then on the following Monday I'd sit down at my desk with my notes,
and try to write the review. Even after I'd been doing this for years, panic
would set in. I'd try to write a lead, but instead I'd write a couple of dreadful
sentences, xx them out, try again, xx everything out, and then feel despair and
worry settle on my chest like an x-ray apron. It's over, I'd think, calmly. I'm not
going to be able to get the magic to work this time. I'm ruined. I'm through.
I'm toast. Maybe, I'd think, I can get my old job back as a clerk-typist. But
probably not. I'd get up and study my teeth in the mirror for a while. Then I'd
stop, remember to breathe, make a few phone calls, hit the kitchen and chow
down. Eventually I'd go back and sit down at my desk, and sigh for the next
ten minutes. Finally I would pick up my one-inch picture frame, stare into it
as if for the answer, and every time the answer would come: All I had to do
was to write a really crummy first draft of, say, the opening paragraph. And no
one was going to see it.

So I'd start writing without reining myself in. It was almost just typing,   4
just making my fingers move. And the writing would be *terrible*. I'd write a lead
paragraph that was a whole page, even though the entire review could only
be three pages long, and then I'd start writing up descriptions of the food, one
dish at a time, bird by bird, and the critics would be sitting on my shoulders,
commenting like cartoon characters. They'd be pretending to snore, or rolling
their eyes at my overwrought descriptions, no matter how hard I tried to tone
those descriptions down, no matter how conscious I was of what a friend said
to me gently in my early days of restaurant reviewing. "Annie," she said, "it is
just a piece of *chicken*. It is just a bit of *cake*."

But because by then I had been writing for so long, I would eventually let   5
myself trust the process — sort of, more or less. I'd write a first draft that was
maybe twice as long as it should be, with a self-indulgent and boring beginning,
stupefying descriptions of the meal, lots of quotes from my black-humored
friends that made them sound more like the Manson girls[1] than food lovers,
and no ending to speak of. The whole thing would be so long and incoherent
and hideous that for the rest of the day I'd obsess about getting creamed by a

---

[1] The Manson girls were young, troubled members of the cult led by Charles
Manson (born 1934). In 1969 Manson and some of his followers were convicted of murder in
California. — Eds.

car before I could write a decent second draft. I'd worry that people would read what I'd written and believe that the accident had really been a suicide, that I had panicked because my talent was waning and my mind was shot.

The next day, though, I'd sit down, go through it all with a colored pen, take out everything I possibly could, find a new lead somewhere on the second page, figure out a kicky place to end it, and then write a second draft. It always turned out fine, sometimes even funny and weird and helpful. I'd go over it one more time and mail it in.   6

Then, a month later, when it was time for another review, the whole process would start again, complete with the fears that people would find my first draft before I could rewrite it.   7

Almost all good writing begins with terrible first efforts. You need to start somewhere. Start by getting something — anything — down on paper. A friend of mine says that the first draft is the down draft — you just get it down. The second draft is the up draft — you fix it up. You try to say what you have to say more accurately. And the third draft is the dental draft, where you check every tooth, to see if it's loose or cramped or decayed, or even, God help us, healthy.   8

What I've learned to do when I sit down to work on a crummy first draft is to quiet the voices in my head. First there's the vinegar-lipped Reader Lady, who says primly, "Well, *that's* not very interesting, is it?" And there's the emaciated German male who writes these Orwellian[2] memos detailing your thought crimes. And there are your parents, agonizing over your lack of loyalty and discretion; and there's William Burroughs,[3] dozing off or shooting up because he finds you as bold and articulate as a houseplant; and so on. And there are also the dogs: Let's not forget the dogs, the dogs in their pen who will surely hurtle and snarl their way out if you ever *stop* writing, because writing is, for some of us, the latch that keeps the door of the pen closed, keeps those crazy, ravenous dogs contained. . . .   9

Close your eyes and get quiet for a minute, until the chatter starts up. Then isolate one of the voices and imagine the person speaking as a mouse. Pick it up by the tail and drop it into a mason jar. Then isolate another voice, pick it up by the tail, drop it in the jar. And so on. Drop in any high-maintenance parental units, drop in any contractors, lawyers, colleagues, children, anyone who is whining in your head. Then put the lid on, and watch all these mouse people clawing at the glass, jabbering away, trying to make you feel crummy because you won't do what they want — won't give them more money, won't   10

---

[2] In his novel *1984*, the British writer George Orwell (1903–50) depicts a futuristic world in which a totalitarian government controls citizens' behavior and thoughts. — Eds.

[3] The American novelist William Burroughs (1914–97) wrote experimental and often surreal works on drug addiction and other aspects of contemporary life. — Eds.

be more successful, won't see them more often. Then imagine that there is a volume-control button on the bottle. Turn it all the way up for a minute, and listen to the stream of angry, neglected, guilt-mongering voices. Then turn it all the way down and watch the frantic mice lunge at the glass, trying to get to you. Leave it down, and get back to your crummy first draft.

A writer friend of mine suggests opening the jar and shooting them all in   11
the head. But I think he's a little angry, and I'm sure nothing like this would ever occur to you.

Journal Writing

Describe what usually happens when you begin a writing project. Is the blank paper or screen an invitation or an obstacle? Do the words flow freely or haltingly or not at all? Do you feel creative? competent? helpless? tortured?

Questions on Meaning

1. What is Lamott's THESIS? Which sentences best convey her main idea?

2. According to Lamott, what role can other people, real or imaginary, play in the writing process? Are they helpful?

3. Review the comment by Lamott's friend (par. 8) that "the first draft is the down draft. . . . The second draft is the up draft. . . . And the third draft is the dental draft. . . ." What do you think is the difference in the writer's approach and focus at each stage? In what ways, if any, do these stages relate to your own approach to writing?

4. What do you think Lamott means when she says that "writing is, for some of us, the latch that keeps the door of the pen closed, keeps those crazy, ravenous dogs contained" (par. 9)? What might the dogs and control of them stand for in this IMAGE?

5. What is the PURPOSE of Lamott's piece? To advise inexperienced writers? To relate her own difficulties with writing? Both, or something else? How do you know?

Questions on Writing Strategy

1. Lamott's book *Bird by Bird*, the source of this piece, is subtitled *Some Instructions on Writing and Life.* Who do you believe would find Lamott's advice most useful? Will it be useful to you? Why, or why not?

2. In paragraph 4 Lamott says that she wrote food reviews "one dish at a time" and "bird by bird" (a metaphor from earlier in her book, meaning one step at a time). What steps does her process analysis outline for overcoming obstacles?

3. Process analysis can be directive or explanatory (see p. 254), and Lamott's piece has good examples of both types. In which paragraphs does Lamott use each type? Where does she combine them? What does each type contribute? Is the mixture effective? Why, or why not?

4. What transitions does Lamott use to guide the reader through the steps of her process analysis? Is her use of transitions effective?

5. **OTHER METHODS**   Paragraphs 3–7 NARRATE Lamott's experience writing food reviews for a magazine. What is the effect of this story?

Questions on Language

1. Although trying to be encouraging, Lamott uses many negative adjectives to describe her own first efforts: for example, "terrible" (par. 4) and "incoherent" (5). Find some other examples of negative adjectives. Why do you think Lamott uses so many of them?

2. What is Lamott's TONE? How seriously does she take the difficulties facing the writer?

3. Lamott uses several original images, such as the "vinegar-lipped Reader Lady" (par. 9). List some images that made a particular impression on you, and explain their effect.

4. Be sure you know how to define the following words: overwrought (par. 4); self-indulgent, stupefying, waning (5); emaciated, hurtle, ravenous (9); guilt-mongering (10).

Suggestions for Writing

1. **FROM JOURNAL TO ESSAY**   Write an essay that explains your own writing process (in general or on a specific project) as you progress from idea to final draft. Enliven the process with specific methods and incidents — techniques of procrastination, ripping up draft after draft, listening to and silencing (or not) your own imagined voices, and so on. Try to draw some conclusions about what the writing process means to you.

2. Writing is, of course, only one way to communicate ideas. Other forms of communication can also be difficult: speaking up in class, making a presentation to a group of people, meeting with a teacher, interviewing for a job, making an important telephone call. Write a process analysis in which you first examine an oral encounter that was particularly difficult for you and then offer advice about how best to tackle such a situation.

3. **CRITICAL WRITING**   We are usually taught to respect our parents and other authority figures, but Lamott advises writers to ignore them while composing. Is her advice justified in your view? Are there times when we can, even should, disregard authority? Write an essay about a time when you felt you could accomplish something only by disregarding the advice of someone you would normally listen

to — or, in contrast, when you heeded advice even though it held you back or ignored advice and eventually regretted doing so. How difficult was your action? How did the situation turn out? Looking back, do you believe you did the right thing?

4. **CONNECTIONS**   Lamott stresses the importance of ignoring the perspectives of others in order to hear your own voice, and in the next essay, Koji Frahm (satirically) encourages writers to be hostile toward their readers. Citing examples from your own experience and from Lamott's and Frahm's essays, write an essay that examines writers' obligations to others versus obligations to themselves. When are we justified in following our own paths regardless of what readers think, and when are we not?

KOJI FRAHM

Koji Frahm was born in 1987 and grew up in Palo Alto, California, a suburb of San Francisco. In high school he competed on the swim team and spent much of his time playing video games. After enrolling at the University of California, Davis, as a biomechanical engineering student, he found himself getting up early to write short stories before classes, and so switched his major to creative writing. He graduated in 2009 and currently lives in Brooklyn, New York, where he runs a makerspace for artists and continues to write.

How to Write an *A* Paper

"How to Write an *A* Paper" was written in response to an assignment given in a freshman composition class. Like Anne Lamott in the previous essay, Frahm considers the challenges and frustrations of writing. Focusing on the advice typically offered to college students, his essay is largely a directive process analysis, but it is also a SATIRE: By outwardly showing us one way to approach a writing project, the author implicitly urges us to do the opposite.

Be nebulous. Scratch that, be amphibological. The vaguer, the better. The 1 reader should be thinking, *what the hell does that mean?* right off the bat. The first sentence is key. Make it short, deadly, and impossible to understand. Convoluted is the term to use here. And remember, I'm not talking indiscernible due to stupidity; I'm talking indiscernible due to smarts. You have to sound brilliant. Scratch that, perspicacious. Be as opaque as a dense fog settling in front of a concrete wall — let them see nothing. Make them understand that you're smarter than they are. The sooner you establish this, the better. Hitting them hard and fast on the first sentence is the quickest way to do it. Make them so unsure of their own acumen from the start that they won't question you afterwards. Get them on the ground, and keep them there. Your God-like intelligence should never be questioned by these mere mortals — that's how you should be writing. Look at your first sentence for a moment and consider this: Is it short? Is it vague? Does it tell the reader nothing about what's going on? If so — bingo. You're in the clear. You can't be marked off if they can't understand your higher parlance — and that's exactly what we're going for.

The end of the introduction means it's thesis time. If you really want to 2 pull this off, end the introduction with no clear thesis. That way, they'll assume the thesis is lurking around somewhere later in the paper like a prowling hyena in Serengeti; and before you KNOW it, they'll forget what they were searching for. You never had one anyway. And if they're really keen for it, they'll probably just extrapolate something from the parts they don't understand later in the paper. You're Shakespeare, remember? You know best.

Be choppy. Scratch that, be desultory. Jump around like a rabbit on 3
fire — never let the reader know where you're headed next. The transitions between your paragraphs should be sudden and unexpected; your sentences short and rapid fire. Your teachers always taught you to be smooth and transitional — screw that. Toss your reader around like a paper bag in a tempest; the only thing they should be doing is covering their heads. Confusion is the key term here. If your reader doesn't look flummoxed and bleary-eyed by paragraph three, you aren't trying hard enough. You're smarter, you're faster, and the only thing they can do is try to keep up.

Paragraph four, all right, now we're getting somewhere. This is the part of 4
the essay where you're taught to bring out the big points. The "meat" of the essay is how teachers sometimes refer to it. That's all garbage. You don't need a plethora of in-depth points or solid evidence to fill up your paper — you just need one. One point. That's all you need. Reiteration is the key term here. I can't stress this part enough. All you need to know is this: keep talking. Be the jammed cassette deck on repeat. Write as if you're being paid a dollar a word, and you have only thirty seconds to type. Just keep pushing through the same old stuff with different wording. Dress it up; do its hair; color its nails; I don't care. Repackage the old, make it look new. Novelty sells the car. Write frivolously. Scratch that, farcically. It'll seem like you're getting deeper and deeper into the topic with every word you say, but really you'll JUST be wasting their time. Analysis is overrated — just keep spitting out what you already said. Regurgitation is the key term here. Vomit your words out and eat them back up, then spit them out a minute later. You're the mother eagle, and the reader is your starving chick. To add weight to this empty package, make sure the paragraph you put your half-digested words in is one of the longest. Nothing says "important" like a hefty paragraph. You would know. You're the smartest.

The thesaurus is your friend. Scratch that, your soul-mate. This whole 5
operation is FUELED by perplexing your reader. If you're the matador, the thesaurus is your cape — you're both coaxing the reader to charge through your charade. An essay is just made up of words, and that's the punch-line of this exploitation. Every word can be more sequestered; every syllable can be more ambagious. Make reading your essay more difficult than solving a Rubik's cube in the dark. Don't write *elderly person*, scratch that off. Write *septuagenarian*. That woman isn't pretty; she's *pulchritudinous* for someone possessing your voluminous vocabulary. And don't worry if the definitions aren't totally

the same; it's not as if the reader is going to know what's going on anyway. Obfuscate is the key term here.

Metaphors. It's always good to throw a lot of these in — teachers love this 6 stuff. Make sure they're really random and sporadic, popping up anywhere and everywhere like ferns in the Amazon jungle. Whatever pops into your head at the time, make it a metaphor. Whether it's animals from the Nature Channel you were watching two hours ago, or a Rubik's cube that's sitting on your desk, anything is fair GAME. Forget about clarity or adding depth, your metaphors are there for the same reason neon lights exist — distraction. Your essay should be a patchwork quilt of random metaphors, shrouding your essay from lucidity like the moon blocking the sun during a lunar eclipse. Just stick them everywhere.

Make errors. You heard right. Capitalize some random words throughout 7 your paper. Attach a note to the final document explaining that your computer was on the fritz, and even during printing it was behaving idiosyncratically. *Proofreading couldn't prevent it because it occurred during printing*, the note will say, and how can the teacher blame you? Your computer was haywire,; totally nuts. It was jumping off the walls and banging into the ceiling like a rubber ball fired out of a Civil War cannon, spitting and blasting unnecessary semicolons and punctuation errors into your work. You weren't responsible for what it did. And once you get that across, you can also blame the computer for for any typos or repeated words you may have left in my accident. Just type some OCCASIONAL caps-locked words now and then, and suddenly you're exonerated from all grammatical imperfections. Diabolical is the key term here.

By now you should be closing in like a school of piranha onto a drown- 8 ing ox. You've probably written enough, so you might as well wrap things up. Conclusions are easy. All you need is a quote and your choice of any massive, tear-inducing flaw in society. Take your pick: consumerism consuming our culture, superficiality sucking out our souls, mankind's maniacal instincts, the government's dominance of society's free will, et cetera, et cetera. It doesn't matter. It doesn't even have to pertain to your topic. The beauty with conclusions is you can tie just about anything to anything. If you were writing about the mating habits of rhinos, you could probably conclude with an anecdote about world hunger. The point is that there is no point. Be as random as a herd of buffalo showing up to present the Best Picture award at the Oscars. Just pick something you can rant about for a good half-page and you're in business.

Now for the quote. This is the last thing the reader's nonplussed eyes will 9 see — so make it good. This is the one time in the essay you want them to understand what's going on. After all this confusion they'll be ravenous for something transpicuous — and this is the time to dish it out. What's even better, they'll love you for it. Everyone likes being enlightened. And after your quote, your reader should be more sagacious than Buddha on heroin. Choose one THAT sounds inspirational and profound. Aristotle and Socrates are always solid choices. Once again, it doesn't matter if it actually pertains to your topic. As long as it's half decent, the reader will be grateful. Place this at the end in italics and you're home free.

Congratulations, you're done. Don't worry about proofreading for typos — you took care of the errors, remember? That damn computer of yours. All you have to do now is make sure you turn it in on Wednesday. Sit back and relax; and have a triumphant smile and modest remarks ready for the teacher next week when he praises your work in front of the class. What could go wrong, anyway? We've covered all the bases. An "A" is inevitable. Scratch that, ineluctable . . . which reminds me.   10

I received a paper back this morning and I still haven't checked the grade. Excuse me for a moment; I have to confirm my "A." Consider this a testament to my guide to success. Confidence is the key term here.   11

Be a victim. Scratch that, be a scapegoat. Take the paper and crumple it, throw it away or tuck it away somewhere you won't see it. Who cares anyway? This was a stupid assignment to begin with. It was a puerile assignment with an imbecilic teacher to grade it. What the hell does he know? Confusing Introduction. Lack of Content. Bad Transitions. *Excessive Grammatical Errors?!* You told him the computer was going haywire. Didn't he see the note? What an IDIOT. Obviously it was too much. He probably didn't understand what was going on and decided to take it out on you. What a sucker. Scratch that, a simpleton. His lack of comprehension isn't your fault — the ignoramus. He's taking his confusion out on you, satisfying his own denial by giving you a bad grade. He's just like everybody nowadays. No one takes responsibility for their own problems. People mess up their lives beyond all repair and still have excuses for everything. It's the whole world's fault before anyone will admit it's theirs. *He doesn't like me because* . . . *It's not my fault, she's the one that* . . . *I'm late because this stupid* . . . *blah* . . . *blah* . . . *blah* . . . How about a simple "sorry, it's my fault"? It's like the entire damn world would rather blame its problems on other things rather than fixing them. No one is willing to own up to their actions and take the consequences anymore. That's what this is all about. I'm just the hapless victim for all those ignorant fools out there. Those vainglorious dunderheads. Those egocentric imbeciles. It's like a wise man once said: 12

> *You must not lose faith in humanity.*
> *Humanity is an ocean;*
> *if a few drops of the ocean are dirty,*
> *the ocean does not become dirty.*
> — *Mahatma Gandhi*

Journal Writing

Frahm's essay is SATIRE — that is, an indirect attack on human follies or flaws, using IRONY to urge behavior exactly the opposite of what is really desired. In your journal, explore when you have proposed satirical approaches to challenges that seem overwhelming or ridiculous — for example, suggesting breaking all the dishes so that they don't have to be washed again or barring pedestrians from city streets so that they don't interfere with cars. What kinds of situations might lead you to make suggestions like these?

Questions on Meaning

1. How seriously does Frahm take his subject? Is his main PURPOSE to amuse and entertain, to inform students of ways they can become better writers, to warn about bad teachers, or to make fun of readers? Support your answer with EVIDENCE from the essay.

2. Look closely at Frahm's conclusion (par. 12). Does his writing advice actually promise an A for those who follow it? Why, or why not?

3. Does Frahm have a THESIS? Where in the essay does he explain his reason for not stating it outright?

Questions on Writing Strategy

1. How is Frahm's essay organized? Trace his process analysis carefully to determine whether it happens CHRONOLOGICALLY or follows another order. How effective is this method of organization and presentation?

2. At several points Frahm writes, "___ is the key term here." Find these sentences and underline them. How do they give the essay COHERENCE and UNITY?

3. What is the author's apparent attitude toward readers? What role does he suggest an awareness of AUDIENCE plays in effective writing?

4. Some of the words in Frahm's essay are unnecessarily printed in all-capital letters. What other errors can you find? Why are they there?

5. **OTHER METHODS**   As is the case with any process analysis, "How to Write an A Paper" relies on DIVISION or ANALYSIS of its subject. What does Frahm imply are the elements of good writing?

Questions on Language

1. How do sentences such as "The vaguer, the better" and "Make it short, deadly, and impossible to understand" (par. 1) signal the TONE of this essay from the start? Should they be read literally, ironically, or some other way? How does the tone contribute to Frahm's satire?

2. What consistent sentence subject does Frahm use in "How to Write an A Paper"? Who is to perform the process?

3. Frahm's essay includes many difficult words seemingly plucked from a thesaurus (par. 5), including the following: nebulous, amphibological, perspicacious, acumen, parlance (1); extrapolate (2); desultory, flummoxed (3); plethora, farcically, regurgitation (4); sequestered, ambagious, obfuscate (5); sporadic, lucidity (6); idiosyncratically (7); nonplussed, transpicuous, sagacious (9); ineluctable (10); puerile, hapless, vainglorious (12). Do readers need to know the definitions of these words to understand Frahm's meaning?

4. In paragraph 6 Frahm encourages writers to use "a lot" of metaphors. Point to any metaphors or similes in his essay that strike you as especially imaginative. (See FIGURATIVE LANGUAGE in the Glossary if you need a definition of *metaphor* or *simile*.) What does Frahm say is the purpose of such language? Do you agree?

Suggestions for Writing

1. **FROM JOURNAL TO ESSAY** Choose one of the solutions you wrote about in your journal, or propose a solution to a challenge that your journal entry has suggested. Write an essay detailing this satirical solution, paying careful attention to explaining each step of the process and to maintaining your satiric tone throughout.

2. Write a serious (not satirical) essay that teaches readers how to do something you're good at, such as making fresh guacamole from scratch, writing letters of complaint, or unclogging a sink. You might, like Frahm, imagine a specific group of people as your readers, or you might address your instructions to a more general audience.

3. Try to recall a time when you struggled with or failed at an assignment you thought would be simple. Write a short NARRATIVE about your difficulties. What went wrong? How did the struggle affect you? Did you learn anything?

4. **CRITICAL WRITING** In a brief essay, pick apart Frahm's advice and the ways he applies it to his own writing in "How to Write an A Paper." Consider, for instance, how his first paragraph illustrates the function of his first sentence, or why he includes the quotation by Mahatma Gandhi at the end of the essay. Where else in this essay does Frahm commit the very sins of bad writing that he implicitly identifies? How effective are his choices?

5. **CONNECTIONS** What does Frahm gain or lose by using satire and irony to make his point? What would be the comparative strengths and weaknesses of an essay that straightforwardly and sincerely approached the challenges writers face, such as Anne Lamott's "The Crummy First Draft" (p. 262)?

Koji Frahm on Writing

Asked to reflect on the experience of writing "How to Write an A Paper," Koji Frahm offered the following comments.

I'm still not sure if I like this essay. But with that said, I will admit it was a ton of fun to write. This assignment was to write a parody of another essay. And so, using observation from over the years of all the garbage and terrible techniques people cram into their essays (the idea actually came while discussing Poli Sci papers with a friend), I molded the most ridiculous and multilayered piece I've ever attempted — this being the result. I still have qualms with it; it still doesn't measure up to what I had in mind. But for what it's worth, it's made people chuckle, and that, for me, was the greatest reward of writing this piece.

The Bedford Reader on Writing

Although his essay is a lot of fun for readers, too, Frahm admits that his advice to student writers is "ridiculous and multilayered." For simple and straightforward guidelines on how to write an effective paper, see Chapter 2 of this book.

FIROOZEH DUMAS

Born in Abadan, Iran, in 1966, Firoozeh Dumas immigrated with her family to Whittier, California, at the age of seven, moved back to Iran two years later, then finally settled in the United States two years after that. She earned her bachelor's degree from the University of California at Berkeley in 1988. Dumas, who has said that the worst misconception about Iranians is "that we are completely humorless," took up writing partly to correct such assumptions. Her popular first book, *Funny in Farsi: A Memoir of Growing Up Iranian in America* (2003), portrays the humor in her family's experiences as Middle Eastern immigrants to the United States. Her second book, *Laughing without an Accent: Adventures of an Iranian American, at Home and Abroad* (2008), continues the theme with essays about trying to sell a cross-shaped potato on *eBay* and taking a cruise with fifty-one family members, among other topics. Dumas has written a novel for young readers, *It Ain't So Awful, Falafel* (2016) and contributes to several periodicals — including the *New York Times*, the *Wall Street Journal*, the *Los Angeles Times*, and *Lifetime*. She is also an occasional commentator on National Public Radio.

Sweet, Sour, and Resentful

In this 2009 essay from *Gourmet* magazine, Dumas outlines her mother's pains-taking process of preparing a traditional Persian meal for the dozens of distant relatives and friends of friends who descended on the family's California condo every weekend. Through her mother's weekly routine — from hunting down ingredients to chopping herbs to refusing praise — Dumas reveals much about family, culture, and humility.

My mother's main ingredient in cooking was resentment — not that I   1
can blame her. In 1979, my family was living temporarily in Newport Beach, California. Our real home was in Abadan, a city in the southwest of Iran. Despite its desert location and ubiquitous refineries, Abadan was the quintessential small town. Everybody's father (including my own) worked for the National Iranian Oil Company, and almost all the moms stayed home. The employees' kids attended the same schools. No one locked their doors. Whenever I hear John Mellencamp's "Small Town," I think of Abadan, although I'm guessing John Mellencamp was thinking of somewhere else when he wrote that song.

By the time of the Iranian revolution,[1] we had adjusted to life in California. We said "Hello" and "Have a nice day" to perfect strangers, wore flip-flops, and grilled cheeseburgers next to our kebabs. We never understood why Americans put ice in tea or bought shampoo that smelled like strawberries, but other than that, America felt like home.

When the revolution happened, thousands left Iran for Southern California. Since we were one of the few Iranian families already there, our phone did not stop ringing. Relatives, friends, friends of relatives, friends of friends, and people whose connection we never quite figured out called us with questions about settling into this new land. Displaying the hospitality that Iranians so cherish, my father extended a dinner invitation to everyone who called. As a result, we found ourselves feeding dozens of people every weekend.

The marathon started on Monday, with my mother planning the menu while letting us know that she was already tired. Fortunately, our rice dishes were made to be shared; our dilemma, however, was space. Our condo was small. Our guests squeezed onto the sofa, sat on the floor, or overflowed onto the patio. We eventually had to explain to our American neighbors why there were so many cars parked in front of our place every weekend. My mother, her diplomatic skills in full swing, had me deliver plates of Persian food, decorated with radish roses and mint sprigs, to them. In time, we learned not to share *fesenjan*, pomegranate stew with ground walnuts. "Yes, now that you mention it, it does look like mud, but it's really good," I'd explain, convincing no one.

Because my mother did not drive, my father took her to buy ingredients every Tuesday after work. In Abadan, my mother and I had started most days in the market, going from vendor to vendor looking for herbs, vegetables, and fruits. The fish came from the Karun and Arvand (Shatt al Arab) Rivers, the *lavash* and the *sangak* breads were freshly baked, and the chickens were still alive. We were locavores by necessity and foodies without knowing it. In America, I learned that the time my parents spent shopping was in direct correlation to the degree of my mother's bad mood. An extra-long trip meant that my mother could not find everything she needed, a point she would make loud and clear when she got home: "Why don't they let fruit ripen here?" "Why are the chickens so huge and flavorless?" "I couldn't find fresh herbs." "My feet hurt." "How am I supposed to get everything done?"

The first step was preparing the herbs. My mother insisted that the parsley, cilantro, and chives for *qormeh sabzi*, herb stew, had to be finely chopped by hand. The food processor, she explained, squished them. As she and my father sat across the table wielding huge knives, they argued incessantly.

---

[1] In 1979 fundamentalist rebels led by Ayatollah Ruhollah Khomeini overthrew the Iranian monarchy and established the Islamic Republic of Iran, a theocratic dictatorship. — EDS.

My father did his best to help her. It wasn't enough. As soon as the mountain of herbs was chopped, my mother started frying them. At any given time, my mother was also frying onions. Every few days, while my father was watching the six o'clock news, my mother would hand him a dozen onions, a cutting board, and a knife. No words were exchanged. Much to my father's relief, I once volunteered for this task, but apparently my slices were neither thin enough nor even. It took my father's precision as an engineer to slice correctly.

While all four burners were in use, my mother mixed the ground beef, rice, split peas, scallions, and herbs for stuffed grape leaves. I chopped the stems of the grape leaves. I had tried stuffing them once, but my rolls, deemed not tight enough, were promptly unrolled and then rerolled by my mother.

In between cooking, my mother made yogurt — the thick, sour variety that we couldn't find in America. She soaked walnuts and almonds in water to plump them up; fried eggplants for *kashk-e bademjan*, a popular appetizer with garlic, turmeric, mint, and whey; made *torshi-e limo*, a sour lemon condiment; and slivered orange peels. I had been fired from this task also, having left on far too much pith.

By the time our guests arrived, my mother was exhausted. But the work was not finished. Rice, the foundation of the Persian meal, the litmus test of the cook's ability, cannot be prepared ahead of time. To wit, one day in Abadan, the phone rang when my mother was about to drain the rice. During the time it took her to answer the phone and tell her sister that she would call her back, the rice overcooked. Almost forty years later, I still remember my mother's disappointment and her explaining to my father that her sister had time to talk because my aunt's maid did all the cooking. My aunt did not even drain her own rice.

We certainly did not have a table big enough to set, so we simply stacked dishes and utensils, buffet-style. As the guest list grew, we added paper plates and plastic utensils. It was always my job to announce that dinner was ready. As people entered the dining room, they gasped at the sight of my mother's table. Her *zereshk polow*, barberry rice, made many emotional. There are no fresh barberries in America (my mother had brought dried berries from Iran in her suitcase), and the sight of that dish, with its distinct deep red hue, was a reminder of the life our guests had left behind.

Our dinners took days to cook and disappeared in twenty minutes. As our guests heaped their plates and looked for a place to sit, they lavished praise on my mother, who, according to tradition, deflected it all. "It's nothing," she said. "I wish I could've done more." When they told her how lucky she was to have me to help her, my mother politely nodded, while my father added, "Firoozeh's good at math."

On Sundays, my mother lay on the sofa, her swollen feet elevated, fielding   12
thank-you phone calls from our guests. She had the same conversation a
dozen times; each one ended with, "Of course you can give our name to your
cousins." As I watched my mother experience the same draining routine week
after week, I decided that tradition is good only if it brings joy to all involved.
This includes the hostess. Sometimes, even our most cherished beliefs must
evolve. Evolution, thy name is potluck.

Journal Writing

Many people have unique rituals, like Dumas's parents' practice of serving elaborate Persian meals to distant acquaintances every weekend. List some rituals that are
unique to your family, to another group you belong to, or to you alone — for instance,
a holiday celebration, a vacation activity, a way of decompressing after a stressful
week.

Questions on Meaning

1. Why were weekend dinners so important to the author's parents and their guests?
   Consider not just the meals themselves but the larger context that prompted
   them.

2. In which sentence or sentences does Dumas state her THESIS most directly?

3. What would you say is Dumas's PURPOSE in this essay? Is it primarily to entertain readers by describing her family's weekly routine, or does she seem to have
   another purpose in mind?

4. What solution to her mother's exhausting role as hostess does Dumas propose
   in paragraph 12? Do you think her mother would have agreed to it? Why, or
   why not?

Questions on Writing Strategy

1. Why does Dumas begin her essay with an overview of life in Abadan and an
   ALLUSION to the Iranian revolution (pars. 1–3)? What purpose does this opening
   serve?

2. How does Dumas seem to imagine her AUDIENCE? To what extent could she
   ASSUME that readers would appreciate her mother's situation?

3. What steps does Dumas identify in the process of hosting Iranian guests every
   weekend? How does she ensure that her analysis has COHERENCE?

4. **OTHER METHODS**   What role does COMPARISON AND CONTRAST play in paragraph 5?

Questions on Language

1. Explain how Dumas's TONE contributes to the humor in her essay.

2. Where in this essay does Dumas use Persian words? What is their EFFECT?

3. In paragraph 9, Dumas says that rice is "the litmus test" for Iranian cooks. What does she mean? What is a litmus test, and how does the phrase connect to the focus (and title) of her essay?

4. Be sure you know the meanings of the following words: ubiquitous, quintessential (par. 1); Persian (4); locavores, correlation (5); pith (8); lavished, deflected (11); potluck (12).

Suggestions for Writing

1. **FROM JOURNAL TO ESSAY**   Write an essay explaining one of the rituals you listed in your journal. Focus on the details and steps of the ritual itself as well as on the significance it holds for you and for any others who participate in it with you.

2. Research the influx of Iranian families into California during the 1970s. What prompted this migration? What quality of life did newcomers face on arrival? What tensions did their arrival create? In an essay, consider these questions and others your research may lead you to. You may prefer to focus on a different migration from the nineteenth or twentieth century — such as that of Irish to the eastern United States, Chinese to the western United States, or African Americans from the southern to the northern United States.

3. **CRITICAL WRITING**   What impression of herself does Dumas create in this essay? What adjectives would you use to describe the writer as she reveals herself on the page? Cite specific language from the essay to support your ANALYSIS.

4. **CONNECTIONS**   Both Firoozeh Dumas and Amy Tan, in "Fish Cheeks" (p. 74), hint at how as children they felt ashamed of their families because of certain foods. Write an essay in which you COMPARE AND CONTRAST the ways the two writers describe food and how each writer uses food to make a larger point about the need to fit in.

Firoozeh Dumas on Writing

In a 2004 interview with Khaled Hosseini (author of *The Kite Runner* and *A Thousand Splendid Suns*), Firoozeh Dumas explained how writing awakens her memory. As a girl growing up in Iran and the United States, Dumas says she "was always that quiet kid in a room full of adults" who carefully "listened and observed." When she started writing as an adult, her collected observations "just flooded back." Unlike those who experience writer's block, Dumas was easily inspired: "Every time I finished a story, another popped up in its place. It was like using a vending machine: The candy falls down and is immediately replaced by another."

In order to keep up with her vending machine of ideas — and to accommodate her busy family life — Dumas writes "in spurts," often waking at four in the morning. "Once a story is in my head, I'm possessed, and the only thing I can do is write like mad," she told Hosseini. "This means the house gets very messy and dinner is something frozen. I do not read or go to the movies when I am writing, because I can't concentrate on anything else. I also keep writing in my head when I'm not actually writing, which means that I become a terrible listener."

The Bedford Reader on Writing

Have you ever found that the act of writing triggers your memory, as it does for Dumas? Try FREEWRITING (p. 33) and see if it works for you. Many writers find that simply sitting down and writing, even for just a few minutes at a time, can yield surprising results.

DAN KOEPPEL

Journalist and outdoors enthusiast Dan Koeppel is best known for his expertise on extreme sports, such as sky diving and wave running. Born in 1962, he studied at Hampshire College and is a contributing editor at *Popular Mechanics* and *Bicycling*. He was inducted into the Mountain Bike Hall of Fame in 2003 and for a time was a commentator on the Public Radio International program *Marketplace*. A productive and eclectic writer, Koeppel has published columns and articles in a wide array of magazines, including *Audubon*, *Mountain Bike*, *Outside*, *Elle*, *Martha Stewart Living*, and, on a regular basis, *Wired* and *Popular Science*. His books include *Extreme Sports Almanac* (2000), *To See Every Bird on Earth: A Father, a Son, and a Lifelong Obsession* (2005), and *Banana: The Fate of the Fruit That Changed the World* (2008). Koeppel lives in Los Angeles, California, where he is also an occasional film and television screenwriter and a professional roller derby referee.

Taking a Fall

Could you survive a six-mile drop from an airplane? The answer, says Koeppel, is a guarded *yes*. In "Taking a Fall," originally published in *Popular Mechanics* in 2010 and selected for *Best American Science and Nature Writing*, he uses a combination of humor and basic physics to explain the process of long-distance falling and to show how survival is possible, if unlikely.

6:59:00 a.m., 35,000 Feet

1   You have a late night and an early flight. Not long after takeoff, you drift to sleep. Suddenly you're wide awake. There's cold air rushing everywhere, and sound. Intense, horrible sound. *Where am I?* you think. *Where's the plane?*

2   You're six miles up. You're alone. You're falling.

3   Things are bad. But now's the time to focus on the good news. (Yes, it goes beyond surviving the destruction of your aircraft.) Although gravity is against you, another force is working in your favor: time. Believe it or not, you're better off up here than if you'd slipped from the balcony of your high-rise hotel room after one too many drinks last night.

4   Or at least you will be. Oxygen is scarce at these heights. By now, hypoxia is starting to set in. You'll be unconscious soon, and you'll cannonball at least a mile before waking up again. When that happens, remember what you are about to read. The ground, after all, is your next destination.

5   Granted, the odds of surviving a six-mile plummet are extraordinarily slim, but at this point you've got nothing to lose by understanding your situation.

There are two ways to fall out of a plane. The first is to free-fall, or drop from the sky with absolutely no protection or means of slowing your descent. The second is to become a wreckage rider, a term coined by the Massachusetts-based amateur historian Jim Hamilton, who developed the *Free Fall Research Page* — an online database of nearly every imaginable human plummet. That classification means you have the advantage of being attached to a chunk of the plane. In 1972 a Serbian flight attendant, Vesna Vulovic, was traveling in a DC-9 over Czechoslovakia when it blew up. She fell 33,000 feet, wedged between her seat, a catering trolley, a section of aircraft, and the body of another crew member, landing on — then sliding down — a snowy incline before coming to a stop, severely injured but alive.

Surviving a plunge surrounded by a semiprotective cocoon of debris is   6
more common than surviving a pure free-fall, according to Hamilton's statistics; thirty-one such confirmed or "plausible" incidents have occurred since the 1940s. Free-fallers constitute a much more exclusive club, with just thirteen confirmed or plausible incidents, including perennial *Ripley's Believe It or Not* superstar Alan Magee, blown from his B-17 on a 1943 mission over France. The New Jersey airman, more recently the subject of a *MythBusters* episode, fell 20,000 feet and crashed into a train station; he was subsequently captured by German troops, who were astonished at his survival.

Whether you're attached to crumpled fuselage or just plain falling, the   7
concept you'll be most interested in is *terminal velocity*. As gravity pulls you toward the earth, you go faster. But like any moving object, you create drag — more as your speed increases. When downward force equals upward resistance, acceleration stops. You max out.

Depending on your size and weight, and factors such as air density, your   8
speed at that moment will be about 120 mph — and you'll get there after a surprisingly brief bit of falling: just 1,500 feet, about the same height as Chicago's Sears (now Willis) Tower. Equal speed means you hit the ground with equal force. The difference is the clock. Body meets Windy City sidewalk in twelve seconds. From an airplane's cruising altitude, you'll have almost enough time to read this entire article.

7:00:20 a.m., 22,000 Feet

By now, you've descended into breathable air. You sputter into conscious-   9
ness. At this altitude you've got roughly two minutes until impact. Your plan is simple. You will enter a Zen state and decide to live. You will understand, as Hamilton notes, "that it isn't the fall that kills you — it's the landing."

Keeping your wits about you, you take aim.   10

But at what? Magee's landing on the stone floor of that French train   11
station was softened by the skylight he crashed through a moment earlier.
Glass hurts, but it gives. So does grass. Haystacks and bushes have cushioned
surprised-to-be-alive free-fallers. Trees aren't bad, though they tend to skewer.
Snow? Absolutely. Swamps? With their mucky, plant-covered surface, even
more awesome. Hamilton documents one case of a sky diver who, upon total
parachute failure, was saved by bouncing off high-tension wires. Contrary to
popular belief, water is an awful choice. Like concrete, liquid doesn't com-
press. Hitting the ocean is essentially the same as colliding with a sidewalk,
Hamilton explains, except that pavement (perhaps unfortunately) won't
"open up and swallow your shattered body."

With a target in mind, the next consideration is body position. To slow   12
your descent, emulate a sky diver. Spread your arms and legs, present your
chest to the ground, and arch your back and head upward. This adds friction
and helps you maneuver. But don't relax. This is not your landing pose.

The question of how to achieve ground contact remains, regrettably,   13
given your predicament, a subject of debate. A 1942 study in the journal *War
Medicine* noted "distribution and compensation of pressure play large parts in
the defeat of injury." Recommendation: wide-body impact. But a 1963 report
by the Federal Aviation Agency argued that shifting into the classic sky diver's landing stance — feet together, heels up, flexed knees and hips — best
increases survivability. The same study noted that training in wrestling and
acrobatics would help people survive falls. Martial arts were deemed especially
useful for hard-surface impacts: "A 'black belt' expert can reportedly crack
solid wood with a single blow," the authors wrote, speculating that such skills
might be transferable.

The ultimate learn-by-doing experience might be a lesson from the   14
Japanese parachutist Yasuhiro Kubo, who holds the world record in the activity's banzai category. The sky diver tosses his chute from the plane and then
jumps out after it, waiting as long as possible to retrieve it, put it on, and pull
the ripcord. In 2000, Kubo — starting from 9,842 feet — fell for fifty seconds
before recovering his gear. A safer way to practice your technique would be
at one of the wind-tunnel simulators found at about a dozen US theme parks
and malls. But neither will help with the toughest part: sticking the landing.
For that you might consider — though it's not exactly advisable — a leap
off the world's highest bridge, France's Millau Viaduct; its platform towers
891 feet over mostly spongy farmland.

Water landings — if you must — require quick decision making. Studies   15
of bridge-jump survivors indicate that a feet-first, knifelike entry (aka "the
pencil") best optimizes your odds of resurfacing. The famed cliff divers of

Acapulco, however, tend to assume a head-down position, with the fingers of each hand locked together, arms outstretched, protecting the head. Whichever you choose, first assume the free-fall position for as long as you can. Then, if a feet-first entry is inevitable, the most important piece of advice, for reasons both unmentionable and easily understood, is to *clench your butt*.

No matter the surface, definitely don't land on your head. In a 1977   16 "Study of Impact Tolerance through Free-Fall Investigations," researchers at the Highway Safety Research Institute found that the major cause of death in falls — they examined drops from buildings, bridges, and the occasional elevator shaft (oops!) — was cranial contact. If you have to arrive top-down, sacrifice your good looks and land on your face rather than the back or top of your head. You might also consider flying with a pair of goggles in your pocket, Hamilton says, since you're likely to get watery eyes — impairing accuracy — on the way down.

7:02:19 a.m., 1,000 Feet

Given your starting altitude, you'll be just about ready to hit the ground   17 as you reach this section of instruction (based on the average adult reading speed of 250 words per minute). The basics have been covered, so feel free to concentrate on the task at hand. But if you're so inclined, here's some supplemental information — though be warned that none of it will help you much at this point.

Statistically speaking, it's best to be a flight crew member, a child, or   18 traveling in a military aircraft. Over the past four decades, there have been at least a dozen commercial airline crashes with just one survivor. Of those documented, four of the survivors were crew like the flight attendant Vulovic, and seven were passengers under the age of eighteen. That includes Mohammed el-Fateh Osman, a two-year-old wreckage rider who lived through the crash of a Boeing jet in Sudan in 2003, and, more recently, fourteen-year-old Bahia Bakari, the sole survivor of last June's Yemenia Airways plunge off the Comoros Islands.

Crew survival may be related to better restraint systems, but there's no   19 consensus on why children seem to pull through falls more often. The Federal Aviation Agency study notes that kids, especially those under the age of four, have more flexible skeletons, more relaxed muscle tonus, and a higher proportion of subcutaneous fat, which helps protect internal organs. Smaller people — whose heads are lower than the seat backs in front of them — are better shielded from debris in a plane that's coming apart. Lower body weight reduces terminal velocity, and reduced surface area decreases the chance of impalement upon landing.

7:02:25 a.m., 0 Feet

The ground. Like a Shaolin[1] master, you are at peace and prepared. *Impact.*   20
You're alive. What next? If you're lucky, you might find that your injuries are
minor, stand up, and smoke a celebratory cigarette, as the British tail gun-
ner Nicholas Alkemade did in 1944 after landing in snowy bushes following
an 18,000-foot plummet. (If you're a smoker, you're *super extra lucky*, since
you've technically gotten to indulge during the course of an airliner trip.)
More likely, you'll have tough work ahead.

Follow the example of Juliane Koepcke. On Christmas Eve, 1971, the   21
Lockheed Electra she was traveling in exploded over the Amazon. The next
morning the seventeen-year-old German awoke on the jungle floor, strapped
into her seat, surrounded by fallen holiday gifts. Injured and alone, she pushed
the death of her mother, who'd been seated next to her on the plane, out of
her mind. Instead, she remembered advice from her father, a biologist: To find
civilization when lost in the jungle, follow water. Koepcke waded from tiny
streams to larger ones. She passed crocodiles and poked the mud in front of
her with a stick to scare away stingrays. She had lost one shoe in the fall and
was wearing a ripped miniskirt. Her only food was a bag of candy, and she had
nothing but dark, dirty water to drink. She ignored her broken collarbone
and her wounds, infested with maggots.

On the tenth day, she rested on the bank of the Shebonya River. When   22
she stood up again, she saw a canoe tethered to the shoreline. It took her hours
to climb the embankment to a hut, where, the next day, a group of lumber-
jacks found her. The incident was seen as a miracle in Peru, and free-fall statistics seem to support those arguing for divine intervention: According to the
Geneva-based Aircraft Crashes Record Office, 118,934 people died in 15,463
plane crashes between 1940 and 2008. Even when you add failed-chute sky
divers, Hamilton's tally of confirmed or plausible lived-to-tell-about-it incidents is only 157, with 42 occurring at heights over 10,000 feet.

But Koepcke never saw survival as a matter of fate. She can still recall the   23
first moments of her fall from the plane, as she spun through the air in her seat.
That wasn't under her control, but what happened when she regained consciousness was. "I had been able to make the correct decision — to leave the
scene of the crash," she says now. And because of experience at her parents'
biological research station, she says, "I did not feel fear. I knew how to move
in the forest and the river, in which I had to swim with dangerous animals like
caimans and piranhas."

---

[1] A style of Kung Fu associated with the Shaolin Temple, a Buddhist monastery in
China. — EDS.

Or, by now, you're wide awake, and the aircraft's wheels have touched   24
safely down on the tarmac. You understand that the odds of any kind of accident on a commercial flight are slimmer than slim and that you will likely
never have to use this information. But as a courtesy to the next passenger,
consider leaving your copy of this guide in the seat-back pocket.

Journal Writing

Koeppel writes about the force of gravity from an unusual perspective. In your journal,
write about a powerful natural phenomenon that you have witnessed — for example,
a thunderstorm, a blizzard, an earthquake, a hurricane, a tornado, a fire. What was
your emotional response to the experience?

Questions on Meaning

1. Is Koeppel's PURPOSE to instruct, to explain, or to entertain? Why, then, do you
   suppose he addresses readers directly, using the second-PERSON *you*? How, if at all,
   does he intend for readers to use the information he provides?

2. What does it mean to be a "wreckage rider" (par. 5)? Why is that preferable to
   free-fall?

3. Explain what Koeppel means by *terminal velocity* (pars. 7, 19). Why does he say
   it's "the concept you'll be most interested in" (7)?

4. How much time elapses between explosion and landing in Koeppel's analysis?
   How does that relate to the time it takes to read his essay? What connection does
   the writer make between these two processes, and why?

5. Does Koeppel have a THESIS? What is the point of his process analysis?

Questions on Writing Strategy

1. Take particular notice of Koeppel's INTRODUCTION and CONCLUSION. What do
   they have in common? What is the EFFECT of this strategy?

2. What function is served by the headings in this essay?

3. "Taking a Fall" originally appeared in *Popular Mechanics*. How can you tell that
   the magazine is intended for general readers, not for a specialized AUDIENCE of
   professional engineers, physicists, or statisticians? What else can you assume
   about the magazine's audience?

4. **OTHER METHODS**   How does Koeppel use EXAMPLES to develop his process analysis?
   What is the effect of the particular examples he provides?

Questions on Language

1. Be sure you know how to define the following words: hypoxia (par. 4); plausible, constitute, perennial, subsequently (6); fuselage (7); Zen (9); skewer (11); emulate, friction (12); banzai (14); cranial (16); consensus, tonus, subcutaneous, impalement (19); tethered (22); caimans (23); tarmac (24).

2. How would you characterize Koeppel's DICTION in this essay? What does the diction contribute to his TONE? How effective do you find this use of language, given his subject and purpose?

3. What does Koeppel ALLUDE to with the phrase "sticking the landing" (par. 14)?

4. Point to a few sentences in the essay that use vivid IMAGES and FIGURES OF SPEECH to describe the process of surviving a fall from an airplane.

Suggestions for Writing

1. **FROM JOURNAL TO ESSAY** Write an essay exploring the natural phenomenon that you wrote about in your journal. Like Koeppel, you might begin and end your essay by grounding readers in an imagined experience of it, but focus on analyzing the general process by which it occurs and reflecting on its significance. What makes this force of nature so deadly? What impact does it have on people? How can they improve the odds of survival if they encounter it? Use vivid images that will make the process come to life for your readers.

2. Koeppel writes that "the odds of any kind of accident on a commercial flight are slimmer than slim" (par. 24), but fears of terrorism have led to increasingly tight airport security measures — to the point that all passengers are subject to physical pat-downs or x-ray scans that reveal blurry outlines of their bodies. To the minds of many, intense screening of airplane passengers is an excessive and ineffective violation of personal liberties, while others argue that such scrutiny is necessary to ensure safety. Do some research to learn more about the ARGUMENTS on both sides of the issue. Then, in an essay, argue your own position on the subject of airport security.

3. **CRITICAL WRITING** Take a close look at the nature of Koeppel's SOURCES and at his use of SUMMARY, PARAPHRASE, and direct QUOTATION. In an essay, analyze the way he SYNTHESIZES and integrates information and ideas. Why does he quote directly where he does? How effective are his summaries and paraphrases? How does he combine source materials to develop a thesis of his own?

4. **CONNECTIONS** "Everybody Jump," by Randall Munroe (p. 410), is another selection about physics written for nonspecialists. In an essay, COMPARE AND CONTRAST Koeppel's essay with Munroe's. Do the authors present complex concepts in ways that most readers can understand? What strategies do their works have in common? Where do the works diverge? Use quotations and paraphrases from both selections to support your ideas.

JESSICA MITFORD

Born in Batsford Mansion, England, in 1917, the daughter of Lord and Lady Redesdale, Jessica Mitford devoted much of her early life to defying her aristocratic upbringing. In her autobiography *Daughters and Rebels* (1960), she tells how she received a genteel schooling at home, then as a young woman moved to Loyalist Spain during the violent Spanish Civil War. Later she immigrated to the United States, where for a time she worked in Miami as a bartender. She obtained US citizenship in 1944 and became one of her adopted country's most noted reporters: *Time* called her "Queen of the Muckrakers." Exposing with her typewriter what she regarded as corruption, abuse, and absurdity, Mitford wrote *The American Way of Death* (1963, revised as *The American Way of Death Revisited* in 1998), *Kind and Unusual Punishment: The Prison Business* (1973), and *The American Way of Birth* (1992). *Poison Penmanship* (1979) collects articles from *The Atlantic Monthly, Harper's,* and other magazines. *A Fine Old Conflict* (1977) is the second volume of Mitford's autobiography. Her biography of a Victorian lighthouse keeper's daughter, *Grace Had an English Heart* (1989), examines how the media transform ordinary people into celebrities. Mitford died at her home in Oakland, California, in 1996.

Behind the Formaldehyde Curtain

The most famous (or infamous) thing Jessica Mitford wrote is *The American Way of Death*, a critique of the funeral industry. In this selection from the book, Mitford analyzes the twin processes of embalming and restoring a corpse, the practices she finds most objectionable. You may need a stable stomach to enjoy the selection, but you'll find it a clear, painstaking process analysis, written with masterly style and outrageous wit. (For those who want to know, Mitford herself was cremated after her death.)

The drama begins to unfold with the arrival of the corpse at the mortuary.   1
    Alas, poor Yorick! How surprised he would be to see how his counterpart   2
of today is whisked off to a funeral parlor and is in short order sprayed, sliced, pierced, pickled, trussed, trimmed, creamed, waxed, painted, rouged, and neatly dressed — transformed from a common corpse into a Beautiful Memory Picture. This process is known in the trade as embalming and restorative art, and is so universally employed in the United States and Canada that the funeral director does it routinely, without consulting corpse or kin. He regards as eccentric those few who are hardy enough to suggest that it might be dispensed with. Yet no law requires embalming, no religious doctrine commends it, nor is it dictated by considerations of health, sanitation, or even of personal

daintiness. In no part of the world but in Northern America is it widely used. The purpose of embalming is to make the corpse presentable for viewing in a suitably costly container; and here too the funeral director routinely, without first consulting the family, prepares the body for public display.

Is all this legal? The processes to which a dead body may be subjected are   3
after all to some extent circumscribed by law. In most states, for instance, the signature of next of kin must be obtained before an autopsy may be performed, before the deceased may be cremated, before the body may be turned over to a medical school for research purposes; or such provision must be made in the decedent's will. In the case of embalming, no such permission is required nor is it ever sought.[1] A textbook, *The Principles and Practices of Embalming*, comments on this: "There is some question regarding the legality of much that is done within the preparation room." The author points out that it would be most unusual for a responsible member of a bereaved family to instruct the mortician, in so many words, to "embalm" the body of a deceased relative. The very term *embalming* is so seldom used that the mortician must rely upon custom in the matter. The author concludes that unless the family specifies otherwise, the act of entrusting the body to the care of a funeral establishment carries with it an implied permission to go ahead and embalm.

Embalming is indeed a most extraordinary procedure, and one must won-   4
der at the docility of Americans who each year pay hundreds of millions of dollars for its perpetuation, blissfully ignorant of what it is all about, what is done, how it is done. Not one in ten thousand has any idea of what actually takes place. Books on the subject are extremely hard to come by. They are not to be found in most libraries or bookshops.

In an era when huge television audiences watch surgical operations in   5
the comfort of their living rooms, when, thanks to the animated cartoon, the geography of the digestive system has become familiar territory even to the nursery school set, in a land where the satisfaction of curiosity about almost all matters is a national pastime, the secrecy surrounding embalming can, surely, hardly be attributed to the inherent gruesomeness of the subject. Custom in this regard has within this century suffered a complete reversal. In the early days of American embalming, when it was performed in the home of the deceased, it was almost mandatory for some relative to stay by the embalmer's

---

[1] Partly because of Mitford's attack, the Federal Trade Commission now requires the funeral industry to provide families with itemized price lists, including the price of embalming, to state that embalming is not required, and to obtain the family's consent to embalming before charging for it. Shortly before her death, however, Mitford observed that the FTC had "watered down" the regulations and "routinely ignored" consumer complaints about the funeral industry. — EDS.

side and witness the procedure. Today, family members who might wish to be in attendance would certainly be dissuaded by the funeral director. All others, except apprentices, are excluded by law from the preparation room.

A close look at what does actually take place may explain in large mea-   6
sure the undertaker's intractable reticence concerning a procedure that has become his major *raison d'être*. Is it possible he fears that public information about embalming might lead patrons to wonder if they really want this service? If the funeral men are loath to discuss the subject outside the trade, the reader may, understandably, be equally loath to go on reading at this point. For those who have the stomach for it, let us part the formaldehyde curtain. . . .

The body is first laid out in the undertaker's morgue — or rather,   7
Mr. Jones is reposing in the preparation room — to be readied to bid the world farewell.

The preparation room in any of the better funeral establishments has the   8
tiled and sterile look of a surgery, and indeed the embalmer–restorative artist who does his chores there is beginning to adopt the term *dermasurgeon* (appropriately corrupted by some mortician-writers as "demi-surgeon") to describe his calling. His equipment, consisting of scalpels, scissors, augers, forceps, clamps, needles, pumps, tubes, bowls, and basins, is crudely imitative of the surgeon's, as is his technique, acquired in a nine- or twelve-month post-high-school course in an embalming school. He is supplied by an advanced chemical industry with a bewildering array of fluids, sprays, pastes, oils, powders, creams, to fix or soften tissue, shrink or distend it as needed, dry it here, restore the moisture there. There are cosmetics, waxes, and paints to fill and cover features, even plaster of Paris to replace entire limbs. There are ingenious aids to prop and stabilize the cadaver: a Vari-Pose Head Rest, the Edwards Arm and Hand Positioner, the Repose Block (to support the shoulders during the embalming), and the Throop Foot Positioner, which resembles an old-fashioned stocks.

Mr. John H. Eckels, president of the Eckels College of Mortuary Science,   9
thus describes the first part of the embalming procedure: "In the hands of a skilled practitioner, this work may be done in a comparatively short time and without mutilating the body other than by slight incision — so slight that it scarcely would cause serious inconvenience if made upon a living person. It is necessary to remove the blood, and doing this not only helps in the disinfecting, but removes the principal cause of disfigurements due to discoloration."

Another textbook discusses the all-important time element: "The ear-   10
lier this is done, the better, for every hour that elapses between death and embalming will add to the problems and complications encountered. . . ." Just how soon should one get going on the embalming? The author tells us, "On the basis of such scanty information made available to this profession through

its rudimentary and haphazard system of technical research, we must conclude that the best results are to be obtained if the subject is embalmed before life is completely extinct — that is, before cellular death has occurred. In the average case, this would mean within an hour after somatic death." For those who feel that there is something a little rudimentary, not to say haphazard, about this advice, a comforting thought is offered by another writer. Speaking of fears entertained in early days of premature burial, he points out, "One of the effects of embalming by chemical injection, however, has been to dispel fears of live burial." How true; once the blood is removed, chances of live burial are indeed remote.

To return to Mr. Jones, the blood is drained out through the veins and replaced by embalming fluid pumped in through the arteries. As noted in *The Principles and Practices of Embalming*, "every operator has a favorite injection and drainage point — a fact which becomes a handicap only if he fails or refuses to forsake his favorites when conditions demand it." Typical favorites are the carotid artery, femoral artery, jugular vein, subclavian vein. There are various choices of embalming fluid. If Flextone is used, it will produce a "mild, flexible rigidity. The skin retains a velvety softness, the tissues are rubbery and pliable. Ideal for women and children." It may be blended with B. and G. Products Company's Lyf-Lyk tint, which is guaranteed to reproduce "nature's own skin texture . . . the velvety appearance of living tissue." Sun-tone comes in three separate tints: Suntan; Special Cosmetic Tint, a pink shade "especially indicated for female subjects"; and Regular Cosmetic Tint, moderately pink.

About three to six gallons of a dyed and perfumed solution of formaldehyde, glycerin, borax, phenol, alcohol, and water is soon circulating through Mr. Jones, whose mouth has been sewn together with a "needle directed upward between the upper lip and gum and brought out through the left nostril," with the corners raised slightly "for a more pleasant expression." If he should be bucktoothed, his teeth are cleaned with Bon Ami and coated with colorless nail polish. His eyes, meanwhile, are closed with flesh-tinted eye caps and eye cement.

The next step is to have at Mr. Jones with a thing called a trocar. This is a long, hollow needle attached to a tube. It is jabbed into the abdomen, poked around the entrails and chest cavity, the contents of which are pumped out and replaced with "cavity fluid." This done, and the hole in the abdomen sewn up, Mr. Jones's face is heavily creamed (to protect the skin from burns which may be caused by leakage of the chemicals), and he is covered with a sheet and left unmolested for a while. But not for long — there is more, much more, in store for him. He has been embalmed, but not yet restored, and the best time to start the restorative work is eight to ten hours after embalming, when the tissues have become firm and dry.

11

12

13

The object of all this attention to the corpse, it must be remembered,   14
is to make it presentable for viewing in an attitude of healthy repose. "Our
customs require the presentation of our dead in the semblance of normality . . . unmarred by the ravages of illness, disease, or mutilation," says
Mr. J. Sheridan Mayer in his *Restorative Art.* This is rather a large order since
few people die in the full bloom of health, unravaged by illness and unmarked
by some disfigurement. The funeral industry is equal to the challenge: "In
some cases the gruesome appearance of a mutilated or disease-ridden subject
may be quite discouraging. The task of restoration may seem impossible and
shake the confidence of the embalmer. This is the time for intestinal fortitude
and determination. Once the formative work is begun and affected tissues are
cleaned or removed, all doubts of success vanish. It is surprising and gratifying
to discover the results which may be obtained."

The embalmer, having allowed an appropriate interval to elapse, returns   15
to the attack, but now he brings into play the skill and equipment of sculptor
and cosmetician. Is a hand missing? Casting one in plaster of Paris is a simple
matter. "For replacement purposes, only a cast of the back of the hand is necessary; this is within the ability of the average operator and is quite adequate."
If a lip or two, a nose, or an ear should be missing, the embalmer has at hand a
variety of restorative waxes with which to model replacements. Pores and skin
texture are simulated by stippling with a little brush, and over this cosmetics
are laid on. Head off? Decapitation cases are rather routinely handled. Ragged
edges are trimmed, and head joined to torso with a series of splints, wires, and
sutures. It is a good idea to have a little something at the neck — a scarf or a
high collar — when time for viewing comes. Swollen mouth? Cut out tissue
as needed from inside the lips. If too much is removed, the surface contour
can easily be restored by padding with cotton. Swollen necks and cheeks are
reduced by removing tissue through vertical incisions made down each side
of the neck. "When the deceased is casketed, the pillow will hide the suture
incisions . . . as an extra precaution against leakage, the suture may be painted
with liquid sealer."

The opposite condition is more likely to present itself — that of emacia-   16
tion. His hypodermic syringe now loaded with massage cream, the embalmer
seeks out and fills the hollowed and sunken areas by injection. In this procedure the backs of the hands and fingers and the under-chin area should not
be neglected.

Positioning the lips is a problem that recurrently challenges the ingenuity   17
of the embalmer. Closed too tightly, they tend to give a stern, even disapprov-
ing expression. Ideally, embalmers feel, the lips should give the impression
of being ever so slightly parted, the upper lip protruding slightly for a more
youthful appearance. This takes some engineering, however, as the lips tend

to drift apart. Lip drift can sometimes be remedied by pushing one or two straight pins through the inner margin of the lower lip and then inserting them between the two front upper teeth. If Mr. Jones happens to have no teeth, the pins can just as easily be anchored in his Armstrong Face Former and Denture Replacer. Another method to maintain lip closure is to dislocate the lower jaw, which is then held in its new position by a wire run through holes which have been drilled through the upper and lower jaws at the midline. As the French are fond of saying, *il faut souffrir pour être belle*.[2]

If Mr. Jones has died of jaundice, the embalming fluid will very likely turn   18 him green. Does this deter the embalmer? Not if he has intestinal fortitude. Masking pastes and cosmetics are heavily laid on, burial garments and casket interiors are color-correlated with particular care, and Jones is displayed beneath rose-colored lights. Friends will say "How *well* he looks." Death by carbon monoxide, on the other hand, can be rather a good thing from the embalmer's viewpoint: "One advantage is the fact that this type of discoloration is an exaggerated form of a natural pink coloration." This is nice because the healthy glow is already present and needs but little attention.

The patching and filling completed, Mr. Jones is now shaved, washed,   19 and dressed. Cream-based cosmetic, available in pink, flesh, suntan, brunette, and blond, is applied to his hands and face, his hair is shampooed and combed (and, in the case of Mrs. Jones, set), his hands manicured. For the horny-handed son of toil special care must be taken; cream should be applied to remove ingrained grime, and the nails cleaned. "If he were not in the habit of having them manicured in life, trimming and shaping is advised for better appearance — never questioned by kin."

Jones is now ready for casketing (this is the present participle of the verb   20 "to casket"). In this operation his right shoulder should be depressed slightly "to turn the body a bit to the right and soften the appearance of lying flat on the back." Positioning the hands is a matter of importance, and special rubber positioning blocks may be used. The hands should be cupped slightly for a more life-like, relaxed appearance. Proper placement of the body requires a delicate sense of balance. It should lie as high as possible in the casket, yet not so high that the lid, when lowered, will hit the nose. On the other hand, we are cautioned, placing the body too low "creates the impression that the body is in a box."

Jones is next wheeled into the appointed slumber room where a few last   21 touches may be added — his favorite pipe placed in his hand or, if he was a great reader, a book propped into position. (In the case of little Master Jones a Teddy bear may be clutched.) Here he will hold open house for a few days, visiting hours 10 a.m. to 9 p.m.

---

[2] You have to suffer to be beautiful. — Eds.

All now being in readiness, the funeral director calls a staff conference   22
to make sure that each assistant knows his precise duties. Mr. Wilber Kriege
writes: "This makes your staff feel that they are a part of the team, with a
definite assignment that must be properly carried out if the whole plan is to
succeed. You never heard of a football coach who failed to talk to his entire
team before they go on the field. They have drilled on the plays they are to
execute for hours and days, and yet the successful coach knows the importance of making even the benchwarming third-string substitute feel that he
is important if the game is to be won." The winning of *this* game is predicated
upon glass-smooth handling of the logistics. The funeral director has notified
the pallbearers whose names were furnished by the family, has arranged for the
presence of clergyman, organist, and soloist, has provided transportation for
everybody, has organized and listed the flowers sent by friends. In *Psychology
of Funeral Service* Mr. Edward A. Martin points out, "He may not always do as
much as the family thinks he is doing, but it is his helpful guidance that they
appreciate in knowing they are proceeding as they should. . . . The important
thing is how well his services can be used to make the family believe they are
giving unlimited expression to their own sentiment."

The religious service may be held in a church or in the chapel of the   23
funeral home; the funeral director vastly prefers the latter arrangement, for
not only is it more convenient for him but it affords him the opportunity to
show off his beautiful facilities to the gathered mourners. After the clergyman
has had his say, the mourners queue up to file past the casket for a last look
at the deceased. The family is *never* asked whether they want an open-casket
ceremony; in the absence of their instruction to the contrary, this is taken for
granted. Consequently well over 90% of all American funerals feature the
open casket — a custom unknown in other parts of the world. Foreigners are
astonished by it. An English woman living in San Francisco described her
reaction in a letter to the writer:

> I myself have attended only one funeral here — that of an elderly fellow
> worker of mine. After the service I could not understand why everyone was
> walking towards the coffin (sorry, I mean casket), but thought I had better
> follow the crowd. It shook me rigid to get there and find the casket open and
> poor old Oscar lying there in his brown tweed suit, wearing a sun-tan makeup
> and just the wrong shade of lipstick. If I had not been extremely fond of the
> old boy, I have a horrible feeling that I might have giggled. Then and there
> I decided that I could never face another American funeral — even dead.

The casket (which has been resting throughout the service on a Classic   24
Beauty Ultra Metal Casket Bier) is now transferred by a hydraulically operated device called Porto-Lift to a balloon-tired, Glide Easy casket carriage

which will wheel it to yet another conveyance, the Cadillac Funeral Coach. This may be lavender, cream, light green — anything but black. Interiors, of course, are color-correlated, "for the man who cannot stop short of perfection."

At graveside, the casket is lowered into the earth. This office, once   25
the prerogative of friends of the deceased, is now performed by a patented mechanical lowering device. A "Lifetime Green" artificial grass mat is at the ready to conceal the sere earth, and overhead, to conceal the sky, is a portable Steril Chapel Tent ("resists the intense heat and humidity of summer and the terrific storms of winter . . . available in Silver Gray, Rose, or Evergreen"). Now is the time for the ritual scattering of earth over the coffin, as the solemn words "earth to earth, ashes to ashes, dust to dust" are pronounced by the officiating cleric. This can today be accomplished "with a mere flick of the wrist with the Gordon Leak-Proof Earth Dispenser. No grasping of a handful of dirt, no soiled fingers. Simple, dignified, beautiful, reverent! The modern way!" The Gordon Earth Dispenser (at $5) is of nickel-plated brass construction. It is not only "attractive to the eye and long wearing"; it is also "one of the 'tools' for building better public relations" if presented as "an appropriate noncommercial gift" to the clergyman. It is shaped something like a saltshaker.

Untouched by human hand, the coffin and the earth are now united.   26

It is in the function of directing the participants through this maze of   27
gadgetry that the funeral director has assigned to himself his relatively new role of "grief therapist." He has relieved the family of every detail, he has revamped the corpse to look like a living doll, he has arranged for it to nap for a few days in a slumber room, he has put on a well-oiled performance in which the concept of *death* has played no part whatsoever — unless it was inconsiderately mentioned by the clergyman who conducted the religious service. He has done everything in his power to make the funeral a real pleasure for everybody concerned. He and his team have given their all to score an upset victory over death.

Journal Writing

Presumably, morticians embalm and restore corpses, and survivors support the work, because the practices are thought to ease the shock of death. Now that you know what goes on behind the scenes, how do you feel about a loved one's undergoing these procedures?

Questions on Meaning

1. What was your emotional response to this essay? Can you analyze your feelings?

2. To what does Mitford attribute the secrecy surrounding the embalming process?

3. What, according to Mitford, is the mortician's intent? What common obstacles to fulfilling it must be surmounted?

4. What do you understand from Mitford's remark in paragraph 10, on dispelling fears of live burial: "How true; once the blood is removed, chances of live burial are indeed remote"?

5. Do you find any implied PURPOSE in this essay? Does Mitford seem primarily out to rake muck, or does she offer any positive suggestions to Americans?

Questions on Writing Strategy

1. What is Mitford's TONE? In her opening two paragraphs, exactly what shows her attitude toward her subject?

2. Why do you think Mitford goes into so much grisly detail in analyzing the processes of embalming and restoration? How does the detail serve her purpose?

3. What is the EFFECT of calling the body Mr. Jones?

4. Paragraph by paragraph, what TRANSITIONS does the author employ?

5. To whom does Mitford address her process analysis? How do you know she isn't writing for an AUDIENCE of professional morticians?

6. Choose one of the quotations from the journals and textbooks of professionals and explain how it serves the author's general purpose.

7. Why do you think Mitford often uses the PASSIVE VOICE to describe the actions of embalmers — for instance, "the blood is drained," "If Flextone is used," and "It may be blended" in paragraph 11? Are the verbs in passive voice effective or ineffective? Why?

8. **OTHER METHODS**   In paragraph 8, Mitford uses CLASSIFICATION in listing the embalmer's equipment and supplies. What groups does she identify, and why does she bother sorting the items at all?

Questions on Language

1. Explain the ALLUSION to Yorick in paragraph 2.

2. What IRONY do you find in this statement in paragraph 7: "The body is first laid out in the undertaker's morgue — or rather, Mr. Jones is reposing in the preparation room"? Pick out any other words or phrases in the essay that seem ironic. Comment especially on those you find in the essay's last two sentences.

3. Why is it useful to Mitford's purpose that she cites the brand names of morticians' equipment and supplies (the Edwards Arm and Hand Positioner, Lyf-Lyk tint)? List all the brand names in the essay that are memorable.

4. Define the following words or terms: counterpart (par. 2); circumscribed, decedent, bereaved (3); docility, perpetuation (4); inherent (5); intractable, reticence, *raison d'être*, formaldehyde (6); "derma-" (in *dermasurgeon*), augers, forceps, distend, stocks (8); somatic (10); carotid artery, femoral artery, jugular vein, subclavian vein, pliable (11); glycerin, borax, phenol (12); trocar, entrails (13); stippling, sutures (15); emaciation (16); jaundice (18); predicated (22); queue (23); hydraulically (24); sere, cleric (25).

Suggestions for Writing

1. **FROM JOURNAL TO ESSAY**   Drawing on your personal response to Mitford's essay in your journal (p. 295), write a brief essay that ARGUES either for or against embalming and restoration. Consider the purposes served by these practices, both for the mortician and for the dead person's relatives and friends, as well as their costs and effects.

2. ANALYZE some other process whose operations may not be familiar to everyone. (Have you ever held a job, or helped out in a family business, that has taken you behind the scenes? How is fast food prepared? How are cars serviced? How is a baby sat? How is a house constructed?) Detail it step by step, including transitions to clarify the steps.

3. **CRITICAL WRITING**   In attacking the funeral industry, Mitford also, implicitly, attacks the people who pay for and comply with the industry's attitudes and practices. What ASSUMPTIONS does Mitford seem to make about how we ought to deal with death and the dead? (Consider, for instance, her statements about the "docility of Americans . . . , blissfully ignorant" [par. 4] and the funeral director's making "the funeral a real pleasure for everybody concerned" [27].) Write an essay in which you interpret Mitford's assumptions and agree or disagree with them, based on your own reading and experience. If you like, defend the ritual of the funeral, or the mortician's profession, against Mitford's attack.

4. **CONNECTIONS**   In "Vampires Never Die" (p. 330), Guillermo del Toro and Chuck Hogan also comment on fears of death, noting that "we have no true jurisdiction over our bodies." Taken together, what do Mitford's and del Toro and Hogan's essays say about the importance of the body in Western culture? Write an essay either defending or criticizing the desire for physical immortality, whether real or imagined.

Jessica Mitford on Writing

"Choice of subject is of cardinal importance," declared Jessica Mitford in *Poison Penmanship.* "One does by far one's best work when besotted by and absorbed in the matter at hand." After *The American Way of Death* was published, Mitford received hundreds of letters suggesting alleged rackets that ought to be exposed, and to her surprise, an overwhelming majority of these letters complained about defective and overpriced hearing aids. But Mitford never wrote a book blasting the hearing aid industry. "Somehow, although there may well be need for such an exposé, I could not warm up to hearing aids as a subject for the kind of thorough, intensive, long-range research that would be needed to do an effective job." She once taught a course at Yale on muckraking, with each student choosing a subject to investigate. "Those who tackled hot issues on campus, such as violations of academic freedom or failure to implement affirmative-action hiring policies, turned in some excellent work; but the lad who decided to investigate 'waste in the Yale dining halls' was predictably unable to make much of this trivial topic."

The hardest problem Mitford faced in writing *The American Way of Death*, she recalled, was doing her factual, step-by-step account of the embalming process. She felt "determined to describe it in all its revolting details, but how to make this subject palatable to the reader?" Her solution was to cast the whole process analysis in the official JARGON of the mortuary industry, drawing on lists of taboo words and their EUPHEMISMS (or acceptable synonyms), as published in the trade journal *Casket & Sunnyside*: "Mr., Mrs., Miss Blank, not corpse or body; preparation room, not morgue; reposing room, not laying-out room. . . ." The story of Mr. Jones thus took shape, and Mitford's use of jargon, she found, added macabre humor to the proceedings.

The Bedford Reader on Writing

We aren't sure that the topic of "waste in the Yale dining halls" is necessarily trivial, but obviously not everyone would burn to write about it. How do you find a topic worth investigating? Something that will engage you and keep you interested "for the kind of thorough, intensive, long-range research that would be needed to do an effective job"? See our tips in Chapter 2 ("Subject," p. 30) and the Appendix ("Conducting Research," pp. 624–28).

ADDITIONAL WRITING TOPICS

Process Analysis

1. Write a *directive* process analysis (a "how-to" essay) in which, drawing on your own knowledge, you instruct someone in doing or making something. You might choose to take a serious approach or a light TONE. Either way, divide the process into steps, and be sure to detail each step thoroughly. Here are some possible subjects (any of which may be modified or narrowed):

   How to protect one's privacy online
   How to enlist people's confidence
   How to teach a person to ski
   How to book a ride through *Uber* or *Lyft*
   How to compose a photograph
   How to judge a dog show
   How to organize your own rock group
   How to eat an artichoke
   How to shear a sheep
   How to build (or fly) a kite
   How to start weight training
   How to aid a person who is choking
   How to kick a habit
   How to win at poker
   How to make an effective protest or complaint

   Or, if you don't like any of those topics, what else do you know that others might care to learn from you?

2. Working in chronological order, write a careful *informative* (explanatory, not "how-to") analysis of any one of the following processes. Make use of DESCRIPTION where necessary, and be sure to include TRANSITIONS. If one of these topics gives you a better idea for a paper, go with your own subject.

   How a student is processed during orientation or registration
   How the student newspaper gets published
   How a particular Web site generates revenue
   How employers find and screen job applicants
   How a Bluetooth speaker or an MP3 player works
   How fracking extracts natural gas from shale
   How a professional umpire (or any other professional) does the job
   How an air conditioner (or other household appliance) works
   How birds teach their young (or some other process in the natural world: how sharks feed, how a snake swallows an egg, how tsunamis form, how the human liver works)
   How police control crowds
   How people make up their minds when shopping for cars (or clothes)

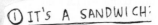

© Roz Chast The New Yorker Collection/The Cartoon Bank

8

DIVISION OR ANALYSIS

Slicing into Parts

◄ **Division or analysis in a cartoon**

The cartoonist Roz Chast is well known for witty and perceptive comments on the everyday, made through words and simple, almost childlike drawings. Dividing or analyzing, this cartoon identifies the elements of a boy's sandwich to discover what they can tell about the values and politics of the parent who made the sandwich. The title, "Deconstructing Lunch," refers to a type of analysis that focuses on the multiple meanings of a subject and especially its internal contradictions. Summarize what the sandwich reveals about the boy's parent. What contradictions do you spot in his or her values or politics? What might Chast be saying more generally about food choices?

THE METHOD

A chemist working for a soft-drink company is asked to improve on a competitor's product, Hydra Sports Water. To do the job, the chemist first has to figure out what's in the drink. She smells the stuff and tastes it. Then she tests a sample chemically to discover the actual ingredients: water, corn syrup, sodium citrate, potassium chloride, coloring. Methodically, the chemist has performed DIVISION or ANALYSIS: She has separated the beverage into its components. Hydra Sports Water stands revealed, understood, and ready to be bettered.

Division or analysis (the terms are interchangeable) is a key skill in learning and in life. It is an instrument allowing you to slice a large and complicated subject into smaller parts that you can grasp and connect to one another. In fact, it is so fundamental that it underlies every other method of development discussed in this book — for instance, it helps you identify features for DESCRIPTION, spot similarities for COMPARISON AND CONTRAST, or sort out the steps for a PROCESS ANALYSIS (as our chemist did in the previous chapter). With analysis you can comprehend — and communicate — the structure of things. And when it works, you find in the parts an idea or conclusion about the subject that makes it clearer, truer, more comprehensive, or more vivid than it was before you started.

Kinds of Division or Analysis

Although division or analysis always works the same way — separating a whole, singular subject into its elements — the method can be more or less difficult depending on how unfamiliar, complex, or abstract the subject is. Obviously, it's going to be easier to analyze a chicken (wings, legs, thighs, . . .) than a speech by John F. Kennedy (this image, that allusion, . . .), and easier to analyze the structure of a small business than that of a multinational conglomerate.

There are always multiple ways to divide or analyze a subject. One historian, for instance, might study an era by looking at its elections, protest movements, wars, and so forth — following its political components — while another might examine the daily experiences of the people who lived in that period — explaining events in their social context. In other words, the outcome of an analysis depends on the rule or *principle* used to conduct it. This fact accounts for some of the differences among academic disciplines: A psychologist may look at the individual person primarily as a bundle of drives and needs, whereas a sociologist may emphasize the individual's roles in society. Even within a discipline, different factions analyze differently, using different principles of division or analysis. Some psychologists are interested mainly in perception, others mainly in behavior; some focus mainly on emotional development, others mainly on brain chemistry.

Analysis and Critical Thinking

Analysis plays a fundamental role in CRITICAL THINKING, READING, AND WRITING, topics discussed in Chapters 1 and 2. In fact, *analysis* and *criticism* are deeply related: The first comes from a Greek word meaning "to undo"; the second from a Greek word meaning "to separate."

Critical thinking, reading, and writing go beneath the surface of the object, word, image, or whatever the subject is. When you work critically, you divide the subject into its elements, INFER the buried meanings and ASSUMPTIONS that define its essence, and SYNTHESIZE the parts into a new whole that is now informed by your perspective. Say a campaign brochure quotes a candidate for election to the city council as being in favor of "reasonable government expenditures on reasonable highway projects." The candidate will support new roads, right? Wrong. As a critical reader of the brochure, you quickly sense something fishy in the use (twice) of *reasonable*. As an informed reader, you might know (or find out) that the candidate has consistently opposed new roads, so the chances of her finding a highway project "reasonable" are slim. At the same time, her stand has been unpopular, so of course she wants to seem "reasonable" on the issue. Read critically, then, a campaign statement that seems to offer mild support for highways is actually a slippery evasion of any such commitment.

Analysis (a convenient term for the overlapping operations of analysis, inference, and synthesis) is very useful for exposing such evasiveness, but that isn't its only function. You've already done quite a bit of analytical thinking as you critically read the selections in this book. The method will also help you understand a sculpture, perceive the importance of a case study in sociology, or form a response to an environmental impact report. And the method can be invaluable for straight thinking about popular culture, from TV to toys.

THE PROCESS

Subject and Purpose

Keep an eye out for writing assignments requiring division or analysis — in college and work, they won't be hard to find. They will probably include the word *analyze* or a word implying analysis, such as *evaluate, examine, explore, interpret, discuss,* or *criticize.* Any time you spot such a term, you know your job is to separate the subject into its elements, to infer their meanings, to explore the relations among them, and to draw a conclusion about the subject.

Almost any coherent entity — object, person, place, concept — is a fit subject for analysis *if* the analysis will add to the subject's meaning or significance. Little is deadlier than the rote analytical exercise that leaves the parts neatly dissected and the subject comatose on the page. As a writer, you have to animate the subject, and that means finding your interest. What about your subject seems curious? What's appealing? or mysterious? or awful? And what will be your PURPOSE in writing about the subject: Do you simply want to explain it, or do you want to argue for or against it?

Such questions can help you find the principle or framework you will use to divide the subject into parts. Say you've got an assignment to write about a sculpture in a nearby park. Why do you like the sculpture, or why don't you? What elements of its creation and physical form make it art? What is the point of such public art? What does this sculpture do for this park, or what does the park do for the sculpture? Any of these questions could suggest a slant on the subject, a framework for analysis, and a purpose for writing, getting your analysis moving.

Principle of Analysis and Thesis

Finding your principle of analysis will lead you to your essay's THESIS as well — the main point you want to make about your subject. Expressed in a THESIS STATEMENT, this idea will help keep you focused and help your readers see your subject as a whole rather than as a bundle of parts. Here are the thesis statements in two of this chapter's selections:

> Boys — and more and more girls — who accept Jock Culture values often go on to flourish in a competitive sports environment that requires submission to authority, winning by any means necessary, and group cohesion.
> — Robert Lipsyte, "Jock Culture"

> Monsters, like angels, are invoked by our individual and collective needs. Today, much as during that gloomy summer in 1816 [when Dracula was conceived], we feel the need to seek their cold embrace.
> — Guillermo del Toro and Chuck Hogan, "Vampires Never Die"

Readers will have an easier time following your analysis — and will more likely appreciate it — if they have a hook on which to hang the details. Your thesis statement can be that hook if you use it to establish your framework, your principle of analysis. A well-focused thesis statement can help you as well, because it gives you a yardstick to judge how complete, consistent, and supportive your analysis is. Don't be discouraged, though, if your thesis statement doesn't come to you until *after* you've written a first draft and had a chance to discover your interest. Writing about your subject may be the best way for you to find its meaning and significance.

Evidence

Making a valid analysis is chiefly a matter of giving your subject thought, but for the result to seem useful and convincing to your readers, it will have to refer to the real world. The method, then, requires open eyes and a willingness to provide EVIDENCE. The nature of the evidence will depend entirely on what you are analyzing — physical details for a sculpture, quotations for a speech, financial data for a business review, statistics for a psychology case study, and so forth. The idea is to supply enough evidence to justify and support your particular slant on the subject.

In developing an essay by analysis, having an outline at your elbow can be a help. You don't want to overlook any parts or elements that should be included in your framework. You needn't mention every feature in your final draft or give them all equal treatment, but any omissions or variations should be conscious. And you want to use your framework consistently, not switching carelessly (and confusingly) from, say, the form of the sculpture to the cost of public art.

A final caution: It's possible to get carried away with one's own analysis, to become so enamored of the details that the subject itself becomes dim or distorted. You can avoid this danger by keeping the subject literally in front of you as you work (or at least imagining it vividly). It often helps to reassemble your subject at the end of the essay, placing it in a larger context, speculating on its influence, or affirming its significance. By the end of the essay, your subject must be a coherent whole truly represented by your analysis, not twisted, inflated, or obliterated. The reader should be intrigued by your subject, yes, but also able to recognize it on the street.

FOCUS ON PARAGRAPH COHERENCE

Because several elements contribute to the whole of a subject, your analysis will be easier for readers to follow if you frequently clarify what element you are discussing and how it fits with your principle of analysis. Two techniques,

(continued)

especially, can help you guide readers through your analysis: transitions and repetition or restatement.

- **Use TRANSITIONS as signposts to tell readers where you, and they, are headed.** Among other uses, transitions may specify the relations between your points and your principle of analysis (*first, second, another feature*) or may clarify the relations among the points themselves (*even more important, similarly*). Consider how transitions keep readers focused in the following paragraph:

> Many television comedies, even some that boast live audiences, rely on laugh tracks to fill too-quiet moments. To create a laugh track, an editor uses four overlapping elements of a laugh. The first is style, from titter to belly laugh. The second is intensity, the volume, ranging from mild to medium to earsplitting. The third ingredient is duration, the length of the laugh, whether quick, medium, or extended. And finally, there's the number of laughers, from a lone giggler to a roaring throng. When creating a canned laugh, the editor draws from a bank of hundreds of prerecorded laugh files and blends the four ingredients as a maestro weaves a symphony out of brass, woodwinds, percussion, and strings.

- **Use repetition and restatement to link sentences and tie them to your principle of analysis.** In the preceding paragraph, two threads run through the sentences to maintain the focus: *laugh tracks, laugh track, laugh, laughers,* and *canned laugh;* and *editor, editor,* and *maestro.*

CHECKLIST FOR REVISING A DIVISION OR ANALYSIS ESSAY

✔ **Principle of analysis and thesis.** What is your particular slant on your subject, the rule or principle you have used to divide your subject into its elements? Do you specify it in your thesis statement?

✔ **Completeness.** Have you considered all the subject's elements required by your principle of analysis?

✔ **Consistency.** Have you applied your principle of analysis consistently, viewing your subject from a definite slant?

✔ **Evidence.** Is your division or analysis well supported with concrete details, quotations, data, or statistics, as appropriate?

✔ **Significance.** Why should readers care about your analysis? Have you told them something about your subject that wasn't obvious on its surface?

✔ **Truth to subject.** Is your analysis faithful to the subject, not distorted, exaggerated, or deflated?

DIVISION OR ANALYSIS IN ACADEMIC WRITING

A Political Science Textbook

In this paragraph adapted from *Government by the People*, an introductory political science textbook focused on American government, authors David B. Magleby, Paul C. Light, and Christine L. Nemacheck divide the US Constitution into its essential elements. The careful analysis supports their admiration for the document's simplicity and flexibility.

Despite its brevity, the Constitution firmly established the Framers' experiment in free-government-in-the-making that each generation reinterprets and renews. That is why after more than 225 years we have not had another written Constitution — let alone two, three, or more, like other countries around the world. Part of the reason is the public's widespread acceptance of the Constitution. But the Constitution has also endured because it is a brilliant structure for limited government and one that the Framers designed to be adaptable and flexible. Article I establishes a bicameral Congress, with a House of Representatives and a Senate, and empowers it to enact legislation — for example, governing foreign and interstate commerce. Article II vests the executive power in the president, and Article III vests the judicial power in the Supreme Court and other federal courts that Congress may establish. Article IV guarantees the privileges and immunities of citizens and specifies the conditions for admitting new states. Article V provides for the methods of amending the Constitution, and Article VI specifies that the Constitution and all laws made under it are the supreme law of the land. Finally, Article VII provides that the Constitution had to be ratified by nine of the original thirteen states to go into effect. In 1791, the first ten amendments, the Bill of Rights, were added, and another seventeen amendments have been added since.

Annotations (right margin):

Principle of analysis: "brilliant" structure of the Constitution
1. Legislative branch
2. Executive branch
3. Judicial branch
4. Protections for citizens
5. Procedures for amendment
6. Authority
7. Ratification
8. Bill of Rights and later amendments

A Critical Reading

The study of literature — poetry, novels, short fiction, even essays — regularly involves analysis in the form of close readings. Interpretations vary, of course, depending on the reader's chosen principle of analysis. One literary critic, for instance, might divide a poem by looking at its rhymes, meter, imagery, and so forth — following its internal components — while another might examine a short story or novel as an artifact of the author's time and place — connecting its components to its context. In either case, such close readings draw on the text itself for evidence: summarizing, paraphrasing, and quoting the work to give readers the flavor of its content and to support the critic's analysis.

For a composition course using *The Bedford Reader* at Seton Hall University in New Jersey, Rachel O'Connor, a dual major in biology and English, wrote an analysis of Shirley Jackson's short story "The Lottery" (p. 100). She chose to focus on Jackson's use of literary techniques, following MLA style to cite evidence from the story. We excerpt her close reading here to avoid spoilers.

Shirley Jackson's "The Lottery" appears simple on a first read, but close analysis reveals a tale packed with dark social commentary. The story takes place on a glorious summer day, in a small and seemingly docile rural town where an annual lottery is about to take place. It is unclear at first what this lottery entails, but since the term typically has positive connotations, the reader does not suspect the morbidity that lies beneath the surface or the horrors unleashed in the last few lines . . . .

Thesis statement

What makes "The Lottery" so brilliant are the subtle clues Jackson embeds in the text and the deeper moral themes to which they point. The narrative flows smoothly and is compelling enough to consume readers and distract them from noticing the tactics strategically set in place. For example, the first sentence describes the setting as "clear and sunny, with the fresh warmth of a full-summer day" (100). This line is ironic: What appears to be a pleasant community gathering on a beautiful day turns out to be something much more sinister. . . .

Principle of analysis: literary technique

1. Irony

Another early clue is the description, in the second paragraph, of boys gathering stones in their pockets. Although it is not clear what these stones might be used for, the reader is not inclined to think anything of it — until he or she becomes aware of the story's ending. At the same time, the fact that some boys "made a great pile of stones . . . and guarded it against the raids of the other boys" (101) exposes the inherent distrust and hostility the townspeople have for one another despite the appearance of being a close-knit community. . . .

2. Foreshadowing

The gravity of the situation is further suggested through the description of the men, whose "jokes were quiet" and who "smiled rather than laughed" (101). The townspeople's conspicuous efforts to make conversation and act normal hint to the reader that something may be awry. The children's attitude

3. Characterization

toward the lottery is especially troubling. They seem to view
it as a game although they are aware of the perverse reality,
which indicates their desensitization to violence and loss of
innocence. . . . Finally, the winner's insistence that the lottery
"isn't fair" and "isn't right" (107) underscores the story's latent
theme of the evil often lurking in societal norms.

Jackson, through irony, foreshadowing, and characterization, spins a flawless tale that both entertains and makes
readers think. She subtly yet powerfully questions a society
that complies with abhorrent practices simply because they are
traditional. . . . She challenges readers to make their own moral
judgments rather than fall victim to the often unjust mentality
of the majority in charge, while simultaneously pulling off a
surprise ending wild enough to catch the attention of almost
anyone.

Reassembly of elements
with a comment on
significance

Work Cited

Jackson, Shirley. "The Lottery." *The Bedford Reader*, edited by
    X. J. Kennedy et al., 13th ed., Bedford/St. Martin's, 2017,
    pp. 100-107.

List of Works Cited with
publication information
for the text (see
pp. 631–45)

Division or Analysis

JUDITH ORTIZ COFER

A native of Puerto Rico who has lived most of her life in the United States, Judith Ortiz Cofer writes poetry, fiction, and essays about her heritage and the balancing of two cultures. Born in Hormingueros, Puerto Rico, in 1952, she earned a BA from Augusta College in 1974 and an MA from Florida Atlantic University in 1977. Cofer started out as a bilingual teacher in the schools of Palm Beach County, Florida, and taught English and creative writing at the University of Georgia. Her publications include the poetry collections *Peregrina* (1986) and *Terms of Survival* (1987); the novels *The Line of the Sun* (1989), *The Meaning of Consuelo* (2003), and *If I Could Fly* (2011); the essay collections *Silent Dancing* (1990) and *Woman in Front of the Sun* (2000); mixes of nonfiction, fiction, and poetry in *The Latin Deli* (1993) and *The Year of Our Revolution* (1998); and several children's books, most recently *Animal Jamboree: Latino Folktales* and *The Poet Upstairs* (both 2012). As a native Spanish speaker who challenged herself to learn English, she is always experimenting, she says, with "the 'infinite variety' and power of language."

The Cruel Country

Cofer moved to New Jersey from Puerto Rico with her parents and siblings when she was three years old; the family made frequent visits back to the island and (with the exception of Cofer's father) always considered it home. In this excerpt from her memoir *The Cruel Country* (2015), Cofer draws on a theory of French philosopher Roland Barthes (1915–80) to make sense of why a photograph of her mother moves her as it does. The essay first appeared in *Brevity* magazine in 2012.

In the selection following this one, "The Capricious Camera," student writer Laila Ayad also uses division or analysis to tease out the meanings of a photograph, in her case an image of a little girl in World War II Poland.

> *"Mourning: a cruel country where I'm no longer afraid."*
> — Roland Barthes, *Mourning Diary*

I study a photograph of my mother taken on her return to the Island as a   1
widow in her forties. What do I see? A woman in a bright red top and black
pants, neither smiling nor frowning, posed in front of a painted canvas. Her

back is very straight and her hands, showing signs of arthritis in the slightly swollen crooked fingers, are spread flat on her lap.

Something draws the eyes to this woman's face. The camera has caught her in between emotions. We do not know whether she is about to smile or cry.

In his book on photography as memorial, *Camera Lucida*, Roland Barthes talks about the two planes in a photograph that interest him. The first he calls the *studium*, and it represents the actual occasion, meaning, or intent of the photograph. But it is the detail that defies analysis, what Barthes calls the *punctum*, that interests him the most.

The punctum is the point of intersection between viewer and image, that detail that draws us into the picture as a shared human event. It is the thing, whether intended by the photographer or not, that touches you or triggers a quickening of the pulse, an irresistible impulse to look closer.

When I was asked for photos to be displayed at the funeral home, I looked through her albums and found dozens of pictures, but I could not find one that had the right tone, the "air," as Barthes calls it.

My brother had visited our mother several months before her final illness and had found a photo that he scanned and sent to me. She had told him that she did not like it, but had not given a reason. She had kept it put away in a box. I looked at it occasionally, drawn to her haunting look of almost-revelation. It had been taken when she first returned to the Island after my father's death. She looked younger in this photo than I remembered her, maybe because she had taken to wearing conservative, matronly clothes and her hair pulled back while she spent her years as a Navy wife-in-waiting in the United States, the time she always called her *exilio*.[1]

But in this photo she has regained her true age. Her hair is shiny with only a hint of gray at the part, her tan arms are bare, and she looks slim and fit. But in spite of her rejuvenation there is a seriousness that belies the outfit, clearly donned for an evening out.

The punctum of this photo for me is the little spray of white flowers adorning her hair. Doesn't a woman have to be thinking of something celebratory or someone special to put flowers in her hair? I had never seen my mother indulge in anything quite as impractical and frivolous. In fact, she was as concerned about bugs on her body as any child who had experienced the parasite scares of her childhood on a tropical island. I looked at the photo for other signs of her transformation, but kept coming back to the two disparate qualities: the hidden grief in her expression, and the flirtatiousness of the little white flowers in her hair.

[1] Spanish, "exile." — EDS.

On the painted canvas behind her there is an idealized seashore scene at   9
dusk: a background of sinuous palm trees, placid ocean, and a black mountain range. Perhaps this is how our beaches looked once, before the litter, the
hotels and condos, and the tourists. It may have been the image my mother
carried in her mind all those years when she yearned for return.

An ordinary woman, she was a muse to me. It was her ineffable air of timid-   10
ity and even fear, precariously balanced by passionate desires and dreams, of living on her own terms, that I had been trying all of my years as a writer to capture.

But I could not create the visual image I had in my mind's eye. I had to   11
show that photo taken by an anonymous photographer of a woman in the
midst of a struggle, a new widow, alone in a place that had grown strange over
the many years of her absence.

Journal Writing

Flip through a family photo album or scroll through a personal collection of pictures
and pick an image that has a special meaning for you, or one that simply grabs your
attention for some reason. DESCRIBE this photograph in your journal. What is the
"actual occasion, meaning, or intent of the photograph," its "studium," as Roland
Barthes calls it (par. 3)? Who or what is depicted? What are the people wearing? What
are the expressions on their faces? Where was the photo taken? On what elements
does the picture focus? What aspects can be seen in the background? What details
puzzle you, and why?

Questions on Meaning

1. What does Cofer suggest was the reason for her parents' move to the US mainland? Why did her mother return to Puerto Rico?

2. What about the photograph of her mother intrigues Cofer as it does?

3. Cofer says her mother "was a muse" (par. 10) to her. What does she mean?

4. What do you think is Cofer's PURPOSE in this essay? Does she have something
specific she wants the reader to understand?

Questions on Writing Strategy

1. Cofer opens her essay with an epigraph, a short quotation that forecasts a theme.
How do you interpret the line by Roland Barthes? What theme does it forecast?

2. How does Cofer seem to imagine her AUDIENCE? How reasonable are her
ASSUMPTIONS about her readers' backgrounds and knowledge?

3. What principle of analysis does Cofer use to interpret her mother's photograph? How does she SYNTHESIZE another writer's ideas to find new meaning in her subject?

4. **OTHER METHODS** How well can you picture the photograph of Cofer's mother, based on her DESCRIPTION of it? What dominant impression does she create?

Questions on Language

1. What is the double meaning of Cofer's title?

2. How would you describe Cofer's overall TONE? Why is this tone appropriate for her purpose?

3. Consult a dictionary if you need help in defining the following: memorial, planes (par. 3); revelation, matronly (6); rejuvenation, belies, donned (7); disparate (8); sinuous, placid (9); ineffable, precariously (10).

Suggestions for Writing

1. **FROM JOURNAL TO ESSAY** In an essay, describe the photograph you wrote about in your journal, but also do more: Try to analyze the photo in the contexts of the time it was taken and the impact it has on you now. What was the occasion behind the picture? Who took it, and why? What, for you, is the "punctum" (par. 3) of the image? What meanings can you draw from it?

2. Research the current situation of Puerto Ricans in the United States: citizenship, population, incomes, living conditions, education levels, occupations, and so forth. Then write an essay in which you present your findings.

3. **CRITICAL WRITING** In an essay, analyze the parallels between Cofer's emotional state after her mother's death and her mother's apparent emotional state when she first became widowed. What point, overall, does Cofer seem to make about the experience of grieving?

4. **CONNECTIONS** In "The Capricious Camera" (the next essay) Laila Ayad describes a photograph of a young girl and attempts to interpret its historical meanings. Using Cofer's and Ayad's essays for examples, write an essay of your own in which you discuss how writers can create meaning through description and analysis of visual images.

Judith Ortiz Cofer on Writing

Cofer told *Contemporary Authors* in the 1980s why she so often chooses her family as her SUBJECT for writing. She was speaking of her poetry, but the same could be said of her stories and essays as well. "My family is one of the main topics of my poetry," Cofer explained, "the ones left behind on the island of Puerto Rico, and the ones who came to the United States. In tracing their lives, I discover more about mine. The place of birth itself becomes a metaphor for the things we all must leave behind; the assimilation of a new culture is the coming into maturity by accepting the terms necessary for survival. My poetry is the study of this process of change, assimilation, and transformation."

The Bedford Reader on Writing

What is Cofer's apparent PURPOSE in writing about her family as often as she does? For advice on using writing to facilitate your own personal reflection, whether in a JOURNAL or in an essay for others to read, see our notes on pages 19 and 31–32.

LAILA AYAD

Born in 1981, Laila Ayad grew up in Columbia, Maryland, a planned community based on ideals of racial, social, and economic diversity and balance. "Being exposed at an early age to such a diverse community and coming from a multiethnic family have given me great insight into different cultures and perspectives," says Ayad. After graduating from New York University in 2003 with a degree in theater and English literature, Ayad embarked on a successful acting career. When not on stage or screen, she paints and draws and continues to write.

The Capricious Camera

Ayad began college as an art major and produced this essay for a writing class in her sophomore year. Like Judith Ortiz Cofer in the previous selection, Ayad explores the elements of a photograph to find its meaning. The analysis takes her to Nazi Germany before and during World War II.

This essay first appeared in 2001 in *Mercer Street*, a journal of writing by New York University students. Notice that it follows MLA style for in-text parenthetical citations and a list of works cited, as discussed on pages 631–45.

In the years between 1933 and 1945, Germany was engulfed by the rise of a powerful new regime and the eventual spoils of war. During this period, Hitler's quest for racial purification turned Germany not only at odds with itself, but with the rest of the world. Photography as an art and as a business became a regulated and potent force in the fight for Aryan domination, Nazi influence, and anti-Semitism. Whether such images were used to promote Nazi ideology, document the Holocaust, or scare Germany's citizens into accepting their own changing country, the effect of this photography provides enormous insight into the true stories and lives of the people most affected by Hitler's racism. In fact, this photography has become so widespread in our understanding and teaching of the Holocaust that often other factors involved in the Nazis' racial policy have been undervalued in our history textbooks — especially the attempt by Nazi Germany to establish the Nordic Aryans as a master race through the *Lebensborn* experiment, a breeding and adoption program designed to eliminate racial imperfections. It is not merely people of

Mounted Nazi troops on the lookout for likely Polish children.

other persecuted races who can become victims in a racial war, but also those we would least expect — the persecuting race itself.

To understand the importance of this often shrouded side of Nazi Germany 2 we might look at the photograph captioned "Mounted Nazi troops on the lookout for likely Polish children." Archived by Catrine Clay and Michael Leapman, this black-and-white photo depicts a young girl in the foreground, carrying two large baskets and treading across a rural and snow-covered countryside, while three mounted and armed Nazi soldiers follow closely behind her. In the distance, we can see farmhouses and a wooden fence, as well as four other uniformed soldiers or guards. Though the photograph accompanies the text without the name of the photographer, year, or information as to where it was found, Clay and Leapman suggest that the photo was taken in Poland between 1943 and 1945.

Who is this young white girl surrounded by armed soldiers? Is she being 3 protected, watched, persecuted? It would be easy enough to assume that she is Jewish, but unlike photos documenting the Holocaust, with *this* image the intent is uncertain. In our general ignorance of the events surrounding this photo, the picture can be deceiving, and yet it is the picture that can also be used to shed light on the story.

Looking just at the photo, and ignoring the descriptive caption, there are 4 some interesting visual and artistic effects that help a viewer better understand the circumstances surrounding the image. One of its most prominent features is the way the photographer decides to focus on only one young child in the foreground, while including seven Nazi soldiers behind her. The effect is overwhelming, and in gazing at the image, one is struck by the magnitude and force of the oppressing men in sharp contrast to the innocence and helplessness of the lone girl. By juxtaposing one child with seven men, the image comes across strongly as both cruel and terribly frightening. In addition, the child in the foreground is a young girl, which only adds to the potency of the image. The photographer makes the soldiers appear far more menacing and unjust, in that there appears to be no physical way in which a young girl could possibly defend herself against these men.

What is additionally interesting about this particular aspect of the photo 5 is that the seven men are not grouped together, or in any way concentrated right next to the child. There are three directly behind the girl, one a little farther behind and to the left, one even slightly farther behind and to the right, and two very far off in the distance, walking in the opposite direction. This placement of the soldiers not only gives the photo an excellent sense of depth, but also conveys to the viewer a sense that the entire surroundings, not just the little girl, are being controlled and surveyed. It allows the viewer to imagine and wonder in what way other children, or perhaps just the other parts of the village, are being similarly restricted. For the young girl, and the viewer, it allows no way out; all angles and directions of the photo are covered by symbols of oppression, producing an eerily suffocating effect.

The child is the only person in the photo looking directly at the pho-   6
tographer. Whether this technique was manipulated on purpose remains to be seen, but it goes without saying that the effect is dramatic. Her gaze is wistful and innocent. In contrast, the men occupying the rest of the photo, and most prominently the three mounted ones in the foreground, are gazing either away or down. While it is uncertain what the soldiers behind the child are staring at, their downward stare causes their heads to hang in almost shameful disgrace. They do not look at the child, and yet they do not look at the photographer, who is quite obviously standing in front of them. Is this because they do not see that there is a picture being taken, or perhaps the photographer is another soldier, and this picture is simply routine in recording the progress of their work?

If not a Nazi soldier, the photographer could be a Polish citizen; if this   7
were the case, it might change our interpretation of the photo. Suddenly, the girl's facial expression and direct gaze seem pleading, while, for fear of being caught, the photographer snaps the picture quickly, in the exact moment the soldiers are looking away. Perhaps the soldiers did not mind having their picture taken. Many Polish were considered, after all, their racial equals, and maybe they would have respected and appreciated an amateur photographer's interest in their work.

While all of these scenarios are seemingly plausible, the purpose of the   8
photograph is still uncertain. There are also several possibilities. One is that the Nazis commissioned the photograph, as they did others at the time, to properly record the events surrounding the development of their plan. In an article entitled "The Camera as Weapon: Documentary Photography and the Holocaust," Sybil Milton describes the ways in which Nazi photographers worked:

> Nazi professional photographers produced in excess of one-quarter million images. Their work was officially regulated and licensed. . . . All photos were screened by military censors subservient to official directives of the Propaganda Ministry. . . . Press photographers of World War II rarely showed atrocities and seldom published prints unfavorable to their own side. (1)

However, while the evidence is compelling, Milton recognizes another possibility that significantly changes the motive for the photo: "Portable cameras, and other technical innovations like interchangeable lenses and multiple exposure film, meant that nonprofessionals owned and used cameras with ease. Many soldiers carried small Leica or Ermanox cameras in their rucksacks or pillaged optical equipment from the towns they occupied" (2). While it *is* possible that the photograph was taken by a soldier seeking to document the work in Poland for his own interests, this probability, against the numerous commissioned photographs and the nature of the subject matter being documented, is unlikely. The photo alone, while intriguing in its image, tells only half of the story, and without a definitive context can become akin to a "choose your own adventure" novel. In other words, the possibilities for a photographic purpose are all laid out, but the true meaning or end remains undetermined. Unlike hand-made art, which in its very purpose begs to be viewed through various interpretations, photography, and particularly photojournalism, captures a certain moment in time, featuring specific subject matter, under a genuine set of circumstances. The picture is not invented, it is real life, and in being so demands to be viewed alongside its agenda, for without this context, it may never be fully understood.

When we turn to the caption describing the photograph, "Mounted Nazi troops on the lookout for likely Polish children," the book *Master Race* and its accompanying story can now properly be discussed. Instead of typically dealing with the issues of a racist Nazi Germany as it relates to the Holocaust, and the other forms of racial extermination and discrimination that were subsequently involved, Clay and Leapman's book looks at the other side of the coin. It is important in dealing with and understanding the concept of racism to realize that racists are not simply those who dislike others; they are also those who worship themselves. In *Mein Kampf* Hitler outlined the inspiration for his racial tyranny by saying, "The products of human culture, the achievements in art, science and technology . . . are almost exclusively the creative product of the Aryan" (ch. 3). He was heavily influenced by the work of racially charged popular science writers, such as H. F. K. Gunther, who in his *Ethnology of the German Nation* wrote: "The man of Nordic race is not only the most gifted but also the most beautiful. . . . The man's face is hard and chiseled, the woman's tender, with rose-pink skin and bright triumphant eyes" (qtd. in Clay and Leapman 17). Through the course of the book, the topic of racism in Nazi Germany focuses intently on the concept of racial purification. By following the work of the carefully selected (meaning those of impeccable Aryan ancestry) members of Himmler's elite SS corps, Clay and Leapman introduce the history of Germany's failed *Lebensborn* experiment and the homes that were created by the Third Reich to breed and raise "perfect Aryans" (ix).

In a disturbing segment on Hitler's racial utopia, Clay and Leapman describe the practice of eugenics, improving humankind by eliminating undesirable genetic traits and breeding those that were considered superior. The SS soldiers who are commonly known for forcing the Jews into concentration camps are mentioned, but this time they are discussed as the same men who were ordered to father white babies with volunteer German and Norwegian mothers. However, it is the final fact, the story of the SS soldiers who occupied surrounding countries and then stole children "who looked as if they might further improve the breed," that becomes the focus and ultimate subject matter of the photograph (ix).

Looking at the photograph in this context, the soldier no longer appears   11 to be protecting the Polish children, but hunting them. The word "likely" in the caption denotes this. Children who possessed strong Nordic or Aryan qualities were systematically taken from their native countries, adopted by German parents (who were paid by the Nazi regime), taught to forget their families and former lives, and raised to breed not only many children of their own but, above all, families that would uphold Nazi ideology. For Hitler and Heinrich Himmler, who was appointed Commissar for Consolidating German Nationhood, exterminating the racially impure was merely preparation. It was the process of breeding and stealing children that Himmler considered central and key in the ultimate goal for racial purification:

> Obviously in such a mixture of peoples there will always be some racially good types. Therefore I think that it is our duty to take their children with us, to remove them from their environment, if necessary by robbing or stealing them. . . . My aim has always been the same, to attract all the Nordic blood in the world and take it for ourselves. (qtd. in Clay and Leapman 91)

Additionally, Himmler's objective in targeting children, rather than adults, was a planned and strategic tool. Through teachings at school, children were used to control their parents by being encouraged to report what they did and said. Himmler realized that older people would be less enthusiastic about his ideas, so he made every effort to win the minds of the next generation.

What is perhaps most compelling about the *Lebensborn* experiment   12 and thus most poignant when viewing the photograph is the reminder that for every child that was stolen from nations like Poland, his or her family was being equally betrayed. One Polish girl recounted the events of her kidnapping years later, describing both her and her father's reaction to the incident:

> Three SS men came into the room and put us up against a wall. . . . They immediately picked out the fair children with blue eyes — seven altogether, including me. . . . My father, who tried to stop my being taken away, was threatened by the soldiers. They even said he would be taken to a concentration camp. But I have no idea what happened to him later. (qtd. in Clay and Leapman 95)

The girl who spoke above just as easily could have been the young girl being followed by soldiers in the photograph, only moments after she was taken. Such incidents force us to broaden our sense of whom the Nazis victimized. While there is no mistaking the victimization of the Jewish population and other races in Germany, amidst these better-known hate crimes the Nazis were also perpetrating a horrific exploitation of the so-called "white" race.

The complexities surrounding this photograph remind us that the story of   13
any photograph is liable to contain ambiguity. As an art, photography relies on the imagination of the viewer; not *knowing* provides the viewer with a realm of interesting possibilities. Context matters even with art, and playing with possible contexts gives a photograph diverse meanings. It is in these various viewpoints that we find pleasure, amusement, fear, or wonder. It is perhaps in the shift to photojournalism that determining a particular context becomes even more important. In fact, even if the original photographer saw the image as artistic, subsequent events compel us to try to see the image of the Polish girl with Nazis as journalism. In this endeavor, we must uncover as much as possible about the surrounding context. As much as we can, we need to know this girl's particular story. Without a name, date, place, or relevant data, this girl would fall even further backward into the chapters of unrecorded history.

Works Cited

Clay, Catrine, and Michael Leapman. *Master Race: The Lebensborn Experiment in Nazi Germany*. Hodder & Stoughton, 1995.

Hitler, Adolf. *Mein Kampf*. Vol. 2, Eher Verlag, 1926. *Hitler Historical Museum, 1996–2000*, www.hitler.org/writings/Mein_Kampf/. Accessed 1 Dec. 2000.

Milton, Sybil. "The Camera as Weapon: Documentary Photography and the Holocaust." *Annual Scholars' Conference*, Proceedings of the National Conference of Christians and Jews, New York, March 1983. *The Museum of Tolerance*, Simon Wiesenthal Center, 2000, motlc.wiesenthal.com/site/pp.asp?c=gvKVLcMVIuG&b=394975. Accessed 6 Dec. 2000.

"Mounted Nazi Troops on the Lookout for Likely Polish Children." Clay and Leapman, p. 87.

Journal Writing

Ayad uncovers an aspect of Nazi history that is not well known and may seem startling. Think of a time when you learned something that surprised you about history, science, or culture — either in a class or through independent research. In your journal, write about your discovery and how it affected you.

Questions on Meaning

1. Ayad's essay pursues two threads: certain events in German history and certain characteristics of photography, especially photojournalism. Each thread in essence has its own THESIS, stated in paragraphs 1 and 8. What are these theses? Where in the essay does Ayad bring them together?

2. Ayad writes about events in history that she thinks some readers do not know about. What are these events?

3. What do you see as Ayad's PURPOSE in this essay?

Questions on Writing Strategy

1. Why does Ayad devote so much of her essay to discussing the photograph? What is the EFFECT of her speculations about its content and creation?

2. Ayad's AUDIENCE was originally the teacher and students in her writing class. What does she ASSUME readers already know about Nazi Germany? What does she assume they may not know?

3. What is the effect of Ayad's last two sentences? Why does Ayad end this way?

4. **OTHER METHODS**   Where in the essay does Ayad draw on DESCRIPTION? Why is description crucial to her analysis?

Questions on Language

1. What words and phrases does Ayad use in paragraphs 4–6 to communicate her own feelings about the photograph? What are those feelings?

2. Why does Ayad quote Adolf Hitler and H. F. K. Gunther (par. 9), Heinrich Himmler (11), and the Polish woman who was kidnapped as a child (12)? What does Ayad achieve with these quotations?

3. What is the effect of the word *targeting* in paragraph 11?

4. Consult a dictionary if you are unsure of the meanings of any of the following: capricious (title); Aryan, anti-Semitism, ideology, Nordic (par. 1); shrouded (2); juxtaposing (4); suffocating (5); scenarios, plausible, pillaged, definitive (8); extermination, tyranny, impeccable (9); poignant (12); ambiguity, subsequent (13).

Suggestions for Writing

1. **FROM JOURNAL TO ESSAY**   Using your journal writing as a starting point, draft an essay about a surprising discovery you made in a class or on your own. If it will be helpful, do some research to extend your knowledge of the subject. Involve your readers in the essay by distinguishing general knowledge — that is, what they probably know already — from the new information.

2. Locate a photograph that you find especially striking, perhaps in a library book or through an online photo collection such as Instagram or Corbis (*corbisimages.com*).

Write an essay that describes and analyzes the image, using a thesis statement and vivid language to make your interpretation clear.

3. **CRITICAL WRITING**   Some of Ayad's paragraphs are long, especially 1, 8, 9, and 11. How COHERENT are these long paragraphs? Write a brief essay in which you analyze two of them in terms of their organization, the TRANSITIONS or other devices that connect sentences, and any problems with coherence that you see.

4. **CONNECTIONS**   Examine the visual subject of Ayad's essay using the principle of analysis Judith Ortiz Cofer employs in "The Cruel Country" (p. 310). To what extent does Ayad try to establish what Cofer (and Roland Barthes) calls the "studium," or the "actual occasion, meaning, or intent of the photograph"? What for her seems to be the "punctum" of the image, "that detail that draws us into the picture as a shared human event"? What is it for you? Explain your answers in an essay.

ROBERT LIPSYTE

Robert Lipsyte is a sportswriter and broadcast journalist who is equally well known for his young-adult novels. Born in 1938 in the Bronx, he grew up feeling bullied and outcast in the Queens borough of New York City, earned a BA in English from Columbia University at the age of nineteen, and received an MA from the Columbia School of Journalism in 1959. As a reporter and writer for the *New York Times*, Lipsyte published more than five hundred columns; he is also the author of nearly thirty books, including *The Masculine Mystique* (1966), *Free to Be Muhammad Ali* (1978), *An Accidental Sportswriter: A Memoir* (2011), and novels such as *The Contender* (1967) and *The Twin Powers* (2015). Lipsyte was a sports commentator for National Public Radio from 1976 to 1982, an on-air essayist for CBS and NBC from 1982 to 1988, and the host of the public television show *The Eleventh Hour* in the late 1980s, for which he won an Emmy for on-camera achievement in 1990. He continues to write both fiction and nonfiction.

Jock Culture

As Lipsyte tells it, he came into his career by happenstance: Fresh out of college, he needed a job and the *Times* gave him one. That his entry-level position morphed into a career immersed in sports continues to surprise him. Long a sportswriter but never a particular fan, Lipsyte is in a unique position to examine what he sees as a damaging obsession with athleticism and competition in American life. "Jock Culture" first appeared in a special 2011 sports issue of *The Nation*, a newsmagazine usually focused on politics.

In the spring of that hard year, 1968, the Columbia University crew coach, 1
Bill Stowe, explained to me that there were only two kinds of men on campus, perhaps in the world — Jocks and Pukes. He explained that Jocks, such as his rowers, were brave, manly, ambitious, focused, patriotic, and goal-driven, while Pukes were woolly, distractible, girlish, and handicapped by their lack of certainty that nothing mattered as much as winning. Pukes could be found among "the cruddy weirdo slobs" such as hippies, pot smokers, protesters, and, yes, former English majors like me.

I dutifully wrote all this down, although doing so seemed kind of Puke-ish. 2
But Stowe was such an affable *ur*-Jock,[1] twenty-eight years old, funny and articulate, that I found his condescension merely good copy. He'd won an Olympic gold medal, but how could I take him seriously, this former Navy officer who had spent his Vietnam deployment rowing the Saigon River and

---

[1] The German prefix *ur*- means "thorough" or "perfect." — EDS.

running an officers' club? Not surprisingly, he didn't last long at Columbia after helping lead police officers through the underground tunnels to roust the Pukes who had occupied buildings during the antiwar and antiracism demonstrations.

As a thirty-year-old *New York Times* sports columnist then, I was not handicapped by as much lack of certainty about all things as I am now. It was clear to me then that Bill Stowe was a "dumb jock," which does not mean stupid; it means ignorant, narrow, misguided by the values of Jock Culture, an important and often overlooked strand of American life.

These days, I'm not so sure he wasn't right; the world may well be divided into Jocks and Pukes. Understanding the differences and the commonalities between the two might be one of the keys to understanding, first, the myths of masculinity and power that pervade sports, and then why those myths are inescapable in everyday life. Boys — and more and more girls — who accept Jock Culture values often go on to flourish in a competitive sports environment that requires submission to authority, winning by any means necessary, and group cohesion. They tend to grow up to become our political, military, and financial leaders. The Pukes — those "others" typically shouldered aside by Jocks in high school hallways and, I imagine, a large percentage of those who are warily reading this special issue of *The Nation* — were often turned off or away from competitive sports (or settled for cross-country). They were also more likely to go on to question authority and seek ways of individual expression.

This mental conditioning of the Jocks was possible because of the intrinsic joy of sports. Sports is good. It is the best way to pleasure your body in public. Sports is entertaining, healthful, filled with honest, sustaining sentiment for warm times and the beloved people you shared them with. At its simplest, think of playing catch at the lake with friends.

Jock Culture is a distortion of sports. It can be physically and mentally unhealthy, driving people apart instead of together. It is fueled by greed and desperate competition. At its most grotesque, think killer dodgeball for prize money, the Super Bowl. (The clash between sports and the Jock Culture version is almost ideological, at least metaphorical. Obviously, I am for de-emphasizing early competition and redistributing athletic resources so that everyone, throughout their lives, has access to sports. But then, I am also for world peace.)

Kids are initiated into Jock Culture when youth sports are channeled into the pressurized arenas of elite athletes on travel teams driven by ambitious parents and coaches. A once safe place to learn about bravery, cooperation, and respect becomes a cockpit of bullying, violence, and the commitment to a win-at-all-costs attitude that can kill a soul. Or a brain. It is in Pee Wee football, for example, that kids learn to "put a hat on him" — to make tackles head first rather than the older, gentler way of wrapping your arms around a ball carrier's legs and dragging him down. Helmet-to-helmet hits start the trauma cycle early. No wonder the current concussion discussion was launched by the discovery of dementia and morbidity among former pro players.

There is no escape from Jock Culture. You may be willing to describe   8 yourself as a Puke, "cut" from the team early to find your true nature as a billionaire geek, Grammy-winning band fag, wonkish pundit, but you've always had to deal with Jock Culture attitudes and codes, and you have probably competed by them. In big business, medicine, the law, people will be labeled winners and losers, and treated like stars or slugs by coachlike authority figures who use shame and intimidation to achieve short-term results. Don't think symphony orchestras, university philosophy departments, and liberal magazines don't often use such tactics.

Jock Culture applies the rules of competitive sports to everything. Boys,   9 in particular, are taught to be tough, stoical and aggressive, to play hurt, to hit hard, to take risks to win in every aspect of their lives. To dominate. After 9/11, I wondered why what seemed like a disproportionate number of athletic women and men were killed. From reading their brief *New York Times* memorials, it seemed as though most were former high school and college players, avid weekend recreationists, or at least passionate sports fans. When I called executives from companies that had offices in the World Trade Center, I discovered it was no coincidence; stock-trading companies in particular recruited athletes because they came to work even if they were sick, worked well in groups, rebounded quickly from a setback, pushed the envelope to reach the goal, and never quit until the job was done. They didn't have to be star jocks, but they did have to have been trained in the codes of Jock Culture — most important, the willingness to subordinate themselves to authority.

The drive to feel that sense of belonging that comes with being part of   10 a winning team — as athlete, coach, parent, cheerleader, booster, fan — is a reflection of Jock Culture's grip on the male psyche and on more and more women. Men have traditionally been taught to pursue their jock dreams no matter the physical, emotional, or financial cost. Those who realized those dreams have been made rich and famous; at the least, they were waved right through many of the tollbooths of ordinary life. Being treated like a celebrity at twelve, freed from normal boundaries, excused from taking out the garbage and from treating siblings, friends, girls responsibly, is no preparation for a fully realized life. No wonder there are so many abusive athletes, emotionally stunted ex-athletes, and resentful onlookers.

At a critical time when masculinity is being redefined, or at least re-   11 examined seriously, this sports system has become more economically, culturally, and emotionally important than ever. More at service to the empire. More dangerous to the common good.

Games have become our main form of mass entertainment (including   12
made-for-TV contests using sports models). Winners of those games become
our examples of permissible behavior, even when that includes cheating, sexual crimes, or dog torturing. And how does that lead us to the cheating, the
lying, the amorality in our lives outside the white lines? It's not hard to connect the moral dots from the field house to the White House.

The recent emergence of girls as competitors of boys has also raised the   13
ante. Boys have traditionally been manipulated by coaches, drill sergeants, and
sales managers by the fear of being labeled a girl ("sissy" and "faggot" have less to
do with homophobia than misogyny). Despite the many ways males can identify themselves as "real men" in our culture — size, sexuality, power, money,
fame — nothing seems as indelible as the mark made in childhood when the
good bodies are separated from the bad bodies, the team from the spectators.
The designated athletes are rewarded with love, attention, and perks. The leftovers struggle with their resentments and their search for identity.

Of course, the final score is not always a sure thing. There are sensitive   14
linebackers and CEOs, domineering shrinks and violinists. Who won in the
contest between the *Facebook* Puke Mark Zuckerberg and his fiercest competitors, the Olympic rowing Jocks Tyler and Cameron Winklevoss?[2]

"I don't follow that stuff these days," says Bill Stowe, now living in Lake   15
Placid, New York, after retiring as crew coach and fundraiser for the Coast
Guard Academy, a far more comfortable fit than Columbia. "And I have to
tell you, I don't remember separating the world into Jocks and Pukes, although
it sounds good. I liked good brains in my boats, as long as they were willing to
concentrate and pay the price."

Stowe, at seventy-one, is still a conservative Republican. But he doesn't   16
like to talk politics. "It's time to give up the torch," he says. "People are still
living in ignorance, but I'm not running it up the flagpole anymore. Life's too
short to fight." He surprises me when we talk sports. "The big-league thing,
that's a circus. I don't understand how anyone could look up to those guys. But
the real issue is with the kids. Did you read where they're building a $60 mil-
lion football stadium for a high school in Texas? Just for the Jocks. Have you
got any idea how much good you could do, even just in athletics, for all the
other kids with that much money?"

I dutifully write all this down, which doesn't at all seem Puke-ish now.   17
We're on the same page, the coach and I. There's hope.

[2] Mark Zuckerberg (born 1984) is the founder and CEO of *Facebook*. Tyler and Cameron
Winklevoss (born 1981) are twins who accused Zuckerberg, once a fellow Harvard student, of
stealing their idea and computer codes to create his social network. After a protracted legal
battle, the brothers settled for a deal valued at $65 million. — Eds.

Journal Writing

Are you a "Jock" or a "Puke"? Do you play on any athletic teams, or are you content to stay on the sidelines? Did you ever experience or witness any of the aspects of youth sports that Lipsyte describes, whether positive or negative? How did you respond? In your journal, reflect on one such memory.

Questions on Meaning

1. Reread the first three paragraphs of this essay. What do you make of Lipsyte's INTRODUCTION? What event is he reporting, and why is it relevant to his subject?

2. What does Lipsyte mean by "Jock Culture"? How is it distinct from sports in general?

3. What is Lipsyte's THESIS? For whom is Jock Culture harmful, and why?

4. How would you describe the apparent PURPOSE of this essay?

Questions on Writing Strategy

1. What, according to Lipsyte, are the "codes" (par. 8), or elements, of Jock Culture — both positive and negative? What principle of analysis does he apply to his subject?

2. To whom does Lipsyte seem to be writing? Athletes, coaches, students, business leaders, someone else? What ASSUMPTIONS does he make about his readers?

3. Lipsyte brings up the terrorist attacks of September 11, 2001, commenting that "a disproportionate number of athletic women and men were killed" at the World Trade Center (par. 9). Why? What does this detail contribute to his analysis?

4. Why does Lipsyte quote crew coach and former Olympian Bill Stowe in his opening and closing paragraphs? What is the EFFECT of using Stowe's words to frame the essay?

5. **OTHER METHODS**   How does Bill Stowe use CLASSIFICATION to categorize people? How does Lipsyte? What characteristics do "Jocks" have that "Pukes" lack?

Questions on Language

1. What are the CONNOTATIONS of the words *Jock* and *Puke*? Why do you suppose the author chose to repeat these labels coined by Bill Stowe?

2. How would you characterize Lipsyte's TONE? Is it appropriate, given his purpose and AUDIENCE?

3. Point to a few of the metaphors Lipsyte uses to enliven his prose. (See FIGURES OF SPEECH in the Glossary for a definition of *metaphor*.) What do they have in common? What is their effect?

4. Consult a dictionary if any of the following words are unfamiliar: affable, deployment, roust (par. 2); cohesion (4); dementia, morbidity (7); wonkish, pundit (8); stoical (9); psyche (10); amorality (12); ante, misogyny (13).

Suggestions for Writing

1. **FROM JOURNAL TO ESSAY**   Respond to Lipsyte's concerns about the effects of Jock Culture. Do you agree that pressures to compete and a "win-at-all-costs attitude" (par. 7) are destructive forces in society, or do you believe that the values taught by team sports bring positive effects? Why? Start your response with the experience you recounted in your journal, adding additional examples from your observations of others.

2. The concussion crisis that Lipsyte ALLUDES to in paragraph 7 has led some to call for an end to football altogether, or at least for new regulations intended to protect players from brain damage. Research the main arguments for and against such regulations. Then write an essay in which you SUMMARIZE your findings. If your research — or your own experience — leads you to form an opinion favoring one side of the issue, present and support that as well.

3. **CRITICAL WRITING**   Based on this essay, analyze Lipsyte's apparent attitude toward masculinity and the feminist movement. How does he characterize attempts to shift cultural assumptions about men's and women's competitive abilities? Does he believe that gender equity is possible or even desirable? What does he suggest have been (or will be) the effects of feminism? Support your ideas with EVIDENCE from the essay.

4. **CONNECTIONS**   "Jock Culture" is one of several pieces in this book that touch on sports, albeit the only one that's overtly critical. Read as many of the following that interest you: Maya Angelou's "Champion of the World" (p. 94), Brad Manning's "Arm Wrestling with My Father" (p. 121), Brian Doyle's "A Note on Mascots" (p. 178), Dan Koeppel's "Taking a Fall" (p. 281), and E. B. White's "Once More to the Lake" (p. 604). How well does Lipsyte's thesis hold up when compared with the feelings others have derived from watching or participating in sporting activities? How do the other writers' experiences support or contradict his analysis of the implications of Jock Culture for individuals and society?

GUILLERMO DEL TORO AND CHUCK HOGAN

Guillermo del Toro and Chuck Hogan are coauthors of *The Strain* (2009), *The Fall* (2010), and *The Night Eternal* (2011) — a trilogy of vampire novels. Although they share an interest in telling a new kind of story about vampires, the authors arrived at their collaboration from very different backgrounds. Born in Guadalajara, Mexico, del Toro began his career as a cinematic makeup artist. He debuted as a director with *Cronos* (1993) and has directed more than a dozen other movies, including both *Hellboy* films (2004, 2008); *Pan's Labyrinth* (2006), which won three Academy Awards; and *Crimson Peak* (2015). Hogan, by contrast, is a Boston-based novelist who was working as a video-store manager when he made his breakthrough with *The Standoff* (1995), a thriller about a tense hostage negotiation. Hogan has since written *The Blood Artists* (1998), *Prince of Thieves* (2004), *The Killing Moon* (2007), *Devils in Exile* (2010), and the screenplay for *13 Hours* (2016). *Prince of Thieves* won the 2005 Hammett Award for literary crime writing and was the basis for the 2010 motion picture *The Town*.

Vampires Never Die

Filmmaker del Toro and novelist Hogan bonded over their fascination with how ancient myths about vampires have been adapted and readapted in popular culture. In this 2009 essay, first published in the *New York Times*, they trace the perpetual craving for vampire stories back to its historical, literary, and scientific roots.

Tonight, you or someone you love will likely be visited by a vampire — on cable television or the big screen, or in the bookstore. Our own novel describes a modern-day epidemic that spreads across New York City. 1

It all started nearly two hundred years ago. It was the "Year without a Summer" of 1816, when ash from volcanic eruptions lowered temperatures around the globe, giving rise to widespread famine. A few friends gathered at the Villa Diodati on Lake Geneva and decided to engage in a small competition to see who could come up with the most terrifying tale — and the two great monsters of the modern age were born. 2

One was created by Mary Godwin, soon to become Mary Shelley, whose Dr. Frankenstein gave life to a desolate creature. The other monster was less created than fused. John William Polidori stitched together folklore, personal 3

resentment and erotic anxieties into "The Vampyre," a story that is the basis
for vampires as they are understood today.

With "The Vampyre," Polidori gave birth to the two main branches of   4
vampiric fiction: the vampire as romantic hero, and the vampire as undead
monster. This ambivalence may reflect Polidori's own, as it is widely accepted
that Lord Ruthven, the titular creature, was based upon Lord Byron — literary
superstar of the era and another resident of the lakeside villa that fateful summer. Polidori tended to Byron day and night, both as his doctor and most
devoted groupie. But Polidori resented him as well: Byron was dashing and
brilliant, while the poor doctor had a rather drab talent and unremarkable
physique.

But this was just a new twist to a very old idea. The myth, established   5
well before the invention of the word "vampire," seems to cross every culture, language and era. The Indian Baital, the Ch'ing Shih in China, and the
Romanian Strigoi are but a few of its names. The creature seems to be as old
as Babylonia and Sumer.[1] Or even older.

The vampire may originate from a repressed memory we had as primates.   6
Perhaps at some point we were — out of necessity — cannibalistic. As soon as
we became sedentary, agricultural tribes with social boundaries, one seminal
myth might have featured our ancestors as primitive beasts who slept in the
cold loam of the earth and fed off the salty blood of the living.

Monsters, like angels, are invoked by our individual and collective needs.   7
Today, much as during that gloomy summer in 1816, we feel the need to seek
their cold embrace.

Herein lies an important clue: In contrast to timeless creatures like the   8
dragon, the vampire does not seek to obliterate us, but instead offers a peculiar
brand of blood alchemy. For as his contagion bestows its nocturnal gift, the
vampire transforms our vile, mortal selves into the gold of eternal youth and
instills in us something that every social construct seeks to quash: primal lust.
If youth is desire married with unending possibility, then vampire lust creates
within us a delicious void, one we long to fulfill.

In other words, whereas other monsters emphasize what is mortal in us,   9
the vampire emphasizes the eternal in us. Through the panacea of its blood it
turns the lead of our toxic flesh into golden matter.

In a society that moves as fast as ours, where every week a new "block-   10
buster" must be enthroned at the box office, or where idols are fabricated by
consensus every new television season, the promise of something everlasting,

---

[1] Countries of ancient Mesopotamia (in the vicinity of modern-day Iraq), dating back to
approximately 4000 BC and 2000 BC, respectively. They are generally considered the origins of
Western civilization. — EDS.

something truly eternal, holds a special allure. As a seductive figure, the vampire is as flexible and polyvalent as ever. Witness its slow mutation from the pansexual, decadent Anne Rice[2] creatures to the current permutations — promising anything from chaste eternal love to wild nocturnal escapades — and there you will find the true essence of immortality: adaptability.

Vampires find their niche and mutate at an accelerated rate now — in the   11
past one would see, for decades, the same variety of fiend, repeated in multiple storylines. Now, vampires simultaneously occur in all forms and tap into our every need: soap opera storylines, sexual liberation, noir detective fiction, etc. The myth seems to be twittering promiscuously to serve all avenues of life, from cereal boxes to romantic fiction. The fast pace of technology accelerates its viral dispersion in our culture.

But if Polidori remains the roots in the genealogy of our creature, the most   12
widely known vampire was birthed by Bram Stoker in 1897.

Part of the reason for the great success of his "Dracula" is generally   13
acknowledged to be its appearance at a time of great technological revolution. The narrative is full of new gadgets (telegraphs, typing machines), various forms of communication (diaries, ship logs), and cutting-edge science (blood transfusions) — a mash-up of ancient myth in conflict with the world of the present.

Today as well, we stand at the rich uncertain dawn of a new level of sci-   14
entific innovation. The wireless technology we carry in our pockets today was the stuff of the science fiction in our youth. Our technological arrogance mirrors more and more the Wellsian[3] dystopia of dissatisfaction, while allow-ing us to feel safe and connected at all times. We can call, see or hear almost anything and anyone no matter where we are. For most people then, the only remote place remains within. "Know thyself" we do not.

Despite our obsessive harnessing of information, we are still ultimately   15
vulnerable to our fates and our nightmares. We enthrone the deadly virus in the very same way that "Dracula" allowed the British public to believe in monsters: through science. Science becomes the modern man's superstition. It allows him to experience fear and awe again, and to believe in the things he cannot see.

And through awe, we once again regain spiritual humility. The current   16
vampire pandemic serves to remind us that we have no true jurisdiction over our bodies, our climate or our very souls. Monsters will always provide the

---

[2] Anne Rice (born 1941) is an American novelist best known for *Interview with the Vampire* (1976), *The Vampire Lestat* (1985), and *The Queen of the Damned* (1988). — Eds.

[3] H. G. Wells (1866–1946) was an influential English science fiction writer whose works include *The Time Machine* (1895), *The Island of Doctor Moreau* (1896), and *War of the Worlds* (1898). — Eds.

possibility of mystery in our mundane "reality show" lives, hinting at a larger spiritual world; for if there are demons in our midst, there surely must be angels lurking nearby as well. In the vampire we find Eros and Thanatos[4] fused together in archetypal embrace, spiraling through the ages, undying.

Forever.   17

Journal Writing

Do you enjoy vampire stories, whether in books, in movies, or on television? Of the vampire characters in popular culture (past or present), who is your favorite? Why do you think this character appeals to you? In your journal, explore what vampires mean to you. If you don't care for vampire fiction, consider why it leaves you cold.

Questions on Meaning

1. Why do you suppose del Toro and Hogan wrote this essay? Are they merely promoting their novels, or do they have a more serious PURPOSE as well?

2. What is the THESIS of "Vampires Never Die"? Where, if at all, is it stated succinctly?

3. How do del Toro and Hogan explain the appeal of vampires in contemporary culture? In what ways has that appeal changed across time and geography? In what ways has it remained consistent?

4. What is a "social construct" (par. 8)? How is the concept central to the authors' interpretation of vampires?

5. In paragraph 15, del Toro and Hogan say, "Science becomes the modern man's superstition." What do they mean? How do you explain the PARADOX in that statement?

Questions on Writing Strategy

1. "Vampires Never Die" uses advanced academic vocabulary and contains several literary, historical, scientific, and psychological references. How, then, do the authors imagine their AUDIENCE? Are their ASSUMPTIONS reasonable in your case?

2. What principle of analysis do del Toro and Hogan use in examining vampire stories? What enduring elements do they perceive in the characters?

3. Why do del Toro and Hogan speculate in their introduction about the "resentment and erotic anxieties" (par. 3) felt by John William Polidori, the author of

---

[4] Greek gods of love (Eros) and death (Thanatos). — EDS.

the first modern vampire story? What do his personal conflicts have to do with how we think about vampires today?

4. What is the EFFECT of the essay's final paragraph?

5. **OTHER METHODS**   Del Toro and Hogan COMPARE AND CONTRAST new technologies from the late nineteenth and early twenty-first centuries. What similarities do they find?

Questions on Language

1. Make sure you know the meanings of the following words: desolate (par. 3); ambivalence, titular, dashing (4); repressed, sedentary, seminal, loam (6); invoked (7); obliterate, primal (8); panacea (9); consensus, polyvalent, pansexual, permutations, chaste (10); noir, promiscuously, dispersion (11); mash-up (13); dystopia (14); pandemic, mundane, archetypal (16).

2. Explain the double meaning of "twittering" in paragraph 11. Why do you think del Toro and Hogan chose this particular word?

3. What do the authors mean by "a peculiar brand of blood alchemy" (par. 8)? Where else do they use this metaphor? Why is it particularly appropriate for their subject? (For a definition of *metaphor*, see FIGURES OF SPEECH in the Glossary.)

Suggestions for Writing

1. **FROM JOURNAL TO ESSAY**   Expanding on your journal entry, write an essay that analyzes one vampire character from popular culture — such as Bram Stoker's Dracula, Edward from the *Twilight* series, Yvette from Anne Rice's novels, Bill Compton from *True Blood*, or The Master from del Toro and Hogan's trilogy. Break the character down into his (or her) elements, considering backstory as well as personality, and reassemble the parts into a new whole of your understanding.

2. Write an essay that analyzes several examples of another type of writing by examining their shared characteristics and hidden meanings. You may choose any narrowly defined GENRE that's familiar to you: food blog, parenting-advice column, amateur film review, gay romance, alternative-history science fiction, and so on. Be sure to make your principle of analysis clear to your readers.

3. Some cultural analysts have said that the resurgence of vampire stories in the last quarter century can be attributed to the AIDS epidemic that emerged in the 1980s. In your library's database of scholarly journal articles, conduct a keyword search with "vampires and AIDS," and read one or two of the arguments in favor of this theory. (If you prefer, you may search for other academic analyses of vampire lore.) How do you respond to the articles? Do alternate interpretations undermine del Toro and Hogan's analysis, or do they simply complicate it?

4. **CRITICAL WRITING**   Del Toro and Hogan explore CAUSES AND EFFECTS to explain the prevalence of vampires in popular culture. How persuasive is their analysis? Do you agree with them that vampire legends fill psychological and spiritual

voids that have been created by advances in science and technology? Why, or why not?

5. **CONNECTIONS**   In this essay Guillermo del Toro and Chuck Hogan examine how vampires serve as SYMBOLS of human anxieties. Likewise, Brian Doyle, in "A Note on Mascots" (p. 178), observes that animals take on a symbolic function when they're adopted as sports icons. What similarities, if any, do you see between team mascots and long-held myths such as vampires? Is either more culturally significant? Do they represent related fears and needs? Write an essay of your own that examines the deeper implications of such symbols. (You need not choose vampires or sports mascots as your subject: If you've noticed some other symbol that captures your interest, such as zombies or angels, feel free to analyze that instead.) Consider, as well, your own thoughts about interpretations of this sort: Is popular culture worthy of serious inquiry?

Guillermo del Toro and Chuck Hogan on Writing

"Vampires Never Die" was by no means Guillermo del Toro and Chuck Hogan's first experience working together as writers. In 2006 they began collaborating on a trilogy of horror novels about vampires. The project started when Hogan's literary agent sent him a twelve-page outline of del Toro's story idea, originally conceived for the small screen, and told him the director was thinking about trying a novel. "I got a page and a half in before calling [my agent] back and essentially telling him that I would do anything to be involved," Hogan gushed in a 2009 interview with blogger Sarah Weinman. In lieu of a publishing deal or any kind of contract, the authors made a pact on a handshake — "actually more of a bro-hug," according to Hogan — and agreed to join forces. They finished the first installment of the trilogy, *The Strain*, after three years.

Hogan admits to being apprehensive about writing with del Toro, whom he calls "a god of the genre," especially since the storyline was the director's. However, he says that del Toro "completely opened up his story," giving Hogan the freedom to expand and change the NARRATIVE in the drafting stage. In a separate interview with Rick Kleffel on KUSP Central Coast Public Radio, del Toro praised Hogan's contributions to the shape of the story: "The book is full of intimate moments of terror that come from personal experience, and others that Chuck created. . . . Some of the best, most disturbing moments in the book come from his imagination, curiously enough."

Both authors note that, though their drafting processes were loose, revising the book was "rigorous." Exchanging drafts by e-mail, they commented extensively on each other's chapters, a practice that del Toro calls "riffing." As he explains, "I was merciless with his chapters; he was merciless with my chapters." Revisions involved moving or cutting large portions of text. Del Toro often rearranged chapters, and Hogan sometimes scrapped entire sections. Speaking of Hogan's editing style, del Toro jokes that some changes were made "subverticiously" (a word of his own invention): "All of a sudden I would get the manuscript and it was missing one chapter I wrote or half a chapter I wrote." However, it was this kind of harsh revision that in the end made for the "seamless blending" of two writers' talents.

The Bedford Reader on Writing

As collaborators, del Toro and Hogan find distinct advantages in drafting freely, but revising rigorously. Such an approach is not at all unique to team projects, however. For advice on applying the same techniques to your own writing, see pages 34–42 ("Drafting" and "Revising").

BARBARA B. PARSONS

A teacher of composition and literature at Tacoma Community College and at Pierce College Puyallup, Barbara B. Parsons has also taught at Green River Community College and Arizona State University. As a freelance writer she has published essays and op-ed articles in *The Tacoma News Tribune* and *Post Defiance*, among other publications, and she has completed drafts of several novels. Born in 1963 and raised in Phoenix, Arizona, Parsons became enamored of literature, particularly nineteenth-century British literature, early on and read ("in air-conditioned rooms") as much as she could whenever she could. She studied briefly at the University of Colorado and at the American Academy of Dramatic Arts, and then completed her bachelor's and master's degrees in English at Arizona State University. Parsons lives in Tacoma, Washington, where she keeps herself busy researching genealogy and attempting to restore her historic Victorian home "to its former statuesque beauty."

Whistling in the Dark

"Whistling in the Dark" is a formal academic analysis of Brent Staples's now classic "Black Men and Public Space" (p. 166). Parsons wrote it as a model to show her students what she expects of them when she assigns a critical essay. (The assignment reads, in part, "Write a [brief] analysis of an article in terms of whether or not it is successful in convincing the reader.") She has since written multiple analyses of Staples's essay for multiple purposes; this one she revised specifically for inclusion in *The Bedford Reader* in 2016.

Brent Staples has an ax to grind in "Black Men and Public Space," but he doesn't grind it. The article, about stereotypes of black men as dangerous, suggests not that society change, but rather that black men themselves change in order to elicit less fear from others, particularly white women. Staples delivers almost endless examples of black men being mistaken for criminals, convinces us that a problem exists, and describes his creative personal solutions. However, his tone of determined self-control hits a false note. While the well-structured essay does make general readers aware of the issue, ultimately it fails to convince us that Staples's solution is the best one possible.

Staples catches the reader's attention immediately by referring to the first woman he noticed cross the street to avoid walking close to him as a "victim" (166). This woman "cast back a worried glance. To her, the youngish black man . . . seemed menacingly close" (166). This opening example does an excellent job of alerting the reader to the issue at hand and even eliciting sympathy and understanding toward the woman, who, after all, is legitimately afraid, though unnecessarily so. Staples himself appears sympathetic: "It was clear that she thought herself the quarry of a mugger, a rapist, or worse" (166), he says. Rather than condemn her false fears, Staples explains carefully, "I was stalking sleep, not defenseless wayfarers. As a softy who is scarcely able to take a knife to raw chicken — let alone hold one to a person's throat — I was surprised, embarrassed, and dismayed all at once" (167). Staples's perception of the situation and the perceptions of wary pedestrians are thus set up from the beginning as equally genuine and innocent, but in opposition. One perception must be false.

Subsequent examples, of people who lock their car doors when Staples   3
passes, of an office manager who calls security when he does not recognize his own employee, and of a storekeeper who threatens a shopper with a guard dog (167–68), adequately prove that public perceptions of black men are often negative and false. Surprisingly, over and over, Staples seems to sympathize with those who mistake him for a menace, saying things like "I understand, of course, that the danger they perceive is not a hallucination" (167). Staples seems determined to take the high road. While those around him jump to frightening conclusions, Staples models tolerance and thoughtful reflection.

The author's sympathetic tone may strike the reader as somewhat false,   4
however. There must be more than sympathy in Staples's reactions. Indeed, he tells us that he has "learned to smother the rage [he] felt at so often being taken for a criminal" (168) and that he long ago began to use careful, non-assertive behavior to counteract the situation. What may trouble some readers, however, is the thought that a smothered rage is likely to become enflamed again at any moment. Rather than combat the problem in any controlled yet assertive manner, Staples chooses to "take precautions to make [him]self less threatening" (168). These precautions — staying at a distance from others in subway stations, avoiding entering a building behind a frightened group of people, whistling classical music when walking late at night (168–69) — seem both excessive and ridiculous. Nor do they seem successful, since Staples himself states that he has kept up this system for "more than a decade" (166) with no change in the situation.

Staples is clear on one point: He is not guilty of anything. He tells us   5
that he "grew up one of the good boys" (168), but that he has lost too many loved ones to street violence to advocate an assertive stance. He is "timid, but a survivor" (168). This retiring position will do nothing to stop a problem that seems to be rampant in American cities. Staples compares his whistling to "the cowbell that hikers wear when they know they are in bear country" (169). But this analogy, while thought-provoking, isn't sound. While those cowbells are intended to keep bears away, Staples's whistles are supposed to

soothe fearful pedestrians and encourage them to stick around. The analogy would be more apt if the pedestrians were making a noise to keep Staples away — perhaps by blowing a police whistle.

Staples hopes to encourage us all to be tolerant and nonaggressive, but he takes the biggest portion of the responsibility onto his own broad shoulders, and by extension, onto the backs of other black men with the same "unwieldy inheritance" (166) as he. Some may find his solution frustrating; others may even believe it is unjust. Despite excellent examples and thoughtful commentary, Staples ultimately fails to convince readers that tolerance and timidity are the best response to the problem of racism on the streets. While violence and hate are self-perpetuating and should be avoided, Staples and other black men should be able to go about their lives without undue concern that they are frightening other people or putting themselves in danger. We need a solution that doesn't require anyone to "smother" a negative emotion, be it fear or rage. That is not too much to ask, and Staples should be asking. 6

Work Cited

Staples, Brent. "Black Men and Public Space." *The Bedford Reader*, edited by X. J. Kennedy et al., 13th ed., Bedford/St. Martin's, 2017, pp. 166–69.

Journal Writing

Parsons is disappointed in Brent Staples's "response to the problem of racism on the streets" (par. 6) and wishes he had proposed a more aggressive solution. Think back to a time when you, or someone around you, responded to a situation in a way that you ultimately determined was not helpful. What was the situation? Why might the initial response have seemed appropriate in the moment? How would you change it now, if you could? Reflect on the problem in your journal.

Questions on Meaning

1. To what end(s) does Parsons analyze Brent Staples's essay? What is her PURPOSE?
2. Why, to Parsons, does Staples's "tone of determined self-control" (par. 1) feel false? Cite evidence from her essay to support your answer.
3. Parsons does not appreciate that Staples is sympathetic to the pedestrians who shy away from him on the street. Why not?
4. What is the THESIS of "Whistling in the Dark"? Where does Parsons state her main idea?

Questions on Writing Strategy

1. As we explain in the note on page 337, Parsons wrote "Whistling in the Dark" as a model for her students. How is her writing appropriate for this AUDIENCE? What other readers might be receptive to her essay, and why?

2. To what extent does Parsons ASSUME that her readers are familiar with "Black Men and Public Space"? How does she ensure that readers can follow her analysis even if they haven't read Brent Staples's essay?

3. What important shift occurs in the TRANSITION between paragraphs 3 and 4?

4. **OTHER METHODS**   Parsons uses analysis to illuminate Staples's social commentary. How does she reassemble the parts of his essay to present her own ARGUMENT about a broader subject? What call to action is she making?

Questions on Language

1. Where in her essay does Parsons use FIGURES OF SPEECH to enliven her academic writing? Choose one of her metaphors or similes and explain its meaning.

2. Check a dictionary if any of the following words are unfamiliar to you: elicit (par. 1); opposition (2); menace (3); advocate, rampant (5); self-perpetuating (6).

3. Parsons uses some words — such as "false," "negative," "perception," and "sympathy" — repeatedly. Why? What does this strategy contribute to the overall effectiveness of her essay?

Suggestions for Writing

1. **FROM JOURNAL TO ESSAY**   Building on your journal reflections, write an essay that analyzes the problem you recorded, particularly the flaws in your (or someone else's) response to a difficult situation. Be sure to cite specific EXAMPLES and to suggest a response that might have been more productive.

2. Consider a challenging issue facing society today, such as income inequality or clean energy. Write an essay that analyzes the problem, using EXAMPLES to capture its many facets or manifestations. You may, if you wish, propose a solution as well, one that addresses the details you discuss in your essay.

3. **CRITICAL WRITING**   Turn to page 166 of this book and read "Black Men and Public Space" for yourself. Then write an essay that responds to Parsons's analysis. Was your initial reaction to Brent Staples's examples similar to hers, or different? How did reading her essay change your understanding of his? Do you agree with her interpretations, or do you read Staples's essay differently? Why?

4. **CONNECTIONS**   Janelle Asselin's "Superhuman Error: What Dixon and Rivoche Get Wrong" (p. 505) is also a model of close analysis of another essay in this book. Review her essay side by side with "Whistling in the Dark" and try to identify the components that make up a strong critical reading. What features do these selections have in common? How do the authors differ in their approaches? Do you find one approach more effective or revealing than the other? Why?

Barbara B. Parsons on Writing

We asked Barbara B. Parsons what advice she would offer to student writers using this book. Here is what she had to say.

The transition to college reading, writing, and learning is hard.

I grew up a reader, but it was hard for me anyway.

There are still kids who, as I did, read novels under their desktops and write four-page book reports when the teacher only asks for a page. My love of literature and youthful success writing made me certain going into college that I already wrote well, so I took a writing-heavy load my first semester. Sitting in my freezing dorm room in the early 1980s, I typed every essay three times. I reread my own phrasing, loving the way the words sounded. I turned in the Wite-Out-crusted pages with a smirk of self-confidence.

That first round of college papers earned Bs and Cs. After a good cry, I pulled the essays out of the waste bin and reread them, along with what was written in the margins. "Comma issues," "Attend to gross mechanical errors," "Fuzzy thinking," and, worst of all, at the end of one essay: "What is a comma splice? What is a run-on? I do not care what you say unless you can say it clearly!"

It gets better, as they say.

That year, I began the lifelong task of learning to write. I forced myself to see the errors in my writing. I reluctantly let go of the literary flourishes. In literature classes, for the first time, I paid conscious attention to the way strong writers put words and phrases together. I began to try tricks, like removing all adjectives and adverbs, just to see how a paragraph sounded without them. If a sentence wasn't working, I started it again in the middle, twisting the clauses to test my emphasis.

Now, I teach college students who face the same challenges I did, but with an additional burden: They grew up with technology. Words spell themselves; grammar checkers highlight incorrect sentences. Yet, just as when I use my GPS system too often I forget the order of my city's streets, some students become so reliant on technology that they don't remember the difference between *their* and *they're*. And just as my GPS occasionally leads me to take a wrong turn, spelling and grammar aids sometimes steer writers to the wrong word choice or sentence structure. They can encourage false confidence, which, like my smug attitude my freshman year, can be a barrier to clear expression in English.

When I was eighteen, a few honest professors had the guts to tell me that what I had produced was garbage. Once I faced that, my childhood spent with J. R. R. Tolkien and Jane Austen gave me the tools to become a strong writer. Students who have grown up reading quickly produced novels full of usage errors, who read only poorly edited online material, or who read only when forced, have a greater challenge than I had. I worry about the writers who haven't been exposed to enough good writing to recognize excellence and to test out different styles and tones. For them, I have only one piece of advice: *Read.*

The Bedford Reader on Writing

When Barbara Parsons advises student writers to "*Read*," she means high-quality, well-written works specifically — like the essays collected in this book. For concrete guidelines on how to read them critically, see Chapter 1. And for help with using such reading to become a better writer yourself, see Chapter 2, where you'll learn, among other things, what a comma splice and a run-on sentence are.

ADDITIONAL WRITING TOPICS
Division or Analysis

Using the method of division or analysis, write an essay on one of the following subjects (or choose your own subject). In your essay, make sure your purpose and your principle of division or analysis are clear to your readers. Explain the parts of your subject so that readers know how each relates to the others and contributes to the whole.

The slang or technical terminology of a group such as stand-up comedians or online gamers

An especially *bad* movie, television show, or book

A doll, action figure, or other toy from childhood

A typical sidebar ad for a product such as clothing, deodorant, beer, a luxury car, or an economy car

A machine or an appliance, such as a drone, a motorcycle, a microwave oven, or a camera

An organization or association, such as a social club, a sports league, or a support group

The characteristic appearance of an indie folk singer or a classical violinist

A day in the life of a student

Your favorite poem

A short story, an essay, or another work that made you think

The government of your community

The most popular restaurant (or other place of business) in town

The Bible, Q'uran, or another religious text

An urban legend: hitchhiking ghosts, flickering orbs, gas-station carjackings, haunted cemeteries, buried treasures, and so forth

A painting or a statue

How the Poor, the Middle Class, and the Rich Spend Their Money

Type of Spending	Household Income		
	$15,000–$19,999	$50,000–$69,999	Above $150,000
Food at Home	10.2%	7.7%	5.4%
Food at Restaurants, etc.	4.7%	5.4%	5.4%
Housing	29.2%	26.7%	27.5%
Utilities	11.1%	8.2%	4.8%
Clothes & Shoes	3.6%	3.2%	3.7%
Transportation & Gasoline	20.4%	21.3%	15.5%
Health Care & Health Insurance	8.2%	7.1%	4.5%
Entertainment	4.8%	5.1%	5.7%
Education	1.5%	1.3%	4.4%
Saving for Retirement	2.6%	9.6%	15.9%

Source: Bureau of Labor Statistics. Credit: Lam Thuy Vo / NPR

9

CLASSIFICATION

Sorting into Kinds

◀ **Classification in a table**

How do you spend your money? Does most of it go for rent and utilities, for instance, or is the bulk of your budget earmarked for tuition, fees, and books? How do your income and expenses compare to those of your peers? In this infographic, National Public Radio's *Planet Money* translates data from the Bureau of Labor Statistics to show how household budgets in the United States typically sort out. NPR's table classifies spending patterns for three economic groups: "the Poor, the Middle Class, and the Rich." Notice, first, how NPR defines each class. Then examine the data. The column on the left identifies ten types of spending; the three other columns compare the percentages of household income devoted to each category by the groups. What similarities and differences among the categories strike you? Are you surprised by any of the numbers? Why, or why not?

THE METHOD

To CLASSIFY is to make sense of some aspect of the world by arranging many units — trucks, chemical elements, wasps, students — into more manageable groups. Zoologists classify animals, botanists classify plants — and their classifications help us understand a vast and complex subject: life on earth. To help us find books in a library, librarians classify books into categories: fiction, biography, history, psychology, and so forth. For the convenience of readers, newspapers run classified advertising, grouping many small ads into categories such as "Services" and "Cars for Sale."

Subjects and Reasons for Classification

The subject of a classification essay is always a number of things, such as peaches or political systems. (In contrast, DIVISION or ANALYSIS, the topic of the preceding chapter, usually deals with a solitary subject, a coherent whole, such as *a* peach or *a* political system.) The job of classification is to sort the things into groups or classes based on their similarities and differences. Say, for instance, you're going to write an essay about how people write. After interviewing a lot of writers, you determine that writers' processes differ widely, mainly in the amount of planning and rewriting they entail. (Notice that this determination involves analyzing the PROCESS of writing, separating it into steps. See Chapter 7.) On the basis of your findings, you create groups for planners, one-drafters, and rewriters. Once your groups are defined, and assuming they are valid, your subjects (the writers) almost sort themselves out.

Just as you can analyze a subject in many ways, you can classify a subject according to many principles. One travel guide, for instance, might group places to stay by style of accommodation: resorts, hotels, motels, bed-and-breakfasts, boarding houses, and hostels. A different guidebook might classify options according to price: grand luxury, luxury, moderate, bargain, fleabag, and flophouse.

The principle used in classifying things depends on the writer's PURPOSE. A guidebook classifies accommodations by price to match visitors with hotels that fit their pocketbooks. A linguist might explain the languages of the world by classifying them according to their origins (Romance languages, Germanic languages, Asian languages, Coptic languages . . .), but a student battling with a college language requirement might try to entertain fellow students by classifying languages into three groups: hard to learn, harder to learn, and unlearnable.

Kinds of Classification

Classification schemes vary in complexity, depending on the groups being sorted and the basis for sorting them. In classifying methods of classification, we find two types: binary and complex.

- **Binary classification.** The simplest classification is binary (or two-part), in which you sort things out into (1) those with a certain distinguishing feature and (2) those without it. You might classify a number of persons, let's say, into smokers and nonsmokers, runners and nonrunners, believers and nonbelievers. Binary classification is most useful when your subject is easily divisible into positive and negative categories.

- **Complex classification.** More often, a classification will sort things into multiple categories, sometimes putting members into subcategories. Such is the case with a linguist who categorizes languages by origin. Writing about the varieties of one Germanic language, such as English, the writer could identify the subclasses of British English, North American English, Australian English, and so on.

As readers, we enjoy classifications that strike us as true and familiar. This pleasure may account for the appeal of magazine and Web articles that classify things ("Seven Common Varieties of Moocher," "The Top Ten Most Embarrassing Social Blunders"). Usefulness as well as pleasure may explain the popularity of classifications that EVALUATE things. The magazine *Consumer Reports* sorts products as varied as space heaters and frozen dinners into groups based on quality (excellent, very good, good, fair, and poor), and then, using analysis, discusses each product (of a frozen pot pie: "Bottom crust gummy, meat spongy when chewed, with nondescript old-poultry and stale-flour flavor").

THE PROCESS

Purposes and Theses

Classification will usually come into play when you want to impose order on a complex subject that includes many items. In one essay in this chapter, for instance, Deborah Tannen tackles the seemingly endless opportunities for men and women to miscommunicate with each other. Sometimes you may use classification humorously, as Russell Baker does in another essay in this chapter, to give a charge to familiar experiences.

Classification

Whatever use you make of classification, do it for a reason: The files of composition instructors are littered with essays in which nothing was ventured and nothing was gained. Classifications can reveal truth or amuse us, but they can also reveal nothing and bore us. To sort ten North American cities according to their relative freedom from air pollution or their cost of living or the range of services offered to residents might prove highly informative and useful to someone looking for a new place to live. But to sort the cities according to a superficial feature such as the relative size of their cat and dog populations wouldn't interest anyone, probably, except a veterinarian looking for a job.

Your purpose, your THESIS, and your principle of classification will all overlap with your interest in your subject. Say you're curious about how other students write. Is your interest primarily in the materials they use (keyboard, pencil, voice recorder), in where and when they write, or in how much planning and rewriting they do? Any of these could lead to a principle for sorting the students into groups. And that principle should be revealed in your THESIS STATEMENT, letting readers know why you are classifying. Here, from the essays in this chapter, are three examples of classification thesis statements:

> Many of the conversational rituals common among women are designed to take the other person's feelings into account, while many of the conversational rituals common among men are designed to maintain the one-up position, or at least avoid appearing one-down. As a result, when men and women interact — especially at work — it's often women who are at the disadvantage.
> — Deborah Tannen, "But What Do You Mean?"

> Inanimate objects are classified into three major categories — those that don't work, those that break down and those that get lost.
> — Russell Baker, "The Plot against People"

> [T]hree types [of stars] stand out as the most potentially beneficial to humankind and prolonging its existence: supergiants, yellow dwarfs, and red dwarfs. . . . The red dwarf, however, is or at least will be the most important star because of its incredibly long life span and relative abundance in our immense universe.
> — Jean-Pierre De Beer, "Stars of Life"

Categories

For a workable classification, make sure that the categories you choose don't overlap. If you were writing a survey of popular magazines for adults and you were sorting your subject into categories that included women's magazines and sports magazines, you might soon run into trouble. Into which

category would you place *Women's Sports?* The trouble is that both categories take in the same item. To avoid this problem, you'd need to reorganize
your classification on a different principle. You might sort out the magazines
by their audiences: magazines intended for women, magazines intended for
men, magazines intended for both women and men. Or you might group
them according to subject matter: sports magazines, political magazines,
fashion magazines, celebrity magazines, and so on. *Women's Sports* would fit
into either of those classification schemes, but into only *one* category in each
scheme.

When you draw up a scheme of classification, be sure that you include all
essential categories. Omitting an important category can weaken the effect of
your essay, no matter how well written it is. It would be a major oversight, for
example, if you were to classify the residents of a dormitory according to their
religious affiliations and not include a category for the nonaffiliated.

Some form of outline can be helpful to keep the classes and their members straight as you develop and draft ideas. You might experiment with a
diagram in which you jot down headings for the groups, with plenty of space
around them, letting each heading accumulate members as you think of them.
This kind of diagram offers more flexibility than a vertical list or an outline,
and is a good aid for keeping categories from overlapping or disappearing.

FOCUS ON PARAGRAPH DEVELOPMENT

A crucial aim of classification is to make sure each group is clear: what's
counted in, what's counted out, and why. You'll provide examples and other
details to make the groups clear as you develop the paragraph(s) devoted to
each.

The following paragraph barely outlines one group in a four-part classification of ex-smokers into zealots, evangelists, the elect, and the serene:

> The second group, evangelists, does not condemn smokers but encourages
> them to quit. Evangelists think quitting is easy, and they preach this message,
> often earning the resentment of potential converts.

Contrast this bare-bones adaptation with the actual paragraphs written by
Franklin E. Zimring in his essay "Confessions of a Former Smoker":

> By contrast, the antismoking evangelist does not condemn smokers. Unlike
> the zealot, he regards smoking as an easily curable condition, as a social disease,
> and not a sin. The evangelist spends an enormous amount of time seeking and
> preaching to the unconverted. He argues that kicking the habit is not *that* dif-
> ficult. After all, *he* did it; moreover, as he describes it, the benefits of quitting are
> beyond measure and the disadvantages are nil.

(continued)

Classification

The hallmark of the evangelist is his insistence that he never misses tobacco. Though he is less hostile to smokers than the zealot, he is resented more. Friends and loved ones who have been the targets of his preachments frequently greet the resumption of smoking by the evangelist as an occasion for unmitigated glee.

In the second sentence of each paragraph, Zimring explicitly contrasts evangelists with zealots, the group he previously defined. And he does more as well: He provides specific examples of the evangelist's message (first paragraph) and of others' reactions to him (second paragraph). These details pin down the group, making it distinct from other groups and clear in itself.

CHECKLIST FOR REVISING A CLASSIFICATION

✔ **Purpose.** Have you classified for a reason? Will readers be able to see why you bothered?

✔ **Principle of classification.** Will readers also see what rule or principle you used for sorting individuals into groups? Is this principle apparent in your thesis sentence?

✔ **Consistency.** Does each representative of your subject fall into one category only, so that categories don't overlap?

✔ **Completeness.** Have you mentioned all the essential categories suggested by your principle of classification?

✔ **Paragraph development.** Have you provided enough information, examples, and other details so that readers can easily distinguish each category from the others?

CLASSIFICATION IN ACADEMIC WRITING

An Anthropology Textbook

This paragraph comes from *Humankind Emerging*, a textbook on human physical and cultural evolution by Bernard Campbell. The author offers a standard classification of hand grips in order to explain one of several important differences between human beings and their nearest relatives, apes and monkeys.

There are two distinct ways of holding and using tools: the *power grip* and the *precision grip*, as John Napier termed them. Human infants and children begin with the power grip and progress to the precision grip. Think of how a child holds a spoon: first in the power grip, in its fist or between its fingers and palm, and later between the tips of the thumb and first two fingers, in the precision grip. Many primates have the power grip also. It is the way they get firm hold of a tree branch. But neither a monkey nor an ape has a thumb long enough or flexible enough to be completely *opposable* through rotation at the wrist, able to reach comfortably to the tips of all the other fingers, as is required for our delicate yet strong precision grip. It is the opposability of our thumb and the independent control of our fingers that make possible nearly all the movements necessary to handle tools, to make clothing, to write with a pencil, to play a flute.

Topic sentence names the principle of classification

Two categories explained side by side

Second category explained in greater detail

A Résumé

Sooner or later, every college student needs a résumé: a one-page overview of skills and experiences that will appeal to a potential employer. Part of the challenge in drafting a résumé is to bring order to what seems a complex and unwieldy subject, a life. The main solution is to classify activities and interests into clearly defined groups: typically work experience, education, and special skills.

The group that poses the biggest challenge is usually work experience: Some résumés list jobs with the most recent first, detailing the specifics of each one; others sort experience into skills (such as computer skills, administrative skills, and communication skills) and then list job specifics under each subcategory. The first arrangement tends to be more straightforward and potentially less confusing to readers. However, college students and recent graduates with few previous jobs often find the second arrangement preferable because it downplays experience and showcases abilities.

The résumé on the following page was prepared by Kharron Reid, who was seeking a paid internship in the field of information systems for the summer between his junior and senior years of college. After experimenting with different organizational strategies, he decided to put the category of work experience first because it related directly to the internships he sought. And he chose to organize his work experience by jobs rather than skills because the companies he had worked for were similar to the companies he was applying to.

For the job-application cover letter Reid wrote to go with the résumé, see page 165 of Chapter 5.

Classification

Kharron Reid
137 Chester Street, Apt. E
Allston, MA 02134
(617) 555-4009
kreid@bu.edu

OBJECTIVE

An internship that offers experience in information systems

EXPERIENCE

NBS Systems Corp., Denniston, MI, June to September 2016

As an intern, helped install seven WANs using Windows
Server 2016

- Planned layout for WANs
- Installed physical platform and configured servers

Pioneer Networking, Damani, MI, May to September 2015

As an intern, worked as a LAN specialist using a Unix-based
server

- Connected eight workstations onto a LAN by laying physical
  platform and configuring software
- Assisted network engineer in monitoring operations of LAN

SPECIAL SKILLS

Computer proficiency:

Windows 10/8	Adobe Photoshop	XML
Unix	JIRA	JavaScript
Red Hat Enterprise Linux	HTML	Python

Internet research

EDUCATION

Boston University, School of Management, 2014 to present

Double major: business administration and information
systems

Courses: organizational behavior, computer science, advanced
programming, networking and data communications

Lahser High School, Bloomfield Hills, MI, 2010 to 2014

Similar to a thesis statement, an objective expresses the applicant's purpose

First major category: work experience

A subcategory for each job includes summaries and specific details

Second major category: special skills

Specific skills

Third major category: education

Specific information relevant to job objective

DEBORAH TANNEN

Deborah Tannen is a linguist who is best known for her popular studies of communication between men and women. Born and raised in New York City, Tannen earned a BA from Harpur College (now part of Binghamton University), MAs from Wayne State University and the University of California at Berkeley, and a PhD in linguistics from Berkeley. She is University Professor at Georgetown University, has published many scholarly articles and books, and lectures on linguistics all over the world. But her renown is more than academic: With television talk-show appearances, speeches to businesspeople and senators, and best-selling books, Tannen has become, in the words of one reviewer, "America's conversational therapist." The books include *You Just Don't Understand* (1990), *The Argument Culture* (1998), *I Only Say This Because I Love You* (2001), and *You Were Always Mom's Favorite!* (2009), the last about communication between sisters. Tannen sits on the board of the PEN/Faulkner Foundation, a nonprofit organization devoted to building audiences for literature.

But What Do You Mean?

Why do men and women so often communicate badly, if at all? This question has motivated much of Tannen's research and writing. Excerpted in *Redbook* magazine from Tannen's book *Talking from 9 to 5* (1994), the essay reprinted here classifies the conversational areas where men and women have the most difficulty communicating in the workplace.

William Lutz's "The World of Doublespeak," the essay following Tannen's, also uses classification to examine communication problems, in the form of misleading verbal substitutions that make "the bad seem good, the negative appear positive."

Conversation is a ritual. We say things that seem obviously the thing to say, without thinking of the literal meaning of our words, any more than we expect the question "How are you?" to call forth a detailed account of aches and pains.

Unfortunately, women and men often have different ideas about what's appropriate, different ways of speaking. Many of the conversational rituals common among women are designed to take the other person's feelings into account, while many of the conversational rituals common among men are designed to maintain the one-up position, or at least avoid appearing one-down. As a result, when men and women interact — especially at work — it's often women who are at the disadvantage. Because women are not trying to avoid the one-down position, that is unfortunately where they may end up.

Here, the biggest areas of miscommunication.   3

1. Apologies

Women are often told they apologize too much. The reason they're told   4
to stop doing it is that, to many men, apologizing seems synonymous with putting oneself down. But there are many times when "I'm sorry" isn't self-deprecating, or even an apology; it's an automatic way of keeping both speakers on an equal footing. For example, a well-known columnist once interviewed me and gave me her phone number in case I needed to call her back. I mis-placed the number and had to go through the newspaper's main switchboard. When our conversation was winding down and we'd both made ending-type remarks, I added, "Oh, I almost forgot — I lost your direct number, can I get it again?" "Oh, I'm sorry," she came back instantly, even though she had done nothing wrong and *I* was the one who'd lost the number. But I understood she wasn't really apologizing; she was just automatically reassuring me she had no intention of denying me her number.

Even when "I'm sorry" *is* an apology, women often assume it will be the   5
first step in a two-step ritual: I say "I'm sorry" and take half the blame, then you take the other half. At work, it might go something like this:

A: When you typed this letter, you missed this phrase I inserted.

B: Oh, I'm sorry. I'll fix it.

A: Well, I wrote it so small it was easy to miss.

When both parties share blame, it's a mutual face-saving device. But if one   6
person, usually the woman, utters frequent apologies and the other doesn't, she ends up looking as if she's taking the blame for mishaps that aren't her fault. When she's only partially to blame, she looks entirely in the wrong.

I recently sat in on a meeting at an insurance company where the sole   7
woman, Helen, said "I'm sorry" or "I apologize" repeatedly. At one point she said, "I'm thinking out loud. I apologize." Yet the meeting was intended to be an informal brainstorming session, and *everyone* was thinking out loud.

The reason Helen's apologies stood out was that she was the only person   8
in the room making so many. And the reason I was concerned was that Helen felt the annual bonus she had received was unfair. When I interviewed her colleagues, they said that Helen was one of the best and most productive workers — yet she got one of the smallest bonuses. Although the problem

might have been outright sexism, I suspect her speech style, which differs from that of her male colleagues, masks her competence.

Unfortunately, not apologizing can have its price too. Since so many women use ritual apologies, those who don't may be seen as hard-edged. What's important is to be aware of how often you say you're sorry (and why), and to monitor your speech based on the reaction you get. 9

2. Criticism

A woman who cowrote a report with a male colleague was hurt when she read a rough draft to him and he leapt into a critical response — "Oh, that's too dry! You have to make it snappier!" She herself would have been more likely to say, "That's a really good start. Of course, you'll want to make it a little snappier when you revise." 10

Whether criticism is given straight or softened is often a matter of convention. In general, women use more softeners. I noticed this difference when talking to an editor about an essay I'd written. While going over changes she wanted to make, she said, "There's one more thing. I know you may not agree with me. The reason I noticed the problem is that your other points are so lucid and elegant." She went on hedging for several more sentences until I put her out of her misery: "Do you want to cut that part?" I asked — and of course she did. But I appreciated her tentativeness. In contrast, another editor (a man) I once called summarily rejected my idea for an article by barking, "Call me when you have something new to say." 11

Those who are used to ways of talking that soften the impact of criticism may find it hard to deal with the right-between-the-eyes style. It has its own logic, however, and neither style is intrinsically better. People who prefer criticism given straight are operating on an assumption that feelings aren't involved: "Here's the dope. I know you're good; you can take it." 12

3. Thank-Yous

A woman manager I know starts meetings by thanking everyone for coming, even though it's clearly their job to do so. Her "thank-you" is simply a ritual. 13

A novelist received a fax from an assistant in her publisher's office; it contained suggested catalog copy for her book. She immediately faxed him her suggested changes and said, "Thanks for running this by me," even though her contract gave her the right to approve all copy. When she thanked the assistant, she fully expected him to reciprocate: "Thanks for giving me such a quick response." Instead, he said, "You're welcome." Suddenly, rather than an 14 equal exchange of pleasantries, she found herself positioned as the recipient of a favor. This made her feel like responding, "Thanks for nothing!"

Many women use "thanks" as an automatic conversation starter and closer; there's nothing literally to say thank you for. Like many rituals typical of women's conversation, it depends on the goodwill of the other to restore the balance. When the other speaker doesn't reciprocate, a woman may feel like someone on a seesaw whose partner abandoned his end. Instead of balancing in the air, she has plopped to the ground, wondering how she got there. 15

4. Fighting

Many men expect the discussion of ideas to be a ritual fight — explored through verbal opposition. They state their ideas in the strongest possible terms, thinking that if there are weaknesses someone will point them out, and by trying to argue against those objections, they will see how well their ideas hold up. 16

Those who expect their own ideas to be challenged will respond to another's ideas by trying to poke holes and find weak links — as a way *of helping.* The logic is that when you are challenged you will rise to the occasion: Adrenaline makes your mind sharper; you get ideas and insights you would not have thought of without the spur of battle. 17

But many women take this approach as a personal attack. Worse, they find it impossible to do their best work in such a contentious environment. If you're not used to ritual fighting, you begin to hear criticism of your ideas as soon as they are formed. Rather than making you think more clearly, it makes you doubt what you know. When you state your ideas, you hedge in order to fend off potential attacks. Ironically, this is more likely to *invite* attack because it makes you look weak. 18

Although you may never enjoy verbal sparring, some women find it helpful to learn how to do it. An engineer who was the only woman among four men in a small company found that as soon as she learned to argue she was accepted and taken seriously. A doctor attending a hospital staff meeting made a similar discovery. She was becoming more and more angry with a male colleague who'd loudly disagreed with a point she'd made. Her better judgment told her to hold her tongue, to avoid making an enemy of this powerful senior colleague. But finally she couldn't hold it in any longer, and she rose to her feet and delivered an impassioned attack on his position. She sat down in a panic, certain she had permanently damaged her relationship with him. To her amazement, he came up to her afterward and said, "That was a great rebuttal. I'm really impressed. Let's go out for a beer after work and hash out our approaches to this problem." 19

5. Praise

A manager I'll call Lester had been on his new job six months when he   20
heard that the women reporting to him were deeply dissatisfied. When he
talked to them about it, their feelings erupted; two said they were on the verge
of quitting because he didn't appreciate their work, and they didn't want to
wait to be fired. Lester was dumbfounded: He believed they were doing a fine
job. Surely, he thought, he had said nothing to give them the impression he
didn't like their work. And indeed he hadn't. That was the problem. He had
said *nothing* — and the women assumed he was following the adage "If you
can't say something nice, don't say anything." He thought he was showing
confidence in them by leaving them alone.

Men and women have different habits in regard to giving praise. For   21
example, Deirdre and her colleague William both gave presentations at a conference. Afterward, Deirdre told William, "That was a great talk!" He thanked
her. Then she asked, "What did you think of mine?" and he gave her a lengthy
and detailed critique. She found it uncomfortable to listen to his comments.
But she assured herself that he meant well, and that his honesty was a signal
that she, too, should be honest when he asked for a critique of his performance.
As a matter of fact, she had noticed quite a few ways in which he could have
improved his presentation. But she never got a chance to tell him because he
never asked — and she felt put down. The worst part was that it seemed she
had only herself to blame, since she *had* asked what he thought of her talk.

But had she really asked for his critique? The truth is, when she asked for   22
his opinion, she was expecting a compliment, which she felt was more or less
required following anyone's talk. When he responded with criticism, she figured, "Oh, he's playing 'Let's critique each other'" — not a game she'd initiated,
but one which she was willing to play. Had she realized he was going to criticize
her and not ask her to reciprocate, she would never have asked in the first place.

It would be easy to assume that Deirdre was insecure, whether she was   23
fishing for a compliment or soliciting a critique. But she was simply talking
automatically, performing one of the many conversational rituals that allow us
to get through the day. William may have sincerely misunderstood Deirdre's
intention — or may have been unable to pass up a chance to one-up her when
given the opportunity.

6. Complaints

"Troubles talk" can be a way to establish rapport with a colleague. You   24
complain about a problem (which shows that you are just folks) and the other
person responds with a similar problem (which puts you on equal footing).

But while such commiserating is common among women, men are likely to hear it as a request to *solve* the problem.

One woman told me she would frequently initiate what she thought would   25
be pleasant complaint-airing sessions at work. She'd talk about situations that bothered her just to talk about them, maybe to understand them better. But her male office mate would quickly tell her how she could improve the situation. This left her feeling condescended to and frustrated. She was delighted to see this very impasse in a section in my book *You Just Don't Understand*, and showed it to him. "Oh," he said, "I see the problem. How can we solve it?" Then they both laughed, because it had happened again: He short-circuited the detailed discussion she'd hoped for and cut to the chase of finding a solution.

Sometimes the consequences of complaining are more serious: A man   26
might take a woman's lighthearted griping literally, and she can get a reputation as a chronic malcontent. Furthermore, she may be seen as not up to solving the problems that arise on the job.

7. Jokes

I heard a man call in to a talk show and say, "I've worked for two women   27
and neither one had a sense of humor. You know, when you work with men, there's a lot of joking and teasing." The show's host and the guest (both women) took his comment at face value and assumed the women this man worked for were humorless. The guest said, "Isn't it sad that women don't feel comfortable enough with authority to see the humor?" The host said, "Maybe when more women are in authority roles, they'll be more comfortable with power." But although the women this man worked for *may* have taken themselves too seriously, it's just as likely that they each had a terrific sense of humor, but maybe the humor wasn't the type he was used to. They may have been like the woman who wrote to me: "When I'm with men, my wit or cleverness seems inappropriate (or lost!) so I don't bother. When I'm with my women friends, however, there's no hold on puns or cracks and my humor is fully appreciated."

The types of humor women and men tend to prefer differ. Research has   28
shown that the most common form of humor among men is razzing, teasing, and mock-hostile attacks, while among women it's self-mocking. Women often mistake men's teasing as genuinely hostile. Men often mistake women's mock self-deprecation as truly putting themselves down.

Women have told me they were taken more seriously when they   29
learned to joke the way the guys did. For example, a teacher who went to a national conference with seven other teachers (mostly women) and a group of administrators (mostly men) was annoyed that the administrators always found reasons to leave boring seminars, while the teachers felt they had to stay

and take notes. One evening, when the group met at a bar in the hotel, the principal asked her how one such seminar had turned out. She retorted, "As soon as you left, it got much better." He laughed out loud at her response. The playful insult appealed to the men — but there was a trade-off. The women seemed to back off from her after this. (Perhaps they were put off by her using joking to align herself with the bosses.)

There is no "right" way to talk. When problems arise, the culprit may be   30
style differences — and *all* styles will at times fail with others who don't share or understand them, just as English won't do you much good if you try to speak to someone who knows only French. If you want to get your message across, it's not a question of being "right"; it's a question of using language that's shared — or at least understood.

Journal Writing

Tannen's ANECDOTE about the newspaper columnist (par. 4) illustrates that much of what we say is purely automatic. Do you excuse yourself when you bump into inanimate objects? When someone says, "Have a good trip," do you answer, "You, too," even if the other person isn't going anywhere? Do you find yourself overusing certain words or phrases such as "like" or "you know"? Pay close attention to these kinds of verbal tics in your own and others' speech. Over the course of a few days, note as many of them as you can in your journal.

Questions on Meaning

1. What is Tannen's PURPOSE in writing this essay?
2. What does Tannen mean when she writes, "Conversation is a ritual" (par. 1)?
3. What does Tannen see as the fundamental difference between men's and women's conversational strategies?
4. Why is "You're welcome" not always an appropriate response to "Thank you"?

Questions on Writing Strategy

1. This essay has a large cast of characters: twenty-three to be exact. What function do these characters serve? How does Tannen introduce them to the reader? Does she describe them in sufficient detail?
2. Whom does Tannen see as her primary AUDIENCE? ANALYZE her use of the pronoun *you* in paragraphs 9 and 19. Whom does she seem to be addressing? Why?

3. Analyze how Tannen develops the category of apologies in paragraphs 4–9. Where does she use EXAMPLE, DEFINITION, and COMPARISON AND CONTRAST?

4. How does Tannen's characterization of a columnist as "well-known" (par. 4) contribute to the effectiveness of her example?

5. **OTHER METHODS**   For each of her seven areas of miscommunication, Tannen compares and contrasts male and female communication styles and strategies. SUMMARIZE the main source of misunderstanding in each area.

Questions on Language

1. What is the EFFECT of "I put her out of her misery" (par. 11)? What does this phrase usually mean?

2. What does Tannen mean by a "right-between-the-eyes style" (par. 12)? What is the FIGURE OF SPEECH involved here?

3. What is the effect of Tannen's use of figurative verbs, such as "barking" (par. 11) and "erupted" (20)? Find at least one other example of the use of a verb in a non-literal sense.

4. Look up any of the following words whose meanings you are unsure of: synonymous, self-deprecating (par. 4); lucid, tentativeness (11); intrinsically (12); reciprocate (14); adrenaline, spur (17); contentious, hedge (18); sparring, rebuttal (19); adage (20); soliciting (23); commiserating (24); initiate, condescended, impasse (25); chronic, malcontent (26); razzing (28); retorted (29).

Suggestions for Writing

1. **FROM JOURNAL TO ESSAY**   Write an essay classifying the examples from your journal entry (p. 359) into categories of your own devising. You might sort out the examples by context ("phone blunders," "faulty farewells"), by purpose ("nervous tics," "space fillers"), or by some other principle of classification. Given your subject matter, you might want to adopt a humorous TONE.

2. How true do you find Tannen's assessment of miscommunication between the sexes? Consider the conflicts you have experienced yourself or observed — between your parents, among fellow students or coworkers, in fictional portrayals in books and movies. You could also go beyond your personal experiences and observations by researching the opinions of other experts (linguists, psychologists, sociologists, and so on). Write an essay confirming or questioning Tannen's GENERALIZATIONS, backing up your (and perhaps others') views with your own examples.

3. **CRITICAL WRITING**   Tannen insists that "neither [communication] style is intrinsically better" (par. 12), that "[t]here is no 'right' way to talk" (30). What do you make of this refusal to take sides in the battle of the sexes? Is Tannen always successful? Is absolute neutrality possible, or even desirable, when it comes to such divisive issues?

4. **CONNECTIONS**   Tannen offers some of her own experiences as examples of communication blunders, and she often uses the first-person *I* or *we* in explaining her categories. In contrast, the author of the next essay, William Lutz, takes a more distant approach in classifying types of misleading language called *doublespeak*. Which of these approaches, personal or more distant, do you find more effective, and why? When, in your view, is it appropriate to inject yourself into your writing, and when is it not?

Deborah Tannen on Writing

Though "But What Do You Mean?" is written for a general audience, Deborah Tannen is a linguistics scholar who does considerable academic writing. One debate among scholarly writers is whether it is appropriate to incorporate personal experiences and biases into their papers, especially given the goal of objectivity in conducting and reporting research. The October 1996 *PMLA (Publications of the Modern Language Association)* printed a discussion of the academic uses of the personal, with contributions from more than two dozen scholars. Tannen's comments, excerpted here, focused on the first-person *I*.

When I write academic prose, I use the first person, and I instruct my students to do the same. The principle that researchers should acknowledge their participation in their work is an outgrowth of a humanistic approach to linguistic analysis. . . . Understanding discourse is not a passive act of decoding but a creative act of imagining a scene (composed of people engaged in culturally recognizable activities) within which the ideas being talked about have meaning. The listener's active participation in sense making both results from and creates interpersonal involvement. For researchers to deny their involvement in their interpreting of discourse would be a logical and ethical violation of this framework. . . .

[O]bjectivity in the analysis of interactions is impossible anyway. Whether they took part in the interaction or not, researchers identify with one or another speaker, are put off or charmed by the styles of participants. This one reminds you of a cousin you adore; that one sounds like a neighbor you despise. Researchers are human beings, not atomic particles or chemical elements. . . .

Another danger of claiming objectivity rather than acknowledging and correcting for subjectivity is that scholars who don't reveal their participation in interactions they analyze risk the appearance of hiding it. "Following is an exchange that occurred between a professor and a student," I have read in articles in my field. The speakers are identified as "A" and "B." The reader is not told that the professor, A (of course the professor is A and the student B), is the author. Yet that knowledge is crucial to contextualizing the author's interpretation. Furthermore, the impersonal designations A and B are another means of constructing a false objectivity. They obscure the fact that human interaction is being analyzed, and they interfere with the reader's understanding. The letters replace what in the author's mind are names and voices and personas that are the basis for understanding the discourse. Readers, given only initials, are left to scramble for understanding by imagining people in place of letters.

Avoiding self-reference by using the third person also results in the depersonalization of knowledge. Knowledge and understanding do not occur in abstract isolation. They always and only occur among people. . . . Denying that scholarship is a personal endeavor entails a failure to understand and correct for the inevitable bias that human beings bring to all their enterprises.

The Bedford Reader on Writing

In arguing for the use of the first-person *I* in scholarly prose, Tannen is speaking primarily about its use in her own field, linguistics. From your experience with ACADEMIC WRITING, is her argument applicable to other disciplines, such as history, biology, psychology, or government? What have your teachers in other courses advised you about writing in the first person? For our guidelines on choosing an appropriate POINT OF VIEW for your writing and using it consistently, check pages 48, 65–66, and 258.

WILLIAM LUTZ

William Lutz was born in 1940 in Racine, Wisconsin. He received a BA from Dominican College, an MA from Marquette University, a PhD from the University of Nevada at Reno, and a JD from Rutgers School of Law. For much of his career, Lutz's interest in words and composition has made him an active campaigner against misleading and irresponsible language. For fourteen years he edited the *Quarterly Review of Doublespeak*, and he has written three popular books on such language, the last being *Doublespeak Defined: Cut through the Bull**** and Get to the Point!* (1999). He has also written for many periodicals, including the *Los Angeles Times*, the *London Times*, and *USA Today*. In 1996 Lutz received the George Orwell Award for Distinguished Contribution to Honesty and Clarity in Public Language. He is professor emeritus at Rutgers University in Camden, New Jersey.

The World of Doublespeak

In the previous essay, Deborah Tannen examines the ways gender differences in speaking can cause innocent misunderstandings. But what if misunderstandings are the result of speech crafted to obscure meaning? Such intentional fudging, or *doublespeak*, is the sort of language Lutz specializes in, and here he uses classification to expose its many guises. "The World of Doublespeak" abridges the first chapter in Lutz's book *Doublespeak: From Revenue Enhancement to Terminal Living* (1989); the essay's title is the chapter's subtitle.

There are no potholes in the streets of Tucson, Arizona, just "pavement deficiencies." The Reagan Administration didn't propose any new taxes, just "revenue enhancement" through new "user's fees." Those aren't bums on the street, just "non–goal oriented members of society." There are no more poor people, just "fiscal underachievers." There was no robbery of an automatic teller machine, just an "unauthorized withdrawal." The patient didn't die because of medical malpractice, it was just a "diagnostic misadventure of a high magnitude." The US Army doesn't kill the enemy anymore, it just "services the target." And the doublespeak goes on.

Doublespeak is language that pretends to communicate but really doesn't. It is language that makes the bad seem good, the negative appear positive, the unpleasant appear attractive or at least tolerable. Doublespeak is language that avoids or shifts responsibility, language that is at variance with its real or purported meaning. It is language that conceals or prevents thought; rather than extending thought, doublespeak limits it.

Doublespeak is not a matter of subjects and verbs agreeing; it is a matter of words and facts agreeing. Basic to doublespeak is incongruity, the incongruity between what is said or left unsaid, and what really is. It is the incongruity between the word and the referent, between seem and be, between the essential function of language — communication — and what doublespeak does — mislead, distort, deceive, inflate, circumvent, obfuscate.   3

How to Spot Doublespeak

How can you spot doublespeak? Most of the time you will recognize doublespeak when you see or hear it. But, if you have any doubts, you can identify doublespeak just by answering these questions: Who is saying what to whom, under what conditions and circumstances, with what intent, and with what results? Answering these questions will usually help you identify as doublespeak language that appears to be legitimate or that at first glance doesn't even appear to be doublespeak.   4

First Kind of Doublespeak

There are at least four kinds of doublespeak. The first is the euphemism, an inoffensive or positive word or phrase used to avoid a harsh, unpleasant, or distasteful reality. But a euphemism can also be a tactful word or phrase which avoids directly mentioning a painful reality, or it can be an expression used out of concern for the feelings of someone else, or to avoid directly discussing a topic subject to a social or cultural taboo.   5

When you use a euphemism because of your sensitivity for someone's feelings or out of concern for a recognized social or cultural taboo, it is not doublespeak. For example, you express your condolences that someone has "passed away" because you do not want to say to a grieving person, "I'm sorry your father is dead." When you use the euphemism "passed away," no one is misled. Moreover, the euphemism functions here not just to protect the feelings of another person, but to communicate also your concern for that person's feelings during a period of mourning. When you excuse yourself to go to the "restroom," or you mention that someone is "sleeping with" or "involved with" someone else, you do not mislead anyone about your meaning, but you do respect the social taboos about discussing bodily functions and sex in direct terms. You also indicate your sensitivity to the feelings of your audience, which is usually considered a mark of courtesy and good manners.   6

However, when a euphemism is used to mislead or deceive, it becomes   7
doublespeak. For example, in 1984 the US State Department announced that
it would no longer use the word "killing" in its annual report on the status of
human rights in countries around the world. Instead, it would use the phrase
"unlawful or arbitrary deprivation of life," which the department claimed
was more accurate. Its real purpose for using this phrase was simply to avoid
discussing the embarrassing situation of government-sanctioned killings in
countries that are supported by the United States and have been certified by
the United States as respecting the human rights of their citizens. This use of
a euphemism constitutes doublespeak, since it is designed to mislead, to cover
up the unpleasant. Its real intent is at variance with its apparent intent. It is
language designed to alter our perception of reality.

The Pentagon, too, avoids discussing unpleasant realities when it refers   8
to bombs and artillery shells that fall on civilian targets as "incontinent ord-
nance." And in 1977 the Pentagon tried to slip funding for the neutron bomb
unnoticed into an appropriations bill by calling it a "radiation enhancement
device."

Second Kind of Doublespeak

A second kind of doublespeak is jargon, the specialized language of a   9
trade, profession, or similar group, such as that used by doctors, lawyers, engineers, educators, or car mechanics. Jargon can serve an important and useful
function. Within a group, jargon functions as a kind of verbal shorthand that
allows members of the group to communicate with each other clearly, efficiently, and quickly. Indeed, it is a mark of membership in the group to be able
to use and understand the group's jargon.

But jargon, like the euphemism, can also be doublespeak. It can be — and   10
often is — pretentious, obscure, and esoteric terminology used to give an
air of profundity, authority, and prestige to speakers and their subject matter. Jargon as doublespeak often makes the simple appear complex, the ordinary profound, the obvious insightful. In this sense it is used not to express
but impress. With such doublespeak, the act of smelling something becomes
"organoleptic analysis," glass becomes "fused silicate," a crack in a metal support beam becomes a "discontinuity," conservative economic policies become
"distributionally conservative notions."

Lawyers, for example, speak of an "involuntary conversion" of property   11
when discussing the loss or destruction of property through theft, accident,
or condemnation. If your house burns down or if your car is stolen, you have
suffered an involuntary conversion of your property. When used by lawyers in
a legal situation, such jargon is a legitimate use of language, since lawyers can
be expected to understand the term.

However, when a member of a specialized group uses its jargon to communicate with a person outside the group, and uses it knowing that the nonmember does not understand such language, then there is doublespeak. For example, on May 9, 1978, a National Airlines 727 airplane crashed while attempting to land at the Pensacola, Florida, airport. Three of the fifty-two passengers aboard the airplane were killed. As a result of the crash, National made an after-tax insurance benefit of $1.7 million, or an extra 18¢ a share dividend for its stockholders. Now National Airlines had two problems: It did not want to talk about one of its airplanes crashing, and it had to account for the $1.7 million when it issued its annual report to its stockholders. National solved the problem by inserting a footnote in its annual report which explained that the $1.7 million income was due to "the involuntary conversion of a 727." National thus acknowledged the crash of its airplane and the subsequent profit it made from the crash, without once mentioning the accident or the deaths. However, because airline officials knew that most stockholders in the company, and indeed most of the general public, were not familiar with legal jargon, the use of such jargon constituted doublespeak.

Third Kind of Doublespeak

A third kind of doublespeak is gobbledygook or bureaucratese. Basically, such doublespeak is simply a matter of piling on words, of overwhelming the audience with words, the bigger the words and the longer the sentences the better. Alan Greenspan, then chair of President Nixon's Council of Economic Advisors, was quoted in *The Philadelphia Inquirer* in 1974 as having testified before a Senate committee that "It is a tricky problem to find the particular calibration in timing that would be appropriate to stem the acceleration in risk premiums created by falling incomes without prematurely aborting the decline in the inflation-generated risk premiums."

Nor has Mr. Greenspan's language changed since then. Speaking to the meeting of the Economic Club of New York in 1988, Mr. Greenspan, now Federal Reserve chair, said, "I guess I should warn you, if I turn out to be particularly clear, you've probably misunderstood what I've said." Mr. Greenspan's doublespeak doesn't seem to have held back his career.[1]

Sometimes gobbledygook may sound impressive, but when the quote is later examined in print it doesn't even make sense. During the 1988 presidential campaign, vice-presidential candidate Senator Dan Quayle explained the need for a strategic-defense initiative by saying, "Why wouldn't an enhanced deterrent, a more stable peace, a better prospect to denying the ones who

---

[1] Greenspan retired from the Federal Reserve in 2006. He is now a private consultant. — EDS.

enter conflict in the first place to have a reduction of offensive systems and an introduction to defense capability? I believe this is the route the country will eventually go."

The investigation into the *Challenger* disaster in 1986 revealed the doublespeak of gobbledygook and bureaucratese used by too many involved in the shuttle program. When Jesse Moore, NASA's associate administrator, was asked if the performance of the shuttle program had improved with each launch or if it had remained the same, he answered, "I think our performance in terms of the liftoff performance and in terms of the orbital performance, we knew more about the envelope we were operating under, and we have been pretty accurately staying in that. And so I would say the performance has not by design drastically improved. I think we have been able to characterize the performance more as a function of our launch experience as opposed to it improving as a function of time." While this language may appear to be jargon, a close look will reveal that it is really just gobbledygook laced with jargon. But you really have to wonder if Mr. Moore had any idea what he was saying.

Fourth Kind of Doublespeak

The fourth kind of doublespeak is inflated language that is designed to make the ordinary seem extraordinary; to make everyday things seem impressive; to give an air of importance to people, situations, or things that would not normally be considered important; to make the simple seem complex. Often this kind of doublespeak isn't hard to spot, and it is usually pretty funny. While car mechanics may be called "automotive internists," elevator operators members of the "vertical transportation corps," used cars "preowned" or "experienced cars," and black-and-white television sets described as having "non-multicolor capability," you really aren't misled all that much by such language.

However, you may have trouble figuring out that, when Chrysler "initiates a career alternative enhancement program," it is really laying off five thousand workers; or that "negative patient-care outcome" means the patient died; or that "rapid oxidation" means a fire in a nuclear power plant.

The doublespeak of inflated language can have serious consequences. In Pentagon doublespeak, "pre-emptive counterattack" means that American forces attacked first; "engaged the enemy on all sides" means American troops were ambushed; "backloading of augmentation personnel" means a retreat by American troops. In the doublespeak of the military, the 1983 invasion of Grenada was conducted not by the US Army, Navy, Air Force, and Marines, but by the "Caribbean Peace Keeping Forces." But then, according to the Pentagon, it wasn't an invasion, it was a "predawn vertical insertion." . . .

The Dangers of Doublespeak

Doublespeak is not the product of carelessness or sloppy thinking. Indeed,   20
most doublespeak is the product of clear thinking and is carefully designed
and constructed to appear to communicate when in fact it doesn't. It is language designed not to lead but mislead. It is language designed to distort reality
and corrupt thought. . . . In the world created by doublespeak, if it's not a tax
increase, but rather "revenue enhancement" or "tax base broadening," how
can you complain about higher taxes? If it's not acid rain, but rather "poorly
buffered precipitation," how can you worry about all those dead trees? If that
isn't the Mafia in Atlantic City, but just "members of a career-offender cartel,"
why worry about the influence of organized crime in the city? If Supreme Court
Justice William Rehnquist wasn't addicted to the pain-killing drug his doctor
prescribed, but instead it was just that the drug had "established an interrela-
tionship with the body, such that if the drug is removed precipitously, there is a
reaction," you needn't question that his decisions might have been influenced
by his drug addiction. If it's not a Titan II nuclear-armed intercontinental bal-
listic missile with a warhead 630 times more powerful than the atomic bomb
dropped on Hiroshima, but instead, according to air force colonel Frank Hor-
ton, it's just a "very large, potentially disruptive reentry system," why be concerned about the threat of nuclear destruction? Why worry about the neutron
bomb escalating the arms race if it's just a "radiation enhancement weapon"?
If it's not an invasion, but a "rescue mission" or a "predawn vertical insertion,"
you won't need to think about any violations of US or international law.

Doublespeak has become so common in everyday living that many people   21
fail to notice it. Even worse, when they do notice doublespeak being used on
them, they don't react, they don't protest. Do you protest when you are asked
to check your packages at the desk "for your convenience," when it's not for
your convenience at all but for someone else's? You see advertisements for
"genuine imitation leather," "virgin vinyl," or "real counterfeit diamonds,"
but do you question the language or the supposed quality of the product? Do
you question politicians who don't speak of slums or ghettos but of the "inner
city" or "substandard housing" where the "disadvantaged" live and thus avoid
talking about the poor who have to live in filthy, poorly heated, ramshackle
apartments or houses? Aren't you amazed that patients don't die in the hospital anymore, it's just "negative patient-care outcome"?

Doublespeak such as that noted earlier that defines cab drivers as "urban   22
transportation specialists," elevator operators as members of the "vertical
transportation corps," and automobile mechanics as "automotive internists"
can be considered humorous and relatively harmless. However, when a fire in
a nuclear reactor building is called "rapid oxidation," an explosion in a nuclear
power plant is called an "energetic disassembly," the illegal overthrow of a

legitimate government is termed "destabilizing a government," and lies are seen as "inoperative statements," we are hearing doublespeak that attempts to avoid responsibility and make the bad seem good, the negative appear positive, something unpleasant appear attractive; and which seems to communicate but doesn't. It is language designed to alter our perception of reality and corrupt our thinking. Such language does not provide us with the tools we need to develop, advance, and preserve our culture and our civilization. Such language breeds suspicion, cynicism, distrust, and, ultimately, hostility.

Doublespeak is insidious because it can infect and eventually destroy the 23 function of language, which is communication between people and social groups. This corruption of the function of language can have serious and far-reaching consequences. We live in a country that depends upon an informed electorate to make decisions in selecting candidates for office and deciding issues of public policy. The use of doublespeak can become so pervasive that it becomes the coin of the political realm, with speakers and listeners convinced that they really understand such language. After a while we may really believe that politicians don't lie but only "misspeak," that illegal acts are merely "inappropriate actions," that fraud and criminal conspiracy are just "miscertification." President Jimmy Carter in April of 1980 could call the aborted raid to free the American hostages in Teheran an "incomplete success" and really believe that he had made a statement that clearly communicated with the American public. So, too, could President Ronald Reagan say in 1985 that "ultimately our security and our hopes for success at the arms reduction talks hinge on the determination that we show here to continue our program to rebuild and refortify our defenses" and really believe that greatly increasing the amount of money spent building new weapons would lead to a reduction in the number of weapons in the world. If we really believe that we understand such language and that such language communicates and promotes clear thought, then the world of *1984*,[2] with its control of reality through language, is upon us.

Journal Writing

Now that you know the name for it, when have you read or heard examples of doublespeak? Over the next few days, jot down examples of doublespeak that you recall or that you read and hear — from politicians or news commentators; in the lease for your

---

[2] In a section omitted from this abridgement of his chapter, Lutz discusses *Nineteen Eighty-Four*, the 1949 novel by George Orwell in which a frightening totalitarian state devises a language, called *newspeak*, to shape and control thought in politically acceptable forms. — EDS.

dwelling or your car; in advertising and catalogs; from bosses, teachers, or other figures of authority; in overheard conversations.

Questions on Meaning

1. What is Lutz's THESIS? Where does he state it?

2. According to Lutz, four questions can help us identify doublespeak. What are they? How can they help us distinguish between truthful and misleading language?

3. What, according to Lutz, are "the dangers of doublespeak"?

4. What ASSUMPTIONS does the author make about his readers' educational backgrounds and familiarity with his subject?

Questions on Writing Strategy

1. What principle does Lutz use for creating his four kinds of doublespeak — that is, what mainly distinguishes the groups?

2. How does Lutz develop the discussion of euphemism in paragraphs 5–8?

3. Lutz quotes Alan Greenspan twice in paragraphs 13–14. What is surprising about the comment in paragraph 14? Why does Lutz include this second quotation?

4. Lutz uses many quotations that were quite current when he first published this piece in 1989 but that now may seem dated — for instance, references to Presidents Carter and Reagan or to the nuclear arms race. Do these EXAMPLES undermine Lutz's essay in any way? Is his discussion of doublespeak still valid today? Explain your answers.

5. **OTHER METHODS**   Lutz's essay is not only a classification but also a DEFINITION of *doublespeak* and an examination of CAUSE AND EFFECT. Where are these other methods used most prominently? What do they contribute to the essay?

Questions on Language

1. How does Lutz's own language compare with the language he quotes as doublespeak? Do you find his language clear and easy to understand?

2. ANALYZE Lutz's language in paragraphs 22 and 23. How do the CONNOTATIONS of words such as "corrupt," "hostility," "insidious," and "control" strengthen the author's message?

3. The following list of possibly unfamiliar words includes only those found in Lutz's own sentences, not those in the doublespeak he quotes. Be sure you can define variance (par. 2); incongruity, referent (3); taboo (5); esoteric, profundity (10); condemnation (11); ramshackle (21); cynicism (22); insidious (23).

Suggestions for Writing

1. **FROM JOURNAL TO ESSAY** Choose at least one of the examples of doublespeak noted in your journal (p. 369), and write an essay explaining why it qualifies as doublespeak. Which of Lutz's categories does it fit under? How did you recognize it? Can you understand what it means?

2. Just about all of us have resorted to doublespeak at one time or another — when making an excuse, when trying to wing it on an exam, when trying to impress a potential employer. Write a NARRATIVE about a time you used deliberately unclear language, perhaps language that you yourself didn't understand. What were the circumstances? Did you consciously decide to use unclear language, or did it just leak out? How did others react to your use of this language?

3. **CRITICAL WRITING** Can you determine from his essay who Lutz believes is responsible for the proliferation of doublespeak? Whose responsibility is it to curtail the use of doublespeak: just those who use it? the schools? the government? the media? we who hear it? Write an essay that considers these questions, citing specific passages from the essay and incorporating your own ideas.

4. **CONNECTIONS** While Lutz looks at language "carefully designed and constructed to appear to communicate when in fact it doesn't," Deborah Tannen, in the previous essay, takes the position that "conversation is a ritual" — that we don't often think about what we're saying and miscommunicate as a result. How do you resolve the apparent contradictions in these two writers' underlying assumptions about language? Is most of our speech deliberate, or is it automatic? Why do you think so? In an essay that draws on examples and EVIDENCE from each of these two essays as well as from your own experience, explain what you see as the major causes of miscommunication.

William Lutz on Writing

In 1989 C-SPAN aired an interview between Brian Lamb and William Lutz. Lamb asked Lutz about his writing process. "I have a rule about writing," Lutz answered, "which I discovered when I wrote my dissertation: You never write a book, you write three pages, or you write five pages. I put off writing my dissertation for a year, because I could not think of writing this whole thing. . . . I had put off doing this book [*Doublespeak*] for quite a while, and my wife said, 'You've got to do the book.' And I said, 'Yes, I am going to, just as soon as I . . . ,' and, of course, I did every other thing I could possibly think of before that, and then I realized one day that she was right, I had to start writing. . . . So one day, I sit down and say, 'I am going to write five pages — that's all — and when I am done with five pages, I'll reward myself.'

So I do the five pages, or the next time I will do ten pages or whatever number of pages, but I set a number of pages."

Perhaps wondering just how high Lutz's daily page count might go, Lamb asked Lutz how much he wrote at one time. "It depends," Lutz admitted. "I always begin a writing session by sitting down and rewriting what I wrote the previous day — and that is the first thing, and it does two things. First of all, it makes your writing a little bit better, because rewriting is the essential part of writing. And the second thing is to get you flowing again, get back into the mainstream. Truman Capote[1] once gave the best piece of advice for writers ever given. He said, 'Never pump the well dry; always leave a bucket there.' So, I never stop writing when I run out of ideas. I always stop when I have something more to write about, and write a note to myself, 'This is what I am going to do next,' and then I stop. The worst feeling in the world is to have written yourself dry and have to come back the next day, knowing that you are dry and not knowing where you are going to pick up at this point."

The Bedford Reader on Writing

You aren't writing whole books for your classes, of course, but Lutz's advice, scaled down, should remind you that you needn't write an essay all at once, only a few paragraphs at a time. Do you think Lutz's REVISION strategy — of rewriting before he starts writing about the idea he didn't develop on the previous day — is a good one? For other ways to approach the sometimes daunting tasks of drafting and revising, see Chapter 2 of this book, especially pages 34–42.

---

[1] Truman Capote (1924–84) was an American journalist and fiction writer. — EDS.

RUSSELL BAKER

Russell Baker is one of America's notable humorists and political satirists. Born in 1925 in Virginia, Baker was raised in New Jersey and Maryland by his widowed mother. After serving in the navy during World War II, he earned a BA from Johns Hopkins University in 1947. He became a reporter for the *Baltimore Sun* that year and then joined the *New York Times* in 1954, covering the State Department, the White House, and Congress. From 1962 until he left the *Times* in 1998, he wrote a popular syndicated column that ranged over the merely bothersome (unreadable menus) and the serious (the Cold War). Many of Baker's columns and essays have been collected in books, such as *There's a Country in My Cellar* (1990). Baker has twice received the Pulitzer Prize, once for distinguished commentary and again for the first volume of his autobiography, *Growing Up* (1982). He has also written fiction and children's books, edited *Russell Baker's Book of American Humor* (1993), and served as host of *Masterpiece Theatre* on public television. Now retired, Baker lives in Leesburg, Virginia.

The Plot against People

The critic R. Z. Sheppard has commented that Baker can "best be appreciated for doing what a good humorist has always done: writing to preserve his sanity for at least one more day." In this piece from the *New York Times* in 1968, Baker uses classification for that purpose, taking aim, as he has often done, at inanimate objects. In the decades since this piece was written, the proliferation of electronic devices has, if anything, intensified the plot Baker imagines.

1   Inanimate objects are classified into three major categories — those that don't work, those that break down and those that get lost.

2   The goal of all inanimate objects is to resist man and ultimately to defeat him, and the three major classifications are based on the method each object uses to achieve its purpose. As a general rule, any object capable of breaking down at the moment when it is most needed will do so. The automobile is typical of the category.

3   With the cunning typical of its breed, the automobile never breaks down while entering a filling station with a large staff of idle mechanics. It waits until it reaches a downtown intersection in the middle of the rush hour, or until it is fully loaded with family and luggage on the Ohio Turnpike.

Thus it creates maximum misery, inconvenience, frustration and irritabil- 4
ity among its human cargo, thereby reducing its owner's life span.

Washing machines, garbage disposals, lawn mowers, light bulbs, auto- 5
matic laundry dryers, water pipes, furnaces, electrical fuses, television tubes,
hose nozzles, tape recorders, slide projectors — all are in league with the automobile to take their turn at breaking down whenever life threatens to flow
smoothly for their human enemies.

Many inanimate objects, of course, find it extremely difficult to break 6
down. Pliers, for example, and gloves and keys are almost totally incapable of
breaking down. Therefore, they have had to evolve a different technique for
resisting man.

They get lost. Science has still not solved the mystery of how they do it, 7
and no man has ever caught one of them in the act of getting lost. The most
plausible theory is that they have developed a secret method of locomotion
which they are able to conceal the instant a human eye falls upon them.

It is not uncommon for a pair of pliers to climb all the way from the cellar 8
to the attic in its single-minded determination to raise its owner's blood pressure. Keys have been known to burrow three feet under mattresses. Women's
purses, despite their great weight, frequently travel through six or seven rooms
to find hiding space under a couch.

Scientists have been struck by the fact that things that break down virtu- 9
ally never get lost, while things that get lost hardly ever break down.

A furnace, for example, will invariably break down at the depth of the 10
first winter cold wave, but it will never get lost. A woman's purse, which after
all does have some inherent capacity for breaking down, hardly ever does; it
almost invariably chooses to get lost.

Some persons believe this constitutes evidence that inanimate objects are 11
not entirely hostile to man, and that a negotiated peace is possible. After all,
they point out, a furnace could infuriate a man even more thoroughly by getting lost than by breaking down, just as a glove could upset him far more by
breaking down than by getting lost.

Not everyone agrees, however, that this indicates a conciliatory attitude 12
among inanimate objects. Many say it merely proves that furnaces, gloves and
pliers are incredibly stupid.

The third class of objects — those that don't work — is the most curious 13
of all. These include such objects as barometers, car clocks, cigarette lighters,
flashlights and toy-train locomotives. It is inaccurate, of course, to say that
they never work. They work once, usually for the first few hours after being
brought home, and then quit. Thereafter, they never work again.

In fact, it is widely assumed that they are built for the purpose of not work- 14
ing. Some people have reached advanced ages without ever seeing some of
these objects — barometers, for example — in working order.

Science is utterly baffled by the entire category. There are many theories   15
about it. The most interesting holds that the things that don't work have
attained the highest state possible for an inanimate object, the state to which
things that break down and things that get lost can still only aspire.

They have truly defeated man by conditioning him never to expect any-   16
thing of them, and in return they have given man the only peace he receives
from inanimate society. He does not expect his barometer to work, his electric
locomotive to run, his cigarette lighter to light or his flashlight to illuminate,
and when they don't it does not raise his blood pressure.

He cannot attain that peace with furnaces and keys and cars and women's   17
purses as long as he demands that they work for their keep.

Journal Writing

What other ways can you think of to classify inanimate objects? In your journal, try
expanding on Baker's categories, or create new categories of your own based on a
different principle — for example, objects no student can live without or objects no
student would want to be caught dead with.

Questions on Meaning

1. What is Baker's THESIS?

2. Why don't things that break down get lost, and vice versa?

3. Does Baker have any PURPOSE other than to make his readers smile?

4. How have inanimate objects "defeated man" (par. 16)?

Questions on Writing Strategy

1. What is the EFFECT of Baker's principle of classification? What categories are
   omitted here, and why?

2. In paragraphs 6–10, how does Baker develop the category of things that get lost?
   Itemize the strategies he uses to make the category clear.

3. Find three places where Baker uses hyperbole. (See FIGURES OF SPEECH in the
   Glossary if you need a definition.) What is the effect of the hyperbole?

4. How does the essay's INTRODUCTION help set its TONE? How does the CONCLUSION
   reinforce the tone?

5. **OTHER METHODS**   How does Baker use NARRATION to portray inanimate objects
   in the act of "resisting" people? Discuss how these mini-narratives make his
   classification more persuasive.

Questions on Language

1. Look up any of these words that are unfamiliar: plausible, locomotion (par. 7); invariably, inherent (10); conciliatory (12).

2. What are the CONNOTATIONS of the word "cunning" (par. 3)? What is its effect in this context?

3. Why does Baker use such expressions as "man," "some people," and "their human enemies" rather than *I* to describe those who come into conflict with inanimate objects? How might the essay have been different if Baker had relied on *I*?

Suggestions for Writing

1. **FROM JOURNAL TO ESSAY**   Write a brief, humorous essay based on one classification system from your journal entry (p. 375). It may be helpful to use narration or DESCRIPTION in your classification. Figures of speech, especially hyperbole and understatement, can help you establish a comic tone.

2. Think of a topic that would not generally be considered appropriate for a serious classification (some examples: game-show winners, body odors, stupid pet tricks, knock-knock jokes). Select a principle of classification, and write a brief essay sorting the subject into categories. You may want to use a humorous tone; then again, you may want to approach the topic "seriously," counting on the contrast between subject and treatment to make your IRONY clear.

3. **CRITICAL WRITING**   In a short essay, discuss the likely AUDIENCE for Baker's essay. (Recall that it first appeared in the *New York Times*.) What can you INFER from his EXAMPLES about Baker's own age and economic status? Does he ASSUME his audience is similar? How do the connections between author and audience help establish the essay's humor? Does this humor exclude some readers?

4. **CONNECTIONS**   Baker's essay bears comparison with "Remembering My Childhood on the Continent of Africa" by another humorist, David Sedaris (p. 206). Each man writes about himself with a self-deprecating, mock-serious tone. Read both works closely, and write an essay in which you COMPARE AND CONTRAST the words the authors use to present themselves and their situations.

JEAN-PIERRE DE BEER

Jean-Pierre (JP) De Beer was born in Pittsburgh, Pennsylvania, in 1999 and grew up in suburban Ohio and Illinois, rural South Carolina, and remote Queensland, Australia. He is currently a senior at Jefferson Township High School in northern New Jersey and hopes to embark to Paris, France, for college. A dual citizen of the United States and Belgium, De Beer has also had occasion to visit parts of Europe, New Zealand, and Japan. In addition to world travel he enjoys snowboarding, acting, massive multiplayer online games, and science fiction.

Stars of Life

De Beer wrote this essay especially for *The Bedford Reader* in 2016. His original intention was to classify computer games, but, he tells us, he quickly realized that his categories were hopelessly overlapped. In a burst of inspiration, he composed a rough draft of "Stars of Life," a curious investigation of the possibilities for life on other planets, in a matter of a few hours. De Beer then devoted a week or so to revising it — refining his purpose, locating sources of information, fleshing out the details, and shaping the organization — and then another day to editing.

Notice that the finished essay is based on Web research. In accordance with MLA style (see pp. 631–45), De Beer names his sources in the text and lists them at the end. Most of his parenthetical citations do not include page numbers because most of his sources do not have them.

"I don't think the human race will survive the next thousand years, unless we spread into space."

— Stephen Hawking

Sooner than later humanity will need to abandon the small asteroid it lives on and find a place to live out among the stars. While most stars could potentially have Earth-like planets orbiting within their habitable zones, many are too short-lived, too unpredictable, or too uncommon to support human life in the long term. Moreover, in the years of the great move people will need to acquire and harness an abundant source of energy to power the space-age contraptions that will be required to reach and colonize a new home. If we wish to survive, humanity will need to find a long-term solution by identifying stars that can support our endeavors and last trillions of years.

Ranging from the runt OGLE-TR-122b to the enormous VY Canis Majoris, there are some 100 billion burning gas balls in our galaxy and 1 billion trillion of them in the observable universe (Howell). Astronomers generally classify these stars into seven major categories and fifty-six subcategories

("Star Types"). Of these, three types stand out as the most potentially beneficial to humankind and prolonging its existence: supergiants, yellow dwarfs, and red dwarfs. Each kind of star varies in different aspects such as temperature, life span, and number, and each offers distinct contributions should humanity succeed in spreading to space. The red dwarf, however, is or at least will be the most important star because of its incredibly long life span and relative abundance in our immense universe.

Supergiants earned their name because they are some of the largest and hottest stars known to science. With temperatures that can exceed 20,000 kelvin (about five times hotter than the sun), supergiants are among the stars with the greatest energy output. With this massive energy comes a cost, though: Where our sun will last about 10 billion years, supergiants tend to last only 10 to 50 million years. Because of their relatively short lifespan supergiants are extremely rare; they account for less then .0001% of all stars still alive, or about one in a million (Lang 140). Nonetheless, supergiant stars could be an immense source of energy for the future. Assuming that scientists could tap into that energy, an entire new world of possibility arises. 3

Intergalactic relocation will likely require an extraordinary amount of energy to power a range of demanding devices: space crafts, terraforming machines, life-support systems, and more. Harnessing the energy released by supergiant stars could theoretically accelerate development, power deep-space missions to other galaxies, and provide a basically infinite supply of fuel to sustain life on other planets. Studying and eventually applying the vast amount of heat and force a supergiant generates could lead to a range of new and stronger tools, materials, and matter that would be otherwise unobtainable. When humankind needs to acquire new forms of energy in any quantity and store it, the universe's greatest power source — the supergiant star — should be able to provide. 4

While supergiants promise to be of assistance in the future, yellow dwarfs deserve special appreciation because they have already been a massive help to humankind: Our current sun is a yellow dwarf. Yellow dwarf stars typically hit a surface temperature of around 5,600 kelvin (about 15 times hotter than boiling water), causing a relatively stable energy output. The low energy gives dwarf stars a longer life span than that of supergiants, commonly about 10 billion years (Cain). Should humanity need to find a new home quickly and nearby, a yellow dwarf would be our best bet. Approximately 20% of the stars in the known universe are yellow dwarfs, and it is likely that at least some host inhabitable planets for humankind to colonize on, at least for a little while. 5

Because of a yellow dwarf's mass and the amount of energy it releases, any rock planet that is in the habitable zone (like Earth) would be relatively safe from solar flares. The long life span of a yellow dwarf star ensures that once the 6 big move is finished, humanity will have plenty of time to colonize, develop, and adapt to the new landscape and solar system. In the event that we find a new home near a yellow dwarf star, we will have a workable base of operations — at least until a more long-term solution can be found.

Red dwarfs, the real stars of the show, are the most likely to help out   7
humankind in the long run. They are the smallest known stars in the universe (but still massive) and consistently hit a temperature of around 4,000 kelvin — a very low energy output in the spectrum of the stars. Because of their relative size and slow release of energy they will last for a cool ten trillion years, give or take a few billion ("Last Star"). Red dwarfs are also abundant, making up about 70% of all the stars in the universe. What's more, NASA's Kepler space telescope mission has found that at least half of the observable red dwarfs host a rock planet near the size of Earth, and many of them are in the "Goldilocks zone" of moderate temperature, atmospheric pressure, and the possibility of water. In the Milky Way alone about 5% of red dwarfs host roughly Earth-sized, inhabitable planets — that's more than four billion potential homes nearby!

The renowned cosmologist Stephen Hawking once said that humanity will   8
not survive unless we relocate. While all types of stars have the potential to host or at least help us, supergiants, yellow dwarfs, and red dwarfs especially will prove to be invaluable in the not-so-distant future. Supergiants and their unparalleled source of energy will power the devices needed to move and rebuild. Yellow dwarfs provide a viable alternative to Earth's sun should we need to evacuate quickly. Red dwarfs, however, give humanity a nearly infinite amount of space to grow, colonize, and hunker down for the long haul. Because of their immense life span, they will provide a place to live after all other stars have died out. And because of how common they are, they offer practically endless amounts of prime real estate just waiting to be claimed. If we look to them for our future, the entire universe will be at our fingertips for trillions of years to come.

Works Cited

Cain, Fraser. "What Kind of Star Is the Sun?" *Universe Today*, 1 Aug. 2008, www.universetoday.com/16350/what-kind-of-star-is-the-sun/.

Hawking, Stephen. "Colonies in Space May Be Only Hope." Interview by Roger Highfield. *The Telegraph*, 16 Oct. 2001, www.telegraph.co.uk/news/uknews/1359562/Colonies-in-space-may-be-only-hope-says-Hawking.html.

Howell, Elizabeth. "How Many Stars Are in the Milky Way?" *Space.com*, Purch, 21 May 2014, www.space.com/25959-how-many-stars-are-in-the-milky-way.html.

Lang, Kenneth R. *The Life and Death of Stars.* Cambridge UP, 2013. *Google Books,* books.google.com/books/about/The_Life_and_Death_of_ Stars.html?id=MN-UCkUK9pcC.

"The Last Star in the Universe: Red Dwarfs Explained." *Kurzgesagt — In a Nutshell,* 31 Jan. 2016. *YouTube,* www.youtube.com/watch?v= LS-VPyLaJFM.

NASA. *Kepler: A Search for Habitable Planets.* Ames Research Center, 18 Jan. 2016, kepler.nasa.gov/.

"Star Types." *All about Astronomy,* Enchanted Learning, 2015, www .enchantedlearning.com/subjects/astronomy/stars/startypes.shtml.

Journal Writing

Do you think there could be life on other planets? If no, why not? If yes, what forms might such extraterrestrial life take: intelligent beings with social structures and civilizations akin to ours, or something more basic, like flora and fauna — or simple microbes? Or perhaps you imagine beings and societies far more evolved than our own? In your journal, ponder the possibilities.

Questions on Meaning

1. How seriously does De Beer take his subject? What seems to be his PURPOSE in classifying stars?

2. What is a planet's "Goldilocks zone" (par. 7)? Where does the term come from?

3. Where does De Beer state his THESIS? Is any part of his main idea left unsaid?

Questions on Writing Strategy

1. "Stars of Life" opens with a short quotation from Stephen Hawking. Why? What is the function of this epigraph? Where in the essay does De Beer return to it, and to what EFFECT?

2. For whom would you say De Beer is writing? What ASSUMPTIONS does he make about his AUDIENCE?

3. Identify the principle of classification De Beer uses to organize types of stars. What does each type have in common?

4. What consistent pattern does De Beer use to develop the paragraphs for each of his categories? How effective do you find this approach?

5. **OTHER METHODS** What role does CAUSE-AND-EFFECT analysis play in De Beer's classification?

Questions on Language

1. How would you describe De Beer's general DICTION? Why is — or isn't — his language appropriate for his subject, his purpose, and his audience?

2. Locate some FIGURES OF SPEECH and COLLOQUIAL EXPRESSIONS in De Beer's writing and explain what they contribute to his essay.

3. Look up any of the following words whose meanings you are unsure of: asteroid, habitable, harness, contraptions, endeavors (par. 1); runt (2); kelvin (3); intergalactic, terraforming (4); spectrum (7); cosmologist (8).

Suggestions for Writing

1. **FROM JOURNAL TO ESSAY**   Taking off from your speculations in your journal, respond to De Beer's proposal that humanity will need to move to another planet to survive. Is such a move really necessary, or possible? And if so, what are the ethical implications of colonizing habitable planets, especially if they already host some forms of life? Do we have the right to "spread into space"? What could happen if we did? Might there be wars and fights over resources, perhaps, the spread of disease, changes to human biology, interspecies development, some other consequences? Be as lighthearted or as serious as you wish, but be as imaginative as you can.

2. Look into the mission, history, and findings to date of the Kepler space telescope team (you might start with the home page De Beer identifies in his works-cited list). What are NASA's goals for the program? What has it achieved? How supportive of its budget has Congress been? Based on your findings, write an essay defending and justifying the use of government funding for the Kepler mission or another program such as the Hubble telescope or the New Horizons spacecraft. This essay will require some research because you will need to argue that the benefits of NASA's programs outweigh their costs, and you will need to support your claims with factual evidence. Or approach the issue from a skeptic's point of view and argue against using taxpayers' money for space exploration. Substantiate your argument with data, and be sure to propose alternative methods for exploring the cosmos and funding such investigations.

3. **CRITICAL WRITING**   Most of the information De Beer provides comes from general-interest space and astronomy sites, and all of it comes from the Web. How convincing do you find this EVIDENCE? Does the nature of De Beer's sources weaken his essay in any way, or does his classification remain valid? Why do you think so? (You might, if time allows, look for more scholarly works on astronomy or the search for habitable planets, and consider how they apply to De Beer's conclusions.) Explain your evaluation in a brief essay.

4. **CONNECTIONS**   Jean-Pierre De Beer's "Stars of Life" and Diane Ackerman's "Black Marble" (p. 138) both deal with space travel and the ultimate fate of the Earth. In an essay, COMPARE AND CONTRAST the two writers' treatment of their subjects. What strategies do De Beer and Ackerman have in common, and where do their perspectives diverge? How does the TONE of each essay contribute to its effect?

MARION WINIK

Born in 1958 in New York City, Marion Winik received a BA from Brown University in 1978 and an MFA from Brooklyn College in 1983. She is the author of *The Lunch Box Chronicles* (1998), which *Child* magazine voted the best parenting book of the year. *First Comes Love* (1996), a memoir of her marriage to a "sexually ambiguous" man with AIDS, was a *New York Times* Notable Book. Winik's essays have appeared in *Ladies' Home Journal*, *Cosmopolitan*, the *Los Angeles Times*, and other periodicals. She currently teaches at the University of Baltimore and writes a regular column, "Bohemian Rhapsody," for the city's newspaper. Winik has been a commentator on National Public Radio since 1991, broadcasting short essays on *All Things Considered*. "I think it is unusual and worth noting," Winik says, "that I actually prefer reading out loud to an audience to writing. The act of speaking is central to my work. I am all about voice."

The Things They Googled

In "The Things They Googled," Winik uses classification to sort through the varieties of searches different kinds of people — young, old, lonely, forgetful — conduct online. The essay first appeared in her column for the *Baltimore Sun* in 2011 and was then reprinted in the *Utne Reader* at the end of 2012.

1   If they were young, they googled the things they didn't know. Some were things they were supposed to know, like the habits of the hammerhead shark. The perfect squares under a hundred, the phrase "rite of passage." When they got bored, they googled images of peace signs, photographs of rainbows, a video of a girl singing about Friday, and another of a baby laughing and laughing. They googled Anne Hathaway. If they were boys, they googled how to build a bomb. If they could get on the computer when their parents weren't home they googled things they weren't supposed to know, things like "sodomy" and "lesbian." Then they cleared the search history and googled "hammerhead shark."

2   If they were old, they googled the things they had forgotten: names of actors and movies and hurricanes, old sports scores, the vice president under Carter, the ingredients in a Manhattan, the hours of the liquor store, "liquor stores open Sunday," directions. They googled things that had escaped them: the definition of *feckless*, a synonym for *regime*, most of the answers to the Sunday crossword puzzle. They googled remedies for burns and bee stings.

3   If they were lonely, they googled "sex." They googled "sex xxx." They googled long-lost lab partners, old boyfriends, their ex-husband's new girlfriend.

They googled cute pictures of baby koalas. They googled the word *lonely*. They googled "distended stomach" "nosebleed that won't stop" "numbness" "insomnia" and "cancer symptoms."

The things they googled were determined by forgetfulness, by need, by   4
desire, by curiosity, and by the endless availability of information. In fact, there was no point in remembering anything except how to google. They didn't even have to remember what they were googling: As soon as they'd typed "When does g — ," just that much, *Google* already knew the question was when *Glee* Season Three would begin. When they googled "pleonism," *Google* quietly looked up pleonasm. *Google* never made them feel bad about not knowing.

So they googled how to lose weight and pictures of psoriasis and checklists   5
for diagnosing attention-deficit disorder. If they were pregnant, there was no end to their googling. Others googled when it would rain and how much it would rain and when to plant their gardens. They googled the tides and the seasons. They googled the times of sunrise and sunset. They googled births and deaths. They googled themselves, which was sometimes unsettling, turning up Boston Marathon times and class reunions and even obituaries not their own.

How did they live before *Google*, they wondered. How did anyone know   6
anything? How did anyone remember, while driving through Mohntown, Pennsylvania, the name of the young blond actress in the movie *Witness* who was from that town?

When they were hungry, they googled "recipe chard cannellini beans,"   7
"recipe apple gingersnap," or "recipe rice noodle salad." How to freeze tomatoes. How to peel and seed tomatoes. Whether you can add grated zucchini to cornbread mix. How to tell if an egg is rotten, and if one egg is rotten, are all the others rotten too? "Best no-egg cornbread." "Best no-egg omelette." "Best restaurant brunch."

Plagued by the familiarity of an essay they had read, they googled "The   8
Things They Googled," and again *Google* was there before they finished typing. It was the short story "The Things They Carried" they were thinking of, the beautiful Vietnam War story by Tim O'Brien. *Google* showed them where to read it online, and some dove in right away, while others ordered the book used for $.99 plus shipping, and still others reserved a copy at their local libraries.

But after all that searching and finding, all the slapped foreheads and the   9
ahas, after all of it, there was still something missing. It was the size of a gingersnap, a two-week-old koala, a liquor store. It looked a bit like Kelly McGillis or Walter Mondale. It was excellent for soothing burns and heartaches. It was not in their computer or their phone or on any file server anywhere. Older search engines would be required.

Journal Writing

How well do your search habits conform to that of your peer group as portrayed by Winik? Check your search history to recall what terms you have looked up lately and list the ten or fifteen most recent in your journal.

Questions on Meaning

1. What does Winik attempt to accomplish with this essay? What is her PURPOSE?

2. Who are Kelly McGillis and Walter Mondale (par. 9)? Where in the essay does Winik first introduce them?

3. What does Winik mean by "[o]lder search engines" in the final sentence? To what, exactly, is she referring?

4. Does Winik have a point? Express her underlying THESIS in your own words.

Questions on Writing Strategy

1. What ASSUMPTIONS does Winik seem to make about her AUDIENCE? How can you tell? Do those assumptions hold true in your case?

2. What is Winik's principle of classification? Into what general categories and more particular subcategories does she sort people who search the Internet?

3. **OTHER METHODS**   What do most of Winik's EXAMPLES of search terms have in common? If you're at all familiar with "The Things They Carried," what implicit COMPARISON does Winik seem to make with people using *Google* and the soldiers in Tim O'Brien's story?

Questions on Language

1. Winik sometimes prints *Google* in italics with a capital G and other times all lowercase and not italicized. Why?

2. Using *Google* or another online search tool, find definitions of the following: perfect squares (par. 1); feckless, regime (2); distended (3); pleonasm (4); psoriasis (5); gingersnap (7); plagued (8).

3. Take note of the progression of search terms Winik cites in paragraph 7. What FIGURE OF SPEECH does she use to gain humor, here and elsewhere in the essay?

Suggestions for Writing

1. **FROM JOURNAL TO ESSAY**   From your own experience and what you have seen of young and old people using the Internet, do you agree with Winik's characterization of the two groups (see Writing Strategy question 2)? Starting with the search

history you recorded in your journal, write an essay comparing and contrasting children's and adults' assumptions about the process of building and retrieving knowledge. (You will have to GENERALIZE, of course, but try to keep your broad statements grounded in a reality your readers will share.)

2. Search the Web or a periodical index for information about services, like *Eternime*, that are attempting to build artificial-intelligence avatars capable of simulating the entire store of a person's memories and saving them online. ("Forever Memory" by Simon Parkin, in the December 2015/January 2016 issue of *Reader's Digest*, is a good starting point.) In an essay, explain how these services work, and ponder their implications. Is memory something that can — or should be — outsourced? Would you want your own memories collected on the Internet for others to experience, even after you're gone? Why, or why not?

3. Contemporary culture seems obsessed with celebrities, as evidenced by the frequency with which they are googled and by the popularity of magazines, tabloids, and TV programs that track the slightest comings and goings of actors, political figures, musicians, models, and even those who are famous simply for being famous. Write an essay in which you speculate about the causes of this obsession with celebrities. What is it about the lives of ordinary people that makes them so interested in the lives of famous people?

4. **CRITICAL WRITING**   Take Winik's suggestion and google "The Things They Carried" by Tim O'Brien. What does Winik accomplish with her ALLUSION to this short story? Read the story and ANALYZE Winik's effort to emulate the style and TONE of O'Brien's most famous work.

5. **CONNECTIONS**   Writing a century and a half ago, Henry David Thoreau, in "What I Lived For" (p. 587), also criticizes new technologies, especially new communication technologies. Unlike Winik, however, he praises isolation. Read his essay, and then, in an essay of your own, compare and contrast these two very different writers' attitudes toward human connection.

Marion Winik on Writing

As a regular columnist and the author of several books, Marion Winik is used to working with editors. But she still has trouble taking their advice. They "usually make . . . revision sound like a lot more work than it actually will be," she says. "Often the cover letter describing a revision will make you shudder. It sounds like everything is wrong, they hate the piece and you have to rewrite it from scratch. Then, after you've torn out your hair, gnashed your teeth and turned in an overhaul, it turns out they liked the first version pretty well and just wanted a few specific changes. Somehow the prose description of what's wrong with the article always makes it sounds much worse" than it really is. Winik's advice? "Push for specifics about what to do and where to do it."

The Bedford Reader on Writing

Do you detect any similarities between the "cover letter describing a revision" that fills Winik with dread and the kinds of comments your instructors or peers might make on your drafts? Criticism, even constructive criticism, can feel overwhelming or discouraging at first. For "specifics" on how to revise and edit your work, whether on your own or in response to comments, see pages 39–42 and 47–53.

ADDITIONAL WRITING TOPICS
Classification

Write an essay by the method of classification, in which you sort one of the following subjects into categories of your own. Make clear your PURPOSE in classifying and the basis of your classification. Explain each class with DEFINITIONS and EXAMPLES (you may find it helpful to make up a name for each group). Check your classes to be sure they neither gap nor overlap.

People who use public transportation

Urban wildlife

Smartphone users or apps

Gym members

Late-night television shows

The drawbacks or benefits of small-town life

Your playlists

Families

Health-care providers

Politicians

Internships

College students

Movies for teenagers or men or women

Difficult coworkers

Graphic novels

Monsters

Sports announcers

Inconsiderate people

Social media platforms

Sources of energy

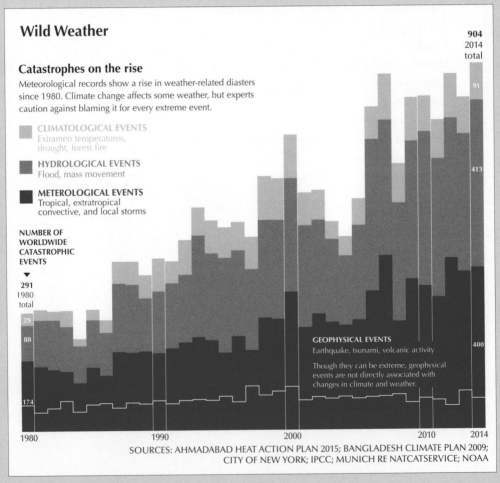

Wild Weather

904
2014
total

Catastrophes on the rise

Meteorological records show a rise in weather-related diasters
since 1980. Climate change affects some weather, but experts
caution against blaming it for every extreme event.

CLIMATOLOGICAL EVENTS
Extramen temperatures,
drought, forest fire

HYDROLOGICAL EVENTS
Flood, mass movement

METEROLOGICAL EVENTS
Tropical, extratropical
convective, and local storms

NUMBER OF
WORLDWIDE
CATASTROPHIC
EVENTS
▼
291
1980
total

29

88

174

91

413

GEOPHYSICAL EVENTS
Earthquake, tsunami, volcanic activity

Though they can be extreme, geophysical
events are not directly associated with
changes in climate and weather.

400

1980   1990   2000   2010   2014

SOURCES: AHMADABAD HEAT ACTION PLAN 2015; BANGLADESH CLIMATE PLAN 2009;
CITY OF NEW YORK; IPCC; MUNICH RE NATCATSERVICE; NOAA

Credit: Matt Twombly and Lawson Parker.

10

CAUSE AND EFFECT

Asking Why

◀ **Cause and effect in a bar graph**

With simple visuals and perhaps a few words, infographics often make striking comments on events and trends. This bar graph by *National Geographic*, published in a 2015 special issue devoted to climate change, proposes some disturbing effects of a well-known but sometimes disputed cause. What is the cause? What, according to the authors, have been three of the major effects, and how are they related? What other effects might result from the cause depicted here? Why do "experts caution against blaming it for every extreme event"? Do you agree or disagree with *National Geographic*'s claims? Why?

THE METHOD

Press the button of a doorbell and, inside the house or apartment, chimes sound. Why? Because the touch of your finger on the button closed an electrical circuit. But why did you ring the doorbell? Because you were sent by your dispatcher: You are a bill collector calling on a customer whose payments are three months overdue.

The touch of your finger on the button is the *immediate cause* of the chimes: the event that precipitates another. That you were ordered by your dispatcher to go ring the doorbell is a *remote cause*: an underlying, more basic reason for the event, not apparent to an observer. Probably, ringing the doorbell will lead to some results: The door will open, and you may be given a check — or have the door slammed in your face.

To figure out reasons and results is to use the method of CAUSE AND EFFECT. Either to explain events or to argue for one version of them, you try to answer the question "Why did something happen?" or "What were the consequences?" or "What might be the consequences?" Seeking causes, you can ask, for example, "Why do birds migrate?" "What led to America's involvement in the war in Vietnam?" Looking for effects, you can ask, "How has legalization of gay marriage changed the typical American family?" "What impact have handheld computers had on the nursing profession?" You can look to a possible future and ask, "Of what use might a course in psychology be to me if I become an office manager?" "Suppose an asteroid the size of a sofa were to strike Philadelphia — what would be the probable consequences?"

Don't confuse cause and effect with the method of PROCESS ANALYSIS (Chap. 7). Some process analysis essays, too, deal with happenings; but they focus more on repeatable events (rather than unique ones) and they explain *how* (rather than why) something happened. If you were explaining the process by which the doorbell rings, you might break the happening into stages — (1) the finger presses the button; (2) the circuit closes; (3) the current travels the wire; (4) the chimes make music — and you'd set forth the process in detail. But why did the finger press the button? What happened because the doorbell rang? To answer those questions, you need cause and effect.

In trying to explain why things happen, you can expect to find a whole array of causes — interconnected, perhaps, like the strands of a spiderweb. To produce a successful essay, you'll want to do an honest job of unraveling, and this may take time. Before you start to write, devote some extra thought to seeing which facts are the causes and which matter most. To answer the questions "Why?" and "What followed as a result?" may sometimes be hard, but it can be satisfying — even illuminating. Indeed, to seek causes and effects is one way for the mind to discover order in a reality that otherwise might seem random and pointless.

THE PROCESS

Subject and Purpose

The method of cause and effect tends to suggest itself: If you have a subject and soon start thinking "Why?" or "What results?" or "What if?" then you are on the way to analyzing causation. Your subject may be impersonal — like a change in voting patterns or the failure or success of a business — or it may be quite personal. Indeed, an excellent cause-and-effect paper may be written on a subject very near to you. You can ask yourself why you behaved in a certain way at a certain moment. You can examine the reasons for your current beliefs and attitudes. Writing such a paper, you might happen upon a truth you hadn't realized before.

Whether your subject is personal or impersonal, make sure it is manageable: You should be able to get to the bottom of it, given the time and information available. For a 500-word essay due Thursday, the causes of teenage rebellion would be a less feasible topic than why a certain thirteen-year-old you know ran away from home.

Before rushing to list causes or effects, stop a moment to consider what your PURPOSE might be in writing. Much of the time you'll seek simply to explain what did or might occur, discovering and laying out the connections as clearly and accurately as you can. But when reasonable people could disagree over causes or effects, you'll want to go further, arguing for one interpretation over others. You'll still need to be clear and accurate in presenting your interpretation, but you'll also need to treat the others fairly. (See Chap. 12 on argument and persuasion.)

Thesis

When you have a grip on your subject and your purpose, you can draft a tentative THESIS STATEMENT to express the main point of your analysis. The essays in this chapter provide good examples of thesis statements that put across, concisely, the author's central finding about causes and effects. Here are two examples:

> A bill like the one we've just passed [to ban imports from factories that use child labor] is of no use unless it goes hand in hand with programs that will offer a new life to these newly released children.
> — Chitra Divakaruni, "Live Free and Starve"

> To begin to solve the problem [of the illegal drug trade], we need to understand what's happening in drug-source countries, how the United States can and can't help there, and what, instead, can be done at home.
> — Marie Javdani, *"Plata o Plomo:* Silver or Lead"

Your own thesis statement may be hypothetical at the discovery stage, before you have gathered EVIDENCE and sorted out the complexity of causes and effects. Still, a statement framed early can help direct your later thinking and research.

Causal Relations

Your toughest job in writing a cause-and-effect essay may be figuring out what caused what. Sometimes one event will appear to trigger another, and it in turn will trigger yet another, and another still, in an order we call a *causal chain*. Investigators at the scene of a ten-car pileup, for instance, might determine that a deer ran across the highway, causing a driver to slam on the brakes suddenly, causing another driver to hit the first car, causing the next driver to swerve and hit the embankment, and so on.

In reality, causes are seldom so easy to find as that stray deer: They tend to be many and complicated. Even a simple accident may happen for more than one reason. Perhaps the deer was flushed out of the woods by a hunter. Perhaps the first driver was distracted by a crying child in the back seat. Perhaps winter had set in and the road was icy. Perhaps the low glare of the setting sun made it difficult for any of the drivers to see clearly. Still, one event precedes another in time, and in discerning causes you don't ignore chronological order; you pay attention to it.

When you can see a number of apparent causes, weigh them and assign each a relative importance. Which do you find matter most? Often, you will see that particular causes are more important or less so: major or minor. If you seek to explain why your small town has fallen on hard times, you might note that two businesses shut down: a factory employing three hundred and a drugstore employing six. The factory's closing is a *major cause*, leading to significant unemployment in the town, while the drugstore's closing is perhaps a *minor cause* — or not a cause at all but an effect. In writing about the causes, you would emphasize the factory and mention the drugstore only briefly if at all.

When seeking remote causes, look only as far back as necessary. Explaining your town's misfortunes, you might see the factory's closing as the immediate cause. You could show what caused the shutdown: a dispute between union and management. You might even go back to the cause of the dispute (announced layoffs) and the cause of the layoffs (loss of sales to a competitor). A paper showing effects might work in the other direction, moving from the factory closing to its impact on the town: unemployment, the closing of stores (including the drugstore), people packing up and moving away.

Two cautions about causal relations are in order here. One is to beware of confusing coincidence with cause. In the logical FALLACY called *post hoc* (short for the Latin *post hoc, ergo propter hoc,* "after this, therefore because of this"), one assumes, erroneously, that because A happened before B, A must have caused B. This is the error of the superstitious man who decides that he lost his job because a black cat walked in front of him. Another fallacy is to oversimplify causes by failing to recognize their full number and complexity — claiming, say, that violent crime is simply a result of "all those first-person shooter games." Avoid such wrong turns in reasoning by patiently looking for evidence before you write, and by giving it careful thought. (For a fuller list of logical fallacies, or errors in reasoning, see pp. 486–87.)

Discovery of Causes

To help find causes of actions and events, you can ask yourself a few searching questions. These have been suggested by the work of the literary critic Kenneth Burke:

1. **What act am I trying to explain?**
2. **What is the character, personality, or mental state of whoever acted?**
3. **In what scene or location did the act take place, and in what circumstances?**
4. **What instruments or means did the person use?**
5. **For what purpose did the person act?**

Burke calls these elements a *pentad* (or set of five): the *act*, the *actor*, the *scene*, the *agency*, and the *purpose*. If you were a detective trying to explain why a liquor store burned down, you might ask these questions:

1. **Act:** Was the fire deliberately set by someone, or was there an accident?
2. **Actors:** If the fire was arson, who set it: the store's worried, debt-ridden owner? a mentally disturbed antialcohol crusader? a drunk who had been denied a purchase?
3. **Scene:** Was the store near a church? a mental hospital? a fireworks factory?
4. **Agency, or means of the act:** Was the fire caused by faulty electrical wiring? a carelessly tossed cigarette? a flaming torch? rags soaked in kerosene?
5. **Purpose:** If the fire wasn't accidental, was it set to collect insurance? to punish drinkers? to get revenge?

You can further deepen your inquiry by seeing relationships between the terms of the pentad. Ask, for instance, what does the actor have to do with this scene? (Is he or she the neighbor across the street, who has been staring at the liquor shop resentfully for years?)

Don't worry if not all the questions apply or if not all the answers are immediately forthcoming. Burke's pentad isn't meant to be a grim rigmarole; it is a means of discovery, to generate a lot of possible material for you — insights, observations, hunches to pursue. It won't solve each and every human mystery, but sometimes it will helpfully deepen your thought.

Educated Guesses

In stating what you believe to be causes and effects, don't be afraid to voice a well-considered hunch. Your instructor doesn't expect you to write, in a short time, a definitive account of the causes of an event or a belief or a phenomenon — only to write a coherent and reasonable one. To discern all causes — including remote ones — and all effects is beyond the power of any one human mind. Still, admirable and well-informed writers on matters such as politics, economics, and world and national affairs are often canny guessers and brave drawers of inferences. At times, even the most cautious and responsible writer has to leap boldly over a void to strike firm ground on the far side. Consider your evidence. Focus your thinking. Look well before leaping. Then take off.

FOCUS ON CLARITY AND CONCISENESS

While drafting a cause-and-effect analysis, you may need to grope a bit to discover just what you think about the sequence and relative importance of reasons and consequences. Your sentences may grope a bit, too, reflecting some initial confusion or a need to circle around your ideas in order to find them. The following draft passage reveals such difficulties:

WORDY AND UNCLEAR   Employees often worry about suggestive comments from others. The employee may not only worry but feel the need to discuss the situation with coworkers. One thing that is an effect of sexual harassment, even verbal harassment, in the workplace is that productivity is lost. Plans also need to be made to figure out how to deal with future comments. Engaging in these activities is sure to take time and concentration from work.

Drafting this passage, the writer seems to have built up to the idea about lost productivity (third sentence) after providing support for it in the first two sentences. The fourth sentence then adds more support. And sentences 2–4 all show a writer working out his ideas: Sentence subjects and verbs do not focus on the main actors and actions of the sentences, words repeat unnecessarily, and word groups run longer than needed for clarity.

These problems disappear from the edited version below, which moves the idea of the passage up front, uses subjects and verbs to state what the sentences are about (underlined), and cuts unneeded words.

> CONCISE AND CLEAR Even verbal sexual <u>harassment</u> in the workplace <u>causes</u> a loss of productivity. Worrying about suggestive comments from <u>others</u>, discussing those comments with coworkers, planning how to deal with future comments — these <u>activities</u> <u>consume</u> time and concentration that a harassed employee could spend on work.

CHECKLIST FOR REVISING A CAUSE-AND-EFFECT ESSAY

✔ **Subject.** Have you been able to cover your subject adequately in the time and space available? Should you perhaps narrow the subject so that you can fairly address the important causes and/or effects?

✔ **Thesis.** For your readers' benefit, have you focused your analysis by stating your main idea succinctly in a thesis statement?

✔ **Completeness.** Have you included all relevant causes or effects? Does your analysis reach back to locate remote causes or forward to locate remote effects?

✔ **Causal relations.** Have you presented a clear pattern of causes or effects? Have you distinguished the remote from the immediate, the major from the minor?

✔ **Accuracy and fairness.** Have you avoided the *post hoc* fallacy, assuming that A caused B just because A preceded B? Have you also avoided oversimplifying and instead covered causes or effects in all their complexity?

✔ **Clarity and conciseness.** Have you edited your draft to foreground your main points and tighten your sentences?

CAUSE AND EFFECT IN ACADEMIC WRITING

A History Textbook

These paragraphs from Alan Brinkley's *American History: A Survey* explain the causes behind President Lyndon Johnson's decision in the 1960s to escalate the ongoing conflict in Vietnam into "a full-scale American war" — a decision that, as the author's text goes on to explain, had grave and far-reaching consequences for the United States.

Many factors played a role in Johnson's decision. But the most obvious explanation is that the new president faced many pressures to expand the American involvement and very few to limit it. As the untested successor to a revered and martyred president, he felt obliged to prove his worthiness for the office by continuing the policies of his predecessor. Aid to South Vietnam had been one of the most prominent of those policies. Johnson also felt it necessary to retain in his administration many of the important figures of the Kennedy years. In doing so, he surrounded himself with a group of foreign policy advisers — Secretary of State Dean Rusk, Secretary of Defense Robert McNamara, National Security Adviser McGeorge Bundy, and others — who firmly believed that the United States had an important obligation to resist Communism in Vietnam. A compliant Congress raised little protest to, and indeed at one point openly endorsed, Johnson's use of executive powers to lead the nation into war. And for several years at least, public opinion remained firmly behind him — in part because Barry Goldwater's bellicose remarks about the war during the 1964 campaign made Johnson seem by comparison to be a moderate on the issue.

Above all, intervention in South Vietnam was fully consistent with nearly twenty years of American foreign policy. An anti-Communist ally was appealing to the United States for assistance; all the assumptions of the containment doctrine, as it had come to be defined by the 1960s, seemed to require the nation to oblige. Vietnam, Johnson believed, was a test of American willingness to fight Communist aggression, a test he was determined not to fail.

Topic sentence: summary of causes to be discussed

Causes:
- *Need to prove worthiness*

- *Advisers urging involvement*

- *Congressional cooperation*

- *Support of public opinion*

- *Consistency with American foreign policy against Communism*

A Letter to the Editor

To encourage interaction between readers and writers, most newspapers, magazines, and journals, as well as some Web sites, solicit and publish letters to the editor. Unlike the anonymous comments readers may attach to news and opinion articles online, letters to the editor are signed by their authors and screened by editors. To be published, such letters generally must take a calm tone and express ideas rationally. In most cases, the writer refers to the original article or other piece that prompted the letter and responds by agreeing or disagreeing (or a little of both). The point is to add a new perspective and move a conversation forward.

An ardent supporter of her school's track team, Kate Krueger was a sophomore during the team's first winning season in many years. At the end of the season, the student newspaper published a sports column crediting the successes to a new coach. Krueger found this explanation inadequate and wrote her own cause-and-effect analysis in the following letter to the newspaper's editor. Notice that because Krueger actually agreed with the original writer that the coach had helped the team, she acknowledged the coach's contributions while also detailing the other causes she saw at work.

May 2, 2016

To the Editor:

I take issue with Tom Boatz's column that was printed in the April 30 *Weekly*. Boatz attributes the success of this year's track team solely to the new coach, John Barak. I have several close friends who are athletes on the track team, so as an interested observer and fan I believe that Boatz oversimplified the causes of the team's recent success.

> Reason for writing: Original author oversimplified a cause-and-effect relationship

To be sure, Coach Barak did much to improve the training regimen and overall morale, and these have certainly contributed to the winning season. Both Coach Barak and the team members themselves can share credit for an impressive work ethic and a sense of camaraderie unequaled in previous years. However, several factors outside Coach Barak's control were also influential.

> Point of agreement: The new coach was one cause of the team's success

> Thesis statement: Other causes played a role

This year's team gained several phenomenal freshman athletes, such as Kristin Hall, who anchored the 4x400 and 4x800 relays and played an integral part in setting several school records, and Eric Montgomery-Asper, who was undefeated in the shot put.

> Other causes:
> • Talented new team members

Even more important, and also unmentioned by Tom Boatz, is the college's increased funding for the track program. Last year the school allotted fifty percent more for equipment, and the results have been dramatic. For example, the new vaulting poles are now the correct length and correspond to the weights of the individual athletes, giving them more power and height. Some vaulters have been able to vault as much as a foot higher than their previous records. Similarly, new starting blocks have allowed the team's sprinters to drop valuable seconds off their times.

> • Financial support from the college

> Examples of positive effects:
> • Improved vaulting performance

> • Improved sprinting times

I agree with Tom Boatz that Coach Barak deserves some credit for the track team's successes. But the athletes do, too, and so does the college for at last supporting its track program.

> Conclusion summarizes Krueger's analysis

— Kate Krueger '18

Cause and Effect

CHITRA DIVAKARUNI

Born in 1956 in Calcutta, India, Chitra Banerjee Divakaruni spent nineteen years in her homeland before immigrating to the United States. She holds a BA from the University of Calcutta, an MA from Wright State University, and a PhD from the University of California, Berkeley. Her books, often addressing the immigrant experience in America, include the novels *The Mistress of Spice* (1997), which was named one of the best books of the twentieth century by the *San Francisco Chronicle*, *One Amazing Thing* (2009), and *Oleander Girl* (2013); the story collections *Arranged Marriage* (1995) and *The Unknown Errors of Our Lives* (2001); and the poetry collections *Leaving Yuba City* (1997) and *Black Candle* (2000). Divakaruni has received a number of prizes for her work including the Before Columbus Foundation's 1996 American Book Award; in 2015, the *Economic Times* listed her among the twenty most globally influential Indian women. She teaches creative writing at the University of Houston and serves on the boards of several organizations that help women and children.

Live Free and Starve

Many of the consumer goods sold in the United States — shoes, clothing, toys, rugs — are made in countries whose labor practices do not meet US standards for safety and fairness. Americans have been horrified at tales of children put to work by force or under contracts (called *indentures*) with the children's parents. Some in the US government have tried to stop or at least discourage such practices: For instance, the bill Divakaruni cites in her first paragraph, which was signed into law, requires the Customs Service to issue a detention order on goods that are suspected of having been produced by forced or indentured child labor. In this essay from *Salon* in 1997, Divakaruni argues that such efforts, however well intentioned, can mean dreadful consequences for the very people they are designed to protect.

For a different perspective on the effects of globalization, see the next essay, Marie Javdani's "*Plata o Plomo:* Silver or Lead."

Some days back, the House passed a bill that stated that the United States 1 would no longer permit the import of goods from factories where forced or indentured child labor was used. My liberal friends applauded the bill. It was a triumphant advance in the field of human rights. Now children in Third World countries wouldn't have to spend their days chained to their posts in

factories manufacturing goods for other people to enjoy while their childhoods slipped by them. They could be free and happy, like American children.

I am not so sure.   2

It is true that child labor is a terrible thing, especially for those children   3
who are sold to employers by their parents at the age of five or six and have
no way to protect themselves from abuse. In many cases it will be decades —
perhaps a lifetime, due to the fines heaped upon them whenever they make
mistakes — before they can buy back their freedom. Meanwhile these children,
mostly employed by rug-makers, spend their days in dark, ill-ventilated rooms
doing work that damages their eyes and lungs. They aren't even allowed to
stand up and stretch. Each time they go to the bathroom, they suffer a pay cut.

But is this bill, which, if it passes the Senate and is signed by President   4
Clinton, will lead to the unemployment of almost a million children, the
answer? If the children themselves were asked whether they would rather work
under such harsh conditions or enjoy a leisure that comes without the benefit
of food or clothing or shelter, I wonder what their response would be.

It is easy for us in America to make the error of evaluating situations in the   5
rest of the world as though they were happening in this country and propose
solutions that make excellent sense — in the context of our society. Even we
immigrants, who should know better, have wiped from our minds the memory
of what it is to live under the kind of desperate conditions that force a parent
to sell his or her child. Looking down from the heights of Maslow's pyramid,[1] it
seems inconceivable to us that someone could actually prefer bread to freedom.

When I was growing up in Calcutta, there was a boy who used to work in   6
our house. His name was Nimai, and when he came to us, he must have been
about ten or so, just a little older than my brother and I. He'd been brought
to our home by his uncle, who lived in our ancestral village and was a field
laborer for my grandfather. The uncle explained to my mother that Nimai's
parents were too poor to feed their several children, and while his older
brothers were already working in the fields and earning their keep, Nimai
was too frail to do so. My mother was reluctant to take on a sickly child who
might prove more of a burden than a help, but finally she agreed, and Nimai
lived and worked in our home for six or seven years. My mother was a good
employer — Nimai ate the same food that we children did and was given
new clothes during Indian New Year, just as we were. In the time between his
chores — dusting and sweeping and pumping water from the tube-well and
running to the market — my mother encouraged him to learn to read and

---

[1] The psychologist Abraham Maslow (1908–70) proposed a "hierarchy of needs" in the
shape of a five-level pyramid with survival needs at the bottom and "self-actualization" and
"self-transcendence" at the top. According to Maslow, one must satisfy the needs at each level
before moving up to the next. — Eds.

write. Still, I would not disagree with anyone who says that it was hardly a desirable existence for a child.

But what would life have been like for Nimai if an anti–child-labor law   7
had prohibited my mother from hiring him? Every year, when we went to visit our grandfather in the village, we were struck by the many children we saw by the mud roads, their ribs sticking out through the rags they wore. They trailed after us, begging for a few paise.[2] When the hunger was too much to bear, they stole into the neighbors' fields and ate whatever they could find — raw potatoes, cauliflower, green sugar cane and corn torn from the stalk — even though they knew they'd be beaten for it. Whenever Nimai passed these children, he always walked a little taller. And when he handed the bulk of his earnings over to his father, there was a certain pride in his eye. Exploitation, you might be thinking. But he thought he was a responsible member of his family.

A bill like the one we've just passed is of no use unless it goes hand in   8
hand with programs that will offer a new life to these newly released children. But where are the schools in which they are to be educated? Where is the money to buy them food and clothing and medication, so that they don't return home to become the extra weight that capsizes the already shaky raft of their family's finances? Their own governments, mired in countless other problems, seem incapable of bringing these services to them. Are we in America who, with one blithe stroke of our congressional pen, rendered these children jobless, willing to shoulder that burden? And when many of these children turn to the streets, to survival through thievery and violence and begging and prostitution — as surely in the absence of other options they must — are we willing to shoulder that responsibility?

Journal Writing

Write a journal response to Divakaruni's argument against legislation that bans goods produced by forced or indentured child laborers. Do you basically agree or disagree with the author? Why?

Questions on Meaning

1. What do you take to be Divakaruni's PURPOSE in this essay? When was it clear?

2. What is Divakaruni's THESIS? Where is it stated?

---

[2] *Paise* (pronounced "pie-say") are the smallest unit of Indian currency, worth a fraction of an American penny. — EDS.

3. What are "Third World countries" (par. 1)?

4. From the further information given in the footnote on page 399, what does it mean to be "[l]ooking down from the heights of Maslow's pyramid" (par. 5)? What point is Divakaruni making here?

5. In paragraph 8 Divakaruni suggests some of the reasons that children in other countries may be forced or sold into labor. What are they?

Questions on Writing Strategy

1. In her last paragraph, Divakaruni asks a series of RHETORICAL QUESTIONS. What is the EFFECT of this strategy?

2. How does the structure of paragraph 3 clarify causes and effects?

3. **OTHER METHODS**   What does the extended EXAMPLE of Nimai (pars. 6–7) contribute to Divakaruni's argument? What, if anything, does it add to Divakaruni's authority? What does it tell us about child labor abroad?

Questions on Language

1. Divakaruni says that laboring children could otherwise be "the extra weight that capsizes the already shaky raft of their family's finances" (par. 8). How does this metaphor capture the problem of children in poor families? (See FIGURES OF SPEECH in the Glossary for a definition of *metaphor*.)

2. What do the words in paragraph 7 tell you about Divakaruni's attitude toward the village children? Is it disdain? pity? compassion? horror?

3. Consult a dictionary if you need help in defining the following: indentured (par. 1); inconceivable (5); exploitation (7); mired, blithe (8).

Suggestions for Writing

1. **FROM JOURNAL TO ESSAY**   Starting from your journal entry, write a letter to your congressional representative or one of your senators who takes a position for or against laws such as that opposed by Divakaruni. You can use quotations from Divakaruni's essay if they serve your purpose, but the letter should center on your own views of the issue. When you've finished your letter, send it. (You can find your representative's and senators' names and addresses on the Web at *house.gov/ representatives/* and *senate.gov.*)

2. David Parker, a photographer and doctor, has documented child laborers in a series of powerful photographs (*childlaborphotographs.com*). He asks viewers, "Under what circumstances and conditions should children work?" Look at Parker's photographs, and answer his question in an essay. What kind of paid work, for how many hours a week, is appropriate for, say, a ten- or twelve-year-old child? Consider: What about children working in their family's business? Where do you draw the line between occasional babysitting or lawn mowing and

full-time factory work? You might want to research the history of child labor in the United States, including the development of child labor laws, to help support your answer.

3. **CRITICAL WRITING**   Divakaruni's essay depends significantly on appeals to readers' emotions (see p. 483). Locate one emotional appeal that either helps to convince you of the author's point or, in your mind, weakens the argument. What does the appeal ASSUME about the reader's feelings or values? Why are the assumptions correct or incorrect in your case?

4. **CONNECTIONS**   In the next essay, *"Plata o Plomo:* Silver or Lead," Marie Javdani examines another global relationship that can harm children: the international traffic in cocaine, heroin, and other drugs. To what extent do you think the people in one country are responsible for what happens in other countries as a result of their actions? Write a brief essay that answers this question, explaining clearly the beliefs and values that guide your answer.

Chitra Divakaruni on Writing

Chitra Divakaruni is also a community worker, reaching out through organizations such as Maitri, a refuge for abused women that she helped to found. In a 1998 interview in *Atlantic Unbound*, Katie Bolick asked Divakaruni how her activism and writing affected each other. Here is Divakaruni's response.

Being helpful where I can has always been an important value for me. I did community work in India, and I continue to do it in America, because being involved in my community is something I feel I need to do. Activism has given me enormous satisfaction — not just as a person, but also as a writer. The lives of people I would have only known from the outside, or had stereotyped notions of, have been opened up to me. My hotline work with Maitri has certainly influenced both my life and my writing immensely. Overall, I have a great deal of sensitivity that I did not have before, and a lot of my preconceptions have changed. I hope that translates into my writing and reaches my readers.

The Bedford Reader on Writing

Do you have a project or an activity comparable to Divakaruni's activism that you believe positively affects your writing? What is it? How does it help you as you write? For additional help with having your "preconceptions" challenged, or CRITICAL THINKING, turn to pages 16–18.

MARIE JAVDANI

Marie Javdani was born in Albuquerque, New Mexico, and attended the University of Oregon, where she earned a BA and an MA in geography and was published in *Harvest*, the university's annual writing publication. As an undergraduate Javdani became interested in international development. She worked as a research assistant for Harvard's Center for International Development and traveled to Malawi to conduct research on the connection between fertilizer subsidies and food security. Currently involved with a nonprofit organization devoted to bringing clean water to communities in Kenya, Javdani is also a musician whose instrument of choice is the marimba, an African percussion device similar to the xylophone.

Plata o Plomo: Silver or Lead

Like Chitra Divakaruni in the previous selection, Javdani is concerned in this essay with how actions taken in the United States can affect people in other countries, often without our realizing it. To make her argument concrete, Javdani tells the stories of two boys, Eric, an American, and Miguel, a Colombian. (Colombia is a country in South America.) Reminding us that global problems start and end with people, the boys represent cause and effect at their most specific. Javdani wrote this paper for a freshman writing course and revised it for us in 2004. It is documented in MLA style, described on pages 631–45.

At 8:00 on a Friday night, Eric walks down the street in his American   1
hometown whistling. Tonight, for the first time in almost a week, Eric does not have to do homework or chores. Tonight Eric is a free spirit. Best of all, tonight Eric has scored some drugs. He and his friends will trade their bland, controlled existence for some action and a little bit of fun.

At 8:00 on a Friday night, Miguel creeps down the road in his Colombian   2
village praying. Tonight, for the last time in his life, Miguel will have to watch where he is going and listen anxiously for distant gunshots. Tonight Miguel will die. The guerillas who have been threatening him and his father will end his life for some coca and a lot of money.

Eric and Miguel represent opposite poles in what the United States gov-   3
ernment refers to as the "war on drugs." Miguel's home is where it starts. In his little village, drug production is the only possible way of life. Eric's home is where it ends. In his suburban paradise, the stress of homework and

ex-girlfriends requires weekend breaks for drugs. All but ignoring both youths, congresspeople, governors, and presidents talk about how their actions will combat the flow of drugs into our homeland. In an attempt to find the quickest route around a complicated problem, the United States sends billions in aid dollars every year to the governments of Latin American "drug-source" countries such as Colombia, Ecuador, Bolivia, and Peru (Carpenter 205). But the solution isn't working: Political turmoil and violence continue to plague the countries to which we are sending aid, and illegal drug use in the United States remains fairly constant (Vásquez 571–75). To begin to solve the problem, we need to understand what's happening in drug-source countries, how the United States can and can't help there, and what, instead, can be done at home.

Miguel's country, Colombia, is one of the top recipients of US money 4 and military weaponry and equipment. According to the US Department of State, Colombia produces nearly 80% of the world's cocaine as well as a significant amount of the US heroin supply. Drug production has become a way of life for Colombians. Some call it the *plata o plomo* mentality. As Gonzalo Sanchez explains it, *plata o plomo* is literally translated as "silver or lead" and means that one can either take the money — drug money, bribe money, and so on — or take a bullet (7). Since 1964, the country has been essentially run by drug lords and leftist extremists, mainly the FARC (the military wing of the Colombian Communist Party), whose guerilla presence is much stronger and more threatening than that of the actual government. In response, extreme right-wing paramilitary forces act in an equally deadly manner. Both of these groups raid villages continually, looking to root out "traitors" and executing whomever they please (Sanchez 12–15).

According to the humanitarian organization Human Rights Watch, US 5 aid money has helped fund, supply, and train Colombian military units that maintain close alliances with paramilitary groups (*World Report*). Although Colombia has recently taken a tougher stance toward the paramilitaries and peace negotiations are in progress, the US State Department, major human rights organizations, and the United Nations claim that the Colombian government is still linked to illicit paramilitary activities. For example, government forces have often invaded, emptied, and then left a guerilla-held area, clearing the way for paramilitary fighters to take control (Carpenter 162). Human rights groups also criticize what Adam Isacson calls a "forgive and forget" government policy toward paramilitary leaders accused of crimes, including promises of amnesty in return for gradual demobilization (251–52). Although the US has threatened to suspend aid if Colombia does not break such ties with paramilitary groups, the full amount of promised aid continues to be granted (*World Report*).

For the past forty years, the people of Colombia have found themselves   6
between a rock and a hard place over the production of coca, the plant used
for making cocaine and heroin. Under threats from the rebel drug lords, who
now control many areas, civilians must either allow their land to be cultivated
for the growth of coca or put themselves and their families at deadly risk. At
the same time, however, the consequence of "cooperation" with the rebels
is execution by paramilitary groups or even by the Colombian government.
Some coca farmers, fearful of the government, willingly form alliances with
rebels who offer to protect their farms for a fee (Vásquez 572).

Entire villages get caught in the crossfire between paramilitaries and reb-   7
els. In the past ten years, over 35,000 civilians have lost their lives in the
conflict and hundreds of thousands have been forced from their homes (Carpenter 215). A terrible incident in the town of Bellavista was reported in the
New York Times in 2002 (Forero, "Colombian War"). Paramilitary forces took
over the town in an attempt to gain control of jungle smuggling routes. When
leftist rebels arrived ready to fight a battle, the paramilitaries fled, leaving the
civilians trapped and defenseless. Most of the villagers huddled together in
their church, and 117 were killed when a stray rocket destroyed the church.

What is to be done to prevent such atrocities? The United States rushes   8
aid to Colombia, hoping to stop the violence and the drugs. Unfortunately,
the solutions attempted so far have had their own bad results. For instance,
eradicating coca fields has alienated peasants, who then turn to the rebels
for support, and it has also escalated violence over the reduced coca supply
(Vásquez 575). Money intended to help peasants establish alternative crops
has ended up buying weapons for branches of the military that support paramilitary operations (*World Report*). Not long ago $2 million intended for the
Colombian police just disappeared (Forero, "Two Million").

Obviously, the United States needs to monitor how its dollars are used   9
in Colombia. It can continue to discourage the Colombian government
from supporting the paramilitaries and encourage it to seek peace among the
warring factions. But ultimately the United States is limited in what it can
do by international law and by the tolerance of the US people for foreign
intervention.

Instead, the United States should be looking to its home front and should   10
focus on cutting the demand for drugs. Any economist will affirm that where
there is demand, there will be supply. A report by the United Nations Office
on Drugs and Crime connects this basic economic principle to illegal drugs:

> Production of illicit drugs is market driven. In the United States alone, illicit
> drugs are an $80 billion market. More than $70 billion of that amount goes
> to traffickers, those who bring the drugs to market. Stopping the demand
> would stop their business. (26)

The United States should reduce demand by dramatically increasing both treatment and education. The first will help people stop using drugs. The second will make users aware of the consequences of their choices.

The war on drugs is not fought just in the jungles of some distant country.   11
It takes place daily at our schools, in our homes, and on our streets. People my age who justify their use of illegal drugs by saying "It's my life, and I can do with it what I please" should be made aware that they are funding drug lords and contributing to the suffering of people across the globe, including in Colombia. Eric's "little bit of fun" is costing Miguel his life.

Works Cited

Carpenter, Ted Galen. *Peace and Freedom: Foreign Policy for a Constitutional Republic*. Cato Institute, 2002.

Forero, Juan. "Colombian War Brings Carnage to Village Altar." *The New York Times*, 9 May 2002, www.nytimes.com/2002/05/09/world/colombia-war-brings-carnage-to-village-altar.html.

– – –. "Two Million in US Aid to Colombia Missing from Colombian Police Fund." *The New York Times*, 11 May 2002, www.nytimes.com/2002/05/11/world/2-million-in-us-aid-is-missing-from-colombian-police-fund.html.

Isacson, Adam. "Optimism, Pessimism, and Terrorism: The United States and Colombia in 2003." *The Brown Journal of World Affairs*, vol. 10, no. 2, 2004, pp. 245–55.

Sanchez, Gonzalo. *Violence in Colombia*. Scholarly Resources, 1992.

United Nations. *Drug Consumption Stimulates Cultivation and Trade*. UN Office on Drugs and Crime, 2003.

United States, Department of State. *International Narcotics Control Strategy Report, 2003*. Government Printing Office, 2004.

Vásquez, Ian. "The International War on Drugs." *Cato Handbook for Congress: Policy Recommendations for the 108th Congress*, edited by Edward H. Crane and David Boaz, Cato Institute, 2003, pp. 567–76. *Cato Institute*, www.cato.org/cato-handbook-policymakers/cato-handbook-congress-policy-recommendations-108th-congress-2003.

World Report 2003. Human Rights Watch, 2004, www.hrw.org/legacy/wr2k3/.

Journal Writing

What do you think about Javdani's solution to the twin problems of violence in drug-producing countries and drug use in the United States (pars. 10–11)? Do you think her solution would work? Why, or why not?

Questions on Meaning

1. Where does Javdani state her THESIS? How does she develop the thesis?
2. Why do the Colombian peasants often support the Communist rebels rather than the government?
3. What, according to Javdani, are the problems caused by the US government's sending "billions in aid dollars every year to the governments of Latin American 'drug-source' countries" (par. 3)? What does Javdani offer as a solution?

Questions on Writing Strategy

1. Who seems to be Javdani's intended AUDIENCE for this essay? How does she appeal to this audience?
2. With whom do Javdani's sympathies lie? What EVIDENCE in the essay supports your answer?
3. Javdani cites a variety of outside sources throughout the essay. What is the EFFECT of her use of these sources?
4. **OTHER METHODS** Why does Javdani use COMPARISON AND CONTRAST in her opening paragraphs? What is the effect of her returning to this comparison in her conclusion?

Questions on Language

1. In paragraph 6 Javdani describes the people of Colombia as "between a rock and a hard place over the production of coca." What does she mean?
2. How and why does Javdani use IRONY to describe Eric in paragraph 3?
3. Why does Javdani use quotation marks around *traitors* (par. 4) and *cooperation* (6)?
4. Consult a dictionary if you are unsure of the meanings of any of the following words: guerillas (par. 2); turmoil, plague (3); paramilitary (4); humanitarian, amnesty, demobilization (5); atrocities, eradicating, alienated (8).

Suggestions for Writing

1. **FROM JOURNAL TO ESSAY** Working from your journal writing and, like Javdani, drawing on research, develop an essay that lays out your view of the most effective ways to curtail either the production or the consumption of illegal drugs. Which current US government efforts are successful, and which fall short? What more could be done?
2. Write a report on the use of illegal drugs by US adolescents, focusing on an aspect of the problem that interests you, such as how widespread it is, what groups it affects most and least, or what drugs are involved. An excellent starting place for your research is Monitoring the Future, a long-term study of "the behavior, attitudes, and values" of students and young adults. Its annual report, *Monitoring the Future Results,* is available at *drugabuse.gov/related-topics /trends-statistics/monitoring-future.*

3. **CRITICAL WRITING**   Is Javdani's essay an effective ARGUMENT? Consider the thesis development, the organization, the evidence, and the clarity of the presentation. What would you say are the strengths and weaknesses of this argument?

4. **CONNECTIONS**   Javdani's essay and Chitra Divakaruni's "Live Free and Starve" (p. 398) both look at effects of globalization, the increasing economic, cultural, and political connections among nations and their people. Write a brief essay discussing what you see as the main advantages and the main disadvantages of globalization. For instance, advantages might include the availability in this country of varied ethnic foods or of relatively inexpensive consumer goods that were produced elsewhere, while disadvantages might include the loss of American manufacturing jobs to foreign factories or the strong international drug trade.

Marie Javdani on Writing

In an interview for this book, we asked Marie Javdani to describe her writing process. She also offered suggestions for college writers based on her own experiences as a student.

Depending on my writing topic, it can often take a while to get a good start. If it's a topic I chose myself and am interested in or am at least somewhat knowledgeable about, the first steps are usually much easier. I usually start by brainstorming an outline by just writing things as I think of them. What questions do I want to answer? How does this topic actually affect people? Once I get a start, the writing process usually goes fairly quickly. I try to write in a way that I would speak if I were, for instance, teaching on the subject. That tends to make my work more readable. As for the introduction, I try to stay away from prescribed formats. I try to think of what would make me want to read more about a topic or to put a spin on it that makes it stand out. Also, I tend to write my introduction last. I've found that if I write it first it typically doesn't match what I write once I get "on a roll." If I plan ahead properly, I don't usually have to do more than two drafts unless I come upon new research that makes me need to rearrange my arguments. I try to write early enough to leave it alone for a few days before I go back and proofread it. . . .

From a student's perspective, the best thing you can do to improve your writing is to be interested in your topic. On the same note, however, don't soapbox. Just say what you want to say, support it, and move on. If you're writing for an assignment for which you weren't able to choose the topic, try to take an angle that you think no one else will take. . . . Do take the time to spell-check and edit your writing. The spelling checker on the computer is not sufficient. You're (not *your*) in college and you know (not *no*) better. Try reading your writing out loud to yourself. If it doesn't sound good when you say it, it doesn't sound good on paper either.

The Bedford Reader on Writing

Do you share Javdani's experience that it's usually easier to write when you're interested in your topic? For tips on finding your interest in a subject, your own personal angle, before you start writing, refer to "Focusing on a Thesis" on pages 35–36 and to "Developing Ideas" on pages 36–37. And for some of those "prescribed formats" Javdani avoids when she turns to her opening paragraphs (they can be quite helpful, really) see "Shaping the Introduction and Conclusion" (pp. 37–39).

RANDALL MUNROE

Randall Munroe (born 1984) is the creator of *xkcd*, a stick-figure "Web comic of romance, sarcasm, math, and language" that has gained a cult following since the author first started uploading his doodles on a whim in 2005. He graduated from Christopher Newport University in Newport News, Virginia, with a degree in physics and worked for a while as a roboticist at NASA's Langley Research Center. When his contract with NASA ended in 2006 he turned to writing the comic full time. Munroe now lives in Somerville, Massachusetts, and earns his living selling T-shirts and other *xkcd* merchandise online. When not drawing or writing, he likes to "climb things, open strange doors, and go to goth clubs dressed as a frat guy so [he] can stand around and look terribly uncomfortable."

Everybody Jump

In 2012, Munroe started a corollary to *xkcd* called "What If?" Once a week, he answers a fan's question about physics with his trademark mix of knowledge, wit, and graphing paper; a collection of his carefully researched posts was published in the book *What If? Serious Scientific Answers to Absurd Hypothetical Questions* in 2015. The illustrated entry we include here offers Munroe's take on what would happen if everybody on the planet got together and jumped at the same time. (He cites his sources in APA style, explained on pages 651–661.)

> **Q.** What would happen if everyone on Earth stood
> as close to each other as they could and jumped,
> everyone landing on the ground at the same instant?
> — Thomas Bennett (and many others)

A. This is one of the most popular questions submitted through my Web site. It's been examined before, including by *ScienceBlogs* (2010) and *The Straight Dope* (1984). They cover the kinematics pretty well. However, they don't tell the whole story. [1]

Let's take a closer look. [2]

At the start of the scenario, the entire Earth's population has been magically transported together into one place. [3]

This crowd takes up an area the size of Rhode Island. But there's no reason   4
to use the vague phrase "an area the size of Rhode Island." This is our scenario;
we can be specific. They're *actually* in Rhode Island.

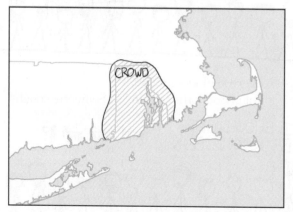

At the stroke of noon, everyone jumps.   5

As discussed elsewhere, it doesn't really affect the planet. Earth outweighs   6
us by a factor of over ten trillion. On average, we humans can vertically jump
maybe half a meter on a good day. Even if the Earth were rigid and responded
instantly, it would be pushed down by less than an atom's width.

Next, everyone falls back to the ground.   7

Technically, this delivers a lot of energy into the Earth, but it's spread out   8
over a large enough area that it doesn't do much more than leave footprints in
a lot of gardens. A slight pulse of pressure spreads through the North American continental crust and dissipates with little effect. The sound of all those
feet hitting the ground creates a loud, drawn-out roar lasting many seconds.

Eventually, the air grows quiet.   9

Seconds pass. Everyone looks around.   10
There are a lot of uncomfortable glances. Someone coughs.   11

A cell phone comes out of a pocket. Within seconds, the rest of the   12
world's five billion phones follow. All of them — even those compatible with
the region's towers — are displaying some version of "NO SIGNAL." The cell
networks have all collapsed under the unprecedented load. Outside Rhode
Island, abandoned machinery begins grinding to a halt.

The T. F. Green Airport in Warwick, Rhode Island, handles a few thou- 13
sand passengers a day. Assuming they got things organized (including sending
out scouting missions to retrieve fuel), they could run at 500% capacity for
years without making a dent in the crowd.

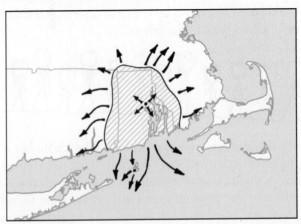

The addition of all the nearby airports doesn't change the equation much. 14
Nor does the region's light rail system. Crowds climb on board container ships

in the deep-water port of Providence, but stocking sufficient food and water for a long sea voyage proves a challenge.

Rhode Island's half-million cars are commandeered. Moments later, I-95, I-195, and I-295 become the sites of the largest traffic jam in the history of the planet. Most of the cars are engulfed by the crowds, but a lucky few get out and begin wandering the abandoned road network. 15

Some make it past New York or Boston before running out of fuel. Since the electricity is probably not on at this point, rather than find a working gas pump, it's easier to just abandon the car and steal a new one. Who can stop you? All the cops are in Rhode Island. 16

The edge of the crowd spreads outward into southern Massachusetts and Connecticut. Any two people who meet are unlikely to have a language in common, and almost nobody knows the area. The state becomes a chaotic patchwork of coalescing and collapsing social hierarchies. Violence is common. Everybody is hungry and thirsty. Grocery stores are emptied. Fresh water is hard to come by and there's no efficient system for distributing it. 17

Within weeks, Rhode Island is a graveyard of billions. 18

The survivors spread out across the face of the world and struggle to build a new civilization atop the pristine ruins of the old. Our species staggers on, but our population has been greatly reduced. Earth's orbit is completely unaffected — it spins along exactly as it did before our species-wide jump. 19

But at least now we know. 20

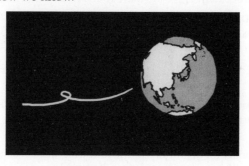

References

Science Blogs, Dot Physics. (26 August 2010). What if everyone jumped? Retrieved from http://scienceblogs.com/dotphysics/2010/08/26/what-if -everyone-jumped/

Straight Dope, The. (6 April 1984). If everyone in China jumped off chairs at once, would the Earth be thrown out of its orbit? Retrieved from http://www.straightdope.com/columns/read/142/if-all-chinese-jumped-at -once-would-cataclysm-result

Journal Writing

Have you recently been struck by curiosity, perhaps because of a question someone asked you, as happened to Munroe, or because of something you've read, or because of a phenomenon you've noticed? What question has been raised in your mind, and why does it interest you? Make note of the question, and your thoughts about it, in your journal.

Questions on Meaning

1. What does Munroe mean by "kinematics" (par. 1)? Why does he not focus on that aspect of the reader's question in his answer?

2. Does Munroe have a THESIS? What does he claim *would* happen if everybody on the planet got together and jumped at the same time?

Questions on Writing Strategy

1. For whom is Munroe writing? What clues in the text reveal how he imagines his AUDIENCE?

2. What is the point in paragraphs 12–18? How does the causal chain Munroe describes there relate to his thesis?

3. What EVIDENCE does Munroe offer to support his analysis of causes and effects? How seriously does he take his subject?

4. What do Munroe's drawings contribute to his essay?

5. **OTHER METHODS**   Why do you think Munroe chose Rhode Island to serve as the EXAMPLE for his scenario?

Questions on Language

1. How would you describe the overall TONE of this essay: academic? detached? amused? something else? Point to some words and phrases that support your answer.

2. Check a dictionary for definitions of the following words: scenario (par. 3); factor (6); dissipates (8); commandeered, engulfed (15); coalescing, hierarchies (17); pristine (19).

3. In speculating about future events, Munroe writes in the present tense. Why? What is the EFFECT of this choice?

Suggestions for Writing

1. **FROM JOURNAL TO ESSAY**   Follow Munroe's lead and look for answers to the question (or questions) you posed in your journal. Try searching the Internet for

information, as well as researching published scholarly works or interviewing an expert or two. Then write an essay that presents your findings, providing plenty of EVIDENCE to support your thesis.

2. Munroe observes that the "five billion" (par. 12) people who populate the Earth (as of 2016 the number is closer to seven billion) consume a lot of resources — "machinery" (12), "food and water" (14), "fuel" (16), and so forth — and his scenario concludes with a human "population [that] has been greatly reduced" (19). Is that a bad thing? In an essay, consider the problem of overpopulation and its effects on the environment. How many people can the planet reasonably hold? Do those in some regions (North America, for instance, or China) consume more than their fair share of resources? To what extent are human beings responsible for changes in the environment? What, if anything, can be done to make human life on Earth more sustainable? How do you envision the future of the planet, and of humanity?

3. **CRITICAL WRITING**   The "kinematics" explanations that Munroe cites at the start of his post and in his list of References are still available online. Read them both for yourself and in an essay, weigh Munroe's use of evidence: Does he represent the math and science accurately and fairly? How well does he adapt technical information for an audience of nonspecialists? What stylistic cues does he seem to take from his sources? Is his approach successful? Why, or why not?

4. **CONNECTIONS**   While Munroe jokes that the collapse of civilization would have no real effect on the Earth itself, Joan Didion, in "Earthquakes" (p. 557), writes about civilization's feelings of powerlessness in the face of natural disasters. What ASSUMPTIONS about human impacts on the Earth (and vice versa) do these writers seem to share, and where do they diverge? How might the apparent contradictions between their two perspectives be resolved?

CHRISTOPHER BEAM

Christopher Beam is a reporter for *Slate* who specializes in politics and crime. His writing has also been published in *New York* magazine, *Business Week*, the *New Republic*, *Gentlemen's Quarterly*, and other magazines. The son of a *Boston Globe* columnist, Beam grew up in Newton, Massachusetts, attended the Roxbury Latin school, and in 2006 completed a degree in American history at Columbia University. With his friend Nick Summers he cofounded *IvyGate*, a popular college news and gossip blog. Beam currently lives in Beijing, China, where he is studying as a Luce Scholar with the Asia Foundation and, by his own account, performing miserably at table tennis.

Blood Loss

Television crime dramas regularly feature plots in which a series of murders are committed by the same person. But how common are such characters in real life? In this 2011 article for *Slate*, Beam reports a surprising trend: Serial killings occur much less often than they did a generation ago. He suggests that shifting cultural anxieties, not just police work, can explain the decline.

When it came to serial killing, Stephen Griffiths did everything by the book. He targeted prostitutes in the slums of Bradford, a city in Northern England. He chose a unique murder weapon: a crossbow. He claimed to have eaten parts of his victims — two of them cooked, one of them raw. "I'm misanthropic," he told police investigators when he was finally caught in 2010. "I don't have much time for the human race." When he appeared in court, he gave his name as the "crossbow cannibal." It was as if he'd studied up on the art of serial murder. (In fact, he had: Griffiths was a part-time PhD student at Bradford University, where he was studying criminology.) And yet, for all his efforts, he got only one short blurb in the *New York Times* when he was sentenced last month.

Serial killers just aren't the sensation they used to be. They haven't disappeared, of course. Last month, Suffolk County, New York, police found the bodies of four women dumped near a beach in Long Island. Philadelphia police have attributed the murders of three women in the city's Kensington neighborhood to one "Kensington Strangler." On Tuesday, an accused serial stabber in Flint, Michigan, filed an insanity plea.

But the number of serial murders seems to be dwindling, as does the public's fascination with them. "It does seem the golden age of serial murderers is probably past," says Harold Schechter, a professor at Queens College of the City University of New York who studies crime.

Statistics on serial murder are hard to come by — the FBI doesn't keep   4
numbers, according to a spokeswoman — but the data we do have suggests
serial murders peaked in the 1980s and have been declining ever since. James
Alan Fox, a criminology professor at Northeastern University and coauthor
of *Extreme Killing: Understanding Serial and Mass Murder*, keeps a database of
confirmed serial murderers starting in 1900. According to his count, based on
newspaper clippings, books, and Web sources, there were only a dozen or so
serial killers before 1960 in the United States. Then serial killings took off:
There were 19 in the 1960s, 119 in the '70s, and 200 in the '80s. In the '90s,
the number of cases dropped to 141. And the 2000s saw only 61 serial murderers. (Definitions of *serial murder* vary, but Fox defines it as "a string of four or
more homicides committed by one or a few perpetrators that spans a period
of days, weeks, months, or even years." To avoid double-counting, he assigns
killers to the decade in which they reached the midpoint of their careers.)

There are plenty of structural explanations for the rise of reported serial   5
murders through the 1980s. Data collection and record-keeping improved,
making it easier to find cases of serial murder. Law enforcement developed
more sophisticated methods of investigation, enabling police to identify link-
ages between cases — especially across states — that they would have otherwise ignored. The media's growing obsession with serial killers in the 1970s and
'80s may have created a minor snowball effect, offering a short path to celebrity.

But those factors don't explain away the decline in serial murders since   6
1990. If anything, they make it more significant. Then why the downtrend?

Trends in Serial Killing

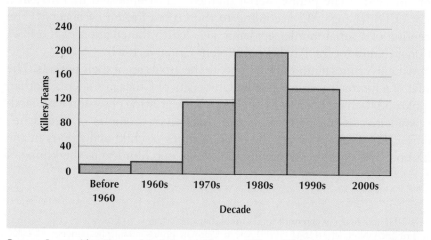

Source: James Alan Fox and Jack Levin. *Extreme Killing: Understanding Serial and Mass
Murder.* Sage Publications, 2011.

It's hard to say. Better law enforcement could have played a role, as police catch would-be serial killers after their first crime. So could the increased incarceration rate, says Fox: "Maybe they're still behind bars." Whatever the reason, the decline in serial murders tracks with a dramatic drop in overall violent crime since the '80s. (One caveat: The numbers for the 2000s may skew low, since some serial killers haven't been caught yet.)

As the raw numbers have declined, the media have paid less attention, too. Sure, you've still got the occasional Beltway sniper or Grim Sleeper who terrorizes a community. But nothing in the last decade has captured the popular imagination like the sex-addled psychopaths of the '70s and '80s, such as Ted Bundy (feigned injuries to win sympathy before killing women; about thirty victims), John Wayne Gacy (stored bodies in his ceiling crawl-space; thirty-three victims), or Jeffrey Dahmer (kept body parts in his closet and freezer; seventeen victims). These crimes caused media frenzies in part because of the way they tapped into the obsessions and fears of the time: Bundy, a golden boy who worked on Nelson Rockefeller's presidential campaign in Seattle, seemed to represent the evil lurking beneath America's cheery exterior. Gacy, who dressed up as a clown and preyed on teenage boys, was every parent's nightmare. "Son of Sam" David Berkowitz milked — and, in so doing, mocked — the media's obsession with serial killers by sending a letter to *New York Daily News* reporter Jimmy Breslin.

The media returned the favor, inflating the perception that serial killers were everywhere and repeating the erroneous statistic that there were five thousand serial murder victims every year. These horror stories were not exactly discouraged by the FBI, one of whose agents coined the term "serial killer" in 1981. (The phrase "serial murderer" first appeared in 1961, in a review of Fritz Lang's M,[1] according to the *Oxford English Dictionary*.) The perception of a serial murder epidemic also led to the creation of the FBI's National Center for the Analysis of Violent Crime in 1981.

Infamous crimes almost always needle the anxieties of their periods. The murder of a fourteen-year-old boy by University of Chicago students Nathan Leopold and Richard Loeb in 1924 captured the growing obsession with modern psychiatry, as the pair considered themselves examples of Nietzsche's *Übermensch*,[2] unbound by moral codes. A series of child abductions in the 1920s and '30s, from the Wineville Chicken Coop Murders to the killing of

7

8

9

---

[1] A 1931 movie about the hunt for a child killer in Germany. — Eds.

[2] Friedrich Nietzsche (1844–1900) was a German philosopher. The concept of *Übermensch*, loosely translated as "superhuman," embodies his idea that human beings should strive for God-like perfection. — Eds.

Charles Lindbergh's son, became a symbol of societal decay during the Depression. Charles Manson, who presided over the Tate murders in 1969, embodied a sexual revolution gone mad. The Columbine massacre preyed on parental fears of the effects of violent movies and video games.

Conversely, sensational crimes that *don't* play into a larger societal narrative fade away. In 1927, Andrew Kehoe detonated three bombs at a school in Bath Township, Michigan, killing thirty-eight children and seven adults, including Kehoe — one of the largest cases of domestic terrorism before the Oklahoma City bombing in 1995. The disaster made headlines, but was soon eclipsed by Charles Lindbergh's trans-Atlantic flight. "It was a crime that was ahead of its time," says Schechter.   10

Indeed, if something like the Bath School massacre happened today, it would probably resonate more deeply than it did in the 1920s. What child abductors were to the '20s and serial killers were to the '70s and '80s, terrorists are to the early twenty-first century. After 9/11, fear of social unraveling has been replaced by anxiety over airplanes, bombs, and instant mass annihilation. Stephen Griffiths isn't the new Jeffrey Dahmer. The Times Square bomber is.   11

Journal Writing

Since Beam wrote this essay, "something like the Bath School massacre" (par. 11) *did* occur. On December 14, 2012, a shooter forced his way into Sandy Hook Elementary School in Newtown, Connecticut, murdering twenty children and six adults before turning the gun on himself. And as Beam predicted, the slaughter of innocents touched a nerve in the national consciousness. How did you react to the news? In your journal, write down what you recall most vividly about your emotions in the wake of the shooting.

Questions on Meaning

1. What seems to be Beam's primary PURPOSE in this piece? Does he want to inform his readers about a trend? express relief that serial killings are on the decline? expose a new threat to public safety? propose a theory? How can you tell?

2. Although Beam gives details about some of the killers he discusses, he mentions others — such as the Beltway sniper, the Grim Sleeper, David Berkowitz, the Times Square bomber — without explaining who they are or what they did. Why? What ASSUMPTIONS does he make about his readers' interests and knowledge? Must one be familiar with the particulars of the crimes Beam cites to understand his point?

3. According to Beam, what role do the media play in the rise and fall of certain types of crime? Does he really mean to suggest that journalists are at least partly to blame for the spike in serial murders in the 1980s?

4. How would you summarize Beam's THESIS? Where in the essay does he state it most directly?

Questions on Writing Strategy

1. Why do you think Beam opens his essay as he does? What is the EFFECT of this opening?

2. What does Beam mean by "structural explanations" (par. 5)? What point is he making here?

3. How does Beam explain the drop in serial killings over the past two decades? What possible causes does he dismiss?

4. In paragraph 4 and the bar graph on page 421, Beam cites a number of statistics, or facts expressed numerically. How reliable are these statistics? What do they accomplish?

5. **OTHER METHODS**   Where in the essay does Beam use DEFINITION to clarify the meaning of *serial murder*?

Questions on Language

1. Find some examples of formal and informal DICTION in the essay. What is the effect of Beam's word choice?

2. What does Beam mean by "golden boy" in paragraph 7? What are the CONNOTATIONS of this term, especially as applied to Ted Bundy?

3. If any of the following words are new to you, look them up in a dictionary: crossbow, misanthropic, criminology (par. 1); incarceration, caveat (6); feigned (7); erroneous, epidemic (8); needle (9); conversely, eclipsed (10); annihilation (11).

Suggestions for Writing

1. **FROM JOURNAL TO ESSAY**   The horror at Newtown, and several mass shootings since then, has sparked a movement to stop publicizing the names of shooters, as the media attention is thought to encourage others to seek a similar limelight. Research the major ARGUMENTS that have taken shape on both sides of the issue since December 2012. Then build on the emotions you described in your journal entry (p. 419) to argue your position on some aspect of the debate. Do mass murderers kill for the attention, or do other motives come into play? Can their actions be considered a form of terrorism? How has the continued threat of such attacks affected your life and the lives of others you know? How has the threat affected the country more generally? Do journalists have an obligation to identify

mass shooters by name, or should they focus solely on the victims? Why do you think so? Make appropriate emotional APPEALS as you draft your essay, but be sure to keep your argument grounded in reason.

2. Choose a subject that has seen significant change in the past twenty years or so — for example, gender roles, communication technology, fashion, manners, a particular sport, ideals of beauty, or attitudes toward a particular group such as gays and lesbians, African Americans, Muslims, or immigrants. Do some research on the topic, and then write an essay that examines the causes and effects of the change. Support your essay with specific EVIDENCE from your experience, observation, and research.

3. **CRITICAL WRITING** Take a close look at Beam's use of SUMMARY, PARAPHRASE, and direct QUOTATION. In an essay, analyze the way he SYNTHESIZES information and ideas from SOURCES. Why does he quote directly where he does? How effective are his summaries and paraphrases? How does he combine source materials to develop a thesis of his own?

4. **CONNECTIONS** Like Christopher Beam, Guillermo del Toro and Chuck Hogan, in "Vampires Never Die" (p. 330), and Alain de Botton, in "Tragedy" (p. 240), also examine mass media. What do news outlets have in common with popular culture productions such as movies and TV dramas? How are they different? Drawing on the ideas presented in all three essays as well as your own experience and observations, write an essay of your own that considers the ways in which the media both reflect and shape cultural anxieties, whether for good or bad.

MALCOLM GLADWELL

Malcolm Gladwell is a celebrated staff writer at the *New Yorker*, where he has earned a reputation for producing highly readable articles that synthesize complex research in the social sciences. Born in 1963 to an English mathematics professor and a Jamaican psychotherapist, he emigrated from England to Canada with his parents in 1969. After receiving his bachelor's degree in history from the University of Toronto, Gladwell worked for the *Washington Post* as a science and medicine reporter and later as chief of the *Post*'s New York bureau. In 2000 he published *The Tipping Point*, an examination of how trends catch on. The book was a breakout success and landed Gladwell on *Time* magazine's list of the hundred most influential people in the world. He has since followed it with four more best-sellers: *Blink* (2005), an argument for acting impulsively; *Outliers* (2008), an exploration of what makes some people more successful than others; *What the Dog Saw* (2009), a collection of his *New Yorker* essays; and *David and Goliath* (2013), a look at the advantages of being disadvantaged.

Little Fish in a Big Pond

Do the "best" universities provide the best opportunities? In "Little Fish in a Big Pond" (editors' title), abridged from a chapter in *David and Goliath*, Gladwell focuses on the experience of one Ivy League biology major to detail the implications of several studies conducted by sociologists, psychologists, and education specialists. Dropped into a competitive environment, he discovers, many of the best students will fail — but only if they perceive that others are winning. Understanding this paradox, Gladwell suggests, could be the key to curbing the shortage of scientists and engineers in the United States.

Note that Gladwell uses a combination of footnotes and end notes to provide citations for the academic studies he refers to and quotes. He does not follow any widely used documentation system (such as MLA or APA), but nonetheless provides clear information about each of the sources that inform his analysis.

Caroline Sacks[1] grew up on the farthest fringes of the Washington, DC, metropolitan area. She went to public schools through high school. Her mother is an accountant and her father works for a technology company. As a child she sang in the church choir and loved to write and draw. But what really excited her was science.

"I did a lot of crawling around in the grass with a magnifying glass and a sketchbook, following bugs and drawing them," Sacks says. She is a thoughtful

---

[1] I've changed her name and identifying details.

and articulate young woman, with a refreshing honesty and directness. "I was really, really into bugs. And sharks. So for a while I thought I was going to be a veterinarian or an ichthyologist. Eugenie Clark was my hero. She was the first woman diver. She grew up in New York City in a family of immigrants and ended up rising to the top of her field, despite having a lot of 'Oh, you're a woman, you can't go under the ocean' setbacks. I just thought she was great. My dad met her and was able to give me a signed photo and I was really excited. Science was always a really big part of what I did."

Sacks sailed through high school at the top of her class. She took a political science course at a nearby college while she was still in high school, as well as a multivariant calculus course at the local community college. She got As in both, as well as an A in every class she took in high school. She got perfect scores on every one of her Advanced Placement pre-college courses.   3

The summer after her junior year in high school, her father took her on a whirlwind tour of American universities. "I think we looked at five schools in three days," she says. "It was Wesleyan, Brown, Providence College, Boston College, and Yale. Wesleyan was fun but very small. Yale was cool, but I definitely didn't fit the vibe." But Brown University, in Providence, Rhode Island, won her heart. It is small and exclusive, situated in the middle of a nineteenth-century neighborhood of redbrick Georgian and Colonial buildings on the top of a gently sloping hill. It might be the most beautiful college campus in the United States. She applied to Brown, with the University of Maryland as her backup. A few months later, she got a letter in the mail. She was in.   4

"I expected that everyone at Brown would be really rich and worldly and knowledgeable," she says. "Then I got there, and everybody seemed to be just like me — intellectually curious and kind of nervous and excited and not sure whether they'd be able to make friends. It was very reassuring." The hardest part was choosing which courses to take, because she loved the sound of everything. She ended up in Introductory Chemistry, Spanish, a class called the Evolution of Language, and Botanical Roots of Modern Medicine, which she describes as "sort of half botany class, half looking at uses of indigenous plants as medicine and what kind of chemical theories they are based on." She was in heaven.   5

Did Caroline Sacks make the right choice? Most of us would say that she did. When she went on that whirlwind tour with her father, she ranked the colleges she saw, from best to worst. Brown University was number one. The University of Maryland was her backup because it was not in any way as good a school as Brown. Brown is a member of the Ivy League. It has more resources, more academically able students, more prestige, and more accomplished faculty than the University of Maryland. In the rankings of American colleges published every year by the magazine *US News & World Report*,   6

Brown routinely places among the top ten or twenty colleges in the United States. The University of Maryland finishes much farther back in the pack.

But let's think about Caroline's decision. . . . [Hers] was a choice between two very *different* options, each with its own strengths and drawbacks. . . . She could be a Big Fish at the University of Maryland, or a Little Fish at one of the most prestigious universities in the world. She chose the [latter] — and she ended up paying a high price.

7

The trouble for Caroline Sacks began in the spring of her freshman year, when she enrolled in chemistry. She was probably taking too many courses, she realizes now, and doing too many extracurricular activities. She got her grade on her third midterm exam, and her heart sank. She went to talk to the professor. "He ran me through some exercises, and he said, 'Well, you have a fundamental deficiency in some of these concepts, so what I would actually recommend is that you drop the class, not bother with the final exam, and take the course again next fall.'" So she did what the professor suggested. She retook the course in the fall of her sophomore year. But she barely did any better. She got a low B. She was in shock. "I had never gotten a B in an academic context before," she said. "I had never *not* excelled. And I was taking the class for the second time, this time as a sophomore, and most of the kids in the class were first-semester freshmen. It was pretty disheartening."

8

She had known when she was accepted to Brown that it wasn't going to be like high school. It couldn't be. She wasn't going to be the smartest girl in the class anymore — and she'd accepted that fact. "I figured, regardless of how much I prepared, there would be kids who had been exposed to stuff I had never even heard of. So I was trying not to be naive about that." But chemistry was beyond what she had imagined. The students in her class were *competitive.* "I had a lot of trouble even talking with people from those classes," she went on. "They didn't want to share their study habits with me. They didn't want to talk about ways to better understand the stuff that we were learning, because that might give me a leg up."

9

In spring of her sophomore year, she enrolled in organic chemistry — and things only got worse. She couldn't do it: "You memorize how a concept works, and then they give you a molecule you've never seen before, and they ask you to make another one you've never seen before, and you have to get from this thing to that thing. There are people who just think that way and in five minutes are done. They're the curve busters. Then there are people who through an amazing amount of hard work trained themselves to think that way. I worked *so* hard and I never got it down." The teacher would ask a question, and around her, hands would go up, and Sacks would sit in silence and listen to everyone else's brilliant answers. "It was just this feeling of overwhelming inadequacy."

10

One night she stayed up late, preparing for a review session in organic   11
chemistry. She was miserable and angry. She didn't want to be working on
organic chemistry at three in the morning, when all of that work didn't seem
to be getting her anywhere. "I guess that was when I started thinking that
maybe I shouldn't pursue this any further," she said. She'd had enough.

The tragic part was that Sacks *loved* science. As she talked about her   12
abandonment of her first love, she mourned all the courses she would have
loved to take but now never would — physiology, infectious disease, biology,
math. In the summer after her sophomore year, she agonized over her decision: "When I was growing up, it was a subject of much pride to be able to say
that, you know, 'I'm a seven-year-old girl, and I love bugs! And I want to study
them, and I read up on them all the time, and I draw them in my sketchbook
and label all the different parts of them and talk about where they live and
what they do.' Later it was 'I am so interested in people and how the human
body works, and isn't this amazing?' There is definitely a sort of pride that goes
along with 'I am a science girl,' and it's almost shameful for me to leave that
behind and say, 'Oh, well, I am going to do something easier because I can't
take the heat.' For a while, that is the only way I was looking at it, like I have
completely failed. This has been my goal and I can't do it."

And it shouldn't have mattered how Sacks did in organic chemistry,   13
should it? She never wanted to be an organic chemist. It was just a course.
Lots of people find organic chemistry impossible. It's not uncommon for pre-
med students to take organic chemistry over the summer at another college
just to give themselves a full semester of practice. What's more, Sacks was
taking organic chemistry at an extraordinarily competitive and academically
rigorous university. If you were to rank all the students in the world who are
taking organic chemistry, Sacks would probably be in the 99th percentile.

But the problem was, Sacks wasn't comparing herself to all the students   14
in the world taking organic chemistry. She was comparing herself to her fellow students at Brown. She was a Little Fish in one of the deepest and most
competitive ponds in the country — and the experience of comparing herself
to all the other brilliant fish shattered her confidence. It made her feel stupid,
even though she isn't stupid at all. "Wow, other people are mastering this,
even people who were as clueless as I was in the beginning, and I just can't
seem to learn to think in this manner."

Caroline Sacks was experiencing what is called "relative deprivation," a   15
term coined by the sociologist Samuel Stouffer during the Second World War.
Stouffer was commissioned by the US Army to examine the attitudes and
morale of American soldiers, and he ended up studying half a million men and
women, looking at everything from how soldiers viewed their commanding

officers to how black soldiers felt they were being treated to how difficult soldiers found it to serve in isolated outposts.

But one set of questions Stouffer asked stood out. He quizzed both soldiers   16
serving in the Military Police and those serving in the Air Corps (the forerunner of the Air Force) about how good a job they thought their service did in
recognizing and promoting people of ability. The answer was clear. Military
Policemen had a far more positive view of their organization than did enlisted
men in the Air Corps.

On the face of it, that made no sense. The Military Police had one of   17
the worst rates of promotion in all of the armed forces. The Air Corps had
one of the best. The chance of an enlisted man rising to officer status in the
Air Corps was *twice* that of a soldier in the Military Police. So, why on earth
would the Military Policemen be more satisfied? The answer, Stouffer famously
explained, is that Military Policemen compared themselves only to other Military Policemen. And if you got a promotion in the Military Police, that was
such a rare event that you were very happy. And if you didn't get promoted,
you were in the same boat as most of your peers — so you weren't *that* unhappy.

"Contrast him with the Air Corps man of the same education and longev-   18
ity," Stouffer wrote. His chance of getting promoted to officer was greater than
50%. "If he had earned a [promotion], so had the majority of his fellows in the
branch, and his achievement was less conspicuous than in the MP's. If he had
failed to earn a rating while the majority had succeeded, he had more reason
to feel a sense of personal frustration, which could be expressed as criticism of
the promotion system."

Stouffer's point is that we form our impressions not globally, by placing   19
ourselves in the broadest possible context, but locally — by comparing ourselves to people "in the same boat as ourselves." Our sense of how deprived
we are is *relative*. . . .

Caroline Sacks's decision to evaluate herself, then, by looking around her   20
organic chemistry classroom was not some strange and irrational behavior. It
is what human beings do. We compare ourselves to those in the same situation
as ourselves, which means that students in an elite school — except, perhaps,
those at the very top of the class — are going to face a burden that they would
not face in a less competitive atmosphere. . . . Students at "great" schools look
at the brilliant students around them, and how do you think they feel?

The phenomenon of relative deprivation applied to education is   21
called — appropriately enough — the "Big Fish–Little Pond Effect." The more
elite an educational institution is, the worse students feel about their own academic abilities. Students who would be at the top of their class at a good school
can easily fall to the bottom of a really good school. Students who would feel
that they have mastered a subject at a good school can have the feeling that

they are falling farther and farther behind in a *really* good school. And that feeling — as subjective and ridiculous and irrational as it may be — *matters.* How you feel about your abilities — your academic "self-concept" — in the context of your classroom shapes your willingness to tackle challenges and finish difficult tasks. It's a crucial element in your motivation and confidence.

The Big Fish–Little Pond theory was pioneered by the psychologist Herbert Marsh, and to Marsh, most parents and students make their school choices for the wrong reasons. "A lot of people think that going to an academically selective school is going to be good," he said. "That's just not true. The reality is that it is going to be *mixed.*" . . .

What happened to Caroline Sacks is all too common. More than half of all American students who start out in science, technology, and math programs (or STEM, as they are known) drop out after their first or second year. Even though a science degree is just about the most valuable asset a young person can have in the modern economy, large numbers of would-be STEM majors end up switching into the arts, where academic standards are less demanding and the coursework less competitive. That's the major reason that there is such a shortage of qualified American-educated scientists and engineers in the United States.

To get a sense of who is dropping out — and why — let's take a look at the science enrollment of a school in upstate New York called Hartwick College. It's a small liberal arts college of the sort that is common in the American Northeast.

Here are all the Hartwick STEM majors divided into three groups — top third, middle third, and bottom third — according to their test scores in mathematics. The scores are from the SAT, the exam used by many American colleges as an admissions test. The mathematics section of the test is out of 800 points.[2]

STEM majors	Top Third	Middle Third	Bottom Third
Math SAT	569	472	407

If we take the SAT as a guide, there's a pretty big difference in raw math ability between the best and the poorest students at Hartwick.

Now let's look at the portion of all science degrees at Hartwick that are earned by each of those three groups.

STEM degrees	Top Third	Middle Third	Bottom Third
Percent	55.0	27.1	17.8

[2] These statistics are derived from a paper entitled "The Role of Ethnicity in Choosing and Leaving Science in Highly Selective Institutions" by the sociologists Rogers Elliott and A. Christopher Strenta et al. The SAT scores are from the early 1990s, and may be somewhat different today.

The students in the top third at Hartwick earn well over half of the school's science degrees. The bottom third end up earning only 17.8% of Hartwick's science degrees. The students who come into Hartwick with the poorest levels of math ability are dropping out of math and science in droves. This much seems like common sense. Learning the advanced mathematics and physics necessary to become an engineer or scientist is really hard — and only a small number of students clustered at the top of the class are smart enough to handle the material.

Now let's do the same analysis for Harvard, one of the most prestigious universities in the world.   27

STEM degrees	Top Third	Middle Third	Bottom Third
Math SAT	753	674	581

Harvard students, not surprisingly, score far higher on the math SAT than their counterparts at Hartwick. In fact, the students in Harvard's bottom third have higher scores than the *best* students at Hartwick. If getting a science degree is about how smart you are, then virtually everyone at Harvard should end up with a degree — right? At least on paper, there is no one at Harvard who lacks the intellectual firepower to master the coursework. Well, let's take a look at the portion of degrees that are earned by each group.

STEM degrees	Top Third	Middle Third	Bottom Third
Percent	53.4	31.2	15.4

Isn't that strange? The students in the bottom third of the Harvard class drop out of math and science just as much as their counterparts in upstate New York. *Harvard has the same distribution of science degrees as Hartwick.*

Think about this for a moment. We have a group of high achievers at   28
Hartwick. Let's call them the Hartwick All-Stars. And we've got another group of lower achievers at Harvard. Let's call them the Harvard Dregs. Each is studying the same textbooks and wrestling with the same concepts and try-ing to master the same problem sets in courses like advanced calculus and organic chemistry, and according to test scores, they are of roughly equal aca-demic ability. But the overwhelming majority of Hartwick All-Stars get what they want and end up as engineers or biologists. Meanwhile, the Harvard Dregs — who go to the far more prestigious school — are so demoralized by their experience that many of them drop out of science entirely and transfer to some nonscience major. The Harvard Dregs are Little Fish in a Very Big and Scary Pond. The Hartwick All-Stars are Big Fish in a Very Welcoming Small Pond. What matters, in determining the likelihood of getting a science degree, is not just how smart you are. It's how smart you *feel* relative to the other people in your classroom. . . .

Let's go back, then, and reconstruct what Caroline Sacks's thinking should 29 have been when faced with the choice between Brown and the University of Maryland. By going to Brown, she would benefit from the prestige of the university. She might have more interesting and wealthier peers. The connections she made at school and the brand value of Brown on her diploma might give her a leg up on the job market. These are all classic Big Pond advantages. . . .

But she would be taking a risk. She would dramatically increase her chances 30 of dropping out of science entirely. How large was that risk? According to research done by Mitchell Chang of the University of California, the likelihood of someone completing a STEM degree — all things being equal — rises by 2 percentage points for every 10-point decrease in the university's average SAT score.[3] The smarter your peers, the dumber you feel; the dumber you feel, the more likely you are to drop out of science. Since there is roughly a 150-point gap between the average SAT scores of students attending the University of Maryland and Brown, the "penalty" Sacks paid by choosing a great school over a good school is that she reduced her chances of graduating with a science degree by 30%. *Thirty percent!* At a time when students with liberal arts degrees struggle to find jobs, students with STEM degrees are almost assured of good careers. Jobs for people with science and engineering degrees are plentiful and highly paid. That's a very large risk to take for the prestige of an Ivy League school. . . .

Parents still tell their children to go to the best schools they possibly can, 31 on the grounds that the best schools will allow them to do whatever they wish. We take it for granted that the Big Pond expands opportunities, just as we take it for granted that a smaller class is always a better class. We have a definition in our heads of what an advantage is — and the definition isn't right. And what happens as a result? It means that we make mistakes. It means that we misread battles between underdogs and giants. It means that we underestimate

---

[3] This is a crucial enough point that it is worth spelling out in more detail. Chang and his coauthors looked at a sample of several thousand first-year college students and measured which factors played the biggest role in a student's likelihood of dropping out of science. The most important factor? How academically able the university's students were. "For every 10-point increase in the average SAT score of an entering cohort of freshmen at a given institution, the likelihood of retention decreased by two percentage points," the authors write. Interestingly, if you look just at students who are members of ethnic minorities, the numbers are even higher. Every 10-point increase in SAT score causes retention to fall by *three* percentage points. "Students who attend what they considered to be their first-choice school were less likely to persist in a biomedical or behavioral science major," they write. You think you want to go to the fanciest school you can. You don't.

how much freedom there can be in what looks like a disadvantage. It's the Little Pond that maximizes your chances to do whatever you want.

At the time she was applying to college, Caroline Sacks had no idea   32
she was taking that kind of chance with the thing she loved. Now she does. At the end of our talk, I asked her what would have happened if she had chosen instead to go to the University of Maryland — to be, instead, a Big Fish in a Little Pond. She answered without hesitation: "I'd still be in science."

Notes

The first academic paper to raise the issue of relative deprivation with respect to school choice was James Davis's "The Campus as Frog Pond: An Application of the Theory of Relative Deprivation to Career Decisions of College Men," *The American Journal of Sociology* 72, no. 1 (July 1966). Davis concludes:

> At the level of the individual, [my findings] challenge the notion that getting into the "best possible" school is the most efficient route to occupational mobility. Counselors and parents might well consider the drawbacks as well as the advantages of sending a boy to a "fine" college, if, when doing so, it is fairly certain he will end up in the bottom ranks of his graduating class. The aphorism "It is better to be a big frog in a small pond than a small frog in a big pond" is not perfect advice, but it is not trivial.

Stouffer's study (coauthored with Edward A. Suchman, Leland C. De Vinney, Shirley A. Star, and Robin M. Williams Jr.) appears in *The American Soldier: Adjustment During Army Life*, vol. 1 of *Studies in Social Psychology in World War II* (Princeton University Press, 1949), 251.

Herbert Marsh teaches in the Department of Education at Oxford University. His academic output over the course of his career has been extraordinary. On the subject of "Big Fish/Little Pond" alone, he has written countless papers. A good place to start is H. Marsh, M. Seaton, et al., "The Big-Fish-Little-Pond-Effect Stands Up to Critical Scrutiny: Implications for Theory, Methodology, and Future Research," *Educational Psychology Review* 20 (2008): 319–50.

For statistics on STEM programs, see Rogers Elliott, A. Christopher Strenta, et al., "The Role of Ethnicity in Choosing and Leaving Science in Highly Selective Institutions," *Research in Higher Education* 37, no. 6 (December 1996), and Mitchell Chang, Oscar Cerna, et al., "The Contradictory Roles of Institutional Status in Retaining Underrepresented Minorities in Biomedical and Behavioral Science Majors," *The Review of Higher Education* 31, no. 4 (Summer 2008).

Journal Writing

Are you enrolled in the college of your top choice, or did you have to settle for a "backup" (par. 6) school? Have you taken, or do you plan to take, any difficult courses of the sort Gladwell describes? How do you respond to his characterizations of STEM majors and liberal arts students? Are you reassured, insulted, thankful for his advice? Why? Express your reactions to his cause-and-effect analysis in your journal.

Questions on Meaning

1. What would you say is the author's PURPOSE in this essay?

2. What is "relative deprivation" (par. 15), as Gladwell explains it?

3. SUMMARIZE what Gladwell means by the "Big Fish–Little Pond Effect" (par. 21). How does this effect apply to college students in general? How, if at all, does it apply to you?

4. Gladwell states his THESIS near the end of his essay. What is it? Why doesn't he include it in his introduction?

Questions on Writing Strategy

1. Does Gladwell expect that readers will actually be able to use the information he provides? How can you tell?

2. Why, according to Gladwell, do "[m]ore than half of all American students who start out in science, technology, and math programs . . . drop out after their first or second year" (par. 23)? How does he support this claim?

3. Gladwell is known for weaving together multiple strands of apparently unrelated materials in his work, and this excerpt from *David and Goliath* is no exception (in fact, the ellipsis marks you see throughout it show where we've omitted some of the original chapter's other strands). To better understand Gladwell's method, sketch an outline of the cause-and-effect analysis offered here. How effective do you find his ORGANIZATION? How does Gladwell integrate the strands to achieve UNITY?

4. **OTHER METHODS**   How does Gladwell use a single extended EXAMPLE to support his explanation of why smart students struggle?

Questions on Language

1. How would you characterize Gladwell's DICTION and TONE? Are they appropriate for a formal analysis? Why, or why not?

2. What does Gladwell mean when he says "Sacks sailed through high school" (par. 3)? Where else does he return to this metaphor? (See FIGURES OF SPEECH in

the Glossary if you need a definition of *metaphor*.) What makes it a particularly effective use of figurative language, given his subject?

3. Consult a dictionary if you are unsure of the meanings of any of the following terms: articulate, ichthyologist (par. 2); multivariant calculus (3); Georgian, Colonial (4); botanical/botany, indigenous (5); latter (7); disheartening (8); naive (9); rigorous, percentile (13); forerunner (16); conspicuous (18); subjective (21); droves (26); distribution (27); demoralized (28); reconstruct (29).

4. Gladwell uses words like *elite* and *prestigious*, and also words like *deficiency* and *inadequacy*, several times in this essay. What are the usual CONNOTATIONS of these words? How does the repetition of key terms help emphasize the author's point?

Suggestions for Writing

1. **JOURNAL TO ESSAY**   What is the purpose of a liberal arts education? Building on your journal writing (p. 431), draft an essay in which you explain what you expect to learn in college and how you might apply your education as a working adult. Does it matter what school you attend or what subject you major in? What kinds of classes are most useful, and why? You might expand your thinking to include advice you would give a friend or relative who was considering what colleges to apply to and what subject to major in.

2. Rising tuition rates and accompanying rates of student debt have sparked significant controversy in recent years. Research explanations for the increases and some of the solutions that policy makers and pundits have proposed. Then write an essay in which you SUMMARIZE your findings. If your research — or your experience as a tuition-paying student — leads you to form an opinion for or against any of the proposals for change, present and support that as well.

3. **CRITICAL WRITING**   Gladwell's cause-and-effect analysis relies on a series of interviews he conducted with one student as well as expert opinion and other EVIDENCE from published sources. Write an essay in which you discuss how effective, or ineffective, you find his SYNTHESIS of source materials to be. You might examine, for instance, his use of SUMMARY, PARAPHRASE, and QUOTATION; consider why he provides source notes at the end but doesn't use formal citations in his text; or explore what else, if anything, he might have brought in to support his analysis.

4. **CONNECTIONS**   In "The Undercurrent" (p. 189), Kellie Young writes about the emotional pressures of being a first-year student at the Massachusetts Institute of Technology, another elite school on a par with Harvard or Brown. Read her reflections, and then write an essay that considers how her experiences compare to those of Caroline Sacks as portrayed by Malcolm Gladwell — as well as to your own experiences and those of your classmates. How do Gladwell's theories hold up when applied to a broader cross-section of people? Besides dropping out, what are some other consequences of the pressure faced by contemporary college students — including positive consequences, if you think there are any?

Malcolm Gladwell on Writing

As a professional researcher, Malcolm Gladwell has tackled a dizzying array of subjects, among them dogs, football, homelessness, ketchup, police tactics, professional success, and decision making. In a 2015 interview for the entrepreneurial podcast *Dorm Room Tycoon*, host William Channer asked Gladwell how he decides what to write about. "I tend to start with a puzzle," Gladwell answered. "Something that I don't entirely understand or can't entirely explain or some kind of story that poses a really interesting question. There are many, many ways into that. Sometimes the puzzle is sparked by someone you meet, someone you read about, something you read, some piece of research you stumble across. . . . A lot of stumbling goes on. In fact I depend on the stumbling. One of the things I like to do in my writing is to put together things that are quite different in many respects but have a surprising similarity. I do that a lot. That is the direct fruit of stumbling on to things."

The stumbling continues throughout Gladwell's writing process. "Like most serious writers," Gladwell explains, he puts in "many, many, many, many drafts." He goes on: "I might do at least four or five or maybe six or seven serious drafts" of a piece. "I have an expectation when I'm writing that it's all going to change. There's no necessity of getting it right the first time. In fact the first drafts I write are often not just in terms of the sentences a long way from where I end up but in the arguments as well. I expect the arguments to change. I'm getting a version of the argument in place and then when I think about it, I adjust it as I go because the process of writing an argument and the process of formulating an argument . . . happens at the same time. It's not a matter that you figured it all out then you write it down. I think as you're writing it down, you're figuring it out."

The Bedford Reader on Writing

Gladwell's work depends on researching the answers to interesting questions, a process we explain on pages 624–28 of the Appendix. You'll find advice on stumbling into and refining what Gladwell calls an "argument" and we call a THESIS on pages 35–36 and 40–41 of Chapter 2.

ADDITIONAL WRITING TOPICS

Cause and Effect

1. In *Blue Highways* (1982), an account of his rambles around the United States, William Least Heat-Moon explains why Americans, and not the British, settled the vast tract of northern land that lies between the Mississippi and the Rockies. He traces what he believes to be the major cause in this paragraph:

   > Were it not for a web-footed rodent and a haberdashery fad in eighteenth-century Europe, Minnesota might be a Canadian province today. The beaver, almost as much as the horse, helped shape the course of early American history. Some *Mayflower* colonists paid their passage with beaver pelts; and a good fur could bring an Indian three steel knives or a five-foot stack could bring a musket. But even more influential were the trappers and fur traders penetrating the great Northern wilderness between the Mississippi River and the Rocky Mountains, since it was their presence that helped hold the Near West against British expansion from the north; and it was their explorations that opened the heart of the nation to white settlement. These men, by making pelts the currency of the wilds, laid the base for a new economy that quickly overwhelmed the old. And all because European men of mode simply had to wear a beaver hat.

   In a Heat-Moon–like paragraph of your own, explain how a small cause produced a large effect. You might generate ideas by browsing in a history book—where you might find, for instance, that a cow belonging to Mrs. Patrick O'Leary is believed to have started the Great Chicago Fire of 1871 by kicking over a lighted lantern—or a collection of *Ripley's Believe It or Not*. If some small event in your life has had large consequences, you might care to write instead from personal experience.

2. In an essay, explain *either* the causes *or* the effects of a situation that concerns you. Narrow your topic enough to treat it in some detail, and provide more than a mere list of causes or effects. If you focus on causes, you will have to decide carefully how far back to go in your search for remote causes. If stating effects, fill your essay with examples. Here are some topics to consider:

   Labor strikes in professional sports
   Rising hostility in partisan politics
   State laws mandating the use of seat belts in cars or the wearing of helmets when riding motorcycles
   Efforts to make police forces more ethnically diverse
   The fact that women increasingly take jobs formerly regarded as being for men only, and vice versa
   Some quirk in your personality, or a friend's
   Income inequality
   The invention of 3D printing
   The popularity of a particular TV program, comic strip, or performer
   The steady increase in college costs

The absence of a military draft

The fact that many couples are choosing to have only one child, or none at all

Being "born again"

The emphasis on competitive sports in high school and college

The pressure on students to get a good grade

The scarcity of people training for employment as skilled workers: plumbers, tool and die makers, electricians, masons, and carpenters, to name a few

I have amazing eyes, an
infectious laugh, and I
always know when
you need
a hug.

INTERNATIONAL DOWN SYNDROME COALITION
www.idscforlife.org

I also have Down syndrome.
It's a part of me, not a
definition of who I am.

International Down Syndrome Coalition

11

DEFINITION

Tracing Boundaries

◀ **Definition in a poster**

This social media poster doesn't define *Down syndrome*. Instead, it invites viewers to rethink their assumptions about people who have the condition. The poster is part of a "photo campaign" launched by the International Down Syndrome Coalition, a volunteer support and advocacy group. Family members submit pictures of their loved ones and work with the IDSC to create captions that highlight the dignity and achievements of people with Down syndrome; the group then distributes the posters on *Twitter, Facebook*, and *Pinterest*. Who seem to be the intended viewers of such photos? What goals of the advocacy group does the campaign seem meant to address? What needs and concerns in viewers might the poster appeal to? What does the photograph of the girl contribute to the appeal? What does the text contribute, and why are some words printed in color? At the same time, what concerns in viewers does the poster ignore or even reject?

THE METHOD

As a rule, when we hear the word DEFINITION, we immediately think of a
dictionary. In that helpful storehouse — a writer's best friend — we find the
literal and specific meaning (or meanings) of a word. The dictionary supplies
this information concisely: in a sentence, in a phrase, or even in a *synonym* — a
single word that means the same thing ("**narrative** [năr-e-tǐv] *n*. **1:** story . . .").

Stating such a definition is often a good way to begin an essay when basic
terms may be in doubt. A short definition can clarify your subject to your
reader, and perhaps help you limit what you have to say. If, for instance, you
are writing a psychology paper about schizophrenia, you might offer a short
definition at the outset, clarifying your subject and your key term.

In constructing a short definition, the usual procedure is to state the
general class to which the subject belongs and then add any particular features that distinguish it. You could say: "Schizophrenia is a brain
disease" — the general class — "whose symptoms include hallucinations,
disorganized behavior, incoherence, and, often, withdrawal." Short definitions are useful whenever you introduce a technical term that readers may
not know.

When a term is central to your essay or likely to be misunderstood, a
stipulative definition may be more helpful. This fuller explanation stipulates,
or specifies, the particular way you are using a term. The following paragraph,
defining *TV addiction*, could serve as a stipulative definition in an essay about
the causes and cures of the addiction.

> Who is addicted to television? According to Marie Winn, author of *The
> Plug-in Drug: Television, Children, and Family Life*, TV addicts are similar to
> drug or alcohol addicts: They seek a more pleasurable experience than they
> can get from normal life; they depend on the source of this pleasure; and
> their lives are damaged by their dependency. TV addicts, says Winn, use tele-
> vision to screen out the real world of feelings, worries, demands. They watch
> compulsively — four, five, even six hours on a work day. And they reject
> (usually passively, sometimes actively) interaction with family or friends,
> work at hobbies or chores, and chances for change and growth.

In this chapter we are mainly concerned with *extended definition*, a kind
of expository writing that relies on a variety of other methods. Suppose you
wanted to write an essay to make clear what *poetry* means. You would specify its
elements — rhythm, IMAGES, and so on — by using DIVISION or ANALYSIS. You'd
probably provide EXAMPLES of each element. You might COMPARE AND CONTRAST
poetry with prose. You might discuss the EFFECT of poetry on the reader. In fact,
extended definition is perhaps less a method in itself than the application of a
variety of methods to achieve a purpose. Like DESCRIPTION, extended definition
tries to *show* a reader its subject. It does so by establishing boundaries, as its

writer tries to differentiate a subject from anything that might be confused with it.

An extended definition can define a word (like *poetry*), a thing (a laser beam), a condition (schizophrenia), a concept (TV addiction), or a general phenomenon (the popularity of *SnapChat*). Unlike a sentence definition or any you would find in a dictionary, an extended definition takes room: at least a paragraph, often an entire essay. Also unlike a dictionary definition, which sets forth meaning in an unimpassioned manner, an extended definition often reflects or champions the author's bias. When Tal Fortgang, in his essay in this chapter, seeks to define the word *privilege*, he examines his experiences as a white male, specifying the meaning of his subject in a particular political context.

THE PROCESS

Discovery of Meanings

The purpose of almost any extended definition is to explore a topic in its full complexity, to explain its meaning or sometimes to argue for (or against) a particular meaning. To discover this complexity, you may find it useful to ask yourself the following questions. To illustrate how the questions might work, at least in one instance, let's say you plan to write a paper defining *sexism*.[1]

- **Is this subject unique, or are there others of its kind? If it resembles others, in what ways? How is it different?** These questions invite you to compare and contrast. Applied to the concept of sexism, they might prompt you to compare sexism with one or two other -isms, such as racism or ageism. Or the questions might remind you that sexists can be both women and men, leading you to note the differences.

- **In what different forms does it occur, while keeping its own identity?** Specific examples might occur to you: a story you read about a woman's experiences in the army and a girlfriend who is nastily suspicious of all men. Each form — the soldier and the girlfriend — might rate a description.

- **When and where do we find it? Under what circumstances and in what situations?** Well, where have you been lately? at any parties where sexism reared its ugly head? in any classroom discussions? Consider other areas of your experience: Did you encounter any sexists while holding a job?

---

[1] The six questions that follow are freely adapted from those first stated by Richard E. Young, Alton L. Becker, and Kenneth L. Pike in *Rhetoric: Discovery and Change* (1970).

Definition

- **What is it at the present moment?** Perhaps you might make the point that sexism was once considered an exclusively male preserve but is now an attribute of women as well. Or you could observe that many men have gone underground with their sexism, refraining from expressing it blatantly while still harboring negative attitudes about women. In either case you might care to draw examples from life.

- **What does it do? What are its functions and activities?** Sexists stereotype and sometimes act to exclude or oppress people of the opposite sex. These questions might also invite you to reply with a PROCESS ANALYSIS: You might show, for instance, how a personnel director who determines pay scales systematically eliminates women from better-paying jobs.

- **How is it put together? What parts make it up? What holds these parts together?** You could apply analysis to the various beliefs and assumptions that, all together, make up sexism. This question might work well in writing about an organization: the personnel director's company, for instance, with its unfair hiring and promotion policies.

Not all these questions will fit every subject under the sun, and some may lead nowhere, but you will usually find them well worth asking. They can make you aware of points to notice, remind you of facts you already know. They can also suggest interesting aspects you need to find out more about.

Methods of Development

The preceding questions will give you a good start in using whatever method or methods of writing can best answer the overall question "What is the nature of this subject?" You will probably find yourself making use of much that you have learned earlier in this book. A short definition like the one for *schizophrenia* on page 438 may be a good start for an essay, especially if readers need a quick grounding in the subject. (But feel no duty to place a dictionaryish definition in the INTRODUCTION of every essay you write: The device is overused.) In explaining schizophrenia, if your readers already have at least a vague idea of the meaning of the term and need no short, formal definition of it, you could open your extended definition with a description of the experiences of a person who has the disease:

> On his twenty-fifth birthday, Michael sensed danger everywhere. The voices in his head argued loudly about whether he should step outside. He could see people walking by who he knew meant him harm — the trick would be to wait for a break in the traffic and make a run for it. But the arguing and another noise — a clanging like a streetcar bell — made it difficult to concentrate, and Michael paced restlessly most of the day.

You could proceed from this opening to explain how Michael's experiences illustrate some symptoms of schizophrenia. You could provide other examples of symptoms. You could, through process analysis, explain how the disease generally starts and progresses. You could use CAUSE AND EFFECT to explore some theories of why schizophrenia develops.

Thesis

Opening up your subject with questions and developing it with various methods are good ways to see what it has to offer, but you might be left with a welter of ideas and a blurred focus. As in description, when all your details build to a DOMINANT IMPRESSION, so in definition you want to center all your ideas and evidence about the subject on a single controlling idea, a THESIS. It's not essential to state this idea in a THESIS STATEMENT, but it is essential that the idea govern.

Here, from the essays in this chapter, are two thesis statements. Notice how each makes an assertion about the subject, and how we can detect the author's bias toward the subject.

> I have checked my privilege. And I apologize for nothing.
> — Tal Fortgang, "Checking My Privilege"

> If you are reading this essay, you have some kind of privilege. It may be hard to hear that, I know, but if you cannot recognize your privilege, you have a lot of work to do; get started.
> — Roxane Gay, "Peculiar Benefits"

Evidence

Writing an extended definition, you are like a mapmaker charting a territory, taking in what lies within the boundaries and ignoring what's outside. The boundaries, of course, may be wide; and for this reason, drafting an extended definition sometimes tempts a writer to sweep across a continent and to soar off into abstract clouds. Like any other method of expository writing, though, definition will work only for the writer who remembers the world of the senses and supports every GENERALIZATION with concrete evidence.

Never lose sight of the reality you are attempting to enclose, even if its frontiers are as inclusive as those of *psychological burnout* or *human economic rights*. Give examples, narrate an illustrative story, bring in specific description — whatever method you use, keep coming back inside. Without your eyes on the world, you will define no reality. You might define *animal husbandry* till the cows come home and never make clear what it means.

Definition

FOCUS ON UNITY

When drafting a definition, you may find yourself being pulled away from your subject by the narratives, descriptions, examples, comparisons, and other methods you use to specify meaning. Let yourself explore the byways of your subject — doing so will help you discover what you think. But in revising you'll need to make sure that all paragraphs focus on your thesis and, within paragraphs, that all sentences focus on the paragraph topic, generally expressed in a TOPIC SENTENCE. In other words, you'll need to ensure the UNITY of your essay and its paragraphs.

Meghan Daum's "Narcissist — Give It a Rest" (p. 460), for instance, opens with a complaint that "a whole lot of people" (par. 1) are misusing the word as a general insult, then proceeds methodically to specify the word's meaning as Daum understands it. As shown in the following outline, the paragraphs begin with topic sentences that state parts of the definition, which Daum then illustrates with examples and analyses.

PARAGRAPH 2   The concept of narcissism as a broad cultural condition, and the word's use as an everyday term, goes back several decades. . . .

PARAGRAPH 3   But lately the word seems to be enjoying a resurgence, often among people who give the impression that they just discovered it. . . .

PARAGRAPH 5   Here's the problem with the charge of narcissism. . . .

PARAGRAPH 7   So perhaps it's time to declare a moratorium on the indiscriminate use of this particular n-word. . . .

CHECKLIST FOR REVISING A DEFINITION

✔ **Meanings.** Have you explored your subject fully, turning up both its obvious and its not-so-obvious meanings?

✔ **Methods of development.** Have you used an appropriate range of other methods to develop your subject?

✔ **Thesis.** Have you focused your definition and kept within that focus, drawing clear boundaries around your subject?

✔ **Evidence.** Is your definition specific? Do examples, anecdotes, and concrete details both pin the subject down and make it vivid for readers?

✔ **Unity.** Do all paragraphs focus on your thesis, and do individual paragraphs or groups of paragraphs focus on parts of your definition?

DEFINITION IN ACADEMIC WRITING

A Biology Textbook

This paragraph from *Life: The Science of Biology*, by William K. Purves and Gordon H. Orians, defines a term, *homology*, that is useful in explaining the evolution of different species from a common ancestor (the topic at this point in the textbook). The paragraph provides a brief definition, a more extensive one, and finally examples of the concept.

When the character traits found in any two species owe their resemblance to a common ancestry, taxonomists say the states are *homologous*, or are *homologues* of each other. *Homology* is defined as correspondence between two structures due to inheritance from a common ancestor. Homologous structures can be identical in appearance and can even be based on identical genes. However, such structures can diverge until they become very different in both appearance and function. Nevertheless, homologous structures usually retain certain basic features that betray a common ancestry. Consider the forelimbs of vertebrates. It is easy to make a detailed, bone-by-bone, muscle-by-muscle comparison of the forearm of a person and a monkey and to conclude that the forearms, as well as the various parts of the forearm, are homologous. The forelimb of a dog, however, shows marked differences from those of primates in both appearance and function. The forelimb is used for locomotion by dogs but for grasping and manipulation by people and monkeys. Even so, all of the bones can still be matched. The wing of a bird and the flipper of a seal are even more different from each other or from the human forearm, yet they too are constructed around bones that can be matched on a nearly perfect one-to-one basis.

Definition of homology *and related words*

Short definition

Refined definition

Examples:
- *Similar appearance, function, and structure*
- *Dissimilar appearance and function, but similar structure*

An Essay Exam

You might worry about essay exams — many students do — but take heart: Instructors who assign timed essays don't expect prize-winning compositions. They expect students to demonstrate their knowledge and critical thinking about important concepts covered in lectures and assignments.

Often you'll need to interpret the wording of an exam question to figure out what kind of response is appropriate. Questions that ask *why*, for example, might call for CAUSE-AND-EFFECT analysis, while those that ask *how* might lead to a PROCESS ANALYSIS. Keep in mind that an essay you write for an in-class exam will be less polished than one you write at home.

Definition

That's fine — as long as you draft an accurate, detailed, and coherent answer to the question asked.

The midterm exam for Martin Ward's introductory government class included multiple-choice questions, a short-answer section, and one essay question: "Explain the meaning of *civil liberties*, including an explanation of how civil liberties differ from civil rights." Ward quickly recognized that "explain the meaning of" called for a definition and that "differ" called for an element of COMPARISON AND CONTRAST. Following the advice of the teaching assistant in the exam review session, Ward quickly outlined the points he needed to cover before he started writing. Then he composed the following response.

Civil liberties are the freedoms that individuals have against state intrusion. Laws protecting civil liberties limit or prohibit government action. The Constitution's Bill of Rights guarantees many of these liberties, including freedom of expression, freedom of religion, and freedom from unreasonable searches and seizures. Historically, the protection of civil liberties was established before the US Constitution in documents such as the English Magna Carta (1215). Since that time, free countries have defined themselves against authoritarian countries by their respect for — and legal protections of — these freedoms.

Short definition of civil liberties

Examples

Brief history of the concept

While most people agree that civil liberties are essential to a free state, there is some controversy surrounding their meaning. People don't always agree which rights are civil liberties. For example, the debate over abortion reflects a dispute over whether the Constitution protects privacy rights that include the right to have an abortion. There is also disagreement about what constitutes a violation of civil liberties. As the federal government has taken measures to protect the country from terrorism, many have questioned whether practices such as warrantless wiretapping violate privacy rights, speech rights, or the prohibition of unreasonable searches and seizures.

Extended definition considers issues that complicate meaning:

• Which rights are civil liberties?

• What violates civil liberties?

People often confuse civil liberties with civil rights. Civil liberties are freedoms from government intrusion protected primarily by the Bill of Rights. Civil rights, however, concern the equal treatment of individuals in society and are established mainly by the Equal Protection Clause of the Fourteenth

Point-by-point contrast with civil rights

Amendment. An example is the right of citizens to attend public schools regardless of their color or gender. Civil liberties and civil rights differ in another important way as well: While protections of civil liberties prohibit government action, the government must often act to protect civil rights, as in the creation of antidiscrimination laws.

TAL FORTGANG

Tal Fortgang is a student at Princeton University, majoring in politics. Born in 1994, he grew up in New Rochelle, New York, graduated from SAR High School (an Orthodox Jewish academy) in the Bronx, and then studied the Talmud for a year in Israel. After college he plans to attend law school and pursue a career that combines his two major passions: American political thought and hockey.

Checking My Privilege

Fortgang wrote this essay as a freshman and published it in *The Princeton Tory*, a conservative campus journal, in 2014. Shortly thereafter, *Time* magazine reprinted it for a national audience, generating a flurry of discussion online. As you'll see, Fortgang was inspired by a criticism leveled at him in class to examine his own experiences and to question the intent of an accusation that he believes is heard on campus all too often.

    The essay following this one, Roxane Gay's "Peculiar Benefits," responds indirectly to Fortgang and counters his point about context and meaning.

There is a phrase that floats around college campuses, Princeton being no exception, that threatens to strike down opinions without regard for their merits, but rather solely on the basis of the person that voiced them. "Check your privilege," the saying goes, and I have been reprimanded by it several times this year. The phrase, handed down by my moral superiors, descends recklessly, like an Obama-sanctioned drone, and aims laser-like at my pinkish-peach complexion, my maleness, and the nerve I displayed in offering an opinion rooted in a personal Weltanschauung.[1] "Check your privilege," they tell me in a command that teeters between an imposition to actually explore how I got where I am, and a reminder that I ought to feel personally apologetic because white males seem to pull most of the strings in the world.

I do not accuse those who "check" me and my perspective of overt racism, although the phrase, which assumes that simply because I belong to a certain ethnic group I should be judged collectively with it, toes that line. But I do condemn them for diminishing everything I have personally accomplished, all the hard work I have done in my life, and for ascribing all the fruit I reap

---

[1] German word meaning, roughly, worldview or philosophy. — EDS.

not to the seeds I sow but to some invisible patron saint of white maleness who places it out for me before I even arrive. Furthermore, I condemn them for casting the equal protection clause, indeed the very idea of a meritocracy, as a myth, and for declaring that we are all governed by invisible forces (some would call them "stigmas" or "societal norms"), that our nation runs on racist and sexist conspiracies. Forget "you didn't build that";[2] check your privilege and realize that nothing you have accomplished is real.

But they can't be telling me that everything I've done with my life can be credited to the racist patriarchy holding my hand throughout my years of education and eventually guiding me into Princeton. Even that is too extreme. So to find out what they are saying, I decided to take their advice. I actually went and checked the origins of my privileged existence, to empathize with those whose underdog stories I can't possibly comprehend. I have unearthed some examples of the privilege with which my family was blessed, and now I think I better understand those who assure me that skin color allowed my family and me to flourish today.

Perhaps it's the privilege my grandfather and his brother had to flee their home as teenagers when the Nazis invaded Poland, leaving their mother and five younger siblings behind, running and running until they reached a Displaced Persons camp in Siberia, where they would do years of hard labor in the bitter cold until World War II ended. Maybe it was the privilege my grandfather had of taking on the local Rabbi's work in that DP camp, telling him that the spiritual leader shouldn't do hard work, but should save his energy to pass Jewish tradition along to those who might survive. Perhaps it was the privilege my great-grandmother and those five great-aunts and uncles I never knew had of being shot into an open grave outside their hometown. Maybe that's my privilege.

Or maybe it's the privilege my grandmother had of spending weeks upon weeks on a death march through Polish forests in subzero temperatures, one of just a handful to survive, only to be put in Bergen-Belsen concentration camp where she would have died but for the Allied forces who liberated her and helped her regain her health when her weight dwindled to barely eighty pounds.

Perhaps my privilege is that those two resilient individuals came to America with no money and no English, obtained citizenship, learned the language and met each other; that my grandfather started a humble wicker basket business with nothing but long hours, an idea, and an iron will — to paraphrase the man I never met: "I escaped Hitler. Some business troubles are going to ruin me?"

---

[2] Phrase from a 2012 campaign speech in which President Barack Obama argued that individual successes arise from the support of others. — Eds.

Maybe my privilege is that they worked hard enough to raise four children, and to send them to Jewish day school and eventually City College.

Perhaps it was my privilege that my own father worked hard enough in 7 City College to earn a spot at a top graduate school, got a good job, and for twenty-five years got up well before the crack of dawn, sacrificing precious time he wanted to spend with those he valued most — his wife and kids — to earn that living. I can say with certainty there was no legacy involved in any of his accomplishments. The wicker business just isn't that influential. Now would you say that we've been really privileged? That our success has been gift-wrapped?

That's the problem with calling someone out for the "privilege" which 8 you assume has defined their narrative. You don't know what their struggles have been, what they may have gone through to be where they are. Assuming they've benefitted from "power systems" or other conspiratorial imaginary institutions denies them credit for all they've done, things of which you may not even conceive. You don't know whose father died defending your freedom. You don't know whose mother escaped oppression. You don't know who conquered their demons, or may still be conquering them now.

The truth is, though, that I have been exceptionally privileged in my life, 9 albeit not in the way any detractors would have it.

It has been my distinct privilege that my grandparents came to America. 10 First, that there was a place at all that would take them from the ruins of Europe. And second, that such a place was one where they could legally enter, learn the language, and acclimate to a society that ultimately allowed them to flourish.

It was their privilege to come to a country that grants equal protection 11 under the law to its citizens, that cares not about religion or race, but the content of your character.

It was my privilege that my grandfather was blessed with resolve and an 12 entrepreneurial spirit, and that he was lucky enough to come to the place where he could realize the dream of giving his children a better life than he had.

But far more important for me than his attributes was the legacy he sought 13 to pass along, which forms the basis of what detractors call my "privilege," but which actually should be praised as one of altruism and self-sacrifice. Those who came before us suffered for the sake of giving us a better life. When we similarly sacrifice for our descendents by caring for the planet, it's called "environmentalism," and is applauded. But when we do it by passing along property and a set of values, it's called "privilege." (And when we do it by raising questions about our crippling national debt, we're called Tea Party radicals.) Such sacrifice of any form shouldn't be scorned, but admired.

My exploration did yield some results. I recognize that it was my parents' 14
privilege and now my own that there is such a thing as an American dream
which is attainable even for a penniless Jewish immigrant.

I am privileged that values like faith and education were passed along 15
to me. My grandparents played an active role in my parents' education, and
some of my earliest memories included learning the Hebrew alphabet with
my Dad. It's been made clear to me that education begins in the home, and
the importance of parents' involvement with their kids' education — from
mathematics to morality — cannot be overstated. It's not a matter of white or
black, male or female or any other division which we seek, but a matter of the
values we pass along, the legacy we leave, that perpetuates "privilege." And
there's nothing wrong with that.

Behind every success, large or small, there is a story, and it isn't always 16
told by sex or skin color. My appearance certainly doesn't tell the whole story,
and to assume that it does and that I should apologize for it is insulting. While
I haven't done everything for myself up to this point in my life, someone
sacrificed themselves so that I can lead a better life. But that is a legacy I am
proud of.

I have checked my privilege. And I apologize for nothing. 17

Journal Writing

As a college student, have you ever been told, or heard someone else be told, "Check
your privilege"? What was your reaction? In your journal, reflect on the advantages
and disadvantages you believe may have helped or hindered you in establishing your
current position in life. How do you think others perceive your background?

Questions on Meaning

1. How does Fortgang define the customary use of "Check your privilege" (par. 1)?
   What does he interpret the phrase to mean?

2. Fortgang acknowledges that he has "been exceptionally privileged in [his] life,
   albeit not in the way any detractors would have it" (par. 9). In what way (or ways)
   does he consider himself privileged? Why does he resent implications that his
   color and gender have given him any advantages?

3. To what is Fortgang referring when he mentions the "equal protection clause"
   (par. 2) and "equal protection under the law" (11)? Why does he invoke this
   concept?

4. What would you say is Fortgang's primary PURPOSE in this essay? How well does
   he succeed?

Questions on Writing Strategy

1. Who was Fortgang's intended AUDIENCE? How do you suppose he expected readers to respond? What do you think he hoped they would take away from their reading? What in the essay supports your answer?

2. In his first three paragraphs Fortgang discusses privilege in the ABSTRACT. How are these paragraphs connected to his stories about his family's history? Why do you think he begins the essay this way? Is this INTRODUCTION effective or not? Why?

3. Identify the TRANSITIONS Fortgang repeats in paragraphs 4–7 and 9–12. How do they create UNITY and COHERENCE in his definition?

4. Look back at the last two sentences of Fortgang's essay. What is the EFFECT of ending on this idea?

5. **OTHER METHODS**   Fortgang's definition is based largely on EXAMPLES and CAUSE-AND-EFFECT. Does his analysis seem sound to you? Do you think he overemphasizes any causes or effects or overlooks others? Explain.

Questions on Language

1. Give some examples of FIGURES OF SPEECH in Fortgang's essay. Do any *metaphors* or *similes* strike you as particularly fresh and inventive?

2. Why does Fortgang put quotation marks around "privilege" at some points in his essay? What other words and phrases does he single out this way?

3. The phrase "content of your character" (par. 11) comes from the famous civil rights speech "I Have a Dream" by Martin Luther King, Jr.: "I have a dream," he said, "that my four little children will one day live in a nation where they will not be judged by the color of their skin but by the content of their character." How does this ALLUSION serve Fortgang?

4. If you don't know the meanings of the following words, look them up in a dictionary: reprimanded, imposition (par. 1); overt, condemn, ascribing, meritocracy, stigmas, conspiracies (2); patriarchy, empathize (3); resilient (6); legacy (7); conspiratorial, conceive, oppression (8); detractors (9); acclimate (10); resolve, entrepreneurial (12); attributes, altruism, descendents (13); perpetuates (15).

Suggestions for Writing

1. **FROM JOURNAL TO ESSAY**   Based on your journal writing (p. 449), compose an essay in which you define your own privilege (or lack thereof). What advantages and disadvantages do you share with other people like you, and which are particular to yourself or your family? Be sure your essay has a clear THESIS and plenty of examples to make your definition precise.

2. Think about the values Fortgang cites in paragraphs 13 and 15: "altruism," "self-sacrifice," "faith," "education," "morality." Choose one of these words, or another

of the values Fortgang mentions in the essay, and write an essay that explains its meanings for you. Use examples from your own experience, observations, and reading to make the definition complete.

3. Research the history of Jewish immigration to the United States. When and why did the initial wave of immigration occur? What forces have led to other patterns of immigration over the years? Have Jewish Americans faced different kinds of discrimination or enjoyed different opportunities than other immigrants have? In an essay, answer these or other questions that occur to you.

4. **CRITICAL WRITING** Evaluate Fortgang's TONE in this essay. What contributes to this tone, and to what extent does it serve his purpose in writing? How might a different tone have changed your response to the essay?

5. **CONNECTIONS** The next essay, Roxane Gay's "Peculiar Benefits," examines privilege from the perspective of a woman born to Haitian immigrants. Write an essay that COMPARES AND CONTRASTS Fortgang's understanding of the concept with Gay's. How does context and personal background help to shape each writer's definition? Whose ARGUMENT do you find more persuasive, and why?

Tal Fortgang on Writing

Tal Fortgang garnered a lot of media attention — both positive and negative — with "Checking My Privilege," but he stands by his argument. In comments he wrote for this book, he reflects on his writing process and considers how being passionate about a belief can lead to a strong thesis.

I distinctly remember how the idea for this piece came to me. I was in the shower (all good ideas start in the shower; the best piece of advice I can give you is if you're stuck or out of good ideas, take a hot shower and let your mind wander) and thinking about how certain things, like money or values, are passed from generation to generation. So I started thinking about possible arguments against estate taxes, wherein I might contend that governments were taking too much money from parents who saved up in hopes of passing down to their children. This tax, to me, was antithetical to the "American dream." That got me thinking about "privilege" and how it was being framed on my campus: Is there something wrong with my parents' and grandparents' hard work being passed along? Not that my family is fabulously wealthy by any stretch, but should I be embarrassed that someone before me wanted to give me a better life, and was successful in allowing me to be born into comfort? And that's how I got to talking about privilege, which is way more interesting than estate taxes, in my opinion.

My method of writing is pretty unusual. I can focus on one thing really well for about forty-five minutes at a time, so I'll usually sit down and pour out everything in my head for that long (again, usually while wearing only a towel and sopping wet because if I took the time to get dressed I'd forget all my deep shower thoughts). Then I'll step away and do something else for a while before coming back an hour or few later. I still do this. I'm writing this piece the same way. I don't know if I recommend it for everyone, but if whatever you've been doing isn't working, don't be afraid to try it out.

More important than how you go about getting your writing done is the content. (I don't think anyone would disagree with that, but it seemed like a nicely authoritative topic sentence.) Central to your content is your thesis, or the thing you know you always need to have but aren't quite sure if you do or don't yet have. I think there's a way of thinking about thesis development that really simplifies the process. Here goes: Making arguments is tough, but the good news is that you probably think things. You may even believe things you think! So you're well on your way to arguing for something you think and/or believe. When you're presented with a prompt or a question or a topic, try to capture your gut-reaction answer. Now channel your inner five-year-old and ask "why?" Then ask "why?" again. And again. As many "whys" as you need to whittle your gut reaction down to its fundamental parts. When you've reached something fundamental — the "nuclear argument" is what I like to call it — you can argue that you think it is true, and is the basis of what you believe.

I'll add that it helps to argue something you deeply, truly, believe from the bottom of your heart and the entirety of your soul. Just ask yourself why you believe it. Your writing will be stronger and you might even learn something about yourself in the process.

The Bedford Reader on Writing

Aside from the "sopping wet" part, Tal Fortgang's DRAFTING process isn't unusual at all. We certainly recommend you try writing freely in concentrated spurts, as time and focus allow (but you might want to put on some clothes). For additional thoughts on how you can narrow a subject until you reach your point of interest, try turning to pages 32–36 of this book. And for help developing your own "nuclear argument" with specifics — the "whys" — see "Supporting the Thesis" (pp. 36–37).

ROXANE GAY

Roxane Gay describes herself as just a "bad feminist . . . trying to make sense of this world we live in," but she is a rising star admired for crafting sharp critiques that bridge academia and popular culture with a solid sense of humor. She was born in 1974 to Haitian immigrants and grew up "a loner, shy and awkward." Shuttled around the suburbs of Nebraska, New Jersey, Colorado, Illinois, and Virginia, she read voraciously for company and wrote to entertain herself. Raped by classmates at the age of twelve, she retreated into herself and deliberately turned to overeating as a way of shielding her body and surviving the trauma. Gay graduated from Phillips Exeter Academy in New Hampshire in 1992, earned an MA in English from the University of Nebraska, Lincoln, and completed a PhD in rhetoric and technical communication at Michigan Technological University in 2010. While teaching at Eastern Illinois University and blogging innumerable essays for sites ranging from *Jezebel* to the *New York Times*, she put together her first book, *Ayiti* (2011), a mixture of poetry, fiction, and prose focused on the experiences of Haitian emigrants. In 2014 she published both *An Untamed State*, a novel, and *Bad Feminist*, a collection of essays. *Hunger*, a critical memoir of obesity, followed in 2016. Currently an associate professor at Purdue University, Gay is also an aggressive Scrabble player who regularly competes in tournaments and the founder of Tiny Hardcore Press, an experimental publishing house.

Peculiar Benefits

As a Haitian American woman "who has been queer identified at varying points in her life," Gay nonetheless considers herself extraordinarily fortunate in the opportunities that have been afforded her. In "Peculiar Benefits," she thoughtfully examines her own privilege, mildly chastising those who cannot or will not acknowledge theirs. The essay first appeared on the online forum *The Rumpus* in 2012 and was revised for inclusion in *Bad Feminist* in 2014, just as the Internet was buzzing with debate over Tal Fortgang's "Checking My Privilege" (p. 446).

When I was young, my parents took our family to Haiti during the summers. For them, it was a homecoming. For my brothers and me it was an adventure, sometimes a chore, and always a necessary education on privilege and the grace of an American passport. Until visiting Haiti, I had no idea what poverty really was or the difference between relative and absolute poverty. To see poverty so plainly and pervasively left a profound mark on me.

To this day, I remember my first visit, and how at every intersection, men 2
and women, shiny with sweat, would mob our car, their skinny arms stretched
out, hoping for a few gourdes[1] or American dollars. I saw the sprawling slums,
the shanties housing entire families, the trash piled in the streets, and also the
gorgeous beach and the young men in uniforms who brought us Coca-Cola
in glass bottles and made us hats and boats out of palm fronds. It was hard for
a child to begin to grasp the contrast of such inescapable poverty alongside
almost repulsive luxury, and then the United States, a mere eight hundred
miles away, with its gleaming cities rising out of the landscape and the well-
maintained interstates stretching across the country, the running water and
the electricity. It wasn't until many, many years later that I realized my education on privilege began long before I could appreciate it in any meaningful way.

Privilege is a right or immunity granted as a peculiar benefit, advantage, or 3
favor. There is racial privilege, gender (and identity) privilege, heterosexual
privilege, economic privilege, able-bodied privilege, educational privilege,
religious privilege, and the list goes on and on. At some point, you have to
surrender to the kinds of privilege you hold. Nearly everyone, particularly in
the developed world, has something someone else doesn't, something someone else yearns for.

The problem is, cultural critics talk about privilege with such alarming fre- 4
quency and in such empty ways, we have diluted the word's meaning. When
people wield the word "privilege," it tends to fall on deaf ears because we hear
that word so damn much it has become white noise.

One of the hardest things I've ever had to do is accept and acknowledge 5
my privilege. It's an ongoing project. I'm a woman, a person of color, and the
child of immigrants, but I also grew up middle class and then upper middle
class. My parents raised my siblings and me in a strict but loving environment.
They were and are happily married, so I didn't have to deal with divorce or
crappy intramarital dynamics. I attended elite schools. My master's and doc-
toral degrees were funded. I got a tenure-track position my first time out. My
bills are paid. I have the time and resources for frivolity. I am reasonably well
published. I have an agent and books to my name. My life has been far from
perfect, but it's somewhat embarrassing for me to accept just how much privilege I have.

It's also really difficult for me to consider the ways in which I lack privi- 6
lege or the ways in which my privilege hasn't magically rescued me from a
world of hurt. On my more difficult days, I'm not sure what's more of a pain in
my ass — being black or being a woman. I'm happy to be both of these things,

---

[1] Official paper currency of Haiti. One Haitian gourde is worth approximately two American
cents. — Eds.

but the world keeps intervening. There are all kinds of infuriating reminders of my place in the world — random people questioning me in the parking lot at work as if it is unfathomable that I'm a faculty member, the persistence of lawmakers trying to legislate the female body, street harassment, strangers wanting to touch my hair.

7   We tend to believe that accusations of privilege imply we have it easy, which we resent because life is hard for nearly everyone. Of course we resent these accusations. Look at white men when they are accused of having privilege. They tend to be immediately defensive (and, at times, understandably so). They say, "It's not my fault I am a white man," or "I'm [insert other condition that discounts their privilege]," instead of simply accepting that, in this regard, yes, they benefit from certain privileges others do not. To have privilege in one or more areas does not mean you are wholly privileged. Surrendering to the acceptance of privilege is difficult, but it is really all that is expected. What I remind myself, regularly, is this: The acknowledgment of my privilege is not a denial of the ways I have been and am marginalized, the ways I have suffered.

8   You don't necessarily *have* to do anything once you acknowledge your privilege. You don't have to apologize for it. You need to understand the extent of your privilege, the consequences of your privilege, and remain aware that people who are different from you move through and experience the world in ways you might never know anything about. They might endure situations you can never know anything about. You could, however, use that privilege for the greater good — to try to level the playing field for everyone, to work for social justice, to bring attention to how those without certain privileges are disenfranchised. We've seen what the hoarding of privilege has done, and the results are shameful.

9   When we talk about privilege, some people start to play a very pointless and dangerous game where they try to mix and match various demographic characteristics to determine who wins at the Game of Privilege. Who would win in a privilege battle between a wealthy black woman and a wealthy white man? Who would win a privilege battle between a queer white man and a queer Asian woman? Who would win in a privilege battle between a working-class white man and a wealthy, differently abled Mexican woman? We could play this game all day and never find a winner. . . .

10   Too many people have become self-appointed privilege police, patrolling the halls of discourse, ready to remind people of their privilege whether those people have denied that privilege or not. In online discourse, in particular, the specter of privilege is always looming darkly. When someone writes from experience, there is often someone else, at the ready, pointing a trembling finger, accusing that writer of having various kinds of privilege. How dare someone speak to a personal experience without accounting for every possible

configuration of privilege or the lack thereof? We would live in a world of silence if the only people who were allowed to write or speak from experience or about difference were those absolutely without privilege.

When people wield accusations of privilege, more often than not, they   11
want to be heard and seen. Their need is acute, if not desperate, and that need rises out of the many historical and ongoing attempts to silence and render invisible marginalized groups. Must we satisfy our need to be heard and seen by preventing anyone else from being heard and seen? Does privilege automatically negate any merits of what a privilege holder has to say? Do we ignore everything, for example, that white men have to say?

We need to get to a place where we discuss privilege by way of obser-   12
vation and acknowledgment rather than accusation. We need to be able to argue beyond the threat of privilege. We need to stop playing Privilege or Oppression Olympics because we'll never get anywhere until we find more effective ways of talking through difference. We should be able to say, "This is my truth," and have that truth stand without a hundred clamoring voices shouting, giving the impression that multiple truths cannot coexist. Because at some point, doesn't privilege become beside the point?

Privilege is relative and contextual. Few people in the developed world, and   13
particularly in the United States, have no privilege at all. Among those of us who participate in intellectual communities, privilege runs rampant. We have disposable time and the ability to access the Internet regularly. We have the freedom to express our opinions without the threat of retaliation. We have smartphones and iProducts and desktops and laptops. If you are reading this essay, you have some kind of privilege. It may be hard to hear that, I know, but if you cannot recognize your privilege, you have a lot of work to do; get started.

Journal Writing

Gay's "bills are paid," she notes, and she has a good job and is "reasonably well published" (par. 5). In your journal, consider the meaning of *success*, focusing on these questions: Whom do you consider to be successful, and why? Where do your ideas of success come from — your parents? your friends? your schooling? the media?

Questions on Meaning

1. In your own words, SUMMARIZE Gay's definition of *privilege*.
2. What does Gay mean by "the difference between relative and absolute poverty" (par. 1)? How does that difference apply to her understanding of privilege?

3. What does Gay believe to be the most basic reason people object when they're "accused of having privilege" (par. 7)?

4. In paragraph 7, Gay says that acknowledging her privilege "is not a denial of the ways [she has] been and [is] marginalized." What does she mean? How do you explain this contradiction?

5. What seems to be Gay's PURPOSE in this essay? What solution to the problem of privilege does she propose? Is she optimistic or pessimistic that people can be encouraged to be more empathetic to others?

Questions on Writing Strategy

1. Why does Gay open by detailing her first family trip to Haiti? How does this INTRODUCTION lead into her subject?

2. What does Gay assume about her AUDIENCE? To what extent do you fit her assumptions?

3. Why is Gay so careful to enumerate her own privileges in paragraph 5? What is the EFFECT of her admissions?

4. **OTHER METHODS** How does Gay use CLASSIFICATION to sort out the types of privilege she sees in the contemporary world? What categories does she identify? What, if any, forms of privilege might you add to her lists?

Questions on Language

1. Find some examples of both formal and informal DICTION in the essay. What is the effect of Gay's word choices?

2. Why does Gay capitalize the phrases "Game of Privilege" and "Oppression Olympics" in paragraphs 9 and 12? What does she mean by these terms?

3. What is "white noise" (par. 4)? Why is this metaphor particularly apt, given Gay's subject and purpose? (For a definition of *metaphor*, see FIGURES OF SPEECH in the Glossary.)

4. Notice that Gay shifts POINT OF VIEW in paragraph 8 and again in her conclusion, addressing readers directly as *you*. What is the effect of the last two sentences of the essay in particular?

5. Be sure you know the meanings of the following words, checking a dictionary if necessary: pervasively (par. 1); shanties (2); immunity, peculiar (3); intramarital, frivolity (5); intervening, unfathomable, legislate (6); marginalized (7); disenfranchised (8); demographic (9); discourse, specter, configuration (10); acute (11); clamoring (12).

Suggestions for Writing

1. **FROM JOURNAL TO ESSAY** Compose an extended definition of *success* that includes an examination of the sources of your definition, as you explored them in your

journal writing. The sources could be negative as well as positive — that is, your ideas of success may have formed in reaction *against* others' ideas and privileges as well as in agreement with or appreciation of them.

2. Propose some course of action in a situation you consider an injustice. Racial privilege is one possible area, or unfairness to any disenfranchised group, such as women, children, the elderly, ex-convicts, the disabled, the poor. If possible, narrow your subject to a particular incident or a local situation on which you can write knowledgeably.

3. As Gay suggests in the introduction to her essay, Haiti is the poorest country in the Americas. Do some research to learn about the natural disasters and decades of social and political upheaval — including violent conflicts between the government and rebels — that have plagued the country, prompted intervention by the United Nations, and encouraged many Haitians to seek asylum in the United States. In an essay, report your findings, considering in particular the CAUSES and EFFECTS of poverty in the Caribbean islands.

4. **CRITICAL WRITING**   Write an essay examining the organization of Gay's essay. What does the author accomplish in each paragraph? How effectively does she use TRANSITIONS to move from paragraph to paragraph?

5. **CONNECTIONS**   In some ways Gay's essay is an admonition to readers to "check your privilege," the phrase that Tal Fortgang, in the previous essay (p. 446), finds so maddening. Read or reread Fortgang's essay and consider the extent to which he fits Gay's understanding of why white men in particular react badly "when they are accused of having privilege" (par. 7). How well do Gay's characterizations describe Fortgang? How might he respond to her definition?

Roxane Gay on Writing

Gay is known for writing regularly in multiple genres on any number of subjects — personal essays on her *Tumblr* blog, scholarly analyses of culture for her *New York Times* column, pithy Tweets on current events, poetry and fiction for a general audience. In a 2014 interview with Tina Essmaker for *The Great Discontent,* she explained why she writes as much as she does.

Writing is not a tortured act for me. I don't have any angst about it, and I don't find it to be a painful misery. Writing is the one endeavor that makes me purely happy, and it comes fairly easily to me. I don't know why I'm that lucky, but it's true.

There are definitely times when I have writer's block, and it's infuriating, but writers love to dramatize the suffering of the writer. I don't judge them on that, because it's their truth, but I'm suffering when I'm *not* writing: It's what

I do for fun. When people say I'm prolific, I think, "Well, it's kind of my self-medication, and it doesn't feel like work."

I'm a happy writer, and although that hasn't always been the case, I count my blessings. I'm finally in the place I've always dreamed of. Maybe my dreams weren't that big, but I just wanted to write and have people read what I had to say one way or another. I have that.

The Bedford Reader on Writing

It seems that Roxane Gay's unassuming PURPOSE for writing — simply expressing herself and reaching an AUDIENCE — makes the task easy for her. How can knowing your readers and having something to say to them work for you? Turn to pages 30–32 to find out.

MEGHAN DAUM

Born in 1970 in Palo Alto, California, Meghan Daum is a writer known for provocative, witty essays on American life. Daum graduated from Vassar College with a BA in English in 1992 and earned an MA in writing from Columbia University in 1996. A former contributing editor for *Harper's Bazaar* and since 2005 a syndicated columnist for the *Los Angeles Times*, Daum has published her work in a variety of newspapers and magazines, including *The New Yorker*, *Gentlemen's Quarterly*, *Vogue*, and the *New York Times Book Review*. She is the author of a number of books, including *The Quality of Life Report* (2003), a novel; *Life Would Be Perfect If I Lived in That House* (2011), a humorous memoir; and *My Misspent Youth* (2001) and *The Unspeakable* (2014), essay collections. Winner of the 2015 PEN Center USA award for creative nonfiction, Daum is also an occasional guest on National Public Radio and has contributed to *Marketplace*, *Morning Edition*, and *This American Life*. She lives in Los Angeles.

Narcissist — Give It a Rest

In this column first published in the *Los Angeles Times* in 2011, Daum takes issue with the current usage of one particular word. We might be a nation of narcissists, she concedes, except we're not. As far as Daum is concerned, Americans are something else entirely.

At any given moment a whole lot of people are accusing a whole lot of other people of being narcissists. In recent years, the term for a self-destructive "personality disorder" has become the insult of choice for almost anyone doing almost anything. [1]

The concept of narcissism as a broad cultural condition, and the word's use as an everyday term, goes back several decades. Christopher Lasch published *The Culture of Narcissism* in 1979, three years after Tom Wolfe[1] declared the era the "me decade." The 1980s turned out to be even more "me" than the '70s had been, and by the 1990s, the rise of identity politics, the birth of reality television and the proliferation of the language of self-help (remember Wendy Kaminer's *I'm Dysfunctional, You're Dysfunctional?*[2]) effectively elevated self-absorption from a passing (if protracted) trend to, well, pretty much just the way things were. To accuse someone of being a narcissist was kind of like accusing them of breathing. In other words, what was the point? [2]

---

[1] American journalist (born 1931) best known for *The Electric Kool-Aid Acid Test* (1968) and *The Right Stuff* (1979). — EDS.

[2] An excerpt from *I'm Dysfunctional, You're Dysfunctional* (1992) appears on page 527 of this book. — EDS.

But lately the word seems to be enjoying a resurgence, often among people   3
who give the impression that they just discovered it. Professional pundits love
it, as do bloggers, politicians, religious leaders, celebrity shrinks, cultural critics, Internet commenters and blowhards at parties. And why shouldn't we?
(Yes, I include myself in this mix; I am, after all, a you-know-what.) It's the
handiest weapon in our arsenal: a derogatory *apercu*[3] that's one-size-fits-all.

Democrats, Republicans, red state folks, blue state folks, baby boomers,   4
Gen Xers, millennials: all narcissists! Parents, nonparents, vegans, meat eaters, city dwellers, rural dwellers, people who travel a lot, people who refuse to
travel, writers who use the first person: all vectors in the national scourge of
self-involvement. In practice, any behavior you don't like can be dismissed
as abrasively, idiotically, dangerously self-centered, with a $10, three-syllable
word that has a way of making even a nincompoop feel like he's saying something intellectual. . . .

Here's the problem with the charge of narcissism. The term has been mis-   5
used and overused so flagrantly that it's now all but meaningless when it comes
to labeling truly destructive tendencies. These days, you can be called a narcissist
merely by having self-esteem and showing a little ambition — in other words,
for trying to survive in the world. In fact, so fluid has the definition become that
narcissism's true home for the last forty-four years, the *Diagnostic and Statistical
Manual of Mental Disorders*, has dropped the diagnosis from its roster.

As for anyone still itching to attribute our collective addiction to *Face-   6
book* and e-mail and other self-referential forms of communication to a
narcissism epidemic, I beg to differ. That stuff hasn't made us into egomaniacs;
it's made us into boring, semi-verbal zombies who bang into each other when
we exit movie theaters because we're buried in our iPhones.

So perhaps it's time to declare a moratorium on the indiscriminate use   7
of this particular n-word. After all, we're not a nation of narcissists. We're a
nation of jerks. Which also happens to be a lot easier to spell.

Journal Writing

Daum writes that "baby boomers, Gen Xers, [and] millennials" (par. 4) have all been
characterized as narcissists. To what generation do you belong? How do you and your
peers tend to be described in the media? Do you agree that people in your age group
are "dangerously self-centered" (4) or otherwise unpleasant to others? In your journal,
write down your own characterization of members of your generation.

[3] French, "perception" or "insight." Daum uses the word in its colloquial sense of linguistic
shorthand. — EDS.

Questions on Meaning

1. When, according to Daum, did people start misusing the word *narcissist*? Why is the timing significant to her?

2. What would you say is Daum's PURPOSE in this essay?

3. Does Daum have a THESIS? In which sentence or sentences does she state her main idea most directly?

Questions on Writing Strategy

1. What AUDIENCE probably would not like this essay? Why would they not like it?

2. Daum defines mostly by negation. In your own words, SUMMARIZE her implied definition of *narcissist*. How does it differ from the meanings commonly attached to the word?

3. Analyze the organization of this essay. What does Daum discuss in each of her paragraphs? How does she create UNITY among them?

4. **OTHER METHODS** Where in the essay does Daum list some of the people and attitudes that have been called narcissistic? What seems to be the intended EFFECT of these EXAMPLES?

Questions on Language

1. How would you describe the TONE of this essay?

2. Be sure you know the meanings of the following words, checking a dictionary if necessary: proliferation, protracted (par. 2); resurgence (3); vegans, vectors, scourge (4); flagrantly, roster (5); moratorium, indiscriminate (7).

3. What is the effect of "you-know-what" in paragraph 3 and "this particular n-word" in paragraph 7? Why doesn't Daum just say "narcissist" in these instances?

Suggestions for Writing

1. **FROM JOURNAL TO ESSAY** Write an essay giving an extended definition of the age group of which you consider yourself a member, drawing on your journal entry (p. 461), Daum's essay, and any other sources that offer ideas. You might use one of the labels Daum cites (baby boomers, Gen Xers, millennials) or come up with a name of your own. Keep in mind that characterizing such a large and diverse group requires GENERALIZATION. How does your definition compare with other definitions you have heard in the media? Does any attempt to characterize an age group necessarily oversimplify? Do you find value or interest in the exercise?

2. Think of another word or phrase that is commonly misused or overused (or both). Examples might include *literally, amazing, hero, like, LOL, I could care less*, or *beg the question*. Following Daum's essay as a model, write an essay of your own explaining your objections and imploring people to stop using the word or phrase.

3. Daum suggests that, thanks to "self-referential forms of communication" (par. 6) such as social media and smartphones, Americans have become increasingly self-absorbed and rude. Write an essay in which you offer your own viewpoint on this idea. Are we, in fact, "a nation of jerks" (7)? If you generally agree, offer specific examples and speculate about the causes of this change. If you generally disagree, challenge Daum's assumptions with examples that counter her claim.

4. **CRITICAL WRITING**   The decision to remove narcissistic personality disorder from the *Diagnostic and Statistical Manual of Mental Disorders* raised some controversy when it was announced in late 2010 — just a few weeks before Daum wrote her essay. Research the controversy so that you understand the views for and against retaining narcissism as a psychiatric diagnosis. In an essay, briefly summarize the controversy, and then analyze Daum's essay as a contribution to the conversation. On which side of the debate does her position seem to fall? Does she agree with the decision to drop the disorder from the psychiatrists' manual? Or does she seem to think it should have stayed? Use PARAPHRASES and QUOTATIONS from the essay to support your conclusions.

5. **CONNECTIONS**   In her essay "An Obligation to Prevent Trauma on Campus" (p. 513), Brianne Richson examines another type of psychiatric diagnosis that seems often misunderstood. How does Richson define *post-traumatic stress disorder*? Does she portray it as a personality trait on a par with Daum's *narcissism*, or as more of a medical problem? Write an essay that COMPARES AND CONTRASTS post-traumatic stress disorder and narcissism as Richson and Daum define them. Why might some people argue that trauma victims deserve special treatment, for instance? Is it possible that people accused of narcissism suffer from mental illness? Should either condition be formally classified as a disorder? Why, or why not?

Meghan Daum on Writing

At least once a week, Daum claims, she hears from a "student who's been assigned a paper about my writing and wants me to tell her what to say." In this excerpt from a 2011 *Los Angeles Times* column, she explains why those students should not expect a response.

I know, I know. I should be flattered. I should be heartened that the youth of America are reading newspapers (albeit under duress) and, for that matter, that anyone's reading my column at all. . . . Still, I find myself consistently irked over this whole phenomenon, and not just because I feel guilty when I don't answer these e-mails and resentful when I do. It's because in a world of hyper-accessibility, writers are expected not only to write things but then engage with readers via e-mail or comment boards or book festival Q&As about why they wrote it and what they meant. Nothing is ever considered enough. Readers don't want to simply read stuff and mull it over on their own; they want a personal dialog with the writer about what they were supposed to get out of it.

Students, especially, should be figuring out the how and why of a piece of writing based not on what the author explains to them in an Internet chat room but by tapping into the pure recesses of their own minds. That kind of approach is the highest compliment a reader can give a writer. It's also, by definition, the one we just can't offer any help on.

The Bedford Reader on Writing

What does Daum mean when she says that students should be "tapping into the pure recesses of their own minds" instead of asking writers what they meant? To learn how to "simply read stuff and mull it over on [your] own," also known as CRITICAL THINKING, read (or reread) Chapter 1 of this book, especially "Developing an Understanding" and "Analyzing Essays," pages 15–22.

DAGOBERTO GILB

Dagoberto Gilb was born in Los Angeles in 1950 to a Mexican mother and a German American father. Though he admits to getting in trouble as a teen and says that he "wasn't the best student at all," he enrolled in junior college and went on to earn a BA in philosophy and an MA in religion from the University of California at Santa Barbara. From 1976 to 1991 Gilb pursued a dual career as a writer and journeyman carpenter. The stories he wrote then and later, often focusing on working-class Latinos in the Southwest, have been collected in *Winners on the Pass Line* (1985), *The Magic of Blood* (1993), *Woodcuts of Women* (2001), and *Before the End, After the Beginning* (2011). Gilb has also written two novels, *The Last Known Residence of Mickey Acuña* (1994) and *The Flowers* (2008), and a collection of essays, *Gritos* (2003). Most recently he edited, with his son Ricardo Angel Gilb, *Mexican American Literature: A Portable Anthology* (2016). Gilb has been a visiting writer at several universities and the recipient of many honors and prizes, including the Hemingway Foundation/PEN award, a *New York Times* Notable Books designation, and a Guggenheim Fellowship. He currently teaches at the University of Houston–Victoria, where he is director of the CentroVictoria Center for Mexican American Literature and Culture, artist-in-residence, and founding editor of *Huizache*, a literary magazine focused on Latino works.

Pride

Gritos, Gilb's essay collection and the source of this piece, takes its title from a Spanish word that translates loosely as "shouts" but more precisely, Gilb explains, as exclamations of "defiance and freedom," "joy and support." All these feelings figure in Gilb's definition of *pride* through the lives of Mexican Americans in El Paso, Texas.

It's almost time to close at the northwest corner of Altura and Copia in   1
El Paso. That means it is so dark that it is as restful as the deepest unremembering sleep, dark as the empty space around this spinning planet, as a black star. Headlights that beam a little cross-eyed from a fatso American car are feeling around the asphalt road up the hill toward the Good Time Store, its yellow plastic smiley face bright like a sugary suck candy. The loose muffler holds only half the misfires, and, dry springs squeaking, the automobile curves slowly into the establishment's lot, swerving to avoid the new self-serve gas pump island. Behind it, across the street, a Texas flag — out too late this and all the nights — pops and slaps in a summer wind that finally is cool.

A good man, gray on the edges, an assistant manager in a brown starched   2
and ironed uniform, is washing the glass windows of the store, lit up by as

many watts as Venus, with a roll of paper towels and the blue liquid from a spray bottle. Good night, m'ijo![1] he tells a young boy coming out after playing the video game, a Grande Guzzler the size of a wastebasket balanced in one hand, an open bag of Flaming Hot Cheetos, its red dye already smearing his mouth and the hand not carrying the weight of the soda, his white T-shirt, its short sleeves reaching halfway down his wrists, the whole XXL of it billowing and puffing in the outdoor gust.

A plump young woman steps out of that car. She's wearing a party dress, wide scoops out of the top, front, and back, its hemline way above the knees.   3

Did you get a water pump? the assistant manager asks her. Are you going   4
to make it to Horizon City? He's still washing the glass of the storefront, his hand sweeping in small hard circles.

The young woman is patient and calm like a loving mother. I don't know   5
yet, she tells him as she stops close to him, thinking. I guess I should make a call, she says, and her thick-soled shoes, the latest fashion, slap against her heels to one of the pay phones at the front of the store.

Pride is working a job like it's as important as art or war, is the happiness   6
of a new high score on a video arcade game, of a pretty new black dress and shoes. Pride is the deaf and blind confidence of the good people who are too poor but don't notice.

A son is a long time sitting on the front porch where he played all those   7
years with the squirmy dog who still licks his face, both puppies then, even before he played on the winning teams of Little League baseball and City League basketball. They sprint down the sidewalk and across streets, side by side, until they stop to rest on the park grass, where a red ant, or a spider, bites the son's calf. It swells, but he no longer thinks to complain to his mom about it — he's too old now — when he comes home. He gets ready, putting on the shirt and pants his mom would have ironed but he wanted to iron himself. He takes the ride with his best friend since first grade. The hundreds of moms and dads, abuelos y abuelitas, the tios and primos,[2] baby brothers and older married sisters, all are at the Special Events Center for the son's high school graduation. His dad is a man bigger than most, and when he walks in his dress eel-skin boots down the cement stairs to get as close to the hardwood basket-ball-court floor and ceremony to see — m'ijo! — he feels an embarrassing sob bursting from his eyes and mouth. He holds it back, and with his hands, hides the tears that do escape, wipes them with his fingers, because the chavalitos[3] in his aisle are playing and laughing and they are so small and he is so big next

---

[1] Spanish slang, "my son." — EDS.
[2] Spanish, "grandfathers and grandmothers," "aunts and uncles," and "cousins." — EDS.
[3] Spanish slang, "little kids." — EDS.

to them. And when his son walks to the stage to get his high school diploma and his dad wants to scream his name, he hears how many others, from the floor in caps and gowns and from around the arena, are already screaming it — could be any name, it could be any son's or daughter's: Alex! Vanessa! Carlos! Veronica! Ricky! Tony! Estella! Isa! — and sees his boy waving back to all of them.

Pride hears gritty dirt blowing against an agave whose stiff fertile stalk, so tall, will not bend — the love of land, rugged like the people who live on it. Pride sees the sunlight on the Franklin Mountains in the first light of morning and listens to a neighbor's gallo[4] — the love of culture and history. Pride smells a sweet, musky drizzle of rain and eats huevos con chile[5] in corn tortillas heated on a cast-iron pan — the love of heritage.   8

Pride is the fearless reaction to disrespect and disregard. It is knowing the future will prove that wrong.   9

Seeing the beauty: Look out there from a height of the mountain and on the north and south of the Rio Grande, to the far away and close, the so many miles more of fuzz on the wide horizon, knowing how many years the people have passed and have stayed, the ancestors, the ones who have medaled, limped back on crutches or died or were heroes from wars in the Pacific or Europe or Korea or Vietnam or the Persian Gulf, the ones who have raised the fist and dared to defy, the ones who wash the clothes and cook and serve the meals, who stitch the factory shoes and the factory slacks, who assemble and sort, the ones who laugh and the ones who weep, the ones who care, the ones who want more, the ones who try, the ones who love, those ones with shameless courage and hardened wisdom, and the old ones still so alive, holding their grandchildren, and the young ones in their glowing prime, strong and gorgeous, holding each other, the ones who will be born from them. The desert land is rock-dry and ungreen. It is brown. Brown like the skin is brown. Beautiful brown.   10

Journal Writing

In your journal, jot down images of pride that occur to you based on your own experiences and observations. Then try briefly to create your own definition — or definitions — of *pride*.

---

[4] Spanish, "rooster." — Eds.
[5] Traditional Mexican dish of eggs and peppers. — Eds.

Questions on Meaning

1. What does Gilb take *pride* to mean? SUMMARIZE his definition as you understand it.

2. How do paragraphs 8–10 contribute to Gilb's definition?

3. What point does Gilb make in his concluding paragraph? How does his final IMAGE serve as a sort of summary?

4. How would you describe the writer's PURPOSE in this essay? What DOMINANT IMPRESSION does Gilb create?

Questions on Writing Strategy

1. Why do you think Gilb opens the essay as he does? What impression does he create with the three people in the Good Time Store parking lot?

2. Following paragraphs 1–5, Gilb specifically defines the pride of the people about whom he has just written; however, after paragraph 7 his definition does not apply specifically to the father and son he just described. Why do you think he varies his strategy here?

3. Closely examine Gilb's development of paragraph 7. How would you describe its movement? its ultimate EFFECT?

4. How does Gilb achieve UNITY and COHERENCE in paragraph 8?

5. **OTHER METHODS** The INTRODUCTION to "Pride" (paragraphs 1–5) relies on DESCRIPTION. Why do you think Gilb portrays this scene in such detail?

Questions on Language

1. In paragraph 1 how does Gilb use specific language to create a distinct impression of the car that pulls into the store's parking lot?

2. What is striking about the verbs Gilb uses in paragraph 8?

3. The first sentence of paragraph 10 is unusually long. How does Gilb manage to maintain its clarity and readability?

Suggestions for Writing

1. **JOURNAL TO ESSAY** Using your journal writing (p. 467) as a springboard, write an essay in which you develop your own definition of *pride*. Like Gilb, present specific images and examples in addition to statements of your definition.

2. In focusing on a Mexican American community in Texas, "Pride" hints at, but doesn't specifically address, the issue of immigration, especially illegal immigration. (Gilb's own mother, he has written elsewhere, "crossed the border without papers.") Research how US immigration officials determine which would-be immigrants to the United States will be granted or denied entrance, based on country of origin and other factors. In an essay, explain these policies and evaluate their fairness as you see it.

3. **CRITICAL WRITING**   In an essay, ANALYZE Gilb's combination of lyrical language and concrete images. How does the concept of pride inform and complicate his depictions of one particular community? Use specific examples of the language he uses and the scenes he describes.

4. **CONNECTIONS**   In "Champion of the World" (p. 94), Maya Angelou writes about the experiences of another ethnic group in the United States, African Americans. Write an essay in which you COMPARE AND CONTRAST Gilb's presentation of Mexican Americans with Angelou's of African Americans.

AUGUSTEN BURROUGHS

Augusten Burroughs was born Christopher Robison in Pittsburgh, Pennsylvania, in 1965 and raised in western Massachusetts. He dropped out of school in the sixth grade, earned a GED, and legally changed his name when he turned eighteen. By his own account Burroughs has been repeatedly victimized by circumstances, many of them recounted in a series of best-selling memoirs. In *Running with Scissors* (2002) he tells of being raised by his mother's psychiatrist and becoming trapped in a relationship with a pedophile. In *Dry* (2003) he examines a period of alcoholism worsened after losing a boyfriend to AIDS. And in *A Wolf at the Table* (2008) he recalls childhood abuse at the hands of his father. Critics sometimes question the details of Burroughs's tales, yet most admire the emotional honesty and gothic humor that pervade his work. In addition to memoirs, Burroughs has also written a novel, *Sellevision* (2000); two collections of essays, *Magical Thinking* (2004) and *Possible Side Effects* (2006); a compilation of Christmas stories, *You'd Better Not Cry* (2009); and, most recently, a self-help book, *This Is How: Proven Aid in Overcoming Shyness, Molestation, Fatness, Spinsterhood, Grief, Disease, Lushery, Decrepitude and More* (2012). He lives in rural Connecticut.

How to Identify Love
by Knowing What It's Not

In *This Is How,* the book Burroughs says he "was born to write," the author draws on his life experiences to offer straightforward if unconventional advice on topics ranging from riding elevators to changing the world. "How to Identify Love by Knowing What It's Not," a chapter from the book, explores the delusions that can lead people to mistake cruelty for caring.

Love doesn't use a fist. 1

Love never calls you fat or lazy or ugly. 2

Love doesn't laugh at you in front of friends. 3

It is not in Love's interest for your self-esteem to be low. 4

Love is a helium-based emotion; Love always takes the high road. 5

Love does not make you beg. 6

Love does not make you deposit your paycheck into its bank account. 7

Love certainly never, never, never brings the children into it. 8

Love does not ask or even want you to change. But if you change, Love is 9
as excited about this change as you are, if not more so. And if you go back to
the way you were before you changed, Love will go back with you.

Love does not maintain a list of your flaws and weaknesses. 10

Love believes you.   11

Love is patient; Love does not make a point of showing you how patient   12
it is. It is critical to understand the distinction.

Patience is like donating a large sum of money to a charity anonymously.   13
What matters to you as the donor is that the charity receives the funding, not
who wrote the check, even if knowing who donated such a huge check would
wildly impress the world.

So, patience is exhibited only by a lack of pressure. This is how you know   14
it's there.

But when you see on the face of your partner or spouse an expression that   15
reads, "I'm being very patient with you," this could be the single detail that
alerts you to the fact that you are in an abusive relationship.

You can be in such a relationship and not even know it. You can receive   16
so many black eyes, you forget it's abnormal to have even one.

Physical violence is one kind of abuse. Emotional violence is another   17
kind of abuse. These assaults are delivered with concepts. People usually say,
emotional abuse is about words: fat, ugly, stupid, lazy. But it's not about words
because an emotionally abusive person doesn't always resort to using the verbal club, but rather the verbal untraceable poison.

They may, in fact, speak very kind words to you. And appear nothing but   18
supportive to those around you: Their covert abuse is administered in small, cunning ways. Over time. So the impact is gradual, not fist-to-the-eye immediate.

An abusive partner is controlling. They are manipulative. They might   19
make a special point of coyly sharing information that they actually know will
upset you. They might supply reasonable arguments as to why they and not
you should make important decisions.

If you possess talent or a natural ease and comfort with a particular ability   20
and your abusive partner is resentful, abuse might arrive in the form of sub-
traction: no remark at all, not a compliment or a gesture of support. Perhaps
one small, internally flawless diamond of a criticism will be presented.

Silence when there should be discussion to resolve an issue is another   21
method of abuse if the silence is used as a tool to frustrate or sadden or otherwise intentionally manipulate the emotions of another.

I knew of somebody . . . who was many years into an abusive relationship   22
but did not know it. She knew only that she had been so happy when they
met and that it seemed to her this feeling was bled out of her year after year,
and she found that she now resembled her partner, whom she had once seen
as strong and silent and loving but had come to understand was emotionally
disturbed and was not silent in his mind, but roiling.

When she finally left him she did so still loving him. She had been more   23
financially stable so she had given him their home. He had admitted to her

that for the last couple of years, he had been occupied with planning his suicide. He told her he'd worked out all the details and would do it in a quaint West Coast town right on the Pacific that they had frequently spoken of visiting but never seen.

When she left him she left their beloved dog with him because she worried a totally empty house would be dangerous. 24

Their plan had been to share the dog but he wanted nothing more to do with her. And the regular updates and photographs he had sent when they first parted stopped now completely. 25

Months passed and she heard nothing until he sent a brief email informing her that the dog now had a potential serious health problem and that he would take care of it. 26

She could not help but feel that he had taken a small measure of satisfaction knowing how brutal the news would be to her ears and how helpless she would feel being able to do nothing, not even see this dog she had loved for so long. 27

Emotional abuse is the process of breaking the spirit or shattering the confidence of another for one's own purpose. 28

Abusive people never change. There is no point of pursuing couples' therapy when one member of the relationship is abusive. A therapist may tell you otherwise. But I'm telling you the not-for-profit truth. Abusers do not change. 29

It will only get worse. 30

The difference between physical violence like a slap on the face or a shove and homicide can be as small as a few centimeters or the angle of approach. 31

Also, abusers are always very, very sorry. Men who abuse women probably shed more tears in one year than the combined tears of all the girls in the audience of a Renée Zellweger movie opening weekend at the Paris Theatre in Manhattan. 32

That's how sorry he is. 33

Or so he says, with his tears. 34

Of course, he's not sorry. She is. 35

Unless the roles are reversed. And the abuser is a woman, not a man. 36

Women can and do physically and emotionally abuse their partners. The perception that the abuser is always a man is false. . . . 37

People remain in abusive relationships for the same reasons they remain in loving ones: they've built a life together, they have children, financial interests, habit, nothing better. Lots of reasons. 38

But probably the number-one reason is simply not knowing they're in one. 39

You think of domestic violence and you think of a character and a weak victim: macho, powerful bully and a passive, frail woman and you don't recognize that. So it can't be you. 40

It might help, then, for me to show you in clinical terms what domestic   41
violence actually looks like on the printed page. This checklist is from the
National Domestic Violence Hotline. Ask yourself, does your partner:

- Embarrass you with put-downs
- Look at you or act in ways that scare you
- Control what you do, who you see or talk to, or where you go
- Stop you from seeing your friends or family members
- Take your money or Social Security check, make you ask for money, or refuse to give you money
- Make all of the decisions
- Tell you that you're a bad parent or threaten to take away or hurt your children
- Prevent you from working or attending school
- Act like the abuse is no big deal, it's your fault, or even deny doing it
- Destroy your property or threaten to kill your pets
- Intimidate you with guns, knives, or other weapons
- Shove you, slap you, choke you, or hit you
- Force you to try and drop charges
- Threaten to commit suicide
- Threaten to kill you

Think about the answers before you answer. Does he prevent you from   42
working? No, he encourages you, that's terrific.

Or does he?   43

Does he *maybe* prevent you a little by getting drunk and then, say, being   44
unable to find a certain pair of shoes so he turns the house upside down, creating such a scene, a ME, ME, ME moment that you can't possibly work?

Might he always, over and over, bring it all back to himself? Leaving no   45
room or time for you to work on your crafts, aka possible future home business
aka threat to him?

Domestic violence is extremely difficult to detect when it is happening to   46
you because domestic violence always only happens to other people, and you
are too smart and sophisticated to ever, for one moment, be with somebody
abusive. The thought is absurd. Domestic violence is a lower-class problem,
something that afflicts only those whose homes are clad in aluminum siding.

Besides, you would know if you were being abused.   47

Except the truth is, some things are too terrible to know; too impossible   48
to see; too painful to realize; too heartbreaking to face.

You could be in an abusive relationship and be unaware that you are,   49
unable to see the abuse for what it is.

Sometimes the truth must unspool slowly. It's simply impossible to grasp   50
it all at once. Perhaps, one day, you will be able to see a glimpse of abuse in
your relationship.

In time, you'll be able to see more.   51

Because if you allow yourself to have one small serving of reality, the hard   52
part, the opaque part, is over. And eventually, you'll be able to see the rest.

Also, the more unlikely it is that you would ever be in an abusive relation-   53
ship, the closer you need to look at your relationship. Not because you want
to try to see something sinister that simply isn't there, but because you're more
likely to be blind to abuse if it is there.

Just, you know, pay attention. To all those familiar, everyday things they say   54
to you or do to you. Ask, "If he said that to my friend, would I think it was mean?"

Try to actually hear what the person says to you. Try to hear it fresh. Try   55
to see if what they say to you might, in a way, also be a kind of steering wheel.

It's a spectrum, too. Maybe your partner isn't exactly "abusive" so much as   56
a little controlling. This is fairly easy to see.

What's difficult to see is when you're with somebody who is a full-strength   57
abuser. And maybe one reason it's so difficult to see something that to the rest
of the world — at least on paper — is so obvious is because there's no contrast. They are controlling and abusive and this is what they are.

If you realize you are in an abusive relationship, you may want to call this   58
phone number — it's toll-free so it won't cost you anything and it won't show
up on your phone bill. If possible, take the number with you and call from
somewhere else:

National Domestic Violence Hotline 1-800-799-SAFE (7233)   59

Seventy-nine-nine, seventy-two, thirty-three.   60

If you have children and your spouse is abusing them physically, mentally,   61
or sexually, leave now.

It never takes courage to leave.   62

It takes love.   63

Journal Writing

Anybody could be in an abusive relationship, Burroughs insists, although recognizing
the abuse can be difficult or even impossible. Do you agree? Have you witnessed any of
the behaviors he describes, whether in one of your relationships or in someone else's?

In your journal, describe the troubling aspects of that relationship. Did you recognize the behavior as abusive? Who was the victim, and who the abuser? Has the relationship ended, or is it still in place?

Questions on Meaning

1. What exactly does Burroughs define in this essay? Is his subject love, as the title suggests it will be, or something else entirely?

2. Where does Burroughs first state his THESIS? At what points does he restate his main idea? Why do you suppose he repeats himself as he does?

3. What do you make of the essay's final sentence? What, to the author, is the true measure of love? How and where does he define it?

4. How do you suppose Burroughs hoped readers would respond to this essay? What is his PURPOSE? What is your response, and why?

Questions on Writing Strategy

1. Many of Burroughs's paragraphs consist of a single sentence. Do you recognize the ALLUSION in paragraphs 1–12? What is the EFFECT of this allusion and of the other very short paragraphs in the essay?

2. This essay is a model of an *extended* definition, yet it also includes several *stipulative* definitions (see p. 438). Locate at least two of these. What do they contribute to Burroughs's meaning?

3. Examine the organization of the essay. What major sections does it fall into? Why do you think Burroughs chose to order the essay as he did?

4. Why does Burroughs provide a checklist from the National Domestic Violence Hotline in paragraph 41 and give the organization's phone number in paragraphs 60 and 61?

5. **OTHER METHODS**   How does Burroughs use a single extended EXAMPLE to clarify his point about emotional abuse?

Questions on Language

1. In much of the essay, Burroughs addresses readers directly, using the second-PERSON *you*. What does this language choice reveal about how he imagines his AUDIENCE?

2. Burroughs often uses the plural pronoun *they* to refer back to a singular *he, partner*, or *person*, as in "An abusive partner is controlling. They are manipulative" (par. 19). Where else does he do this? Does Burroughs seem to break the rules of pronoun-antecedent agreement for a reason, or is he guilty of using bad grammar? Why do you think so? (If necessary, refer to p. 52 for an explanation of pronoun-antecedent agreement.)

3. Consult a dictionary if you don't know the meaning of any of the following words: helium (par. 5); covert, cunning (18); coyly (19); roiling (22); clinical (41); unspool (50); opaque (52); sinister (53); spectrum (56).

4. How would you characterize the TONE of this essay: serious? detached? earnest? angry? compassionate? something else? Point to some words and phrases that support your answer.

Suggestions for Writing

1. **FROM JOURNAL TO ESSAY**   Expand your journal writing (pp. 474–75) into an essay explaining why and how a specific someone should leave an abusive relationship. You might write about somebody you know, about yourself, about a public figure, or about a fictional abuse victim, but take care to protect the person's anonymity. In your essay, draw on Burroughs's definitions and advice as appropriate to support your points, but be sure to develop a unique thesis of your own and to offer plenty of specifics to support your claims.

2. Write an essay that defines *love* or another strong feeling, such as *hate, compassion, happiness,* or *fear*. You might, like Burroughs, choose to focus on what the feeling is *not*, or you might prefer to define it by explaining what it *is*. In either case, be sure to provide a wide range of examples to suggest the various aspects of your subject.

3. **CRITICAL WRITING**   ANALYZE Burroughs's use of FIGURES OF SPEECH in this essay. How does the author combine *personification, metaphor, simile, paradox,* and similar devices to add meaning and a sense of empathy to his definition of abuse? In your analysis, pay particular attention to those figures of speech you find especially fresh or compelling.

4. **CONNECTIONS**   Compare Burroughs's "How to Identify Love by Knowing What It's Not" with Junot Díaz's "The Dreamer" (p. 88). Of these two highly subjective essays dealing with abuse, which is more personal? Write a brief essay answering this question, and support your answer with quotations and PARAPHRASES from Burroughs and Díaz.

ADDITIONAL WRITING TOPICS

Definition

1. Write an essay in which you define an institution, trend, phenomenon, or abstraction as specifically and concretely as possible. Following are some suggestions designed to stimulate ideas. Before you begin, limit your subject.

Responsibility	Fairness
Fun	Leadership
Empathy	Leisure
Plagiarism	Originality
Community	Integrity
Education	Imagination
Progress	Socialism
Advertising	A smile
Happiness	A classic (of music, literature, art, or film)
Fads	Success
Feminism	Meditation
Marriage	Friendship

2. In a brief essay, define one of the following. In each instance, you have a choice of something good or something bad to talk about.

    A good or bad boss
    A good or bad parent
    A good or bad host
    A good or bad athlete
    A good or bad physician
    A good or bad nurse
    A good or bad minister, priest, rabbi, or imam
    A good or bad roommate
    A good or bad driver
    A good or bad business

3. In a paragraph, define a slang expression or specialized term for someone who has never heard it. Possible expressions include *cisgender, sick, hook up, vaping, clickbait, wicked, poser, vine, swag, chill, hot mess.*

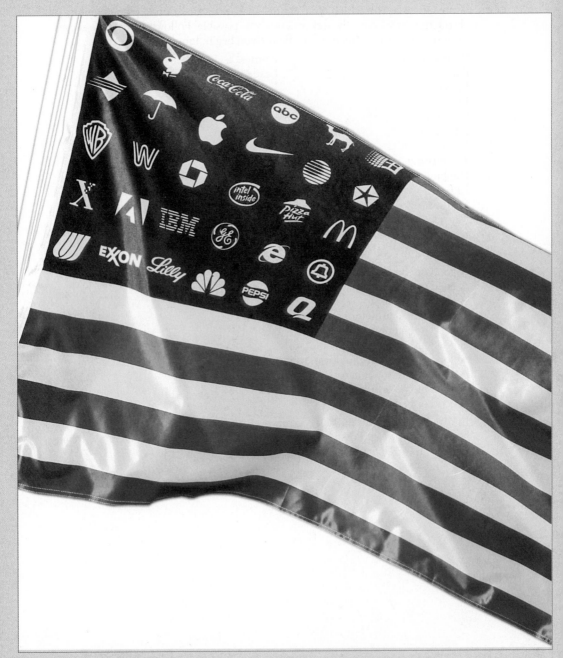

Courtesy of Adbusters Media Foundation

12

ARGUMENT AND PERSUASION

Stating Opinions and Proposals

◀ **Argument and persuasion in an image**

Adbusters Media Foundation, an activist group "concerned about the erosion of our physical and cultural environments by commercial forces," launched its Corporate America flag in 1999. This version appeared in a full-page advertisement in the *New York Times*. Showing the American flag's stars replaced by well-known corporate logos, the image adapts a symbol that many Americans revere to make a strong argument about the United States. What is the argument? How do you respond to the image: Are you offended? persuaded? amused? Why? Whatever your view, do you understand why others might think differently?

THE METHOD

Practically every day, we try to persuade ourselves or someone else. We usually attempt such persuasion without being aware that we follow any special method at all. Often, we'll state an *opinion*: We'll tell someone our way of viewing things. We say to a friend, "I'm starting to like Senator Clark. Look at all she's done to help people with disabilities. Look at her voting record on the minimum wage." And, having stated these opinions, we might go on to make a *proposal*, to recommend that some action be taken. Addressing our friend, we might suggest, "Hey, Senator Clark is speaking on campus at four-thirty. Want to come with me and listen to her?"

Sometimes you try to convince yourself that a certain way of interpreting things is right. You even set forth your opinion in writing — as in a post to a social media site complaining about unreasonable return policies at a certain retailer. You might write an e-mail of protest to a landlord who wants to raise your rent, pointing out that the bathroom hot water faucet doesn't work. As a concerned citizen, you may wish to speak your mind in an occasional letter to an editor or to an elected representative.

Many professions involve persuading people in writing as well. Before arguing a case in court, lawyers prepare briefs setting forth all the points in favor of their sides. Businesspeople regularly put in writing their ideas for new products and ventures, for improvements in cost control and job efficiency. Researchers write proposals for grants to obtain money to support their work. Scientists write and publish papers to persuade the scientific community that their findings are valid, often stating hypotheses, or tentative opinions.

Even if you never produce a single persuasive work (which is very unlikely), you will certainly encounter such works directed at you. We live our lives under a steady rain of opinions and proposals. Organizations that work for causes campaign with broadcast media and direct mail, all hoping that we will see things their way. Moreover, we are bombarded with proposals from people who wish us to act. Religious leaders urge us to lead more virtuous lives. Advertisers urge us to rush right out and buy the large economy size.

Small wonder, then, that argument and persuasion — and CRITICAL THINKING about argument and persuasion — may be among the most useful skills a college student can acquire. Time and again, your instructors will ask you to criticize or to state opinions, either in class or in writing. You may be asked to state your view of anything from the Electoral College to animal rights. You may be asked to judge the desirability or undesirability of compulsory testing for drugs or revision of the existing immigration laws. Critically reading other people's arguments and composing your own, you will find, helps you discover what you think, refine it, and share what you believe.

Be aware that the terms *argument* and *persuasion* have somewhat different meanings: PERSUASION aims to influence readers' actions, or their support for

an action, by engaging their beliefs and feelings, while ARGUMENT aims to win
readers' agreement with an assertion or claim by engaging their powers of reasoning. However, most effective argument or persuasion contains elements of
both methods. In this book we tend to use the terms interchangeably.

One other point: We tend to talk here about *writing* arguments, but most
of what we say has to do with *reading* them as well. When we discuss your
need, as a writer, to support your claims, we are also discussing your need, as a
reader, to question the support other authors provide for their claims. In reading arguments critically, you apply the critical-thinking skills we discussed in
Chapter 1 — ANALYSIS, INFERENCE, SYNTHESIS, and EVALUATION — to a particular
kind of writing.

Audience and Common Ground

Unlike some advertisers, responsible writers of argument do not try to
storm people's minds. In writing a paper for a course, you persuade by gentler
means: by sharing your view with an AUDIENCE willing to consider it. You'll
want to learn how to express your view clearly and vigorously. But to be fair
and persuasive, it is important to understand your readers' views as well.

In stating your opinion, you present the truth as you see it: "The immigration laws discourage employers from hiring nonnative workers," perhaps, or
"The immigration laws protect legal aliens." To persuade your readers that your
view makes sense, you need not begin by proclaiming that your view is absolutely right and should prevail. Instead, you might begin by trying to state what
your readers probably think, as best you can infer it. You don't consider views
that differ from your own merely to flatter your readers. You do so to balance
your own view and make it more accurate. Writer and reader become two sen-
sible people trying to find COMMON GROUND, or points on which both can agree.
This approach will relieve you, whenever you have to state your opinions in
writing, of the terrible obligation to be one hundred percent right at all times.

Elements of Argument

The British philosopher Stephen Toulmin has proposed a useful division
of argument into distinct elements. Adapted to the terminology of this book,
they are *claims, evidence, appeals,* and *assumptions.*

Claims and Thesis Statements

A CLAIM is an assertion that requires support. It is what an argument tries
to convince readers to accept. The central claim — the main point — is
almost always stated explicitly in a THESIS STATEMENT like one of the following:

A CLAIM ABOUT REALITY   The war on drugs is not winnable because laws can-not eradicate demand or the supply to meet it.

A CLAIM OF VALUE   Drug abuse is a personal matter that should not be subject to government interference.

A CLAIM FOR A COURSE OF ACTION   The United States must intensify its efforts to reduce production of heroin in Afghanistan.

Usually, but not always, you'll state your thesis at the beginning of your essay, making a play for readers' attention and clueing them in to your pur-pose. But if you think readers may have difficulty accepting your thesis until they've heard some or all of your argument, then you might save the thesis statement for the middle or end.

The essays in this chapter provide a variety of thesis statements as models. Here are four examples:

> The fact that so many illegal immigrants are intertwined with American citi-zens or legal residents, either as spouses or parents, should give pause to those who'd like to see all illegal immigrants rounded up and deported or their lives made so miserable they leave on their own.
> — Linda Chavez, "Supporting Family Values"

> Such measures [calling for "trigger warnings" on college syllabi] certainly have a potential to be taken too far, but our obligation to prevent a trauma survivor's class time becoming a living hell outweighs concerns about a stunted learning environment.
> — Brianne Richson, "An Obligation to Prevent Trauma on Campus"

> My main gripe with trigger warnings . . . is that while they aim to be sensi-tive to people suffering from afflictions like post-traumatic stress disorder, they threaten to stifle some of the most important conversations and lessons in college.
> — Jon Overton, "Beware the Trigger Warning"

> Ads that pop up on your screen might seem useful, or at worst, a nuisance. But they are much more than that. The bits and bytes about your life can easily be used against you. . . . We need a do-not-track law, similar to the do-not-call one.
> — Lori Andrews, "*Facebook* Is Using You"

Evidence

Claims are nothing without the EVIDENCE to make them believable and convincing. Toulmin calls evidence *data* or *grounds*, using terms that convey how specific and fundamental it is. Depending on your subject, your evidence may include facts, statistics (facts expressed in numbers), expert opinions, examples, and reported experiences. These kinds of evidence should meet certain criteria.

- **Accuracy:** Facts, examples, and opinions should be taken from reliable sources and presented without error or distortion.

- **Representation:** The evidence should reflect reality, neither slanting nor exaggerating it.

- **Relevance:** All evidence should apply directly to the claims, reflecting current thinking by recognized experts.

- **Adequacy:** The evidence should be sufficient to support the claims entirely, not just in part.

Appeals

To strengthen the support for your claims, you can also make APPEALS to readers either directly or indirectly, in the way you present your evidence. In classical argument these appeals are often referred to as *logos, ethos,* and *pathos;* we refer to them as RATIONAL APPEALS, ETHICAL APPEALS, and EMOTIONAL APPEALS, respectively.

- **Rational appeals** rely on sound reasoning (*logos*) and marshal evidence that meets the criteria above. See pages 484–87 for more on reasoning.

- **Ethical appeals** show readers that you are a well-informed person of goodwill, good sense, and good moral character — and, therefore, to be believed (*ethos*). Strengthen your ethical appeal by collecting ample evidence, reasoning carefully, demonstrating respect for opposing views, using an appropriate emotional appeal (see below), and minding your TONE (see p. 490).

- **Emotional appeals** acknowledge what you know of readers' sympathies and beliefs and show how your argument relates to them (*pathos*). An example in this chapter appears in Linda Chavez's "Supporting Family Values": The author argues for immigration reform by appealing to readers' respect for intact families and fear of cultural disintegration. Carefully used, an emotional appeal can stir readers to constructive belief and action by engaging their feelings as well as their minds, as long as the appeal is appropriate for the audience and the argument.

Assumptions

Another element of argument, the ASSUMPTION, is in Toulmin's concep-tion the connective tissue between grounds, or evidence, and claims: An assumption explains why the evidence leads to and justifies a claim. Called a *warrant* by Toulmin, an assumption is usually a belief, a principle, or an inference whose truth the writer takes for granted. Here is how an assumption might figure in an argument for one of the claims given earlier:

CLAIM   The United States must intensify its efforts to reduce the production of heroin in Afghanistan.

EVIDENCE   Afghanistan is the world's largest heroin producer and a major supplier to the United States.

ASSUMPTION   The United States can and should reduce the production of heroin in other countries when its own citizens are affected.

As important as they are, the assumptions underlying an argument are not always stated. As we will see in the discussion of deductive reasoning, which begins on the next page, unstated assumptions can sometimes pitch an argu-ment into trouble.

Reasoning

When we argue rationally, we reason — that is, we make statements that lead to a conclusion. Two reliable methods of rational argument date back to the classical Greek philosopher Aristotle, who identified the complementary processes of inductive and deductive reasoning.

Inductive Reasoning

In INDUCTIVE REASONING, the method of the sciences, we collect bits of evidence on which to base a GENERALIZATION, the claim of the argument. The assumption linking evidence and claim is that what is true for some cir-cumstances is true for others as well. For instance, you might interview a hun-dred representative students about their attitudes toward changing your school's honor code. You find that 65% of the interviewees believe that the code should remain as it is, 15% believe that the code should be toughened, 10% believe that it should be loosened, and 10% have no opinion. You then assume that these statistics can be applied to the student body as a whole and make a claim against changing the code because 65% of students don't want change.

The more evidence you have, the more trustworthy your claim will be, but it would never be airtight unless you interviewed every student on campus. Since such thoroughness is almost always impractical if not impossible, you

assume in an *inductive leap* that the results can be generalized. The smaller the leap — the more evidence you have — the better.

Deductive Reasoning

DEDUCTIVE REASONING works the opposite way of inductive reasoning: It moves from a general statement to particular cases. The basis of deduction is the SYLLOGISM, a three-step form of reasoning practiced by Aristotle:

> All men are mortal.
>
> Socrates is a man.
>
> Therefore, Socrates is mortal.

The first statement, called a *major premise*, is an assumption: a fact, principle, or inference that you believe to be true. The second statement, or *minor premise*, is the evidence — the new information about a particular member of the larger group named in the major premise. The third statement, or *conclusion*, is the claim that follows inevitably from the premises. If the premises are true, then the conclusion must be true. Following is another example of a syllogism. You may recognize it from the discussion of assumptions on page 484, only here the statements are simplified and arranged differently:

> MAJOR PREMISE (ASSUMPTION)   The United States can and should reduce heroin production when its own citizens are affected.
>
> MINOR PREMISE (EVIDENCE)   A major producer of heroin for the US market is Afghanistan.
>
> CONCLUSION (THESIS)   The United States can and should reduce heroin production in Afghanistan.

Problems with deductive reasoning start in the premises. Consider this untrustworthy syllogism: "To do well in school, students must cheat a little. Jolene wants to do well in school. Therefore, she must cheat." This is bad deductive reasoning, and its flaw is in its major premise, which is demonstrably untrue: Plenty of students do well without cheating. Because the premise is false, the conclusion is necessarily false as well.

When they're spelled out neatly, bad syllogisms are pretty easy to spot. But many deductive arguments are not spelled out. Instead, one of the premises goes unstated, as in this statement: "Mayor Perkins was humiliated in his recent bid for reelection, winning only 2,000 out of 5,000 votes." The unstated assumption here, the major premise, is "Winning only two-fifths of the votes humiliates a candidate." (The rest of the syllogism: "Mayor Perkins received only two-fifths of the votes. Thus, Mayor Perkins was humiliated.")

The unstated premise isn't necessarily a problem in argument — in fact, it's quite common. But it *is* a problem when it's wrong or unfounded. For instance,

in the statement "She shouldn't be elected mayor because her husband has bad ideas on how to run the city," the unstated assumption is that the candidate cannot form ideas independently of her husband. This is a possibility, perhaps, but it requires its own discussion and proof, not concealment behind other assertions.

Logical Fallacies

In arguments we read and hear, we often meet logical FALLACIES: errors in reasoning that lead to wrong conclusions. From the time you start thinking about your thesis and claims and begin planning your paper, you'll need to watch out for them. To help you recognize logical fallacies when you see them or hear them, and so guard against them when you write, here is a list of the most common.

- **Non sequitur** (from the Latin, "it does not follow"): stating a conclusion that doesn't follow from one or both premises.

   I've lived in this town a long time — why, my great-grandfather was one of the first settlers — so I'm against putting fluoride in the drinking water.

- **Oversimplification:** supplying neat and easy explanations for large and complicated phenomena.

   No wonder drug abuse is out of control. Look at how the courts have hobbled police officers.

   Oversimplified solutions are also popular:

   All these teenage kids that get in trouble with the law — why, they ought to put them in work camps. That would straighten them out!

- **Post hoc, ergo propter hoc** (from the Latin, "after this, therefore because of this"), or *post hoc* for short: a form of oversimplification assuming that because B follows A, B was caused by A.

   Ever since the city suspended height restrictions on skyscrapers, the city budget has been balanced.

   (For more on *post hoc* and oversimplification, see the discussion in Chapter 10 on cause-and-effect analysis, pp. 392–93.)

- **Either/or reasoning:** assuming that a reality may be divided into only two parts or extremes or assuming that a given problem has only one of two possible solutions.

   What's to be done about the trade imbalance with Asia? Either we ban all Asian imports, or American industry will collapse.

   Obviously, either/or reasoning is a kind of extreme oversimplification.

- **Hasty generalization:** leaping to a generalization from inadequate or faulty evidence. The most familiar hasty generalization is the stereotype.

  Men aren't sensitive enough to be day-care providers.
  Women are too emotional to fight in combat.

- **Argument from doubtful or unidentified authority:** citing an unreliable source.

  Uncle Oswald says that we ought to imprison all sex offenders for life.
  According to an anonymous informant, my opponent is lying.

- **Argument ad hominem** (from the Latin, "to the man"): attacking a person's views by attacking his or her character.

  Mayor Burns is divorced and estranged from his family. How can we listen to his pleas for a city nursing home?

- **Begging the question:** taking for granted from the start what you set out to demonstrate. When you reason in a *logical* way, you state that because something is true, then, as a result, some other truth follows. When you beg the question, however, you repeat that what is true is true.

  Dogs are a menace to people because they are dangerous.

  This statement proves nothing, because the idea that dogs are dangerous is already assumed in the statement that they are a menace. Beggars of questions often just repeat what they already believe, only in different words. This fallacy sometimes takes the form of arguing in a circle, or demonstrating a premise by a conclusion and a conclusion by a premise.

  I am in college because that is the right thing to do. Going to college is the right thing to do because it is expected of me.

- **False analogy:** the claim of persuasive likeness when no significant likeness exists. An ANALOGY asserts that because two things are comparable in some respects, they are comparable in other respects as well. Analogies cannot serve as evidence in rational arguments because the differences always outweigh the similarities; but analogies can reinforce such arguments *if* the subjects are indeed similar in some ways. If they aren't, the analogy is false. Many observers see the "war on drugs" as a false and damaging analogy because warfare aims for clear victory over a specific, organized enemy, whereas the complete eradication of illegal drugs is probably unrealistic and, in any event, the "enemy" isn't well defined: the drugs themselves? users? sellers? producers? the producing nations? (These critics urge approaching drugs as a social problem to be skillfully managed and reduced.)

THE PROCESS

Finding a Subject

Your way into a subject will probably vary depending on whether you're writing an argument that supports an opinion or one that proposes a change. In stating an opinion, you set forth and support a claim — a truth you believe. You may find such a truth by thinking and feeling, by reading, by talking to your instructors or fellow students, by listening to a discussion of some problem or controversy. Before you run with a subject, take a minute to weigh it: Is this something about which reasonable people disagree? Arguments go nowhere when they start with ideas that are generally accepted (pets should not have to endure physical abuse from their owners) or are beyond the pale (pet owners should be able to hurt their animals if they want).

In stating a proposal, you already have an opinion in mind, and from there, you go on to urge an action or a solution to a problem. Usually, these two statements will take place within the same piece of writing: You will first set forth a view ("The campus honor code is unfair to first offenders"), provide the evidence to support it, and then present your proposal as a remedy ("The campus honor code should be revised to give more latitude to first offenders").

Whatever your subject, resist the temptation to make it big. If you have two weeks to prepare, an argument about the litter problem in your town is probably manageable: In that time you could conduct your own visual research and talk to town officials. But an argument about the litter problem in your town compared with that in similar-sized towns across the state would surely demand more time than you have.

Organizing

There's no one right way to organize an argument because so much depends on how your readers will greet your claim and your evidence. Below we give some ideas for different situations.

Introduction

In your opening paragraph or two, draw readers in by connecting them to your subject if possible, showing its significance, and providing any needed background. End the INTRODUCTION with your thesis statement if you think readers will entertain it before they've seen the evidence. Put the thesis statement later, in the middle or even at the end of the essay, if you think readers need to see some or all of the evidence in order to be open to the idea.

Body

The BODY of the essay develops and defends the points that support your thesis. Generally, start with your least important point and build in a crescendo to your strongest point. However, if you think readers may resist your ideas, consider starting strong and then offering the more minor points as reinforcement.

For every point you make, give the evidence that supports it. The methods of development can help here, providing many options for injecting evidence. Say you were arguing for or against further reductions in welfare funding. You might give EXAMPLES of wasteful spending, or of neighborhoods where welfare funds are still needed. You might spell out the CAUSES of social problems that call for welfare funds, or foresee the likely EFFECTS of cutting welfare programs or of keeping them. You could use NARRATION to tell a pointed story; you could use DESCRIPTION to portray certain welfare recipients and their neighborhoods.

Response to Objections

Part of the body of the essay, but separated here for emphasis, a response to probable objections is crucial to effective argument. If you are arguing fairly, you should be able to face potential criticisms fairly and give your critics due credit, reasoning with them, not dismissing them. This is the strategy Linda Chavez uses later in this chapter in "Supporting Family Values" (p. 495) by conceding, more than once, that arguments against immigration have some merit ("But the greater concern for some opponents," "It is true that," and so on) before she points out what she sees as their logical flaws. As Chavez does, you can tackle possible objections throughout your essay, as they pertain to your points. You can also field objections near the end of the essay, an approach that allows you to draw on all of your evidence. But if you think that readers' own opposing views may stiffen their resistance to your argument, you may want to address those views very early, before developing your own points.

Conclusion

The CONCLUSION gives you a chance to gather your points, restate your thesis in a fresh way, and leave readers with a compelling final idea. In an essay with a strong emotional component, you may want to end with an appeal to readers' feelings. But even in a mostly rational argument, try to involve readers in some way, showing why they should care or what they can do.

FOCUS ON TONE

Readers are most likely to be persuaded by an argument when they sense that the writer is reasonable, trustworthy, and sincere. Sound reasoning, strong evidence, and acknowledgment of opposing views do much to convey these attributes, but so does tone, the attitude implied by choice of words and sentence structures.

Generally, you should try for a tone of moderation in your view of your subject and a tone of respectfulness and goodwill toward readers and opponents.

- **State opinions and facts calmly:**

  OVEREXCITED   One clueless administrator was quoted in the newspaper as saying she thought many students who claim learning disabilities are "faking" their difficulties to obtain special treatment! Has she never heard of dyslexia, attention deficit disorders, and other well-established disabilities?

  CALM   Particularly worrisome was one administrator's statement, quoted in the newspaper, that many students who claim learning disabilities may be "faking" their difficulties to obtain special treatment.

- **Replace arrogance with deference:**

  ARROGANT   I happen to know that many students would rather party or just bury their heads in the sand than get involved in a serious, worthy campaign against the school's unjust learning-disabled policies.

  DEFERENTIAL   Time pressures and lack of information about the issues may be what prevent students from joining the campaign against the school's unjust learning-disabled policies.

- **Replace sarcasm with plain speaking:**

  SARCASTIC   Of course, the administration knows even without meeting students what is best for every one of them.

  PLAIN   The administration should agree to meet with each learning-disabled student to learn about his or her needs.

- **Choose words whose CONNOTATIONS convey reasonableness** rather than anger, hostility, or another negative emotion:

  HOSTILE   The administration coerced some students into dropping their lawsuits. [*Coerced* implies the use of threats or even violence.]

  REASONABLE   The administration convinced some students to drop their lawsuits. [*Convinced* implies the use of reason.]

  (For more on connotations and tone in general, refer to the Glossary and to pages 48–49 in Chapter 2.)

CHECKLIST FOR REVISING ARGUMENT AND PERSUASION

✔ **Audience.** Have you taken account of your readers' probable views? Have you reasoned with readers, not attacked them? Are your emotional appeals appropriate to readers' likely feelings? Do you acknowledge opposing views?

✔ **Thesis.** Does your argument have a thesis, a claim about how your subject is or should be? Is the thesis narrow enough to argue convincingly in the space and time available? Is it stated clearly? Is it reasonable?

✔ **Evidence.** Is your thesis well supported with facts, statistics, expert opinions, and examples? Is your evidence accurate, representative, relevant, and adequate?

✔ **Assumptions.** Have you made sound connections between your evidence and your thesis and other claims?

✔ **Logical fallacies.** Have you avoided common errors in reasoning, such as oversimplifying or begging the question? (See pp. 486–87 for a list of fallacies.)

✔ **Structure.** Does your organization lead readers through your argument step by step, building to your strongest ideas and frequently connecting your evidence to your central claim?

✔ **Tone.** Is the tone of your argument reasonable and respectful?

ARGUMENT AND PERSUASION IN ACADEMIC WRITING

A Public Relations Textbook

Taken from *Public Relations: Strategies and Tactics,* by Dennis L. Wilcox, Phillip H. Ault, and Warren K. Agee, the following paragraph argues that lobbyists (who work to persuade public officials on behalf of a cause) are not slick manipulators but something else. The paragraph falls in the textbook's section on lobbying as a form of public relations, and its purpose is to correct a mistaken definition.

Although the public stereotypes a lobbyist as a fast-talking person twisting an elected official's arm to get special concessions, the reality is quite different. Today's lobbyist, who may be fully employed by one industry or represent a variety of clients, is often a quiet-spoken, well-educated man or woman armed with statistics and research reports. Robert Gray, former head of Hill and Knowlton's Washington office and a public affairs expert for thirty years, adds, "Lobbying is no longer a booze and buddies business. It's presenting

Topic sentence: the claim

Evidence:
• Expert opinion

Argument and Persuasion

honest facts and convincing Congress that your side has more merit than the other." He rejects lobbying as being simply "influence ped-dling and button-holing" top administration officials. Although the public has the perception that lobbying is done only by big business, Gray correctly points out that a variety of special interests also do it. These may include such groups as the Sierra Club, Mothers Against Drunk Driving, the National Association of Social Workers, the American Civil Liberties Union, and the American Federation of Labor. Even the American Society of Plastic and Reconstructive Surgeons hired a Washington public relations firm in their battle against restrictions on breast implants. Lobbying, quite literally, is an activity in which widely diverse groups and organizations engage as an exercise of free speech and representation in the marketplace of ideas. Lobbyists often balance each other and work toward leg-islative compromises that benefit not only their self-interests but society as a whole.

• Facts and examples

A Proposal

In many courses and occupations, you'll be expected to write proposals that identify specific problems or related sets of problems and argue for rea-sonable solutions. A proposal usually addresses clearly defined readers who are in a position to take action or approve an action. It addresses those readers' unique needs and concerns, anticipating objections and offering evidence to demonstrate the benefits of the solution.

As a nursing student in California as well as a mother, Adrianne Silver knew that school districts across the nation had been struggling with an escalating problem of bullying and that many states had recently insti-tuted new laws to address the issue. Eager to see her own state government improve its response, she researched possible changes and also attitudes toward change on the part of schoolteachers and administrators. The fol-lowing paragraphs come from her longer proposal for a law mandating pros-ecution and counseling for bullies. Before this section, Silver opened with an overview of the problem and of recent laws that had been passed in response to bullied students' suicides. After this section, Silver explained her solution in greater detail, suggested steps for implementing it, and addressed objections more fully.

Yet with all the anti-bullying policies, procedures, and training being implemented nationwide, not much is being done to address the behavior before it reaches the level of violence. Unfortunately, many teachers have the opinion that teasing

Transition from discussion of problem

and taunting is just "kids being kids" and that nothing needs to be done. But these kids grow up to become teenagers with destructive behaviors. If we are to reduce aggression, we must understand the cause and deal with the offender while the behavior can still be corrected.

Acknowledgment of objections

In order to reduce the problem of school bullying, I propose to establish a new law . . . to make bullying or discrimination and harassment a summary offense, which does not require a jury trial. Unlike existing laws that provide only guidelines to protect students from acts of bullying, this new law will take the course of action one step further: If a student is accused of bullying, it will be mandatory for the incident to be reported to the police. The student will be charged and must appear in juvenile court for disciplinary action.

Solution: new law making bullying a "summary offense"

The penalty for this offense will include court-mandated counseling to determine the severity of the student's behavior. In accordance with the California Education Code, suspension from school may be recommended, and family counseling may also be imposed. The student's parents or guardians will be responsible for adhering to all treatment(s) as recommended by the court counselor. . . . If the student commits a second offense, he or she will receive a one-week suspension and family counseling will be required as a condition of returning to school. A third offense will result in mandatory expulsion. Each incident and court ruling will be noted in the student's permanent school records and police record.

Elements of the solution:

• Criminal charges

• Court-mandated counseling

• Consequences (suspension, expulsion) for additional offenses

Enforcement of this new anti-bullying law will be the key to its success. It will be the responsibility of the teachers, school counselors, school administrators, and parents or guardians of each student to ensure that all claims of discrimination and harassment are reported and investigated. Failure of a school administrator to investigate any complaint can be reported to the school board, and the school board will be obligated to compel an immediate investigation.

• Enforcement

Once a student is found guilty of discrimination and harassment, the police and juvenile court will enforce the penalty. The court will monitor the individual's progress through

family counseling, and the school administrator will be advised
of the student's status.

Each day another bully becomes empowered when his or   Response to objections
her actions are dismissed and the victim's cries are ignored.
We must be more proactive in dealing with these offenders
before more young lives are needlessly lost.

LINDA CHAVEZ

An outspoken commentator on issues of civil rights and affirmative action, Linda Chavez was born in 1947 in Albuquerque, New Mexico, to a Spanish American family long established in the Southwest. She graduated from the University of Colorado (BA, 1970) and did graduate work at the University of California at Los Angeles and at the University of Maryland. She has held a number of government positions, including director of the White House Office of Public Liaison under President Ronald Reagan and chair of the National Commission on Migrant Education under President George H. W. Bush. She has published three books: *Out of the Barrio: Toward a New Politics of Hispanic Assimilation* (1991), which argues against affirmative action and bilingual education; *An Unlikely Conservative: The Transformation of an Ex-Liberal (Or How I Became the Most Hated Hispanic in America)* (2002); and *Betrayal: How Union Bosses Shake Down Their Members and Corrupt American Politics* (with Daniel Gray, 2004). Chavez currently directs the Becoming American Institute, a nonprofit public policy organization. She also writes a syndicated newspaper column and is a political analyst for Fox News. She lives in Purcellville, Virginia.

Supporting Family Values

In this piece written in 2009 for *townhall.com*, a conservative news and information site, Chavez makes an unusual case in favor of immigration, legal or not. Presenting evidence that challenges the stereotype of immigrants as unstable and unable to adapt to life in the United States, she argues that established American citizens should be taking life lessons from their newest neighbors.

A new report out this week from the Pew Hispanic Center confirms what many observers already suspected about the illegal immigrant population in the United States: It is made up increasingly of intact families and their American-born children. Nearly half of illegal immigrant households consist of two-parent families with children, and 73% of these children were born here and are therefore US citizens.

The hard-line immigration restrictionists will, no doubt, find more cause for alarm in these numbers. But they should represent hope to the rest of us. One of the chief social problems afflicting this country is the breakdown in the traditional family. But among immigrants, the two-parent household is alive and well.

"Supporting Family Values" from *townhall.com*, Friday, April 17, 2009. Reprinted by permission of Linda Chavez and Creators Syndicate, Inc.

Only 21% of native households are made up of two parents living with   3
their own children. Among legal immigrants, the percentage of such households jumps to 35%. But among the illegal population, 47% of households
consist of a mother, a father and their children.

Age accounts for the major difference in household composition between   4
the native and foreign-born populations: Immigrants, especially illegal
immigrants, tend to be younger, while the native population includes large
numbers of older Americans whose children have already left home. But out-
of-wedlock births and divorce, which are more common among the native
born — especially blacks, but also Hispanics and whites — also mean that
even young native households with children are more likely to be headed by
single women than immigrant households are.

But the greater concern for some opponents of immigration — legal and   5
illegal — is the fear that these newcomers will never fully adapt, won't learn
English, will remain poor and uneducated, and transform the United States
into a replica of Mexico or some other Latin American country. The same
fears led Americans of the mid-nineteenth century to fear German and Irish
immigrants, and in the early twentieth century to fear Italians, Jews, Poles and
others from Eastern and Southern Europe.

Such worries are no more rational today — or born out of actual   6
evidence — than they were a hundred years ago. It is true that Hispanic
immigrants today take a while to catch up with the native born just as their
European predecessors did, and illegal immigrants never fully do so in terms
of education or earnings. But there is still some room for optimism in the
Pew Hispanic report. Nearly half of illegal immigrants between the ages of
18 and 24 who have graduated from high school attend college. A surprising
25% of illegal immigrant adults have at least some college, with 15% having
completed college.

And although earnings among illegal immigrants are lower than among   7
either the native population or legal immigrants, they are far from destitute.
The median household income for illegal immigrants was $36,000 in 2007
compared with $50,000 for native-born households. And illegal immigrant
males have much higher labor force participation rates than the native born,
94% compared with 83% for US-born males.

The inflow of illegal immigrants has slowed substantially since the peak,   8
which occurred during the economic boom of the late 1990s, not in recent
years, contrary to popular but uninformed opinion. The Pew Hispanic Center
estimates there are nearly 12 million illegal immigrants living in the United
States now, a number that has stabilized over the last few years as a result both
of better border enforcement and the declining job market. As a result, there

might never be a better time to grapple with what to do about this population than right now.

The fact that so many illegal immigrants are intertwined with American   9
citizens or legal residents, either as spouses or parents, should give pause to those who'd like to see all illegal immigrants rounded up and deported or their lives made so miserable they leave on their own. A better approach would allow those who have made their lives here, established families, bought homes, worked continuously and paid taxes to remain after paying fines, demonstrating English fluency and proving they have no criminal record. Such an approach is as much about supporting family values as it is granting amnesty.

Journal Writing

How do you feel about illegal immigrants? Are they criminals who should be punished? victims of circumstance who should be helped? something in between? In your journal, explore your thoughts on illegal immigration. Why do you feel as you do?

Questions on Meaning

1. What seems to have prompted Chavez's essay? How can you tell?

2. What distinctions, if any, does Chavez make between legal and illegal immigrants? Are such distinctions important to her?

3. What is Chavez's point in paragraphs 5 and 6, and how does this point fit into her larger argument?

4. At what point does Chavez reveal her PURPOSE in writing? Why do you suppose she chose not to state her THESIS in the introduction?

Questions on Writing Strategy

1. How does Chavez characterize those who hold opposing views? What does this characterization suggest about how she imagines her AUDIENCE?

2. On what underlying ASSUMPTION does Chavez base her argument? Is that assumption reasonable?

3. As a whole, is Chavez's essay an appeal to emotion or a reasoned argument, or both? Give EVIDENCE to support your answer.

4. **OTHER METHODS**   Where and how does Chavez use CLASSIFICATION to support her argument?

Questions on Language

1. Consult a dictionary if you are unsure of the meaning of any of the following: restrictionists (par. 2); wedlock (4); replica (5); predecessors (6); destitute, median (7); stabilized, grapple (8); intertwined, amnesty (9).

2. What does Chavez mean by "native" households and populations? Do you detect any IRONY in her use of the word?

3. How would you describe Chavez's TONE in this essay?

Suggestions for Writing

1. **FROM JOURNAL TO ESSAY** Based on your journal entry (p. 497), draft an essay in which you respond directly to Chavez, explaining why you agree or disagree with her position. If you wish, write your essay as a letter to the editor of *townhall. com*, the online journal in which Chavez's essay was published. (See p. 396 for an example of a letter to the editor.)

2. Write an essay in which you present your view on an aspect of US immigration policy or practice that you have strong opinions about — for example, amnesty for illegal immigrants, treatment of asylum seekers, border control, or restrictions on immigration. Before beginning your draft, do some research to support your position and also to explore opposing views so that you answer them squarely and fairly.

3. Identify a current controversy over national policy — raising taxes for the wealthy, the right to carry a concealed weapon, government funding for private schools, and so on. Read newspaper and weekly magazine editorials, letters to the editor, and other statements on the subject of the controversy. You could also discuss the issue with your friends and family. Based on your research, write a classification essay in which you group people according to their stand on the issue. Try to be as objective as possible.

4. **CRITICAL WRITING** Write an essay in which you ANALYZE the main CLAIMS of Chavez's argument. What evidence does she provide to back up these claims? Do you find the evidence adequate? (You may wish to track down and examine the source Chavez cites in her introduction: Published by the Pew Hispanic Center on April 14, 2009, its title is *A Portrait of Unauthorized Immigrants in the United States*.)

5. **CONNECTIONS** While defending the status of some illegal immigrants, Chavez stresses the need for all immigrants to "fully adapt," or assimilate, to American culture. Read Tal Fortgang's "Checking My Privilege" (p. 446), which touches on the author's grandparents' experiences as Polish refugees during World War II. What does it mean to be "American" in a country as diverse as the United States? In an essay, define, defend, or dispute the concept of assimilation. To what extent should recent immigrants be expected to trade ethnic or national identity for a new American identity? What might such an identity encompass, and how could it be obtained? What is gained, or lost, when immigrants become "Americanized"?

Linda Chavez on Writing

To Linda Chavez, telling writers they don't need to know the rules of grammar is like "telling aerospace engineers they don't need to learn the laws of physics." In a 2002 article for *The Enterprise*, Chavez writes about her affection for the lost art of diagramming sentences — using a branching structure to identify sentence parts and map their relationships. She fondly recalls her years in elementary school, then called "grammar school," when learning "where to place a modifier and whether to use an adverb or adjective" was an essential part of the curriculum. Abandoning grammar instruction, she writes, is leaving students scrambled.

Chavez criticizes recent classroom practices of emphasizing creativity over accuracy in composition: "For years now, schools have been teaching students to 'express' themselves, without worrying about transmitting the finer points of grammar and syntax. . . . But effective communication always entails understanding the rules. There are no short-cuts to good writing." According to Chavez, self-expression and grammar are not at odds with each other at all. As she sees it, a solid grasp of grammar is what allows a writer to clearly communicate meaning. In her own writing, Chavez follows the adage of her childhood teacher: "If you can't diagram it, don't write it."

The Bedford Reader on Writing

Like many of the educators Chavez criticizes, we, too, suggest setting sentence-level concerns aside when you begin to write, because doing so is an important tool in getting that first draft done (see p. 34). A finished essay needs a different set of tools, however, and we have to agree with Chavez that grammar is a useful one. For a rundown of ways to bring polish to your writing, and to correct common grammatical errors in particular, check out "Editing" in Chapter 2 (pp. 47–53).

CHUCK DIXON AND PAUL RIVOCHE

Born in Philadelphia in 1954, comics legend Chuck Dixon has written graphic novels — most notably an adaption of J. R. R. Tolkien's *The Hobbit* (1990) — and several installations of *The Punisher*, *The Green Lantern*, and *Superman*, among other titles, but he is best known for his long run at DC Comics with *Batman*, which included cocreating the villain Bane and the series *Nightwing*. Toronto native Paul Rivoche was born in 1959 and studied at the Ontario College of Art and Design. He began his career as one of the developers of *Mister X* and has since done graphic work for advertising agencies and magazines; illustrated covers and stories for DC Comics, Marvel, and Boom Studios; and created design for several Warner Brothers animated series, including *Batman*, *Superman*, *Justice League*, and *X-Men*. Together, the writer and the illustrator are coauthors of *The Forgotten Man* (2014), a best-selling graphic novel adapted from a conservative history of the Great Depression.

How Liberalism Became Kryptonite for Superman

In this essay published in the *Wall Street Journal* in 2014, Dixon and Rivoche set forth their reasons for creating *The Forgotten Man*. A culture of political correctness in the comics industry, they claim, has corrupted our heroes — and therefore threatens to corrupt our children. Conservatives, they say, need to make their voices heard if they hope to protect "truth, justice, and the American way."

The selection that follows this one offers a (liberal) comic-book editor's direct response to Dixon and Rivoche's argument.

In the nine-hundredth issue of *Action Comics*, Superman decides to go before the United Nations and renounce his US citizenship. "'Truth, justice and the American way' — it's not enough anymore," he despairs. That issue, published in April 2011, is perhaps the most dramatic example of modern comics' descent into political correctness, moral ambiguity and leftist ideology.

We are comic-book artists and comics are our passion. But more important, they've inspired and shaped many millions of young Americans. Our fear is that today's young comic-book readers are being ill-served by a medium that often presents heroes as morally compromised or no different from the criminals they battle. With the rise of moral relativism, "truth, justice and the American way" have lost their meaning.

This story commences way back in the 1930s. Superman, as he first   3
appeared in early comics and later on radio and TV, was not only "able to
leap tall buildings in a single bound," he was also good, just and wonderfully
American. Superman and other "superheroes" like Batman went out of their
way to distinguish themselves from villains like Lex Luthor or the Joker. Superman even battled Nazi Germany and Imperial Japan during World War II.

Cover illustration for *World's Finest Comics*, with Superman, Batman and Robin selling US War Bonds to sink the
"Japanazis." — Hulton Archive/Getty Images

Superman also led domestic crusades, the most famous against the Ku Klux   4
Klan. A man familiar with the Klan, Stetson Kennedy, approached radio show
producers in the mid-1940s with some of the Klan's secret codes and rituals.
The radio producers developed more than ten anti-Klan episodes of *The Clan of
the Fiery Cross*, which aired in June 1946. The radio show's unmistakable opposition to bigotry sharply reduced respect of young white Americans for the Klan.

The family of one of us, Paul Rivoche, fled Soviet Russia. The fact that   5
Superman's creators, Jerry Siegel and Joe Shuster, were themselves immigrants,
inspired Paul. Superman was a kind of immigrant, having come to Earth from
Krypton, a planet "far far away." Paul grew up in Canada, but he wanted to depict
through his art and illustrations appreciation for both North America and the
United States. Similar idealism drew Chuck, the writer in our team, into comics.

In the 1950s, the great publishers, including DC and what later became   6
Marvel, created the Comics Code Authority, a guild regulator that issued rules
such as "Crimes shall never be presented in such a way as to create sympathy for

the criminal." The idea behind the CCA, which had a stamp of approval on the cover of all comics, was to protect the industry's main audience — kids — from story lines that might glorify violent crime, drug use or other illicit behavior.

In the 1970s, our first years in the trade, nobody really altered the super- 7
hero formula. The CCA did change its code to allow for "sympathetic depiction of criminal behavior . . . [and] corruption among public officials" but only "as long as it is portrayed as exceptional and the culprit is punished." In other words, there were still good guys and bad guys. Nobody cared what an artist's politics were if you could draw or write and hand work in on schedule. Comics were a brotherhood beyond politics.

The 1990s brought a change. The industry weakened and eventually 8
threw out the CCA, and editors began to resist hiring conservative artists. One of us, Chuck, expressed the opinion that a frank story line about AIDS was not right for comics marketed to children. His editors rejected the idea and asked him to apologize to colleagues for even expressing it. Soon enough, Chuck got less work.

The superheroes also changed. Batman became dark and ambiguous, a 9
kind of brooding monster. Superman became less patriotic, culminating in his decision to renounce his citizenship so he wouldn't be seen as an extension of US foreign policy. A new code, less explicit but far stronger, replaced the old: a code of political correctness and moral ambiguity. If you disagreed with mostly left-leaning editors, you stayed silent.

The political-correctness problem stretches beyond traditional comics 10
into graphic novels. These works, despite the genre title, are not all fiction. For years a graphic novel of *A People's History of American Empire* by Howard Zinn has been taught in US schools. There's even a cartoon version of *Working* by Studs Terkel. Che Guevara, the Marxist Cuban revolutionary, is the subject of several graphic novels, as is the anarchist Emma Goldman.

Yet not all comics and graphic novels parrot the progressive line. *Maus* 11
and *Persepolis* have both sold many hundreds of thousands of copies, and are taught in schools. Neither of these two mega-successes can be called left- or right-wing. Pixar's *The Incredibles* is a parable about the evils of bringing down great people merely because they feature special talents. You can, if you choose to, find libertarian content in *X-Men*. Still the general message most modern comics send is — in a morally ambiguous world largely created by American empire — head left.

This would matter less if comics were fading away. But comics are more 12
popular than ever, as evidenced by Hollywood megahits like *X-Men*. One third of English-as-a-second-language teachers in the US use comics. If you doubt the future of this medium, look to Amazon, which bought comiXology, a company that translates comics to e-books. Or try getting a booth this July at Comic-Con, the mob scene that is the annual comics convention.

As a peer of ours recently wrote on *comicsbeat.com*, when it comes to   13
catching up to the left in modern comics, "Conservatives are taking the
remedial course." As our contribution to that course, the two of us poured
years into a graphic novel of *The Forgotten Man*, conservative writer Amity
Shlaes's new history of the Great Depression. But ours is one book. We hope
conservatives, free-marketeers and, yes, free-speech liberals will join us. It's
time to take back comics.

Journal Writing

Do you agree with Dixon and Rivoche that children are strongly influenced by the
comics they read? In your journal, list particular books and magazines from your childhood that stand out in your memory. What made these works come alive so that
you still remember them today — the stories, the characters, the illustrations, the
language?

Questions on Meaning

1. What do you take to be the authors' PURPOSE in writing this essay? Of what major
   claim, or THESIS, do they attempt to convince readers?

2. What do Dixon and Rivoche mean by "political correctness" (pars. 1, 9) and
   "moral relativism" (2)? How are these concepts central to their point?

3. Why do the authors focus their criticism of modern comics on Superman? What
   other works do they cite, and to what end? How effective do you find their EXAMPLES?

4. Why do Dixon and Rivoche bemoan the switch to "dark and ambiguous" (par. 9)
   characters that began in the 1990s? What ASSUMPTIONS about the function of
   comics in popular culture are evident in their preference for earlier superheroes?

Questions on Writing Strategy

1. For whom do Dixon and Rivoche seem to be writing? Liberals, conservatives,
   historians, comic book fans, editors, another group? How can you tell?

2. Identify the primary APPEALS Dixon and Rivoche make in the essay. Do you find
   them effective?

3. What kinds of EVIDENCE do the authors provide to support their claims, and how
   do they ORGANIZE it? Is their evidence convincing? Why, or why not?

4. Take a close look at the visual image that appears with this essay. Why do the
   authors include it? What does the illustration contribute to their meaning?

5. **OTHER METHODS**   Much of the authors' argument is developed by CAUSE-AND-
   EFFECT analysis. What do they say has been the result of liberal politics in the
   comics industry? Who is affected?

Questions on Language

1. How do Dixon and Rivoche characterize conservative and liberal values? Point to a few words that SUMMARIZE their attitude toward adherents of their own political ideology and toward their opponents.

2. How would you describe the writers' TONE in this essay — for instance, worried, condescending, frustrated, dismissive, optimistic, angry, defensive, reassuring, serious, irritated? Is the tone appropriate, given their audience and purpose?

3. Consult a dictionary if you are unsure of the meanings of any of the following: ambiguity, ideology (par. 1); compromised (2); commences, Imperial (3); domestic (4); guild (6); culminating, renounce (9); Marxist, anarchist (10); progressive, libertarian (11).

Suggestions for Writing

1. **FROM JOURNAL TO ESSAY**   Working from your journal entry (p. 503), write a brief essay that explores the messages sent by one of your childhood books or magazines. Did it contain positive role models? negative ones? moral messages? values that you now embrace or reject? Did you learn anything in particular from this text? Based on your recollections, come to your own conclusions about what's appropriate or not in children's literature, comics especially.

2. At a library or online, locate a sampling of Superman comics from the original *Action Comics #1* (1938) through the current day. Write an essay that traces the evolution of Superman's personality and behavior over the years. You might also consider his stature as the anchor character of multiple television and film franchises, or his position as a SYMBOL of American values. For more information on Superman and a selection of recent comics and graphic novels, visit his character page, *www.dccomics.com/characters/superman*, maintained by DC Comics.

3. Dixon and Rivoche suggest that, for a variety of reasons, comics have been ruined — they're no longer as good as they once were. Write an essay in which you offer your view of this idea, arguing for or against some recent change in a particular realm of popular culture. If you generally support the change, offer specific examples and speculate about the benefits. If you generally disapprove, challenge supporters with examples that counter their arguments.

4. **CRITICAL WRITING**   Based on this essay, ANALYZE Dixon and Rivoche's view of the state of national politics. In what ways has the political climate changed in recent decades, according to the writers? How do they portray conservative and liberal philosophies, as well as disagreements among political parties? How meaningful do they find "political correctness," for instance, or the distinction between "immigrants" and "aliens"? Which groups do Dixon and Rivoche consider most powerful and which most disadvantaged? Why? What problems do they identify, and what solutions, if any, do they propose?

5. **CONNECTIONS**   In the next essay, "Superhuman Error: What Dixon and Rivoche Get Wrong," Janelle Asselin analyzes the authors' argument and finds that it comes up short. Before you read her response, EVALUATE the success of Dixon and Rivoche's essay for yourself, considering especially how well their evidence supports their GENERALIZATIONS. Are there important examples they overlook, exceptions they do not account for, gaps in definitions? Offer specific evidence for your own view, whether positive or negative.

JANELLE ASSELIN

A self-described geek and feminist, Janelle Asselin is a freelance writer and the publisher of Rosy Press and *Fresh Romance* comics. She has also worked as an editor for the *Batman* franchise at DC Comics and for Disney Publishing Worldwide, whose subsidiaries include Marvel. Asselin was born in 1983, grew up in the Midwest, and earned a BA in English from Southern New Hampshire University (2009) and an MA in publishing from Pace University (2011). A life-long fan of comics, Asselin has devoted her "entire career," she has said, to "the study of broadening . . . readership to wider, more diverse demographics," particularly girls and young women. Her essays, reviews, and criticism have appeared in *Shotgun Reviews*, *Newsarama*, *XOJane*, *Bitch*, *TheMarySue*, and *ComicsAlliance*, the last "an online community of comic book fans" where Asselin worked as a senior editor. She has also published several comics of her own, including strips for *Mickey Mouse Mickey Shorts* (2013) and *Don't Be a Dick* with the Ladydrawers Comics Collective (2014). In addition to writing, Asselin has contributed her editorial talents to humanitarian efforts, among them the Homeless Shift Project and Architecture for Humanity in New York City. She lives outside Los Angeles.

Superhuman Error:
What Dixon and Rivoche Get Wrong

As a working comics editor, Janelle Asselin wrote "Superhuman Error" in heated response to Chuck Dixon and Paul Rivoche's "How Liberalism Became Kryptonite for Superman" (p. 500) and posted it to *ComicsAlliance* two days after their article appeared in the *Wall Street Journal*. In her essay, which she revised for print publication in *The Bedford Reader*, Asselin methodically analyzes Dixon and Rivoche's claims, questioning in particular their assumptions and their evidence.

Asselin's argument is based on her interpretation of multiple texts, so she acknowledges those sources in the body of her essay and in a works-cited list at the end. In accordance with MLA style, she includes page numbers for the one source that has them but not for unpaginated online documents, films, or references to entire works.

Comics creators Chuck Dixon and Paul Rivoche have written a frustrat-   1
ing piece for the *Wall Street Journal* titled "How Liberalism Became Kryptonite

for Superman." Beating familiar conservative pundit drums like jingoistic nostalgia and referencing a lot of demonstrably incorrect information, these two experienced pros manage to paint a picture of an industry tottering on the edge of moral collapse to an audience that knows little about what's actually going on in cape comics and the American comics industry in general.

The goal here, of course, is to sell comics. By complaining to the *Wall* 2 *Street Journal*'s ostensibly conservative audience about how liberals have taken over the American medium, conservatives Dixon and Rivoche attempt to persuade non-comics readers to buy their new book, an adaptation of Amity Shlaes's *The Forgotten Man*, as an exercise in political activism.

For those unfamiliar with their accomplishments, Dixon and Rivoche 3 have created great and enduring work in comics. While writing one of the most popular and fan-favorite eras of Batman comics in the 1990s (including *Detective Comics*, *Robin*, *Birds of Prey*, and *Nightwing*), Dixon and artist Graham Nolan cocreated the villain Bane, now a household name. Working with Dean Motter, artist Rivoche developed the hugely influential *Mister X*, whose creative progeny includes, most notably, *Batman: The Animated Series*. Both have numerous other credits to their names.

Like many conservative comics fans, Dixon and Rivoche bemoan the lack 4 of conservative comics being published today, and a perceived liberal bent of the industry, while limiting their definition of comics primarily to superhero books published by Marvel and DC Comics. The problem is not with their politics; it's with their misrepresentation of the industry and its history.

To begin, Dixon and Rivoche start their piece by citing *Action Comics* 5 #900, in which "Superman decides to go before the United Nations and renounce his US citizenship," explaining, "'Truth, justice and the American way [is] not enough anymore. . . .'" They go on to claim that "[w]ith the rise of moral relativism, 'truth, justice and the American way' have lost their meaning." Dixon and Rivoche have drawn their line in the sand, then, by characterizing *conservative* as American with a sense of right and wrong and *liberal* as morally ambiguous. The charge of "moral relativism" is beloved by conservatives when talking about liberals. The term is often used incorrectly, however, or misunderstood.

There are different kinds of moral relativism, including descriptive moral 6 relativism — the idea that there are widespread moral disagreements across different societies as a fact, and that those disagreements are more significant than agreements — and meta-ethical moral relativism — the idea that moral judgments are not absolute, but instead relative to individual groups. Just using the term "moral relativism" is actually not all that helpful or accurate.

The way this idea gets tied into liberalism for conservatives seems to be 7 twofold. One: Many liberals preach tolerance and acceptance for cultures and people whose ideals differ from our own. This is often assumed to be related to moral relativism, but is not in fact considered such by actual philosophers who write about these things. Two: Moral relativism leads to moral ambiguity. Accepting the morals of other cultures will lead to the downfall of American society, which has for hundreds of years been primarily Judeo-Christian in its moral view. In other words: dogs and cats living together — mass hysteria.

Now, to be fair, the issue of *Action Comics* that Dixon and Rivoche cite   8
is a particularly political one, but since when has it been okay to claim that only conservatives are patriotic? Or that it's "politically correct" for someone to care about what happens beyond the boundaries of their own country? Why wouldn't an alien from another planet want to help his entire adopted home *planet*, versus just his home country? You could argue, as this issue of *Action* does implicitly, that limiting Superman to just America is like limiting Green Lantern to one half of a planet in his sector (Goyer and Sepulveda 77).

But the merits of David S. Goyer and Miguel Sepulveda's comic are a dis-   9
cussion for another time, really. The problem here is that Dixon and Rivoche are pretending before an ignorant audience that within the story, Superman has forsworn his home country because of those darn liberals — and in a particularly dramatic way. The truth is that this was one short story in an anniversary issue filled with them, and a story that really didn't matter in the long run. Was it a political story? Yes. Did it ultimately impact the tone of other Superman stories? Not at all. Indeed, Goyer's own *Man of Steel* movie script goes out of its way to identify Superman as a firmly American charac-ter when he tells a military commander, "I'm from Kansas; I'm as American as it gets."

Superman is "wonderfully American," say Dixon and Rivoche, but their   10
criteria for that judgment ignore other pieces of the Superman mythos that would seem to be at odds with contemporary conservative values. Is Super-man not the ultimate "illegal alien"? He wasn't born in the United States, his biological parents weren't born in the United States, and he didn't enter the country in any state-approved way — plus he's literally an alien. Yet he's built his life in the US, continues to work in the country, and, one short story not-withstanding, identifies as a proud American. Real-life humans whose stories reflect that dimension of Superman are as a group frequently targeted by con-servative politics, so it's interesting that the Man of Steel is the figure being upheld by Dixon and Rivoche as the conservative ideal.

The greater and more damaging implication in Dixon and Rivoche's piece   11
is that only American conservatives can perceive right and wrong. The two authors attempt to draw a correlation between the idea of accepting or even just respecting other viewpoints and understanding right and wrong at all. This position is limiting both to our society and to our entertainment, and it

is incredibly flawed. People who tolerate other folks with different opinions do not, as a rule, lack a moral compass — they simply are willing to listen to others. It's not as if tolerance is a solely liberal trait, either. Why draw that comparison? When America entered World War II and "Superman even battled Nazi Germany and Imperial Japan," were all of our soldiers conservatives? Or is the rise of what the authors call moral relativism (again, most likely meaning "tolerance") only a recent phenomenon, and prior to that, liberals were okay? There are a lot of people in this country today who are "good, just and wonderfully American" and plenty of those people are not conservatives. Or even citizens.

As well as hailing Superman as a (fictional) war hero, Dixon and Rivoche 12 cite some radio episodes in which Superman led a crusade against the Ku Klux Klan, which they reference in the context of conservatives' allegedly stronger understanding of justice. To be fair, the KKK did in its earliest incarnation target Republicans, and Southern Democrats had plenty of racists and bigots among them. But it seems odd to bring up race in regards to liberals versus conservatives, as Republicans consistently tolerate racism within their party and block legislation meant to address racial injustice. It's a very cool thing that Superman was employed as anti-racist propaganda, but it would seem, based on their own track record on civil rights for minorities, that contemporary conservative politicians have more to learn from the Man of Steel's example than modern-day liberals do.

"How Liberalism Became Kryptonite for Superman" transcends mere 13 wrongness into weirdness when the authors write about comics from the 1950s to the 1970s. In that section of their argument, they speak of the loathsome Comics Code Authority (CCA) with what sounds like teary-eyed nostalgia.

That's right. In an article bemoaning the lack of free speech in comics 14 because of oppressive liberal values, two men who presumably share a political ideology that believes in minimizing government manage to talk with admiration about a literally oppressive set of censoring regulations that the comics industry imposed on itself following actual government hearings about whether comics — even superhero comics — were corrupting children. When Dixon and Rivoche say of one of the CCA's rules that "there were still good guys and bad guys," it's like they're pointing to the Code as a kind of proper morality that they wish comics still had. This is not longing for free speech. This is longing for a limited kind of morality that matches the authors' own particular set of morals.

Dixon and Rivoche also bemoan the dark and gritty turn superheroes 15 have taken, and a new "code of political correctness and moral ambiguity." Again, this is just factually inaccurate. The tonal shift from black-and-white morality of older comics to the pervasive "grim and gritty" aesthetic of the

1990s was not ushered in solely by liberal creators. It's true that Alan Moore and Frank Miller[1] (now an outspoken right-winger) wrote popular works in this vein (Ronald Reagan was actually a villain in Miller's *Batman: The Dark Knight Returns*), but then again, so did Chuck Dixon, whose *Punisher* comics — where the protagonist circumvents the law to murder anyone he thinks deserves it — are remembered as some of the most intensely dark and violent anti-hero comics of the era. The shift had less to do with politics and more to do with fashion and an aging audience. To assign a political bent towards these changes because of "political correctness and moral ambiguity" is like accusing anyone who believes in tolerance of actively encouraging crime. Tolerating other viewpoints does not equal anarchy or a lack of morals.

Later in their piece, Dixon and Rivoche hold up the graphic novels   16 *Persepolis* and *Maus* as examples of popular comic books that do not fall on either side of the political divide. This is just completely incorrect. The story of author Marjane Satrapi's growing up in Iran during the Islamic Revolution, *Persepolis* is a manifestly anti-fascist work. Likewise, Art Spiegelman's *Maus* dramatized his father's ordeal during the Holocaust. These comics may not, in Dixon and Rivoche's minds, "parrot the progressive line," but the truth is that these are political comics that Dixon and Rivoche happen accidentally to have enjoyed.

There are a lot of other issues in the phrasing chosen by Dixon and Rivoche   17 that help spread incorrect facts to newspaper readers who likely wouldn't know any better. Simple things like saying comics are for kids, referring to comiXology as a company that "translates comics to e-books," or describing San Diego Comic-Con International as "the annual comics convention" are misleading at best. Perhaps most crucially, Dixon and Rivoche's pretending that American comics are made up entirely of superhero comics, rather than discussing the wide range of work that exists and is successful today, ignores the fact that there *is* room in the comics market for a book like the one they have produced. If the only comics that existed were the superhero books and graphic novels they discuss, they would never have had the chance to create *The Forgotten Man*.

Dixon and Rivoche are right that there should be more conservative com-   18 ics. They're both talented creators who have written some amazing and influential comics and created some important characters, and they deserve the

---

[1] English writer Alan Moore (born 1953) is best known for the graphic novels *Watchmen, V for Vendetta,* and *From Hell.* American writer, artist, and director Frank Miller (born 1957) has written episodes of *Daredevil, Sin City, 300, Batman: The Dark Knight Returns,* and *Batman: The Dark Knight Strikes Again.* — EDS.

opportunity to produce work that accurately represents their world view. It's good that they've taken the advice so many Internet commenters are eager to throw at feminist fans: "If you don't like what's being made, make your own comics." However, two accomplished pros should know the facts about their industry and be able to speak to an audience beyond that industry in an accurate way. The authors' use of rose-colored glasses of nostalgia and political fallacies may help them sell books to readers inclined to accept such notions without further investigation; it won't do the industry any good. In the end, that is the issue — Dixon and Rivoche have misrepresented American comics to an audience that probably doesn't care in the first place, but now will be kept away from any future contemplation of the work and medium and community we all love.

Works Cited

Dixon, Chuck, and Paul Rivoche. "How Liberalism Became Kryptonite for Superman." *The Wall Street Journal*, 8 June 2014, www.wsj.com/articles/dixon-and-rivoche-how-liberalism-became-kryptonite-for-superman-1402265792.

Goyer, David S., writer. *Man of Steel*. Directed by Zack Snyder, performance by Henry Cavill, Warner Brothers, 2013.

Goyer, David S., and Miguel Sepulveda. "The Incident." *Action Comics*, no. 900, DC Comics, 2011, pp. 70–78.

Miller, Frank. *Batman: The Dark Night Returns*. DC Comics, 1996.

Satrapi, Marjane. *Persepolis*. Pantheon Books, 2003.

Spiegelman, Art. *Maus: A Survivor's Tale*. Penguin Books, 2003.

Journal Writing

How do you access various kinds of popular culture, and what GENRES do you like the most? Make a list of what you've read, seen, or heard over the past month or so and what the medium was — whether the Internet or more traditional channels such as magazines, books, TV, radio, or theaters.

Questions on Meaning

1. What does Asselin claim is the PURPOSE of Dixon and Rivoche's essay? What seems to be hers? Why, that is, do you think she was compelled to write "Superhuman Error"?

2. What is Asselin's THESIS? Where does she state it directly?

3. Why does Asselin dwell on the meanings of "moral relativism" and "moral ambiguity" (pars. 5–7, 11)? What is her point?

4. In what sense, according to Asselin, can Superman be considered both "the ultimate 'illegal alien'" and a "proud American" (par. 10)? Why is this SYMBOLISM important to her?

5. How does Asselin explain the "dark and gritty turn superheroes have taken" (par. 15)? What general ASSUMPTION about comics is she disputing here?

Questions on Writing Strategy

1. Does Asselin seem to be writing mainly for readers familiar with the comics industry or for a wider AUDIENCE? Cite passages from the essay to support your answer.

2. From where does Asselin draw her EVIDENCE? What strategies does she use to SYNTHESIZE information and ideas from multiple sources?

3. Why does Asselin highlight Dixon's and Rivoche's accomplishments in paragraph 3 and admit in paragraphs 8, 12, and 18 that they are correct on some points? How do these concessions affect her argument?

4. In her conclusion, Asselin accuses Dixon and Rivoche of using "fallacies" (par. 18) but doesn't specify which logical errors she has in mind. What do you think she means? Does Asselin slip into any fallacies herself? (For an overview, refer to pp. 486–87 and to FALLACIES in the Glossary.)

5. **OTHER METHODS**   Asselin's essay is also a model of DIVISION or ANALYSIS, in that she picks apart the elements of another essay. What principle of analysis does she use to ORGANIZE her argument?

Questions on Language

1. Asselin says that Dixon and Rivoche define "*conservative* as American with a sense of right and wrong and *liberal* as morally ambiguous" (5). How does *she* characterize liberal and conservative values? In a few words, SUMMARIZE her depictions.

2. At what points in her essay, and how, does Asselin adopt a sarcastic TONE? What does her use of sarcasm contribute to (or take away from) her argument? (For a definition of *sarcasm*, see IRONY in the Glossary.)

3. Consult a dictionary if you are unsure of the meanings of any of the following: pundit, jingoistic (par. 1); ostensibly (2); progeny (3); bemoan, bent (4); renounce, ambiguous (5); meta-ethical, absolute (6); Judeo-Christian (7); implicitly (8); forsworn (9); mythos (10); correlation (11); incarnation, propaganda (12); transcends, loathsome (13); aesthetic, circumvents, anti-hero, anarchy (15); manifestly, fascist (16).

4. How would you describe Asselin's DICTION? Is it appropriate, given her purpose and audience? Is it effective? Why, or why not?

Suggestions for Writing

1. **FROM JOURNAL TO ESSAY** Write an essay in which you explain and defend your own relationship with one medium of popular culture — Internet, TV, books, radio, and so on. Which genres do you prefer, and why? Have your preferences changed over time? Give specific examples to support your explanation.

2. Asselin notes that "feminist fans" are often told, "If you don't like what's being made, make your own comics" (par. 18). Why should that be? Although the entertainment media have come a long way in the portrayal of female characters in recent decades, some critics complain that there is still much progress to be made. Write an essay in which you EVALUATE the depictions of women in comics today. Base your analysis on your own experiences with graphic novels or with franchises such as *Superman*, *Supergirl*, *Batman*, *The Avengers*, *Wonder Woman*, *Jessica Jones*, and the like — whether online or in magazines, books, TV, or film. Overall, do you find the portrayals to be negative or positive? What messages do these portrayals send to audiences? How might the portrayals be improved?

3. Censorship is a controversial issue with arguments and strong feelings on both sides. In a page or so of preliminary writing, respond to Asselin's remarks on the Comics Code Authority (pars. 13–14) with your own gut feelings on the issue. Then do some library research to extend, support, or refute your views. In a well-reasoned and well-supported essay, give your opinion on whether or not the media and publishing industries should censor themselves to avoid "corrupting children" or for any other reasons.

4. **CRITICAL WRITING** Select any essay in *The Bedford Reader* that inspires a strong response for you. Using Asselin's argument as a model, write a rhetorical analysis of the essay you have chosen, breaking down what makes it effective or ineffective or why you agree or disagree with the author (or authors) in some fundamental way. As Asselin did, be sure to carefully examine the author's claims and evidence and to include citations for any summaries, paraphrases, and quotations you decide to integrate into your essay. (See the Appendix for more on citing sources in MLA or APA style.)

5. **CONNECTIONS** In "How Liberalism Became Kryptonite for Superman" (p. 500), Chuck Dixon and Paul Rivoche use a method similar to that taken by Janelle Asselin in "Superhuman Error," synthesizing ideas from popular culture and academics to develop an argument, but the two essays' approaches are markedly different and their conclusions are squarely opposed. Write an essay of your own in which you analyze how these writers adapt their evidence and tone for their audience and purpose, using quotations from both essays to support your analysis. Which essay, in your opinion, is more successful? Why?

BRIANNE RICHSON

Brianne Richson was born in 1992 in Wisconsin and as a teenager moved to New Jersey and attended Summit High School. Richson returned to the Midwest to study English, journalism, and psychology at the University of Iowa, where she also competed on the swim team and wrote a regular opinion column for the *Daily Iowan*. She graduated in 2015 and plans to pursue a PhD in clinical psychology.

An Obligation to Prevent Trauma on Campus

"An Obligation to Prevent Trauma on Campus" (editors' title) first appeared, in slightly different form, in Richson's column for the *Daily Iowan*, the student newspaper of the University of Iowa. Showing empathy toward classmates who may be suffering from post-traumatic stress disorder (PTSD), Richson urges her readers to support the inclusion of "trigger warnings," or advance notices of potentially upsetting material, in all class syllabi.

In the essay following this one, "Beware the Trigger Warning," fellow University of Iowa student Jon Overton shares Richson's concerns for trauma victims but argues against adopting trigger warnings on campus.

We all have that one memory that we'd prefer people not bring up because we want to block it from our consciousness forever. Hopefully, such memories become more vague as we grow further removed from them with time, but what about a memory that has legitimately traumatized a person? A memory that has even made its holder a victim of post-traumatic stress disorder (PTSD)? 1

Students at colleges across the country are taking a term originating from the world of blogs, "trigger warning," and calling for its direct use on class syllabi, to alert them to potential adverse reactions to sensitive academic material. This might include anything from sexual assault — a prominent issue on college campuses — to eating disorders, violent graphic content, or topics of race. The list goes on. 2

One might consider such measures as dramatic and symptomatic of what I have often heard my father refer to as the "every kid gets a trophy" generation: a generation full of coddling and cushioning when things go wrong. It isn't fair, however, to compare modern parents' affinity for sheltering their children from failure with the generation's demand to be protected from reliving that which was traumatic. 3

Is it too much to ask that a rape survivor be forewarned when a profes-   4
sor is about to cover material on the topic or to ask that a person who was
confronted with a racial slur and beaten up be allowed to leave the lecture
hall before course material sends her or him into a tizzy of hypervigilance, a
hallmark characteristic of PTSD?

A great difficulty that goes along with PTSD is that it can surface at any   5
given time following a traumatic event — in weeks or years. It is one thing to
be aware of what sensory elements could trigger an episode for you, but it is
another to have the ability to actively avoid these potentially toxic situations.

University of California–Santa Barbara has passed a resolution that profes-   6
sors should indicate in syllabi when emotionally or physically stressful material
would be presented in class, prompting a *Los Angeles Times* editorial to stamp
the measure as "antithetical to college life." The same editorial suggests that
trigger warnings are a cop-out for students not wishing to engage with a diverse
set of subject material or to face traditionally uncomfortable issues head-on.

Victims of PTSD do not have more to learn about the academic subject   7
matter that is traumatic for them; they have lived it. Not everyone has the
luxury of dealing with issues upfront and immediately after a trauma. And no
one has the right to force you to do so. In Ohio, Oberlin College has gone so
far as to suggest that trigger material should not even be included in a course
if it is not clear how the students might learn from the material.

Such measures certainly have a potential to be taken too far, but our   8
obligation to prevent a trauma survivor's class time becoming a living hell
outweighs concerns about a stunted learning environment.

Journal Writing

As a student yourself, you've probably had at least one experience with the sort of
uncomfortable course materials Richson describes, whether as the person upset or as a
witness to someone else's negative reaction. Do you agree with Richson that students
should be "forewarned" of such materials so they can avoid them, or do you think it's
more beneficial to confront disturbing materials directly? Or are your feelings mixed?
In your journal, explore your thoughts on the inclusion of "traumatizing" subject matters in a college education.

Questions on Meaning

1. What is Richson's PURPOSE for writing? What problem does she identify, and
   what solution does she propose?
2. What is a "trigger warning," as Richson explains it? Where did the practice originate?

3. What is the THESIS of Richson's argument? Where is this thesis stated most clearly?

4. Richson mentions, in paragraph 7, that "Oberlin College has gone so far as to suggest that trigger material should not even be included in a course if it is not clear how the students might learn from the material." How does she seem to feel about this suggestion?

Questions on Writing Strategy

1. "An Obligation to Prevent Trauma on Campus" was directed at a very specific AUDIENCE. Who were Richson's intended readers? What ASSUMPTIONS does she make about them?

2. Where and how does Richson address opposing points of view? Do her concessions seem adequate to you? Why, or why not?

3. Clearly Richson's argument relies on EMOTIONAL APPEAL, but it is nonetheless based on an implied SYLLOGISM. Tease out her major claim, minor claim, and conclusion, and express them in your own words. (For help, refer to pp. 485–86 on deductive reasoning.)

4. **OTHER METHODS**   Discuss how Richson uses EXAMPLES to explain the experiences of people suffering from post-traumatic stress disorder, or PTSD. Why do you suppose she highlights just a few potential reactions?

Questions on Language

1. Find some COLLOQUIAL EXPRESSIONS in Richson's essay. What is the effect of such language? Does it strike you as appropriate for an academic argument?

2. Be sure you are familiar with the following words, checking a dictionary if necessary: traumatized (par. 1); adverse (2); coddling (3); forewarned, hypervigilance, hallmark (4); sensory, toxic (5); resolution (6).

3. Examine the language Richson uses to describe people who suffer from PTSD. Is it OBJECTIVE? sympathetic? negative?

Suggestions for Writing

1. **FROM JOURNAL TO ESSAY**   Working from your journal entry, write an essay that responds to Richson's argument, putting forth your own position on calls for trigger warnings in college syllabi. Under what circumstances (if any) is it acceptable, or even necessary, to study potentially traumatic subjects? Are some subjects more likely to trigger negative responses than others? Do the benefits of preventing discomfort indeed outweigh the drawbacks? Why do you think so? Like Richson, you may arrange your thoughts into an argument for or against using trigger warnings, or you may prefer to structure your essay as a personal NARRATIVE focused on your own experiences.

2. Do some research on another issue related to free speech on campus. For example: Should schools adopt codes banning speech that might offend any group based on race, gender, ethnicity, religion, or sexual orientation? Should administrators have control over what students publish in school newspapers? What is the proposed Academic Bill of Rights, and how would its enactment affect the exchange of ideas on campus? Write an essay in which you give background information on the issue and support your own view in a well-reasoned argument.

3. CRITICAL WRITING   Find the original version of Richson's *Daily Iowan* column online and compare it to the version we present here (titled "Colleges Should Adopt Trigger Warnings," it was first published on May 6, 2014). What REVISION and EDITING strategies did Richson use to improve her essay? What additional changes might you suggest?

4. CONNECTIONS   In the next essay Jon Overton writes about what he sees as the problem with trigger warnings. Write an essay in which you COMPARE AND CONTRAST the ways Richson and Overton present their cases. Which argument do you find more effective? Why?

Brianne Richson on Writing

As a recent graduate, Brianne Richson tells us that she enjoyed having "the privilege of studying creative nonfiction, the punchy world of journalism, and the research-driven writing of clinical psychology" while in school. In this reflection on her own writing process, written especially for *The Bedford Reader*, Richson stresses the importance of having something to say and then saying it clearly, whatever the subject.

I find that my writing is most successful when I have a thorough handle on what it is exactly that I'm trying to get across. One thing most disciplines have in common is that no matter what, it is very important that each sentence drives home your point. This is not to say that I don't include contradictions or sentences in which I play the devil's advocate. However, if I am struggling with a particular piece, I will often write my thesis last, after reading what I have managed to flesh out. It is easy when drafting a thesis to write something that misses the mark of what you're trying to say, and it's a tricky position to write an entire piece feeling obligated to what you thought was your original stance. Saving the thesis sentence for later ensures that it encompasses your true, unencumbered thoughts.

When I write, I try to think about my thesis (or what it might ultimately be) and also about my audience, but I have spent a lot of time caught up in trying to impress readers with fancy words or experimental prose.

With experience, I have realized that the most authentic pieces say what they really mean and do not need the excess dressings to do so. I think that oftentimes writers like to fluff up their writing with strange words or unconventional style because saying what they are really trying to say can be scary, particularly in the context of nonfiction or opinion pieces. Nevertheless, it is your duty to your stance and to your readers to say what you mean.

The Bedford Reader on Writing

Richson's practice of putting off writing a THESIS STATEMENT until she has worked out her ideas is one that many writers find helpful, as we discuss on pages 35–36. For suggestions on how to "say what you mean" as directly as possible, refer to "Clear and Engaging Sentences" (pp. 49–50) and "Focus on Clarity and Conciseness" (pp. 394–95).

JON OVERTON

Born in Marshalltown, Iowa, in 1993, Jon Overton first got involved with journalism in high school, reporting for his school paper. As a student at the University of Iowa, he served as media editor for the Iowa Peace Network and wrote editorials and opinion columns for *The Daily Iowan*. Overton earned degrees in sociology and in ethics and public policy (BA, 2015) and is now a graduate student at Kent State University. His interests include social psychology, politics, inequality, and science.

Beware the Trigger Warning

Overton first published "Beware the Trigger Warning" in his *Daily Iowan* column, one day after Brianne Richson's argument (p. 513) appeared. Responding directly to her claims, Overton counters that adopting trigger warnings in course syllabi threatens to undermine the very purpose of a college education.

Brianne Richson suggests that US colleges and universities should adopt 1 trigger warnings on syllabi, on the grounds that people who've suffered traumatic experiences may be exposed to course material that would trigger memories of those events.

I agree that we should be considerate toward people who suffer from psy- 2 chological illnesses. My main gripe with trigger warnings more broadly, however, is that while they aim to be sensitive to people suffering from afflictions like post-traumatic stress disorder, they threaten to stifle some of the most important conversations and lessons in college.

Trigger warnings run into the same problem as proposed hate-speech laws: 3 Where do they stop? Anything can be a trigger, from hot dogs to Nazis to Mike Tyson[1] to the color yellow. The right smell, sound, word, or image can initiate a painful flashback for a particular person, who can't always anticipate them. The triggers don't have to be traditionally traumatic words, phrases, or concepts, so you can't easily predict what will set someone off.

And yet in Ohio, Oberlin College recently issued a policy that advised 4 instructors to "remove triggering material when it does not contribute directly

---

[1] Tyson (born 1966) is an American boxer with a history of violent behavior both in and out of the ring, including a rape conviction in 1992. — Eds.

to the course learning goals." This implies that professors ought to go through their syllabi line by line to consider what might trigger a traumatic memory for some students.

Students at the University of California–Santa Barbara also passed a res- 5 olution encouraging faculty to include a list of potential triggers on course syllabi and not punish students for leaving early if triggering content arises. Some of the most extreme trigger warning advocates have even attacked classical literature like *Things Fall Apart* and *The Great Gatsby*.[2]

Thanks to some highly vocal faculty at Oberlin, the attack on academic 6 freedom there was shot down, but these examples illustrate perfectly what is so dangerous about trigger warnings. They threaten to transform higher education into a horrific nightmare in which political correctness on steroids allows students to avoid any information with which they disagree. One of the great things about colleges and universities is that they challenge your worldview. They force you to confront information that makes you rethink cherished beliefs. This can be distressing, but that's the point: to expose yourself to new ideas and points of view.

The motivations behind trigger warnings are undoubtedly admirable. 7 They reflect the pinnacle of empathy and compassion. However, it's up to the students who suffer from PTSD to tell their instructors in advance if they're concerned about a potential trigger from specific course material. As much as we'd like to help trauma victims, we can't know what's going to initiate a panic attack, and trying to prevent any and all of them endangers academic discourse.

Journal Writing

Think of a proposal or development that some people view positively but that you view differently because of its risks, unintended effects, or ethical implications: space travel? stem-cell research? wind farms? an everyday convenience such as Bitcoin or location tracking? In your journal, explore your thoughts about this proposal or development.

Questions on Meaning

1. What do you take to be Overton's main PURPOSE in writing? What is his THESIS, and where does he state it?

2. Why, according to Overton, are trigger warnings a bad idea? What exactly are "triggers," as he explains them? What's wrong with listing them in syllabi?

[2] Chinua Achebe's *Things Fall Apart* (1958) has been singled out for themes of racial conflict and colonialism; F. Scott Fitzgerald's *The Great Gatsby* (1925) includes violence against women. — EDS.

3. What does Overton believe to be the purpose of a college education? Where does he spell out the primary ASSUMPTION behind his argument?

4. What alternative solution to the problem identified by Richson does Overton propose?

Questions on Writing Strategy

1. Why does Overton open and close his essay by saying he agrees with Richson and admires her motivations (pars. 2, 7)? Do you think he fully understands the issue she addresses?

2. Does Overton seem to expect his AUDIENCE to agree or disagree with his position? In answering this question, consider his TONE and his use of pronouns (*we* and *you* especially). What audience reaction does he seem to be seeking?

3. To what extent does Overton use rational, emotional, and ethical APPEALS in his argument? Identify examples of each kind of appeal in your answer.

4. **OTHER METHODS** Examine the way Overton uses EXAMPLE to develop his response to Richson. From where does he draw his examples? How persuasive are they as EVIDENCE for his claim about trigger warnings' potential to "stifle some of the most important conversations and lessons in college" (par. 2)?

Questions on Language

1. Check a dictionary if you are unfamiliar with the meanings of any of the following words: traumatic (par. 1); afflictions, stifle (2); initiate, flashback (3); resolution (5); distressing (6); pinnacle, empathy, discourse (7).

2. What does Overton mean by "political correctness on steroids" (par. 6)? Do you notice any other FIGURES OF SPEECH that underscore his attitude toward trigger warnings?

3. How do the ALLUSIONS to *Things Fall Apart* and *The Great Gatsby* in paragraph 5 support (or undermine) Overton's point?

Suggestions for Writing

1. **FROM JOURNAL TO ESSAY** Compose an essay in which you explain why you believe that the proposal or development you wrote about in your journal has or may have negative consequences ignored by others. Be sure to acknowledge what others see as the benefits. Also keep in mind that some readers may not immediately agree with you, so you will need to defend your views carefully and fully.

2. In paragraph 6 Overton asserts that the purpose of higher education is to "challenge your worldview [and] force you to . . . rethink cherished beliefs." When has your mind been expanded by exposure to a view that was different from your own? Perhaps you attended a religious service with a friend, visited another country, took a course with an instructor whose political views you disagreed with, or

learned something interesting from a book you thought you would hate. What did you gain from the experience? Write an essay about the importance of challenging your worldview, using concrete examples (or a single extended example) to support your point.

3. Expand your knowledge about post-traumatic stress disorder (PTSD) by researching the condition. You might start with its definition in the *Diagnostic and Statistical Manual of Mental Disorders*, Fifth Edition, published by the American Psychiatric Association and available in most college libraries. Look also for scholarly articles in a periodical database, and perhaps some personal accounts by people who have the condition. What causes PTSD, and what are some of its symptoms? How is it treated? How do "triggers" come into play? In an essay SYNTHESIZE what you discover.

4. **CRITICAL WRITING**   In an essay, EVALUATE Overton's argument. How truly does it resonate with your own experience? How persuasive do you find his evidence? How well does he convince you of the threats posed by trigger warnings? How well do you think he develops his proposed solutions?

5. **CONNECTIONS**   On what points does Overton seem to agree with *Daily Iowan* columnist Brianne Richson (p. 513)? On what points does he disagree? To what extent do the two writers' perspectives explain their difference of opinion? What are *your* thoughts on the issue they debate, and how does your own perspective influence your opinion? Answer these questions in an essay.

Jon Overton on Writing

Asked to tell us about his experience writing arguments, Jon Overton took it upon himself to do some research to learn more about the method and how to be effective at persuading readers. Here he shares his findings.

Effective persuasion requires empathy.

It's hard to build an argument that actually changes someone's opinion, especially when your stance contradicts audience members' firmly held beliefs. Social psychologists have long known that once people form an opinion, and especially if that opinion is important to their identity, it's incredibly hard to change.

To a degree, you can still reason with people. But you have to understand why they think the way they do. It helps if you can establish common ground with opponents from the beginning. This makes them more likely to listen to you once you lay out your case.

From there, your argument should appeal not only to your moral intuitions, but to the moral intuitions of those who disagree with you. Recent research by Feinberg and Willer (2015) illustrated that arguments that appeal to ideological opponents' values are far more persuasive than arguments that simply rely on your sides' values.

The more you consider the opposing side's position, the more persuasive your argument will be.

Reference

Feinberg, M., & Willer, R. (2015). From gulf to bridge: When do moral arguments facilitate political influence? *Personality and Social Psychology Bulletin, 41*(12), 1665–1681. doi:10.1177/0146167215607842

The Bedford Reader on Writing

Overton's quick research follows APA style, outlined on pages 651–61 of the Appendix. You can find additional suggestions for building COMMON GROUND with readers on page 481 of this chapter.

WENDY KAMINER

Wendy Kaminer (born 1949) is a lawyer and writer known for fiercely libertarian social criticism grounded in an insistence on personal freedom and individual accountability. She graduated from Smith College (BA, 1971) and Boston University Law School (JD, 1975) and then briefly practiced as an attorney in New York City before fully embarking on her career as a critic. Kaminer is a contributing editor for the *Atlantic Monthly* and has written for many other periodicals, among them the *American Prospect*, the *Washington Post*, the *Wall Street Journal*, the *Nation*, *Mirabella*, *Dissent*, and *Newsweek*. She has published eight books on subjects related to the politics of victimhood, including *I'm Dysfunctional, You're Dysfunctional: The Recovery Movement and Other Self-Help Fashions* (1992), *Sleeping with Extraterrestrials: The Rise of Irrationalism and Perils of Piety* (1999), and *Worst Instincts: Cowardice, Conformity, and the ACLU* (2010). A frequent commentator on National Public Radio and guest lecturer on college campuses, Kaminer has also taught writing at Radcliffe College and Tufts University.

The Danger of Playing It Safe

What is happening on college campuses? In this 2014 essay for National Public Radio's *Cognoscenti* series on WBUR in Boston, Kaminer challenges the notion that any student's mental health should need protection. Looking past the question of "trigger warnings" debated by Brianne Richson (p. 513) and Jon Overton (p. 518), the professional educator examines instead several related — and to her mind, disturbing — trends involving student demands for emotional safety.

At Hampshire College, a predominantly white band playing Afrobeat music is condemned as an act of cultural appropriation that makes some students feel "unsafe." At Brown University, students feel unsafe when contemplating a debate between two feminists about rules governing alleged sexual assaults on campus. At Smith College, my alma mater, I make some feel "unsafe" by questioning our growing list of forbidden words and uttering one or two, instead of referencing them by initials, during a panel discussion on free speech. At Oxford University, a debate about abortion is characterized, in part, as a threat to the "mental security" of female students.

Is it reasonable for students to fear for their safety when confronted with "offensive" speech or entertainments? That is likely to be deemed an irrelevant, if not an insulting, question on many campuses today, where verbal or musical "assaults" are defined by the subjective reactions of offended listeners. A student who feels threatened by a word, a song or an argument is threatened and deserves protection: "Safe spaces" must be made available to those who feel "attacked by viewpoints."

People who require protection from viewpoints on attack probably   3
shouldn't go to college. Education is, or was, supposed to expose us to opposing views. But these days, speech and harassment codes shield presumptively vulnerable students from language or ideas that the students consider offensive, demeaning or psychologically threatening. In part, this reflects their devolution from students to customers of corporate educational institutions. In part, it's a legacy of late twentieth-century political and cultural trends: the feminist crusade against pornography and the pop therapeutic recovery movement, both of which equated offensive words with harmful actions.

Pornography was an actual assault on women, anti-porn activists insisted;   4
pornographic speech should be considered a civil rights violation — an actionable threat to equality. "Words wound," best-selling pop therapists agreed, defining abuse broadly to include verbal affronts as well as physical attacks. Self-appointed codependency experts declared that virtually all of us were victims or survivors of abuse, still fragile and vulnerable to whatever we considered unwelcome speech.

These notions of victimization, verbal abuse and discrimination by word   5
as well as action helped shape a campus climate today that's increasingly hostile to free speech. Colleges and universities are steeped in a therapeutic culture that effectively treats students as patients, as well as consumers, and frames censorship as a moral and political necessity — an essential shield against abuse, as well as a civil right.

Censorship is anathema to education. How do you ensure your safety   6
when you feel "attacked by viewpoints"? You shut down or avoid debates about controversial subjects that feature perspectives you don't share. You demand enforcement of expansive speech and civility codes. You befriend or associate with only those people who share your ideology and sensibilities. You learn nothing apart from the "fact" that you're always entirely and self-evidently right, while everyone else is entirely and self-evidently wrong.

For me, in a free and open society, safety means protection from physical,   7
not emotional harm. Besides, strangers and ideological opponents can't hurt my feelings. Only family members and close friends can wound or threaten me emotionally. And no laws can or should try to stop them from doing so.

Outside our circles of intimates, freedom requires a willingness to hear   8
and tolerate wildly divergent, dissenting ideas as well as insults. If we have a right not to be offended, then we have no right to give offense. That means we

have no reliable, predictable right to speak, because in diverse societies there are no universal opinions or beliefs that are universally inoffensive. If we have a legal right to feel emotionally safe and unoffended, we have a legal obligation to keep silent, which we violate at our peril. Emotionally safe societies are dangerous places for people who speak.

Journal Writing

"People who require protection from viewpoints on attack probably shouldn't go to college," Kaminer writes in paragraph 3. How do you respond to this assertion? Write in your journal about your thoughts on higher education — not necessarily who should go to college or what you see as the ideal learning environment, but rather why you think people go to college in the first place. What do they hope to gain? What do they give up? What kinds of risks are they taking? To what extent is a college degree necessary for a happy, successful life? Base your entry on your observations and experiences.

Questions on Meaning

1. What seems to have prompted Kaminer to compose this essay? What does her opening paragraph reveal about her PURPOSE for writing?

2. What is cultural appropriation (par. 1)? pop therapeutic recovery (3)? codependency (4)? From what discipline or disciplines does Kaminer seem to pick up this JARGON? Is it necessary to understand the meaning of such phrases to follow her point?

3. What, according to Kaminer, is the common understanding among college students of what safety is? What is Kaminer's own attitude toward safety? What is yours?

4. What is Kaminer's THESIS? Does she state her main idea anywhere, or is it implied?

Questions on Writing Strategy

1. Why does Kaminer address readers directly as *you* in paragraph 6 but nowhere else in the essay? What about college students are evident in what she has to say?

2. Where and how does Kaminer address objections or opposing arguments? Do you find her strategy of counterargument effective? Why, or why not?

3. Notice the PARALLELISM and repetition in the passage beginning "If we have a right not to be offended . . ." in Kaminer's concluding paragraph. What is the EFFECT of the writing here? What is distinctive about the final sentence?

4. Kaminer's overall argument relies on a SYLLOGISM. Express the author's major premise, minor premise, and conclusion in your own words. Is her reasoning valid, in your opinion?

5. **OTHER METHODS**   What role does CAUSE-AND-EFFECT analysis play in the essay?

Questions on Language

1. What is Kaminer's point in putting so many terms (in pars. 1 and 2 especially) in quotation marks?

2. What are the CONNOTATIONS of *assault* and *attack*? How do these and similar words reinforce the EMOTIONAL APPEAL of Kaminer's argument?

3. Use a dictionary if necessary to help you define any of the following words: condemned, alleged, alma mater (par. 1); deemed, subjective (2); presumptively, devolution, legacy, therapeutic (3); actionable, affronts, codependency (4); steeped (5); anathema, expansive, sensibilities (6); ideological (7); intimates, divergent, dissenting, peril (8).

Suggestions for Writing

1. **FROM JOURNAL TO ESSAY**   Using your journal writing as a starting point, write an essay that presents a detailed view of the function of a college education in contemporary society. Refer to specific examples from your experience as appropriate. If you wish, use your observations and reflections to make a point about who should (or should not) go to college, and why.

2. Does your school "demand enforcement of expansive speech and civility codes" (par. 6)? Are such codes as common as Kaminer suggests? Using the Internet, research the current state of speech codes on campus, both at your current institution and at a small sampling of other colleges and universities in the United States. In an essay, summarize the content of such codes, which may include definitions of offensive language, harassment policies, or lists of penalties for noncompliance. Then discuss whether you approve or disapprove of the implementation of speech codes in college settings. Do you feel they infringe on individuals' First Amendment rights, for instance, or do you think they're a necessary tool in protecting the rights of minority students? Or perhaps your opinion lies somewhere in between the two extremes. (You may need to narrow your discussion to a particular aspect of the codes you investigate.)

3. **CRITICAL WRITING**   Based on what you know about the context of this piece — that it was written to be read out loud on public radio in Boston — analyze how Kaminer's AUDIENCE and purpose seem to have shaped her essay. In particular, you might focus on the essay's length, TONE, DICTION, ORGANIZATION, and uses of EVIDENCE.

4. **CONNECTIONS**   In the previous two essays, "An Obligation to Prevent Trauma on Campus" (p. 513) and "Beware the Trigger Warning" (p. 518), University of Iowa students Brianne Richson and Jon Overton debate one particular form

of the demands for emotional safety that Wendy Kaminer opposes. How might Richson and Overton respond to Kaminer's attitude toward college students and their "devolution . . . to customers of corporate educational institutions" (par. 3)? How do you respond? In an essay, bring these three writers together, considering what they have in common as well as what they do not.

Wendy Kaminer on Writing

As "The Danger of Playing It Safe" might suggest, Wendy Kaminer has a long history of criticizing the self-help and recovery industries that gained traction with the feminist movement. In this passage from the introduction to her best-selling book *I'm Dysfunctional, You're Dysfunctional* (1992), she expounds on why that is.

Some will call me an elitist for disdaining popular self-help literature and the popular recovery movement; but a concern for literacy and critical thinking is only democratic. The popularity of books comprising slogans, sound bites, and recipes for success is part of a larger, frequently bemoaned trend blamed on television and the failures of public education and blamed for political apathy. Intellectuals, right and left, complain about the debasement of public discourse the way fundamentalist preachers complain about sex. Still, to complain just a little — recently the fascination with self-help has made a significant contribution to the dumbing down of general interest books and begun changing the relationship between writers and readers; it is less collegial and collaborative than didactic. Today, even critical books about ideas are expected to be prescriptive, to conclude with simple, step-by-step solutions to whatever crisis they discuss. Reading itself is becoming a way out of thinking.

The Bedford Reader on Writing

Do you agree with Kaminer that the "dumbing down" of popular works will lead to the demise of CRITICAL THINKING, READING, AND WRITING in the general population? It certainly doesn't have to. For our own "step-by-step solutions" for maintaining an active "relationship between writers and readers," turn to Chapter 1 of this book.

NICHOLAS CARR

Nicholas Carr was born in 1959 and educated at Dartmouth College and Harvard University. He worked as a management consultant for a private firm and as executive editor for *Harvard Business Review* and is currently an editorial advisor for *Encyclopaedia Britannica*. Carr is best known, however, for his worrisome insights into computers and culture. He has stirred controversy with his books, all skeptical of the benefits of technology: *Does IT Matter? Information Technology and the Corrosion of Competitive Advantage* (2004), *The Big Switch: Rewiring the World, from Edison to Google* (2008), *The Shallows: What the Internet Is Doing to Our Brains* (2011), and *The Glass Cage: How Our Computers Are Changing Us* (2014). Carr's writing has also appeared in several newspapers and magazines, including *The Atlantic Monthly*, *Financial Times*, *Wired*, the *New York Times*, and *Advertising Age*. He is a sought-after speaker on the business lecture circuit and a regular commentator on television and radio.

Tracking Is an Assault on Liberty

Carr is a leading critic of the Internet and often writes about the dangers of spending time online. In this 2010 essay for the *Wall Street Journal*, he cites examples of how corporations collect and use our personal information, warns of potential abuses of such data mining, and advocates new rules protecting consumer privacy. The essays following this one — Jim Harper's "Web Users Get as Much as They Give" (p. 535) and Lori Andrews's "*Facebook* Is Using You" (p. 541) — address the same issue.

In a 1963 Supreme Court opinion, Chief Justice Earl Warren observed that "the fantastic advances in the field of electronic communication constitute a great danger to the privacy of the individual." The advances have only accelerated since then, along with the dangers. Today, as companies strive to personalize the services and advertisements they provide over the Internet, the surreptitious collection of personal information is rampant. The very idea of privacy is under threat.

Most of us view personalization and privacy as desirable things, and we understand that enjoying more of one means giving up some of the other. To have goods, services and promotions tailored to our personal circumstances and desires, we need to divulge information about ourselves to corporations, governments or other outsiders.

This tradeoff has always been part of our lives as consumers and citizens. 3
But now, thanks to the Net, we're losing our ability to understand and control
those tradeoffs — to choose, consciously and with awareness of the consequences, what information about ourselves we disclose and what we don't.
Incredibly detailed data about our lives are being harvested from online databases without our awareness, much less our approval.

Even though the Internet is a very social place, we tend to access it in 4
seclusion. We often assume that we're anonymous as we go about our business
online. As a result, we treat the Net not just as a shopping mall and a library
but as a personal diary and, sometimes, a confessional. Through the sites we
visit and the searches we make, we disclose details not only about our jobs,
hobbies, families, politics and health, but also about our secrets, fantasies,
even our peccadilloes.

But our sense of anonymity is largely an illusion. Pretty much everything 5
we do online, down to individual keystrokes and clicks, is recorded, stored
in cookies and corporate databases, and connected to our identities, either
explicitly through our user names, credit-card numbers and the IP addresses
assigned to our computers, or implicitly through our searching, surfing and
purchasing histories.

A few years ago, the computer consultant Tom Owad published the results of 6
an experiment that provided a chilling lesson in just how easy it is to extract sensitive personal data from the Net. Mr. Owad wrote a simple piece of software that
allowed him to download public wish lists that *Amazon.com* customers post to
catalog products that they plan to purchase or would like to receive as gifts. These
lists usually include the name of the list's owner and his or her city and state.

Using a couple of standard-issue PCs, Mr. Owad was able to download 7
over 250,000 wish lists over the course of a day. He then searched the data for
controversial or politically sensitive books and authors, from Kurt Vonnegut's
Slaughterhouse-Five[1] to the Koran. He then used *Yahoo!* People Search to identify addresses and phone numbers for many of the list owners.

Mr. Owad ended up with maps of the United States showing the locations 8
of people interested in particular books and ideas, including George Orwell's
Nineteen Eighty-Four.[2] He could just as easily have published a map showing the residences of people interested in books about treating depression or
adopting a child. "It used to be," Mr. Owad concluded, "you had to get a
warrant to monitor a person or a group of people. Today, it is increasingly easy
to monitor ideas. And then track them back to people."

---

[1] A 1969 novel about alien abduction, time travel, and the bombing of Dresden, Germany,
in World War II. — Eds.

[2] A 1949 novel critical of communism and mind control. — Eds.

What Mr. Owad did by hand can increasingly be performed automatically, 9 with data-mining software that draws from many sites and databases. One of the essential characteristics of the Net is the interconnection of diverse stores of information. The "openness" of databases is what gives the system much of its power and usefulness. But it also makes it easy to discover hidden relationships among far-flung bits of data.

In 2006, a team of scholars from the University of Minnesota described 10 how easy it is for data-mining software to create detailed personal profiles of individuals — even when they post information anonymously. The software is based on a simple principle: People tend to leave lots of little pieces of information about themselves and their opinions in many different places on the Web. By identifying correspondences among the data, sophisticated algorithms can identify individuals with extraordinary precision. And it's not a big leap from there to discovering the people's names. The researchers noted that most Americans can be identified by name and address using only their ZIP code, birthday and gender — three pieces of information that people often divulge when they register at a website.

The more deeply the Net is woven into our work lives and leisure activities, 11 the more exposed we become. Over the last few years, as social-networking services have grown in popularity, people have come to entrust ever more intimate details about their lives to sites like *Facebook* and *Twitter*. The incorporation of GPS transmitters into cellphones and the rise of location-tracking services like *Foursquare* provide powerful tools for assembling moment-by-moment records of people's movements. As reading shifts from printed pages onto networked devices like the Kindle and the Nook, it becomes possible for companies to more closely monitor people's reading habits — even when they're not surfing the Web.

"You have zero privacy," Scott McNealy remarked back in 1999, when 12 he was chief executive of Sun Microsystems. "Get over it." Other Silicon Valley CEOs have expressed similar sentiments in just the last few months. While Internet companies may be complacent about the erosion of personal privacy — they, after all, profit from the trend — the rest of us should be wary. There are real dangers.

First and most obvious is the possibility that our personal data will fall into 13 the wrong hands. Powerful data-mining tools are available not only to legitimate corporations and researchers, but also to crooks, con men and creeps. As more data about us is collected and shared online, the threats from unsanctioned interceptions of the data grow. Criminal syndicates can use purloined information about our identities to commit financial fraud, and stalkers can use locational data to track our whereabouts.

The first line of defense is, of course, common sense. We need to take personal 14 responsibility for the information we share whenever we log on. But no amount of caution will protect us from the dispersal of information collected without our

knowledge. If we're not aware of what data about us are available online, and how they're being used and exchanged, it can be difficult to guard against abuses.

A second danger is the possibility that personal information may be used   15
to influence our behavior and even our thoughts in ways that are invisible to us. Personalization's evil twin is manipulation. As mathematicians and marketers refine data-mining algorithms, they gain more precise ways to predict people's behavior as well as how they'll react when they're presented with online ads and other digital stimuli. Just this past week, *Google* CEO Eric Schmidt acknowledged that by tracking a person's messages and movements, an algorithm can accurately predict where that person will go next.

As marketing pitches and product offerings become more tightly tied to our   16
past patterns of behavior, they become more powerful as triggers of future behavior. Already, advertisers are able to infer extremely personal details about people by monitoring their Web-browsing habits. They can then use that knowledge to create ad campaigns customized to particular individuals. A man who visits a site about obesity, for instance, may soon see a lot of promotional messages related to weight-loss treatments. A woman who does research about anxiety may be bombarded with pharmaceutical ads. The line between personalization and manipulation is a fuzzy one, but one thing is certain: We can never know if the line has been crossed if we're unaware of what companies know about us.

Safeguarding privacy online isn't particularly hard. It requires that software makers and site operators assume that people want to keep their information   17
private. Privacy settings should be on by default and easy to modify. And when companies track our behavior or use personal details to tailor messages, they should provide an easy way for us to see what they're doing.

The greatest danger posed by the continuing erosion of personal privacy   18
is that it may lead us as a society to devalue the concept of privacy, to see it as outdated and unimportant. We may begin to see privacy merely as a barrier to efficient shopping and socializing. That would be a tragedy. As the computer security expert Bruce Schneier has observed, privacy is not just a screen we hide behind when we do something naughty or embarrassing; privacy is "intrinsic to the concept of liberty." When we feel that we're always being watched, we begin to lose our sense of self-reliance and free will and, along with it, our individuality. "We become children," writes Mr. Schneier, "fettered under watchful eyes."

Privacy is not only essential to life and liberty; it's essential to the pursuit   19
of happiness, in the broadest and deepest sense. We human beings are not just social creatures; we're also private creatures. What we don't share is as important as what we do share. The way that we choose to define the boundary between our public self and our private self will vary greatly from person to person, which is exactly why it's so important to be ever vigilant in defending everyone's right to set that boundary as he or she sees fit.

Journal Writing

"The more deeply the Net is woven into our work lives and leisure activities, the more exposed we become," Carr writes (par. 11). Do you agree? Draft a narrative account of an experience you have had of feeling exposed while using a medium such as *Google*, *Facebook*, or *Instagram*. If you've never felt exposed, explain why not.

Questions on Meaning

1. What problem does Carr identify? What solution, if any, does he propose?

2. How, according to Carr, do "corporations, governments or other outsiders" (par. 2) obtain personal information about individual Internet users?

3. "There are real dangers" to losing privacy online, says Carr (par. 12). What are those dangers, as he sees them?

4. What seems to be Carr's PURPOSE? Is he writing to express a concern, offer a solution, influence government regulations, change attitudes, or do something else? What details from the essay support your answer?

Questions on Writing Strategy

1. What does the author accomplish by opening with a discussion of the "tradeoff" (par. 3) between privacy and personalization?

2. Is this essay an appeal to emotion or a reasoned argument, or both? Give evidence for your answer.

3. Why is Carr so concerned about "manipulation" (pars. 15–16)? What exactly does he think could happen if advertisers customize their messages to individual Internet users' interests and behaviors? Do you think his concerns are valid? What does he seem to ASSUME about his readers' CRITICAL-THINKING abilities?

4. **OTHER METHODS**   How does Carr use DEFINITION to clarify the meaning of *privacy*? By what means does he bring his argument around to the subject of liberty?

Questions on Language

1. How would you describe Carr's attitude toward his subject? What is the overall TONE of his argument?

2. Who are Earl Warren (par. 1), Tom Owad (6), Scott McNealy (12), Eric Schmidt (15), and Bruce Schneier (18)? What does Carr achieve by quoting and paraphrasing them?

3. Be sure you are familiar with the following words, checking a dictionary if necessary: surreptitious (par. 1); peccadilloes (4); algorithms (10); complacent (12); syndicates, purloined (13); dispersal (14); stimuli (15); intrinsic, fettered (18).

Suggestions for Writing

1. **FROM JOURNAL TO ESSAY**   Expand on the narrative account you drafted in your journal to write an essay that assesses the CAUSE-AND-EFFECT relationship between the Internet and loss of privacy, being sure to define what you mean by *privacy*. Do you believe that online tools encourage people to share "ever more intimate details about their lives" (par. 11)? Do you think such exposure is a problem? Why, or why not?

2. Both of the novels Carr mentions — *Slaughterhouse-Five* and *Nineteen Eighty-Four* — present pessimistic visions of imagined societies in which governments control individual citizens' minds and behaviors. Choose one novel and read it (or a reputable synopsis of it), keeping Carr's argument in mind. Why do searches for these novels represent especially apt examples of the issues surrounding data tracking? What might a government agency in particular infer about a person who reads one of these works?

3. **CRITICAL WRITING**   Write an essay in which you analyze and evaluate any one of Carr's ideas. Some possibilities: Do "[m]ost of us view personalization and privacy as desirable things" (par. 2)? Are the dangers of online exposure as "real" (12) as he claims? Are we becoming resigned to a lack of privacy as he says (18)? Do we really need privacy in the first place (19)? Support your view with evidence from your experience, observation, or reading.

4. **CONNECTIONS**   While Carr expresses deep concern about the theoretical implications of data mining, and Lori Andrews (p. 541) argues that tracking poses serious practical risks for Internet users, Jim Harper, the author of the next essay, sees little reason to worry. On what major point do these authors agree and disagree? How do the tones of the three essays compare? Does any one writer seem more convinced of being in the right than the others do? Which essay do you find most convincing, and why?

Nicholas Carr on Writing

Carr is well known for his concern that constant exposure to electronic stimuli shortens one's attention span. In a 2010 blog post for both the *Futurist* and *Encyclopaedia Britannica,* he offers a dour prediction of how new technologies will continue to affect not only reading but also writing.

I have little doubt that in 2050 — or 2100, for that matter — we'll still be happily reading and writing. Even if we come to be outfitted with nifty Web-enabled brain implants, most of the stuff that's beamed into our skulls will likely take the form of text. Even our robots will probably be adept at reading.

What will change — what already is changing, in fact — is *the way we read and write*. In the past, changes in writing technologies, such as the shift from scroll to book, had dramatic effects on the kind of ideas that people put down on paper and, more generally, on people's intellectual lives. Now that we're leaving behind the page and adopting the screen as our main medium for reading, we'll see similarly far-reaching changes in the way we write, read, and even think.

Our eager embrace of a brand new verb — *to text* — speaks volumes. We're rapidly moving away from our old linear form of writing and reading, in which ideas and narratives wended their way across many pages, to a much more compressed, nonlinear form. What we've learned about digital media is that, even as they promote the transmission of writing, they shatter writing into little, utilitarian fragments. They turn stories into snippets. They transform prose and poetry into quick, scattered bursts of text.

Writing will survive, but it will survive in a debased form. It will lose its richness. We will no longer read and write words. We will merely process them, the way our computers do.

The Bedford Reader on Writing

Do you share Carr's concern that new technologies will diminish our talent for CRITICAL THINKING? To hone your own analytic skills, read Chapter 1, especially pages 16–18. And for tips on developing "quick, scattered bursts of text" into writing that has UNITY and COHERENCE, see pages 41–42 of Chapter 2.

JIM HARPER

Jim Harper is the Web master of *WashingtonWatch*, a site that tracks federal spending; the editor of *Privacilla*, a Web-based think tank; and the director of information policy studies at the Cato Institute in Washington, DC. He is also a founding member of the Data Privacy and Integrity Advisory Committee for the Department of Homeland Security. Harper studied political science at the University of California at Santa Barbara and in 1994 received a law degree from Hastings College of the University of California. His articles about privacy and security have appeared in *Administrative Law Review*, the *Minnesota Law Review*, the *Hastings Constitutional Law Quarterly*, the *Blaze*, and the *Technology Liberation Front*. He has also published two books: *Identity Crisis: How Identification Is Overused and Misunderstood* (2006) and *Terrorizing Ourselves: Why US Counterterrorism Policy Is Failing and How to Fix It* (2010), coedited with Benjamin H. Friedman and Christopher A. Preble. As an expert in the legal complications surrounding new technologies, Harper has testified at several congressional hearings and lectured widely.

Web Users Get as Much as They Give

With so much useful (and not so useful) material available free of charge, some might say that privacy is a fair price for Web users to pay. In this essay published in the *Wall Street Journal* alongside the previous selection, Nicholas Carr's "Tracking Is an Assault on Liberty" (p. 528), Harper argues that contemporary business models and opportunities to customize advertising justify the use of data mining. The next essay, "*Facebook* Is Using You," by Lori Andrews (p. 541), offers a third perspective on the subject.

If you surf the Web, congratulations! You are part of the information economy. Data gleaned from your communications and transactions grease the gears of modern commerce. Not everyone is celebrating, of course. Many people are concerned and dismayed — even shocked — when they learn that "their" data are fuel for the World Wide Web.

Who is gathering the information? What are they doing with it? How might this harm me? How do I stop it?

These are all good questions. But rather than indulging the natural reaction to say "stop," people should get smart and learn how to control personal information. There are plenty of options and tools people can use to protect privacy — and a certain obligation to use them. Data about you are not "yours" if you don't do anything to control them. Meanwhile, learning about the information economy can make clear its many benefits.

It's natural to be concerned about online privacy. The Internet is an inter-   4
active medium, not a static one like television. Every visit to a Web site sends information out before it pulls information in. And the information Web surfers send out can be revealing.

Most Web sites track users, particularly through the use of cookies, little   5
text files placed on Web surfers' computers. Sites use cookies to customize a visitor's experience. And advertising networks use cookies to gather information about users. A network that has ads on a lot of sites will recognize a browser (and by inference the person using it) when it goes to different Web sites, enabling the ad network to get a sense of that person's interests. Been on a site dealing with SUVs? You just might see an SUV ad as you continue to surf. Most Web sites and ad networks do not "sell" information about their users. In targeted online advertising, the business model is to sell space to advertisers — giving them access to people ("eyeballs") based on their demographics and interests. If an ad network sold personal and contact info, it would undercut its advertising business and its own profitability.

Some people don't like this tracking, for a variety of reasons. For some, it   6
feels like a violation to be treated as a mere object of commerce. Some worry that data about their interests will be used to discriminate wrongly against them, or to exclude them from information and opportunities they should enjoy. Excess customization of the Web experience may stratify society, some believe. If you are poor or from a minority group, for example, the news, entertainment and commentary you see on the Web might differ from others', preventing your participation in the "national" conversation and culture that traditional media may produce. And tied to real identities, Web-surfing data could fall into the hands of government and be used wrongly. These are all legitimate concerns that people with different worldviews prioritize to differing degrees.

"Surreptitious" use of cookies is one of the weaker complaints. Cookies   7
have been integral to Web browsing since the beginning, and their privacy consequences have been a subject of public discussion for over a decade. Cookies are a surreptitious threat to privacy the way smoking is a surreptitious threat to health. If you don't know about it, you haven't been paying attention. But before going into your browser settings and canceling cookies, Web users should ask another question about information sharing in the online world. What am I getting in return?

The reason why a company like *Google* can spend millions and millions   8
of dollars on free services like its search engine, Gmail, mapping tools, *Google*

Groups and more is because of online advertising that trades in personal information. And it's not just *Google*. *Facebook, Yahoo!*, MSN and thousands of blogs, news sites, and comment boards use advertising to support what they do. And personalized advertising is more valuable than advertising aimed at just anyone. Marketers will pay more to reach you if you are likely to use their products or services. (Perhaps online tracking makes everyone special!)

If Web users supply less information to the Web, the Web will supply   9
less information to them. Free content won't go away if consumers decline to allow personalization, but there will be less of it. Bloggers and operators of small Web sites will have a little less reason to produce the stuff that makes our Internet an endlessly fascinating place to visit. As an operator of a small government-transparency Web site, *WashingtonWatch*, I add new features for my visitors when there is enough money to do it. More money spent on advertising means more tools for American citizens to use across the Web.

Ten years ago — during an earlier round of cookie concern — the Federal   10
Trade Commission asked Congress for power to regulate the Internet for privacy's sake. If the FTC had gotten authority to impose regulations requiring "notice, choice, access, and security" from Web sites — all good practices, in varying measure — it is doubtful that *Google* would have had the same success it has had over the past decade. It might be a decent, struggling search engine today. But, unable to generate the kind of income it does, the quality of search it produces might be lower, and it may not have had the assets to produce and support all its fascinating and useful products. The rise of *Google* and all the access it provides was not fated from the beginning. It depended on a particular set of circumstances in which it had access to consumer information and the freedom to use it in ways that some find privacy-dubious.

Some legislators, privacy advocates and technologists want very badly to   11
protect consumers, but much "consumer protection" actually invites consumers to abandon personal responsibility. The *caveat emptor*[1] rule requires people to stay on their toes, learn about the products they use, and hold businesses' feet to the fire. People rise or fall to meet expectations, and consumer advocates who assume incompetence on the part of the public may have a hand in producing it, making consumers worse off. If a central authority such as Congress or the FTC were to decide for consumers how to deal with cookies, it would generalize wrongly about many, if not most, individuals' interests, giving them the wrong mix of privacy and interactivity. If the FTC ruled that third-party cookies required consumers to opt in, for example, most would not, and the wealth of "free" content and services most people take for granted would quietly fade from view. And it would leave consumers unprotected

---

[1] Latin, "buyer beware." — Eds.

from threats beyond their jurisdiction (as in Web tracking by sites outside the United States). Education is the hard way, and it is the only way, to get consumers' privacy interests balanced with their other interests.

But perhaps this is a government vs. corporate passion play, with government as the privacy defender. The *Wall Street Journal* reported last week that engineers working on a new version of Microsoft's Internet Explorer browser thought they might set certain defaults to protect privacy better, but they were overruled when the business segments at Microsoft learned of the plan. Privacy "sabotage," the Electronic Frontier Foundation called it. And a *Wired* news story says Microsoft "crippled" online privacy protections. But if the engineers' plan had won the day, an equal, opposite reaction would have resulted when Microsoft "sabotaged" Web interactivity and the advertising business model, "crippling" consumer access to free content. The new version of Microsoft's browser maintained the status quo in cookie functionality, as does *Google*'s Chrome browser and *Firefox*, a product of the nonprofit Mozilla Foundation. The "business attacks privacy" story doesn't wash.

This is not to say that businesses don't want personal information — they do, so they can provide maximal service to their customers. But they are struggling to figure out how to serve all dimensions of consumer interest, including the internally inconsistent consumer demand for privacy along with free content, custom Web experiences, convenience and so on.

Only one thing is certain here: Nobody knows how this is supposed to come out. Cookies and other tracking technologies will create legitimate concerns that weigh against the benefits they provide. Browser defaults may converge on something more privacy-protective. (Apple's *Safari* browser rejects third-party cookies unless users tell it to do otherwise.) Browser plug-ins will augment consumers' power to control cookies and other tracking technologies. Consumers will get better accustomed to the information economy, and they will choose more articulately how they fit into it. What matters is that the conversation should continue.

Journal Writing

Harper acknowledges, in paragraph 6, that some people are concerned that by narrowing the kinds of information certain segments of the population are exposed to, customized news outlets limit "participation in the 'national' conversation and culture that traditional media may produce." What kind of news do you follow, and how do you gain access to it? Why do you choose to follow the stories you do on the outlets you do?

Questions on Meaning

1. What connection does Harper make between personal data and the "information economy" (par. 1)? Express his THESIS in a sentence or two of your own.

2. What are cookies, and how are they used? Why is Harper not bothered by them?

3. Where does Harper ultimately place the blame for the average American's loss of privacy online? What solution does he suggest?

4. What seems to be the author's primary PURPOSE in this essay: to discredit critics of Internet tracking? to reassure Web users that their personal information is safe? to advance an economic theory? Do you think Harper accomplishes his purpose? Why, or why not?

Questions on Writing Strategy

1. To understand Harper's strategy, make an outline of the main points in his argument. Which of these points directly counter points made by Nicholas Carr in the previous essay (pp. 528–531)? Which of Carr's points does Harper not address directly? In what ways is his emphasis different from Carr's?

2. What ASSUMPTIONS does Harper seem to make about the readers of this essay? (Recall that it was first published in the *Wall Street Journal*.) Are the assumptions correct in your case?

3. In paragraph 9 Harper discusses his role as "an operator of a small government-transparency Web site." What persuasive tactic is he employing here? Does it work, in your opinion?

4. What examples of past efforts to protect consumer privacy does Harper present? What do these examples contribute to his point?

5. **OTHER METHODS**   Much of Harper's argument is developed by CAUSE-AND-EFFECT analysis. What does he claim would be the result of new regulations protecting privacy online?

Questions on Language

1. Harper uses FIGURES OF SPEECH throughout his essay, such as the metaphor "grease the gears of modern commerce" (par. 1), and the personification "advertising that trades in personal information" (8). Locate a few more figures of speech and comment on their effectiveness. What do they contribute to Harper's TONE?

2. Check a dictionary if you are unfamiliar with the meanings of any of the following words: gleaned (par. 1), demographics (5), stratify (6), surreptitious (7), jurisdiction (11), status quo (12), augment (14).

3. A "passion play" (par. 12) is a traditional Christian pageant that celebrates the death and resurrection of Jesus. What does Harper accomplish by making an ALLUSION to this particular dramatic GENRE? Does it strengthen his argument, or weaken it? Why?

Suggestions for Writing

1. **JOURNAL TO ESSAY**   Beginning with an analysis of your own preferences in news reporting and sources, write an essay in which you consider how important you think it is for people to stay informed about what's happening in the world around them. In your essay, also consider the kinds of news you believe people should follow and what you see as the best sources for gaining access to such news.

2. Write an essay in which you compare and contrast two related types of communication or entertainment media: for example, print books and e-readers, television and *YouTube*, radio and streaming music services, laptops and tablets. Your approach may be either lighthearted or serious, but make sure you come to some conclusion about your subjects. Which technology do you favor? Why?

3. **CRITICAL WRITING**   Harper writes that "[s]ome people don't like . . . tracking, for a variety of reasons" (par. 6). He then lists several of these reasons and acknowledges that such concerns are legitimate, but doesn't go into them in any detail. Pick one of the issues he raises and explore it in an essay. Does it, for instance, "feel like a violation to be treated as a mere object of commerce" (6)? Could data mining lead to discrimination or stratification in society? What might happen if information falls into the wrong hands? You may wish to think broadly about this issue, but bring your essay down to earth by focusing on one specific concern — perhaps one that you've experienced or witnessed yourself.

4. **CONNECTIONS**   Jim Harper and Nicholas Carr (p. 528) both assume that Internet tracking is used to collect data so that advertisers can customize their messages to a targeted audience. But Lori Andrews, in the next essay ("*Facebook* Is Using You"), asserts that data mining is conducted for a much different — and more disturbing — purpose. What is that purpose, and why do you suppose neither Harper nor Carr dwell on it? How does Andrews's perspective affect your understanding of the issue? Should the uses to which data may be put affect people's willingness (or refusal) to sacrifice privacy online? Why, or why not? Answer these questions in an essay.

LORI ANDREWS

Lori Andrews was born in Chicago, Illinois, in 1952 and earned her under-graduate and law degrees from Yale University. She has published ten books on the legal issues associated with subjects ranging from infertility and cloning to genetic screening. Her most recent book, *I Know Who You Are and I Saw What You Did* (2012), looks at the cultural and political consequences of online social networking. Considered a leading expert on bioethics and emerging tech-nologies, Andrews is a frequent contributor to newspapers and magazines and a popular guest on TV news programs, including *Good Morning America*, *Night-line*, and *60 Minutes*. She is also the author of three mystery novels. Andrews teaches at the Illinois Institute of Technology's Chicago–Kent College of Law, where she is director of the Institute of Science, Law, and Technology.

Facebook Is Using You

In this 2012 essay for the *New York Times*, Andrews extends the debate between Nicholas Carr and Jim Harper in the previous two essays. Despite the many opportunities and advantages offered by the Internet, Andrews warns, data-collection technologies also pose practical threats to Web users. As she sees it, individual privacy settings are insufficient. What we need, she insists, are new laws to protect us from harm.

Last week, *Facebook* filed documents with the government that will allow   1
it to sell shares of stock to the public. It is estimated to be worth at least $75 billion. But unlike other big-ticket corporations, it doesn't have an inven-tory of widgets or gadgets, cars or phones. *Facebook*'s inventory consists of personal data — yours and mine.

Facebook makes money by selling ad space to companies that want to reach   2
us. Advertisers choose key words or details — like relationship status, loca-tion, activities, favorite books and employment — and then *Facebook* runs the ads for the targeted subset of its 845 million users. If you indicate that you like cupcakes, live in a certain neighborhood and have invited friends over, expect an ad from a nearby bakery to appear on your page. The magnitude of online information *Facebook* has available about each of us for targeted mar-keting is stunning. In Europe, laws give people the right to know what data companies have about them, but that is not the case in the United States.

Facebook made $3.2 billion in advertising revenue last year, 85% of its   3
total revenue. Yet *Facebook*'s inventory of data and its revenue from advertising are small potatoes compared to some others. *Google* took in more than
ten times as much, with an estimated $36.5 billion in advertising revenue
in 2011, by analyzing what people sent over Gmail and what they searched
on the Web, and then using that data to sell ads. Hundreds of other companies have also staked claims on people's online data by depositing software
called cookies or other tracking mechanisms on people's computers and in
their browsers. If you've mentioned anxiety in an e-mail, done a *Google* search
for "stress" or started using an online medical diary that lets you monitor your
mood, expect ads for medications and services to treat your anxiety.

Ads that pop up on your screen might seem useful, or at worst, a nuisance.   4
But they are much more than that. The bits and bytes about your life can easily be used against you. Whether you can obtain a job, credit or insurance can
be based on your digital doppelgänger — and you may never know why you've
been turned down.

Material mined online has been used against people battling for child   5
custody or defending themselves in criminal cases. LexisNexis has a product
called Accurint for Law Enforcement, which gives government agents
information about what people do on social networks. The Internal Revenue
Service searches *Facebook* and *MySpace* for evidence of tax evaders' income
and whereabouts, and United States Citizenship and Immigration Services
has been known to scrutinize photos and posts to confirm family relationships or weed out sham marriages. Employers sometimes decide whether to
hire people based on their online profiles, with one study indicating that 70%
of recruiters and human resource professionals in the United States have
rejected candidates based on data found online. A company called Spokeo
gathers online data for employers, the public and anyone else who wants it.
The company even posts ads urging "HR Recruiters — Click Here Now!" and
asking women to submit their boyfriends' e-mail addresses for an analysis of
their online photos and activities to learn "Is He Cheating on You?"

Stereotyping is alive and well in data aggregation. Your application for   6
credit could be declined not on the basis of your own finances or credit history,
but on the basis of aggregate data — what other people whose likes and dislikes
are similar to yours have done. If guitar players or divorcing couples are more
likely to renege on their credit-card bills, then the fact that you've looked at
guitar ads or sent an e-mail to a divorce lawyer might cause a data aggregator
to classify you as less credit-worthy. When an Atlanta man returned from his
honeymoon, he found that his credit limit had been lowered to $3,800 from
$10,800. The switch was not based on anything he had done but on aggregate
data. A letter from the company told him, "Other customers who have used

their card at establishments where you recently shopped have a poor repayment history with American Express."

Even though laws allow people to challenge false information in credit 7
reports, there are no laws that require data aggregators to reveal what they
know about you. If I've Googled "diabetes" for a friend or "date rape drugs"
for a mystery I'm writing, data aggregators assume those searches reflect my
own health and proclivities. Because no laws regulate what types of data these
aggregators can collect, they make their own rules.

In 2007 and 2008, the online advertising company NebuAd contracted with 8
six Internet service providers to install hardware on their networks that monitored users' Internet activities and transmitted that data to NebuAd's servers for
analysis and use in marketing. For an average of six months, NebuAd copied every
e-mail, Web search or purchase that some 400,000 people sent over the Internet.
Other companies, like Healthline Networks Inc., have in-house limits on which
private information they will collect. Healthline does not use information about
people's searches related to HIV, impotence or eating disorders to target ads to
people, but it will use information about bipolar disorder, overactive bladder and
anxiety, which can be as stigmatizing as the topics on its privacy-protected list.

In the 1970s, a professor of communication studies at Northwestern 9
University named John McKnight popularized the term *redlining* to describe
the failure of banks, insurers and other institutions to offer their services to
inner city neighborhoods. The term came from the practice of bank officials
who drew a red line on a map to indicate where they wouldn't invest. But use
of the term expanded to cover a wide array of racially discriminatory practices,
such as not offering home loans to African-Americans, even those who were
wealthy or middle class.

Now the map used in redlining is not a geographic map, but the map 10
of your travels across the Web. The term *Weblining* describes the practice
of denying people opportunities based on their digital selves. You might be
refused health insurance based on a *Google* search you did about a medical
condition. You might be shown a credit card with a lower credit limit, not
because of your credit history, but because of your race, sex or ZIP code or the
types of Web sites you visit.

Data aggregation has social implications as well. When young people in 11
poor neighborhoods are bombarded with advertisements for trade schools, will
they be more likely than others their age to forgo college? And when women
are shown articles about celebrities rather than stock market trends, will they
be less likely to develop financial savvy? Advertisers are drawing new redlines,
limiting people to the roles society expects them to play.

Data aggregators' practices conflict with what people say they want. 12
A 2008 *Consumer Reports* poll of two thousand people found that 93% thought

Internet companies should always ask for permission before using personal information, and 72% wanted the right to opt out of online tracking. A study by Princeton Survey Research Associates in 2009 using a random sample of one thousand people found that 69% thought that the United States should adopt a law giving people the right to learn everything a Web site knows about them. We need a do-not-track law, similar to the do-not-call one. Now it's not just about whether my dinner will be interrupted by a telemarketer. It's about whether my dreams will be dashed by the collection of bits and bytes over which I have no control and for which companies are currently unaccountable.

———————

Journal Writing

What does your online self look like? Consider not just any profiles you have created but also records of searches you have conducted, transactions you have completed, and information others may have posted about you. (You may wish to search the Web for your name to see what comes up.) In your journal, create two lists of adjectives: one for how you think you appear to others online and one for how you think you really are.

Questions on Meaning

1. In which sentence or sentences does Andrews state her THESIS most directly?

2. What is a "data aggregator" (par. 6)? How are data aggregators different from advertisers? Why is the distinction important?

3. How, according to Andrews, do data aggregators stereotype Web users? Why does the practice concern her?

4. What would you say is the PURPOSE of this essay? What, specifically, does Andrews propose, and why?

Questions on Writing Strategy

1. Despite the title and the INTRODUCTION, this essay is not concerned exclusively with *Facebook*. What does Andrews accomplish by opening with a discussion of the company's initial stock offering and business earnings?

2. As a whole, is this essay an APPEAL to emotion or a reasoned argument, or both? What ASSUMPTIONS does Andrews seem to make about her readers? Give evidence for your answer.

3. In her final paragraph, Andrews cites the results of two surveys. How convincing do you find this EVIDENCE? Why?

4. Where in the essay does Andrews write about herself? What is the point of her doing so?

5. **OTHER METHODS**   How does Andrews use EXAMPLES to support her argument?

Questions on Language

1. How would you characterize Andrews's prevailing DICTION? Why does she also use COLLOQUIAL EXPRESSIONS? Find at least three examples of everyday speech and explain their EFFECT.

2. Andrews writes, "Whether you can obtain a job, credit or insurance can be based on your digital doppelgänger" (par. 4). What does she mean? What is a *doppelgänger*?

3. What is *Weblining* (par. 10)? What is the source of this term?

4. Use a dictionary if necessary to help you define any of the following words: magnitude (par. 2); revenue, mechanisms (3); scrutinize (5); renege (6); proclivities (7); stigmatizing (8); bombarded, forgo (11).

Suggestions for Writing

1. **FROM JOURNAL TO ESSAY**   Based on the list you created in your journal, write an essay in which you COMPARE AND CONTRAST how you view yourself with how you think the digital world views you. You might focus on a single aspect of your identity (for example, you may see yourself as fun-loving, while you're careful to appear serious online) or on a number of characteristics that make up your persona as a whole.

2. Andrews bases much of her argument on objections to stereotyping. Have you ever witnessed or been the object of unfair treatment based on race, ethnicity, marital status, medical history, shopping habits, or something else? What happened, and what was your reaction? Write an essay discussing stereotypes and how they can harm people. Use vivid details to re-create the incident and your reaction to it, but also reflect on its larger significance. Do you view the incident as fairly unusual, or do you think it is symptomatic of widespread stereotyping? What are the causes of this stereotyping, and how does it affect the people it is directed against?

3. **CRITICAL WRITING**   In an essay, examine the organization of Andrews's argument. What does Andrews accomplish in each paragraph? How effectively does she use TRANSITIONS to move from one idea to the next?

4. **CONNECTIONS**   Write an essay in which you establish your own position on the debate over Internet privacy. Are new laws necessary, or unwise? Do you agree with Andrews that loss of privacy causes real damage to people's lives? Do you take Nicholas Carr's (p. 528) view that privacy is a fundamental right not to be given up lightly? Or do you accept Jim Harper's (p. 535) position that privacy is

a reasonable price to pay for the content available online? Perhaps your opinion falls somewhere in between? As much as possible, use examples from your own experience (or from the experiences of those close to you) to support your argument.

Lori Andrews on Writing

"I love to write," says Lori Andrews in a faculty interview for the Chicago–Kent College of Law, "and in fact, I put myself through college and law school writing magazine articles and other things that I published in legal literature." As a lawyer and bioethicist, she has since written hundreds of articles and legal briefs and more than a dozen books of nonfiction. But when she started work on her first mystery novel, a project inspired by the human dramas she witnessed as an ethics advisor for the Human Genome Project, Andrews discovered her writing had room for improvement.

"I found," she explains, that "since I had written things that were almost always conceptual and oriented on the mind . . . I had to learn the way to describe things in a totally different context that had to do with people's bodies, not just with their ideas." In another faculty interview, for *Illinois Institute of Technology Magazine*, she continues: "I realized that I had no sense of physicality. For example, someone can't get shot and talk normally five seconds later. That was the biggest issue — leading an academic life of the mind, and then writing about very physical, tangible things."

The Bedford Reader on Writing

Andrews reflects here on the impact that GENRE can have on readers' expectations. Writing for a scientific or legal AUDIENCE, she discovered, requires an approach that doesn't work with fiction. You may make a similar discovery when writing for classes in different disciplines. Refer back to "Assessing the Writing Situation" (pp. 30–32) for advice on adapting your style to your SUBJECT and PURPOSE.

ADDITIONAL WRITING TOPICS
Argument and Persuasion

1. Write a persuasive essay in which you express a deeply felt opinion. In it, address a particular person or audience. For instance, you might direct your essay to any of the following readers:

    A friend unwilling to attend a ballet performance (or a car race) with you on the grounds that such an event is a waste of time

    A teacher who asserts that the prevalence of texting has led to a decline in students' writing skills

    A developer who plans to tear down a historic building

    Someone who sees no purpose in studying a foreign language

    A high-school class whose members don't want to commit to public service

    An older generation insistent on the value of home ownership

    A skeptic who asserts that religion is a leading cause of violence

    The members of a community organization who want to ban pit bulls or another breed of dog

2. Write a letter to your campus newspaper or a city newspaper in which you argue for or against a certain cause or view. You may wish to object to a particular feature or editorial in the paper. Send your letter and see if it is published.

3. Write a short letter to your congressional or state representative, arguing in favor of (or against) the passage of some pending legislation. Look in a news magazine or a newspaper for a worthwhile bill to write about. Or else write in favor of some continuing cause: for instance, requiring (or not requiring) cities to provide shelter for homeless people, reducing (or increasing) military spending, providing (or refusing) aid to the arts, solving (or ignoring) income inequality.

4. Write an essay arguing that something you feel strongly about should be changed, removed, abolished, enforced, repealed, revised, reinstated, or reconsidered. Be sure to propose some plan for carrying out whatever suggestions you make. Possible topics, listed to start you thinking, are these:

    Drug laws
    Unpaid internships
    Women in combat
    Police brutality
    Graffiti
    Fraternities and sororities
    Genetically modified organisms (GMOs) in food
    Public transportation

PART THREE

MIXING THE METHODS

Everywhere in this book, we have tried to prove how flexible the methods of development are. All the preceding essays offer superb examples of DEFINITION or CLASSIFICATION or ARGUMENT, but every one illustrates other methods, too — DESCRIPTION in PROCESS ANALYSIS, NARRATION in COMPARISON, ANALYSIS and EXAMPLES in CAUSE AND EFFECT.

In this part of the book, we take this point even further by presenting a collection of essays that share a significant feature: All the authors draw on whatever methods of development, at whatever length, will help them achieve their PURPOSES. To show how the writers combine methods, we highlight the most significant ones in the notes preceding each essay.

You have already begun to command the methods by focusing on them individually, making each a part of your kit of writing tools. Now, when you face a writing assignment, you can consider whether and how each method may help you sharpen your focus, develop your ideas, and achieve your aim. Indeed, one way to approach a subject is to apply each method to it, one by one. The following list offers a set of questions that you can ask about any subject.

- **Narration:** Can you tell a story about the subject?
- **Description:** Can you use your senses to illuminate the subject?
- **Example:** Can you point to instances that will make the subject concrete and specific?
- **Comparison and contrast:** Will setting the subject alongside another one generate useful information?
- **Process analysis:** Will a step-by-step explanation of how the subject works add to readers' understanding?
- **Division or analysis:** Can slicing the subject into parts produce a clearer vision of it?
- **Classification:** Is it worthwhile to sort the subject into kinds or groups?
- **Cause and effect:** Does it help to ask why something happened or what its results are?
- **Definition:** Can you trace boundaries that will clarify the meaning of the subject?
- **Argument and persuasion:** Can you back up an opinion or make a proposal about the subject?

Rarely will every one of these questions produce fruit for a given essay, but inevitably some will. Try the whole list when you're stuck at the beginning of an assignment or when you're snagged in the middle of a draft. You'll find the questions are as good at removing obstacles as they are at generating ideas.

JUDY BRADY

Judy Brady was born in 1937 in San Francisco, where she now lives, and earned a BFA in painting from the University of Iowa in 1962. Drawn into political action by her work in the feminist movement, she went to Cuba in 1973, where she studied class relationships as a way of understanding change in a society. When she was diagnosed with cancer in 1980, Brady became an activist against what she calls "the cancer establishment." ("Cancer is, after all, a multibillion-dollar business," she says.) In 1991 she published *One in Three: Women with Cancer Confront an Epidemic*, an anthology of writings by women. She is a board member of Greenaction, an environmental justice organization, and a founding member of the Toxic Links Coalition, which seeks to educate people about the links between environmental toxins and public health. She provided a chapter for the book *Sweeping the Earth: Women Taking Action for a Healthy Planet* (1999), and she writes articles for Breast Cancer Action in San Francisco. Brady is also featured in the 2011 movie *Pink Ribbons, Inc.*, a documentary critiquing corporate breast cancer philanthropy.

I Want a Wife

After reading "I Want a Wife" aloud at a 1970 women's meeting in San Francisco, Brady submitted the essay for the Spring 1972 issue of *Ms.* magazine, which had started the year before as a vehicle for the modern feminist movement, then in its first decade. "I Want a Wife" became one of the best-known manifestos in popular feminist writing. In the essay Brady trenchantly examines the multiple duties and functions expected of a wife, leading to an inescapable conclusion.

On the whole a definition (Chap. 11) of *wife* that relies on division or analysis (Chap. 8) to identify the parts of the role, "I Want a Wife" uses several other methods of development to show both how Brady sees her expected duties in marriage and why she resents them:

Example (Chap. 5): paragraphs 2–4
Comparison and contrast (Chap. 6): paragraphs 5, 7
Process analysis (Chap. 7): paragraphs 4, 6
Classification (Chap. 9): paragraphs 3–7
Cause and effect (Chap. 10): paragraph 3

I belong to that classification of people known as wives. I am A Wife. And, not altogether incidentally, I am a mother.

Not too long ago a male friend of mine appeared on the scene fresh from a recent divorce. He had one child, who is, of course, with his ex-wife. He is looking for another wife. As I thought about him while I was ironing one evening, it suddenly occurred to me that I, too, would like to have a wife. Why do I want a wife?

I would like to go back to school so that I can become economically independent, support myself, and, if need be, support those dependent upon me. I want a wife who will work and send me to school. And while I am going to school I want a wife to take care of my children. I want a wife to keep track of the children's doctor and dentist appointments. And to keep track of mine, too. I want a wife to make sure my children eat properly and are kept clean. I want a wife who will wash the children's clothes and keep them mended. I want a wife who is a good nurturant attendant to my children, who arranges for their schooling, makes sure that they have an adequate social life with their peers, takes them to the park, the zoo, etc. I want a wife who takes care of the children when they are sick, a wife who arranges to be around when the children need special care, because, of course, I cannot miss classes at school. My wife must arrange to lose time at work and not lose the job. It may mean a small cut in my wife's income from time to time, but I guess I can tolerate that. Needless to say, my wife will arrange and pay for the care of the children while my wife is working.   3

I want a wife who will take care of my physical needs. I want a wife who will keep my house clean. A wife who will pick up after my children, a wife who will pick up after me. I want a wife who will keep my clothes clean, ironed, mended, replaced when need be, and who will see to it that my personal things are kept in their proper place so that I can find what I need the minute I need it. I want a wife who cooks the meals, a wife who is a *good* cook. I want a wife who will plan the menus, do the necessary grocery shopping, prepare the meals, serve them pleasantly, and then do the cleaning up while I do my studying. I want a wife who will care for me when I am sick and sympathize with my pain and loss of time from school. I want a wife to go along when our family takes vacation so that someone can continue to care for me and my children when I need a rest and change of scene.   4

I want a wife who will not bother me with rambling complaints about a wife's duties. But I want a wife who will listen to me when I feel the need to explain a rather difficult point I have come across in my course of studies. And I want a wife who will type my papers for me when I have written them.   5

I want a wife who will take care of the details of my social life. When my wife and I are invited out by my friends, I want a wife who will take care of the babysitting arrangements. When I meet people at school that I like and want to entertain, I want a wife who will have the house clean, will prepare a special meal, serve it to me and my friends, and not interrupt when I talk   6 about things that interest me and my friends. I want a wife who will have arranged that the children are fed and ready for bed before my guests arrive so that the children do not bother us. I want a wife who takes care of the needs of my guests so that they feel comfortable, who makes sure that they have an ashtray, that they are passed the hors d'oeuvres, that they are offered a second helping of the food, that their wine glasses are replenished when necessary, that their coffee is served to them as they like it. And I want a wife who knows that sometimes I need a night out by myself.

I want a wife who is sensitive to my sexual needs, a wife who makes love   7 passionately and eagerly when I feel like it, a wife who makes sure that I am satisfied. And, of course, I want a wife who will not demand sexual attention when I am not in the mood for it. I want a wife who assumes the complete responsibility for birth control, because I do not want more children. I want a wife who will remain sexually faithful to me so that I do not have to clutter up my intellectual life with jealousies. And I want a wife who understands that *my* sexual needs may entail more than strict adherence to monogamy. I must, after all, be able to relate to people as fully as possible.

If, by chance, I find another person more suitable as a wife than the wife I   8 already have, I want the liberty to replace my present wife with another one. Naturally, I will expect a fresh, new life; my wife will take the children and be solely responsible for them so that I am left free.

When I am through with school and have a job, I want my wife to quit   9 working and remain at home so that my wife can more fully and completely take care of a wife's duties.

My God, who *wouldn't* want a wife?   10

Journal Writing

Brady addresses the traditional obligations of a wife and mother. In your journal, jot down what you perceive to be the parallel obligations of a husband and father.

Questions on Meaning

1. Sum up the duties of a wife as Brady sees them.
2. To what inequities in the roles traditionally assigned to men and to women does "I Want a Wife" call attention?
3. What is the THESIS of this essay? Is it stated or implied?
4. Is Brady unfair to men?

Questions on Writing Strategy

1. What EFFECT does Brady obtain with the title "I Want a Wife"?

2. What do the first two paragraphs accomplish?

3. What is the TONE of this essay?

4. How do you explain the fact that Brady never uses the pronoun *she* to refer to a wife? Does this make her prose unnecessarily awkward?

5. Knowing that this essay was first published in Ms. magazine in 1972, what can you guess about its intended readers? Does "I Want a Wife" strike a college AUDIENCE today as revolutionary?

6. **OTHER METHODS**   What principle of ANALYSIS does Brady use to analyze the role of wife? Can you think of some other principle for analyzing the role?

7. **OTHER METHODS**   Although she mainly divides or analyzes the role of wife, Brady also creates a DEFINITION by using CLASSIFICATION to sort the many duties and responsibilities into manageable groups. What are the groups?

Questions on Language

1. What is achieved by the author's frequent repetition of the phrase "I want a wife"?

2. Be sure you know how to define the following words as Brady uses them: nurturant (par. 3); replenished (6); adherence, monogamy (7).

3. In general, how would you describe the DICTION of this essay? How well does it suit the essay's intended audience?

Suggestions for Writing

1. **FROM JOURNAL TO ESSAY**   Working from your journal entry (p. 553), write an essay titled "I Want a Husband" in which, using examples as Brady does, you enumerate the roles traditionally assigned to men in our society.

2. Imagining that you want to employ someone to do a specific job, divide the task into its duties and functions. Then, guided by your analysis, write an accurate job description in essay form.

3. **CRITICAL WRITING**   As indicated in the note introducing it, Brady's essay was first published in 1972 in Ms., a feminist magazine. Do some research about the women's movement of the 1960s and '70s. Where did women stand in higher education (studying and teaching), in medicine and other professions, in the workforce, as wives and mothers, as homemakers, and so on? What kinds of change did feminists seek, and how did they go about demanding those changes? How did society as a whole seem to respond? Based on your research, write an essay in which you SUMMARIZE Brady's view as you understand it and then EVALUATE her essay. Consider: Is Brady fair? If not, is unfairness justified? Provide specific EVIDENCE from your experience, observation, and research.

4. **CONNECTIONS**   Both "I Want a Wife" and Augusten Burroughs's "How to Identify Love by Knowing What It's Not" (p. 470) address domestic partnerships and traditional expectations of spouses. However, Brady's STYLE is fast paced and her tone is sarcastic, while Burroughs's is more methodical and earnest. Which method of addressing relationship issues do you find more effective? Why? Write an essay that COMPARES AND CONTRASTS the essays' tones, styles, POINTS OF VIEW, and language. What conclusions can you draw about the connection between the writers' strategies and their messages?

5. **CONNECTIONS**   In "But What Do You Mean?" (p. 353), Deborah Tannen looks at some of the ways in which women and men communicate. In a brief essay, consider how Tannen's discussion of gender differences, particularly in instances of "Troubles Talk," might add another layer of meaning to Brady's complaints about traditional roles for husbands and wives.

Judy Brady on Writing

Before Judy Brady penned "I Want a Wife" in 1970, she had never considered being a writer. In a 2007 interview with Dick Gordon on American Public Media, Brady recalled that the idea of writing the essay was planted at a women's movement gathering at Glide Memorial Church in San Francisco: "Well, I was complaining at one of the consciousness-raising group meetings and somebody just said, 'Why don't you write it?' Which hadn't occurred to me. And I went home and did."

Brady says that although writing the essay took her only a couple of hours, its inspiration had been brewing for the decade of marriage and motherhood that preceded it. Brady remembers feeling spitefully awakened when she began to speak with other women about their position in the home and in society: "There was tremendous anger when I began to understand how I had been . . . how can I say this? . . . how I had been *molded* by forces about which I was totally unconscious."

At a rally celebrating the fiftieth anniversary of American women's right to vote, Brady read "I Want a Wife" aloud (and "totally terrified") to a gathering of both supporters and hecklers. Her now ex-husband bought her flowers after the event, a gesture that Brady describes as "bizarre." "He meant it well, but he sort of didn't get it," she says.

Inspired by the response to her essay, Brady became an active supporter of social and political causes, volunteering in Cuba, advocating for cancer patients, and getting involved in the environmental movement while continuing to work for women's rights. Reflecting on the impact of "I Want a

Wife" forty years later, Brady is still frustrated by what she sees as a lack of meaningful change for women and for underprivileged people in general. Writing the piece did, however, affect her personally: "I've had a much more interesting life than I would have had had I not found the women's movement and not . . . done this essay."

The Bedford Reader on Writing

Judy Brady discovered her subject matter long before she ever considered writing about it, and her hastily written speech became a component of her activism — a public ARGUMENT against expectations for women. For tips on finding a subject for an argument of your own, see page 488. Then, consider the revision checklist on page 491. In your estimation, does "I Want a Wife" meet all of the criteria for an effective argument? If Brady were to revise her essay to make a case for modern women, what changes would you suggest?

JOAN DIDION

A writer whose fame is fourfold — as novelist, essayist, journalist, and screen-writer — Joan Didion was born in 1934 in California, where her family had lived for five generations. After graduation from the University of California at Berkeley, she spent a few years in New York, working as a feature editor for the fashion magazine *Vogue*. She gained wide notice in the 1960s and 1970s with the publication of the essay collections *Slouching towards Bethlehem* (1968) and *The White Album* (1979) and the novels *River Run* (1963), *Play It as It Lays* (1971), and *A Book of Common Prayer* (1977). *Salvador* (1983), her book-length essay based on a visit to war-torn El Salvador, and *Miami* (1987), a study of Cuban exiles in Florida, also received close attention. With her late husband, John Gregory Dunne, Didion coauthored a number of screenplays, notably for *A Star Is Born* (1976), *True Confessions* (1981), and *Up Close and Personal* (1996). Her latest books are *The Year of Magical Thinking* (2005), an examination of her reactions to Dunne's sudden death, and *Blue Nights* (2011), an emotional memoir of losing their adult daughter after an extended illness.

Earthquakes

Long a resident of California, Didion knows firsthand the experience of earth-quakes and the peculiar blend of dread and denial with which most Californians view seismic catastrophe. This piece is a self-contained excerpt from a longer essay, "Los Angeles Days," that appeared first in 1988 in *The New Yorker* and then in Didion's collection *After Henry* (1992).

"Earthquakes" relies on a range of methods to depict the attitudes of Didion herself and of her fellow Californians toward "the Big One":

Narration (Chap. 3): paragraphs 1, 2–7, 8, 9
Description (Chap. 4): paragraphs 1, 2, 9
Example (Chap. 5): paragraphs 1, 2, 8, 9
Process analysis (Chap. 7): paragraph 2
Cause and effect (Chap. 10): paragraphs 1, 7–9
Definition (Chap. 11): paragraphs 1, 8, 9

During one of the summer weeks I spent in Los Angeles in 1988 there was a cluster of small earthquakes, the most noticeable of which, on the Garlock Fault, a major lateral-slip fracture that intersects the San Andreas in the Tehachapi range north of Los Angeles, occurred at six minutes after four on a Friday after-noon when I happened to be driving in Wilshire Boulevard from the beach. People brought up to believe that the phrase *terra firma*[1] has real meaning often

---

[1] Latin, "solid earth." — Eds.

find it hard to understand the apparent equanimity with which earthquakes are accommodated in California, and tend to write it off as regional spaciness. In fact it is less equanimity than protective detachment, the useful adjustment commonly made in circumstances so unthinkable that psychic survival precludes preparation. I know very few people in California who actually set aside, as instructed, a week's supply of water and food. I know fewer still who could actually lay hands on the wrench required to turn off, as instructed, the main gas valve; the scenario in which this wrench will be needed is a catastrophe, and something in the human spirit rejects planning on a daily basis for catastrophe. I once interviewed, in the late sixties, someone who did prepare: a Pentecostal minister who had received a kind of heavenly earthquake advisory, and on its quite specific instructions was moving his congregation from Port Hueneme, north of Los Angeles, to Murfreesboro, Tennessee. A few months later, when a small earthquake was felt not in Port Hueneme but in Murfreesboro, an event so novel that it was reported nationally, I was, I recall, mildly gratified.

A certain fatalism comes into play. When the ground starts moving all bets are off. Quantification, which in this case takes the form of guessing where the movement at hand will rank on the Richter scale, remains a favored way of regaining the illusion of personal control, and people still crouched in the nearest doorjamb will reach for a telephone and try to call Caltech, in Pasadena, for a Richter reading. "Rock and roll," the DJ said on my car radio that Friday afternoon at six minutes past four. "This console is definitely shaking . . . no word from Pasadena yet, is there?"   2

"I would say this is a three," the DJ's colleague said.   3

"Definitely a three, maybe I would say a little higher than a three."   4

"Say an eight . . . just joking."   5

"It felt like a six where I was."   6

What it turned out to be was a five-two, followed by a dozen smaller   7 after-shocks, and it had knocked out four of the six circuit breakers at the A. D. Edmonston pumping plant on the California Aqueduct, temporarily shutting down the flow of Northern California water over the Tehachapi range and cutting off half of Southern California's water supply for the weekend. This was all within the range not only of the predictable but of the normal. No one had been killed or seriously injured. There was plenty of water for the weekend in the system's four southern reservoirs, Pyramid, Castaic, Silverwood, and Perris lakes. A five-two earthquake is not, in California, where the movements people remember tend to have Richter numbers well over six, a major event, and the probability of earthquakes like this one had in fact been built into the aqueduct: The decision to pump the water nineteen hundred feet over the Tehachapi was made precisely because the aqueduct's engineers rejected the idea of tunneling through an area so geologically complex, periodically wrenched by opposing displacements along the San Andreas and the Garlock, that it has been called California's structural knot.

Still, this particular five-two, coming as it did when what Californians call   8 "the Big One" was pretty much overdue (the Big One is the eight, the Big One is the seven in the wrong place or at the wrong time, the Big One could even be the six-five centered near downtown Los Angeles at nine on a weekday morning), made people a little uneasy. There was some concern through the weekend that this was not merely an ordinary five-two but a "foreshock," an earthquake prefiguring a larger event (the chances of this, according to Caltech seismologists, run about one in twenty), and by Sunday there was what seemed to many people a sinister amount of activity on other faults: a three-four just east of Ontario at twenty-two minutes past two in the afternoon, a three-six twenty-two minutes later at Lake Berryessa, and, four hours and one minute later, northeast of San Jose, a five-five on the Calaveras Fault. On Monday, there was a two-three in Playa del Rey and a three in Santa Barbara.

Had it not been for the five-two on Friday, very few people would have   9 registered these little quakes (the Caltech seismological monitors in Southern California normally record from twenty to thirty earthquakes a day with magnitudes below three), and in the end nothing came of them, but this time people did register them, and they lent a certain moral gravity to the way the city happened to look that weekend, a temporal dimension to the hard white edges and empty golden light. At odd moments during the next few days people would suddenly clutch at tables, or walls. "Is it going," they would say, or "I think it's moving." They almost always said *it*, and what they meant by *it* was not just the ground but the world as they knew it. I have lived all my life with the promise of the Big One, but when it starts going now even I get the jitters.

Journal Writing

What potential threat or threats in your life most give you "the jitters"? Write a journal entry exploring your specific worries.

Questions on Meaning

1. What does Didion mean by "protective detachment" in referring to Californians' attitude toward earthquakes (par. 1)?

2. How, according to Didion, do Californians maintain the illusion of personal control during earthquakes?

3. Why was the earthquake Didion writes about a cause of special concern, even though it was not a major disturbance?

4. What is the ultimate threat of "the Big One"? Why does its possibility give Didion "the jitters" (par. 9)?

Questions on Writing Strategy

1. Why in paragraphs 1 and 8 is Didion so specific about the times of the earthquakes?

2. How does Didion use IRONY in paragraph 1?

3. Why do you suppose Didion quotes the on-air conversation between the radio DJ and his associate in paragraphs 2–6?

4. **MIXED METHODS** What other method does Didion use in paragraph 8 to DEFINE "the Big One"?

5. **MIXED METHODS** What CAUSE-AND-EFFECT relationship does Didion explore in paragraph 9?

Questions on Language

1. What is the effect of Didion's use of "as instructed" twice in the middle of paragraph 1?

2. Throughout the essay Didion refers to specific Richter-scale numbers when describing earthquakes. Why does she do so?

3. What does Didion mean by the phrase "temporal dimension" in paragraph 9? What does *temporal* mean?

4. Check a dictionary if any of the following are unfamiliar to you: equanimity, precludes, scenario (par. 1); fatalism (2); displacements (7); seismologists (8); magnitudes (9).

Suggestions for Writing

1. **FROM JOURNAL TO ESSAY** Expand your journal entry (p. 559) into an essay in which you explore your concerns about a potential threat in your life. What has led you to feel the way you do? Do you think many other people share your concern? How do you cope with your feelings? What might you do if the threat became real?

2. Do some research about the incidence and probability of earthquakes in the United States. (A good starting point would be the Geologic Hazards Team of the US Geological Survey: *geohazards.usgs.gov*.) Is California the only state vulnerable to earthquakes? (The answer may surprise you.) What kinds of damage and loss of life have been caused by earthquakes in this country? Write a report about earthquakes in which you answer these questions and others that interest you.

3. **CRITICAL WRITING**   Didion is noted for a distinctive STYLE of writing. In an essay, ANALYZE her style in "Earthquakes." What seems notable about the words Didion chooses and the ways she structures her sentences? What is her TONE? What does her style say about her? How do you respond to it?

4. **CONNECTIONS**   In "Stars of Life" (p. 377), student writer Jean-Pierre De Beer also speculates about the end of the world as we know it. Write an essay that COMPARES AND CONTRASTS Didion's and De Beer's essays. How are the authors' assumptions, conclusions, self-presentations, and attitudes toward catastrophe similar and different?

5. **CONNECTIONS**   Like that in "Earthquakes," Didion's reporting often involves herself as part of the story. In "Live Free and Starve" (p. 398) Chitra Divakaruni is also involved in the situation she reports. Write an essay that considers how the presence of the writer affects each essay. How would the essays be different if they had been written from a completely OBJECTIVE perspective?

Joan Didion on Writing

In "Why I Write," an essay published by the *New York Times Book Review*, adapted from her Regents' Lecture at the University of California at Berkeley, Joan Didion writes, "I stole the title for this talk, from George Orwell. One reason I stole it was that I like the sound of the words: Why I Write. There you have three short unambiguous words that share a sound, and the sound they share is this:

I

I

I

In many ways writing is the act of saying I, of imposing oneself upon other people, of saying *listen to me, see it my way, change your mind.* . . ."

Didion's "way," though, comes not from notions of how the world works or should work but from its observable details. She writes, "I am not in the least an intellectual, which is not to say that when I hear the word 'intellectual' I reach for my gun, but only to say that I do not think in abstracts. During the years when I was an undergraduate at Berkeley I tried, with a kind of hopeless late-adolescent energy, to buy some temporary visa into the world of ideas, to forge for myself a mind that could deal with the abstract. . . . In short, I tried to think. I failed. My attention veered inexorably back to the specific, to the tangible, to what was generally considered, by everyone I knew then and for that matter have known since, the peripheral. I would try to contemplate the Hegelian dialectic and would find myself concentrating instead on the flowering pear tree outside my window and the particular way the petals fell on my floor."

Later in the essay, Didion writes, "During those years I was traveling on what I knew to be a very shaky passport, forged papers: I knew that I was no legitimate resident in any world of ideas. I knew I couldn't think. All I knew then was what I wasn't, and it took me some years to discover what I was.

"Which was a writer.

"By which I mean not a 'good' writer or a 'bad' writer but simply a writer, a person whose most absorbed and passionate hours are spent arranging words on pieces of paper. Had my credentials been in order I would never have become a writer. Had I been blessed with even limited access to my own mind there would have been no reason to write. I write entirely to find out what I'm thinking, what I'm looking at, what I see, and what it means. What I want and what I fear. . . . *What is going on in these pictures in my mind?*"

In the essay, Didion emphasizes that these mental pictures have a grammar. "Grammar is a piano I play by ear, since I seem to have been out of school the year the rules were mentioned. All I know about grammar is its infinite power. To shift the structure of a sentence alters the meaning of that sentence, as definitely and inflexibly as the position of a camera alters the meaning of the object photographed. Many people know about camera angles now, but not so many know about sentences. The arrangement of the words matters, and the arrangement you want can be found in the picture in your mind. The picture dictates the arrangement. The picture dictates whether this will be a sentence with or without clauses, a sentence that ends hard or a dying-fall sentence, long or short, active or passive. The picture tells you how to arrange the words and the arrangement of the words tells you, or tells me, what's going on in the picture."

The Bedford Reader on Writing

Didion writes, she says, to make sense of her observations and to learn what she thinks. That is, she doesn't start with a THESIS but works her way into it, as we suggest you try when you draft your own essays (see pp. 34–36). For quick guidelines on how to harness the "infinite power" of grammar and sentences for yourself, turn to "Editing" in Chapter 2 (pp. 47–53).

MAXINE HONG KINGSTON

Maxine Hong Kingston grew up caught between two complex and very different cultures: the China of her parents and the America of her surroundings. In her first two books, *The Woman Warrior: Memoirs of a Girlhood among Ghosts* (1976) and *China Men* (1980), Kingston combines Chinese myth and history with family tales to create a dreamlike world that shifts between reality and fantasy. Born in 1940 in Stockton, California, Kingston was the first American-born child of a scholar and a medical practitioner who became laundry workers in this country. After graduating from the University of California at Berkeley (BA, 1962), Kingston taught English at California and Hawaii high schools, at the University of Hawaii, and for many years at UC Berkeley. She has contributed essays, poems, and stories to many periodicals, including *The New Yorker*, the *New York Times Magazine*, and *Ms.* Other books by Kingston include a collection of essays, *Hawaii One Summer* (1987); a novel, *Tripmaster Monkey: His Fake Book* (1989); a blend of fiction and nonfiction, *The Fifth Book of Peace* (2003); and a memoir in verse, *I Love a Broad Margin to My Life* (2011). She also edited *Veterans of War, Veterans of Peace* (2006), a collection of essays written in workshops she holds for military veterans. In 2013 Kingston was awarded the National Medal of Arts for her lifelong contributions to the written word.

No Name Woman

"No Name Woman" is part of *The Woman Warrior.* Like much of Kingston's writing, it blends the "talk-stories" of Kingston's elders, her own vivid imaginings, and the reality of her experience — this time to discover why her Chinese aunt drowned herself in the family well.

Kingston develops "No Name Woman" with four main methods, all intertwined: In the context of narrating her own experiences, she seeks the causes of her aunt's suicide by comparing various narratives of it, and she employs description to make the narratives concrete and vivid. The main uses of these methods appear below:

Narration (Chap. 3): paragraphs 1–8, 14, 16–20, 23, 28–30, 34–35, 37–46
Description (Chap. 4): paragraphs 4–8, 21, 23–27, 31, 37, 40–46
Comparison and contrast (Chap. 6): paragraphs 15–18, 20–24, 27–28, 31
Cause and effect (Chap. 10): paragraphs 10–11, 15–18, 21–25, 29–31, 33–39, 44–48

"You must not tell anyone," my mother said, "what I am about to tell   1
you. In China your father had a sister who killed herself. She jumped into the family well. We say that your father has all brothers because it is as if she had never been born.

"In 1924 just a few days after our village celebrated seventeen hurry-up   2
weddings — to make sure that every young man who went 'out on the road'
would responsibly come home — your father and his brothers and your grandfather and his brothers and your aunt's new husband sailed for America, the
Gold Mountain. It was your grandfather's last trip. Those lucky enough to get
contracts waved good-bye from the decks. They fed and guarded the stow-
aways and helped them off in Cuba, New York, Bali, Hawaii. 'We'll meet in
California next year,' they said. All of them sent money home.

"I remember looking at your aunt one day when she and I were dressing;   3
I had not noticed before that she had such a protruding melon of a stomach.
But I did not think, 'She's pregnant,' until she began to look like other pregnant women, her shirt pulling and the white tops of her black pants showing.
She could not have been pregnant, you see, because her husband had been
gone for years. No one said anything. We did not discuss it. In early summer
she was ready to have the child, long after the time when it could have been
possible.

"The village had also been counting. On the night the baby was to be   4
born the villagers raided our house. Some were crying. Like a great saw, teeth
strung with lights, files of people walked zigzag across our land, tearing the
rice. Their lanterns doubled in the disturbed black water, which drained away
through the broken bunds. As the villagers closed in, we could see that some
of them, probably men and women we knew well, wore white masks. The
people with long hair hung it over their faces. Women with short hair made
it stand up on end. Some had tied white bands around their foreheads, arms,
and legs.

"At first they threw mud and rocks at the house. Then they threw eggs   5
and began slaughtering our stock. We could hear the animals scream their
deaths — the roosters, the pigs, a last great roar from the ox. Familiar wild
heads flared in our night windows; the villagers encircled us. Some of the faces
stopped to peer at us, their eyes rushing like searchlights. The hands flattened
against the panes, framed heads, and left red prints.

"The villagers broke in the front and the back doors at the same time,   6
even though we had not locked the doors against them. Their knives dripped
with the blood of our animals. They smeared blood on the doors and walls.
One woman swung a chicken, whose throat she had slit, splattering blood in
red arcs about her. We stood together in the middle of our house, in the family hall with the pictures and tables of the ancestors around us, and looked
straight ahead.

"At that time the house had only two wings. When the men came back, we   7
would build two more to enclose our courtyard and a third one to begin a second
courtyard. The villagers pushed through both wings, even your grandparents'

rooms, to find your aunt's, which was also mine until the men returned. From this room a new wing for one of the younger families would grow. They ripped up her clothes and shoes and broke her combs, grinding them underfoot. They tore her work from the loom. They scattered the cooking fire and rolled the new weaving in it. We could hear them in the kitchen breaking our bowls and banging the pots. They overturned the great waist-high earthenware jugs; duck eggs, pickled fruits, vegetables burst out and mixed in acrid torrents. The old woman from the next field swept a broom through the air and loosed the spirits-of-the-broom over our heads. 'Pig.' 'Ghost.' 'Pig,' they sobbed and scolded while they ruined our house.

"When they left, they took sugar and oranges to bless themselves. They   8
cut pieces from the dead animals. Some of them took bowls that were not broken and clothes that were not torn. Afterward we swept up the rice and sewed it back up into sacks. But the smells from the spilled preserves lasted. Your aunt gave birth in the pigsty that night. The next morning when I went up for the water, I found her and the baby plugging up the family well.

"Don't let your father know that I told you. He denies her. Now that you   9
have started to menstruate, what happened to her could happen to you. Don't humiliate us. You wouldn't like to be forgotten as if you had never been born. The villagers are watchful."

Whenever she had to warn us about life, my mother told stories that ran   10
like this one, a story to grow up on. She tested our strength to establish realities. Those in the emigrant generations who could not reassert brute survival died young and far from home. Those of us in the first American generations have had to figure out how the invisible world the emigrants built around our childhoods fit in solid America.

The emigrants confused the gods by diverting their curses, misleading   11
them with crooked streets and false names. They must try to confuse their offspring as well, who, I suppose, threaten them in similar ways — always trying to get things straight, always trying to name the unspeakable. The Chinese I know hide their names; sojourners take new names when their lives change and guard their real names with silence.

Chinese-Americans, when you try to understand what things in you are   12
Chinese, how do you separate what is peculiar to childhood, to poverty, insanities, one family, your mother who marked your growing with stories, from what is Chinese? What is Chinese tradition and what is the movies?

If I want to learn what clothes my aunt wore, whether flashy or ordinary, I   13
would have to begin, "Remember Father's drowned-in-the-well sister?" I cannot ask that. My mother has told me once and for all the useful parts. She will add nothing unless powered by Necessity, a riverbank that guides her life.

She plants vegetable gardens rather than lawns; she carries the odd-shaped tomatoes home from the fields and eats food left for the gods.

Whenever we did frivolous things, we used up energy; we flew high kites. 14
We children came up off the ground over the melting cones our parents brought home from work and the American movie on New Year's Day — *Oh, You Beautiful Doll* with Betty Grable one year, and *She Wore a Yellow Ribbon* with John Wayne another year. After the one carnival ride each, we paid in guilt; our tired father counted his change on the dark walk home.

Adultery is extravagance. Could people who hatch their own chicks and 15
eat the embryos and the heads for delicacies and boil the feet in vinegar for party food, leaving only the gravel, eating even the gizzard lining — could such people engender a prodigal aunt? To be a woman, to have a daughter in starvation time was a waste enough. My aunt could not have been the lone romantic who gave up everything for sex. Women in the old China did not choose. Some man had commanded her to lie with him and be his secret evil. I wonder whether he masked himself when he joined the raid on her family.

Perhaps she encountered him in the fields or on the mountain where the 16
daughters-in-law collected fuel. Or perhaps he first noticed her in the market-place. He was not a stranger because the village housed no strangers. She had to have dealings with him other than sex. Perhaps he worked an adjoining field, or he sold her the cloth for the dress she sewed and wore. His demand must have surprised, then terrified her. She obeyed him; she always did as she was told.

When the family found a young man in the next village to be her husband, 17
she stood tractably beside the best rooster, his proxy, and promised before they met that she would be his forever. She was lucky that he was her age and she would be the first wife, an advantage secure now. The night she first saw him, he had sex with her. Then he left for America. She had almost forgotten what he looked like. When she tried to envision him, she only saw the black and white face in the group photograph the men had had taken before leaving.

The other man was not, after all, much different from her husband. They 18
both gave orders: She followed. "If you tell your family, I'll beat you. I'll kill you. Be here again next week." No one talked sex, ever. And she might have separated the rapes from the rest of living if only she did not have to buy her oil from him or gather wood in the same forest. I want her fear to have lasted just as long as rape lasted so that the fear could have been contained. No drawn-out fear. But women at sex hazarded birth and hence lifetimes. The fear did not stop but permeated everywhere. She told the man, "I think I'm pregnant." He organized the raid against her.

On nights when my mother and father talked about their life back home, 19
sometimes they mentioned an "outcast table" whose business they still seemed

to be settling, their voices tight. In a commensal tradition, where food is precious, the powerful older people made wrongdoers eat alone. Instead of letting them start separate new lives like the Japanese, who could become samurais and geishas, the Chinese family, faces averted but eyes glowering sideways, hung on to the offenders and fed them leftovers. My aunt must have lived in the same house as my parents and eaten at an outcast table. My mother spoke about the raid as if she had seen it, when she and my aunt, a daughter-in-law to a different household, should not have been liv- ing together at all. Daughters-in-law lived with their husbands' parents, not their own; a synonym for marriage in Chinese is "taking a daughter-in-law." Her husband's parents could have sold her, mortgaged her, stoned her. But they had sent her back to her own mother and father, a mysterious act hint- ing at disgraces not told me. Perhaps they had thrown her out to deflect the avengers.

She was the only daughter; her four brothers went with her father, husband, 20 and uncles "out on the road" and for some years became western men. When the goods were divided among the family, three of the brothers took land, and the youngest, my father, chose an education. After my grandparents gave their daughter away to her husband's family, they had dispensed all the adventure and all the property. They expected her alone to keep the traditional ways, which her brothers, now among the barbarians, could fumble without detection. The heavy, deep-rooted women were to maintain the past against the flood, safe for returning. But the rare urge west had fixed upon our family, and so my aunt crossed boundaries not delineated in space.

The work of preservation demands that the feelings playing about in one's 21 guts not be turned into action. Just watch their passing like cherry blossoms. But perhaps my aunt, my forerunner, caught in a slow life, let dreams grow and fade and after some months or years went toward what persisted. Fear at the enormities of the forbidden kept her desires delicate, wire and bone. She looked at a man because she liked the way the hair was tucked behind his ears, or she liked the question-mark line of a long torso curving at the shoulder and straight at the hip. For warm eyes or a soft voice or a slow walk — that's all — a few hairs, a line, a brightness, a sound, a pace, she gave up family. She offered us up for a charm that vanished with tiredness, a pigtail that didn't toss when the wind died. Why, the wrong lighting could erase the dearest thing about him.

It could very well have been, however, that my aunt did not take subtle 22 enjoyment of her friend, but, a wild woman, kept rollicking company. Imagin- ing her free with sex doesn't fit, though. I don't know any women like that, or men either. Unless I see her life branching into mine, she gives me no ancestral help.

To sustain her being in love, she often worked at herself in the mirror, 23 guessing at the colors and shapes that would interest him, changing them frequently in order to hit on the right combination. She wanted him to look back.

On a farm near the sea, a woman who tended her appearance reaped a 24 reputation for eccentricity. All the married women blunt-cut their hair in flaps about their ears or pulled it back in tight buns. No nonsense. Neither style blew easily into heart-catching tangles. And at their weddings they displayed themselves in their long hair for the last time. "It brushed the backs of my knees," my mother tells me. "It was braided, and even so, it brushed the backs of my knees."

At the mirror my aunt combed individuality into her bob. A bun could 25 have been contrived to escape into black streamers blowing in the wind or in quiet wisps about her face, but only the older women in our picture album wear buns. She brushed her hair back from her forehead, tucking the flaps behind her ears. She looped a piece of thread, knotted into a circle between her index fingers and thumbs, and ran the double strand across her forehead. When she closed her fingers as if she were making a pair of shadow geese bite, the string twisted together catching the little hairs. Then she pulled the thread away from her skin, ripping the hairs out neatly, her eyes watering from the needles of pain. Opening her fingers, she cleaned the thread, then rolled it along her hairline and the tops of her eyebrows. My mother did the same to me and my sisters and herself. I used to believe that the expression "caught by the short hairs" meant a captive held with a depilatory string. It especially hurt at the temples, but my mother said we were lucky we didn't have to have our feet bound when we were seven. Sisters used to sit on their beds and cry together, she said, as their mothers or their slaves removed the bandages for a few minutes each night and let the blood gush back into their veins. I hope that the man my aunt loved appreciated a smooth brow, that he wasn't just a tits-and-ass man.

Once my aunt found a freckle on her chin, at a spot that the almanac said 26 predestined her for unhappiness. She dug it out with a hot needle and washed the wound with peroxide.

More attention to her looks than these pullings of hairs and pickings at 27 spots would have caused gossip among the villagers. They owned work clothes and good clothes, and they wore good clothes for feasting the new seasons. But since a woman combing her hair hexes beginnings, my aunt rarely found an occasion to look her best. Women looked like great sea snails — the corded wood, babies, and laundry they carried were the whorls on their backs. The Chinese did not admire a bent back; goddesses and warriors stood straight. Still there must have been a marvelous freeing of beauty when a worker laid down her burden and stretched and arched.

Such commonplace loveliness, however, was not enough for my aunt. She   28
dreamed of a lover for the fifteen days of New Year's, the time for families
to exchange visits, money, and food. She plied her secret comb. And sure
enough she cursed the year, the family, the village, and herself.

Even as her hair lured her imminent lover, many other men looked at her.   29
Uncles, cousins, nephews, brothers would have looked, too, had they been
home between journeys. Perhaps they had already been restraining their curiosity, and they left, fearful that their glances, like a field of nesting birds, might
be startled and caught. Poverty hurt, and that was their first reason for leaving.
But another, final reason for leaving the crowded house was the never-said.

She may have been unusually beloved, the precious only daughter, spoiled   30
and mirror gazing because of the affection the family lavished on her. When
her husband left, they welcomed the chance to take her back from the in-
laws; she could live like the little daughter for just a while longer. There are
stories that my grandfather was different from other people, "crazy ever since
the little Jap bayoneted him in the head." He used to put his naked penis on
the dinner table, laughing. And one day he brought home a baby girl, wrapped
up inside his brown western-style greatcoat. He had traded one of his sons,
probably my father, the youngest, for her. My grandmother made him trade
back. When he finally got a daughter of his own, he doted on her. They must
have all loved her, except perhaps my father, the only brother who never went
back to China, having once been traded for a girl.

Brothers and sisters, newly men and women, had to efface their sexual   31
color and present plain miens. Disturbing hair and eyes, a smile like no other,
threatened the ideal of five generations living under one roof. To focus blurs,
people shouted face to face and yelled from room to room. The immigrants
I know have loud voices, unmodulated to American tones even after years
away from the village where they called their friendships out across the
fields. I have not been able to stop my mother's screams in public libraries
or over telephones. Walking erect (knees straight, toes pointed forward, not
pigeontoed, which is Chinese-feminine) and speaking in an inaudible voice,
I have tried to turn myself American-feminine. Chinese communication was
loud, public. Only sick people had to whisper. But at the dinner table, where
the family members came nearest one another, no one could talk, not the
outcasts nor any eaters. Every word that falls from the mouth is a coin lost.
Silently they gave and accepted food with both hands. A preoccupied child
who took his bowl with one hand got a sideways glare. A complete moment of
total attention is due everyone alike. Children and lovers have no singularity
here, but my aunt used a secret voice, a separate attentiveness.

She kept the man's name to herself throughout her labor and dying; she   32
did not accuse him that he be punished with her. To save her inseminator's
name she gave silent birth.

He may have been somebody in her own household, but intercourse with 33
a man outside the family would have been no less abhorrent. All the village
were kinsmen, and the titles shouted in loud country voices never let kinship
be forgotten. Any man within visiting distance would have been neutralized
as a lover — "brother," "younger brother," "older brother" — one hundred
and fifteen relationship titles. Parents researched birth charts probably not so
much to assure good fortune as to circumvent incest in a population that has
but one hundred surnames. Everybody has eight million relatives. How useless
then sexual mannerisms, how dangerous.

As if it came from an atavism deeper than fear, I used to add "brother" 34
silently to boys' names. It hexed the boys, who would or would not ask me to
dance, and made them less scary and as familiar and deserving of benevolence
as girls.

But, of course, I hexed myself also — no dates. I should have stood up, 35
both arms waving, and shouted out across libraries, "Hey, you! Love me back."
I had no idea, though, how to make attraction selective, how to control its
direction and magnitude. If I made myself American-pretty so that the five
or six Chinese boys in the class fell in love with me, everyone else — the
Caucasian, Negro, and Japanese boys — would too. Sisterliness, dignified and
honorable, made much more sense.

Attraction eludes control so stubbornly that whole societies designed to 36
organize relationships among people cannot keep order, not even when they
bind people to one another from childhood and raise them together. Among
the very poor and the wealthy, brothers married their adopted sisters, like
doves. Our family allowed some romance, paying adult brides' prices and providing dowries so that their sons and daughters could marry strangers. Marriage
promises to turn strangers into friendly relatives — a nation of siblings.

In the village structure, spirits shimmered among the live creatures, bal- 37
anced and held in equilibrium by time and land. But one human being flar-
ing up into violence could open up a black hole, a maelstrom that pulled in
the sky. The frightened villagers, who depended on one another to maintain
the real, went to my aunt to show her a personal, physical representation
of the break she made in the "roundness." Misallying couples snapped off the
future, which was to be embodied in true offspring. The villagers punished her
for acting as if she could have a private life, secret and apart from them.

If my aunt had betrayed the family at a time of large grain yields and peace, 38
when many boys were born, and wings were being built on many houses, perhaps she might have escaped such severe punishment. But the men — hungry,
greedy, tired of planting in dry soil, cuckolded — had been forced to leave the
village in order to send food-money home. There were ghost plagues, bandit
plagues, wars with the Japanese, floods. My Chinese brother and sister had

died of an unknown sickness. Adultery, perhaps only a mistake during good times, became a crime when the village needed food.

The round moon cakes and round doorways, the round tables of grad-   39 uated size that fit one roundness inside another, round windows and rice bowls — these talismans had lost their power to warn this family of the law: A family must be whole, faithfully keeping the descent line by having sons to feed the old and the dead who in turn look after the family. The villagers came to show my aunt and lover-in-hiding a broken house. The villagers were speeding up the circling of events because she was too shortsighted to see that her infidelity had already harmed the village, that waves of consequences would return unpredictably, sometimes in disguise, as now, to hurt her. This roundness had to be made coin-sized so that she would see its circumference: punish her at the birth of her baby. Awaken her to the inexorable. People who refused fatalism because they could invent small resources insisted on culpability. Deny accidents and wrest fault from the stars.

After the villagers left, their lanterns now scattering in various directions   40 toward home, the family broke their silence and cursed her. "Aiaa, we're going to die. Death is coming. Death is coming. Look what you've done. You've killed us. Ghost! Dead Ghost! Ghost! You've never been born." She ran out into the fields, far enough from the house so that she could no longer hear their voices, and pressed herself against the earth, her own land no more. When she felt the birth coming, she thought that she had been hurt. Her body seized together. "They've hurt me too much," she thought. "This is gall, and it will kill me." With forehead and knees against the earth, her body convulsed and then relaxed. She turned on her back, lay on the ground. The black well of sky and stars went out and out and out forever; her body and her complexity seemed to disappear. She was one of the stars, a bright dot in blackness, without home, without a companion, in eternal cold and silence. An agoraphobia rose in her, speeding higher and higher, bigger and bigger; she would not be able to contain it; there would be no end to fear.

Flayed, unprotected against space, she felt pain return, focusing her body.   41 This pain chilled her — a cold, steady kind of surface pain. Inside, spasmodically, the other pain, the pain of the child, heated her. For hours she lay on the ground, alternately body and space. Sometimes a vision of normal comfort obliterated reality: She saw the family in the evening gambling at the dinner table, the young people massaging their elders' backs. She saw them congratulating one another, high joy on the mornings the rice shoots came up. When these pictures burst, the stars drew out further apart. Black space opened.

She got to her feet to fight better and remembered that old-fashioned   42 women gave birth in their pigsties to fool the jealous, pain-dealing gods, who do not snatch piglets. Before the next spasms could stop her, she ran to the pigsty, each step a rushing out into emptiness. She climbed over the fence and knelt in the dirt. It was good to have a fence enclosing her, a tribal person alone.

Laboring, this woman who had carried her child as a foreign growth that   43
sickened her every day, expelled it at last. She reached down to touch the hot, wet, moving mass, surely smaller than anything human, and could feel that it was human after all — fingers, toes, nails, nose. She pulled it up onto her belly, and it lay curled there, butt in the air, feet precisely tucked one under the other. She opened her loose shirt and buttoned the child inside. After resting, it squirmed and thrashed and she pushed it up to her breast. It turned its head this way and that until it found her nipple. There, it made little snuffling noises. She clenched her teeth at its preciousness, lovely as a young calf, a piglet, a little dog.

She may have gone to the pigsty as a last act of responsibility: She would   44
protect this child as she had protected its father. It would look after her soul, leaving supplies on her grave. But how would this tiny child without family find her grave when there would be no marker for her anywhere, neither in the earth nor the family hall? No one would give her a family hall name. She had taken the child with her into the wastes. At its birth the two of them had felt the same raw pain of separation, a wound that only the family pressing tight could close. A child with no descent line would not soften her life but only trail after her, ghostlike, begging her to give it purpose. At dawn the villagers on their way to the fields would stand around the fence and look.

Full of milk, the little ghost slept. When it awoke, she hardened her   45
breasts against the milk that crying loosens. Toward morning she picked up the baby and walked to the well.

Carrying the baby to the well shows loving. Otherwise abandon it. Turn   46
its face into the mud. Mothers who love their children take them along. It was probably a girl; there is some hope of forgiveness for boys.

"Don't tell anyone you had an aunt. Your father does not want to hear her   47
name. She has never been born." I have believed that sex was unspeakable and words so strong and fathers so frail that "aunt" would do my father mysterious harm. I have thought that my family, having settled among immigrants who had also been their neighbors in the ancestral land, needed to clean their name, and a wrong word would incite the kinspeople even here. But there is more to this silence: They want me to participate in her punishment. And I have.

In the twenty years since I heard this story I have not asked for details nor   48
said my aunt's name; I do not know it. People who comfort the dead can also chase after them to hurt them further — a reverse ancestor worship. The real

punishment was not the raid swiftly inflicted by the villagers, but the family's deliberately forgetting her. Her betrayal so maddened them, they saw to it that she would suffer forever, even after death. Always hungry, always needing, she would have to beg food from other ghosts, snatch and steal it from those whose living descendants give them gifts. She would have to fight the ghosts massed at crossroads for the buns a few thoughtful citizens leave to decoy her away from village and home so that the ancestral spirits could feast unharassed. At peace, they could act like gods, not ghosts, their descent lines providing them with paper suits and dresses, spirit money, paper houses, paper automobiles, chicken, meat, and rice into eternity — essences delivered up in smoke and flames, steam and incense rising from each rice bowl. In an attempt to make the Chinese care for people outside the family, Chairman Mao encourages us now to give our paper replicas to the spirits of outstanding soldiers and workers, no matter whose ancestors they may be. My aunt remains forever hungry. Goods are not distributed evenly among the dead.

My aunt haunts me — her ghost drawn to me because now, after fifty   49
years of neglect, I alone devote pages of paper to her, though not origamied into houses and clothes. I do not think she always means me well. I am telling on her, and she was a spite suicide, drowning herself in the drinking water. The Chinese are always very frightened of the drowned one, whose weeping ghost, wet hair hanging and skin bloated, waits silently by the water to pull down a substitute.

Journal Writing

Most of us have heard family stories that left lasting impressions — ghost stories like Kingston's, biographies of ancestors, explanations for traditions, family superstitions, and so on. Write in your journal about a family story you remember vividly from your childhood.

Questions on Meaning

1. What PURPOSE does Kingston have in telling her aunt's story? How does this differ from her mother's purpose in relating the tale?

2. According to Kingston, who could have been the father of her aunt's child? Who could not?

3. Kingston says that her mother told stories "to warn us about life" (par. 10). What warning does this story provide?

4. Why is Kingston so fascinated by her aunt's life and death?

Questions on Writing Strategy

1. Whom does Kingston seem to include in her AUDIENCE: her family and other older Chinese? second-generation Chinese Americans like herself? other Americans? How might she expect each of these groups to respond to her essay?

2. Why is Kingston's opening line — her mother's "You must not tell anyone" — especially fitting for this essay? What secrets are being told? Why does Kingston divulge them?

3. As Kingston tells her tale of her aunt, some events are based on her mother's story or her knowledge of Chinese customs, while others are wholly imaginary. What is the EFFECT of blending these several threads of reality, perception, and imagination?

4. **MIXED METHODS**   Examine the details in the two contrasting NARRATIVES of how Kingston's aunt became pregnant: one in paragraphs 15–18 and the other in paragraphs 21–28. How do the details create different realities? Which version does Kingston seem more committed to? Why?

5. **MIXED METHODS**   Kingston COMPARES AND CONTRASTS various versions of her aunt's story, trying to find the CAUSES that led her aunt to drown in the well. In the end, what causes does Kingston seem to accept?

Questions on Language

1. How does Kingston's language — lyrical, poetic, full of FIGURES OF SPEECH and other IMAGES — reveal her relationship to her Chinese heritage? Find phrases that are especially striking.

2. Look up any of these words you do not know: bunds (par. 4); acrid (7); frivolous (14); tractably, proxy (17); hazarded (18); commensal (19); delineated (20); depilatory (25); plied (28); miens (31); abhorrent, circumvent (33); atavism (34); maelstrom (37); talismans, inexorable, fatalism, culpability (39); gall, agoraphobia (40); spasmodically (41).

3. Sometimes Kingston indicates that she is reconstructing or imagining events through verbs like "would have" and words like "maybe" and "perhaps" ("Perhaps she encountered him in the fields," par. 16). Other times she presents obviously imaginary events as if they actually happened ("Once my aunt found a freckle on her chin," 26). What effect does Kingston achieve with these apparent inconsistencies?

Suggestions for Writing

1. **FROM JOURNAL TO ESSAY**   Develop the family story from your journal (p. 573) into a narrative essay. Build in the context of the story as well: Who told it to you? What purpose did he or she have in telling it to you? How does it illustrate your family's beliefs and values?

2. Write an essay explaining the role of ancestors in Chinese family and religious life, supplementing what Kingston says with research in the library or on the Web or (if you are Chinese or Chinese American) drawing on your own experiences.

3. **CRITICAL WRITING**   ANALYZE the ideas about gender roles revealed in "No Name Woman," both in China and in the Chinese American culture Kingston grew up in. How have these ideas affected Kingston? Do you perceive any semblance of them in contemporary American culture?

4. **CONNECTIONS**   Both Maxine Hong Kingston and Brad Manning, in "Arm Wrestling with My Father" (p. 121), examine communication within their families. Relate an incident or incidents from your own childhood that portray something about communication within your family. You might want to focus on the language of communication, such as the words used to discuss (or not discuss) a taboo topic, the special family meanings for familiar words, a misunderstanding between you and an adult about something the adult said. Use dialog and as much CONCRETE detail as you can to clarify your experience and its significance.

5. **CONNECTIONS**   Like Kingston, several other authors in this book write about relationships between immigrant parents and their American-raised children. These include Amy Tan in "Fish Cheeks" (p. 74), Junot Díaz in "The Dreamer" (p. 88), Kellie Young in "The Undercurrent" (p. 189), Andrea Roman in "We're Not . . ." (p. 215), Firoozeh Dumas in "Sweet, Sour, and Resentful" (p. 275), and Judith Ortiz Cofer in "The Cruel Country" (p. 310). Select two or three of these essays and read or reread them. Then, in an essay of your own, analyze what the authors you have chosen suggest about the experiences of the children of immigrants to the United States. Do any expectations, supports, or conflicts strike you as common, even universal? How do your own experiences with your parents (or grandparents) compare? Do particular cultures seem to influence family relationships in particular ways? Why do you think so?

Maxine Hong Kingston on Writing

In an interview with Jean W. Ross published in *Contemporary Authors* in 1984, Maxine Hong Kingston discusses the writing and revising of *The Woman Warrior*. Ross asks Kingston to clarify an earlier statement that she had "no idea how people who don't write endure their lives." Kingston replies: "When I said that, I was thinking about how words and stories create order. Some of the things that happen to us in life seem to have no meaning, but when you write them down you find the meanings for them; or, as you translate life into words, you force a meaning. Meaning is intrinsic in words and stories."

Ross then asks if Kingston used an outline and planned to blend fact with legend in *The Woman Warrior*. "Oh no, no," Kingston answers. "What I have at the beginning of a book is not an outline. I have no idea of how stories will end or where the beginning will lead. Sometimes I draw pictures. I draw a blob and then I have a little arrow and it goes to this other blob, if you want to call that an outline. It's hardly even words; it's like a doodle. Then when it turns into words, I find the words lead me to various scenes and stories which I don't know about until I get there. I don't see the order until very late in the writing and sometimes the ending just comes. I just run up against it. All of a sudden the book's over and I didn't know it would be over."

A question from Ross about whether her emotions enter her writing leads Kingston to talk about revision. "Well, when I first set something down I feel the emotions I write about. But when I do a second draft, third draft, ninth draft, then I don't feel very emotional. The rewriting is very intellectual; all my education and reading and intellect are involved. The mechanics of sentences, how one phrase or word goes with another one — all that happens in later drafts. There's a very emotional first draft and a very technical last draft."

The Bedford Reader on Writing

Blending memory with fiction, as Kingston did, can be similar to drawing outside research into your writing. In the beginning, you might work with general ideas similar to Kingston's doodles, and then refine them as you go. As Kingston notes, it's important to pay close attention to how you weave in the details. After getting everything down on the page, don't forget to check back and make sure everything works in the way you intended, revising as necessary. For more advice on integrating source material, see pages 42–47 in Chapter 2 and 628–30 in the Appendix.

JONATHAN SWIFT

Jonathan Swift (1667–1745), the son of English parents who had settled in Ireland, divided his energies among literature, politics, and the church. He was educated at Trinity College in Dublin (BA, 1686) and Oxford University (MA, 1692). In 1695 he was ordained a priest in the Church of Ireland, part of the Anglican Church. Dissatisfied with the quiet life of a parish priest, Swift spent much of his time in London hobnobbing with writers and producing pamphlets in support of the Tory Party. In 1713 Queen Anne rewarded his political services with an assignment the London-loving Swift didn't want: to supervise St. Patrick's Cathedral in Dublin. There, as Dean Swift, he ended his days — beloved by the Irish, whose interests he defended against the English government. Although Swift's chief works include the remarkable satires *The Battle of the Books* and *A Tale of a Tub* (both 1704) and scores of fine poems, he is best remembered for *Gulliver's Travels* (1726), an account of four imaginary voyages. This classic is abridged when it is given to children because of its frank descriptions of human filth and viciousness. In *Gulliver's Travels*, Swift pays tribute to the reasoning portion of "that animal called man," and delivers a stinging rebuke to the rest of him.

A Modest Proposal

Three consecutive years of drought and sparse crops had worked hardship upon the Irish when Swift wrote this ferocious essay in the summer of 1729. At the time, there were said to be thirty-five thousand wandering beggars in the country: Whole families had quit their farms and had taken to the roads. Large landowners, of English ancestry, preferred to ignore their tenants' sufferings and lived abroad to dodge taxes and payment of church duties. Swift had no special fondness for the Irish, but he hated the inhumanity he witnessed.

Although printed as a pamphlet in Dublin, Swift's essay is clearly meant for English readers as well as Irish ones. When circulated, the pamphlet caused a sensation in both Ireland and England and had to be reprinted seven times in the same year. Swift is an expert with plain, vigorous English prose, and "A Modest Proposal" is a masterpiece of SATIRE and IRONY. (If you are uncertain what Swift argues for, see the discussion of these devices in the Glossary.)

"A Modest Proposal" is an argument developed chiefly by process analysis and cause and effect, with notable uses of description, example, and comparison.

Description (Chap. 4): paragraphs 1–2, 19
Example (Chap. 5): paragraphs 1–2, 6, 10, 14, 18, 32
Comparison and contrast (Chap. 6): paragraph 17
Process analysis (Chap. 7): paragraphs 4, 6–7, 10–17
Cause and effect (Chap. 10): paragraphs 4–5, 13, 21–29, 31, 33
Argument and persuasion (Chap. 12): throughout

For Preventing the Children of Poor People in Ireland from Being a Burden to Their Parents or Country, and for Making Them Beneficial to the Public

It is a melancholy object to those who walk through this great town[1] or travel in the country, when they see the streets, the roads, and cabin doors, crowded with beggars of the female sex, followed by three, four, or six children, all in rags and importuning every passenger for an alms. These mothers, instead of being able to work for their honest livelihood, are forced to employ all their time in strolling to beg sustenance for their helpless infants, who, as they grow up, either turn thieves for want of work, or leave their dear native country to fight for the Pretender in Spain, or sell themselves to the Barbados.[2]

I think it is agreed by all parties that this prodigious number of children in the arms, or on the backs, or at the heels of their mothers, and frequently of their fathers, is in the present deplorable state of the kingdom a very great additional grievance; and therefore whoever could find out a fair, cheap, and easy method of making these children sound, useful members of the commonwealth would deserve so well of the public as to have his statue set up for a preserver of the nation.

But my intention is very far from being confined to provide only for the children of professed beggars; it is of a much greater extent, and shall take in the whole number of infants at a certain age who are born of parents in effect as little able to support them as those who demand our charity in the streets.

As to my own part, having turned my thoughts for many years upon this important subject, and maturely weighed the several schemes of other projectors,[3] I have always found them grossly mistaken in their computation. It is true, a child just dropped from its dam may be supported by her milk for a solar year, with little other nourishment; at most not above the value of two shillings, which the mother may certainly get, or the value in scraps, by her lawful occupation of begging; and it is exactly at one year that I propose to provide for them in such a manner as instead of being a charge upon their parents or the parish, or wanting food and raiment for the rest of their lives, they shall on the contrary contribute to the feeding, and partly to the clothing, of many thousands.

There is likewise another great advantage in my scheme, that it will prevent those voluntary abortions, and that horrid practice of women murdering

1

2

3

4

5

---

[1] Dublin. — EDS.

[2] The Pretender was James Stuart, exiled in Spain; in 1718 many Irishmen had joined an army seeking to restore him to the English throne. Others wishing to emigrate had signed papers as indentured servants, agreeing to work for a number of years in the Barbados or other British colonies in exchange for their ocean passage. — EDS.

[3] Planners. — EDS.

their bastard children, alas, too frequent among us, sacrificing the poor inno-cent babes, I doubt, more to avoid the expense than the shame, which would move tears and pity in the most savage and inhuman breast.

The number of souls in this kingdom being usually reckoned one million   6
and a half, of these I calculate there may be about two hundred thousand cou-ples whose wives are breeders; from which number I subtract thirty thousand couples who are able to maintain their own children, although I apprehend there cannot be so many under the present distress of the kingdom; but this being granted, there will remain an hundred and seventy thousand breeders. I again subtract fifty thousand for those women who miscarry, or whose chil-dren die by accident or disease within the year. There only remain an hundred and twenty thousand children of poor parents annually born. The question therefore is, how this number shall be reared and provided for, which, as I have already said, under the present situation of affairs, is utterly impossible by all the methods hitherto proposed. For we can neither employ them in handi-craft or agriculture; we neither build houses (I mean in the country) nor cul-tivate land. They can very seldom pick up a livelihood stealing till they arrive at six years old, except where they are of towardly parts;[4] although I confess they learn the rudiments much earlier, during which time they can however be looked upon only as probationers, as I have been informed by a principal gentleman in the country of Cavan, who protested to me that he never knew above one or two instances under the age of six, even in a part of the kingdom so renowned for the quickest proficiency in that art.

I am assured by our merchants that a boy or a girl before twelve years old   7
is no salable commodity; and even when they come to this age they will not yield above three pounds, or three pounds and half a crown at most on the Exchange; which cannot turn to account either to the parents or the kingdom, the charge of nutriment and rags having been at least four times that value.

I shall now therefore humbly propose my own thoughts, which I hope will   8
not be liable to the least objection.

I have been assured by a very knowing American of my acquaintance in   9
London, that a young healthy child well nursed is at a year old a most deli-cious, nourishing, and wholesome food, whether stewed, roasted, baked, or boiled; and I make no doubt that it will equally serve in a fricassee or a ragout.[5]

I do therefore humbly offer it to public consideration that of the hundred   10
and twenty thousand children, already computed, twenty thousand may be reserved for breed, whereof only one fourth part to be males, which is more than we allow to sheep, black cattle, or swine; and my reason is that these

---

[4] Teachable wits, innate abilities. — EDS.
[5] Stew. — EDS.

children are seldom the fruits of marriage, a circumstance not much regarded by our savages, therefore one male will be sufficient to serve four females. That the remaining hundred thousand may at a year old be offered in sale to the persons of quality and fortune through the kingdom, always advising the mother to let them suck plentifully in the last month, so as to render them plump and fat for a good table. A child will make two dishes at an entertainment for friends; and when the family dines alone, the fore or hind quarter will make a reasonable dish, and seasoned with a little pepper or salt will be very good boiled on the fourth day, especially in winter.

I have reckoned upon a medium that a child just born will weigh twelve pounds, and in a solar year if tolerably nursed increaseth to twenty-eight pounds. 11

I grant this food will be somewhat dear, and therefore very proper for landlords, who, as they have already devoured most of the parents, seem to have the best title to the children. 12

Infant's flesh will be in season throughout the year, but more plentiful in March, and a little before and after. For we are told by a grave author, an eminent French physician,[6] that fish being a prolific diet, there are more children born in Roman Catholic countries about nine months after Lent than at any other season; therefore, reckoning a year after Lent, the markets will be more glutted than usual, because the number of popish infants is at least three to one in this kingdom; and therefore it will have one other collateral advantage, by lessening the number of Papists among us. 13

I have already computed the charge of nursing a beggar's child (in which list I reckon all cottagers, laborers, and four-fifths of the farmers) to be about two shillings per annum, rags included; and I believe no gentleman would repine to give ten shillings for the carcass of a good fat child, which, as I have said, will make four dishes of excellent nutritive meat, when he hath only some particular friend or his own family to dine with him. Thus the squire will learn to be a good landlord, and grow popular among the tenants; the mother will have eight shillings net profit, and be fit for work till she produces another child. 14

Those who are more thrifty (as I must confess the times require) may flay the carcass; the skin of which artificially[7] dressed will make admirable gloves for ladies, and summer boots for fine gentlemen. 15

As to our city of Dublin, shambles[8] may be appointed for this purpose in the most convenient parts of it, and butchers we may be assured will not be wanting; although I rather recommend buying the children alive, and dressing them hot from the knife as we do roasting pigs. 16

---

[6] Swift's favorite French writer, François Rabelais, sixteenth-century author; not "grave" at all, but a broad humorist. — EDS.

[7] With art or craft. — EDS.

A very worthy person, a true lover of his country, and whose virtues I   17
highly esteem, was lately pleased in discoursing on this matter to offer a refinement upon my scheme. He said that many gentlemen of his kingdom, having of
late destroyed their deer, he conceived that the want of venison might be well
supplied by the bodies of young lads and maidens, not exceeding fourteen years
of age nor under twelve, so great a number of both sexes in every county being
now ready to starve for want of work and service; and these to be disposed of by
their parents, if alive, or otherwise by their nearest relations. But with due deference to so excellent a friend and so deserving a patriot, I cannot be altogether
in his sentiments; for as to the males, my American acquaintance assured me
from frequent experience that their flesh was generally tough and lean, like
that of our schoolboys, by continual exercise, and their taste disagreeable; and
to fatten them would not answer the charge. Then as to the females, it would, I
think with humble submission, be a loss to the public, because they soon would
become breeders themselves; and besides, it is not improbable that some scrupulous people might be apt to censure such a practice (although indeed very
unjustly) as a little bordering upon cruelty; which, I confess, hath always been
with me the strongest objection against any project, how well soever intended.

But in order to justify my friend, he confessed that this expedient was put   18
into his head by the famous Psalmanazar,[9] a native of the island Formosa, who
came from thence to London above twenty years ago, and in conversation
told my friend that in his country when any young person happened to be
put to death, the executioner sold the carcass to persons of quality as a prime
dainty; and that in his time the body of a plump girl of fifteen, who was cruci-
fied for an attempt to poison the emperor, was sold to his Imperial Majesty's
prime minister of state, and other great mandarins of the court, in joints from
the gibbet, at four hundred crowns. Neither indeed can I deny that if the same
use were made of several plump young girls in this town, who without one
single groat to their fortunes cannot stir abroad without a chair, and appear at
the playhouse and assemblies in foreign fineries which they never will pay for,
the kingdom would not be the worse.

Some persons of a desponding spirit are in great concern about that vast num-   19
ber of poor people who are aged, diseased, or maimed, and I have been desired to
employ my thoughts what course may be taken to ease the nation of so grievous
an encumbrance. But I am not in the least pain upon that matter, because it is
very well known that they are every day dying and rotting by cold and famine,
and filth and vermin, as fast as can be reasonably expected. And as to the younger

---

[8] Butcher shops or slaughterhouses. — Eds.

[9] Georges Psalmanazar — a Frenchman who pretended to be Japanese, the author of a
completely imaginary *Description of the Isle Formosa* (1705) — had become a well-known figure
in gullible London society. — Eds.

laborers, they are now in almost as hopeful a condition. They cannot get work, and consequently pine away for want of nourishment to a degree that if any time they are accidentally hired to common labor, they have not strength to perform it; and thus the country and themselves are happily delivered from the evils to come.

I have too long digressed, and therefore shall return to my subject. I think   20
the advantages by the proposal which I have made are obvious and many, as well as of the highest importance.

For first, as I have already observed, it would greatly lessen the number of   21
Papists, with whom we are yearly overrun, being the principal breeders of the nation as well as our most dangerous enemies; and who stay at home on pur-pose to deliver the kingdom to the Pretender, hoping to take their advantage by the absence of so many good Protestants, who have chosen rather to leave their country than to stay at home and pay tithes against their conscience to an Episcopal curate.

Secondly, the poorer tenants will have something valuable of their own,   22
which by law may be made liable to distress,[10] and help to pay their landlord's rent, their corn and cattle being already seized and money a thing unknown.

Thirdly, whereas the maintenance of an hundred thousand children, from   23
two years old and upwards, cannot be computed at less than ten shillings a piece per annum, the nation's stock will be thereby increased fifty thousand pounds per annum, besides the profit of a new dish introduced to the tables of all gentlemen of fortune in the kingdom who have any refinement in taste. And the money will circulate among ourselves, the goods being entirely of our own growth and manufacture.

Fourthly, the constant breeders, besides the gain of eight shillings sterling   24
per annum by the sale of their children, will be rid of the charge of maintain-ing them after the first year.

Fifthly, this food would likewise bring great custom to taverns, where the   25
vintners will certainly be so prudent as to procure the best receipts for dressing it to perfection, and consequently have their houses frequented by all the fine gentlemen, who justly value themselves upon their knowledge in good eating; and a skillful cook, who understands how to oblige his guests, will contrive to make it as expensive as they please.

Sixthly, this would be a great inducement to marriage, which all wise   26
nations have either encouraged by rewards or enforced by laws and penalties. It would increase the care and tenderness of mothers toward their children, when they were sure of a settlement for life to the poor babes, provided in some sort by the public, to their annual profit instead of expense. We should see an honest emulation among the married women, which of them could

[10] Subject to seizure by creditors. — Eds.

bring the fattest child to the market. Men would become as fond of their wives during the time of their pregnancy as they are now of their mares in foal, their cows in calf, or sows when they are ready to farrow; nor offer to beat or kick them (as is too frequent a practice) for fear of a miscarriage.

Many other advantages might be enumerated. For instance, the addition of some thousand carcasses in our exportation of barreled beef, the propagation of swine's flesh, and improvements in the art of making good bacon, so much wanted among us by the great destruction of pigs, too frequent at our tables, which are no way comparable in taste or magnificence to a well-grown, fat, yearling child, which roasted whole will make a considerable figure at a lord mayor's feast or any other public entertainment. But this and many others I omit, being studious of brevity.

Supposing that one thousand families in this city would be constant customers for infants' flesh, besides others who might have it at merry meetings, particularly weddings and christenings, I compute that Dublin would take off annually about twenty thousand carcasses, and the rest of the kingdom (where probably they will be sold somewhat cheaper) the remaining eighty thousand.

I can think of no one objection that will possibly be raised against this proposal, unless it should be urged that the number of people will be thereby much lessened in the kingdom. This I freely own, and it was indeed one principal design in offering it to the world. I desire the reader will observe, that I calculate my remedy for this one individual kingdom of Ireland and for no other that ever was, is, or I think ever can be upon earth. Therefore let no man talk to me of other expedients: of taxing our absentees at five shillings a pound: of using neither clothes nor household furniture except what is of our own growth and manufacture: of utterly rejecting the materials and instruments that promote foreign luxury: of curing the expensiveness of pride, vanity, idleness, and gaming in our women: of introducing a vein of parsimony, prudence, and temperance: of learning to love our country, in the want of which we differ even from Laplanders and the inhabitants of Topinamboo:[11] of quitting our animosities and factions, nor acting any longer like the Jews, who were murdering one another at the very moment their city was taken:[12] of being a little cautious not to sell our country and conscience for nothing: of teaching landlords to have at least one degree of mercy toward their tenants: lastly, of putting a spirit of honesty, industry, and skill into our shopkeepers; who, if a resolution could now be taken to buy only our native goods, would immediately unite to cheat and exact upon us in the price, the measure, and

27

28

29

[11] A district of Brazil. — Eps.
[12] During the Roman siege of Jerusalem (AD 70), prominent Jews were executed on the charge of being in league with the enemy. — Eps.

the goodness, nor could ever yet be brought to make one fair proposal of just dealing, though often and earnestly invited to it.

Therefore I repeat, let no man talk to me of these and the like expedients, till he hath at least some glimpse of hope that there will ever be some hearty and sincere attempt to put them in practice. 30

But as to myself, having been wearied out for many years with offering vain, idle, visionary thoughts, and at length utterly despairing of success, I fortunately fell upon this proposal, which, as it is wholly new, so it hath something solid and real, of no expense and little trouble, full in our own power, and whereby we can incur no danger in disobliging England. For this kind of commodity will not bear exportation, the flesh being of too tender a consistence to admit a long continuance in salt, although perhaps I could name a country which would be glad to eat up our whole nation without it. 31

After all, I am not so violently bent upon my own opinion as to reject any offer proposed by wise men, which shall be found equally innocent, cheap, easy, and effectual. But before something of that kind shall be advanced in contradiction to my scheme, and offering a better, I desire the author or authors will be pleased maturely to consider two points. First, as things now stand, how they will be able to find food and raiment for an hundred thousand useless mouths and backs. And secondly, there being a round million of creatures in human figure throughout this kingdom, whose sole subsistence put into a common stock would leave them in debt two millions of pounds sterling, adding those who are beggars by profession to the bulk of farmers, cottagers, and laborers, with their wives and children who are beggars in effect; I desire those politicians who dislike my overture, and may perhaps be so bold to attempt an answer, that they will first ask the parents of these mortals whether they would not at this day think it a great happiness to have been sold for food at a year old in this manner I prescribe, and thereby have avoided such a perpetual scene of misfortunes as they have since gone through by the oppression of landlords, the impossibility of paying rent without money or trade, the want of common sustenance, with neither house nor clothes to cover them from the inclemencies of the weather, and the most inevitable prospect of entailing the like or greater miseries upon their breed forever. 32

I profess, in the sincerity of my heart, that I have not the least personal interest in endeavoring to promote this necessary work, having no other motive than the public good of my country, by advancing our trade, providing for infants, relieving the poor, and giving some pleasure to the rich. I have no children by which I can propose to get a single penny; the youngest being nine years old, and my wife past childbearing. 33

Journal Writing

Swift's proposal is aimed at a serious social problem of his day. In your journal, consider a contemporary problem that — like the poverty and starvation Swift describes — seems to require drastic action. For instance, do you believe that a particular group of people is neglected, mistreated, or victimized? Turn to the news media for ideas if no problem comes immediately to mind.

Questions on Meaning

1. On the surface, what is Swift proposing?
2. Beneath his IRONY, what is Swift's argument?
3. What do you take to be the PURPOSE of Swift's essay?
4. How does the introductory paragraph serve Swift's purpose?
5. Comment on the statement "I can think of no one objection that will possibly be raised against this proposal" (par. 29). What objections can you think of?

Questions on Writing Strategy

1. Describe the mask of the personage through whom Swift writes.
2. By what means does the writer attest to his reasonableness?
3. At what point in the essay did it become clear to you that the proposal isn't modest but horrible?
4. **MIXED METHODS**   As an ARGUMENT, does "A Modest Proposal" appeal primarily to reason or to emotion? (See p. 483 for a discussion of the distinction.)
5. **MIXED METHODS**   What does Swift's argument gain by his careful attention to PROCESS ANALYSIS and to CAUSE AND EFFECT?

Questions on Language

1. How does Swift's choice of words enforce the monstrousness of his proposal? Note especially words from the vocabulary of breeding and butchery.
2. Consult your dictionary for the meanings of any of the following words not yet in your vocabulary: importuning, sustenance (par. 1); prodigious, commonwealth (2); computation, raiment (4); apprehend, rudiments, probationers (6); nutriment (7); fricassee (9); repine (14); flay (15); scrupulous, censure (17); mandarins (18); desponding, encumbrance (19); per annum (23); vintners (25); emulation, foal, farrow (26); expedients, parsimony, animosities (29); disobliging, consistence (31); overture, inclemencies (32).

Suggestions for Writing

1. **FROM JOURNAL TO ESSAY**   Write an essay in which you propose a solution to the problem raised in your journal (p. 585). Your essay may be either of the following:

   a. A straight argument, giving EVIDENCE, in which you set forth possible solutions to the problem.

   b. An ironic proposal in the manner of Swift. If you do this one, find a device other than cannibalism to eliminate the victims or their problems. You don't want to imitate Swift too closely; he is probably inimitable.

2. In an encyclopedia, look into what has happened in Ireland since Swift wrote. Choose a specific contemporary aspect of Irish-English relations, research it in books and periodicals, and write a report on it.

3. **CRITICAL WRITING**   Choose several examples of irony in "A Modest Proposal" that you find particularly effective. In a brief essay, ANALYZE Swift's use of irony. Do your examples of irony depend on understating, overstating, or saying the opposite of what is meant? How do they improve on literal statements? What is the value of irony in argument?

4. **CONNECTIONS**   Read Jessica Mitford's "Behind the Formaldehyde Curtain" (p. 288) alongside "A Modest Proposal," and analyze the use of irony and humor in these two essays. How heavily does each author depend on irony and humor to make his or her argument? Do these elements strengthen both authors' arguments? What evidence does each offer that would also work in a more straightforward argument?

5. **CONNECTIONS**   Analyze the strategies that Jonathan Swift and N. Scott Momaday, in "The Way to Rainy Mountain" (p. 129), use to create sympathy for the oppressed groups they are concerned about. Concentrate not only on what they say but also on the words they use and their TONE. Then write a process analysis explaining techniques for portraying oppression so as to win the reader's sympathy. Use quotations or PARAPHRASES from Swift's and Momaday's essays as EXAMPLES. If you can think of other techniques that neither author uses, by all means include and illustrate them as well.

HENRY DAVID THOREAU

Henry David Thoreau (1817–62) was born in Concord, Massachusetts, where, excerpt for short excursions, he remained for the whole of his life. After his graduation from Harvard College, he taught school briefly, worked irregularly as a surveyor and house painter, and for a time labored in his father's pencil factory. The small sales of his first, self-published book, *A Week on the Concord and Merrimac Rivers* (1849), led him to remark, "I have now a library of nearly nine hundred volumes, over seven hundred of which I wrote myself." The lecturer Ralph Waldo Emerson befriended his neighbor Thoreau; but although these leading figures of Transcendentalism shared a faith in instinct and agreed that a unity exists between humankind and nature, they did not always see eye to eye on matters of politics. Unlike Emerson, Thoreau was an activist. He helped escaped slaves flee to Canada; he publicly renounced the church; he went to jail rather than pay his poll tax to a government that made war against Mexico. He recounts these brushes with the law in his essay "Civil Disobedience" (1849), in which later readers (including Mahatma Gandhi and Martin Luther King, Jr.) have found encouragement for their own nonviolent resistance. One other book appeared in Thoreau's lifetime: *Walden* (1854), a searching account of his time in (and around, and beyond) the one-room cabin he built for himself on the edges of Concord. When the famously solitary Thoreau lay dying, an aunt asked whether he had made his peace with God. "I did not know we had quarreled," he replied.

What I Lived For

At Walden Pond, Thoreau mercilessly scaled back his existence. Making himself almost fully self-reliant, he proved to his own satisfaction that he could build a home, grow beans, read classics in the original Greek and Latin, indulge the occasional visitor, and observe in minute detail the glories of the natural world.

Thoreau wrote with equal attentiveness: To revise *Walden*, a relatively short book, took him seven years. The following excerpt — the second half of the second chapter — is foremost an earnest argument for simplicity, but the poet-philosopher relies on multiple methods to develop and give significance to his artful commentary:

Narration (Chap. 3): paragraphs 4, 6
Description (Chap. 4): paragraphs 6, 7–8
Example (Chap. 5): paragraphs 3, 4, 5

Comparison and contrast (Chap. 6): paragraphs 2, 3, 4–5, 6
Process analysis (Chap. 7): paragraphs 2, 7, 8
Division or analysis (Chap. 8): paragraphs 1–2, 8
Cause and effect (Chap. 10): paragraphs 1–3, 6
Definition (Chap. 11): paragraphs 3, 4–5
Argument (Chap. 12): throughout

I went to the woods because I wished to live deliberately, to front only   1
the essential facts of life, and see if I could not learn what it had to teach,
and not, when I came to die, discover that I had not lived. I did not wish to
live what was not life, living is so dear; nor did I wish to practice resignation,
unless it was quite necessary. I wanted to live deep and suck out all the marrow of life, to live so sturdily and Spartan-like as to put to rout all that was
not life, to cut a broad swath and shave close, to drive life into a corner, and
reduce it to its lowest terms, and, if it proved to be mean, why then to get the
whole and genuine meanness of it, and publish its meanness to the world; or
if it were sublime, to know it by experience, and be able to give a true account
of it in my next excursion. For most men, it appears to me, are in a strange
uncertainty about it, whether it is of the devil or of God, and have *somewhat
hastily* concluded that it is the chief end of man here to "glorify God and enjoy
him forever."

Still we live meanly, like ants; though the fable tells us that we were long   2
ago changed into men; like pygmies we fight with cranes; it is error upon error,
and clout upon clout, and our best virtue has for its occasion a superfluous and
evitable wretchedness. Our life is frittered away by detail. An honest man has
hardly need to count more than his ten fingers, or in extreme cases he may
add his ten toes, and lump the rest. Simplicity, simplicity, simplicity! I say, let
your affairs be as two or three, and not a hundred or a thousand; instead of a
million count half a dozen, and keep your accounts on your thumb nail. In the
midst of this chopping sea of civilized life, such are the clouds and storms and
quicksands and thousand-and-one items to be allowed for, that a man has to
live, if he would not founder and go to the bottom and not make his port at
all, by dead reckoning, and he must be a great calculator indeed who succeeds.
Simplify, simplify. Instead of three meals a day, if it be necessary eat but one;
instead of a hundred dishes, five; and reduce other things in proportion. Our
life is like a German Confederacy, made up of petty states, with its boundary
forever fluctuating, so that even a German cannot tell you how it is bounded
at any moment. The nation itself, with all its so-called internal improvements,
which, by the way are all external and superficial, is just such an unwieldy and
overgrown establishment, cluttered with furniture and tripped up by its own
traps, ruined by luxury and heedless expense, by want of calculation and a

worthy aim, as the million households in the land; and the only cure for it as for them is in a rigid economy, a stern and more than Spartan simplicity of life and elevation of purpose. It lives too fast. Men think that it is essential that the *Nation* have commerce, and export ice, and talk through a telegraph, and ride thirty miles an hour, without a doubt, whether *they* do or not; but whether we should live like baboons or like men, is a little uncertain. If we do not get out sleepers,[1] and forge rails, and devote days and nights to the work, but go to tinkering upon our *lives* to improve *them*, who will build railroads? And if railroads are not built, how shall we get to heaven in season? But if we stay at home and mind our business, who will want railroads? We do not ride on the railroad; it rides upon us. Did you ever think what those sleepers are that underlie the railroad? Each one is a man, an Irishman, or a Yankee man. The rails are laid on them, and they are covered with sand, and the cars run smoothly over them. They are sound sleepers, I assure you. And every few years a new lot is laid down and run over; so that, if some have the pleasure of riding on a rail, others have the misfortune to be ridden upon. And when they run over a man that is walking in his sleep, a supernumerary sleeper in the wrong position, and wake him up, they suddenly stop the cars, and make a hue and cry about it, as if this were an exception. I am glad to know that it takes a gang of men for every five miles to keep the sleepers down and level in their beds as it is, for this is a sign that they may sometime get up again.

Why should we live with such hurry and waste of life? We are determined to be starved before we are hungry. Men say that a stitch in time saves nine, and so they take a thousand stitches today to save nine tomorrow. As for *work*, we haven't any of any consequence. We have the Saint Vitus's dance,[2] and cannot possibly keep our heads still. If I should only give a few pulls at the parish bell-rope, as for a fire, that is, without setting the bell, there is hardly a man on his farm in the outskirts of Concord, notwithstanding that press of engagements which was his excuse so many times this morning, nor a boy, nor a woman, I might almost say, but would forsake all and follow that sound, not mainly to save property from the flames, but, if we will confess the truth, much more to see it burn, since burn it must, and we, be it known, did not set it on fire — or to see it put out, and have a hand in it, if that is done as handsomely; yes, even if it were the parish church itself. Hardly a man takes a half hour's nap after dinner, but when he wakes he holds up his head and asks, "What's the news?" as if the rest of mankind had stood his sentinels. Some give directions to be waked every half hour, doubtless for no other purpose; and then, to

3

---

[1] Railroad ties. — EDS.
[2] Colloquial term for Sydenham's chorea, an acute neurological condition often preceded by rheumatic fever and characterized by uncontrolled jerking movements. — EDS.

pay for it, they tell what they have dreamed. After a night's sleep the news is as indispensable as the breakfast. "Pray tell me anything new that has happened to a man anywhere on this globe" — and he reads it over his coffee and rolls, that a man has had his eyes gouged out this morning on the Wachito River; never dreaming the while that he lives in the dark unfathomed mammoth cave of this world, and has but the rudiment of an eye himself.

For my part, I could easily do without the post-office. I think that there are very few important communications made through it. To speak critically, I never received more than one or two letters in my life — I wrote this some years ago — that were worth the postage. The penny-post is, commonly, an institution through which you seriously offer a man that penny for his thoughts which is so often safely offered in jest. And I am sure that I never read any memorable news in a newspaper. If we read of one man robbed, or murdered, or killed by accident, or one house burned, or one vessel wrecked, or one steamboat blown up, or one cow run over on the Western Railroad, or one mad dog killed, or one lot of grasshoppers in the winter — we never need read of another. One is enough. If you are acquainted with the principle, what do you care for a myriad instances and applications? To a philosopher all *news*, as it is called, is gossip, and they who edit and read it are old women over their tea. Yet not a few are greedy after this gossip. There was such a rush, as I hear, the other day at one of the offices to learn the foreign news by the last arrival, that several large squares of plate glass belonging to the establishment were broken by the pressure — news which I seriously think a ready wit might write a twelvemonth or twelve years beforehand with sufficient accuracy. As for Spain, for instance, if you know how to throw in Don Carlos and the Infanta, and Don Pedro and Seville and Granada, from time to time in the right proportions — they may have changed the names a little since I saw the papers — and serve up a bull-fight when other entertainments fail, it will be true to the letter, and give us as good an idea of the exact state or ruin of things in Spain as the most succinct and lucid reports under this head in the newspapers: and as for England, almost the last significant scrap of news from that quarter was the revolution of 1649; and if you have learned the history of her crops for an average year, you never need attend to that thing again, unless your speculations are of a merely pecuniary character. If one may judge who rarely looks into the newspapers, nothing new does ever happen in foreign parts, a French revolution not excepted.

What news! how much more important to know what that is which was never old! "Kieou-he-yu (great dignitary of the state of Wei) sent a man to Khoung-tseu to know his news. Khoung-tseu caused the messenger to be seated near him, and questioned him in these terms: What is your master doing? The messenger answered with respect: My master desires to diminish

4

5

the number of his faults, but he cannot come to the end of them. The messenger being gone, the philosopher remarked: What a worthy messenger! What a worthy messenger!" The preacher, instead of vexing the ears of drowsy farmers on their day of rest at the end of the week — for Sunday is the fit conclusion of an ill-spent week, and not the fresh and brave beginning of a new one — with this one other draggle-tail of a sermon, should shout with thundering voice — "Pause! Avast! Why so seeming fast, but deadly slow?"

Shams and delusions are esteemed for soundest truths, while reality is fabulous. If men would steadily observe realities only, and not allow themselves to be deluded, life, to compare it with such things as we know, would be like a fairy tale and the Arabian Nights' Entertainments.[3] If we respected only what is inevitable and has a right to be, music and poetry would resound along the streets. When we are unhurried and wise, we perceive that only great and worthy things have any permanent and absolute existence — that petty fears and petty pleasures are but the shadow of the reality. This is always exhilarating and sublime. By closing the eyes and slumbering, and consenting to be deceived by shows, men establish and confirm their daily life of routine and habit everywhere, which still is built on purely illusory foundations. Children, who play life, discern its true law and relations more clearly than men, who fail to live it worthily, but who think that they are wiser by experience, that is, by failure. I have read in a Hindu book that "there was a king's son, who, being expelled in infancy from his native city, was brought up by a forester, and, growing up to maturity in that state, imagined himself to belong to the barbarous race with which he lived. One of his father's ministers, having discovered him, revealed to him what he was, and the misconception of his character was removed, and he knew himself to be a prince. So soul," continues the Hindu philosopher, "from the circumstances in which it is placed, mistakes its own character, until the truth is revealed to it by some holy teacher, and then it knows itself to be *Brahme*." I perceive that we inhabitants of New England live this mean life that we do because our vision does not penetrate the surface of things. We think that that *is* which *appears* to be. If a man should walk through this town and see only the reality, where, think you, would the "Mill-dam" go to? If he should give us an account of the realities he beheld there, we should not recognize the place in his description. Look at a meeting-house, or a courthouse, or a jail, or a shop, or a dwelling-house, and say what that thing really is before a true gaze,

6

---

[3] Thoreau is referring to *One Thousand and One Nights*, a medieval collection of Middle Eastern and Indian folktales narrated by a bride whose new husband (a king) has had each of his previous wives killed on their wedding night. Scheherazade staves off her own execution by telling him stories but withholding their endings to the next evening, until he spares her life for good. — Eds.

and they would all go to pieces in your account of them. Men esteem truth remote, in the outskirts of the system, behind the farthest star, before Adam and after the last man. In eternity there is indeed something true and sublime. But all these times and places and occasions are now and here. God himself culminates in the present moment, and will never be more divine in the lapse of all the ages. And we are enabled to apprehend at all what is sublime and noble only by the perpetual instilling and drenching of the reality that surrounds us. The universe constantly and obediently answers to our conceptions; whether we travel fast or slow, the track is laid for us. Let us spend our lives in conceiving then. The poet or the artist never yet had so fair and noble a design but some of his posterity at least could accomplish it.

Let us spend one day as deliberately as Nature, and not be thrown off the   7
track by every nutshell and mosquito's wing that falls on the rails. Let us rise early and fast, or break fast, gently and without perturbation; let company come and let company go, let the bells ring and the children cry — determined to make a day of it. Why should we knock under and go with the stream? Let us not be upset and overwhelmed in that terrible rapid and whirlpool called a dinner, situated in the meridian shallows. Weather this danger and you are safe, for the rest of the way is down hill. With unrelaxed nerves, with morning vigor, sail by it, looking another way, tied to the mast like Ulysses.[4] If the engine whistles, let it whistle till it is hoarse for its pains. If the bell rings, why should we run? We will consider what kind of music they are like. Let us settle ourselves, and work and wedge our feet downward through the mud and slush of opinion, and prejudice, and tradition, and delusion, and appearance, that alluvion which covers the globe, through Paris and London, through New York and Boston and Concord, through church and state, through poetry and philosophy and religion, till we come to a hard bottom and rocks in place, which we can call *reality*, and say, This is, and no mistake; and then begin, having a *point d'appui*,[5] below freshet and frost and fire, a place where you might found a wall or a state, or set a lamppost safely, or perhaps a gauge, not a Nilometer,[6] but a Realometer, that future ages might know how deep a freshet of shams and appearances had gathered from time to time. If you stand right fronting and face to face to a fact, you will see the sun glimmer on both its surfaces, as if it were a cimeter, and feel its sweet edge dividing you through the heart and marrow, and so you will happily conclude your mortal career.

---

[4] In a memorable scene from the ancient Greek epic poem *The Odyssey* by Homer, Ulysses must pass his ship through a strait populated by sirens, whose songs were known to lure sailors and cause them to crash into the rocky shore. Ulysses asks his crew to restrain him to save them all from a deadly fate. — EDS.

[5] French, "point of support," or foundation. — EDS.

[6] An ancient Egyptian device for measuring the depth and clarity of the Nile River. — EDS.

Be it life or death, we crave only reality. If we are really dying, let us hear the rattle in our throats and feel cold in the extremities; if we are alive, let us go about our business.

Time is but the stream I go a-fishing in. I drink at it; but while I drink I see the sandy bottom and detect how shallow it is. Its thin current slides away, but eternity remains. I would drink deeper; fish in the sky, whose bottom is pebbly with stars. I cannot count one. I know not the first letter of the alphabet. I have always been regretting that I was not as wise as the day I was born. The intellect is a cleaver; it discerns and rifts its way into the secret of things. I do not wish to be any more busy with my hands than is necessary. My head is hands and feet. I feel all my best faculties concentrated in it. My instinct tells me that my head is an organ for burrowing, as some creatures use their snout and forepaws, and with it I would mine and burrow my way through these hills. I think that the richest vein is somewhere hereabouts; so by the divining rod and thin rising vapors I judge; and here I will begin to mine.

Journal Writing

In your journal, respond to Thoreau's contention that we should all simplify our existence and become attuned to nature for the sake of leading more purposeful lives. How persuaded are you by his argument? Do you agree that forsaking the world of business and commerce, for instance, could make you a happier person, or do you think meaningful work (or religion, or building relationships, or something else) is the purpose of living? Why do you feel the way you do?

Questions on Meaning

1. Notice the first sentence of this excerpt from *Walden*: "I went to the woods because I wished to live deliberately," Thoreau writes. What does he mean by "live deliberately"? What does this statement reveal about his PURPOSE for writing?

2. Why did Thoreau choose to live in isolation? What, to his mind, were the major problems with society at the time? Do his criticisms still apply?

3. In two or three words, what would you say is Thoreau's THESIS?

4. What can you INFER from this piece about Thoreau's attitude toward organized religion? Does he seem to believe in God or some other divinity?

5. How does Thoreau explain the relationship between perception and reality? Does he think it's possible to know truth?

6. "I have always been regretting that I was not as wise as the day I was born," Thoreau writes in his conclusion (par. 8). How do you account for this PARADOX?

Questions on Writing Strategy

1. For whom does Thoreau seem to be writing: general readers? politicians? business owners? religious leaders? some other group? What influence does he apparently hope to have on his readers' behavior? To what extent did he influence your opinion about simple living?

2. Thoreau's writing feels impressionistic — even transcendent, one might say. What strategies does he use to give his musings UNITY and COHERENCE?

3. **MIXED METHODS**   How does Thoreau use EXAMPLES to DEFINE *news* (par. 4)? How does the news COMPARE to gossip, as far as he's concerned?

4. **MIXED METHODS**   What role does NARRATION play in Thoreau's ARGUMENT? What do the ANECDOTES in paragraphs 5 and 6 contribute to his point? To what other works of literature does Thoreau ALLUDE? Must readers be familiar with these stories to appreciate his meaning?

Questions on Language

1. Thoreau was a poet as well as a philosopher, and his writing is, accordingly, rich in FIGURES OF SPEECH. Point to the two or three metaphors or similes you find most lyrical or compelling (or confounding) and explain their meaning.

2. Explain how and why Thoreau gives human qualities to railroads. What is the effect of these uses of PERSONIFICATION?

3. What is the TONE of this selection? In his chosen solitude does Thoreau seem grim, pleased, appalled, disgusted, mocking, or what? How can you tell?

4. You may find Thoreau's vocabulary more difficult than that of some other writers in this book. Look up, as necessary, definitions for any of these words you aren't sure of: dear, Spartan, rout, mean, sublime (par. 1); superfluous, founder, heedless, forge, supernumerary (2); forsake, unfathomed, rudiment (3); jest, myriad, lucid, pecuniary (4); vexing, avast (5); barbarous, Brahme, culminates, lapse, posterity (6); perturbation, meridian, alluvion, freshet, cimeter (7); rifts, faculties (8).

Suggestions for Writing

1. **FROM JOURNAL TO ESSAY**   Expand your journal writing into an essay in which you respond personally to Thoreau's plea: "Simplify, simplify" (par. 2). What do you think is the purpose of life? If you generally agree with Thoreau's assessment, what can you add to convince others who do not? If you generally disagree, how do you counter his argument?

2. Are your thoughts and actions a matter of habit or of deliberate choice? Write an essay about the importance (or unimportance) of self-awareness and conscious decision making, using several concrete examples or a single extended example to support your point. You may refer to some of Thoreau's ideas if you wish, but be sure to develop a unique thesis of your own.

3. If Thoreau objected so strongly to the rapid growth of the newspaper business enabled by the telegraph and the construction of railroads in the mid-nineteenth century, what do you think he would make of today's online news feeds and twenty-four-hour broadcast cycles? What do *you* make of them? Do new technologies necessarily advance civilization, or might they also hinder it? Why do you think so? Can you think of other recent technologies that might be said to do more harm than good? Ponder these questions in a short essay.

4. **CRITICAL WRITING**   When Thoreau decamped to the woods to write *Walden* in 1845, the United States (and indeed much of the world) was experiencing a period of immense social, cultural, and political upheaval. The economy was shifting from one of home-based subsistence and informal trade to paid labor in structured workplaces. Abolitionists were pushing for an end to slavery, and women's rights activists were demanding equal protection under the law. The church was losing its influence and its place in local government. Social workers were seeking reforms in charitable, penal, and psychiatric institutions; others were calling for universal education and a new approach to schooling. Even Transcendentalism was a reform movement of sorts. Choose any one of these developments that interests you and do some research to learn more about it. Then, in an essay, explain how and why Thoreau incorporates critiques of that change into his argument in "What I Lived For."

5. **CONNECTIONS**   Colson Whitehead, in "Loving Las Vegas" (p. 612), blends narration and description to explore his own conceptions of the meaning of life. In an essay, COMPARE AND CONTRAST Whitehead's purpose and method with Thoreau's. What similarities and differences do you find in the two writers' approaches to the subject of deliberate living? To what extent do Whitehead's conclusions fit with Thoreau's ideas about simplicity?

6. **CONNECTIONS**   Recalling his own pilgrimage to Walden Pond, the author of the next essay, Luis Alberto Urrea, comments that as a teenager he had thought he understood what Thoreau meant when he wrote "Time is but the stream I go a-fishing in" (par. 8), but suggests that he didn't, really. What is your understanding of this famous line? In a paragraph or two, PARAPHRASE Thoreau's extended metaphor in plain language. What exactly is Thoreau saying here?

LUIS ALBERTO URREA

Often praised as a significant "voice of the border," writer Luis Alberto Urrea has explained the reason for his persistent focus on life at the edge: "The border runs down the middle of me," he says. "I have a barbed-wire fence neatly bisecting my heart." He was born in Tijuana in 1955 and raised in San Diego, torn between the conflicting cultures of his father's Mexico and his mother's America. Urrea earned writing degrees from the University of California at San Diego (BA, 1977) and the University of Colorado at Boulder (MA, 1994), and for a decade pursued a dual career as a relief worker and investigative journalist in the slums surrounding Tijuana. He wrote four books exposing the horrors of extreme poverty that he encountered, all of them acclaimed for their combination of stark realism and lyrical voice: *Across the Wire* (1993); *By the Lake of Sleeping Children* (1996); *Nobody's Son* (1998), winner of the American Book Award; and *The Devil's Highway* (2004), nominated for a Pulitzer Prize. A popular fiction writer as well, Urrea has published many novels, including *The Hummingbird's Daughter* (2005) and *Queen of America* (2011), and multiple collections of short stories and poems, most recently *The Water Museum* and *The Tijuana Book of the Dead* (both 2015). Currently a professor at the University of Illinois at Chicago, he has taught expository and creative writing at Harvard University, Massachusetts Bay Community College, and the University of Colorado. Urrea also contributes an occasional column to *Orion* magazine.

Barrio Walden

Growing up, Urrea witnessed the effects of involuntary poverty in the neighborhoods of San Diego and Tijuana both. In this 2013 essay for *Orion*, he recounts, with a mix of mirth and embarrassment, a youthful pilgrimage to the site of Henry David Thoreau's famous experiment in self-imposed simplicity (p. 587) in Concord, Massachusetts.

"Barrio Walden" is foremost a narrative, but Urrea also uses description, example, comparison and contrast, and definition to develop and give significance to his story.

Narration (Chap. 3): throughout
Description (Chap. 4): paragraphs 4–5, 9–12, 27–35
Example (Chap. 5): paragraphs 1, 3
Comparison and contrast (Chap. 6): paragraphs 10–26, 27–35
Definition (Chap. 11): paragraphs 3, 9

Imagine my shock. I was living in Massachusetts for the first time. Adjust-   1
ing. The first time I saw snow falling past my Somerville[1] apartment window,
I told a woman on the phone that a neighbor was on the roof shaking out a
pillow. Not many snowstorms in my desertified homeland. The first time I saw
ice on the sidewalk, I thought a prankster had smeared Vaseline on the bricks
to watch businessmen fall down.

This old world was all new to me. I was manhandled by quotidian revela-   2
tions, wrenched by the duende of Yankee cultural hoodoo. So when I realized
I could walk over to Porter Square[2] (where the porterhouse steak was first
hacked out of some Bostonian cow) and catch a commuter train to Concord,
to Walden freakin' Pond, I was off and running.

Perhaps I was a barrio Transcendentalist. Well, I was certainly one by the   3
time I hit the San Diego 'burbs in my tweens. I loved me some Thoreau. "Civil
Disobedience," right? What Doors fan couldn't get behind that? I also had
copied passages of "Self Reliance" by Emerson and pasted them to my walls
amid posters of hot rods and King Kong and John Lennon and trees. Even in
the '70s, I was deeply worried about trees.

So I trudged to the T stop and went down to the suburban rail level and   4
caught the Purple Line.[3] I, and all the rambunctious Concord high school kids,
were deeply plugged into our Walkmans.[4] I was all Screaming Blue Messiahs
and class rage, scribbling in my notebooks about rich bastards giggling self-
indulgently and shrieking "Eau my GWOD!" at each other as they ignored the
woods and the mangy deer outside. For me, it was a Disneyland train ride,
all this stuff I had only experienced robotically before. I was imagining the
ditch diggers from my old neighborhood tripping out over all this water. These
damned New Englanders had water everywhere. And deer.

We pulled into Concord as if it were a normal thing, and I detrained   5
and stepped into the Friendly's. At the time, if I could have had deep-tissue
grafts of Americana I would have, and a striped-awning ice cream place where
the happy lady called me "Deah" was just about the shiniest moment of my
Americanness to date.

"I'm looking for Walden," I announced. "Pond." Helpful-like, as if she   6
didn't know.

"Right out the door." Doah. "Go out and walk about a mile."   7

---

[1] A small city adjacent to Boston and Cambridge, Somerville has a large population of
college students and recent graduates. — Eds.

[2] A section of Cambridge less than a mile north of Harvard University. — Eds.

[3] "The T" is local shorthand for the MBTA, or the Massachusetts Bay Transportation
Authority. — Eds.

[4] Portable cassette players. — Eds.

I drank some soda. She called it "tonic." And I was off. She didn't tell me   8
I had to turn south. I turned north. And walked away.

Before we proceed much farther on our first New England early autumn   9
country walk, before we grow dizzy with red maples actually turning red in
a natural psychedelic blowmind, we might consider the dearth of what you
might call "ponds" where I come from. To me, a pond was a muddy hole you
could jump across, and it housed six or seven crawdads and some tadpoles.
(My friend Mark put dead polliwogs in a jar with hand lotion and charged kids
a nickel to look at "elephant sperm." We were guttersnipe naturalists.) When
Thoreau said, "Time is but the stream I go a-fishing in," I thought I knew what
he was talking about, though my stream was rain-shower runoff in an alley. I
had been fishing exactly once in my life, and I felt guilt about the poor worm
that came out of the water not only impaled on the hook but stiff as a twig.

So there I was, marching at a splendid pace! Away to Walden Pond! Or,   10
as my homeboys would have spelled it, GUALDENG! Delighted by every
tree! White fences! Orange and yellow and scarlet leaves! Concord thinned
and vanished and I was suddenly among farms! Huzzah! Well-met, shrieking
farm dogs threatening me! Bonjour, paranoiac farm wives hanging laundry
and glaring at me from fields of golden, uh, barley! Eau my gwod! I saw stacks
of lobster pots. I saw pumpkins. It was a shock to me that pumpkins grew
somewhere. Next to lobster pots! And a red tractor to boot.

Behold the festive black-and-white New England moo-cow. Scenes   11
bucolic and poetic — scenes the Alcotts[5] might have penned. Sad autumn
light, what a hipster pal in Harvard Square had called "Irish light," slanted
through the trees to make everything tremble with the most delicious melancholy I have yet to see again. I was bellowing along to Sisters of Mercy: "Oh
Marian, this world is killing me." Cows regarded me. Goths in paradise.

Right about then, I beheld it. In a field of mown hay. Next to a small   12
house and a slanty barn. Walden Pond. It was about twenty feet across and
surrounded by meditative heifers. I removed my headphones and went to the
fence and leaned upon the topmost rail and communed with the transcendent. I wrestled with man's fate and the epic movements of the universe and
the natural splendour of the Creator's delight in the temple of His Creation.

The farmer came out of his house and stared at me. I waved. He jumped   13
in his truck and banged over ruts in his field. He wasn't smiling.

"I help you?" he shouted.   14

---

[5] Bronson Alcott (1799–1888) and his daughter Louisa May Alcott (1832–88) were both
writers and Transcendentalists friendly with Henry David Thoreau. For a short time in 1843
the Alcotts hosted an experimental utopian community in Concord called Fruitlands. — EDS.

"Just looking at the pond," said I. 15

"What pond?" 16

"Walden Pond!" 17

"Jesus Christ!" he reasoned. He looked back at his cows. He looked at me. 18
He looked at the cows. He said, "You're not from around here, are ya?"

"California," I said. 19

"That explains it." 20

What ho, my good fellow! 21

"You walked the wrong damned direction. It's about four mile that way." 22

I looked back, as though the great pond would reveal itself in the autum- 23
nal haze.

"Could you give me a ride?" I asked. 24

"Hell no!" 25

He smoked as he watched me trudge back toward Concord with a slightly 26
less splendid cadence.

Yeah, whatever. Barking dogs. Screw you. Farm wives gawking. What's 27
your problem? My feet hurt. Past Friendly's. Don't do me any favors, Deah.
And south, out of town again, across the crazed traffic on the highway, and
past a tumbledown trailer park and a garbage dump. What is this? Tijuana?

Gradually, I became aware of a bright blue mass to my right. A sea. A 28
Great Lake. This deal wasn't a pond, man. Are you kidding? Who called this
Sea of Cortez[6] a pond?

Down to the water. A crust of harlequin leaves lay along the shore. It was 29
dead silent. Thin wisps of steam rode the far shoreline. I squatted and watched
and fancied myself living in a shack, smoking my pipe, scratching out one-
liners with a quill, changing the world.

An ancient Dalmatian came along. He was stiff and arthritic, walking at an 30
angle, grinning and making horking sounds. His tag said his name was Jason.

"Jason," I said. "I'm looking for Thoreau." 31

"Snork," he said, and headed out. I followed. We walked past cove and 32
bog and found ourselves at Henry's stone floor. The cairn of stones left by travelers. I was glad my homeys did not see me cry over mere rocks.

The shack was about the size of my small bedroom back home in San 33
Diego. I put my hand on the old pines and felt Henry's bark against my palm.
Jason sneezed and thumped along to his own meditations. The pond moved
in slow motion before us, Henry and me. A train rolled past the far trees like
some strange dream.

Crows went from shadow to shadow, arguing. 34

---

[6] The Gulf of California, in the upper west of Mexico. — Eds.

Was it just me, or did I smell pipe tobacco burning?   35

I placed my stone on the cairn. I tipped my collar to my chin. Fall turned   36
cold fast in those days. "Adios, Enrique," I said. Then I headed back to town
for a hot cup of coffee and a ride home on a dark train.

Journal Writing

What works of literature hold a special place in your memory? In your journal, recall
as much as you can about a text or a writer that had a strong influence on you.

Questions on Meaning

1. Why is Urrea drawn to Walden Pond? What does it represent to him?

2. What one sentence best SUMMARIZES Urrea's understanding of Thoreau's Transcendentalist philosophy?

3. What does Urrea mean by "guttersnipe naturalists" (par. 9)? In what ways does
   this term seem to encapsulate his own philosophy?

4. Why does Urrea cry over the pile of rocks at Thoreau's cabin?

5. What would you say is Urrea's PURPOSE in this piece? How would you express his
   unstated THESIS?

Questions on Writing Strategy

1. Why might Urrea have chosen to open his NARRATIVE as he does? What is the
   function of his first three paragraphs?

2. For whom does Urrea seem to be writing? (Hint: Look up *Orion* magazine's mission and history online.) What ASSUMPTIONS does the author make about his
   readers' knowledge and interests? Does one need to be familiar with the works of
   Henry David Thoreau or Ralph Waldo Emerson to understand Urrea's meaning?

3. Most of Urrea's essay moves in SPATIAL ORDER, from the streets of Somerville to
   the center of Concord to an outlying farm and then to Walden Pond. Paragraph
   9, however, jumps back to San Diego, as Urrea explains what "ponds" were like
   in the neighborhood where he grew up. Why do you think Urrea places this paragraph in the middle of his essay, instead of at the beginning?

4. What is the EFFECT of the last sentence of the essay?

5. **MIXED METHODS**   Which of the five senses does Urrea mainly appeal to in his
   DESCRIPTIONS? Point to some sensory IMAGES that seem especially concrete. What
   DOMINANT IMPRESSION does the author create?

6. **MIXED METHODS**   Where does Urrea use COMPARISON AND CONTRAST? What do
   these passages contribute to the essay?

Questions on Language

1. Notice that Urrea mixes urban slang, teenage colloquialisms, academic vocabulary, regional pronunciations, and a few words and phrases that sound as though he transported them from the nineteenth century. What does this DICTION contribute to the author's TONE?

2. "Barrio Walden" is riddled with sentence fragments (see p. 51 if you need an explanation). Identify four or five of them. Does Urrea need a better copy editor, or does he use sentence fragments for a reason? If so, what is it?

3. Contrast Urrea's DIALOG with the farmer (pars. 13–26) with his conversation with Jason the dog (30–33). What FIGURE OF SPEECH is he using here, and does he use it anywhere else? What point is he getting at, do you think?

4. How does Urrea seem to define *barrio* as it's used in his title and paragraph 3? What CONNOTATIONS can the word have?

5. Define any of these other words you may have doubts about: quotidian, duende (par. 2); Transcendentalist (3); rambunctious, mangy (4); grafts, Americana (5); psychedelic, dearth, polliwogs, impaled (9); paranoiac (10); bucolic, melancholy (11); heifers, communed, transcendent (12); harlequin, quill (29); cairn (32).

Suggestions for Writing

1. **FROM JOURNAL TO ESSAY** In an essay, describe the effect one of the written works you discussed in your journal has had on you, but also do more: Like Urrea, focus not just on the text itself but also on its larger context. Why is it so special? What does it represent to you? How has it influenced your take on the world and the way you live your life? Be sure to infuse your writing with vivid IMAGES evoking concrete sensory experiences.

2. Have you ever had the experience of feeling caught between two worlds, whether because of region or culture or "class rage" (par. 4) or because of some other sense of disconnection — being new in town, struggling with neighbors, feeling friendless, or returning home after being away? Describe the experience in an essay to be read out loud, using plenty of details to help your listeners understand your feelings.

3. According to the National Institute of Food and Agriculture, 17% of Americans live in rural areas and fewer than 2% farm for a living. Research a current issue with small farms in the United States: Timely topics include competition with agribusiness, federal regulations and subsidies, financial stability, and opportunities. Then write an essay that presents your findings.

4. **CRITICAL WRITING** In an essay, ANALYZE the image that Urrea presents of himself. Consider in particular his language and tone, as well as how thoroughly he develops his narrative with details, images, and dialog. How seriously does he take himself and his subject?

5. **CONNECTIONS** Closely read or reread Henry David Thoreau's "What I Lived For" (p. 587), which is excerpted from *Walden*. What similarities do you notice between it and Urrea's essay? Why is it significant, for instance, that Urrea takes a commuter train to visit Thoreau's cabin? Do you notice any other themes in

common? In an essay, explain how and why Urrea incorporates Thoreau's Transcendentalist philosophy into his own writing.

6. **CONNECTIONS**   Urrea writes of feeling "dizzy" from "a natural psychedelic blowmind" (par. 9) when he walks the New England countryside in the fall. Similarly, Diane Ackerman, in "Black Marble" (p. 138), expresses astonishment at a video showing the unexpected beauty of the Earth as viewed at night from space. What else do these two writers' experiences have in common? In an essay that combines narration and description, write about a time when observing your environment filled you with awe and made you feel connected to the natural world.

Luis Alberto Urrea on Writing

Luis Alberto Urrea is a prolific and diverse writer: Even while teaching he has published volumes of poetry, short stories, novels, investigative journalism, and essays, and he promises to "write a bunch more." In a 2011 interview for the journal *Bookslut*, reviewer Terry Hong asked him, "When you get stuck — do you get stuck? — what do you do for inspiration?" Here we give you Urrea's ebullient answer.

I do get stuck! I think everyone gets stuck! Here's the thing, and this is a part of my belief system that continues to grow over the years: I have to thank the ancient Chinese poets and writers, and especially the Japanese haiku poets. Through them, I've come to realize that writing is not a product, but a process. Writing is a life style, a life choice, a path. Writing is part of my process of sacredness and prayer even. What I do is writing; that's how I've chosen to understand and process the world, as a writer.

When I feel stuck, then that season has taken a bit of a pause. The garden has already grown many different blossoms, and my task is to know when not to force something more. It would be a mistake to do battle with the writing spirit. Writer's block is like a stop sign; it's a warning. So sometimes I just think for a while, sometimes I drive cross-country, sometimes I read something. That's the time to do something fascinating that's outside of myself, and there's *always* something fascinating going on. If I get all wrapped up in myself, I'll grind to a halt eventually. If nothing else, I'm just not that interesting.

The world is full of hilarious, upsetting, entertaining, disturbing stuff out there — that well just never runs dry. That's a great gift for all of us. We just have to go out and look.

The Bedford Reader on Writing

We have to agree with Urrea that the world around you can be fascinating and inspiring. And as he suggests, looking with a critical eye can help you turn such inspiration into concrete ideas for writing. For help with delving into the meanings of the images you encounter — online, on television, in advertisements and the movies — see pages 22–26 of Chapter 1. For additional inspiration, you might also heed Urrea's advice to "read something," such as one of the other essays in this book. Any of them might spark fresh ideas for you.

E. B. WHITE

For half a century Elwyn Brooks White (1899–1985) was a regular contributor to *The New Yorker,* and his essays, editorials, anonymous features for "The Talk of the Town," and fillers helped build the magazine a reputation for wit and good writing. If as a child you read *Charlotte's Web* (1952), you have met E. B. White before. The book reflects some of his own life on a farm in North Brooklin, Maine. White wrote other children's books, including *Stuart Little* (1945), and in 1970 he received the Laura Ingalls Wilder Award for his "substantial and lasting contribution to literature for children." He is also widely known for revising and expanding *The Elements of Style* (50th anniversary edition, 2008), a writer's guide by his college professor William Strunk, Jr. White's *Letters* were collected in 1976, his *Essays* in 1977, and his *Poems and Sketches* in 1981. On July 4, 1963, President Kennedy named White in the first group of Americans to receive the Presidential Medal of Freedom, with a citation that called him "an essayist whose concise comment . . . has revealed to yet another age the vigor of the English sentence."

Once More to the Lake

"Once More to the Lake" first appeared in *Harper's* magazine in 1941. Perhaps if a duller writer had written the essay, or an essay with the same title, we wouldn't much care about it, for at first its subject seems as personal and ordinary as a letter home. White's loving and exact portrayal, however, brings this lakeside camp to life for us. In the end, the writer arrives at an awareness that shocks him — shocks us, too, with a familiar sensory detail.

"Once More to the Lake" is a stunning mixture of description and narration, but it is also more. To make his observations and emotions clear and immediate, White relies extensively on several methods of development.

Narration (Chap. 3): throughout
Description (Chap. 4): throughout
Example (Chap. 5): paragraphs 2, 7–8, 11, 12
Comparison and contrast (Chap. 6): paragraphs 4–7, 9–10, 11–12
Process analysis (Chap. 7): paragraphs 9, 10, 12

August 1941

One summer, along about 1904, my father rented a camp on a lake in 1 Maine and took us all there for the month of August. We all got ringworm from some kittens and had to rub Pond's Extract on our arms and legs night and morning, and my father rolled over in a canoe with all his clothes on; but outside of that the vacation was a success and from then on none of us ever thought there was any place in the world like that lake in Maine. We returned summer after summer — always on August 1 for one month. I have since become a salt-water man, but sometimes in summer there are days when the restlessness of the tides and the fearful cold of the sea water and the incessant wind that blows across the afternoon and into the evening make me wish for the placidity of a lake in the woods. A few weeks ago this feeling got so strong I bought myself a couple of bass hooks and a spinner and returned to the lake where we used to go, for a week's fishing and to revisit old haunts.

I took along my son, who had never had any fresh water up his nose and who had seen lily pads only from train windows. On the journey over to the lake I began to wonder what it would be like. I wondered how time would have marred this unique, this holy spot — the coves and streams, the hills that the sun set behind, the camps and the paths behind the camps. I was sure that the tarred road would have found it out, and I wondered in what other ways it would be desolated. It is strange how much you can remember about places like that once you allow your mind to return into the grooves that lead back. You remember one thing, and that suddenly reminds you of another thing. I guess I remembered clearest of all the early mornings, when the lake was cool and motionless, remembered how the bedroom smelled of the lumber it was made of and of the wet woods whose scent entered through the screen. The partitions in the camp were thin and did not extend clear to the top of the rooms, and as I was always the first up I would dress softly so as not to wake the others, and sneak out into the sweet outdoors and start out in the canoe, keeping close along the shore in the long shadows of the pines. I remembered being very careful never to rub my paddle against the gunwale for fear of disturbing the stillness of the cathedral.

The lake had never been what you would call a wild lake. There were cottages sprinkled around the shores, and it was in farming country although the shores of the lake were quite heavily wooded. Some of the cottages were owned by nearby farmers, and you would live at the shore and eat your meals at the farmhouse. That's what our family did. But although it wasn't wild, it was a fairly large and undisturbed lake and there were places in it that, to a child at least, seemed infinitely remote and primeval.

I was right about the tar: It led to within half a mile of the shore. But when I got back there, with my boy, and we settled into a camp near a farmhouse and into the kind of summertime I had known, I could tell that it was going to be pretty much the same as it had been before — I knew it, lying in bed the first morning smelling the bedroom and hearing the boy sneak quietly out and go off along the shore in a boat. I began to sustain the illusion that he was I, and therefore, by simple transposition, that I was my father. This sensation persisted, kept cropping up all the time we were there. It was not an entirely new feeling, but in this setting it grew much stronger. I seemed to be living a dual existence. I would be in the middle of some simple act, I would be picking up a bait box or laying down a table fork, or I would be saying something and suddenly it would be not I but my father who was saying the words or making the gesture. It gave me a creepy sensation.

We went fishing the first morning. I felt the same damp moss covering the worms in the bait can, and saw the dragonfly alight on the tip of my rod as it hovered a few inches from the surface of the water. It was the arrival of this fly that convinced me beyond any doubt that everything was as it always had been, that the years were a mirage and that there had been no years. The small waves were the same, chucking the rowboat under the chin as we fished at anchor, and the boat was the same boat, the same color green and the ribs broken in the same places, and under the floorboards the same fresh water leavings and debris — the dead hellgrammite, the wisps of moss, the rusty discarded fishhook, the dried blood from yesterday's catch. We stared silently at the tips of our rods, at the dragonflies that came and went. I lowered the tip of mine into the water, tentatively, pensively dislodging the fly, which darted two feet away, poised, darted two feet back, and came to rest again a little farther up the rod. There had been no years between the ducking of this dragon-fly and the other one — the one that was part of memory. I looked at the boy, who was silently watching his fly, and it was my hands that held his rod, my eyes watching. I felt dizzy and didn't know which rod I was at the end of.

We caught two bass, hauling them in briskly as though they were mackerel, pulling them over the side of the boat in a businesslike manner without any landing net, and stunning them with a blow on the back of the head. When we got back for a swim before lunch, the lake was exactly where we had left it, the same number of inches from the dock, and there was only the merest suggestion of a breeze. This seemed an utterly enchanted sea, this lake you could leave to its own devices for a few hours and come back to, and find that it had not stirred, this constant and trustworthy body of water. In the shallows, the dark, water-soaked sticks and twigs, smooth and old, were undulating in clusters on the bottom against the clean ribbed sand, and the track of the mussel was plain. A school of minnows swam by, each minnow with its small individual shadow, doubling the attendance, so clear and sharp in the sunlight. Some of the other campers were in swimming, along the shore, one of them with a cake of soap, and the water felt thin and clear and unsubstantial. Over the years there had been this person with the cake of soap, this cultist, and here he was. There had been no years.

Up to the farmhouse to dinner through the teeming dusty field, the road under our sneakers was only a two-track road. The middle track was missing, the one with the marks of the hooves and the splotches of dried, flaky manure. There had always been three tracks to choose from in choosing which track to walk in; now the choice was narrowed down to two. For a moment I missed terribly the middle alternative. But the way led past the tennis court, and something about the way it lay there in the sun reassured me; the tape had loosened along the backline, the alleys were green with plantains and other weeds, and the net (installed in June and removed in September) sagged in the dry noon, and the whole place steamed with midday heat and hunger and emptiness. There was a choice of pie for dessert, and one was blueberry and one was apple, and the waitresses were the same country girls, there having been no passage of time, only the illusion of it as in a dropped curtain — the waitresses were still fifteen; their hair had been washed, that was the only difference — they had been to the movies and seen the pretty girls with the clean hair.

Summertime, oh, summertime, pattern of life indelible, the fade-proof   8 lake, the woods unshatterable, the pasture with the sweetfern and the juniper forever and ever, summer without end; this was the background, and the life along the shore was the design, the cottages with their innocent and tranquil design, their tiny docks with the flagpole and the American flag floating against the white clouds in the blue sky, the little paths over the roots of the trees leading from camp to camp and the paths leading back to the outhouses and the can of lime for sprinkling, and at the souvenir counters at the store the miniature birchbark canoes and the postcards that showed things looking a little better than they looked. This was the American family at play, escaping the city heat, wondering whether the newcomers in the camp at the head of the cove were "common" or "nice," wondering whether it was true that the people who drove up for Sunday dinner at the farmhouse were turned away because there wasn't enough chicken.

It seemed to me, as I kept remembering all this, that those times and those   9 summers had been infinitely precious and worth saving. There had been jollity and peace and goodness. The arriving (at the beginning of August) had been so big a business in itself, at the railway station the farm wagon drawn up, the first smell of the pine-laden air, the first glimpse of the smiling farmer, and the great importance of the trunks and your father's enormous authority in such matters, and the feel of the wagon under you for the long ten-mile haul, and at the top of the last long hill catching the first view of the lake after eleven months of not seeing this cherished body of water. The shouts and cries of the other campers when they saw you, and the trunks to be unpacked, to give up their rich burden. (Arriving was less exciting nowadays, when you sneaked up in your car and parked it under a tree near the camp and took out the bags and in five minutes it was all over, no fuss, no loud wonderful fuss about trunks.)

Peace and goodness and jollity. The only thing that was wrong now, really,   10 was the sound of the place, an unfamiliar nervous sound of the outboard motors. This was the note that jarred, the one thing that would sometimes break the illusion and set the years moving. In those other summertimes all motors were inboard; and when they were at a little distance, the noise they made was a sedative, an ingredient of summer sleep. They were one-cylinder and two-cylinder engines, and some were make-and-break and some were jump-spark, but they all made a sleepy sound across the lake. The one-lungers throbbed and fluttered, and the twin-cylinder ones purred and purred, and that was a quiet sound, too. But now the campers all had outboards. In the daytime, in the hot mornings, these motors made a petulant irritable sound; at night in the still evening when the afterglow lit the water, they whined about one's ears like mosquitoes. My boy loved our rented outboard, and his great desire was to achieve single-handed mastery over it, and authority, and he soon learned the trick of choking it a little (but not too much), and the adjustment of the needle valve. Watching him I would remember the things you could do with the old one-cylinder engine with the heavy flywheel, how you could have it eating out of your hand if you got really close to it spiritually. Motorboats in those days didn't have clutches, and you would make a landing by shutting off the motor at the proper time and coasting in with a dead rudder. But there was a way of reversing them, if you learned the trick, by cutting the switch and putting it on again exactly on the final dying revolution of the flywheel, so that it would kick back against compression and begin reversing. Approaching a dock in a strong following breeze, it was difficult to slow up sufficiently by the ordinary coasting method, and if a boy felt he had complete mastery over his motor, he was tempted to keep it running beyond its time and then reverse it a few feet from the dock. It took a cool nerve, because if you threw the switch a twentieth of a second too soon you would catch the flywheel when it still had speed enough to go up past center, and the boat would leap ahead, charging bull-fashion at the dock.

We had a good week at the camp. The bass were biting well and the sun   11
shone endlessly, day after day. We would be tired at night and lie down in the accumulated heat of the little bedrooms after the long hot day and the breeze would stir almost imperceptibly outside and the smell of the swamp drift in through the rusty screens. Sleep would come easily and in the morning the red squirrel would be on the roof, tapping out his gay routine. I kept remembering everything, lying in bed in the mornings — the small steamboat that had a long rounded stern like the lip of a Ubangi, and how quietly she ran on the moonlight sails, when the older boys played their mandolins and the girls sang and we ate doughnuts dipped in sugar, and how sweet the music was on the water in the shining night, and what it had felt like to think about girls then. After breakfast we would go up to the store and the things were in the same place — the minnows in a bottle, the plugs and spinners disarranged and pawed over by the youngsters from the boys' camp, the Fig Newtons and

the Beeman's gum. Outside, the road was tarred and cars stood in front of the store. Inside, all was just as it had always been, except there was more Coca-Cola and not so much Moxie and root beer and birch beer and sarsaparilla. We would walk out with a bottle of pop apiece and sometimes the pop would backfire up our noses and hurt. We explored the streams, quietly, where the turtles slid off the sunny logs and dug their way into the soft bottom; and we lay on the town wharf and fed worms to the tame bass. Everywhere we went I had trouble making out which was I, the one walking at my side, the one walking in my pants.

One afternoon while we were at the lake a thunderstorm came up. It was   12
like the revival of an old melodrama that I had seen long ago with childish awe. The second-act climax of the drama of the electrical disturbance over a lake in America had not changed in any important respect. This was the big scene, still the big scene. The whole thing was so familiar, the first feeling of oppression and heat and a general air around camp of not wanting to go very far away. In midafternoon (it was all the same) a curious darkening of the sky, and a lull in everything that had made life tick; and then the way the boats suddenly swung the other way at their moorings with the coming of a breeze out of the new quarter, and the premonitory rumble. Then the kettle drum, then the snare, then the bass drum and cymbals, then crackling light against the dark, and the gods grinning and licking their chops in the hills. Afterward the calm, the rain steadily rustling in the calm lake, the return of light and hope and spirits, and the campers running out in joy and relief to go swimming in the rain, their bright cries perpetuating the deathless joke about how they were getting simply drenched, and the children screaming with delight at the new sensation of bathing in the rain, and the joke about getting drenched linking the generations in a strong indestructible chain. And the comedian who waded in carrying an umbrella.

When the others went swimming my son said he was going in, too. He   13
pulled his dripping trunks from the line where they had hung all through the shower and wrung them out. Languidly, and with no thought of going in, I watched him, his hard little body, skinny and bare, saw him wince slightly as he pulled up around his vitals the small, soggy, icy garment. As he buckled the swollen belt, suddenly my groin felt the chill of death.

Journal Writing

White strongly evokes the lake camp as a place that was important to him as a child. What place or places were most important to you as a child? In your journal, jot down some memories.

Questions on Meaning

1. How do you account for the distortions that creep into the author's sense of time?

2. What does the discussion of inboard and outboard motors (par. 10) have to do with the author's divided sense of time?

3. To what degree does White make us aware of his son's impression of this trip to the lake?

4. What do you take to be White's main PURPOSE in the essay? At what point do you become aware of it?

Questions on Writing Strategy

1. In paragraph 4 the author first introduces his confused feeling that he has gone back in time to his own childhood, an idea that he repeats and expands throughout his account. What is the function of these repetitions?

2. Try to describe the impact of the essay's final paragraph. By what means is it achieved?

3. To what extent is this essay written to appeal to any but middle-aged readers? Is it comprehensible to anyone whose vacations were never spent at a Maine summer cottage?

4. What is the TONE of White's essay?

5. **MIXED METHODS**   White's DESCRIPTION depends on many IMAGES that are not FIGURES OF SPEECH but literal translations of sensory impressions. Locate four such images.

6. **MIXED METHODS**   Within White's description and NARRATION of his visit to the lake, what purpose is served by the COMPARISON AND CONTRAST between the lake now and when he was a boy?

Questions on Language

1. Be sure you know the meanings of the following words: incessant, placidity (par. 1); gunwale (2); primeval (3); transposition (4); hellgrammite (5); undulating, cultist (6); indelible, tranquil (8); petulant (10); imperceptibly (11); premonitory (12); languidly (13).

2. Comment on White's DICTION in his reference to the lake as "this unique, this holy spot" (par. 2).

3. Explain what White is describing in the sentence that begins, "Then the kettle drum . . ." (par. 12). Where else does the author use figures of speech?

Suggestions for Writing

1. **FROM JOURNAL TO ESSAY**   Choose one of the places suggested by your journal entry (p. 609), and write an essay describing the place now, revisiting it as an adult. (If you haven't visited the place since childhood, you can imagine what

seeing it now would be like.) Your description should draw on your childhood memories, making them as vivid as possible for the reader, but you should also consider how your POINT OF VIEW toward the place differs now.

2. In a descriptive paragraph about a real or imagined place, try to appeal to each of your reader's five senses.

3. **CRITICAL WRITING**   While on the vacation he describes, White wrote to his wife, "This place is as American as a drink of Coca-Cola. The white collar family having its annual liberty." Obviously, not everyone has a chance at the lakeside summers White enjoyed. To what extent, if at all, does White's privileged point of view deprive his essay of universal meaning and significance? Write an essay answering this question. Back up your ideas with EVIDENCE from White's essay.

4. **CONNECTIONS**   In White's "Once More to the Lake" and Brad Manning's "Arm Wrestling with My Father" (p. 121), the writers reveal a changing sense of what it means to be a father. Write an essay that examines the similarities and differences in their definitions of fatherhood. How does a changing idea of what it means to be a son connect with this redefinition of fatherhood?

5. **CONNECTIONS**   White's essay is full of images that place readers in an important setting of his childhood. David Sedaris, in "Remembering My Childhood on the Continent of Africa" (p. 206), also uses vivid images to evoke childhood, both his own and that of his partner. After reading these two essays, write an essay of your own ANALYZING four or five images from each that strike you as especially evocative. What sense impression does each image draw on? What does each one tell you about the author's feelings?

COLSON WHITEHEAD

Hailed by *Contemporary Black Biography* as "one of the most promising — and certainly one of the hippest — young writers on the literary scene today," Colson Whitehead is a popular author of fiction, essays, and offbeat journalism. Born in 1969 and raised in Manhattan, he (just barely) graduated from Harvard University with a degree in English in 1991 and took an entry-level job with the *Village Voice* in New York City. While sorting the mail and learning to write book reviews and television criticism on deadline, Whitehead began working in his spare time on the experimental and conceptual novels that have earned him a Pulitzer nomination, a MacArthur "genius" grant, and a devoted following: *The Intuitionist* (1999), *John Henry Days* (2001), *Apex Hides the Hurt* (2006), *Sag Harbor* (2009), *Zone One* (2011), and, most recently, *The Underground Railroad* (2016). His nonfiction works include *The Colossus of New York* (2003), a collection of essays, and *The Noble Hustle: Poker, Beef Jerky, and Death* (2014), a chronicle of the author's effort, on a magazine assignment, to compete in the 2011 World Series of Poker in Las Vegas and see how far an amateur player could rise. Currently residing in Brooklyn, Whitehead has never learned to drive.

Loving Las Vegas

"Loving Las Vegas" is extracted from *The Noble Hustle* and was first published in *Harper's* magazine as a self-contained essay in 2013. In this piece, Whitehead relates with precision and nostalgia his first impressions, formed on a postgraduation road trip with aimless college friends, of "what the prudes get wrong about Sin City."

Primarily a blend of narration and description, Whitehead's essay mixes in several other methods of development to reveal the hopes and anxieties of a recent college graduate with an uncertain future.

Narration (Chap. 3): throughout
Description (Chap. 4): throughout
Example (Chap. 5): paragraphs 1, 2, 5, 14, 15–20
Comparison and contrast (Chap. 6): paragraphs 15–20
Process analysis (Chap. 7): paragraphs 3–4, 19
Division or analysis (Chap. 8): paragraphs 10, 15–20
Cause and effect (Chap. 10): paragraphs 2, 8–12, 23
Definition (Chap. 11): paragraph 2

I pity people who've never been to Vegas. Who dismiss the city without setting foot on its carpeted sidewalks. I recognized myself in the town the first time I laid eyes on it, during a cross-country trip the summer after college. 1

My friend Darren had a gig writing for Let's Go, the student-produced series of travel guides. *Let's Go: USA*, *Let's Go: Europe*, *Let's Go: North Korea* (they always lost a few freshmen updating that one). The previous year his beat had been New York City. We'd spent the summer eating 50¢ hot dogs at Gray's Papaya for breakfast, lunch, and dinner and "researching" dive bars like Downtown Beirut and King Tut's Wah Wah Hut, which were beacons of pure, filthy truth in a city still years away from its Big Cleanup. This summer he was assigned the Southwest. The subways didn't run that far out, but his roommate Dan had a car, a brown '83 Toyota Tercel, and the idea was we'd hit the open road and split the writing duties and the money three ways.

It was 1991. We'd just been diagnosed as Generation X, and certainly we   2
had all the symptoms, our designs and life plans as scrawny and undeveloped as our bodies. Sure, we had dreams. Dan had escaped college with a degree in visual arts, was a cartoonist en route to becoming an animator. Darren was an anthro major who'd turned to film, fancying himself a Lynchian[1] auteur in those early days of the indie art-house wave. I considered myself a writer but hadn't got much further than wearing black and smoking cigarettes. I wrote two five-page short stories, two five-page epics, to audition for my college's creative-writing workshops and was turned down both times. I was crushed, but in retrospect it was perfect training for being a writer. You can keep "write what you know" — for a true apprenticeship, internalize the world's indifference and accept rejection and failure into your very soul.

First thing, Dan hooked up our ride with new speakers. We didn't have   3
money or prospects, but we had our priorities straight. I couldn't drive. That spring I'd sworn I'd get my license so I could contribute my fair share, but no.

I promised to make it up to Dan and Darren by being a Faithful Naviga-   4
tor, wrestling with the Rand McNally[2] and feeding the cassette deck with dub.[3] Dub, Lee "Scratch" Perry, deep deep cuts off side six of *Sandinista!* — let these be indicators of the stoner underpinnings of our trip out west. As if our eccentric route were not enough. From New York down to Lancaster, Pennsylvania, to visit a college pal. He took me to my first mall. Even then, I had a weakness for those prefab palaces. "I asked Andy why there were no security guards around," I wrote in my notebook. "He told me I had a New Yorker's mentality."

Then hundreds of miles to Chicago for a disappointing pilgrimage too   5
complicated and inane to detail here. We bought two tiny replicas of the Sears

---

[1] David Lynch (1946–) is an American director known for gritty, surrealist films. — Eds.
[2] Rand McNally publishes printed foldout roadmaps and atlases. — Eds.
[3] A subgenre of electronic dancehall music, emerged from reggae. — Eds.

Tower as consolation. Veered south, taking in the territory, cooking up plots. Inspiration: "discussing the plot of the movie Darren wants to write, about 7-Elevens that land in cornfields." Down to New Orleans, where we slept in a frat house, on mattresses still moldy and damp from the spring floods. One of Darren's childhood friends belonged to the frat. His brothers wanted to know why he was "bringing niggers and Jews" into their chill-space. We sure were seeing a lot of America on this trip.

Then west to tackle our Let's Go assignment proper. We wrote up the   6 Grand Canyon and Lake Mead. Decided to keep driving so we could spend the night in Las Vegas, the camping thing not really taking. ("Hours of agony. Impossible to sleep. Bugs. A consistent feeling of itchiness.") Miles and miles of black hills and winding roads, and then at one crest it manifested, this smart white jellyfish flopping on the desert floor. We suited up in a cheap motel downtown. Anticipating all the sweaty, laundryless days and nights we'd spend in the Tercel, we'd hit Domsey's, the famous Brooklyn thrift store, before we left New York City. We required proper gear for our Vegas debut. Dead men's spats, ill-fitting acrylic slacks and blazers with stiff fibers sticking out of the joints and seams. Roll up the sleeves of the sports jacket to find the brown stains corresponding to the previous owner's track marks. We looked great.

The whole trip out I'd maintained that I wasn't going to gamble. Gam-   7 bling was a weakness of the ignorant masses, the suckers inhabiting the Great American Middle we'd just driven through. I was an intellectual, see, could quote Beckett[4] on the topic of the abyss, had a college degree and everything. I can't remember the name of our hotel — the place was long ago demolished to make way for the Fremont Street Experience.[5] It wasn't a proper casino, just a grim box with rooms upstairs, but the first floor had rows of low-stakes gam- bling apparatuses to keep the reception desk company. On our way to check- in, we passed the geriatric zombies in tracksuits installed at the slots, empty coin buckets overturned on their oxygen tanks. These gray-skinned doomed tugged on the levers, blinked, tugged again. Blink. Tug. Blink.

Grisly. We were about to get our first glimpse of the hurly-burly of down-   8 town Vegas. Before we pushed open the glass doors, what the heck, I dropped a nickel into a one-armed bandit and won two dollars.

In a dank utility room deep in the sub-basements of my personality, a little   9 man wiped his hands on his overalls and pulled the switch: *More*. Remember- ing it now, I hear a sizzling sound, like meat being thrown into a hot skillet. I didn't do risk, generally. So I thought. But I see now I'd been testing the House Rules the previous few years. I'd always been a goody-goody. Study

---

[4] Samuel Beckett (1906–89), Irish author and playwright. — EDS.
[5] A pedestrian mall and "entertainment district" covered by a five-block long LED video canopy. — EDS.

hard, obey your parents, hut-hut-hut through the training exercises of decent society. Then, in college, now that no one was around, I started to push the boundaries, a little more each semester. I was an empty seat in lecture halls, slept late in a depressive funk, handed in term papers later and later to see how much I could get away with before the House swatted me down.

Push it some more. We go to casinos to tell the everyday world that we will not submit. There are rules and codes and institutions, yes, but for a few hours in this temple of pure chaos, of random cards and inscrutable dice, we are in control of our fates. My little gambles were a way of pretending that no one was the boss of me. I hadn't had time for driving lessons before our trip because I'd been too busy cramming a semester of work into exam period. It had been touch and go whether I'd graduate, as I'd barely shown up for my final semester's religion course. The last thing I'd wanted to hear about was some sucker notion of the Divine. There's a man in the sky who watches over everything you do, as all-seeing as the thousands of security cameras embedded in casino ceilings. So what? Nothing escapes his attention, and nothing will move him to intervene.   10

After a few phone calls, the administration released me into the world with a D minus. What was it to them? My passive-aggressive rebellion against the system was meaningless. The House doesn't care if you piss away your chances, are draining the college fund, letting the plumber's bill slide until next month. Ruin yourself. The cameras above record it all, but you're just another sap passing in the night.   11

The nickels poured into the basin, sweet music. If it worked once, it will work again.   12

We hit the street.   13

Before we left town, we bought dozens of tiny plastic slot machines from a trinket shop. Pink, red, lime green. They joined the Museum of Where We'd Been. Everybody's a walking Museum of Where They've Been, but we decided to make it literal. We had serious epoxy. Each place we stopped, we picked up souvenirs and glued them to the Tercel. Two Sears Towers sticking up over the engine, a row of small turquoise stones just above the windshield, toy buffalo stampeding across the great brown plain of the hood. Bull's horns from Arizona, in case we needed to gore someone at ramming speed, you never know, and four refrigerator magnets with Elvis's face on the front grille, to repel ghosts. We dotted the hood with glue and stuck the slot machines on, the polyethylene totems marking us as goofball heathens.   14

Weeks later, we were in Berkeley,[6] sleeping on a friend's floor. The friend was catsitting for a drug dealer, weed mostly. I didn't approve of the drug dealer's lifestyle choices — for vacation, he went camping. We wrote up our time in the   15

---

[6] City in northern California. — Eds.

land of Circus Circus and the El Cortez, the cheap steaks and watered-down drinks. Let's Go's previous correspondent had been a prissy little [thing], filling his/her copy with snobby asides. ("But what do you *do* there?") He/she wrote:

> Forget Hollywood images of Las Vegas glamor, the city at base is nothing but a desert Disneyland. As a small, small world of mild, middle-aged debauchery, Vegas simply replaces Mickey and Minnie with overbright neon marquees, monolithic hotel/casinos, besequinned Ziegfieldesque [sic] entertainers, quickly marrying them in rococo wedding chapels.

Percy, where are my smelling salts?

And what's wrong with Disneyland? It brings joy to millions of people and tutors children about the corporate, overbranded world they've been born into. "It's a Small World" is a delightful ditty, an ode to that quality of everyday existence by which the soul is crushed, diminished, *made entirely small*. No need to denigrate it. Better to worry about the lack of a clear antecedent for "them" in that last sentence. I would protect Vegas. How about: 16

> The magic formula of this oasis of mild, middle-aged debauchery — offer everything but the gambling cheaply, and if you gild it, they will come — was hit upon by Bugsy Siegel in the 1940s. Das Kapital is worshipped here, and sacrifices from all major credit cards are happily accepted.

Much more upbeat, although I apologize if some readers were tricked into thinking the city is devoted to Karl Marx's book.[7] I think we were just trying to get fancy with "capital."

Some of the classic joints we wrote about are gone now, and we captured a time before Las Vegas made a science of demography, but most of the basic observations in our Let's Go entry remain solid. In between games of Risk (board-game version), we cut up the previous year's text, discarded what we disliked, and glued (more glue) what remained onto white paper alongside our revisions and additions. "But remember that casinos function on the basis of most tourists leaving considerably closer to the poverty line than when they arrived; don't bring more than you're prepared to lose cheerfully" became "But always remember: *In the long run, chances are you're going to lose money*. Don't bring more than you're prepared to lose cheerfully." No, casinos are not out to destroy you. The destroyed do not return to redeem reward-card perks and lose more money. No one forces doom upon you, folks. You need to seek it out.   17

---

[7] German philosopher Karl Marx (1818–83) was a revolutionary socialist and the author (with Friedrich Engels, 1820–95) of *The Communist Manifesto* (1848) and *Das Kapital* (1894), a three-volume critique of capitalist society. — Eds.

We kept "Drinks in most casinos cost 75¢–$1, free to those who look like   18
they're playing" but added "Look like you're gambling; acting skills will stretch
your wallet, but don't forget to tip that cocktail waitress in the interesting get-
up." Out with the general tsk-tsking and upper-middle-class disdain, in with
"For best results, put on your favorite loud outfit, bust out the cigar and pinky
rings, and begin." You have been granted a few days' reprieve from who you
are. Celebrate the gift of a place that allows you to be someone else for a time.

Then Darren wigged out and caught a plane home. He still had his child-   19
hood room. Dan was going to drive back east in August, maybe get a Eurail
pass that autumn and check out some . . . castles or whatever. I was out of
money when Dan set off, and I asked whether he had any room in the car, as
the guy we'd been crashing with, the catsitter, was bailing out of California,
too, and bringing all his stuff. After all, I was a good navigator. As luck would
have it, they intended to stop off in Vegas on the way back.

No one laid a hand on the Museum when we were on the road. Odd,   20
moonfaced kids — a motel owner's brood — gawked at it when we stopped at
night but dared not touch. A cop pulled us over for speeding in Massachusetts
the last day of our return trip. "What's all this?" We shrugged. What to say? He
wrote us a ticket. The Museum lasted a few days in Cambridge before teenagers or disaffected housewives or whoever stripped everything. We'd made it
home, and the spell had worn off.

We grew up. Our generational symptoms faded bit by bit. I got a job work-   21
ing for the books section of a newspaper. We ran fiction sometimes, mixed in
with reviews. When the writing teacher who had rejected my work in college submitted a story, I passed on it. Not out of revenge; it just wasn't up to
snuff. As in cards, it was business, not personal. I badgered one editor for an
assignment, that assignment led to another, and soon enough I was paying
my bills freelancing. Played poker at Dan's house every Sunday for a couple
years, and one day we picked up Hold'em. Dan got into computer animation
and founded a visual-effects company, rendering animation for movies such as
Requiem for a Dream and *Black Swan*, which Darren directed. We'd waited for
cards, and then we played them.

Journal Writing

Do you find the Las Vegas gambling industry and its visitors, as described by Whitehead, to be ridiculous, depressing, amusing, criminal, harmless, something else? Why?
Compose a one- or two-paragraph answer in your journal.

Questions on Meaning

1. Against what did the author rebel as a college student? What forms did his rebellion take, and what was the result?

2. Why does Whitehead "pity people who've never been to Vegas" (par. 1)? What does the place represent to him?

3. How does Whitehead explain the SYMBOLISM of the trinkets he and his friends glued to their car? What, to him, do the souvenirs signify?

4. What do you take to be Whitehead's PURPOSE in writing this piece? How well does he accomplish it?

5. What would you say is Whitehead's implied THESIS?

Questions on Writing Strategy

1. Closely examine how Whitehead appeals to each of the five senses in his descriptions of his trip to Las Vegas. Choose two or three particularly effective sensory IMAGES, and explain their purpose and their effect.

2. Identify some of the TRANSITIONS throughout the essay. How do they create COHERENCE among the different episodes that Whitehead recounts?

3. Where, and why, does Whitehead quote passages from the JOURNAL he kept in 1991?

4. **MIXED METHODS** How does Whitehead use CAUSE AND EFFECT to explain the appeal of gambling?

5. **MIXED METHODS** What role does DIVISION or ANALYSIS play in paragraphs 15–18? How do the revisions to the *Let's Go* guidebook made by Whitehead and his friends COMPARE with the original text?

Questions on Language

1. Find examples of both formal and informal DICTION in the essay and consider their intent. What do Whitehead's word choices reveal about the way he imagines his AUDIENCE?

2. Identify some FIGURES OF SPEECH in Whitehead's essay, especially metaphors and understatements, and explain their effect. Why do some of the stories of failure, in particular, come off as slightly funny?

3. What are the implications of Whitehead's ALLUSIONS to the works of Samuel Beckett (par. 7) and Karl Marx (16)?

4. In quoting the *Let's Go* passage in paragraph 15, what does Whitehead intend by the use of *sic* in brackets?

5. Why do you suppose Whitehead chose to capitalize "Faithful Navigator" (par. 4), "Great American Middle" (7), and "Museum of Where We'd Been" (14)?

6. Define en route, auteur, retrospect, apprenticeship (par. 2); prospects (3); pilgrimage, inane (5); manifested (6); abyss, apparatuses, geriatric (7); hurly-burly (8); inscrutable (10); passive-aggressive (11); literal, polyethylene, totems, heathens (14); denigrate, antecedent (16); demography (17); brood, disaffected (20); rendering (21).

Suggestions for Writing

1. **FROM JOURNAL TO ESSAY**   Write an essay, drawn from your journal entry (p. 617), in which you spell out and explain your response to Whitehead's essay. If you find it depressing, for instance, what depresses you — the elderly gamblers? the casino workers? the aimless college students? Why do they depress you? What do you think these people say about American culture? If you find the essay reassuring, on the other hand, explain what exactly in Whitehead's observations cheers you, and why.

2. Like Los Angeles, New York, and some other American cities, Las Vegas is a place with a reputation. What does Las Vegas mean to you? Base your answer on firsthand experience if you can, but also on information in the media (TV, movies, books, magazines). In an essay giving specific examples, describe the city as you understand it.

3. Whitehead writes of experiencing a "depressive funk" (par. 9) in his last year of college in 1991. Has the problem of depression (or anxiety) among college students improved or worsened since then? Research the problem in several studies published since 1991 — the more recent the better. Then write an essay in which you explain current trends in mental illness in college, what you think causes it, and how it might be addressed.

4. **CRITICAL WRITING**   How serious is Whitehead when he counsels young readers and aspiring writers to "internalize the world's indifference and accept rejection and failure into your very soul" (par. 2)? Where else does he return to this notion or something like it? In an essay, analyze Whitehead's TONE. How does the writer present himself and his apparent attitude toward life, risk, and writing? How appropriate do you find this tone, given Whitehead's subject and purpose? How do you respond to it?

5. **CONNECTIONS**   Both Whitehead and Naomi Shihab Nye, in "Museum" (p. 78), write many years later about the emotions they felt while visiting a new place. Write an essay in which you COMPARE AND CONTRAST how the two writers describe their travels and how each writer uses the arts to make a larger point about desire.

6. **CONNECTIONS**   Like "Loving Las Vegas," E. B. White's "Once More to the Lake" (p. 604) also blends narration and description. Examine the two essays together, not so much on their purposes, which are somewhat different, but on this blending. What senses do the authors rely on? How do they keep their narratives moving? How much of themselves do they inject into their essays?

Colson Whitehead on Writing

As a successful and popular novelist, Colson Whitehead often gives creative writing workshops. He has been the writer in residence at the University of Richmond, the University of Wyoming, and Vassar College; and he has also taught aspiring writers at Brooklyn College, the University of Houston, Princeton, Columbia, and Wesleyan, to name just a few appointments. In 2012 Whitehead published "How to Write," a breakdown of the "rules" he stresses with his students, in *The New York Times*. A condensed version of the essay appears below.

The art of writing can be reduced to a few simple rules. I share them with you now.

Rule No. 1: Show and Tell. Most people say, "Show, don't tell," but I stand by Show and Tell, because when writers put their work out into the world, they're like kids bringing their broken unicorns and chewed-up teddy bears into class in the sad hope that someone else will love them as much as they do. . . . Show and Tell, followed by a good nap.

Rule No. 2: Don't go searching for a subject, let your subject find you. You can't rush inspiration. . . . Once your subject finds you, it's like falling in love. It will be your constant companion. Shadowing you, peeping in your windows, calling you at all hours to leave messages like, "Only you understand me." Your ideal subject should be like a stalker with limitless resources, living off the inheritance he received after the suspiciously sudden death of his father. He's in your apartment pawing your stuff when you're not around, using your toothbrush and cutting out all the really good synonyms from the thesaurus. Don't be afraid. . . .

Rule No. 3: Write what you know. . . . How do you make that which is your everyday into the stuff of literature? Listen to your heart. Ask your heart, Is it true? And if it is, let it be. Once the lawyers sign off, you're good to go.

Rule No. 4: Never use three words when one will do. Be concise. Don't fall in love with the gentle trilling of your mellifluous sentences. Learn how to "kill your darlings," as they say. . . . and don't be shy about softening them up in the hostage pit for a few days before you do.

Rule No. 5: Keep a dream diary.

Rule No. 6: What isn't said is as important as what is said. . . . Try to keep all the good stuff off the page. Some "real world" practice might help. The next time your partner comes home, ignore his or her existence for thirty minutes, and then blurt out "That's it!" and drive the car onto the neighbor's lawn. When your children approach at bedtime, squeeze their shoulders meaningfully and, if you're a woman, smear your lipstick across your face with the back of your wrist, or, if you're a man, weep violently until they say, "It's okay, Dad." Drink out of a chipped mug, a souvenir from a family vacation or weekend getaway in better times, one that can trigger a two-paragraph compare/contrast description later on. It's a bit like Method acting. Simply let this thought guide your every word and gesture: "Something is wrong — can you guess what it is?" If you're going for something a little more postmodern, repeat the above, but with fish.

Rule No. 7: Writer's block is a tool — use it. When asked why you haven't produced anything lately, just say, "I'm blocked." . . . Being blocked is the perfect cover for when you just don't feel like working. The gods of creativity bless you, they forsake you, it's out of your hands and whatnot. Writer's block is like "We couldn't get a baby sitter" or "I ate some bad shrimp," an excuse that always gets you a pass. . . . But don't overdo it. In the same way the baby-sitter bit loses credibility when your kids are in grad school, there's an expiration date. . . .

Rule No. 8: Is secret.

Rule No. 9: Have adventures. . . . Get out and see the world. It's not going to kill you to butch it up a tad. Book passage on a tramp steamer. Rustle up some dysentery; it's worth it for the fever dreams alone. Lose a kidney in a knife fight. You'll be glad you did.

Rule No. 10: Revise, revise, revise. I cannot stress this enough. Revision is when you do what you should have done the first time, but didn't. It's like washing the dishes two days later instead of right after you finish eating. Get that draft counter going. Remove a comma and then print out another copy — that's another draft right there. Do this enough times and you can really get those numbers up, which will come in handy if someone challenges you to a draft-off. When the ref blows the whistle and your opponent goes, "26 drafts!," you'll bust out with "216!" and send 'em to the mat.

Rule No. 11: There are no rules. If everyone jumped off a bridge, would you do it, too? No. There are no rules except the ones you learned during your Show and Tell days. Have fun. If they don't want to be friends with you, they're not worth being friends with. Most of all, just be yourself.

The Bedford Reader on Writing

Whitehead offers a lot of advice on writing, most of it tongue in cheek yet useful nonetheless. Two of our favorites are "let your subject find you" (Rule No. 2) and "Revise, revise, revise" (Rule No. 10). If you find yourself stuck for something to write about, revisit the suggestions under "Discovering Ideas" (pp. 32–34). And for details on how revision is the key to successful writing, check out "Revising" on pages 39–42. Whitehead may lean otherwise, but we keep no secrets.

APPENDIX

FINDING AND DOCUMENTING SOURCES

Responding to the readings in this book — thinking critically about them and synthesizing the writers' ideas with your own — prepares you for the researched writing that will occupy you for much of your college career. The academic disciplines — history, psychology, chemistry, and the like — examine different subjects and take different approaches, but they share the common goal of using reading and writing to build and exchange knowledge.

Reading critically and writing effectively are both key skills for this kind of ACADEMIC WRITING, which calls on your ability to think critically about what you read. Part One of this book shows you how to read and write in response to a single SOURCE, such as any of the selections in Part Two. This appendix covers the essentials of using multiple sources in your writing: finding and evaluating them (below), synthesizing source material without plagiarizing (p. 628), and documenting sources using the styles of the Modern Language Association (MLA) for papers in English and most humanities (p. 631) or the

American Psychological Association (APA) for papers in the social sciences and business (p. 651).

CONDUCTING RESEARCH

Research is a process of inquiry, driven by curiosity. Whatever discipline you are working in, the process is most productive when you start with a specific question that interests you enough to spend some time investigating. Often such questions will be provided for you, as is the case with many of the writing suggestions that accompany the essays in this book. Other times, you will need to come up with intriguing questions for yourself. In either case, try to focus on a question you care about, because you will put a good deal of effort into finding and examining sources that can help you answer it.

Using the Library

You have two paths to sources for a research project: your school's library and a public search engine such as *Google* or *Bing*. Although it may seem easier to turn to the open Internet first, always start with the library: Its Web portal will lead you to books, scholarly journals, reputable newspapers, and other quality sources that information professionals have deemed worthwhile. Furthermore, some of the most useful source material is not freely available or online at all. Your library can link you to online resources that are accessible only to paid subscribers, and it can provide periodicals and specialized reference works that exist only in print.

The Internet is home to many valuable sources as well, but finding them requires ingenuity and an extra degree of caution. Tapping a question into a search engine will not lead you to the best materials as if by magic. A quick keyword search can give you an overview of your subject and generate ideas, but it can just as easily direct you to the rantings of extremists, advertisements posing as science, and dubious claims in anonymous posts. It will also generally bring up an unwieldy number of hits, with little indication of which ones are worthy of your attention. Most of the quality material you can find on the Web is indexed on your library's home page; searching from there will save you time and trouble in the long run.

Evaluating Sources

When examining multiple works for possible use in your paper, you of course want each one to be relevant to your subject and to your question. But you also want it to be reliable — that is, based on good evidence and carefully reasoned. To evaluate relevance and reliability, you'll depend on your critical-reading skills of analysis, inference, and synthesis (see pp. 16–18). Use the questions for evaluating sources in the box below and the following discussion of the criteria. Take extra care when evaluating Internet sources you have reached directly, for those materials have not been filtered and are therefore inherently less reliable.

QUESTIONS FOR EVALUATING SOURCES

ALL SOURCES

✔ What is the PURPOSE of the source?

✔ Who is the intended AUDIENCE?

✔ Is the material a primary or a secondary source?

✔ Is the author an expert? What are his or her credentials?

✔ Does the author's bias affect his or her argument?

✔ Is the argument supported with EVIDENCE that is complete and up to date?

INTERNET SOURCES

✔ What is the origin of the source? Can you identify the author?

✔ Who created the Web site? Does the sponsor have any biases or agendas?

✔ Does the site contain links to sources used as evidence? Is the evidence credible?

✔ How current is the source?

Purpose and Audience

The potential sources you find may have been written for a variety of reasons — for instance, to inform the public, to publish new research, to promote a product or service, to influence readers' opinions about a particular issue. The first two of these purposes might lead to a balanced approach to the subject, one that treats all sides fairly. The second two are likely to be biased toward one view, and you'll need to weigh what they say accordingly.

A source's intended audience can suggest relevance. Was the work written for general readers? Then it may provide a helpful overview but not much detail. Was the work written for specialists? Then it will probably cover the topic in depth, but understanding it may require careful reading or consulting additional sources for clarification.

Primary versus Secondary Sources

Primary sources are works by people who conducted or saw events firsthand. They include research reports, eyewitness accounts, diaries, and personal essays as well as novels, poems, and other works of literature. *Secondary sources*, in contrast, present and analyze the information in primary sources and include histories, reviews, and surveys of a field. Both types of sources can be useful in research writing. For example, if you were writing about the debate over the assassination of President John F. Kennedy, you might seek an overview in books that discuss the evidence and propose theories about what happened — secondary sources. But you would be remiss if you did not also consult eyewitness accounts and law-enforcement documents — the primary sources.

Author's Credentials and Bias

Before you use a source to support your ideas, investigate the author's background to be sure that he or she is trustworthy. Look for biographical information in the introduction or preface of a book or in a note at the beginning or end of an article. Is the author an expert on the topic? Do other writers cite the author of your source in their work?

Often you won't be able to tell easily, or at all, who put a potential source on the Internet and thus whether that author is credible and reliable. Specific background may require digging. On Web sites, look for pages that have information about the author or sponsor or links to such information on other sites. On blogs and social media, ask anonymous writers for information about themselves. If you can't identify an author or a sponsor at all, you probably should not use the source.

Investigating an author's background and credentials will likely also uncover any bias — that is, the author's preference for a particular view of an issue. Bias itself is not a problem: Everyone has a unique outlook created by experience, training, and even research techniques. What does matter is whether the author deals frankly with his or her bias and argues reasonably despite it. (See Chap. 12 for a discussion of reasoning.)

Evidence

Look for strong and convincing evidence to support the ideas in a source: facts, examples, reported experience, expert opinions. A source that doesn't muster convincing evidence, or much evidence at all, is not a reliable source. For very current topics, such as in medicine or technology, the source's ideas and evidence should be as up to date as possible.

The most reliable sources acknowledge borrowed evidence and ideas and tell you where they came from, whether with general mentions in the case of journalism, with formal references in scholarly works, or (sometimes online) with links to the borrowed material. Check out references or links to be sure they represent a range of views. Be suspicious of any work that doesn't acknowledge sources at all.

Currency

If you are writing about a current topic, you want your sources to be up to date. Online sources tend to be more current than print sources, but they also have some potential disadvantages. Very current information may not have been tested by others and therefore may not be reliable. And because Web sites change constantly, information you locate one day could be missing or altered the next. Finally, sites that seem current may actually be dated because their authors or sponsors have not tended them. Look for a date of copyright, publication, or last revision to gauge currency. If you don't find a date (and you may not), compare the source with others you know to be recent before using its information.

Preparing an Annotated Bibliography

Whether for your own use or as part of an assignment, preparing an annotated bibliography during research can help you keep track of your sources and your evaluation of them, ensuring that you use them effectively.

A common form of annotated bibliography contains a two-part entry for every potential source: (1) full publication information for the source, so that you can find it again and cite it accurately in your paper; and (2) your own comments on the source, including an overview and a brief ANALYSIS that identifies its contents, addresses its value in its field, and considers its usefulness to you. One student, for instance, researched and wrote a literary analysis about revenge in the works of Edgar Allan Poe, focusing on the parallels in Poe's life and fiction. She read and reread several of Poe's short stories and then searched her school's library and the Internet for critical analyses of the author's work. At her instructor's request, she compiled an annotated bibliography that listed and commented on the sources she thought would be most helpful in writing her paper, using MLA style (p. 631) to format the publication information. Here are two of her entries:

> Allen, Brooke. "The Tell-Tale Artist: Edgar Allan Poe Turns   Source: magazine
>   200." *The Weekly Standard*, 28 Sept. 2009, pp. 28–31.   article
> A literary critic's view of Poe's place in literary history and   Contents of article
> popular culture on the 200th anniversary of his birth. Allen
> claims that Poe essentially invented horror fiction, science   1. Poe's influence

fiction, and the detective story. She also sees parallels between Poe himself and the characters in his fiction. Allen's focus on Poe's mental instability and its effects on his creativity is helpful in understanding some themes in his work, particularly revenge. Poe's sensitivity to insults, for example, connects to Montressor in "The Cask of Amontillado," who kills to avenge an unnamed slight.

> 2. Parallels between Poe's life and work
>
> Potential use of source

The Edgar Allan Poe Society of Baltimore. 1997–2016, www .eapoe.org/. Accessed 26 Feb. 2016.
A comprehensive online collection of all of Poe's works, including letters and other documents, as well as links to critical articles from the journal *Poe Studies/Dark Romanticism*. The site's most useful features are essays by scholars that address common misconceptions about Poe, particularly that his poems and stories about anger, loss, fear, and vengeance mirror events and relationships in his own life. This perspective is valuable to balance Allen and other writers who make a great deal of the connections between Poe's life and work. At the same time, the site seems somewhat defensive about Poe and protective of him, so information about Poe and his life needs to be verified in other sources.

> Source: Web site
>
> Contents of Web site
> 1. Collection of Poe's works
>
> 2. Scholarly criticism
>
> 3. Balancing perspectives
>
> Potential use of source

You may or may not be required to include an annotated bibliography with the final draft of a research paper. But if you do, the annotations along with the publication information can help readers locate and assess your sources for themselves.

WRITING WITH SOURCES

In researched writing, you test and support a THESIS by exploring and orchestrating a range of opinions and evidence found in multiple sources. The writing is source *based* but not source *dominated*: As when responding to a single work, your critical reading and your views set the direction and govern the final presentation.

Integrating Source Material

Writing with sources, you have an opportunity and an obligation to think critically — to analyze, infer, evaluate, and synthesize as described on pages 16–18. Key to SYNTHESIS is first deciding how to present evidence from your research and then working the evidence into your paper smoothly and informatively so it flows with your own ideas.

Depending on what the source material contributes to your thesis, you might use summary, paraphrase, or quotation to integrate it with your text. When you SUMMARIZE or PARAPHRASE a source, you express its ideas in your own words; when you QUOTE, you use the source's exact words, in quotation marks. See pages 42–47 in Chapter 2 for guidelines and examples. And remember that *all summaries, paraphrases, and quotations must be acknowledged with source citations*, as modeled in the sections on MLA and APA documentation later in this appendix (pp. 631–67).

Synthesizing Multiple Sources

In research writing as in response writing, your views should predominate over those of others. You decide which sources to use, how to treat them, and what conclusions to draw from them in order to test and support your thesis. In your writing, this thinking about sources' merits and relevance should be evident to readers. Here, for example, is a paragraph from a student writer's research paper about the problem of mental illness in college. Notice how the writer states her idea at the outset, guides us through the presentation of evidence from three sources, and finally concludes by tying the evidence back to her idea.

> Despite the prevalence of depression and related disorders on campus, however, most students avoid seeking help when they need it. The American Psychiatric Association maintains that most mental-health issues can be managed or overcome with treatment by therapy and/or medication. But among students with a history of depression, according to the American College Health Association, a mere 10% currently receive any kind of treatment (35). One reason for such low numbers can be found in a study published in *Journal of Mental Health Counseling:* Four in five American students are unwilling to ask for help even when they are certain they need it, because they perceive mental illness as embarrassing or shameful (Aegisdóttir et al. 327–28). Thus students who need help suffer additional pain — and no treatment — because they fear the stigma of mental illness.

Writer's idea

Evidence from a Web site

Evidence from a survey

Evidence from a scholarly journal

Writer's interpretation of the evidence

This paragraph illustrates the techniques of synthesis detailed in pages 42–47 of Chapter 2:

- **Summarize and paraphrase data and ideas from sources,** stressing your own voice and your mastery of the source material.

- **Integrate each summary or paraphrase into your sentences.** Use SIGNAL PHRASES that name the source authors, and tell readers how the borrowed material relates to your idea.
- **Clearly indicate what material is borrowed and where it is borrowed from.** Such source citation is crucial to avoid plagiarism, discussed in the next section.

Avoiding Plagiarism

Academic knowledge building depends on the integrity and trust of its participants. PLAGIARISM — the theft of someone's ideas or written work — violates that trust. Most students know that passing off another writer's work as their own, or copying long passages from published texts, are unacceptable practices that can bring severe punishments. Such intentional plagiarism is obviously cheating and is easily detected.

But plagiarism is often more subtle, the result of carelessness or misunderstanding. Writers of researched papers must be cautious in their use of sources to avoid instances of unintentional plagiarism, such as poorly handled paraphrases or missing quotation marks. As you synthesize the information and ideas gathered through research in your writing, it is essential that you make clear to readers what ideas are your own and what ones are borrowed, *always citing the sources of borrowed material.* Avoid plagiarism by following these guidelines:

- **Identify the sources of all borrowed information and ideas.** Introduce every summary, paraphrase, or quotation and name the author in a signal phrase or a parenthetical citation. See pages 42–47 on integrating source material.
- **Indicate where the material can be found.** Follow any information or idea taken from a source with a parenthetical citation that provides the name of the author (if not mentioned in a signal phrase) and the page number(s), if available. (If you are using APA style, give the year of publication as well.) See pages 631–35 on MLA parenthetical citations and pages 652–54 on APA parenthetical text citations.
- **Mark direct quotations.** Whether sentences, phrases, or distinctive words, another writer's language must be clearly distinguished from your own. (See p. 45.) Enclose brief quotations in quotation marks. Set off longer quotations with an indentation. See page 647 for an example in MLA style.

- **Take care to express all paraphrases and summaries in your own words.** Check your sentences against the original sources, making sure that you haven't picked up any of the writers' phrasings or sentence structures. For examples of acceptable and unacceptable summary and paraphrase, see pages 43–44.
- **Include a list of sources.** On a separate page (or pages) at the end, provide a complete list of the sources cited within your paper, with full publication information for each. See pages 635–45 for guidelines on creating an MLA list of works cited and see pages 654–61 for guidelines on creating an APA references list.
- **Recognize common knowledge.** Not all information from sources must be cited. Some falls under the category of common knowledge — facts so widely known or agreed upon that they are not attributable to a specific source. You may not know that President Dwight Eisenhower coined the term *military-industrial complex* during his 1961 farewell address, for example, but because anyone can easily find that fact in encyclopedias, in books, and in articles about Eisenhower, it requires no citation (as long as you express it in your own words). In contrast, a scholar's argument that Eisenhower waited too long to criticize the defense industry, or the president's own comments, would need to be credited because each remains the property of its author.

Be especially cautious about plagiarism when you are working online. Whether accidentally or deliberately, you can download source material directly into your own document with a few clicks. And you might be tempted to buy complete papers from term-paper sites. Don't. *It is plagiarism to use downloaded material without credit, even accidentally, and it is plagiarism to submit someone else's work as your own, even if you paid for it.* Getting caught is more than likely, too, because anything from the Internet is easy to trace.

SOURCE CITATION USING MLA STYLE

In this section we explain the documentation style of the Modern Language Association, as described in the *MLA Handbook*, 8th edition (2016). This style — used in English, foreign languages, and some other humanities — involves providing a citation in your text that names the author of borrowed material and gives the page number(s) in the source where the material appears. Readers can use the name to locate the full source information in a list of works cited at the end of your text, and they can find the location of the borrowed material in the source itself.

In your text, the author's name may appear in a SIGNAL PHRASE, or it may appear in parentheses. In either case, put any page numbers in parentheses:

TEXT CITATION, AUTHOR NAMED IN SIGNAL PHRASE

As Quindlen suggests, people's dwellings seem to have lost their emotional hold and to have become just investments (185).

TEXT CITATION, AUTHOR NAMED IN PARENTHESES

People's dwellings seem to have lost their emotional hold and to have become just investments (Quindlen 185).

ENTRY IN LIST OF WORKS CITED

Quindlen, Anna. "Homeless." *The Bedford Reader*, edited by X. J. Kennedy
    et al., 13th ed., Bedford/St. Martin's, 2017, pp. 184-86.

MLA Parenthetical Citations

The following examples of MLA text citations show the author named in a signal phrase or named in parentheses.

MLA Parenthetical Citations

A work with two authors 632
A work with three or more
  authors 632
A work with a group author 633
A work with no identified
  author 633
Two or more works by the same
  author(s) 633
A source without page numbers 634

An entire work or a work with no
  reference numbers 634
A work in more than one
  volume 634
An indirect source 634
A literary work 634
More than one work in the same
  citation 635

A work with two authors

By shortening the time to product-in-hand, 3D printing enables designers and engineers to create prototypes quickly and cheaply (Lipson and Kurman 30).

A work with three or more authors

With three or more authors, name only the first author followed by et al. (*et alii*, "and others").

Gilman herself created the misconception that doctors tried to ban her story "The Yellow Wallpaper" when it appeared in 1892 (Dock et al. 61).

A work with a group author

For a work that lists an organization as author — for instance, a government agency or a corporation — treat the group's name as the author name.

> In a tongue-in-cheek graphic novel, the Centers for Disease Control and Prevention invokes the threat of a zombie apocalypse to encourage Americans to gather materials for an all-purpose emergency kit and keep them readily at hand (United States 5).

If the group author is also the publisher of the work, however, you will need to alphabetize it by title in your works-cited list (see pp. 636–37), so provide the title in a parenthetical citation.

> According to the National Coalition for the Homeless, several city governments have passed legislation meant to discourage individuals and charitable organizations from providing food to homeless people (*Share No More* 4).

A work with no identified author

Cite an unsigned work by its title. In a signal phrase, use the full title. In a parenthetical citation, shorten a long title to the first one, two, or three main words.

> A growing number of national chain hotels allow guests to bring dogs and cats with them — a welcome relief for travelers whose pets require specialized care ("Rooming" 10).

Two or more works by the same author(s)

If you cite more than one work by the same author or authors, include a short version of each work's title. The full titles for the citations below are "The Case for Reparations" and "The Black Family in the Age of Mass Incarceration."

> Ta-Nehisi Coates argues that a long history of systemic oppression, discrimination, and racial injustice has inflicted "practical damage" that can only be repaired with government payments of cash to African Americans ("Case" 55).

> One example of such oppression can be found in contemporary imprisonment rates: At least 25% of black men living in America today have been jailed, affecting not only those incarcerated but also their families and their larger communities (Coates, "Black Family" 66).

A source without page numbers

Cite an unpaginated source, such as an HTML document, a sound recording, or a DVD, as you would any printed source: by author's name or, if there is no author specified, by title. If a source numbers paragraphs instead of pages, give the reference number after par. (one paragraph) or pars. (more than one paragraph). If a source's numbering system is unstable, as is often the case with e-books, refer to section or chapter numbers (sec., secs.; ch., chs.) instead of page numbers. For a source with no reference numbers at all, use the model for an entire work below.

> One nurse questions whether doctors are adequately trained in tending patients' feelings (Van Eijk, pars. 6–7).

> Kozol believes that most people do not understand the effect that tax and revenue policies have on the quality of urban public schools (ch. 2).

An entire work or a work with no reference numbers

Omit page numbers when you cite an entire work or cite a work that does not number pages, paragraphs, or other parts.

> Vogel recommends that new entrants into the job market strive to create their own professional roles, rather than search for existing positions.

A work in more than one volume

If you cite two or more volumes of a multivolume work, identify the volume number before the page number. Separate volume number and page number with a colon and a space.

> According to Gibbon, during the reign of Gallienus "every province of the Roman world was afflicted by barbarous invaders and military tyrants" (1: 133).

An indirect source

Use qtd. in ("quoted in") to indicate that you found the source you quote within another source.

> Despite his tendency to view human existence as an unfulfilling struggle, Schopenhauer disparaged suicide as "a vain and foolish act" (qtd. in Durant 248).

A literary work

Because novels, poems, and plays may be published in various editions, the page number may not be enough to lead readers to the quoted line or passage. For a novel, specify the chapter number after the page number and a semicolon.

> Among South Pacific islanders, the hero of Conrad's *Lord Jim* found "a totally
> new set of conditions for his imaginative faculty to work upon" (160; ch. 21).

For a verse play or a poem, omit the page number in favor of line numbers.

> In "Dulce et Decorum Est," Wilfred Owen undercuts the heroic image of
> warfare by comparing suffering soldiers to "beggars" and "hags" (lines 1-2)
> and describing a man dying in a poison-gas attack as "guttering, choking,
> drowning" (17).

If the work has parts, acts, or scenes, cite those as well (below: act 1, scene 5,
lines 16–17).

> Lady Macbeth worries about her husband's ambition: "Yet I do fear thy
> nature; / It is too full o' the milk of human kindness" (1.5.16-17).

More than one work in the same citation

> In the post-Watergate era, journalists have often employed aggressive
> reporting techniques not for the good of the public but simply to advance
> their careers (Fallows 64; Gopnik 92).

MLA List of Works Cited

Your list of works cited is a complete record of your sources. Follow these
guidelines for the list:

- **Title the list** Works Cited.
- **Double-space the entire list.**
- **Arrange the sources alphabetically** by the last name of the first author or
  by the first main word of the title if the source has no named author.
- **Begin the first line of each entry at the left margin,** and indent subsequent
  lines one-half inch.

Following are the essentials of a works-cited entry:

- **Reverse the names of the author,** last name first, with a comma between.
  (If there are two authors, give the second name in normal order.) Conclude
  the author name(s) with a period.
- **Give the full title of the work,** capitalizing the first, last, and all important words. Italicize the titles of books, periodicals, and Web sites; use
  quotation marks for the titles of parts of books, articles in periodicals, and
  pages on Web sites. Place a period after the title.

- **Give publication information.** For this information, MLA style operates on a principle of nested "containers." For a scholarly article, for instance, the journal that published it is the primary container; if you accessed the article through a periodicals database, the database is a second container. In each container, list as many of the following elements that apply to the source, in the order listed: Title of the container, names and functions of additional contributors, version of the material (a revised edition of a book, for example), sequence numbers (such as volumes and issues for journals), publisher or sponsor, date of publication, and location details (typically page numbers or a URL). Separate the elements within a container with commas, and separate each container with a period.

- **Include any additional information that might help clarify the nature of the source.** Optional elements include descriptive labels such as Review, Letter, or Address; access dates for some online sources; and original publication information for republished works.

In the pages that follow, we demonstrate how the MLA system works when applied to several common types of sources. You may need to combine the following models for a given source — for instance, combine "Three or more authors," "An article in a scholarly journal," and "A short work on a Web site" for an online journal article with five authors.

Authors

One author

Olson, W. Scott. "Nine Variations on the Idea of Street Music." *Utne Reader*,
      Winter 2015, pp. 80-83.

Two authors

Ansari, Aziz, and Eric Klinenberg. *Modern Romance*. Penguin Press, 2016.

Three or more authors

List only the first author followed by et al. (*et alii*, "and others").

DiGiovanni, Janine, et al. "The New Exodus." *Newsweek*, 3 Apr. 2015, pp. 24-33.

A group author

For a publication by an organization, corporation, or government agency, use the group name as the author name. If the group is also the publisher, omit the author name and start with the title of the work.

Associated Press. "Civil Rights Leaders Press NBA on Diversity." *Sports Illustrated*, 4 June 2014, www.si.com/nba/2014/06/04/ap-bkn-clippers-sharpton.

Share No More: The Criminalization of Efforts to Feed People in Need. National Coalition for the Homeless, 2014, nationalhomeless.org/wp-content/uploads/2014/10/Food-Sharing2014.pdf. Accessed 5 Apr. 2016.

MLA List of Works Cited

Authors

One author 636
Two authors 636
Three or more authors 636
A group author 636
No identified author 638
More than one work by the same author(s) 638

Periodicals: Journals, Magazines, and Newspapers

An article in a scholarly journal 638
An article in a magazine 638
An article in a newspaper 639
A review 639
A periodical article from a database 639

Books

A book with an author 639
A book with an editor or editors 639
A book with an author and an editor 640
A later edition 640
A work in a series 640
An anthology or collection 640
A selection from an anthology or collection 640

A reference work 640
A book on the Web 641

Visual, Audio, and Multimedia Sources

A photograph, painting, sculpture, or other work of art 641
A map, graph, or chart 641
An advertisement 641
A television or radio broadcast 642
A television program on the Web 642
A podcast or sound recording 642
A film or video 642

Other Online Sources

A short work on a Web site 643
An entire Web site 643
A government publication on the Web 643
A wiki 643
A blog post or comment 644
A posting to a discussion group 644
Twitter and social media 644

Personal Communications

E-mail 645
A letter 645
An interview 645

No identified author

"Sit Down and Shut Up." *Outside*, Mar. 2016, p. 51.

More than one work by the same author(s)

Coates, Ta-Nehisi. "The Black Family in the Age of Mass Incarceration." *The Atlantic*, Oct. 2015, pp. 60-84.

---. "The Case for Reparations." *The Atlantic*, June 2014, www.theatlantic .com/magazine/archive/2014/06/the-case-for-reparations/361631/.

Periodicals: Journals, Magazines, and Newspapers

An article in a scholarly journal

After the journal title, give the volume and issue numbers, the date of publication, and the page numbers of the article. If the journal numbers issues but not annual volumes, give just the issue number after the title.

Hansen, Luke O., et al. "'You Get Caught Up': Youth Decision-Making and Violence." *The Journal of Primary Prevention*, vol. 35, no. 1, Feb. 2014, pp. 21-31.

Rogoss, Jay. "The Paris Diet." *Able Muse*, no. 19, 2015, pp. 24-25.

For journals published online, provide a location where the article can be accessed. If the article has been assigned a DOI (digital object identifier), use that as its locator; if there is no DOI, provide the URL.

Resane, Thomas. "The Theological Responses to the Socio-Economic Activities that Undermine Water as a Resource." *HTS Teologiese Studies / Theological Studies*, vol. 66, no. 1, June 2010, doi:10.4102/hts.v66i1.328.

Zhou, Coco. "Magical Girl as a Shōjo: Genre and the Male Gaze." *Flow*, vol. 22, no. 4, Feb. 2016, www.flowjournal.org/2016/02/magical-girl-as-a-shojo-genre/.

An article in a magazine

Acocella, Joan. "The Lure of the Fairytale." *The New Yorker*, 23 July 2012, pp. 73-78.

McWilliams, James. "Vegan Feud." *Slate*, 7 Sept. 2012, www.slate.com/ articles/life/food/2012/09/hsus_vs_abolitionists_vs_the_meat_ industry_why_the_infighting_should_stop_.html.

Nolan, Rachel. "Displaced in the Dominican Republic: A Country Strips 210,000 of Citizenship." *Harper's Magazine*, May 2015, pp. 38-47.

An article in a newspaper

Boylan, Jennifer Finney. "The Year of the Angry Voter." *The New York Times*,
10 Feb. 2016, www.nytimes.com/2016/02/11/opinion/the-year-of-the-
angry-voter.html?_r=0.

Gasper, Christopher L. "Hopefully, Optimism Pays Off." *The Boston Globe*,
greater Boston ed., 4 Mar. 2016, pp. D1+.

The page number D1+ in the second example means that the article begins
on page 1 of section D and continues on a later page. If the newspaper has an
edition, such as greater Boston ed. in the example, it will be labeled at the top
of the first page.

A review

Tóibín, Colm. "She Played Hard with Happiness." Review of *The Complete
Stories*, by Clarice Lispector. *The New York Review of Books*, 17 Dec. 2015,
pp. 61-63.

A periodical article from a database

For an article that you obtain from a library or online database, provide
publication information using the models above. Add the database title and
the DOI (if available) or URL.

Conway, Daniel W. "Reading Henry James as a Critic of Modern Moral Life."
Inquiry, vol. 45, no. 3, Aug. 2002, pp. 319-30. *Academic Search Elite*,
doi:10.1080/002017402760258169.

Wortham, Stanton, et al. "Scattered Challenges, Singular Solutions: The
New Latino Diaspora." *The Phi Delta Kappan*, vol. 94, no. 6, Mar. 2013,
pp. 14-19. *JSTOR*, www.jstor.org/stable/23611744.

Books

A book with an author

Oldstone-Moore, Christopher. *Of Beards and Men*. U of Chicago P, 2015.

A book with an editor or editors

Clarke, Jaime, editor. *Don't You Forget about Me: Contemporary Writers on the
Films of John Hughes*. Simon & Schuster, 2007.

Gessen, Keith, and Stephen Squibb, editors. *City by City: Dispatches from the
American Metropolis*. N+1 / Farrar, Straus and Giroux, 2015.

A book with an author and an editor

Austen, Jane. *Northanger Abbey: An Annotated Edition*. Edited by Susan J. Wolfson, Harvard UP, 2014.

A later edition

Friedan, Betty. *The Feminine Mystique*. 50th anniversary ed., W. W. Norton, 2015.

A work in a series

Macleod, Jenny. *Gallipoli*. Oxford UP, 2015. Great Battles.

An anthology or collection

Kennedy, X. J., et al., editors. *The Bedford Reader*. 13th ed., Bedford/St. Martin's, 2017.

Cite an entire anthology only when you are citing the work of the editor(s) or you are cross-referencing it, as in the Doyle and Lipsyte models below.

A selection from an anthology or collection

The numbers at the end of the following entry identify the pages on which the entire cited selection appears.

Doyle, Brian. "A Note on Mascots." *The Bedford Reader*, edited by X. J. Kennedy et al., 13th ed., Bedford/St. Martin's, 2017, pp. 178-80.

If you cite more than one selection from the same anthology, you may give the anthology as a separate entry and cross-reference it by the editor's or editors' last name(s) in the entries for the selections. Place each entry in its proper alphabetical place in the list of works cited.

Doyle, Brian. "A Note on Mascots." Kennedy et al., pp. 178-80.

Kennedy, X. J., et al., editors. *The Bedford Reader*. 13th ed., Bedford/St. Martin's, 2017.

Lipsyte, Robert. "Jock Culture." Kennedy et al., pp. 324-27.

A reference work

Cheney, Ralph Holt. "Coffee." *Collier's Encyclopedia*, 2007 ed.

"Seagrass Beds." *Ocean: A Visual Encyclopedia*, Dorling Kindersley, 2015.

A book on the Web

Addington, H. Bruce. *Historic Ghosts and Ghost Hunters*. Moffat, Yard, 1908.
    Project Gutenberg, www.gutenberg.org/files/28699/28699-h/28699-h
    .htm. Accessed 6 Apr. 2016.

Visual, Audio, and Multimedia Sources

A photograph, painting, sculpture, or other work of art

For a work of art that you see in the original, follow this format:

van Gogh, Vincent. *The Starry Night*. 1889, Museum of Modern Art,
    New York.

For a work of art that you see online or in a reproduction, provide the publication information for the source you used:

Doble, Rick. *Spring Rain Abstraction*. 2009. *Digital Art Photography*, 2010,
    www.rickdoble.net/. Accessed 18 Dec. 2015.

Hockney, David. *Nichols Canyon*. 1980. *David Hockney: A Retrospective*, edited
    by Maurice Tuchman and Stephanie Barron, Los Angeles County Museum
    of Art, 1988, p. 205.

If the image originally or simultaneously appeared in another medium, you may provide the information for the other medium before the publication information:

Matisse, Henri. *La Musique*. 1939, Albright-Knox Gallery, Buffalo. *WebMuseum*,
    www.ibiblio.org/wm/paint/auth/matisse/matisse.musique.jpg. Accessed
    3 Mar. 2016.

A map, graph, or chart

If the title doesn't make the type of visual clear, provide a label describing it at the end of the entry.

Fisk, Charles. "Las Vegas Annual Precipitation, 1949-2015." *Climate Stations*,
    www.climatestations.com/wp-content/uploads/2016/01/lvannp.gif.
    Graph.

An advertisement

Maxwell House. Advertisement. *Rolling Stone,* 18 Jun. 2015, p. 35.

A television or radio broadcast

What information you provide, and in what order, depends on your focus in using the source. If your emphasis is on a particular contributor, start with that person's name and function:

> Chase, Zoe, performer. "That's One Way to Do It." *This American Life*, hosted
>   by Ira Glass, episode 580, Chicago Public Media, 19 Feb. 2016.

If your focus is on an episode or the series as a whole, start with the relevant title and list any significant contributors:

> "That's One Way to Do It." *This American Life*, hosted by Ira Glass, perfor-
>   mances by Zoe Chase and Sigrid Frye-Revere, episode 580, Chicago
>   Public Media, 19 Feb. 2016.
>
> *This American Life*. Hosted by Ira Glass, Chicago Public Media, 1995-2016.

A television program on the Web

Cite the program using one of the models above, followed with information about the Web source.

> "Breath Play." *Criminal Minds*, season 10, episode 17, CBS, 11 Mar. 2015.
>   *Netflix*, www.netflix.com/search/criminalminds. Accessed 19 July 2015.
>
> Joubert, Beverly, and Dereck Joubert, narrators. "Soul of the Elephant."
>   *Nature*, season 34, episode 4, WNET, 14 Oct. 2015. *PBS*, www.pbs.org/
>   wnet/nature/soul-elephant-full-episode/12956/.

A podcast or sound recording

> "The Alibi." *Serial*, narrated by Sarah Koenig, season 1, episode 1, WBEZ
>   Chicago, 3 Oct. 2014. *iTunes*, itunes.apple.com/us/podcast/serial/
>   id917918570?mt=2.
>
> Mendelssohn, Felix. *A Midsummer Night's Dream*. Conducted by Erich Leinsdorf,
>   Boston Symphony Orchestra. RCA, 1982.
>
> Roosevelt, Franklin D. Inaugural address. 20 Jan. 1941. *Vincent Voice Library*,
>   Michigan State University, 2015, www.lib.msu.edu/cs/branches/vvl/
>   presidents/fdr.html.

A film or video

For untitled works, provide a generic description of the content. If a video recording originally or simultaneously appeared in another medium, you may provide the information for the other medium before the publication information:

> Edison, Thomas A. Gordon sisters boxing. Edison Manufacturing, 1901.
>   *American Memory*, Library of Congress, NCN046321, memory.loc.gov/
>   mbrs/varsmp/1628.mpg.

Manufacturing Consent: Noam Chomsky and the Media. Directed by Mark
    Achbar and Peter Wintonick, Humanist Broadcasting Foundation, 1992.
    Zeitgeist Video, 2002.

vlogbrothers. *Is the Gender Pay Gap Real? YouTube,* 2 Feb. 2016, www
    .youtube.com/watch?v=it0EYBBl5LI.

Other Online Sources

Online sources vary greatly, and they may be and often are updated. Your
aim in citing such a source should be to tell what version you used and how
readers can find it for themselves. If you don't see a model for the type of
source you used, follow a model that comes close. If you can't find all the
information shown in a model, give what you can find.

A short work on a Web site

The following example shows the basic elements to include when citing
a source from the Web: (1) author's name, (2) title of the work, (3) title of
the site, (4) sponsor or publisher of the site, (5) date of the online publication
or last update, (6) URL (omitting "http://"), and (7) date you consulted the
source (optional).

Speer, Cindy Lynn. "Neil Gaiman's Film Work." *Neil Gaiman,* Harper Collins
    Publishers, Aug. 2007, www.neilgaiman.com/Cool_Stuff/Essays/Essays
    _About_Neil/Neil_Gaiman's_Film_Work. Accessed 28 Apr. 2016.

An entire Web site

Civic Engagement. University of Chicago, civicengagement.uchicago.edu/.
    Accessed 10 Feb. 2016.

A government publication on the Web

United States, Department of Education. "Teaching Academic Content and
    Literacy to English Learners in Elementary and Middle School." *What
    Works Clearinghouse,* Institute of Education Sciences, Feb. 2010, ies
    .ed.gov/ncee/wwc/pdf/practice_guides/english_learners_pg_040114
    .pdf. Accessed 2 Mar. 2016.

A wiki

"Carnival." *Wikipedia,* 10 Feb. 2016, en.wikipedia.org/wiki/Carnival. Accessed
    26 Feb. 2016.

A blog post or comment

Allan, Patrick. "The Power of Going It Alone." *Life Hacker*, Gawker Media,
16 May 2016, lifehacker.com/the-power-of-going-it-alone-1776843438.

EasyBakeGirl. Comment on "The Power of Going It Alone," by Patrick Allen.
Life Hacker, Gawker Media, 17 May 2016, lifehacker.com/the-power-of-
going-it-alone-1776843438.

Sullivan, Andrew. "The Years of Writing Dangerously." *The Dish*, 6 Feb. 2015,
dish.andrewsullivan.com/2015/02/06/the-years-of-writing-dangerously/.

A posting to a discussion group

Olney, Alexandra. "First-Person Pronouns." *Teaching and Learning Forum*, National
Council of Teachers of English, 4 Nov. 2015, ncte.connectedcommunity
.org/communities/community-home/digestviewer/viewthread
?GroupId=757&MID=24714&CommunityKey=6e95458a-28cf-448e-b907-
7974ab61b95c&tab=digestviewer#bm0.

Peckham, Irvin. "RE: First-Person Pronouns." *Teaching and Learning
Forum*, National Council of Teachers of English, 5 Nov. 2015, ncte
.connectedcommunity.org/communities/community-home/digestviewer/
viewthread?GroupId=757&MID=24714&CommunityKey=6e95458a-28cf-
448e-b907-7974ab61b95c&tab=digestviewer#bm6.

If the posting has no title, use the label Online posting in the place of a
title.

Twitter and social media

Provide the user name or pseudonym as the author name; you may follow
it with the writer's real name (if known) in parentheses. If a posting has a title,
use it. Otherwise, quote the entire content of a tweet or a short message, citing the date and time of the post. End with the URL.

@NASA (United States, National Aeronautics and Space Administration).
"Newly discovered Kepler-452b is first near-Earth-size planet in
'habitable zone' around a sun-like star." *Twitter*, 23 Jul. 2015, 7:32
p.m., twitter.com/NASA/status/624406765707268097?lang=en.

Reich, Robert. "An Open Letter to the Republican Establishment." *Facebook*,
29 Feb. 2016, 12:22 p.m., www.facebook.com/RBReich/.

Sedaris, David. "I Am 'America's Most Beloved Author' David Sedaris. AMA."
Reddit, 8 Oct. 2014, www.reddit.com/r/IAmA/comments/2iokd7/i_am_
americas_most_beloved_author_david_sedaris/.

Personal Communications

E-mail

Dove, Chris. "Re: Bishop's Poems." Received by Rhonda Blake, 7 May 2016.

A letter

For a letter that you receive, list the source under the writer's name, use the label Letter to the author, and provide the date of the correspondence.

Dove, Chris. Letter to the author. 14 May 2016.

List a published letter under the author's name, and provide full publication information.

Stetson, James A. Letter to Dolly W. Stetson. 8 Feb. 1845. *Letters from an American Utopia: The Stetson Family and the Northampton Association, 1843-1847*, edited by Christopher Clark and Kerry W. Buckley, U of Massachusetts P, 2004, pp. 133-34.

An interview

Arnaldo, Donald. Personal interview. 13 May 2016.

Brownstein, Carrie. Interview by Rachel Brodsky. *Spin*, 27 Oct. 2015, www.spin.com/2015/10/carrie-brownstein-hunger-makes-me-a-modern-girl-memoir-interview/.

A SAMPLE RESEARCH PAPER IN MLA STYLE

Margaret Lundberg wrote the following research paper for a first-year writing course at Tacoma Community College in Washington State and revised and updated it for *The Bedford Reader*. We present Lundberg's paper for three reasons: It illustrates many techniques of using and documenting sources, which are highlighted in the marginal comments; it demonstrates elements of effective ARGUMENT, also noted in the margins; and it shows a writer working with a topic that interests her in a way that arouses the readers' interest as well.

Lundberg's advice to other writers is straightforward: "Keep a notebook handy at all times," she says. "You never know when that 'perfect' idea will show up."

Margaret Lundberg

Professor Fox

English 101

12 April 2016

Eating Green

When I was a child, our family's diet was important to
my mother. We had two vegetables with every meal, ate plain
yogurt for breakfast, and exercised with Jack LaLanne. Later, as
a young mom myself, I learned to cook meals from scratch, froze
and canned fresh produce, and did aerobics with Jane Fonda.
I was concerned with my sons' nutrition, having learned early
that good health didn't just happen — you had to work for it.
Now that my family circle has widened to include grandchildren,
I find that my concerns go beyond just the health of my own
family, to the health of the planet we live on. I believe that our
personal and global health is tightly interconnected, and what
benefits one will benefit the other.

I became a vegetarian about three years ago, and "went
vegan" last spring. I could tout all sorts of reasons, but suffice
it to say that I look and feel better at fifty-two than I did five
years ago. For *my* health and well-being, becoming a vegetarian
was the best thing I could have done. Which got me thinking —
what if we could establish that a vegetarian diet would benefit
not only our personal health, but the health of the planet as
well? Between pollution, greenhouse gases, and dependence on
a dwindling supply of fossil fuels, our little blue planet isn't feeling too well. If all of us adopting a vegetarian diet could slow
or stop all of these ills, shouldn't we consider it? The idea is not
as far-fetched as it might sound: A vegetarian diet could be just
what the doctor ordered for our global health.

Eating meat is such a big part of the American way of life
that it almost feels unpatriotic to spurn it. Would it still be
Thanksgiving without the turkey, the Fourth of July without the
hamburgers, a baseball game without the hotdogs? All of these
things seem to be permanently interwoven into our culture.
But the great American love affair with burgers and fries also
has a dark side. Just as the standard American diet is killing us
individually — with skyrocketing rates of obesity, diabetes, heart

Title arouses readers' curiosity.

Introduction provides context and establishes Lundberg's purpose.

Evidence from personal experience. No source citation needed for Lundberg's generalizations.

Thesis statement.

Acknowledgment of opposing viewpoint (see p. 489).

Refutation of opposing viewpoint.

disease, and a host of other ills — it is also having devastating effects on our planet. Pollution, global warming, and an alarming dependence on fossil fuels can all be traced back, in large part, to the agricultural practices that are required to feed our ever-growing craving for meat. Dietician Kate Geagan compares the environmental impact of the American diet with that of "our love affair with SUVs," warning that the energy use involved in the "production, transport, processing, packaging, storing, and preparation [of food] is now the single largest contributor to global warming" (x).

> Quotation integrated into Lundberg's text. Brackets indicate change to original wording (see p. 45).
>
> Citation includes page number only because author (Geagan) is named in the text.

Livestock production in this country and throughout the Western world has come a long way from the era of the American cowboy. The days of cattle grazing serenely on huge expanses of prairie pasture land are pretty much over. As journalist Michael Pollan points out in his book *The Omnivore's Dilemma*, raising cattle and other livestock is a multi-billion dollar operation that is now more manufacturing plant than traditional ranching. Cows no longer spend their lives grazing the hillsides until they are ready for slaughter. They are warehoused and fed a diet that is contrary to their very physiology — intended to eat grass, they are now fattened on corn, in as short a time as possible. In the early 1900s it took four to five years to ready a steer for slaughter; it now takes fourteen to sixteen months (ch. 4).

> Citation for summary uses a chapter number because the source, an e-book, does not have stable page numbers.

The corn-based diet they are fed leads to a variety of health issues for the cattle. In his article "The Ecology of Eating: The Power of the Fork," Mark Hyman offers an example:

> Of the 24 million pounds of antibiotics produced each year in this country, 19 million are put in the factory-farmed animals' feed to prevent infection, which results from overcrowding, and to prevent the cow's stomach from exploding with gas from the fermentation of the corn. (15)

> Quotation of more than four lines is indented one-half inch.
>
> Parenthetical citation for set-off quotation falls outside final period.

As a result of what is basically indigestion, Hyman explains, cattle belch vast amounts of methane, which is twenty-three times more potent at trapping heat than carbon dioxide. Livestock manure is the source of two-thirds of the man-made nitrous oxide now circulating in our atmosphere — a greenhouse gas that is three hundred times more potent than carbon dioxide (14).

> Citation of a paraphrase. Citation includes only page number because author (Hyman) is named in the text.

Other statistics are equally grim. Kate Geagan reports that livestock raised for meat production are responsible for 18% of greenhouse gas emissions — more than the cars we drive. The food sector is responsible for 20% of the total energy use in the United States every year, and most of that comes from the raising and packaging of livestock animals (30). The average household could make a bigger impact on greenhouse gas emissions by cutting their meat consumption in half than by cutting their driving in half!

A nonvegetarian diet requires 2.9 times more water, 2.5 times more energy, 13 times more fertilizer (also made from petroleum products), and 1.4 times more pesticides than does a vegetarian diet — and the greatest difference comes from beef consumption (Marlow et al. 1699). Less than half of the harvested acreage in the United States is used to grow food for people, and it takes sixteen pounds of grain and soybeans fed to cattle to get one pound of meat ready for us to eat. Ten times as much land is required for meat-protein production than is required for plant-protein production, and producing one pound of animal protein uses almost a hundred times more water than it takes to produce one pound of plant protein ("Land").

As a population's income rises, its people have traditionally eaten more meat and dairy foods, replacing wheat and rice in their diets — exactly what we have been experiencing over the last fifty years (Bittman). Nevertheless, between global warming and decreased natural resources such as farmable land and water, the earth simply can't support any greater increase in meat production. In my lifetime, the world population has doubled, and it is still growing exponentially. Yet, with finite resources, how will we continue to feed us all? Factory farming is simply unsustainable. Even Dennis Avery, director of the Centre for Global Food Issues (a very pro-livestock organization), has commented that "[t]he world must create 5 billion vegans in the next several decades, or triple its total farm output without using more land" (qtd. in "Land"). If *he* thinks so, it *must* be time to rethink our diet!

But what about our burgers? For far too many of us, giving up meat seems like an unreasonable thing to ask.

Statistics provided as evidence.

Author's name above and parenthetical page number clearly indicate the beginning and end of paraphrased material.

Lundberg's interpretation of the evidence.

Paragraph synthesizes information from two sources to support Lundberg's argument (see pp. 629–30).

Citation includes author's name and page number; "et al." ("and others") indicates more than two authors.

Citation includes title of source published by a group author. Online source has no page or reference numbers.

Paragraph synthesizes information from two sources to support Lundberg's argument.

Lundberg's interpretation of the evidence.

Expert opinion offered as evidence. Brackets indicate change to original passage (see p. 45).

Source quoted in another source.

Acknowledgment of opposing viewpoint.

Meat is good for us, isn't it? Maybe. But the average American consumes nearly 200 pounds of meat a year — 33% more than five decades ago. We eat about 110 grams of protein a day (more than three-quarters of which is animal protein), while the USDA's Food Pyramid recommends less than half that — an amount still nearly twice the 30 grams most other experts say we actually *need* (Bittman). Since the advent of products like McDonald's Quarter Pounder with Cheese (30 grams of protein all by itself!), it has become entirely too easy to eat much more meat than any of us could ever need ("USA Nutrition"). Our expanding waistlines and rising levels of diabetes and heart disease prove that any benefit we might gain from a modest amount of meat in our diet is being overcome by the sheer amount we are eating on a daily basis.

> **Refutation of opposing viewpoint.**
>
> **Citation uses shortened version of title for work with corporate author and no page numbers.**
>
> **Lundberg's interpretation of the evidence.**

With growing evidence that human activities in general — and livestock production in particular — are causing large-scale environmental effects, many major corporations are attempting to make changes and "do their part" for the environment. A group of dairy farmers in New York State, for example, is teaming with General Electric to produce renewable energy from cow manure. Apparently manure from 2,500 cows can generate enough electricity for 200 homes. In a state with over 600,000 dairy cows, that's a lot of potential kilowatts. "We've estimated that this could generate $38 million in new revenue for dairy farmers around the country and offset 2 million tons of carbon dioxide equivalents annually by 2020," says Rick Naczi, executive vice president at Dairy Management Inc., in a press release ("GE"). Naczi reports that the dairy industry has committed to reducing greenhouse gas emissions by 25% by 2020 — the equivalent of getting "1.25 million passenger cars off the road every year." That's a lot of gas.

> **Acknowledgment of opposing viewpoint.**
>
> **Citation uses shortened version of title for work with no named author. Online source has no page numbers.**
>
> **Lundberg's comment on the evidence.**

But even if we *can* make electricity from "cow pies," does that make up for the fact that we in the Western world are using far more than our fair share of the earth's limited resources? We use substantial amounts of fossil fuels and other nonrenewable resources to grow a "crop" that many in our global population cannot access; one that pollutes and sickens the planet — and its inhabitants — in ways we are only beginning to comprehend.

> **Refutation of opposing viewpoint.**
>
> **No source citation for common knowledge.**

Lundberg 5

In the face of a looming worldwide crisis where food prices are rising and nearly 3 billion people earn less than two dollars a day, two of every three people in the world already subsist on a vegetarian diet (Clemmit 1). Yet in the industrialized world over 50% of the grain that we grow is used to fatten livestock (Hyman 14). Peter Timmer, a fellow at the Washington-based Center for Global Development, states, "There's still plenty of food for everyone, but only if everyone eats a grain and legume-based diet. If the diet includes large . . . amounts of animal protein . . . , food demand is running ahead of global production" (qtd. in Clemmit 3).

> Citation of a quotation from an indirect source. Ellipses indicate omission from quotation (see p. 45).

With finite resources already being stretched thin by a growing global population, is it rational for us to continue on as we are? Our food systems are not sustainable, and today's livestock production methods make potential food crises more likely every day. If greenhouse gases continue to build as they have over the last fifty years, the effects on today's farmlands may be irreversible. As global temperatures continue to rise, Alaska may become the new "Corn Belt" and the Midwest could become a desert. How much of the land we now depend on to feed us could be lost to agriculture? A vegetarian diet would enable us to healthfully feed many more people, and make much better use of the resources we have. Do we really want to wait until it's too late to change our way of eating?

> Conclusion summarizes Lundberg's main points and restates her thesis.

> Paper ends with a provocative question.

Works Cited

> List of works cited provided at end of paper.

Bittman, Mark. "Rethinking the Meat-Guzzler." *The New York Times*, 27 Jan. 2008, www.nytimes.com/2008/01/27/weekinreview/27bittman.html?_r=0. Accessed 2 Apr. 2016.

> An article in the Web version of a newspaper.

Clemmit, Marcia. "Global Food Crisis: What's Causing the Rising Prices?" *Social Problems: Selections from* CQ Researcher, Sage, 2010, pp. 1-24.

> A selection in an anthology.

Geagan, Kate. *Go Green Get Lean: Trim Your Waistline with the Ultimate Low-Carbon Footprint Diet*. Rodale, 2009.

> A print book.

"GE, US Dairy Industry Shine Light on Potential of 'Cow Power' in New York." *Business Wire*, 29 Oct. 2009, www.businesswire.com/news/home/20091029006166/en/GE-U.S.-Dairy-Industry-Shine-Light-Potential. Accessed 4 Apr. 2016.

> A newspaper article posted on the Web.

Hyman, Mark. "The Ecology of Eating: The Power of the Fork." | An article from a print journal.
Alternative Therapies in Health and Medicine, vol. 15, no.
4, July/Aug. 2009, pp. 14-15.

"Land." *Information Resources*, The Vegan Society, www.vegansociety | A short work from a Web site published by a group author.
.com/resources. Accessed 18 Mar. 2016.

Marlow, Harold J., et al. "Diet and the Environment: Does What | Journal article from a database. "Et al." ("and others") indicates more than two authors.
You Eat Matter?" *American Journal of Clinical Nutrition*,
vol. 89, no. 5, May 2009, pp. 1699-1703. *General One File*,
doi:10.3945/.

Pollan, Michael. *The Omnivore's Dilemma: A Natural History of* | An e-book.
Four Meals. Penguin Books, 2006.

"USA Nutrition Facts for Popular Menu Items." *Nutrition Choices*, | A short work from a Web site published by a corporate author.
McDonald's, nutrition.mcdonalds.com/getnutrition/
nutritionfacts.pdf. Accessed 25 Mar. 2016.

SOURCE CITATION USING APA STYLE

In this section we explain the documentation style of the American Psychological Association, as described in the *Publication Manual of the American Psychological Association*, 6th edition (2010). This style — used in psychology, sociology, business, education, economics, and other social sciences — involves a citation within the text that identifies the author and date of a source, as well as the page number(s) for a quotation or paraphrase (page numbers are not required for a summary).

In your text, the author's name may appear in a SIGNAL PHRASE, or it may appear in parentheses along with the date and any page numbers. Either way, the citation information directs readers to the source's full publication information in a list of references at the end of the text:

TEXT CITATION, AUTHOR NAMED IN SIGNAL PHRASE

As Quindlen (2017) has suggested, people's dwellings seem to have lost their emotional hold and to have become just investments (p. 185).

TEXT CITATION, AUTHOR NAMED IN PARENTHESES

One observer has suggested that people's dwellings seem to have lost their emotional hold and to have become just investments (Quindlen, 2017, p. 185).

ENTRY IN REFERENCE LIST

Quindlen, A. (2017). Homeless. In X. J. Kennedy, D. M. Kennedy, J. E. Aaron, & E. K. Repetto (Eds.), *The Bedford Reader* (13th ed., pp. 184-86). Boston: Bedford.

APA Parenthetical Citations

The following examples of APA text citations show the author named in a signal phrase or named in parentheses.

APA Parenthetical Citations

A work with two authors 652	Two or more works by exactly the
A work with three to five	same author(s) 653
authors 652	A source without page numbers 653
A work with six or more authors 652	An indirect source 654
A work with a group author 653	More than one work in the same
A work with no identified	citation 654
author 653	Personal communications 654

A work with two authors

Comer and White (2016) reported that a mere 1.5% of writing students enrolled in their Massive Open Online Course earned a certificate of accomplishment, presumably because only a small number of enrollees intended to complete the work in the first place (p. 320).

A work with three to five authors

With more than two but fewer than six authors, list all of the authors in the first parenthetical citation. Separate the names with commas, and precede the final name with &.

Emergency room visitors over 65 years old are twice as likely as younger patients to be admitted for a hospital stay (Murdoch, Turpin, Johnston, MacLullich, & Losman, 2015, p. 1).

In later references to the same source, shorten the citation to the first author's name followed by et al. (*et alii*, "and others").

Murdoch et al. (2015) have suggested that all medical personnel need to be better trained in recognizing and addressing the unique needs of a growing elderly population (p. 6).

A work with six or more authors

Name only the first author followed by et al. (*et alii*, "and others").

In the midst of a global economic downturn in the early twenty-first century, household spending in the United States actually increased (Thiel et al., 2010, p. 26).

A work with a group author

For a work published under the name of an organization, such as a government agency or a corporation, use the name of the group as the author.

> The United States Conference of Mayors (2015) reported that most cities do not have enough emergency shelter beds to accommodate the needs of homeless residents (p. 2).

A work with no identified author

Cite an unsigned work by using the first one or two main words of the title (excluding any initial "A," "An," or "The").

> A full decade after Hurricane Katrina devastated New Orleans, some six thousand families remain unable to rebuild their homes ("Long Way," 2015, p. 39).

Two or more works by exactly the same author(s)

If you cite more than one work by the same author or authors, in most cases the year of publication will indicate which work you're referring to. If two or more works were published in the same year, assign lowercase letters to the years in your list of references (see p. 657) and include the same letters in your parenthetical citations.

> Gladwell (2011a) has argued that although popular wisdom held that Apple founder "[Steve] Jobs stole the personal computer from Xerox," the reality was that he refined ideas that Xerox showed little interest in pursuing (p. 48).

> According to Gladwell (2011b), Jobs's most significant personality trait— more so than his perfectionism, his aggressiveness, or his resilience—was his preference to "tweak" other people's inventions instead of innovate from scratch.

A source without page numbers

Cite an unpaginated source, such as an HTML document, a sound recording, or a DVD, as you would any print source: by author's name or, if there is no author indicated, by title. If a source numbers paragraphs instead of pages, give the appropriate number(s) as in the following model, after para. (one paragraph) or paras. (more than one paragraph).

> For six years in the 1970s, folk singer Joni Mitchell occasionally appeared on stage disguised as a black man, a deviant practice that Grier (2012) has claimed gave her "legitimacy and authority" among rock musicians (para. 1).

For a source with no page or paragraph numbers, provide a heading for the section in which the cited material appears (abbreviated if it is long), followed by the paragraph number within the section, as determined by your own count.

> One patient developed a painful, swollen rash that dermatologists attributed to an exclusive diet of fast food; in the months he abstained from such meals, his condition improved (Sundhar et al., 2012, Case section, para. 1).

An indirect source

Use as cited in to indicate that you found the source you quote within another source.

> Of the many difficulties of living in space, astronaut Norm Thagard felt that "boredom was the most common problem" (as cited in Roach, 2010, p. 28).

More than one work in the same citation

List the names in alphabetical order and separate the entries with a semicolon.

> Moving welfare recipients out of blighted neighborhoods has been shown to increase their happiness, if not their earning potential (Edsall, 2014; Rothwell, 2015).

Personal communications

Interviews you conduct and letters, e-mails, and messages you receive should be cited in your text with the correspondent's initials and last name, the words personal communication, and the full date. Because readers cannot retrieve such materials, they are not included in the list of references.

> A county health inspector explained that meat must be shelved at the bottom of refrigeration units to reduce the risk of contaminating vegetables and dairy products with bacteria (M. K. Edwards, personal communication, May 30, 2016).

APA Reference List

Your reference list is a complete record of your sources. Follow these guidelines for the list:

- **Title the list** References.
- **Double-space the entire list.**
- **Arrange the sources alphabetically** by the last name of the first author or by the first main word of the title if the source has no named author.

- **Begin the first line of each entry at the left margin.** Indent the subsequent lines of the entry one-half inch or five spaces.

Following are the essentials of a reference-list entry:

- **Reverse the names of the authors,** last name first, followed by a comma and initials for first and middle names (even if the names are given in full on the source), with another comma after the initials.

- **Provide a publication date** in parentheses after the name or names.

- **Give the full title of the work.** For titles of books, use italics and capitalize only the first word of the title and subtitle and any proper nouns. Use the same capitalization style for titles of articles, but don't italicize them or enclose them in quotation marks. For titles of periodicals, capitalize all major words and italicize the title.

- **Give publication information.** For books, include the city and state of publication and the publisher's name. For periodicals, include the volume number and sometimes the issue number along with the page numbers for the article you cite. For print periodical articles, also include a digital object identifier (DOI) if one is available. Always include the DOI or a URL for online periodical articles. (See pp. 657–58 for more on DOIs and URLs.)

- **Use periods between parts of each entry,** but do not include a period at the end of a DOI or URL.

You may need to combine some of the following models to document a particular source — for instance, combine "Eight or more authors" and "A periodical article from a database" for an online database article with twelve listed authors.

Authors

One author

Jordan, J. A. (2015). *Edible memory: The lure of heirloom tomatoes and other forgotten foods.* Chicago, IL: University of Chicago Press.

Two to seven authors

McFadden, J., & Al-Khalili, J. (2014). *Life on the edge: The coming of age of quantum biology.* New York, NY: Crown.

Murdoch, I., Turpin, S., Johnston, B., Maclullich, A., & Losman, E. (2015). *Geriatric emergencies.* Malden, MA: Wiley-Blackwell.

APA Reference List

Authors

One author 655
Two to seven authors 655
Eight or more authors 656
A group author 656
No identified author 656
More than one work by exactly
  the same author(s) 657

*Periodicals: Journals, Magazines,
and Newspapers*

An article in a journal 657
An article in a magazine 658
An article in a newspaper 658
A periodical article from a data-
  base 658

Books

A book with an author 659
A book with an editor or
  editors 659
A later edition 659
A selection from an anthology 659
A book on the Web 659
A book on an e-reader 660

*Other Online and Multimedia
Sources*

A document from a Web site 660
A video or audio recording 660
A podcast 661
A posting to a blog or discussion
  group 661

Eight or more authors

Name the first six authors, insert ellipses, and end with the name of the last listed author.

> Adams, J. D., Kavouras, S. A., Robillard, J. I., Bardis, C. N., Johnson, E. C.,
> Ganio, M. S., . . . White, M. A. (2016). Fluid balance of adolescent
> swimmers during training. *Journal of Strength and Conditioning Research,*
> *30,* 621-25.

A group author

> U.S. Department of Justice, Cybersecurity Unit. (2015). *Best practices for*
> *victim response and reporting of cyber incidents.* Retrieved from http://
> www.justice.gov/sites/default/files/criminal-ccips/legacy/2015/04/30
> /04272015reporting-cyber-incidents-final.pdf

No identified author

Start the entry with the title of the work, followed by the date and publication information.

> If you can't stand the heat. (2015, November 28). *The Economist, 417*(8966),
> 10-13.

More than one work by exactly the same author(s)

When you cite two or more works by the same author that were published in *different* years, include the author's name in each entry and list the entries in chronological order by publication date.

> Turkle, S. (2011). *Alone together: Why we expect more from technology and less from each other.* New York, NY: Basic Books.
>
> Turkle, S. (2015). *Reclaiming conversation: The power of talk in a digital age.* New York, NY: Penguin Press.

When you cite two or more works by the same author that were published in the *same* year, list the works in alphabetical order by title and add lowercase letters (a, b, c, etc.) to the date. Use the same letters with the date in the corresponding parenthetical citations (see p. 653).

> Gladwell, M. (2011a, May 16). Creation myth: Xerox PARC, Apple, and the truth about innovation. *The New Yorker, 87*(13), 44-53.
>
> Gladwell, M. (2011b, November 14). The tweaker: The real genius of Steve Jobs. *The New Yorker, 87*(36), 32-35.

Periodicals: Journals, Magazines, and Newspapers

An article in a journal

Most journals number issues consecutively throughout the year, so that the first page of issue 3, for instance, might begin on page 409. In such cases, follow the journal title with the volume number (italicized), a comma, the inclusive page numbers of the article, and a period. If a journal starts each issue with page 1, include the issue number in parentheses (not italicized) after the volume number. APA strongly recommends listing the digital object identifier (DOI) for any article that has one assigned to it.

> Conti, R. (2015). Compassionate parenting as a key to satisfaction, efficacy and meaning among mothers of children with autism. *Journal of Autism and Developmental Disorders, 45*, 2008-2018. doi:10.1007/s10803-015-2360-6
>
> Ryan, C. (2014). Empowering teachers and students through formative assessment. *Council Chronicle, 23*(3), 6-9.

Base an entry for an online journal article on one of the above models for print journals. Include the DOI if one is provided.

> Yu, Z., Day, D. A., Connal-Nicolaou, A., & Enders, F. T. (2011). Early food allergen exposure may be protective against food allergies: An extension of the hygiene hypothesis. *Internet Journal of Epidemiology, 10*(1). doi:10.5580/243a

If no DOI is provided, give the URL of the journal's home page after Retrieved from.

> Peel, M. (2015). Assessing fitness to detain in police custody. *Nursing Standard, 30*(11), 43-49. Retrieved from http://nursingstandard .rcnpublishing.co.uk

(If you must break a DOI or URL, do it after the two slashes following http:// or before a single slash, a period, or another punctuation mark. Do not add a hyphen.)

An article in a magazine

Include the complete date in parentheses and provide volume and issue numbers.

> Fallows, J. (2015, November). The (planet-saving, capitalism-subverting, surprisingly lucrative) investment secrets of Al Gore. *The Atlantic, 316*(4). Retrieved from http://www.theatlantic.com
>
> Helgoe, L. (2010, October). Revenge of the introvert. *Psychology Today, 43*(5), 54-61.
>
> Von Drehle, D. (2015, April 20). Line of fire. *Time, 185*(14), 24-28.

An article in a newspaper

Include the year, month, and day in the date. List all page numbers, preceded by p. (for one page) or pp. (for multiple pages).

> Kaplan, S. (2016, March 3). Whose advice is it? Doctors promoting treatments on social media routinely fail to disclose ties to drug makers. *The Boston Globe*, pp. C1, C7.

For an article from the Web version of a newspaper, replace page numbers with the URL for the full site.

> Ferdman, R. A. (2016, March 4). The magical thing eating chocolate does to your brain. *The Washington Post*. Retrieved from https://www .washingtonpost.com/

A periodical article from a database

For an article that you obtain from a library or online database, provide print publication information using the models for journals, magazines, and newspapers above. Add the DOI or, if there is none, the URL of the periodical's home page. Do not include the name of the database.

Reed, M. G., & George, C. (2011). Where in the world is environmental justice? *Progress in Human Geography, 35,* 835-842. doi:10.1177 /0309132510388384

Scudellari, M. (2015, July 31). The kids aren't all right. *Newsweek, 165*(5), 44-47. Retrieved from http://www.newsweek.com

Books

A book with an author

Sacks, O. (2012). *Hallucinations.* New York, NY: Knopf.

A book with an editor or editors

Masih, T. L. (Ed.). (2012). *The chalk circle: Intercultural prizewinning essays.* Deadwood, OR: Wyatt-MacKenzie.

Zeigler-Hill, V., & Marcus, D. K. (Eds.). (2016). *The dark side of personality: Science and practice in social, personality, and clinical psychology.* Washington, DC: American Psychological Association.

A later edition

Patterson, K., Grenny, J., McMillan, R., & Switzler, A. (2012). *Crucial conversations: Tools for talking when stakes are high* (2nd ed.). New York, NY: McGraw-Hill.

A selection from an anthology

Use the anthology's publication year after the author's name, even if the selection was originally published earlier. In the page numbers in parentheses, give the location of the cited selection within the anthology.

Barnet, R. (2010). Why didn't the boat sink? How a kindertransportee kept afloat. In S. Kriger (Ed.), *Marking humanity: Stories, poems, and essays by Holocaust survivors* (pp. 64-67). Toronto, Canada: Soul Inscriptions Press.

A book on the Web

Instead of print publication information, provide the URL you used to retrieve the book. In this example, the final parenthesis provides the date of the book's original publication:

Barker, C. H. (2004). *Wanted, a young woman to do housework: Business principles applied to housework.* Retrieved from http://www.gutenberg.org /files/14117/14117-h/14117-h.htm (Original work published 1915)

A book on an e-reader

For an electronic book on an e-reader such as a Kindle, Nook, or iPad, add the type of file in brackets after the title, followed by the URL where you retrieved the book.

> Cohen, A. (2016). *Imbeciles: The Supreme Court, American eugenics, and the sterilization of Carrie Buck* [iBooks version]. Retrieved from http://www
> .itunes.apple.com
>
> Urrea, L. A. (1996). *By the lake of sleeping children: The secret life of the Mexican border* [Kindle version]. Retrieved from http://www.amazon.com

Other Online and Multimedia Sources

Online sources vary greatly, and they may be and often are updated. Your aim in citing such a source should be to tell what version you used and how readers can find it for themselves. Include the date on which you accessed the source only if the source is likely to change or if it lacks a publication date or version number (see the first model below for an example). Substitute n.d. (for "no date") in parentheses if a source is undated. If you don't see a model for the type of source you used, follow a model that comes close. If you can't find all the information shown in a model, give what you can find.

A document from a Web site

Include as much of the following information as you can find: author's name, date of publication or last update, title, and URL.

> Rigoglioso, M. (2012, April 17). *The psychology around voter turnout.*
> Retrieved from http://csi.gsb.stanford.edu/getting-out-vote

If no author is listed, begin the entry with the title followed by the date in parentheses. The following example also includes the date of retrieval because the source has no publication date and is likely to change.

> *Lyme disease.* (n.d.). Retrieved September 18, 2015, from http://www.webmd
> .com/rheumatoid-arthritis/arthritis-lyme-disease

A video or audio recording

Include a description of the medium or file type in brackets after the title of the work.

> Campbell, M. (Director). (2011). *Green lantern* [DVD]. Burbank, CA: Warner Bros.

Fraser, S. (2012, May). Why eyewitnesses get it wrong [Video file]. Retrieved
   from http://www.ted.com/talks/scott_fraser_the_problem_with
   _eyewitness_testimony.html

Montgomery, S. (2014, November/December). Predators in the barnyard
   [Audio file]. Retrieved from https://orionmagazine.org/article
   /sy-montgomery-reads-predators-in-the-barnyard/

Waits, T. (1976). The piano has been drinking (not me). On *Small change*
   [CD]. New York, NY: Elektra/Asylum Records.

A podcast

Crespi, S., & Grimm, D. (Hosts). (2016, January 8). Dancing dinosaurs, naked
   black holes, and more [Audio podcast]. *Science podcasts*. Retrieved from
   http://www.sciencemag.org/podcasts

A posting to a blog or discussion group

HypnoToad72. (16 July 2012). Re: Go mobile or go home: From augmented
   reality to language learning to virtual classrooms, the word is mobile
   [Blog comment]. Retrieved from http://www.zdnet/article/go-mobile
   -or-go-home

Northrup, L. (2016, February 16). Our growing e-commerce addiction means
   mountains of cardboard [Blog post]. Retrieved from http://consumerist.com

SAMPLE PAPER IN APA STYLE

As a bioengineering major and pre-med student at the University of Pennsylvania in Philadelphia, Eric Kim enrolled in the sophomore-level composition seminar "The Novelist and the Neuroscientist" to fulfill a critical writing requirement. "Writing has always been difficult" for him, Kim says, but he enjoyed the course because "it was nice to write on a topic he is interested in." The paper we present on the following pages explores Kim's interest in one recently discovered aspect of the human brain; it also demonstrates the uses of APA documentation style in a brief yet thoroughly developed sample of researched writing. Kim revised and updated the essay for *The Bedford Reader*.

Notice that in accordance with APA style, the writer provides a title page with an (optional) author note and a running head that continues through the paper; he also follows the American Psychological Association's convention of using past tense or past perfect tense in signal phrases that introduce the findings of other researchers.

Running head: BRAIN   1   Title page provides a
                                                                               shortened version of
                                                                               title used as a running
                                                                               head throughout paper.

                          The Brain That Changes   Title, author name, and
                                Eric Kim   school are centered on
                        University of Pennsylvania   page.

Author Note: This paper was prepared for *Critical Writing Seminar in Psychology:*   Optional author note
The Novelist and the Neuroscientist, taught by Professor Charbonnier.   provides additional
                                                                                          information about
                                                                                          course and lists any
                                                                                          acknowledgements.

Until recently, neuroscientists held the notion that the structure of the brain was fixed after infancy; neurons could never regenerate or form new networks. Less than two decades ago, however, researchers documented neural cell division in adult primates (Gould, Tanapat, McEwen, Flügge, & Fuchs, 1998). A flurry of subsequent experiments illustrated that the brain continuously changes throughout life. This property has been termed *neuroplasticity* and it involves modifying neural connections, building new neural networks, destroying old neurons, and generating new neurons. Through neuroplasticity, everything from experiences, injuries, and even thoughts can change the fabric of the brain (Carr, 2011, p. 27). In fact, if this concept is new to you, your brain is undergoing reorganization as you read. For some, this might be a startling notion: Are these structural changes in the brain taking place for better or worse? After all, in a system as complex as the brain, any changes might disrupt a natural balance. On the other hand, neuroplasticity implies an opportunity to improve the brain. Human experience shows both results can occur. For the most part, however, neuroplasticity is beneficial.

It would be wrong to ignore that, in some cases, neuroplasticity can lead to harmful conditions. For example, neuroplasticity may malfunction in response to injury. Normal injuries rearrange nerve cells to help enforce a feeling of pain. These neural changes eventually revert, and the pain subsides. With severe injuries, however, the neural changes may become irreversible, leading to many cases of chronic pain. Amputees often develop this problem in their severed limbs, a disorder known as "phantom limb" pain (Carr, 2011, p. 30). Many other harmful results of neuroplasticity have been documented. For example, writers who used hand muscles frequently strengthened corresponding networks in the motor cortex. In some cases, this development led to a hyperactive motor cortex that caused painful, involuntary contractions of hand muscles (Johnston, 2009, p. 99). Likewise, drug use can overstimulate and change neural pathways, ultimately leading to addiction (Rácz, 2014). While

---

Margin annotations:

Citation of a source with five authors not named in the text. No page number required for a summary.

Citation of a source with one author not named in the text. Page number provided for paraphrase.

Introduction engages readers' interest and identifies Kim's research question.

Thesis statement answers research question.

Acknowledgment of opposing viewpoint (see p. 489).

Paragraph synthesizes information from four sources (see pp. 629–30).

Page numbers provided for quotations (Carr) and paraphrases (Johnston), but not for summaries (Rácz and Wilson & Hunt [on next page]).

neuroplasticity can have harmful results, virtually all biological functions have some negative effects. Errors in nuclear division, for example, can lead to Down syndrome; likewise, faulty protein synthesis can result in diabetes, cystic fibrosis, cancer—the list goes on (Wilson & Hunt, 2015). However, normal functioning of nuclear division and protein synthesis are both critical for human life. Similarly, while neuroplasticity can have some problems, it still plays an overall positive role in our biology.

> Refutation of opposing viewpoint.

For one, neuroplasticity allows the brain to improve useful mental functions. When the brain engages in a challenging mental task, it structures a network of neurons to perform the task. With repetition, the neurons thicken, and new connections are added to the network to make it more advanced. To study this role of neuroplasticity, a research team at the University of Dokuz Eylül in Turkey examined the parietal lobes of mathematicians; this part of the brain helps process the abstract creativity used in advanced mathematics. The results showed that the density of neurons and neural connections in the parietal lobes "were strongly correlated with the time spent [training] as an academician" (Aydin et al., 2007, p. 1859). Other studies found similar correlations between violinists and the motor and auditory cortexes, as well as taxi cab drivers and brain regions that store spacial information (Wilson, Conyers, & Rose, 2015, Redefining section, para. 2). In other words, practicing a skill, such as mathematicians do when repeatedly solving difficult problems, leads to lasting changes in the brain that make a person better at that skill. Just like physical exercises that can strengthen specific body parts, mental exercises can literally reshape the brain to suit different functions as needed. Without neuroplasticity, the brain would be a fixed structure and any improvements would be impossible.

> Paragraph synthesizes information from two sources.

> Quotation integrated into Kim's text. Brackets indicate word added for clarity (see p. 45).

> Citation of a source with eight authors not named in the text; page number required for quotation.

> Citation of source with three authors not named in the text; abbreviated section heading and paragraph number for paraphrase from an unpaged document.

> Kim's interpretation of the evidence.

Beyond improving the usual roles of brain regions, neuroplasticity allows brain regions to adopt radically new functions. This mechanism plays a critical role in compensating for the disruption or loss of a function. The first experiment to illustrate this notion was conducted by MIT neuroscientists von Melchner,

Pallas, and Sur (2000), who disturbed retinal connections in newborn ferrets by redirecting them to the auditory cortex. Because the structure of the auditory cortex cannot process light, the ferrets should have been completely blind. Remarkably, the ferrets still responded to light stimuli. Brain imaging showed that neurons in the auditory cortex had reorganized to resemble networks normally present in the visual cortex (pp. 874-875). Thus, neuroplasticity can adapt brain regions to suit new needs. Later studies have found numerous parallels in humans. Deaf subjects, for instance, can use the auditory cortex to interpret sign language, while blind people can use the visual cortex to read Braille; if a finger is lost, its brain area can be taken over by the remaining fingers to make them more efficient (Carr, 2011, p. 29; Johnston, 2009, pp. 96-97). These studies have shown that when regions of the brain can no longer be used for their normal functions, they are adapted for other purposes. In this context, neuroplasticity operates to constantly make the most of the brain's neural real estate. This efficiency cushions the impact when normal processes are compromised.

   Moreover, neuroplasticity helps patients recover from physical brain injuries. Because the brain is such an integral part of normal functioning, brain injuries often have devastating consequences. Strokes, for example, can destroy an entire hemisphere of the brain, leading to paralysis in half of the body. Other brain injuries can occur from surgeries, tumors, and blood vessel disorders; these commonly result in severe speech impairments, disrupted vision, and memory problems. Luckily, neuroplasticity acts as a built-in healing mechanism. When the brain senses injury, it forms new neurons and synapses to repair the damaged networks, often leading to dramatic improvements. Stroke patients, for example, can recover almost full speech and motor function (Johnston, 2009). In this way, neuroplasticity prevents brain damage from leading to permanent disability.

   In a related manner, neuroplasticity assists in recovery from psychological disorders. Insight into this process was first gained by studying the brains of Buddhist monks after

Names and date here and date number later in the paragraph frame evidence paraphrased from a source.

Two sources cited in a single citation.

Kim's interpretation of the evidence.

No citation needed for common knowledge, or generally accepted information that cannot be traced to any single source.

No page numbers for a summary.

meditation (Kaufman, 2005). The results indicated that brain regions associated with positive attitudes and happiness underwent lasting changes during meditation that made them more active. In other words, conscious thoughts (such as the positive ones common during meditation) can fundamentally alter the brain, and these thoughts can be controlled. Thus, it is not surprising that in many cases of depression and anxiety, patients reported marked improvements by simply thinking positive thoughts (Marx, 2013). In this context, neuroplasticity allows us to actively improve our mental health. When something goes wrong, we have the power to fix it.

Neuroplasticity has shattered the concept of a static brain. Within less than twenty years of its discovery, numerous benefits of neuroplasticity have been identified. Such broad implications are beginning to change old notions. In education, for example, neuroplasticity has strongly swung the nature-nurture debate in favor of the nurturists; educators are helping children overcome learning difficulties and actually improve their intelligence through training programs that restructure the brain (Wilson, Conyers, & Rose, 2015). Neuroplasticity is impacting the adult population as well. As news of a malleable brain spreads, people are engaging in mental exercises to proactively improve themselves (Marx, 2013). Meditation, anyone?

Paragraph synthesizes information from two sources.

Kim's interpretation of the evidence.

Conclusion considers implications of the research.

Citation for a source with three authors not named in the text; no page numbers for a summary.

References

Aydin, K., Ucar, A., Oguz, K. K., Okur, O. O., Agayev, A., Unal, Z., . . . Ozturk, C. (2007). Increased gray matter density in the parietal cortex of mathematicians: A voxel-based morphometry study. *Neuroradiology, 28*, 1859-64. Retrieved from http://link.springer.com/journal/234

Carr, N. (2011). *The shallows: What the Internet is doing to our brains.* New York, NY: Norton.

Gould, E., Tanapat, P., McEwen, B. S., Flügge, G., & Fuchs, E. (1998). Proliferation of granule cell precursors in the dentate gyrus of adult monkeys is diminished by stress. *Proceedings of the National Academy of Sciences of the United States of America, 95*, 3168-71.

Johnston, M. V. (2009). Plasticity in the developing brain: Implications for rehabilitation. *Developmental Disabilities Research Reviews, 15*(2), 94-101. doi:10.1002/ddrr.64

Kaufman, M. (2005, January 3). Meditation gives brain a charge, study finds. *The Washington Post.* Retrieved from http://www.washingtonpost.com

Marx, P. (2013, July 29.) Mentally fit: Workouts at the brain gym. *The New Yorker, 89*(22), 24-28.

Rácz, I. (2014). Neuroplastic changes in addiction. *Frontiers in Molecular Neuroscience, 6*(56). doi:10.3389/fnmol2013.00056

von Melchner, L., Pallas, S. L., & Sur, M. (2000). Visual behavior mediated by retinal projections directed to the auditory pathway. *Nature, 404*, 871-75.

Wilson, D., Conyers, M., & Rose, K. (2015). Rethinking learning potential. *Independent School, 75*(1). Retrieved from https://www.nais.org

Wilson, J. H., & Hunt, T. (2015). *Molecular biology of the cell* (6th ed.). New York, NY: Garland Science.

Reference list begins on a new page.

An article with eight authors and no DOI from a database.

A print book with one author.

An article with five authors from a print journal.

A journal article with a DOI from a database.

A newspaper article on the Web.

A print article from a weekly magazine.

An online scholarly journal without page numbers.

An article with three authors from a print journal.

A journal article without page numbers or a DOI from a database.

A print book with two authors in a later edition.

GLOSSARY OF
USEFUL TERMS

Abstract and concrete Two kinds of language. *Abstract* words refer to ideas, conditions, and qualities we cannot directly perceive: *truth, love, happiness, courage, evil, poverty, progressive.* *Concrete* words indicate things we can know with our senses: *tree, chair, bird, pen, courthouse, motorcycle, perfume, thunderclap.* Concrete words lend vigor and clarity to writing, for they help a reader to picture things. See IMAGE.

    Writers of expository and argumentative essays tend to shift back and forth from one kind of language to the other. They often begin a paragraph with a general statement full of abstract words ("There is *hope* for the *future* of *driving*"). Then they usually go on to give examples and present evidence in sentences full of concrete words ("Inventor *Jones* claims his *car* will go from *Fresno* to *Los Angeles* on a *gallon* of *peanut oil*"). Inexperienced writers often use too many abstract words and not enough concrete ones. See also pages 48 and 118.

Academic writing The kind of writing generally undertaken by scholars and students, in which a writer responds to another's work or uses multiple SOURCES to develop and support an original idea. Typically based on one or more TEXTS, all academic writing calls on a writer's CRITICAL THINKING, READING, AND WRITING abilities and shares the common goal of using reading and writing to build and exchange knowledge. See Chapter 2, pp. 42–47, and the Appendix, pp. 628–31.

Active voice The form of the verb when the sentence subject is the actor: *Trees* [subject] *shed* [active verb] *their leaves in autumn.* Contrast PASSIVE VOICE.

Allude, allusion To refer to a person, place, or thing believed to be common knowledge (*allude*), or the act or result of doing so (*allusion*). An allusion may point to a famous event, a familiar saying, a noted personality, or a well-known story or song. Usually brief, an allusion is a space-saving way to convey much meaning. For example, the statement "The game was Coach Johnson's Waterloo" informs the reader that, like Napoleon meeting defeat in a celebrated battle, the coach led a confrontation resulting in his downfall and that of his team. If the writer is also showing Johnson's character, the allusion might further tell us that the coach is a man of Napoleonic ambition and pride. To make an effective allusion, you have to ensure that it will be clear to your audience. Not every reader, for example, would understand an allusion to a neighbor, to a seventeenth-century Russian harpsichordist, or to a little-known stock-car driver.

Analogy An extended comparison based on the like features of two unlike things: one familiar or easily understood, the other unfamiliar, abstract, or complicated. For instance, most people know at least vaguely how the human eye works: The pupil adjusts to admit light, which registers as an image on the retina at the back of the eye. You might use this familiar information to explain something less familiar to many people, such as how a camera works: The aperture (like the pupil) adjusts to admit light, which registers as an image on the film (like the retina) at the back of the camera. Analogies are especially helpful for explaining technical information in a way that is nontechnical, more easily grasped. For example, the spacecraft *Voyager 2* transmitted spectacular pictures of Saturn to Earth. To explain the difficulty of their achievement, NASA scientists compared their feat to a golfer sinking a putt from five hundred miles away. Because it can make abstract ideas vivid and memorable, analogy is also a favorite device of philosophers, politicians, and preachers.

Analogy is similar to the method of COMPARISON AND CONTRAST. Both identify the distinctive features of two things and then set the features side by side. But a comparison explains two obviously similar things — two Civil War generals, two responses to a mess — and considers both their differences and their similarities. An analogy yokes two apparently unlike things (eye and camera, spaceflight and golf) and focuses only on their major similarities. Analogy is thus an extended *metaphor*, the FIGURE OF SPEECH that declares one thing to be another — even though it isn't, in a strictly literal sense — for the purpose of making us aware of similarity: "Hope," writes the poet Emily Dickinson, "is the thing with feathers / That perches in the soul."

In an ARGUMENT, analogy can make readers more receptive to a point or inspire them, but it can't prove anything because in the end the subjects are dissimilar. A false analogy is a logical FALLACY that claims a fundamental likeness when none exists. See page 487.

Analyze, analysis To separate a subject into its parts (*analyze*), or the act or result of doing so (*analysis*, also called *division*). Analysis is a key skill in CRITICAL THINKING, READING, AND WRITING; see pages 16, 18–22, and 24–25. It is also considered a method of development; see Chapter 8.

Anecdote   A brief NARRATIVE, or retelling of a story or event. Anecdotes have many uses: as essay openers or closers, as examples, as sheer entertainment. See Chapter 3.

Appeals   Resources writers draw on to connect with and persuade readers:

- A **rational appeal** *(logos)* asks readers to use their intellects and their powers of reasoning. It relies on established conventions of logic and evidence.
- An **emotional appeal** *(pathos)* asks readers to respond out of their beliefs, values, or feelings. It inspires, affirms, frightens, angers.
- An **ethical appeal** *(ethos)* asks readers to look favorably on the writer. It stresses the writer's intelligence, competence, fairness, morality, and other qualities desirable in a trustworthy debater or teacher.

See also page 483.

Argument   A mode of writing intended to win readers' agreement with an assertion by engaging their powers of reasoning. Argument often overlaps PERSUASION. See Chapter 12.

Assume, assumption   To take something for granted (*assume*), or a belief or opinion taken for granted (*assumption*). Whether stated or unstated, assumptions influence a writer's choices of subject, viewpoint, EVIDENCE, and even language. See also pages 17 and 484.

Audience   A writer's readers. Having in mind a particular audience helps the writer in choosing strategies, such as which method(s) to use, what details to include, and how to shape an ARGUMENT. You can increase your awareness of your audience by asking yourself a few questions before you begin to write. Who are to be your readers? What is their age level? background? education? Where do they live? What are their beliefs and attitudes? What interests them? What, if anything, sets them apart from most people? How familiar are they with your subject? Knowing your audience can help you write so that your readers will not only understand you better but care more deeply about what you say. See also pages 20, 30–31, 115–16, and 481.

Body   The part of an essay, usually several PARAGRAPHS, that develops the writer's main idea. See pages 36–37.

Cause and effect   A method of development in which a writer ANALYZES reasons for an action, event, or decision, or analyzes its consequences. See Chapter 10. See also EFFECT.

Chronological order   The arrangement of events as they occurred or occur in time, first to last. Most NARRATIVES and PROCESS ANALYSES use chronological order.

Claim   The proposition that an ARGUMENT demonstrates, generally expressed in a THESIS STATEMENT. See pages 481–82.

Classification   A method of development in which a writer sorts out multiple things (contact sports, college students, kinds of music) into categories. See Chapter 9.

Cliché   A worn-out, trite expression that a writer employs thoughtlessly. Although at one time the expression may have been colorful, from heavy use it has lost its luster. It is now "old as the hills." In conversation, most of us sometimes use clichés, but in writing they "stick out like sore thumbs." Alert writers, when they revise, replace a cliché with a fresh, CONCRETE expression. Writers who have trouble recognizing clichés should be suspicious of any phrase they've heard before and should try to read more widely. Their problem is that, because so many expressions are new to them, they do not know which ones are full of moths.

Climactic order   The arrangement of points from least to most important, weakest to strongest. Essays organized by EXAMPLE and CAUSE AND EFFECT often use climactic order, as do many ARGUMENTS.

Coherence   The clear connection of the parts in effective writing so that the reader can easily follow the flow of ideas between sentences, paragraphs, and larger divisions, and can see how they relate successively to one another.

In making your essay coherent, you may find certain devices useful. TRANSITIONS, for instance, can bridge ideas. Reminders of points you have stated earlier are helpful to a reader who may have forgotten them — as readers tend to do sometimes, particularly if an essay is long. However, a coherent essay is not one merely pasted together with transitions and reminders. It derives its coherence from the clear relationship between its THESIS (or central idea) and all its parts. See also pages 41–42 and 305–06.

Colloquial expressions   Words and phrases occurring primarily in speech and in informal writing that seeks a relaxed, conversational tone. "I need a burger and a shake" or "This mess is making me twitchy" may be acceptable in talking to a roommate, in corresponding with a friend, or in writing a humorous essay for general readers. Such choices of words, however, would be out of place in formal writing — in, say, a laboratory report or a letter to your senator. Contractions (*let's, don't, we'll*) and abbreviated words (*pic, sales rep, ad*) are the shorthand of spoken language. Good writers use such expressions with an awareness that they produce an effect of casualness.

Common ground   One or more aspects of an ARGUMENT on which both writer and reader can agree. A writer arguing in favor of raising highway speed limits might, for example, start by acknowledging the importance of safe driving before citing evidence showing that higher average speeds would have little effect on accident rates. By conceding the validity of opposing points or identifying ASSUMPTIONS shared by people on both sides of an issue, the writer establishes the fairness of his or her position and helps to win over readers who may otherwise be inclined to reject the argument outright. See page 481.

Comparison and contrast   Two methods of development usually found together. Using them, a writer examines the similarities and differences between two things to reveal their natures. See Chapter 6.

Conclusion   The sentences or paragraphs that bring an essay to a satisfying and logical end. See pages 38–39.

Concrete   See ABSTRACT AND CONCRETE.

Connotation and denotation   Two types of meanings most words have. *Denotation* is the explicit, literal, dictionary definition of a word. *Connotation* refers to a word's implied meaning, resonant with associations. The denotation of *blood* is "the fluid that circulates in the vascular system." The connotations of *blood* range from *life force* to *gore* to *family bond*. A doctor might use the word *blood* for its denotation, and a mystery writer might rely on the word's connotations to heighten a scene.

Because people have different experiences, they bring to the same word different associations. A conservative's emotional response to the word *welfare* is not likely to be the same as a liberal's. And referring to your senator as a *diplomat* evokes a different response, from the senator and from others, than would *baby-kisser, political hack,* or even *politician*. The effective use of words involves knowing both what they mean literally and what they are likely to suggest.

Critical thinking, reading, and writing A group of interlocking skills that are essential for college work and beyond. Each seeks the meaning beneath the surface of a statement, poem, editorial, picture, advertisement, Web site, or other TEXT. Using ANALYSIS, INFERENCE, SYNTHESIS, and often EVALUATION, the critical thinker, reader, and writer separates a text into its elements in order to see and judge meanings, relations, and ASSUMPTIONS that might otherwise remain buried. See also pages 12, 15–26, 303, and 480–81.

Data A name for EVIDENCE favored by philosopher Stephen Toulmin in his conception of ARGUMENT. See pages 482–83.

Deductive reasoning, deduction The method of reasoning from the general to the particular: From information about what we already know, we deduce what we need or want to know. See Chapter 12, pages 485–86.

Definition A statement of the literal and specific meaning or meanings of a word or a method of developing an essay. In the latter, the writer usually explains the nature of a word, a thing, a concept, or a phenomenon. Such a definition may employ NARRATION, DESCRIPTION, or any other method. See Chapter 11.

Denotation See CONNOTATION AND DENOTATION.

Description A mode of writing that conveys the evidence of the senses: sight, hearing, touch, taste, smell. See Chapter 4.

Dialog The quoted speech of participants in a story. Dialog is commonly included in a NARRATIVE, especially fiction, but it can also be useful in bringing any form of reported writing to life. See page 68.

Diction The choice of words. Every written or spoken statement uses diction of some kind. To describe certain aspects of diction, the following terms may be useful:

- **Standard English:** the common American language, words, and grammatical forms that are used and expected in schools, businesses, and other formal sites.
- **Nonstandard English:** words and grammatical forms such as *theirselves* and *ain't* that are used mainly by people who speak a dialect other than standard English.
- **Dialect:** a variety of English based on differences in geography, education, or social background. Dialect is usually spoken but may be written. Shirley Jackson's story in Chapter 3 transcribes the words of dialect speakers ("'I looked out the window and the kids was gone, and then I remembered it was the twenty-seventh and came a-running'").
- **Slang:** certain words in highly informal speech or writing, or in the speech of a particular group — for example, *blow off, dweeb, wack.*
- **Colloquial expressions:** words and phrases from conversation. See COLLOQUIAL EXPRESSIONS for examples.
- **Regional terms:** words heard in a certain locality, such as *spritzing* for "raining" in Pennsylvania Dutch country.
- **Technical terms:** words and phrases that form the vocabulary of a particular discipline (*monocotyledon* from botany), occupation (*drawplate* from die-making), or avocation (*interval training* from running). See also JARGON.
- **Archaisms:** old-fashioned expressions, once common but now used to suggest an earlier style, such as *ere* and *forsooth.*
- **Obsolete diction:** words that have passed out of use (such as the verb *werien,* "to protect or defend," and the noun *isetnesses,* "agreements"). *Obsolete* may

also refer to certain meanings of words no longer current (*fond* for foolish, *clipping* for hugging or embracing).

- **Pretentious diction:** use of words more numerous and elaborate than necessary, such as *institution of higher learning* for "college," and *partake of solid nourishment* for "eat."

Archaic, obsolete, and pretentious diction usually have no place in good writing unless for ironic or humorous effect: The journalist and critic H. L. Mencken delighted in the hifalutin use of *tonsorial studio* instead of barber shop. Still, any diction may be the right diction for a certain occasion: The choice of words depends on a writer's PURPOSE and AUDIENCE.

Discovery   The stage of the writing process before the first draft. It may include deciding on a topic, narrowing the topic, creating or finding ideas, doing reading and other research, defining PURPOSE and AUDIENCE, or planning and arranging material. Discovery may follow from daydreaming or meditation, reading, or perhaps carefully ransacking memory. In practice, though, it usually involves considerable writing and is aided by the act of writing. The operations of discovery — reading, research, further idea creation, and refinement of subject, purpose, and audience — may all continue well into drafting as well. See also pages 32–34.

Division   See ANALYZE, ANALYSIS.

Dominant impression   The main idea a writer conveys about a subject through DESCRIPTION — that an elephant is gigantic, for example, or an experience scary. See Chapter 4.

Drafting   The stage of the writing process during which a writer expresses ideas in complete sentences, links them, and arranges them in a sequence. See also pages 34–39 and 53–54.

Editing   The final stage of the writing process, during which a writer corrects errors and improves stylistic matters by, for example, using the ACTIVE VOICE and reworking sentences to achieve PARALLEL STRUCTURE. Contrast with REVISION. And see pages 47–53 and 58.

Effect   The result of an event or action, usually considered together with CAUSE as a method of development. See the discussion of cause and effect in Chapter 10. In discussing writing, the term *effect* also refers to the impression a word, a sentence, a paragraph, or an entire work makes on the reader: how convincing it is, whether it elicits an emotional response, what associations it conjures up, and so on.

Emotional appeal (*pathos*)   See APPEALS.

Emphasis   The stress or special importance given to a certain point or element to make it stand out. A skillful writer draws attention to what is most important in a sentence, a paragraph, or an essay by controlling emphasis in any of the following ways:

- **Proportion:** Important ideas are given greater coverage than minor points.
- **Position:** The beginnings and ends of sentences, paragraphs, and larger divisions are the strongest positions. Placing key ideas in these spots helps draw attention to their importance. The end is the stronger position, for what stands last stands out. A sentence in which less important details precede the main point is called a **periodic sentence**: "Having disguised himself as a guard and walked through the courtyard to the side gate, the prisoner made his escape."

A sentence in which the main point precedes less important details is a **loose sentence**: "Autumn is orange: gourds in baskets at roadside stands, the harvest moon hanging like a pumpkin, and oak leaves flashing like goldfish."

- **Repetition:** Careful repetition of key words or phrases can give them greater importance. (Careless repetition, however, can cause boredom.)
- **Mechanical devices:** Italics (underlining), capital letters, and exclamation points can make words or sentences stand out. Writers sometimes fall back on these devices, however, after failing to show significance by other means. Italics and exclamation points can be useful in reporting speech, but excessive use makes writing sound exaggerated or bombastic.

For additional ways to emphasize ideas at the sentence level, see pages 49–50.

Essay A short nonfiction composition on one central theme or subject in which the writer may offer personal views. Essays are sometimes classified as either formal or informal. In general, a **formal essay** is one whose DICTION is that of the written language (not colloquial speech), whose TONE is serious, and whose focus is on a subject the writer believes is important. (For example, see Alain de Botton's "Tragedy.") An **informal essay**, in contrast, is more likely to admit COLLOQUIAL EXPRESSIONS; the writer's tone tends to be lighter, perhaps humorous, and the subject is likely to be personal, sometimes even trivial. (See Naomi Shihab Nye's "Museum.") These distinctions, however, are rough ones: An essay such as Judy Brady's "I Want a Wife" uses colloquial language and speaks of personal experience, but its tone is serious and its subject important. See also EXPOSITION.

Ethical appeal (*ethos*) See APPEALS.

Euphemism The use of inoffensive language in place of language that readers or listeners may find hurtful, distasteful, frightening, or otherwise objectionable — for instance, a police officer's announcing that someone *passed on* rather than *died*, or a politician's calling for *revenue enhancement* rather than *taxation*. Writers sometimes use euphemism out of consideration for readers' feelings, but just as often they use it to deceive readers or shirk responsibility. (For more on euphemism, see William Lutz's "The World of Doublespeak" in Chap. 9.)

Evaluate, evaluation To judge the merits of something (*evaluate*) or the act or result of doing so (*evaluation*). Evaluation is often part of CRITICAL THINKING, READING, AND WRITING. In evaluating a work of writing, you base your judgment on your ANALYSIS of it and your sense of its quality or value. See also pages 17–18, 23, 26, and 624–27.

Evidence The details that support an argument or an explanation, including facts, examples, and expert opinions. A writer's opinions and GENERALIZATIONS must rest upon evidence. See pages 482–83.

Example Also called **exemplification** or **illustration**, a method of development in which the writer provides instances of a general idea. See Chapter 5. An *example* is a verbal illustration.

Exposition The mode of prose writing that explains (or exposes) its subject. Its function is to inform, to instruct, or to set forth ideas: the major trade routes in the Middle East, how to make a dulcimer, why the United States consumes more energy than it needs. Exposition may call various methods to its service: EXAMPLE, COMPARISON AND CONTRAST, PROCESS ANALYSIS, and so on. Most college writing is at least partly exposition, and so are most of the ESSAYS in this book.

Fallacies   Errors in reasoning. See pages 486–87 for a list and examples.

Figures of speech   Expressions that depart from the literal meanings of words for the sake of emphasis or vividness. To say "She's a jewel" doesn't mean that the subject of praise is literally a kind of shining stone; the statement makes sense because the CONNOTATIONS of *jewel* come to mind: rare, priceless, worth cherishing. Some figures of speech involve comparisons of two objects apparently unlike:

- A **simile** (from the Latin, "likeness") states the comparison directly, usually connecting the two things using *like, as,* or *than:* "The moon is like a snowball"; "He's as lazy as a cat full of cream"; "My feet are flatter than flyswatters."
- A **metaphor** (from the Greek, "transfer") declares one thing to *be* another: "A mighty fortress is our God"; "The sheep were bolls of cotton on the hill." (A **dead metaphor** is a word or phrase that, originally a figure of speech, has come to be literal through common usage: "the *hands* of a clock.")
- **Personification** is a simile or metaphor that assigns human traits to inanimate objects or abstractions: "A stoop-shouldered refrigerator hummed quietly to itself"; "The solution to the math problem sat there winking at me."

Other figures of speech consist of deliberate misrepresentations:

- **Hyperbole** (from the Greek, "throwing beyond") is a conscious exaggeration: "I'm so hungry I could eat a saddle"; "I'd wait for you a thousand years."
- The opposite of hyperbole, **understatement**, creates an ironic or humorous effect: "I accepted the ride. At the moment, I didn't feel like walking across the Mojave Desert."
- A **paradox** (from the Greek, "conflicting with expectation") is a seemingly self-contradictory statement that, on reflection, makes sense: "Children are the poor person's wealth" (wealth can be monetary, or it can be spiritual). *Paradox* may also refer to a situation that is inexplicable or contradictory, such as the restriction of one group's rights in order to secure the rights of another group.

Flashback   A technique of NARRATION in which the sequence of events is interrupted to recall an earlier period.

Focus   The narrowing of a SUBJECT to make it manageable. Beginning with a general subject, you concentrate on a certain aspect of it. For instance, you may select crafts as a general subject, then decide your main interest lies in weaving. You could focus your essay still further by narrowing it to operating a hand loom. You also focus your writing according to who will read it (AUDIENCE) or what you want it to achieve (PURPOSE).

General and specific   Terms that describe the relative number of instances or objects included in the group signified by a word. *General* words name a group or class (*flowers*); *specific* words limit the class by naming its individual members (*rose, violet, dahlia, marigold*). Words may be arranged in a series from more general to more specific: *clothes, pants, jeans, Levis.* The word *cat* is more specific than *animal,* but less specific than *tiger,* or *Garfield.* See also ABSTRACT AND CONCRETE and pages 48 and 118.

Generalization   A statement about a class based on an examination of some of its members: "Lions are fierce." The more members examined and the more representative they are of the class, the sturdier the generalization. The statement

"Solar energy saves home owners money" would be challenged by home owners who have yet to recover their installation costs. "Solar energy can save home owners money in the long run" would be a sounder generalization. Insufficient or nonrepresentative EVIDENCE often leads to a hasty generalization, such as "All freshmen hate their roommates" or "Men never express their feelings." Words such as *all, every, only, never,* and *always* have to be used with care: "Some men don't express their feelings" is more credible. Making a trustworthy generalization involves the use of INDUCTIVE REASONING (discussed on pp. 84–85).

Genre   The category into which a piece of writing fits. Shaped by PURPOSE, AUDI-ENCE, and context, genres range from broad types (such as fiction and nonfiction) to general groups (novel, essay) to narrower groups (science fiction novel, personal narrative) to specific document formats (steampunk graphic novel, post on a retail workers' forum) — and they tend to overlap. The genres of college writing vary widely. Examples appear on pages 71 (police log), 119 (field observation), 164 (job-application letter), 204 (review), 260 (lab report), 307 (critical analysis), 351 (résumé), 396 (letter to the editor), 443 (essay exam), and 492 (proposal).

   Most readers are instinctively aware of individual genres and the characteristics that distinguish them, and they expect writers to follow the genre's conventions for POINT OF VIEW, structure and organization, types of EVIDENCE, language, TONE, length, appearance, and so forth. Consider, for instance, a daily newspaper: Readers expect the news articles to be objective statements of fact, with none of the reporters' personal thoughts and little rhetorical flourish; but when they turn to the op-ed page or their favorite columnists, such opinions and clever turns of phrase are precisely what they're looking for. Similar expectations exist for every kind of writing, and good writers make a point of knowing what they are. See also pages 10, 32, and 40 and the individual chapter introductions in Part Two.

Grounds   A name for EVIDENCE favored by philosopher Stephen Toulmin in his conception of ARGUMENT. See pages 482–83.

Hyperbole   See FIGURES OF SPEECH.

Illustration   Another name for EXAMPLE. See Chapter 5.

Image   A word or word sequence that evokes a sensory experience. Whether literal ("We picked two red apples") or figurative ("His cheeks looked like two red apples, buffed and shining"), an image appeals to the reader's memory of seeing, hearing, smelling, touching, or tasting. Images add concreteness to fiction — "The farm looked as tiny and still as a seashell, with the little knob of a house surrounded by its curved furrows of tomato plants" (Eudora Welty in a short story, "The Whistle") — and are an important element in poetry. But writers of essays, too, use images to bring ideas down to earth. See also FIGURES OF SPEECH.

Inductive reasoning, induction   The process of reasoning to a conclusion about an entire class by examining some of its members. See pages 484–85.

Infer, inference   To draw a conclusion (*infer*), or the act or result of doing so (*inference*). In CRITICAL THINKING, READING, AND WRITING, inference is the means to understanding a writer's meaning, ASSUMPTIONS, PURPOSE, fairness, and other attributes. See also pages 16–17, 23, and 25.

Introduction   The opening of a written work. Often it states the writer's subject, narrows it, and communicates the writer's main idea (THESIS). See page 38.

Irony   A manner of speaking or writing that does not directly state a discrepancy, but implies one. **Verbal irony** is the intentional use of words to suggest a meaning other than literal: "What a mansion!" (said of a shack); "There's nothing like sunshine" (said on a foggy morning). (For more examples, see the essays by Jessica Mitford and Judy Brady.) If irony is delivered contemptuously with an intent to hurt, we call it **sarcasm**: "Oh, you're a real friend!" (said to someone who refuses to lend the speaker the coins to operate a clothes dryer). With **situational irony**, the circumstances themselves are incongruous, run contrary to expectations, or twist fate: Juliet regains consciousness only to find that Romeo, believing her dead, has stabbed himself. See also SATIRE.

Jargon   Strictly speaking, the special vocabulary of a trade or profession. The term has also come to mean inflated, vague, meaningless language of any kind. It is characterized by wordiness, ABSTRACT terms galore, pretentious DICTION, and needlessly complicated word order. Whenever you meet a sentence that obviously could express its idea in fewer words and shorter ones, chances are that it is jargon. For instance: "The motivating force compelling her to opt continually for the most labor-intensive mode of operation in performing her functions was consistently observed to be the single constant and regular factor in her behavior patterns." Translation: "She did everything the hard way." (For more on such jargon, see William Lutz's "The World of Doublespeak" in Chap. 9.)

Journal   A record of one's thoughts, kept daily or at least regularly. Keeping a journal faithfully can help a writer gain confidence and develop ideas. See also page 33.

Logos   See APPEALS.

Metaphor   See FIGURES OF SPEECH.

Narration, narrative   The mode of writing (*narration*) that tells a story (*narrative*). See Chapter 3.

Narrator   The teller of a story, usually either in the first PERSON (*I*) or in the third (*he, she, it, they*). See pages 65–66.

Nonstandard English   See DICTION.

Objective and subjective   Kinds of writing that differ in emphasis. In *objective* writing the emphasis falls on the topic; in *subjective* writing it falls on the writer's view of the topic. Objective writing occurs in factual journalism, science reports, certain PROCESS ANALYSES (such as recipes, directions, and instructions), and logical arguments in which the writer attempts to downplay personal feelings and opinions. Subjective writing sets forth the writer's feelings, opinions, and interpretations. It occurs in friendly letters, journals, bylined feature stories and columns in periodicals, personal essays, and ARGUMENTS that appeal to emotion. Few essays, however, contain one kind of writing exclusive of the other.

Organization   The way ideas and supporting evidence are structured in the BODY of an essay. The methods of development typically lend themselves to different approaches, discussed in the introductions to Chapters 3–12. Independent of the methods, a successful writer orders subpoints and details in whatever way will best get the main idea across. While a NARRATIVE or a PROCESS ANALYSIS typically follows a CHRONOLOGICAL ORDER, for instance, the writer may need to step back to relate previous or concurrent events. DESCRIPTION often uses a SPATIAL ORDER, arranging details the way one's eyes might take them in. And the writer of an essay that presents EXAMPLES or an ARGUMENT may choose to move from most compelling points to least, or vice versa with a CLIMACTIC ORDER, depending on the desired EFFECT. See pages 20–21, 37, 68–69 (narration), 116–17 (description), 200–01 (COMPARISON AND CONTRAST), 256 (process analysis), 305 (DIVISION OR ANALYSIS), 348–49 (CLASSIFICATION), and 488–89 (argument or persuasion).

Paradox   See FIGURES OF SPEECH.

Paragraph   A group of closely related sentences that develop a central idea. In an essay, a paragraph is the most important unit of thought because it is both self-contained and part of the larger whole. Paragraphs separate long and involved ideas into smaller parts that are more manageable for the writer and easier for the reader to take in. Good paragraphs, like good essays, possess UNITY and COHERENCE. The central idea is usually stated in a TOPIC SENTENCE, often found at the beginning of the paragraph and related directly to the essay's THESIS. All other sentences in the paragraph relate to this topic sentence, defining it, explaining it, illustrating it, providing it with evidence and support. If you come across a unified and coherent paragraph that has no topic sentence, it will contain a central idea that no sentence in it explicitly states, but that every sentence in it clearly implies. See also pages 41–42, 305–06 (paragraph coherence); 41, 349–50 (paragraph development); and 41, 442 (paragraph unity).

Parallelism, parallel structure   A habit of good writers: keeping related ideas of equal importance in similar grammatical form. A writer may place nouns side by side (*"Trees* and *streams* are my weekend tonic") or in a series ("Give me *wind, sea,* and *stars"*). Phrases, too, may be arranged in parallel structure (*"Out of my bed, into my shoes, up to my classroom* — that's my life"), as may clauses ("Ask not what your country can do for you; ask what you can do for your country").

Parallelism may be found not only in single sentences but in larger units as well. A paragraph might read: "Rhythm is everywhere. It throbs in the rain forests of Brazil. It vibrates ballroom floors in Vienna. It snaps its fingers on street corners in Chicago." In a whole essay, parallelism may be the principle used to arrange ideas in a balanced or harmonious structure. See the famous speech given by Judy Brady (p. 551), in which paragraphs 4–7 all begin with the words "I want a wife who will" and describe an imagined partner. Not only does such a parallel structure organize ideas, but it also lends them force. See also pages 50 and 202–03.

Paraphrase   Putting another writer's thoughts into your own words. In writing a research paper or an essay containing EVIDENCE gathered from your reading, you will find it necessary to paraphrase — unless you are using another writer's very words with quotation marks around them — and to acknowledge your sources. Contrast SUMMARY. And see page 44.

Passive voice   The form of the verb when the sentence subject is acted upon: *The report* [subject] *was published* [passive verb] *anonymously.* Contrast ACTIVE VOICE.

Pathos   See APPEALS.

Person   A grammatical distinction made between the speaker, the one spoken to, and the one spoken about. In the first person (*I, we*), the subject is speaking. In the second person (*you*), the subject is being spoken to. In the third person (*he, she, it*), the subject is being spoken about. The point of view of an essay or work of fiction is often specified according to person: "This short story is told from a first-person point of view." See also POINT OF VIEW.

Personification   See FIGURES OF SPEECH.

Persuasion   A mode of writing intended to influence people's actions by engaging their beliefs and feelings. Persuasion often overlaps ARGUMENT. See Chapter 12.

Plagiarism   The use of someone else's ideas or words as if they were your own, without acknowledging the original author. See pages 42–45 and 630–31.

Point of view   In an essay, the physical position or the mental angle from which a writer beholds a SUBJECT. On the subject of starlings, the following three writers would likely have different points of view: An ornithologist might write OBJEC-TIVELY about the introduction of these birds into North America, a farmer might advise other farmers how to prevent the birds from eating seed, and a bird watcher might SUBJECTIVELY describe a first glad sighting of the species. Whether objective or subjective, point of view also encompasses a writer's biases and ASSUMPTIONS. For instance, the scientist, farmer, and bird watcher would likely all have different perspectives on starlings' reputation as nuisances: Although such perspectives may or may not be expressed directly, they would likely influence each writer's approach to the subject. See also PERSON.

Premise   A proposition or ASSUMPTION that leads to a conclusion. See pages 485–86 for examples.

Process analysis   A method of development that most often explains step by step how something is done or how to do something. See Chapter 7.

Purpose   A writer's reason for trying to convey a particular idea (THESIS) about a particular subject to a particular AUDIENCE of readers. Though it may emerge gradually during the writing process, in the end, purpose should govern every element of a piece of writing.

In trying to define the purpose of an essay you read, ask yourself, "Why did the writer write this?" or "What was this writer trying to achieve?" Even though you cannot know the writer's intentions with absolute certainty, an effective essay will make some purpose clear. See also pages 19, 31–32, and 40.

Rational appeal   See APPEALS.

Revision   The stage of the writing process during which a writer "re-sees" a draft from the viewpoint of a reader. Revision usually involves rethinking fundamental matters such as PURPOSE and organization as well as rewriting to ensure COHER-ENCE and UNITY. See pages 39–42 and 55–57. See also EDITING.

Rhetoric   The study (and the art) of using language effectively. *Rhetoric* also has a negative CONNOTATION of empty or pretentious language meant to waffle, stall, or even deceive. This is the meaning in "The president had nothing substantial to say about taxes, just the usual rhetoric."

Rhetorical question   A question posed for effect, one that requires no answer. Instead, it often provokes thought, lends emphasis to a point, asserts or denies something without making a direct statement, launches further discussion, introduces an opinion, or leads the reader where the writer intends. Sometimes a writer throws one in to introduce variety in a paragraph full of declarative sentences. The following questions are rhetorical: "When will the United States learn that sending people into space does not feed them on the earth?" "Shall I compare thee to a summer's day?" "What is the point of making money if you've no one but yourself to spend it on?" Both reader and writer know what the answers are supposed to be: (1) Someday, if the United States ever wises up. (2) Yes. (3) None.

Sarcasm   See IRONY.

Satire   A form of writing that employs wit to attack folly. Unlike most comedy, the purpose of satire is not merely to entertain, but to bring about enlightenment — even reform. Usually, satire employs irony — as in Koji Frahm's "How to Write an A Paper" and Jonathan Swift's "A Modest Proposal." See also IRONY.

Scene   In a NARRATION, an event retold in detail to re-create an experience. See Chapter 3.

Sentimentality   A quality sometimes found in writing that fails to communicate. Such writing calls for an extreme emotional response on the part of an AUDIENCE, although its writer fails to supply adequate reason for any such reaction. A sentimental writer delights in waxing teary over certain objects: great-grandmother's portrait, a lock of hair from baby's first trip to the barber, an empty popcorn box saved from the World Series of 1996. Sentimental writing usually results when writers shut their eyes to the actual world, preferring to snuffle the sweet scents of remembrance.

Signal phrase   Words used to introduce a quotation, PARAPHRASE, or SUMMARY, often including the source author's name and generally telling readers how the source material should be interpreted: "Nelson argues that the legislation will backfire." See also page 47.

Simile   See FIGURES OF SPEECH.

Slang   See DICTION.

Source   Any outside TEXT or material that a writer uses to develop and support ideas. Often found through the process of researching a subject, a single source might be the focus of an essay (as when you write about a selection in this book), or a writer might SYNTHESIZE multiple sources as EVIDENCE for one or more points. Any source referred to in an essay must be documented with an in-text citation and an entry in a works-cited or references list. See Chapter 2 on academic writing, especially pages 42–47, and the Appendix on research and documentation.

Spatial order   An organizational technique in which a writer DESCRIBES an object or scene by presenting details parallel to the way people normally view them — for instance, near to far, top to bottom, left to right. See also pages 116–17.

Specific   See GENERAL AND SPECIFIC.

Standard English   See DICTION.

Strategy   Whatever means a writer employs to write effectively. The methods set forth in this book are strategies; but so are narrowing a SUBJECT, organizing ideas clearly, using TRANSITIONS, writing with an awareness of your AUDIENCE, and other effective writing practices.

Style   The distinctive manner in which a writer writes. Style may be seen especially in the writer's choice of words and sentence structures. Two writers may write on the same subject, even express similar ideas, but it is style that gives each writer's work a personality.

Subject   What a piece of a writing is about. The subject of an essay starts with a general topic, but because writers narrow their FOCUS on a subject until they have a specific point to make about it, multiple works on the same topic will typically be very different from one another. See also page 30, PURPOSE, and THESIS.

Subjective   See OBJECTIVE AND SUBJECTIVE.

Summarize, summary   To condense a work (essay, movie, news story) to its essence (*summarize*), or the act or result of doing so (*summary*). Summarizing a piece of writing in one's own words is an effective way to come to understand it. (See pp. 15–16.) Summarizing (and acknowledging) others' writing in your own text is a good way to support your ideas. (See pp. 43–44 and 46.) Contrast PARAPHRASE.

Suspense   Often an element in NARRATION: the pleasurable expectation or anxiety we feel that keeps us reading a story. In an exciting mystery story, suspense is constant: How will it all turn out? Will the detective get to the scene in time to prevent another murder? But there can be suspense in less melodramatic accounts as well.

Syllogism   A three-step form of reasoning that employs DEDUCTION. See page 485 for an illustration.

Symbol   A visible object or action that suggests further meaning. The flag suggests country; the crown suggests royalty — these are conventional symbols familiar to us. Life abounds in such clear-cut symbols. Football teams use dolphins and rams for easy identification; married couples symbolize their union with a ring.

In writing, symbols usually do not have such a one-to-one correspondence, but evoke a whole constellation of associations. In Herman Melville's *Moby-Dick*, the whale suggests more than the large mammal it is. It hints at evil, obsession, and the untamable forces of nature. Such a symbol carries meanings too complex or elusive to be neatly defined.

Although more common in fiction and poetry, symbols can be used to good purpose in nonfiction because they often communicate an idea in a compact and concrete way.

Synthesize, synthesis   To link elements into a whole (*synthesize*), or the act or result of doing so (*synthesis*). In CRITICAL THINKING, READING, AND WRITING, synthesis is the key step during which you use your own perspective to reassemble a work you have ANALYZED or to connect the work with others. (See pp. 17 and 25.) Synthesis is a hallmark of ACADEMIC WRITING in which you respond to others' work or use multiple sources to support your ideas. (See pp. 46–47 and 629–30.)

Text   Any creation — written, visual, auditory, physical, or experiential — that can be interpreted or used as a SOURCE for writing. The starting point for most ACADEMIC WRITING, texts include written documents such as essays, articles, and books, of course, but also photographs, paintings, advertisements, Web sites, performances, musical scores, experiments, conversations, lectures, field observations, interviews, dreams, jokes — anything that invites a response, sparks an idea, or lends itself to CRITICAL THINKING, READING, AND WRITING. See pages 26–28.

Thesis, thesis statement   The central idea in a work of writing (*thesis*), to which everything else in the work refers; one or more sentences that express that central idea (*thesis statement*). In some way, each sentence and PARAGRAPH in an effective essay serves to support the thesis and to make it clear and explicit to readers. Good writers, while writing, often set down a thesis statement to help them define their purpose. They also often include this statement in their essay as a promise and a guide to readers. See pages 19, 35–36, 40–41, and the introductions to Chapters 3–12.

Tone   The way a writer expresses his or her regard for subject, AUDIENCE, or self. Through word choice, sentence structures, and what is actually said, the writer conveys an attitude and sets a prevailing spirit. Tone in writing varies as greatly as tone of voice varies in conversation. It can be serious, distant, flippant, angry, enthusiastic, sincere, sympathetic. Whatever tone a writer chooses, usually it informs an entire essay and helps a reader decide how to respond. For examples of strong tone, see the essays by Diane Ackerman, Brian Doyle, Jessica Mitford, David Sedaris, Russell Baker, Chitra Divakaruni, Tal Fortgang, and Judy Brady. See also page 490.

Topic sentence   The statement of the central idea in a PARAGRAPH, usually asserting one aspect of an essay's THESIS. Often the topic sentence will appear at (or near) the beginning of the paragraph, announcing the idea and beginning its development. Because all other sentences in the paragraph explain and support this central idea, the topic sentence is a way to create UNITY.

Transitions   Words, phrases, sentences, or even paragraphs that relate ideas. In moving from one topic to the next, a writer has to bring the reader along by showing how the ideas are developing, what bearing a new thought or detail has on an earlier discussion, or why a new topic is being introduced. A clear purpose, strong ideas, and logical development certainly aid COHERENCE, but to ensure that the reader is following along, good writers provide signals, or transitions.

To bridge sentences or paragraphs and to point out relationships within them, you can use some of the following devices of transition:

- Repeat or restate words or phrases to produce an echo in the reader's mind.
- Use PARALLEL STRUCTURES to produce a rhythm that moves the reader forward.
- Use pronouns to refer back to nouns in earlier passages.
- Use transitional words and phrases. These may indicate a relationship of time (*right away, later, soon, meanwhile, in a few minutes, that night*), proximity (*beside, close to, distant from, nearby, facing*), effect (*therefore, for this reason, as a result, consequently*), comparison (*similarly, in the same way, likewise*), or contrast (*yet, but, nevertheless, however, despite*). Some words and phrases of transition simply add on: *besides, too, also, moreover, in addition to, second, last, in the end.*

Understatement   See FIGURES OF SPEECH.

Unity   The quality of good writing in which all parts relate to the THESIS. In a unified essay, all words, sentences, and PARAGRAPHS support the single central idea. Your first step in achieving unity is to state your thesis; your next step is to organize your thoughts so that they make your thesis clear. See also pages 41 and 442.

Voice   In writing, the sense of the author's character, personality, and attitude that comes through the words. See TONE.

Warrant   The name for ASSUMPTION favored by philosopher Stephen Toulmin in his conception of ARGUMENT. See page 484.

DIRECTORY TO THE WRITERS ON WRITING

DESCRIPTION

Lori Andrews, comments from faculty interviews   546
Joan Didion, from "Why I Write"   561
Colson Whitehead, from "How to Write"   620

DETAILS

Lori Andrews, comments from faculty interviews   546
Joan Didion, from "Why I Write"   561
Firoozeh Dumas, from "A Reader's Guide"   279
Jessica Mitford, from *Poison Penmanship*   297
Andrea Roman (student), comments written for *The Bedford Reader*   219
David Sedaris, from "Day In, Day Out"   212
Brent Staples, comments written for *The Bedford Reader*   170

DISCOVERING IDEAS

Maya Angelou, from an interview for *Intellectual Digest*   98
Judy Brady, from an interview on American Public Media   555
Suzanne Britt, comments written for *The Bedford Reader*   225
Alain de Botton, from an interview for the *Deloitte Review*   249
Firoozeh Dumas, from "A Reader's Guide"   279
Tal Fortgang (student), comments written for *The Bedford Reader*   451
Shirley Jackson, from "Biography of a Story"   109
Marie Javdani (student), comments written for *The Bedford Reader*   408
Maxine Hong Kingston, from *Contemporary Authors*   575
Anne Lamott, "The Crummy First Draft"   262
Brent Staples, comments written for *The Bedford Reader*   170
Luis Alberto Urrea, from an interview for *Bookslut*   602

DRAFTING

Alain de Botton, from an interview for the *Deloitte Review*   249
Firoozeh Dumas, from "A Reader's Guide"   279
Guillermo del Toro and Chuck Hogan, from interviews with Sarah Weinman
     and Rick Kleffel   335
Junot Díaz, from "Becoming a Writer"   92
Tal Fortgang (student), comments written for *The Bedford Reader*   451
Malcolm Gladwell, from an interview for *Dorm Room Tycoon*   433
Shirley Jackson, from "Biography of a Story"   109
Marie Javdani (student), comments written for *The Bedford Reader*   408
Maxine Hong Kingston, from *Contemporary Authors*   575
Anne Lamott, "The Crummy First Draft"   262
William Lutz, from an interview on C-SPAN   371
Brad Manning (student), comments written for *The Bedford Reader*   127
Naomi Shihab Nye, from an interview for *Pif Magazine*   82
Brianne Richson (student), comments written for *The Bedford Reader*   516

OBSERVATION

ORGANIZATION

PLANNING

POETRY

POINT OF VIEW

PROCRASTINATION

SELF-DISCOVERY

SENTENCES

STYLE

SUBJECT

Acknowledgments

Ackerman, Diane. "Black Marble," from *The Human Age: The World Shaped by Us.* © 2014 by Diane Ackerman. Used by permission of W. W. Norton Company, Inc. and HarperCollins Publishers Ltd. All rights reserved.

Andrews, Lori. "*Facebook* is Using You" from *The New York Times*, Feb. 5, 2012. Copyright © 2012 by The New York Times. All rights reserved. Used by permission and protected by the Copyright Laws of the United States. The printing, copying, redistribution, or retransmission of this Content without express written permission is prohibited.

Angelou, Maya. Chapter 19 ("Champion of the World") from *I Know Why the Caged Bird Sings* by Maya Angelou, copyright © 1969 and renewed 1997 by Maya Angelou. Used by permission of Random House, an imprint and division of Penguin Random House LLC. All rights reserved.

Asselin, Janelle. "Superhuman Error: What Dixon and Rivoche Get Wrong." Comics Alliance, June 10, 2014.

Baker, Russell. "The Plot against People" from *The New York Times*, June 18, 1968. Copyright © 1968 by The New York Times. All rights reserved. Used by permission and protected by the Copyright Laws of the United States. The printing, copying, redistribution, or retransmission of the Material without express written permission is prohibited.

Beam, Christopher. "Blood Loss" from *Slate*, Jan. 5, 2011. Copyright © 2011 by The Slate Group. All rights reserved. Used by permission and protected by the Copyright Laws of the United States. The printing, copying, redistribution, or retransmission of the Material without express written permission is prohibited.

Birkerts, Sven. "Ladder" from *The Other Walk: Essays.* Copyright © 2011 by Sven Birkerts. Reprinted with the permission of The Permissions Company, Inc. on behalf of Graywolf Press, Minneapolis, Minnesota, *www.graywolfpress.org.*

Brady, Judy. "I Want a Wife." Copyright © 1970 by Judy Brady. Reprinted with the permission of the author.

Britt, Suzanne. "Neat People vs. Sloppy People" from *Show and Tell* (1982). Reprinted by permission of the author.

Britt, Suzanne. "On Writing." Reprinted by permission of the author.

Burroughs, Augusten. "How to Identify Love by Knowing What It's Not" from *This Is How: Surviving What You Think You Can't* (St. Martin's Press). Copyright © 2012 by Augusten Inc., published by permission of Augusten Burroughs c/o Selectric Artists LLC.

Carr, Nicholas. "The Great Privacy Debate: Tracking Is an Assault on Liberty, With Real Dangers" from *The Wall Street Journal*, Aug. 6, 2010. Reprinted with permission of The Wall Street Journal. Copyright © 2010 Dow Jones & Company, Inc. All Rights Reserved Worldwide. Used under license.

Carr, Nicholas. "The Rapid Evolution of Text" was originally published in *The Futurist*, vol. 43, no. 6, Nov.–Dec. 2009. Used with permission from the author.

Catton, Bruce. "Grant and Lee: A Study in Contrasts," copyright © 1956 by United States Capitol Historical Society. All rights reserved. Reprinted with permission.

Chavez, Linda. "Supporting Family Values," *townhall.com*, Friday, April 17, 2009. By permission of Linda Chavez and Creators Syndicate, Inc.

Cofer, Judith Ortiz. "The Cruel Country," first published in *Brevity* magazine, Issue 40, Fall 2012. Reprinted by permission of University of Georgia Press.

Daum, Meghan. "Narcissist — Give It a Rest" from *The Los Angeles Times*, Jan. 6, 2011. Reprinted by permission of the author.

Daum, Meghan. "On Writing" from "Kids, Do Your Own Homework," *The Los Angeles Times*, April 21, 2011. Reprinted by permission of the author.

de Botton, Alain. "Tragedy" from *The News: A User's Manual.* Copyright © 2014 by Alain de Botton. Used by permission of Pantheon Books, an imprint of the Knopf Doubleday Publishing Group, a division of Penguin Random House LLC. All rights reserved.

INDEX

Page numbers in boldface refer to definitions in the Glossary of Useful Terms.

NOTES AND RESOURCES FOR TEACHING

2016
MLA
Update

The
BEDFORD
READER

THIRTEENTH EDITION

X. J. Kennedy • Dorothy M. Kennedy
Jane E. Aaron • Ellen Kuhl Repetto

NOTES AND RESOURCES
FOR TEACHING

THE
BEDFORD
READER

THIRTEENTH EDITION

X. J. Kennedy • Dorothy M. Kennedy

Jane E. Aaron • Ellen Kuhl Repetto

bedford/st.martin's
Macmillan Learning

Boston | New York

PREFACE

In finding your way to this preface, you may already have discovered the innovations in the thirteenth edition of *The Bedford Reader*. (If not, they are summed up in the text's own preface.) Here we describe the various resources for teachers provided in this manual.

"Teaching with Journals and Collaboration" (p. 1). *The Bedford Reader* includes quite a bit on journal writing and many opportunities for small-group collaboration, and here we support the text with background on these popular techniques—benefits, pitfalls, suggestions.

"Teaching Visual and Multimodal Literacy" (p. 4). We suggest ways to use an engaging feature of *The Bedford Reader*: the introductory material on critical reading of visuals and the many images and multimedia selections appearing throughout the book and suggested in the manual.

"Academic Reading and Writing" (p. 7). This section gives an overview of the text's crucial chapters on critical reading and the writing process in Part One, as well as the Appendix on finding and documenting sources in MLA and APA style.

Chapter introductions. For each rhetorical chapter we preview the method, predicting difficulties that students may have with it and suggesting various uses for the selections that illustrate the method.

Selection introductions. For each selection we highlight what students may like (or dislike) about the piece, suggest topics for discussion and collaboration, and mark connections to other selections or media resources.

Answers to questions. For each selection we also give answers to the questions on meaning, writing strategy, and language that follow the selection in the text.

Comments on the "Writers on Writing." For each comment by a selection author on his or her process, we suggest how the author's reported experience may be instructive for students. Note that a directory at the back of the text lists each of these comments under the topics it addresses, such as choosing a subject or organizing or revising.

As always, these resources are intended not as a pedagogic *CliffsNotes* but as the notes of colleagues with whom you might care to hold a dialog. The answers to questions, especially, are necessarily brief, and undoubtedly you and your students will find much to disagree with. We hope you will also find views to test and enlarge your own questions to prompt better answers.

CONTENTS

SYLLABUS—RHETORICAL APPROACH

Ten-week term, three classes per week. Instructors can tailor readings to suit their own students' abilities and interests.

Week   Activities

1   **Introduction: How (and Why) to Use This Book**

Chapter 1: Critical Reading

In-Class Peer-Review Workshop
    Draft Thesis for Nancy Mairs, *Disability*

Chapter 2: The Writing Process

    Revise *Disability* Thesis and Draft Outline

2   **Chapter 3: Narration**

Narration in Academic Writing
Amy Tan, *Fish Cheeks*
Jonathan Bethards, *Code Three*
    Journal Response

Chapter 4: Description

Description in Academic Writing
Brad Manning, *Arm Wrestling with My Father*
    Journal Response

Chapter 4: Description

Diane Ackerman, *Black Marble*
Sven Birkerts, *Ladder*
    Draft of First Paper

3   **Chapter 5: Example**

Examples in Academic Writing
Kellie Young, *The Undercurrent*
     Journal Response

Chapter 5: Example

Brent Staples, *Black Men and Public Space*
     Journal Response

Chapter 5: Example

Anna Quindlen, *Homeless*
     Turn In First Paper

4   **Chapter 6: Comparison and Contrast**

David Sedaris, *Remembering My Childhood on the Continent of Africa*
     Journal Response
In-Class Peer-Review Workshop

Chapter 6: Comparison and Contrast

Andrea Roman, *"We're Not . . ."*
     Revised Final Draft of First Paper

5   **Chapter 7: Process Analysis**

Processes in Academic Writing
Koji Frahm, *How to Write an A Paper*
     Journal Response

Chapter 7: Process Analysis

Anne Lamott, *The Crummy First Draft*
     Journal Response

Chapter 7: Process Analysis

Dan Koeppel, *Taking a Fall*
     Rough Draft of Second Paper

9 **Chapter 11: Definition**

Definition in Academic Writing
Tal Fortgang, *Checking My Privilege*
Journal Response

Chapter 11: Definition

Roxane Gay, *Peculiar Benefits*
Journal Response

Chapter 11: Definition

Augusten Burroughs, *How to Identify Love by Knowing What It's Not*
Turn In Final Paper

10 **Chapter 12: Argument and Persuasion**

Argument and Persuasion in Academic Writing
Brianne Richson, *An Obligation to Prevent Trauma on Campus*
Jon Overton, *Beware the Trigger Warning*
Journal Response

Chapter 12: Argument and Persuasion

Chuck Dixon and Paul Rivoche, *How Liberalism Became Kryptonite for Superman*
Janelle Asselin, *Superhuman Error: What Dixon and Rivoche Get Wrong*
In-Class Peer-Review Workshop

PART THREE: MIXING THE METHODS

Judy Brady, *I Want a Wife*
Revised Final Paper

SYLLABUS—THEMATIC APPROACH

Fourteen-week term, three classes per week

Week   **Activities**

1   **Introduction to the Writing Process**

Chapter 1: Critical Reading

> Draft Thesis for Nancy Mairs, *Disability*

Chapter 2: The Writing Process

In-Class Peer-Review Workshop
> Revise *Disability* Thesis and Draft Outline

2   **Experiencing Places**

Chapter 4: Description

Description in Academic Writing
N. Scott Momaday, *The Way to Rainy Mountain*
> Journal Response

Chapter 4: Description

Diane Ackerman, *Black Marble*
> Journal Response

**Writing Workshop: Thesis Statements
and Outlines**

> Rough Draft of First Paper

Chapter 11: Definition

Dagoberto Gilb, *Pride*
    Writing Reflection Essay

Chapter 11: Definition

Augusten Burroughs, *How to Identify Love by Knowing What It's Not*
    Reflect on Happiness and Enjoy the End of Term

TEACHING WITH JOURNALS
AND COLLABORATION

Our users report that they often employ journal writing and small-group collaboration in their writing classes. *The Bedford Reader* and this instructor's manual support these techniques in several ways.

JOURNALS

The Bedford Reader includes discussions of journal writing in Chapters 1 and 2 (see pp. 15 and 33) and a journal-writing assignment just after every selection in the printed book (for example, p. 86).

Many instructors use the journal as a teaching tool because it offers students a place to experiment with their ideas without the pressure of producing a crafted, polished essay. This opportunity for creative thinking can also lead to more provocative classroom discussions and formal essays.

One advantage of journals from the teacher's perspective is that they encourage students to share the responsibility of preparing for discussion. You can require a journal entry as part of every assignment, as the first step of writing a paper, or as an integrated part of class discussion. You can allow students to keep their entries on loose pages for easy submission or ask them to keep a paper or electronic notebook so they (and you) have all their entries in one place. You can use the structured journal prompts at the end of each selection, or you can allow students to write anything at all, in any direction, as long as they write something. Most instructors find that journal writing, like any other teaching technique, requires trial and error in the classroom. One teacher's pleasure is another's pain, after all; and some classes will sit slack-jawed before the same assignment that fires others into animated participation. Following are some general guidelines for those who do or want to use journals.

However often or seldom you require journal entries, try to present them in the context of other writing and discussion in the course; the danger of using journals in an unstructured way is that they can become busywork. Explain to students that it's in their best interest to use their journals as idea books: safe places to record notes and impressions, grapple with difficult issues, respond to the essays in *The Bedford Reader*, and generate ideas for more formal writing assignments. They'll find that papers, discussions, and tests are easier because of the time they spend responding to what they read. Your promise not to grade the entries will guarantee more experimentation. However, you may need scheduled or surprise checks to ensure that writing is actually being committed to paper, and of course some students will be disappointed if you don't personally respond to their personal entries. One productive system is to schedule one or two submissions—emphasizing that they're just for a check in the gradebook toward a discussion grade—while encouraging unscheduled submissions for your comments on a particular entry whenever a student wants them. A student who is worried about a paper can get your early feedback, or a student who prefers writing to speaking can have a conversation with you.

Many students will be unfamiliar, even uncomfortable, with required writing that is informal and ungraded, so you may want to coax and guide them into writing. For those who are anxious about your expectations, emphasize that a journal provides a free space where there are no right answers and where organization and sentence structure may simply reflect the student's train of thought. For everyone, make use of the open-ended journal assignment after every selection in the book: It asks students for personal recollections or gut responses to the selection in an effort to help them recognize their own connection to it. Farther on, a "From Journal to Essay" writing topic asks students to hone their personal responses into structured essays, sometimes personal, often critical. You can use the journal prompt by itself to get students writing and talking. Even if you don't build journals into your course, you might find some of the prompts useful as in-class free-writing prompts or as remedies for dull discussions. Try assigning a journal entry for a particular selection and then asking volunteers to read theirs aloud and lead a discussion for five minutes or so. Try asking pairs of students to trade journals, read each other's entries on a given topic, and write responses. Try giving the journal assignments as starting points for small-group discussions.

Some students will have strong responses to the essays in *The Bedford Reader* and will not need any prompting to come up with "something to write about." Definitely encourage students to stray from our suggested avenues of response if they have another idea to explore. The main purpose of journals, after all, is to challenge students to articulate their own ideas more fully.

COLLABORATION

Working in small groups creates unique opportunities for students to examine the concepts of a course and the process of writing. Like journals, small groups are a useful testing ground for ideas and a means for exploring the nuances of issues. Often less intimidating than a whole-class discussion, a small group can provide students with a more collaborative forum for voicing their opinions. In fact, many teachers find that a major benefit of small groups is that they require all students to participate actively both as talkers and as listeners.

Small groups can augment learning in a variety of ways. Discussions might center on an opinion presented in a selection on writing style or rhetorical strategy or on solving a problem raised by an author. (This manual's introductions to the selections often suggest possible directions.) The result could be a collaborative written response that you collect or a series of brief presentations in which groups explain their responses to the rest of the class. Or, keeping it more informal, you may choose simply to roam and eavesdrop throughout the group sessions to see that groups stay focused and to discover what kinds of conclusions they are reaching.

Groups can also enhance whole-class discussions. Try having small groups spend the first fifteen minutes of class brainstorming answers to difficult questions as a precursor to a whole-class discussion. Have groups do outside research related to upcoming essays and report their findings to the class as a whole. Toward the end of the semester, you may feel confident enough in your groups to allow them to take turns planning and running class discussions.

Small groups can also be invaluable as writing workshops, to help students learn to become better readers and revisers of their own essays. Once students get to know members of their group well, they will begin to trust the feedback they receive. From brainstorming on an essay topic to providing suggestions on drafts, peer readers are often uniquely able to point out what works in an essay, what is confusing, what needs expanding, and so on.

You may have to teach students how to give this kind of feedback. Toward that end, Chapter 2 sets the stage with ideas about what problems to look for in a draft and suggestions for revising effectively. With the general checklists for revision and editing in hand (see pp. 40 and 47), try modeling a workshop process for the class, beginning with a conversation about what *constructive criticism* means. Ask a volunteer to bring copies of a draft paper to class, copy a paper from a previous term, or even copy something of your own. Distribute copies to the class. Have the author read the paper aloud, as would occur in the small group. (If the author isn't present, ask a volunteer to read.) Ask the author to explain his or her main concerns about the essay (introduction doesn't seem to fit rest of paper, organization feels choppy, transitions awkward, and so on)—or if there is no author, take this role yourself. Then lead the whole class in a discussion of the essay, starting with what works particularly well and moving to what doesn't work. (Often students will shy away from criticizing a peer, and you may need to get the discussion going.) Give the author (you, if you're role-playing) plenty of opportunities to respond to people's comments. During the discussion, point out what works in workshopping and what doesn't. The most useful feedback will reflect the reader's understanding of the essay ("I got confused when you . . ." or "I wish you would give more details so I could see this place better" or "I don't follow your logic in paragraph 3"). *Discussion* of how to solve such problems will be more fruitful than blunt suggestions like "This passage should be cut" or "You should just rewrite this sentence like this."

Of course, negotiating personality conflicts and overcoming shyness and other qualities that can silence a small group can sometimes be tricky. To minimize these problems, have students compose a "personals" ad on an index card at the beginning of the term, explaining that they're searching for their workshop soul mates. Write a few questions on the board, such as what their strengths and weaknesses are as writers, readers, and talkers or how they respond to constructive criticism. Such self-portraits may not be entirely accurate, but they can help you group students according to complementary abilities and attitudes: You can group some who like to do research with others who like to talk in front of a large group; some who struggle to organize essays with others who feel that organizing is their biggest strength; some who are experienced in collaboration with others who aren't.

Small groups give students a chance to practice the ideas and strategies gleaned from lectures and reading. And such collaborative learning eases some of the burden on you, too: Students will not only gain a great sense of authority over their learning but also share the hot seat at the front of the room.

TEACHING VISUAL
AND MULTIMODAL LITERACY

Throughout *The Bedford Reader* we provide many opportunities to incorporate visuals and multimedia into writing classes: A section in Chapter 1 extends critical thinking from texts to illustrations; every rhetorical chapter opens with an image along with a caption that prompts students' critical responses; a few of the written selections center on illustrations that we also reprint; and in this manual we often suggest multimedia resources—video, audio, visual, or textual—that can enhance the possibilities for engaging students with the readings and the rhetorical methods.

THINKING CRITICALLY ABOUT VISUAL IMAGES

In Chapter 1 on reading we offer a detailed approach to thinking critically about visuals (pp. 22–26). Paralleling the method for evaluating written texts, the approach involves five steps: getting the big picture, analyzing, inferring, synthesizing, and evaluating. A photograph provides a rich opportunity to apply the method.

Students generally like looking at images, and they often form immediate, almost visceral responses to what they see. The challenge, then, may be to guide their responses along critical pathways. For instance, they may need coaching to perceive the value of information about artists or advertisers or historical and cultural contexts—and they may need help gathering such information. In analyzing an image, they often benefit from small-group discussions in which they hear several points of view. Similarly, in the inference phase they can listen to the meanings attributed by others with different backgrounds and outlooks. Finally, as they evaluate images, they may need encouragement to step back from their natural emotional responses and judge the worthiness of the image's purpose and its success in fulfilling that purpose.

CHAPTER-OPENING IMAGES

Each rhetorical chapter in Part Two opens with a visual representation of the chapter's method at work, accompanied by background information and questions about the image(s).

- A drawing tells a story of romantic disappointment (narration, Chap. 3)
- A photograph depicts a riverside shanty (description, Chap. 4)

- A cartoon proposes "low-energy drinks" that could counteract today's trendy jolters (example, Chap. 5)
- A panel from Alison Bechdel's graphic memoir *Fun Home* plays off a disarming family resemblance (comparison and contrast, Chap. 6)
- A photograph makes a telling comment on a doll-making factory (process analysis, Chap. 7)
- A cartoon deconstructs a kid's bologna sandwich (division or analysis, Chap. 8)
- A table categorizes typical household budgets by income status (classification, Chap. 9)
- A bar graph examines some effects of global climate change (cause and effect, Chap. 10)
- A social media poster probes the realities of Down syndrome (definition, Chap. 11)
- An alternative version of the Stars and Stripes makes a strong argument about the United States (argument and persuasion, Chap. 12)

We anticipate that these images will inspire you and your students in several possible ways:

- Because each chapter opener shows a rhetorical method at work, it provides an additional way to introduce the method. The images may especially help students who resist or struggle with reading.
- The caption accompanying each chapter opener provides background on the image so that students have essential information for a critical response. The questions in each caption encourage reflection and discourage a snap judgment such as "I like it" or "I don't like it" or "I don't get it," and they can serve as journal or discussion prompts. Using the caption questions or your own assignments, you can devise various class or small-group projects centered on the chapter openers. For instance, the *National Geographic* graphic in Chapter 10 open up worlds to investigate—the assumptions and interests of the graphic artists, the effects of warming temperatures on oceans and marine life, the uses of data. For another example, the poster in Chapter 11 practically begs for a more detailed and substantiated examination of the problem of stereotyping and presents an opportunity to discuss the nuances of personal identity.

ILLUSTRATIONS ACCOMPANYING TEXT SELECTIONS

Six of *The Bedford Reader*'s text selections include illustrations. In each case, the juxtaposition deepens the meaning of both the written text and the illustration.

- Joyce Carol Oates's poem "Edward Hopper's *Nighthawks*, 1942" (p. 150) describes and interprets Hopper's famous urban scene, which we show in full view and in a detail. "Joyce Carol Oates on Writing" (p. 154) comments on the making of the poem and further interprets the painting.
- "Tragedy" (p. 240) reproduces images from a television news story and an ancient Greek vase to support Alain de Botton's unexpected take on the similarities between contemporary journalism and classical drama.
- Student Laila Ayad's "The Capricious Camera" (p. 315) models the close analysis of a photograph. Examining an arresting image from World War II, Ayad makes a point about the Nazis' agenda of racial purification and about the ambiguities of photography.

- "Everybody Jump" (p. 410) incorporates several of Randall Munroe's trademark stick-figure drawings to illustrate the author's comical answer to a theoretical question about physics.
- Christopher Beam's "Blood Loss" (p. 416), about changing trends in murder and mayhem, includes a bar graph interpreted by the author.
- In "How Liberalism Became Kryptonite for Superman" (p. 500), Chuck Dixon and Paul Rivoche present a comic book cover from the 1940s to support their claim that superheroes used to embody "wonderfully American" values.

MULTIMEDIA SUGGESTIONS

Notes and Resources for Teaching The Bedford Reader now includes suggestions for multimedia materials—such as videos, audio selections, comics, graphics, and essays accessible online—that may prove to enhance students' engagement with the essays in the book. Accompanying the notes on Naomi Shihab Nye's "Museum" (p. 78), for instance, we offer the link to an audio recording of Nye reading her essay to a live audience; and in the introduction to Issa Rae's "The Struggle" (p. 173), we point to the author's popular Web series *Awkward Black Girl*. Additional suggestions include film versions of "The Lottery," multimodal oral histories, an interactive emotional intelligence quiz, DC Comics' character page for Superman, and much more.

In some cases you might wish to share these pieces in class, viewing or listening with your students as a group; or you could assign them just as you would the traditional essays in the book. They are all the work of quality writers or artists and will reward close examination; each of them is not only entertaining but also thought-provoking.

PART ONE

ACADEMIC READING AND WRITING

The first two chapters of *The Bedford Reader* provide a substantial and well-illustrated discussion of critical reading and the writing process (with a focus on writing from reading), and an Appendix offers guidelines for researching and citing sources using MLA and APA style. The outline of this material (below) is followed by a description of the contents.

Chapter 1 gives step-by-step instructions on attentive, critical reading, including examples of annotating a text, summarizing, and using analysis, interpretation, synthesis, and evaluation. A sample essay by Nancy Mairs and a student's marginal notes along with our commentary illustrate the steps. Then a section shows students, again by example, how to apply their faculties for critical thinking to visual images. (For more on this topic, see p. 4 of this manual.) Finally, a discussion of responding to texts previews the uses of reading as a foundation for writing.

Chapter 2 aims to help students surmount one of their biggest hurdles: learning to write critically about what they have read. The chapter details the stages of the writing process, including aids to discovery (journals, freewriting, and the rhetorical methods themselves); a stress on the thesis and thesis statement; suggestions for drafting the introduction, body, and conclusion of an essay; careful explanations of integrating summaries, paraphrases, and quotations from reading (without plagiarizing); and detailed advice on and examples of revising and editing. This section also includes the stages of a student's response to Mairs's essay, from first journal entry through annotated final draft. This paper also serves as an example of writing in response to reading.

An Appendix, "Finding and Documenting Sources," covers the basics of researched writing. Designed as a reference tool, it includes sections on finding and evaluating sources, synthesizing ideas in writing, and documenting sources in MLA and APA styles. Featured in the Appendix are two annotated student papers to model both documentation systems in practice.

You can use Part One and the Appendix in various ways, depending on your students' needs and, of course, your own inclinations. Many instructors teach directly from this material, especially when students are unfamiliar with the processes of critical reading and writing, have little experience with academic writing or with research, or have no other text to rely on. Other instructors ask their students to read the material on their own—it does not assume previous knowledge and so can be self-teaching. Still others select for classwork the parts they wish to stress (summary, say, or the thesis statement) and ask students to cover the remaining sections on their own.

PART TWO

THE METHODS

3
NARRATION
Telling a Story

To write a short account of a personal experience is, for many students, a first assignment that looks reassuring and possible to fulfill. Instructors who wish to begin in this way may assign for reading one or more of this chapter's essays by Amy Tan, Naomi Shihab Nye, Jonathan Bethards, and Maya Angelou: These writers give students a sense of what a good writer can do with material perhaps much like their own: recollections and observations of ordinary experience from daily life. Junot Díaz takes a different approach and shares a story told to him by his mother, expressing with awe what another person experienced in another time. The chapter ends with a short story. By juxtaposing Shirley Jackson's "The Lottery" with the fictional and nonfictional narratives of the other selections, this chapter gives you a chance to ask, "How does fiction differ from nonfiction?"

Not all freshmen feel comfortable writing in the first person. Some may writhe under a burden of self-consciousness. Some may feel guilty about not following the doctrine of a high-school teacher who once urged them to avoid *I*. A few members of the composition staff at Chapel Hill reported encountering this problem, and because of it, some preferred to begin their courses with *The Bedford Reader*'s chapter on description. Writing in the third person seems to give some students greater assurance about constructing that crucial first paper in which they're trying hard to please.

AMY TAN
Fish Cheeks

(*p. 74*)

Amy Tan remains one of the best-known Chinese American writers on the current scene. This brief, amusing piece about a shock between two cultures is a good example of how much can be accomplished in very little space. Every detail contributes to the contrast between the two families and their cultures.

We have paired Tan's essay with Naomi Shihab Nye's recent story of another kind of embarrassment, but instructors who wish to continue teaching Tan together with Angelou can certainly do so—both essays illuminate the experience of being an outsider in America and the ways family can ameliorate or exacerbate a child's grappling with social identity. Be aware that some students may take offense at Tan's use of stereotypes for humor, while others may see her Asian Americanness as exempting her from criticism on those grounds. If this issue is controversial in your class, consider setting up small-group debates on the "political correctness" of the essay. Another valuable look at the Chinese American experience is Maxine Hong Kingston's *The Woman Warrior* (1976), a portion of which is reprinted on page 563.

Media resources: Tan discussed the influences of her own childhood experiences on her work as a writer with Roger Rosenblatt as part of the 2008 Chautauqua Institution morning lecture series; a video of their conversation, "Finding Meaning through Writing," is available on *YouTube*. Students who enjoy "Fish Cheeks" should be encouraged to look further into Tan's works—such as *The Joy Luck Club* (1989), *The Kitchen God's Wife* (1991), *The Hundred Secret Senses* (1995), *The Bonesetter's Daughter* (2001), *The Opposite of Fate* (2003), and *The Valley of Amazement* (2013).

QUESTIONS ON MEANING

1. Tan believes that her family will embarrass her.
2. Tan's mother wants to teach her not to be ashamed of her Chineseness, not to become completely Americanized. "Your only shame is to have shame" (par. 7).
3. Tan is ashamed of her background, referring to her family's "shabby Chinese Christmas" and "noisy Chinese relatives who lacked proper American manners" (par. 2). She resents her mother at the time but eventually learns to appreciate the lesson she has taught her.
4. Tan's purpose is to amuse and entertain, yes, but possibly also to thank her mother and to impart her lesson to the reader.

QUESTIONS ON WRITING STRATEGY

1. Tan sets us up for a story right away. We know immediately that we're going to hear an anecdote about the minister's cute son—and an ethnic conflict.

2. The narrative progression is straightforward; each paragraph starts with a transition that places us in time: "the winter I turned fourteen" (par. 1); "When I found out" (2); "On Christmas Eve" (3); "And then" (4); "Dinner" (5); "At the end of the meal" (6); "After everyone had gone" (7); "And even though I didn't agree with her then" (8). This gives a sense of constant forward momentum to the story.
3. The irony lies in the narrator's inability to acknowledge or realize that the dishes she has described with such disgust in paragraph 3 are in fact her favorites. The Chinese Tan and the American Tan conflict with each other.
4. The descriptive paragraph is meant to be humorous and entertaining, and it will probably have the desired effect on non-Chinese readers: to make clear the culture shock the narrator thinks the minister's family will experience. (Some readers, though, may relish the description.)

QUESTIONS ON LANGUAGE

1. The comparison is amusing because the minister's son is compared to a chaste female figure even though it's a first crush and the narrator is "in love"; it also underscores both the cultural and nonsexual nature of her love.
2. Tan's language is typical of a young adolescent girl: "my mother had outdone herself" (par. 3); "Robert grunted hello, and I pretended he was not worthy of existence" (4); "Dinner threw me deeper into despair," "I wanted to disappear" (5).
3. Students' opinions may differ, but Tan's use of verbs in paragraph 5 is especially strong.
4. Tofu (a curd of soybean milk) comes from the Chinese *dòu*, "bean," and *fu*, "curdled." Once exotic in the United States, tofu is now a staple of many American diets.

NAOMI SHIHAB NYE

Museum

(p. 78)

Nye's quick, unassuming story of a teenage misadventure packs a surprising punch. Gleefully recounting the "mortifying" mistake of wandering into a private San Antonio residence thinking it was a public museum, she discovers, thirty years later, that her fleeting embarrassment had a lasting impact on a stranger's life.

The narration of the incident itself offers an accessible model for students' own narrative writing. Point out that Nye's sentences and narrative structure are very simple yet very effective. They should see that writers don't need to bog down in complicated prose to get their points across. The story is also a good example of how narration can be used in the service of a larger theme, with implications that go beyond the events recounted. Nye does more than simply tell a story; she makes an interesting observation about the hidden ways people affect each other.

Nye's essay is paired with Amy Tan's narrative "Fish Cheeks" (p. 74) for discussion and writing. Both writers tell good-natured tales of misunderstanding and forgiveness.

Media resources: Nye read this story in 2012 for a live audience at the Four Souls symposium in Fargo, North Dakota, as part of the program "The Stories That Tell Us Who We Are." Prairie Public Broadcasting's audio recording of her performance is available for free at *soundcloud.com/ndhumanities/ true-story-by-naomi-shihab-nye.*

QUESTIONS ON MEANING

1. Nye seems to want to show that people of means often take their privileges for granted but also that it's possible to have a lasting impact on someone's life without intending to—or even knowing it.
2. Nye and her friend thought they were entering a formerly private residence that had been bequeathed to the community as an art museum; the house was so full of fine art, architecture, and furnishings that they didn't catch on that they were at the wrong address and in someone's home. We can only imagine what the residents thought they were up to, but the homeowner's friendly questions and directions to the actual museum (and the fact that he let them wander the house for as long as they did) suggest the family were mostly bemused by their presence.
3. For Nye and her friend, the incident was simply a "mortifying" but laughable mistake not to be revealed to anyone else—until she learned that for the other teenager the incident was an epiphany deserving of gratitude. The uninvited visitors' belief that the girl's home was a museum opened her eyes to how "lucky" (par. 8) she was and led her to appreciate what her parents had given her.
4. The moral of the story is easily felt but not so easily expressed— precisely why narration is an ideal vehicle for Nye to make her point. Students' attempts to express Nye's main idea will surely vary. We might say her thesis is that sometimes one's own experiences can best be appreciated through someone else's eyes.

QUESTIONS ON WRITING STRATEGY

1. "Museum" consists of one extended scene (pars. 1–5) followed by one brief summary (6–8). The scene carries readers along with Nye as her mistake slowly reveals itself; the summary brings us to the moral of her story.
2. Nye's narration combines the sophistication of an adult interpreter with a teenager's view of the events as they unfold.
3. *Honeybee* is sometimes categorized as a children's book, but we think Nye intended this story for adults who can relate to her experience as well as to the lesson learned by the unnamed girl. Despite the simple sentences and language, Nye seems to assume some sophistication in her readers. She rattles off the names of modern artists (Klee, van Gogh, Picasso, Tamayo) without explanation, for instance, and tells the tale as an adult looking back thirty years. As is often the case with Nye's writing, however, children could just as easily follow her story without feeling condescended to.

4. Although the family was clearly wealthy and Nye and her friend were not, both the parents and the visitors had a taste for modern art and fine furnishings, even to the point that a print by Nye's favorite artist was hanging on the wall. The daughter of the household, on the other hand, took such luxuries for granted until strangers showed their admiration.

QUESTIONS ON LANGUAGE

1. Students might not realize that *mortifying* has at its root the Latin word *mors*, or "death." By calling the experience mortifying Nye implies, ironically, that it is killing her.
2. The simple sentences are partly a product of Nye's career of working with and writing for children; the accessibility of her style is one of the writer's trademarks. In the case of "Museum," the simplicity and lack of variety create a trance-like rhythm that carries readers along with the narrator's perspective of events. Some students may reasonably complain, however, that the language lends a childish feel to the story.
3. "Museum" is short on transitions, but Nye uses dialog to keep the story moving. In quoting the father in particular, she is also to hint at the family's perspective of events by revealing their thoughts and feelings.
4. The essay is full of ironic understatements, which together give Nye's story its distinct humor. Additional examples include "She was a good friend that way" (par. 1); "The parking lot under the palm trees was pretty empty" (1); "There weren't very good tags in this museum" (2); "This would be a good place for reading" (2); "we didn't have a word for this" (3); and "We never told anyone" (5).

NAOMI SHIHAB NYE ON WRITING

Nye's advice is aimed at budding poets, but her imploration to read voraciously applies to all writers, of course. Reading, as we stress throughout *The Bedford Reader*, is the foundation of good writing. Other Writers on Writing who reinforce the point include Brian Doyle (p. 182), Suzanne Britt (p. 225), Alain de Botton (p. 249), Barbara B. Parsons (p. 341), Malcolm Gladwell (p. 433), Meghan Daum (p. 463), Wendy Kaminer (p. 527), Nicholas Carr (p. 533), and Colson Whitehead (p. 620).

JONATHAN BETHARDS

Code Three

(p. 84)

As a former emergency medical technician turned community college student, Jonathan Bethards is in the enviable position of having a heroic tale to tell. Some students might object that they have nothing comparable in their pasts to write about, but it's worth pointing out that the success of this essay is not in the action but in the telling. Bethards relates his story with skill, captivating readers' interest from the start and holding it to the end, drawing on fast-paced scenes and remembered dialog to capture the tension of the call and carry readers along to its satisfying conclusion.

You may want to spend some time considering Bethards's diction, specifically his mixture of medical jargon and colloquialism (see question 2 on language). Such usage is generally frowned upon in formal writing, but in the case of this narrative it works quite well, creating a strong writer's voice and clearly opening a window into an EMT's mindset.

QUESTIONS ON MEANING

1. Although he surely means to entertain, Bethards seems to have a higher purpose in mind: He writes to give readers a taste of what it's like to be an emergency worker, sharing the mix of tedium and tension involved with shouldering responsibility for other people's lives.
2. Bethards tells us that the man "was in respiratory arrest and ventricular fibrillation" (par. 4)—essentially he wasn't breathing and his heart wasn't beating—but he doesn't tell us why. We might infer that he had a heart attack or collapsed from the heat "in the low 100s" (3), but readers—like the EMTs and firefighters themselves—can't really know for sure. What's important to the story isn't what caused the condition but the condition itself and the first responders' attempts to resolve it.
3. The wife was attacking the fire chief, it seems, out of instinct and fear. She and the rest of the family were agitated and becoming aggressive because they believed her husband was dying, and as Bethards empathetically explains, "when panic and love combine, a situation can change from stressful to violent in an instant" (par. 6).
4. The main point of the story seems to be that an EMT's job can be highly stressful but profoundly rewarding.

QUESTIONS ON WRITING STRATEGY

1. Bethards is both an active participant and an observer of the events he recounts. His point of view is highly subjective, culminating in tears of relief.
2. By opening *in medias res* at the most dramatic part of the story—the point when the EMTs are getting ready to call time of death—Bethards grabs readers' attention and draws them in.
3. After starting the narrative with the patient on the verge of death and the EMTs thinking "This isn't going to work" (par. 1), Bethards builds suspense by quoting the family's screams (pars. 5, 7) and by suggesting repeatedly that he and the other responders would fail to revive the man: "This was not going to be an easy call" (4); "non-responsive" (4); "I had been in this situation before" (5); "This was not an easy job" (6).
4. Bethards briefly sketches the medical procedures followed by his team—specifically, defibrillation and intubation—in paragraphs 5 and 6.

QUESTIONS ON LANGUAGE

1. Students might be surprised to realize that the French term *en route*, for "on the way" or "along the way," has worked its way into regular English usage. If it had not, Bethards would have needed to italicize it.

2. Some examples of jargon and occupational vocabulary: "call it" (par. 1); "Dispatch," "'man down'" (3); "SFD," "rig" (4); "non-responsive," "respiratory arrest and ventricular fibrillation" (4); "defibrillation paddles," "chest compressions," (5); "get an airway into the lungs," "clear the patient," "sinus rhythm" (6); "crashed" (8). Some colloquial expressions: "hanging out," "get slammed" (2); "gunned the engine," "flipped the sirens," "numbskulls and space cadets" (3); "sweetest sound" (6); "out of the woods" (8). Considering Bethards's purpose of giving readers a taste of an EMT's job, the mixed diction does seem appropriate; it is certainly effective at revealing the need to keep a clinical distance from events while highlighting the responders' humanity.

3. The statement expresses humility and pride at the same time, much as the job can be both dull and stressful.

JUNOT DÍAZ
The Dreamer

(p. 88)

In this brief, personal story, the author captures the desperation of a young girl in a developing country while expressing the influence she had on him as a writer. For students accustomed to taking their own education for granted, the lengths to which Díaz's mother went to secure her schooling is likely to come as a shock.

Some discussion should certainly focus on Díaz's unique voice as a writer (see the questions on language and the critical-writing prompt). He is known for his loose, conversational style and a predilection for sentence fragments; this is the only work of his we have encountered that isn't also riddled with profanity. Although his style is unusual, it has won Díaz legions of admirers, not to mention a MacArthur grant and multiple literary prizes.

Students can be expected to know little or nothing about Dominican history, and so they may tend to gloss over the essay's hints at the brutalities inflicted by Trujillo. You may want to encourage them to do some research on the subject, but at least have them focus on those details in the story that suggest what it was like to live in the Dominican Republic under a harsh dictatorship (see the last question on meaning). Díaz tells readers just enough for them to understand why a girl would court sickness and abuse for a dream of a better life.

Media resources: Readers who enjoy "The Dreamer" might be directed to Junot Díaz's story collections *Drown* (1996) and *This Is How You Lose Her* (2012) as well as to the author's works archived in *The New Yorker* (*www.newyorker.com*). The novel undertaking Díaz describes in his comments on writing, *The Brief Wondrous Life of Oscar Wao* (2007), is a challenging but deeply engaging read that offers additional insights into Dominican life under Trujillo's reign. Peter Sagal (host of NPR's *Wait Wait Don't Tell Me*) interviewed Díaz for the Chicago Humanities Festival in 2013: Video of their hour-long conversation, titled "Junot Díaz: Immigrants, Masculinity, Nerds, and Art," is available on *YouTube*. And Díaz discusses the impacts of immigration and reading on his work as a writer in a short clip for *The Big Think* at *bigthink.com/videos/junot-diaz-on-immigration*.

QUESTIONS ON MEANING

1. It seems that Díaz admires his mother for her defiance and determination in the face of impossible odds. That she would, as a young child, make herself physically ill and risk violence for an education is impressive. And as he explains in his conclusion, she represents desire and "courage" (par. 11)—a source of inspiration for his work and life. (We see evidence of his own determination and stubbornness in his comments on writing, p. 92.)
2. Díaz states his main idea in his conclusion: "I do believe that who I am as an artist, everything that I've ever written, was possible because a seven-year-old girl up in the hills of Azua knelt before a puddle, found courage in herself and drank" (par. 11).
3. Díaz writes to inspire his readers and to encourage them to take risks. He also wants to explain his sense of who he is as a writer.
4. The line suggests that Trujillo and his government inflicted great harm on the people of the Dominican Republic. Much can be inferred from the writer's casual remarks. We can tell, for instance, that rural Dominicans were desperately poor and generally uneducated (to the point of resisting education for their children). We know that they were "brutalized" (par. 1)—not only by the demands of field labor but also by the police (2)—and that they feared Trujillo (3). We can guess that political dissenters were jailed and also that prison conditions were extremely bad. We see that some "idealistic educators" did what they could and that even the police were afraid of Trujillo (8). All told, Díaz paints a portrait of a nation suffering extreme oppression and violence at the hands of a cruel dictator.

QUESTIONS ON WRITING STRATEGY

1. By opening his essay with "I think of my mother" (par. 1) and closing it with "I think of her" (11), he frames his narrative in a dreamlike state of admiration. The device of introducing and closing the essay with variations on the same sentence creates a satisfying coherence.
2. Although he is telling someone else's story and relates the bulk of it in the third person, Díaz writes from a very subjective point of view: He imagines his mother's feelings as well as those of his grandmother, and he allows his own feelings to infuse most every line of the story. Given that the point of the story is the effect it had on him (par. 11), the choice seems highly appropriate.
3. He focuses almost exclusively on female characters and stresses the difficulties faced by girls in the Dominican Republic. Although male readers can certainly appreciate the story, Díaz's obvious admiration for women in general and the resilience of a young girl in particular seems intended to appeal to a female readership.
4. A convergence of circumstances opened the possibility of education for the author's mother: Trujillo decreed mandatory education for children her age, a teacher accepted her into the school when she "should

have laughed and sent her poor ass back to the hills" (par. 8), and the
police intervened when her mother tried to pull her out of school—but
it was his mother's own action, Díaz stresses, that saved her. Astonish-
ingly, she deliberately ingested dirty water to make herself so sick that
her family would have to leave her behind, and then she walked to the
school and demanded an education. Although the education didn't help
her much and she did not realize her dream of becoming a nurse, she
passed her values on to her son, who did benefit from her daring by
becoming a successful writer.

QUESTIONS ON LANGUAGE

1. Our dictionary doesn't define the idiomatic *ironwill*, but students
    should appreciate the implications of Díaz's adjective: It creates an im-
    age of his mother as a strong, stubborn woman.
2. *Horizon* can refer to the apparent convergence of earth and sky in the
    distance; it can also mean a person's goals and interests. Díaz uses the
    word in the second sense, but for most readers it will conjure an image
    of open space in the distance. By stressing the word, Díaz effectively
    creates a metaphor equating his mother's dreams with distant realities
    that are, eventually, illusions.
3. Fragments can be found throughout the essay. Díaz knows what he's
    doing: His heavy use of deliberately incomplete sentences—especially
    in paragraph 1—creates a brooding tone and rhythm; it also creates
    emphasis and, in some cases, a sense of indignation.
4. The second quotation is from a direct conversation Díaz had with his
    mother. The first is something he might have been told or have imagined
    she said, but because he didn't witness the conversation he reports it as
    dialog the way fiction writers often do, without quotation marks.

JUNOT DÍAZ ON WRITING

We like Díaz's comments both for the reassurance they offer struggling
writers and for their raw honesty. A writer, as he defines it, is someone who
feels compelled to write, even when the effort seems futile. You might ask
students to discuss a time when they were frustrated with projects of their
own, writing or otherwise. What inspired them to persist? Or if they quit, how
did the failure affect them? Incidentally, Díaz's comments bear comparison
with Brian Doyle's (p. 182). Both portray the writing process as something of
a painful compulsion that nonetheless has healing qualities.

MAYA ANGELOU

Champion of the World

(p. 94)

A story within a story, Maya Angelou's suspenseful narrative invites attention to both its method and its matter. Inside the story of what happens in the general store (told in the first person, as Angelou looks back to her childhood), we follow the story of the Louis-Carnera fight. Suspense builds from the beginning, in the introductory glimpse of the people crowding in eagerly, in the "apprehensive mood" compared to a sky "streaked with lightning" (par. 2), and in the scraps of conversation. Larger events of the history of civil rights form a background to this narrative—for example, the fact that African Americans were not safe at night, although we learn this only at the end of the story.

You might begin by asking students what they know of the career of Joe Louis. (In some classes no one may know of him.) You could break the class into groups of three or four and have them research what it meant in the 1930s for an African American to become a prominent and universally admired athlete. Come up with a few contextual categories: Louis's career overall; other firsthand reminiscences of boxing in the 1930s; African American life in the 1930s. Each group could then present its findings for five to ten minutes, ending with a whole-class discussion of Angelou's memoir. (Note: If this sort of background research is something you'd like to have students do fairly regularly, you might consider rotating the responsibility so that just one group works and reports on any given essay.)

Media resources: Angelou reads excerpts from *I Know Why the Caged Bird Sings* on a set of CDs with the same title, produced by Random House Audiobooks. The recordings may be ordered or downloaded from *Amazon.com.* Video of her reading of "On the Pulse of Morning" for President Clinton's inauguration is available on *biography.com.*

QUESTIONS ON MEANING

1. Like the rest of the autobiography from which this selection is taken, "Champion of the World" seems written for a dual purpose: to recall vivid and significant moments of the author's life and to reveal the ironic situation of African Americans in the United States in the 1930s—able to become world champions but not able to walk a country road at night. This irony is given great weight by being placed at the end of the story.

2–3. As Angelou indicates in much of her story, and especially in paragraphs 16 and 17, the pride of the race depends on the fight. Not only pride but a whole future rides on the outcome: "If Joe lost we were back in slavery. . . ." Everyone in the store believes this, but the author's view is not so simple. Obviously she doesn't share the notion that if Joe Louis lost it would be clear that "God Himself hated us"; she is exaggerating the assumptions of the people in the store to emphasize the ideological importance of the fight.

4. The error makes untrue a small corner of the story (and might distract people who recognize it), but the fact that Angelou mixed up Louis's fights does not discredit what she reports experiencing.

QUESTIONS ON WRITING STRATEGY

1. Every sentence in the first paragraph contributes to our sense of the importance of the coming events. Note that, with space inside the store at such a premium, children (except infants and toddlers who could fit on a lap) are banished to the porch outside.
2. From paragraph 1 we feel anticipation and a tension that mounts to a crisis in paragraph 15, when the contender rains blows on Louis and staggers him. Short, punchy sentences add speed and force to Angelou's account: "We didn't breathe. We didn't hope. We waited" (par. 18—and, incidentally, a good example of parallelism). The whole device of telling the story of the fight through a radio announcer's spiel is particularly effective because, as Angelou makes clear, the listeners in the store hang on the announcer's every word. Using radio as a medium in story-telling can increase suspense by leaving much to the imagination.
     Anyone familiar with the history of boxing will predict the winner as soon as the name of Joe Louis emerges; others may not be sure until Louis rallies in paragraph 20.
3. Students who sense the irony will probably express it in any of several ways. Some will say that despite all the hopes and dreams bound up in the fight, Louis's victory hasn't delivered his people. Maybe Louis is the strongest man in the ring, but African Americans in rural Arkansas are still vulnerable. Angelou's irony in the final line is so strong that it is practically sarcasm. Isn't there a suggestion, too, that on this particular night some whites, resenting the Louis victory, will be out to punish any African Americans they can find alone or in small numbers?
4. Here, as everywhere, direct quotation lends immediacy to any scene an author creates.
5. The descriptive details in paragraph 27—drinking Coke "like ambrosia," eating candy "like Christmas," boys "blowing their breath in front of themselves like proud smokers"—move the story ahead and re-create the special joy and pride of the occasion.

QUESTIONS ON LANGUAGE

1. Singing commercials for razor blades; sales pitches designed to "string" the listener along. It is possible that Angelou finds irony in the sponsor's product, too, since a racist, stereotypical view of poor African Americans might have them fighting with razors or razor blades.
2. Examples of strong verbs include "perched" (par. 1); "grunted" (6); "poured" (10); "pushed" (12); "groaned," "ambushed," "raped," "whipped," "maimed," "slapping" (16); "clutched" (17); "slid" (21); and "shouted" (23).
3. Nonstandard English here makes the people gathered in the store come alive for us. (This story offers a great opportunity to point out the occasional high value of nonstandard English. The comments in pars. 4 and 8 are so well put that they're hard to forget.)
4. The definition of *white lightning* is hard to find in standard dictionaries. *The Dictionary of American Slang* defines it as "cheap, inferior, homemade, or bootleg whisky, usually uncolored corn whisky."

MAYA ANGELOU ON WRITING

What Angelou means by *rhythm* might be difficult for students to grasp. She means (we'd guess) getting a sense of the size and shape of a subject—or perhaps working up some feeling for it. For Angelou, it seems, finding the rhythm of a subject is that early stage all writers go through when first preparing to write.

SHIRLEY JACKSON

The Lottery

(p. 100)

Still holding the ability to shock decades after its initial publication, this powerful short story is sure to capture your classroom's attention. Some students may know of Stanley Milgram's psychological experiments in obedience to authority. (We've directed them to Milgram's book in writing suggestion 2.) For the skeptics in your class, a brief discussion of Milgram's work could make Jackson's fiction more worthy of serious discussion.

Media resources: "The Biography of a Story" by Shirley Jackson appeared in *Come Along with Me* (1968), a posthumous collection of sixteen stories, part of a novel, and three lectures, edited by Jackson's husband, S. E. Hyman. In the lecture Jackson discusses the writing and publishing of and the public reaction to "The Lottery." We have used excerpts in "Shirley Jackson on Writing," but you may find the entire lecture worth investigating.

Jackson reads "The Lottery" (and "The Demon Lover") on a Folkways recording made in 1963. Carol Jordan Stewart reads "The Lottery" on an Audio Partners cassette made in 1998. You can purchase and download the latter recording from *audible.com*. If you wish to screen a viewing of the story, a twenty-minute film version, produced by the Encyclopaedia Britannica Educational Corporation in 1968, is freely available on *YouTube* and *Brittanica.com*.

QUESTIONS ON MEANING

1. "The Lottery" makes sharp statements on human nature and the nature of society. It attempts to warn about the consequences of unthinking conformity to social practices.
2. The reader senses a problem in paragraph 45, when Mrs. Hutchinson objects. Full knowledge comes in paragraph 74 and is confirmed when Tessie is hit in paragraph 77.
3. It is a close-knit, rural community of farmers (pars. 3, 4). The villagers know each other well—all questions and instructions are mere formalities (13, 20, 50). It is a hardworking community—the lottery is rushed so that people can get back to work (10).

4. Villagers hesitate before touching the box (par. 4). They won't replace it, no matter how shabby it is (5). It is ignored throughout the year (6). And Mr. Summers gains in importance by resting his hand on it (7). It seems that the villagers respect their tradition but also fear it and feel ashamed of it.

QUESTIONS ON WRITING STRATEGY

1. By keeping her distance, Jackson heightens the suspense, for relating even one character's thoughts would doubtless reveal the lottery's nature. This point of view also emphasizes the complacency and hypocrisy of the townspeople—we mostly see and hear only their cheerful, bland interaction—and it intensifies the mystery of the lottery itself.
2. The references to rocks are puzzling but not the least alarming because of the conviviality and playfulness—the normalcy—surrounding them. By the end of the story, the reader has forgotten all about the rocks until he or she is suddenly reminded in paragraph 74.
3. Through the characters' discussion of giving up the lottery, we get a hint that not everyone likes the ritual (some villages have stopped it), and we hear the most vehement defense of the practice from Old Man Warner.
4. The lottery is now merely tradition. It may have originated as a superstition to ensure a good corn harvest (par. 32), but it has long since lost that meaning even for its staunchest supporters.

QUESTIONS ON LANGUAGE

1. We would not know that the lottery is losing ground in some places or the more conservative defense of the ritual (pars. 31–34, 67), how Tessie Hutchinson feels about her fate (45, 49, 51, 59, 79), and how others feel (46, 47, 50, 67, 75). Other examples are possible.
2. The vocabulary in this story should not present much of a stumbling block to students. Even if they don't know all the words, contextual clues are numerous, and the suspense pulls the reader through any barriers.
3. "Snatched" suggests Mrs. Hutchinson's anger that her family has been chosen. She is following the rules but at the same time showing her defiance.
4. All the names seem British except for Delacroix and Zanini: Evidently, we are to think this is a British town or an American New England town. The non-British names indicate perhaps that immigrants have settled in the town, have been accepted (though the pronunciation of the Delacroix name has been altered in par. 2), and have in turn accepted the tradition. "Zanini," of course, gives a clear signal that the alphabet has ended (par. 42).
5. Figurative writing might have contradicted the plainness of the people and would certainly have mitigated the distance that Jackson establishes between herself and the story.

SHIRLEY JACKSON ON WRITING

We heartily recommend the rest of "The Biography of a Story" for the grace and humor of its author and for the numerous quotations from hostile readers. Is Jackson's surprise at readers' reactions naive or even disingenuous? Perhaps. Some students, even many, will think she asked for a harsh response.

4
DESCRIPTION
Writing with Your Senses

Because most instructors make much of descriptive writing, this chapter offers an ample choice of illustrations. Students tend to think of descriptive writing as a kind of still-life painting in words: An apple or a banana sits on a table, and you write about it. In this chapter we strive to demonstrate that, on the contrary, description can involve the testimony of all the senses. All the writers employ description in fresh and engaging ways. And the poet—Joyce Carol Oates—examines with careful eyes the smallest details of a painting, Edward Hopper's *Nighthawks* (reproduced along with the poem).

For our pairing in this chapter, we have chosen Brad Manning's "Arm Wrestling with My Father" (Manning wrote the essay as a college freshman) and N. Scott Momaday's "The Way to Rainy Mountain." Both authors look at members of their families, but otherwise their views (and their descriptions) are quite different. Note that each essay is followed by a "Connections" writing suggestion involving the other.

BRAD MANNING

Arm Wrestling with My Father

(p. 121)

Manning's essay specifically addresses the male experience by exploring how masculine ideals (such as strong, silent, athletic) can affect father-son relations. Most students will have something to say about the general difficulties of parent-child communication, and you may want to extend discussion to how Manning's personal experience represents larger issues. That men communicate nonverbally and women verbally is a commonly held belief. Ask students whether they agree with this gender generalization. Is it easier, more common, or more acceptable for mothers to talk openly with their daughters than for fathers to do so with their sons? What about for mothers and sons, for fathers and daughters, for grandparents and grandchildren? (For a take on the latter relationship, see N. Scott Momaday's "The Way to Rainy Mountain," the essay following this one.) Students may need encouragement to complicate their answers to these questions with specific reasons for their generalizations.

To enhance class discussion, small groups could initially be asked to spend ten to fifteen minutes brainstorming stereotypes about a particular gendered parent-child relationship: one group working with fathers and sons, one with mothers and daughters, and so on (you could even throw stepparents into the mix). When the class reassembles, groups should both respond to each other's ideas and connect their claims to the relationship and standard of communication that Manning describes with his father.

QUESTIONS ON MEANING

1. Manning's father communicates through gestures rather than words.
2. They have learned primarily that they don't have to compete to express affection and that there are many different kinds of communication.
3. Clearly Manning has always felt loved, but he recognizes that these challenges *show* that his father loves him.
4. His purpose is definitely to express love for his father. In a larger context he also wants to suggest the strength of a nonverbal relationship between fathers and sons.

QUESTIONS ON WRITING STRATEGY

1. Manning begins with his bitterness to set us up for the emotional progress of the essay, which moves from frustration and anger to acceptance (all responses to various arm-wrestling competitions).
2. These options suggest that he believes they have both learned something about new avenues of communication. We aren't supposed to predict anything; just knowing options exist shows progress is being made.
3. Manning compares the thrill of hooking his first big fish (par. 10) to the sense of accomplishment he initially felt when he realized that he was going to win his first arm-wrestling match with his father. Although both events are exciting firsts that suggest the approach toward manhood, Manning is a little sorry in both cases to know that he can defeat (kill?) a worthy and longtime foe: "I wanted to win but I did not want to see him lose" (9); "when you finally think you've got him, you want to let him go, cut the line, keep the legend alive" (10). Still, these poetic and self-sacrificing impulses stand in contrast to the end of this wrestling match, which Manning, despite his regrets, won't lose on purpose (11).
4. The narrative progresses through events that demonstrate Manning's boyish powerlessness: his "whole upper body pushing down in hope of winning," his father would "grin with his eyes fixed on me," Manning would "start to cheat and use both hands," his brother once even tried to help, and yet "the man would win." The description emphasizes the contrast between the boy and the man in terms of size ("tiny shoulders" are no match for the man's "calm, unmoving forearm"); effort (the father "not seeming to notice his own arm" while the boy's "greatest efforts" were useless); and power (the father's arm moves "steadily . . . regardless of the opposition").

QUESTIONS ON LANGUAGE

1. *Competition* suggests sportsmanship, organized rivalry with a goal, rather than the discordant clash of wills that *conflict* suggests.

2. This reduces the father to just the arm, giving the reader a greater sense of how large a role the father's arms play in characterizing the man as a whole. The image of him as "the arm" suggests both his competitiveness and his protectiveness (par. 4).
3. Manning still feels competitive with his father but is loath to sacrifice his sense of being protected by a father who is stronger than he is.
4. *Mononucleosis* is a disease involving a high white-blood-cell count, causing fever, weakness, swollen lymph nodes, and a sore throat.

BRAD MANNING ON WRITING

Students who struggle to write may dispute Manning's claim that writing can be a better means of self-expression than speaking. You might reinforce Manning's message that writing, unlike speaking, provides a chance to build and shape thought.

N. SCOTT MOMADAY
The Way to Rainy Mountain
(p. 129)

Students may have difficulty with this complex essay: Although the language is accessible, Momaday weaves together description, personal memoir, history, and social commentary in subtle ways. Even in determining what the essay is about, students may offer differing views: Some will say it's about the death of Momaday's grandmother, some will say it's about the death of the Kiowa culture, and others may say it's about a place of great spiritual importance to the writer. It is, of course, about all these things as well as the relationship between the individual and his or her community and the relationship between minority and majority cultures.

You might ask a small group of students to do some outside research on Kiowa culture and to present their findings to the whole class. The background they provide can give other students a context for establishing their own understandings of this essay.

Media resources: In an extraordinarily ambitious undertaking, Aaron Huey, *National Geographic*, and *Cowbird.com* have collaborated with the residents of the Pine Ridge Reservation in South Dakota to create an extensive archive of multimodal oral histories documenting the lives, frustrations, and hopes of one group of Oglala Lakota Sioux. Nearly 250 submissions have been uploaded to date, all with the goal of letting American Indians speak for themselves and express the full complexities of their experiences in ways that no reporters or essayists could ever hope to accomplish. We encourage you to visit the project's home page at *cowbird.com/collection/pineridge/* or at *ngm.nationalgeographic.com/2012/08/pine-ridge/community-project* and take in as many stories as time and interest allow. We have no doubt that your students will be fascinated and fully engaged by what's there.

QUESTIONS ON MEANING

1. Ultimately the Kiowas could not see far enough: the forces that weakened and restricted them came from beyond the horizon.
2. Despite the suffering of the Kiowas (pars. 3, 9), hope appears in the grandmother's prayers and in her ability to love "without bitterness" despite her "vision of deicide" (9). The prayer half-resembles the "urgency in the human voice" and also positions the grandmother "beyond the reach of time" (10). The grandmother's condition is the human condition.
3. Momaday equates the loneliness he feels at the loss of his grandmother with the expansive loneliness of the landscape, especially in the absence of the Kiowas who once thrived in it.
4. Momaday implies his purpose in paragraph 5: "I wanted to see in reality what [my grandmother] had seen more perfectly in the mind's eye." What he saw—of the land and the Kiowa's place in it—he wants to convey in this essay. The essay speaks to and preserves a way of life long past, and it attempts to immortalize the Kiowa tribe, history, and legend.
5. The audience includes both descendants and non-Indians, as the piece functions to preserve the past and teach about it. It is also universal in reflecting on the loss of a close relative and on what that individual's life represented.

QUESTIONS ON WRITING STRATEGY

1. Loneliness is a constant of the essay: the loneliness of Rainy Mountain and the whole landscape as well as Momaday's own loneliness because of his grandmother's death and the absence of the Kiowa from the place and from his life.
2. Momaday begins and ends with himself in the present at Rainy Mountain (pars. 1–2, 14–15). In between he tells how the Kiowas were defeated by the US Cavalry (3) and how they had migrated from the north and settled on the plain and seen their culture undermined (4–9), and he recalls his grandmother and summers at her house (10–13). In framing the Kiowas' story with the present, Momaday stresses the discrepancy of past and present and the loneliness he feels.
3. The essay is clearly subjective. For example, note the language used to describe the Kiowas' condition in Fort Sill in paragraph 3 ("humiliation," "affliction of defeat," "dark brooding") and to describe the Kiowas before their surrender in paragraph 4 ("suddenly free," "destiny . . . courage and pride," "lordly and dangerous").
4. The paragraphs poignantly contrast the vibrant life of his grandmother's house in the past with its "funereal silence" now. The absence of life sharpens Momaday's point about loss and loneliness.

QUESTIONS ON LANGUAGE

1. Our English word *affliction*, "a pain, calamity, grief, or distress," comes through the Old French *aflicion* from the Latin *affligere*, "disturbed" or "frightened." *Affliction* originally referred to the self-infliction of religious discipline.
2. Metaphor: "the prairie is an anvil's edge" (par. 1); "it was a journey toward the dawn, and it led to a golden age" (4); "Yellowstone . . . was the top of the world" (6). Simile: "popping up like corn to sting the flesh" (1); "the continental interior lay like memory in her blood" (5); "shadows

that move upon the grain like water" (7). Hyperbole: "going nowhere in the plenty of time" (1); "she seemed beyond the reach of time" (10). Students' interpretations of Momaday's meanings will surely vary.

3. The contrast reflects the contrasts in the essay between harsh isolation and hope. The opening images set the dominant mood, but the ending ones convey continuity and strength as well.

4. The parallelism in this paragraph creates a jaunty, festive, even ceremonial rhythm, contributing to what the words say about the mood of this occasion.

N. Scott Momaday on Writing

Momaday's observations about whether he speaks for his group may resonate with students who are also members of racial or ethnic minorities. Not only in their writing but in discussions of all kinds, some of these students may feel that they are viewed as spokespeople, whether they see themselves that way or not.

DIANE ACKERMAN
Black Marble

(p. 138)

In this stunning work of description, the second chapter of *The Human Age: The World Shaped by Us* (2014), poet and naturalist Diane Ackerman brings her trademark exuberance for the natural world to a subject of great importance to her and, probably, to many of your students. Using highly evocative imagery and gorgeously figurative language, she portrays the world at night as seen from space, marveling at the glittering wonder of it. And surprisingly, Ackerman finds reason for optimism and cheer in a phenomenon that has most science and nature writers wringing their hands with worry.

The biggest stumbling block for students might be the essay's densely crafted introduction. Steering an imaginary spaceship toward the Earth, Ackerman puts her poetic license in overdrive. You might want to spend some time in class picking the images apart one by one until students grasp the author's spirit and meaning, as we encourage them to do with the first question on writing strategy (for more on that, see below). More so than is often the case with nonfiction, especially science nonfiction, the first four paragraphs of "Black Marble" reward repeated close reading.

Media resources: Don Pettit's Space Station video montage, which Ackerman uses as the basis for much of her description, is just over ten minutes long and well worth watching with your students; titled "City Lights from International Space Station (2002–2008)," it can be found at *youtube .com/watch?v=U7WuSP663uU*. NASA's 1972 "Blue Marble" photograph, shot by the Apollo 17 crew, is available at *earthobservatory.nasa.gov/IOTD/ view.php?id=1133*. The 2012 "Black Marble" composite image, acquired by satellite, can be downloaded from *earthobservatory.nasa.gov/IOTD/view .php?id=79803.* NASA offers additional space shots of the Earth at night at *earthobservatory.nasa.gov/Features/NightLights/.*

QUESTIONS ON MEANING

1. The dominant impression of "Black Marble" is one of awe, wonder, and glittering beauty. Some students might characterize it as admiring of civilization or hopeful for the future.

2. With *The Human Age*, the book from which this essay is drawn, Ackerman means to persuade readers that although "our relationship with nature has changed . . . radically, irreversibly," such changes are "by no means all for the bad." (We identify this purpose for students in the note preceding the essay.) In the case of "Black Marble," she seems to want readers to accept that light pollution, urbanization, and energy consumption are reassuring signs of civilization, progress, and human ingenuity rather than visible evidence of an environmental problem. She comes closest to stating her thesis in the one-sentence final paragraph: "Our shimmering cities tell all (including us) that Earth's inhabitants are thinkers, builders and rearrangers who like to bunch together in hivelike settlements, and for some reason — bad night vision, primal fear, sheer vanity, to scare predators, or as a form of group adornment — we bedeck them all with garlands of light."

3. Ackerman is citing here the general assumption that living creatures adapt to their environments. But as she sees it, human beings have done the reverse: We whittled the world to fit our lives. She returns to this paradox in paragraphs 9 and 10, when she writes that the lights are "humanity's electric fingerprints on the planet. . . . The silent message of this spectacle is timely, strange, and wonderful. We've tattooed the planet with doings. Our handiwork is visible everywhere . . ." She stresses it again in paragraph 13 when she says, "In a little over two hundred years we've wired up the world and turned on the lights, as if we signed the planet in our luminous ink. In another forty years our scrawl won't look the same." Ackerman repeats these variations on her idea to stress her point that human ingenuity has brought beneficial changes to our environment and will continue to do so.

4. Whether natural or artificial, light, to Ackerman, reveals human industry, accomplishment, and community — but, most of all, "hope" (par. 1). The sprawling urban lightscapes she describes represent everything that is good and special about civilization.

QUESTIONS ON WRITING STRATEGY

1. Ackerman's experience as a poet is particularly evident in this introduction. Somewhat out of character with the rest of the essay, the first four paragraphs read more like a prose poem than like science. Highly impressionistic, imaginative, and entranced — and rich in metaphor and sci-fi imagery — the introduction invites readers to mentally position themselves as space travelers encountering the Earth for the first time, and to be as filled with awe at the sight as Ackerman is. As artful as the writing is, however, the language and structure of these first paragraphs may prove difficult for students, even discouraging them from reading on. They may need to read the introduction several times, and slowly,

before they come to understand its meaning and appreciate what the writer is doing. The rest of the essay is much easier to follow.

2. The essay opens with a poetic introduction in the first four paragraphs (see question 1 on writing strategy, above), approaching the Earth from space. Ackerman continues to use a spatial organization with a moving point of view as she follows astronaut Don Pettit's "orbital tour of Earth's cities at night" as viewed from the International Space Station (pars. 5–9). The essay then takes a fixed view as Ackerman compares and contrasts NASA's 2012 "Black Marble" photograph with its 1972 "Blue Marble" photograph (10–14), focusing on their most telling elements and analyzing their implications for environmental consciousness. Finally, Ackerman concludes with her thesis (15).

3. The author assumes, first, that her readers are concerned for the environment but willing to be reassured that human activities aren't necessarily harmful to the planet. Students will also notice that she assumes a good deal of familiarity with global geography, feeling no need to specify where the many cities and landmarks she names are located or to detail their histories and cultures. Students will probably fit the former part of her assumptions if not the latter. Ultimately, however, lacking knowledge of particular landscapes and features should not impede readers from understanding the point Ackerman is trying to make with her description (which is why we chose not to clutter the essay with gloss notes explaining the abundance of references).

4. The author bases her description on a *YouTube* video stitched together from images taken from the International Space Station and on two photographs taken for NASA: "Blue Marble" (1972) and "Black Marble" (2012). Ackerman paraphrases and quotes the videographer Don Pettit (pars. 5–6, 8) to capture the astronaut's enthusiasm and awe as well as her own, and she summarizes what she sees in the video and the photos from her own point of view (7, 10–14), seamlessly synthesizing the sources' information and ideas with her personal take on their implications.

5. Ackerman compares NASA's iconic "Blue Marble" and "Black Marble" photographs in paragraphs 10–14. As she sees it, both images of the Earth taken from space spurred major shifts in environmental consciousness. "Blue Marble" (1972) implied the insignificance of individual human beings relative to the planet as a whole; "Black Marble" (2012) reveals the extent to which those same human beings have altered the planet to fit their own needs, real and perceived.

QUESTIONS ON LANGUAGE

1. Just a few of the almost overwhelming quantity of metaphors in "Black Marble" include the following: "As our spaceship enters the roulette wheel of a new solar system, hope starts building its fragile crystals once again" (par. 1); "sequins sparkle everywhere . . . embroidery of gold and white lights . . ." (4); "dragon-shaped lights of Hong Kong flutter under us" (7); "we've created our own constellations on the ground. . . ." (9); "the lagoon of the mind's eye" (12). Some *similes*: "this sun resembles our own middle-aged star" (1); "as if we too were peering out of a Space Station window" (5); "village lights dotted over the countryside, softly glowing as through a veil" (7); "as if we signed the planet in luminous ink" (13). Some *personifications* of the Earth as itself human: "a strange assortment of siblings, with many small straggling hangers-on, but we've

encountered odder night-fellows" (1); "we've tattooed the planet with our doings" (10); "this radical new self-portrait" (10); "We could paste the image into our *Homo sapiens* family album" (12). Every one of Ackerman's figures of speech is fresh, imaginative, and highly evocative.

2. As in much of her writing, Ackerman's diction mixes scientific vocabulary and poetic language with a tone of wonder. Students might be startled by the unusual combination, but we would say that given Ackerman's purpose in finding reasons for hope in human impacts on the planet, her diction and tone are not only appropriate but also effective in making a scientific subject accessible for a general audience.

3. Notice how many of Ackerman's words hail from astronomy and geology: *hyperglide, hydrocarbon, magma, auroras, orbital, xenon, lunar, solstice, ozone.*

SVEN BIRKERTS

Ladder

(p. 144)

Anybody who suffers from a fear of heights, and of ladders in particular, will nod knowingly as they read Birkerts's amusing account of the physical and emotional panic he experienced as a hired painter. But his description is so precise and vivid that even readers who have no issues with wobbling up high on a narrow contraption can imagine his terrors for themselves.

The symbolism of the ladder as career trajectory and the deeper points of the essay will likely escape students on a first (or even second or third) reading. Encourage them to think carefully about and discuss the writer's meaning, focusing on the third and fourth questions on meaning and the fourth writing suggestion, labeled "Critical Writing."

QUESTIONS ON MEANING

1. The writer means to entertain but also to mull over a defining moment in his life. The dominant impression he creates is a mixed sense of deep fear and shame as a young man.

2. He means that by abandoning his determination not to look down he suddenly lost his focus and became aware of the precariousness of his position. In other words, he panicked. (Some readers may recognize the somewhat vulgar slang usage of "breaking the seal," referring to the first trip to a bathroom in a night of drinking, which supposedly causes a person to need to urinate more frequently afterward. There's a slight implication that Birkerts may have wet himself in fear.)

3. As Birkerts explains in paragraph 1, he was young and unemployed. He sought out short-term menial tasks because he was broke but also, he suggests, because he didn't want or hadn't settled on a permanent job. The background details establish an aimlessness that sets up the ladder's function as a symbol (see the next question).

4. As we see it, the ladder symbolizes an adult career path (the proverbial "ladder to success"). Birkerts is afraid of responsibility. He is also afraid of getting old (like his employer) and dying.

QUESTIONS ON WRITING STRATEGY

1. Birkerts makes repeated self-deprecating remarks to establish humor and to make readers sympathize with and even like him. We think he succeeds quite well.
2. The essay is only four paragraphs long, with no formal introduction or conclusion. Birkerts takes a point of view that is simultaneously spatial and moving, and he arranges his description chronologically (with the exception of the end of paragraph 1, where he flashes back to provide the background to the story).
3. The unfocused structure of the last paragraph—and especially of the nearly 200-word sentence within it—conveys the author's feelings of panic, creating for readers the same sense of disembodiment and breathlessness that Birkerts experienced.
4. Birkerts compares the old man's appearance with and without teeth at the beginning of paragraph 1 and the end of paragraph 2. The striking difference creates humor; it also suggests that appearances can be deceiving and implies a not-so-flattering comparison between the employer (a successful man at the end of his career) and the author (an unsuccessful man at the beginning of his adult life).

QUESTIONS ON LANGUAGE

1. Notice the connotations of *lapping* in paragraph 3. Rather than describing the shingles with the more commonly used *overlapping*, Birkerts deftly chooses a word that also hints at competitive racing, wagging tongues, and the waves of the nearby ocean.
2. *Lady-killer* is a colloquial term for a man so attractive that women swoon over him. In using the term in both his introduction and conclusion, however, Birkerts seems to suggest that his employer's attractiveness and competence, especially compared to his own, left him feeling emasculated.
3. Students should have no difficulty finding examples: Birkerts masterfully employs vivid details and fresh figures of speech to render his sensations unmistakably clear. Some of our favorites include "a bump in my stomach" (par. 1); the "mouth . . . crimped like the top of a string bag" (2), "that first nervous heaviness in my legs" (3); "the time stream balked, then stopped and started backing up" (4); "the other hand feeling in its joints the cut of the handle, the weight of the bucket, the weathered shingles mere inches away" (4); and "shuddering my torso inch by inch down along the rungs" (4).

JOYCE CAROL OATES
Edward Hopper's *Nighthawks*, 1942

(p. 150)

When assigning this poem, also ask students to look carefully at the reproduction and detail of Hopper's painting that accompany it. You might even ask students to complete a variation of the "Journal Writing" suggestion in which they jot down their own responses to the painting before reading the poem.

In class discussion, a central question for students is what they see as Oates's larger theme in the poem. Oates goes well beyond simply describing the scene of the painting and those peopling it—and even beyond imagining its characters' thoughts and feelings (although these are presented quite vividly). Implicitly, she is contemplating the painting as a work of art in which "time is never going to budge" (line 37), in which the word *still* has the connotations both of "not moving" and of "not changing," even being trapped in the moment the artist has created. In Oates's hands the image could be a metaphor for the human condition ("so why isn't he happier?" [60]).

Media resources: Your library can probably provide you with other works by Hopper either in books about the artist or on slides, and numerous Hopper images can be found online. You may also want to bring to class a color reproduction of *Nighthawks* to share with students.

QUESTIONS ON MEANING

1. The couple are in the midst of an extramarital affair. The man has apparently left his wife (line 7), but he's done that before and gone back (15–19, 28–30, 39–41). He's relieved but, in the end, not happy (60). The woman's thoughts dwell on her mistrust of the man (7–8) as she works herself up not to be hurt by him again (37–41, 45–47).
2. Various interpretations are possible, of course. Perhaps the poem's speaker poses the question about the painting itself; none of the figures in the painting would seem to have this wider perspective. The setting of the picture seems to have the characteristics of a dream—"so much that's wide, still, mute, horizontal" (lines 23–24).
3. Two possible interpretations stand out. The figures in any painting are caught forever in a particular moment, still and silent, so Oates could be urging her readers to contemplate the larger idea of art and its permanency. And Oates also pictures a relationship that is stagnant, going nowhere (although the man is blind to this fact at the moment), which may be interpreted as a fact of the human condition.

QUESTIONS ON WRITING STRATEGY

1. Oates uses concrete language to describe the painting in lines 1–6, 8–10, 22–27, and 54–56. She uses these specific details as a springboard, imagining what they reveal about the characters or how the characters

respond to them: for instance, "And she's thinking / the light in this place is too bright, probably / not very flattering, she hates it when her lipstick / wears off and her makeup gets caked" (30–34). Oates's purpose is not so much to render the physical details of the painting as to describe the situation those details could be illuminating as well as to parallel the situation with the idea of artistic creation.

2. In lines 14–15 the woman thinks of her lover's guilt as "an actual smell, sweaty, rancid, like / dirty socks," and in lines 52–53 she recalls him "burying his hot face in her neck, between her cool / breasts." The man, in contrast, is "not the kind to talk much" (20), and his thoughts lack imagery: "he's thinking / thank God he made the right move at last" (20–21), "he's feeling pretty good, . . . this time he's sure / as hell going to make it work, he owes it to her / and to himself" (27–30), "he's thinking he's the luckiest man in the world" (59).

3. Oates runs sentences and phrases together with few pauses, in a stream of consciousness that builds to the italicized sentence ending line 44.

4. The man's thoughts and, particularly, the woman's thoughts are essentially narrative, and through them the reader can infer the larger narrative of their past relationship. The painting suggests a story to Oates, so she needs narration to relate it.

QUESTIONS ON LANGUAGE

1. *Rancid*, from the Latin *rancēre* ("to have a rank, unpleasant smell"), is a particularly effective word, its sound mimicking its meaning. One almost curls one's lip when saying it.

2. Oates clearly sees these two as a couple of tough characters, not at all refined or even admirable. Who else would be sitting in a cheap restaurant on a deserted street in the middle of the night?

3. "Relief" implies escape from a bad situation, whether from his unhappy home life or from his girlfriend's anger. It suggests looking back at something unpleasant rather than looking forward to something good.

JOYCE CAROL OATES ON WRITING

Both the prolific and the protean Joyce Carol Oates reveal themselves in her essay about her poem about a painting: Oates likes to communicate, and she has much to say in many different ways. This explicit analysis illuminates the painting and also Oates's description of it in her poem. Some students may at first have difficulty penetrating Oates's brief essay, but they should get the point that she wrote the poem for just the reason that most people write anything: to find meaning ("The poem enters the painting as a way of animating what cannot be animated; a way of delving into the painting's mystery").

5
EXAMPLE
Pointing to Instances

Some essays in this chapter use only a few examples; others use many. They all show the ways examples can pin down and give meaning to generalizations.

Brent Staples's and Issa Rae's essays are connected by theme as well as by method: Both treat perceptions of race—where they come from and how to deal with them. Brian Doyle takes a lighter touch, looking at college sports and pondering why so many mascots take the form of animals, some of them mythical. Anna Quindlen explores with a moving case the problem of homelessness. And student writer Kellie Young, in a personal essay, considers her mother's worries and the ways they shape her own behavior.

Some students find difficulty in seeing the difference between giving an example and giving evidence to support a general statement. The latter is a larger concern, in which example is only one strategy. It may help to explain that, usually, an example backs up a general statement ("There have been many fine woman runners: Joan Benoit Samuelson . . ."), but not everything supporting a general statement is an example. Statistics and other data, factual statements, expert opinions, and quotations also serve as evidence. The distinction may not be worth losing sleep over, but if a class has trouble seeing it, ask them to take a more painstaking look at "The Method" at the beginning of this chapter.

BRENT STAPLES
Black Men and Public Space

(p. 166)

This classic essay forms a pair with the next, recent one, "The Struggle." Both Brent Staples and Issa Rae examine problems of stereotype and public perceptions, but the authors write from very different perspectives and draw nearly opposing conclusions about the meanings of race (and gender) in America.

As Brent Staples demonstrates, the most gripping and convincing examples are often brief anecdotes. His personal memoir provides instances when the author aroused suspicion simply because of his skin color—anecdotes that generally arouse keen interest and lively discussion. Examples of Staples's major discovery—of the "alienation that comes of being ever the suspect"—take up most of the room. In addition, Staples gives examples of "tough guys" who died in street violence (par. 7) and precautions he takes to appear less threatening (11–12). His vivid opening paragraph, with its first sentence pretending that he is a killer, deserves special scrutiny.

For collaborative work on this essay, we suggest focusing on just what public space is and what happens to us when we enter it. Students might try to define *public space* by coming up with examples and discovering what the examples have in common. How do they feel different in private and in public space? Once they have their examples and definitions, the groups could reassemble as a class to arrive at a generally accepted definition.

As an alternative, you could encourage students to explore their own feelings about public space. Are there places they feel more or less welcome, safe, at home? The "Journal Writing" prompt after the essay gives students an opportunity to explore such questions. They might also find it helpful to generate a list of generalizations in small groups. What does it mean to be a student, a woman, a man, a member of a particular religious or ethnic group, and so on, in American public spaces? Working in small groups, students will probably feel freer to discuss their experiences; you might even consider dividing the groups along gender lines for those women and men who might be reluctant to speak up otherwise.

Media resources: College teacher Barbara B. Parsons has done us the invaluable service of writing a rhetorical analysis of "Black Men and Public Space" to model the commonly assigned genre for students; we present it in Chapter 8 on division or analysis (p. 337). As an editor for the *New York Times* Staples continues to write on matters of race and, recently, the #blacklivesmatter movement. In a 2015 blog post for the *Times*, for instance, he analyzes some disturbing videos of police interactions with students: *takingnote .blogs.nytimes.com/2015/10/27/south-carolina-video-reveals-the-problem -with-zero-tolerance/?_r=0.*

QUESTIONS ON MEANING

1. Students will state the author's purpose variously. Staples writes to communicate his experience as a black man of whom others are needlessly frightened. He writes to explain his discovery that, when mistaken for a criminal, it is wiser not to react with rage but to take precautions to appear less threatening. However the writer's purpose is put, this is personal experience and observation; we do not see Staples trying to predict the future or proposing any long-term solutions.

2. If we keep on reading, we find Staples acknowledging that women are often the victims of street violence, some of it perpetrated by young African American males. He believes, though, that reports have been exaggerated. He takes pains to make clear that he isn't dangerous. He considers himself not a tough guy but a "softy" who hates to cut up a raw chicken (par. 2); he has shrunk from street fights (6); his own brother and others have been killed in "episodes of bravado" (7).

3. By using it in this context, Staples gives the word *survivor* fresh connotations. Usually it suggests rugged strength, ability to endure, and so on, but here Staples helps us to understand that, in an area of gang warfare, knifings, and murders, timidity is a form of self-preservation.

QUESTIONS ON WRITING STRATEGY

1. Staples convinces by giving examples: anecdotes from his own experience (pars. 1, 5, 8, 9) and that of another African American male (10).
2. The examples are set forth in detail too rich to seem a mere bare-bones list. The similar nature of all the examples lends the essay coherence, and to give it even more Staples uses transitions skillfully. In nearly every paragraph, the opening sentence is transitional, and transitional phrases indicate time: "One day," "Another time," "a couple of summers ago."
3. Beginning with the scene of a near-empty street at night and a frightened woman fleeing him, Staples dramatizes his thesis and immediately sets forth a typical, recurrent situation.

QUESTIONS ON LANGUAGE

1. As we have seen, Staples's essay uses a narrative hook at the start, and to make the hook grab hard, the writer deliberately misleads us. The word *victim* leads us to take him for a self-confessed criminal. By the end of the paragraph, we doubt our impression, and in his second paragraph, Staples explains that he is harmless; he can hardly take a knife to a chicken. If we look back on the opening paragraph, we see the discrepancy between the word *victim* and reality. In truth, the fleeing woman is mistaken and fearful, a person on whom the innocent narrator has no designs. This discrepancy makes clear the writer's ironic attitude. As the essay proceeds, he expresses a mingling of anger, humor, and resignation.
2. We admire Staples's use of that fine old formal word *constitutionals*, "walks taken for health." Like the expression "robust constitution," though, it seems a throwback to another era.
3. Students will have fun defining *dicey* ("risky, unpredictable"), recalling that shooting dice is, of course, a game of chance.

BRENT STAPLES ON WRITING

The story of how Staples wrote "Black Men and Public Space" should help students to see that the process of writing on a subject can help a person come to understand it. In setting down examples of his experiences, Staples discovered what they meant to him. His comparison of essay and news writing is related: The work begins in the details, in the data, the observations, the feelings—in the facts, as Staples says. The big picture depends on the details.

_____

ISSA RAE
The Struggle

(p. 173)

In this personal reflection on what it means to be a black woman in America, Web personality Issa Rae offers a contemporary—and pointed—female response to Brent Staples's decades-old complaint in "Black Men and Public Space" regarding misperceptions of African American men.

Sick of discussions about race, Rae nonetheless joins the conversation, examining multiple episodes when her "blackness" was called into question and concluding that her racial identity is a badge of honor rather than the source of oppression Staples finds it to be. In class, you might want to emphasize the differences in the writers' points of view and how those perspectives influence their ideas about race (the "Connections" questions after each essay encourage this approach). Has the problem Staples identified changed with time, or does something else explain Rae's pride in her "blackness"?

Media resources: Rae's award-winning Web comedy, *The Misadventures of Awkward Black Girl*, follows a semi-autobiographical character as she deals with the frustrations of interpersonal relationships; students can watch episodes at *awkwardblackgirl.com* or on *YouTube* (but be warned: the language can sometimes be graphic and uncomfortable). The first season of her HBO series, *Insecure*, is in production and likely to be released in 2017. The Puff Daddy song Rae and her eighth-grade cohort battled over (as described in "The Struggle") is "Been Around the World," featuring Ma$e and Notorious B.I.G., from the record *No Way Out* (1997).

QUESTIONS ON MEANING

1. Rae states her thesis in paragraphs 6 and 7: "The truth is, I slip in and out of my black consciousness, as if I'm in a racial coma. Sometimes, I'm so deep in my anger, my irritation, my need to stir change, that I can't see anything outside of the lens of race. At other times I feel guilty about my apathy." Her primary purpose seems to be personal reflection: She writes to try to understand why she "demilitarized from [her] blackness" (par. 1) and what being black means to her personal and public identity. At the same time, she seems to want readers to think about why the issue of race feels so inescapable in public discourse, even for those who have reached a level of comfort in their own skin.

2. As her examples specify, Rae feels she needs to prove her blackness to "'down' white people" (par. 19)—that is, those who have appropriated black culture for themselves—and to "blacks in the so-called know" (19). But Rae acknowledges that many of the examples she points to were only partially about proving her "blackness" to those around her: She "was trying to prove it to [herself] just as much as [she] was to everyone" else (16).

3. The "(mostly negative) stereotypes" (par. 16) held for black women, as Rae sees them, boil down to "knowledge of hip-hop culture" (13). To be "black," in her youthful estimation, was to talk a certain way (9, 16), to dance a certain way (9), to know obscure rappers (11–13); it was also to stay out of the water (9), to eat chicken (9), to "feel oppressed" and "marginalized" (18). Rae blames the media and pop culture, particularly rap culture, for the "specific, limited definition" (19) of blackness that she has come to reject.

QUESTIONS ON WRITING STRATEGY

1. By providing a detailed and vivid anecdote about the bus-ride rap battle in her youth as "Situation 1," Rae gives readers a sense that it was a moment that has stayed with her and truly affected her perception of herself and others. The multiple examples grouped as "Situation 2" are less detailed and vivid, diminishing the reader's sense of their personal impact and implying that perhaps Rae has grown not to be so concerned with how others perceive her. The organization and differences in these examples contribute to the reader's sense that Rae has matured and gained a deeper understanding of her own identity.

2. Rae's references to Kanye West (par. 5), Puff Daddy (10–12), "Random Underground Rapper[s]" (12), the "Bad Boy" recording label (13), and Ma$e (14) indicate that she is writing for an audience already familiar with hip-hop culture. Her allusions to black leaders in paragraph 2, to the Rainbow Coalition in paragraph 8, and to CNN stories and non-black rappers appropriating "the N-word" in paragraph 19 further indicate that she is writing for a politically aware American audience. Her use of *we* in the concluding paragraph, finally, suggests that she assumes most of her readers are, like her, "black."

3. Rae uses examples to define by negation, coming to self-understanding through an exploration of what her own "blackness" is not.

QUESTIONS ON LANGUAGE

1. It would seem that Rae hasn't quite abandoned her seventh-grade attempt to "prove that [she] could talk *and* write 'black'" (par. 16). By peppering her essay with urban slang and colloquialisms—such as "It's all good" (5), "Oreo girl" (9), "down" (10, 16, 19), "fool" (11), "I give no f%^&s" (18)—she positions herself as a member of the culture she criticizes.

2. The quotation marks make the words stand out and call into immediate question whether they are sufficient terms for the larger identity question with which the author is grappling. Without them, the words in question would not stand out as much for readers and it would be less immediately apparent that the author is taking issue with generally held definitions and stereotypes associated with the two terms.

3. *Ebonics*, or the formal study of African American dialect as a language in its own right, remains a controversial subject, particularly among linguists and educators. The word is a blend of *ebony*, or black, with *phonics*, or sound.

BRIAN DOYLE
A Note on Mascots

(p. 178)

Brian Doyle's style is unconventional, but there's a reason his works are so consistently selected for *Best American Essays* and writing anthologies. His is a voice that stands out on its own merit and practically dares readers not to be engaged with what he has to say, whatever that may be. This selection from *Children and Other Wild Animals* (originally published in the *American Scholar* as "Go-o-o-o Lemmings!") is no exception. In just four paragraphs, Doyle manages to amuse readers with increasingly ridiculous (but true) examples of college and high school sports mascots, surprising them with a bittersweet and clearly heartfelt interpretation at the end.

Some discussion should surely center on the author's sentence choices. At least a few students will notice that despite our own exhortations (on pages 162 and 163 of the book) to vary their sentences and to avoid example essays that read like lists, Doyle does neither. Yet his essay is very effective, even moving. Why is that? We offer some possible explanations in our comments on the first question on writing strategy below.

Another potential avenue for discussion is an issue Doyle hints at ever so slightly but doesn't address. For some people, sports mascots like the "Fighting Irish" and "Knickerbockers" (par. 1)—and, more to the point, anything related to American Indians, most notably the Washington Redskins—can be not only stereotypical but downright offensive. Doyle focuses on the positive associations of animal symbolism while noting the losses and anxieties they underscore: To what extent could similar insights be applied to human mascots? Why do students think so?

Media resources: Doyle occasionally delivers lectures and readings at high schools and colleges as a visiting author. A one-hour video of his 2013 appearance at Wabash College in Indiana can be accessed at *youtube.com/watch?v=If8MBl2Tw6c*. His enthusiastic lecture on the essay as nourishment, for the 2015 NonfictionNOW conference, is at *youtube.com/watch?v=Oz4Uypy3aFg*.

QUESTIONS ON MEANING

1. As we hint at in the note preceding the selection, "A Note on Mascots" strikes us as one of Doyle's "proems." Essentially, it's a prose poem—not quite poetry, not quite exposition. Evidence for this classification can be found in Doyle's rhythmic sentence structure (particularly the first nine sentences of par. 2) and in his extensive use of figurative language, such as the hyperbole and personification of "I know a man in North Carolina who once lost a fistfight with a heron" (1) and, of course, the metaphors, including but not limited to "on which image we had better pull this whole essay to the side of the road . . ." (3) and "electric jolt in the heart" (4).

2. The primary purpose for quoting Franklin's disdain for eagles seems to be sarcastic humor. (Franklin famously objected to the choice of bald eagle as national symbol and would have preferred the wild turkey as mascot for the country.) Selecting a naturalist might have given greater credence to Doyle's final point about the loss of animals in our immediate surroundings, while including a quote from a sports enthusiast could have served many purposes, among them giving insight into the energy and determination that these mascots inspire.

3. The author is suggesting there is something sinister in sports in general and college sports in particular; he also trying to inject some humor with understatement. Students might also observe that Doyle, a graduate of Notre Dame, is an openly Catholic writer and concerned with matters of religion; he seems to be glancing sideways at the tendency of some sports fans to worship their teams.

4. Doyle's thesis appears in paragraph 4: "I think we love animals as images because we miss them in the flesh, and I think we love them as images because they matter to us spiritually in ways we cannot hope to articulate." He believes, in other words, that animal mascots remind us of the lost vitality of those real-life animals that are no longer with us, either due to extinction or to urban dislocation. By choosing to withhold his melancholy point until the end of the piece, Doyle allows readers to appreciate the vibrancy and humor of the animal mascots on their own merit, deepening their understanding of the power these symbols hold when he finally points to it directly.

QUESTIONS ON WRITING STRATEGY

1. Students might or might not notice that paragraphs 1 and 3 each consist of a single long sentence, somewhat tortured in their structure and deliberately guilty of the "listing" effect we caution against in the method introduction but grammatically correct. The first nine sentences of paragraph 2, on the other hand, are deliberately repetitive: Each one begins with "There is" or "There are" and rattles off an example or two. The combination creates a sense of lushness and quantity. Doyle's long lists of animals imply a multitude of possibilities—in mascots and in nature in general. This sense of endless supply makes it all the more jarring when he concludes with an observation on the present scarcity of the animals we revere. By the time readers reach the final paragraph, Doyle's almost compulsive listing takes on the cadence of a dirge, a roll call of what has been lost rather than the enumeration of plenty it initially seems to be.

2. Doyle ends each of the first three paragraphs with a metaphoric aside that personifies his subject and injects wry humor into the piece: Paragraph 2 ends with "But the two schools that Franklin helped establish are nicknamed the Quakers and the Diplomats, so we can safely ignore Ben on this matter"; paragraph 3 comes to a screeching halt with " . . . on which image we had better pull this whole essay to the side of the road and sit silently for a moment." (He abandons the joke in the final paragraph for the sake of ending on a serious note.) Taken together, these lines suggest that he imagines an audience consisting primarily of students on a field trip.

3. Doyle opens the essay with examples of human mascots ("Fighting Irish," "Metropolitans," "Knickerbockers," "Rangers," "Islanders," par. 1) before introducing his subject of animal mascots. In paragraph 2 he

attempts a scientific classification ("canids . . ., felids . . ., ruminants . . ., mustelids . . ., denizens of the deep") but derails when he gets to the category of the strange and inexplicable, beginning with the "aggrieved camel" and ending with "bearcat of Asia"; he then shifts to birds, especially the eagle (2), and on to "the mysterious world of fantastical fauna" (3), concluding the classification with plants as mascots (3). The classification helps not only to organize the examples but also to set up the faux-scientific feel of the piece before Doyle goes on to make his deeper ecological point.

QUESTIONS ON LANGUAGE

1. The *American Heritage Dictionary*, Second College Edition, tells us that a *totem* is "an animal, plant, or natural object serving among *certain primitive peoples* as the emblem of a clan or family by virtue of an asserted ancestral relationship" (emphasis ours). In the redundancy of the phrase "tribal totems" (par. 4), Doyle seems to be nodding at the controversy over American Indian sports mascots even as he skips over it.

2. Doyle's decision to use the first person allows him to add personality and his own wry humor to what could otherwise be a very dry recitation. In many ways, his use of scientific language feels tongue-in-cheek, removing the necessity of immediate comprehension and replacing it with an appreciation of the sound and flow of the words themselves. If he had stuck with the more academic third person throughout, he might have been able to retain the subtle humor, but the piece as a whole would be more difficult and less inviting. Additionally, the speculation at the end would feel distinctly unsupported in a third-person narrative, while the first-person pronoun allows readers to feel that they are inside the author's head.

3. Beyond the "Fighting Irish" (par. 1), Doyle lists the "Fighting Turtles of the College of Insurance in New York" (2), "the fighting Stormy Petrels of Oglethorpe University in Georgia" (2), and "the Fighting Violets of New York University" (3). The names are inherently ironic. Although one could argue that the "Fighting Irish" reveals negative stereotypes and one could stretch to imagine fighting birds, turtles are generally considered both slow and very mild—leading to an absurd visualization of a fight taking place in slow motion. Trying to imagine a violent violet is even more ridiculous, given that they are rooted to the ground and are more commonly associated with mildness and frailty (shrinking violet).

4. A few examples of Doyle's strong verbs: "hatched," "coddled," "shuffled," "snarling," "roaring," "plopped," "roar and fly and spring and lope and canter and gallop and prowl" (par. 1); "reels" (3); "shivers," "shouting," "grinning" (4). They work because they're vigorous and precise; most convey animal action as well.

BRIAN DOYLE ON WRITING

Readers might be interested to know that the "best ever" question Doyle brings up in this short essay on writing also factors in the NonfictionNOW lecture we recommend viewing on page 39 of this manual, as do several of the other points he makes here. Notice, too, that like Brent Staples (p. 170) and Anna Quindlen (p. 187) in this chapter, Doyle emphasizes the similarities

between personal writing and journalism, especially crime reports. You
might ask your students why they think that is. What can essay writers learn
from reading short, factual accounts in newspapers?

ANNA QUINDLEN

Homeless

(p. 184)

In this direct, personal essay, Quindlen uses detailed examples to explore
what it is to be without a home. The third question on meaning provides a
likely occasion for class discussion of the importance of a home and what a
home is.

If you think your students may need more background on the issue
of homelessness, the third writing suggestion gives them a chance to do
research into and write about the rights of the homeless—to supplement
the evidence of their own experience with facts, expert opinions, and so on.
Students could research collaboratively, with small groups focusing on each
of the following questions to cover more ground: How widespread is homelessness in your area? What are local attitudes toward homeless people?
What provisions are made for the homeless? Is homelessness thought of
differently on the national level? Each group could report its findings back
to the class. (If this sort of research is something you'd like to have students
do fairly regularly, you might consider rotating the responsibility so that just
one group works and reports on any given essay.)

If students already have enough background on the issue, you might
use Quindlen's essay as a springboard for discussing practical measures to
help solve the problem. Working in groups of three or four, students could
discuss the practicalities of Quindlen's claim that nothing but a home will
solve the problems of the homeless: With this as a premise, what can be done
to achieve this goal? Fifteen minutes of collaborative brainstorming on this
question should give students enough time to prepare for a whole-class discussion of the issues Quindlen raises.

Media resources: For a BookTV interview in 2012, Quindlen discussed
her writing process on camera. Her comments and advice for writers can be
watched at *c-span.org/video/?306425-1/anna-quindlen-writing.*

QUESTIONS ON MEANING

1. Quindlen's thesis (in pars. 8–9) is that abstraction from particular human beings to "issues" may distance us from problems and impede
   their solution—in this case, solving homelessness with homes.
2. The key is in paragraph 8: Use of the term "the homeless" distances us
   from the problem suffered by particular people with particular needs.

3. Having a place to live makes you "somebody" (par. 2); it provides "certainty, stability, predictability, privacy" (4), and "pride of ownership" (7). Students' opinions about the importance of a home will vary. This question and the fourth writing suggestion provide good opportunities to discuss just what a home is, anyway: a house or an apartment? a room in a dorm? a heating grate?

QUESTIONS ON WRITING STRATEGY

1. Quindlen might have begun with a statement of her opinion (among other options), but the story of Ann draws the reader in and illustrates Quindlen's point. It also, perhaps even more importantly, reinforces Quindlen's argument that we should focus more on particular people with particular problems.
2. The examples bring Quindlen to earth and magnify the loss suffered by the homeless.
3. The author assumes that the reader has a home and feels strongly about it. Some students may not feel as strongly about having a home as Quindlen does. In paragraph 7 she addresses readers' likely assumption that shelters are better than the streets.
4. The second through fourth sentences enumerate examples and could be parallel simple sentences, but Quindlen varies their structures and complexity (notice the distribution of subordinate clauses), building to the brief, poignant fragment spoken by the mother.
5. She wants readers to agree that nothing short of homes will solve the problems of homeless people.

QUESTIONS ON LANGUAGE

1. It invests her opinion with passion and urgency.
2. Not only do our hearts reside in and take nourishment from our homes, but we can show heart by providing homes for those who lack them.
3. *Crux* is a Latin word meaning "cross." In English it is a critical point or essential feature.

ANNA QUINDLEN ON WRITING

Notice the advantages and disadvantages of reporting, as Quindlen presents them. Analyzing the differences between her essay and a conventional news report may engage students. To us, the myriad differences come down to "My God" (par. 9): Such a fervently personal exclamation would never appear in straight news, not even in feature writing. (Other examples include statements of belief, such as "You are where you live" [par. 2] and "That [a home] is everything" [4], or personal details, such as the Irish grandfather [3] and the beloved hot-water heater [4].) It may be worth pointing out, too, that while Brian Doyle in his comments on writing calls *catharsis* "the lowest form of writing," for Quindlen it's the whole point. How might students characterize her relief at being able to express her emotions in writing?

KELLIE YOUNG

The Undercurrent

(p. 189)

Students should enjoy Young's entertaining reflections on her anxious mother's incessant worries and their effects on her. For a generation raised by "helicopter parents," many will undoubtedly have similar tales to tell of overprotectiveness and nagging reminders. A good way to begin classroom discussion might be to ask students how Young's experience compares with their own. Why do parents worry so much about their children, especially after they leave home? Are they right to be concerned?

Media resources: For students interested in learning more about emotional intelligence for the second writing suggestion (or simply for their own edification), the tenth anniversary edition of Daniel Goleman's *Emotional Intelligence: Why It Can Matter More Than IQ* (2006) is an obvious starting point.

QUESTIONS ON MEANING

1. An *undercurrent* is a marine phenomenon in which a strong stream of water under the surface pulls back from the shore, often catching swimmers off guard and pulling them under and out to sea. (Warning signs on beaches usually advise bathers not to fight the current but to swim with it until it subsides.) According to Merriam-Webster's online dictionary, the word also refers to "a hidden opinion, feeling, or tendency often contrary to the one publicly shown." Young, a surfer, uses the concept as a metaphor for the nagging warnings from her mother that she hears in her head and struggles to overcome. As a swimmer must, she finds that the best approach is to follow the flow.
2. We outline Young's purpose in the essay headnote: Her essay is a response to a college composition assignment that specified she should reflect on events or emotions that shaped her into the person she is.
3. Her grandparents' relationship was not unusual for immigrant families in the mid-twentieth century. Young's widowed grandfather went to China to find a new wife to take care of his four teenage children; the wife brought a daughter from a previous relationship with her. Young doesn't make it terribly clear, but it seems that the couple had three children together after marriage. Because Young's grandmother was occupied with caring for her husband and his older children (the "first family," par. 12), it fell to her daughter to care for their younger children. Young's point is that her mother was laden with adult responsibilities from a young age and through hardships learned early the dangers of living.
4. Young seems to consider the influence somewhat mixed, as she states in paragraph 16: "My mother's voice in my head is something I cannot shake or hide from, but neither is it confining or oppressing. . . . Although at times her/my fears catch me, freezing me momentarily before I leap, she is me, and her voice steers me clear of jumps I realize I cannot make."

QUESTIONS ON WRITING STRATEGY

1. Young's description of surfing in the dark (pars. 1–3) and of the warnings in her head (4) is entertaining, surprising, and thoroughly engaging—a hook practically guaranteed to grab readers' interest in a personal topic that might otherwise seem irrelevant or abstract. At the same time, the story's focus, fears of injury or death while participating in an obviously risky endeavor, sets an ironic tone and establishes Young's overarching point that while her mother's worries may sometimes seem overblown, the writer has learned that it's best to heed them.

2. The writer assumes an audience of peers: college students familiar with the struggles and ambivalent feelings that accompany growing up and away from a parent as they try to become independent.

3. Young covers a lot of ground in "The Undercurrent"; she maintains unity by ensuring that each paragraph includes a clear topic sentence that makes a generalization related to the thesis. Young is also careful to mark transitions among her paragraphs and to repeat key words such as *mother, hear, life,* and *danger.*

4. Young provides three anecdotes: the morning of pre-dawn surfing (pars. 1–5), the afternoon locked out in the rain (8), and the departure to Boston at the airport (15). The stories are meant both to amuse readers and to illustrate Young's point that her mother has good reason to worry about her.

QUESTIONS ON LANGUAGE

1. The quotations—both real and imagined—are essential examples of the voice and the warnings that have become engrained in Young's mind. Without them, the essay would contain only vague generalizations and would lose its effectiveness entirely.

2. "The Undercurrent" is loaded with examples of hyperbole, whether from Young's and her mother's overstatements of the dangers facing her—"*Get one shard in your toe and you're going to have to chop it off—the entire thing!*" (par. 4); "what if someone starts a mosh pit and you get crushed? (6); "if I were unfortunate enough to touch the seat with my bare skin, I would contract a disease and die too quickly for doctors to make a saving diagnosis" (10)—or from Young's predilection for exaggerated phrases, such as "risks that could (and would!) prematurely cut short our lives" (6), "lightning bolts of doom" (9), "utter depths of poverty" (10), and "'twenty seat covers and yards of toilet paper'" (10). The abundance of hyperbole is amusing, of course, but it also establishes a wry, self-mocking tone that lets readers know Young doesn't take herself or her worries too seriously.

3. *The American Heritage Dictionary* tells us that *maverick* can mean not only a stubbornly independent person but also an "unbranded range animal, especially a calf that has become separated from its mother." We don't know if Young intended the second meaning, but it seems especially fitting for her subject.

4. The repetition points out the parallels between her mother's behavior and Young's own.

6
COMPARISON AND CONTRAST
Setting Things Side by Side

Many students dread the method of comparison and contrast, perhaps because of meeting it on essay examinations. We do our best to reassure them (in "The Method") that it is manageable with a little planning. The chapter offers extra help with outlining; we try to take some of the mystique out of it, and we urge the student not to feel a slave to a mere charting of letters and numerals. For a short paper, the formal outline—of the Roman numeral *I*, capital *A* variety—is surely more trouble than it's worth. But in writing any paper that compares and contrasts, a plan to follow, at least a rough plan, is especially useful.

For introducing the method of comparison and contrast, here's a lightweight illustration possibly worth reading to your class. At least it suggests that in comparing and contrasting, a writer has to consider a whole series of points. Craig Hosmer, a Republican and, at the time, representative from California's thirty-second district, introduced the following advice into the *Congressional Record* for October 1, 1974. (We found this item in *American Humor: An Interdisciplinary Newsletter*, Fall 1983, and offer it in a slightly abbreviated version, the better to illustrate comparison and contrast.)

How to Tell Republicans from Democrats

Republicans employ exterminators.
Democrats step on bugs.

Democrats name their children after popular sports figures, politicians, and entertainers.
Republican children are named after their parents or grandparents, according to where the money is.

Republicans tend to keep their shades drawn, although there is seldom any reason why they should.
Democrats ought to, but don't.

Republicans study the financial pages of the newspaper.
Democrats put them in the bottom of the bird cage.

Democrats buy most books that have been banned somewhere.
Republicans form censorship committees and read them as a group.

Democrats give their worn-out clothes to those less fortunate.
Republicans wear theirs.

Democrats raise Airedales, kids, and taxes.
Republicans raise dahlias, Dalmatians, and eyebrows.

Democrats eat the fish they catch.
Republicans hang them on the wall.

Republicans sleep in twin beds—some even in separate rooms.
That is why there are more Democrats.

The essays we present in this chapter are no less illuminating of the possibilities inherent in comparing and contrasting. David Sedaris amusingly considers his dull life in an American suburb compared with his partner's garishly textured life as the child of a nomadic diplomat. We've paired it with a more serious piece on growing up, "We're Not . . . ," in which student writer Andrea Roman contrasts her Bolivian heritage with her American upbringing.

Coming back to humor, Suzanne Britt's "Neat People vs. Sloppy People" is easy reading, but it makes sharp comments on human behavior. The remaining selections in this chapter are more serious though not somber. Bruce Catton's "Grant and Lee: A Study in Contrasts" remains a classic example of a method clearly serving a writer's purpose. Fatema Mernissi's "Size 6: The Western Women's Harem" uses comparison to argue that the Muslim harem has its parallels among supposedly liberated Western women. And in "Tragedy," Alain de Botton finds intriguing similarities between contemporary tabloid journalism and ancient Greek drama.

DAVID SEDARIS

Remembering My Childhood on the Continent of Africa

(p. 206)

This essay is humorist David Sedaris's account of the exotic childhood and adolescent experiences of his partner Hugh—who grew up in various African outposts as the son of a US diplomat—as contrasted with Sedaris's far more mundane youth in suburban North Carolina. The essay that follows it, Andrea Roman's "We're Not . . . ," also considers an upbringing shaped by the culture of a distant country.

Students may initially have some trouble with Sedaris's subtle irony. You could begin discussion by asking class members whether they think Sedaris truly wishes he could have traded places with Hugh, whose youth, while "fascinating" in retrospect (par. 13), was in fact marked by some pretty gruesome and dangerous events. Sedaris admits that he can't acknowledge this fact because it means "I should have been happy with what I had" (21). Instead he retreats into fantasy, safely appropriating the stories he has heard from Hugh as memories of his own.

To pursue this question further, you could divide the class into small groups and have each group analyze the essay for evidence of Sedaris's clear awareness that Hugh's childhood was "not as glamorous as it sounds" (12). In reporting back their findings to the class, each group could consider what Sedaris seems to be suggesting about his own personality.

Media resources: Sedaris's reading of *Me Talk Pretty One Day*, from which this essay comes, is available on CD and for download. Students may enjoy his distinctive delivery, familiar to anyone who has heard him on National Public Radio.

QUESTIONS ON MEANING

1. Sedaris contrasts his own "unspeakably dull" middle-class American childhood (par. 8) with the much more exotic and eventful childhood of his partner Hugh, who, as the son of a diplomat, grew up in various countries in Africa.
2. The thesis might seem to be that Sedaris's life was dull compared with Hugh's (par. 8) or that Sedaris makes up for his dull life by appropriating Hugh's (21). But hovering over all, just hinted, is the larger idea that Hugh's childhood, while much more exciting than Sedaris's and food for resentment and imagination, had terrible costs that Sedaris would not have wanted to pay.
3. Sedaris's envy is essentially ironic because many of Hugh's childhood experiences seem pretty lonely and harrowing, beginning with the field trip to the slaughterhouse. This is true even when Sedaris writes of something that one might indeed be envious of: For example, Hugh's family had servants, but they included guards with machetes (par. 11), suggesting that the family was always in danger. In paragraph 21 Sedaris notes that while he was longing for more exotic adventures as a child, Hugh ("[s]omeone unknown to me" at the time) was probably longing for something more normal.

QUESTIONS ON WRITING STRATEGY

1. Sedaris's point-by-point organization can be outlined as follows: comparison of field trips (pars. 1–7); of daily life (8); of access to popular culture, specifically movies and the circumstances of viewing them (9–10); of servants and security (11); of dangerous experiences (12–13); of meeting a celebrity (14); of Sedaris's ten-day visit with his senile grandmother and Hugh's two years living with strangers (15–19); and of vacations (20–21).
2. Transitions include "[w]hen I was in elementary school" (par. 7), "[w]hen I was seven years old" and "[w]hen he was seven years old" (8), "[u]nlike me" (10), "but" (11), and "[a]bout the same time" (16).
3. A monkey is a particularly exotic pet that many children might long to own. Hugh's monkey comes to represent for Sedaris everything that he envies about Hugh's childhood.
4. The opening conversation establishes the relationship between Sedaris and Hugh and particularly the fact that Hugh seems unfazed by his odd experiences. This opening also makes clear that Sedaris has had many such conversations with Hugh, on which he bases his knowledge of Hugh's experiences.
5. Sedaris narrates stories from his own life and from Hugh's to point out how different their experiences have been.

QUESTIONS ON LANGUAGE

1. The second and third, fourth and fifth, and sixth and seventh sentences in the paragraph are parallel in structure, which highlights the contrast that concludes each sentence. As Sedaris wittily puts it, "The verbs are the same, but [Hugh] definitely wins the prize when it comes to nouns and objects."
2. The term "petty thief" emphasizes the self-deprecating portrait that Sedaris has presented throughout. His use of Hugh's memories represents no "spiritual symbiosis" but is merely a way for Sedaris to live vicariously through the other man's experiences.
3. Almost any paragraph will provide examples of specific, concrete language. In paragraph 6 examples include "low-ceilinged concrete building," "small white piglet," "its dainty hooves clicking against the concrete floor," "class gathered in a circle," "turned from face to face," "drew a pistol from his back pocket, held it against the animal's temple, and shot the piglet, execution-style," "Blood-spattered, frightened children wept."
4. *Symbiosis*, from the Greek word for "living together," implies the intimate union of two dissimilar types.

DAVID SEDARIS ON WRITING

You might take a poll of the students in your class: How many keep a diary or a journal? And what do they make of Sedaris's sometime regret that he doesn't record enough details? Do they agree that too much note-taking gets in the way of living, or do they find as writers that it's more productive to gather as much evidence as possible from the start? Why?

ANDREA ROMAN

"We're Not ..."

(p. 215)

A natural companion piece to David Sedaris's "Remembering My Childhood on the Continent of Africa," this engaging and well-written student essay is sure to resonate with many students who have struggled to shape their own identities as well as those who may have shared Roman's frustrations with a parent's oppositions to their quest for independence. For students who are children of immigrants, the essay may be especially affecting because cultural differences often exacerbate the normal parent-child conflicts, as Roman demonstrates.

Two possible approaches to discussing this essay: Focus on how your students define *American* and the degree to which their families contribute to that definition, directly or indirectly; or focus on how differences between parents and children nourish or thwart the children. For either approach, students will be drawing on their own experiences, so small groups may encourage freer discussion than a whole-class setting. Hearing their classmates'

experiences and ideas will broaden students' own perspectives and prepare
them for work on the second, third, and fourth writing suggestions.

Media resources: Students are likely to be unfamiliar with the Bolivian
flag that Roman so proudly displays on her dorm room wall, and many will
not know where the country is located. You might wish to share an image
of the flag or a map, such as those available at *worldatlas.com/webimage/
countrys/samerica/bolivia/boflags.htm.*

QUESTIONS ON MEANING

1. Roman states her thesis in paragraph 1: "One would think that language
   would create the biggest barriers for immigrants but in my mother's
   case, the biggest obstacles were the small cultural differences." The
   last sentence of the paragraph reiterates that idea.
2. Roman's purpose is to explain the differences between her mother's
   Bolivian cultural assumptions and her own American assumptions. She
   makes it clear in her conclusion that she considers neither cultural
   heritage superior to the other: "Through my mother's multiple rules,
   I had become comfortable enough with my identity and culture that
   showing pride in another country would not take away from my heritage" (par. 27).
3. To her mother's Bolivian eye, borrowing clothing indicated to others
   that the Roman family was too poor to provide for their children. It was,
   in other words, a source of shame. She punished Roman not for the borrowing but for having the audacity to question her mother's rules, for
   "talking back."
4. Each flag—one Bolivian, one American—represents an important part
   of the author's identity.

QUESTIONS ON WRITING STRATEGY

1. Although we have included Roman's essay as a model of comparison
   and contrast, it is also an episodic narrative (see question 5 below), an
   assignment we have noticed is becoming increasingly popular in college
   writing courses. The blank spaces separate the three major episodes
   Roman recounts, breaking the essay into its parts and lending a reflective quality to her story.
2. Roman's basis of comparison, identified in her introduction, is "that
   certain unacceptable acts in [Bolivian] culture were quite acceptable
   here in the States" (par. 1). Her points of comparison focus on three of
   those acts: borrowing clothing (2–3), attending sleepover parties (4–11),
   and working on Sundays (12–24).
3. Roman is writing for her peers—other students at Boston College, specifically her hall mates who asked why she displayed a large American
   flag in her dorm room. The essay answers their question, which had become her own. To some extent, then, Roman is also writing for herself.
4. In her concluding paragraph Roman not only explains the significance
   of her thesis but circles back neatly to each of the major points in her
   essay without resorting to dull summary: "I now borrow clothes, have
   sleepovers, and do a ton of work on Sundays, but I have not left behind that little Bolivian girl who received the mouth-washing with dishwasher soap, no matter what flag hangs on my wall."

5. Dialog lends immediacy and vibrancy to each episode and expresses each participant's lack of understanding better than summary or explanation could. In Roman's case it also reveals the linguistic and cultural differences she asserts in her introduction. The conversations mingle English and Spanish for both mother and daughter.

QUESTIONS ON LANGUAGE

1. In almost every instance Roman restates the Spanish phrase in English, usually within the space of a sentence or two. There are two exceptions. The opening quotation from her mother is translated in paragraph 3 (we provide it in a gloss note as well because students may not recognize the relationship). She doesn't translate "*Te dije que no*," but most readers can figure out its meaning by context.
2. "We're not poor, Andrea. Why do you have to borrow clothes?" (par. 3); "We're not American, Andrea. Why do you want a sleepover?" (4); "We're not American, Andrea. We don't do that in Bolivia" (10). The repetition gives the essay coherence, but it also does more: In repeating her mother's continued assertion that she's not American, Roman emphasizes the cultural conflict she felt and is able to conclude with some defiance that she is, indeed, American.
3. Notice the paradox in Roman's statement that the specifics of her mother's objections "invariably changed" (par. 1): *invariable* means unchanging, constant.

ANDREA ROMAN ON WRITING

Although Andrea Roman may not have thought she's "all that interesting," we have to disagree. Her comments offer useful points about the personal benefits to be derived from writing—and from seeking and accepting feedback. Her advice to draft from the heart should prove especially useful to other students struggling with the pressures of writing for an audience. Being "true" to themselves and then letting others help refine their work can help them work through their own difficulties, as Roman illustrates.

SUZANNE BRITT
Neat People vs. Sloppy People

(p. 221)

Whatever Suzanne Britt believes, she believes wholeheartedly. Then she merrily sets out to convince her readers that she's right. A danger in teaching this essay, perhaps, is that students without Britt's skill may be inspired to emulate her slapdash unreasonableness without quite achieving the desired effect. Some students, though, just might surprise you with the delightful writing they can produce with this essay as their inspiration.

Small groups can be useful for helping students through the brainstorming part of writing an essay. Students might appreciate having time to talk about the points of comparison they have come up with in preparing to write an essay for either of our first two writing suggestions. Group members can help each other expand their lists of comparative points and find the details that will bring these points to life.

QUESTIONS ON MEANING

1. Whoever said it failed to perceive Britt's humor.
2. Britt is hardly impartial. It's easy to see that her sympathies lie with sloppy people and that she considers herself one of them. Mostly, she writes to amuse and entertain.
3. "As always" means what it says. Yes, Britt is saying—with tongue only partially in cheek—the distinctions among people are moral.

QUESTIONS ON WRITING STRATEGY

1. Britt's tone is blunt, assured, and, of course, hyperbolic. The tone is established from the start: "Neat people are lazier and meaner than sloppy people." Words and phrases that illustrate the tone abound throughout the essay.
2. Britt finds no similarities at all between the two. Had she mentioned any, her essay would be less exaggerated and would therefore lose some of its force. Writers who aren't exaggerating might give short shrift to similarities, too, if they are obvious or irrelevant.
3. These broad statements are generalizations because they make conclusive assertions on the basis of some evidence—although, of course, Britt is deliberately exaggerating whatever evidence she has. By using so many generalizations, Britt compounds the outrageous nature of her essay. Her humor derives from her being unfair to neat people and finding no fault at all with their opposites.
4. Britt constantly clarifies her subjects by repeating *sloppy people* and *neat people*.
5. The examples do specify the kinds of behavior Britt has in mind, but they are themselves generalizations about the two kinds of people. They illustrate behavior but not particular persons.

QUESTIONS ON LANGUAGE

1. *The American Heritage Dictionary* tells us that *métier* is a word that began as the Latin *ministerium* ("occupation") and then became the Vulgar Latin *misterium* and the Old French *mestier* before assuming its present spelling and meaning ("specialty") in modern French and English.
2. The word is not to be understood literally, but humorously, as are *rectitude, stupendous* (par. 2), *excavation* (5), and *vicious* (9). Students may argue for one or two others that they perceive are not to be taken literally.

SUZANNE BRITT ON WRITING

Suzanne Britt's comments on writing, written for *The Bedford Reader*, are artfully crafted and could easily stand alone as an essay in themselves. Though she regards writing with humor and zest and doesn't take it in grim earnest, clearly she deeply cares about it. Notice, for instance, her many figures of speech: The first paragraph yields at least two metaphors ("you have to suck out all the marrow of whatever you do" and "My answer is rock bottom and hard") and a simile ("silence falls like prayers across the room"). More colorful still are the similes two paragraphs later, in which the student is advised to gather "your life around you as a mother hen gathers her brood, as a queen settles the folds in her purple robes." There's hyperbole, too, in the next paragraph: "an interminable afternoon in a biology lab." In the end, Britt equates writing with an act of faith.

BRUCE CATTON

Grant and Lee: A Study in Contrasts

(p. 227)

If ever that weary term *classic* applied to an essay, this is it. Where can you find a neater illustration of comparison and contrast? First Catton contrasts the two generals, then he compares them—gracefully moving from broad generalizations to specific evidence. Introducing the essay, you might remind students that they know a good deal about Grant and Lee already (or reveal that they need more knowledge). If your campus is far from Virginia, you may wish to acquaint the class with the connotations of *tidewater Virginia* (old family name, wealth, landowning, patrician). (See the third question on language.) A small group of students could research Virginia, the generals, and the Civil War and present their findings as a counterpoint to Catton's observations. (Note: If this sort of research is something you'd like to have students do fairly regularly, you might consider rotating the responsibility so that just one group works and reports on any given essay.)

Media resources: Ken Burns's documentary series *The Civil War* features a comparison of Grant and Lee in episode 6, "Valley of the Shadow of Death." The video can be viewed on *PBS.org* or streamed through *Netflix.*

QUESTIONS ON MEANING

1. Catton's central purpose is to explain how Grant and Lee stood for opposing social forces. Though he remarks in paragraph 13 that the two generals differed in personality, he doesn't expand on this observation. The qualities he cites (daring, resourcefulness, and so on) seem traits not of personality but of character.
2. Lee, an aristocrat from tidewater Virginia, believed in a leisure class of landowners responsible to their community and obliged to be models of strength and virtue. Grant, son of a frontier tanner, held with self-reliance, competition, and a society in which the most resourceful will rise. Lee's first loyalty was to his native soil; Grant's was to the nation. Lee's commitment was to the agrarian society of the past; Grant's, to an urban industrial future.

3. Both had "utter tenacity and fidelity," "daring and resourcefulness." Most important, both possessed the ability to turn quickly from war to peace. They made possible a reconciliation of North and South, for which all later Americans are indebted to them.

4. Each by nature was a warrior of "utter tenacity and fidelity" (par. 14), who fought for the ideals of his people (10–11).

QUESTIONS ON WRITING STRATEGY

1. *The American Story* is a collection addressed to general readers with a special interest in American history. Catton doesn't assume a profound knowledge of the Civil War on their part, but he does assume that the campaigns of Petersburg, Second Manassas, Chancellorsville, and Vicksburg (in pars. 14–15) will be at least somewhat familiar to his readers.

2. Catton rounds out his essay by so doing; he stresses his point (made in his opening paragraph) that at Appomattox "a great new chapter" in American life began.

3. By arranging the essay to show that Grant and Lee, despite their profound differences of background and outlook, agreed on one essential, Catton saves his most important point for last. This structure makes the point more effectively than if Catton had begun by asserting that Grant and Lee were much alike and had then spent the body of his essay differentiating between them. Important points often stand out more when the reader is left with them.

4. Nearly every paragraph begins with a sentence containing some transition: sometimes no more than a word or phrase, such as "these men," "they," "each man," referring back to both Grant and Lee. Some transitions are explicitly comparative, such as "on the other hand" (par. 11). The most crucial sentence of transition is the one that opens paragraph 13: "Yet it was not all contrast, after all"—announcing the start of Catton's comparison.

5. The tone is sympathetic, admiring, and respectful. By imagining Lee with lance and banner, Catton hints that he finds the general's chivalric ideals a bit preposterous. But he is referring back to the point he makes in paragraph 5: Lee's way of life descended from "the age of knighthood." That he thinks its values outdated doesn't mean he finds them silly nor that he mocks Lee for being their representative.

6. The classification broadens the significance of the comparison from two generals to the whole population. The analysis provides Catton with his points of comparison, his differences and similarities.

QUESTIONS ON LANGUAGE

1. Like most figures of speech, Catton's add vigor and concreteness to his prose. They include the metaphor of "two conflicting currents" (par. 3); the metaphor of an age "transplanted" (5); the metaphor of the "past that had settled into grooves" (8); the metaphors of the nation's expanding horizons and of the "dollars-and-cents stake" (9); the metaphor of Grant's seeing the Union as the ground under his feet (11); the personification of Grant as "the modern man emerging," the metaphor of the stage, and that of Lee as a knight with banner and lance (12); the metaphor of Grant and Lee as two battered boxers, each able to "remain on his feet and lift his two fists" (14).

2. *Poignant*, from the French verb *poindre* ("to sting"), means "sharply painful to the feelings; piercing or wounding." Clearly it is a stronger and more energetic word here than *touching, sad,* or *teary.* You might care to remind students (if you aren't tired of it) of Twain's remark about the right word being the lightning; the almost right word, the lightning bug.

3. Eastern Virginia's tidewater region, the low-lying coastal plain bisected by Chesapeake Bay, is so named because tidal water flows up its bays, inlets, and rivers. It is the area of the oldest colonial settlements (including Jamestown, Yorktown, and Williamsburg), where large plantations were established.

4. *Aristocratic* refers to a privileged class responsible for the well-being of the people it served as leaders.

5. Context will supply these meanings almost as well as a dictionary. This might be an opportune moment to point out that you don't expect students to interrupt their reading of an essay fourteen times to rummage through a dictionary. They usually can figure out the sense of words they don't know if they pay attention to other words in the neighborhood. Those they can't figure out they can circle and save up for a one-time trip to the dictionary.

FATEMA MERNISSI

Size 6: The Western Women's Harem

(p. 233)

Mernissi, a Moroccan intellectual, comes to a rather startling conclusion in this essay. Discovering that she is overweight by American standards, she suggests that the invisibility imposed on women in Muslim cultures—being housebound in harems and completely veiled in public—has its counterpart in Western norms of female attractiveness: Western women who don't conform to an ideal of youthful beauty are ignored and devalued.

If your classes are ethnically diverse, you could have students discuss how standards of attractiveness differ among cultures, not only internationally but within the United States as well.

Media resources: Encourage students to discuss the extent to which the "norm is everywhere," as the saleswoman encountered by Mernissi says in paragraph 9. How often do TV shows, movies, or fashion or cosmetics ads feature obviously mature or heavyset women? What examples can they think of?

QUESTIONS ON MEANING

1. Mernissi compares attitudes toward women in Western and Muslim cultures. She first states her thesis in paragraph 1 ("That distressing experience made me realize how the image of beauty in the West can hurt and humiliate a woman as much as the veil does when enforced by the state police in extremist nations such as Iran, Afghanistan, or Saudi

Arabia"). She repeats it in paragraph 13 ("I realized for the first time that maybe 'size 6' is a more violent restriction imposed on women than is the Muslim veil"), elaborates on it in paragraph 14 ("Unlike the Muslim man, who uses space to establish male domination by excluding women from the public arena, the Western man manipulates time and light. He declares that in order to be beautiful, a woman must look fourteen years old"), repeats it in paragraph 15 ("This Western time-defined veil is even crazier than the space-defined one enforced by the ayatollahs"), and again elaborates on it in paragraph 17 ("Framing youth as beauty and condemning maturity is the weapon used against women in the West just as limiting access to public space is the weapon used in the East"). For Mernissi the objective is the same in both situations: "to make women feel unwelcome, inadequate, and ugly" (par. 17).

2. The saleswoman is initially superior and condescending. She later takes an interest in Mernissi's life and finally seems almost envious of a culture where size 6 is not the norm. Her change in attitude suggests the tyranny of size 6 for Western women.

3. Western attitudes are "more dangerous and cunning" because aging is inevitable ("that normal unfolding of the years," par. 15) and the Western stricture is "masked as an aesthetic choice" rather than "attacked directly" (16).

QUESTIONS ON WRITING STRATEGY

1. In paragraphs 6–7 Mernissi depicts herself as self-confident, impervious to attitudes about the way she looks within her own culture. It is only within Western culture that she feels humiliated by her physical attributes.

2. In paragraph 16 Mernissi first compares the Chinese custom of foot binding with the expectation that she shrink her hips (the transition here is "Similarly"). She then compares the month of fasting for the Muslim holy time of Ramadan with the perpetual dieting of the Western woman ("but").

3. The narrative (pars. 1–5, 8–13) draws readers into Mernissi's complex comparison and confronts them, as she was confronted, with the physical ideal imposed on Western women. She may have considered, too, that many of her readers might have had similarly humiliating experiences shopping for clothes.

QUESTIONS ON LANGUAGE

1. *Deviant* suggests not just a differing from the norm but also shamefulness, even immorality.

2. The veil is figurative in Western cultures, "wrapping [mature women] in shrouds of ugliness." In Muslim cultures, of course, it is literal, masking women in public.

3. Students may be unfamiliar with the sense of *generous* to mean "amply proportioned." Note that in context the word also has positive connotations.

ALAIN DE BOTTON
Tragedy

(p. 240)

As a populizer of philosophy and a generalist, Alain de Botton is some-times accused of oversimplifying his subjects, dumbing them down for a nonspecialist audience. But he is just as often praised for making complex ideas accessible and applying insights in fresh ways. Such is certainly the case with this selection from *The News: A User's Manual.* Comparing mod-ern tabloid news to classical Greek drama, the author surprises us with the notion that they both serve the same civilizing function: to encourage audi-ences to reflect on their own violent impulses and, one hopes, to squelch them. His analogy is sophisticated, to be sure, but it is quite effective.

The essay also gives an opportunity to talk to students about control: What parts of their lives do they have direct control over? What lies beyond their control? What can they gain from the latter? What do they lose?

Media resources: A screening of all or parts of any of the plays de Botton cites in his essay—*Oedipus Rex, Iphigenia, Medea*—could prove instruc-tive to students, who may not be familiar with classical drama; professional productions for all three are easily found online. Students interested in de Botton's School of Life project might be directed to the educational videos hosted at *youtube.com/theschooloflifetv.* The author has also given two TED talks, "A Kinder, Gentler Philosophy of Success" and "Atheism 2.0," both available to watch at *ted.com/speakers/alain_de_botton.*

QUESTIONS ON MEANING

1. As with everything he does (and as we stress in the headnotes), de Botton's purpose mixes self-help and critical analysis. In evaluating tabloid news stories and finding that they come up short of their potential to civilize readers, he means to help his readers become critical consumers of newspapers and broadcast journalism and at the same to open their eyes to their own vulnerabilities as human beings and "learn from the experiences . . . of those whose behavior should profoundly scare, horrify and warn us" (par. 25).

2. As a trained philosopher, de Botton clearly has an appreciation for clas-sic Greek dramas and for Aristotle's notion that gruesome stories, told well, "function as civilizing forces" (par. 9). Although he asserts that the ancient plays accomplished that task more successfully, de Botton be-lieves that contemporary news holds the potential to do the same—but only if we "tweak how they are reported" (7). His depictions of both genres are necessarily subjective, focusing on empathy for the charac-ters portrayed and the emotions such portrayals bring forth for their audiences.

3. The author states his thesis at the end of his introduction: "Rather than just inveigh moralistically against our fascination with heinous events, the challenge should be to tweak how they are reported—in order that

they better release their important, yet too often latent, emotional and societal benefits" (par. 7). The basis for comparing news and Greek tragedy is the "civilizing" function de Botton finds in each genre.

4. Both genres, de Botton informs us, tell stories of lives gone horribly wrong in an instant. But the Greek playwrights put those stories in context and stressed to their audiences that similar fates could easily befall them, thereby leading to empathy and personal growth, while modern reporters rush through the graphic details and treat their subjects as isolated cases, missing the opportunity for readers and viewers to reflect. He'd like to see the news give more space to context and implications when telling such stories, elevating them from voyeuristic "*horror*" to instructive "*tragedy*" (par. 10).

5. De Botton seems to assume a somewhat sophisticated audience that will understand his allusions, although he does offer just enough summary and comment in each case to explain their significance. Readers familiar with the works he cites, however, will likely appreciate his points even more.

QUESTIONS ON WRITING STRATEGY

1. A subject-by-subject organization would have undermined de Botton's examples, which depend on the interplay of fact and fiction to make his point.

2. He puts extra space between paragraphs.

3. The visuals and their captions underscore de Botton's point, in paragraph 8, that classic Greek dramas had plot lines remarkably similar to the stories reported in today's news. The still image from a 2012 BBC news report shows a man crashing into his own house "to punish his wife"; the Greek vase shows Medea stabbing her own child "to punish her husband." In both cases, de Botton suggests in his caption, the stories reveal that "[o]ur fascination with crimes may be part of an unconscious effort to make sure we never commit them."

4. As de Botton explains it, Aristotle's elements of tragedy require a carefully laid out plot, close examination of the characters' "motives and personalities" (par. 10), and skill in bringing the audience to the "terrifying conclusion" that given the right circumstances, they might unwittingly commit similar atrocities themselves. While horror is mere spectacle, tragedy teaches by "demonstrat[ing] the ease with which an essentially decent and likeable person could end up generating hell" (10).

QUESTIONS ON LANGUAGE

1. A *crucible* is a furnace pot; it seems likely that in using the word de Botton is also alluding to Arthur Miller's 1953 play about the Salem witch trials.

2. The images, of a man's body splattered on a sidewalk, of dead children, of rape, of beheadings, and so on, are meant to shock readers and grab their attention, certainly, but also to depict in no uncertain terms the nature of the stories (both modern and classical) de Botton intends to investigate. We are drawn to such images, de Botton says, not only because they're "tasteless" and "prurient" but also because they "get at something important" on a subconscious level (par. 5).

3. He quotes the news stories because the passages are essential to his analysis of their content and their failings. Quoting from the plays (in translation, of course) would have distracted from his purpose.

4. The author combines formal, academic vocabulary with casual words and phrases. The mixture of objective, almost scholarly language—such as "the most appalling eventualities that can befall our species" (par. 1) and "inveigh moralistically against our fascination with heinous events" (7)—with lively (if macabre) terms such as "blood-soaked narratives" (5), "tweak" (7), "dismissed as nothing but a maniac" (10), and "never actually fling our children off a bridge" (12) shows that de Botton is knowledgeable about his subject but not stiff or impersonal; it helps him to connect with his readers.

ALAIN DE BOTTON ON WRITING

Delivered off the cuff, this comparison of writing and building is both clever and illuminating. Students could have fun elaborating on the similarities between the processes. Some, for instance, might comment that a thesis is like a foundation; others might invoke vocabulary as building blocks or grammar as framing. Encourage them to be creative. To go in another direction, you might ask students to invent their own analogies that compare writing with other kinds of creative projects, perhaps cooking, painting, film-making, or something else entirely.

7
PROCESS ANALYSIS
Explaining Step by Step

This chapter provides a good sampling of process analyses, ranging from the paired directions in Anne Lamott's "The Crummy First Draft" and Koji Frahm's "How to Write an *A* Paper" (albeit directions that are not to be followed) to the informative analyses in Dan Koeppel's "Taking a Fall" and Jessica Mitford's "Behind the Formaldehyde Curtain." Mixing both types is Firoozeh Dumas's personal reflection in "Sweet, Sour, and Resentful," which treats processes of food preparation for houseguests.

Incidentally, the opening of this chapter explains the *analysis* part of process analysis. We continue to introduce process analysis *before* analysis (Chap. 8) because we expect that many students find the former easier to understand. Process analysis thus becomes a way into analysis. But if you'd rather cover analysis itself first, nothing in the text discussion or essays will impede you.

ANNE LAMOTT

The Crummy First Draft

(p. 262)

This piece comes from Lamott's popular writing guide, *Bird by Bird*, where it was originally titled "Shitty First Drafts." The toned-down title reduces the risk of offending some readers and, worse, distracting them from Lamott's immensely valuable advice. The change does nothing to diminish Lamott's description of that all-too-familiar feeling of helplessness and despair that we call writer's block—or the author's ingenious remedy.

Lamott's piece is sure to find a sympathetic audience among students, many of whom probably face a similar predicament on a weekly basis. Her advice on how to salvage the situation will certainly promote class discussion and may even lead to those breakthroughs that all writers yearn for.

We pair this essay with the work of another humorist, student writer Koji Frahm, because both "The Crummy First Draft" and "How to Write an *A* Paper" touch on the frustrations and rewards of the writing process in telling and insightful ways without prescribing strict rules or condescending to students.

Media resources: Lamott keeps up a very active and humorous *Twitter* feed, which students might find entertaining. She talks more about her writing process in an interview for *The Big Think*; the video is at *bigthink.com/videos/on-being-a-tough-writer*.

QUESTIONS ON MEANING

1. Lamott's thesis appears in paragraph 8: "Almost all good writing begins with terrible first drafts. You need to start somewhere." In other words, once you get over the "crummy first draft," your writing will only get better.
2. People can be inspiring or encouraging (Lamott's friends offer words of support in pars. 4 and 8), but they are obstacles when a writer imagines them judging his or her work (2, 4, 9, 10). Some of these obstacles are imaginary ("the vinegar-lipped Reader Lady" and the "emaciated German male," 9), while some are more real ("high-maintenance parental units" and "contractors, lawyers, colleagues, children," 10).
3. The focus shifts from expressing meaning to pinning it down to polishing—in the context of *The Bedford Reader*'s Chapter 2, from discovery and drafting to revising to editing. Many students will probably just be learning this approach for their own work.
4. The image of the ravenous dogs is ambiguous, and students' responses may vary. One possibility: The dogs stand for psychological demons—deep conflicts, fears, desires—that can devour a person. By quelling the demons, writing preserves sanity.
5. Lamott is a writing teacher, and *Bird by Bird* is an instruction book for writers, so the purpose of the piece is to help other, less experienced writers get over a major hurdle: producing a first draft. Revealing many of her own difficulties with writing, she grounds her advice in reality.

QUESTIONS ON WRITING STRATEGY

1. Presumably Lamott's book would appeal most to writers or would-be writers and this piece to those who face obstacles such as difficulty drafting. Many students will be reassured to learn that even a professional like Lamott can struggle to compose, and her advice ("You need to start somewhere. Start by getting something—anything—down on paper," par. 8) may be the permission they need to let go.
2. Lamott recommends writing about a topic one part at a time ("bird by bird," par. 4); writing whatever comes to mind, just "getting something—anything—down on paper" (8); and "quiet[ing] the voices [one's] head" (9) by enclosing the speakers, like mice, in a jar and turning down the volume (10). Only when the first draft is finished should one do the "up draft" (fixing the first draft) and then the "dental draft" (editing) (8).
3. Explanatory process analysis: paragraphs 3–7. Directive process analysis: 2, 8, 10. Combined types: 9. The explanatory passages show Lamott's advice to be based on extensive experience. The directive passages, with their lively examples, tell readers how to use her approach. Some students may find the shifts distracting or confusing, but the mixture seems effective overall to give a rounded, convincing analysis of process.

4. Transitions include "first" (pars. 1, 2, 3); "Then," "Even after," "Eventually," "Finally" (3); "then" (4); "by then," "eventually," "for the rest of the day" (5); "then," "one more time" (6); "The next day," "a month later" (7); "the first," "The second," "And the third" (8); "First," "And" (9); "Then" (10). The transitions help to clarify the sequence and duration of steps.

5. Lamott's story pulls the reader in and establishes rapport by revealing some of the author's own insecurities as a writer. It sets the stage for the advice on overcoming these difficulties.

QUESTIONS ON LANGUAGE

1. Other negative adjectives are "crazy" (par. 2) and "self-indulgent," "boring," "stupefying," "long," and "hideous" (3). These words reinforce the idea that a first draft is not meant to be good—just get it written, no matter how bad. Mistakes can be remedied in a second draft, which in Lamott's case "always turned out fine, sometimes even funny and weird and helpful" (6).

2. Lamott's tone is partly serious and partly humorous. She is sincere and straightforward when she advises writers struggling with writer's block to just start somewhere, "getting something—anything—down on paper" (8). Yet she lightens the tone with a good dollop of self-deprecating humor about her imaginary censoring voices and her terrible first drafts. There is a distinct strain of black humor to Lamott's writing, particularly in paragraphs 9 and 11: "there's William Burroughs, dozing off or shooting up because he finds you as bold and articulate as a houseplant"; "[a] writer friend of mine suggests opening the jar and shooting them all in the head."

3. The sentimental, weepy inner child (par. 2), the "worry settl[ing] on my chest like an x-ray apron" (3), the critics "sitting on my shoulders [. . .] pretending to snore" (4), the chattering people becoming mice in jars (10)—these and other images are all fresh and evocative. Most of these images characterize the distracting voices that block writing, and with them Lamott makes the abstract concept of inner voices both concrete and memorable.

4. *Overwrought* can mean both nervous and overdone. In the context of Lamott's anxiety over writing descriptions of food, the adjective seems especially well chosen.

KOJI FRAHM

How to Write an *A* Paper

(p. 268)

It shouldn't take most readers long to realize that Frahm's essay is a tongue-in-cheek plea for other students to take their writing assignments more seriously and to put more effort into their work. One risk in teaching this essay is that some students may nonetheless fail to catch the irony and not notice in the final paragraph that the essay's narrator receives a bad grade for following the advice Frahm offers. Though it is mainly a directive process analysis, no one is expected to follow his directions. Clearly what the author hopes is just the reverse: that readers will learn what *not* to do when they write.

Frahm's satire—giving advice precisely opposite to what he really hopes to impart—is so effective that students may find themselves inspired to imitate him. While the technique can be particularly forceful, duplicating his flippant irony and metacognitive applications will not be so simple. You can give students practice at managing the task by asking them to work in pairs or threes to write a short how-to essay of their own. Have them consider carefully *why* Frahm's essay works so well and then try their own hands at giving advice in this backward way. (You may need to remind them that they will likely be more successful if they choose a subject they know a lot about.)

Media resources: Frahm is starting to establish himself as a successful writer and artist. Students who enjoyed "How to Write an *A* Paper" might be directed to his Web site *kojifrahm.com*, where they will find additional essays, short films, sculptures, photography, and more. "Beyond the Red Ink: Teachers' Comments through Student's Eyes," a free Macmillan Learning video of college students talking about their own responses to instructor remarks on their papers, is also available at *youtube.com/watch?v=PKfLRz7h7gs* and could resonate with members of your class.

QUESTIONS ON MEANING

1. Frahm is writing primarily to entertain his readers (and himself), but he does take the subject of writing seriously, as his satire reveals. Students might notice that Frahm cleverly commits every sin of *bad* writing that he cites, from the first "short, deadly, and impossible to understand" (par. 1) sentence to the irrelevant quotation at the end. He clearly knows and cares what the elements of *good* writing are: a clear thesis (2), transitions (3), solid evidence (4), and so forth (see the "Other Methods" question under Writing Strategy for more on Frahm's analysis of good writing).
2. No. The essay is a satire, and it proposes, despite appearances, how *not* to write an *A* paper. As the poor grade that surfaces in his conclusion reveals, Frahm has been outlining in each paragraph of his essay how bad writing happens.
3. Frahm's implied thesis might be expressed as something like "Writing an *A* paper is a process of finding a thesis, introducing it clearly, supporting it with evidence, incorporating transitions and figurative language, and making your ideas easy for readers to follow." All of paragraph 2 is a satirical claim that he has no thesis and expects readers to provide it for themselves.

QUESTIONS ON WRITING STRATEGY

1. Frahm does not follow a chronological order. Writing is a recursive process, after all, as his organization suggests. He traces the process of writing a paper paragraph by paragraph and element by element, from global concerns down the small details and then back again: First the introduction ending in a thesis, or lack thereof (pars. 1–2); then the body paragraphs ("If your reader doesn't look flummoxed and bleary-eyed by paragraph 3, you aren't trying hard enough" [3]; "Paragraph four . . . is

the part of the essay where you're taught to bring out the big points" [4]); followed by word choice and figurative language (5–6), proofreading (7, 10), and the conclusion (8–9). The essay then concludes with Frahm's surprise, in the form of a narrative, that his process results in a "bad grade" (12).

2. "Convoluted is the term to use here" (par. 1); "Confusion is the key term here" (3); "Reiteration is the key term here" (4); "Regurgitation is the key term here" (4); "Obfuscate is the key term here" (5); "Diabolical is the key term here" (7); "Confidence is the key term here" (11). These short summaries of his points serve as Frahm's topic sentences. In addition, their parallel structure, along with the author's repetition and restatement of "key terms" (twice in par. 4) focus readers on his subject and the connections among his points.

3. On the surface Frahm appears rather hostile to readers, teachers especially. But in satirically and repeatedly insisting that the writer is smarter than his readers and that the goal of writing is to confuse them, he implies that awareness of and respect for a particular audience are in fact key elements of effective writing.

4. Other typographical errors (an errant semicolon, the repetition of "for for," and "by accident" mistyped as "my accident") are all contained within paragraph 7, where Frahm explains the reason for their inclusion: They're red herrings. By deliberately inserting a few errors and claiming they occurred during a printing malfunction, a writer can supposedly get away with not proofreading.

5. The elements of good writing, as Frahm satirically outlines them, are precisely what we outline in Chapter 2 of *The Bedford Reader*: a clear introduction ending with a thesis (pars. 1–2), unity and coherence in the body paragraphs (3), ample evidence (4), effective word choice (5–6), editing and proofreading (7), and a solid conclusion (8–9).

QUESTIONS ON LANGUAGE

1. All of Frahm's sentences are dripping with irony. Typically, satire depends on such irony to attack its subject.

2. "How to Write an *A* Paper" is a directive process analysis, so Frahm appropriately uses *you* (directly or understood) as the subject of his sentences.

3. No. Frahm makes it clear to readers that he intends for the words to be incomprehensible for readers, and he deliberately misuses many of them, claiming that it doesn't matter "if the definitions [of synonyms] aren't totally the same" (par. 5).

4. Frahm seems to be a master at metaphor and simile. Just a few of the many examples from the essay include "Be as opaque as a dense fog settling in front of a concrete wall" (par. 1); "they'll assume the thesis is lurking around somewhere later in the paper like a prowling hyena in Serengeti" (2); "Jump around like a rabbit on fire" (3); "Toss your reader around like a paper bag in a tempest" (3); "Be the jammed cassette deck on repeat" (4); "Vomit your words out and then eat them back up" (4); "You're the mother eagle, and the reader is your starving chick" (4); "If you're the matador, the thesaurus is your cape" (5); "Your computer . . . was jumping off the walls and banging into the ceiling like a rubber ball fired out of a Civil War cannon" (7); "you should be closing in like a school of piranha onto a drowning ox" (8). He claims the purpose of figurative language is mere "distraction" (par. 6); we hope students will disagree.

Koji Frahm on Writing

Frahm makes a good point that the success of an essay lies in the effect it has on readers. Students who insist they don't have anything to write about might be reminded that many of the best efforts revolve around having fun with a subject. Whether they realize it or not, readers can be captivated by voice and style more than by subject matter.

FIROOZEH DUMAS
Sweet, Sour, and Resentful

(p. 275)

Popular humorist Firoozeh Dumas has made it her mission to humanize Iranian people in the American consciousness, a mission that seems especially important in the context of political unrest and wars in the Middle East, nuclear proliferation, and terrorism.

Younger readers may not be familiar with the Iranian revolution to which Dumas refers or with the ensuing exodus of Iranian families to America and Americans' distrust of them in the 1970s and 1980s. We encourage students to research this background in the second writing suggestion, but you may also want to flesh out the basic outline provided in the gloss note on page 276: In the late 1970s fundamentalist Muslims fostered political and religious unrest in the country, culminating in a coup and the exile of American-backed Shah Reza Pahlavi. In his place revolutionaries installed Ayatollah Ruhollah Khomeini, who was determined to jettison Western influence and restructure Iranian culture and politics around strict interpretation of Islamic religious rule. In 1979, Khomeini supporters captured fifty-three Americans at the US embassy in Tehran, precipitating a hostage crisis that lasted 444 days and ended in a botched rescue attempt and embarrassment for the Carter administration; the hostages were released upon Ronald Reagan's inauguration in 1981. (During the same period Iran was attacked by Iraq, leading to a brutal war that lasted until 1988.) Backlash against Iranians in the United States—the vast majority of whom had fled the violence and repression in their country—was severe and included general hostility, physical attacks, and demands for universal deportation.

If you assign Amy Tan's "Fish Cheeks" (p. 74), another short piece about a family tradition surrounding food, you might wish to have students compare and contrast Dumas's essay with Tan's. Both writers, whose families immigrated to the United States in the wake of political unrest, explore the difficulty of keeping a tradition alive in their new country. Whereas Tan's difficulty stems from a desire to fit in with her American peers, Dumas's mother's difficulty is purely logistic. Nevertheless, the two essays make a similar point about the importance of maintaining family tradition and cultural ties. And although both writers focus on the difficulty of adjusting to American life, Dumas states her thesis explicitly while Tan leaves it up to readers to work out the significance of her story.

Media resources: Readers who like "Sweet, Sour, and Resentful" will certainly enjoy the humorous essays collected in Firoozeh Dumas's *Funny in Farsi* and *Laughing without an Accent*. Both are available as audiobooks, narrated by the author herself.

QUESTIONS ON MEANING

1. The dinners provided an opportunity to orient recent Iranian immigrants to life in California; they also allowed the hosts to share "the hospitality that Iranians so cherish" (par. 3) as well as stay connected to their roots. For both the hosts and the guests, the elaborate and traditional Persian meals helped to maintain a sense of community; they also served as a bittersweet "reminder of the life [they] had left behind" (10).

2. "As I watched my mother experience the same draining routine week after week, I decided that tradition is good only if it brings joy to all involved. . . . Sometimes, even our most cherished beliefs must evolve" (par. 12).

3. Dumas wants to share a belief that she developed as a witness to her mother's exhaustion and resentment—the importance of adapting tradition and beliefs when circumstances demand it. To some extent, she is also relating the impetus behind her own assimilation into American culture.

4. Dumas suggests potluck, or requiring guests to contribute to the meals by bringing food with them. Based on the way Dumas characterizes her (traditional, diplomatic, judgmental of inadequate or lazy cooks, perfectionist, and controlling), we doubt her mother would have relinquished the role of hostess, no matter how much it strained her. However, Dumas does relate the process in the past tense, so it's possible that her mother did, indeed, scale back her efforts—or that the number of guests dwindled after the first wave of Iranian immigration in the late 1970s and early 1980s.

QUESTIONS ON WRITING STRATEGY

1. The introductory paragraphs establish the context behind the elaborate weekly meals: The guests who came to the author's parents' condo every weekend were reluctant immigrants, possibly even refugees, displaced from their "real home" (par. 1) by war. At the same time, the introduction indicates the parallels between Iranian culture and American culture to help make Iranians seem less "foreign" to readers—one of Dumas's overriding goals as a writer.

2. "Sweet, Sour, and Resentful" was, as the introduction to the essay indicates, first published in the now-defunct *Gourmet*, an upscale magazine for "foodies" (par. 5) that often featured complicated recipes and travel essays. Dumas could reasonably assume, then, that her readers held a strong interest in food and culture. Most readers of the magazine would have had some experience preparing elaborate dishes, hunting down elusive ingredients, and hosting large gatherings, so it's likely they could empathize with the difficulties and stresses the author's mother endured—if not, perhaps, her resentment.

3. Although Dumas identifies the "first step" as "preparing the herbs" (par. 6), the process actually began with her father taking phone calls and extending invitations to near strangers. Next came menu planning

(on Mondays) and softening the neighbors with gifts of food (par. 4), followed by Tuesday shopping trips that usually ended in frustration. With all ingredients corralled, by midweek the author's parents began the simultaneous tasks of chopping by hand and frying herbs and onions (6); mixing, cooking, and rolling the contents of stuffed grape leaves (7); and preparing homemade yogurt and other side dishes (8). The guests would arrive on the weekends, at which time Dumas's mother cooked and drained the rice. The meals would then be served "buffet-style" (10) and consumed in a matter of minutes (11). The final step was "fielding thank-you phone calls from . . . guests" (12) and extending more invitations. With several overlapping stages occurring over the course of a week, Dumas ensures coherence by providing clear time-markers and transitions throughout her analysis, then circling back to the first stage in her conclusion, implying that the process never ended.

4. By comparing bucolic local market days in Abadan with frustrating car-dependent shopping trips in California, Dumas harkens back to her introduction and underscores her point that adjusting to life in the United States was challenging and unpleasant for Iranian immigrants. At the same time, she emphasizes how much additional trouble her mother went to in order to give her guests a taste of home.

QUESTIONS ON LANGUAGE

1. Characteristically, Dumas's ironic tone in this essay borders on sarcasm but is nonetheless good-natured and appreciative. She tempers the implied criticism of her parents' and guests' behavior with several self-deprecating remarks, which is where most of her humor lies. You might ask students how the writer's attitude toward her parents would have come across without the mocking comments about her own abilities.

2. Dumas provides the Persian names for most of the dishes her mother prepared and served to guests every week. In doing so, she emphasizes the sense of home those meals provided for both her family and their guests. She ensures that American readers will understand the meaning by renaming each dish in an appositive phrase, such as "*fesenjan*, pomegranate stew with ground walnuts" (par. 4) or "*qormeh sabzi*, herb stew" (6).

3. In its literal sense a "litmus test" is a chemical process that measures the pH level of a substance to determine where it falls within a range from base to acid; colloquially, the phrase refers to a basis for making a judgment. Dumas uses the term in its colloquial meaning, but we like the echo of "sweet" (base) and "sour" (acidic) with the title and the concept's effectiveness in evoking her mother's bitterness about performing her tasks.

4. *Locavore*—a combination of *local* and the Latin *vorare*, "to eat"—is a recent coinage and does not appear in all dictionaries. The word refers to a politically and environmentally motivated movement advocating a preference for organic, local foods, rather than those that have been processed or shipped long distances.

FIROOZEH DUMAS ON WRITING

Many students may identify with Dumas's childhood memory of soaking up observations in a room full of adults. Fewer will relate to her experience of feeling almost intoxicated with the inspiration to write them down. One way to simulate the experience is to have students write for ten minutes from observation or from a prompt. Try having them write about their favorite Halloween costume or the first time they can remember feeling guilty. The only rule is to keep the pencil moving (or the fingers typing) until you call time.

DAN KOEPPEL
Taking a Fall

(p. 281)

Students should enjoy Koeppel's highly entertaining romp into survival strategies for those unlucky enough to fall from an airplane unexpectedly. In just a few pages the author traces the physical and biological processes of free-fall, at the same time providing details from physics and aviation history and showing what research has taught us about statistical probabilities. It sounds unreadable, but Koeppel pulls it off wonderfully. In his hands what could be dry, impenetrable science turns amusing and informative, even life saving.

At the same time, Koeppel offers glorious proof that researched writing need not be dull or mechanical (we encourage students to analyze his use of sources in the third writing topic). Drawing on sources both popular (*Mythbusters*, even!) and scholarly, his essay is a model of synthesis. Koeppel paraphrases and summarizes materials in such a way that anybody can follow their ideas and quotes only the most delectable language. At no point does he lose his delightfully insouciant voice.

In case some of your students resist science writing, even comical science writing, you might start off by dividing the class into small groups to work on the first and third questions on meaning. When they see clearly *why* Koeppel goes the trouble of explaining the intricacies of terminal velocity, students will be able to relax and enjoy the ride.

Media resources: Many of the works Koeppel draws on for this essay—including *The Free Fall Research Page*, *Mythbusters* (Episode 69), and "Study of Impact Tolerance through Free-Fall Investigations"—are freely available online. Students might be encouraged to check his research for themselves, evaluating Koeppel's sources and drawing their own conclusions about his subject and technique.

QUESTIONS ON MEANING

1. Koeppel writes to explain and to entertain. His use of the second person for an informative process analysis is unusual, but by addressing readers directly he engages them in a process that might otherwise come across as theoretical and dry. He doesn't expect that readers will actually need to use the information, as he makes clear in his thesis and in the middle of the essay: "Granted, the odds of surviving a six-mile

plummet are extraordinarily slim, but at this point you've got nothing to lose by understanding your situation" (par. 5); "here's some supplemental information, though be warned that none of it will help you at this point" (17).

2. A "wreckage rider" is somebody whose fall is cushioned and slowed by virtue of "being attached to a chunk of the plane" (par. 5). Such crash victims have a higher chance of survival.

3. As Koeppel explains it, *terminal velocity* is the point at which a faller reaches the highest speed of descent. (The word *terminal*, in this case, refers to a limit rather than an end.) If a person hits that limit while still falling, the possibility of slowing ("drag") and reducing the intensity of impact comes into play. This is why, Koeppel says, a person is more likely to survive a fall from an airplane than a fall from, say, a tall building.

4. Judging by the time-markers in the essay's headings, the fall Koeppel analyzes takes three minutes and twenty-five seconds—almost as much time as he estimates it should take a person to read the essay (pars. 8, 17). (Note that a few minutes might be enough for a first quick read, but we would argue that students should take significantly more time to fully digest his work.) The connection helps make it clear just how long three and a half minutes actually is while also stressing to readers that Koeppel is unfolding events in (almost) real time.

5. Koeppel's straightforward thesis appears in paragraph 5: "Granted, the odds of surviving a six-mile plummet are extraordinarily slim, but at this point you've got nothing to lose by understanding your situation." One might say that his point is to have fun with some useless information.

QUESTIONS ON WRITING STRATEGY

1. Koeppel opens and closes his essay by having readers imagine themselves sleeping on an airplane. By putting them in the situation he means to explore, he makes a potentially abstract concept concrete and understandable. At the same time, the framing device reassures readers that the rare horrors he examines were nothing but a dream.

2. The headings break the process into its stages, both in terms of time and height.

3. Koeppel's analysis of what a person endures in a six-mile fall shows that he assumes a general audience. He explains the process carefully and with no small amount of cheek, using simple language and humor to convey complicated scientific concepts. He defines certain physics terms, such as *terminal velocity* (par. 7), and he draws comparisons to sports, such as martial arts (13) and cliff diving (15), to help clarify his points. He does assume, however, that his audience is well educated and somewhat knowledgeable about science, using terms such as *hypoxia* (4), *friction* (12), *cranial* (16), *tonus* (19), and *subcutaneous* (19) without defining them.

4. Koeppel cites eight examples of people who have survived falls from airplanes: Vesna Vulovic (pars. 5, 18), Alan Magee (6, 11), an unnamed sky diver (11), Yasuhiro Kubo (14), Mohammed el-Fateh Osman (18), Bahia Bakari (18), Nicholas Alkemade (20), and Juliane Koepcke (21–23). Ranging in detail from quick mention to extended consideration, the examples prove his claim that survival is possible and help him to illustrate each of his recommended moves; they're also quite gripping and morbidly entertaining.

QUESTIONS ON LANGUAGE

1. The connotations of *banzai* for most readers will bring up images of reckless attack, as Koeppel intends. Students may enjoy learning that according to *The American Heritage Dictionary*, the Japanese battle cry translates into "(may you live) ten thousand years!"—a nice touch of irony, we think.
2. Koeppel deftly overshadows formal, scientific language and technical terms with giddily colloquial expressions, conversational sentence structures, and black humor. Taken together, the writer's language choices clearly communicate the details of a complicated scientific process while making that process surprisingly entertaining and easily understandable, even for general readers with no background in science.
3. The allusion is to acrobatics, which Koeppel first brings up as good training for fall survival in paragraph 13. In gymnastics (and also in figure skating) "sticking the landing" means completing a jump gracefully, without wobbling or falling down.
4. Although Koeppel uses a few figures of speech, such as the metaphor "a semiprotective cocoon of debris" (par. 6) and the simile "[h]itting the ocean is essentially the same as colliding with a sidewalk" (11), he relies much more heavily on literal images which are no less vivid (although admittedly gruesome) for being real. Some of our favorites include Vesna Vulovic "wedged between her seat, a catering trolley, a section of aircraft, and the body of another crew member, landing on—then sliding down—a snowy incline" (5); "Magee's landing on the stone floor of that French train station . . . softened by the skylight he crashed through" (11); the "mucky, plant-covered surface" of swamps (11); the clear description of the classic sky diver pose (12); and Juliane Koepcke waking "on the jungle floor, strapped into her seat, surrounded by fallen holiday gifts" (21).

JESSICA MITFORD

Behind the Formaldehyde Curtain

(p. 288)

For that soporific class that sits and looks at you, here is a likely rouser. If Mitford can't get any response out of them, they're in a league with her Mr. Jones, and you might as well devote the rest of the course to silent study periods. Sometimes, it is true, a class confronted with this essay will just sit there like people in whose midst a large firecracker has been hurled, watching it sputter. Give them time to respond with five or ten minutes to freewrite about whatever Mitford's essay first inspires them to say. Then have them trade papers in groups of three or four, read the papers, and discuss their responses with each other. You can turn these smaller group discussions into a whole-class conversation whenever it seems appropriate.

Teaching Mitford's essay invites one possible danger: that someone in the class, having recently experienced the death of a loved one, will find

Mitford's macabre humor cruel and offensive. We once received a painful letter from a student in Wenatchee, Washington, who complained bitterly about this "hideous" essay. "My husband was crushed in a logging accident," she wrote. "If Mitford also learned a little about grief, she would know that those people who view a body have an easier time with grief than those who don't. She wouldn't hate funeral directors. I guess Mitford would have had me view my husband's mangled body, but I'm glad the funeral director prepared his body for viewing."

How can you answer such a protest? Before assigning this essay for reading, you might ask the class whether anyone present has suffered a death in the family. At least warn students what to expect. Anyone recently bereaved might be given the option of skipping both Mitford's essay and the class discussion. If a student in mourning reads Mitford's essay anyway and protests its seeming callousness, you might see whether that student feels impelled to write a personal response to Mitford and her essay—as our correspondent did so effectively. The first and fourth writing suggestions may be helpful.

Media resources: The painstaking legwork that Mitford did before she wrote *The American Way of Death* is documented in *Poison Penmanship: The Gentle Art of Muckraking* (1979). Much of her information came from professional journals, such as *Casket & Sunnyside, Mortuary Management,* and *Concept: The Journal of Creative Ideas for Cemeteries*. While laying stress on the value of such research, Mitford adds that a muckraker profits from sheer luck. A friend happened to recall a conversation with an undertaker when she was arranging for her brother-in-law's funeral. She had insisted on the cheapest redwood coffin available, but the undertaker objected. The deceased was too tall to fit into it; a costly coffin was required. When she continued to insist, the undertaker said, "Oh, all right, we'll use the redwood, but we'll have to cut off his feet." This grim example of high-pressure sales tactics supplied Mitford's book with one of its "more shining jewels."

When Mitford first showed her analysis of the embalming process (as a manuscript chapter for *The American Way of Death*) to her British and her American publishers, "it was met with instantaneous and thunderous disapproval from the editors on both sides of the Atlantic; this chapter is too revolting—it must go, they said." She insisted on keeping it and lost the publishers. A year after Simon & Schuster brought out the book, she recalls, "those self-same embalming passages were chosen for inclusion in a college textbook on writing. Well! Of course I felt vindicated. The obvious moral is that although *some* editors can *sometimes* perform wonders in improving your work, in the last analysis your own judgment must prevail" (from *Poison Penmanship*, pp. 22–23).

QUESTIONS ON MEANING

1. In case anyone finds this essay repulsive and resents your assigning it, we suggest you begin by inviting reactions of all kinds. Let students kick the essay about, and, if they hate it, encourage them to say why. Almost certainly some will find it hilarious and will defend it as humor. Others will probably say that they didn't like it, that it's unpleasant, but that it tells truths we ought to know. You'll usually get more reactions if you are slow to advance your own. If the sense of the meeting should be vehemently against this essay, you may care to stick up for it (or you may want to skip on to the next selection in a hurry). But if, as is likely,

most students are intrigued by it, they'll indicate this by their reactions, and your ensuing class discussion can ride on this momentum.

2. She speculates that perhaps undertakers keep it secret for fear that patrons, knowing what it is, wouldn't want it done (par. 6).

3. "To make the corpse presentable for viewing in a suitably costly container" (par. 2). Most of the usual obstacles to presentability are itemized in paragraphs 14–18: the effects of mutilation, emaciation, and disease.

4. If the subject was not dead, the undertaker will have killed him.

5. Her purpose is to attack the custom of embalming (and to chide the society that permits it). Mitford finds Americans "docile" and "ignorant" in tolerating such a procedure (par. 4). From her concluding paragraphs (23–27), we infer that she would urge Americans not to embalm, to admit the fact of death, and to bury the dead in closed coffins, as is done in much of the rest of the Western world.

QUESTIONS ON WRITING STRATEGY

1. Mitford's tone is cheerful scorn. Her verbs for the treatments inflicted on the corpse—"sprayed," "sliced," "pierced," "pickled," and so on—clearly show that she regards the process as ridiculous. The ironic phrase "suitably costly container" strongly hints that she regards morticians as racketeers.

2. She is determined to show that if we knew what embalming and restoration entailed—its every detail—we wouldn't stand for it.

3. The body becomes a character in her drama—whether it is that of an adult or a child.

4. Mitford's opening sentence indicates the start of a time sequence, and students should easily be able to find the ensuing time-markers. Her favorites are the small words "next" and "now," and most of the paragraphs about Mr. Jones contain one or the other.

5. Her audience is American general readers, whom she distinguishes from "funeral men" in paragraph 6.

6. The quotation in paragraph 3 suggests that embalming (and all it entails) may be illegal; the one in paragraph 10 suggests that dolling up the corpse is more important to the mortician than possibly saving a life. Mr. Kriege (quoted in par. 22) makes the undertaker sound like a funeral football coach, in whose hands the corpse is a helpless ball. In offering these quotations, Mitford hangs the ethics and professional behavior of morticians by their own words and once more questions the desirability of embalming.

7. Mitford's passive verbs are to us very effective. They keep the focus on the grisly process, and they undermine her target actors, funeral directors.

8. The groups are "surgery" tools, tissue chemicals, restorative cosmetics and plasters, and props and stabilizers. The groups make the catalog of equipment and supplies more intelligible and reinforce Mitford's point about the pretentions and absurdities of the process.

QUESTIONS ON LANGUAGE

1. By alluding to the Prince of Denmark's speech with skull in hand (*Hamlet* 5.1), Mitford suggests that perhaps Yorick's "counterpart of today" is another luckless jester or clown. This theatrical allusion also enforces her metaphor of the drama that begins and the curtain that must be lifted.

2. Mitford delights in citing undertakers' euphemisms. The morticians, she implies, dislike plain words—in paragraph 20 she quotes one who warns against creating the impression "that the body is in a box" (which, of course, is fact). There seems an ironic discrepancy between the attitudes expressed in the last two sentences and Mitford's own view. A funeral, she implies, shouldn't be a "real pleasure" but an occasion for grief. Death isn't an opposing football team.

3. To the general reader, these brand names carry unpleasant connotations, and a lively class discussion may be devoted to unraveling what these are. Lyf-Lyk tint seems cutesy in its spelling, like some drugstore cosmetic item. Other brand names seem practical and unfeeling: Throop Foot Positioner, Armstrong Face Former, and Denture Replacer. Porto-Lift and the Glide Easy casket carriage stress slickness and efficiency. Classic Beauty Ultra Metal Casket Bier seems absurdly grand. Mitford's purpose is to attack our sympathy and tolerance for the undertaker's art, and certainly these names rub us the wrong way.

4. "Dermasurgeon" (par. 8) is a euphemism Mitford especially relishes. Although it tries to dignify the mortician, Mitford points out how (unlike the surgeon he imitates) the embalmer acquired his training in a quick post–high-school course.

JESSICA MITFORD ON WRITING

Surprisingly often, authors are in total agreement when they discuss the art of writing. Mitford takes the common view that to write well, you have to care deeply about your subject. (We love that British phrase "besotted by.") Like so many other writers, both amateur and professional, she knows that writing is hard work. Like George Orwell, muckraker Mitford sees writing as a valuable tool for righting the world's wrongs.

From what Mitford says about her research for *The American Way of Death*, students can learn how important it is to get the facts straight when doing an exposé. The author makes clear as well that in writing, as in most other activities, a sense of humor is a valuable asset.

8
DIVISION OR ANALYSIS
Slicing into Parts

Division and classification have long been combined and confused in composition textbooks, so it is no wonder that some authors, some teachers, and many students cannot tell them apart. The true loser has seemed to be division. Indeed, some texts dispose of division as the mere servant of classification, the operation required to sort (divide) things into classes.

At the same time, first-year writing classes are absorbed in critical thinking, reading, and writing. Scholarly journals, textbooks, and teachers are inventing and experimenting with ways to teach these crucial skills. Yet all along we have had the means to introduce the skills through the Cinderella of the division and classification pair. Though generally treated, when treated at all, as a simple cutting operation, division is of course *analysis*. And what is analysis but the basis of criticism?

We have tried to rescue division/analysis and give it useful work in the composition course. We have, most noticeably, given the method its own chapter (and classification its own), in which we stress analytic thinking and discuss critical thinking. We have also made much more explicit the analytical underpinnings of the other methods of development, including (but not only) classification. (Two of these related methods—comparison/contrast and process analysis—continue to be covered before this chapter on the theory that they may be more familiar and accessible to students, even without explicit discussion of analysis. Of course, you may change the order of chapters if you see it differently.)

We now pair "The Cruel Country" by Judith Ortiz Cofer with "The Capricious Camera" by Laila Ayad, for what students should find an intriguing look at the meanings that can be gleaned from photographs. Robert Lipsyte's "Jock Culture" forms a bridge from visual division to textual analysis, illustrated by Guillermo del Toro and Chuck Hogan's "Vampires Never Die" and Barbara B. Parsons's "Whistling in the Dark."

JUDITH ORTIZ COFER
The Cruel Country

(p. 310)

Judith Ortiz Cofer's moving essay uses academic theory to navigate complicated emotional terrain—the conflicting senses of grief and liberation upon a loved one's death. Students should be inspired, we hope, to see how effectively writers can adapt ideas from scholarly works to make sense of their own lives and feelings. They might also be inspired to conduct their own analyses of family photographs, a project we suggest in the journal prompt and the first writing suggestion.

Media resources: It seems likely that Cofer's musings on her mother's life were inspired at least in part by the posthumous publication of Roland Barthes's unfinished *Mourning Diary*, which was curated and translated with much fanfare in 2010. Like Cofer, Barthes examines his deeply conflicted emotions upon the death of his mother after a long illness. Unlike Cofer, he was writing solely for himself. *The New Yorker* published excerpts from the book in its September 13, 2010, issue; you may wish to share some bits of it with your class.

Students who are intrigued by Cofer's Latina perspective may want to read more of her writing, such as the books *Silent Dancing* (1990) and *The Meaning of Consuelo* (2003), or one of the following: *Reclaiming Medusa: Short Stories by Contemporary Puerto Rican Women*, edited by Diana Velez (1988); Julia Alvarez's *How the Garcia Girls Lost Their Accents* (1991); or Laura Esquivel's *Like Water for Chocolate* (1992). A film based on Esquivel's book was released in 1993 and is available for download or on DVD.

QUESTIONS ON MEANING

1. The family moved to New Jersey, Cofer suggests, because her father joined the US Navy and was stationed there. Her mother returned to Puerto Rico as soon as he died: The reason behind her "*exilio*," or exile (par. 6), passed, she was no longer tied to the States and could return home.
2. Cofer is mystified by what Roland Barthes calls the "*punctum*" (par. 3) of the photograph, "the point of intersection between viewer and image, that detail" that draws the viewer in (4). In this case that detail is "the little spray of white flowers adorning her [mother's] hair" (8). It intrigues Cofer because, although her mother would have been in mourning, the flowers suggest celebration or flirtation (8). The photograph suggests to Cofer that her mother felt ambivalent in her grief, possibly even relieved by her husband's death, much as Cofer seems to feel in her grief for her mother. (We encourage students to explore this implication in the third writing suggestion.)
3. Students may need to look up *muse* in a dictionary to understand Cofer's allusion. In Greek mythology, each of the nine Muses—daughters of Zeus and Mnemosyne—presided over one of the arts or sciences.

The word has come to mean a guiding spirit or any source of creative inspiration. What Cofer is saying is that most of her work as a writer has been inspired and guided by a desire to understand her mother.

4. Cofer wants to memorialize her mother and express how the woman influenced her career as a writer. At the same time, she seems to want to examine her own "struggle" (par. 11) with mixed feelings upon a parent's death.

QUESTIONS ON WRITING STRATEGY

1. The line expresses a paradox: Mourning, Barthes suggests, is a mental state that is at once painful and liberating. The quotation forecasts a theme of grief mixed with a twinge of relief.

2. Cofer assumes an audience familiar with the running themes in her work and with the philosophy of Roland Barthes — essentially well-educated readers versed in literature and theory. She also assumes some familiarity with the cultural shifts that accompanied Puerto Ricans' migration to the mainland United States in the 1950s and 1960s, a subject she has written about extensively. While citing Barthes might seem esoteric to most first-year college students, we think Cofer does an effective job of giving her readers credit for intelligence while also offering accessible examples to help ground both his and her ideas.

3. The conflicting details Cofer provides — bright clothing (par. 1), "shiny" hair (7), bared tan arms (7), the spray of flowers (8), and a painting of "an idealized seashore scene at dusk" (9), alongside a stiff posture (1), a face "neither smiling nor frowning" (1), a "hint of gray" (7), a sense of "seriousness that belies the outfit" (7), and a feeling of being "alone in a place that had grown strange" (11) — create a dominant impression of a confused, struggling woman "caught . . . between emotions" (2).

4. Cofer uses Barthes's concept of the "*punctum*" (par. 3) of a photograph as her principle of analysis. Drawing on his theory, she examines that one aspect of the photograph that "touches you or triggers a quickening of the pulse" (4).

QUESTIONS ON LANGUAGE

1. The title borrows Roland Barthes's metaphor for mourning (see the first question on writing strategy) and adds an implication that living in the United States, for Cofer's mother anyway, was an unpleasant experience of exile.

2. Using formal, academic language and concepts to explore her mother's and her own emotions, Cofer's tone might best be described as ambivalent. She is at once detached from and immersed in her grief.

3. Cofer uses the word *planes* in its geometrical sense of intersecting lines, whereas students may know it only as an abbreviation of *airplanes*. The word comes from the Latin *plānum*, "flat surface."

JUDITH ORTIZ COFER ON WRITING

This is a brief but powerful statement on family as a source of growth *and* of material for writing. The transformation from one's origins to maturity may be more marked for an immigrant because it corresponds to a cultural sea change, but "accepting the terms necessary for survival" is essential to anyone's successful adulthood.

LAILA AYAD
The Capricious Camera
(p. 315)

This documented student essay is complex in both its ideas and its organization. It analyzes a photograph taken during the Nazi occupation of Poland during World War II: an image of a young girl surrounded by soldiers. Ayad makes two overlapping points—one about the Nazis' *Lebensborn* experiment (the attempt to create a master race through breeding and adoption) and another about the ambiguities of photography.

Media resources: Ayad assumes her readers will have some familiarity with the Nazi agenda, so before you begin discussion you may want to explore what students know about Nazi Germany, its occupations, and the Holocaust. Showing students photographs from the era could help them put Ayad's analysis in context. Your library may even have the book by Clay and Leapman that was Ayad's source.

Incidentally, some of your students might recognize Laila Ayad's name. Our former student has appeared on *Grey's Anatomy* and currently has a recurring role in the popular TV series *Scandal*.

QUESTIONS ON MEANING

1. Ayad's dual theses are as follows: "It is not merely people of other persecuted races who can become victims in a racial war, but also those we would least expect—the persecuting race itself" (par. 1); and "Unlike hand-made art, which in its very purpose begs to be viewed through various interpretations, photography, and particularly photojournalism, . . . demands to be viewed alongside its agenda, for without this context, it may never be fully understood" (par. 8). The two come together in the final paragraph: "[E]ven if the original photographer saw the image as artistic, subsequent events compel us to try to see the image of the Polish girl with Nazis as journalism. In this endeavor, we must uncover as much as possible about the surrounding context. As much as we can, we need to know this girl's particular story."
2. Ayad focuses on the Nazi *Lebensborn* experiment, in which "[c]hildren who possessed strong Nordic or Aryan qualities were systematically taken from their native countries, adopted by German parents (who were paid by the Nazi regime), taught to forget their families and former lives, and raised to breed not only many children of their own but, above all, families that would uphold Nazi ideology" (par. 11). Thus the Nazis persecuted their own "race" as well as others.
3. Ayad seems to want to show both the limitations of and the opportunities in photojournalism. It must be viewed in context, but that analysis can be very revealing.

QUESTIONS ON WRITING STRATEGY

1. Ayad focuses extensively on the photograph to show the ways it can be interpreted out of context and to demonstrate that without context we cannot truly understand the image.
2. Ayad seems to assume a general familiarity with Nazi Germany: In paragraph 1, for example, she uses "Hitler," "Aryan," "anti-Semitism," and "Holocaust" without explanation. However, she does not assume familiarity with the *Lebensborn* program, which she explains in detail (pars. 1, 9–12).
3. The conclusion brings the essay full circle and (as noted in the answer to the first question on meaning) weaves together the essay's two threads. The last two sentences freeze the image of the girl in readers' minds, capturing the poignancy of her unknown fate.
4. Ayad uses description in paragraphs 2–6, giving readers the information they need to see the photograph as she does.

QUESTIONS ON LANGUAGE

1. Ayad is clearly moved by the girl's plight, as evident in language such as "overwhelming," "the magnitude and force of the oppressing men," "innocence and helplessness of the lone girl," "both cruel and terribly frightening," "menacing and unjust" (par. 4), "symbols of oppression, producing an eerily suffocating effect" (5), "dramatic," "wistful and innocent," and "heads . . . hang in almost shameful disgrace" (6).
2. The quotations from Hitler, Gunther, and Himmler chillingly prove the Nazis' racism and their goals of racial purification. The quotation from the Polish woman provides an eyewitness account of what happened to many children, including, perhaps, the girl in the photograph.
3. *Targeting* conveys a sinister intent, as in targeting prey.
4. *Aryan* originally referred to a Northern tribe that conquered much of Asia around 2000 BC. German racialists began—some spuriously—to trace Northern Europeans back to these ancestors in the nineteenth century, and the Nazis found further reason to apply the term to themselves because of that people's idealization of conquest.

ROBERT LIPSYTE

Jock Culture

(p. 324)

While sports are an integral part of American culture, Robert Lipsyte argues in this compelling essay, the values instilled by competition are harmful and counterproductive, both for those who embrace them and those who don't.

The sports fans in your class will likely have a strong reaction against the writer's negative assessment of "Jock Culture," while the indifferent will probably be relieved to find a sympathetic friend—especially if your school has a vibrant athletic program. It may be worth reminding both camps that although Lipsyte self-identifies as a "Puke," he has made his career writing about sports. To appease students hostile to Lipsyte's criticisms, you may also wish to assign his analysis in conjunction with one or more of the sports-positive selections included in *The Bedford Reader*; we list them in the "Connections" question that follows his essay.

QUESTIONS ON MEANING

1. Lipsyte describes an interview he held with Columbia University's crew coach in the midst of student occupations of the school's buildings in protest of the Vietnam War. It would seem that Stowe was involved in breaking up the demonstrations. The student occupations are relevant to Lipsyte's subject for several reasons. First, his interview with Stowe introduced him to the concept of Jocks and Pukes: Stowe, of course, is an example of the former and Lipsyte (and the protesting students) of the latter. By placing his analysis in the context of the Vietnam War, Lipsyte also highlights the conflicts between athleticism and intellectualism and previews his claim that Jock Culture can be blamed, at least in part, for violence and warfare.

2. Jock Culture is the set of values instilled by devotion to overly competitive team sports: "submission to authority, winning by any means necessary, and group cohesion" (par. 4). Sports themselves, Lipsyte acknowledges, are beneficial (5), but Jock Culture debases them through "greed and desperate competition" (6) that turn people against each other in other aspects of life, particularly business, school, and government. It pits aggression against cooperation and results in "the cheating, the lying, the amorality" (12) that seem to mark contemporary society.

3. Lipsyte introduces his thesis in paragraph 4: "Boys—and more and more girls—who accept Jock Culture values often go on to flourish in a competitive sports environment that requires submission to authority, winning by any means necessary, and group cohesion." Implied in this statement and developed in the rest of the essay is Lipsyte's claim that those values are damaging to society as a whole. In a culture focused on winning, everybody—Jocks, Pukes, men, women, business leaders, workers, professionals, artists, intellectuals, and children especially—loses.

4. "Jock Culture" is an argument against aggressive, competitive values in American business and leisure. Lipsyte aims to persuade his readers to question those values and, perhaps, to support "de-emphasizing early competition and redistributing athletic resources" (par. 6), especially in schools (16).

QUESTIONS ON WRITING STRATEGY

1. Using the "myths of masculinity and power" (par. 4) instilled by competitive team sports as his principle of analysis, Lipsyte identifies several elements of Jock Culture, among them "greed and desperate competition" (6); "bullying, violence, and the commitment to a win-at-all-costs attitude that can kill a soul" (7); division into "winners and losers" (8); "coachlike authority figures who use shame and intimidation to achieve short-term results (8); expectations for people "to be tough, stoical, and

aggressive, to play hurt, to hit hard, to take risks to win in every aspect of their lives" (9); desires to "pursue . . . jock dreams no matter the physical, emotional, or financial cost" (10); and "misogyny" (13). The positive aspects of sports—"entertaining, healthful, filled with honest, sustaining sentiments for warm times and the beloved people you shared them with" (5); "a once safe place to learn about bravery, cooperation, and respect" (7); learning teamwork and developing the ability to reach a goal despite setbacks (9)—are completely overshadowed by the damaging effects of Jock Culture.

2. As he indicates, Lipsyte is writing to other Pukes like himself—educated, politically aware readers of *The Nation* who "were often turned off or away from competitive sports" (par. 4). He assumes his audience consists of liberals who "question authority and seek ways of individual expression" (4) and anticipates that many of them identify as artsy misfits, whether they work in "business, medicine, the law" or in "symphony orchestras, university philosophy departments, and liberal magazines" like *The Nation* (8). He seems to want them to understand that even if they think they live apart from Jock Culture, it permeates every aspect of their lives and affects them more than they may realize.

3. Although the 9/11 example may seem gratuitous to some readers, it neatly encapsulates the entirety of Lipsyte's analysis. It shows, first of all, that Jocks—both male and female—have an advantage in business yet also are harmed by that advantage. It reinforces his implication, in paragraphs 1–4, that competitive values lead to military action and outright war. It hints at why "submission to authority" (4) is a dangerous trait. And it lets Lipsyte show empathy for those who embrace the values he disdains.

4. By quoting the "affable *ur*-Jock" (par. 2) in his introduction, Lipsyte establishes the position that he intends to counter while simultaneously distancing himself from terms that some readers will find offensive. Returning to Stowe four decades later in his conclusion, Lipsyte circles back to his introduction (creating unity) and reveals that even a devoted athlete has changed his mind about the value of sports and come around to the author's way of thinking.

5. Lipsyte starts off with Bill Stowe's binary classification, which ascribes positive characteristics to Jocks: They are, he claims, "brave, manly, ambitious, focused, patriotic, and goal-driven" (par. 1). Pukes are exactly the opposite: "wooly, distractible, girlish, and handicapped by their lack of certainty that nothing mattered as much as winning" (1). In Lipsyte's own reckoning, however, the characteristics are different. As he presents them, Pukes "question authority and seek ways of individual expression," while Jocks are conformists who do whatever is asked of them (4).

QUESTIONS ON LANGUAGE

1. Although Stowe uses the word *Jock* approvingly, both words have derogatory connotations, especially *Puke*, which brings up images of sickliness and weakness. If nothing else, the labels capture readers' attention and stress the different personalities more colorfully than *athlete* and *intellectual* would.

2. No doubt Lipsyte himself would describe his tone as "Puke-ish" (par. 2)—in a good way. His words are calm, reasoned, intellectual, and infused with empathy.

3. Lipsyte's invective against sport mentality is riddled with sport metaphors. Some examples: "mental conditioning" (par. 4); "arenas of elite athletes," "cockpit of bullying" (7); "'cut' from the team early" (8); "pushed the envelope" (9); "our lives outside the white lines" (12). Taken together with Bill Stowe's mixed metaphors/clichés in paragraph 16 ("It's time to give up the torch. . . . I'm not running it up the flagpole anymore"), they show that while the author might reject Jock Culture, he understands it fully—and probably better than Jocks do.

4. *Wonkish* is a relatively new coinage and could be counted as slang. The word refers to a student or analyst (a *wonk*) who focuses excessively on a particular subject.

GUILLERMO DEL TORO AND CHUCK HOGAN

Vampires Never Die

(p. 330)

Students may be surprised to discover that the creators of such pulp fiction as *Hell Boy*, *Blade II*, and *Prince of Thieves* are also capable of writing a poetic, sophisticated, and seriously academic literary analysis of a trend in popular culture. In just a few pages, del Toro and Hogan survey the complete history of vampire lore and offer a fresh take on what it reveals about the human condition, especially within contemporary culture. Some of their literary and philosophical allusions, as well as their unstated reliance on the psychological theories of Carl Jung, may wash over students, yet the analysis as a whole remains compelling and understandable. (We've glossed those allusions that seem most important to following the authors' ideas; others we leave to students to investigate if they're so inclined.) Fans of current vampire stories will surely be interested to learn of the legacy behind them and be intrigued by the idea that those stories could mean anything more than just good entertainment.

You may wish to begin class discussion with the question likely to be on many students' minds: Does popular culture, especially something as seemingly trivial as vampire fiction, merit academic study? Why, or why not? What can we learn from analyses such del Toro and Hogan's?

Media resources: As an alternative, you might consider encouraging students to find and share criticism of del Toro's and Hogan's own literary and filmic productions, many of which are listed in the author headnote preceding the essay. To what extent has their creative work been the subject of similar kinds of interpretation? And does "Vampires Never Die" make readers more—or less—inclined to read the authors' collaborative vampire novels for pleasure?

QUESTIONS ON MEANING

1. There's no question that "Vampires Never Die" serves as clever and well-conceived publicity for the authors' vampire trilogy. However, the authors also examine the larger cultural meanings of vampire stories

in general, over time and across cultures. The essay is a sophisticated psychological analysis of one particular literary genre.

2. "Monsters, like angels, are invoked by our individual and collective needs. Today, much as during that gloomy summer in 1816, we feel the need to seek their cold embrace" (par. 7).

3. The authors posit that the concept of vampiric immortality fills a universal psychological and spiritual void. By tapping into deep-seated fears and desires, vampire stories both reassure us and "provide the possibility of mystery in our mundane . . . lives" (par. 16). The particulars of those fears and desires might change over time and across cultures, but the basic truths of death and sexuality do not. Vampires, say del Toro and Hogan, represent a powerful mixture of the two most profound aspects of human existence.

4. Students should be able to infer from the context that a *social construct* is any custom, taboo, philosophy, or law designed to govern human conduct by repressing base urges. (The idea also refers to any cultural infusion of meaning onto abstractions, but the authors aren't using it that way.) The concept is important to del Toro and Hogan's analysis because they see the vampire character as one released from the pressures of civilization who allows human beings to reconnect vicariously with their primal instincts.

5. Although science appears to be rational and objective, new technologies can seem mysterious, even ominous to laypersons. Even those with a scientific mindset tend to embrace innovation and understanding as a faith in itself and, in so doing, to "experience fear and awe again, and to believe in the things [they] cannot see" (par. 15).

QUESTIONS ON WRITING STRATEGY

1. Writing for the *New York Times*, del Toro and Hogan assume an audience of well-educated readers with wide-ranging interests. At the same time, they assume a familiarity with popular culture, from classic novels to *American Idol*, and an immersion in communication technologies. Some students may object that several of the authors' allusions go above readers' heads, but other students will surely appreciate the apparent respect for their intelligence.

2. Their principle of analysis is the question of what makes vampires appeal across time and culture. The two basic elements identified by del Toro and Hogan are lust and death, introduced as "romantic hero" and "undead monster" (par. 4) and reiterated in the conclusion as "Eros and Thanatos fused together in archetypal embrace" (16). Subsets of those elements include primal fear (6), immortality (8), adaptability (10), uncertainty (13–14), superstition (15), and spirituality (16).

3. Their point is that the folklore taps into something deeply personal—yet primal and universal. That the first written story might have stemmed from deep-seated emotional, psychological, and sexual tensions is therefore highly significant (even if students don't recognize Jung's theory of the collective unconscious lurking behind the authors' assumptions).

4. The single word *forever* evokes immortality, both of vampires as individual characters and as a universal cultural need. Coming on the heels of a paragraph about faith and spirituality, it also echoes the concluding sentiment of Christian prayers: *Amen.*

5. The authors compare two eras "of great technical revolution" in paragraphs 13–15. Both in the early nineteenth century and now, people were confronted with "new gadgets . . ., various forms of communication . . ., and cutting-edge science" (par. 13). Del Toro and Hogan name those new technologies in the case of the nineteenth century but leave it to readers to fill in the details for the twenty-first. In either case, such innovations were both liberating and disorienting, leaving us "still ultimately vulnerable to our fates and our nightmares" (15).

QUESTIONS ON LANGUAGE

1. For a definition of *mash-up*, students may need to turn to the Internet or to a recent dictionary of slang. The term, similar in meaning to *remix*, applies to the creative process that combines elements of multiple existing productions (songs, film clips, video clips, and the like) to create something new, a technique often used by avant-garde musicians and filmmakers. We find it interesting that del Toro and Hogan manage to apply a cutting-edge (and controversial) creative trend to "ancient myth" and folklore.
2. Traditionally, *twitter* means to chirp or speak excitedly, but the word also refers to the recent and fast-growing social networking application. The verb is especially effective, given that del Toro and Hogan are writing about the psychological effects of fast-paced technology and overwhelming torrents of communication.
3. *Alchemy* refers to medieval beliefs that an as-yet-undiscovered chemical process could transform base metals, lead in particular, into gold; the hope was that such transformations would form the foundation for an elixir for everlasting youth. The metaphor fits the vampire subject very well, both in the idea that commingling of blood would transform both biter and victim into something better and that the transformation would enable immortality; it also reinforces? the suggestion that science is superstition (see par. 15). The authors return to the metaphor in the next paragraph (9).

GUILLERMO DEL TORO AND CHUCK HOGAN ON WRITING

Del Toro and Hogan provide valuable insight into their collaborative writing process. Their committal "bro-hug" and their banter during the interview indicate a rapport between the two men. Is a friendly relationship a prerequisite for the deep (and sometimes ruthless) revision del Toro and Hogan do? Students may want to discuss best practices for giving feedback and ways to approach suggested revisions with an open mind, especially if peer revision is part of your course.

BARBARA B. PARSONS
Whistling in the Dark

(p. 337)

We are indebted to Barbara Parsons for writing a critical analysis of an essay to model the genre for her students and for generously sharing her work with us. In just a few short pages she breaks down the elements of "Black Men and Public Space" by Brent Staples while also highlighting how relevant that 1986 essay still is. Examining the implications of Staples's tone, evidence, and assumptions, Parsons dissects his work for a larger purpose, imploring those on the receiving end of racist encounters to speak up for themselves and to demand change. Her astute reading and adept writing are sure to reassure students that they, too, are capable of producing similar efforts.

Students who want to read "Black Men and Public Space" can find it in Chapter 5 of *The Bedford Reader* (p. 166). The critical writing topic following Parsons's analysis invites students to read the essay and then respond to Parsons's interpretation. This topic could also spark class discussion as students share their responses to Parsons and to Staples's essay itself.

Media resources: Parsons questions the usefulness of Staples's habit of whistling Vivaldi to calm those around him. Students may appreciate hearing a bit of *The Four Seasons* for context: Check if your campus library holds recordings for loan; you can also find clips online.

QUESTIONS ON MEANING

1. The author has a dual purpose. Her essay is, first, intended as a model of critical analysis for her students (as we explain in the note preceding the essay), but it is also an evaluation of Brent Staples's implied argument in "Black Men and Public Space." Although she admires his essay and his patience, Parsons concludes that Staples "fails to convince readers that tolerance and timidity are the best response to the problem of racism on the streets" (par. 6).

2. Parsons praises Staples for "mak[ing] general readers aware of the issue" (par. 1) of subtle and not-so-subtle racism against black men in public as well as for being "determined to take the high road" (3) in laying out his case. But the tone strikes her as having "a false note" (par. 1) because Staples himself, she points out, admits "that he has 'learned to smother the rage [he] felt at so often being taken for a criminal'" (4). Lurking beneath his calm demeanor, she notices, is repressed anger, an emotion that threatens to "become enflamed again" (4), likely at the wrong moment.

3. Parsons feels that in taking the responsibility for tolerance onto himself rather than demanding it of those who do not tolerate his presence, Staples unfairly pressures other black men to be equally passive in the face of injustice (par. 6). She would prefer that he "condemn [the] false fears" of female pedestrians and others whose negative (and often hostile) reactions he cites (2).

4. The thesis appears at the end of the introduction and is reiterated in the conclusion: "While [Staples's] well-constructed essay does make general readers aware of the issue [of casual racism], ultimately it fails to convince us that Staples's solution is the best one possible" (par. 1); "Despite excellent examples and thoughtful commentary, Staples ultimately fails to convince readers that tolerance and timidity are the best response to the problem of racism on the streets" (6).

QUESTIONS ON WRITING STRATEGY

1. Parsons takes care to make her essay both academic and accessible to first-year college students. She writes in the third person and uses formal diction, yet she keeps her vocabulary relatively simple and her analysis brief. Even as she criticizes Staples's argument and expresses a passion for justice, she remains objective and level-headed, citing her evidence meticulously and keeping her emotions in check—just as we all hope students will do when they write. Additional potential readers include *your* students, other teachers of English composition, and, perhaps, Staples himself.

2. Of course she assumes some familiarity with "Black Men and Public Space" among her students, but Parsons integrates extensive evidence from her source to ensure that any reader can follow her analysis. She opens by summarizing Staples's essay and establishing her point of contention. Each paragraph in the body of her essay paraphrases Staples's examples as appropriate to her interpretation and quotes his exact words to give readers a clear idea of the emotions she detects in his writing, always providing in-text citations in MLA style. And in every case she makes a point of synthesizing his argument with her own. Even those who have never read "Black Men and Public Space" learn enough about it from Parsons's essay to follow her examination of its examples and its thesis. (And we hope that those who have not yet been introduced to Staples's classic work will be inspired to turn to Chapter 5 and read it for themselves.)

3. With the transition "however" in paragraph 4, Parsons shifts her attention from what works in Staples's essay to what, to her mind, does not.

4. Parsons ties her analysis together in her conclusion: " . . . Staples and other black men should be able to go about their lives without undue concern that they are frightening other people or putting themselves in danger. We need a solution that doesn't require anyone to 'smother' a negative emotion, be it fear or rage. That is not too much to ask, and Staples should be asking" (par. 6). She is calling for social justice in the form of racial tolerance.

QUESTIONS ON LANGUAGE

1. *Metaphors*: "Whistling in the Dark" (title); "Brent Staples has an ax to grind in 'Black Men and Public Space,' but he doesn't grind it" (par. 1); "hits a false note" (1); "determined to take the high road" (3); "a smothered rage is likely to become enflamed again at any moment" (4); "retiring position" (5); "he takes the biggest portion of the responsibility onto his own broad shoulders, and by extension, onto the backs of other black men with the same 'unwieldy inheritance'" (6). *Simile*: "While those cowbells are intended to keep bears away, Staples's whistles are supposed to soothe fearful pedestrians and encourage them to stick

around. The analogy would be more apt if the pedestrians were making a noise to keep Staples away—perhaps by blowing a police whistle" (5). Students' choices and explanations will, of course, vary.

2. A *self-perpetuating* phenomenon, such as racism, is one that feeds on itself to continue growing. By avoiding "violence and hate," Parsons implies, one can starve them into nonexistence.

3. The repetition and restatement of key terms gives the essay unity and coherence.

BARBARA B. PARSONS ON WRITING

Students who find themselves struggling in a composition class should, we hope, take comfort in the knowledge that even a published writing teacher earned Bs and Cs in her first year of college. We appreciate, too, that Parsons shares our conviction that reading and writing are interconnected processes. Her love of reading as a child, she notes, helped to make her a better writer by exposing her to models of quality prose. Students might be surprised by her worry that they are being poorly served by technology and the materials they encounter online. It may be worth pointing out that computer skeptic Nicholas expresses similar concerns in his own comments on writing (p. 533).

9
CLASSIFICATION
Sorting into Kinds

In our general comments on Chapter 8 (p. 74 of this manual), we explain our reasons for divorcing the hoary pair of division and classification. Our reasons have mainly to do with salvaging division/analysis, but benefits accrue to classification, too. For one thing, it doesn't have to compete for attention (ours, yours, students'), so it's much clearer. For another, we can provide more illustrations.

The selections in this chapter range from humorous to serious, reflecting the classifications we find in the publications we read. Deborah Tannen and William Lutz look at miscommunications inadvert and deliberate, respectively. Russell Baker contributes a well-known humorous piece of curmudgeonly confusion over our material possessions. Student writer Jean-Pierre De Beer imaginatively examines the possibilities for colonizing space. And the always popular Marion Winik considers the implications of our online search habits. *Troubleshooting*: All our efforts to keep division/analysis and classification separate and equal are hampered by the inescapable fact that *divide* is sometimes taken to mean *classify*, as in "Divide the students into groups." You might want to point out this issue directly to students if you think the terminology will confuse them. We maintain that division/analysis treats a singular, whole, coherent subject (a camera, a theory, a poem), whereas classification treats a plural, numerous subject (cameras, theories, poems).

The confusion between division and classification may account for the tendency of some students to "classify" by taking a single item (say, the television show *Survivor*) and placing it in a category (say, reality shows). We'd explain that they haven't classified anything; they have just filed an item in a pigeonhole. If they'll remember that classification begins not with one thing but with several things, they may avoid much perplexity.

DEBORAH TANNEN

But What Do You Mean?

(p. 353)

The linguist Deborah Tannen came to national prominence with *You Just Don't Understand*, a book about misunderstandings between men and women in conversation. Since then, she has continued to disseminate much of her research through the mass media, trying to help people solve the communication problems of daily life. The late Oliver Sacks, another intellectual who often addressed a general audience, wrote of *You Just Don't Understand*: "Deborah Tannen combines a novelist's ear for the way people speak with a rare power of original analysis. It is this that makes her an extraordinary sociolinguist, and it is this that makes her book such a fascinating look at that crucial social cement, conversation."

This is one essay that students should be able to apply easily to their own lives, although the men in your class may be more resistant than the women. The essay will certainly evoke a wide range of student response, which should lead to lively class discussion. Here is an in-class exercise to test Tannen's theories: Ask students to bring in dialogs that illustrate conflict from novels, plays, or movie scripts, deleting characters' names and direct references to gender. Have students read the dialogs out loud and try to guess characters' genders, justifying their choices. Encourage students to look for instances of Tannen's seven categories of miscommunication in the dialogs. (A variation is to cross-cast the dialogs, with women reading men's lines, and vice versa, and see if they are still believable.)

While Tannen examines innocent misunderstandings, William Lutz, in the next essay, takes on language that misleads on purpose. The "Connections" questions following both essays will help students consider what both kinds of miscommunication have in common as well as how such confusions might be avoided.

Media resources: Not only does Tannen frequently address the general public through mass media, she archives many of her talks on her personal Web site. A comprehensive menu of lectures, presentations, interviews, and commentaries—including a 2015 discussion of women's speaking in the workplace for NPR's *Here and Now*—is available at *deborahtannen .com/in-the-media/*.

QUESTIONS ON MEANING

1. Tannen is pointing out the areas of communication in which misunderstandings between the sexes are most frequent. She seems to hope that a better understanding of how men's and women's communication styles differ will help eliminate such misunderstandings. A secondary purpose is to show women how their problems in the workplace may be linked to their style of communication.
2. Much of what we say is based on pure protocol, which serves as a kind of social cement. We're not so much communicating facts as establishing

a rapport with the other person. This speech is often so automatic and predictable that we aren't even aware of what we're saying. (See also the journal prompt and the first writing suggestion.)

3. "Many of the conversational rituals common among women are designed to take the other person's feelings into account, while many of the conversational rituals common among men are designed to maintain the one-up position, or at least avoid appearing one-down" (par. 2).

4. "Thank you" is not always used as an expression of gratitude but is simply a ritual, "an automatic conversation starter and closer" (par. 15). An answer of "You're welcome" results in an imbalance between the speakers.

QUESTIONS ON WRITING STRATEGY

1. Tannen uses these characters as examples of the points she is making. She adds variety to the essay by referring to people alternately by their first names (real or fictitious) and by their functions ("a well-known columnist," par. 4; "[a] woman manager I know," 13). These characters are ciphers, empty vessels in the service of Tannen's argument, and as such do not need to be described in detail. Tannen reveals only what is relevant to her point. (See also question 4.)

2. Because the essay appeared in *Redbook*, a women's magazine, Tannen uses *you* to address women readers: "What's important is to be aware of how often you say you're sorry (and why), and to monitor your speech based on the reaction you get" (par. 9); "Although you may never enjoy verbal sparring, some women find it helpful to learn how to do it" (19). (Tannen takes a broader approach for a male *and* female audience in *Talking from 9 to 5*, the book from which this essay was excerpted.)

3. Tannen begins by redefining women's apologizing not as self-deprecation but as a "way of keeping both speakers on an equal footing." She then offers an extended example of this redefinition and expands on it further through a brief dialog that reveals apologizing as "a mutual face-saving device." In paragraphs 6 and 7, she gives an example of a woman whose constant apologies may have limited others' perceptions of her competence. Finally, she poses a contrast: the negative response women may get if they don't use "ritual apologies."

4. That the columnist is well known makes her apology all the more unexpected, less likely to be chalked up to insecurity.

5. (1) *Apologies*: Women apologize more than men do. They see apology as a way of keeping both speakers on an equal footing, of sharing responsibility. Men take apologies at face value, seeing them as self-deprecating. (2) *Criticism*: Women tend to soften criticism more than men do. Men prefer "straight answers." (3) *Thank-yous*: Women say "thank you" more often, as a ritual. Men take "thank you," like "I'm sorry," more literally. (4) *Fighting*: Men see conversation as a battleground, stating their ideas and criticizing those of others in the strongest possible terms. Women often perceive this approach as a personal attack. (5) *Praise*: Women often assume that the absence of praise is the equivalent of criticism. For men, in contrast, praise is often implied when no criticism is given. Women who ask for criticism may really be asking for praise, but men will give them what they ask for. (6) *Complaints*: Women complain as a way of bonding with others. Men see these complaints as a call for a solution. (7) *Jokes*: "[T]he most common form of

humor among men is razzing, teasing, and mock-hostile attacks, while among women it's self-mocking. Women often mistake men's teasing as genuinely hostile. Men often mistake women's mock self-deprecation as truly putting themselves down."

QUESTIONS ON LANGUAGE

1. The humor here relies on exaggeration. It usually refers to finishing off a suffering animal.
2. Tannen uses the metaphor of a gun: criticism as shooting.
3. These verbs liven up the essay and inspire a strong visual or auditory impression. Other examples are "*leapt* into a critical response" (par. 10) and "*poke* holes" (17).
4. Note Tannen's vocabulary of physical and verbal conflict: "contentious," "hedge," "sparring," "rebuttal," "retorted," and "disadvantage" (par. 2) as well as "attack" (18) and "enemy" (19). You might discuss whether Tannen loads her case with such words, perhaps exaggerating the conflicts between genders.

DEBORAH TANNEN ON WRITING

Students may not be aware of the debate about the personal in scholarly writing, but many have probably been told at some time not to use *I* in their academic papers. Tannen suggests why and also argues in favor of the first person on scholarly grounds. Students in the natural and applied sciences may be more likely than others in the class to resist Tannen's argument, contending that they don't write about personal interactions. Try this experiment on the effects of the first person and third person (*he, she, they*): Have students write a passage of academic prose in one person or the other. (Tannen's example of professor A and student B can perhaps suggest a direction for a passage, or they may have one already written in a paper they've submitted.) Next, have them rewrite the passage in the other person and analyze the two versions. Does one sound more academic than the other? What are the advantages and disadvantages of each one? Collaboration in small groups is ideal: Working together, students will find it easier to draft the third-person or first-person passage and then revise it, seeing firsthand what the differences are.

WILLIAM LUTZ
The World of Doublespeak

(p. 363)

William Lutz is a leading figure in the campaign against the dishonest language that he (and others) call doublespeak. This essay, extracted from the first chapter of his book-length treatment of the subject, both defines the term and classifies its varieties. The many, many examples will leave students in no doubt about the meaning of doublespeak and should make it relatively easy for them to spot it.

One problem with doublespeak is that it often relies on multisyllabic words and complicated syntax. As a result, the most example-heavy parts of Lutz's essay may be difficult reading for some students. Lutz himself practices what he preaches, writing clearly and concisely, but you may want to warn students that some passages in the essay require patience.

Probably the best way to make this essay immediate and significant for students is to have them locate doublespeak in what they read and hear. Indeed, you may want to ask them to try the journal-writing assignment as soon as they've read the essay and to bring their examples to class. Even if each student contributes only one or two examples, you'll have a good collection. Working as a whole class or in small groups to sort their examples into Lutz's categories, students will be writing a continuation of the essay.

We pair Lutz's essay with the previous one, Deborah Tannen's "But What Do You Mean?" While Tannen deals with gender communications and Lutz with a subtle form of deception, both authors look at how our uses of language can hinder understanding. The final writing suggestion following each essay can be used as an assignment or to spark discussion.

Media resources: Although the *Quarterly Review of Doublespeak,* which Lutz once edited, is now defunct, your library may carry back issues of the journal or offer access through a database. You might have students select and read a few related articles from the journal and based on them write an essay in which they challenge, expand, or add more examples to Lutz's categories. The 1989 CSPAN interview with Brian Lamb, from which we have extracted William Lutz's comments on writing, is available to watch in full at *youtube.com/watch?v=91ka2s9Ubs0.*

QUESTIONS ON MEANING

1. Lutz's thesis might be stated briefly as follows: The four kinds of doublespeak all include language "that avoids or shifts responsibility, language that is at variance with its real or purported meaning" (par. 2). The thesis accumulates over paragraphs 2–3, with the addition of the intention to classify in paragraph 5.
2. Paragraph 4 offers the following questions: "Who is saying what to whom, under what conditions and circumstances, with what intent, and with what results?" These questions locate the motivation for dishonesty that would indicate doublespeak.
3. The greatest danger is that, as in Orwell's *Nineteen Eighty-Four,* doublespeak will lead to the "control of reality through language" (par. 23). Doublespeak "alter[s] our perception of reality and corrupt[s] our thinking. . . . [It] breeds suspicion, cynicism, distrust, and, ultimately, hostility" (22). It can "infect and eventually destroy the function of language" (23).
4. Lutz clearly assumes an educated reader, someone able to perceive the fundamental dishonesty in his examples. At the same time, his careful classification, scores of examples, and extensive discussion of the dangers indicate that he believes his reader probably is not sensitive to doublespeak and needs help to recognize it.

QUESTIONS ON WRITING STRATEGY

1. Lutz's principle of classification is the intention of doublespeakers. Those who use euphemisms are trying to "mislead or deceive" (par. 7) with inoffensive words. Those who use jargon seek to give their words "an air of profundity, authority, and prestige" (10). Those who use gobble-dygook or bureaucratese are bent on "overwhelming the audience with words" (13). And those who use inflated language seek "to make the ordinary seem extraordinary; . . . to make the simple seem complex" (17).
2. Lutz begins by offering a definition of the category. Then he offers examples of euphemisms used to spare others' feelings or to avoid language regarded as taboo—euphemisms he finds acceptable. Finally, he contrasts these kinds of euphemism with three examples of euphemism used by government agencies to "mislead or deceive"—in which case it becomes doublespeak.
3. Greenspan's second comment is surprising because he acknowledges that he is deliberately unclear. With the quotation Lutz shows that doublespeak is intentional.
4. Many of Lutz's examples are dated, and some students may at first think that doublespeak is an old, not a current, problem. The first writing suggestion, asking students to find current examples of their own, should help them see that doublespeak is no less a problem now than it was more than two decades ago.
5. Definition appears mainly in paragraphs 2 and 3 and in the explanations of each kind of doublespeak (pars. 5, 7, 9–10, 13, 17). Cause and effect also figures in the explanation of categories, as Lutz gives the intentions of doublespeakers, but mainly it develops the last section of the essay (20–23). The definition, of course, clarifies Lutz's subject and his categories. The cause-and-effect analysis shows what is at stake with this dishonest language.

QUESTIONS ON LANGUAGE

1. Lutz's language provides a good foil to the quotations of doublespeak: He uses plain language and relatively simple syntax.
2. The words listed all have negative connotations, suggesting undesirable or even dangerous effects of doublespeak. More neutral language would not make Lutz's point as sharply. For just a few examples, see paragraph 1.
3. *Taboo* now refers to a prohibition against the use or practice of something. The word comes from the Tongan word *tabu*, an adjective meaning "set apart, consecrated to a special use or purpose." Captain Cook traveled to Tonga in 1777; his widely read narrative of his experiences, including an explanation of *tabu*, brought the term into common use in England.

WILLIAM LUTZ ON WRITING

Students may be encouraged to see recognizable behaviors, particularly procrastination, in a successful writer. Though his work is devoted to words and writing, Lutz admits that he once spent a great deal of time avoiding writing. The writer and humorist Fran Lebowitz once joked that being a writer was a bit like being a perpetual student . . . except you can't write a book the night before it is due. "I know," Lebowitz deadpanned, "because I tried twice."

RUSSELL BAKER

The Plot against People

(p. 373)

In this essay, the well-known humorist Russell Baker makes a common use of classification—for humor. Baker takes a wry look at the universal human feeling that the material world is conspiring against us. Ask the class to come up with more examples of things that "have it in" for people.

Writing humor is difficult, as students who have tried can attest. Give students an opportunity to try their hands at a collaborative essay modeled on Baker's. What conspiracy theories can the class generate? (These might include the school's conspiracy to keep students from registering for any of the classes they most need, the local market's conspiracy to run out of Diet Coke when you most need one, and so on.) Make a list of ideas on the board, and have small groups of students write a short essay describing this conspiracy in detail. You might ask the groups to read their finished products.

Media resources: Students who enjoy Baker's approach can be encouraged to look into some of his collections, such as *Poor Russell's Almanac* (1972) and *So This Is Depravity* (1980).

QUESTIONS ON MEANING

1. Baker's thesis is stated in paragraph 1. His larger meaning is that inanimate objects conspire to frustrate humans.
2. The reason may be that objects are doing humans a favor (par. 11) or that they are "incredibly stupid" (12).
3. He may also want to point out how ridiculous we are when we become infuriated with inanimate things.
4. By not working, thus "conditioning him never to expect anything of them" (par. 16).

QUESTIONS ON WRITING STRATEGY

1. Baker classifies objects by the ways they thwart human wishes. He might have included things that work for a while and then break or even things that work fine, but his use of extreme cases adds to the essay's humor.
2. Baker begins by contrasting the category with the previous category. Next he provides two examples (pliers and keys) and then an additional example (women's purses). Finally, he again contrasts things that break down with things that get lost, using the examples of a furnace and a woman's purse.
3. "[A]ny object capable of breaking down at the moment when it is most needed will do so" (par. 2); "A furnace . . . will invariably break down . . ." (10); "Thereafter, they never work again" (13). (Students will, of course, find others.) Hyperbole establishes Baker's comic tone of exasperation.

4. His pseudoscientific classification, with its dogmatic assertion of the three categories of objects, is a parody of intellectual authority. The pseudophilosophical discussion of spiritual "peace" in the conclusion reinforces the essay's mock-serious tone.

5. Baker's little stories (the cunning automobile of par. 3 or par. 8's climbing pliers) capture the reader's attention. Shared experiences provide a sense of recognition and help make the essay funny.

QUESTIONS ON LANGUAGE

1. The vocabulary words highlighted here all contribute to the essay's mock-serious tone. In general, the essay's diction is quite simple.
2. Clever, malicious, plotting. Its effect is to personify the automobile.
3. The general terms make the shared experiences more universal. Had Baker used *I*, he might have seemed more of a crank, less persuasive.

JEAN-PIERRE DE BEER

Stars of Life

(p. 377)

Full disclosure: Student writer Jean-Pierre De Beer is Ellen Kuhl Repetto's nephew. In writing this classification of stars that hold the greatest potential to support human life, he received our feedback for revision and some help with editing—but the subject, the research, the development of the details, and the language are all his own work. A fan of hard science as well as of science fiction, De Beer was inspired to write after watching a *YouTube* channel he enjoys—specifically, the Kurzgesagt video on red dwarfs presented in his list of works cited. "Stars of Life" shows him to be open to the idea of colonizing other planets and eager to explore the possibilities offered by distant stars, even those beyond our own galaxy. And De Beer does it with an academic yet accessible point of view—while managing to avoid resorting to the all-too-common classifier's crutch of headings or lists.

"Stars of Life" is one of several selections in this book that use humor to impart scientific information to a general audience. We point to one, Diane Ackerman's "Black Marble," in the writing suggestion labeled "Connections." Others include Dan Koeppel's "Taking a Fall" (p. 281), Jessica Mitford's "Behind the Formaldehyde Curtain" (p. 288), Randall Munroe's "Everybody Jump" (p. 410), and Joan Didion's "Earthquakes" (p. 557). You might want to ask students what it is about hard science that leads some writers to look to irreverence as a way to hook readers in.

Media resources: Students who enjoy De Beer's cheeky take on space research might also enjoy the initial source of inspiration for his essay. "Kurzgesagt—In a Nutshell" is a *YouTube* channel showcasing a German design studio's animated educational videos (one a month) on scientific subjects ranging from astronomy to zoology.

QUESTIONS ON MEANING

1. De Beer's primary purpose was, simply, to model classification for students using *The Bedford Reader*: We asked him for an essay "on types of things—anything—that interest" him. In choosing space exploration (verging on science fiction) as his topic, he takes a lighthearted approach to examining the possibilities for colonizing other planets. But in researching specific kinds of stars and presenting his findings in scientific detail, De Beer makes it clear that he does take the study of astronomy seriously.

2. As De Beer explains, the "Goldilocks," or "habitable" (pars. 1, 6), zone refers to a combination "of moderate temperature, atmospheric pressure, and the possibility of water" enjoyed by a planet near enough, but not too near, to a long-lasting host star. The term, used by NASA and many astronomers, refers of course to the story of "Goldilocks and the Three Bears"—the conditions on such a planet are, by allusion, "just right" for sustaining human life.

3. De Beer's relatively simple thesis appears in his introduction: "[T]hree types [of stars] stand out as the most potentially beneficial to humankind and prolonging its existence: supergiants, yellow dwarfs, and red dwarfs. . . . The red dwarf, however, is or at least will be the most important star because of its incredibly long life span and relative abundance in our immense universe" (par. 2). He repeats this main idea in his conclusion: "If we look to [red stars] for our future, the entire universe will be at our fingertips for trillions of years to come" (8). However, De Beer would be among the first to acknowledge that (as he himself told us) "this paper assumes *a lot*" and leaves much to readers' imaginations. He doesn't, for instance, specify *how* humanity would locate red dwarfs hosting habitable planets, let alone get there and subsequently colonize them, nor does he explain *why* such a move would be necessary in the first place, other than to quote Stephen Hawking's assertion that "the human race will [not] survive the next thousand years, unless we spread into space" (in the epigraph and final paragraph) and to hint (in pars. 5 and 6) that our own sun will eventually die. Some readers may find that such omissions weaken the overall effectiveness of De Beer's short essay, but given his speculative purpose and the space available to him, we'd say he does an admirable job of presenting his main idea clearly and succinctly.

QUESTIONS ON WRITING STRATEGY

1. As they often do, the epigraph forecasts the theme of the essay. In this case it also does more: In citing Stephen Hawking, De Beer evokes expert opinion to support his otherwise fantastical-seeming claim that "humanity will need to abandon the small asteroid it lives on and find a place to live out among the stars" (par. 1). He alludes to the epigraph in his introduction when he writes of the possibility that we might "succeed in spreading to space" (2). Finally, he circles back to Hawking in his conclusion, effectively giving the essay a sense of closure with a flourish.

2. As we mention in the note introducing his essay, De Beer wrote "Stars of Life" especially for *The Bedford Reader*. Accordingly, he assumes an audience of college (and high school) students who, like himself, share a concern for the fate of the Earth and the survival of humanity as well as

at least a passing interest in astronomy and space exploration. He seems also to expect that they will unquestionably accept his assertion that evacuating our planet will be necessary "[s]ooner than later" (par. 1)—and perhaps they will—but some readers may object to the basic assumption that underlies his purpose for writing, countering that the prediction is mere speculation and not rooted in established facts.

3. De Beer establishes his principle of classification in his introduction: He is exploring types of stars that "stand out as the most potentially beneficial to humankind and prolonging its existence" (par. 2)—whether as sources of power to fuel relocation (supergiants, 3–4) or as hosts to habitable planets for colonization (yellow dwarfs, 5–6, and red dwarfs, 7–8).

4. De Beer gives each category two paragraphs. The first establishes what kind of star he's looking at and offers researched details about its temperature, lifespan, and relative abundance (in the form of a percentage); the second speculates how he imagines that kind of star could be beneficial to humanity. Readers might notice, as well, that he is careful to provide transitions between the categories, referring either back to previous paragraphs or forward to the next.

5. "Stars of Life" builds on an implied cause-and-effect analysis. Although De Beer doesn't come right out and say it, he suggests that in the short term (geologically speaking) the Earth will become uninhabitable—perhaps because of environmental destruction or a catastrophic event. (Stephen Hawking, in the interview De Beer cites in his opening epigraph and closing paragraph, suggested the reasons would be "biological," essentially human destruction of the Earth and its ability to sustain life.) Even if that turns out not to be the case, De Beer notes in paragraph 5, our sun won't live much longer than 10 billion years (a relatively short time, galactically speaking), so we'd do well to look for a "long-term solution" to its inevitable end. Otherwise, the human race won't survive.

QUESTIONS ON LANGUAGE

1. Although he enlivens his essay with some figures of speech (see the next question), De Beer's diction is primarily academic. He is careful to write objectively, in the third person, and he uses scientific vocabulary sparingly but appropriately.

2. De Beer's colloquial figures of speech include the metaphors "Stars of Life" (title), "our best bet" (par. 5), "the real stars of the show" (7), "a cool ten trillion years" (7), "hunker down for the long haul" (8), "prime real estate" (8), and "at our fingertips" (8) and understatements such as "the years of the great move" (1) and "at least for a little while" (5). Although not terribly inventive, such language lends freshness and accessibility to a scientific essay that might otherwise prove dull or unreadable to a nonspecialist audience of high school and college students.

3. Notice that most of the words that might be difficult for some students—*asteroid, kelvin, intergalactic, terraforming, spectrum, cosmologist*—hail from astronomers' vocabulary. Any science (or science fiction) enthusiasts in your class will likely have no trouble with them.

MARION WINIK
The Things They Googled
(p. 382)

In this pleasantly bittersweet essay, classifier extraordinaire Marion Winik cleverly channels the ghosts of a classic short story to ponder the burdens of memory in the information age. Even readers unfamiliar with Timothy O'Brien's "The Things They Carried" should feel a jolt of recognition at the problems of isolation and forgetting that Winik explores.

For such a short work, "The Things They Googled" follows a sophisticated classification scheme. Beginning with a binary classification of young and old Internet users, Winik then moves into complex classifications of the types of Google searches each group might employ. Whether "young" or "old" themselves, students should have fun applying her categories to their own experiences, a project we suggest in the paired journal writing prompts.

Media resources: Readers who share a concern over Winik's implied question—"Is Google making us stupid?"—might be referred to Nicholas Carr's famous *Atlantic* article by that title (*theatlantic.com/magazine/archive/2008/07/is-google-making-us-stupid/306868/*) as well as to his comments on writing on page 533 of *The Bedford Reader*. Those inspired by Winik's essay to read "The Things They Carried" can find it in any library, whether in print or as an e-book. Dylan Baker has also read O'Brien's story for Public Radio International's *Selected Shorts*; audio of the reading can be obtained by subscribing to the podcast at *selectedshorts.org/2011/09/the-things-they-carried-shorts-for-september-16-2011/*.

QUESTIONS ON MEANING

1. "The Things They Googled" is Winik's reflection on memory and human connection; as she reveals in paragraph 8, it is also an effort to emulate the style and tone of Tim O'Brien's haunting short story.
2. Kelly McGillis is "the name of the young blond actress in the movie *Witness* who was from [Mohntown, Pennsylvania]" (par. 6) and Walter Mondale was "the vice president under Carter" (2). Students might note that every description of the "something missing" in Winik's final paragraph refers back to an example used earlier in the essay: "recipe apple gingersnap" (7), "baby koalas" (3), "liquor stores open Sunday" (2), "burns and bee stings" (2), "lonely" (3). Some might also sense that each of these examples is a metaphor for nostalgia.
3. "Older search engines" is Winik's metaphor for actual, human memory.
4. Winik's thesis might be expressed as some combination of the recent concerns that "*Google* is making us stupid" and "The Internet is making us lonely." In abandoning memory to machines, she argues subtly, we lose something important, some sense of ourselves and our connections with other human beings.

QUESTIONS ON WRITING STRATEGY

1. Winik assumes an audience much like herself and the "old" she cites in her second paragraph: probably forgetful, maybe lonely, but certainly familiar with O'Brien's story about the Vietnam War. Most of your students will not fit this assumption; instead they might fall somewhere along the spectrum between her intended audience and the "young" (1) readers Winik describes.
2. The two major categories are the "young" (par. 1) and the "old" (2). The first group includes the curious (1, 4), the bored (1), and possibly the pregnant (5); within the second group fall the forgetful (2, 4, 6), the lonely (3), and the hungry (7).
3. Both works suggest that memory is a burden. But while nearly all of the search subjects Winik invokes are trivial, O'Brien's "beautiful Vietnam War story" (par. 8) is about love, death, and responsibility. Even if students know nothing about the story, Winik offers just enough information about it to get her implied comparison across. Those who know the story will better appreciate her suggestion that American culture has become more narcissistic and shallow over the past few decades.

QUESTIONS ON LANGUAGE

1. Like many of us do, Winik is using "google" as a verb. She treats it as a title (capitalized and italics) only when she's referring to the search engine proper.
2. In citing a search for the word *pleonasm*, which means "redundancy" or "using more words than necessary to get meaning across," Winik makes a sly little joke at her own expense.
3. Throughout the essay, Winik establishes a bittersweet humor with deadpan understatement. Other examples include the search for a liquor store in paragraph 2, the fear of cancer in paragraph 3, and the discovery of "obituaries not their own" in paragraph 5.

MARION WINIK ON WRITING

Your students might not have experience working with professional editors, but surely they've experienced the dread of revising that Winik describes. We hope they will find encouragement in knowing that even a professional writer can feel overwhelmed by a reviewer's comments on a draft and follow her lead in pushing through the work anyway.

10
CAUSE AND EFFECT
Asking Why

As you know, the matter of cause and effect can plunge a class into many complexities, and it can sometimes lead to fruitless wrangles. Still, many instructors find that this chapter leads to unusually satisfying results.

We start off with two complementary essays, Chitra Divakaruni's "Live Free and Starve" and student Marie Javdani's "*Plata o Plomo*: Silver or Lead" (Javdani's essay is documented), both examining effects of globalization. Then Randall Munroe's "Everybody Jump" irreverently answers a hypothetical question about physics, and Christopher Beam's "Blood Loss" considers interrelated trends in crime and journalism. The chapter concludes with "Little Fish in a Big Pond," Malcolm Gladwell's take on why excellent students so often struggle in college.

We have endeavored to clarify the difference between process analysis and cause-and-effect analysis, a frequent source of confusion. Process asks *how*; cause and effect asks *why*. Further, process deals with events that are repeated or repeatable or even just theoretically repeatable (like the creation of the Grand Canyon); cause and effect deals with singular events, one-time happenings.

Studying cause and effect can lead to a discussion of common errors in reasoning, as we indicate in this chapter when we touch on the fallacy of *post hoc*. If you wish to bring up logical fallacies, a few are listed, defined, and illustrated in Chapter 12, on argument and persuasion (pp. 486–87). Perhaps it is enough at this point merely to call students' attention to them. Cause and effect may be complicated enough without trying to tackle logical fallacies at the same time.

CHITRA DIVAKARUNI
Live Free and Starve

(p. 398)

Both Chitra Divakaruni's "Live Free and Starve" and the essay we pair it with, Marie Javdani's *"Plata o Plomo,"* tackle globalization—specifically, the effects that policies or actions in the United States can have on those in the developing world.

Divakaruni focuses on the drastically limited choices of child laborers: If they don't work, even under terrible conditions, they starve. Divakaruni argues that Americans should not try to stop child labor abroad without also taking responsibility for the terrible deprivation that sends children into labor in the first place. That "without also" is crucial for students to understand: Divakaruni may show the unintended consequences of a bill banning goods produced with child labor, but she certainly does not argue *for* child labor. For readers inclined to favor US action on unjust labor practices and similar issues of human rights around the world, Divakaruni's paragraph 5 presents a warning not to evaluate others' situations from a strictly American perspective. In the end, the author suggests the kinds of measures Americans would need to take if they really want to help child laborers.

We have previously included Divakaruni's essay in the argument chapter, and it could still be taught as an argument. It provides an excellent chance to discuss emotional appeals. Ask students to mark places in the essay where Divakaruni works to touch the emotions of readers, and then in class spend some time at the board noting the relevant passages. Small groups of students could each analyze one of the passages: What beliefs and values does Divakaruni appeal to? How accurate is she in gauging her readers' sympathies? Do the appeals work to strengthen her argument? (If you would like students to write on Divakaruni's emotional appeals, see the fourth writing suggestion.)

Media resources: In the second suggestion for writing, we direct students to *childlaborphotographs.com* for an essay assignment. It could be worthwhile to examine some of David Parker's photographs of child laborers in class. The interview from which Divakaruni's comments on writing are drawn—along with several others—can be heard in full at the author's Web site: *chitradivakaruni.com/videos/*; the site also features videos of Divakaruni's frequent speaking engagements.

QUESTIONS ON MEANING

1. Divakaruni wants to make her readers think with greater complexity about the solutions available—or not available—for the problem of child labor in developing countries. The title alerts the readers that the author's perspective is perhaps unusual. The brief paragraph 2 makes it clear that she disagrees with the House's solution. Then in paragraph 4 she begins to explain why.

2. Divakaruni's thesis is stated in paragraph 8: "A bill like the one we've just passed is of no use unless it goes hand in hand with programs that will offer a new life to these newly released children."
3. Third World countries are the developing nations of Asia, Africa, and Latin America. The term comes from the Cold War: The First and Second Worlds were the non-Communist and Communist industrialized nations.
4. Divakaruni means that most Americans have already met their survival needs (for "bread," as she puts it) and thus can afford the relative luxury of seeking freedom and other needs at the top of the pyramid.
5. The children lack "food and clothing and medication," there are no schools for them, their governments can't provide these things, and ultimately no one takes responsibility for them.

QUESTIONS ON WRITING STRATEGY

1. The rhetorical questions expand on the opening (thesis) sentence. They push readers to think hard about the negative effects the legislation could have on child laborers and to consider their willingness to "shoulder the responsibility" for the children when they are jobless.
2. Divakaruni explains in this paragraph how child labor affects children. The first words ("It is true that child labor is a terrible thing") establish the idea of the paragraph, and the remainder concisely itemizes the effects.
3. In telling the detailed story of one child, Divakaruni grounds her essay in a specific case. She establishes her authority as an observer of child labor abroad, and an open-eyed and sympathetic observer at that. Though Nimai had a life that was "hardly a desirable existence for a child," he still was better off, Divakaruni contends, than the nonworking children in his village.

QUESTIONS ON LANGUAGE

1. The survival of the families is so borderline that caring for their own children could ruin them.
2. The words show compassion—"ribs sticking out," "hunger was too much to bear," "ate whatever they could find," "knew they'd be beaten for it."
3. *Blithe* has roots in Old Saxon, Middle Dutch, Old High German, and Old Norse. It earlier referred to the outward expression of a kindly feeling but has come to mean "heedless or careless, unaware of the full implications of an act."

CHITRA DIVAKARUNI ON WRITING

For Divakaruni, social activism broadens and sensitizes her and is thus a boon to her writing. Our note following her comments prompts students to consider just what a writer gains from having her or his "preconceptions" challenged and from understanding the lives of others. The author's remarks could open up a discussion of critical thinking, not just about others' ideas but about one's own as well.

MARIE JAVDANI

Plata o Plomo: Silver or Lead

(p. 403)

Paired with the previous essay—Chitra Divakaruni's look at child labor in developing countries—this essay focuses on another problem that affects children in the Third World: drug production and trafficking. In a good example of student research writing, Marie Javdani explores the plight of Colombian peasants caught between rebels who finance their cause through drug trafficking and government-condoned forces who battle the rebels. Extensive financial aid to the Colombian government from the United States has done little to stem the production and flow of drugs from the country, largely because of government corruption. Javdani argues that US money would be better spent drastically reducing US demand for drugs, which would, in turn, significantly decrease the profitability of the drug trade and thus improve the situation in places like Colombia.

Students may be surprised by the connection Javdani makes between young Americans' use of illegal drugs and the death of a young Colombian. Class discussion might focus on this connection, which brings the abstractions of globalization down to concrete cases. Do students accept the connection? Do they accept Javdani's conclusion that Americans have a responsibility to change their own behavior in order to help improve conditions in developing countries?

Media resources: The second writing prompt following Javdani's essay suggests that students research drug use among US adolescents. The report we recommend as a starting point, *Monitoring the Future Results,* is updated annually and published by the National Institute on Drug Abuse at *drugabuse .gov/related-topics/trends-statistics/monitoring-future.*

QUESTIONS ON MEANING

1. Javdani states her thesis at the end of paragraph 3, forecasting the organization of the essay. In paragraphs 4–7 she describes "what's happening in drug-source countries," in paragraphs 8–9 she covers "how the United States can and cannot help there," and in paragraphs 10–11 she makes a case for "what, instead, can be done at home."
2. Many peasants fear the government more than the rebels, in part because the rebels can provide protection from the government whereas the government provides little protection from the rebels. Also, the peasants evidently receive money from the rebel drug lords to farm coca.
3. As Javdani writes in paragraph 8, money used to eradicate coca fields has "alienated peasants" and "escalated violence," and money intended to "help peasants establish alternative crops" and further legitimate police efforts has wound up helping arm paramilitary forces or simply disappearing. Javdani argues that greater efforts must be made to reduce the US market for drugs.

QUESTIONS ON WRITING STRATEGY

1. Students may have different thoughts about Javdani's intended audience, but in her final paragraph she clearly appeals to people her own age to recognize the extent to which their use of and tolerance for drug use in this country has harmful effects elsewhere. Javdani wrote the essay in a freshman writing class, so she may have had in mind an audience of her classmates.
2. Javdani's sympathies seem to lie with the Colombian peasants. For evidence, students might point to her opening description of Miguel and her discussion throughout of the Colombians' plight and the atrocities they face.
3. Javdani's extensive use of sources backs up her claims and gives her writing authority. The source citations are particularly effective in the detailed descriptions of the situation in Colombia.
4. The contrast Javdani sets up in her opening paragraphs is between a suburban teenager scoring drugs in the United States and a peasant boy facing execution because of his family's resistance to drug trafficking in Colombia. She creates a connection between the two that she returns to in her conclusion: It is the demand for drugs in the United States, typified by Eric, that endangers peasants in Colombia, typified by Miguel.

QUESTIONS ON LANGUAGE

1. The phrase "between a rock and a hard place" means being stuck between two equally bad choices with no alternative. The peasants can either work with the government and face torture and execution by the rebel drug lords or work with the drug lords and face the same fate from government-condoned paramilitary forces.
2. Javdani writes that Eric lives in a "suburban paradise" and yet still faces the "stress of homework and ex-girlfriends"; obviously, she intends readers to see his life as not terribly stressful at all and certainly not an excuse to use drugs. Students should see immediately that Javdani has no sympathy for Eric.
3. The peasants are "traitors" to one side or the other no matter what their choice, so they are not literally traitors, and the "cooperation" the peasants are accused of is not voluntary but forced, so it is not literally cooperation.
4. *Guerilla* comes from the Spanish word for war, *guerra*, with the diminutive ending *-illa*; it might be translated literally as "small war." The word was coined in the early nineteenth century to describe the Spanish resistance movement against the French regime established by Napoleon Bonaparte. The Spanish word for "guerilla fighter" is *guerillero*, but in English *guerilla* has long referred to those who participate in guerilla warfare as well as to the warfare itself.

MARIE JAVDANI ON WRITING

Javdani offers much useful advice for other student writers. We emphasize her counsel to care about one's topic because inexperienced writers, especially reluctant ones, often don't make the effort to find their own angle on a subject. We also like Javdani's warning that interest doesn't justify the speechifying of a soapbox orator: Moderation is the key.

RANDALL MUNROE
Everybody Jump

(p. 410)

It's easy to see why Randall Munroe has developed such a devoted following of self-professed "geeks" of all stripes. A trained physicist, the writer knows his science but doesn't take himself (or his subjects) seriously at all.

Students should, we hope, take inspiration from Munroe's inquisitive approach to writing. As he explained in an interview with Megan Garber for the *Atlantic*, he takes great pleasure in researching his "What If?" blog posts. Faced with an interesting question, he can't help but look into the answer, he says: "It's just like, once it gets in my brain, it keeps bugging me, and I don't know the answer, but I'm really curious. What really happens is: I have an idea for what the answer is, but then I want to figure out if I'm right or not. So I have to keep working to find out. And oftentimes, in the process of learning I'm wrong, I'll run into something even cooler. And then once I find that, I just want to tell everyone about it." You might use this statement as a starting point for discussion: What role does curiosity play in research and in writing? To what extent does Munroe's blog post convey his own joy in learning something new?

Media resources: Readers who enjoy "Everybody Jump" will surely also enjoy the many cartoons at *xkcd.com* and likely want to spend some time with other *What If?* posts archived on the site. We encourage students to check Munroe's online sources, the science blogs *Dot Physics* and *The Straight Dope*, for themselves in the third writing suggestion after the essay. They (and you) might also be interested in the author's March 2014 TED talk, available at *ted.com/talks/randall_munroe_comics_that_ask_what _if?language=en#t-212571*.

QUESTIONS ON MEANING

1. Kinematics is the branch of mechanical physics that examines bodies in motion; Munroe is referring to the question of whether a large mass of human bodies impacting the Earth at a concentrated point would affect the planet's orbit in any way (it would not, he explains). Although the implied intent of his readers' question, Munroe acknowledges that other writers have already covered it; he turns to what he sees as a more interesting, less commonly considered effect—of the entire global population gathering in one place and then attempting to disperse.
2. The scenario would result in the collapse of modern civilization. Billions would die, the survivors would move on, and the planet itself (or its orbit, anyway) would be unaffected.

QUESTIONS ON WRITING STRATEGY

1. Munroe is writing for fans of *xkcd* and his *What If* blog, specifically to those who have written in with "one of the most popular questions submitted through [his] Web site" (par. 1). Those fans are at least somewhat

knowledgeable about physics, as his unexplained reference to "kinematics" suggests, but they also have a sense of humor. They might be characterized as, in a word, geeks—but in a good way.

2. The absurd causal chain *is* Munroe's thesis. Although he starts the essay by purporting to answer a scientific question, he turns the subject on its head and examines, instead, the chain of events that might happen after the event in question has concluded.

3. For his explanation of the physics of kinematics and the *cause* of billions of people jumping at once, Munroe summarizes information from two science blogs. But his consideration of *effects* is purely speculative and entertainingly irreverent.

4. The illustrations bring life and humor to a scientific explanation and extend Munroe's meaning by helping readers to visualize the scenario as he imagines it.

5. As Munroe explains his choice, he doesn't want to be vague. Since the world's population would fill a space the size of Rhode Island, he decides to go ahead and place his scenario *in* Rhode Island. The specificity anchors a theoretical analysis and helps readers to better understand Munroe's explanations by attaching them to a real place.

QUESTIONS ON LANGUAGE

1. Munroe's tone is ironic to the point of absurdity. He presents himself as not very serious and more than a little cheeky, yet his essay is infused with obvious appreciation for physics and natural science.

2. In mathematics, a *factor* (par. 6) is a multiplier. The Earth, Munroe is saying, weighs ten trillion times as much as the weight of all human beings combined.

3. The present tense gives the scenario he describes a sense of immediacy, letting readers imagine themselves as active participants.

CHRISTOPHER BEAM

Blood Loss

(p. 416)

Prompted to write by the lackluster media response to a serial killer's conviction and sentencing, Christopher Beam comes up with an interesting theory to explain a decline in serial killings over the past few decades. Drawing on examples of sensational crimes throughout the twentieth century (and the early twenty-first), he concludes that we are most caught up with those misdoings that tap into generalized anxieties. Ignored by the media because more pressing concerns have moved to the forefront of the national consciousness, serial killers have less incentive to do what they do. And in their place, it seems, we have an epidemic of mass murders.

Students may have a hard time accepting Beam's suggestion that media coverage contributes to the incidence of some types of crime. The author is, after all, a crime reporter. You may want to begin discussion by asking the class to recall examples of recent "media frenzies" over sensational crimes. What elements do the big stories have in common? Did the perpetrators, in fact, seem to want the notoriety their actions brought them? Could they have been motivated by a desire for fame? If so, what responsibility do the media bear for their actions?

QUESTIONS ON MEANING

1. As the structure of the essay suggests, Beam has a dual purpose: to report that serial killings have declined significantly since their peak in the 1980s and to propose a theory explaining why. In the first four paragraphs he establishes the fact of the trend, showing that the number of serial murders has dropped dramatically and with it the public's fascination with serial killers. The next two paragraphs examine possible explanations for the drop but dismiss them, and the remainder of the essay develops the idea, introduced in paragraph 7, that media coverage of serial killers "tapped into the obsessions and fears of the time."

2. Beam assumes an audience of true-crime buffs, it seems. At the very least, he expects that readers will have a passing knowledge of the events and cases he cites, whether recent or historic. Even if they don't, however, Beam's interest is not in the individual crimes but in their accumulation and their cultural symbolisms. The details are not necessary to get his point across.

3. Yes, he does. Beam suggests a correlation between sensational crimes and media coverage, claiming that the "short path to celebrity" offered by the "media's growing obsession with serial killers in the 1970s and '80s" (par. 5) helped to fuel such killings. He adds, in paragraph 7, that one serial killer (David Berkowitz) went as far as to contact the news media directly. His point seems to be that by sensationalizing certain kinds of crimes, the media give criminals an added incentive to commit them.

4. Beam's thesis is that the crimes that attract the most media attention are those that resonate with or somehow symbolize prevailing cultural fears—such as kidnappings and "societal decay during the Depression" (par. 9), serial murders by "sex-addled psychopaths" (7) in the 1970s and 1980s, and terrorism today. Serial killings don't capture our attention anymore because we're worried about "instant mass annihilation" (11). He comes closest to stating his general idea in paragraph 9: "Infamous crimes almost always needle the anxieties of their periods."

QUESTIONS ON WRITING STRATEGY

1. The gruesome details in Beam's story about an archetypal serial killer grab readers' interest. That the "crossbow cannibal" was more or less ignored by the media starts the essay on an ironic note and sets up Beam's claim that serial killers murder partly for the media attention.

2. Beam uses the word *structural* in its sense of "related to or concerned with systematic structure in a particular field of study" (*The American Heritage Dictionary*). His point in paragraph 5 is that serial killings didn't necessarily increase in the 1970s and 1980s: It's possible, he acknowledges, that they were simply better documented. But as he goes on to say in paragraph 6, that questionable cause-and-effect relationship is not relevant to his inquiry. Regardless of whether there was an actual rise in serial killings four decades ago, the number has declined since then.

3. In paragraph 6 Beam considers the possibility that police work and longer jail terms for captured killers might have contributed to the decline in serial killings. But he has a different explanation: He suggests that serial killings have dropped off the radar because the public isn't as fascinated by them as it once was, giving "psychopaths" (par. 7) less reason to kill.

4. The statistics support Beam's claim that "serial murders peaked in the 1980s and have been declining ever since" (par. 4). Readers may reasonably question their reliability: The data were gathered by a single scholar and represent cases reported in popular sources. But there is little other data available, according to Beam.

5. Beam cites James Alan Fox's definition in paragraph 4: "a string of four or more homicides committed by one or a few perpetrators that spans a period of days, weeks, months, or even years." He also identifies the first recorded instance of "serial murderer" (as cited in *The Oxford English Dictionary*) and the source of the synonym "serial killer" (it was coined by an FBI agent in 1981) in paragraph 8.

QUESTIONS ON LANGUAGE

1. Beam uses complex, formal words and phrases—such as *incarceration* and *caveat* (par. 6), *conversely* (10), "structural explanations for the rise of reported serial murders" (5), and "As the raw numbers have declined" (7)—alongside colloquial expressions, including "just aren't the sensation they used to be" (1), "hard to come by" (4), and "returned the favor" (8). The informal language helps him connect with readers and build a casual tone; the formal language emphasizes that he has studied his subject thoroughly and takes his argument seriously.

2. "Golden boy" carries with it a sense of resentment for somebody who appears to be perfect; it also implies that such a person is an insincere sycophant. Applied to Ted Bundy, a wealthy political supporter, the term also hints at Americans' distrust of the greedy and powerful in the 1980s.

3. Beam uses *needle* as a transitive verb ("needle the anxieties of their periods"), whereas students may know it only as a noun (a sewing implement). The informal use creates a compelling image, implying both a prick of conscience and the lethal injection of a death sentence.

MALCOLM GLADWELL

Little Fish in a Big Pond

(p. 422)

Students of any level of ability at any level of institution will, we expect, take heart in Malcolm Gladwell's probing explanation of why even the best students, at the best universities, might unexpectedly find themselves flailing. The problem is not in their abilities, he argues, but in their perceptions. And most of them, he argues, would do better for themselves to lower their sights and pick a less competitive school, one that lets them soar.

Gladwell is clear in the assumption that the sciences are more rigorous and more rewarding, career-wise, than the humanities—a bias that could raise some hackles in your class. Discussion might open with the question that will be on many students' minds: What is the purpose of a college education? (See the journal prompt and the first writing suggestion.) Are your students in school simply to earn a degree or to gain a particular set of marketable skills, or have they enrolled for other reasons, such as developing critical-thinking abilities and enhancing their personal development? Is it worthwhile to study the liberal arts, or do more "practical" disciplines—such as math, science, or a technical trade—seem more useful? Why?

We have highlighted Kellie Young's "The Undercurrent" (p. 189) in the "Connections" question following Gladwell's essay, but note that several of the student writers in *The Bedford Reader* offer an opportunity to assess his analysis against Caroline Sacks's experience, most notably Andrea Roman (p. 215), Koji Frahm (p. 268), Tal Fortgang (p. 446), Brianne Richson (p. 513), and Jon Overton (p. 518). Your own students' perspectives, of course, will be invaluable in supporting their evaluation of Gladwell's argument.

Media resources: Gladwell's contribution is one of several recent books and articles that argue for changes to what has become a hyper-competitive college selection and application process. Others include *Excellent Sheep: The Miseducation of the American Elite and the Way to a Meaningful Life* by William Deresiewicz (2014), *Where You Go Is Not Who You'll Be: An Antidote to the College Admissions Mania* by Frank Bruni (2015), *Our Kids: The American Dream in Crisis* by Robert D. Putnam (2015), and "The Poisonous Reach of the College-Admissions Process" by Matt Feeney (*The New Yorker*, January 28, 2016). Gladwell also discussed his argument in "Little Fish in a Big Pond" with public radio host Brian Lehrer when *David and Goliath* was first released in 2015; audio can be retrieved at *wnyc.org/story/malcolm-gladwell-battling-giants/*.

QUESTIONS ON MEANING

1. As Gladwell often does (and as we mention in the author headnote), he is writing to synthesize academic research for a general audience. In this case he seems also to hope to persuade anxious parents and potential college students that less elite schools are often the better choice.

2. As Gladwell explains in paragraphs 15–20, "relative deprivation" is sociologist Samuel Stouffer's term for the natural outcome of the human tendency to compare oneself to one's peers. Rather than measure success or failure objectively, he found in multiple studies, people tend to judge themselves *relative* to the accomplishments of those around them. We tend to feel more deprived if we perceive others as doing better; more satisfied if we perceive others as doing the same or worse.

3. The "Big Fish–Little Pond effect" is the concept of "relative deprivation" (see question 2 above) applied to education. The analogy comes courtesy of psychologist Herbert Marsh, who contends that students in a selective school, or "Big Fish," naturally feel inadequate because they're surrounded by peers who are as just as talented as they—or more so. That feeling of inadequacy, in turn, has a negative effect on "motivation and confidence" (par. 21), discouraging otherwise talented students from pursuing their goals. Those same students in a "Little Pond," or a merely "good" school, tend to feel superior to their peers and are therefore more motivated and more likely to succeed. Where your students

place themselves in this scheme will depend, of course, on the relative selectivity of your school and their own "academic 'self-concept'" (21) within it.

4. Gladwell summarizes the main idea of this selection, which reinforces the general thesis of *David and Goliath*, in paragraph 31: "We take it for granted that the Big Pond expands opportunities. . . . We have a definition in our heads of what an advantage is — and the definition isn't right. And what happens as a result? It means that we make mistakes. . . . It's the Little Pond that maximizes your chances to do whatever you want." More specifically, Gladwell is arguing that is it not necessarily a good idea for students to strive to attend the "best" schools.

QUESTIONS ON WRITING STRATEGY

1. Although Gladwell's *subject* is college students, they're not necessarily counted among his intended general audience. All the same, in couching the start of his conclusion (par. 31) as advice to anxious parents and to prospective students addressed as "you," he makes it clear that he absolutely expects that readers can use the information he provides in making their own choices. Your students are already in school, of course, but his analysis may help them live with their choice if they're feeling out of water — or reassure them that they're in the right place.

2. In typical Gladwellian fashion, the author presents tables of seemingly impenetrable data and interprets them for readers (pars. 25–28). To support his claim that STEM students often "drop out" (he means from the majors, not from school), he compares incoming SAT scores and degree completion rates at Hartwick College, a "small liberal arts college" (24), and Harvard University, one of the most "prestigious universities in the world" (27). Gladwell finds, counterintuitively, that students of higher ability are less likely to finish a STEM program at the elite school than are students of lower ability at the "easier" college. Noticing that science students at both schools give up at the same rate, he extrapolates this evidence to apply to all STEM majors everywhere, concluding that they quit not because of lack of ability but because of feelings of relative deprivation.

3. Gladwell starts by relating the background of Caroline Sacks and her decision to be a science major at an Ivy League school (pars. 1–5). He briefly turns to contrast schools like Brown and the University of Maryland, explaining how they're different and bringing in the "Big Fish . . . Little Fish" concept (7), then he returns to Sacks's story, examining how and why she gave up on science (8–14). Gladwell pauses to introduce the theory of "relative deprivation" and its scholarly origins (15–19) and apply it to Sacks's example (20). Next he delves into consideration of the "Big Fish–Little Pond Effect," again explaining its academic source (21–22). Briefly invoking Sacks again, he goes on to compare data from two schools to consider why so many STEM students in general tend to switch majors (23–28), bringing back the theory of "relative deprivation" to explain his interpretation. He then applies that interpretation to Sacks's experience (29–30). Finally, Gladwell concludes by presenting his thesis, a summary of the implications of his analysis, and returning, one more time, to Sacks. Many readers will be entranced by the way Gladwell weaves disparate notions together; others may express frustration and a suspicion (voiced often by critics) that he oversimplifies.

4. By focusing his analysis on the experiences of one student in particular, Gladwell grounds the academic theories he discusses and makes them relatable.

QUESTIONS ON LANGUAGE

1. Gladwell mixes academic vocabulary and colloquial expressions with a dose of figurative language (see the next question); his tone might be described as reportorial. Given that he's writing for a general audience rather than an academic one, his choices are not only appropriate but effective.
2. Other boating metaphors include "whirlwind tour" (pars. 4, 6), "finishes much farther back in the pack" (6), "her heart sank" (8), "you were in the same boat as your peers" (17), and "comparing ourselves to people 'in the same boat as ourselves'" (19). They work so well because Sacks wanted to be an ichthyologist, or fish scientist, and presumably would have spent much of her life on the water—and also of course because they neatly float with the "Big Fish–Little Pond" analogy that informs and runs through Gladwell's entire analysis.
3. From its context in this essay, some readers might mistakenly assume that an *ichthyologist* (par. 2) is a scientist who studies bugs (properly known as an *entomologist*). In truth, the word refers to a scientist who studies fish, or a marine biologist. "Shark Lady" Eugenie Clark (1922–2015), whom Sacks idolized, was a pioneer in the field.
4. *Elite* and *prestigious* usually carry positive connotations; *deficiency* and *inadequacy* are usually considered negative qualities. Gladwell turns these assumptions on their head, ironically stressing that the "best" schools are not the best choices, that the worst students are smarter than they get credit for.

MALCOM GLADWELL ON WRITING

We like Gladwell's point that crafting an argument or supporting a thesis is not a process of working out an idea and then writing it down but is rather a process of working out an idea *by* writing it down. That the process depends on "stumbling"—asking questions, looking for answers, reshaping ideas as new information comes to light, and revising many times over—seems equally important and a point that beginning writers often resist.

11
DEFINITION
Tracing Boundaries

"When they come to definition," said the late Richard Beal, an author of textbooks, a director of composition, and our sage adviser, "most authors of rhetorically organized readers seem not to know what it is nor what to do about it."

Definition, he suggested, is not in itself a distinct and separate expository method but a catchall name for a kind of explaining that involves whatever method or methods it can use. It would break with tradition, Beal said, to place definition last among methods of exposition. Then the instructor might use it to review all the rest.

We hope that this ordering of the book's contents proves useful to you. You will also find the book carefully distinguishing a short definition (the kind found in a dictionary), a stipulative definition (the kind that pins down an essential term in a paragraph or two), and an extended definition (the kind found in whole essays).

All the essays in this chapter trace the shape of a definite territory and attempt to set forth its nature. In the paired selections, Tal Fortgang and Roxane Gay demonstrate how a word can change meaning depending on who's using it: Each explores the concept of *privilege*, coming to remarkably different conclusions about their respective advantages. Meghan Daum takes issue with popular usage of *narcissist*, insisting on the value of the psychological term's clinical meaning. Dagoberto Gilb defines what *pride* means for one community of Mexican Americans. And Augusten Burroughs strives to help victims of domestic abuse learn to love themselves.

TAL FORTGANG
Checking My Privilege

(p. 446)

When *Time* magazine re-published Tal Fortgang's provocative student essay, they gave it the sensationalistic headline "Why I'll Never Apologize for My White Male Privilege"—and a firestorm erupted. Predictably, conservative pundits hailed Fortgang as a hero; liberals (and at least one student at Princeton) criticized him harshly. He was interviewed on Fox News, the *New York Times* and the *Washington Post* jumped on the claim that students across the country were being told to "check" their privilege, and outlets ranging from *The Huffington Post* to *The Guardian* weighed in.

We have no doubt your students will have their own strong reactions to Fortgang's defensive insistence that being white and male has had nothing to do with what he's accomplished so far or will accomplish in the future. We pair his essay with "Peculiar Benefits," an exploration of the subtleties of privilege by Haitian American college teacher and cultural critic Roxane Gay, at least in part to help temper their responses.

Readers intrigued or otherwise affected by Fortgang's discussion of the Holocaust in Poland might be pointed to "The Capricious Camera" in Chapter 8 (p. 315 of the book). In that carefully researched essay, student writer Laila Ayad closely examines a photograph from a Polish site, unearthing a relatively unknown aspect of the Nazi agenda.

Media resources: For an entertaining and eye-opening check of their own privileges, students might want to take Charles Murray's famous "bubble" quiz, hosted by *PBS Newshour* at *www.pbs.org/newshour/making-sense/do-you-live-in-a-bubble-a-quiz-2/.* Fortgang's Fox News interview can be watched at *video.foxnews.com/v/3529042337001/princeton-student-why-i-dont-apologize-for-white-privilege/?#sp=show-clips.* You might also ask students to locate and read any of the dozens of responses to his argument available online, particularly Princeton student Briana Payton's "Dear Privileged-at-Princeton: You. Are. Privileged. And Meritocracy Is a Myth" (*time.com/89482/dear-privileged-at-princeton-you-are-privileged-and-meritocracy-is-a-myth/*).

QUESTIONS ON MEANING

1. Fortgang considers "Check your privilege" to be an accusation of unearned advantage based on race and gender, a "reminder that [he] ought to feel personally apologetic because white males seem to pull most of the strings in the world" (par. 1).

2. After outlining his family's struggles as ironic examples of privilege in paragraphs 4–7, Fortgang shifts focus in paragraph 9, turning to notions of privilege he does accept. He considers himself lucky that his grandparents immigrated to the United States (10–11), that his grandfather was a hard worker (12–14), that his family stressed faith and education in the home (15), and that he has enjoyed a "legacy" (15, 16) of support and strong values. He does not accept, however, that this legacy has given him any advantages or that he should apologize for it.

3. The "equal protection clause" is an element of the Fourteenth Amendment of the US Constitution, which promises that all American citizens have the same rights. Fortgang invokes the idea of a "meritocracy" (par. 2) and the "American Dream" (14) to insist that everyone has equal opportunities. Essentially, he's denying the existence of institutional racism or white male privilege.

4. The author's primary purpose seems to be to publicly defend himself against accusations of privilege. On another level, he attempts to persuade fellow students to reconsider the assumptions they make about each other. And since he is writing for a conservative audience, another

purpose could be to take a visible stance in the debate on white male privilege. Estimations of how well he has succeeded will vary, depending on readers' own biases.

QUESTIONS ON WRITING STRATEGY

1. As we point out in the introductory note to the essay, Fortgang's original audience was very specific: He was writing for politically conservative students at Princeton. That expected readership is evident in his mention of Princeton (par. 1) and in his cheeky references to President Obama (par. 1), "meritocracy" and "conspiracies" (2), and "Tea Party Radicals" (14). We expect he anticipated a positive response of hearty agreement and recognition. When the essay was distributed to a wider audience, he did indeed get much of that, but he was also excoriated by liberals for missing the meaning of privilege and failing to acknowledge the invisible benefits it confers.
2. The generalizations in Fortgang's introductory paragraphs are essential to his purpose of defining. The stories about his family offer specifics to bring his proposed definition down to earth and show "the problem with calling someone out for the 'privilege' which you assume has defined their narrative" (par. 8).
3. "Perhaps it's the privilege my grandfather . . ." (par. 4); "Or maybe it's the privilege my grandmother . . ." (5); "Perhaps my privilege is that . . ." (6); "Perhaps it was my privilege that . . ." (7). Steeped in irony verging on sarcasm, these phrases introduce specific elements of his Jewish family's difficult history, reiterate the subject of Fortgang's definition for emphasis, and underscore his hostile attitude toward "detractors" (9).
4. Fortgang concludes with his thesis statement, which will likely strike readers as angry and defiant.
5. Answers will vary. Some readers will find Fortgang's analysis of causes and effects—particularly his examination of the Holocaust and its decimation of his family—provocative and insightful, while others will surely call him out for denying the existence of institutionalized forms of oppression or refusing to acknowledge that his own "legacy" (a supportive family, a decent standard of living, educational opportunities, and so forth) may indeed have conferred some advantages.

QUESTIONS ON LANGUAGE

1. We find one *simile*—"The phrase . . . descends recklessly, like an Obama-sanctioned drone, and aims laser-like" (par. 1)—and several *metaphors*, including "a phrase that floats around college campuses" (1), "strike down opinions" (1), "pull most of the strings in the world" (1), "toes that line" (2), "ascribing all the fruit I reap not to the seeds I sow but some invisible patron saint" (2), "racist patriarchy holding my hand" (3), "underdog stories" (3), "iron will" (6), "our success has been gift-wrapped" (7), "conquered their demons" (8), and "American dream" (14). The "fruit I reap . . ." metaphor, with its Old Testament connotations, strikes us as the most clever: Fortgang returns to it when he says he "unearthed some examples" (3) and speaks of the ability to "flourish" (3, 10).
2. Fortgang puts quotation marks around "privilege" in paragraphs 8, 13, and 15 to indicate that he takes issue with the word and conventional understandings of its meaning. Other examples of liberal words and phrases Fortgang questions include "check," "stigmas," "societal norms" (par. 2), "power systems" (8), and "environmentalism" (13).

3. In alluding to the most influential African American leader of the civil rights movement, Fortgang seems to intend to align his Jewish identity with that of other oppressed minorities. Some readers are sure to find the implication jarring, or at least disingenuous, particularly because while King was stressing that Americans *are* judged by race, Fortgang is insisting that they're not.

4. *Acclimate* is not quite a synonym of *assimilate*. While *assimilation* implies subsuming one's native culture to the dominant culture of a new country, *acclimation* refers simply to growing accustomed to a new environment. Students might notice that the word also picks up again on Fortgang's "fruit I reap . . . seeds I sow" metaphor from the second paragraph.

TAL FORTGANG ON WRITING

Any student who has ever struggled to narrow a subject down to an arguable thesis should find Fortgang's advice helpful. His notion of "channel[ing] your inner five-year-old" and asking yourself "why" over and over again is, we think, not only inventive but also practical. In illustrating how Fortgang came to the "nuclear argument" of his own essay, the metaphor further reveals how he developed the support for his controversial point. Students should see that those who pick a subject about which they care passionately tend to write well, and writers who know that are off to a running start.

ROXANE GAY

Peculiar Benefits

(p. 453)

Roxane Gay's honest and thoughtful look at the loaded concept of privilege serves as both a stinging retort to the essay by Tal Fortgang that precedes it and an example of the sort of teacherly injunction he so vehemently resents.

How do your own students respond to Gay's assertion, at multiple points, that they, too, are privileged? We suspect that some will nod in agreement, while others, like Fortgang, will resist the idea. It will surely be worthwhile to spend some time picking apart the nuances of Gay's definition, which appears sophisticated but is at heart pretty simple. Privilege, as she sees it, is any personal attribute that carries a social or economic advantage; that's it. Whatever form(s) it takes, it's nothing to be ashamed of and nothing to apologize for.

Students interested in learning more about poverty in Haiti, the research project proposed in the third writing topic, might be pointed to Junot Díaz's narrative about his mother (p. 88) as a starting point. His story takes place in the Dominican Republic, which shares an island with Haiti, if not a government— and at the moment some rather contentious immigration policies.

Media resources: For readers who enjoy Gay's voice and writing, any of the author's critical essays collected in *Bad Feminist* rewards careful reading, and much of her prolific output (fiction and nonfiction) is archived on the author's Web site, *roxanegay.com*. She also offers an entertaining and insightful definition of *feminist* in a 2015 TED talk: The eleven-minute video is available at *ted.com/talks/roxane_gay_confessions_of_a_bad_feminist*.

QUESTIONS ON MEANING

1. Gay offers a brief summary of her own in paragraph 3. As she defines it, "Privilege is a right or immunity granted as a peculiar benefit, advantage, or favor. . . . Nearly everyone, particularly in the developed world, has something someone else doesn't, something someone else yearns for." Her point is that privilege is not necessarily determined by race, gender, or income—it's whatever aspects of a person's demographic profile give them opportunities others don't have.

2. The author is saying that even the poorest person in America is better off than the average person in Haiti, where poverty is extreme and widespread. And like poverty, she says, "Privilege is relative and contextual" (par. 10): That is, both are determined in comparison to others.

3. "We tend to believe that accusations of privilege imply we have it easy, which we resent because life is hard for nearly everyone" (par. 7). Gay goes on to explain that such implications are not, in fact, intended; that the idea of calling out a person's privilege is to get that person to acknowledge his or her advantages and develop empathy for those who don't share them.

4. For Gay, privilege is something of a paradox. The same person can have advantages in some respects but disadvantages in others.

5. Although she says "You don't necessarily *have* to do anything once you acknowledge your privilege" (par. 8), Gay proposes that readers at the very least acknowledge it. Even better, she suggests, they should use that knowledge "for the greater good—to try to level the playing field for everyone, to work for social justice, to bring attention to how those without certain privileges are disenfranchised" (8)—precisely what she (optimistically) attempts to do with this essay.

QUESTIONS ON WRITING STRATEGY

1. Even in Haiti, Gay notes, "inescapable poverty [exists] alongside almost repulsive luxury" (par. 2). She wants to make the point that because privilege is relative, understanding it is difficult for everybody, "particularly in the developed world" (3) and the United States. The childhood trip, she explains, started her "education on privilege . . . long before [she] could appreciate it in any meaningful way" (par. 2). She goes on in the rest of the essay to attempt to impart that education on readers.

2. As she states in her concluding sentences, Gay assumes that her readers—all of them—are privileged in some way. Some students (like Tal Fortgang in the previous essay) might reject that assumption, but we hope that Gay has made a strong enough case to persuade them to consider its validity.

3. By acknowledging the ways in which she, herself, is privileged ("one of the hardest things [she's] ever had to do," par. 5), Gay practices what she preaches. The "embarrassing" admissions of her class status, family

support, and professional success establish her ethical appeal and at the same time lend credibility to her complaints, in the next paragraph, about being treated poorly for "being black or being a woman" (6).

4. Gay identifies seven (or eight) "kinds of privilege" in paragraph 3: "racial privilege, gender (and identity) privilege, heterosexual privilege, economic privilege, able-bodied privilege, educational privilege, religious privilege, and the list goes on and on" (3). (What students might add to this list will of course vary but should be very interesting.) In paragraph 9 Gay extends her classification by mixing types of privilege and pitting them against each other: "Who would win a privilege battle between a wealthy black woman and a wealthy white male? Who would win a privilege battle between a queer white man and a queer Asian woman? Who would in a privilege battle between a working-class white man and a wealthy, differently abled Mexican woman?" Nobody wins, she determines.

QUESTIONS ON LANGUAGE

1. Although a rhetoric PhD and a college teacher, Gay is fond of informal—and sometimes mildly off-color—language, such as "so damn much" (par. 4), "crappy" (5), "my first time out" (5), "a world of hurt" (6), "pain in my ass" (6), and "smartphones and iProducts" (13). But she also uses complex, formal words and phrases—such as "immunity" (3), "intra-marital dynamics" (5), "surrendering to the acceptance of privilege" (7), "marginalized" (7, 11), "disenfranchised" (8), "demographic characteristics" (9), "halls of discourse" (10), and "relative and contextual" (13). The informal language helps her connect with readers and build an earnest tone; the formal language lends her academic credibility as a cultural critic.

2. The capital letters indicate both that Gay invented these terms and that she is using them ironically.

3. Colloquially, "white noise" is any low, repetitive sound that drowns out the ambient noise in one's environment. Gay's metaphorical use of the term carries racial connotations in the context of cultural criticism, particularly hinting at white male privilege as the usual locus of the meaning of *privilege*.

4. The final sentences are Gay's thesis statement, which she builds to throughout the essay. She holds it, a call to action, for the end because readers would have been unreceptive to her plea until reading through and absorbing the complexity of her argument. Even so, some readers might find the unexpected command a little jarring.

5. *Shanties* (par. 2) are, of course, ramshackle constructions hastily built. Students who need help visualizing just how little shelter such structures provide might be pointed to the photograph of a New York City shanty that opens Chapter 4, "Doug and Mizan's House, East River."

ROXANE GAY ON WRITING

Simply expressing oneself to be heard, Gay observes in these comments, is reason enough to write. Students might be interested to know that in the TED talk we recommend on p. 115 of this manual, Gay offers additional thoughts on how, and why, she became a writer: Feminism, she says, gave her a voice after it had been stolen, and writing gave her a use for that voice. We hope that students will be inspired by Gay's example to find their own voices.

MEGHAN DAUM

Narcissist—Give It a Rest

(p. 460)

In Greek mythology Narcissus was a handsome Greek youth who, as punishment for ignoring the advances of the nymph Echo, was made to fall in love with his own image. He then pined away, changing into the flower that bears his name. *Narcissism* has come to mean excessive self-love, and Daum has a problem with that. In this column abridged from the *Los Angeles Times*, she examines popular usage of the word, explains why such usage is inappropriate, and begs people to stop.

Students may not catch the significance of this essay's timing and context, although Daum hints at it in paragraph 5. She published "Narcissist—Give It a Rest" about a month after the American Psychiatric Association announced the controversial decision to drop narcissistic personality disorder from the latest edition of the *Diagnostic and Statistical Manual of Mental Disorders*, or DSM-V, psychologists' official catalog of mental illness. We point that out in the writing suggestion labeled "Critical Writing" and encourage students to learn why the decision sparked debate.

QUESTIONS ON MEANING

1. Daum asserts that the misuse of the word began in the 1970s and by the 1990s became so overused as to become meaningless, apparently dropping out of popular use in the first decade of the twenty-first century. As she sees it, however, people have just recently begun flinging it around again as an insult, giving "the impression that they just discovered it" (par. 3) when in fact it's been around for decades.
2. Daum's essay goes beyond defining *narcissist*. She is writing to explain how others use the word inappropriately, to complain vocally about the misuse, and to implore people to stop.
3. Daum divides her thesis between paragraphs 5 and 7: "The term has been misused and overused so flagrantly that it's now all but meaningless when it comes to labeling truly destructive tendencies. . . . So perhaps it's time to declare a moratorium on the indiscriminate use of this particular n-word."

QUESTIONS ON WRITING STRATEGY

1. The "[p]rofessional pundits . . ., bloggers, politicians, religious leaders, celebrity shrinks, cultural critics, Internet commenters and blowhards at parties" (par. 3) whom Daum criticizes would likely take umbrage at her accusations and her tone. Actual narcissists probably would not care what she thinks, one way or the other.
2. While popular usage of *narcissist* treats the word as a synonym for "any behavior you don't like" (par. 4), Daum argues for the American Psychiatric Association's clinical definition as it appeared in the *Diagnostic and*

Statistical Manual of Mental Disorders for more than four decades—a serious disorder that causes "self-destructive" (pars. 1, 5) behavior.

3. Daum opens with her complaint that "a whole lot of people" (par. 1) are using the word *narcissist* as a general insult. In paragraph 2 she establishes the history of the popular usage. Paragraphs 3 and 4 rattle off examples of people who use the word and people to whom it's applied. In paragraph 5 Daum explains her objection to the usage. Her conclusion (6–7) offers her alternate characterization of Americans' behavior. Each paragraph relates directly to Daum's thesis, includes a topic sentence, and is developed with details.

4. Daum gives examples of "narcissistic" people in paragraph 4: "Democrats, Republicans, red state folks, blue state folks, baby boomers, Gen Xers, millennials . . ., [p]arents, nonparents, vegans, meat eaters, city dwellers, rural dwellers, people who travel a lot, people who refuse to travel, writers who use the first person. . . ." By setting up most of her examples as diametrically opposed pairs (implicitly comparing and contrasting the two groups) in a breathless string, she emphasizes her point that *everybody* can be accused of narcissism, usually by someone whose tendencies are different.

QUESTIONS ON LANGUAGE

1. The writer is clearly annoyed.
2. A *vector*, from the Latin *vehere*, "to carry," is an organism that transmits disease. Given that Daum is arguing to preserve the clinical meaning of *narcissist*, readers should appreciate her implication that people casually refer to the disorder as though it's contagious, even though it's not.
3. Both phrases connote shame and taboo (especially the latter); Daum is taking her own advice and refusing to use the word.

MEGHAN DAUM ON WRITING

Daum's comments on a reader's responsibilities reinforce our own advice about reading actively and critically as well as about writing being a transaction between writer and reader. In the note following her complaint, we encourage students to explore in more detail what a reader brings to that transaction.

DAGOBERTO GILB

Pride

(p. 465)

In this lyrical essay, Gilb defines the concept of pride by focusing specifically on the experiences of Mexican Americans—"good people who are too poor but don't notice" (par. 6). Based almost wholly on examples, the definition is beautifully developed in language that is poetic and highly concrete. The language is also deceptively simple. Gilb creates striking effects using words that will be familiar to students (we couldn't think of any difficult enough for a vocabulary question, though we did gloss the Spanish words). He provides an excellent example for students to see that effective definition and description do not require sophisticated words, just specific, fresh language.

If you enjoy reading aloud, you might read the final paragraph to your students. Carefully wrought, it builds to a wonderfully satisfying conclusion.

Media resources: Gilb read from his essay collection *Gritos* for the 2003 author series at the Yarborough branch of the Austin Public Library in Austin, Texas. C-SPAN aired the reading on BookTV and has archived it online at *www.c-span.org/video/?177726-1/book-discussion-gritos-essays*. The full video is one hour long; Gilb's reading of "Pride" begins at the thirty-seven-minute mark and is immediately followed by a Q&A session in which Gilb offers his insights on the writing process.

QUESTIONS ON MEANING

1. Here is a possible summary: Pride is hard work, respect for landscape and history, fearlessness—all despite poverty.
2. Paragraphs 8–10 expand the definition outside particular lives to the landscape and heritage of Mexican Americans.
3. Gilb's final paragraph offers a panoply of images of Mexican Americans: heroes, workers, human beings with the same feelings and needs as anyone else—all of whom feel a pride in who they are. The very brownness of their skin ("Beautiful brown") is a source of pride.
4. Gilb's purpose here goes well beyond defining *pride* and creating a dominant impression of hardscrabble dignity. The essay is a hymn to the lives, history, and culture of Mexican Americans. Gilb wants to share his vision with readers from all kinds of backgrounds.

QUESTIONS ON WRITING STRATEGY

1. Gilb's opening establishes diversity—an older man in a "starched and ironed uniform" hard at work, a boy in an oversized T-shirt hard at play, and a young woman in a wreck of a car dressed for a party—and it conveys camaraderie among these three people, together in a lighted parking lot surrounded by the deepest darkness.
2. Gilb may vary his strategy because in the first instance the sources of pride are not immediately obvious and he wants to make them clear. In the second instance, the source of pride goes without saying, and he can move on.
3. The development of paragraph 7 is sophisticated. It begins with the image of the son sitting "a long time . . . on the front porch" (we don't know why until later). Then we see the boy in a brief flashback as a youngster with his dog ("both puppies"). His exuberance leads him to the park, where his response to an insect bite shows how he has matured into a proud young man. Back home, he puts on the clothes "he wanted to iron himself"—another sign of his pride—for, it turns out, his graduation. We don't know until two sentences later that these clothes are for his graduation. Now the focus shifts to the father (whose "eel-skin boots" are an especially effective detail), embarrassed by the emotion he feels because

of his pride in his son. Finally, the son accepts his diploma to the cheers of classmates and families, who could be calling "any name . . . any son's or daughter's," an image of their communal pride.

4. The unity and coherence of paragraph 8 come from the common topics of the sentences (sensory experience), their identical subjects ("Pride"), and their parallel structures.

5. Gilb works for a specific mood in this opening, as discussed in the answer to question 1. He wants readers to *see* these people and the landscape they inhabit.

QUESTIONS ON LANGUAGE

1. The description is a good example of showing, not telling. Gilb doesn't just say the car is a big wreck. No, it is a "fatso American car" with "cross-eyed" headlights, a misfiring muffler, and "dry springs squeaking."

2. While the subject of the sentences in paragraph 8 is pride, an abstract concept, Gilb uses verbs referring to the senses: "hears," "sees," "listens," "smells," "eats." He personifies pride.

3. Students should see that the repetition of "the ones who" keeps this long sentence under control. They may also note that when he needs to, Gilb varies this phrase.

AUGUSTEN BURROUGHS

How to Identify Love by Knowing What It's Not

(p. 470)

Augusten Burroughs's essay imploring abuse victims to recognize their problem and leave their abusers is likely to strike a painful chord for at least a few people in your class. According to the National Coalition Against Domestic Violence, one in five college students is currently in an abusive relationship, and more than a third were abused in previous relationships. We include "How to Identify Love by Knowing What It's Not" not to make students uncomfortable but to help them recognize the scope of the problem of domestic violence: If they see themselves or someone they care for in Burroughs's descriptions, we hope his essay will prompt the affected students to get the help they need. Accordingly, we encourage you to be prepared to refer students to counseling services if your school offers them; it's possible one or two will identify themselves as abuse victims in response to the journal prompt or bring up the issue during office hours.

In preparation for discussing the essay, students could collaboratively devise a portrait of the ideal romantic relationship in America today. What qualities do we find most valuable or important in men? in women? Is gender relevant? What do your students expect of romantic partners? What do they offer in return? Are there different sets of standards? Who decides them? Who might be said to represent the perfect couple? In groups of four or five, students should be able to generate a list of the behaviors and attitudes that offer the best hope of a happy relationship.

Media resources: Augusten Burroughs presents an unusual character as a writer. Students might enjoy his comments on writing, offered in video format at *bigthink.com/ideas/867*. No doubt they'll be surprised by both his appearance and voice. But hearing Burroughs speak may give them a better appreciation of the tone and urgency of his writing.

QUESTIONS ON MEANING

1. Although the title suggests that Burroughs will define *love* in the essay, his true subject is abusive relationships.
2. The thesis first appears in paragraph 16: "You can be in [an abusive] relationship and not even know it." Burroughs includes variations of this statement in paragraphs 22, 39, 46, 49, 53, and 57: "I knew of somebody . . . who was many years into an abusive relationship but did not know it"; "But probably the number-one reason [for people not leaving abusive relationships] is simply not knowing they're in one"; "Domestic violence is extremely difficult to detect when it is happening to you"; "You could be in an abusive relationship and be unaware that you are, unable to see the abuse for what it is"; "you're more likely to be blind to abuse if it is there"; "What's difficult to see is when you're with somebody who is a full-strength abuser." The relentless repetition lends emphasis and urgency to Burroughs's idea; it also gives the essay unity and coherence.
3. Burroughs presents his definition of love in the introductory paragraphs (1–12) and comes back to it in his conclusion (60–62). His negative examples imply that love is a combination of selfless caring, support, acceptance, and patience. And as he suggests in the paradox of his closing sentence, it starts with self-love.
4. Clearly, Burroughs wants readers to feel empathy for victims of domestic abuse, especially those who stay with their abusers, but even more so, he wants readers to examine their own relationships carefully and honestly and, if they realize they're being abused, to get out. (He expects no response from abusers because they "do not change," par. 29.) Students' own responses, of course, will vary.

QUESTIONS ON WRITING STRATEGY

1. The very short paragraphs give the essay a clipped, urgent feel and emphasize the importance of Burroughs's major points. The single-sentence paragraphs in the introduction also create the feel of a homily, specifically invoking Corinthians 13:4–8, which is commonly recited at weddings: "Love is patient and kind; love is not jealous or boastful; it is not arrogant or rude. Love does not insist on its own way; it is not irritable or resentful; it does not rejoice at wrong, but rejoices in the right. Love bears all things, believes all things, hopes all things, endures all things. Love never ends. . . ." That sense that Burroughs is offering a sermon carries through the rest of the essay.
2. Stipulative definitions in the essay include those of "Love" (pars. 1–12), "patience" (12–15), "physical violence" (16–17), and "emotional violence" (17–28). With each definition, Burroughs emphasizes that abuse comes in many forms and can be difficult to recognize.

3. Burroughs begins with a stipulative definition of "Love" (pars. 1–12), then moves on to definitions of "patience," "physical violence," and "emotional violence" (see the previous question). Once he's established his meanings, Burroughs describes the mentality of abusers, arguing that they won't change (29–37), then moves on to consideration of why victims don't leave (38–40). Because the main reason they stay is not knowing they're abused, Burroughs goes on to characterize the symptoms of abuse, citing evidence from the National Domestic Violence Hotline and elaborating on one symptom, preventing the partner from working (41–45). Finally, he acknowledges (again) that victims often don't recognize abuse and outlines the process by which they may come to see it for themselves, imploring readers to leave if they discover they're being victimized (46–62). The structure allows Burroughs to carry readers through the process he describes toward the end: understanding, recognizing, acknowledging, and then doing something about abuse.

4. Citing an authoritative source lends authority to Burroughs's claims. Perhaps more important, he provides the information as a service to victims of domestic violence. Burroughs is quite sincere in his desire to help, and including the checklist and phone number is a concrete way for him to do that.

5. In paragraphs 22–28 Burroughs relates the experience of a friend who suffered emotional abuse. The anecdote not only illustrates what the author means by emotional abuse with concrete details but also works as evidence to support his claim. At the same time, his friend's success in leaving the relationship offers inspiration and hope for readers who may be thinking about leaving an abuser.

QUESTIONS ON LANGUAGE

1. Burroughs clearly assumes that many (if not most) of his readers are victims of domestic abuse, whether physical or emotional, and that they do not recognize it.

2. The essay is riddled with inappropriate use of *they* and *their*, but the choice seems deliberate. Burroughs takes great pains to stress that abusers and their victims come in all genders and sexualities; he doesn't want to stereotype with masculine or feminine pronouns or be accused of using sexist language. All the same, the resulting poor grammar will be jarring for many readers. We suggest you take the opportunity to discuss the effects of faulty agreement with your class, asking how they might edit the essay for better readability.

3. In a usage note for the verb *roil*, the editors of *The American Heritage Dictionary* write, the word "means literally 'to make muddy or cloudy by stirring up sediment,' and this meaning has given rise to a number of figurative uses. *Roil* can also mean 'to be or cause to be agitated.'" Given that the turbulence in Burroughs's example's mind caused agitation for both himself and his wife, clouding and fouling the relationship in the process, we find the unusual word choice here especially effective.

4. The tone might best be described as *empathetic*. Throughout the essay Burroughs hints that he, too, has been the victim of abuse (which, as we point out in the author's headnote, is in fact the case) and that he is pulling examples from his own experience. The hint is especially strong when he writes about victims who, like himself, "possess talent" but are prevented from pursuing their "crafts" (pars. 20, 42–45).

12
ARGUMENT AND PERSUASION
Stating Opinions and Proposals

Argument and persuasion are often difficult for students to master, so the introduction to this chapter is more detailed than the others. We spell out the elements of argument, integrating the Rogerian and Toulmin methods and the more traditional inductive and deductive reasoning. Then we cover the most common fallacies and (in the section headed "The Process") discuss possible structures for arguments. We also give emphasis to anticipating likely objections when conceiving and writing an argument.

This chapter's selections start with one piece that flies solo: Linda Chavez's "Supporting Family Values," a liberal argument by a conservative writer. Then we present three casebooks:

- Chuck Dixon and Paul Rivoche on political correctness in the comics industry, followed by Janelle Asselin's pointed response
- Brianne Richson and Jon Overton (both students) and then Wendy Kaminer on trigger warnings in syllabi and emotional safety on campus
- Nicholas Carr, Jim Harper, and Lori Andrews on Internet tracking, the practice of mining personal data and analyzing the information to customize Web users' experiences

---

LINDA CHAVEZ

Supporting Family Values

(p. 495)

Chavez, a politically conservative writer who hails from a Spanish-speaking background, insists in this essay that Hispanic immigrants are both willing and able to adapt to American life and culture. Even more, Chavez suggests, that same group of immigrants so often vilified as lazy, uneducated, or criminal are in fact exemplars of virtue and should be honored, even rewarded, for their moral contributions to American society.

This essay is notable for using conservative ideals (family values) to argue for liberal policy (amnesty for illegal immigrants). Students may have some difficulty reconciling two points of view that would seem almost mutually exclusive, but we find it quite clever of Chavez to intertwine them in such a way that neither position can be easily refuted: As Chavez presents her argument, readers on either side of the conservative-liberal divide have little choice but to accept at least part of their opponents' way of thinking.

Media resources: The report that Chavez cites as evidence for her argument, and which we suggest that students check for themselves in the "Critical Writing" prompt following her essay, is posted at *www.pewhispanic.org/ 2009/04/14/a-portrait-of-unauthorized-immigrants-in-the-united-states/*. The Pew Hispanic Center published an updated report on the subject in 2015: Titled "Unauthorized Immigrant Population Stable for Half a Decade," it can be found at *www.pewresearch.org/act-tank/2015/07/22/unauthorized -immigrant-population-stable-for-half-a-decade/*. For an overview of US immigration trends in general, you might want to share with your students the Census Bureau infographic that was previously included in the now-defunct e-Pages for the *Bedford Reader*; it is freely available online at *www.census .gov/library/infographics/foreign_born.html*.

QUESTIONS ON MEANING

1. Chavez opens her essay by noting it was prompted by a "new report out this week from the Pew Hispanic Center" (par. 1), but perceptive readers will notice from her remarks in the final two paragraphs that her argument was inspired as well by the ongoing conflict between efforts to aggressively identify and deport illegal immigrants and proposals to offer amnesty to illegal immigrants who meet certain criteria.

2. Although she mentions slight differences in family structure, education level, and income among illegal and legal immigrants, the only real distinction Chavez makes between the two groups is their legal status. Especially because so many immigrant families consist of both illegal and legal residents, Chavez suggests, the distinctions are practically meaningless.

3. Chavez's comparison of attitudes toward current Mexican and "other Latin American" immigrants with attitudes toward European immigrants of a century ago is a commonly used argument in favor of relaxed immigration controls. Her point is that a century of experience has shown that immigrants do assimilate into the larger culture over time and that fears of unfamiliar ethnic groups are unfounded. At the same time, because most of her readers are presumably of European heritage, Chavez subtly chides them for perpetuating the same hostilities that were once directed at their own ancestors—and reassures them that Spanish-speaking immigrants will, indeed, become an integral part of American culture if given the opportunity.

4. Chavez's purpose is revealed in the last two paragraphs: She is writing to argue in favor of granting amnesty" to a qualified category of illegal immigrants. Her thesis might best be expressed in the penultimate sentence: "A better approach [to deportation] would allow those who have made their lives here, established families, bought homes, worked continuously and paid taxes to remain after paying fines, demonstrating English fluency, and proving they have no criminal record." By withholding her thesis and purpose until the end, Chavez acknowledges that her position will be difficult for readers to accept; she therefore fully makes her case before letting them in on what she wants them to believe.

QUESTIONS ON WRITING STRATEGY

1. Chavez characterizes opponents as unreasonable to the point of hysteria, referring to "hard-line immigration restrictionists," "alarm" (par. 2); "fear" (5); "worries [that] are no more rational today—or born out of actual evidence—than they were a hundred years ago" (6); and "popular but uninformed opinion" (8). In doing so, Chavez suggests that some readers may hold these views, yet she forces them to reexamine their beliefs by portraying them as irrational. She seems to trust that most of her readers—"the rest of us" (2)—are reasonable people who can be persuaded to change their minds if presented with sufficient information.

2. Chavez states her main assumption in paragraph 2: "One of the chief social problems afflicting this country is the breakdown in the traditional family." Many readers, especially those of a conservative medium like *townhall.com*, will presumably share the writer's concern about family values; others will reject it outright. In either case readers are likely to find Chavez's approach creative at the very least.

3. Chavez appeals to both reason and emotion. She is careful to base her argument on statistical evidence from a published report in paragraphs 1, 3, 6, 7, and 8, using the numbers to draw inferences about the character, values, and potential for success of undocumented Spanish-speaking immigrants, especially as they compare to legal immigrants and native-born families. But she appeals to emotion throughout, citing both family values and fears of cultural disintegration as she makes her case.

4. Chavez names three categories of American "households" in paragraph 3: native, legal, and illegal. As she explains, native families are the least likely to be "made up of two parents living with their own children," while a third of legal immigrant households and nearly half of all illegal immigrant households consist of traditional nuclear families. The point is central to her argument that immigrant families represent a positive influence on the rest of the country and should therefore be supported and encouraged, not broken apart by deportation or harassment.

QUESTIONS ON LANGUAGE

1. *Amnesty* is a political term for a government's pardon of illegal activities; in Chavez's essay, it refers explicitly to ongoing proposals to grant legal status to illegal residents who have nonetheless established themselves successfully. The word comes from the same Latin and Greek roots as *amnesia*, or forgetting.

2. By "native" Chavez means those born in the United States and thus automatically granted citizenship. There are at least two layers of irony in her use of the term: First is the subtle reference to Native Americans, the peoples who were displaced with the first wave of European settlement in the fifteenth century, but Chavez also points out that nearly three-quarters of the children of illegal immigrants are "American-born" (par. 1) and thus citizens—a fact that complicates the issue of deportation, especially for readers with a strong interest in family values.

3. Most students will likely find Chavez's tone reasonable and levelheaded, even appealing. The diction is for the most part plain; Chavez avoids sarcasm and hectoring, and in her conclusion she becomes somewhat informal, saying her evidence "should give pause to those who'd like to see all illegal immigrants rounded up and deported or their lives made so miserable they leave on their own" (par. 9).

LINDA CHAVEZ ON WRITING

Chavez's nostalgia for the old days of sentence diagramming might prompt students to reflect on their own grammatical education. How were they taught the rules? You might point out that understanding the rules is different from following them. Plenty of writers occasionally write "incorrect" sentences, but they do so on purpose and for a particular effect. Readers can tell the difference between intentional rule breaking and error.

CHUCK DIXON AND PAUL RIVOCHE

How Liberalism Became Kryptonite for Superman

(p. 500)

This heartfelt essay is the first of a pair of arguments that both take the form of textual analysis. In "How Liberalism Became Kryptonite for Superman," Chuck Dixon and Paul Rivoche assess the successes and failures of comics in the United States today. Janelle Asselin, in the next essay, evaluates the successes and failures of their argument.

Although Dixon and Rivoche's argument is focused on the comics industry and on Superman in particular, it's worth noting that in many ways their essay is a lament of the divisiveness of partisan politics (even as they indulge in it) as well as an objection to the limits on free expression they assert have been imposed by a culture of political correctness. Students' own political leanings are sure to influence their receptiveness to the authors' claims.

One way to begin discussion might be to gauge your students' familiarity with the kinds of comics and graphic novels Dixon and Rivoche examine. Chances are that a good number of your students are fans (even Comic-Con–attending superfans) of such works; others may dismiss them as so much fluff. What is it that draws so many adults to increasingly popular genres that were originally intended for children?

Media resources: In the second writing prompt we encourage students to check DC Comics's *Superman* page at *www.dccomics.com/characters /superman* to get a sense of the character's evolution over time. In addition, any of the comics, graphic novels, radio shows, and movies that Dixon and Rivoche invoke in their argument could be worth examining in class—whether in part or in full. *Action Comics #900* can be purchased for $5.99 at *dccomics.com* or $4.99 for an e-book version in *iTunes*; all sixteen episodes of *The Clan of the Fiery Cross* have been uploaded to *You-Tube*; *A People's History of the American Empire* (Howard Zinn), *Working* (Studs Terkel), *Maus* (Art Spiegelman), *Persepolis* (Marjane Satrapi), and of course *The Forgotten Man* (Chuck Dixon, Paul Rivoche, and Amity Shlaes) are likely to be included among your school library's holdings; and *The Incredibles* and *X-Men* should be available for loan through a local library or any streaming service.

QUESTIONS ON MEANING

1. In the essay following this one, Janelle Asselin accuses Dixon and Rivoche of writing purely to sell copies of *The Forgotten Man*, but they do seem to have a larger purpose in mind. The authors, both self-proclaimed conservatives, claim that liberal politics have infiltrated the comics industry and compromised the integrity of the genre—and of superheroes in particular. They state their purpose in the final sentence of the essay: "It's time," they say, for conservatives "to take back comics."

2. The authors use both terms as a kind of shorthand for "moral ambiguity and leftist ideology" (par. 1)—or what they perceive as liberals' acceptance of immoral behavior and failure to distinguish right from wrong. Liberalism in comics corrupts children, Dixon and Rivoche contend, and so they want to see it replaced with conservative values.

3. Dixon and Rivoche explain that they chose Superman as their focus because the episode they cite in their introduction is "the most dramatic example of modern comics' descent into political correctness, moral ambiguity and leftist ideology" (par. 1). To bolster their claim that superheroes were once positive role models, they cite Superman and Batman comics "during World War II" (3), the 1946 Superman radio show *The Clan of the Fiery Cross* (4), and the censorship guidelines of the Comics Code Authority from the 1950s to the '70s (6–7). To prove their point that liberalism has infected the genre they cite left-leaning graphic histories by Howard Zinn and Studs Terkel and claim the existence of graphic novels about Marxists and anarchists (10). They then assert that "not all comics and graphic novels parrot the progressive line" (11), pointing to Art Spiegelman's *Maus*, Marjane Satrapi's *Persepolis*, and the movies *The Incredibles* and *X-Men* as evidence. And finally, they quote an unnamed peer to support their claim that conservatives need to do more to make their voices heard. Janelle Asselin argues in "Superhuman Error: What Dixon and Rivoche Get Wrong" (p. 505) that most of these examples are odd, misleading, or outright false; students' own assessment of their effectiveness will naturally vary, depending in large part on how familiar they are with the works alluded to.

4. The authors assume that comics are for children and that superheroes are role models. As such, Dixon and Rivoche believe the characters should be "wonderfully American" (par. 3)—that is, patriotic and of high moral caliber (read, conservative).

QUESTIONS ON WRITING STRATEGY

1. "How Liberalism Became Kryptonite for Superman" is aimed at general readers of the *Wall Street Journal*, a traditionally conservative publication with well-educated, well-off readers. Presumably some of these readers are passingly familiar with superhero comics and graphic novels (as the allusions to particular authors and titles in pars. 10–11 suggest)—although not necessarily avid fans of the genre. But as Dixon and Rivoche make clear in their conclusion, they hope that even "free-speech liberals" (par. 13) will heed their words.

2. While Dixon and Rivoche's argument is based primarily on emotional appeal and fear for children's moral education, students might sense the implied syllogism of their deductive argument: Liberal politics promote "moral ambiguity" (par. 1). The comics industry has been taken over by liberals. Therefore, comic books promote moral ambiguity. Readers

might take issue with either the major or minor premise. They might also note that the authors make a concerted effort to build their *ethos* as concerned artists with decades of experience on the issue. They point out in their introduction, for instance, that "comics are [their] passion" (par. 2) and establish Rivoche's status as the son of Russian emigrants and a Canadian who is nonetheless staunchly pro-American (5). They further assert that they (or at least Dixon) have been personally punished for their politics (8) and "poured years" of effort into making their own contribution to the solution they propose (13).

3. The authors support their claims with a mix of personal experience, analysis of textual examples (print comics, radio, film, and the Comics Code Authority guidelines), and the opinion of one unnamed expert (par. 13)—mostly in chronological order. How convinced readers are may depend on the degree to which they align with Dixon and Rivoche's politics as well as how familiar they are with their subject.

4. The cover illustration, from an issue of *World's Finest Comics* sometime in World War II, provides evidence for the writers' claim that superheroes were patriots who even "battled Nazi Germany and Imperial Japan" (par. 3) and is meant to support their assertions that the Superman of the past was pro-American and anti-racist (3–4). Students might note, however, the incongruity of the vaguely racist term *Japanazis* in the image and its caption.

5. Liberal politics, according to Dixon and Rivoche, have turned superheroes into "morally compromised" characters "no different from the criminals they battle" (par. 2); liberalism has also resulted in a rash of leftist propaganda, particularly in graphic novels taught in schools (10, 12), and a stifling of free speech (13). The primary victims of the trend, as the authors see it, are children but also conservative artists.

QUESTIONS ON LANGUAGE

1. Conservative values, as Dixon and Rivoche portray them, might be summed up as "Truth, justice and the American way" (pars. 1, 2): patriotism, virtue, "idealism" (5). Conversely, they characterize liberal values as a disheartening embrace of "moral relativism" (2): ambiguity (1) compromise (2), corruption (7), "weakened" (8), "dark" (9).

2. Of the given adjectives, *worried* and *defensive* seem the most appropriate to describe the authors' tone. At times Dixon and Rivoche sound condescending, particularly when they refer to morality and patriotism; at other times they seem cautiously optimistic, as when they speak of the future of the industry (pars. 12–13). Readers who share their conservative outlook might appreciate their tone; those further to the left might report being put off by it.

3. Objectively, an *anarchist* (from the Greek *anarkhia*, "without a ruler") seeks absence of political authority and a *Marxist* prefers a socialist structure. Both terms have come to carry sinister connotations, however (especially for conservatives), and in using them to describe the subjects of graphic novels, Dixon and Rivoche certainly intend to send shivers down their readers' spines.

JANELLE ASSELIN

Superhuman Error: What Dixon and Rivoche Get Wrong

(p. 505)

Like Chuck Dixon and Paul Rivoche (p. 500), Janelle Asselin is a veteran comics-industry insider who takes her job seriously and personally. Although "How Liberalism Became Kryptonite for Superman" was published in the *Wall Street Journal*, Asselin's essay, posted two days later on *ComicsAlliance.com*, is a direct—and unabashedly angry—response to her colleagues. (Her revisions for *The Bedford Reader* involved adapting the original Web formatting to linear prose, removing some admittedly entertaining digressions and personal attacks, and adding in-text citations and a Works Cited list.)

Read together, these essays should help students recognize that ideas need not be dual opposites or rigid pro/con debates to merit argument. Asselin's strong reaction to Dixon and Rivoche's article also shows students how an intelligent and knowledgeable reader like Asselin can counter what may have seemed an airtight argument—while it models the possibilities for their own critical readings of any writing they might encounter, in *The Bedford Reader* or elsewhere. Following Asselin's example, students may in turn question some of her arguments, evidence, or assumptions.

Media resources: Asselin's original blog post includes a panel from *Action Comics #900* to support her analysis of the story Dixon and Rivoche cite. We were unable to obtain permission to reprint it in *The Bedford Reader*, but you can share it with your students at *comicsalliance.com/chuck-dixon-paul -rivoche-conservative-politics-comic-industry-response-superman/*; the post also includes some samples of Dixon and Rivoche's own comics and additional images of Superman. (It could also be interesting to have students take note of Asselin's revisions to her piece and examine how genre and medium shape a writer's options.) Students interested in her feminist approach to comics might be directed to the *Fresh Romance* series published by Asselin's Rosy Press (*rosypress.com*) or to her contributions to the *Don't Be a Dick* series (*bitchmedia.org/post/dont-be-a-dick-a-comic-about-how-to-talk -about-comics*).

QUESTIONS ON MEANING

1. According to Asselin, Dixon and Rivoche's purpose in "How Liberalism Became Kryptonite for Superman" was promotional. "The goal here, of course," she says, "is to sell comics" (par. 2). Her own purpose, in contrast, seems to be to inform comics fans of their article and to defend her peers in the comics industry, particularly editors like herself, from the accusations lobbed against them.

2. Asselin states her thesis in her introduction and restates it in her conclusion: "The problem is not with their politics; it's with their misrepresentation of the industry and its history" (par. 4); "In the end, that is the

issue—Dixon and Rivoche have misrepresented American comics to an audience that probably doesn't care in the first place, but now will be kept away from any future contemplation of the work and medium and community we all love" (18).

3. Asselin devotes several passages to the meaning of "moral relativism" because she disputes Dixon and Rivoche's use of a "term [that] is often used incorrectly . . . or misunderstood" (par. 5). Although Dixon and Rivoche equate "moral relativism" and "moral ambiguity" as the same slippery slope to immoral behavior and a failure to distinguish right from wrong, Asselin asserts that "moral relativism" is a positive trait—one of tolerance, respect for other viewpoints, and understanding of other cultures. Her point is that liberals are not the oppressors of free expression that Dixon and Rivoche portray them to be.

4. As Asselin portrays him, Superman is technically an illegal immigrant: "He wasn't born in the United States, his biological parents weren't born in the United States, and he didn't enter the country in any state-approved way—plus he's literally an alien" (par. 10). But like many of the immigrants "targeted by conservative politics" (10), he's fully assimilated to American culture: "[H]e's built his life in the US, continues to work in the country, and . . . identifies as a proud American" (10). Superman's immigration status and patriotism matter to her because they put him more in line with traditionally liberal values than the conservative ones Dixon and Rivoche attribute to the character.

5. Asselin attributes the shift in tone not to politics but to "fashion and an aging audience" (par. 15), subtly undermining the notion (expressed by Dixon and Rivoche) that comics are for children.

QUESTIONS ON WRITING STRATEGY

1. Asselin is writing primarily for her peers, as her allusions to the "industry" and "the work and medium and community we all love" in her concluding sentence (par. 18) reveal. At the same time, she does seem to assume the possibility of a wider readership and stresses the importance of audience throughout her essay. She refers, for instance, to "an audience that knows little about what's actually going on in cape comics" (par. 1) and offers information "[f]or those unfamiliar with [Dixon and Rivoche's] accomplishments" (3). Later she criticizes Dixon and Rivoche for "pretending before an ignorant audience" (9) and refers to "newspaper readers who likely wouldn't know any better" (17). And finally, she notes that writers in the comics industry should "be able to speak to an audience beyond that industry in an accurate way" (18).

2. The main source for "Superhuman Error: What Dixon and Rivoche Get Wrong" is, of course, Dixon and Rivoche's essay "How Liberalism Became Kryptonite for Superman" (p. 500), which Asselin quotes and paraphrases extensively. She paraphrases a panel from "The Incident" in *Action Comics* #900—the same episode Dixon and Rivoche cite in their essay as particularly troubling—to dispute their characterization of the episode and offer her own interpretation of its deeper meanings. She also quotes a line from *Man of Steel* (in par. 9) to support her contention that the episode had no long-term effect on Superman's character, summarizes the basic story arcs of Frank Miller's *Batman: The Dark Knight Returns* and Dixon's own *Punisher* comics to counter Dixon and Rivoche's claim that liberals were responsible for the "dark and gritty turn

superheroes have taken" (15), and summarizes the subjects of *Persepolis* and *Maus* to disprove their assertion that Marjane Satrapi's and Art Spiegelman's creations were not political in their intents.

3. The concessions help to build common ground and make Asselin sound reasonable. Still, with each concession to opposing viewpoints, she goes on to argue that the point conceded is not really relevant.

4. If asked to put names to the fallacies she mentions, Asselin would likely accuse Dixon and Rivoche of hasty generalization and either/or reasoning, possibly also non sequitur or even begging the question. Students might note that Asselin could be accused of using ad hominem attacks, such as in her characterizations of conservatives as hostile to immigrants and racist (pars. 11, 12), in her depiction of Chuck Dixon's *Punisher* comics "as some of the most intensely dark and violent anti-hero comics of the era" (15), and in her questioning of the authors' motives (2, 18).

5. Asselin's principle for analysis seems identical to the criteria for effective evidence that we cite on page 483 of the book: accuracy, representation, relevance, and adequacy. In picking apart Dixon and Rivoche's claims and their evidence point by point, she disputes the truth of everything they say in the order that they said it.

QUESTIONS ON LANGUAGE

1. Most succinctly, Asselin might characterize *liberal* as tolerant and *conservative* as intolerant.

2. Sarcastic elements begin with Asselin's title "Superhuman Error" and continue throughout the essay, often in the form of figurative language. Some examples: "Beating familiar conservative pundit drums like jingoistic nostalgia . . . these two experienced pros manage to paint a picture of an industry tottering on the edge of moral collapse" (par. 1); "This is often assumed to be related to moral relativism, but is not in fact considered such by actual philosophers who write about these things" (7); "In other words: dogs and cats living together — mass hysteria" (7); "those darn liberals" (9); "teary-eyed nostalgia" (13); "these are political comics that Dixon and Rivoche happen accidentally to have enjoyed" (16). Such sarcastic moments express the writer's frustration with the politics she describes. They also add some humor to the essay and (assuming readers agree with it) strengthen Asselin's bond with her audience.

3. *Correlation* (par. 11) is not the same as *causation*, as we all know. In using the word to portray Dixon and Rivoche's slippery slope argument that moral relativism leads to moral ambiguity, Asselin explained to us in an e-mail, she means that "Dixon and Rivoche are trying to say that if you respect other viewpoints then you don't understand right and wrong."

4. Appropriately for an audience of comic-book "geeks" like herself, the author mixes formal academic terminology with highly casual language to analyze her subject.

BRIANNE RICHSON

An Obligation to Prevent Trauma on Campus

(p. 513)

Richson's essay is the first of a pair on the current issue of whether college instructors should include "trigger warnings," or notices of potentially upsetting subject matter, on their syllabi. She takes the "pro" position. Jon Overton, in the next essay, takes the "con." Following the two student pieces comes an argument by libertarian Wendy Kaminer, who extends the issue to student sensitivity in general, making a case that a recent surge in student demands for protections defeats the purpose of a college education.

Referring to student movements across the country, Richson adds her voice to the crusade for heightened sensitivity to the needs of trauma survivors on campus. Dismissing opponents' concerns that devices like trigger warnings diminish the rigor of a college education and threaten to stifle free expression, Richson passionately—and compassionately—insists that protecting victims takes first priority, and she does so in just five hundred words. Even students who do not agree with her position should be able to learn from her model.

Media resources: The *Los Angeles Times* editorial Richson refers to in her argument is "Warning: College Students, This Article May Upset You." Published on March 31, 2014, it is available online at *www.latimes.com/nation/la-ed-trigger-warnings-20140331-story.html*. Richson's original column, which we encourage students in the third writing suggestion to find and compare with the version we reprint, is at *www.dailyiowan.com/2014/05/06/Opinions/37824.html*.

QUESTIONS ON MEANING

1. The problem, as Richson presents it, is many college students are legitimate trauma survivors, and some suffer from PTSD. Arguing that these students deserve protection from "reliving that which was traumatic" (par. 3), she proposes that college professors include trigger warnings on their syllabi and let students opt out of encountering or discussing "sensitive" (2) or potentially upsetting material.

2. Richson describes a trigger warning as a printed notice on a syllabus that indicates "when emotionally or physically stressful material would be presented in class" (par. 4)—something like the ratings notices that pop up in television programming to identify sexual, violent, or otherwise objectionable material. She states that the practice started in "the world of blogs" (2) but doesn't specify the exact origins. Students may or may not know that the term originated on feminist discussion boards as a way of warning rape survivors about graphic content.

3. Richson states her thesis in her conclusion: "Such measures [calling for "trigger warnings" on syllabi] certainly have the potential to be taken too far, but our obligation to prevent a trauma survivor's class time becoming a living hell outweighs concerns about a stunted learning environment."

4. Despite her acknowledgement that such proposals "certainly have a potential to be taken too far" (par. 8), Richson seems to approve.

QUESTIONS ON WRITING STRATEGY

1. Writing in the student newspaper, Richson assumes an audience of her peers at the University of Iowa (a large public research university in Iowa City): primarily other students, especially trauma survivors, but also teachers and administrators. She characterizes the students as emotionally fragile, raised by overprotective parents, and sensitive to the needs of others; she also seems to assume that the authority figures on campus are, if not indifferent to students' suffering, at the very least unaware of it.
2. Richson raises objections to her argument and dismisses them at several points in the body of the essay. She acknowledges in paragraph 3 that some people "consider such measures dramatic and symptomatic" of overprotective parenting but insists that such comparisons are unfair. She further acknowledges, in paragraph 5, that opponents have suggested that students with PTSD are responsible for knowing their own triggers, countering that such awareness leaves out the option of avoiding those triggers. In paragraph 6 Richson cites a *Los Angeles Times* editorial and characterizes it as dismissive of valid concerns, going on in paragraph 7 to stress the severity of the traumas at issue and to question the educational value of sensitive course materials. And finally, in her conclusion, Richson admits that adopting trigger warnings carries "a potential to be taken too far" (8) but asserts that such overreaches are preferable to causing students to suffer. Some readers may wish she addressed the counterarguments in more detail; others may have different objections that she failed to address; still others might suggest that her argument, as a whole, begs the question.
3. We might express Richson's syllogism as follows: Colleges have an obligation to protect students from trauma. A major source of trauma for some students is sensitive course material. Therefore, colleges have an obligation to protect students from sensitive course material. How valid readers find her conclusion depends on whether they accept her major and minor claims.
4. Richson offers, in paragraph 4, two vivid depictions of the types of trauma victims she has in mind: a survivor of rape and a target of racial violence. Although readers might wish for more examples to support her generalization, in paragraph 2, that the "list" of potentially traumatizing material "might include anything," the examples she does provide are specific and clear and help to dispel negative assumptions that PTSD is imagined or trivial.

QUESTIONS ON LANGUAGE

1. Examples of colloquial language include "The list goes on" (par. 2), "the 'every kid gets a trophy generation'" (3), "beaten up" (4), "tizzy" (4), "cop-out" (6), and "living hell" (8). The expressions help to build rapport with the students in her audience, but they might strike teachers and administrators as overly casual and inconsistent with an academic subject and purpose.
2. Richson, a psychology student as well as an English and journalism major, borrows a few specialized terms from the social sciences in making

her argument. *Hypervigilance* is one such term. *Merriam Webster's Medical Dictionary* defines it as "the condition of maintaining an abnormal awareness of environmental stimuli" and explains that it is a common condition of PTSD involving "heightened startle responses and flashbacks."

3. Richson opens her essay with the claim that "We all have one memory we'd prefer people not bring up because we want to block it from our consciousness forever" (par. 1), implying that she herself has experienced trauma. Her descriptions of people afflicted with post-traumatic stress disorder, accordingly, are highly empathetic.

BRIANNE RICHSON ON WRITING

Students might be surprised by Richson's suggestion that saving the thesis statement for last can keep a writer out of trouble, but she makes a good point that the act of writing often leads to the main idea rather than the other way around. We appreciate her observation that writers sometimes turn to ornate prose as a way of shielding their ideas from criticism and that being direct can be "scary" but is more effective. We also appreciate her point that experience helps, a lesson that other students may learn themselves as they gain more practice writing.

JON OVERTON
Beware the Trigger Warning

(p. 518)

The second in a trio of essays devoted to issues of free speech on campus, Jon Overton's argument is a direct retort of his *Daily Iowan* colleague's call for the adoption of trigger warnings on course syllabi. Proposals such as Brianne Richson's, as Overton sees it, might be well intentioned, but they ask too much of instructors and carry unintended consequences. The essay following Overton's, "The Danger of Playing It Safe" by Wendy Kaminer, adds another perspective on cultures of victimhood and what Overton calls "political correctness on steroids" (par. 6).

Discussion of "Beware the Trigger Warning" might begin with the author's tone. Although Overton claims to agree with Richson that people with mental illness deserve consideration, he seems at points to mock her—and them. (The first two questions on writing strategy point students to this potential contradiction.) Or, for an interesting classroom exercise, you might take Overton's point that trigger warnings can easily go too far by using *The Bedford Reader* as an example. Ask your students to look over the book's table of contents and identify any readings (such as, say, Jessica Mitford's "Behind the Formaldehyde Curtain") that they think should come with explicit warnings about potentially upsetting material: What triggers would they list, and why?

Media resources: Like Brianne Richson, Jon Overton revised his essay for inclusion in a textbook. His original column can be found at *www.dailyiowan .com/2014/05/07/Opinions/37841.html*. Students across the country continue to debate the merits and drawbacks of trigger warnings. *USA Today* reporter Dan Reimold published a useful roundup of student writing on the subject shortly after Overton wrote his response to Richson: "Students Debate 'Trigger Warnings': Excessive Coddling or a Useful System?" quotes Richson among others and can be read at *college.usatoday.com/2014/05/09/students -debate-trigger-warnings-excessive-coddling-or-a-useful-system/*.

QUESTIONS ON MEANING

1. Overton's purpose, put simply, is to publicly respond to another columnist's argument—and in this case to refute it. He states his thesis in his introduction: "My main gripe with trigger warnings more broadly . . . is that they threaten to stifle some of the most important conversations and lessons in college" (par. 2). He restates the thesis in his conclusion: "As much as we'd like to help trauma victims, we can't know what's going to initiate a panic attack, and trying to prevent any and all of them endangers academic discourse" (7).

2. Triggers, as Overton understands them, are "[a]nything" (par. 3) that might bring up memories of "traumatic experiences" (1) and thus "set someone off" (3). Because there's no way to anticipate what "smell, sound, word, or image" (3) might serve as a trigger for any particular person, it's unreasonable and unproductive to expect instructors to single them out on a syllabus. More to the point, Overton argues, even if it were possible to identify "any and all" (7) possible triggers in advance, attempts to shield the feelings of a few traumatized students would amount to censorship for the rest.

3. The "point" of college, as Overton sees it, is "to challenge your worldview . . ., to confront information that makes you rethink cherished beliefs . . ., [and] to expose yourself to new ideas and points of view" (par. 6). Essentially, he is championing the benefits of a liberal arts education for personal enrichment.

4. Overton offers his solution in the final paragraph, asserting that "it's up to the students who suffer from PTSD to tell their instructors in advance if they're concerned about a potential trigger from specific course material" (par. 7).

QUESTIONS ON WRITING STRATEGY

1. By agreeing with Richson that "we should be considerate toward people who suffer from psychological illnesses" (par. 2) and admiring the "empathy and compassion" that she and her supporters show to those people, Overton is attempting to build common ground—both with his opponent and with their shared readership. Students might voice suspicion, however, that he is actually dismissive of the problem she stresses: He trivializes triggers as "[a]nything . . . from hot dogs to Nazis to Mike Tyson to the color yellow" (3), for instance, ignoring the legitimate forms of trauma Richson cites, and he is somewhat condescending to PTSD sufferers in his chastisements about the purpose of college in paragraph 6.

2. In responding to Richson, Overton takes a somewhat mocking tone, assuming that most readers at the University of Iowa will share his attitude toward trigger warnings as a well-intentioned but ultimately foolish, even counterproductive, idea. He includes those readers (presumably students who do not "suffer from PTSD," par. 7) as *we* in his introduction and conclusion, but in addressing those readers who might disagree as *you* in paragraph 6, he comes close to mocking them as well while accusing them of missing the point of being in college.

3. In citing examples of other colleges where students pushed for trigger warnings, Overton uses deductive reasoning (a rational appeal) to "illustrate . . . what is so dangerous about trigger warnings" (par. 6)—but the emphasis on such dangers throughout the essay is an emotional appeal to readers' fears. Overton's ethical appeal, in contrast, relies on his presentation of himself as an open-minded person (6) supposedly concerned for students with "psychological illnesses" (2) but even more concerned for the integrity of "academic discourse" (7).

4. Overton picks up Richson's own examples of colleges that have adopted trigger warnings, but to the opposite effect. While she intended them as something of a bandwagon appeal (other colleges are using trigger warnings so we should, too), he cites them as instances of failed "attack[s] on academic freedom" (6).

QUESTIONS ON LANGUAGE

1. The word *stifle* is often understood to mean simply "suppress" or "cut off," but Overton uses it in its most aggressive sense (and the primary definition in *The American Heritage College Dictionary*): "To kill by preventing respiration; smother or suffocate."

2. By "political correctness," Overton is referring to conservative accusations that liberals expect people to police their own speech to avoid giving offense to any minority group; putting that idea "on steroids" creates an image of a bulked-up beast ready to attack. Students might or might not notice that Overton uses related metaphors of violence and warfare throughout his essay: "triggers" themselves hint at guns, and he repeats words like "threaten" (pars. 2, 6), "flashback" (3), "punish" (5), "attacked" (5, 6), "shot down" (6), "horrific" (6), "nightmare" (6), "confront" (6), and "endangers" (7).

3. Overton holds the novels up as examples of "classical literature" that has been "attacked" by trigger-warning advocates, but he neglects to inform his readers *why* they've been singled out (we offer some hints in a gloss note). He seems to assume that his peers at the University of Iowa will be familiar with both works and their content and that they'd be aghast at efforts to censor them.

JON OVERTON ON WRITING

When asked to comment for *The Bedford Reader* on writing arguments, Overton, now a graduate student, immediately turned to informal research to learn more about the subject and to develop his thoughts. You might encourage your students to do the same when faced with a potentially daunting assignment, regardless of length or formality.

WENDY KAMINER
The Danger of Playing It Safe

(p. 523)

Libertarian social critic Wendy Kaminer certainly likes to provoke, as this essay makes unmistakably clear. Writing for the notoriously liberal NPR, and more specifically the station run out of Boston University, Kaminer puts forth her objections to the liberal politics typical on college campuses and seems to question the integrity of college students in general—particularly those who, like Brianne Richson (p. 513) and Jon Overton (p. 518) in the essays preceding hers, express concern for the feelings of others. No matter your own students' political leanings, Kaminer's complaints are sure to get a rise out of your class.

Students might want to share in small groups their reactions to Kaminer's characterizations of demands for protections like trigger warnings on syllabi (as Richson and Overton debate), "safe spaces" on campus, and speech and harassment codes. Some may find Kaminer's description of college students overly cynical and her portrait of what education used to be romanticized. Others may report that they themselves expected something different from college, that their hopes of educational possibility and campus debate were greater than what they're experiencing. (Or they may have experienced moments when they caught themselves unexpectedly offended.)

Students might also be asked to do a little research into the issues Kaminer addresses—questioning why speech and harassment codes exist, for instance, whether they truly stifle discussion, and what the alternatives might be. (The second writing suggestion can be helpful in this regard.) If students are themselves well informed about the issues, the discussion that results might be one of the liveliest of the year.

Media resources: Kaminer is but one of many journalists, educators, and scholars to have jumped into the trigger warning and campus climate debates of recent years. Other notable contributions include "The Coddling of the American Mind" by Greg Lukianoff and Jonathan Haidt (*The Atlantic Monthly*, September 2015), "That's Not Funny! Today's College Students Can't Seem to Take a Joke" by Caitlin Flanagan (*The Atlantic Monthly*, September 2015), "A New Trigger Warning for College Kids: How to Prepare Them for the Intellectual Discomforts of a University" by Jonathan Rauch (*New York Daily News*, November 11, 2015), "Why I Use Trigger Warnings" by Kate Manne (*New York Times*, September 19, 2015), "The Trigger Warning Myth" by Aaron R. Hanlon (*The New Republic*, August 14, 2015), and "College Is Not a Commodity: Stop Treating It Like One" by Hunter Rawlings (*The Washington Post*, June 19, 2015). All are easily accessed online or through a periodicals database. Students might also be interested in Kaminer's "Testimony on 'First Amendment Protections on Public Colleges and Universities' before the House Judiciary Sub-Committee on the Constitution and Civil Justice," published by the Foundation for Individual Rights in Education at *www.thefire*.org; the site also offers resources and case information for multiple issues related to students' rights.

QUESTIONS ON MEANING

1. In her opening paragraph Kaminer cites several examples of student claims that arts or academic events made them feel "unsafe." One of those instances involved Kaminer herself, who was criticized for speaking "forbidden words" (par. 1). That personal incident in particular would seem to be what prompted her to write; the essay is meant as a defense of free speech — on college campuses specifically.

2. *Cultural appropriation* refers to arguments that members of a dominant culture ("a predominantly white band" in Kaminer's example) have no right to adopt or participate in practices or norms originated by a minority group (such as "Afrobeat music"). The *pop therapeutic recovery* movement Kaminer alludes to was a string of works in popular (i.e., not professional) psychology: books, television, radio, and lectures that "equated offensive words with harmful actions" (par. 3) and, as Kaminer sees it, encouraged women especially to view themselves as survivors of abuse (she has more to say on the subject in "Wendy Kaminer on Writing," p. 527). *Codependent* relationships involve one person encouraging or supporting another person's destructive behaviors. Kaminer uses these terms from sociology and psychology ironically, highlighting her disdain for "notions of victimization" (5).

3. Kaminer argues that today's students think of *safety* in terms of emotions or negative reactions to feeling offended in some way, especially when "attacked by viewpoints" (2). This, to her, is both ridiculous and dangerous: As far as she is concerned, "safety means protection from physical, not emotional harm" (7). Kaminer is not a proponent of emotional safety, believing that demands for "safe spaces" on campus undermine education and harm everybody — educators and students alike. Students' own attitudes will vary.

4. Kaminer comes closest to stating her thesis in paragraph 6: "Censorship is anathema to education." The major claim of her argument is, essentially, that student demands for protections (such as trigger warnings) amount to an assault on free speech that shields them from encountering differing points of view and thus prevents them from learning.

QUESTIONS ON WRITING STRATEGY

1. Kaminer's primary audience is not college students but general listeners of National Public Radio, presumably educated adults who may have children of their own in school. In addressing students as *you* toward the end of her essay, she seems to be chiding them for foolishness. Current students will surely be put off by her negative opinion of them: She seems to assume, among other things, that students are overprotected, consumer-oriented, self-righteous, immature, and unreasonably fearful of ideas.

2. Kaminer's entire essay is an exasperated rejection of opposing arguments. She opens with examples of student objections to free speech and then characterizes students as easily offended (par. 2). She cites the proliferation of "speech and harassment codes" (3) as evidence that students embrace "censorship as a moral and political necessity" (5), openly criticizing the "feminist crusade against pornography and the pop therapeutic recovery movement" (4) as the cause. Kaminer goes on to characterize opponents who "feel 'attacked by viewpoints'" (6) as missing the point of college and concludes by presenting her case in defense of offensive speech (7–8).

3. The parallelism and repetition stress the contrast between student demands for "a right not to be offended" and Kaminer's insistence on the right to freedom of speech, setting up the paradox expressed in the final sentence: "Emotionally safe societies are dangerous places for people who speak" (par. 8).

4. The syllogism runs something like this: In a "free and open society" (par. 7), all speech should be protected. Some speech is offensive. Offensive speech should be protected.

5. Paragraphs 4 and 5 trace "late twentieth-century political and cultural trends" (3), blaming feminists and self-help writers for creating a culture of victimhood, particularly among women, and "a campus climate today that's increasingly hostile to free speech" (5). On a broader scale, the essay as a whole examines the broader effects of that hostility, warning that censorship, even self-censorship, is a threat to freedom.

QUESTIONS ON LANGUAGE

1. The quotation marks suggest that Kaminer is quoting the actual words and phrases students have used to complain about offensive speech and subject matters. But in repeatedly putting such words in quotation marks, she also distances herself from them and shows her disdain for the very concepts they convey.

2. Kaminer repeatedly uses words that connote physical violence—not only variations on *assault* and *attack* but also words such as *unsafe*, *threat*, *fear*, *shield*, *harmful*, *abuse*, and *hurt*—to highlight what she perceives as students' fragile emotional state and underscore her opinion that their fears are irrational.

3. From the Latin *devolutus*, "to roll down," *devolution* means simply a passing down by stages. Kaminer uses the word as an antonym of *evolution*, suggesting that college students have degenerated into something less than they once were.

WENDY KAMINER ON WRITING

Kaminer seems to share our view that effective writing is a *transaction* between a writer and a reader. Although we don't necessarily agree that reading "is becoming a way out of thinking," as she asserts, students might be asked to debate the merits of her claim.

NICHOLAS CARR

Tracking Is an Assault on Liberty

(p. 528)

Nicholas Carr's is the first essay in a three-selection casebook focusing on the problem of Internet tracking. This essay pairs specifically with the following one by Jim Harper: The two were published together as a debate in the

Wall Street Journal. The essay following Harper's, by Lori Andrews, extends the debate with a third perspective.

Students may be surprised to learn how much information is gathered about them on the Web and what can be done with that information, although having grown up online as they have, many may not see why they should care. Carr tries to make readers care about the issue by revealing surprising facts to support his argument and by suggesting that by failing to safeguard their privacy, Americans risk losing civil liberties.

You might want to start discussion by asking students about their personal experiences with targeted online advertising. How open are they about sharing personal information online? Have they noticed any ads on their computers or mobile devices that seemed eerily connected to something they had posted or researched? Do they find such customized marketing helpful or creepy, and why?

Media resources: Students for whom Carr's essay strikes a chord will certainly be interested in the article for which he is best known: "Is Google Making Us Stupid?" *The Atlantic* continues to provide it free of charge online. Carr gave an earnest twenty-minute talk on the subject at the 2015 *IdeaCity* conference; video of the event is housed at *www.ideacity.ca/video/ nicholas-carr-what-the-internet-is-doing-to-our-brians/*. For a lighter approach, he appeared as a guest on *The Colbert Report* in 2008: The entertaining interview is archived on *Comedy Central* at *www.cc.com/video-clips/ bqde8h/the-colbert-report-nicholas-carr*.

QUESTIONS ON MEANING

1. The problem, for Carr, is the "surreptitious collection of personal information" (par. 1) online by companies and government agencies, a practice that he believes not only poses practical dangers to individual Web users (13, 15–16, and 18) but also threatens their liberties and "pursuit of happiness" (19). He suggests two mostly undeveloped solutions: Individual Web users should be more cautious about sharing information (14), and "software makers and site operators" should offer more control and transparency to users who wish to safeguard their information (17). Implied, but not stated outright, is that regulations should require such controls and transparency of technology providers.

2. Information might be disclosed voluntarily by individual users (par. 2) and through shopping hubs (4, 6, 11), social-networking sites (11), and "location-tracking services like *Foursquare*" (11), often with the false assumption that such sharing is anonymous or in forgetfulness of how public such services are (4). Perhaps more worrisome to Carr are the growth of data-tracking software (5) and the ease with which researchers can analyze disparate bits of supposedly anonymous cookies and data not only to identify individual users (6–10) but also to anticipate and manipulate their behaviors (15–16).

3. Carr lists three distinct dangers. The first is practical: Criminals can access and analyze data as easily as anybody else can, creating a risk that Web users will be subjected to cons, theft, stalking, and the like (par. 13). The second is the problem of "manipulation" (15), Carr's concern that personalized marketing will influence people's knowledge and behaviors in ways they don't necessarily recognize (15–16). The final

danger is more theoretical: Carr worries that as privacy continues to be lost, society will cease to value it, leading individuals to feel constantly monitored and forever on guard and therefore less free (18).

4. Carr's purpose is to sound an alarm, to warn readers that their privacy is at risk and to persuade them to care about it. He is careful to establish the existence of a problem and to examine its scope, but he has little to say in the way of proposing a solution.

QUESTIONS ON WRITING STRATEGY

1. By acknowledging data tracking's practical benefits before raising concerns about its personal and political dangers, Carr simultaneously addresses an opposing viewpoint and enhances his ethical appeal by establishing himself as a reasonable observer.

2. Carr's argument appeals to both reason and emotion. The closest reasoning appears in paragraphs 5–12, where the author draws on published research and expert opinion to forge a connection between new technologies and loss of privacy. He appeals to emotion throughout, but especially when discussing the dangers of exposure (13–16) and the potential tragic effects on "life and liberty" (18–19).

3. Carr seems to imagine that the more advertisers (and, presumably, governments) know about individual consumers, the more they'll be able to direct those individuals' choices through subliminal mind control, subtly altering messages and available information to influence people's thoughts and behaviors. Many readers, fully confident in their own free will, will likely dismiss his concerns as overblown, maybe even a little ridiculous. Others more skilled at critical media consumption may find that his concerns ring true.

4. Carr warns that Americans' ability to protect their rights is threatened by the devaluation of privacy in an online culture that assumes "privacy is . . . just a screen we hide behind when we do something naughty or embarrassing" (par. 18). Privacy is more than that, he insists: It is a "boundary" (19) between ourselves and others, and it provides a sense of individuality that is "intrinsic to the concept of liberty" (18). The less privacy we have as individuals, he argues, the more we resign ourselves to the possibility of corporate and government manipulation. The definition allows him to state his conviction that privacy is a foundational American right and to explain how it protects civil liberties.

QUESTIONS ON LANGUAGE

1. Carr accepts that some loss of privacy online is inevitable and even desirable (par. 2), but he worries that Internet exposure is moving beyond individual users' control, creating "real dangers" for them and for society in general (12). His tone, while balanced, is one of deep concern and mild alarm; some readers might even characterize it as paranoid.

2. Earl Warren was Chief Justice of the US Supreme Court from 1953 to 1969; Tom Owad is a computer consultant and experimental researcher; Scott McNealy is the former chief executive of Sun Microsystems, an information technology company; Eric Schmidt heads *Google*; and Bruce Schneier is a computer-security expert. By quoting and paraphrasing expert opinion on both sides of the issue, Carr enhances his credibility while offering reliable evidence to support his ideas.

3. Jim Harper, in the next essay, takes issue with Carr's use of *surreptitious,* meaning "secret or stealthy," to describe the "collection of personal information" online. Anybody who doesn't know about such data collection, says Harper, "hasn't been paying attention" (par. 7).

NICHOLAS CARR ON WRITING

Carr addresses an issue that many writing teachers face: how to get students to write thoughtfully and carefully when they're used to dashing off text messages with little attention to critical thinking, rhetorical craft, or, for that matter, grammar, spelling, and mechanics. Carr's insistence that texting is the first stage of a "debased form" of writing provides an occasion to discuss with students "our old linear form of reading and writing" and how it may differ between, say, text messaging and academic writing.

JIM HARPER

Web Users Get as Much as They Give

(p. 535)

In a pointed response to Nicholas Carr's argument for safeguarding privacy online, Jim Harper shifts the focus of the debate to business and commerce. In today's "information economy" (par. 1), he insists, personal information is a commodity that has monetary value for businesses and consumers alike. Whether your students agree with him will be a matter of both their personal perspectives and their evaluation of his argumentative technique. For some readers, the essay will smack of pro-business bias; others will surely find it very persuasive.

You might want to start a discussion by asking students about their positions on recent calls for privacy legislation such as those made by Nicholas Carr, in "Tracking Is an Assault on Liberty" (p. 528), and by Lori Andrews, in "*Facebook* Is Using You" (p. 541). Do they favor tighter restrictions on data tracking, do they think that individual Web users are responsible for protecting their own privacy, do they think that information should be freely shared, or do they view privacy as a nonissue? Why?

Media resources: In "Privacy, Regulation, and the Internet," a 2013 video primer for *Libertarianism.org*'s *Exploring Liberty* series on *YouTube*, Harper draws on his legal background to offer a complex definition of *privacy* in the digital age. Students can watch it at *youtube.com/watch?v=KFks0whismk.*

QUESTIONS ON MEANING

1. Harper's thesis is best summed up in his title: "Web Users Get as Much as They Give." The trade in personal data drives Internet commerce (advertising especially) and makes it possible for sites to produce and

distribute free content; if Web users restrict access to their personal information, businesses will have less incentive and fewer resources to give anything in return.

2. *Cookies* are small files downloaded to Web users' computers by the sites they visit. Those files then send information from the users' computers back to the sites as well as to third parties, enabling site producers to "customize a visitor's experience" (par. 5). Most sites share aggregate data with advertising networks, which use demographics and individual visitors' interests and habits to personalize marketing messages. As far as Harper is concerned, this data mining and sharing is a good thing because it increases profitability for businesses and enables them to provide free services and content to consumers.

3. He places the blame on the average American for failing to use the privacy tools that are available and for failing to understand how the "information economy" (par. 1) works. His solution is to use those tools to control the spread of personal information as well as to be willing to give up a certain amount of privacy in exchange for the services and materials provided online.

4. Harper's purpose is twofold: He wants to educate readers about the workings of the "information economy" (par. 1); he also wants to persuade them to allow their own data to be tracked because such tracking, as he sees it, is for their benefit. Whether he succeeds in persuading readers will depend on their individual perspectives and concerns about business and privacy.

QUESTIONS ON WRITING STRATEGY

1. Harper previews the organization of his argument with the series of questions he asks in paragraph 2: "Who is gathering this information? What are they doing with it? How might this harm me? How do I stop it?" A rough outline:

    a. Web sites and advertising networks gather Internet users' information (par. 5).
    b. They use this information to personalize Web content and target advertising to individual interests, not to discriminate against people or harm them in any way (5).
    c. Cookies and tracking in general have been in use for a long time; expressing concern about them is disingenuous and beside the point (6–7).
    d. Trying to stop data tracking would harm both businesses and consumers (8–10).
    e. It is not the government's job to protect privacy (11).

    All but point e counter points Carr makes, although Harper's emphasis is decidedly different: While Carr's focus is on individual liberties, Harper's focus is on business and commerce. He does not directly address Carr's arguments about manipulation and potential loss of personal freedoms. Harper concentrates on issues of free trade.

2. The *Wall Street Journal* is a business newspaper with a conservative slant; Harper assumes that his readers are affluent, influential professionals whose primary interest is making money. As businesspeople, Harper's readers may have a vested interest in Web commerce especially and so are likely to be biased in favor of his claims. Harper also assumes that his readers—business professionals or not—are consumers who enjoy the free content and services provided online and expect

unfettered access to such products. Students will likely fit the latter assumption if not the former.

3. Harper is attempting to establish ethical appeal by disclosing that he is one of those Web producers who relies on data tracking to generate advertising revenue and produce new content for viewers; in other words, he attempts to show readers that he knows what he's talking about. At the same time, by mentioning that his site monitors the government, he implies that the government can't be trusted to protect privacy. Although some readers might feel that Harper's admission increases his credibility, others might find that it reveals a conflict of interest.

4. Harper offers two examples: the Federal Trade Commission's failed bid more than a decade ago "for power to regulate the Internet for privacy's sake" (pars. 10–11) and Microsoft engineers' more recent attempt to tighten the privacy settings on Internet Explorer (12). In both cases Harper argues that had the efforts succeeded, businesses would have been harmed and consumers would have been given less "access to free content" (12): *Google,* he claims, would not have grown to the powerhouse it is today (10), and Microsoft would have been accused of damaging "interactivity and the advertising business model" (12). The implication is that any efforts to protect privacy are ultimately counterproductive.

5. Harper believes strongly that tighter privacy regulations would hurt business and consumers. "If Web users supply less information to the Web," he claims, "the Web will supply less information to them" (par. 9). Businesses would have less opportunity to grow and innovate (10), and consumers' interests would be both misinterpreted and thwarted (11), limiting their access to "free content, custom Web experiences, convenience and so on" (13).

QUESTIONS ON LANGUAGE

1. The mixed metaphors of Harper's first paragraph (surfing, gleaning, gears, and fuel, all at once) might make students' heads spin, but in general Harper uses figures of speech, especially personifications of businesses and technologies, to establish a friendly and reassuring (if sometimes condescending) tone. Other examples include the simile "[c]ookies are a surreptitious threat to privacy the way smoking is a surreptitious threat to health" (par. 7); the metaphors "eyeballs" (5), "hold businesses' feet to the fire" (11), "fade from view" (11), and "passion play" (12); and the personifications throughout, such as "[a] network . . . will recognize a browser" (5), "enabling the ad network to get a sense of that person's interests" (5), "if the engineers' plan had won the day" (12), and "[t]his is not to say that businesses don't want personal information—they do" (13).

2. The Latin phrase *status quo* means literally "state in which." It has come to mean "the way things are."

3. The allusion seems meant to imply that even if government regulators succeed in passing privacy protections, thereby destroying a successful business model, companies will find a way to resurrect the practices of tracking and data mining or put something similar in their place. Some readers will surely find the reference to Christian tradition unsettling if not offensive.

LORI ANDREWS
Facebook Is Using You
(p. 541)

Lori Andrews is both a renowned legal scholar and an engaging story-teller. In "*Facebook* Is Using You," her narrative skill enlivens and helps support her argument that in systematically violating Web users' privacy, large corporations and government agencies can and do inflict real harm on individual American citizens.

With the previous two essays by Nicholas Carr and Jim Harper, this essay rounds out an argumentative trio on the pros and cons of Internet tracking and data mining. In teaching the three arguments together, you may want to help students see how different each author's argumentative strategies are on the surface: Andrews writes personally and appeals to readers' emotions with examples of data-mining practices and their consequences for real people, whereas Carr and Harper take a more distanced, impersonal, and logical approach. And while Carr's argument is largely theoretical, Harper's and Andrews's essays focus more on practical realities. You might ask students to consider why the subject of privacy lends itself to both emotional and rational appeals on both sides of the issue.

Media resources: Andrews has her own *YouTube* channel, *youtube.com/user/loriandrewsauthor*, where she sometimes uploads video of her many media interviews and public appearances. Her Web site, *The Social Network Constitution*, proposes an Internet bill of rights and features several more videos, articles, listings of upcoming events, and the author's blog.

QUESTIONS ON MEANING

1. Andrews introduces her thesis in paragraph 4: "Ads that pop up on your screen might seem useful, or at worst, a nuisance. But they are much more than that. The bits and bytes about your life can easily be used against you." She states the implications of her thesis, her proposal, in the conclusion of her argument: "We need a do-not-track law, similar to the do-not-call one" (12).
2. Data aggregators are for-profit companies, such as LexisNexis, Spokeo, and NebuAd, that gather personal information about Web users and sell it to interested parties such as law enforcement agencies, the IRS, and insurance companies. Unlike advertisers, who gather or purchase the data to customize messages that "might seem useful, or at worst, a nuisance" (par. 4), data aggregators have a vested interest in using data against individuals and can cause people real harm.
3. Aggregators analyze data from hundreds of thousands of users to predict individual behaviors, relying on broad patterns to make assumptions that are often incorrect. Many people, she asserts, have been treated unfairly as a result, and many more will be.
4. The writer's purpose is to expose a problem and to offer a solution. Andrews calls for new laws that "give people the right to know what

data companies have about them" (par. 2) and that allow Web users to prevent companies from tracking them (12).

QUESTIONS ON WRITING STRATEGY

1. By setting her argument in the context of *Facebook*'s initial public offering, Andrews emphasizes the relevance of her subject (data aggregation in general) while grounding it in a concrete example and establishing the size of the stakes at hand. *Facebook* and other companies such as *Google*, Andrews points out, gather "stunning" (par. 2) amounts of personal information and stand to make enormous profits from it. Web users, by implication, are at risk of being exploited.
2. Andrews appeals primarily to emotion. Although she offers statistics and examples to support her claims, her emphasis is on readers' desires for privacy, distrust of large corporations, and fear of personal harm. The focus on "stereotyping" (pars. 6–11) and the reference to racial discrimination (9) in particular seem designed to stoke indignation and concern.
3. The sources Andrews cites, *Consumer Reports* and Princeton Survey Research Associates, will seem reliable or authoritative to most readers. Some, however, might feel that in citing the opinions of three thousand survey respondents relative to the hundreds of millions *Facebook* subscribers and *Google* users, Andrews makes a big inductive leap.
4. Andrews writes about herself at three points: She notes that her own personal data are included in "*Facebook*'s inventory" (par. 1), she describes the kinds of potentially damaging Web searches she has conducted and why (7), and she concludes with an image of herself being "interrupted by a telemarketer" at dinner contrasted with "whether my dreams will be dashed by the collection of bits and bytes over which I have no control" (12). Injecting herself shows that Andrews is not a disinterested bystander but is affected directly by the practices she argues against.
5. Andrews's evidence is almost entirely anecdotal, consisting of examples of companies and government agencies that track personal information and sell it as well as of people who have experienced or could experience the negative consequences of such tracking.

QUESTIONS ON LANGUAGE

1. A lawyer, Andrews relies primarily on formal, academic language through most of her essay. But being a mystery writer as well, she frequently slips into everyday speech that any reader could understand. A few examples: "big-ticket corporations" (par. 1); "widgets or gadgets" (1); "small potatoes" (3); "bits and bytes" (4); "'Is He Cheating on You?'" (5); "alive and well" (6); "Googled" (7); "make their own rules" (7); "whether my dreams will be dashed" (12); and the direct appeal to readers as "you" throughout. The colloquialisms inject a dose of lightheartedness into what might otherwise become an overly academic or theoretical argument; they also humanize the author and help readers follow her ideas.
2. A *doppelgänger*, as *The American Heritage Dictionary* tells us, is a "ghostly double of a living person, especially one that haunts its fleshly counterpart." The word is also used colloquially to describe an uncanny likeness between two distinct people, usually strangers. Andrews is

saying that digital selves are not identical to their real-world counter-parts and also that those digital selves can haunt us in unpleasant ways.

3. *Weblining* is the virtual equivalent of redlining, the discriminatory practice—now outlawed—of mapping out neighborhoods to deny finan-cial services to predefined classes (and races).

4. *Scrutinize* comes from the Latin *scrutinum,* "close search," which came from the Latin *scruta,* "old clothes." Thus, *to scrutinize* is to perform a minute search, such as a used-clothing vendor might conduct in a pile of old clothes.

LORI ANDREWS ON WRITING

Andrews's difficulty with fiction writing, it would seem, was an academic tendency toward abstraction. Her need to "learn the way to describe things" in a physical context offers two useful reminders to students: First, con-crete and specific language, along with plenty of examples, brings specificity to a writer's work and anchors ideas to reality; and second, all writers can improve.

PART THREE

MIXING THE METHODS

In this part of the book we provide an anthology, arranged alphabetically by author, of eight works by very well-known writers. The collection has a dual purpose. First, we want to widen the tight focus of the previous ten chapters so that students see the methods as a kit of tools to be used *in combination* as the need arises. All eight selections demonstrate just this flexibility in approach, narrating here, comparing there, analyzing a process for a couple of paragraphs, defining a term when helpful. The headnote to each selection lists the methods the author most relies on, pointing to specific paragraphs. And the introduction to Part Three gives students a list of questions—a kind of crib sheet of the methods—that they can use to explore or focus any subject.

The second goal of this anthology is to give you more leeway in your assignments. You can teach this part as a "mixing the methods" unit, of course, but you can also pluck out individual selections for any number of uses. If you want to show how a particular method works with other methods, you can point to, say, the examples in Joan Didion's "Earthquakes" or the description in E. B. White's "Once More to the Lake." If you're just seeking another example of a particular method, you can turn to, say, Judy Brady's "I Want a Wife" for definition or Colson Whitehead's "Loving Las Vegas" for narration. If you think students will respond to the thematic pairing of White's "Once More to the Lake" with Brad Manning's "Arm Wrestling with My Father" (in Chap. 5), you can assign them together.

We have highlighted the possible links in several ways. As we mentioned above, the headnote to each essay in this part itemizes the main methods used by the author. Among the writing suggestions for each selection in this part is at least one "Connections" topic that pulls in an essay from Part Two. For more general thematic links among selections, we provide a "Table of Contents by Theme and Discipline" just after the book's main contents.

JUDY BRADY
I Want a Wife

(p. 551)

In the late 1980s newspapers and magazines quoted an instantly famous remark attributed to the actress Joan Collins after her divorce from musician Peter Holm. Declaring that her bitter public divorce battle had soured her on remarrying, Collins is also said to have quipped, "I don't need a husband, I need a wife." But we suspect that the credit for originating this epigram belongs to Judy Brady.

Instructors who have taught this essay in earlier editions report that it's a trusty class-rouser, evoking lively comments and a few intense disputes. Does Brady overstate her case in "I Want a Wife"? Some students, reading her essay in the new millennium, may think so. Perhaps their skepticism indicates real advances in the status of women since Brady first wrote in 1972. Do wives today play roles as humble and exacting as the one Brady details here? Are men as well as women freer today to depart from prescribed patterns of behavior? Are women still as angry as Brady was? Note that similar questions are addressed in the third writing suggestion.

Give students some time to consider the above questions by having them collaboratively update Brady's essay: What are the requirements of a wife these days? Students can replace "wife" with "husband," "girlfriend," or "boyfriend" if they prefer. You might ask a few groups to read their responses aloud to the class as a way to open discussion of Brady's essay.

Media resources: Dick Gordon's full interview with Judy Brady, in which they discuss "I Want a Wife" and from which we extracted her comments for "Judy Brady on Writing," can be heard at *www.thestory.org/stories/2007-09/why-i-want-wife*. Still, the context of the women's liberation movement in the 1970s is likely to seem almost impossibly remote for most of your students. To give them a sense of the atmosphere Brady was railing against, try showing them a sampling of some of the sexist (and sometimes outright misogynist) advertising of the era. *Buzzfeed* has collected a few at *buzzfeed.com/patricksmith/unbelievably-sexist-adverts-from-classic-magazines*, and Megan Garber has discussed them in "'You've Come a Long Way, Baby': The Lag between Advertising and Feminism" (*The Atlantic*, June 15, 2015).

QUESTIONS ON MEANING

1. The essay lists them all. In general, the duties of a wife seem to entail making life easy and comfortable for everyone in the family—except the wife herself.
2. What it all boils down to, in Brady's view, is that husbands shoulder whatever responsibilities they want to assume. All others they assign to their wives.
3. The thesis is implied: Wives are not persons but conveniences whose subservient roles have been fashioned by husbands.

4. Answers will vary. Are all men as demanding and insensitive as the composite male chauvinist Brady draws? Are there fewer who resemble him nowadays than there were in 1972, when the essay was first published? The class might like to consider the extent to which traditional roles have changed in the past decades.

QUESTIONS ON WRITING STRATEGY

1. Because the author's name clearly indicates that she is a woman, the title is a surefire attention-getter.
2. The first two paragraphs establish Brady's credentials, position her essay in the real world, and show from the outset that wishing for a wife is not uncommon—among men.
3. Brady's tone is sardonic.
4. Avoiding the pronoun, though a bit awkward here and there, contributes greatly to the irony of "I Want a Wife." It dehumanizes a wife; she is not a woman but a thing to be used.
5. Readers of *Ms.* have feminist leanings. To us, the essay's observations of husbands and wives remain fresh: "Supermom" is, after all, a recent coinage. However, not everyone will agree.
6. The principle of analysis is determined by the thesis: The role of a wife can be divided into jobs that serve others, especially the husband. Other principles of analysis might be the jobs a wife does that require brainpower or the satisfactions of the role of wife—but these, of course, would produce entirely different essays.
7. The groups of duties are nurse-governess (par. 3), maid (4), confidante (5), social planner (6), and sex object (7). Today, "*bread winner*" might get more play than Brady gives it (par. 3).

QUESTIONS ON LANGUAGE

1. It emphasizes the selfishness and the demanding tone of the words. The words themselves reduce a wife to the level of a possession.
2. You might be able to elicit a definition of *monogamy* by asking your class to list other words they know that contain *mono-* and to list what all the definitions have in common.
3. The essay's diction is appropriate, the words easy for any intelligent reader to understand. The repetition of "I want a wife" and the author's use of short sentences give the essay a staccato beat that underscores the anger behind it.

JUDY BRADY ON WRITING

Brady's essay is a perfect example of writing derived from the rhetorical situation. She went from "complaining" at a meeting of frustrated women to reading her essay in front of a crowd to, later, publishing it. Students should be made aware of their own opportunities to turn their private gripes into coherent and audience-appropriate public arguments, perhaps in the form of an opinion piece for the campus newspaper.

JOAN DIDION
Earthquakes

(p. 557)

One of the most admired essayists of our time, Joan Didion often focuses her attention on the vagaries of life in her home state of California. Here, she depicts the aftermath of a relatively minor Los Angeles earthquake and reflects on living with the constant threat of "the Big One" still to come.

One hallmark of Didion's writing—and this essay provides a good example—is its specificity. You might ask students in small groups to look at how Didion uses very specific nouns, including many proper nouns, to create a sense in the reader of actually being where she is, observing what she does. Alternatively, explore Didion's concept of "protective detachment" (it's asked about in the first meaning question). Ask students: Has living with the threat of terrorism—or of global climate change—produced a sense of protective detachment in you?

Media resources: In her acceptance speech for the National Book Foundation's lifetime achievement award in 2007, Didion recounts her early writing process and hallowed career with humility and grace *(youtube.com/ watch?v=845yE6v23dg)*. And if there was any doubt about the lasting relevance of her work, Diane Keaton's 2012 reading of *Slouching Towards Bethlehem* should remove it. In a review of the audiobook for *Salon*, Kyle Minor exclaims that Keaton's performance reminds us that the value of Didion's writing "has only deepened with time." Didion remains, he says, "the most consistently interesting and quotable essayist in the English language." We tend to agree.

QUESTIONS ON MEANING

1. By "protective detachment," Didion means that Californians do not think about or prepare for a major earthquake because the thought of the potential catastrophe is too much to consider. They protect themselves emotionally.
2. According to Didion, Californians maintain the illusion of control when an earthquake strikes by "[q]uantification . . . guessing where the movement at hand will rank on the Richter scale" (par. 2)
3. Because it was closely followed by a series of similar earthquakes, the earthquake seemed potentially a foreshock, "an earthquake prefiguring a larger event" (par. 9).
4. "The Big One" threatens the destruction of life as Californians know it. What gives Didion the jitters is that the lifelong "promise of the Big One" (par. 9) could yet be fulfilled.

QUESTIONS ON WRITING STRATEGY

1. Didion's specificity about the times of the earthquakes gives a sense of their immediacy.

2. It is, of course, ironic that the Pentecostal minister moved his congrega-
    tion from California to Tennessee to escape a major earthquake, only to
    experience an earthquake in Tennessee a few months later.
3. Student opinion may differ here, but one effect of the conversation is to
    suggest Californians' familiarity and obsession with earthquakes.
4. Didion uses examples of people's expectations to define "the Big One."
5. Didion connects the series of earthquakes described in paragraph 8 to
    anxiety of Southern Californians.

QUESTIONS ON LANGUAGE

1. The repeated phrase suggests that a number of instructions have been
    issued for earthquake preparedness, and its implications of order con-
    trast markedly with the catastrophe envisioned by those receiving the
    instructions.
2. The Richter-scale numbers show how closely attuned Didion and others
    are to the earthquakes and their severity.
3. "Temporal dimension" suggests a heightened awareness of time, a
    sense that the world is not fixed.
4. The root of *seismologist* is the Greek *seismos*, "shock" or "earthquake,"
    which derives from *seiein*, "to shake." Both probably relate to a similar
    word meaning "fear."

JOAN DIDION ON WRITING

Didion's comments on writing seem apt from a writer noted for observation. She has, though, been criticized for lacking a framework, for writing
without a point. Do details as carefully selected and well written as Didion's
make their own point, or does she have some other responsibility as a
writer?

Students may be surprised at Didion's assertion about the relationship
between meaning ("the picture") and grammar, especially if they believe (as
many students seem to) that grammar is somehow extrinsic to meaning, the
frightening "rules" meant to be applied to already-expressed meaning.

MAXINE HONG KINGSTON

No Name Woman

(p. 563)

Students are usually moved by Kingston's evocation of a haunting childhood story. Ask them to describe their own reactions to the tale of Kingston's
aunt. Does it seem completely alien, from a world far away, or more immediate?
Does it hold students' imaginations?

Media resources: Kingston's books *The Woman Warrior* and *China
Men* are sources of further mystery and understanding about Chinese and

American culture. In addition, a number of films have depicted Chinese village life: *Ju Dou*, *Raise the Red Lantern*, and *To Live* are just a few available on DVD or online. Students who are interested in the films might consider writing a comparative paper on the role of women, for example, in Kingston's essay and in one of the films. How important is the medium to the message? What do the two media say in common? Another use of the films, given their complicated imagery, is to assign a collaborative paper. Interested students could watch one film together, discuss it, and prepare a comparison between it and Kingston's essay, addressing the questions above.

QUESTIONS ON MEANING

1. Kingston and her mother share the purpose of telling a riveting story. Kingston's purpose is also self-examination and an inquiry into Chinese cultural attitudes; her mother's is also to instill these cultural attitudes in her.
2. Her aunt's husband could not have been the child's father (par. 3). Kingston posits two possible fathers: a man who "commanded [the aunt] to be with him" (15) and a man she herself was drawn to (21).
3. It is meant to warn her against adultery and, by extension, sexuality.
4. Kingston is haunted by her Chinese heritage; she seeks "ancestral help" (par. 22). Her aunt is a powerful representative of that heritage, an example of its grip on women and their emotions. Her life and death are a profound "family secret" that transcends Kingston's own immediate family.

QUESTIONS ON WRITING STRATEGY

1. Kingston's family and other older Chinese would be unlikely to read the essay: Kingston does address Chinese Americans directly (par. 12), and her detailed descriptions of Chinese and Chinese American cultures indicate that she is trying to explain them to other Americans. Older Chinese, and particularly her family, would be shocked that she is breaking the silence about her aunt. Chinese Americans would see themselves and their own "haunting" in her story. Other Americans might be enlightened about the complexity and power the Chinese heritage holds.
2. The story of the aunt is supposed to be kept secret by the mother. The mother's tale is supposed to be kept secret by Kingston but is instead examined minutely in this essay. Kingston's telling the secret of her aunt's story is an act of rebellion equivalent to her aunt's. Thus, the opening line presages all the themes of the essay (and creates suspense as well).
3. The effect is to intensify the confusion of reality and truth and to show the subjective nature of memory and family history. Kingston creates this effect in passages such as "I want her fear to have lasted just as long as rape lasted" (par. 18), "I hope that the man my aunt loved appreciated a smooth brow" (25), and "She may have gone to the pigsty as a last act of responsibility" (44). You might want to draw students' attention to places where Kingston's different sources are intertwined—for example, "My mother spoke about the raid as if she had seen it, when she and my aunt, a daughter-in-law to a different household, should not have been living together at all" (19).

4. The details in paragraphs 15–18 tell a much bleaker story: "She obeyed him" (par. 16), "No one talked sex, ever" (18). The details in paragraphs 21–28 are those of a more romantic tale: "she often worked at herself in the mirror" (23), "my aunt combed individuality into her bob" (25), "she dreamed of a lover for the fifteen days of New Year's" (28). Kingston seems more caught up in the romantic version of the story, in her aunt's desire and need to rebel.

5. Her aunt might have been "commanded . . . to lie with" the father of her child (par. 15), or she might have "let dreams grow" and "offered us up for a charm that vanished" (21). The raid might have been organized by her rapist (16) or by villagers who were "speeding up the circling of events" (39). She might have killed her child because it was "a foreign growth that sickened her every day" (43) or because "Mothers who love their children take them along" (46). In the end Kingston concludes that her aunt's suicide was caused by her feelings of imprisonment within the conventions of village life.

QUESTIONS ON LANGUAGE

1. Kingston's poetic language shows how deeply she responds to her Chinese heritage and its tales. Some striking phrases include "a protruding melon of a stomach" (par. 3), "the heavy, deep-rooted women were to maintain the past against the flood" (20), "women looked like great sea snails" (27), and "violence could open up a black hole, a maelstrom that pulled in the sky" (37).

2. You might want to explain the "commensal" tradition (par. 19), in which food is shared by the generations of an extended family. The idea of food and its allocation is central to societies, like China's, where resources are stretched to their utmost. Kingston underscores this in paragraph 15, when she describes her ancestors as "people who hatch their own chicks and eat the embryos and the heads for delicacies and boil the feet in vinegar for party food, leaving only the gravel, eating even the gizzard lining."

3. Kingston blurs the distinction between history and her interpretation of it.

MAXINE HONG KINGSTON ON WRITING

In this interview Kingston discloses a profound belief in the power of writing to generate writing, even to bring order and meaning to one's life. Some students may have had this experience of writing, and perhaps they can confirm Kingston's words for students who haven't. (Students often don't realize that the turmoil of writing can actually be productive.) Kingston also slips in a small warning: It's fine to let yourself go in drafting, but eventually the "intellectual" (Kingston seems to mean "critical") side must kick in for revision.

JONATHAN SWIFT
A Modest Proposal

(p. 577)

That Swift is being ironic in proposing this monstrous solution to the problems of Ireland usually dawns slowly on a few students. It will be a highly entertaining class wherein someone thinks Swift is serious. From Swift's essay a perfectly straightforward argument for Christian charity may be inferred. For a contemporary satiric essay that depends on irony, see Koji Frahm's "How to Write an *A* Paper" (p. 268).

The irony of Swift's essay is masterful and inspiring. Students who would like to imitate Swift's tone will benefit from feedback on their attempts. Try assigning the class a single paragraph written in a tone of heavy irony. (You may wish to leave the subject up to students or integrate this with the first writing suggestion.) Give students time in class to read their paragraphs aloud in small groups (it will help if every student in the group has a copy) and to discuss how they might revise their work to improve the tone and the point(s) they are making.

QUESTIONS ON MEANING

1. Swift is proposing that the Irish poor sell their year-old children to the rich for meat.
2. Swift is calling for charity and compassion. Some specific alternatives for relieving poverty are given in Swift's list of "other expedients," paragraph 29.
3. Swift's essay calls attention to both the plight of the poor in Ireland and the hard-heartedness of their oppressors.
4. Swift's image of the begging mothers and their children immediately arouses readers' sympathy and prepares them to react with horror against the "modest" proposal.
5. Objections should be obvious, unless one regards a human being as an animal to be butchered.

QUESTIONS ON WRITING STRATEGY

1. The author writes as a reasonable, kind, serious do-gooder, impatient with the failure of those in power to do anything about the problem.
2. Swift does this effectively by calling his proposal "modest," by citing authorities and experts to back him up (such as the "very knowing American," par. 9), by carefully listing the advantages of the proposal (21–28), by his concern that the flesh would spoil if exported (31), and by professing at the end that he doesn't stand to make a penny himself.
3. Probably not until paragraph 9.
4. Surely to our feelings. Most of the reasonable arguments are deliberately monstrous, although other convincing points appeal to reason in paragraph 29.

5. The process analysis makes us study the proposal in its every gruesome particular. It forces our noses into the proposal, and thus into the plight of the Irish poor, in a way mere generalities would not have. The cause-and-effect analysis specifies the ways in which the proposal will achieve its goals, summarized in paragraph 33 as "advancing our trade, providing for infants, relieving the poor, and giving some pleasure to the rich."

QUESTIONS ON LANGUAGE

1. The words from breeding and butchery include "dam" (par. 4); "breed" (10); "carcass" (14); "flay" (15); "dressing them hot" (16); "mares in foal . . . ready to farrow" (26); "barreled beef . . . bacon" (27); and "customers for infants' flesh" (28).
2. Swift's vocabulary is extensive. When they read "A Modest Proposal," students might have to use their dictionaries more than they usually do when reading an essay. The exercise might increase their vocabularies.

HENRY DAVID THOREAU
What I Lived For

(p. 587)

We brought this oft-anthologized excerpt from *Walden* into the *Bedford Reader* first and foremost as a companion piece to provide context for the marvelously fresh "Barrio Walden" by Luis Alberto Urrea (p. 596). But as Urrea might say himself, who doesn't love a little Henry David Thoreau?

As a concept, a philosophy, or a movement, Transcendentalism can be difficult to pin down. Emerson, for instance, put an emphasis on the new, the idea of internal divinity, and exhortations for self-cultivation and self-reliance, while Thoreau was suspicious of novelty and focused more so than Emerson on nature and intellect. Yet students tend to be drawn to Transcendental thought all the same, perhaps because many of them come to college with romanticized expectations of engaging in heady philosophical debates—and the works of Thoreau and his ilk certainly deliver.

Of course some students will have encountered *Walden* before—it's often taught in high schools—but they likely won't have had the opportunity to examine just one brief section as closely as we encourage them to do here. A foundational and highly literary explanation of Thoreau's philosophy of life, "What I Lived For" demands, and rewards, multiple readings. Each time through, new layers of meaning and artistry emerge from the depths of that "stream" he fishes in.

Media resources: The Walden Woods Project, a nonprofit group dedicated to protecting and preserving the site of Thoreau's experiment in deliberate living, hosts an informative Web site regarding all things *Walden*. At *www.walden.org* you and your students can find biographies of Thoreau, digital collections of his writing, scholarship, and an extensive collection of artwork and photography depicting the location and its history. You might also wish to share with the class a photograph or drawing of the writer's cabin (easily secured through an image search for *Walden*): Most will be surprised to see just how small and Spartan it is. And for any students who grouse that Thoreau lacks relevance to modern American culture, we might point them to "Pond Scum," Kathryn Schulz's scathing analysis of Thoreau's account of his time in the woods, published in the October 19, 2015, *New Yorker*.

QUESTIONS ON MEANING

1. By "deliberately" Thoreau means attentively, consciously, and with purpose. He is writing to examine the meaning of life, and in doing so he mixes reflection and persuasion.

2. A major theme of Transcendentalism is a general tension between the individual and the community. Thoreau's criticisms of his community are numerous, but they all seem to come down to a rejection of modernity. Specifically, he takes issue with an exploitive mercantile economy based on commerce and paid labor (par. 2); unnecessary "internal improvements" (2) such as the newly emerging railroads, telegraphs, and penny press; a harried, fast-paced lifestyle and obsession with the affairs of others (3); and an over-reliance on institutions such as jails, almshouses, and churches (6). As Thoreau portrays it, mid-nineteenth-century America was too focused on "petty" things like money, gossip, speed, and technology and not focused enough on the fine arts (6) or the natural world (7). His complaints certainly do seem to apply today, probably to an even greater degree.

3. "Simplicity, simplicity, simplicity!" or "Simplify, simplify" (both in par. 2).

4. As we mention in the author headnote, Thoreau rejected the church (incidentally, many scholars cite a political schism in the New England Unitarian church as the major precipitator of Transcendentalism). Students should notice that in this excerpt from *Walden* the author mentions religion often and is openly critical of church leaders and those who deem the purpose of life to be to "glorify God and enjoy him forever" (par. 1): Take, for instance, the suggestion of a burning "parish church" in paragraph 3, the "draggle-tail" preacher in paragraph 5, the elitist Hindu minister in paragraph 6, and the image of being mired in the mud of "church and state . . . philosophy and religion" in paragraph 7. As a Transcendentalist, Thoreau finds divinity in human intuition and in nature. "God himself," he asserts in paragraph 6, "culminates in the present moment, and . . . we are enabled to apprehend at all what is sublime and noble only by the perpetual instilling and drenching of the reality that surrounds us."

5. Thoreau addresses the conflicts between perception and reality in paragraph 6. Our perceptions, he says, are filtered through contextual cues and traditions, and we fail to see past "the surface of things." Truth can be known, he believes, but only in consciously striving to look beyond the surface and attempting to see things—the natural elements of the world, particularly—for what they actually are, stripped of their social context. Instinct, he ironically suggests, is superior to intellect.

6. The writer's admiration for the wisdom of children is an extension of his evaluation of perception and reality (see the previous question). Infants have not yet been socialized and therefore are free of the misperceptions

and distractions that plague adults, especially educated adults. "Children, who play life," Thoreau asserts in paragraph 6, "discern its true law and relations more clearly than men, who fail to live it worthily, but who think that they are wiser by experience."

QUESTIONS ON WRITING STRATEGY

1. Writing in the mid-nineteenth century, Thoreau could assume a limited readership consisting mostly of highly educated men (and perhaps a handful of women) who were expected to pursue careers in the clergy, the professions, or business; most would not have been among the laborers whose harried existence Thoreau bemoans, although they may well have been their employers. His goal in writing *Walden*, and this part of it in particular, seems to have been to persuade those readers to scale back and live their lives more "deliberately" (par. 1) and more attuned to the natural world, as he himself chose to do. Students' responses will depend on their openness to his philosophy.

2. Thoreau uses topic sentences as transitions that preview the focus of each paragraph; repeats key words and themes such as *religion, children, nature, sublime, calculation, see,* and *sleepers*; and deftly runs certain metaphors—especially those pertaining to water and to railroads—throughout his argument (see the first question on language).

3. They're one and the same: "To a philosopher," Thoreau writes, "all *news*, as it is called, is gossip" (par. 4). His examples of news items all come down to "petty" (6) concerns: injuries, crimes, accidents, freak occurrences, royal ascensions. The only important news, he implies in citing the French Revolution, is that which pertains to major political or cultural upheaval, and such events are rare.

4. The stories of the Hindu messenger and the Brahmin prince, both taken from world literature, emphasize the importance of self-awareness and self-improvement. In quoting them, Thoreau makes readers aware of his own education and ongoing quest for knowledge, thereby increasing his ethical appeal. In alluding also to *Arabian Nights* (6), a tale of the life-saving powers of storytelling, and to the sirens' songs in *The Odyssey* (7), he also underscores his claim that truth lies in "music and poetry" (par. 6)—or, really, literary pursuits in general. Certainly it helps to be familiar with these works (and his original audience most definitely would have been), but knowing their content isn't necessary; all the same, we hint at their meaning in gloss notes for students.

QUESTIONS ON LANGUAGE

1. Nearly every sentence of "What I Lived For" uses dense figurative language, and students may have difficulty wrestling with Thoreau's meanings on a first (or second or even third) read. The most prominent figure of speech is probably Thoreau's personification of railroads; see the next question. The extended metaphor of the final paragraph, which begins with "Time is but the stream I go a-fishing in" may be the most famous metaphor from this chapter of *Walden*: Luis Alberto Urrea, in "Barrio Walden" (p. 596), refers to it directly, and so we ask students to take special note and tease out its meanings in the "Connections" question that links the two essays. Just a few examples of Thoreau's other metaphors and similes include "cut a broad swath and

shave close," "drive life into a corner" (par. 1); "we live meanly, like ants," "this chopping sea of civilized life," "Our life is like a German Confederacy," (2); "We have the Saint Vitus' dance, and cannot possibly keep our heads still" (3); and "drenching of the reality that surrounds us" (6). Notice, too, that several of the metaphors—particularly those involving railroads and water—thread throughout the essay. Undoubtedly what similes and metaphors students point to and what meanings they extract will vary.

2. Students will likely grasp from Thoreau's treatment that railroads were a new development in the United States when he was writing. They might further grasp that many workers—particularly Irish and Chinese workers—died in their construction, as did pedestrians and passengers once they were running: As Thoreau describes them, the rails themselves are human corpses. In giving the railroads a human quality—most notably with the famous line "We do not ride on the railroad; it rides upon us" (par. 2)—Thoreau characterizes the new transportation system as a menace and an oppressor. That the railroads increased commerce and pressures to commute to jobs as well as facilitated the mass distribution of popular newspapers seems only to enrage Thoreau the more. Beyond the focus in paragraph 2, the railroads return personified toward the end of the essay, with "the track is laid for us" (6), "let us . . . not be thrown off the track" (7), and "If the engine whistles, let it whistle till it is hoarse for its pains" (7). As personifications tend to do, these figures of speech make both the rails and the trains seem alive—and in Thoreau's case terribly threatening.

3. We'd say his tone is transcendental—that disorienting mixture of hectoring and sublime. Students' own characterizations will surely vary.

4. Contemporary readers often trip over *dear* and *mean* in older works because their meanings seem so obvious but wrong in the context. As Thoreau uses them in the nineteenth century, *dear* means "expensive" and *mean* means "cheap" or "stingy."

LUIS ALBERTO URREA

Barrio Walden

(p. 596)

Luis Alberto Urrea is one of the best-loved and most prolific Mexican American writers working today, and his essay makes a perfect companion piece to Henry David Thoreau's "What I Lived For." A contemporary "barrio transcendentalist" known for his disarming ability to portray discouraging circumstances with an uplifting tone, Urrea applies his unique voice in full force to this lyrical essay on the lasting impacts that the works of Thoreau (and Emerson and the Alcotts) have had on him. The philosophies of Transcendentalism, Urrea suggests, are still highly relevant and personally meaningful—even life-changing—and especially so for those who might feel culturally dislocated.

"Barrio Walden" is a good example of how narration can be used in the service of a larger theme, with implications that go beyond the events recounted. Urrea does more than simply tell a story; in responding almost viscerally to another writer's work, he makes an interesting observation about the role of the natural world in individual consciousness. The essay is also wonderful proof that source-inspired writing need not be dry or tedious: In Urrea's hands the academic field of philosophy becomes a source of entertainment.

Media resources: We encourage you and your students to listen to Urrea's audio performance of this piece for *Orion* (*orionmagazine.org/article/luis-alberto-urrea-reads-from-his-may-june-2013-wastelander-column/*); the author's cheerful, unassuming voice brings his work to life. Students interested in *Walden*'s influence on Urrea might also be pointed to his essay "Life on the Mississippi" for the same magazine (*orionmagazine.org/article/the-wastelander-life-on-the-mississippi/*): Just as he borrows many of Thoreau's themes for "Barrio Walden," Urrea explicitly adopts the Transcendentalist's famous "Battle of the Ants" scene from *Walden* for a passage in his own essay about the transformative powers of literature.

QUESTIONS ON MEANING

1. Urrea is drawn to Walden Pond because it's where Henry David Thoreau lived and wrote one of the most influential and enduring works of American philosophy, "scratching out one-liners with a quill, changing the world" (par. 29). The pond and the hut are physical manifestations of the Transcendentalism that so influenced Urrea as a "tween" (3) and seems to influence his life and his writing still.
2. "I wrestled with man's fate and the epic movements of the universe and the natural splendour of the Creator's delight in the temple of His Creation" (par. 12).
3. "Guttersnipe naturalists" is something of a paradox, a contradiction that makes its own sense. The term mixes nineteenth- and twenty-first-century language to reflect Urrea's own way of being a "barrio Transcendentalist" (par. 3): Like Thoreau (and Emerson) he is enamored of nature, but the natural world available to him as an inner-city resident surrounded by poverty is more elemental and less grandiose than the nature at Walden.
4. He is overcome with emotion at being at the conclusion of an intellectual pilgrimage that many others before him have taken. (Students may need to be told that hikers often add rocks to cairns to mark their arrival and to pay respect to a site.)
5. Urrea's primary purpose is to entertain, but he seems to also be reflecting on the transformative power of writing: Literature, he suggests, can not only influence individual readers, it can "chang[e] the world" (par. 29).

QUESTIONS ON WRITING STRATEGY

1. Urrea's first three paragraphs set the context for his pilgrimage. He was a California transplant to Massachusetts and disoriented by the winter environment and the coldness of New Englanders (or what he calls the "duende of Yankee cultural hoodoo," par. 2); he also explains that as a youth in San Diego he had been deeply influenced by Transcendentalism—specifically, the writings of Emerson and

Thoreau. So he was excited at the prospect of visiting the site where *Walden* was hatched.

2. In writing for readers of *Orion* (a magazine devoted to the environment and the arts), Urrea assumes an audience of educated people "deeply worried" (par. 3) about nature and well versed in American history and literature. It's not completely necessary to be familiar with "Civil Disobedience" or "Self Reliance" (the titles of these famous works are almost self-explanatory, and Urrea hints at their influence on him), but it certainly helps to have some knowledge of *Walden*, which is why we provide an excerpt from it ("What I Lived For," p. 587) to accompany Urrea's essay. Urrea wryly picks up on several of Thoreau's themes in that work (see the first "Connections" question following "Barrio Walden"). Readers who miss out on the joke, however, can still enjoy Urrea's transcendent story.

3. The flashback to the San Diego of Urrea's youth establishes what he expected to find and clues readers in that he's about to make an embarrassing mistake (it also suggests that he didn't really understand Thoreau as well as he thought he did). The paragraph serves as a humorously ironic transition between his anticipation and his actual experience.

4. The sentence indicates how long and exhausting (physically and emotionally) the day was for Urrea and helps to bring the reader back down to earth. It is also anticlimactic after the imaginative transcendence of Urrea's experience with nature. It is a typically banal, urban commute.

5. Urrea hits on all five senses in his descriptions. *Sight*, of course, infuses the entire essay with, for instance, his opening descriptions of seeing snow and ice for the first time (par. 1), the scenes viewed from the train (4), the glorified images of a "New England early autumn" (9), and so forth. *Sound* also prefigures early, with Urrea and fellow commuters "plugged into [their] Walkmans" and listening to music (4), and it reappears throughout with the author spelling out the New England pronunciations of words such as "Doah" (7) and "Eau my gwod" (4, 10) as well as his San Diego friends' pronunciation of Walden as "GUALDENG" (10) along with Jason the dog's "horking sounds" (30). He invokes *touch* from the start as well, encouraging readers to imagine shivering in the snow and slipping on ice (1) or jumping across and fishing in muddy street ponds, not to mention "dead polliwogs in a jar with hand lotion" (9), for just two examples. *Taste* figures in his mentions of porterhouse steak (2), ice cream (5), soda (8), pumpkins and lobsters (10), and coffee (36). And Urrea concludes with scent, asking, "did I smell pipe tobacco burning?" (35). Students might well point out additional images of their own. The dominant impression, they might conclude, is one of sensory overload.

6. Urrea compares his anticipatory mood and disappointing experience of the farmer's holding pond (pars. 10–26) with his dejected mood and revelatory experience of Thoreau's Walden Pond (27–35). The contrast is humorous but also indicative of the transcendence he experienced.

QUESTIONS ON LANGUAGE

1. As is the case with nearly everything he writes, Urrea's essay comes across as lyrical, accessible, irreverent, and yet somehow profound.

2. Some fragments: "Not many snowstorms in my desertified homeland" (par. 1); "'Civil Disobedience,' right?" (3); "And deer" (4); "Helpful-like,

as if she didn't know" (6); "And walked away" (8); "Next to lobster pots!"
(10); "Goths in paradise" (11); "Next to a small house and slanty barn"
(12); "Barking dogs" (27); "Farm wives gawking" (27); "And south, out of
town again, across the crazed traffic on the highway, and past a tumbledown trailer park and a garbage dump" (27); "A sea. A Great Lake" (28);
"Down to the water" (29); "The cairn of stones left by travelers" (32). The
fragments are deliberate: They create a detached, conversational effect
and add to Urrea's humor.

3. In personifying animals — not only the dog but also the "crows . . .
   arguing" (par. 34) and even to some extent the "mangy deer" (4) — Urrea
   lends human qualities to the natural world and implies, with the dog,
   that nature is more accommodating and pleasant than human beings are (especially if those human beings are crusty New England
   farmers).

4. A *barrio*, or Spanish-speaking neighborhood, is often associated with
   poverty. But it is just as often associated with heritage and a strong
   sense of community. Students may offer additional connotations of
   their own; you might wish to consult a dictionary of slang and share
   with students the evolution of some of these meanings or ask them to
   do so on their own. Urrea uses the word with pride.

5. *Psychedelic* is commonly used to describe the bright colors and surreal aspects associated with hippie counterculture; its literal meaning
   is "hallucinogenic" and refers to effects of the experimental drugs, especially LSD and psilocybin, that were popular with some intellectuals
   in the 1960s and '70s. Students would probably be surprised to learn
   that at the time, those drugs were legal and touted by researchers for
   their psychological benefits.

LUIS ALBERTO URREA ON WRITING

Urrea's insistence that inspiration comes from without rather than
within is refreshing and, we hope, inspiring. Your students may be surprised
by a professional writer's assertion that he's not that interesting, but his
point, as we see it, is that the best subjects for writing are the observable,
not the personal. Students who worry that they have nothing to write about
should be reassured that even the best writers "get stuck" when looking for
subjects.

E. B. WHITE

Once More to the Lake

(p. 604)

Among White's essays, this is one of the most often reprinted. In
July 1941 White made a pilgrimage back to the Belgrade Lakes, northwest
of Augusta, Maine, together with his young son, Joel. "This place is as
American as a drink of Coca Cola," he wrote to his wife, Katharine. "The

white collar family having its annual liberty. I must say it seems sort of good" (*Letters of E. B. White,* 1976). After his return to civilization, White produced "Once More to the Lake" for a column he was then contributing to *Harper's* magazine. Too marvelous to be a reasonable model for most student writers, the essay can encourage them to believe that their own memories are worth recording and can interest others. "Once More to the Lake" exhibits a whole array of rhetorical methods, too: description, narration, exemplification, comparison and contrast, even process analysis.

Of course, it is White's description — of place, people, feelings — that is most inimitable, but students can try their hand in a small way at first. Give them a one-paragraph writing assignment — even with a word limit, if you desire — to describe a place that is highly familiar to them. Working in small groups, students can read aloud their paragraphs and get feedback on how they might revise them to make the images more vivid, the phrasing more precise, the details more developed. (This will work best if students bring copies of their paragraphs for the other members of their group.) Fine-tuning their own writing on this small scale should give students the confidence to undertake larger writing projects (like those in the writing suggestions).

Media resources: White wrote and narrated a short (eighteen-minute) documentary on lobster fishing for the CBS series *Omnibus* in 1954. Students who wish to hear the writer's voice (or learn about trapping in the '50s) can watch the clip at *The Bangor Daily News*'s Web site: *thinkmaine.bangordailynews .com/2016/03/09/home/watch-this-remarkable-1954-video-narrated-by-e-b -white-of-a-deer-isle-lobsterman/.*

QUESTIONS ON MEANING

1. White senses that nothing essential at the lake has changed; besides, he sustains the illusion that his son is himself as a boy and that he has become his own father (par. 4 and later passages).
2. Once, inboard motors had made a sleepy sound; today, the outboards seem "petulant, irritable." A central detail: "this was the note that jarred, the one thing that would sometimes break the illusion and set the years moving."
3. White's son is engaged by the same attractions: the joy of getting up early and going off by himself in a boat (par. 4), the fun of learning tricks with a motor (10). But the essay sets forth an insight that is White's alone, and the boy is not portrayed in any clear detail until the final paragraph.
4. White's purpose, made explicit in the final paragraph, is to set forth a theme: that although time at the lake seems to have stood still, time for the writer has been passing. He has aged and he will die like his father before him.

QUESTIONS ON WRITING STRATEGY

1. The repetitions help set forth the central theme of the essay. (In the answer to question 4 above we suggest one way of stating it.)
2. Beautifully arranged, this essay doesn't completely unfold its purpose until its final line. By a multitude of details, we have been lulled into accepting the illusion that time stands still. Suddenly, in one

unforgettable image, White invokes reality. The feeling of donning an ice-cold bathing suit is a familiar sensation from childhood, but the cold of the suit also suggests the cold of the grave.

3. Young readers, we trust, will understand and appreciate it, too. Ask them. Students might not be greatly excited by White's slowly unfolding account at first, but most do warm to it.

4. The author's tone, sometimes gently humorous, in general is nostalgic, even dreamlike—as if he were viewing the lake and his early adventures there through a gentle haze.

5. White's images appeal to all five senses. They capture the smells of the bedroom and wet woods (par. 2); the sight of a dragonfly, the boat, and its contents (5); the sounds of motors (10); the taste of donuts dipped in sugar (11); and the tactile sense of damp moss in the bait can (5), of the "soggy, icy" bathing trunks (13).

6. The comparison, notably between White's childhood experiences and his son's, contains the essay's theme of time and mortality.

QUESTIONS ON LANGUAGE

1. For the word *cultist* (par. 6), it might be worth pointing out that White apparently means an enthusiast for cleanliness.

2. The diction might sound exaggerated, but "unique" and "holy" describe the way the lake appears to White in memory.

3. White's description of a thunderstorm is only one of the essay's rich array of figurative language. The lake in early morning preserves "the stillness of the cathedral" (par. 2). Waves keep "chucking the rowboat under the chin" (5). In paragraph 10 a one-cylinder engine was like a wild animal "eating out of your hand," and a boat could approach a dock like a charging bull. In paragraph 11 a steamboat used to look like a Ubangi, and a drink of soda pop would backfire like an engine. In paragraph 12 the storm becomes a wild concert, and the generations are linked "in a strong indestructible chain." The essay ends in a splendid metaphor.

COLSON WHITEHEAD

Loving Las Vegas

(p. 612)

Much as Colson Whitehead saw something in himself the first time he set foot in the fabled city of Las Vegas, we expect that many of your students will recognize something of themselves in the experience he relates of resisting adulthood or of being barely graduated from college and trying to establish himself while having no idea how. Mildly depressed, aimless, and defiant, the writer finds joy, and himself, in a place reputed for its decadence and superficiality. "Loving Las Vegas" has been cited for honorable mention in several "Best Essay" collections and annual reviews, and it's easy to see why. The essay is beautifully written and great fun to read, and it manages to capture something universal about the human condition—even in the midst of despair, Whitehead reveals, we can find hope in the "pure, filthy truth" (par. 1) of who we are.

Class discussion of the essay might open with an exploration of your students' own struggles in college and their hopes and fears for the future. Do they know what they want to do in life? Do they have a plan for making that happen? How, if it all, does Whitehead help to reassure them that it will all turn out okay? If they're not convinced, why not?

Media resources: In "How to Write and the Art of Writing," a presentation at the Chicago Humanities Festival in 2010, Whitehead reads an extended version of "How to Write" (the essay we condensed for "Colson Whitehead on Writing"): *youtube.com/watch?v=vMFwW47HWCM.*

QUESTIONS ON MEANING

1. As Whitehead puts it, he was rebelling "against the system" (par. 11)—that is, the adult world of work and responsibility, of "rules and codes and institutions" (10). His "passive-aggressive rebellions" (11) took the form of pushing the limits and testing authority in small ways: skipping class, sleeping in, handing in assignments late "to see how much [he] could get away with" (9). The result, aside from nearly failing to graduate, was that Whitehead developed a fatalistic attitude, in which he determined that the world ("The House," 11) is indifferent to any one individual's choices or failures and that nothing and no one can be expected to step in and help.

2. Las Vegas, for Whitehead, is an escape from reality, a place that lets people pretend "we are in control of our fates" (par. 10), that offers "a few days' reprieve from who you are . . . [and] allows you to be someone else for a time" (par. 20). For him personally, being there opened his eyes to who he was and who he wanted to be.

3. Whitehead explains that while "[e]verybody's a [metaphoric] walking Museum of Where They've Been" (par. 14), he and his friends "decided to make it literal" (14). In other words, the trinkets symbolized the particular places they visited on their road trip: the "Sears Towers" from Chicago, the "small turquoise stones" presumably from New Mexico, the "toy buffalo" from Colorado perhaps, "Bull's horns from Arizona," Elvis magnets and "tiny plastic slot machines" from Las Vegas. Appropriately, the literal manifestations survived the trip itself but disappeared when the friends returned home "and the spell" of their travels "had worn off" (22).

4. As a stand-alone essay, "Loving Las Vegas" is a memoir in which Whitehead is writing to reflect on his college-age experiences and to share his philosophy of life. As an excerpt from *The Noble Hustle,* the piece seems meant to provide context about Las Vegas for Whitehead's account of the World Series of Poker held there, an argument, even, that the city is more meaningful than readers might assume it to be.

5. Whitehead reveals his thesis in his final metaphoric line: "We'd waited for cards, and then we played them." Students might interpret this to mean that Whitehead is saying life is a gamble, perhaps, or that nobody controls his or her fate.

QUESTIONS ON WRITING STRATEGY

1. Whitehead's essay is rich with sensory images. Here we list some possible choices. *Sight:* "brown stains corresponding to the previous owner's track marks" (6); "geriatric zombies in tracksuits installed at the slots, empty coin buckets overturned on their oxygen tanks" (7); "a man in the sky who watches over everything you do, as all-seeing as the thousands of security cameras embedded in casino ceilings" (10); the souvenirs glued to the car (14). *Sound:* "Dub, Lee 'Scratch' Perry, deep deep cuts off side six of *Sandinista!*" (2); "I hear a sizzling sound, like meat being thrown into a hot skillet" (9, notice this image also invokes taste and smell); "nickels poured into the basin, sweet music" (12). *Touch:* "carpeted sidewalks" (par. 1); "mattresses still moldy and damp from the spring floods" (5); "A consistent feeling of itchiness" (6); "ill-fitting acrylic slacks and blazers with stiff fibers sticking out of the joints and seams" (6). *Taste:* "We'd spent the summer eating 50¢ hot dogs at Gray's Papaya" (1); "the cheap steaks and watered-down drinks" (15). *Smell:* "smoking cigarettes" (2); "sweaty, laundryless days and nights" (6). Often but not always metaphoric, the descriptions help readers to participate themselves in Whitehead's experiences and make his points concrete.

2. Whitehead's transitions indicate shifts in time and in direction, keeping readers on track with the progression of Whitehead's narrative: "The previous year" (par. 1); "This summer" (1); "It was 1991" (2); "First thing" (3); "Then hundreds of miles to Chicago" (5); "Then west to tackle our Let's Go assignment proper" (6); "But I see now I'd been testing the House Rules the previous two years" (9); "After a few phone calls" (11); "Before we left town" (14); "Weeks later" (15); "And what's wrong with Disneyland?" (17); "Some of the classic joints we wrote about are gone now" (19); "Then Darren wigged out and caught a plane home" (21); "We grew up" (23).

3. Whitehead includes snippets from his notebook at a few points in the essay: "I asked Andy why there were no security guards around. . . . He told me I had a New Yorker's mentality" (par. 4); "discussing the plot of the movie Darren wants to write, about 7-Elevens that land in cornfields" (5); "Hours of agony. Impossible to sleep. Bugs. A consistent feeling of itchiness" (6). The passages offer examples of exactly what he was thinking at the time rather than how he might interpret his memories twenty-five years later; they also hint at the banality of the recent graduate's mindset and set up some context for the passages the friends revised in the Let's Go guide and that Whitehead cites in paragraphs 15–20.

4. Whitehead traces cause and effect in paragraphs 7–12. Although he asserts that he hadn't planned to gamble because the pastime "was a weakness of the ignorant masses" (par. 7), Whitehead discovers that the thrill of winning even a handful of nickels is a visceral pleasure and that "little gambles were a way of pretending that no one was the boss of me" (10).

5. As Whitehead characterizes them, the original text was full of "snobby asides" (par. 15) and "upper-middle-class disdain" (20). He and his friends revised the book to be "more upbeat" (18). Some readers might note the irony of this principle of analysis, given the general malaise Whitehead portrays in his attitude toward life at the time, citing "that quality of everyday existence by which the soul is crushed, diminished,

made entirely small" (17). But as he explains his own attitude in this section of the essay, "No one forces doom upon you, folks. You need to seek it out" (19), as he seems to have been doing.

QUESTIONS ON LANGUAGE

1. Whitehead uses complex, formal words and phrases such as "en route" (par. 2), "retrospect" (2), "apprenticeship" (2), "Lynchian auter" (2), "disappointing pilgrimage too complicated and inane to detail here" (5), "manifested" (6), "ignorant masses" (7), "inscrutable" (10), "polyethylene totems" (14), and "demography" (19) alongside colloquial expressions including "gig" (1), "beat" (1), "hooked up" (3), "stoner underpinnings" (4), "chill-space" (5), "suckers" (7), "We had serious epoxy" (14), "Percy, where are my smelling salts?" (16), "joints" (19), and "wigged out" (21). The author also uses sentence fragments liberally to build a sense of brooding. The formal words contribute to Whitehead's pseudoacademic tone, and their juxtaposition with conversational phrases adds to the essay's humor. He seems to assume that his readers are educated and familiar with the travails of being a college graduate with no clear plan for the future.

2. Some metaphors: "We'd just been diagnosed as Generation X, and certainly we had all the symptoms" (par. 2); "this smart white jellyfish flopping on the desert floor" (6); "In a dank utility room deep in the sub-basements of my personality, a little man wiped his hands on his overalls and pulled the switch" (9); "I'd been testing the House Rules the previous few years" (9); "hut hut hut through the training years of decent society" (9); "games of Risk" (19); "As in cards, it was business, not personal" (23). Some understatements: "*Let's Go North Korea* (they always lost a few freshmen updating that one)" (1); "The subways didn't run that far out" (1); "His brothers wanted to know why he was 'bringing niggers and Jews' into their chill-space. We sure were seeing a lot of America on this trip" (5); "the camping thing not really taking" (6); "Blink. Tug. Blink" (7); "Grisly" (8); "I didn't approve of the drug dealer's lifestyle choices—for vacation, he went camping" (15). The metaphors, of course, bring freshness and vibrancy to Whitehead's prose. And as they often do, the understatements lend a sense of [ironic] humor to his subject.

3. The allusions to Beckett and Marx hint at a freshly minted college graduate's pretensions but also at malaise (students may or may not be familiar with *Waiting for Godot*, but Whitehead's "topic of the abyss" suggests a feeling of meaninglessness) and at relative poverty. The misrepresentation of communism's bible *Das Kapital* as something "worshipped" in the hyper-materialized Las Vegas is particularly ironic.

4. Students may not know that *sic*, the Latin for "thus," indicates that a quotation is just as the original author wrote it. Writers often use *sic* to point to errors. Whitehead uses it to mock the previous writers' pretentions in using "Ziegfieldesque" to refer to the famous Ziegfeld Follies.

5. The capital letters impart a comic sense of formality and distance between himself and his subject (which is, of course, himself).

6. An *antecedent*, as students should have learned in Chapter 2 (p. 58), is the noun to which a pronoun refers. We greatly enjoy Whitehead's wry complaint that his predecessors for *Let's Go* committed the common error of vague or implied pronoun reference.

COLSON WHITEHEAD ON WRITING

We find ourselves hard-pressed to disagree with Whitehead's rules for writing, flippant as he may be in putting them forth. Clarity and conciseness are key to communicating with readers, and being passionate about a subject is key to having something to communicate in the first place. You might ask students to expand on what Whitehead has to say: What do *they* think is the "secret" (rule number 8) to good writing?